American Casebook Series
Hornbook Series and Basic Legal Texts
Black Letter Series and Nutshell Series

of

WEST PUBLISHING COMPANY
P.O. Box 64526
St. Paul, Minnesota 55164–0526

Accounting

FARIS' ACCOUNTING AND LAW IN A NUT-SHELL, 377 pages, 1984. Softcover. (Text)

FIFLIS' ACCOUNTING ISSUES FOR LAWYERS, TEACHING MATERIALS, , 706 pages, 1991. Teacher's Manual available. (Casebook)

SIEGEL AND SIEGEL'S ACCOUNTING AND FINANCIAL DISCLOSURE: A GUIDE TO BASIC CONCEPTS, 259 pages, 1983. Softcover. (Text)

Administrative Law

BONFIELD AND ASIMOW'S STATE AND FEDERAL ADMINISTRATIVE LAW, 826 pages, 1989. Teacher's Manual available. (Casebook)

GELLHORN AND LEVIN'S ADMINISTRATIVE LAW AND PROCESS IN A NUTSHELL, Third Edition, 479 pages, 1990. Softcover. (Text)

MASHAW AND MERRILL'S CASES AND MATERIALS ON ADMINISTRATIVE LAW—THE AMERICAN PUBLIC LAW SYSTEM, Second Edition, 976 pages, 1985. (Casebook) 1989 Supplement.

ROBINSON, GELLHORN AND BRUFF'S THE ADMINISTRATIVE PROCESS, Third Edition, 978 pages, 1986. (Casebook)

Admiralty

HEALY AND SHARPE'S CASES AND MATERIALS ON ADMIRALTY, Second Edition, 876 pages, 1986. (Casebook)

MARAIST'S ADMIRALTY IN A NUTSHELL, Second Edition, 379 pages, 1988. Softcover. (Text)

SCHOENBAUM'S HORNBOOK ON ADMIRALTY

AND MARITIME LAW, Student Edition, 692 pages, 1987 with 1989 pocket part. (Text)

Agency—Partnership

DEMOTT'S FIDUCIARY OBLIGATION, AGENCY AND PARTNERSHIP: DUTIES IN ONGOING BUSINESS RELATIONSHIPS, 740 pages, 1991. Teacher's Manual available. (Casebook)

FESSLER'S ALTERNATIVES TO INCORPORATION FOR PERSONS IN QUEST OF PROFIT, Third Edition, 339 pages, 1991. Softcover. (Casebook)

HENN'S CASES AND MATERIALS ON AGENCY, PARTNERSHIP AND OTHER UNINCORPORATED BUSINESS ENTERPRISES, Second Edition, 733 pages, 1985. Teacher's Manual available. (Casebook)

REUSCHLEIN AND GREGORY'S HORNBOOK ON THE LAW OF AGENCY AND PARTNERSHIP, Second Edition, 683 pages, 1990. (Text)

SELECTED CORPORATION AND PARTNERSHIP STATUTES, RULES AND FORMS. Softcover. 937 pages, 1991.

STEFFEN AND KERR'S CASES ON AGENCY-PARTNERSHIP, Fourth Edition, 859 pages, 1980. (Casebook)

STEFFEN'S AGENCY-PARTNERSHIP IN A NUTSHELL, 364 pages, 1977. Softcover. (Text)

Agricultural Law

MEYER, PEDERSEN, THORSON AND DAVIDSON'S AGRICULTURAL LAW: CASES AND MATERIALS, 931 pages, 1985. Teacher's Manual available. (Casebook)

Alternative Dispute Resolution

KANOWITZ' CASES AND MATERIALS ON ALTER-

Alternative Dispute Resolution—Cont'd

NATIVE DISPUTE RESOLUTION, 1024 pages, 1986. Teacher's Manual available. (Casebook) 1990 Supplement.

RISKIN AND WESTBROOK'S DISPUTE RESOLUTION AND LAWYERS, 468 pages, 1987. Teacher's Manual available. (Casebook)

RISKIN AND WESTBROOK'S DISPUTE RESOLUTION AND LAWYERS, Abridged Edition, 223 pages, 1987. Softcover. Teacher's Manual available. (Casebook)

American Indian Law

CANBY'S AMERICAN INDIAN LAW IN A NUTSHELL, Second Edition, 336 pages, 1988. Softcover. (Text)

GETCHES AND WILKINSON'S CASES AND MATERIALS ON FEDERAL INDIAN LAW, Second Edition, 880 pages, 1986. (Casebook)

Antitrust—see also Regulated Industries, Trade Regulation

FOX AND SULLIVAN'S CASES AND MATERIALS ON ANTITRUST, 935 pages, 1989. Teacher's Manual available. (Casebook)

GELLHORN'S ANTITRUST LAW AND ECONOMICS IN A NUTSHELL, Third Edition, 472 pages, 1986. Softcover. (Text)

HOVENKAMP'S BLACK LETTER ON ANTITRUST, 323 pages, 1986. Softcover. (Review)

HOVENKAMP'S HORNBOOK ON ECONOMICS AND FEDERAL ANTITRUST LAW, Student Edition, 414 pages, 1985. (Text)

POSNER AND EASTERBROOK'S CASES AND ECONOMIC NOTES ON ANTITRUST, Second Edition, 1077 pages, 1981. (Casebook) 1984–85 Supplement.

SULLIVAN'S HORNBOOK OF THE LAW OF ANTITRUST, 886 pages, 1977. (Text)

Appellate Advocacy—see Trial and Appellate Advocacy

Architecture and Engineering Law

SWEET'S LEGAL ASPECTS OF ARCHITECTURE, ENGINEERING AND THE CONSTRUCTION PROCESS, Fourth Edition, 889 pages, 1989. Teacher's Manual available. (Casebook)

Art Law

DUBOFF'S ART LAW IN A NUTSHELL, 335 pages, 1984. Softcover. (Text)

Banking Law

BANKING LAW: SELECTED STATUTES AND REGULATIONS. Softcover. 263 pages, 1991.

LOVETT'S BANKING AND FINANCIAL INSTITUTIONS LAW IN A NUTSHELL, Second Edition, 464 pages, 1988. Softcover. (Text)

SYMONS AND WHITE'S BANKING LAW: TEACHING MATERIALS, Third Edition, 818 pages, 1991. Teacher's Manual available. (Casebook)

Statutory Supplement. *See Banking Law: Selected Statutes*

Business Planning—see also Corporate Finance

PAINTER'S PROBLEMS AND MATERIALS IN BUSINESS PLANNING, Second Edition, 1008 pages, 1984. (Casebook) 1990 Supplement.

Statutory Supplement. *See Selected Corporation and Partnership*

Civil Procedure—see also Federal Jurisdiction and Procedure

AMERICAN BAR ASSOCIATION SECTION OF LITIGATION—READINGS ON ADVERSARIAL JUSTICE: THE AMERICAN APPROACH TO ADJUDICATION, 217 pages, 1988. Softcover. (Coursebook)

CLERMONT'S BLACK LETTER ON CIVIL PROCEDURE, Second Edition, 332 pages, 1988. Softcover. (Review)

COUND, FRIEDENTHAL, MILLER AND SEXTON'S CASES AND MATERIALS ON CIVIL PROCEDURE, Fifth Edition, 1284 pages, 1989. Teacher's Manual available. (Casebook)

COUND, FRIEDENTHAL, MILLER AND SEXTON'S CIVIL PROCEDURE SUPPLEMENT. 476 pages, 1991. Softcover. (Casebook Supplement)

FEDERAL RULES OF CIVIL PROCEDURE—EDUCATIONAL EDITION. Softcover. 816 pages, 1991.

FRIEDENTHAL, KANE AND MILLER'S HORNBOOK ON CIVIL PROCEDURE, 876 pages, 1985. (Text)

KANE AND LEVINE'S CIVIL PROCEDURE IN CALIFORNIA: STATE AND FEDERAL 543 pages, 1991. Softcover. (Casebook Supplement)

KANE'S CIVIL PROCEDURE IN A NUTSHELL, Third Edition, 303 pages, 1991. Softcover. (Text)

KOFFLER AND REPPY'S HORNBOOK ON COM-

Civil Procedure—Cont'd

MON LAW PLEADING, 663 pages, 1969. (Text)

LEVINE, SLOMANSON AND WINGATE'S CALIFORNIA CIVIL PROCEDURE, CASES AND MATERIALS, . 546 pages, 1991. (Casebook)

MARCUS, REDISH AND SHERMAN'S CIVIL PROCEDURE: A MODERN APPROACH, 1027 pages, 1989. Teacher's Manual available. (Casebook) 1991 Supplement.

MARCUS AND SHERMAN'S COMPLEX LITIGATION–CASES AND MATERIALS ON ADVANCED CIVIL PROCEDURE, 846 pages, 1985. Teacher's Manual available. (Casebook) 1989 Supplement.

PARK AND MCFARLAND'S COMPUTER-AIDED EXERCISES ON CIVIL PROCEDURE, Third Edition, 210 pages, 1991. Softcover. (Coursebook)

SIEGEL'S HORNBOOK ON NEW YORK PRACTICE, Second Edition, Student Edition, 1068 pages, 1991. Softcover. (Text)

Commercial Law

BAILEY AND HAGEDORN'S SECURED TRANSACTIONS IN A NUTSHELL, Third Edition, 390 pages, 1988. Softcover. (Text)

EPSTEIN, MARTIN, HENNING AND NICKLES' BASIC UNIFORM COMMERCIAL CODE TEACHING MATERIALS, Third Edition, 704 pages, 1988. Teacher's Manual available. (Casebook)

HENSON'S HORNBOOK ON SECURED TRANSACTIONS UNDER THE U.C.C., Second Edition, 504 pages, 1979, with 1979 pocket part. (Text)

MURRAY'S COMMERCIAL LAW, PROBLEMS AND MATERIALS, 366 pages, 1975. Teacher's Manual available. Softcover. (Coursebook)

NICKLES' BLACK LETTER ON COMMERCIAL PAPER, 450 pages, 1988. Softcover. (Review)

NICKLES, MATHESON AND DOLAN'S MATERIALS FOR UNDERSTANDING CREDIT AND PAYMENT SYSTEMS, 923 pages, 1987. Teacher's Manual available. (Casebook)

NORDSTROM, MURRAY AND CLOVIS' PROBLEMS AND MATERIALS ON SALES, 515 pages, 1982. (Casebook)

NORDSTROM, MURRAY AND CLOVIS' PROBLEMS AND MATERIALS ON SECURED TRANSACTIONS,

594 pages, 1987. (Casebook)

RUBIN AND COOTER'S THE PAYMENT SYSTEM: CASES, MATERIALS AND ISSUES, 885 pages, 1989. Teacher's Manual Available. (Casebook)

SELECTED COMMERCIAL STATUTES. Softcover. 1851 pages, 1991.

SPEIDEL'S BLACK LETTER ON SALES AND SALES FINANCING, 363 pages, 1984. Softcover. (Review)

SPEIDEL, SUMMERS AND WHITE'S COMMERCIAL LAW: TEACHING MATERIALS, Fourth Edition, 1448 pages, 1987. Teacher's Manual available. (Casebook)

SPEIDEL, SUMMERS AND WHITE'S COMMERCIAL PAPER: TEACHING MATERIALS, Fourth Edition, 578 pages, 1987. Reprint from Speidel et al., Commercial Law, Fourth Edition. Teacher's Manual available. (Casebook)

SPEIDEL, SUMMERS AND WHITE'S SALES: TEACHING MATERIALS, Fourth Edition, 804 pages, 1987. Reprint from Speidel et al., Commercial Law, Fourth Edition. Teacher's Manual available. (Casebook)

SPEIDEL, SUMMERS AND WHITE'S SECURED TRANSACTIONS: TEACHING MATERIALS, Fourth Edition, 485 pages, 1987. Reprint from Speidel et al., Commercial Law, Fourth Edition. Teacher's Manual available. (Casebook)

STOCKTON'S SALES IN A NUTSHELL, Second Edition, 370 pages, 1981. Softcover. (Text)

STONE'S UNIFORM COMMERCIAL CODE IN A NUTSHELL, Third Edition, 580 pages, 1989. Softcover. (Text)

WEBER AND SPEIDEL'S COMMERCIAL PAPER IN A NUTSHELL, Third Edition, 404 pages, 1982. Softcover. (Text)

WHITE AND SUMMERS' HORNBOOK ON THE UNIFORM COMMERCIAL CODE, Third Edition, Student Edition, 1386 pages, 1988. (Text)

Community Property

MENNELL AND BOYKOFF'S COMMUNITY PROPERTY IN A NUTSHELL, Second Edition, 432 pages, 1988. Softcover. (Text)

VERRALL AND BIRD'S CASES AND MATERIALS ON CALIFORNIA COMMUNITY PROPERTY, Fifth

Community Property—Cont'd

Edition, 604 pages, 1988. (Casebook)

Comparative Law

BARTON, GIBBS, LI AND MERRYMAN'S LAW IN RADICALLY DIFFERENT CULTURES, 960 pages, 1983. (Casebook)

GLENDON, GORDON AND OSAKWE'S COMPARATIVE LEGAL TRADITIONS: TEXT, MATERIALS AND CASES ON THE CIVIL LAW, COMMON LAW AND SOCIALIST LAW TRADITIONS, 1091 pages, 1985. (Casebook)

GLENDON, GORDON AND OSAKWE'S COMPARATIVE LEGAL TRADITIONS IN A NUTSHELL. 402 pages, 1982. Softcover. (Text)

Computers and Law

MAGGS, SOMA AND SPROWL'S COMPUTER LAW—CASES, COMMENTS, AND QUESTIONS, Approximately 725 pages, 1992. Teacher's Manual available. (Casebook)

MAGGS AND SPROWL'S COMPUTER APPLICATIONS IN THE LAW, 316 pages, 1987. (Coursebook)

MASON'S USING COMPUTERS IN THE LAW: AN INTRODUCTION AND PRACTICAL GUIDE, Second Edition, 288 pages, 1988. Softcover. (Coursebook)

Conflict of Laws

CRAMTON, CURRIE AND KAY'S CASES–COMMENTS–QUESTIONS ON CONFLICT OF LAWS, Fourth Edition, 876 pages, 1987. (Casebook)

HAY'S BLACK LETTER ON CONFLICT OF LAWS, 330 pages, 1989. Softcover. (Review)

SCOLES AND HAY'S HORNBOOK ON CONFLICT OF LAWS, Student Edition, approximately 1025 pages, 1992. (Text)

SIEGEL'S CONFLICTS IN A NUTSHELL, 470 pages, 1982. Softcover. (Text)

Constitutional Law—Civil Rights—see also First Amendment and Foreign Relations and National Security Law

ABERNATHY'S CIVIL RIGHTS AND CONSTITUTIONAL LITIGATION, CASES AND MATERIALS, Second Edition, approximately 750 pages, 1992. (Casebook)

BARRON AND DIENES' BLACK LETTER ON CONSTITUTIONAL LAW, Third Edition, 440 pages, 1991. Softcover. (Review)

BARRON AND DIENES' CONSTITUTIONAL LAW IN A NUTSHELL, Second Edition, 483 pages, 1991. Softcover. (Text)

ENGDAHL'S CONSTITUTIONAL FEDERALISM IN A NUTSHELL, Second Edition, 411 pages, 1987. Softcover. (Text)

FARBER AND SHERRY'S HISTORY OF THE AMERICAN CONSTITUTION, 458 pages, 1990. Softcover. Teacher's Manual available. (Text)

GARVEY AND ALEINIKOFF'S MODERN CONSTITUTIONAL THEORY: A READER, Second Edition, 559 pages, 1991. Softcover. (Reader)

LOCKHART, KAMISAR, CHOPER AND SHIFFRIN'S CONSTITUTIONAL LAW: CASES–COMMENTS–QUESTIONS, Seventh Edition, 1643 pages, 1991. (Casebook) 1991 Supplement.

LOCKHART, KAMISAR, CHOPER AND SHIFFRIN'S THE AMERICAN CONSTITUTION: CASES AND MATERIALS, Seventh Edition, approximately 1200 pages, 1991. Abridged version of Lockhart, et al., Constitutional Law: Cases–Comments–Questions, Seventh Edition. (Casebook) 1991 Supplement.

LOCKHART, KAMISAR, CHOPER AND SHIFFRIN'S CONSTITUTIONAL RIGHTS AND LIBERTIES: CASES AND MATERIALS, Seventh Edition, approximately 1375 pages, 1991. Reprint from Lockhart, et al., Constitutional Law: Cases–Comments–Questions, Seventh Edition. (Casebook) 1991 Supplement.

MARKS AND COOPER'S STATE CONSTITUTIONAL LAW IN A NUTSHELL, 329 pages, 1988. Softcover. (Text)

NOWAK AND ROTUNDA'S HORNBOOK ON CONSTITUTIONAL LAW, Fourth Edition, 1357 pages, 1991. (Text)

ROTUNDA'S MODERN CONSTITUTIONAL LAW: CASES AND NOTES, Third Edition, 1085 pages, 1989. (Casebook) 1991 Supplement.

VIEIRA'S CONSTITUTIONAL CIVIL RIGHTS IN A NUTSHELL, Second Edition, 322 pages, 1990. Softcover. (Text)

WILLIAMS' CONSTITUTIONAL ANALYSIS IN A NUTSHELL, 388 pages, 1979. Softcover. (Text)

Consumer Law—see also Commercial Law

EPSTEIN AND NICKLES' CONSUMER LAW IN A NUTSHELL, Second Edition, 418 pages, 1981. Softcover. (Text)

Consumer Law—Cont'd

SELECTED COMMERCIAL STATUTES. Softcover. 1851 pages, 1991.

SPANOGLE, ROHNER, PRIDGEN AND RASOR'S CASES AND MATERIALS ON CONSUMER LAW, Second Edition, 916 pages, 1991. Teacher's Manual available. (Casebook)

Contracts

CALAMARI AND PERILLO'S BLACK LETTER ON CONTRACTS, Second Edition, 462 pages, 1990. Softcover. (Review)

CALAMARI AND PERILLO'S HORNBOOK ON CONTRACTS, Third Edition, 1049 pages, 1987. (Text)

CALAMARI, PERILLO AND BENDER'S CASES AND PROBLEMS ON CONTRACTS, Second Edition, 905 pages, 1989. Teacher's Manual Available. (Casebook)

CORBIN'S TEXT ON CONTRACTS, One Volume Student Edition, 1224 pages, 1952. (Text)

FESSLER AND LOISEAUX'S CASES AND MATERIALS ON CONTRACTS—MORALITY, ECONOMICS AND THE MARKET PLACE, 837 pages, 1982. Teacher's Manual available. (Casebook)

FRIEDMAN'S CONTRACT REMEDIES IN A NUTSHELL, 323 pages, 1981. Softcover. (Text)

FULLER AND EISENBERG'S CASES ON BASIC CONTRACT LAW, Fifth Edition, 1037 pages, 1990. (Casebook)

HAMILTON, RAU AND WEINTRAUB'S CASES AND MATERIALS ON CONTRACTS, Second Edition, approximately 850 pages, May, 1992 Pub. (Casebook)

KEYES' GOVERNMENT CONTRACTS IN A NUTSHELL, Second Edition, 557 pages, 1990. Softcover. (Text)

SCHABER AND ROHWER'S CONTRACTS IN A NUTSHELL, Third Edition, 457 pages, 1990. Softcover. (Text)

SUMMERS AND HILLMAN'S CONTRACT AND RELATED OBLIGATION: THEORY, DOCTRINE AND PRACTICE, Second Edition, approximately 1100, March, 1992 Pub. Teacher's Manual available. (Casebook)

Copyright—see Patent and Copyright Law

Corporate Finance—see also Business Planning

HAMILTON'S CASES AND MATERIALS ON COR-PORATION FINANCE, Second Edition, 1221 pages, 1989. (Casebook)

OESTERLE'S THE LAW OF MERGERS, ACQUISITIONS AND REORGANIZATIONS, 1096 pages, 1991. (Casebook)

Corporations

HAMILTON'S BLACK LETTER ON CORPORATIONS, Second Edition, 513 pages, 1986. Softcover. (Review)

HAMILTON'S CASES AND MATERIALS ON CORPORATIONS—INCLUDING PARTNERSHIPS AND LIMITED PARTNERSHIPS, Fourth Edition, 1248 pages, 1990. Teacher's Manual available. (Casebook) 1990 Statutory Supplement.

HAMILTON'S THE LAW OF CORPORATIONS IN A NUTSHELL, Third Edition, 518 pages, 1991. Softcover. (Text)

HENN'S TEACHING MATERIALS ON THE LAW OF CORPORATIONS, Second Edition, 1204 pages, 1986. Teacher's Manual available. (Casebook)

Statutory Supplement. *See Selected Corporation and Partnership*

HENN AND ALEXANDER'S HORNBOOK ON LAWS OF CORPORATIONS, Third Edition, Student Edition, 1371 pages, 1983, with 1986 pocket part. (Text)

SELECTED CORPORATION AND PARTNERSHIP STATUTES, RULES AND FORMS. Softcover. 937 pages, 1991.

SOLOMON, SCHWARTZ AND BAUMAN'S MATERIALS AND PROBLEMS ON CORPORATIONS: LAW AND POLICY, Second Edition, 1391 pages, 1988. Teacher's Manual available. (Casebook) 1990 Supplement.

Statutory Supplement. *See Selected Corporation and Partnership*

Corrections

KRANTZ' THE LAW OF CORRECTIONS AND PRISONERS' RIGHTS IN A NUTSHELL, Third Edition, 407 pages, 1988. Softcover. (Text)

KRANTZ AND BRANHAM'S CASES AND MATERIALS ON THE LAW OF SENTENCING, CORRECTIONS AND PRISONERS' RIGHTS, Fourth Edition, 619 pages, 1991. Teacher's Manual available. (Casebook)

ROBBINS' CASES AND MATERIALS ON POST-CONVICTION REMEDIES, 506 pages, 1982.

Corrections—Cont'd

(Casebook)

Creditors' Rights

BANKRUPTCY CODE, RULES AND OFFICIAL FORMS, LAW SCHOOL EDITION. 909 pages, 1991. Softcover.

EPSTEIN'S DEBTOR-CREDITOR LAW IN A NUT-SHELL, Fourth Edition, 401 pages, 1991. Softcover. (Text)

EPSTEIN, LANDERS AND NICKLES' CASES AND MATERIALS ON DEBTORS AND CREDITORS, Third Edition, 1059 pages, 1987. Teacher's Manual available. (Casebook)

LoPUCKI'S PLAYER'S MANUAL FOR THE DEBTOR-CREDITOR GAME, 123 pages, 1985. Softcover. (Coursebook)

NICKLES AND EPSTEIN'S BLACK LETTER ON CREDITORS' RIGHTS AND BANKRUPTCY, 576 pages, 1989. (Review)

RIESENFELD'S CASES AND MATERIALS ON CREDITORS' REMEDIES AND DEBTORS' PROTECTION, Fourth Edition, 914 pages, 1987. (Casebook) 1990 Supplement.

WHITE'S CASES AND MATERIALS ON BANK-RUPTCY AND CREDITORS' RIGHTS, 812 pages, 1985. Teacher's Manual available. (Casebook) 1987 Supplement.

Criminal Law and Criminal Procedure—see also Corrections, Juvenile Justice

ABRAMS' FEDERAL CRIMINAL LAW AND ITS ENFORCEMENT, 866 pages, 1986. (Casebook) 1988 Supplement.

AMERICAN CRIMINAL JUSTICE PROCESS: SELECTED RULES, STATUTES AND GUIDELINES. 723 pages, 1989. Softcover.

DIX AND SHARLOT'S CASES AND MATERIALS ON CRIMINAL LAW, Third Edition, 846 pages, 1987. (Casebook)

GRANO'S PROBLEMS IN CRIMINAL PROCEDURE, Second Edition, 176 pages, 1981. Teacher's Manual available. Softcover. (Coursebook)

HEYMANN AND KENETY'S THE MURDER TRIAL OF WILBUR JACKSON: A HOMICIDE IN THE FAMILY, Second Edition, 347 pages, 1985. (Coursebook)

ISRAEL, KAMISAR AND LaFAVE'S CRIMINAL PROCEDURE AND THE CONSTITUTION: LEADING

SUPREME COURT CASES AND INTRODUCTORY TEXT. 767 pages, 1991 Edition. Softcover. (Casebook)

ISRAEL AND LaFAVE'S CRIMINAL PROCEDURE—CONSTITUTIONAL LIMITATIONS IN A NUTSHELL, Fourth Edition, 461 pages, 1988. Softcover. (Text)

JOHNSON'S CASES, MATERIALS AND TEXT ON CRIMINAL LAW, Fourth Edition, 759 pages, 1990. Teacher's Manual available. (Casebook)

JOHNSON'S CASES AND MATERIALS ON CRIMINAL PROCEDURE, 859 pages, 1988. (Casebook) 1991 Supplement.

KAMISAR, LaFAVE AND ISRAEL'S MODERN CRIMINAL PROCEDURE: CASES, COMMENTS AND QUESTIONS, Seventh Edition, 1593 pages, 1990. (Casebook) 1991 Supplement.

KAMISAR, LaFAVE AND ISRAEL'S BASIC CRIMINAL PROCEDURE: CASES, COMMENTS AND QUESTIONS, Seventh Edition, 792 pages, 1990. Softcover reprint from Kamisar, et al., Modern Criminal Procedure: Cases, Comments and Questions, Seventh Edition. (Casebook) 1991 Supplement.

LaFAVE'S MODERN CRIMINAL LAW: CASES, COMMENTS AND QUESTIONS, Second Edition, 903 pages, 1988. (Casebook)

LaFAVE AND ISRAEL'S HORNBOOK ON CRIMINAL PROCEDURE, Second Edition, approximately 1350 pages, 1992. (Text)

LaFAVE AND SCOTT'S HORNBOOK ON CRIMINAL LAW, Second Edition, 918 pages, 1986. (Text)

LOEWY'S CRIMINAL LAW IN A NUTSHELL, Second Edition, 321 pages, 1987. Softcover. (Text)

LOW'S BLACK LETTER ON CRIMINAL LAW, Revised First Edition, 443 pages, 1990. Softcover. (Review)

SALTZBURG AND CAPRA'S CASES AND COMMENTARY ON AMERICAN CRIMINAL PROCEDURE, Fourth Edition, approximately 1300 pages, May, 1992 Pub. Teacher's Manual available. (Casebook)

VORENBERG'S CASES ON CRIMINAL LAW AND PROCEDURE, Second Edition, 1088 pages, 1981. Teacher's Manual available. (Casebook) 1990 Supplement.

Domestic Relations

CLARK'S HORNBOOK ON DOMESTIC RELATIONS, Second Edition, Student Edition, 1050 pages, 1988. (Text)

CLARK AND GLOWINSKY'S CASES AND PROBLEMS ON DOMESTIC RELATIONS, Fourth Edition. 1150 pages, 1990. Teacher's Manual available. (Casebook)

KRAUSE'S BLACK LETTER ON FAMILY LAW, 314 pages, 1988. Softcover. (Review)

KRAUSE'S CASES, COMMENTS AND QUESTIONS ON FAMILY LAW, Third Edition, 1433 pages, 1990. (Casebook)

KRAUSE'S FAMILY LAW IN A NUTSHELL, Second Edition, 444 pages, 1986. Softcover. (Text)

KRAUSKOPF'S CASES ON PROPERTY DIVISION AT MARRIAGE DISSOLUTION, 250 pages, 1984. Softcover. (Casebook)

Economics, Law and—see also Antitrust, Regulated Industries

BARNES AND STOUT'S CASES AND MATERIALS ON LAW AND ECONOMICS, Approximately 550 pages, March, 1992 Pub. (Casebook)

GOETZ' CASES AND MATERIALS ON LAW AND ECONOMICS, 547 pages, 1984. (Casebook)

MALLOY'S LAW AND ECONOMICS: A COMPARATIVE APPROACH TO THEORY AND PRACTICE, 166 pages, 1990. Softcover. (Text)

Education Law

ALEXANDER AND ALEXANDER'S THE LAW OF SCHOOLS, STUDENTS AND TEACHERS IN A NUTSHELL, 409 pages, 1984. Softcover. (Text)

YUDOF, KIRP AND LEVIN'S EDUCATIONAL POLICY AND THE LAW, Third Edition, 860 pages, 1992. (Casebook)

Employment Discrimination—see also Gender Discrimination

ESTREICHER AND HARPER'S CASES AND MATERIALS ON THE LAW GOVERNING THE EMPLOYMENT RELATIONSHIP, 962 pages, 1990. Teacher's Manual available. (Casebook) Statutory Supplement. 1991 Supplement.

JONES, MURPHY AND BELTON'S CASES AND MATERIALS ON DISCRIMINATION IN EMPLOYMENT, (The Labor Law Group). Fifth Edition, 1116 pages, 1987. (Casebook) 1990 Supplement.

PLAYER'S FEDERAL LAW OF EMPLOYMENT DISCRIMINATION IN A NUTSHELL, Third Edition, approximately 270 pages, 1992. Softcover. (Text)

PLAYER'S HORNBOOK ON EMPLOYMENT DISCRIMINATION LAW, Student Edition, 708 pages, 1988. (Text)

PLAYER, SHOBEN AND LIEBERWITZ' CASES AND MATERIALS ON EMPLOYMENT DISCRIMINATION LAW, 827 pages, 1990. Teacher's Manual available. (Casebook)

Energy and Natural Resources Law—see also Oil and Gas

LAITOS' CASES AND MATERIALS ON NATURAL RESOURCES LAW, 938 pages, 1985. Teacher's Manual available. (Casebook)

LAITOS AND TOMAIN'S ENERGY AND NATURAL RESOURCES LAW IN A NUTSHELL, Approximately 525 pages, 1992. Softcover. (Text)

SELECTED ENVIRONMENTAL LAW STATUTES—EDUCATIONAL EDITION. Softcover. 1256 pages, 1991.

Environmental Law—see also Energy and Natural Resources Law; Sea, Law of

BONINE AND MCGARITY'S THE LAW OF ENVIRONMENTAL PROTECTION: CASES—LEGISLATION—POLICIES, Second Edition, approximately 1050 pages, 1992. (Casebook)

FINDLEY AND FARBER'S CASES AND MATERIALS ON ENVIRONMENTAL LAW, Third Edition, 763 pages, 1991. (Casebook)

FINDLEY AND FARBER'S ENVIRONMENTAL LAW IN A NUTSHELL, Third Edition, approximately 375 pages, February, 1992 Pub. Softcover. (Text)

PLATER, ABRAMS AND GOLDFARB'S ENVIRONMENTAL LAW AND POLICY: NATURE, LAW AND SOCIETY, Approximately 950 pages, 1992. Teacher's Manual available. (Casebook)

RODGERS' HORNBOOK ON ENVIRONMENTAL LAW, 956 pages, 1977, with 1984 pocket part. (Text)

SELECTED ENVIRONMENTAL LAW STATUTES—EDUCATIONAL EDITION. Softcover. 1256 pages, 1991.

Equity—see Remedies

Estate Planning—see also Trusts and Estates; Taxation—Estate and Gift

LYNN'S AN INTRODUCTION TO ESTATE PLANNING IN A NUTSHELL, Third Edition, 370 pages, 1983. Softcover. (Text)

Evidence

BROUN AND BLAKEY'S BLACK LETTER ON EVIDENCE, 269 pages, 1984. Softcover. (Review)

BROUN, MEISENHOLDER, STRONG AND MOSTELLER'S PROBLEMS IN EVIDENCE, Third Edition, 238 pages, 1988. Teacher's Manual available. Softcover. (Coursebook)

CLEARY, STRONG, BROUN AND MOSTELLER'S CASES AND MATERIALS ON EVIDENCE, Fourth Edition, 1060 pages, 1988. (Casebook)

FEDERAL RULES OF EVIDENCE FOR UNITED STATES COURTS AND MAGISTRATES. Softcover. 381 pages, 1990.

FRIEDMAN'S THE ELEMENTS OF EVIDENCE, 315 pages, 1991. Teacher's Manual available. (Coursebook)

GRAHAM'S FEDERAL RULES OF EVIDENCE IN A NUTSHELL, Third Edition, approximately 475 pages, 1992. Softcover. (Text)

LEMPERT AND SALTZBURG'S A MODERN APPROACH TO EVIDENCE: TEXT, PROBLEMS, TRANSCRIPTS AND CASES, Second Edition, 1232 pages, 1983. Teacher's Manual available. (Casebook)

LILLY'S AN INTRODUCTION TO THE LAW OF EVIDENCE, Second Edition, 585 pages, 1987. (Text)

McCORMICK, SUTTON AND WELLBORN'S CASES AND MATERIALS ON EVIDENCE, Sixth Edition, 1067 pages, 1987. (Casebook)

McCORMICK'S HORNBOOK ON EVIDENCE, Fourth Edition, Student Edition, approximately 1150 pages, March, 1992 Pub. (Text)

ROTHSTEIN'S EVIDENCE IN A NUTSHELL: STATE AND FEDERAL RULES, Second Edition, 514 pages, 1981. Softcover. (Text)

Federal Jurisdiction and Procedure

CURRIE'S CASES AND MATERIALS ON FEDERAL COURTS, Fourth Edition, 783 pages, 1990. (Casebook)

CURRIE'S FEDERAL JURISDICTION IN A NUTSHELL, Third Edition, 242 pages, 1990.

Softcover. (Text)

FEDERAL RULES OF CIVIL PROCEDURE—EDUCATIONAL EDITION. Softcover. 816 pages, 1991.

REDISH'S BLACK LETTER ON FEDERAL JURISDICTION, Second Edition, 234 pages, 1991. Softcover. (Review)

REDISH'S CASES, COMMENTS AND QUESTIONS ON FEDERAL COURTS, Second Edition, 1122 pages, 1989. (Casebook) 1990 Supplement.

VETRI AND MERRILL'S FEDERAL COURTS PROBLEMS AND MATERIALS, Second Edition, 232 pages, 1984. Softcover. (Coursebook)

WRIGHT'S HORNBOOK ON FEDERAL COURTS, Fourth Edition, Student Edition, 870 pages, 1983. (Text)

First Amendment

SHIFFRIN AND CHOPER'S FIRST AMENDMENT, CASES—COMMENTS—QUESTIONS, 759 pages, 1991. Softcover. (Casebook) 1991 Supplement.

Foreign Relations and National Security Law

FRANCK AND GLENNON'S FOREIGN RELATIONS AND NATIONAL SECURITY LAW, 941 pages, 1987. (Casebook)

Future Interests—see Trusts and Estates

Gender Discrimination—see also Employment Discrimination

KAY'S TEXT, CASES AND MATERIALS ON SEX-BASED DISCRIMINATION, Third Edition, 1001 pages, 1988. (Casebook) 1990 Supplement.

THOMAS' SEX DISCRIMINATION IN A NUTSHELL, Second Edition, 395 pages, 1991. Softcover. (Text)

Health Law—see Medicine, Law and

Human Rights—see International Law

Immigration Law

ALEINIKOFF AND MARTIN'S IMMIGRATION: PROCESS AND POLICY, Second Edition, 1056 pages, 1991. (Casebook)

    Statutory Supplement. *See Immigration and Nationality Laws*

IMMIGRATION AND NATIONALITY LAWS OF THE UNITED STATES: SELECTED STATUTES, REGULATIONS AND FORMS. Softcover. 477 pages,

Immigration Law—Cont'd
1991.

WEISSBRODT'S IMMIGRATION LAW AND PROCEDURE IN A NUTSHELL, Second Edition, 438 pages, 1989, Softcover. (Text)

Indian Law—see American Indian Law

Insurance Law
DEVINE AND TERRY'S PROBLEMS IN INSURANCE LAW, 240 pages, 1989. Softcover. Teacher's Manual available. (Coursebook)

DOBBYN'S INSURANCE LAW IN A NUTSHELL, Second Edition, 316 pages, 1989. Softcover. (Text)

KEETON'S CASES ON BASIC INSURANCE LAW, Second Edition, 1086 pages, 1977. Teacher's Manual available. (Casebook)

KEETON'S COMPUTER-AIDED AND WORKBOOK EXERCISES ON INSURANCE LAW, 255 pages, 1990. Softcover. (Coursebook)

KEETON AND WIDISS' INSURANCE LAW, Student Edition, 1359 pages, 1988. (Text)

WIDISS AND KEETON'S COURSE SUPPLEMENT TO KEETON AND WIDISS' INSURANCE LAW, 502 pages, 1988. Softcover. Teacher's Manual available. (Casebook)

WIDISS' INSURANCE: MATERIALS ON FUNDAMENTAL PRINCIPLES, LEGAL DOCTRINES AND REGULATORY ACTS, 1186 pages, 1989. Teacher's Manual available. (Casebook)

YORK AND WHELAN'S CASES, MATERIALS AND PROBLEMS ON GENERAL PRACTICE INSURANCE LAW, Second Edition, 787 pages, 1988. Teacher's Manual available. (Casebook)

International Law—see also Sea, Law of
BUERGENTHAL'S INTERNATIONAL HUMAN RIGHTS IN A NUTSHELL, 283 pages, 1988. Softcover. (Text)

BUERGENTHAL AND MAIER'S PUBLIC INTERNATIONAL LAW IN A NUTSHELL, Second Edition, 275 pages, 1990. Softcover. (Text)

FOLSOM'S EUROPEAN COMMUNITY LAW IN A NUTSHELL, Approximately 425 pages, 1992. Softcover. (Text)

FOLSOM, GORDON AND SPANOGLE'S INTERNATIONAL BUSINESS TRANSACTIONS—A PROBLEM-ORIENTED COURSEBOOK, Second Edition, 1237 pages, 1991. Teacher's Manual available. (Casebook) 1991 Documents

Supplement.

FOLSOM, GORDON AND SPANOGLE'S INTERNATIONAL BUSINESS TRANSACTIONS IN A NUTSHELL, Third Edition, 509 pages, 1988. Softcover. (Text)

HENKIN, PUGH, SCHACHTER AND SMIT'S CASES AND MATERIALS ON INTERNATIONAL LAW, Second Edition, 1517 pages, 1987. (Casebook) Documents Supplement.

JACKSON AND DAVEY'S CASES, MATERIALS AND TEXT ON LEGAL PROBLEMS OF INTERNATIONAL ECONOMIC RELATIONS, Second Edition, 1269 pages, 1986. (Casebook) 1989 Documents Supplement.

KIRGIS' INTERNATIONAL ORGANIZATIONS IN THEIR LEGAL SETTING, 1016 pages, 1977. Teacher's Manual available. (Casebook) 1981 Supplement.

WESTON, FALK AND D'AMATO'S INTERNATIONAL LAW AND WORLD ORDER—A PROBLEM-ORIENTED COURSEBOOK, Second Edition, 1335 pages, 1990. Teacher's Manual available. (Casebook) Documents Supplement.

Interviewing and Counseling
BINDER AND PRICE'S LEGAL INTERVIEWING AND COUNSELING, 232 pages, 1977. Softcover. Teacher's Manual available. (Coursebook)

BINDER, BERGMAN AND PRICE'S LAWYERS AS COUNSELORS: A CLIENT–CENTERED APPROACH, 427 pages, 1991. Softcover. (Coursebook)

SHAFFER AND ELKINS' LEGAL INTERVIEWING AND COUNSELING IN A NUTSHELL, Second Edition, 487 pages, 1987. Softcover. (Text)

Introduction to Law—see Legal Method and Legal System

Introduction to Law Study
HEGLAND'S INTRODUCTION TO THE STUDY AND PRACTICE OF LAW IN A NUTSHELL, 418 pages, 1983. Softcover. (Text)

KINYON'S INTRODUCTION TO LAW STUDY AND LAW EXAMINATIONS IN A NUTSHELL, 389 pages, 1971. Softcover. (Text)

Judicial Process—see Legal Method and Legal System

Jurisprudence

CHRISTIE'S JURISPRUDENCE—TEXT AND READINGS ON THE PHILOSOPHY OF LAW, 1056 pages, 1973. (Casebook)

Juvenile Justice

FOX'S JUVENILE COURTS IN A NUTSHELL, Third Edition, 291 pages, 1984. Softcover. (Text)

Labor and Employment Law—see also Employment Discrimination, Workers' Compensation

FINKIN, GOLDMAN AND SUMMERS' LEGAL PROTECTION OF INDIVIDUAL EMPLOYEES, (The Labor Law Group). 1164 pages, 1989. (Casebook)

GORMAN'S BASIC TEXT ON LABOR LAW—UNIONIZATION AND COLLECTIVE BARGAINING, 914 pages, 1976. (Text)

LESLIE'S LABOR LAW IN A NUTSHELL, Third Edition, approximately 400 pages, 1992. Softcover. (Text)

NOLAN'S LABOR ARBITRATION LAW AND PRACTICE IN A NUTSHELL, 358 pages, 1979. Softcover. (Text)

OBERER, HANSLOWE, ANDERSEN AND HEINSZ' CASES AND MATERIALS ON LABOR LAW—COLLECTIVE BARGAINING IN A FREE SOCIETY, Third Edition, 1163 pages, 1986. Teacher's Manual available. (Casebook) Statutory Supplement. 1991 Case Supplement.

RABIN, SILVERSTEIN AND SCHATZKI'S LABOR AND EMPLOYMENT LAW: PROBLEMS, CASES AND MATERIALS IN THE LAW OF WORK, (The Labor Law Group). 1014 pages, 1988. Teacher's Manual available. (Casebook) 1988 Statutory Supplement.

Land Finance—Property Security—see Real Estate Transactions

Land Use

CALLIES AND FREILICH'S CASES AND MATERIALS ON LAND USE, 1233 pages, 1986. (Casebook) 1991 Supplement.

HAGMAN AND JUERGENSMEYER'S HORNBOOK ON URBAN PLANNING AND LAND DEVELOPMENT CONTROL LAW, Second Edition, Student Edition, 680 pages, 1986. (Text)

WRIGHT AND GITELMAN'S CASES AND MATERIALS ON LAND USE, Fourth Edition, 1255 pages, 1991. Teacher's Manual available.

(Casebook)

WRIGHT AND WRIGHT'S LAND USE IN A NUTSHELL, Second Edition, 356 pages, 1985. Softcover. (Text)

Legal History—see also Legal Method and Legal System

PRESSER AND ZAINALDIN'S CASES AND MATERIALS ON LAW AND JURISPRUDENCE IN AMERICAN HISTORY, Second Edition, 1092 pages, 1989. Teacher's Manual available. (Casebook)

Legal Method and Legal System—see also Legal Research, Legal Writing

ALDISERT'S READINGS, MATERIALS AND CASES IN THE JUDICIAL PROCESS, 948 pages, 1976. (Casebook)

BERCH AND BERCH'S INTRODUCTION TO LEGAL METHOD AND PROCESS, 550 pages, 1985. Teacher's Manual available. (Casebook)

BODENHEIMER, OAKLEY AND LOVE'S READINGS AND CASES ON AN INTRODUCTION TO THE ANGLO-AMERICAN LEGAL SYSTEM, Second Edition, 166 pages, 1988. Softcover. (Casebook)

DAVIES AND LAWRY'S INSTITUTIONS AND METHODS OF THE LAW—INTRODUCTORY TEACHING MATERIALS, 547 pages, 1982. Teacher's Manual available. (Casebook)

DVORKIN, HIMMELSTEIN AND LESNICK'S BECOMING A LAWYER: A HUMANISTIC PERSPECTIVE ON LEGAL EDUCATION AND PROFESSIONALISM, 211 pages, 1981. Softcover. (Text)

KEETON'S JUDGING, 842 pages, 1990. Softcover. (Coursebook)

KELSO AND KELSO'S STUDYING LAW: AN INTRODUCTION, 587 pages, 1984. (Coursebook)

KEMPIN'S HISTORICAL INTRODUCTION TO ANGLO-AMERICAN LAW IN A NUTSHELL, Third Edition, 323 pages, 1990. Softcover. (Text)

MEADOR'S AMERICAN COURTS, 113 pages, 1991. Softcover. (Text)

REYNOLDS' JUDICIAL PROCESS IN A NUTSHELL, Second Edition, 308 pages, 1991. Softcover. (Text)

Legal Research

COHEN'S LEGAL RESEARCH IN A NUTSHELL, Fourth Edition, 452 pages, 1985. Soft-

Legal Research—Cont'd

cover. (Text)

COHEN, BERRING AND OLSON'S HOW TO FIND THE LAW, Ninth Edition, 716 pages, 1989. (Text)

COHEN, BERRING AND OLSON'S FINDING THE LAW, 570 pages, 1989. Softcover reprint from Cohen, Berring and Olson's How to Find the Law, Ninth Edition. (Coursebook)

Legal Research Exercises, 3rd Ed., for use with Cohen, Berring and Olson, 229 pages, 1989. Teacher's Manual available.

ROMBAUER'S LEGAL PROBLEM SOLVING—ANALYSIS, RESEARCH AND WRITING, Fifth Edition, 524 pages, 1991. Softcover. Teacher's Manual with problems available. (Coursebook)

STATSKY'S LEGAL RESEARCH AND WRITING, Third Edition, 257 pages, 1986. Softcover. (Coursebook)

TEPLY'S LEGAL RESEARCH AND CITATION, Third Edition, 472 pages, 1989. Softcover. (Coursebook)

Student Library Exercises, 3rd ed., 391 pages, 1989. Answer Key available.

Legal Writing and Drafting

CHILD'S DRAFTING LEGAL DOCUMENTS: PRINCIPLES AND PRACTICES, Second Edition, approximately 300 pages, April, 1992 Pub. Softcover. Teacher's Manual available. (Coursebook)

DICKERSON'S MATERIALS ON LEGAL DRAFTING, 425 pages, 1981. Teacher's Manual available. (Coursebook)

FELSENFELD AND SIEGEL'S WRITING CONTRACTS IN PLAIN ENGLISH, 290 pages, 1981. Softcover. (Text)

GOPEN'S WRITING FROM A LEGAL PERSPECTIVE, 225 pages, 1981. (Text)

MARTINEAU'S DRAFTING LEGISLATION AND RULES IN PLAIN ENGLISH, 155 pages, 1991. Softcover. Teacher's Manual available. (Text)

MELLINKOFF'S DICTIONARY OF AMERICAN LEGAL USAGE, Approximately 900 pages, March, 1992 Pub. (Text)

MELLINKOFF'S LEGAL WRITING—SENSE AND

NONSENSE, 242 pages, 1982. Softcover. Teacher's Manual available. (Text)

PRATT'S LEGAL WRITING: A SYSTEMATIC APPROACH, 468 pages, 1990. Teacher's Manual available. (Coursebook)

RAY AND COX'S BEYOND THE BASICS: A TEXT FOR ADVANCED LEGAL WRITING, 427 pages, 1991. Softcover. Teacher's Manual available. (Text)

RAY AND RAMSFIELD'S LEGAL WRITING: GETTING IT RIGHT AND GETTING IT WRITTEN, 250 pages, 1987. Softcover. (Text)

SQUIRES AND ROMBAUER'S LEGAL WRITING IN A NUTSHELL, 294 pages, 1982. Softcover. (Text)

STATSKY AND WERNET'S CASE ANALYSIS AND FUNDAMENTALS OF LEGAL WRITING, Third Edition, 424 pages, 1989. Teacher's Manual available. (Text)

TEPLY'S LEGAL WRITING, ANALYSIS AND ORAL ARGUMENT, 576 pages, 1990. Softcover. Teacher's Manual available. (Coursebook)

WEIHOFEN'S LEGAL WRITING STYLE, Second Edition, 332 pages, 1980. (Text)

Legislation—see also Legal Writing and Drafting

DAVIES' LEGISLATIVE LAW AND PROCESS IN A NUTSHELL, Second Edition, 346 pages, 1986. Softcover. (Text)

ESKRIDGE AND FRICKEY'S CASES AND MATERIALS ON LEGISLATION: STATUTES AND THE CREATION OF PUBLIC POLICY, 937 pages, 1988. Teacher's Manual available. (Casebook) 1990 Supplement.

NUTTING AND DICKERSON'S CASES AND MATERIALS ON LEGISLATION, Fifth Edition, 744 pages, 1978. (Casebook)

STATSKY'S LEGISLATIVE ANALYSIS AND DRAFTING, Second Edition, 217 pages, 1984. Teacher's Manual available. (Text)

Local Government

FRUG'S CASES AND MATERIALS ON LOCAL GOVERNMENT LAW, 1005 pages, 1988. (Casebook) 1991 Supplement.

MCCARTHY'S LOCAL GOVERNMENT LAW IN A NUTSHELL, Third Edition, 435 pages, 1990. Softcover. (Text)

REYNOLDS' HORNBOOK ON LOCAL GOVERN-

Local Government—Cont'd

MENT LAW, 860 pages, 1982, with 1990 pocket part. (Text)

VALENTE AND MCCARTHY'S CASES AND MATERIALS ON LOCAL GOVERNMENT LAW, Fourth Edition, approximately 1150 pages, 1992. Teacher's Manual available. (Casebook)

Mass Communication Law

GILLMOR, BARRON, SIMON AND TERRY'S CASES AND COMMENT ON MASS COMMUNICATION LAW, Fifth Edition, 947 pages, 1990. (Casebook)

GINSBURG, BOTEIN AND DIRECTOR'S REGULATION OF THE ELECTRONIC MASS MEDIA: LAW AND POLICY FOR RADIO, TELEVISION, CABLE AND THE NEW VIDEO TECHNOLOGIES, Second Edition, 657 pages, 1991. (Casebook) Statutory Supplement.

ZUCKMAN, GAYNES, CARTER AND DEE'S MASS COMMUNICATIONS LAW IN A NUTSHELL, Third Edition, 538 pages, 1988. Softcover. (Text)

Medicine, Law and

FISCINA, BOUMIL, SHARPE AND HEAD'S MEDICAL LIABILITY, 487 pages, 1991. Teacher's Manual available. (Casebook)

FURROW, JOHNSON, JOST AND SCHWARTZ' HEALTH LAW: CASES, MATERIALS AND PROBLEMS, Second Edition, 1236 pages, 1991. Teacher's Manual available. (Casebook)

FURROW, JOHNSON, JOST AND SCHWARTZ' BIOETHICS: HEALTH CARE LAW AND ETHICS, Reprint from Furrow et al., Health Law, Second Edition. Softcover. Teacher's Manual available. (Casebook)

FURROW, JOHNSON, JOST AND SCHWARTZ' THE LAW OF HEALTH CARE ORGANIZATION AND FINANCE,Reprint from Furrow et al., Health Law, Second Edition. Softcover. Teacher's Manual available.

FURROW, JOHNSON, JOST AND SCHWARTZ' LIABILITY AND QUALITY ISSUES IN HEALTH CARE, Reprint from Furrow et al., Health Law, Second Edition. Softcover. Teacher's Manual available. (Casebook)

HALL AND ELLMAN'S HEALTH CARE LAW AND ETHICS IN A NUTSHELL, 401 pages, 1990. Softcover (Text)

JARVIS, CLOSEN, HERMANN AND LEONARD'S AIDS LAW IN A NUTSHELL, 349 pages, 1991. Softcover. (Text)

KING'S THE LAW OF MEDICAL MALPRACTICE IN A NUTSHELL, Second Edition, 342 pages, 1986. Softcover. (Text)

SHAPIRO AND SPECE'S CASES, MATERIALS AND PROBLEMS ON BIOETHICS AND LAW, 892 pages, 1981. (Casebook) 1991 Supplement.

Military Law

SHANOR AND TERRELL'S MILITARY LAW IN A NUTSHELL, 378 pages, 1980. Softcover. (Text)

Mortgages—see Real Estate Transactions

Natural Resources Law—see Energy and Natural Resources Law, Environmental Law

Negotiation

GIFFORD'S LEGAL NEGOTIATION: THEORY AND APPLICATIONS, 225 pages, 1989. Softcover. (Text)

TEPLY'S LEGAL NEGOTIATION IN A NUTSHELL, Approximately 250 pages, 1992. Softcover. (Text)

WILLIAMS' LEGAL NEGOTIATION AND SETTLEMENT, 207 pages, 1983. Softcover. Teacher's Manual available. (Coursebook)

Office Practice—see also Computers and Law, Interviewing and Counseling, Negotiation

HEGLAND'S TRIAL AND PRACTICE SKILLS IN A NUTSHELL, 346 pages, 1978. Softcover (Text)

MUNNEKE'S LAW PRACTICE MANAGEMENT: MATERIALS AND CASES, 634 pages, 1991. Teacher's Manual available. (Casebook)

Oil and Gas—see also Energy and Natural Resources Law

HEMINGWAY'S HORNBOOK ON THE LAW OF OIL AND GAS, Third Edition, Student Edition, approximately 700 pages, 1992. (Text)

KUNTZ, LOWE, ANDERSON AND SMITH'S CASES AND MATERIALS ON OIL AND GAS LAW, 857 pages, 1986. Teacher's Manual available. (Casebook) Forms Manual. Revised.

LOWE'S OIL AND GAS LAW IN A NUTSHELL,

Oil and Gas—Cont'd

Second Edition, 465 pages, 1988. Softcover. (Text)

Partnership—see Agency—Partnership

Patent and Copyright Law

CHOATE, FRANCIS AND COLLINS' CASES AND MATERIALS ON PATENT LAW, INCLUDING TRADE SECRETS, COPYRIGHTS, TRADEMARKS, Third Edition, 1009 pages, 1987. (Casebook)

HALPERN, SHIPLEY AND ABRAMS' CASES AND MATERIALS ON COPYRIGHT, Approximately 700 pages, April, 1992 Pub. (Casebook)

MILLER AND DAVIS' INTELLECTUAL PROPERTY—PATENTS, TRADEMARKS AND COPYRIGHT IN A NUTSHELL, Second Edition, 437 pages, 1990. Softcover. (Text)

NIMMER, MARCUS, MYERS AND NIMMER'S CASES AND MATERIALS ON COPYRIGHT AND OTHER ASPECTS OF ENTERTAINMENT LITIGATION—INCLUDING UNFAIR COMPETITION, DEFAMATION, PRIVACY, ILLUSTRATED, Fourth Edition, 1177 pages, 1991. (Casebook) Statutory Supplement. See *Selected Intellectual Property Statutes*

SELECTED INTELLECTUAL PROPERTY AND UNFAIR COMPETITION STATUTES, REGULATIONS AND TREATIES. Softcover.

Products Liability

FISCHER AND POWERS' CASES AND MATERIALS ON PRODUCTS LIABILITY, 685 pages, 1988. Teacher's Manual available. (Casebook)

PHILLIPS' PRODUCTS LIABILITY IN A NUTSHELL, Third Edition, 307 pages, 1988. Softcover. (Text)

Professional Responsibility

ARONSON, DEVINE AND FISCH'S PROBLEMS, CASES AND MATERIALS IN PROFESSIONAL RESPONSIBILITY, 745 pages, 1985. Teacher's Manual available. (Casebook)

ARONSON AND WECKSTEIN'S PROFESSIONAL RESPONSIBILITY IN A NUTSHELL, Second Edition, 514 pages, 1991. Softcover. (Text)

MELLINKOFF'S THE CONSCIENCE OF A LAWYER, 304 pages, 1973. (Text)

PIRSIG AND KIRWIN'S CASES AND MATERIALS ON PROFESSIONAL RESPONSIBILITY, Fourth Edition, 603 pages, 1984. Teacher's Manual available. (Casebook)

ROTUNDA'S BLACK LETTER ON PROFESSIONAL RESPONSIBILITY, Third Edition, approximately 400 pages, 1992. Softcover. (Review)

SCHWARTZ AND WYDICK'S PROBLEMS IN LEGAL ETHICS, Second Edition, 341 pages, 1988. (Coursebook)

SELECTED STATUTES, RULES AND STANDARDS ON THE LEGAL PROFESSION. Softcover. 844 pages, 1991.

SMITH AND MALLEN'S PREVENTING LEGAL MALPRACTICE, 264 pages, 1989. Reprint from Mallen and Smith's Legal Malpractice, Third Edition. (Text)

SUTTON AND DZIENKOWSKI'S CASES AND MATERIALS ON PROFESSIONAL RESPONSIBILITY FOR LAWYERS, 839 pages, 1989. Teacher's Manual available. (Casebook)

WOLFRAM'S HORNBOOK ON MODERN LEGAL ETHICS, Student Edition, 1120 pages, 1986. (Text)

Property—see also Real Estate Transactions, Land Use, Trusts and Estates

BERNHARDT'S BLACK LETTER ON PROPERTY, Second Edition, 388 pages, 1991. Softcover. (Review)

BERNHARDT'S REAL PROPERTY IN A NUTSHELL, Second Edition, 448 pages, 1981. Softcover. (Text)

BOYER, HOVENKAMP AND KURTZ' THE LAW OF PROPERTY, AN INTRODUCTORY SURVEY, Fourth Edition, 696 pages, 1991. (Text)

BROWDER, CUNNINGHAM, NELSON, STOEBUCK AND WHITMAN'S CASES ON BASIC PROPERTY LAW, Fifth Edition, 1386 pages, 1989. Teacher's Manual available. (Casebook)

BRUCE, ELY AND BOSTICK'S CASES AND MATERIALS ON MODERN PROPERTY LAW, Second Edition, 953 pages, 1989. Teacher's Manual available. (Casebook)

BURKE'S PERSONAL PROPERTY IN A NUTSHELL, 322 pages, 1983. Softcover. (Text)

CUNNINGHAM, STOEBUCK AND WHITMAN'S HORNBOOK ON THE LAW OF PROPERTY, Student Edition, 916 pages, 1984, with 1987 pocket part. (Text)

DONAHUE, KAUPER AND MARTIN'S CASES ON PROPERTY, Second Edition, 1362 pages,

Property—Cont'd

1983. Teacher's Manual available. (Casebook)

HILL'S LANDLORD AND TENANT LAW IN A NUTSHELL, Second Edition, 311 pages, 1986. Softcover. (Text)

JOHNSON, JOST, SALSICH AND SHAFFER'S PROPERTY LAW, CASES, MATERIALS AND PROBLEMS, Approximately 925 pages, April, 1992 Pub. (Casebook)

KURTZ AND HOVENKAMP'S CASES AND MATERIALS ON AMERICAN PROPERTY LAW, 1296 pages, 1987. Teacher's Manual available. (Casebook) 1991 Supplement.

MOYNIHAN'S INTRODUCTION TO REAL PROPERTY, Second Edition, 239 pages, 1988. (Text)

Psychiatry, Law and

REISNER AND SLOBOGIN'S LAW AND THE MENTAL HEALTH SYSTEM, CIVIL AND CRIMINAL ASPECTS, Second Edition, 1117 pages, 1990. (Casebook)

Real Estate Transactions

BRUCE'S REAL ESTATE FINANCE IN A NUTSHELL, Third Edition, 287 pages, 1991. Softcover. (Text)

MAXWELL, RIESENFELD, HETLAND AND WARREN'S CASES ON CALIFORNIA SECURITY TRANSACTIONS IN LAND, Fourth Edition, approximately 775 pages, 1992. (Casebook)

NELSON AND WHITMAN'S BLACK LETTER ON LAND TRANSACTIONS AND FINANCE, Second Edition, 466 pages, 1988. Softcover. (Review)

NELSON AND WHITMAN'S CASES ON REAL ESTATE TRANSFER, FINANCE AND DEVELOPMENT, Third Edition, 1184 pages, 1987. (Casebook)

NELSON AND WHITMAN'S HORNBOOK ON REAL ESTATE FINANCE LAW, Second Edition, 941 pages, 1985 with 1989 pocket part. (Text)

Regulated Industries—see also Mass Communication Law, Banking Law

GELLHORN AND PIERCE'S REGULATED INDUSTRIES IN A NUTSHELL, Second Edition, 389 pages, 1987. Softcover. (Text)

MORGAN, HARRISON AND VERKUIL'S CASES AND MATERIALS ON ECONOMIC REGULATION OF BUSINESS, Second Edition, 666 pages, 1985. (Casebook)

Remedies

DOBBS' HORNBOOK ON REMEDIES, 1067 pages, 1973. (Text)

DOBBS' PROBLEMS IN REMEDIES. 137 pages, 1974. Teacher's Manual available. Softcover. (Coursebook)

DOBBYN'S INJUNCTIONS IN A NUTSHELL, 264 pages, 1974. Softcover. (Text)

FRIEDMAN'S CONTRACT REMEDIES IN A NUTSHELL, 323 pages, 1981. Softcover. (Text)

LEAVELL, LOVE AND NELSON'S CASES AND MATERIALS ON EQUITABLE REMEDIES, RESTITUTION AND DAMAGES, Fourth Edition, 1111 pages, 1986. Teacher's Manual available. (Casebook)

O'CONNELL'S REMEDIES IN A NUTSHELL, Second Edition, 320 pages, 1985. Softcover. (Text)

SCHOENBROD, MACBETH, LEVINE AND JUNG'S CASES AND MATERIALS ON REMEDIES: PUBLIC AND PRIVATE, 848 pages, 1990. Teacher's Manual available. (Casebook)

YORK, BAUMAN AND RENDLEMAN'S CASES AND MATERIALS ON REMEDIES, Fifth Edition, approximately 1275 pages, 1992. (Casebook)

Sea, Law of

SOHN AND GUSTAFSON'S THE LAW OF THE SEA IN A NUTSHELL, 264 pages, 1984. Softcover. (Text)

Securities Regulation

HAZEN'S HORNBOOK ON THE LAW OF SECURITIES REGULATION, Second Edition, Student Edition, 1082 pages, 1990. (Text)

RATNER'S SECURITIES REGULATION IN A NUTSHELL, Third Edition, 316 pages, 1988. Softcover. (Text)

RATNER AND HAZEN'S SECURITIES REGULATION: CASES AND MATERIALS, Fourth Edition, 1062 pages, 1991. Teacher's Manual available. (Casebook) Problems and Sample Documents Supplement.

   Statutory Supplement. *See Securities Regulation, Selected Statutes*

SECURITIES REGULATION, SELECTED STATUTES, RULES, AND FORMS. Softcover. Approximately 1375 pages, 1992.

Sports Law

SCHUBERT, SMITH AND TRENTADUE'S SPORTS LAW, 395 pages, 1986. (Text)

Tax Practice and Procedure

GARBIS, RUBIN AND MORGAN'S CASES AND MATERIALS ON TAX PROCEDURE AND TAX FRAUD, Third Edition, approximately 925 pages, 1992. Teacher's Manual available. (Casebook)

MORGAN'S TAX PROCEDURE AND TAX FRAUD IN A NUTSHELL, 400 pages, 1990. Softcover. (Text)

Taxation—Corporate

KAHN AND GANN'S CORPORATE TAXATION, Third Edition, 980 pages, 1989. Teacher's Manual available. (Casebook) 1991 Supplement.

SCHWARZ AND LATHROPE'S BLACK LETTER ON CORPORATE AND PARTNERSHIP TAXATION, 537 pages, 1991. Softcover. (Review)

WEIDENBRUCH AND BURKE'S FEDERAL INCOME TAXATION OF CORPORATIONS AND STOCKHOLDERS IN A NUTSHELL, Third Edition, 309 pages, 1989. Softcover. (Text)

Taxation—Estate & Gift—see also Estate Planning, Trusts and Estates

MCNULTY'S FEDERAL ESTATE AND GIFT TAXATION IN A NUTSHELL, Fourth Edition, 496 pages, 1989. Softcover. (Text)

PEAT AND WILLBANKS' FEDERAL ESTATE AND GIFT TAXATION: AN ANALYSIS AND CRITIQUE, 265 pages, 1991. Softcover. (Text)

PENNELL'S CASES AND MATERIALS ON INCOME TAXATION OF TRUSTS, ESTATES, GRANTORS AND BENEFICIARIES, 460 pages, 1987. Teacher's Manual available. (Casebook)

Taxation—Individual

DODGE'S THE LOGIC OF TAX, 343 pages, 1989. Softcover. (Text)

GUNN AND WARD'S CASES, TEXT AND PROBLEMS ON FEDERAL INCOME TAXATION, Third Edition, approximately 850 pages, May, 1992 Pub. Teacher's Manual available. (Casebook)

HUDSON AND LIND'S BLACK LETTER ON FEDERAL INCOME TAXATION, Third Edition, 406 pages, 1990. Softcover. (Review)

KRAGEN AND MCNULTY'S CASES AND MATERIALS ON FEDERAL INCOME TAXATION—INDIVIDUALS, CORPORATIONS, PARTNERSHIPS, Fourth Edition, 1287 pages, 1985. (Casebook)

MCNULTY'S FEDERAL INCOME TAXATION OF INDIVIDUALS IN A NUTSHELL, Fourth Edition, 503 pages, 1988. Softcover. (Text)

POSIN'S HORNBOOK ON FEDERAL INCOME TAXATION, Student Edition, 491 pages, 1983, with 1989 pocket part. (Text)

ROSE AND CHOMMIE'S HORNBOOK ON FEDERAL INCOME TAXATION, Third Edition, 923 pages, 1988, with 1991 pocket part. (Text)

SELECTED FEDERAL TAXATION STATUTES AND REGULATIONS. Softcover. 1690 pages, 1992.

Taxation—International

DOERNBERG'S INTERNATIONAL TAXATION IN A NUTSHELL, 325 pages, 1989. Softcover. (Text)

KAPLAN'S FEDERAL TAXATION OF INTERNATIONAL TRANSACTIONS: PRINCIPLES, PLANNING AND POLICY, 635 pages, 1988. (Casebook)

Taxation—Partnership

BERGER AND WIEDENBECK'S CASES AND MATERIALS ON PARTNERSHIP TAXATION, 788 pages, 1989. Teacher's Manual available. (Casebook) 1991 Supplement.

BISHOP AND BROOKS' FEDERAL PARTNERSHIP TAXATION: A GUIDE TO THE LEADING CASES, STATUTES, AND REGULATIONS, 545 pages, 1990. Softcover. (Text)

BURKE'S FEDERAL INCOME TAXATION OF PARTNERSHIPS IN A NUTSHELL, Approximately 400 pages, February, 1992 Pub. Softcover. (Text)

SCHWARZ AND LATHROPE'S BLACK LETTER ON CORPORATE AND PARTNERSHIP TAXATION, 537 pages, 1991. Softcover. (Review)

Taxation—State & Local

GELFAND AND SALSICH'S STATE AND LOCAL TAXATION AND FINANCE IN A NUTSHELL, 309 pages, 1986. Softcover. (Text)

HELLERSTEIN AND HELLERSTEIN'S CASES AND MATERIALS ON STATE AND LOCAL TAXATION, Fifth Edition, 1071 pages, 1988. (Casebook)

Torts—see also Products Liability

CHRISTIE AND MEEKS' CASES AND MATERIALS ON THE LAW OF TORTS, Second Edition, 1264 pages, 1990. (Casebook)

DOBBS' TORTS AND COMPENSATION—PERSONAL ACCOUNTABILITY AND SOCIAL RESPONSIBILITY FOR INJURY, 955 pages, 1985. Teacher's Manual available. (Casebook) 1990 Supplement.

KEETON, KEETON, SARGENTICH AND STEINER'S CASES AND MATERIALS ON TORT AND ACCIDENT LAW, Second Edition, 1318 pages, 1989. (Casebook)

KIONKA'S BLACK LETTER ON TORTS, 339 pages, 1988. Softcover. (Review)

KIONKA'S TORTS IN A NUTSHELL, Second Edition, approximately 500 pages, March, 1992 Pub. Softcover. (Text)

MALONE'S TORTS IN A NUTSHELL: INJURIES TO FAMILY, SOCIAL AND TRADE RELATIONS, 358 pages, 1979. Softcover. (Text)

PROSSER AND KEETON'S HORNBOOK ON TORTS, Fifth Edition, Student Edition, 1286 pages, 1984 with 1988 pocket part. (Text)

ROBERTSON, POWERS AND ANDERSON'S CASES AND MATERIALS ON TORTS, 932 pages, 1989. Teacher's Manual available. (Casebook)

Trade Regulation—see also Antitrust, Regulated Industries

MCMANIS' UNFAIR TRADE PRACTICES IN A NUTSHELL, Second Edition, 464 pages, 1988. Softcover. (Text)

SCHECHTER'S BLACK LETTER ON UNFAIR TRADE PRACTICES, 272 pages, 1986. Softcover. (Review)

WESTON, MAGGS AND SCHECHTER'S UNFAIR TRADE PRACTICES AND CONSUMER PROTECTION, CASES AND COMMENTS, Fifth Edition, approximately 975 pages, 1992. Teacher's Manual available. (Casebook)

Trial and Appellate Advocacy—see also Civil Procedure

APPELLATE ADVOCACY, HANDBOOK OF, Second Edition, 182 pages, 1986. Softcover. (Text)

BERGMAN'S TRIAL ADVOCACY IN A NUTSHELL, Second Edition, 354 pages, 1989. Softcover. (Text)

BINDER AND BERGMAN'S FACT INVESTIGATION:

FROM HYPOTHESIS TO PROOF, 354 pages, 1984. Teacher's Manual available. (Coursebook)

CARLSON'S ADJUDICATION OF CRIMINAL JUSTICE: PROBLEMS AND REFERENCES, 130 pages, 1986. Softcover. (Casebook)

CARLSON AND IMWINKELRIED'S DYNAMICS OF TRIAL PRACTICE: PROBLEMS AND MATERIALS, 414 pages, 1989. Teacher's Manual available. (Coursebook) 1990 Supplement.

DESSEM'S PRETRIAL LITIGATION: LAW, POLICY AND PRACTICE, 608 pages, 1991. Softcover. Teacher's Manual available. (Coursebook)

DEVINE'S NON-JURY CASE FILES FOR TRIAL ADVOCACY, 258 pages, 1991. (Coursebook)

GOLDBERG'S THE FIRST TRIAL (WHERE DO I SIT? WHAT DO I SAY?) IN A NUTSHELL, 396 pages, 1982. Softcover. (Text)

HAYDOCK, HERR, AND STEMPEL'S FUNDAMENTALS OF PRE-TRIAL LITIGATION, Second Edition, approximately 700 pages, 1992. Softcover. Teacher's Manual available. (Coursebook)

HAYDOCK AND SONSTENG'S TRIAL: THEORIES, TACTICS, TECHNIQUES, 711 pages, 1991. Softcover. (Text)

HEGLAND'S TRIAL AND PRACTICE SKILLS IN A NUTSHELL, 346 pages, 1978. Softcover. (Text)

HORNSTEIN'S APPELLATE ADVOCACY IN A NUTSHELL, 325 pages, 1984. Softcover. (Text)

JEANS' HANDBOOK ON TRIAL ADVOCACY, Student Edition, 473 pages, 1975. Softcover. (Text)

LISNEK AND KAUFMAN'S DEPOSITIONS: PROCEDURE, STRATEGY AND TECHNIQUE, Law School and CLE Edition. 250 pages, 1990. Softcover. (Text)

MARTINEAU'S CASES AND MATERIALS ON APPELLATE PRACTICE AND PROCEDURE, 565 pages, 1987. (Casebook)

NOLAN'S CASES AND MATERIALS ON TRIAL PRACTICE, 518 pages, 1981. (Casebook)

SONSTENG, HAYDOCK AND BOYD'S THE TRIALBOOK: A TOTAL SYSTEM FOR PREPARATION AND PRESENTATION OF A CASE, 404 pages, 1984. Softcover. (Coursebook)

WHARTON, HAYDOCK AND SONSTENG'S CALI-

Trial and Appellate Advocacy—Cont'd

FORNIA CIVIL TRIALBOOK, Law School and CLE Edition. 148 pages, 1990. Softcover. (Text)

Trusts and Estates

ATKINSON'S HORNBOOK ON WILLS, Second Edition, 975 pages, 1953. (Text)

AVERILL'S UNIFORM PROBATE CODE IN A NUTSHELL, Second Edition, 454 pages, 1987. Softcover. (Text)

BOGERT'S HORNBOOK ON TRUSTS, Sixth Edition, Student Edition, 794 pages, 1987. (Text)

CLARK, LUSKY AND MURPHY'S CASES AND MATERIALS ON GRATUITOUS TRANSFERS, Third Edition, 970 pages, 1985. (Casebook)

DODGE'S WILLS, TRUSTS AND ESTATE PLANNING–LAW AND TAXATION, CASES AND MATERIALS, 665 pages, 1988. (Casebook)

MCGOVERN'S CASES AND MATERIALS ON WILLS, TRUSTS AND FUTURE INTERESTS: AN INTRODUCTION TO ESTATE PLANNING, 750 pages, 1983. (Casebook)

MCGOVERN, KURTZ AND REIN'S HORNBOOK ON WILLS, TRUSTS AND ESTATES–INCLUDING TAXATION AND FUTURE INTERESTS, 996 pages, 1988. (Text)

MENNELL'S WILLS AND TRUSTS IN A NUTSHELL, 392 pages, 1979. Softcover. (Text)

SIMES' HORNBOOK ON FUTURE INTERESTS, Second Edition, 355 pages, 1966. (Text)

TURANO AND RADIGAN'S HORNBOOK ON NEW

YORK ESTATE ADMINISTRATION, 676 pages, 1986 with 1991 pocket part. (Text)

UNIFORM PROBATE CODE, OFFICIAL TEXT WITH COMMENTS. 839 pages, 1990. Softcover.

WAGGONER'S FUTURE INTERESTS IN A NUTSHELL, 361 pages, 1981. Softcover. (Text)

WATERBURY'S MATERIALS ON TRUSTS AND ESTATES, 1039 pages, 1986. Teacher's Manual available. (Casebook)

Water Law—see also Energy and Natural Resources Law, Environmental Law

GETCHES' WATER LAW IN A NUTSHELL, Second Edition, 459 pages, 1990. Softcover. (Text)

SAX, ABRAMS AND THOMPSON'S LEGAL CONTROL OF WATER RESOURCES: CASES AND MATERIALS, Second Edition, 987 pages, 1991. Teacher's Manual available. (Casebook)

TRELEASE AND GOULD'S CASES AND MATERIALS ON WATER LAW, Fourth Edition, 816 pages, 1986. (Casebook)

Wills—see Trusts and Estates

Workers' Compensation

HOOD, HARDY AND LEWIS' WORKERS' COMPENSATION AND EMPLOYEE PROTECTION LAWS IN A NUTSHELL, Second Edition, 361 pages, 1990. Softcover. (Text)

MALONE, PLANT AND LITTLE'S CASES ON WORKERS' COMPENSATION AND EMPLOYMENT RIGHTS, Second Edition, 951 pages, 1980. Teacher's Manual available. (Casebook)

[xviii]

CASES AND MATERIALS ON
CONTRACTS
Second Edition

By

Robert W. Hamilton
Minerva House Drysdale
Regents Chair in Law
The University of Texas at Austin School of Law

Alan Scott Rau
Robert F. Windfohr & Anne Burnett Windfohr Professor
in Oil, Gas & Mineral Law
The University of Texas at Austin School of Law

Russell J. Weintraub
John B. Connally
Chair in Civil Jurisprudence
The University of Texas at Austin School of Law

AMERICAN CASEBOOK SERIES®

WEST PUBLISHING CO.
ST. PAUL, MINN., 1992

COPYRIGHT © 1984 WEST PUBLISHING CO.
COPYRIGHT © 1992 By WEST PUBLISHING CO.
                    610 Opperman Drive
                    P.O. Box 64526
                    St. Paul, MN 55164–0526

Library of Congress Cataloging-in-Publication Data

Hamilton, Robert W., 1931–
   Cases and materials on contracts / by Robert W. Hamilton. Alan Scott Rau, Russell J. Weintraub. — 2nd ed.
     p.   cm. — (American casebook series)
   Includes index.
   ISBN 0–314–00360–6
   1. Contracts—United States—Cases. I. Rau, Alan Scott, 1942–
. II. Weintraub, Russell J. III. Title. IV. Title: Contracts.
V. Series.
KF801.A7H25 1992
346.73'02—dc20
[347.3062]   92–283
                                   CIP

ISBN 0–314–00360–6

Preface

The course in contracts is often viewed as the classic first year law school class, emphasizing careful reading of cases and development of common law principles. Twenty years ago this characterization was doubtless accurate in practically all the law schools throughout the nation. While the contracts course of the 1990s continues to have these attributes, its role in the law school curriculum has changed significantly in many schools. With the enactment of the Uniform Commercial Code, the contracts course has gradually changed from a purely common law course to a course with an increasingly important statutory component. The Code also has had an effect in modifying common law contract doctrine. This change, along with many others, is reflected in The Second Restatement of Contracts. Further, with the growth of the application of economic analysis to contract formation and performance, the course has increasingly become a study of the relationship between regulation of private transactions and broad social goals.

Despite all these changes, the course in contracts must still fulfill its historic function of introducing beginning law students to the study of the common law legal system and the application of legal principles to complex transactions. The casebook we have prepared continues to fulfill this function as well as exposing students to more statutory analysis.

The three of us have each taught contracts for more than twenty years. Our combined experience in teaching this course exceeds seventy years. We each continue to believe that the most appropriate place to begin the study of contracts is with the law of remedies, and that the subject of remedies is central to an understanding of contract law. Cases discussing remedy problems cut across the subject matter of the course and provide an overview of the most important issues in the law of contracts. We have therefore retained essentially the same organizational scheme that was followed in the first edition. During the first days of law school, students are thus exposed to common law development of principles through classic and contemporary remedies cases; yet they are at the same time exposed to the difficulties of interpreting and applying the provisions of the Uniform Commercial Code that attempt to codify and modify the traditional principles in connection with sales of goods. We have, however, attempted to make the Second Edition considerably more "user friendly" by the insertion of section headings and additional notes and questions to reduce the need for instructor exposition. This additional material also helps to focus student analysis before class discussion.

An outstanding feature of both the first and second editions of this book is that Uniform Commercial Code principles are integrated with common law rules throughout the book. We believe that the notion of a separate course in "Sales" is pedagogically unsound and an anachronism, and the interplay between "common law" and "Code" approaches to particular problems is another recurring theme throughout these materials. In addition, an important role of the course is to expose students to the methods and theories of Code interpretation.

Although there are, therefore, many citations to the Uniform Commercial Code in the text and cases, there are no excerpts from the Code in the notes and most Code passages have been edited out of the cases. The reason for this is to encourage reading of the full text and comments of the relevant Code sections. This book is designed for use with one of the statutory collections that contain the Uniform Commercial Code, all official comments to the Code, and other materials. An example is "Selected Commercial Statutes" published by West Publishing Company.

The first edition contained only one short excerpt from a draft of the United Nations Convention on Contracts for the International Sale of Goods. Since then, the Convention has gone into force and has been ratified by 28 countries, including the United States. The new edition contains many more excerpts from and notes on the Convention and invites comparison of the Convention provisions with both common law and UCC rules.

A significant number of modern cases have been substituted for older cases in the first edition in an effort to give students a better "feel" for modern business practices and for the context of the cases with which they will have to deal in the future. Every effort has been made to select new cases that are as interesting and as much fun to teach as the cases they have displaced.

A word about form. In editing the cases, deletions of text are indicated by spaced asterisks; omissions of citations in the text are not indicated, nor are omissions of many footnotes. Where footnotes appear, their original numbers are retained. In a few instances, the locations of footnotes have been changed.

We are grateful to our colleagues and students who provided many helpful suggestions for the revision of these materials. We again wish to thank Mark Yudof, who joined us in teaching from the experimental materials before publication of the First Edition. We have greatly benefitted from Dean Yudof's extensive comments on his experience.

> ROBERT W. HAMILTON
> ALAN S. RAU
> RUSSELL J. WEINTRAUB

January 24, 1992

Acknowledgments

The following authors and publishers gave us permission to reprint excerpts from copyrighted material; we gratefully acknowledge their assistance: The American Bar Association and its Section of Corporation, Banking and Business Law, for excerpts from Davenport, How to Handle Sales of Goods: The Problem of Conflicting Purchase Orders and Acceptances and New Concepts in Contract Law, 19 Bus.Law. 75 (1963); American Society of International Law, for excerpts reprinted with permission from the UN Convention for the International Sale of Goods, 19 I.L.M. 671 (1980), Copyright © 1980 American Society of International Law; Baker, Voorhis & Co., Inc., for excerpts from Williston, Contracts (3d ed. 1957); The California Law Review and Fred B. Rothman & Co., for excerpts from Whittier, The Restatement of Contracts and Mutual Assent, 17 Calif.L.Rev. 441 (1929), and Weiner, The Civil Jury Trial and the Law-Fact Distinction, 54 Calif.L.Rev. 1867 (1966); Cambridge University Press, for excerpts from Searle, Intentionality (1983); The University of Chicago, for excerpts from Epstein, Blackmail, Inc., 50 U.Chi.L.Rev. 553 (1983); Llewellyn, A Lecture on Appellate Advocacy, 29 U.Chi.L.Rev. 627 (1962); Epstein, In Defense of the Contract at Will, 51 U.Chi.L.Rev. 947 (1984); Posner, Gratuitous Promises in Economics and Law, 6 J.Legal Stud. 411 (1977); Joskow, Commercial Impossibility, The Uranium Market and the Westinghouse Case, 6 J.Legal Stud. 119 (1977), and Kronman, Mistake, Disclosure, Information and the Law of Contracts, 7 J.Legal Stud. 1 (1978); Columbia Law Review Association, for excerpts from Fuller, Consideration and Form, 41 Colum.L.Rev. 799 (1941); Columbia Law Review Association and E. Allen Farnsworth, for excerpts from Farnsworth, The Past of Promise: An Historical Introduction to Contract, 69 Colum.L.Rev. 576 (1969); Contemporary Books, Inc., for excerpts from Von Mises, Human Action: A Treatise on Economics (3d ed. 1966); Cornell L.Q. and Fred B. Rothman & Co., for excerpts from Note, 14 Cornell L.Rev. 81 (1928); The Foundation Press, Inc., for excerpts from Dawson, Harvey, & Henderson, Cases and Comments on Contracts (4th ed. 1982), and Teachers Manual; Harvard Law Review Association, for excerpts from McGovney, Irrevocable Offers, 27 Harv.L.Rev. 644 (1914); Williston, The Law of Sales in the Proposed Uniform Commercial Code, 63 Harv.L.Rev. 561 (1950); Cohen, The Basis of Contract, 46 Harv.L.Rev. 553 (1933); Harvard Law Review Association and Arthur Von Mehren, for excerpts from Von Mehren, Civil-Law Analogues to Consideration: An Exercise in Comparative Analysis, 72 Harv.L.Rev. 1009 (1959); Harvard Law Review Association and Melvin A. Eisenberg, for excerpts from Eisenberg, The Bargain Principle and Its Limits, 95 Harv.L.Rev. 741 (1982); Harvard Law

Review Association and Roberto Unger, for excerpts from Unger, The Critical Legal Studies Movement, 96 Harv.L.Rev. 563 (1983); Harvard Law Review Association and Jay M. Feinman, for excerpts from Feinman, Promissory Estoppel and Judicial Method, 97 Harv.L.Rev. 678 (1984); Hofstra Law Review Association, Mary E. Becker and Randy E. Barnett, for excerpts from Becker & Barnett, Beyond Reliance: Promissory Estoppel, Contract Formalities and Another Look at Construction Bidding and Misrepresentations, 15 Hofstra L.Rev. 443 (1987); Journal of Legal Education, for excerpts from Wormser, Review of Cases on Contracts, 3 J.Legal Educ. 145 (1950); Macmillan Publishing Company, for excerpts from Leff, Swindling and Selling (Copyright © 1976 by The Free Press, a Division of Macmillan Publishing Company); New York University Law Review, for excerpts from Childres & Spitz; Status in the Law of Contract, 47 N.Y.U.L.Rev. 1 (1972), and Knapp, Enforcing the Contract to Bargain, 44 N.Y.U.L.Rev. 673 (1969); Oxford University Press, for excerpts from Atiyah, The Rise and Fall of Freedom of Contract (1979); Oxford University Press, for excerpts from Essays on Contract, (1986); The Royal Institute of International Affairs, for excerpts from Sweet-Escott, Greece: A Political and Economic Survey (1954); Sweet & Maxwell, Ltd., for excerpts from Treitel, The Law of Contracts (7th ed. 1987); Tulane Law Review Association, for excerpts from Von Mehren, The French Doctrine of *Lesion* in the Sale of Immovable Property, 49 Tul.L.Rev. 321 (1975); Virginia Law Review and Fred B. Rothman & Co., for excerpts from Henderson, Promises Grounded in the Past: The Idea of Unjust Enrichment and the Law of Contracts, 57 Va.L.Rev. 1115 (1971), and Note, Another Look at Construction Bidding and Contracts at Formation, 53 Va.L.Rev. 1720 (1967); Virginia Law Review Association, Fred B. Rothman, Douglas G. Baird, and Robert Weisberg for excerpts from Rules, Standards, and the Battle of the Forms: A Reassessment of Section 2–207, 68 Va.L.Rev. 1217 (1982); J. White and R. Summers, for excerpts from Uniform Commercial Code (2d ed. 1980); John Wiley & Sons, Inc., for excerpts from Blau, Exchange and Power in Social Life (1964); The Yale Law Journal Company, for excerpts from McCormick, The Parol Evidence Rule as a Procedural Device for Control of the Jury, 41 Yale L.J. 365 (1932); Fuller & Perdue, The Reliance Interest in Contract Damages, 46 Yale L.J. 52 (1936); Corbin, The Effect of Options on Consideration, 34 Yale L.J. 571 (1925), and Wormser, The True Conception of Unilateral Contracts, 26 Yale L.J. 136 (1916); Yale University Press, for excerpts from Dawson, Gifts and Promises (1980).

All extracts from The Death of Contract by Grant Gilmore, ("Law Forum Series of the College of Law of the Ohio State University," No. 8) are copyright © 1974 by the Ohio State University Press. All rights reserved. Reprinted by permission of the publisher.

We wish to express our particular appreciation to The American Law Institute, whose gracious cooperation made possible the many excerpts which appear here from the following sources: Restatement [First] of Contracts, Copyright © 1932 by The American Law Institute;

Restatement, Second, Contracts, Copyright © 1981 by The American Law Institute; Restatement of the Law of Restitution, Copyright © 1937 by The American Law Institute; Restatement, Second, of Trusts, Copyright © 1959 by The American Law Institute; Restatement, Second, Torts, Copyright © 1977 by The American Law Institute; Restatement, Second, Agency, Copyright © 1958 by The American Law Institute; Proceedings, 4th Annual Meeting of The American Law Institute, Copyright © 1926 by The American Law Institute. All reprinted with the permission of The American Law Institute.

*

Summary of Contents

Table of Contents

Table of Cases

The principal cases are in bold type. Cases cited or discussed in the text are roman type. References are to pages. Cases cited in principal cases and within other quoted materials are not included.

CASES AND MATERIALS ON
CONTRACTS
Second Edition

*

Chapter 1

ENFORCEMENT OF PROMISES: INTRODUCTION AND OVERVIEW

SECTION 1: MONETARY RECOVERIES

HAWKINS v. McGEE

Supreme Court of New Hampshire, 1929.
84 N.H. 114, 146 A. 641.

Assumpsit against a surgeon for breach of an alleged warranty of the success of an operation. Trial by jury. Verdict for the plaintiff. The writ also contained a count in negligence upon which a nonsuit was ordered, without exception.

Defendant's motions for a nonsuit and for a directed verdict on the count in assumpsit were denied, and the defendant excepted. During the argument of plaintiff's counsel to the jury, the defendant claimed certain exceptions, and also excepted to the denial of his requests for instructions and to the charge of the court upon the question of damages, as more fully appears in the opinion. The defendant seasonably moved to set aside the verdict upon the grounds that it was (1) contrary to the evidence; (2) against the weight of the evidence; (3) against the weight of the law and evidence; and (4) because the damages awarded by the jury were excessive. The court denied the motion upon the first three grounds, but found that the damages were excessive, and made an order that the verdict be set aside, unless the plaintiff elected to remit all in excess of $500. The plaintiff having refused to remit, the verdict was set aside "as excessive and against the weight of the evidence," and the plaintiff excepted.

The foregoing exceptions were transferred by Scammon, J. The facts are stated in the opinion. * * *

BRANCH, J. 1. The operation in question consisted in the removal of a considerable quantity of scar tissue from the palm of the plaintiff's right hand and the grafting of skin taken from the plaintiff's chest in place thereof. The scar tissue was the result of a severe burn caused by

1

contact with an electric wire, which the plaintiff received about nine years before the time of the transactions here involved. There was evidence to the effect that before the operation was performed the plaintiff and his father went to the defendant's office, and that the defendant, in answer to the question, "How long will the boy be in the hospital?" replied, "Three or four days, not over four; then the boy can go home and it will be just a few days when he will go back to work with a good hand." Clearly this and other testimony to the same effect would not justify a finding that the doctor contracted to complete the hospital treatment in three or four days or that the plaintiff would be able to go back to work within a few days thereafter. The above statements could only be construed as expressions of opinion or predictions as to the probable duration of the treatment and plaintiff's resulting disability, and the fact that these estimates were exceeded would impose no contractual liability upon the defendant. The only substantial basis for the plaintiff's claim is the testimony that the defendant also said before the operation was decided upon, "I will guarantee to make the hand a hundred per cent perfect hand or a hundred per cent good hand." The plaintiff was present when these words were alleged to have been spoken, and, if they are to be taken at their face value, it seems obvious that proof of their utterance would establish the giving of a warranty in accordance with his contention.

The defendant argues, however, that, even if these words were uttered by him, no reasonable man would understand that they were used with the intention of entering "into any contractual relation whatever," and that they could reasonably be understood only "as his expression in strong language that he believed and expected that as a result of the operation he would give the plaintiff a very good hand." It may be conceded, as the defendant contends, that, before the question of the making of a contract should be submitted to a jury, there is a preliminary question of law for the trial court to pass upon, i.e. "whether the words could possibly have the meaning imputed to them by the party who founds his case upon a certain interpretation," but it cannot be held that the trial court decided this question erroneously in the present case. It is unnecessary to determine at this time whether the argument of the defendant, based upon "common knowledge of the uncertainty which attends all surgical operations," and the improbability that a surgeon would ever contract to make a damaged part of the human body "one hundred per cent perfect," would, in the absence of countervailing considerations, be regarded as conclusive, for there were other factors in the present case which tended to support the contention of the plaintiff. There was evidence that the defendant repeatedly solicited from the plaintiff's father the opportunity to perform this operation, and the theory was advanced by plaintiff's counsel in cross-examination of defendant that he sought an opportunity to "experiment on skin grafting," in which he had had little previous experience. If the jury accepted this part of plaintiff's contention, there would be a reasonable basis for the further conclusion that, if defendant spoke the words attributed to him, he did so with the intention that they should be accepted at their face value, as an inducement for the granting of consent to the operation by the plaintiff and his father, and there was ample evidence that they were so accepted by them. The question of the making of the alleged contract was properly submitted to the jury.

2. The substance of the charge to the jury on the question of damages appears in the following quotation: "If you find the plaintiff entitled to anything, he is entitled to recover for what pain and suffering he has been made to endure and for what injury he has sustained over and above what injury he had before." To this instruction the defendant seasonably excepted. By it, the jury was permitted to consider two elements of damage: (1) pain and suffering due to the operation; and (2) positive ill effects of the operation upon the plaintiff's hand. Authority for any specific rule of damages in cases of this kind seems to be lacking, but, when tested by general principle and by analogy, it appears that the foregoing instruction was erroneous.

"By 'damages,' as that term is used in the law of contracts, is intended compensation for a breach, measured in the terms of the contract." Davis v. New England Cotton Yarn Co., 77 N.H. 403, 404, 92 A. 732, 733. The purpose of the law is "to put the plaintiff in as good a position as he would have been in had the defendant kept his contract." 3 Williston Cont. § 1338. The measure of recovery "is based upon what the defendant should have given the plaintiff, not what the plaintiff has given the defendant or otherwise expended." 3 Williston Cont. § 1341. "The only losses that can be said fairly to come within the terms of a contract are such as the parties must have had in mind when the contract was made, or such as they either knew or ought to have known would probably result from a failure to comply with its terms." Davis v. New England Cotton Yarn Co., 77 N.H. 403, 404, 92 A. 732, 733.

The present case is closely analogous to one in which a machine is built for a certain purpose and warranted to do certain work. In such cases, the usual rule of damages for breach of warranty in the sale of chattels is applied, and it is held that the measure of damages is the difference between the value of the machine, if it had corresponded with the warranty and its actual value, together with such incidental losses as the parties knew, or ought to have known, would probably result from a failure to comply with its terms.

The rule thus applied is well settled in this state. "As a general rule, the measure of the vendee's damages is the difference between the value of the goods as they would have been if the warranty as to quality had been true, and the actual value at the time of the sale, including gains prevented and losses sustained, and such other damages as could be reasonably anticipated by the parties as likely to be caused by the vendor's failure to keep his agreement, and could not by reasonable care on the part of the vendee have been avoided." Union Bank v. Blanchard, 65 N.H. 21, 23, 18 A. 90, 91. We therefore conclude that the true measure of the plaintiff's damage in the present case is the difference between the value to him of a perfect hand or a good hand, such as the jury found the defendant promised him, and the value of his hand in its present condition, including any incidental consequences fairly within the contemplation of the parties when they made their contract. 1 Sutherland, Damages (4th Ed.) § 92. Damages not thus limited, although naturally resulting, are not to be given.

The extent of the plaintiff's suffering does not measure this difference in value. The pain necessarily incident to a serious surgical operation was a part of the contribution which the plaintiff was willing to make to his joint undertaking with the defendant to produce a good hand. It was a legal detriment suffered by him which constituted a part of the consideration given by him for the contract. It represented a part of the price which he was willing to pay for a good hand, but it furnished no test of the value of a good hand or the difference between the value of the hand which the defendant promised and the one which resulted from the operation.

It was also erroneous and misleading to submit to the jury as a separate element of damage any change for the worse in the condition of the plaintiff's hand resulting from the operation, although this error was probably more prejudicial to the plaintiff than to the defendant. Any such ill effect of the operation would be included under the true rule of damages set forth above, but damages might properly be assessed for the defendant's failure to improve the condition of the hand, even if there were no evidence that its condition was made worse as a result of the operation.

It must be assumed that the trial court, in setting aside the verdict, undertook to apply the same rule of damages which he had previously given to the jury, and, since this rule was erroneous, it is unnecessary for us to consider whether there was any evidence to justify his finding that all damages awarded by the jury above $500 were excessive.

3. Defendant's requests for instructions were loosely drawn, and were properly denied. A considerable number of issues of fact were raised by the evidence, and it would have been extremely misleading to instruct the jury in accordance with defendant's request No. 2, that "the only issue on which you have to pass is whether or not there was a special contract between the plaintiff and the defendant to produce a perfect hand." Equally inaccurate was defendant's request No. 5, which reads as follows: "You would have to find, in order to hold the defendant liable in this case, that Dr. McGee and the plaintiff both understood that the doctor was guaranteeing a perfect result from this operation." If the defendant said that he would guarantee a perfect result, and the plaintiff relied upon that promise, any mental reservations which he may have had are immaterial. The standard by which his conduct is to be judged is not internal, but external.

Defendant's request No. 7 was as follows: "If you should get so far as to find that there was a special contract guaranteeing a perfect result, you would still have to find for the defendant unless you also found that a further operation would not correct the disability claimed by the plaintiff." In view of the testimony that the defendant had refused to perform a further operation, it would clearly have been erroneous to give this instruction. The evidence would have justified a verdict for an amount sufficient to cover the cost of such an operation, even if the theory underlying this request were correct. * * *

New trial.

––––––––

Background of Hawkins v. McGee

George Hawkins suffered an electrical burn when he was 11 years old. The resulting scar was small and did not significantly affect the use of the hand. Dr. McGee persuaded George to undergo surgery, emphasizing the social problems that the scarred hand might create. The operation was performed shortly after George's 18th birthday. The skin graft was taken from George's chest. There was infection and profuse bleeding. George was hospitalized for three months. The graft covered the thumb and two fingers and soon was matted with hair. Movement of the hand was greatly restricted. The jury awarded George $3,000. After the Supreme Court of New Hampshire ordered a new trial, the case was settled for $1,400. George's father took him to specialists in Montreal to see if the appearance of the hand could be improved, but was advised that nothing could be done.

George was so embarrassed by his hand that he did not return to high school. Throughout his life, he was sensitive about his hand. He worked at various semi-skilled occupations, was a chauffeur for a time, married late in life, and had no children. He died of a heart attack at the age of 54.

Dr. McGee's medical practice flourished. He was very popular and served as mayor of Berlin, New Hampshire, the scene of the events described in the opinion. He formed McGee's Symphony Orchestra as a hobby and performed throughout the region. See Robert Hawkins Case: A Hair-Raising Experience, 66 Harvard Law Record 1, 7, 13 (March 17, 1978).

Dr. McGee had a policy in which the insurer promised to defend and indemnify him against claims resulting from "any malpractice, error or mistake * * * in the practice of his profession." Did this policy cover his liability on the count in assumpsit? What should the attorney employed by the insurer do when the negligence count is dismissed? See McGee v. United States Fidelity & Guaranty Co., 53 F.2d 953 (1st Cir. 1931).

––––––––

Why Start With Remedies?

There are two reasons why the book begins with materials that focus on remedies. First, and more important, cases discussing remedy problems cut across the subject matter of the course. This chapter provides an overview of some of the most important issues in the law of contracts, many of which are treated in more detail in subsequent chapters. Second, a thorough knowledge of contract remedies is essential for the practice of law. It is important to know how to plan transactions and draft documents to minimize enforcement problems. The drafter should be aware of what provisions might be unenforceable or create ambiguity in the light of background remedies law. It is also important to know to what extent the parties are free to craft their own remedies and when and why this is desirable. Moreover, remedies are the bottom line. It is not very useful to know that your client is likely to prevail as a plaintiff in a breach of contract suit unless you also know what remedies are available. A "victory" is not likely to be worth pursuing if the result is an award of only nominal damages.

RESTATEMENT, SECOND, CONTRACTS § 1:

A contract is a promise or a set of promises for the breach of which the law gives a remedy, or the performance of which the law in some way recognizes as a duty.

RESTATEMENT, SECOND, CONTRACTS § 347:

Comment a:

Expectation interest. Contract damages are ordinarily based on the injured party's expectation interest and are intended to give him the benefit of his bargain by awarding him a sum of money that will, to the extent possible, put him in as good a position as he would have been in had the contract been performed.

RESTATEMENT, SECOND, CONTRACTS, CHAPTER 16, INTRODUCTORY NOTE:

Reporter's Note:

Awarding damages on this basis to protect the injured party's "expectation interest" gives the other party an incentive to break the contract if, but only if, he gains enough from the breach that he can compensate the injured party for his losses and still retain some of the benefits from the breach.

The Restatement of Contracts

There are many excerpts from and citations to the Restatement of Contracts in this book. The Restatement of Contracts is one of a series of "Restatements" of various subjects (torts, property, agency, etc.) written by teams of experts under the sponsorship of the American Law Institute. The American Law Institute is an organization of lawyers, judges, and professors devoted to improvement of the legal institution. The Institute's Restatement projects are carried out under the leadership of a Reporter appointed by the Institute. The Reporter and a Committee of Advisers prepare a series of Tentative Drafts of the Restatement sections which are submitted to the Institute for its approval. After revisions and final approval of the Restatement, it is published by the Institute.

The original Restatement of Contracts was approved and promulgated by the Institute in 1932 and was the first Restatement to be published. Professor Samuel Williston of Harvard Law School was the Chief Reporter, and Professor Arthur L. Corbin of Yale Law School was a Special Adviser and Reporter on Remedies. The Restatement, Second, of Contracts was begun in 1962, received final Institute approval in 1979, and was published in 1981. Professor Robert Braucher of Harvard Law School served as Reporter until resigning to accept appointment to the Supreme Judicial Court of Massachusetts in 1971. Professor E. Allan Farnsworth of Columbia University School of Law then served as Reporter until completion of the project.

Originally the Restatements were conceived of as setting forth the true rules. Law was thought of as a science. Given a correct statement of its axioms and theorems, the one correct answer to any legal problem could be derived. Legal rules were either possible or not possible—not wise or foolish, responsive or unresponsive to social realities. This notion of the law is no longer held by most members of the profession. The Restatements are now viewed as statements by scholars in particular subjects of what the most satisfactory response to a particular legal problem is thought to be. The Restatement provisions are usually drawn from case precedent, though they do not always reflect the "majority" view. Sometimes a Restatement provision sets forth what the Reporter and Advisers think the rule should be even though there is little precedent for it. When this occurs, because of the prestige of the persons stating the proposed rule, courts are likely to adopt it. Perhaps a more accurate name in these instances would be "Prestatement" rather than Restatement.

PEEVYHOUSE v. GARLAND COAL & MINING CO.

Supreme Court of Oklahoma, 1962.
382 P.2d 109, modified and rehearing denied, cert. denied,
375 U.S. 906, 84 S.Ct. 196, 11 L.Ed.2d 145 (1963).

JACKSON, JUSTICE.

In the trial court, plaintiffs Willie and Lucille Peevyhouse sued the defendant, Garland Coal and Mining Company, for damages for breach of contract. Judgment was for plaintiffs in an amount considerably less than was sued for. Plaintiffs appeal and defendant cross-appeals.

In the briefs on appeal, the parties present their argument and contentions under several propositions; however, they all stem from the basic question of whether the trial court properly instructed the jury on the measure of damages.

Briefly stated, the facts are as follows: plaintiffs owned a farm containing coal deposits, and in November, 1954, leased the premises to defendant for a period of five years for coal mining purposes. A "stripmining" operation was contemplated in which the coal would be taken from pits on the surface of the ground, instead of from underground mine shafts. In addition to the usual covenants found in a coal mining lease, defendant specifically agreed to perform certain restorative and remedial work at the end of the lease period. It is unnecessary to set out the details of the work to be done, other than to say that it would involve the moving of many thousands of cubic yards of dirt, at a cost estimated by expert witnesses at about $29,000.00. However, plaintiffs sued for only $25,000.00.

During the trial, it was stipulated that all covenants and agreements in the lease contract had been fully carried out by both parties, except the remedial work mentioned above; defendant conceded that this work had not been done.

Plaintiffs introduced expert testimony as to the amount and nature of the work to be done, and its estimated cost. Over plaintiffs' objections, defendant thereafter introduced expert testimony as to the "diminution in value" of plaintiffs' farm resulting from the failure of defendant to render performance as agreed in the contract—that is, the difference between the present value of the farm, and what its value would have been if defendant had done what it agreed to do.

At the conclusion of the trial, the court instructed the jury that it must return a verdict for plaintiffs, and left the amount of damages for jury determination. On the measure of damages, the court instructed the jury that it might consider the cost of performance of the work defendant agreed to do, "together with all of the evidence offered on behalf of either party".

It thus appears that the jury was at liberty to consider the "diminution in value" of plaintiffs' farm as well as the cost of "repair work" in determining the amount of damages.

It returned a verdict for plaintiffs for $5000.00—only a fraction of the "cost of performance", *but more than the total value of the farm even after the remedial work is done.*

On appeal, the issue is sharply drawn. Plaintiffs contend that the true measure of damages in this case is what it will cost plaintiffs to obtain performance of the work that was not done because of defendant's default. Defendant argues that the measure of damages is the cost of performance "limited, however, to the total difference in the market value before and after the work was performed".

It appears that this precise question has not heretofore been presented to this court. In Ardizonne v. Archer, 72 Okl. 70, 178 P. 263, this court held that the measure of damages for breach of a contract to drill an oil well was the reasonable cost of drilling the well, but here a slightly different factual situation exists. The drilling of an oil well will yield valuable geological information, even if no oil or gas is found, and of course if the well is a producer, the value of the premises increases. In the case before us, it is argued by defendant with some force that the performance of the remedial work defendant agreed to do will add at the most only a few hundred dollars to the value of plaintiffs' farm, and that the damages should be limited to that amount because that is all plaintiffs have lost.

Plaintiffs rely on Groves v. John Wunder Co., 205 Minn. 163, 286 N.W. 235, 123 A.L.R. 502. In that case, the Minnesota court, in a substantially similar situation, adopted the "cost of performance" rule as opposed to the "value" rule. The result was to authorize a jury to give plaintiff damages in the amount of $60,000, where the real estate concerned would have been worth only $12,160, even if the work contracted for had been done.

It may be observed that Groves v. John Wunder Co., supra, is the only case which has come to our attention in which the cost of performance rule has been followed under circumstances where the cost of performance greatly exceeded the diminution in value resulting from the breach of contract. Incidentally, it appears that this case was decided by a plurality rather than a majority of the members of the court.

Defendant relies principally upon Sandy Valley & E. R. Co., v. Hughes, 175 Ky. 320, 194 S.W. 344; Bigham v. Wabash-Pittsburg Terminal Ry. Co., 223 Pa. 106, 72 A. 318; and Sweeney v. Lewis Const. Co., 66 Wash. 490, 119 P. 1108. These were all cases in which, under similar circumstances, the appellate courts followed the "value" rule instead of the "cost of performance" rule. Plaintiff points out that in the earliest of these cases (Bigham) the court cites as authority on the measure of damages an earlier Pennsylvania *tort* case, and that the other two cases follow the first, with no explanation as to why a measure of damages ordinarily followed in cases sounding in tort should be used in contract cases. Nevertheless, it is of some significance that three out of four appellate courts have followed the diminution in value rule under circumstances where, as here, the cost of performance greatly exceeds the diminution in value.

The explanation may be found in the fact that the situations presented are artificial ones. It is highly unlikely that the ordinary property owner would agree to pay $29,000 (or its equivalent) for the construction of "improvements" upon his property that would increase its value only about ($300) three hundred dollars. The result is that we are called upon to apply principles of law theoretically based upon reason and reality to a situation which is basically unreasonable and unrealistic.

In Groves v. John Wunder Co., supra, in arriving at its conclusions, the Minnesota court apparently considered the contract involved to be analogous to a building and construction contract, and cited authority for the proposition that the cost of performance or completion of the building as contracted is ordinarily the measure of damages in actions for damages for the breach of such a contract.

In an annotation following the Minnesota case beginning at 123 A.L.R. 515, the annotator places the three cases relied on by defendant (Sandy Valley, Bigham and Sweeney) under the classification of cases involving "grading and excavation contracts".

We do not think either analogy is strictly applicable to the case now before us. The primary purpose of the lease contract between plaintiffs and defendant was neither "building and construction" nor "grading and excavation". It was merely to accomplish the economical recovery and marketing of coal from the premises, to the profit of all parties. The special provisions of the lease contract pertaining to remedial work were incidental to the main object involved.

Even in the case of contracts that are unquestionably building and construction contracts, the authorities are not in agreement as to the factors to be considered in determining whether the cost of performance rule or the value rule should be applied. The American Law Institute's Restatement of the Law, Contracts, Volume 1, Sections 346(1)(a)(i) and (ii) submits the proposition that the cost of performance is the proper measure of damages "if this is possible and does not involve *unreasonable economic waste*"; and that the diminution in value caused by the breach is the proper measure "if construction and completion in accordance with the contract would involve *unreasonable economic waste*". (Emphasis supplied.) In an explanatory comment immediately following the text, the Restatement makes it clear that the "economic waste" referred to consists of the destruction of a substantially completed building or other structure. Of course no such destruction is involved in the case now before us.

On the other hand, in McCormick, Damages, Section 168, it is said with regard to building and construction contracts that " * * * in cases where the defect is one that can be repaired or cured without *undue expense*" the cost of performance is the proper measure of damages, but where " * * * the defect in material or construction is one that cannot be remedied without *an expenditure for reconstruction disproportionate to the end to be attained*" (emphasis supplied) the value rule should be followed. The same idea was expressed in Jacob & Youngs, Inc. v. Kent, 230 N.Y. 239, 129 N.E. 889, 23 A.L.R. 1429, as follows:

"The owner is entitled to the money which will permit him to complete, unless the cost of completion is grossly and unfairly out of proportion to the good to be attained. When that is true, the measure is the difference in value."

It thus appears that the prime consideration in the Restatement was "economic waste"; and that the prime consideration in McCormick, Damages, and in Jacob & Youngs, Inc. v. Kent, supra, was the relationship between the expense involved and the "end to be attained"—in other words, the "relative economic benefit".

In view of the unrealistic fact situation in the instant case, and certain Oklahoma statutes to be hereinafter noted, we are of the opinion that the "relative economic benefit" is a proper consideration here. This is in accord with the recent case of Mann v. Clowser, 190 Va. 887, 59 S.E.2d 78, where, in applying the cost rule, the Virginia court specifically noted that " * * * the defects are remediable from a practical standpoint and the costs *are not grossly disproportionate to the results to be obtained*" (Emphasis supplied).

23 O.S.1961 §§ 96 and 97 provide as follows:

"§ 96. * * * Notwithstanding the provisions of this chapter, no person can recover a greater amount in damages for the breach of an obligation, than he would have gained by the full performance thereof on both sides * * * .

"§ 97. * * * Damages must, in all cases, be reasonable, and where an obligation of any kind appears to create a right to unconscionable and grossly oppressive damages, contrary to substantial justice no more than reasonable damages can be recovered."

Although it is true that the above sections of the statute are applied most often in tort cases, they are by their own terms, and the decisions of this court, also applicable in actions for damages for breach of contract. It would seem that they are peculiarly applicable here where, under the "cost of performance" rule, plaintiffs might recover an amount about nine times the total value of their farm. Such would seem to be "unconscionable and grossly oppressive damages, contrary to substantial justice" within the meaning of the statute. Also, it can hardly be denied that if plaintiffs here are permitted to recover under the "cost of performance" rule, they will receive a greater benefit from the breach than could be gained from full performance, contrary to the provisions of Sec. 96.

An analogy may be drawn between the cited sections, and the provisions of 15 O.S.1961 §§ 214 and 215. These sections tend to render void any provisions of a contract which attempt to fix the amount of stipulated damages to be paid in case of a breach, except where it is impracticable or extremely difficult to determine the actual damages. This results in spite of the agreement of the parties, and the obvious and well known rationale is that insofar as they exceed the actual damages suffered, the stipulated damages amount to a penalty or forfeiture which the law does not favor.

23 O.S.1961 §§ 96 and 97 have the same effect in the case now before us. *In spite of the agreement of the parties*, these sections limit the damages recoverable to a reasonable amount not "contrary to substantial justice"; they prevent plaintiffs from recovering a "greater amount in damages for the breach of an obligation" than they would have "gained by the full performance thereof".

We therefore hold that where, in a coal mining lease, lessee agrees to perform certain remedial work on the premises concerned at the end of the lease period, and thereafter the contract is fully performed by both parties except that the remedial work is not done, the measure of damages in an action by lessor against lessee for damages for breach of contract is ordinarily the reasonable cost of performance of the work; however, where the contract provision breached was merely incidental to the main purpose in view, and where the economic benefit which would result to lessor by full performance of the work is grossly disproportionate to the cost of performance, the damages which lessor may recover are limited to the diminution in value resulting to the premises because of the non-performance.

We believe the above holding is in conformity with the intention of the Legislature as expressed in the statutes mentioned, and in harmony with the better-reasoned cases from the other jurisdictions where analogous fact situations have been considered. It should be noted that the rule as stated does not interfere with the property owner's right to "do what he will with his own" Chamberlain v. Parker, 45 N.Y. 569, or his right, if he chooses, to contract for "improvements" which will actually have the effect of reducing his property's value. Where such result is in fact contemplated by the parties, and is a main or principal purpose of those contracting, it would seem that the measure of damages for breach would ordinarily be the cost of performance.

The above holding disposes of all of the arguments raised by the parties on appeal.

Under the most liberal view of the evidence herein, the diminution in value resulting to the premises because of nonperformance of the remedial work was $300.00. After a careful search of the record, we have found no evidence of a higher figure, and plaintiffs do not argue in their briefs that a greater diminution in value was sustained. It thus appears that the judgment was clearly excessive, and that the amount for which judgment should have been rendered is definitely and satisfactorily shown by the record.

We are asked by each party to modify the judgment in accordance with the respective theories advanced, and it is conceded that we have authority to do so.

We are of the opinion that the judgment of the trial court for plaintiffs should be, and it is hereby, modified and reduced to the sum of $300.00, and as so modified it is affirmed.

WELCH, DAVISON, HALLEY, and JOHNSON, JJ., concur.

WILLIAMS, C.J., BLACKBIRD, V.C.J., and IRWIN and BERRY, JJ., dissent.

IRWIN, JUSTICE (dissenting). * * *

Defendant admits that it failed to perform its obligations that it agreed and contracted to perform under the lease contract and there is nothing in the record which indicates that defendant could not perform its obligations. Therefore, in my opinion defendant's breach of the contract was wilful and not in good faith.

Although the contract speaks for itself, there were several negotiations between the plaintiffs and defendant before the contract was executed. Defendant admitted in the trial of the action, that plaintiffs insisted that the above provisions be included in the contract and that they would not agree to the coal mining lease unless the above provisions were included.

In consideration for the lease contract, plaintiffs were to receive a certain amount as royalty for the coal produced and marketed and in addition thereto their land was to be restored as provided in the contract. * * *

Defendant did not have the right to mine plaintiffs' coal or to use plaintiffs' property for its mining operations without the consent of plaintiffs. Defendant had knowledge of the benefits that it would receive under the contract and the approximate cost of performing the contract. With this knowledge, it must be presumed that defendant thought that it would be to its economic advantage to enter into the contract with plaintiffs and that it would reap benefits from the contract, or it would have not entered into the contract. * * *

In the instant action defendant has made no attempt to even substantially perform. The contract in question is not immoral, is not tainted with fraud, and was not entered into through mistake or accident and is not contrary to public policy. It is clear and unambiguous and the parties understood the terms thereof, and the approximate cost of fulfilling the obligations could have been approximately ascertained. There are no conditions existing now which could not have been reasonably anticipated when the contract was negotiated and executed. The defendant could have performed the contract if it desired. It has accepted and reaped the benefits of its contract and now urges that plaintiffs' benefits under the contract be denied. If plaintiffs' benefits are denied, such benefits would inure to the direct benefit of the defendant.

Therefore, in my opinion, the plaintiffs were entitled to specific performance of the contract and since defendant has failed to perform, the proper measure of damages should be the cost of performance. Any other measure of damage would be holding for naught the express provisions of the contract; would be taking from the plaintiffs the benefits of the contract and placing those benefits in defendant which has failed to perform its obligations; would be granting benefits to defendant without a resulting obligation; and would be completely rescinding the solemn obligation of the contract for the benefit of the defendant to the detriment of the plaintiffs by making an entirely new contract for the parties.

I therefore respectfully dissent to the opinion promulgated by a majority of my associates.

In a petition for rehearing, plaintiff contended that even under a "diminution in value" theory, the damages awarded were not sufficient. Plaintiff pointed out that the farm consisted not only of the 60 acres covered by the coal mining lease but also of at least an equal amount of additional land. If the diminution in value of the entire farm were considered, it would greatly exceed the $300 awarded. At trial, because his theory of recovery was cost of performance and not dimunition in value, plaintiff offered no evidence of the effect of the mining on the neighboring land and objected to any references to that land. The petition for rehearing was denied with the statement:

> "We think plaintiffs' present position is that of a plaintiff in any damage suit who has failed to prove his damages—opposed by a defendant who has proved plaintiff's damages; and that plaintiffs' complaint that the record does not show the total 'diminution in value' to their lands comes too late. It is well settled that a party will not be permitted to change his theory of the case upon appeal.

> "Also, plaintiffs' expressed fear that by introducing evidence on the question of 'diminution in value' they would have waived their objection to similar evidence by defendant was not justified."

"Efficient" Breach

Expectancy damages are intended, in the words of the Restatement, to give the injured party "the benefit of his bargain by awarding him a sum of money that will, to the extent possible, put him in as good a position as he would have been in had the contract been performed." Restatement, Second, Contracts § 347, comment a. This measure of recovery has been defended on the ground that it is "efficient" in the sense that it makes it likely that the goods or services that are the subject of the contract will wind up in the hands of a person who values them most highly. Breach is deterred only if the gain to the promisor does not exceed the loss to the promisee. For example, suppose that there is a contract for the sale of goods and that the promisee will suffer $1,000 in expectancy damages if the goods are not delivered. The promisor, however, can sell the goods to someone else for a profit of $2,000. If the only sanction for breach of contract is expectancy damages, the promisor has an economic incentive to breach the contract. In the view of some scholars, this is as it "should be." R. Posner, Economic Analysis of Law § 4.8 at p. 107 (3d ed. 1986).

There are criticisms of the efficient breach argument even in terms of efficiency. First, the argument assumes that the seller rather than the buyer can more efficiently locate the party who values the goods more than the buyer. This may usually be so, but as Dura–Wood Treating Co. v. Century Forest Industries, p. 37, indicates, this will not always be so. Second, it may be more efficient for the seller to bargain with the buyer for the right to sell the goods to someone else rather than to break the contract. Talk before breach is very likely to be less expensive than talk after breach, because afterwards lawyers usually do the talking.

There are also moral objections to the efficient breach argument. Once the buyer has acquired a contractual right to the goods, should the goods be viewed as belonging to the buyer? If so, the seller's sale to someone who valued them more highly than the buyer is no more justified than if a burglar entered your house and took a painting that he valued more highly than you did. On this view, the seller's "profit" from breaking the contract should belong to the buyer. See Colorado Rev.Stat.Ann. § 5–12–102(1) " ＊ ＊ ＊ creditors shall receive interest as follows:

> "(a) When money or property has been wrongfully withheld, interest shall be in an amount which fully recognizes the gain or benefit realized by the person withholding such money or property from the date of wrongful withholding to the date of payment or to the date judgment is entered, whichever first occurs ＊ ＊ ＊".

Great Western Sugar Co. v. KN Energy, Inc., 778 P.2d 272 (Colo.App. 1989) (applying § 5–12–102 to breach of a contract to sell natural gas).

In 1967, Oklahoma enacted the Open Cut Land Reclamation Act (45 Okla.Stat.Ann. §§ 701–713) replaced in 1971 by the Mining Lands Reclamation Act (45 Okla.Stat.Ann. §§ 721–738). The Act requires mine operators to apply for a permit before engaging in mining. The application must be accompanied by a plan of reclamation of the affected land that meets the requirements of the Act, including grading and revegetation. In 1979, Oklahoma enacted the Coal Reclamation Act (id. §§ 742.1–793) and in 1981 the Abandoned Mine Reclamation Act (id. §§ 740.1–740.7), both keyed to the federal legislation discussed in the next paragraph.

In 1977, Congress enacted the Surface Mining Control and Reclamation Act (30 U.S.C.A. ch. 25). One of the findings on which the legislation is based is that "many surface mining operations result in disturbances of surface areas that burden and adversely affect commerce and the public welfare by destroying or diminishing the utility of land for commercial, industrial, residential, recreational, agricultural, and forestry purposes, by causing erosion and landslides, by contributing to floods, by polluting the water, by destroying fish and wildlife habitats, by impairing natural beauty, by damaging the property of citizens, by creating hazards dangerous to life and property by degrading the quality of life in local communities, and by counteracting governmental programs and efforts to conserve soil, water, and other natural resources." The Act's purposes include assuring "that adequate procedures are undertaken to reclaim surface areas" (30 U.S.C.A. § 1202(e)) and promoting "the reclamation of mined areas left without adequate reclamation prior to August 3, 1977" (30 U.S.C.A. § 1202(h)).

Do these statutes require "economic waste"?

———

JACOB & YOUNGS, INC. v. KENT, 230 N.Y. 239, 129 N.E. 889 (1921). Builder had constructed a large country house for owner. The plumbing specifications required that only Reading pipe be used. Nine months after the house was completed and occupied, it was discovered that pipe of a different manufacture had been used. Owner's architect directed builder to replace the pipe, which would have required destruction and rebuilding of substantial portions of the house. When builder refused, architect did not certify that the final payment was due, and this payment of about $3,500 was not made. Builder sued for this payment. The trial court excluded builder's evidence that there was no difference in value between the pipe used and Reading pipe and directed a verdict for owner. In an opinion by Judge Cardozo, judgment for owner was reversed and judgment ordered for builder: "We must weigh the purpose to be served, the desire to be gratified, the excuse for deviation from the letter, the cruelty of enforced adherence. Then only can we tell whether literal fulfillment is to be implied by law as a condition. This is not to say that the parties are not free by apt and certain words to effectuate a purpose that performance of every term shall be a condition of recovery. That question is not here. This is merely to say that the law will be slow to impute the purpose, in the silence of the parties, where the significance of the default is grievously out of proportion to the oppression of the forfeiture. The willful transgressor must accept the penalty of his transgression. For him there is no occasion to mitigate the rigor of implied conditions. The transgressor whose default is unintentional and trivial may hope for mercy if he will offer atonement for his wrong."

Does this opinion support the result in the principal case? Would Cardozo have reached the same result if owner were the president of Reading pipe company?

ROCKINGHAM COUNTY v. LUTEN BRIDGE CO.

United States Court of Appeals, Fourth Circuit, 1929.
35 F.2d 301.

PARKER, CIRCUIT JUDGE. This was an action at law instituted in the court below by the Luten Bridge Company, as plaintiff, to recover of Rockingham county, North Carolina, an amount alleged to be due under a contract for the construction of a bridge. The county admits the execution and breach of the contract, but contends that notice of cancellation was given the bridge company before the erection of the bridge was commenced, and that it is liable only for the damages which the company would have sustained, if it had abandoned construction at that time. The judge below excluded evidence offered by the county in support of its contentions as to notice of cancellation and damages, and instructed a verdict for plaintiff for the full amount of its claim. From judgment on this verdict the county has appealed.

The facts out of which the case arises, as shown by the affidavits and offers of proof appearing in the record, are as follows: On January 7, 1924, the board of commissioners of Rockingham county voted to award to plaintiff a contract for the construction of the bridge in controversy. * * *

At the regular monthly meeting of the board on March 3d, a resolution was passed directing that plaintiff be notified that any work done on the bridge would be done by it at its own risk and hazard, that the board was of the opinion that the contract for the construction of the bridge was not valid and legal, and that, even if the board were mistaken as to this, it did not desire to construct the bridge, and would contest payment for same if constructed. A copy of this resolution was also sent to plaintiff. At the regular monthly meeting on April 7th, a resolution was passed, reciting that the board had been informed that one of its members was privately insisting that the bridge be constructed. It repudiated this action on the part of the member and gave notice that it would not be recognized. At the September meeting, a resolution was passed to the effect that the board would pay no bills presented by plaintiff or any one connected with the bridge. At the time of the passage of the first resolution, very little work toward the construction of the bridge had been done, it being estimated that the total cost of labor done and material on the ground was around $1,900; but, notwithstanding the repudiation of the contract by the county, the bridge company continued with the work of construction. * * *

Coming, then, to the * * * question * * * as to the measure of plaintiff's recovery—we do not think that, after the county had given notice, while the contract was still executory, that it did not desire the bridge built and would not pay for it, plaintiff could proceed to build it and recover the contract price. It is true that the county had no right to rescind the contract, and the notice given plaintiff amounted to a breach on its part; but, after plaintiff had received notice of the breach, it was its duty to do nothing to increase the damages flowing therefrom. If A enters into a binding contract to build a house for B, B, of course, has no right to rescind the contract without A's consent. But if, before the house is built, he decides that he does not want it, and notifies A to that effect, A has no right to proceed with the building and thus pile up damages. His remedy is to treat the contract as broken when he receives the notice, and sue for the recovery of such damages as he may have sustained from the breach, including any profit which he would have realized upon performance, as well as any other losses which may have resulted to him. In the case at bar, the county decided not to build the road of which the bridge was to be a part, and did not build it. The bridge, built in the midst of the forest, is of no value to the county because of this change of circumstances. When, therefore, the county gave notice to the plaintiff that it would not proceed with the project, plaintiff should have desisted from further work. It had no right thus to pile up damages by proceeding with the erection of a useless bridge.

The contrary view was expressed by Lord Cockburn in Frost v. Knight, L.R. 7 Ex. 111, but, as pointed out by Prof. Williston (Williston on Contracts, vol. 3, p. 2347), it is not in harmony with the decisions in this country. The American rule and the reasons supporting it are well stated by Prof. Williston as follows:

> "There is a line of cases running back to 1845 which holds that, after an absolute repudiation or refusal to perform by one party to a contract, the other party cannot continue to perform and recover damages based on full performance. This rule is only a particular application of the general rule of damages that a plaintiff cannot hold a defendant liable for damages which need not have been incurred; or, as it is often stated, the plaintiff must, so far as he can without loss to himself, mitigate the damages caused by the defendant's wrongful act. The application of this rule to the matter in question is obvious. If a man engages to have work done, and afterwards repudiates his contract before the work has been begun or when it has been only partially done, it is inflicting damage on the defendant without benefit to the plaintiff to allow the latter to insist on proceeding with the contract. The work may be useless to the defendant, and yet he would be forced to pay the full contract price. On the other hand, the plaintiff is interested only in the profit he will make out of the contract. If he receives this it is equally advantageous for him to use his time otherwise."

The leading case on the subject in this country is the New York case of Clark v. Marsiglia, 1 Denio (N.Y.) 317, 43 Am.Dec. 670. In that case defendant had employed plaintiff to paint * certain pictures for him, but countermanded the order before the work was finished. Plaintiff, however, went on and completed the work and sued for the contract price. In reversing a judgment for plaintiff, the court said:

> "The plaintiff was allowed to recover as though there had been no countermand of the order; and in this the court erred. The defendant, by requiring the plaintiff to stop work upon the paintings, violated his contract, and thereby incurred a liability to pay such damages as the plaintiff should sustain. Such damages would include a recompense for the labor done and materials used, and such further sum in damages as might, upon legal principles, be

---

* Plaintiff was employed to clean and repair the pictures. [Ed.]

assessed for the breach of the contract; but the plaintiff had no right, by obstinately persisting in the work, to make the penalty upon the defendant greater than it would otherwise have been."

* * *

This is in accord with the North Carolina decision of Heiser v. Mears, 120 N.C. 443, 27 S.E. 117, in which it was held that, where a buyer countermands his order for goods to be manufactured for him under an executory contract, before the work is completed, it is notice to the seller that he elects to rescind his contract and submit to the legal measure of damages, and that in such case the seller cannot complete the goods and recover the contract price. * * * It follows that there was error in directing a verdict for plaintiff for the full amount of its claim. The measure of plaintiff's damage, upon its appearing that notice was duly given not to build the bridge, is an amount sufficient to compensate plaintiff for labor and materials expended and expense incurred in the part performance of the contract, prior to its repudiation, plus the profit which would have been realized if it had been carried out in accordance with its terms. * * * The judgment below will accordingly be reversed, and the case remanded for a new trial.

Reversed.

HUSSEY v. HOLLOWAY

Supreme Judicial Court of Massachusetts, 1914.
217 Mass. 100, 104 N.E. 471.

Contract for a breach of a contract to employ the plaintiff as trimmer in the defendants' millinery department in Boston for the spring season of 1910 at $18 a week. Writ dated March 24, 1910.

In the Superior Court the case was tried before Fox, J. At the trial the defendants admitted that there had been a breach of the contract, and it was agreed that the only question to be decided was the amount of the damages. The facts which could have been found upon the evidence are stated in the opinion, where also are stated certain instructions given by the judge. At the close of the evidence the defendants asked for the following rulings: * * *

"2. That if the jury find that the plaintiff was offered employment by [defendants] at the same wages and in the same general line of work as was mentioned in the contract, then the plaintiff cannot recover any damages for the alleged breach of the contract which accrued subsequent to the receipt of the offer. * * *

"6. That in order for the plaintiff to recover for the loss of wages as fixed by the contract the jury must find that the plaintiff was unable to procure by the exercise of proper industry other employment of some kind reasonably adapted to her abilities.

"7. That the plaintiff was bound as a matter of law to use due care and diligence after the termination of her employment to secure other employment of some kind reasonably adapted to her abilities. * * *

"9. That the plaintiff was obliged as a matter of law to accept any employment offered her at $15 a week, if the work was of the same general nature as the work which was provided for in the contract. * * *

"C. That the plaintiff's damages must be diminished in the amount that she would have been obliged to pay a nurse to care for her mother or do other work which she was able to do and did do while out of employment during the time covered by this contract."

The judge gave as instructions the sixth and seventh rulings requested by the defendants, but refused to give the remaining rulings, except as incorporated in his charge. The jury returned a verdict for the plaintiff in the sum of $419.04, of which amount $40 afterwards was remitted by requirement of the judge. The defendants alleged exceptions to the refusal of the judge to give the rulings requested and to the admission of evidence of the physical condition of the plaintiff's mother.

De Courcy, J. The defendants agreed to employ the plaintiff for the spring season of 1910 as trimmer in their millinery department. In the Superior Court they admitted that there had been a breach of this contract on their part, and the trial proceeded on the issue of damages. The case is here on exceptions to the refusal of the judge to give several rulings requested by the defendants, and to the admission of certain testimony.

It appeared in evidence that the season began about February 15, 1910. On February 14 the defendants wrote to the plaintiff notifying her that they would not re-engage her. To this she replied that she would treat the letter as a breach of their contract, and would hold them responsible in damages. On February 19 they wrote to her:

"After due consideration of yours of the 16th inst. we beg to advise you we shall expect you to report at the store Monday a.m. February 21st. We have, however, a head trimmer and your work will be under the supervision of this head trimmer, and Mrs. Cooksey."

The plaintiff testified that she regarded this letter as an afterthought and as not written in good faith; that the defendants never kept more than one trimmer, and that she was wanted for the inferior and lower salaried position of a hat maker; and that she believed they would let her go again in a few days. One of the defendants admitted that they needed but one trimmer, and intimated that the plaintiff's work would be that of a maker.

There was also evidence to warrant the finding of the following facts. After her [rejection of the defendants' February 19 offer], the plaintiff applied to the various wholesale houses and to some of the retailers for employment. On March 14, she was offered a position as copyist at $15 a week, but declined it as she had never worked for less

than $18 and sometimes received $20, and was hoping to get employment at her regular pay. On that same day she was employed at
Kornfeld's, and worked there from Tuesday until Saturday night at $3
a day. After that no position was obtainable in Boston, as it was too
late in the season, and she was unable to accept those offered out of
town on account of the condition of her invalid mother.

The presiding judge fully and correctly instructed the jury on the
general rule of damages applicable in such cases. There were two
portions of the evidence that called for more specific instructions,
namely, the defendants' letter of February 19, and the testimony
relating to the plaintiff's refusal to accept certain offers of employment.
As to the letter, the judge expressly said to the jury, "there is no
question that if she had been offered definitely her old employment for
the term and for the wages for which she was engaged, that her
absolute refusal to accept that should be regarded as a bar for any
further claim for damages beyond the date when that refusal was sent
in." And he properly left it to the jury to say as a matter of fact
whether the letter constituted such an offer. If the defendants really
had intended to restore to the plaintiff her old position, they easily
could have said so. The letter, however, did not state what the new
work was to be, nor the wages, nor the term of employment; and the
jury well might regard such an offer, terminable at will, as one not
equivalent to the plaintiff's former contract, which was for a definite
period and in a superior position. The plaintiff was not obliged to
accept a modification of the original agreement.

With reference to the plaintiff's duty to make efforts to secure
other employment after her dismissal from the service of the defendants, the presiding judge, as a portion of his instructions, read the
following from the opinion of this court in Maynard v. Royal Worcester
Corset Co., 200 Mass. 1: "Where one is under contract for personal
service, and is discharged, it becomes his duty to dispose of his time in a
reasonable way, so as to obtain as large compensation as possible, and
to use honest, earnest and intelligent efforts to this end. He cannot
voluntarily remain idle and expect to recover the compensation stipulated in the contract from the other party." He also gave the sixth
ruling requested, namely, "In order for the plaintiff to recover for the
loss of wages as fixed by the contract the jury must find that the
plaintiff was unable to procure by the exercise of proper industry other
employment of some kind reasonably adapted to her abilities." This
fully protected the rights of the defendant. Indeed, it might be regarded as too favorable, unless taken in connection with the further ruling,
given at the request of the plaintiff and not excepted to by the
defendant, that "the plaintiff was not obliged to seek employment in
another locality, or of a substantially lower grade and character than
that from which she was discharged." The principle on which the
plaintiff's damages were allowed was that of compensation. And while
it was her duty to use reasonable diligence to secure other employment
and thereby lessen her loss, it has generally been held that where, as in

this case, a plaintiff was employed in a special service, she is not obliged to engage in a business that is not of the same general character, in order to mitigate the defendant's damages. It was for the jury to determine as questions of fact whether the plaintiff did exercise such reasonable diligence, whether she was justified in declining offers of employment out of town by reason of her mother's illness, and whether the refusal of offers at $15 a week or of work in an inferior position was warranted by her expectation of early employment at her regular occupation and salary.

The specific requests of the defendants, so far as not covered by what has been said, may be disposed of briefly. * * * C was given in substance.

As to the evidence with reference to the condition of the plaintiff's mother, it was at least competent as bearing on the reasonableness of the plaintiff's refusal to accept employment in Fall River.

Exceptions overruled.

The opinion in Hussey v. Holloway states that "[t]he plaintiff was not obliged to accept a modification of the original agreement." If Ms. Hussey had accepted the offer of re-employment and was paid lower wages than originally agreed, would she be entitled to sue for the difference? If it is not clear from Holloway's offer whether accepting re-employment constitutes a settlement of any claims that Ms. Hussey might have for breach of contract, against whom should this ambiguity be construed?

GOLOB v. GEORGE S. MAY INTERNATIONAL CO., 2 Wash.App. 499, 468 P.2d 707 (1970). Golob, engaged in cattle feeding, hired May Company to perform management consulting services. These services included the development of formulas for determining the best time to stop feeding cattle and sell them. May's employees visited Golob's business for eighteen days and Golob paid the full contract price. May then delivered its report to Golob, but the formulas were not included. Golob sued for breach of contract and recovered as damages an amount equal to the cost of paying someone else to perform the services that May had promised. This amount was measured by the payments to May, the court finding that another consultant would have to start "all over again" and that the payments to May established "the reasonable cost of substituted performance." May contended that "it [had] expressed its willingness after action brought to complete performance of the contract and thereby avoid plaintiffs' claimed damages," but the court rejected this argument:

"Assuming the offer was timely, then * * * the defendant failed to show that its belated offer of performance would not involve an undesirable relationship with the plaintiffs. If it would, the offer was immaterial."

———

PARKER v. TWENTIETH CENTURY–FOX FILM CORP., 3 Cal.3d 176, 89 Cal.Rptr. 737, 474 P.2d 689 (1970). Film company signed a contract with Shirley MacLaine to star her in a musical to be made in California, but the company then decided not to produce the picture. It offered MacLaine the starring role in a drama to be made in Australia without the script and director approval that she had for the musical. Otherwise the terms, including compensation, for the two pictures were the same. MacLaine did not accept the offer of substitute employment and sued for breach of contract. A directed verdict in her favor of $750,000 was affirmed on the ground that as a matter of law her refusal did not constitute a failure to use reasonable efforts to mitigate damages.

OLDS v. MAPES–REEVES CONSTRUCTION CO.

Supreme Judicial Court of Massachusetts, 1900.
177 Mass. 41, 58 N.E. 478.

KNOWLTON, J: The only question argued in this case relates to the subject of damages. The defendant, as a contractor had agreed to erect on land of another a large building in Northampton. The plaintiffs, as subcontractors, had agreed with the defendant to furnish and set up all the marble work in the building for $3,000. A controversy afterwards arose between the defendant and the owner of the building, on account of which the defendant ordered the plaintiffs to discontinue the work, and do nothing further under the contract. The defendant, having broken the contract, immediately became liable to the plaintiffs for damages, the measure of which was the difference between the sum which it would cost to complete the work in accordance with the contract, and the sum which the plaintiffs were to receive. This breach which fixed the liability occurred on November 9, 1896, and two days afterwards (on November 11th) this suit was brought. On the same day (whether before or after the commencement of the suit does not appear, and is not material) the plaintiffs made a new contract with the owner of the building, to complete the work called for by their contract with the defendant, and also to do certain other work, for a round sum agreed upon between them. The profits on this last contract, as found by the auditor, were $335.23, and the only question before us is whether the plaintiffs are to allow the amount of these profits in diminution of the damages to which they would otherwise be entitled.

The rule which is applicable to one who is under a contract to render personal services, and who, being discharged without cause before the end of his term, sues for damages, requires him, in estimating the damages, to allow for his services during the unexpired term whatever he is able to obtain for them, or, if damages are assessed before the end of the term, whatever he reasonably can be expected to obtain for them during the time covered by the contract. That is, on the breach of the contract he is left with his personal services as his property, in his own control, and he must allow for them, in the computation, their fair value for such use as he is able reasonably to make of them. In estimating the damages in the present case the auditor found that the actual cost of completing the work after the breach of the contract was $717.27, although, with such allowances as he made for work included in the plaintiffs' contract with the landowner which was not included in their contract with the defendant, he found that the plaintiffs received $1,052.50 for completing the work called for by the original contract. In making this estimate of the cost of completing the work, the auditor charged the plaintiffs with all labor and services which would have entered into it, whether personal to themselves or rendered by agents or employés, just as one under a contract to render personal services, when recovering damages for a broken contract, would be charged with the value of the personal services which remained unused after the breach of the contract. But there is this difference between the case of one who is discharged while under a contract to render personal services and a case like the present: In the former case the person discharged, whose personal services come back to him, is bound to dispose of them in a reasonable way, so as to make the damages to the other party not unreasonably large, while, in a case like the present, one deprived of his contract is under no obligation to enter into new contracts with a view to make profits for the other party. In a contract of the kind before the court, personal services are not necessarily included. The labor or supervision may be personally performed by the contractor, or may be furnished through agents or employees. In either case the value of it is all included, for the benefit of the other party, when the contractor is charged with the whole cost of completing the work, as an amount to be deducted from the contract price in estimating his damages. Since the damages properly are assessable in this way immediately after the breach of the contract, can it make any difference that the contractor afterwards makes a new contract with the owner, which includes the unfinished work? In making this contract the plaintiffs did not include anything which originally belonged to the defendant, in specie, under the original contract. Their agreement was not to render personal services, but only to accomplish a specific result. The plaintiffs were at liberty to leave this work entirely to the care of the hired servants, and to take as many other contracts as they chose elsewhere, and to give their personal time and attention to any occupation that they might choose. The question is whether the profits from the new contract with the landowner were a direct result of the defendant's breach of contract, or whether they came from an independent, intervening cause. It does not appear, and it is not to be assumed, that the plaintiffs were not competent to carry on several contracts at one time, and the making of profits on a new contract does not appear to be because of relief from the obligations of the old one. There is usually plenty of work to be contracted for, and the addition of one more possible job for which contractors may bid does not make the subsequent contract to do the work a direct result of the increase of opportunities for work. The addition of a new piece of work is merely a condition of the subsequent contract to do the work, and not a direct or proximate cause of it. Moreover, the making of such a contract involves many considerations besides the existence of the work to be done. There must be calculations and estimates. In making a contract of this kind there is always a risk of loss, as well as a possibility of gain. To say nothing of the fact that the plaintiffs' new contract included work which was not included in the old one, the cost of which could be fixed only as a matter of estimate, this contract with the landowner was a new undertaking, in which the plaintiffs were under no obligation to engage, and which involved risks that they could assume for themselves alone, if the contract had resulted in a loss to them, they could not have charged the defendant with the loss, to the increase of their damages. As the contract resulted in a gain to them, there is no reason why the defendant should receive this gain in diminution of the damages for which it was liable. There is no privity between the defendant and the plaintiffs, or between the defendant and the landowner, in reference to the new contract. There was an independent arrangement made between the plaintiffs and the landowner, and the only relation which the defendant's breach of the former contract had to it was that it furnished one of the conditions, namely, the work to be done, without which the new contract could not have been made. But the existence of this condition was not the cause of the contract, and the creator of this condition has no title to the fruits of the contract. If another person had taken this contract and made profits on it, as the plaintiffs did, it would hardly have been contended that the plaintiffs' damages were to be diminished on that account; or if the plaintiffs, instead of taking this contract after the breach of the former one, had gone elsewhere, and taken another contract, which afforded them similar profits, there would be no ground for a claim of the defendant to be allowed these profits in diminution of the damages. We are of opinion that the ruling at the trial was erroneous, and that the plaintiffs' damages should have been assessed without reference to their profits obtained under the new contract with the landowner. Exceptions sustained.

MASSENGALE v. TRANSITRON ELECTRONIC CORP., 385 F.2d 83 (1st Cir. 1967). Burck, a real estate broker, arranged a merger between Thermo King and Transitron, Transitron agreeing to pay the broker's commission of $300,000. Transitron repudiated the merger agreement. The broker then arranged a merger between Thermo King and Westinghouse. This merger went through and Thermo King paid the broker a fee of $325,000. The court held that Transitron was liable to the broker for the $300,000 that Transitron had promised to pay the broker:

> "The second ground of the district court's decision—that Thermo King's payment for the Westinghouse transaction satisfied any liability of Transitron—is based on the concept that all that was bargained for was one fee for one transaction. In a sense this is true. Prospectively, Burck and Thermo King contemplated only one completed transaction. There obviously could be only one completed merger. But what is alleged by the complaint to have happened is something beyond the contemplation of the parties, i.e., the unjustifiable refusal by Transitron to consummate the first transaction. This, as we have concluded, gives rise to an obligation. The broker has in such case earned a commission just as if the merger had been completed. When its subsequent services, which it was under no compulsion to render, resulted in a completed transaction, a second commission was earned. This is not, as appellant properly notes, an action against an employer for damages caused by wrongful discharge, in which damages would be mitigated by plaintiff's subsequent earnings."

Problem

Seller agrees to sell and Buyer agrees to buy 100,000 yards of cloth woven by Seller to Buyer's specifications. The contract price is $10 per yard. After Seller has spent $2 per yard in labor and materials to produce partially finished cloth, Buyer countermands. At this time it is likely that the completed cloth will have a market value of $4 per yard.

(a) Despite the countermand, Seller finishes the cloth at an additional cost of $3 per yard in labor and materials. When completed, the cloth has a market value of $2 per yard. What damages can Seller recover from Buyer?

(b) Seller stops production, removes the partially finished cloth from its machines, and sells it for scrap at $0.50 per yard. What damages can Seller recover from Buyer?

(c) Does Seller have a "duty" to finish the cloth if this will reduce damages?

See UCC §§ 2–703, 2–704, 2–706, 2–708, 2–709, 2–710.

R.E. DAVIS CHEMICAL CORP. v. DIASONICS, INC.
United States Court of Appeals, Seventh Circuit, 1987.
826 F.2d 678.

Before BAUER, CHIEF CIRCUIT JUDGE, CUDAHY and FLAUM, CIRCUIT JUDGES.

CUDAHY, CIRCUIT JUDGE.

Diasonics, Inc. appeals from the orders of the district court denying its motion for summary judgment and granting R.E. Davis Chemical Corp.'s summary judgment motion. * * * We * * * reverse the grant of summary judgment in favor of Davis and remand for further proceedings.

I.

Diasonics is a California corporation engaged in the business of manufacturing and selling medical diagnostic equipment. Davis is an Illinois corporation that contracted to purchase a piece of medical diagnostic equipment from Diasonics. On or about February 23, 1984, Davis and Diasonics entered into a written contract under which Davis agreed to purchase the equipment. Pursuant to this agreement, Davis paid Diasonics a $300,000 deposit on February 29, 1984. * * * Davis then breached its contract with Diasonics; it refused to take delivery of the equipment or to pay the balance due under the agreement. Diasonics later resold the equipment to a third party for the same price at which it was to be sold to Davis.

Davis sued Diasonics, asking for restitution of its $300,000 down payment under [§ 2–718(2)] of the Uniform Commercial Code (the "UCC" or the "Code"). Diasonics counterclaimed. Diasonics did not deny that Davis was entitled to recover its $300,000 deposit less $500 as provided in [§ 2–718(2)(b)]. However, Diasonics claimed that it was entitled to an offset under [§ 2–718(3)]. Diasonics alleged that it was a "lost volume seller," and, as such, it lost the profit from one sale when Davis breached its contract. Diasonics' position was that, in order to be put in as good a position as it would have been in had Davis performed, it was entitled to recover its lost profit on its contract with Davis under [§ 2–708(2)] of the UCC. * * *

The district court * * * entered summary judgment for Davis. The court held that lost volume sellers were not entitled to recover damages under [§ 2–708(2)] but rather were limited to recovering the difference between the resale price and the contract price along with incidental damages under [§ 2–706(1)]. * * * Davis was awarded $322,656, which represented Davis' down payment plus prejudgment interest less Diasonics' incidental damages. Diasonics appeals the district court's decision respecting its measure of damages. * * *

II.

We consider first Diasonics' claim that the district court erred in holding that Diasonics was limited to the measure of damages provided in [§ 2–706] and could not recover lost profits as a lost volume seller under [§ 2–708(2)]. Surprisingly, given its importance, this issue has never been addressed by an Illinois court, nor, apparently, by any other court construing Illinois law. Thus, we must attempt to predict how the Illinois Supreme Court would resolve this issue if it were presented to it. Courts applying the laws of other states have unanimously adopted the position that a lost volume seller can recover its lost profits under [§ 2–708(2)]. Contrary to the result reached by the district court, we conclude that the Illinois Supreme Court would follow these other cases and would allow a lost volume seller to recover its lost profit under [§ 2–708(2)].

We begin our analysis with [§ 2–718(2) and (3)]. Under [§ 2–718(2)(b)], Davis is entitled to the return of its down payment less $500. Davis' right to restitution, however, is qualified under [§ 2–718(3)(a)] to the extent that Diasonics can establish a right to recover damages under any other provision of Article 2 of the UCC. Article 2 contains four provisions that concern the recovery of a seller's general damages (as opposed to its incidental or consequential damages): [§ 2–706] (contract price less resale price); [§ 2–708(1)] (contract price less market price); [§ 2–708(2)] (profit); and [§ 2–709] (price). The problem we face here is determining whether Diasonics' damages should be measured under [§ 2–706] or [§ 2–708(2)]. To answer this question, we need to engage in a detailed look at the language and structure of these various damage provisions.

The Code does not provide a great deal of guidance as to when a particular damage remedy is appropriate. The damage remedies provided under the Code are catalogued in [§ 2–703], but this section does not indicate that there is any hierarchy among the remedies. One method of approaching the damage sections is to conclude that [§ 2–708] is relegated to a role inferior to that of [§ 2–706] and [§ 2–709] and that one can turn to [§ 2–708] only after one has concluded that neither [§ 2–706] nor [§ 2–709] is applicable. Under this interpretation of the relationship between [§ 2–706] and [§ 2–708], if the goods have been resold, the seller can sue to recover damages measured by the difference between the contract price and the resale price under [§ 2–706]. The seller can turn to [§ 2–708] only if it resells in a commercially unreasonable manner or if it cannot resell but an action for the price is inappropriate under [§ 2–709]. The district court adopted this reading of the Code's damage remedies and, accordingly, limited Diasonics to the measure of damages provided in [§ 2–706] because it resold the equipment in a commercially reasonable manner. * * *

Those courts that found that a lost volume seller can recover its lost profits under [§ 2–708(2)] implicitly rejected the position adopted by the district court; those courts started with the assumption that [§ 2–708] applied to a lost volume seller without considering whether the seller was limited to the remedy provided under [§ 2–706]. None of those courts even suggested that a seller who resold goods in a commercially reasonable manner was limited to the damage formula provided under [§ 2–706]. * * *

Concluding that Diasonics is entitled to seek damages under [§ 2–708], however, does not automatically result in Diasonics being awarded its lost profit. Two different measures of damages are provided in [§ 2–708]. Subsection [2–708(1)] provides for a measure of damages calculated by subtracting the market price at the time and place for tender from the contract price. The profit measure of damages, for which Diasonics is asking, is contained in [§ 2–708(2)]. However, one applies [§ 2–708(2)] only if "the measure of damages provided in subsection (1) is inadequate to put the seller in as good a position as performance would have done. * * *" Diasonics claims that [§ 2–708(1)] does not provide an adequate measure of damages when the seller is a lost volume seller. To understand Diasonics' argument, we need to define the concept of the lost volume seller. Those cases that have addressed this issue have defined a lost volume seller as one that has a predictable and finite number of customers and that has the capacity either to sell to all new buyers or to make the one additional sale represented by the resale after the breach. According to a number of courts and commentators, if the seller would have made the sale represented by the resale whether or not the breach occurred, damages measured by the difference between the contract price and market price cannot put the lost volume seller in as good a position as it would have been in had the buyer performed. The breach effectively cost the seller a "profit," and the seller can only be made whole by awarding it damages in the amount of its "lost profit" under [§ 2–708(2)].

We agree with Diasonics' position that, under some circumstances, the measure of damages provided under [§ 2–708(1)] will not put a reselling seller in as good a position as it would have been in had the buyer performed because the breach resulted in the seller losing sales volume. However, we disagree with the definition of "lost volume seller" adopted by other courts. Courts awarding lost profits to a lost volume seller have focused on whether the seller had the capacity to supply the breached units in addition to what it actually sold. In reality, however, the relevant questions include, not only whether the seller could have produced the breached units in addition to its actual volume, but also whether it would have been profitable for the seller to produce both units. Goetz & Scott, *Measuring Sellers' Damages: The Lost–Profits Puzzle*, 31 Stan.L.Rev. 323, 332–33, 346–47 (1979). As one commentator has noted, under

> the economic law of diminishing returns or increasing marginal costs[,] * * * as a seller's volume increases, then a point will inevitably be reached where the cost of selling each additional item diminishes the incremental return to the seller and eventually makes it entirely unprofitable to conclude the next sale.

Shanker, [The Case for a Literal Reading of UCC Section 2–708(2) (One Profit for the Reseller), 24 Case W.Res.L.Rev. 697, 705 (1973)]. Thus, under some conditions, awarding a lost volume seller its presumed lost profit will result in overcompensating the seller, and [§ 2–708(2)] would not take effect because the damage formula provided in [§ 2–708(1)] does place the seller in as good a position as if the buyer had performed. Therefore, on remand, Diasonics must establish, not only that it had the capacity to produce the breached unit in addition to the unit resold, but also that it would have been profitable for it to have produced and sold both. Diasonics carries the burden of establishing these facts because the burden of proof is generally on the party claiming injury to establish the amount of its damages; especially in a case such as this, the plaintiff has easiest access to the relevant data. * * *

One final problem with awarding a lost volume seller its lost profits was raised by the district court. This problem stems from the formulation of the measure of damages provided under [§ 2–708(2)] which is "the profit (including reasonable overhead) which the seller would have made from full performance by the buyer, together with any incidental damages provided in this Article [§ 2–710], due allowance for costs reasonably incurred and due credit for payments or *proceeds of resale.*" The literal language of [§ 2–708(2)] requires that the proceeds from resale be credited against the amount of damages awarded which, in most cases, would result in the seller recovering nominal damages. In those cases in which the lost volume seller was awarded its lost profit as damages, the courts have circumvented this problem by concluding that this language only applies to proceeds realized from the resale of uncompleted goods for scrap. Although neither the text of [§ 2–708(2)] nor the official comments limit its application to resale of goods for scrap, there is evidence that the drafters of [§ 2–708] seemed to have had this more limited application in mind when they proposed amending [§ 2–708] to include the phrase "due credit for payments or proceeds of resale." We conclude that the Illinois Supreme Court would adopt this more restrictive interpretation of this phrase rendering it inapplicable to this case.

We therefore reverse the grant of summary judgment in favor of Davis and remand with instructions that the district court calculate Diasonics' damages under [§ 2–708(2)] if Diasonics can establish not only that it had the capacity to make the sale to Davis as well as the sale to the resale buyer, but also that it would have been profitable for it to make both sales. Of course, Diasonics, in addition, must show that it probably would have made the second sale absent the breach.

The Uniform Commercial Code

The materials in this book incorporate discussions of and citations to provisions of the Uniform Commercial Code (UCC), particularly to Articles 1 and 2. The UCC was a joint project of the National Conference of Commissioners on Uniform State Laws and the American Law Institute. The National Conference of Commissioners on Uniform State Laws consists of lawyers, judges, and professors appointed by the states. It was founded in 1890 to draft legislation and recommend it to the state legislatures for adoption. The purpose is to make uniform the law in the United States on certain subjects.

Seven acts promulgated by the Commissioners between 1896 and 1933 concerned aspects of commercial law, including the Uniform Negotiable Instruments Law (1896) and the Uniform Sales Act (1906).

By 1940, there was widespread sentiment that these commercial statutes were in need of revision to take account of changed conditions and that they should be incorporated in a single commercial code. This project was begun as a joint project of the American Law Institute and the Commissioners in 1942. The Chief Reporter was Professor Karl N. Llwellyn of the University of Chicago Law School.

A version of the Code was first promulgated by the Institute and Commissioners in 1952 with the endorsement of the American Bar Association. Pennsylvania adopted it in 1953. The New York legislature referred the Code to the New York Law Revision Commission for study. The New York Commission issued its report in 1956, recommending many revisions. A revised version of the Code was issued by the Code's Editorial Board in late 1956. All states have now adopted a version of the Code, although Louisiana, as of January 1, 1991, has adopted only Articles 1, 3, 4, 4A, 5, 7, 8, and 9.

Many states made changes in the text of the Uniform Commercial Code. Because of this fact and the need for continual revision to meet changing commercial needs, a Permanent Editorial Board has been established for the UCC. This Board issues reports from time to time commenting on nonuniform state enactments and other code developments. The National Conference of Commissioners on Uniform State Laws and the American Law Institute cooperate in planning and executing revisions of the UCC. After the original version in 1952, major revisions were completed in 1956, 1962, 1972, and 1977. Now the process of revision has greatly accelerated. Recent years have seen the promulgation of two new articles (2A for Leases and 4A for Funds Transfers) and the revision or planned revision of almost every other article.

Even if all states eventually adopt a suggested revision, there is a period of time over which these adoptions occur and lack of uniformity results. One of the original concepts that was discarded was to submit the UCC for adoption as federal law. In the light of the lack of uniformity that has resulted from state variations and from lag in adoption of "official" revisions, is it time to dust off this old idea of a uniform federal commercial law?

NOBS CHEMICAL, U.S.A., INC. v. KOPPERS CO., INC.

United States Court of Appeals, Fifth Circuit, 1980.
616 F.2d 212.

HENDERSON, CIRCUIT JUDGE:

Koppers Company contracted with the plaintiffs, Nobs Chemical, U.S.A., Inc. (hereinafter referred to as "Nobs") and Calmon-Hill Trading Corporation (hereinafter referred to as "Calmon-Hill") to purchase

1000 metric tons of cumene.[1] Koppers breached the contract. Nobs and Calmon-Hill brought suit in United States District Court for the Southern District of Texas, and the case was tried before the court sitting without a jury.

The district court found that the plaintiffs had arranged to purchase the cumene in Brazil for $400.00 a ton and to expend $45.00 per ton for the cost of transporting the cumene to the defendant, for a total expense of $445,000.00. Koppers agreed to buy the cumene for $540,000.00. The court applied [UCC § 2–708(2)] and determined that the plaintiffs were entitled to recover their lost profits, $95,000.00 ($540,000.00 minus $445,000.00). The district court ruled that the plaintiffs could not recover the extra $25.00 per ton they allegedly were forced to pay their Brazilian supplier when the price per ton increased because their total order with the supplier was reduced from 4,000 metric tons to 3,000 metric tons because of Koppers' breach. The court decided this lost quantity discount amounted to consequential damages and was, therefore, not recoverable.

Nobs and Calmon-Hill appeal the measure of damages applied by the district court, and, assuming it is correct, they challenge the computation of those damages. The defendant, Koppers, cross-appeals, also claiming that the district court's calculation of damages under the lost profits method was incorrect.

We first turn to the issue of whether the district court was correct in applying the lost profits measure of damages to the plaintiffs' loss.

[The court quotes UCC § 2–708].

The plaintiffs urge that subsection [(1)] should govern in this case. Because the market value of cumene dropped to between $220.40 and $264.48 a metric ton at the time of the breach, the plaintiffs contend that they should recover the difference between the contract price ($540,000.00) and the market price (between $220,400.00 and $264,480.00), substantially more than the $95,000.00 awarded them under subsection [(2)]. * * *

Because there does not appear to be any law directly on point, we take the liberty of looking to those more learned on the subject of the Uniform Commercial Code. Professors White and Summers, recognizing that [§ 2–708(2)] is not the most lucid or best-drafted of the sales article sections, decided that the drafters of the Uniform Commercial Code intended subsection [(2)] to apply to certain sellers whose losses would rarely be compensated by the subsection [(1)] market price-contract price measure of damages, and for these sellers the lost profit formula was added in subsection [(2)]. One such type of seller is a "jobber," who, according to the treatise writers, must satisfy two conditions: "[f]irst, he is a seller who never acquires the contract goods. Second, his decision not to acquire those goods after learning of the

---

1. Cumene is "a colorless oily hydrocarbon * * * used as an additive for high-octane motor fuel. * * *" Webster's   Third New International Dictionary 553 (1966).

breach was not commercially unreasonable. * * *" J. White & R. Summers, Uniform Commercial Code [§ 7–10], at 228 (1972) (hereinafter cited as "White & Summers"). Nobs and Calmon-Hill clearly fit this description. The plaintiffs never acquired the goods from their Brazilian supplier, and, as White and Summers point out, an action for the purchase price or resale was therefore unavailable. See, [§§ 2–703, 2–704, 2–706, 2–709]. See also, American Metal Climax, Inc. v. Essex International, Inc., 16 U.C.C.Rep. 101, 115 (S.D.N.Y.1974) ("[C]ompensatory damages as provided in the contract-market formula of [§ 2–708(1)] are realistic only where the seller continues to be in a position to sell the product to other customers in the market.").

The plaintiffs argue, however, that in this case the measure of damages under subsection [(1)] would adequately compensate them and therefore, according to the terms of subsection [(1)], subsection [(2)] does not control. This is an intriguing argument. It appears that the drafters of [§ 2–708(1)] did not consider the possibility that recovery under that section may be *more than* adequate. White & Summers, supra, § 7–12, at 232–233.

It is possible that the code drafters intended subsection [(1)] as a liquidated damage clause available to a plaintiff-seller regardless of his actual damages. There have been some commentators who agree with this philosophy. See, C. Goetz & R. Scott, Measuring Sellers' Damages: the Lost-Profits Puzzle, 31 Stan.L.Rev. 323, 323–324 n. 2 (1979); E. Peters, Remedies for Breach of Contracts Relating to the Sale of Goods Under the Uniform Commercial Code: A Roadmap for Article Two, 73 Yale L.J. 199, 259 (1963). But, this construction is inconsistent with the code's basic philosophy, announced in [§ 1–106(1)] which provides "that the aggrieved party may be put in as good a position as if the other party had fully performed" but not in a better posture. White & Summers, supra, § 7–12, at 232. * * * Moreover, White and Summers conclude that statutory damage formulas do not significantly affect the practices of businessmen and therefore "breach deterrence," which would be the purpose of the statutory liquidated damages clause, should be rejected in favor of a standard approximating actual economic loss. White & Summers, supra, § 7–12, at 232. No one insists, and we do not think they could, that the difference between the fallen market price and the contract price is necessary to compensate the plaintiffs for the breach. Had the transaction been completed, their "benefit of the bargain" would not have been affected by the fall in market price, and they would not have experienced the windfall they otherwise would receive if the market price-contract price rule contained in [§ 2–708(1)] is followed. Thus, the premise contained in [§ 1–106] and Texas case law is a strong factor weighing against application of [§ 2–708(1)].

Our conclusion that the district court was correct in applying [§ 2–708(2)] brings us to the second issue—was it error for the district court to refuse to award the plaintiffs the additional $75,000.00, which they were required to pay when they lost their quantity discount?

We believe the trial court was correct in declining to award the plaintiffs the extra $75,000.00. Under [§ 2–708(2)], in addition to profit, the seller may recover "incidental damages" and "due allowance for costs reasonably incurred." The code does not provide for the recovery of consequential damages by a seller. [§ 1–106(1).] Petroleo Brasileiro, S. A. v. Ameropan Oil Corp., 372 F.Supp. 503, 508 (E.D.N.Y. 1974); Cf. [§ 2–715] (buyer's remedies). "Incidental damages" are defined in [§ 2–710] as "any commercially reasonable charges, expenses or commissions incurred in stopping delivery, in the transportation, care and custody of goods after the buyer's breach, in connection with return or resale of the goods or otherwise resulting from the breach." The draftsmen's comment to the section states that the purpose is to "authorize reimbursement of the seller for expenses reasonably incurred by him as a result of the buyer's breach." We think it is clear that [§ 2–710] was intended to cover only those expenses contracted by the seller after the breach and occasioned by such things as the seller's need to care for, and, if necessary, dispose of, the goods in a commercially reasonable manner. See, Guy H. James Construction Co. v. L. B. Foster Co., No. 17,473 (Tex.Civ.App.1979) (cost of replacing material in stock for resale recoverable as incidental damages); Cesco Mfg. Corp. v. Norcross, Inc., 7 Mass.App. 837, 391 N.E.2d 270, 27 U.C.C.Rep. 126 (1979) (incidental damages awarded for storage and moving of goods wrongfully rejected); Lee Oldsmobile v. Kaiden, 32 Md.App. 556, 363 A.2d 270, 20 U.C.C.Rep. 117 (1976) (commissions paid to salesman and broker on resale, floor plan interest on cost of car between breach of contract for sale of car and resale, and transportation expenses recoverable as incidental damages); Harlow & Jones, Inc. v. Advance Steel Co., 424 F.Supp. 770 (E.D.Mich.1976) (charges for storage and handling of goods after breach recoverable as incidental damages); Neri v. Retail Marine Corp., 30 N.Y.2d 393, 334 N.Y.S.2d 165, 285 N.E.2d 311, 10 U.C.C.Rep. 950 (1972) (proper incidental damages include storage, upkeep, finance charges and insurance for boat after buyer breached contract for sale); Bache & Co. v. International Controls Corp., 339 F.Supp. 341 (S.D.N.Y.), aff'd 469 F.2d 696 (2d Cir. 1972) (seller can recover as incidental damages commissions due him as result of buyer's breach); Hudgens v. Bain Equip. & Tube Sales, Inc., 459 S.W.2d 873 (Tex.Civ.App.1970) (expense of recovering and transporting goods not paid for awarded); Cf., Industrial Circuits Co. v. Terminal Communications, Inc., 26 N.C.App. 536, 216 S.E.2d 919, 17 U.C.C.Rep. 996 (1975) ("bill back" charges which resulted when buyer failed to order a certain quantity not allowed).

Equally as clear is the premise that this lost discount is not a "cost reasonably incurred" within the meaning of [§ 2–708(2)], which has been defined as "an amount equal to what he [the seller] has expended for performance of the contract that will now be valueless." White & Summers, supra, § 7–13, at 236. The extra $25.00 per ton does not fall within this definition, most obviously because it was not an expense necessary to the performance of the contract. Rather, it was simply an extra benefit the sellers did not receive from their supplier by reason of the buyer's breach. * * *

Affirmed.

———

Do you agree that the Uniform Commercial Code does not permit recovery of the $75,000 lost volume-discount? Can an argument for recovery be based on the concluding words of § 1–106 ("or by other rule of law") coupled with § 1–103?

It is clear that recovery of the discount cannot be had as incidental damages under § 2–710? If the Uniform Commercial Code does not provide for recovery of consequential damages by sellers (cf. § 2–715(2)), is there any way that a seller can overcome this obstacle? See § 2–719(1).

Why does the court say, "[h]ad the transaction been completed [Nob's profit] would not have been affected by the fall in market price"? Does the answer turn on the terms of the Nob's contract with its supplier?

———

TRANS WORLD METALS, INC. v. SOUTHWIRE CO., 769 F.2d 902, 908–909 (2d Cir.1985). The seller was permitted to recover under § 2–708(1) when the market price dropped after the contract had been made. The court said that "nothing in the language or history of § 2–708(2) suggests that it was intended to apply to cases in which § 2–708(1) might overcompensate the seller," but then the court distinguished *Nobs Chemical:* "Whether or not we would have reached the same result in *Nobs,* here the benefit of the bargain under a completed contract would have been affected by the fall in * * * prices."

———

Application of the UCC to "Mixed" Contracts

Does the UCC apply if the contract in issue involves not only a sale of goods, but also the performance of services, or the sale of items that are not goods? Three common situations in which this question arises are (1) a contract for the sale of goods involving substantial installation services by the seller; (2) a sale of a business in which the buyer pays not only for goods in inventory, but also for realty and goodwill; (3) a transaction in which the buyer supplies the seller with all or part of the materials from which the goods are manufactured.

Most courts that have faced the issue of whether the UCC applies to mixed contracts, apply the "Bonebrake predominant purpose test," taken from Bonebrake v. Cox, 499 F.2d 951, 960 (8th Cir.1974):

"The test for inclusion or exclusion [of such contracts under the UCC] is not whether they are mixed, but granting that they are mixed, whether their predominant factor, their thrust, their purpose, reasonably stated, is the rendition of service, with goods incidentally involved (e.g., contract with artist for painting) or is a transaction of sale with labor incidentally involved (e.g., installation of a water heater in a bathroom)."

A minority approach to mixed contracts is to apply Article 2 of the UCC to the sale of goods aspects and other law to other parts of the transaction. See Foster v. Colorado Radio Corp., 381 F.2d 222 (10th Cir. 1967) (sale of a radio station).

THE UNITED NATIONS CONVENTION ON CONTRACTS FOR THE INTERNATIONAL SALE OF GOODS

19 Int'l Legal Mat. 671, 672 (1980):*

ARTICLE 3

(1) Contracts for the supply of goods to be manufactured or produced are to be considered sales unless the party who orders the goods undertakes to supply a substantial part of the materials necessary for such manufacture or production.

(2) This Convention does not apply to contracts in which the preponderant part of the obligations of the party who furnishes the goods consists in the supply of labour or other services.

The United Nations Convention on Contracts for the International Sale of Goods

An important example of a special set of substantive rules for transjurisdictional contracts is the United Nations Convention on Contracts for the International Sale of Goods. The excerpt from the Sale of Goods Convention, set out immediately above, shows that unlike the UCC, the Convention deals expressly with at least some mixed contract problems. Other excerpts from and references to this Convention appear throughout the book.

The United States ratified the Convention in 1986 and it went into force on January 1, 1988 after the necessary ten countries had ratified it. As of January 1, 1991, 28 countries had become parties to the Convention. The Convention is reprinted in the Appendix to 15 U.S.C.A.

The Convention was adopted at a 62–nation United Nations conference in 1980 after twelve years of preparatory work by the U.N. Commission on International Trade Law. The Convention does not apply to consumer sales or to the sales of certain items such as securities. (Art. 2) It covers formation of the contract, but not the validity of its provisions (Art. 4), and it does not apply to the liability of the seller for death or personal injury. (Art. 5). The parties to a contract may exclude the operation of the Convention or "derogate from or vary the effect of any of its provisions." (Art. 6). In the absence of such action by the contracting parties, the "Convention applies to contracts of sales of goods between parties whose places of business are in different [countries]" that have ratified the Convention. (Art. 1).

DURA–WOOD TREATING CO. v. CENTURY FOREST INDUSTRIES, INC.

United States Court of Appeals, Fifth Circuit, 1982.
675 F.2d 745.

SAM D. JOHNSON, CIRCUIT JUDGE:

Plaintiff—Dura-Wood Treating Company, a division of Roy O. Martin Lumber Co., Inc. (Dura-Wood)—brought suit against defendant, Century Forest Industries, Inc. (Century Forest), alleging a breach of contract. The court had jurisdiction by virtue of diversity of citizenship. The district court, holding the parties had entered into a legally binding contract, determined that Century Forest breached the contract and rendered judgment in favor of Dura-Wood for the amount of $100,000. * * *

This Court affirms the district court's judgment as it relates to the determination that Century Forest breached a legally enforceable contract. However, the Court reverses in part the damage award.

I. FACTS

Dura-Wood and Century Forest are both in the business of treating cross-ties for industrial and commercial use, and are both "merchants" within the meaning of [UCC § 2–104(1)]. On October 19, 1977, Dura-Wood contracted to supply a third party—the William A. Smith Company (Smith Company)—with cross-ties. [Dura-Wood and Century Forest agreed that Century Forest would sell Dura-Wood the ties that Dura-Wood needed to keep its contract with Smith Company. Century Forest then repudiated its agreement.]

[F]aced with the prospect that resolution by Century Forest of the matter was not forthcoming, Dura-Wood obtained price quotations for substitute ties from other manufacturers. Upon review of the price quotations, Dura-Wood determined that it could produce the ties internally at a lower price than it could purchase substitute ties from other manufacturers.

Further discussion between Dura-Wood and Century Forest appeared fruitless at the time Dura-Wood was obligated to begin shipping cross-ties to Smith Company. Shipping began in February of 1979 and was concluded in June of 1979. As a result, Dura-Wood manufactured ties in April, May, and June of 1979 specifically to replace the ties it had undertaken to purchase from Century Forest and sell to Smith Company. * * *

III. DAMAGES

The district court's damage award will be addressed in three parts. First, there is a question regarding actual damages as they relate to Dura-Wood's "cover." The second part addresses the so-called "potential profits" allegedly lost as a result of Dura-Wood's method of covering. Finally, there is a question regarding profits that Dura-Wood would have received as a result of its contract with Smith Company, but lost because of Century Forest's breach of contract.

A. *Cover*

When a seller breaches a contract, the buyer "may 'cover' by making in good faith and without unreasonable delay any reasonable purchase of or contract to purchase goods in substitution for those due from the seller." [UCC § 2–712(1)] "Covering" is an optional remedy for the buyer faced with securing a damage award. *See* [UCC § 2–711; § 2–712 and comment 3 to § 2–712]. If he chooses to cover, "The buyer may recover from the seller as damages the difference between the cost of cover and the contract price together with any incidental or consequential damages." [UCC § 2–712(2)].

In the case *sub judice*, Dura-Wood claims—and the district court found—it engaged in a valid method of cover by manufacturing the necessary ties itself. Century Forest argues this is an invalid mechanism for cover. The basis of Century Forest's argument is that the [Code] does not contemplate a buyer's covering by purchasing from itself. Century Forest argues the purchase of or contract to purchase goods in substitution of those due from the seller must be made "on the market."

This Court recognizes the language of [§ 2–712], read literally, appears to contemplate the purchase of cover goods should be from an outside source. However, the [Code] is to be "liberally construed and applied to promote its underlying purposes and policies." [UCC § 1–102(1)]. The [Code] "is drawn to provide flexibility." Comment 1, [§ 1–102]. Consequently, a buyer should be able to cover by manufacturing goods in substitution of those due from the seller, if such a cover otherwise satisfies and promotes the purposes and policies of the [Code].

Comment one to [§ 2–712] states the "section provides the buyer with a remedy aimed at enabling him to obtain the goods he needs thus meeting his essential need." This statement essentially describes two purposes that may be fulfilled by an appropriate cover. First, it puts an aggrieved buyer in the same economic position in which it would have been had the seller actually performed. Second, it allows the buyer to achieve its prime objective, which is acquiring the needed goods.

This Court acknowledges there is some language indicating the purchase of substitute goods should be "on the market." See Kiser v.

Lemco, 536 S.W.2d 585 (Tex.Civ.App.—Amarillo 1976, no writ). However, this language is explained by the Texas courts' interpretations of [§ 2–712]. As Century Forest itself points out, the Texas courts have noted that one policy behind [§ 2–712] is a presumption "that the cost of cover will approximate the market price of the undelivered goods." Jon-T Farms, Inc. v. Good Pasture, Inc., 554 S.W.2d 743, 749 (Tex.Civ. App.—Amarillo 1977, writ ref'd n.r.e.). Indeed, an appropriate cover has the effect of setting the market price so that an aggrieved buyer does not have to prove damages through more onerous means. However, actually purchasing the cover goods from another source is not the exclusive means of satisfying the presumption of [§ 2–712]. In an appropriate situation, internally producing the substitute or cover goods can satisfy the recognized underlying presumptions of [§ 2–712].

Regarding the case *sub judice*, this Court finds no error in the district court's actual damage award based upon Dura-Wood's cover. This Court determines that a buyer, at least in the case *sub judice*, may cover by manufacturing goods internally. The purposes and presumptions of the [Code] can be, and are, fulfilled in those instances—such as in the instant case—when the buyer is already in the marketplace and can produce the goods at a price approximating or lower than the market price. It would defy reason and the [Code's] purposes of flexibility and adaptation to reasonable commercial practice to require a buyer to increase losses by covering through the purchase of goods from another seller, if it could produce the goods itself at a lower price. This is particularly true when it is recognized that such a determination would remove the other advantages that [§ 2–712] contemplates from cover.

As a factual matter, cover by internal manufacturing must be in "good faith." The [Code] provides workable definitions of good faith in at least two pertinent places.[8] Section [1–201(19)] defines good faith as "honesty in fact in the conduct or transaction concerned." Section [2–103(1)(b)] expands this basic definition in order to make it specifically applicable to merchants. "'Good faith' in the case of a merchant means honesty in fact and the observance of reasonable commercial standards of fair dealing in the trade."

Another factual matter concerns the necessity for the aggrieved buyer to cover without "unreasonable delay" and to make a "reasonable purchase." The [Code] provides only limited aid for the court attempting to determine whether a cover purchase is reasonable in the appropriate respects. However, there is some aid. Initially, [§ 1–204(2)] provides guidelines for what a reasonable time within which to cover may be. The section states, "What is a reasonable time for taking any action depends on the nature, purpose and circumstances of such action." Additionally, Comment two to [§ 2–712] dictates, "The

---

8. Section [1–203] of the [Code] expressly establishes that "[e]very contract or duty within this title imposes an obligation of good faith in its performance or enforcement."

test of proper cover is whether at the time and place the buyer acted in good faith and in a reasonable manner, and it is immaterial that hindsight may later prove that the method of cover used was not the cheapest or most effective." At a minimum this "test" suggests a buyer has some time in which to evaluate the situation and attempt to determine what may be the best or most appropriate means to cover.

Finally, there is the factual requirement that the goods be "in substitution for those due from the seller." Comment two to [§ 2–712] points out that "[t]he definition of 'cover' * * * envisages * * * goods not identical with those involved but commercially usable as reasonable substitutes under the circumstances of the particular case."

The record demonstrates good faith on the part of Dura-Wood in choosing to cover by manufacturing the cross-ties internally. Dura-Wood took price quotations and ultimately determined it could produce the ties at a lower price. The district court's finding that Dura-Wood acted in good faith—which is implicit in its determination regarding actual damages—is not clearly erroneous.

Additionally, the district court's finding that Dura-Wood covered within a reasonable time and provided a reasonable substitute was not clearly erroneous. The record reveals Dura-Wood waited to cover in order to evaluate the market for cross-ties. There is evidence demonstrating the cross-tie market is volatile and subject to fluctuations. The price of cross-ties was high during the time Dura-Wood was evaluating the market. Consequently, Dura-Wood's waiting to determine whether a decrease in market price might occur was not unreasonable. In addition, Dura-Wood continued to urge performance, as contemplated by [§ 2–610] of the [Code]. The record also demonstrates the internally produced cover goods were commercially usable as reasonable substitutes for those due from Century Forest.

B. Potential Profits

The district court awarded Dura-Wood $42,000 as "potential profits" that it lost "by using its own facilities to produce cross-ties to replace those which the defendant refused to provide." In other words, the district court found that, when Dura-Wood covered by internally manufacturing the cross-ties, it could have been producing cross-ties and selling them to new or different customers instead of producing them in substitution for goods due from Century Forest.

As a general proposition, lost profits are consequential damages as contemplated by [§ 2–715(2)]. Section [2–715] establishes that consequential damages include "any loss resulting from general or particular requirements and needs of which the seller at the time of contracting had reason to know and which could not reasonably be prevented by cover or otherwise." Of course, [§ 2–712] allows a plaintiff to obtain consequential damages.

However, the district court's damage award for "potential profits" does not fall within the contemplation of [§ 2–715]. It is true Dura-

Wood, by manufacturing its own cross-ties, covered for less money than if it had purchased ties from some other source. It is also true that, while Dura-Wood was producing its cross-ties, its facilities were tied up and Dura-Wood was unable to manufacture goods for new or different contracts. However, Dura-Wood could have minimized its *overall* losses. The cost of producing the ties plus the cost of lost profits resulting from Dura-Wood's inability to enter into new or different contracts was greater than the cost of simply purchasing the cover goods from another source. If Dura-Wood had purchased ties from someone else, its facilities would not have been tied up and Dura-Wood would have been able to enter new or different contracts. As a result, Dura-Wood would have had lower overall costs. Century Forest should not be obligated to pay for Dura-Wood's poor choice.

The so-called loss of potential profits could have reasonably been prevented by a different form of cover or otherwise. In the absence of such preventative measures, the district court's award of consequential damages, as it relates to the loss of potential profits, is not authorized by [§ 2–715].

C. Lost Profits on the Dura-Wood/Smith Contract

The district court also awarded Dura-Wood $13,000 for "lost profits on its contract with the third party [Smith Company]." This amount was computed by determining the amount of profit per tie Dura-Wood would have received from Smith Company had Century Forest performed, and was awarded as consequential damages. However, the award was erroneous since it allows Dura-Wood a double recovery as to the $13,000.

Dura-Wood received an actual damage award that considered the difference between the cost of cover and the contract price. Since Dura-Wood was able to provide Smith Company with cross-ties and received payment, there is no room for the $13,000 award. Stated another way, Dura-Wood already had been compensated for the fact that producing its own cross-ties was more expensive than buying them from Century Forest. * * *

This case is remanded to the district court for entry of a judgment consistent with this opinion.

Affirmed in Part, Reversed in Part, and Remanded.

———

INTERIOR ELEVATOR CO. v. LIMMEROTH, 278 Or. 589, 565 P.2d 1074 (1977). Farmer promised to sell grain elevator 125,801 bushels of wheat at $2.49 per bushel. Farmer delivered only 120,663 bushels. In the meantime, grain elevator had promised to resell 125,000 bushels to Dreyfus, a grain dealer. Grain elevator purchased enough wheat to make up the difference between the amount it had promised to dealer and the amount delivered by farmer (4,337 bushels). Grain elevator paid slightly more than the market price of $5.05 for the wheat it purchased to make up the difference. Grain elevator then sued for

$5.05 minus $2.49 ($2.56) times the difference between the number of bushels farmer promised and the number of bushels he delivered (5,138 bushels). The trial court permitted grain elevator to recover only $2.56 times 4,337. On appeal, elevator was held entitled to recover $2.56 times 5,138:

"Since the contract called for 125,801 bushels, only 125,000 of which were to be sold to Dreyfus, the trial court's determination of damages did not allow recovery on 801 bushels. The trial court appears to have based its reasoning on the 'cover' provisions of [UCC § 2–712]. Plaintiff, however, did not seek damages under the 'cover' provision but rather under [UCC § 2–713], which grants damages as the difference between the market price of the goods on the date of breach and the contract price. Under this section plaintiff would be entitled to damages of $2.56 a bushel times the 5,138 bushels which were not delivered by defendant under the contract. This results in a figure of $13,153.28, which was the amount prayed for by plaintiff.

"Defendant contends that plaintiff elected its remedy at the time it purchased the additional wheat to fulfill its contract with Dreyfus and that since that constitutes 'cover' under [UCC § 2–712], plaintiff cannot now seek to recover damages under [UCC § 2–713]. Defendant relies upon White and Summers, Uniform Commercial Code 191, § 6–4 (1972), where Uniform Commercial Code [§ 2–713 comment 5], is quoted:

> 'The present section provides a remedy which is complete-ly alternative to cover under the preceding section and applies only when *and to the extent that* the buyer has not covered.' (Emphasis added.)

"However, the language emphasized in comment 5 above makes it clear that the drafters of the code contemplated situations in which buyers would only partially cover. This is precisely what occurred here. The plaintiff 'covered' only enough to meet its contract obligation to Drey-fus. It would appear, therefore, that plaintiff would have been entitled to the actual cost of cover, if shown to be reasonable, plus damages measured under [UCC § 2–713] as to the remaining 801 bushels. Plain-tiff did not seek this remedy but rather sought to recover under [UCC § 2–713] as to the entire amount of wheat that defendant failed to deliver. Since market price was less than the cost of cover, plaintiff is entitled to use this measure as to the wheat which was actually purchased. The fact that plaintiff did not cover the entire amount does not bar recovery under [UCC § 2–713]. The trial court therefore was in error and should have granted plaintiff's prayer for $13,153.28, together with interest at the rate of 6 percent per annum from September 6, 1973.

"Reversed and remanded for entry of judgment consistent with this opinion."

––––––––

CHATLOS SYSTEMS, INC. v. NATIONAL CASH REGISTER CORP., 670 F.2d 1304 (3d Cir.1982), reh'g en banc denied, 670 F.2d 1315, cert. dismissed, 457 U.S. 1112, 102 S.Ct. 2918, 73 L.Ed.2d 1323 (1982). Chatlos Systems purchased a computer from National Cash Register for $46,020. The computer failed to operate as National Cash Register had warranted that it would and Chatlos sued for damages. Applying UCC § 2–714(2), the trial judge found that the value of the system delivered was $6,000 and the fair market value of a system that would perform as National Cash Register had warranted was $207,826. A judgment was rendered for Chatlos for $201,826 plus prejudgment interest. National Cash Register appealed contending that basing damages on the value of computers in a much higher price range than the model sold to Chatlos was "substituting a Rolls Royce for a Ford." Held, affirmed: "The correct measure of damages, under [UCC § 2–714(2)], is the difference between the fair market value of the goods accepted and the value they would have had if they had been as warranted. Award of that sum is not confined to instances where there has been an increase in value between date of ordering and date of delivery. It may also include the benefit of a contract price which, for whatever reason quoted, was particularly favorable for the customer. Evidence of the contract price may be relevant to the issue of fair market value, but it is not controlling." Would the result have been different if Chatlos had revoked its acceptance of the computer under UCC § 2–608 and then had purchased a "substitute" computer for $207,826?

OVERSTREET v. NORDEN LABORATORIES, INC.

United States Court of Appeals, Sixth Circuit, 1982.
669 F.2d 1286.

Before ENGEL, KEITH and KENNEDY, CIRCUIT JUDGES.

KEITH, CIRCUIT JUDGE.

This is a direct appeal of a judgment involving a breach of expressed and implied warranty under UCC [§§ 2–313, 2–314] brought pursuant to the district court's diversity jurisdiction 28 U.S.C. § 1332.

Defendant-appellant Norden Laboratories, Inc. ("Norden") appeals from a judgment of $40,500.00, awarded in favor of plaintiff-appellee Dr. Luel P. Overstreet, a Kentucky veterinarian and horse owner.

* * *

FACTS

Dr. Overstreet is a practicing veterinarian and operator of a standard bred horse farm in Henderson County, Kentucky. Equine rhinopneumonitis is a virus which causes horses to exhibit symptoms which generally resemble a common cold. In pregnant mares, however, the virus will cause abortions. Norden Laboratories, Inc., a Nebraska corporation, manufactures and markets various drugs to veterinarians. Rhinomune, one of the drugs manufactured by Norden, is a vaccine designed to inoculate horses against equine rhinopneumonitis.

Rhinomune was first marketed by Norden in the spring of 1973. Norden's marketing program for the new, unique drug utilized magazine advertisements, brochures and sales persons. In the spring of 1973, about the time Norden began marketing Rhinomune, two mares on Dr. Overstreet's farm aborted their foals. Dr. Overstreet became concerned about a possible outbreak of equine rhinopneumonitis virus among his breeding horses. It was later determined that an equine rhinopneumonitis virus caused the abortions.

A Norden sales representative called on Dr. Overstreet's office and spoke with an associate of the doctor's concerning rhinomune. Dr. Overstreet became interested in the drug and allegedly read rhinomune promotional literature. Dr. Overstreet asserts that he then ordered a quantity of rhinomune, because of the representations contained in Norden's advertisements.

The rhinomune vaccine was administered to a number of Dr. Overstreet's horses during the three months prior to November, 1973. Six of the inoculated mares on Dr. Overstreet's farm aborted their foals during the spring of 1974.

Dr. Overstreet instituted this breach of warranty action under [UCC §§ 2–313, 2–314] against Norden to recover losses resulting from the aborted foals. At trial, Dr. Overstreet alleged that Norden breached expressed and implied warranties which Norden made concerning its rhinomune vaccine. A jury returned a verdict of $40,500.00 in favor of Dr. Overstreet.

Norden made motions for judgment n.o.v. and, in the alternative, for a new trial. Both motions were denied. Defendant Norden perfected this appeal. Norden assigns as error jury instructions on the issue of its liability under [UCC §§ 2–313, 2–314]. Norden argues that the trial court should have instructed the jury that in order to recover, plaintiff must establish that he relied on any warranty which Norden made. Appellant's challenge is well founded, but imprecise. As Norden contends, reliance is an element of a breach of an expressed warranty action under Kentucky law, and the jury should have been instructed accordingly. However, the implied warranty of merchantability [UCC § 2–314] is a duty imposed by Kentucky law and plaintiff's reliance thereon is not a requisite to defendant's liability for breach.

The verdict form allowed the jury to award a judgment against Norden without stating which warranty was breached, consequently we cannot determine under which theory appellant's liability was imposed. We find these jury instructions were erroneous. Because the instructions were erroneous and, for the reasons set forth below, we reverse the trial court's judgment and remand for proceedings consistent with this opinion.

A. Implied Warranty of Merchantability

The implied warranty of merchantability as set forth in [UCC § 2–314] * * * arises by operation of law. As such, it does not require reliance as an element of a purchaser's recovery. Consequently, Norden's reliance argument, so far as it relates to the implied warranty of merchantability, is without merit. We find that Judge Gordon properly instructed the jury on the implied warranty theory. However, we hold that there is insufficient evidence on this record to sustain a finding that Norden breached its implied warrant of merchantability.

B. Express Warranty

Appellant contends that the jury instructions and verdict form were improper, because neither required a finding of reliance as an element of recovery under the express warranty. We agree. * * *

Appellant noted above that the jury instructions did not include a charge that Dr. Overstreet must have relied on the express warranty. Moreover, the record before us does not reflect that the trial court properly ascertained whether reliance was an element of appellee's recovery. Accordingly, we hold that these instructions were erroneous. We must now decide, as we think a Kentucky court would decide, the elements of an express warranty action. * * *

An express warranty may be created by any affirmation of fact or promise made by a seller which relates to the goods. [UCC § 2–313(1) (a)]. The language creating an express warranty need not contain special phrases or formal words such as guarantee or warranty. In fact, a seller need not have intended that the language create an express warranty. [UCC § 2–313(2)]. Every statement made by a seller, however, does not create an express warranty. A seller may puff his wares and state his opinion on their value without creating an express warranty.

The existence of an express warranty depends upon the particular circumstances in which the language is used and read. A catalog description or advertisement may create an express warranty in appropriate circumstances. The trier of fact must determine whether the circumstances necessary to create an express warranty are present in a given case. The test is "whether the seller assumes to assert a fact of which the buyer is ignorant, or whether he merely states an opinion or expresses a judgment about a thing as to which they may each be expected to have an opinion and exercise a judgment." Wedding v. Duncan, 310 Ky. 374, 378, 220 S.W.2d 564, 567 (1949).

The mere existence of a warranty is insufficient to sustain an action for breach of an express warranty. The warranty must be "part of the basis of the bargain" between the parties. A warranty is the basis of the bargain if it has been relied upon as one of the inducements for purchasing the product. See Ky.Rev.Stat.Ann. § 355.2–313(1)(a), Comment 1(C) (Baldwin).[5]

---

5. Comment 1(c) states in full:

Materiality of Affirmation, Promise, Description, Sample. Under the Code, the qualification that affirmations, etc. create a warranty if made "as the basis of" the bargain, appears to be substantially the same as the "reliance" qualification in § 12 of the Uniform Sales Act, former KRS 361.120. Van Deren Hard-

A buyer is not under a duty to investigate the seller's representations; he may accept them at face value. However, a buyer may not rely blindly on a statement or affirmation that he knows is incorrect. A buyer does not disregard any special knowledge he possesses or his accumulated experience with a product in determining whether to enter the bargain. Consequently, a statement known to be incorrect cannot be an inducement to enter a bargain. An incorrect representation by the seller which is qualified in any manner may become the basis of a bargain to the extent it is believed and relied upon. For example, a seller represents in its advertising that its product is capable of lifting 100 pounds. The buyer is aware that the product cannot lift the weight claimed in its advertising. Nevertheless, he relies on his subjective belief that the product could lift 75 pounds and purchases the product. The product fails to lift 75 pounds. In an action for breach of express warranty against the seller, the buyer will prevail. The seller cannot complain because his product failed to perform at a level of proficiency lower than that originally claimed in its advertising.

We do not reach the issue of whether an expert may rely on the representations of another expert in his area of specialty. At a minimum, however, an expert may rely on the representations of a seller of a newly marketed, unique product. Butcher v. Garrett–Enumclaw Co., 20 Wash.App. 361, 581 P.2d 1352, 24 UCC Rep. 832, 843 (Ct.App.1978). In *Butcher,* the court held that an expert with many years of experience as a conventional saw mill operator and consultant could rely on the representations of the seller of a newly developed portable small log sawmill. Where the capabilities and properties of a unique, newly developed product are known only to the seller, the expert is in no better position to evaluate the representations of the seller than a layperson. Therefore, he is entitled to reply on representations concerning such a novel product. See Grinnell v. Charles Pfizer & Company, 274 Cal.App.2d 424, 79 Cal.Rptr. 369, 378 (Ct.App.1969) (Physician could rely upon representations of drug manufacturer where manufacturer possessed superior knowledge concerning the properties of the drug.)

C. Damages

Norden contends that the trial court improperly instructed the jury (1) on the issue of causation, and (2) as to the proper measure of damages. Although both Judges Engel and Kennedy agree, I remain unpersuaded. * * *

Measure of Damages

The trial court relied on Schleicher v. Gentry, 554 S.W.2d 884 (Ky. App.1977), and instructed the jury that the proper measure of damages was "the difference between the fair and reasonable market value of

ware Co. v. Preston, 224 Ky. 170, 5 S.W.2d 1052 (1928).

each of the mares with foal and the fair and reasonable market without foal." Trial transcript at 144.

Norden argues that plaintiff's recovery is limited under [UCC § 2–714(2)] to the cost of the vaccine. Norden reasons as follows. Norden's vaccine did not cause the equine rhinopneumonitis in the mares, and plaintiff would not have used any other preventative. Therefore, the cost of the vaccine is the only loss plaintiff has suffered.

Norden relies heavily upon its contention that Dr. Overstreet made conflicting statements concerning whether he would have used another product. However, the resolution of factual disputes lies clearly within the province of the jury. * * *

ALTERNATIVE PRODUCT RULE

Judges Kennedy and Engel reason that Dr. Overstreet must establish that an equally effective alternative product was available and would have been used by Dr. Overstreet before he can recover consequential damages for breach of Norden's express warranty. I disagree. Therefore, I address this question separately. The alternative product rule announced today is not supported by the law or public policy.

First, the proposed rule would require plaintiff to prove that at the time the warranted product was purchased, he was aware that an available alternative product existed. Second, the proposed rule minimizes the purpose and effect of reliance on a product warranty. It is unreasonable to assume that consumers are able to determine the relative effectiveness of a given product. The available alternative product rule, therefore, will penalize consumers because they lack meaningful independent information about the products they purchase. Moreover, warranty actions generally arise where there is a disparity in the relevant information possessed by the consumer and warrantor.

An alternative product will be absent primarily in two situations: either when the product or the consumer is in some way unique. In either of these situations, the commercially available alternative product rule could lead to absurd results. Assume that consumers A and B purchase a particular product and in both instances the product fails to perform as warranted. Consumer B is allergic to all alternative products, while Consumer A has no such allergies. Consumer A recovers consequential damages because alternative products were available to him. Consumer B, however, could only have utilized the one product with success. According to the commercially available alternative rule, Consumer B could only recover incidental damages. I know of no principled basis for enabling manufacturers and other warrantors of products to receive this windfall. The recovery of consequential damages in an action based on an express warranty should not depend upon a mere fortuity, the uniqueness of the consumer.

The other circumstance in which the consumer will not be able to purchase commercially available alternative products will occur when the product itself is unique. A product is unique in two instances. The first occurs when the product allegedly is a new breakthrough. The rule announced today will allow manufacturers of new products to make unsupportable claims concerning product effectiveness; yet insulate the manufacturers from liability for consequential damages. In my view, this approach is tantamount to the licensing of placebos. Moreover, the relative cost of litigation will discourage consumers from initiating valid suits where as here only incidental damages may be recovered. For the foregoing reasons, I regard as unsound the available alternative product rule announced today.

At the second trial of this case, a jury may find: 1) that Norden warranted that the vaccine Rhinomune, would prevent equine rhinopneumonitis, a disease which almost invariably induces abortions in mares; and 2) that Norden breached its warranty when six of Dr. Overstreet's horses, properly inoculated with Rhinomune, contracted the disease and aborted. The essence of Norden's warranty would be the representation that mares inoculated with Rhinomune would not contract equine rhinopneumonitis and abort. It therefore would be foreseeable that if the vaccine failed to perform as warranted, a purchaser would probably sustain losses due to aborted foals. In my view these losses are precisely the type of losses contemplated under [UCC § 2–714(3)].

Norden's liability arose because its product failed to prevent the disease as warranted, not because plaintiff's mares aborted foals. Accordingly, I would allow plaintiff to recover without considering the alternative product rule. * * *

[W]e reverse and remand for proceedings consistent with this opinion. It is so ordered.

ENGEL and CORNELIA G. KENNEDY, CIRCUIT JUDGES, concurring specially.

We agree with Judge Keith that the evidence is insufficient to sustain a finding that appellant breached any implied warranty. We also agree that while there was sufficient evidence for the jury to find that appellant expressly warranted that Rhinomune prevents equine rhinopneumonitis, the trial court's instructions on express warranty erroneously failed to include appellee's reliance on the warranty as a necessary element of the claim. However, we do not agree with Judge Keith that the District Court correctly instructed the jury on the measure of damages.

There was evidence at trial that Rhinomune failed to prevent appellee's mares' contracting equine rhinopneumonitis, thereby failing to prevent the abortions of appellee's foals. The Rhinomune did not cause the equine rhinopneumonitis, and appellee does not here claim that it did. There was conflicting evidence on the efficacy of Rhinomune in general. There was also evidence that no abortion preventive more effective than Rhinomune was available to appellee, and that even if one was available, appellee would not have used it.

The District Court's instruction on damages required the jury to award appellee, after it found a breach of warranty, the difference in value between the mares with foal and the same mares without foal. In directing the jury to award this amount the District Court was holding that the value of the foals was the correct measure of damages in all circumstances which the jury could find. This was error.

*   *   *

The only possible support for the instruction that the District Court did give is [UCC § 2–715(2)]. *   *   * Under this section it is clear that once appellee has demonstrated a breach of warranty he may recover only for damages that are *caused* by the breach. See White & Summers, Uniform Commercial Code § 10–4 (1972); Brown v. Globe Laboratories, Inc., 165 Neb. 138, 84 N.W.2d 151, 160, 163, 167 (1957).

The only item of consequential damages appellee claimed here was the value of the aborted foals. Appellee might have established a causal line between the loss of the foals and the breach in any of several ways. He might have claimed that the abortions were directly due to some effect of the vaccine, or that this batch of Rhinomune was ineffective and a good batch of Rhinomune would better have prevented the abortions. He might have claimed that the warranty induced him to forego some other, effective means of preventing the abortions, or that he acted to his detriment in some other way in reliance on the warranty. Of these possible claims, there is evidence in the present record to support the claims that appellee would have used another abortion preventive but for the Rhinomune warranty or possibly that appellee's lot of Rhinomune was ineffective as compared to other Rhinomune. The evidence on these theories is conflicting. Thus, causation was not established as a matter of law. If neither Rhinomune nor any other product or device would have been effective or could have been used by appellee to prevent the abortions, then any breach of warranty did not cause the abortions. The fact that the abortions were foreseeable if the Rhinomune did not work does not mean the breach of warranty was the *cause* of the abortions. There was simply a failure to prevent an occurrence that nothing would have prevented, and appellee may not recover the value of the foals.

Judge Keith correctly notes that appellant established the conditions of liability when it warranted that Rhinomune would prevent equine rhinopneumonitis. However, the warranty did not further establish, by itself, appellant's liability for particular items of consequential damage in the event of a breach. [UCC § 2–715(2)] clearly requires that the additional element of causation be proved to establish liability for consequential damages. The concern that Judge Engel and I share is that the jury was not permitted to decide whether appellant's promises caused any damage to result from the breach where the evidence on this issue was in dispute.

To our minds the result we reach is a straightforward application to the facts of this case of the well-settled requirement that causation must be proved to recover damages. Judge Keith overstates our contribution to the law by categorizing it with the heady title "Alternative Product Rule." Nonetheless, Judge Keith's concerns about the scope of the result prompt some additional comments. The inquiry is always whether the breach caused the particular harm complained of. The existence or nonexistence of an alternative product aids this inquiry only in those cases where there is no other causal link between the breach and the harm for which consequential damages are sought.

The existence of an alternative product would not be relevant in this case if appellee had had his mares impregnated in reliance on a warranty by appellant and now sought to recover that cost. It would not be relevant had appellant, in reliance on the warranty, entered into contracts for delivery of the foals to another and been sued for failure to deliver. Appellee's reliance on the warranty would have caused him to incur expenses and the breach would have caused those losses, even in the absence of an effective alternative product. * * *

The result we reach does not insulate manufacturers from liability for consequential damages or lead to absurd results, as Judge Keith fears.[3] Liability for truly consequential damages, including damages flowing from reliance on the warrantor's promise, should be a sufficient deterrent to unsupportable claims of performance. If not, a suit alleging fraud might be appropriate, and there are many state and federal agencies that police false advertising. It is not also necessary to award damages where no damage has been caused, in effect imposing absolute liability for a breach of warranty, as Judge Keith would do. This would render the consequential damages provision of Kentucky's statute meaningless. It is not a windfall to the warrantor to be liable only for losses that it causes, nor is it a hardship to the warrantee only to recover for losses caused by the breach.

———

Is the non-uniform comment quoted in note 5 in *Overstreet* correct in assuming that reliance is necessary to create an express warranty under UCC § 2–313? See infra p. 616.

Problem

Seller agrees to sell and Buyer agrees to buy two violins for a total price of $10,000. Seller, in good faith, warrants one violin to be a

---

3. Judge Keith posits Consumer A and Consumer B, both of whom buy a product which fails to perform as warranted. Consumer A could have used an alternative, but Consumer B could not, being allergic to all alternatives. Judge Keith claims that under our analysis Consumer A would be able to recover consequential damages but Consumer B would not, and argues that this distinction between the two is unprincipled. * * * [T]o make Judge Keith's example concrete, assume that the product A and B used was a drug warranted to prevent disease, and the drug proved ineffective. Assume also that both A and B sue to recover for contracting the disease and not for any other damage. The fact is that A's contracting the disease was a consequence of his not using some other drug in reliance on the warranted product, while B could have done nothing else. B's illness was not a consequence of the breach. While A was harmed by the breach, B was not. This is a perfectly principled distinction between A and B.

Stradivarius and the other a Guarnerius. Buyer makes a down payment of $2000, the rest due on delivery. When the violins are delivered to Buyer and before he accepts them, he discovers that they are fakes worth about $1,000. If genuine, the violins would have a combined market value of about $20,000. What remedies does Buyer have? See UCC §§ 2–606, 2–711, 2–712, 2–713, 2–714, 2–715, 2–717.

CARGILL, INC. v. STAFFORD, 553 F.2d 1222 (10th Cir.1977). Stafford repudiated his contract to sell wheat to Cargill. The final date for performance was September 30. Stafford's written repudiation was received by Cargill on August 24. On September 6 Stafford repeated his repudiation in response to Cargill's urging of performance. After Stafford told Cargill on September 6 that he would not perform, Cargill told Stafford that the contract was cancelled and claimed damages. The market price of the wheat fluctuated during this period. To determine the proper measure of damages, the court construed UCC § 2–713(1):

"The basic question is whether 'time when buyer learned of the breach' means 'time when buyer learned of the repudiation' or means 'time of performance' in anticipatory repudiation cases. See discussion in J. White and R. Summers, Uniform Commercial Code, 197–202 (1972). The authors conclude, Ibid. at 201, that the soundest arguments support the interpretation of 'learned of the breach' to mean 'time of performance' in the anticipatory repudiation case. We agree for two reasons.

"First, before the adoption of the [Code] in Colorado and other states, damages were measured from the time when performance was due and not from the time when the buyer learned of repudiation.

"A clear deviation from past law would not ordinarily be accomplished by [Code] ambiguities.

"Second, Code [§ 2–723(1)] discusses when to measure damages in a suit for anticipatory repudiation which comes to trial before the time for performance. That section says:

'[A]ny damages based on market price ([§ 2–708] or [§ 2–713]) shall be determined according to the price of such goods prevailing at the time when the aggrieved party *learned of the repudiation.*' (Emphasis supplied.)

Thus, when the [Code] drafters intended to base damages on the date a party 'learned of the repudiation,' they did so by explicit language. We conclude that under [§ 2–713] damages normally should be measured from the time when performance is due and not from the time when the buyer learns of repudiation. * * *

"This brings us to [§ 2–712] which provides that the buyer may 'cover' by the reasonable purchase of substitute goods. A buyer is allowed to buy substitute goods so long as he does not delay unreasonably. Section [2–713] relates to a buyer's damages for nondelivery or repudiation. The official comment to that section says:

> 'The general baseline adopted in this section uses as a yardstick the market in which the buyer would have obtained cover had he sought that relief.'

"We conclude that under [§ 2–713] a buyer may urge continued performance for a reasonable time. At the end of a reasonable period he should cover if substitute goods are readily available. If substitution is readily available and buyer does not cover within a reasonable time, damages should be based on the price at the end of that reasonable time rather than on the price when performance is due. If a valid reason exists for failure or refusal to cover, damages may be calculated from the time when performance is due.

"Specifically, this means that Cargill had a reasonable time after the August 24 anticipatory repudiation to cover. This reasonable time expired on September 6 when Cargill cancelled the contract. The record does not show that Cargill covered or attempted to cover. Nothing in the record shows the continued availability or nonavailability of substitute wheat. On remand the court must determine whether Cargill had a valid reason for failure or refusal to cover. If Cargill did not have a valid reason, the court's award based on the September 6 price should be reinstated. If Cargill had a valid reason for not covering, damages should be awarded on the difference between the price on September 30, the last day for performance, and the July 31 contract price."

Anticipatory Breach

Cargill raises the problem of the duty to mitigate damages when the other party repudiates the contract before performance is due. The UCC covers the problem of "anticipatory repudiation" in §§ 2–610 and 2–611. Under § 2–610, the party receiving the repudiation has several options including doing nothing and awaiting performance by the repudiating party "for a commercially reasonable time." Is this consistent with *Cargill*?

There is also the question of whether the repudiating party is privileged to withdraw the repudiation and proceed with performance. UCC § 2–611 deals with "retraction of anticipatory repudiation." Under the Restatement, Second, Contracts, the repudiating party may sometimes retract the repudiation even when it is no longer "anticipatory" and an actual failure of performance has occurred. The repudiating party is nevertheless privileged to withdraw the repudiation and proceed with performance if the aggrieved party has not relied on the repudiation or indicated that he regards the repudiation as final, and if the breach that has already occurred is not a "total breach." A "total breach" is one so substantial that it is fair to permit the aggrieved party to refuse to perform the part of the contract that was to be exchanged for the performance that is defective, to refuse to receive any further performance from the party who has committed the breach, and to recover damages resulting from the termination of performance. Restatement, Second, Contracts §§ 243, 256. (But see Glass v. Anderson, 596 S.W.2d 507 (Tex.1980), construing the Restatement provisions to mean that a repudiation could not be withdrawn after the time for the repudiator's performance had arrived.)

Is UCC § 2–611 consistent with the Restatement, or does the UCC make every breach accompanied by repudiation a total breach?

HADLEY v. BAXENDALE

Court of Exchequer, 1854.
9 Exch. 341.

At the trial before Crompton, J., at the last Gloucester Assizes, it appeared that the plaintiffs carried on an extensive business as millers at Gloucester; and that, on the 11th of May, their mill was stopped by a breakage of the crank shaft by which the mill was worked. The steam-engine was manufactured by Messrs. Joyce & Co., the engineers, at Greenwich, and it became necessary to send the shaft as a pattern for a new one to Greenwich. The fracture was discovered on the 12th, and on the 13th the plaintiffs sent one of their servants to the office of the defendants, who are the well-known carriers trading under the name of Pickford & Co., for the purpose of having the shaft carried to Greenwich. The plaintiffs' servant told the clerk that the mill was stopped, and that the shaft must be sent immediately; and in answer to the inquiry when the shaft would be taken, the answer was, that if it was sent up by twelve o'clock any day, it would be delivered at Greenwich on the following day. On the following day the shaft was taken by the defendants, before noon, for the purpose of being conveyed to Greenwich, and the sum of £2,4s. was paid for its carriage for the whole distance; at the same time the defendants' clerk was told that a special entry, if required, should be made to hasten its delivery. The delivery of the shaft at Greenwich was delayed by some neglect; and the consequence was, that the plaintiffs did not receive the new shaft for several days after they would otherwise have done, and the working of their mill was thereby delayed, and they thereby lost the profits they would otherwise have received.

On the part of the defendants, it was objected that these damages were too remote, and that the defendants were not liable with respect to them. The learned Judge left the case generally to the jury, who found a verdict with £25. damages beyond the amount paid into Court.

[Defendants had paid £25 into court in satisfaction of plaintiff's claim.]

Whateley, in last Michaelmas Term, obtained a rule nisi for a new trial, on the ground of misdirection. * * *

Whateley, Willes, and *Phipson,* in support of the rule—

* * * Here the declaration is founded upon the defendants' duty as common carriers, and indeed there is no pretence for saying that they entered into a special contract to bear all the consequences of the non-delivery of the article in question. They were merely bound to carry it safely, and to deliver it within a reasonable time. The duty of the clerk, who was in attendance at the defendants' office, was to enter the article, and to take the amount of the carriage; but a mere notice to him, such as was here given, could not make the defendants, as carriers, liable as upon a special contract. Such matters, therefore, must be rejected from the consideration of the question. If carriers are to be liable in such a case as this, the exercise of a sound judgment would not suffice, but they ought to be gifted also with a spirit of prophecy. "I have always understood," said Patteson, J., in Kelly v. Partington,[c] "that the special damage must be the natural result of the thing done." That sentence presents the true test. * * * This therefore is a question of law, and the jury ought to have been told that these damages were too remote; and that, in the absence of the proof of any other damage, the plaintiffs were entitled to nominal damages. * * * Suppose a manufacturer were to contract with a coal merchant or mine owner for the delivery of a boat load of coals, no intimation being given that the coals were required for immediate use, the vendor in that case would not be liable for the stoppage of the vendee's business for want of the article which he had failed to deliver: for the vendor has no knowledge that the goods are not to go to the vendee's general stock. Where the contracting party is shewn to be acquainted with all the consequences that must of necessity follow from a breach on his part of the contract, it may be reasonable to say that he takes the risk of such consequences. * * *

Cur. adv. vult.

The judgment of the Court was now delivered by

Alderson, B.—We think that there ought to be a new trial in this case; but, in so doing, we deem it to be expedient and necessary to state explicitly the rule which the Judge, at the next trial, ought, in our opinion, to direct the jury to be governed by when they estimate the damages.

It is, indeed, of the last importance that we should do this; for, if the jury are left without any definite rule to guide them, it will, in such cases as these, manifestly lead to the greatest injustice. * * *

Now we think the proper rule in such a case as the present is this:—Where two parties have made a contract which one of them has broken, the damages which the other party ought to receive in respect of such breach of contract should be such as may fairly and reasonably be considered either arising naturally, i.e., according to the usual course of things, from such breach of contract itself, or such as may

c. 5 B. & Ad. 651.

reasonably be supposed to have been in the contemplation of both parties, at the time they made the contract, as the probable result of the breach of it. Now, if the special circumstances under which the contract was actually made were communicated by the plaintiffs to the defendants, and thus known to both parties, the damages resulting from the breach of such a contract, which they would reasonably contemplate, would be the amount of injury which would ordinarily follow from a breach of contract under these special circumstances, so known and communicated. But, on the other hand, if these special circumstances were wholly unknown to the party breaking the contract, he, at the most, could only be supposed to have had in his contemplation the amount of injury which would arise generally, and in the great multitude of cases not affected by any special circumstances, from such a breach of contract. For, had the special circumstances been known, the parties might have specially provided for the breach of contract by special terms as to the damages in that case; and of this advantage it would be very unjust to deprive them. Now the above principles are those by which we think the jury ought to be guided in estimating the damages arising out of any breach of contract. It is said, that other cases, such as breaches of contract in the non-payment of money, or in the not making a good title to land, are to be treated as exceptions from this, and as governed by a conventional rule. But as, in such cases, both parties must be supposed to be cognisant of that well-known rule, these cases may, we think, be more properly classed under the rule above enunciated as to cases under known special circumstances, because there both parties may reasonably be presumed to contemplate the estimation of the amount of damages according to the conventional rule. Now, in the present case, if we are to apply the principles above laid down, we find that the only circumstances here communicated by the plaintiffs to the defendants at the time the contract was made, were, that the article to be carried was the broken shaft of a mill, and that the plaintiffs were the millers of that mill. But how do these circumstances shew reasonably that the profits of the mill must be stopped by an unreasonable delay in the delivery of the broken shaft by the carrier to the third person? Suppose the plaintiffs had another shaft in their possession put up or putting up at the time, and that they only wished to send back the broken shaft to the engineer who made it; it is clear that this would be quite consistent with the above circumstances, and yet the unreasonable delay in the delivery would have no effect upon the intermediate profits of the mill. Or, again, suppose that, at the time of the delivery to the carrier, the machinery of the mill had been in other respects defective, then, also, the same results would follow. Here it is true that the shaft was actually sent back to serve as a model for a new one, and that the want of a new one was the only cause of the stoppage of the mill, and that the loss of profits really arose from not sending down the new shaft in proper time, and that this arose from the delay in delivering the broken one to serve as a model. But it is obvious that, in the great multitude

of cases of millers sending off broken shafts to third persons by a
carrier under ordinary circumstances, such consequences would not, in
all probability, have occurred; and these special circumstances were
here never communicated by the plaintiffs to the defendants. It
follows, therefore, that the loss of profits here cannot reasonably be
considered such a consequence of the breach of contract as could have
been fairly and reasonably contemplated by both the parties when they
made this contract. For such loss would neither have flowed naturally
from the breach of this contract in the great multitude of such cases
occurring under ordinary circumstances, nor were the special circumstances, which, perhaps, would have made it a reasonable and natural
consequence of such breach of contract, communicated to or known by
the defendants. The Judge ought, therefore, to have told the jury that,
upon the facts then before them, they ought not to take the loss of
profits into consideration at all in estimating the damages. There must
therefore be a new trial in this case.

Rule absolute.

———

The principal case mentions a special rule concerning consequential damages for "the non-payment of money, or in the not making good
title to land."

Damages for nonpayment of money were once limited to the sum
owed plus interest from the time performance was due. Restatement
[First] of Contracts § 337(a) (1932). There is some evidence of current
willingness to include additional foreseeable damages, at least if the
payment is not to the promisee but to a third person on behalf of the
promisee. For example, in Mead v. Johnson Group, Inc., 615 S.W.2d
685 (Tex.1981), the buyer of a business had agreed to pay the debts that
the business had acquired while owned by the seller. The buyer did not
pay. The seller was permitted to recover compensation for damage to
seller's credit rating. Cf. UCC § 4–402.

The rule was established in early English cases that if the seller of
land broke his contract to convey good title because he did not have
title, the buyer's remedy was limited to recovery of any payment with
interest. Later English cases permitted recovery of costs that buyer
had incurred in reliance on the contract, such as expenditures for a
title investigation. Most American jurisdictions now permit the buyer
to recover damages for loss of the bargain—the difference between
contract and market prices. See Williston, Contracts § 1399 (3d ed.
Jaeger).

MORROW v. FIRST NATIONAL BANK OF HOT SPRINGS

Supreme Court of Arkansas, 1977.
261 Ark. 568, 550 S.W.2d 429.

GEORGE ROSE SMITH, JUSTICE.

For a number of years before 1971 the two plaintiffs, Morrow and Goslee, collected coins, individually and as partners. In 1971 a substantial part of the collection was kept at Morrow's home in Hot Springs. On September 4 of that year someone broke into the house and stole coins valued at $32,155.17. Almost three years later the plaintiffs brought this action against the defendant bank to recover the value of the stolen coins. The complaint alleges a breach of contract, in that the bank failed to notify the plaintiffs of the availability, on August 30, 1971, of safety-deposit boxes in a new bank building. This appeal is from a summary judgment in favor of the bank.

We state the facts most favorably to the plaintiffs. Morrow collected coins for many years. In about 1964 he had metal cabinets built in a closet in his house, so arranged that a burglar would have to go through eleven sets of locks to reach the coins. In about 1969, as insurance rates were becoming prohibitive, the two plaintiffs began to look for large safety-deposit boxes in which to keep their coins. No boxes were available in Hot Springs. From time to time Morrow discussed the problem with one or more employees of the defendant bank, where he was a regular customer.

In the summer of 1971 the bank was planning to move into its new building. Safety-deposit boxes were advertised. On June 25 the plaintiffs reserved three large boxes in the new building, paying $25 for each box. It was expected that the boxes would be available in from 30 to 60 days. Morrow explained his need for the boxes, adding that he particularly wanted them by September 1, when his husky teenage son would leave for college. The bank was perhaps on notice, through a loan application to a different department, that the coins were worth at least $12,000.

One or two employees of the bank promised to notify Morrow as soon as the boxes were available. The burglary occurred on the evening of Saturday, September 4, while Morrow and his wife were out to dinner. When Morrow inquired about the safety-deposit boxes on the following Tuesday, after Labor Day, he learned that the boxes had become available on August 30. An employee of the bank explained that "we just didn't have time" to notify Morrow that the boxes were ready. The plaintiffs immediately moved the rest of their coins into the safety-deposit boxes. * * *

We consider this case to be controlled by our holding in Hooks Smelting Co. v. Planters' Compress Co., 72 Ark. 275, 79 S.W. 1052 (1904). There we adopted what is now known as the "tacit agreement test" for the recovery of consequential damages for a breach of contract.

By that test the plaintiff must prove more than the defendant's mere knowledge that a breach of contract will entail special damages to the plaintiff. It must also appear that the defendant at least tacitly agreed to assume responsibility. Justice Riddick's entire opinion in *Hooks* is enlightening, but we emphasize this particular language:

> It seems then that mere notice is not always sufficient to impose on the party who breaks a contract damages arising by reason of special circumstances, and the reason why this is so was referred to in a recent decision by the supreme court of the United States. In that case Mr. Justice Holmes, who delivered the opinion of the court, after remarking that one who makes a contract usually contemplates performance, not a breach, of his contract, said: "The extent of liability in such cases is likely to be within his contemplation, and whether it is or not, should be worked out on terms which it fairly may be presumed he would have assented to if they had been presented to his mind." Globe Refining Co. v. Landa Oil Co., 190 U.S. 540, 23 S.Ct. 754, 47 L.Ed. 1171.

> Now, where the damages arise from special circumstances, and are so large as to be out of proportion to the consideration agreed to be paid for the services to be rendered under the contract, it raises a doubt at once as to whether the party would have assented to such a liability had it been called to his attention at the making of the contract unless the consideration to be paid was also raised so as to correspond in some respect to the liability assumed. To make him liable for the special damages in such a case, there must not only be knowledge of the special circumstances, but such knowledge "must be brought home to the party sought to be charged under such circumstances that he must know that the person he contracts with reasonably believes that he accepts the contract with the special condition attached to it." In other words, where there is no express contract to pay such special damages, the facts and circumstances in proof must be such as to make it reasonable for the judge or jury trying the case to believe that the party at the time of the contract tacitly consented to be bound to more than ordinary damages in case of default on his part.

In the case at bar there is no proof to support a finding that the bank, in return for box rentals of $75, agreed in effect to issue a burglary insurance policy to the plaintiffs in the amount of at least $32,155.17 and probably much more, as the actual loss was only partial. The bank's bare promise to notify the plaintiffs as soon as the boxes were available did not amount to a tacit agreement that the bank, for no consideration in addition to its regular rental for the boxes, would be liable for as much as $32,000 if the promised notice was not given.

The tacit agreement rule is a minority rule, but we think it to be sound. We did not lightly adopt it. To the contrary, we relied upon three textbooks and a number of decisions, including one written by

Justice Holmes. This language from the *Hooks* opinion expresses what Holmes described as "common sense":

> Suppose, for instance, that a large manufacturing establishment is driven by power from a single engine, and that, by reason of an accident to some small but important part of the engine or machinery, it becomes necessary to stop the operation of the whole plant until a new part can be made or the old one repaired. If thereupon a blacksmith or machinist is called in, and, for the price of a few dollars, undertakes to make the repairs, but through some mistake or unskillfulness the part supplied by him should fail to fit, requiring it to be remade and entailing still further delay, would any court hold that the blacksmith or machinist could be held liable for all the damages entailed by the delay when they were large, in the absence of a contract on his part to be thus liable, unless the notice and the circumstances under which he made the contract were such that he ought reasonably to have known that in the event of his failure to perform his contract the other party would look to him to make good the loss?

The tacit agreement test, to be sure, has been questioned and was rejected by the draftsmen of the Uniform Commercial Code. Ark.Stat. Ann. § 85–2–715 and Comment 2 (Add.1961); Williston, Contracts, § 1357 (3d ed., 1968); Casenote, 18 Ark.L.Rev. 169 (1964). We do not attach great importance to the Commercial Code provision, simply because the legislature, in adopting a uniform act containing hundreds of sections, certainly did not specifically and consciously decide that the rule of the *Hooks* case should be changed in all situations. We adhere to that decision. * * *

Affirmed.

KERR S.S. CO. v. RADIO CORP. OF AMERICA, 245 N.Y. 284, 157 N.E. 140 (1927), cert. denied, 275 U.S. 557, 48 S.Ct. 118, 72 L.Ed. 424 (1927). Steamship company gave RCA a radiogram in Scott's code to send to steamship company's agent in Manila. The radiogram contained instructions for the loading of cargo. RCA mislaid the radiogram and it was not sent. As a result the cargo was not loaded and steamship company lost the freight charge of over $6,500 that it otherwise would have collected. Steamship company paid $26.78 to send the message. An opinion by Judge Cardozo holds that damages recoverable by steamship company from RCA are limited to the charge for sending:

"The settled doctrine of this court confines the liability of a telegraph company for failure to transmit a message within the limits of the rule in Hadley v. Baxendale (9 Exch. 341). Where the terms of the telegram disclose the general nature of the transaction which is the subject of the message, the company is answerable for the natural consequences of its neglect in relation to the transaction thus known or foreseen. On the other hand, where the terms of the message give no hint of the nature of the transaction, the liability is for nominal damages or for the cost of carriage if the tolls have been prepaid.

"We are now asked to hold that the transaction has been revealed within the meaning of the rule if the length and cost of the telegram or the names of the parties would fairly suggest to a reasonable man that business of moment is the subject of the message. This is very nearly to annihilate the rule in the guise of an exception. The defendant upon receiving from a steamship company a long telegram in cipher to be transmitted to Manila would naturally infer that the message had relation to business of some sort. Beyond that it could infer nothing. The message might relate to the loading of a cargo but equally it might relate to the sale of a vessel or to the employment of an agent or to any one of myriad transactions as divergent as the poles. Notice of the business, if it is to lay the basis for special damages, must be sufficiently informing to be notice of the risk. * * *

"Imputed knowledge, if it exists, must rest upon an assumption less timid and uncertain. The assumption cannot be less than this, that whatever a carrier could ascertain by diligent inquiry as to the nature of the undisclosed transaction, this he should be deemed to have ascertained, and charged with damages accordingly. We do not need to consider whether such a rule might wisely have been applied in the beginning, when the law as to carriers of messages was yet in its infancy. Most certainly it is not the rule announced in our decisions. We cannot accept it now without throwing overboard the doctrine that notice is essential. * * *

"We are not unmindful of the force of the plaintiff's assault upon the rule in Hadley v. Baxendale in its application to the relation between telegraph carrier and customer. The truth seems to be that neither the clerk who receives the message over the counter nor the operator who transmits it nor any other employee gives or is expected to give any thought to the sense of what he is receiving or transmitting. This imparts to the whole doctrine as to the need for notice an air of unreality. The doctrine, however, has prevailed for years, so many that it is tantamount to a rule of property. The companies have regulated their rates upon the basis of its continuance. They have omitted precautions that they might have thought it necessary to adopt if the hazard of the business was to be indefinitely increased. Nor is the doctrine without other foundation in utility and justice. Much may be said in favor of the social policy of a rule whereby the companies have been relieved of liabilities that might otherwise be crushing. The sender can protect himself by insurance in one form or another if the risk of nondelivery or error appears to be too great. The total burden is not heavy since it is distributed among many, and can be proportioned in any instance to the loss likely to ensue. The company, if it takes out insurance for itself, can do no more than guess at the loss to be avoided. To pay for this unknown risk, it will be driven to increase the rates payable by all, though the increase is likely to result in the protection of a few. We are not concerned to balance the considerations of policy that give support to the existing rule against others that weigh against it. Enough for present purposes that there are weights in either scale. Telegraph companies in interstate and foreign commerce are subject to the power of Congress. If the rule of damages long recognized by state and federal decision is to give way to another, the change should come through legislation.

"The plaintiff makes the point that the action is one in tort for the breach of a duty owing from a public service corporation, and that the rule of Hadley v. Baxendale does not protect the carrier unless sued upon the contract. There is much authority the other way. Though the duty to serve may be antecedent to the contract, yet the contract when made defines and circumscribes the duty. Possibly the existing rule of damage would have been rejected at the beginning if the carrier's default had been dissociated from the law of contracts and considered as a tort. As it is, there is little trace of a disposition to make the measure of the liability dependent on the form of action. A different question would be here if the plaintiff were seeking reparation for a wrong unrelated to the contract, as, e.g., for a refusal to accept a message or for an insistence upon the payment of discriminatory rates. The plaintiff alleges in the complaint that the defendant did accept the message and 'promised and agreed' to transmit it, and that the plaintiff has 'duly performed each and every condition of the agreement' on its part to be performed and is willing to pay the charges. We do not stop to inquire whether such a complaint is turned into one in tort by the later allegation that the defendant was negligent in the performance of its promise. Upon the acceptance of the message the defendant's duty was to deliver it in accordance with the contract, and the damages recoverable for nonperformance of the contract are the damages recoverable for nonperformance of the duty.

"The conclusion thus reached makes it unnecessary to consider whether a limitation of liability has been effected by agreement. On the back of the message is the warning, "to guard against mistakes, the sender of every message should order it repeated," followed by these words:

" 'It is agreed between the sender of the message on the face hereof and this company, that said company shall not be liable for mistakes or delays in transmission or delivery, nor for nondelivery to the next connecting telegraph company or to the addressee, of any unrepeated message, beyond the amount of that portion of the tolls which shall accrue to this company; and that this company shall not be liable for mistakes or delays in the transmission or delivery, nor for delay or nondelivery to the next connecting telegraph company, or to the addressee, of any repeated message beyond the usual tolls and extra sum received by this company from the sender for transmitting and repeating such message; and that this company shall not be liable in any case for delays arising from interruption in the working of its system, nor for errors in cipher or obscure messages.' "

RESTATEMENT, SECOND, CONTRACTS § 351:

(1) Damages are not recoverable for loss that the party in breach did not have reason to foresee as a probable result of the breach when the contract was made.

(2) Loss may be foreseeable as a probable result of a breach because it follows from the breach

(a) in the ordinary course of events, or

(b) as a result of special circumstances, beyond the ordinary course of events, that the party in breach had reason to know.

(3) A court may limit damages for foreseeable loss by excluding recovery for loss of profits, by allowing recovery only for loss incurred in reliance, or otherwise if it concludes that in the circumstances justice so requires in order to avoid disproportionate compensation.

Illustrations:

3. A and B make a written contract under which A is to recondition by a stated date a used machine owned by B so that it will be suitable for sale by B to C. A knows when they make the contract that B has contracted to sell the machine to C but knows nothing of the terms of B's contract with C. Because A delays in returning the machine to B, B is unable to sell it to C and loses the profit that he would have made on that sale. B's loss of reasonable profit was foreseeable by A as a probable result of the breach at the time the contract was made. * * *

5. A and B make a contract under which A is to recondition by a stated date a used machine owned by B so that it will be suitable for use in B's canning factory. A knows that the machine must be reconditioned by that date if B's factory is to operate at full capacity during the canning season, but nothing is said of this in the written contract. Because A delays in returning the machine to B, B loses its use for the entire canning season and loses the profit that he would have made had his factory operated at full capacity. B's loss of reasonable profit was foreseeable by A as a probable result of the breach at the time the contract was made.

———

See UCC § 2–715(2).

AINSWORTH v. COMBINED INSURANCE CO. OF AMERICA

Supreme Court of Nevada, 1988.
104 Nev. 587, 763 P.2d 673, cert. denied, 493 U.S. 958, 110 S.Ct. 376, 107
L.Ed.2d 361 (1989).

GUNDERSON, CHIEF JUSTICE.

On January 14, 1982, Thomas Ainsworth was a healthy, working man who also served his community as a member of the Sparks City Council. His only health concerns involved occasional "dizzy spells," which he had experienced at irregular intervals over a period of several years. Within twenty-four hours, Thomas Ainsworth's life was shattered. Because of an accident which occurred during the administration of an angiogram, Thomas suffered a stroke. He immediately went into a coma, which continued for seven days. He was still 100% disabled after six months. The stroke did not kill him, but some of its effects are permanent and devastating. He will never walk or talk as well as he previously did.

While Thomas was fighting for his life, his wife, Evelyn Ainsworth, was fighting a different battle. She attempted to collect benefits for Thomas under two accident policies issued by the respondent. Combined Insurance Company of America (Combined). The Ainsworths had been advised by agents of Combined that their accident policies would protect them in the event of "any conceivable accident." Relying on this promise, and the advice of Thomas' physician, Evelyn sent in an accident claim.

The insurance adjuster who received the claim denied it immediately, without any investigation whatsoever, because the doctor's report hypothesized that the stroke may have been caused by the disruption of atheromatous plaque during the angiogram. The adjuster focused upon this one sentence in the report, and concluded that the development of arterial plaque had contributed to Thomas' stroke. Since the policy excluded any accident which was contributed to by disease, Combined refused to pay benefits under the policies. These benefits amounted to $9,600.

Evelyn was distressed by the denial, but decided to resubmit the claim on advice from her nephew, who was a physician, and from the Combined salesman who came by in June to collect the next biannual premium. Combined's salesman discussed the Ainsworths' financial condition with Evelyn, and encouraged her to resubmit her claim. He even promised to put a hold on the premium check while the matter was cleared up.

The claim was resubmitted, along with a doctor's report which corrected the earlier hypothesis. The doctor stated that the results of the angiogram clearly showed that Thomas' blood vessels were normal and were not built up with atheromatous plaque. He affirmed that the stroke was entirely accidental, and could have resulted from numerous causes.

At this time, Combined sent its file to its medical consultant, Dr. Goldfinger. The consultant was provided, however, only with the first doctor's report and records from Washoe Medical Center, where Thomas had been transferred after the accident. The consultant's one-line report stated that the stroke was the result of disease. After receiving the consultant's report, Combined again denied the claim, without evaluating the second doctor's report or the record summaries from the Veteran's Administration Hospital, where the accident occurred. Combined never made further inquiry into the claim, never telephoned or wrote to the doctors, and never obtained a copy of the operating report or the angiogram.

In November, 1982, Evelyn submitted Thomas' claim for the third time, accompanied by yet another doctor's report explaining that Thomas had been the victim of an accident. By this time, the claim file included more records from the V.A. Hospital. The file was sent to Dr. Goldfinger for a second evaluation, but on the same day Combined sent Evelyn a third denial letter. Two days later, Dr. Goldfinger again recommended denying the claim, because the angiogram had been ordered for the purpose of diagnosing Thomas' dizzy spells. Thus, according to Goldfinger, the loss was not "purely accidental."

In a further effort to obtain the badly-needed policy benefits, Evelyn submitted the claim for the fourth time in February, 1983. With her claim she included a letter from her husband's doctor which confirmed that the angiogram "revealed no pre-existing vascular disease." In response to this claim, Combined offered to "compromise" by paying the Ainsworths $1,940 in exchange for a release of all claims. Evelyn understandably refused this offer, and wrote a fifth letter, requesting payment of the full benefits under the two policies, a total of $9,600. Combined still refused to pay.

The Ainsworths then sued Combined, seeking the payment of benefits and compensatory and punitive damages. The jury awarded the benefits, $200,000 in compensatory damages, and $5,939,500 in punitive damages. Combined moved for a judgment notwithstanding the verdict and for a new trial. The district court denied the latter motion, but granted the former, totally eliminating the award of punitive damages. For the reasons expressed in this opinion, we reverse the judgment of the district court and reinstate the jury's verdict. The denial of the motion for new trial is affirmed. * * *

A jury may award punitive damages where the defendant has been guilty of fraud, malice, or oppression. NRS 42.010. We conclude that the punitive damages award in this case is supported by substantial evidence of oppression on the part of the defendant, Combined. Therefore, we reverse the decision of the district court.

Oppression has been defined as "a conscious disregard for the rights of others which constitute[s] an act of subjecting plaintiffs to cruel and unjust hardship." *Roth v. Shell Oil Company,* 185 Cal.App. 2d 676, 682, 8 Cal.Rptr. 514 (1960). Our decisions have recognized that such a "conscious disregard" may support an award of punitive damages. *Leslie v. Jones Chemical Co.,* 92 Nev. 391, 551 P.2d 234 (1976); *Nevada Cement Co. v. Lemler,* 89 Nev. 447, 514 P.2d 1180 (1973). The Ainsworths presented substantial evidence that Combined had consciously and deliberately ignored their rights to the payment of benefits. * * *

Combined's obstinate and unjustified refusal to pay, in our opinion, constitutes oppression as contemplated by the statute. The evidence establishes that the Ainsworths were in desperate need of funds, and that Combined had reason to know of their dire circumstances. The record clearly supports an inference that Combined consciously disregarded the rights of its insured by clinging to its restrictive definition of "accident" as used in its policy.

This intransigent resistance is remarkable in light of the written inducements offered to obtain renewal premiums from Thomas and Evelyn Ainsworth. As stated above, they had carried insurance with Combined since 1969. At trial, documents were introduced which showed that Combined sent "good news letters" to its insureds, assuring them they were covered in the event of "any conceivable accident," incurred in "any activity whatsoever." When the salesman arrived to collect the premiums, he reminded the Ainsworths of the benefits they were receiving, as explained in the news letters. In fact, the salesman's manual defined "accident" simply as "an event that is unforseen [sic] and unexpected." Given such information, the Ainsworths could reasonably expect that an unforeseeable, unexpected accident which occurred as a result of a medical test would be covered by their policy. *See National Union Fire Ins. v. Reno's Exec. Air,* 100 Nev. 360, 682 P.2d 1380 (1984).

The relationship of an insured to an insurer is one of special confidence. A consumer buys insurance for security, protection, and peace of mind. *Rawlings v. Apodaca,* 151 Ariz. 149, 726 P.2d 565 (1986) (*en banc*). The insurer is under a duty to negotiate with its insureds in good faith and to deal with them fairly. The insurer may not rely on its own ambiguous contract as the sole basis for denial. Rawlings, supra, 726 P.2d at n. 572, *see also Sullivan v. Dairyland Ins. Co.,* 98 Nev. 364, 649 P.2d 1357 (1982). To allow such conduct would only encourage ambiguous contracts. Indeed, our law has held that any ambiguity will be construed against the insurance company, and rightly so. *N. American Life & Cas. Co. v. Gingrich,* 91 Nev. 491, 538 P.2d 163 (1975). Negotiations between a wealthy, sophisticated commercial venturer and a naive consumer cannot be of equal strength. For that reason, the law attempts to render an ambiguous contract fair by making the drafter responsible for ambiguity. The insurance industry is heavily regulated by the state, because it is an important public trust. Along with the profits obtained from insurance premiums, insurers must accept the obligations of good faith and fair dealing imposed by law.

Furthermore, even if the evidence is not sufficient to prove that Combined acted oppressively in avoiding the payment of benefits, we note that in the past we have found malice in fact when the defendant has engaged in wilful and intentional conduct, done in reckless disregard of its possible results. *Nevada Cement, supra,* 89 Nev. at 451, 514 P.2d at 1183; *Nevada National Bank v. Huff,* 94 Nev. 506, 582 P.2d 364 (1978). Combined's conduct was neither accidental nor simply negligent. In spite of five requests made in eighteen months, in spite of the serious nature of its insured's accident, it conducted no independent investigation and utterly failed to evaluate fairly the medical evidence it possessed in its claim file.

Therefore, we conclude that the jury's award of punitive damages was supported by substantial evidence.

PUNITIVE DAMAGES

Traditionally this court has held that the amount of a punitive damages award was subjective, and therefore best left to the jury's determination. *Phillips v. Lynch,* 101 Nev. 311, 704 P.2d 1083 (1985); *Miller v. Schnitzer,* 78 Nev. 301, 371 P.2d 824 (1962). Recently we have attempted to define the allowable limits of punitive damages in a more objective fashion. *Ace Truck v. Kahn,* 103 Nev. 503, 746 P.2d 132 (1987). *Ace Truck* described several factors which contribute to an appellate evaluation of a punitive damages award. We conclude, however, that none of these factors prevent us from affirming the award in this case.

First, we note that the financial position of the defendant is still relevant to the determination of the amount of the punitive damages award. The wealth of a defendant is directly relevant to the size of an award, which is meant to deter the defendant from repeating his misconduct as well as punish him for his past behavior. *See Midwest Supply, Inc. v. Waters,* 89 Nev. 210, 510 P.2d 876 (1973). We note that the award in this case, while large, amounts to only 5% of Combined's 1985 net operating gain. The award constitutes only .4% of Combined's 1985 total assets. Since we find its business conduct totally unacceptable, we are reluctant to disturb the jury's determination that a sizable award is necessary to deter Combined from pursuing its inappropriate methods.

Second, we conclude that the culpability and blameworthiness of Combined is considerable, with few mitigating circumstances. Despite repeated requests by the insured, all of which were accompanied by medical reports, Combined failed to investigate the claim properly. It refused to pay on the basis of one inaccuracy in the initial report, an inaccuracy which was corrected by three later reports. Combined must take full responsibility for the handling of the claim, and its own obstinate refusal to take more appropriate action.

Third, we look to the vulnerability of, and injury suffered by, the offended party. Thomas Ainsworth was in a highly vulnerable position as the result of the devastating consequences of his stroke. Unable to communicate effectively, he depended on the efforts of his wife, a woman who was inexperienced in handling business matters. Sufficient evidence was produced at trial to show that Thomas was permanently impaired in his speaking ability by the lack of crucial funds to pay for speech therapy at the proper time during his recovery. Thomas' injuries prompted the jury to make a substantial award of compensatory damages. These injuries also support an award of punitive damages.

Another factor is the offensiveness of the punished conduct when compared to societal values of justice and propriety. As discussed above, insurance is a special kind of commercial activity. The insurer is under a duty to treat its policyholders fairly. The obstinate, unjustified refusal to pay a legitimate claim is offensive to society, precisely because the consumer pays for insurance to gain security and peace of mind.

Finally, we must evaluate the means judged necessary to deter future misconduct. Combined is a very large, wealthy insurance company which sends its agents out among the innocent citizenry, selling policies door-to-door. Its policyholders are not sophisticated commercial investors; they are ordinary citizens who hope to protect themselves from future calamities. If Combined is to be deterred from its past course of conduct, this can only be done through an assessment of punitive damages. In order to accomplish this purpose, the amount awarded must be sufficient to cause the defendant real concern. We cannot say that an assessment of .4% of the respondent's total assets is unwarranted under the circumstances of this case. The award does not shock our judicial conscience, and it is not clearly excessive. *Hale v. Riverboat Casino, Inc.,* 100 Nev. 299, 682 P.2d 190 (1984).

————

SEAMAN'S DIRECT BUYING SERVICE, INC. v. STANDARD OIL CO. OF CALIFORNIA, 36 Cal.3d 752, 206 Cal.Rptr. 354, 686 P.2d 1158 (1984). Seaman's was in the business of supplying ships with fuel and other necessities. Seaman's and Standard Oil signed a letter setting out the basic terms of an agreement under which Standard would sell marine fuel to Seaman's. The letter concluded "this offer is subject to our mutual agreement on the specific wording of contracts to be drawn." Seaman's then leased space in a marina under construction. Conditions in the oil industry changed in favor of sellers. Standard then denied that it had a binding contract with Seaman's. "Seaman's asked Standard to stipulate to the existence of a contract, explaining that it could not continue in operation throughout the time that a trial would take. In reply, Standard's representative laughed and said, 'See you in court.' " Seaman's discontinued operations and sued Standard on several theories including breach of contract and "breach of the implied covenant of good faith and fair dealing." At trial, the jury awarded Seaman's $397,050 in compensatory damages and over $11 million in punitive damages for "tortious breach of the implied covenant." In order to avoid a new trial, Seaman's consented to the trial court's request that the punitive damages be reduced to $1 million. Judgment was entered for this amount and Standard appealed. The Supreme Court of California held that tort remedies, including punitive damages, are available for "denying, in bad faith and without probable cause" that a contract exists, but reversed the judgment for failure of the trial court to instruct the jury that no tort was committed if Standard's denial of the existence of a binding contract, although erroneous, was made in good faith:

"The principal issue raised by this appeal is whether, and under what circumstances, a breach of the implied covenant of good faith and fair dealing in a commercial contract may give rise to an action in tort. Standard contends that a tort action for breach of the implied covenant has always been, and should continue to be, limited to cases where the underlying contract is one of insurance. Seaman's, pointing to several recent cases decided by this court and the Courts of Appeal, challenges this contention. * * *

"While the proposition that the law implies a covenant of good faith and fair dealing in all contracts is well established, the proposition advanced by Seaman's—that breach of the covenant always gives rise to an action in tort—is not so clear. In holding that a tort action is available for breach of the covenant in an insurance contract, we have emphasized the 'special relationship' between insurer and insured, characterized by elements of public interest, adhesion, and fiduciary responsibility. (*Egan v. Mutual of Omaha Ins. Co.*, 24 Cal.3d at p. 820, 169 Cal.Rptr. 691, 620 P.2d 141.) No doubt there are other relationships with similar characteristics and deserving of similar legal treatment.

"When we move from such special relationships to consideration of the tort remedy in the context of the ordinary commercial contract, we move into largely uncharted and potentially dangerous waters. Here, parties of roughly equal bargaining power are free to shape the contours of their agreement and to include provisions for attorney fees and liquidated damages in the event of breach. They may not be permitted to disclaim the covenant of good faith but they are free, within reasonable limits at least, to agree upon the standards by which application of the covenant is to be measured.[7] In such contracts, it may be difficult to distinguish between breach of the covenant and breach of contract, and there is the risk that interjecting tort remedies will intrude upon the expectations of the parties. This is not to say

---

7. California's Commercial Code section [1–102(3)] prohibits disclaimer of the good faith obligation, as well as the obligations of diligence, reasonableness, and care, but provides that "the parties may by agree- ment determine the standards by which the performance of such obligations is to be measured if such standards are not manifestly unreasonable."

that tort remedies have no place in such a commercial context, but that it is wise to proceed with caution in determining their scope and application.

"For the purposes of this case it is unnecessary to decide the broad question which Seaman's poses. Indeed, it is not even necessary to predicate liability on a breach of the implied covenant. It is sufficient to recognize that a party to a contract may incur tort remedies when, in addition to breaching the contract, it seeks to shield itself from liability by denying, in bad faith and without probable cause, that the contract exists.

"It has been held that a party to a contract may be subject to tort liability, including punitive damages, if he coerces the other party to pay more than is due under the contract terms through the threat of a lawsuit, made ' "without probable cause and with no belief in the existence of the cause of action." ' (*Adams v. Crater Well Drilling, Inc.* (1976) 276 Or. 789, 556 P.2d 679, 681.) There is little difference, in principle, between a contracting party obtaining excess payment in such manner, and a contracting party seeking to avoid all liability on a meritorious contract claim by adopting a 'stonewall' position ('see you in court') without probable cause and with no belief in the existence of a defense. Such conduct goes beyond the mere breach of contract. It offends accepted notions of business ethics. (See *Jones v. Abriani* (1976) 169 Ind.App. 556, 350 N.E.2d 635.) Acceptance of tort remedies in such a situation is not likely to intrude upon the bargaining relationship or upset reasonable expectations of the contracting parties.

"Turning to the facts of this case, the jury was instructed that 'where a binding contract [has] been agreed upon, the law implies a covenant that neither party will deny the existence of a contract, since doing so violates the legal prohibition against doing anything to prevent realization of the promises of the performance of the contract.'

"According to Standard, this instruction erroneously allowed the jury to hold Standard liable if it found that Standard denied the existence of a valid contract, regardless of whether that denial was in good or bad faith."

Since the opinion in *Seaman's,* the California courts have struggled with its implications. In Foley v. Interactive Data Corp., 47 Cal.3d 654, 254 Cal.Rptr. 211, 765 P.2d 373 (1988), a discharged employee sued for breach of an implied-in-fact promise to discharge him only for good cause. Included in the employee's action was a tort claim for breach of the implied covenant of good faith and fair dealing, which was part of the contract of employment. The Supreme Court of California held that a tort remedy was not available for breach of this covenant in employment-contract cases:

"If the covenant is implied in every contract, but its breach does not in every contract give rise to tort damages, attempts to define when tort damages are appropriate simply by interjecting a requirement of "bad faith" do nothing to limit the potential reach of tort remedies or to differentiate between those cases properly and traditionally compensable by contract damages and those in which tort damages should flow. Virtually any firing (indeed any breach of a contract term in any context) could provide the basis for a pleading alleging the discharge was in bad faith under the cited standards.

"Finally, and of primary significance, we believe that focus on available contract remedies offers the most appropriate method of expanding available relief for wrongful terminations. The expansion of tort remedies in the employment context has potentially enormous consequences for the stability of the business community.

"We are not unmindful of the legitimate concerns of employees who fear arbitrary and improper discharges that may have a devastating effect on their economic and social status. Nor are we unaware of or unsympathetic to claims that contract remedies for breaches of contract are insufficient because they do not fully compensate due to their failure to include attorney fees and their restrictions on foreseeable damages. These defects, however, exist generally in contract situations. As discussed above, the variety of possible courses to remedy the problem is well demonstrated in the literature and include increased contract damages, provision for award of attorney fees, establishment of arbitration or other speedier and less expensive dispute resolution, or the tort remedies (the scope of which is also subject to dispute) sought by plaintiff here.

"The diversity of possible solutions demonstrates the confusion that occurs when we look outside the realm of contract law in attempting to fashion remedies for a breach of a contract provision. As noted, numerous legislative provisions have imposed obligations on parties to contracts which vindicate significant social policies extraneous to the contract itself. As Justice Kaus observed in his concurring and dissenting opinion in *White v. Western Title Ins. Co.* (1985) 40 Cal.3d 870, 901, 221 Cal.Rptr. 509, 710 P.2d 309, 'our experience in *Seaman's* surely tells us that there are real problems in applying the substitute remedy of a tort recovery—with or without punitive damages—outside the insurance area. In other words, I believe that under all the circumstances, the problem is one for the Legislature ∗ ∗ ∗.' "

Lynch & Freytag v. Cooper, 218 Cal.App.3d 603, 267 Cal.Rptr. 189 (1990), refused to extend *Seaman's* to a denial of the existence of a contract when the denial was in an answer to a complaint. The majority opinion rested this result, in part, on potential conflict with the statutory right to file a general denial. The concurring opinion remarked: "The general viability of *Seaman's* in view of *Foley* appears to be tenuous at best."

PATTON v. MID–CONTINENT SYSTEMS, INC., 841 F.2d 742 (7th Cir. 1988). A franchisee sued its franchisor for breach of the franchise agreement. The franchisor had allegedly breached the contract by not giving the franchisee sufficient time to provide additional coverage in the franchisee's territory, and then by authorizing someone else to compete with the franchisee in that territory. At trial, the franchisee recovered compensatory and punitive damages. The 7th Circuit, in an opinion by Judge Posner, applying Indiana law, reversed an award of punitive damages:

"Indiana allows punitive damages to be awarded in suits for breach of contract if, 'mingled' with the breach, are 'elements of fraud, malice, gross negligence or oppression.' In trying to give concrete meaning to these terms (especially 'oppression'), it is important to bear in mind certain fundamentals of contractual liability. First, liability for breach of contract is, prima facie, strict liability. That is, if the promisor fails to perform as agreed, he has broken his contract even though the failure may have been beyond his power to prevent and therefore in no way blameworthy. The reason is that contracts often contain an insurance component. The promisor promises in effect either to perform or to compensate the promisee for the cost of nonperformance; and one who voluntarily assumes a risk will not be relieved of the consequences if the risk materializes.

"Even if the breach is deliberate, it is not necessarily blameworthy. The promisor may simply have discovered that his performance is worth more to someone else. If so, efficiency is promoted by allowing him to break his promise, provided he makes good the promisee's actual losses. If he is forced to pay more than that, an efficient breach may be deterred, and the law doesn't want to bring about such a result. Suppose that by franchising Truck–O–Mat in the plaintiffs' territory, Mid–Continent increased its own profits by $150,000 and inflicted damages of $75,000 on the plaintiffs. That would be an efficient breach. But if Mid–Continent had known that it would have to pay in addition to compensatory damages $100,000 in punitive damages, the breach would not have been worthwhile to it and efficiency would have suffered because the difference between Mid–Continent's profits of $150,000 and the plaintiffs' losses of $75,000 would (certainly after the plaintiffs were compensated) represent a net social gain.

"Not all breaches of contract are involuntary or otherwise efficient. Some are opportunistic; the promisor wants the benefit of the bargain without bearing the agreed-upon cost, and exploits the inadequacies of purely compensatory remedies (the major inadequacies being that pre- and post-judgment interest rates are frequently below market levels when the risk of nonpayment is taken into account and that the winning party cannot recover his attorney's fees). * * *

"There is no evidence that the action of Mid–Continent in franchising Truck–O–Mat in the plaintiffs' exclusive territory was opportunistic or even deliberate. So far as can be discerned from the record it was an honest mistake resulting from the ambiguous description of the territory in the franchise agreement with the plaintiffs. However, Mid–Continent's failure to correct the violation year after year after the plaintiffs had called its attention to it—even after it acknowledged the violation—converted an innocent breach into a deliberate one; but no clear and convincing evidence enables the breach to be characterized as malicious, fraudulent, oppressive, or even grossly negligent. * * * "

HAYNES v. DODD, [1990] 2 All E.R. 815 (Ct.App.1988). Plaintiffs operated a motor vehicle repair business. They purchased property on which to conduct the business. Plaintiffs relied on the advice of the defendants, their attorneys, that there was a right of access to the property across adjoining land. In fact, there was no right of access, and when the adjoining landowner refused to permit the plaintiffs to use its land, the plaintiffs were forced to close their business and dispose of the property at a loss. They sued their attorneys for breach of contract recovering compensatory damages and £1,500 for anguish and vexation. On appeal the judgment for anguish and vexation was reversed:

"Like the [trial] judge, I consider that the English courts should be wary or adopting what he called the 'United States practice of huge awards.' Damages awarded for negligence or want of skill, whether against professional men or anyone else, must provide fair compensation, but no more than that. And I would not view with enthusiasm the prospect that every shipowner in the Commercial Court, having successfully claimed for unpaid freight or demurrage, would be able to add a claim for mental distress suffered while he was waiting for his money. * * *

"I am not convinced that it is enough to ask whether mental distress was reasonably foreseeable as a consequence, or even whether it should reasonably have been contemplated as not unlikely to result from a breach of contract. It seems to me that damages for mental distress in contract are, as a matter of policy, limited to certain classes of case. I would broadly follow the classification provided by Dillon LJ in *Bliss v. South East Thames Regional Health Authority* [1987] ICR 700 at 718:

" ' * * * where the contract which has been broken was itself a contract to provide peace of mind or freedom from distress * * * ' "

CLUB MEDITERRANEE, S.A. v. STEDRY, 159 Ga.App. 53, 283 S.E.2d 30 (1981), cert. denied, 159 Ga.App. 53, 283 S.E.2d 30 (1981). Vacationer recovered actual and punitive damages for breach of contract to provide vacation facilities. Actual damages included return of vacationer's down payment and the cost of staying at another hotel until transportation could be arranged back home. Punitive damages were recovered for fraud:

"We do not agree with the appellant that the damages were based on the plaintiff's 'subjective evaluation of defendants' brochure,' or on mere puffing. The line between advertising which merely creates a promise, prophecy or expression of opinion, and advertising, although structured to future results, which conveys a false impression so intentionally overreaching as to rise to the level of an implied contract is often a fine line but it exists nevertheless. 'If by a number of statements you intentionally give a false impression and induce a person to act upon it, it is not the less false although if one takes each statement by itself there may be a difficulty in showing that any specific statement is [deliberately] untrue.' Downey v. Finucane, 205 N.Y. 251, 264, 98 N.E. 391, 395 (1912). * * *

"The trial judge in a lengthy and accurate analysis went over the evidence as it contrasted with the specific promises of the brochures on which the plaintiff acted. Guaranteed air reservations were nonexistent, and the family underwent several days of standby wait both coming and going between Los Angeles and Papeete. On arrival there was also a lengthy wait for a cottage. Promised sports, tennis, scuba, boat transportation to reefs, etc. were unavailable except at undesirable hours and after long waits. The same was true of meals. All facilities were overcrowded. Rooms were bug infested, promised services were not provided, and so on. After numerous complaints the family was offered a transfer to Club Med's other village at Bora Bora. They tried this, found it worse than the first one, and eventually moved to a hotel where they completed their vacation. The judge found the factual evidence a total misrepresentation of the vacation offered: 'The good life * * * A carefree ambiance * * * a casual yet elegant reflection of the local environment * * * facilities with the emphasis on fun * * * uncrowded white beaches * * * active sports * * * The Club gives them all to you * * * first class equipment rent-free and instruction at all levels for sports * * * Tranquility is yours * * * a fun-filled vacation to remember * * * Lots of space to be alone * * * Fall under the spell of our gentle natural lifestyle as you begin discovering the true meaning of the Tahitian saying * * * only happiness is important.' * * *

"The award of punitive damages is supported by some evidence relative to each of the five elements of fraud: that the representations were made, that they were false, that the defendant necessarily knew of their falsity at the time the offer was made to the plaintiff and was intended to deceive him, and that the plaintiff did in fact suffer damages as a result of his reliance on the offers made. It is true that this case differs from the usual fraudulent advertising situation in that the defendant did in fact have an apparent ability to offer each of the factually listed elements of the vacation—the flower filled paths, turquoise reefs, uncrowded white beaches, clean comfortable living quarters, ambiance of relaxation, array of sports, and so on. But the vacation which is what the customer thinks he is buying, was destroyed by lack of services, overcrowding of facilities, and failure to make the individual arrangements guaranteed. Under the evidence offered punitive damages were authorized. It cannot be argued that the plaintiff failed to exercise diligence to discover the true situation ahead of time since he could hardly explore Papeete and Bora Bora personally in advance, nor that he had no right to rely on the representations made, since he had in fact had a prior vacation at the defendant's facilities in Mexico which he had found satisfactory."

LAMM v. SHINGLETON, 231 N.C. 10, 55 S.E.2d 810 (1949). Widow was held entitled to recover damages for mental anguish when an undertaker broke his implied promise to perform the burial service in a good and workmanlike manner. There was evidence that a watertight vault enclosing the casket was not locked, resulting in water seeping into the casket and part of the vault being forced above ground.

RESTATEMENT, SECOND, CONTRACTS, § 353:

Recovery for emotional disturbance will be excluded unless the breach also caused bodily harm or the contract or the breach is of such a kind that serious emotional disturbance was a particularly likely result.

PACIFIC MUTUAL LIFE INSURANCE CO. v. HASLIP, 499 U.S. ___, 111 S.Ct. 1032, 113 L.Ed.2d 1 (1991). Pacific Mutual issued life insurance policies and Union Fidelity issued health insurance policies to city employees. The two companies were not affiliated, but Ruffin was an agent for both companies. Ruffin collected premiums for the health insurance from the city clerk, but misappropriated the money and did not remit the premiums to Union. Before the frauds in this case, Pacific Mutual had received notice that Ruffin had previously misappropriated premiums for other policies. Haslip, a city employee, was hospitalized. Because her premiums had been misappropriated by Ruffin, she was not covered by health insurance, she had to pay her own hospital bill, and her physician was not paid. The doctor placed Haslip's account with a collection agency, which obtained a judgment against Haslip that adversely affected her credit. Haslip and other city employees then sued Pacific Mutual and Ruffin, but not Union, seeking damages for fraud. The claim against Pacific Mutual was based on a theory that the company was liable for its agent's fraud. Haslip sought $200,000 as compensatory damages, including out-of-pocket expenses of less than $4,000, and punitive damages. The jury returned a general verdict for Haslip in the amount of $1,040,000 and general verdicts for three other city employees in amounts ranging from ten to fifteen thousand dollars. After the verdicts were affirmed by the Supreme Court of Alabama, Pacific Mutual petitioned the United States Supreme Court to reverse on the ground that the punitive damages violated due process. The Supreme Court, however, affirmed.

Justice Blackmun, in an opinion joined by four other justices, wrote that "[i]t would be ∗ ∗ ∗ inappropriate to say that, because punitive damages have been recognized for so long, their imposition is never unconstitutional." He expressed "concern about punitive damages that 'run wild,'" and stated "that general concerns of reasonableness and adequate guidance from the court when the case is tried to a jury properly enter into the constitutional calculus." Nevertheless, he found the damages in this case constitutional. He noted that before the trial in this case, the Supreme Court of Alabama had established criteria under which trial courts would scrutinize punitive awards, including "culpability of the defendant's conduct," "desirability of discouraging others from similar conduct," and "the impact upon the parties [and on] innocent third parties." The Supreme Court of Alabama then further reviewed the award to determine whether "the punitive damages are reasonable in their amount [compared with awards in similar cases] and rational in light of their purpose to punish what has occurred and to deter its repetition."

Justices Scalia and Kennedy concurred in the judgment on the ground that the long continued practice of permitting juries, in their discretion, to determine punitive damages, could not violate due process. Justice O'Connor dissented on the ground that "the trial court's instructions in this case provided no meaningful standards to guide the jury's decision to impose punitive damages or to fix the amount."

———

Fourteen days after its decision in *Pacific Mutual Life Insurance,* the United States Supreme Court granted certiorari in seven punitive damages cases, vacated the judgments, and remanded the cases for further consideration under the standards stated in *Pacific Mutual.* ___ U.S. at ___–___, 111 S.Ct. at 1298–1299, 113 L.Ed.2d at 233–235 (1991). In each of the seven cases, an appellate court had affirmed an award of punitive damages, although in one case the award had first been reduced as excessive.

SECURITY STOVE & MANUFACTURING CO. v. AMERICAN RAILWAY EXPRESS CO.

Missouri Court of Appeals, 1932.
227 Mo.App. 175, 51 S.W.2d 572.

BLAND, J.

This is an action for damages for the failure of defendant to transport, from Kansas City to Atlantic City, New Jersey, within a reasonable time, a furnace equipped with a combination oil and gas burner. The cause was tried before the court without the aid of a jury, resulting in a judgment in favor of plaintiff in the sum of $801.50 and interest, or in a total sum of $1,000.00 Defendant has appealed.

The facts show that plaintiff manufactured a furnace equipped with a special combination oil and gas burner it desired to exhibit at the American Gas Association Convention held in Atlantic City in October, 1926. The president of plaintiff testified that plaintiff engaged space for the exhibit for the reason "that the Henry L. Dougherty Company was very much interested in putting out a combination oil and gas burner; we had just developed one, after we got through, better than anything on the market and we thought this show would be the psychological time to get in contact with the Dougherty Company"; that "the thing wasn't sent there for sale but primarily to show"; that at the time the space was engaged it was too late to ship the furnace by freight so plaintiff decided to ship it by express, and, on September 18th, 1926, wrote the office of the defendant in Kansas City, stating that it had engaged a booth for exhibition purposes at Atlantic City, New Jersey, from the American Gas Association, for the week beginning October 11th; that its exhibit consisted of an oil burning furnace, together with two oil burners which weighed at least 1,500 pounds; that, "In order to get this exhibit in place on time it should be in Atlantic City not later than October the 8th. What we want you to do is to tell us how much time you will require to assure the delivery of the exhibit on time."

Mr. Bangs, chief clerk in charge of the local office of the defendant, upon receipt of the letter, sent Mr. Johnson, a commercial representative of the defendant, to see plaintiff. Johnson called upon plaintiff taking its letter with him. Johnson made a notation on the bottom of the letter giving October 4th, as the day that defendant was required to have the exhibit in order for it to reach Atlantic City on October 8th.

On October 1st, plaintiff wrote the defendant at Kansas City, referring to its letter of September 18th, concerning the fact that the furnace must be in Atlantic City not later than October 8th, and stating what Johnson had told it, saying: "Now Mr. Bangs, we want to make doubly sure that this shipment is in Atlantic City not later than October 8th and the purpose of this letter is to tell you that you can *have your truck call for the shipment between 12 and 1 o'clock on Saturday, October 2nd for this.*" (Italics plaintiff's.) On October 2d, plaintiff called the office of the express company in Kansas City and told it that the shipment was ready. Defendant came for the shipment on the last mentioned day, received it and delivered the express receipt to plaintiff. The shipment contained 21 packages. Each package was marked with stickers backed with glue and covered with silica of soda, to prevent the stickers being torn off in shipping. Each package was given a number. They ran from 1 to 21.

Plaintiff's president made arrangements to go to Atlantic City to attend the convention and install the exhibit, arriving there about October 11th. When he reached Atlantic City he found the shipment had been placed in the booth that had been assigned to plaintiff. The exhibit was set up, but it was found that one of the packages shipped was not there. This missing package contained the gas manifold, or that part of the oil and gas burner that controlled the flow of gas in the burner. This was the most important part of the exhibit and a like burner could not be obtained in Atlantic City.

Wires were sent and it was found that the stray package was at the "over and short bureau" of defendant in St. Louis. Defendant reported that the package would be forwarded to Atlantic City and would be there by Wednesday, the 13th. Plaintiff's president waited until Thursday, the day the convention closed, but the package had not arrived at the time, so he closed up the exhibit and left. About a week after he arrived in Kansas City, the package was returned by the defendant.

*   *   *

Plaintiff asked damages, which the court in its judgment allowed as follows: $147.00 express charges (on the exhibit); $45.12 freight on the exhibit from Atlantic City to Kansas City; $101.39 railroad and pullman fares to and from Atlantic City, expended by plaintiff's president and a workman taken by him to Atlantic City; $48.00 hotel room for the two; $150.00 for the time of the president; $40.00 for wages of plaintiff's other employee and $270.00 for rental of the booth, making a total of $801.51.

Defendant contends * * * that the court erred in allowing plaintiff's expenses as damages; that the only damages, if any, that can be recovered in cases of this kind, are for loss of profits and that plaintiff's evidence is not sufficient to base any recovery on this ground.

*   *   *

We think, under the circumstances in this case, that it was proper to allow plaintiff's expenses as its damages. Ordinarily the measure of damages where the carrier fails to deliver a shipment at destination within a reasonable time is the difference between the market value of the goods at the time of the delivery and the time when they should have been delivered. But where the carrier has notice of peculiar circumstances under which the shipment is made, which will result in an unusual loss by the shipper in case of delay in delivery, the carrier is responsible for the real damage sustained from such delay if the notice given is of such character, and goes to such extent, in informing the carrier of the shipper's situation, that the carrier will be presumed to have contracted with reference thereto. *   *   *

Defendant contends that plaintiff "is endeavoring to achieve a return of the status quo in a suit based on a breach of contract. Instead of seeking to recover what he would have had, had the contract not been broken, plaintiff is trying to recover what he would have had, had there never been any contract of shipment"; that the expenses sued for would have been incurred in any event. It is no doubt, the general rule that where there is a breach of contract the party suffering the loss can recover only that which he would have had, had the contract not been broken. But this is merely a general statement of the rule and is not inconsistent with the holdings that, in some instances, the injured party may recover expenses incurred in relying upon the contract, although such expenses would have been incurred had the contract not been breached.

In Sperry et al. v. O'Neill-Adams Co. (C.C.A.) 185 F. 231, the court held that the advantages resulting from the use of trading stamps as a means of increasing trade are so contingent that they cannot form a basis on which to rest a recovery for a breach of contract to supply them. In lieu of compensation based thereon the court directed a recovery in the sum expended in preparation for carrying on business in connection with the use of the stamps. The court said, loc. cit. 239:

"Plaintiff in its complaint had made a claim for lost profits, but, finding it impossible to marshal any evidence which would support a finding of exact figures, abandoned that claim. Any attempt to reach a precise sum would be mere blind guesswork. Nevertheless a contract, which both sides conceded would prove a valuable one, had been broken and the party who broke it was responsible for resultant damage. In order to carry out this contract, the plaintiff made expenditures which otherwise it would not have made. * * * The trial judge held, as we think rightly, that plaintiff was entitled at least to recover these expenses to which it had been put in order to secure the benefits of a contract of which defendant's conduct deprived it." * * *

The case at bar was [not] to recover damages for loss of profits by reason of the failure of the defendant to transport the shipment within a reasonable time, so that it would arrive in Atlantic City for the exhibit. There were no profits contemplated. The furnace was to be shown and shipped back to Kansas City. There was no money loss, except the expenses, that was of such a nature as any court would allow as being sufficiently definite or lacking in pure speculation. Therefore, unless plaintiff is permitted to recover the expenses that it went to, which were a total loss to it by reason of its inability to exhibit the furnace and equipment, it will be deprived of any substantial compensation for its loss. The law does not contemplate any such injustice. It ought to allow plaintiff, as damages, the loss in the way of expenses that it sustained, and which it would not have been put to if it had not been for its reliance upon the defendant to perform its contract. There is no contention that the exhibit would have been entirely valueless and whatever it might have accomplished defendant knew of the circumstances and ought to respond for whatever damages plaintiff suffered. In cases of this kind the method of estimating the damages should be adopted which is the most definite and certain and which best achieves the fundamental purpose of compensation. Had the exhibit been shipped in order to realize a profit on sales and such profits could have been realized, or to be entered in competition for a prize, and plaintiff failed to show loss of profits with sufficient definiteness, or that he would have won the prize, defendant's cases might be in point. But as before stated, no such situation exists here.

While, it is true that plaintiff already had incurred some of these expenses, in that it had rented space at the exhibit before entering into the contract with defendant for the shipment of the exhibit and this part of plaintiff's damages, in a sense, arose out of a circumstance which transpired before the contract was even entered into, yet, plaintiff arranged for the exhibit knowing that it could call upon defendant to perform its common law duty to accept and transport the shipment with reasonable dispatch. The whole damage, therefore, was suffered in contemplation of defendant performing its contract, which it failed to do, and would not have been sustained except for the reliance by plaintiff upon defendant to perform it. It can, therefore, be fairly said that the damages or loss suffered by plaintiff grew out of the breach of the contract, for had the shipment arrived on time, plaintiff would have had the benefit of the contract, which was contemplated by all parties, defendant being advised of the purpose of the shipment.

The judgment is affirmed.

All concur.

RESTATEMENT, SECOND, CONTRACTS § 349:

Comment:

a. [T]he injured party may, if he chooses, ignore the element of profit and recover as damages his expenditures in reliance. He may choose to do this if he cannot prove his profit with reasonable certainty.

———

ANGLIA TELEVISION v. REED, [1971] 3 All E.R. 690 (C.A.) Anglia decided to make a film for television. After spending money to hire a director and other key personnel, Anglia entered into a contract with Robert Reed to play the lead. Reed did not perform because of conflicting commitments. Anglia was unable to find another suitable actor and abandoned the project. Anglia could not prove the profits it would have made on the film and sought instead recovery of the money that had been spent in preparing to make the film. Reed's attorneys objected to Anglia's recovery of money spent before Reed was hired, but Lord Denning held that the recovery was proper:

"It seems to me that a plaintiff in such a case as this had an election: he can either claim for his loss of profits; or for his wasted expenditure. But he must elect between them. He cannot claim both. If he has not suffered any loss of profits—or if he cannot prove what his profits would have been—he can claim in the alternative the expenditure which has been thrown away, that is, wasted, by reason of the breach. * * *

"If the plaintiff claims the wasted expenditure, he is not limited to the expenditure incurred *after* the contract was concluded. He can claim also the expenditure incurred *before* the contract, provided that it was such as would reasonably be in the contemplation of the parties as likely to be wasted if the contract was broken. Applying that principle here, it is plain that, when Mr. Reed entered into this contract, he must have known perfectly well that much expenditure had already been incurred on director's fees and the like. He must have contemplated— or, at any rate, it is reasonably to be imputed to him—that if he broke his contract, all that expenditure would be wasted, whether or not it was incurred before or after the contract. He must pay damages for all the expenditure so wasted and thrown away. * * *"

CHICAGO COLISEUM CLUB v. DEMPSEY, 265 Ill.App. 542 (1932). Jack Dempsey signed a contract to defend his heavyweight championship against Harry Wills. Dempsey refused to fight Wills, and the promoter, which had contracted with Dempsey and Wills for the fight, sued Dempsey. Four items of recovery were sought by the promoter: (1) profits it would have made from the fight; (2) expenditures before signing the contract with Dempsey; (3) expenses incurred in attempting to restrain Dempsey from participating in other fights; (4) expenses after signing the contract with Dempsey. The court held that recovery could be had only under the fourth category:

"*Proposition 1.* Plaintiff offered to prove by one Mullins that a boxing exhibition between Dempsey and Wills held in the City of Chicago on September 22, 1926, would bring a gross receipt of $3,000,000, and that the expense incurred would be $1,400,000, leaving a net profit to the promoter of $1,600,000. The court properly sustained an objection to this testimony. The character of the undertaking was such that it would be impossible to produce evidence of a probative character sufficient to establish any amount which could be reasonably ascertainable by reason of the character of the undertaking. The profits from a boxing contest of this character, open to the public, is dependent upon so many different circumstances that they are not susceptible of definite legal determination. The success or failure of such an undertaking depends largely upon the ability of the promoters, the reputation of the contestants and the conditions of the weather at and prior to the holding of the contest, the accessibility of the place, the extent of the publicity, the possibility of other and counter attractions and many other questions which would enter into consideration. Such an entertainment lacks utterly the element of stability which exists in regular organized business. * * *

"Compensation for damages for a breach of contract must be established by evidence from which a court or jury are able to ascertain the extent of such damages by the usual rules of evidence and to a reasonable degree of certainty. * * *

"*Proposition 2.* Expenses incurred by the plaintiff prior to the signing of the agreement between the plaintiff and Dempsey.

"The general rule is that in an action for a breach of contract a party can recover only on damages which naturally flow from and are the result of the act complained of. The Wills contract was entered into prior to the contract with the defendant and was not made contingent upon the plaintiff's obtaining a similar agreement with the defendant Dempsey. Under the circumstances the plaintiff speculated as to the result of his efforts to procure the Dempsey contract. It may be argued that there had been negotiations pending between plaintiff and Dempsey which clearly indicated an agreement between them, but the agreement in fact was never consummated until sometime later. The action is based upon the written agreement which was entered into in Los Angeles. Any obligations assumed by the plaintiff prior to that time are not chargeable to the defendant. * * *"

SULLIVAN v. O'CONNOR, 363 Mass. 579, 296 N.E.2d 183 (1973). A patient sued a plastic surgeon for failure to improve the patient's appearance as the surgeon had promised. Justice Kaplan discussed the measure of recovery:

"If an action on the basis of contract is allowed, we have next the question of the measure of damages to be applied where liability is found. Some cases have taken the simple view that the promise by the physician is to be treated like an ordinary commercial promise, and accordingly that the successful plaintiff is entitled to a standard measure of recovery for breach of contract—'compensatory' ('expectancy') damages, an amount intended to put the plaintiff in the position he would be in if the contract had been performed, or, presumably, at the plaintiff's election, 'restitution' damages, an amount corresponding to any benefit conferred by the plaintiff upon the defendant in the performance of the contract disrupted by the defendant's breach. See Restatement: Contracts § 329 and comment a, §§ 347, 384(1). Thus in Hawkins v. McGee, 84 N.H. 114, 146 A. 641 (1929), * * * [t]he court, following the usual expectancy formula, would have asked the jury to estimate and award to the plaintiff the difference between the value of a good or perfect hand, as promised, and the value of the hand after the operation. * * *

"Other cases, including a number in New York, without distinctly repudiating the *Hawkins* type of analysis, have indicated that a different and generally more lenient measure of damages is to be applied in patient-physician actions based on breach of alleged special agreements to effect a cure, attain a stated result, or employ a given medical method. This measure is expressed in somewhat variant ways, but the substance is that the plaintiff is to recover any expenditures made by him and for other detriment (usually not specifically described in the opinions) following proximately and foreseeably upon the defendant's failure to carry out his promise. This, be it noted, is not a 'restitution' measure, for it is not limited to restoration of the benefit conferred on the defendant (the fee paid) but includes other expenditures, for example, amounts paid for medicine and nurses; so also it would seem according to its logic to take in damages for any worsening of the plaintiff's condition due to the breach. Nor is it an 'expectancy' measure, for it does not appear to contemplate recovery of the whole difference in value between the condition as promised and the condition actually resulting from the treatment. Rather the tendency of the formulation is to put the plaintiff back in the position he occupied just before the parties entered upon the agreement, to compensate him for the detriments he suffered in reliance upon the agreement. This kind of intermediate pattern of recovery for breach of contract is discussed in the suggestive article by Fuller and Perdue, The Reliance Interest in Contract Damages, 46 Yale L.J. 52, 373, where the authors show that, although not attaining the currency of the standard measures, a 'reliance' measure has for special reasons been applied by the courts in a variety of settings, including noncommercial settings. See 46 Yale L.J. at 396–401.

"For breach of the patient-physician agreements under consideration, a recovery limited to restitution seems plainly too meager, if the agreements are to be enforced at all. On the other hand, an expectancy recovery may well be excessive. * * * Where, as in the case at bar and in a number of the reported cases, the doctor has been absolved of negligence by the trier, an expectancy measure may be thought harsh. We should recall here that the fee paid by the patient to the doctor for the alleged promise would usually be quite disproportionate to the putative expectancy recovery. To attempt, moreover, to put a value on the condition that would or might have resulted, had the treatment succeeded as promised, may sometimes put an exceptional strain on the imagination of the fact finder. As a general consideration, Fuller and Perdue argue that the reasons for granting damages for broken promises to the extent of the expectancy are at their strongest when the promises are made in a business context, when they have to do with the production or distribution of goods or the allocation of functions in the market place; they become weaker as the context shifts from a commercial to a noncommercial field. 46 Yale L.J. at 60–63.

"There is much to be said, then, for applying a reliance measure to the present facts, and we have only to add that our cases are not unreceptive to the use of that formula in special situations. We have, however, had no previous occasion to apply it to patient-physician cases.

"The question of recovery on a reliance basis for pain and suffering or mental distress requires further attention. We find expressions in the decisions that pain and suffering (or the like) are simply not compensable in actions for breach of contract. The defendant seemingly espouses this proposition in the present case. True, if the buyer under a contract for the purchase of a lot of merchandise, in suing for the seller's breach, should claim damages for mental anguish caused by his disappointment in the transaction, he would not succeed; he would be told, perhaps, that the asserted psychological injury was not fairly foreseeable by the defendant as a probable consequence of the breach of such a business contract. See Restatement: Contracts, § 341, and comment a. But there is no general rule barring such items of damage in actions for breach of contract. It is all a question of the subject matter and background of the contract, and when the contract calls for an operation on the person of the plaintiff, psychological as well as physical injury may be expected to figure somewhere in the recovery, depending on the particular circumstances. Suffering or distress resulting from the breach going beyond that which was envisaged by the treatment as agreed, should be compensable on the same ground as the worsening of the patient's condition because of the breach. Indeed it can be argued that the very suffering or distress 'contracted for'—that which would have been incurred if the treatment achieved the promised result—should also be compensable on the theory underlying the New York cases. For that suffering is 'wasted' if the treatment fails. Otherwise stated, compensation for this waste is arguably required in order to complete the restoration of the status quo ante."

The remedy of "restitution" is further dealt with infra, page 88.

In Sullivan v. O'Connor, does Justice Kaplan advocate a reliance measure of damages for a different reason than justified its use in Security Stove?

FREUND v. WASHINGTON SQUARE PRESS, INC.

New York Court of Appeals, 1974.
34 N.Y.2d 379, 357 N.Y.S.2d 857, 314 N.E.2d 419.

SAMUEL RABIN, JUDGE.

In this action for breach of a publishing contract, we must decide what damages are recoverable for defendant's failure to publish plaintiff's manuscript. In 1965, plaintiff, an author and a college teacher, and defendant, Washington Square Press, Inc., entered into a written agreement which, in relevant part, provided as follows. Plaintiff ("author") granted defendant ("publisher") exclusive rights to publish and sell in book form plaintiff's work on modern drama. Upon plaintiff's delivery of the manuscript, defendant agreed to complete payment of a nonreturnable $2,000 "advance". Thereafter, if defendant deemed the manuscript not "suitable for publication", it had the right to terminate the agreement by written notice within 60 days of delivery. Unless so terminated, defendant agreed to publish the work in hardbound edition within 18 months and afterwards in paperbound edition. The contract further provided that defendant would pay royalties to plaintiff, based upon specified percentages of sales. (For example, plaintiff was to receive 10% of the retail price of the first 10,000 copies sold in the continental United States.) If defendant failed to publish within 18 months, the contract provided that "this agreement shall terminate and the rights herein granted to the Publisher shall revert to the Author. In such event all payments theretofore made to the Author shall belong to the Author without prejudice to any other remedies which the Author may have. ✻ ✻ ✻"

Plaintiff performed by delivering his manuscript to defendant and was paid his $2,000 advance. Defendant thereafter merged with another publisher and ceased publishing in hardbound. Although defendant did not exercise its 60-day right to terminate, it has refused to publish the manuscript in any form.

Plaintiff commenced the instant action and initially sought specific performance of the contract. The Trial Term Justice denied specific performance but, finding a valid contract and a breach by defendant, set the matter down for trial on the issue of monetary damages, if any, sustained by the plaintiff. At trial, plaintiff sought to prove: (1) delay of his academic promotion; (2) loss of royalties which would have been earned; and (3) the cost of publication if plaintiff had made his own arrangements to publish. The trial court found that plaintiff had been promoted despite defendant's failure to publish, and that there was no evidence that the breach had caused any delay. Recovery of lost royalties was denied without discussion. The court found, however, that the cost of hardcover publication to plaintiff was the natural and probable consequence of the breach and, based upon expert testimony, awarded $10,000 to cover this cost. It denied recovery of the expenses of paperbound publication on the ground that plaintiff's proof was conjectural.

The Appellate Division, (3 to 2) affirmed, finding that the cost of publication was the proper measure of damages. In support of its conclusion, the majority analogized to the construction contract situation where the cost of completion may be the proper measure of damages for a builder's failure to complete a house or for use of wrong materials. The dissent concluded that the cost of publication is not an appropriate measure of damages and consequently, that plaintiff may recover nominal damages only. We agree with the dissent. In so concluding, we look to the basic purpose of damage recovery and the nature and effect of the parties' contract.

It is axiomatic that, except where punitive damages are allowable, the law awards damages for breach of contract to compensate for injury caused by the breach—injury which was foreseeable, i.e., reasonably within the contemplation of the parties, at the time the contract was entered into. Money damages are substitutional relief designed in theory "to put the injured party in as good a position as he would have been put by full performance of the contract, at the least cost to the defendant and without charging him with harms that he had no sufficient reason to foresee when he made the contract." (5 Corbin, Contracts, § 1002, pp. 31–32; 11 Williston, Contracts [3d ed.], § 1338, p. 198.) In other words, so far as possible, the law attempts to secure to the injured party the benefit of his bargain, subject to the limitations that the injury—whether it be losses suffered or gains prevented—was foreseeable, and that the amount of damages claimed be measurable with a reasonable degree of certainty and, of course, adequately proven. But it is equally fundamental that the injured party should not recover more from the breach than he would have gained had the contract been fully performed.

Measurement of damages in this case according to the cost of publication to the plaintiff would confer greater advantage than performance of the contract would have entailed to plaintiff and would place him in a far better position than he would have occupied had the defendant fully performed. Such measurement bears no relation to compensation for plaintiff's actual loss or anticipated profit. Far beyond compensating plaintiff for the interests he had in the defendant's performance of the contract—whether restitution, reliance or expectation (see Fuller & Perdue, Reliance Interest in Contract Damages, 46 Yale L.J. 52, 53–56) an award of the cost of publication would enrich plaintiff at defendant's expense.

Pursuant to the contract, plaintiff delivered his manuscript to the defendant. In doing so, he conferred a value on the defendant which, upon defendant's breach, was required to be restored to him. Special Term, in addition to ordering a trial on the issue of damages, ordered defendant to return the manuscript to plaintiff and plaintiff's restitution interest in the contract was thereby protected. (Cf. 5 Corbin, Contracts, § 996, p. 15.)

At the trial on the issue of damages, plaintiff alleged no reliance losses suffered in performing the contract or in making necessary preparations to perform. Had such losses, if foreseeable and ascertainable, been incurred, plaintiff would have been entitled to compensation for them.

As for plaintiff's expectation interest in the contract, it was basically two-fold—the "advance" and the royalties. (To be sure, plaintiff may have expected to enjoy whatever notoriety, prestige or other benefits that might have attended publication, but even if these expectations were compensable, plaintiff did not attempt at trial to place a monetary value on them.) There is no dispute that plaintiff's expectancy in the "advance" was fulfilled—he has received his $2,000. His expectancy interest in the royalties—the profit he stood to gain from sale of the published book—while theoretically compensable, was speculative. Although this work is not plaintiff's first, at trial he provided no stable foundation for a reasonable estimate of royalties he would have earned had defendant not breached its promise to publish. In these circumstances, his claim for royalties falls for uncertainty.

Since the damages which would have compensated plaintiff for anticipated royalties were not proved with the required certainty, we agree with the dissent in the Appellate Division that nominal damages alone are recoverable. Though these are damages in name only and not at all compensatory, they are nevertheless awarded as a formal vindication of plaintiff's legal right to compensation which has not been given a sufficiently certain monetary valuation.

In our view, the analogy by the majority in the Appellate Division to the construction contract situation was inapposite. In the typical construction contract, the owner agrees to pay money or other consideration to a builder and expects, under the contract, to receive a completed building in return. The value of the promised performance to the owner is the properly constructed building. In this case, unlike the typical construction contract, the value to plaintiff of the promised performance—publication—was a percentage of sales of the books published and not the books themselves. Had the plaintiff contracted for the printing, binding and delivery of a number of hardbound copies of his manuscript, to be sold or disposed of as he wished, then perhaps the construction analogy, and measurement of damages by the cost of replacement or completion, would have some application.

Here, however, the specific value to plaintiff of the promised publication was the royalties he stood to receive from defendant's sales of the published book. Essentially, publication represented what it would have cost the defendant to confer that value upon the plaintiff, and, by its breach, defendant saved that cost. The error by the courts below was in measuring damages not by the value to plaintiff of the promised performance but by the cost of that performance to defendant. Damages are not measured, however, by what the defaulting party saved by the breach, but by the natural and probable consequences of the breach *to the plaintiff*. In this case, the consequence to plaintiff of defendant's failure to publish is that he is prevented from realizing the gains promised by the contract—the royalties. But, as we have stated, the amount of royalties plaintiff would have realized was not ascertained with adequate certainty and, as a consequence, plaintiff may recover nominal damages only.

Accordingly, the order of the Appellate Division should be modified to the extent of reducing the damage award of $10,000 for the cost of publication to six cents, but with costs and disbursements to the plaintiff.

———

See UCC § 1–106.

———

FERRELL v. ELROD, 63 Tenn.App. 129, 469 S.W.2d 678 (1971), cert. denied, 63 Tenn.App. 129, 469 S.W.2d 678 (1971). Lessor agreed to lease premises to lessee for ten years to conduct a school of cosmetology. Lessor repudiated the agreement. Lessee leased other premises for a term commencing nine months after the original lease. Lessee sued lessor for damages for breach of the lease agreement. One item of damages was the profits lost during the nine months it took to obtain substitute premises. The judgment included these lost profits calculated as the amount of profit earned during the first nine months that the business was in operation on the substitute premises. Defendant appealed, contending that the lost profits from the new business were too speculative. Held, affirmed:

"Defendant also cites Evergreen Amusement Corp. v. Milstead, 206 Md. 610, 112 A.2d 901 (1955) wherein a movie theatre sued a grading contractor for damages for delay in completing a parking lot. It was held in that case that the theatre, as a new enterprise, could not prove anticipated profits by showing profits of other theatres during the period of delay or profits of the same theatre at a subsequent time. Acknowledging the practical difficulty of proving with reasonable certainty the amount of anticipated profits of a new enterprise, this Court is unable to agree with the holding of *Evergreen*, which would effectively exonerate a defaulting contractor from damages suffered by a new business. If, as in the present case, the profits have been shown with reasonable certainty by actual experience, there is no reason to penalize the enterprise of the founder of a new business by denying him his remedy for losses occasioned by the default of the defendant. * * *

"Each particular suit for anticipated profits must be decided upon its own peculiar facts within the broad general rules laid down in prior decisions. In the present case, this Court is satisfied that the anticipated profits, and the evidence thereof, were not matters of speculation or conjecture, but rather of credible experience. * * *

"From this record, there are other bases which might be used in calculating damages to be allowed. For example, the measure of damages for nine months delay in opening a business is not necessarily the profit or loss which would be or actually was realized during the initial and usually profitless operation of a business enterprise. The default of defendant delayed not only the beginning of the initial, low-profit phase of a new enterprise; but it also ultimately delayed the beginning of and shortened the period of the profitable, full-scale, operation. In other words, it could be well insisted and concluded that the first nine months of the business operation would be at a limited profit whenever and wherever the business was begun, and that thereafter, the remaining nine years and three months of established operation would be on a sustained and profitable basis. The delay of nine months actually shortened the period of full profit operations from nine years and three months to eight years and six months. By this reasoning, complainants could have been allowed damages based upon nine months of full-scale operating profits. * * *

"The master and chancellor did not adopt this liberal view of complainants' damages; and in conformity with the rules heretofore cited, this Court has adopted and followed the findings and conclusions of the master and chancellor to the extent that they are supported by competent evidence and comport with applicable rules of law. * * *"

BOLLENBACK v. CONTINENTAL CASUALTY CO.

Supreme Court of Oregon, en banc, 1966.
243 Or. 498, 414 P.2d 802.

HOLMAN, JUSTICE.

Plaintiff was the holder of a policy issued by defendant under a group health and accident plan. The effective date of the policy was August 10, 1954. Premiums were due every six months and were paid by plaintiff. On September 28, 1963, while the policy was in full force and effect, plaintiff was hospitalized for six days with a back injury.

On November 12 he filed a claim with defendant for $107.33. He received no answer. On December 12 he wrote to the defendant calling to its attention that he had filed the claim and had received no acknowledgment. He still received no answer. On January 6, 1964, he wrote to the defendant a third time calling to its attention the filing of his claim and his previous correspondence. On January 20 both plaintiff and defendant wrote to each other. Plaintiff wrote to the assistant to the president of defendant, calling his attention to the plaintiff's payment of premiums, protesting the manner in which he was being ignored, enclosing copies of his previous letters, and asking for action. Defendant's correspondence was an answer to plaintiff's letter of January 6, informing plaintiff that his policy had lapsed in 1959 for nonpayment of premiums. On January 30 defendant wrote again to plaintiff. This letter specified that it was an answer to plaintiff's letter of January 20 to the assistant to the president of defendant. This letter contained the same information previously given plaintiff about the lapse of his policy and called to his attention their previous notification to this effect.

On January 25, plaintiff wrote two more letters to the defendant, one to the accounting department requesting information from its records concerning the premiums it had received from him and the other to the claims department requesting information about the reason for the policy's lapse. Plaintiff had received no answer to these letters when, on February 4, he filed the present case stating that he had elected to rescind the contract because of its repudiation by defendant and requesting judgment against defendant for all premiums previously paid under the policy in the sum of $2,166.50.

To plaintiff's complaint defendant filed an answer denying its repudiation of the contract, pleading the affirmative defense of mistake and tendering the amount of plaintiff's claim into court. A trial without a jury ensued which resulted in findings and conclusions by the judge to the effect that defendant had repudiated the contract by nonpayment of plaintiff's claim, that it had done so because of mistake and that plaintiff was entitled to recover as prayed for in his complaint.

Defendant assigns as error the court's denial of judgment in its favor at the close of testimony, its denial of a conclusion of law that plaintiff was not entitled to rescission, and the entering of the conclusion of law that plaintiff was entitled to recover. * * *

The right to rescind is dependent upon placing the other party to the contract in statu quo ante, with some exceptions not important here. If a suit is brought in equity for rescission, no prior return or offer to return is a prerequisite because equity has the power to require of plaintiff that he return the proceeds of the contract. Before he is entitled to equitable relief the court will require that a plaintiff do equity and return that which he has received. On the other hand, a court of law has no such power, and therefore, before an action may be brought to recover the money or property from the other party, plaintiff must have returned or offered to return that which he has received.
* * *

In the present case the facts disclose a contract which required the payment by plaintiff of premiums in return for the protection of defendant's promise to pay covered claims. This is the first claim plaintiff filed under his policy. He had received no benefits which it was possible for him to return or offer to return to the defendant. Therefore, there was no need for him to tender the return of anything as a prerequisite to bringing an action at law or to resort to the powers of a court of equity in the absence of such tender. * * *

As an action at law, this case is in the nature of an action for money had and received. 5 Corbin, Contracts § 1108 (1964). The following comment is found in 4 Am.Jur. 508–509, Assumpsit § 20 (1936), concerning an action for money had and received:

> "The action for money had and received was invented by the common-law judges to secure relief from the narrower restrictions of the common-law procedure which afforded no remedy in too many cases of merit. The action is a modified form of assumpsit. * * * Though an action at law, it is equitable in its nature, and is said to resemble or to be, in its nature, a substitute for a suit in equity, and to lie wherever a suit in equity would lie. * * * It lies where there is an express promise, if nothing remains to be done but the payment of money, but it is not a proper form of action to recover damages for breach of an actual subsisting or executory contract. The action is not dependent, however, upon an express promise, or even upon one implied in fact, although the action is contractual in form. The action for money had and received is founded upon the principle that no one ought unjustly to enrich himself at the expense of another, and it is maintainable in all cases where one person has received money or its equivalent under such circumstances that in equity and good conscience he ought not to retain it and, ex aequo et bono, it belongs to another.
> * * *"

Therefore, the applicable principles determining whether plaintiff is entitled to the relief he seeks are the same whether at law or in equity.
* * *

Before a party to a contract is justified in rescinding it because of its breach by the other party, the breach must be substantial. Rescission is not warranted when the breach is not substantial and does not defeat the objects of the parties. * * *

The purpose of the contract, in so far as plaintiff was concerned, was to obtain protection in the form of defendant's promise to pay claims in case of his disability. It would hardly seem arguable but that defendant's refusal to pay claims, based upon its position that the policy had lapsed, effectively frustrated this purpose and was a substantial breach.

One of defendant's principal contentions is that rescission of an insurance contract cannot be predicated upon the insurer's breach if the breach is motivated by a mistake of fact. * * *

In the present case, after defendant refused to pay plaintiff's claim on the basis that the policy had lapsed and did not exist, plaintiff notified the defendant of its mistake by informing it that he had faithfully paid his premiums. Because equitable principles apply, it was necessary for plaintiff to call to defendant's attention its mistake. It would be inequitable for plaintiff to take advantage of defendant's mistake without giving it an opportunity to rectify its error. Despite plaintiff's notification, defendant persisted in its position that the policy had lapsed. True, it was still laboring under a mistake of fact, but it was a mistake that was readily ascertainable by a conscientious investigation. It is significant that when plaintiff finally filed this action the error was promptly discovered. An insurer may not blithely disregard a warning that it has made a mistake when its mistake is readily ascertainable and, after a law suit is filed, then avail itself of the armor of ignorance. Under these circumstances the failure to pay is willful because it willfully neglected to ascertain its mistake. If defendant wants to indulge in the luxury of omnipotence, it must be responsible when it commits error. Under these circumstances its mistake was willful and will not serve as an excuse. The plaintiff is entitled to rescind because of defendant's material breach of the contract. * * *

Defendant contends that even if plaintiff is entitled to rescind he is limited in his recovery to the unearned portion of the last six months' premium because each six months' payment period was a separate contract of insurance. It argues that all previous payments had been fully earned. The policy contained the following provisions:

"This policy is issued in consideration of the statements contained in the copy of the application attached hereto and the payment in advance of the first premium stated in the Schedule which includes premium for attached rider, if any; after taking effect this policy continues in force until the first renewal premium due date. All periods of insurance shall begin and end at 12 o'clock noon, Standard Time, at the residence of the Insured. * * *

"The Company reserves the right to decline renewal of this policy under the following circumstances only:

    "(a) nonpayment of premium on or before due date;

    "(b) when the Insured leaves the practice of his profession or occupation;

    "(c) when the Company declines to renew ALL such policies issued to members of the above named organization [Oregon State Bar]. * * *

    "Loss resulting from tuberculosis, heart disease * * * shall be covered only if the sickness or disease causing such loss originates after this policy has been in force for six months after its effective date."

The contract was a continuing one so long as the insured paid the premium. The defendant had a continuing obligation to renew the policy unless plaintiff left the practice of law or the defendant canceled out all members of the Oregon State Bar, neither of which occurred. If, as the defendant contends, each six months' period was a new policy, the provisions for the coverage of tuberculosis and heart disease would never become effective. This group policy was not a policy of term insurance which expired at the end of each six months' period. * * *

The defendant next contends the return of all the premiums is not the proper measure of relief. The law relative to relief that can be secured by the insured when the insurer wrongfully repudiates the contract is in much confusion. One reason is the failure to distinguish an action for restitution upon rescission of the contract from an action for damages for its breach. The first is based on an annulment of the contract, the latter upon an assertion of the contract. As an illustration of the confusion the Annotation, 48 A.L.R. 107 (1927), uses the following language at page 110:

    "As concerns the *measure of damages* for the wrongful cancelation, repudiation, or termination of the contract of insurance by the insurer, there seems to be an irreconcilable conflict between two principal lines of authority, as well as variations from these two rules. The first of these rules is to the effect that the insured may *recover as damages* the amount of premiums paid or premiums, with interest, where there has been a wrongful repudiation of the contract by the insurer, *and the assured has elected to rescind the contract rather than have it enforced.* The other of these two rules is to the effect that, if the assured is still in such a state of health that he can secure other insurance of like nature and kind, his measure of damages would be the difference between the cost of carrying the insurance which he has for the term stipulated for, and the cost of new insurance at the rate he would then be required to pay for a like term. * * *" (Emphasis added.) See also Annotation 107 A.L.R. 1233, at 1235 (1937).

The fact is that recovery in each case is based upon a different theory. The purpose of rescission and restitution is to return the parties as near as possible to their respective positions prior to the formation of the contract so that each of the parties will be free to obtain his desired performance elsewhere. The purpose of an action for damages is to put the injured party as near as possible to the position where he would have been had the contract actually been performed. See 5 Corbin, Contracts § 996 (1964); Federici v. Lehman, supra, 230 Or. at 72–73, 368 P.2d 611. A more consistent adherence by the courts to this distinction would enable a more accurate analysis and classification of cases.

Whether relief for wrongful repudiation of an insurance contract is granted by way of restitution upon rescission or upon an action for damages for breach of contract, there is a split in authority whether or not a proper measure of recovery is the return of *all* premiums. Probably the majority opinion in the United States is that all premiums may be recovered. At least, it is referred to as the majority rule. See Annotation 48 A.L.R. 107, at 111. * * *

There are also cases which hold that upon rescission there should be offset against the recovered premiums the value of the coverage actually received by the insured. * * *

The theory of relief on an action for restitution is placing both parties in statu quo ante. Because insurance protection cannot be returned to defendant, the theory of recovery necessarily means the return to plaintiff of all premiums less the value of any benefits the plaintiff has actually received under the contract. Defendant contends plaintiff received the value of the protection for the ten year period which, upon loss, could have been asserted by plaintiff at any time despite defendant's subsequent disavowal of the contract. Defendant's assertion upon repudiating the contract was that the policy had lapsed in 1959. There is no reason to believe that after that date defendant would have been any more willing to honor claims by plaintiff than it was in 1964 when it refused payment. By its own assertion that the policy lapsed in 1959 defendant demonstrated its unwillingness to meet contractual obligations since that time. Plaintiff therefore could not have been receiving the protection for which his premiums were being paid. * * *

Plaintiff has not claimed that the amount of premiums paid were in excess of the cost to defendant of carrying the risk of his policy. Defendant, on the other hand, has not stated, nor did it prove when in 1959 it terminated plaintiff's policy. Not having shown this, it should be considered as terminated on January 1, 1959, or the time most unfavorable to defendant.

As a result, plaintiff is not entitled to recover for those premiums paid prior to the year 1959 because it appears from the record that he received the protection these payments afforded. It would be inequitable for him to recover them. Defendant having wrongfully terminated plaintiff's policy in 1959, plaintiff is entitled to recover all premiums paid subsequent to January 1, 1959. * * *

The case is remanded to the trial court with directions to modify the judgment to include only those sums paid by plaintiff to defendant subsequent to January 1, 1959. Interest on such payments is to be computed from the time the payments were actually made.   *   *   *

Forms of Action and the Common Counts

The principal case refers to an "action for money had and received" as a "modified form of assumpsit." In order to understand this, a little history concerning the development of contract law is helpful. (The classic short history is Ames, The History of Assumpsit, 2 Harv.L.Rev. 1, 53 (1888).) This note covers several hundred years of development. The changes described occurred slowly and, for the most part, imperceptibly.

In the early English common law courts, a plaintiff seeking relief had to plead his cause in strict conformity with one of a small number of standard forms. These were the "forms of action." If the plaintiff's complaint did not fit one of these forms, he could not obtain relief.

At this time there were two forms of action for what we would now think of as contractual obligations—covenant and debt. These actions, however, had substantive or procedural limitations, or both, which prevented recovery on many meritorious contractual claims. Covenant would lie only if the promise were under seal. Debt could be brought only on an express promise to pay a specific price for goods delivered or services rendered. There was thus no cause of action if the plaintiff performed services for the defendant with the justifiable expectation that defendant would pay a reasonable amount and the defendant refused to pay. Morever, even when debt did lie (an express promise to pay a specific sum of money for goods or services) there was an important procedural barrier to recovery. The defendant was entitled to "wager of law." Under this procedure the defendant could escape his obligation by taking an oath in open court that he did not owe the debt and by having eleven neighbors ("compurgators") swear that they believed he was telling the truth.

The common law forms of recovery for goods or services were thus very unsatisfactory. An important impetus for reform was provided by the separate courts of equity. The equity courts permitted recoveries when the remedy at law was inadequate. The facts that in equity recovery could be had even though there was no express promise to pay a specific price and that there was no wager of law diverted business and fees from the law courts.

To meet the competition, the law courts developed the action of assumpsit. "Assumpsit" means "he promised." The first pleadings to use the term "assumpsit" were in what we would now think of as tort cases. A carrier injured plaintiff's goods by carelessness or a doctor negligently treated plaintiff or plaintiff's animal. The plaintiff would allege that the defendant promised ("assumpsit") to be careful but then negligently injured plaintiff or plaintiff's property. The reason for this allegation of "assumpsit" in tort cases (at common law they were called "actions on the case") was similar to the modern concept of negating assumption of the risk. In early common law the idea of tort was limited to harm by a stranger—battery, trespass to land. If you had entrusted your body or goods to the defendant there was no tort— unless he acted negligently after promising to use due care. The allegation of "assumpsit" in actions on the case was especially useful in overcoming the argument that there could be no recovery if the harm was caused by defendant's failure to act rather than by wrongful action; recovery could be had for misfeasance but not for nonfeasance. With the help of "assumpsit" there was little left to this nonfeasance argument in actions on the case by the middle of the 16th century.

The concept of assumpsit was adapted from tort-like actions on the case to contractual actions by alleging that after the original promise to pay, the defendant made a new promise to pay. This new promise was essential to distinguish the action of assumpsit from debt. One characteristic of early common law that we would now regard as very strange was the doctrine that there was one and only one cause of action (at most) for each fact situation. If debt would lie, no other action would. (This was even true of covenant and debt. Until the 16th century, debt, not covenant, would lie for a promise under seal to pay a specific sum of money. There was not the same pressure for change here, however, because one action of debt in which wager of law was not permitted was debt on a sealed instrument.)

Thus by alleging a new promise to pay the price of goods or services, the action of debt was converted to assumpsit and fact determination was by jury trial rather than by wager of law. For a substantial time, however, the defendant was able to defend the action in assumpsit by showing that no new promise had been made after the original promise to pay. Finally in Slade's Case in 1602 (4 Coke 92b) this defense was abolished. All the Justices of England sat together and decided that an action in assumpsit would lie even though no second promise had been made. The common allegation that, after promising at the time of receipt to pay a specific price for goods or services, the defendant made a subsequent promise to pay ("indebitatus assumpsit"—"being indebted he promised") became irrebutable. It was a fiction to avoid the procedural embarrassment of wager of law and the competition of equity courts.

Once Slade's Case cleared the way for assumpsit to displace the action of debt, other expansions of the remedy in assumpsit followed. Even with the fiction of a subsequent promise, no action in debt would lie when there was no express promise to pay a specific amount, even though justice required a remedy. Two classes of these cases were included in the expanded action of assumpsit.

First were cases involving delivery of goods or services in which the defendant had not promised to pay a specific price, but the plaintiff reasonably interpreted defendant's acceptance of the goods or services as a promise to pay a reasonable price for them. This is an "implied-in-fact" promise derived by realistically applying ordinary standards of interpretation to the non-verbal manifestations of the parties' intentions.

Second were cases in which justice required the defendant to pay the plaintiff, but the defendant had manifested no promise to pay—either verbally or by his actions. A classic example occurred when the plaintiff paid money to the defendant by mistake, either overpaying an amount owed the defendant or paying the defendant an amount the plaintiff owed to someone else. Recovery was based on a fictitious promise by the defendant to return plaintiff's money—a promise "implied-in-law."

Assumpsit thus developed to cover a wide range of situations—the original action of debt through the "indebitatus assumpsit" fiction, and the new actions for reasonable compensation or to prevent unjust enrichment. The term used to describe assumpsit in all its uses was "general assumpsit." Assumpsit to recover on an express promise to pay a particular sum was "special assumpsit."

Forms of complaints were developed to cover the typical situations in which recovery was available in general assumpsit. These forms became known as "the common counts." The common counts included actions to recover reasonable payment for goods sold and delivered ("quantum valebat") and for services rendered ("quantum meruit"), as well as the one referred to in the principal case—"money had and received." The common counts recited a promise to pay, but following the practice established in Slade's Case, this promise could not be disproved. It was a fiction that traced through the history of the common law to debt and covenant, wager of law, and the salutary competition for business by the courts of equity.

RESTATEMENT, SECOND, CONTRACTS § 373:

(1) Subject to the rule stated in Subsection (2), on a breach by non-performance that gives rise to a claim for damages for total breach or on a repudiation, the injured party is entitled to restitution for any benefit that he has conferred on the other party by way of part performance or reliance.

(2) The injured party has no right to restitution if he has performed all of his duties under the contract and no performance by the other party remains due other than payment of a definite sum of money for that performance.

Illustrations:

1. A contracts to sell a tract of land to B for $100,000. After B has made a part payment of $20,000, A wrongfully refuses to transfer title. B can recover the $20,000 in restitution. The result is the same

even if the market price of the land is only $70,000, so that performance would have been disadvantageous to B.

2. A contracts to build a house for B for $100,000, progress payments to be made monthly. After having been paid $40,000 for two months, A commits a breach that is not material by inadvertently using the wrong brand of sewer pipe. B has a claim for damages for partial breach but cannot recover the $40,000 that he has paid A.

12. A contracts to work as a consultant for B for a fee of $50,000, payable at the end of the year. B wrongfully discharges A at the end of eleven months. A can recover in restitution based on the reasonable value of his services. The terms of the contract are evidence of this value but are not conclusive.

––––––

In illustration 12, if the reasonable value of A's service is $60,000, can A recover $60,000?

––––––

See UCC §§ 2–711, 2–608, 2–601, 2–508, 2–612. To what extent do the rights of a buyer of goods who wishes to "cancel" differ from the remedy of restitution as discussed in the principal case? The issue is discussed in the following case.

––––––

RAMIREZ v. AUTOSPORT, 88 N.J. 277, 440 A.2d 1345 (1982). Mr. and Mrs. Ramirez contracted to purchase a camper van from Autosport. They left their old van with Autosport as a trade in. The Ramirezes returned to Autosport on the date specified in the contract for delivery but discovered that the paint was scratched, electric and sewer hookups were missing, and there were no hubcaps. On the advice of one of Autosport's salesmen, they did not accept the camper. They returned two more times during the next month prepared to pick up the van and pay for it. The first time the van was again not ready and the second time they were told to wait and, when no one appeared for an hour and a half, they left in disgust. In the meantime, Autosport had sold the Ramirezes' old van. The Ramirezes sued to rescind the contract and were awarded the fair market value of their trade-in van. The New Jersey Supreme Court affirmed:

"In the nineteenth century, sellers were required to deliver goods that complied exactly with the sales agreement. That rule, known as the 'perfect tender' rule, remained part of the law of sales well into the twentieth century. By the 1920's the doctrine was so entrenched in the law that Judged Learned Hand declared '[t]here is no room in commercial contracts for the doctrine of substantial performance.' Mitsubishi Goshi Kaisha v. J. Aron & Co., Inc., 16 F.2d 185, 186 (2 Cir.1926).

"The harshness of the rule led courts to seek to ameliorate its effect and to bring the law of sales in closer harmony with the law of contracts, which allows rescission only for material breaches. Nevertheless, a variation of the perfect tender rule appeared in the Uniform Sales Act. The chief objection to the continuation of the perfect tender rule was that buyers in a declining market would reject goods for minor nonconformities and force the loss on surprised sellers.

"To the extent that a buyer can reject goods for any nonconformity, the UCC retains the perfect tender rule. Section [2–106] states that goods conform to a contract 'when they are in accordance with the obligations under the contract'. Section [2–601] authorizes a buyer to reject goods if they 'or the tender of delivery fail in any respect to conform to the contract'. The [Code] however, mitigates the harshness of the perfect tender rule and balances the interests of buyer and seller. See Restatement, Second, Contracts, § 241 comment (b)(1981). The [Code] achieves that result through its provisions for revocation of acceptance and cure. [§§ 2–608, 2–508].

"Initially, the rights of the parties vary depending on whether the rejection occurs before or after acceptance of the goods. Before acceptance, the buyer may reject goods for any nonconformity. [§ 2–601]. Because of the seller's right to cure, however, the buyer's rejection does not necessarily discharge the contract. [§ 2–508]. Within the time set for performance in the contract, the seller's right to cure is unconditional. Id., subsec. (1); see id., Official Comment 1. Some authorities recommend granting a breaching party a right to cure in all contracts, not merely those for the sale of goods. Restatement, Second, Contracts, ch. 10, especially §§ 237 and 241. Underlying the right to cure in both kinds of contracts is the recognition that parties should be encouraged to communicate with each other and to resolve their own problems. Id., Introduction p. 193.

"The rights of the parties also vary if rejection occurs after the time set for performance. After expiration of that time, the seller has a further reasonable time to cure if he believed reasonably that the goods would be acceptable with or without a money allowance. [§ 2–508(2)]. The determination of what constitutes a further reasonable time depends on the surrounding circumstances, which include the change of position by and the amount of inconvenience to the buyer. [§ 2–508, Official Comment 3]. Those circumstances also include the length of time needed by the seller to correct the nonconformity and his ability to salvage the goods by resale to others. See Restatement, Second, Contracts, § 241, comment (d). Thus, the [Code] balances the buyer's right to reject nonconforming goods with a 'second chance' for the seller to conform the goods to the contract under certain limited circumstances.

"After acceptance, the [Code] strikes a different balance: the buyer may revoke acceptance only if the nonconformity substantially impairs the value of the goods to him. [§ 2–608]. This provision protects the seller from revocation for trivial defects. It also prevents the buyer from taking undue advantage of the seller by allowing goods to depreciate and then returning them because of asserted minor defects. See

White & Summers, Uniform Commercial Code, § 8–3 at 391 (2 ed. 1980). Because this case involves rejection of goods, we need not decide whether a seller has a right to cure substantial defects that justify revocation of acceptance. See Pavesi v. Ford Motor Co., 155 N.J.Super. 373, 378, 382 A.2d 954 (1978) (right to cure after acceptance limited to trivial defects) and White & Summers, supra, § 8–4 at 319 n. 76 (open question as to the relationship between [§§ 2–608 and 2–508]). * * *

"A further problem, however, is identifying the remedy available to a buyer who rejects goods with insubstantial defects that the seller fails to cure within a reasonable time. The [Code] provides expressly that when 'the buyer rightfully rejects, then with respect to the goods involved, the buyer may cancel.' [§ 2–711]. 'Cancellation' occurs when either party puts an end to the contract for breach by the other. [§ 2–106(4)]. Nonetheless, some confusion exists whether the equitable remedy of rescission survives under the [Code].

"The Code eschews the word 'rescission' and substitutes the terms 'cancellation', 'revocation of acceptance', and 'rightful rejection'. [§ 2–106(4); 2–608; and 2–711 & Official Comment 1]. Although neither 'rejection' nor 'revocation of acceptance' is defined in the Code, rejection includes both the buyer's refusal to accept or keep delivered goods and his notification to the seller that he will not keep them. White & Summers, supra, § 8–1 at 293. Revocation of acceptance is like rejection, but occurs after the buyer has accepted the goods. Nonetheless, revocation of acceptance is intended to provide the same relief as rescission of a contract of sale of goods. [§ 2–608 Official Comment 1]. In brief, revocation is tantamount to rescission. Similarly, subject to the seller's right to cure, a buyer who rightfully rejects goods, like one who revokes his acceptance, may cancel the contract. [§ 2–711 & Official Comment 1]. We need not resolve the extent to which rescission for reasons other than rejection or revocation of acceptance, e.g. fraud and mistake, survives as a remedy outside the [Code]. Compare [§ 1–103] and White & Summers, supra, § 8–1, p. 295, with [§ 2–721]. * * *

"Although the complaint requested rescission of the contract, plaintiffs actually sought not only the end of their contractual obligations, but also restoration to their pre-contractual position. That request incorporated the equitable doctrine of restitution, the purpose of which is to restore plaintiff to as good a position as he occupied before the contract. In UCC parlance, plaintiffs' request was for the cancellation of the contract and recovery of the price paid. [§§ 106(4), 2–711].

"General contract law permits rescission only for material breaches, and the [Code] restates 'materiality' in terms of 'substantial impairment'. The [Code] permits a buyer who rightfully rejects goods to cancel a contract of sale. [§ 2–711]. Because a buyer may reject goods with insubstantial defects, he also may cancel the contract if those defects remain uncured. Otherwise, a seller's failure to cure minor defects would compel a buyer to accept imperfect goods and collect for any loss caused by the nonconformity. [§ 2–714].

"Although the [Code] permits cancellation by rejection for minor defects, it permits revocation of acceptance only for substantial impairments. That distinction is consistent with other [Code] provisions that depend on whether the buyer has accepted the goods. Acceptance creates liability in the buyer for the price, [§ 2–709(1)], and precludes rejection. [§ 2–607(2); § 2–606]. Also, once a buyer accepts goods, he has the burden to prove any defect. [§ 2–607(4)]; White & Summers, supra, § 8–2 at 297. By contrast, where goods are rejected for not conforming to the contract, the burden is on the seller to prove that the nonconformity was corrected.

"Underlying the [Code] provisions is the recognition of the revolutionary change in business practices in this century. The purchase of goods is no longer a simple transaction in which a buyer purchases individually-made goods from a seller in a face-to-face transaction. Our economy depends on a complex system for the manufacture, distribution, and sale of goods, a system in which manufacturers and consumers rarely meet. Faceless manufacturers mass-produce goods for unknown consumers who purchase those goods from merchants exercising little or no control over the quality of their production. In an age of assembly lines, we are accustomed to cars with scratches, television sets without knobs and other products with all kinds of defects. Buyers no longer expect a 'perfect tender'. If a merchant sells defective goods, the reasonable expectation of the parties is that the buyer will return those goods and that the seller will repair or replace them.

"Recognizing this commercial reality, the [Code] permits a seller to cure imperfect tenders. Should the seller fail to cure the defects, whether substantial or not, the balance shifts again in favor of the buyer, who has the right to cancel or seek damages. [§ 2–711]. In general, economic considerations would induce sellers to cure minor defects. Assuming the seller does not cure, however, the buyer should be permitted to exercise his remedies under [§ 2–711]. The Code remedies for consumers are to be liberally construed, and the buyer should have the option of cancelling if the seller does not provide conforming goods. See [§ 1–106].

"To summarize, the UCC preserves the perfect tender rule to the extent of permitting a buyer to reject goods for any nonconformity. Nonetheless, that rejection does not automatically terminate the contract. A seller may still effect a cure and preclude unfair rejection and cancellation by the buyer. [§ 2–508, Official Comment 2; § 2–711, Official Comment 1.]"

----

1. In what ways does Ramirez v. Autosport indicate that the rights of a buyer of goods who wishes to "cancel" differ from the

remedy of restitution, as discussed in Bollenbeck v. Continental Casualty? See UCC §§ 2–508, 2–601, 2–606, 2–608, 2–612, 2–711.

2. In *Ramirez,* the court says that if the seller fails to cure the defects, the buyer "has the right to cancel or seek damages," citing UCC § 2–711. Is this statement inacurate? If so, how would you change it?

DURFEE v. ROD BAXTER IMPORTS, INC., 262 N.W.2d 349 (Minn. 1977). Durfee purchased a new Saab. On the trip home from the dealer, the seatbelt light and buzzer activated. Durfee returned immediately and a salesman silenced the warning device. Durfee again started for home only to have the shift lever come off in his hand, a rattle develop under the dashboard, and the seatbelt warning activate again. During the next 9 months, Durfee returned the car to a Saab dealer five times for the repair of minor and major problems, including repeated stalling. In one instance, the dealer kept the car for almost a month. At the end of 9 months, after having driven the car for 6,300 miles, Durfee informed the United States Saab distributor that he would not submit the car for further repairs and sued to revoke his acceptance and cancel the contract. The only damage to the car from use was to a radio aerial, which was broken off by vandals. The trial court held that the defects in the automobile did not justify rescission and awarded the plaintiff $600 damages for breach of warranty. The Minnesota Supreme Court reversed, holding that revocation of acceptance was proper:

"Section [2–608] prescribes the following requirements for an effective revocation of acceptance: (1) the goods must be nonconforming; (2) the nonconformity must substantially impair the value of the goods to the buyer; (3) the buyer must have accepted the goods on the reasonable assumption that the nonconformity would be cured; (4) the nonconformity must not have been seasonably cured; (5) the buyer must notify the seller of his revocation; (6) revocation must occur within a reasonable time after the buyer discovers or should have discovered the ground for it and before any substantial change in condition of the goods which is not caused by their own defects;[4] and (7) the buyer must take reasonable care of the goods for which he has revoked acceptance. Defendant Saab-Scania contends that the defects in the Saab did not

---

4. See, also [§ 2–607(3)(a)]. Many courts find that the period in which the seller attempts to cure the nonconformity is not part of the time in which the buyer must act.

Apparently the only changes in the car's condition not arising from its defects are the broken radio aerial and the 6,300 miles it logged. The broken aerial is a minor defect and insubstantial. See, [§ 2–608, U.C.C. Comment 6]. The mileage is more troublesome, but we find that in this circumstance it does not constitute a substantial change in condition so as to preclude revocation of acceptance. Although no specific [Code] provision authorizes offsetting the fair and reasonable value of the use the buyer has made of a car, several courts have taken this approach, relying on the equivalent of [§ 1–103]. We do not reach this point because defendant failed to raise it.

substantially impair its value to plaintiff, in part, because the defects already had been repaired or were easily repairable.

"This court has not yet interpreted the substantial-impairment test of [§ 2–608]. The impact of the substantial impairment is measured by the goods' loss of value to the buyer, but in other respects, the language of the statute hardly provides a sensitive gauge to test the justification for any particular revocation. Indeed, two respected commentators suggest that the test ultimately rests on a commonsense perception of substantial impairment, akin to the determination of a material breach under traditional contract law. White & Summers, Uniform Commercial Code, § 8–3, p. 257. The cases that involve revocation of acceptance of defective new automobiles are amenable to classification by this practical criterion. Minor defects not substantially interfering with the automobile's operation or with the comfort and security it affords passengers do not constitute grounds for revocation. On the other hand, if the defect substantially interferes with operation of the vehicle or a purpose for which it was purchased, a court may find grounds for revocation. Indeed, substantial impairment has been found even where the defect is curable, if it shakes the faith of the purchaser in the automobile.

"Plaintiff was plagued by a series of annoying difficulties with the Saab (the recurrent rattle and seatbelt buzz among them) as well as a difficulty that directly interfered with the Saab's operation (the repeated stalling which began 5 months after purchase and which, despite several attempted repairs, was never remedied.) The district court found that the Saab 'apparently could not, or would not, be placed in reasonably good operating condition by the Defendants or their agents or dealers.' Nevertheless, the court concluded that '[s]aid breach of warranty and defects in the vehicle are not such as to constitute grounds for rescission of the contract between the parties.' This conclusion, although not framed in the language of the Code, necessarily suggests that the defects did not substantially impair the value of the car to plaintiff. The determination of substantial impairment necessarily involves factual findings. However, once the basic facts are found, the question of whether they constitute substantial impairment is legal in character, and we need not defer to the ultimate conclusion drawn by the trial court.

"The succession of minor defects, even if considered in total, perhaps might not constitute substantial impairment; however, in combination with the frequent stalling of the Saab, plaintiff has shown substantial impairment. Other courts have recognized that repeated stalling may substantially impair the value of an automobile. * * *

"Defendant Saab-Scania argues that the defects cannot constitute substantial impairment because they are repairable and that defendants should be permitted to make the repairs pursuant to their contractual obligation. The district court found, however, that defendants could not or would not return the Saab to reasonably good operating condition. In light of the opportunities defendants had to repair the vehicle, this finding is not clearly erroneous. Moreover, even if the defects could be repaired, that possibility does not necessarily negate substantial impairment. A seller does not have an unlimited time to deliver conforming goods. [§ 2–608(1)(a)] requires the seller to seasonably cure the nonconformity. [§ 1–204(3)] defines 'seasonably' as 'within a reasonable time.' That period may well have passed in circumstances where the seller has been given several opportunities to cure. * * *

"The evidence demonstrates that the defects substantially impaired the value of the Saab to plaintiff. The district court therefore erred in reaching the contrary conclusion. Thus, plaintiff ordinarily would be entitled to the remedies available to a rejecting buyer pursuant to [§ 2–711(1)]. Defendant Saab-Scania suggests, however, that a provision in the owner's manual limits plaintiff's remedies to the repair or replacement of defective parts.

"[§ 2–719] authorizes a contractual limitation of remedy and specifically sanctions a repair-and-replacement clause, but it also defines the circumstances in which such limitations are valid. * * * A repair-and-replacement clause provides both a remedy to the buyer, whereby he may secure goods conforming to the contract, and a limitation of liability to the seller. If the repair-and-replacement clause as a remedy fails of its essential purpose, [§ 2–719(2)] entails that its function as a limitation of the seller's liability must also fail. In such a circumstance, plaintiff may cancel the contract and recover his purchase price.

"An exclusive remedy fails of its essential purpose if circumstances arise to deprive the limiting clause of its meaning or one party of the substantial value of its bargain. [§ 2–719], U.C.C. Comment 1. So long as the seller repairs the goods each time a defect arises, a repair-and-replacement clause does not fail of its essential purpose. But if repairs are not successfully undertaken within a reasonable time, the buyer may be deprived of the benefits of the exclusive remedy. Commendable efforts and considerable expense alone do not relieve a seller of his obligation to repair.

"In the instant case, the district court implicitly found that the repair-and-replacement clause failed as an exclusive remedy, for it awarded plaintiff damages. Its explicit finding that the car could not or would not be placed in reasonably good operating condition, which was not clearly erroneous, compels the conclusion that the remedy failed of its essential purpose. Thus, revocation of acceptance and cancellation of the contract was a remedy available to plaintiff.

"Plaintiff seeks to recover both consequential and incidental damages in addition to the purchase price. He failed to prove any consequential damages, and the only incidental damages proved involved repair and maintenance costs totalling $116.30. A buyer who justifiably revokes acceptance is entitled to recover incidental damages as defined in [§ 2–715(1)]. The repair and maintenance costs were expenses reasonably incurred in caring for the automobile and thus are recoverable as incidental damages. The validity of the provisions found in the owner's manual which purportedly exclude recovery of incidental damages must therefore be considered.

"[§ 2–719(2)] provides that '[w]here circumstances cause an exclusive or limited remedy to fail of its essential purpose, remedy may be had as provided in this chapter.' Where a buyer has justifiably revoked acceptance, this clause precludes the invocation of a clause limiting liability with respect to the recovery of incidental damages. To withhold incidental damages from a buyer revoking acceptance is to make cancellation of the contract a less than adequate remedy. In these circumstances, plaintiff is entitled to recover both his purchase price and incidental damages."

See UCC §§ 2–610 and comment 3 to that section; 2–302.

For another method of protecting purchasers of automobiles that do not perform satisfactorily after the seller has had a reasonable opportunity to repair, see the note on "Lemon Laws", infra page 731.

COTNAM v. WISDOM
Supreme Court of Arkansas, 1907.
83 Ark. 601, 104 S.W. 164.

Action by F.L. Wisdom and another against T.T. Cotnam, administrator of A.M. Harrison, deceased, for services rendered by plaintiffs as surgeons to defendant's intestate. Judgment for plaintiffs. Defendant appeals. * * *

Instructions 1 and 2, given at the instance of plaintiffs, are as follows: "(1) If you find from the evidence that plaintiffs rendered professional services as physicians and surgeons to the deceased, A.M. Harrison, in a sudden emergency following the deceased's injury in a street car wreck, in an endeavor to save his life, then you are instructed that plaintiffs are entitled to recover from the estate of the said A.M. Harrison such sum as you may find from the evidence is a reasonable compensation for the services rendered. (2) The character and importance of the operation, the responsibility resting upon the surgeon performing the operation, his experience and professional training, and the ability to pay of the person operated upon, are elements to be considered by you in determining what is a reasonable charge for the services performed by plaintiffs in the particular case."

HILL, C.J. The reporter will state the issues and substance of the testimony and set out instructions 1 and 2 given at instance of appellee, and it will be seen therefrom that instruction 1 amounted to a peremptory instruction to find for the plaintiff in some amount.

The first question is as to the correctness of this instruction. As indicated therein the facts are that Mr. Harrison, appellant's intestate, was thrown from a street car, receiving serious injuries which rendered him unconscious, and while in that condition the appellees were notified of the accident and summoned to his assistance by some spectator, and performed a difficult operation in an effort to save his life, but they were unsuccessful, and he died without regaining consciousness. The appellant says: "Harrison was never conscious after his head struck the pavement. He did not and could not, expressly or impliedly, assent to the action of the appellees. He was without knowledge or will power. However merciful or benevolent may have been the intention of the appellees, a new rule of law, of contract by implication of law, will have to be established by this court in order to sustain the recovery." Appellant is right in saying that the recovery must be sustained by a contract by implication of law, but is not right in saying that it is a new rule of law, for such contracts are almost as old as the English system of jurisprudence. They are usually called "implied contracts." More properly they should be called "quasi contracts" or "constructive contracts."

The following excerpts from Sceva v. True, 53 N.H. 627, are peculiarly applicable here: "We regard it as well settled by the cases referred to in the briefs of counsel, many of which have been commented on at length by Mr. Shirley for the defendant, that an insane person, an idiot, or a person utterly bereft of all sense and reason by the sudden stroke of an accident or disease may be held liable, in assumpsit, for necessaries furnished to him in good faith while in that unfortunate and helpless condition. And the reasons upon which this rest are too broad, as well as too sensible and humane, to be overborne by any deductions which a refined logic may make from the circumstances that in such cases there can be no contract or promise, in fact, no meeting of the minds of the parties. The cases put it on the ground of an implied contract; and by this is not meant, as the defendant's counsel seems to suppose, an actual contract—that is, an actual meeting of the minds of the parties, an actual, mutual understanding, to be inferred from language, acts, and circumstances by the jury—but a contract and promise, said to be implied by the law, where, in point of fact, there was no contract, no mutual understanding, and so no promise. The defendant's counsel says it is usurpation for the court to hold, as a matter of law, that there is a contract and a promise, when all the evidence in the case shows that there was not a contract, nor the semblance of one. It is doubtless a legal fiction, invented and used for the sake of the remedy. If it was originally usurpation, certainly it has now become very inveterate, and firmly fixed in the body of the law. Illustrations might be multiplied, but enough has been said to show that when a contract or promise implied by law is spoken of, a very different thing is meant from a contract in fact, whether express or tacit. The evidence of an actual contract is generally to be found either in some writing made by the parties, or in verbal communications which passed between them, or in their acts and conduct considered in the light of the circumstances of each particular case. A contract implied by law, on the contrary, rests upon no evidence. It has no actual existence. It is simply a mythical creation of the law. The law says it shall be taken that there was a promise, when in point of fact, there was none. Of course this is not good logic, for the obvious and sufficient reason that it is not true. It is a legal fiction, resting wholly for its support on a plain legal obligation, and a plain legal right. If it were true, it would not be a fiction. There is a class of legal rights, with their correlative legal duties, analogous to the obligationes quasi ex contractu of the civil law, which seem to lie in the region between contracts on the one hand, and torts on the other, and to call for the application of a remedy not strictly furnished either by actions ex contractu or actions ex delicto. The common law supplies no action of duty, as it does of assumpsit and trespass; and hence the somewhat awkward contrivance of this fiction to apply the remedy of assumpsit where there is no true contract and no promise to support it." * * *

One phase in the law of implied contracts was considered in the case of Lewis v. Lewis, 75 Ark. 191, 87 S.W. 134. In its practical application it sustains recovery for physicians and nurses who render services for infants, insane persons, and drunkards. And services rendered by physicians to persons unconscious or helpless by reason of injury or sickness are in the same situation as those rendered to persons incapable of contracting, such as the classes above described. The court was therefore right in giving the instruction in question.

2. The defendant sought to require the plaintiff to prove, in addition to the value of the services, the benefit, if any, derived by the deceased from the operation, and alleges error in the court refusing to so instruct the jury. The court was right in refusing to place this burden upon the physicians. The same question was considered in Ladd v. Witte, 116 Wis. 35, 92 N.W. 365, where the court said: "That is not at all the test. So that a surgical operation be conceived and performed with due skill and care, the price to be paid therefor does not depend upon the result. The event so generally lies with the forces of nature that all intelligent men know and understand that the surgeon is not responsible therefor. In absence of express agreement, the surgeon, who brings to such a service due skill and care, earns the reasonable and customary price therefor, whether the outcome be beneficial to the patient or the reverse."

3. The court permitted to go to the jury the fact that Mr. Harrison was a bachelor, and that his estate would go to his collateral relatives, and also permitted proof to be made of the value of the estate, which amounted to about $18,500, including $10,000 from accident and life insurance policies. There is a conflict in the authorities as to whether it is proper to prove the value of the estate of a person for whom medical services were rendered, or the financial condition of the person receiving such services. * * *

Whatever may be the true principle governing this matter in contracts, the court is of the opinion that the financial condition of a patient cannot be considered where there is no contract and recovery is sustained on a legal fiction which raises a contract in order to afford a remedy which the justice of the case requires.   *   *   *

In order to admit such testimony, it must be assumed that the surgeon and patient each had in contemplation that the means of the patient would be one factor in determining the amount of the charge for the services rendered. While the law may admit such evidence as throwing light upon the contract and indicating what was really in contemplation when it was made, yet a different question is presented when there is no contract to be ascertained or construed, but a mere fiction of law creating a contract where none existed in order that there might be a remedy for a right. This fiction merely requires a reasonable compensation for the services rendered. The services are the same be the patient prince or pauper, and for them the surgeon is entitled to fair compensation for his time, service, and skill. It was therefore error to admit this evidence, and to instruct the jury in the second instruction that in determining what was a reasonable charge they could consider the "ability to pay of the person operated upon."

It was improper to let it go to the jury that Mr. Harrison was a bachelor and that his estate was left to nieces and nephews. This was relevant to no issue in the case, and its effect might well have been prejudicial. While this verdict is no higher than some of the evidence would justify, yet it is much higher than some of the other evidence would justify, and hence it is impossible to say that this was a harmless error.

Judgment is reversed, and cause remanded.

BATTLE and WOOD, JJ., concur in sustaining the recovery, and in holding that it was error to permit the jury to consider the fact that his estate would go to collateral heirs; but they do not concur in holding that it was error to admit evidence of the value of the estate, and instructing that it might be considered in fixing the charge.

––––––––

SCHNEIDER v. DELWOOD CENTER, INC., 394 S.W.2d 671 (Tex.Civ. App.—Austin, 1965), writ ref'd n.r.e. Delwood leased land to Hall. The lease granted permission for Hall to erect improvements on the land but provided that at the end of the lease, the improvements became the property of Delwood. Hall built apartments on the land but went bankrupt and was not able to pay the contractors or materialmen who had supplied labor and materials for the construction. The court held that the contractors and materialmen could not file liens on the land and had no cause of action against Delwood for the amount that they had increased the value of the land:

"The eighth and last point is that the court erred in holding that appellants are not entitled to recover under the theory of quantum meruit for benefits conferred and to prevent unjust enrichment.

"There is a sufficient showing that appellants have contributed to the value of Delwood's land for which contributions they have not been paid.

"In Cantrell v. Garrett, Tex.Civ.App., 342 S.W.2d 466, Houston, n.w.h., the Court quoted the classic statement of Chief Justice Fly of the San Antonio Court in Barrow v. Booth, Tex.Civ.App., 227 S.W. 1113, n.w.h., setting forth the essentials of a plea of quantum meruit as follows:

> 'The law as to quantum meruit rests on the principle that a person will be compelled to pay for services if he stands by and permits another to render such services, under such circumstances as to convince any reasonable man that they were being done with the expectation of being paid for them, and no effort is made to prevent the rendition of such services. *This proposition of law is based upon the knowledge of the person served that the services were being rendered for him, and not some other person* (emphasis supplied), and liability will depend upon the facts of each case.'

"There is no showing in this record that appellants furnished any materials or labor to Delwood. They dealt with Hall and only with Hall. There is no basis for a recovery on quantum meruit. Point eight is overruled."

Is "quantum meruit" a reason for recovery or is it a measure of recovery? What theory of recovery is described in the *Schneider* court's statement of the "law as to quantum meruit"? What other theories might permit recovery of the reasonable value of goods or services? Would any of these theories justify recovery in *Schneider?*

RESTATEMENT, SECOND, CONTRACTS § 69:

Illustration:

7. A sends B a one-volume edition of Shakespeare with a letter, saying, "If you wish to buy this book send me $6.50 within one week after receipt hereof, otherwise notify me and I will forward postage for return." B examines the book and without replying makes a gift of it to his wife. B owes A $6.50.

What different theories of recovery might explain the conclusion in illustration 7 above, that "B owes A $6.50?" What theory might explain recovery if B never communicated with A, but within one week A learns that B had given the book to his wife, and B knew that A would learn of the gift? What theory might explain recovery if immediately after giving the book to his wife, B wrote to A, "I have given the book to my wife but I refuse to pay you for it"?

Cf. UCC § 2–606(1)(c).

Under 39 U.S.C.A. § 3009, "merchandise mailed without the prior expressed request or consent of the recipient" "may be treated as a gift by the recipient." See infra p. 556.

MICHIGAN CENTRAL RAILROAD v. STATE

Indiana Appellate Court, en banc, 1927.
85 Ind.App. 557, 155 N.E. 50.

REMY, J. On June 10, 1920, and pursuant to section 2 of the Appropriation Act of 1919 (Acts 1919, p. 196, c. 58), the state of Indiana, through its joint purchasing committee, contracted for a year's supply of coal for the Indiana State Prison, a penal institution located at Michigan City, the contract price for the coal being $3.40 per ton, delivered. On October 22, 1920, while the contract was in force, appellant railway company, a carrier of interstate commerce, had in its possession for interstate transportation a carload of coal of the same kind and quality as that contracted for by the state, which coal by mutual mistake of the carrier and agents of the state was delivered to the Indiana State Prison and there consumed. This carload of coal at the time and place of its delivery was of the market value of $6.85 per ton. Upon learning of the misdelivery of the coal and its consumption, appellant paid to the consignee of the coal the market value thereof and demanded of the state that it be reimbursed for the amount so paid. With this demand the state refused to comply. Whereupon appellant commenced this action against the state to recover the market value of the coal. Edward J. Fogarty, superintendent of the Indiana State Prison, was joined as a party defendant. In its complaint, appellant specifically waived any action in tort which it may have had. The cause was submitted to the court upon an agreed statement of facts, the substance of which is as above set forth. The court found against the state, but limited recovery to $3.40 per ton, the price of the year's supply of coal as contracted for by the joint purchasing committee, and judgment was so rendered.

Claiming that the amount of the recovery should have been $6.85 per ton, the market value of the coal, and was therefore too small, the railroad company prosecutes this appeal. The state not having assigned cross-errors, the only question for determination by this court is whether, under the facts stipulated, the measure of recovery is the market value of the coal at the time and place of the misdelivery, or, as held by the trial court, the price at which the joint purchasing committee had purchased the year's supply. A decision of the question will require a consideration of the nature and character of the action.
* * *

That a carrier may recover for a consignment of goods delivered to the wrong person by mistake, in an action against the person who received and retained the goods, is not questioned by appellees, nor can it be. Nor do appellees question the right of appellant to sue the state in an action of this character. The state's obligation which forms the basis of this action is what is termed quasi contractual. Though frequently referred to by the courts as equitable in character, it is a legal obligation on the part of the obligor to make restitution in value— that is, to pay the equivalent of the benefit received and unjustly enjoyed. The legal obligation of the state in this action is to pay to appellant a sum equal to the benefit to the state which resulted from the misdelivery. The benefit is not fixed by any agreement, for there had been no agreement by the state as to this carload of coal; and since this is not an action in tort, the rules governing the measure of damages in actions ex delicto are not controlling. In actions to enforce quasi contractual obligations, the general rule is that the measure of recovery is the value of the benefit received by the defendant but it cannot be said that to this rule there are no exceptions. If, for example, the carrier has settled with the owner of a consignment of goods which had been misdelivered, the settlement being for a sum less than the market value, it would not be contended that the carrier could recover the market value in an action against the person who had received the goods. It is unnecessary, however, to discuss the exceptions to the general rule.

Quasi contractual obligations usually arise between the parties to illegal or unenforceable contracts. This action is between the parties whose mutual mistake resulted in the conversion of the coal. One of the parties to the conversion, having made restitution to the owner of the property converted, is seeking indemnity from the other. Furthermore, the defendant in the action is the state of Indiana, against which an action in tort could not have been maintained. Acts 1889, p. 265, c. 128 (section 1550, Burns' 1926). The obligation forming the basis of the action is essentially an obligation to restore a benefit received by the defendant, and not to compensate the plaintiff for damages sustained. The obligation rests upon the principle that the defendant—the state in this case—cannot be allowed, in equity and good conscience, to keep what it has obtained. Put affirmatively, the state must restore what in good conscience it cannot retain. The state having contracted, in the way provided by the statute, for a year's supply of coal for its penal institution, at the price of $3.40 per ton, the state's representatives could not, by their mistake in receiving from a common carrier coal of a like quality, but which had been sold and consigned to another, obligate the state to pay the carrier for the coal a price in excess of the state's contract price; the carrier having been a party to the mistake. It would be contrary to sound public policy to require the state to pay more for coal delivered and received by mistake than it would be required to pay under a contract resulting from competitive bids.

We hold that the measure of recovery is the state's contract price, and not the market value of the coal at the time and place of the misdelivery.

Affirmed.

BOONE v. COE

Kentucky Court of Appeals, 1913.
153 Ky. 233, 154 S.W. 900.

CLAY, C. Plaintiffs, W.H. Boone and J.T. Coe, brought this action against defendant, J.F. Coe, to recover certain damages, alleged to have resulted from defendant's breach of a parol contract of lease for one year to commence at a future date. It appears from the petition that the defendant was the owner of a large and valuable farm in [Foard] county, Tex. Plaintiffs were farmers, and were living with their families in Monroe county, Ky. In the fall of 1909 defendant made a verbal contract with plaintiffs, whereby he rented to them his farm in Texas for a period of 12 months, to commence from the date of plaintiffs' arrival at defendant's farm. Defendant agreed that if plaintiffs would leave their said homes and businesses in Kentucky, and with their families, horses, and wagons, move to defendant's farm in Texas, and take charge of, manage, and cultivate same in wheat, corn, and cotton for the 12 months next following plaintiffs' arrival at said farm, the defendant would have a dwelling completed on said farm and ready for occupancy upon their arrival, which dwelling plaintiffs would occupy as a residence during the period of said tenancy. Defendant also agreed that he would furnish necessary material at a convenient place on said farm out of which to erect a good and commodious stock and grain barn, to be used by plaintiffs. The petition further alleges that plaintiffs were to cultivate certain portions of the farm, and were to receive certain portions of the crops raised, and that plaintiffs, in conformity with their said agreement, did move from Kentucky to the farm in Texas, and carried with them their families, wagons, horses, and camping outfit, and in going to Texas they traveled for a period of 55 days. It is also charged that defendant broke his contract, in that he failed to have ready and completed on the farm a dwelling house in which plaintiffs and their families could move, and also failed to furnish the necessary material for the erection of a suitable barn; that on December 6th defendant refused to permit plaintiffs to occupy the house and premises, and failed and refused to permit them to cultivate the land or any part thereof; that on the _____ day of December, 1909, they started for their home in Kentucky, and arrived there after traveling for a period of 4 days. It is charged that plaintiffs spent in going to Texas, in cash, the sum of $150; that the loss of time to plaintiffs and their teams in making the trip to Texas was reasonably worth $8 a day for a period of 55 days, or the sum of $440; that the loss of time to them and their teams during the period they remained in Texas was $8 a day for 22 days, or $176; that they paid out in actual cash for transportation for themselves, families, and teams from Texas to Kentucky the sum of $211.80; that the loss of time to them and their teams in making the last-named trip was reasonably worth the sum of $100; that in abandoning and giving up their homes and businesses in Kentucky they had been damaged in the sum of $150, making a total damage of $1,387.80, for which judgment was asked. Defendant's demurrer to the petition was sustained and the petition dismissed. Plaintiffs appeal. * * *

The statute of frauds (section 470, subsecs. 6 and 7, Kentucky Statutes) provides as follows: "No action shall be brought to charge any person: 6. Upon any contract for the sale of real estate, or any lease thereof, for longer term than one year; nor 7. Upon any agreement which is not to be performed within one year from the making thereof, unless the promise, contract, agreement, representation, assurance, or ratification, or some memorandum or note thereof, be in writing, and signed by the party to be charged therewith, or by his authorized agent; but the consideration need not be expressed in the writing; it may be proved when necessary, or disproved by parol or other evidence." A parol lease of land for one year, to commence at a future date, is within the statute. The question sharply presented is: May plaintiffs recover for expenses incurred and time lost on the faith of a contract that is unenforceable under the statute of frauds?

* * * [I]t is the general rule that damages cannot be recovered for violation of a contract within the statute of frauds. To this general rule there are certain well-recognized exceptions. Thus, in a number of * * * cases, it has been held that, where services have been rendered during the life of another, on the promise that the person rendering the service should receive at the death of the person served a legacy, and the contract so made is within the statute of frauds, a reasonable compensation may be recovered for the services actually rendered. It has also been held that the vendee of land under a parol contract is entitled to recover any portion of the purchase money he may have paid, and is also entitled to compensation for improvements.

The doctrine of these cases proceeds upon the theory that the defendant has actually received some benefits from the acts of part performance; and the law therefore implies a promise to pay. In 29 Am. & Eng. Ency. 836, the rule is thus stated: "Although part performance by one of the parties to a contract within the statute of frauds will not, at law, entitle such party to recover upon the contract itself, he may nevertheless recover for money paid by him, or property delivered, or services rendered in accordance with and upon the faith of the contract. The law will raise an implied promise on the part of the other party to pay for what has been done in the way of part performance. But this right of recovery is not absolute. The plaintiff is entitled to compensation only under such circumstances as would warrant a recovery in case there was no express contract; and hence it must appear that the defendant has actually received, or will receive, some benefit from the acts of part performance. It is immaterial that the plaintiff may have suffered a loss because he is unable to enforce his contract." * * *

In the case under consideration the plaintiffs merely sustained a loss. Defendant received no benefit. Had he received a benefit, the law would imply an obligation to pay therefor. Having received no benefit, no obligation to pay is implied. The statute says that the contract of defendant made with plaintiffs is unenforceable. Defendant therefore had the legal right to decline to carry it out. To require him to pay plaintiffs for losses and expenses incurred on the faith of the contract, without any benefit accruing to him, would, in effect, uphold a contract upon which the statute expressly declares no action shall be brought. The statute was enacted for the purpose of preventing frauds and perjuries. That it is a valuable statute is shown by the fact that similar statutes are in force in practically all, if not all, of the states of the Union. Being a valuable statute, the purpose of the lawmakers in its enactment should not be defeated by permitting recoveries in cases to which its provisions were intended to apply. * * *

Judgment affirmed.

See chapter 12 for a discussion of statutes of frauds.

FARASH v. SYKES DATATRONICS, INC., 59 N.Y.2d 500, 465 N.Y.S.2d 917, 452 N.E.2d 1245 (1983). Owner claimed that Tenant had orally agreed that if Owner renovated a building, Tenant would lease it for a period longer than one year. Owner had performed the renovations, but Tenant had not paid Owner, signed a contract, or occupied the building. The court reversed a dismissal of Owner's action:

"Plaintiff pleaded three causes of action in his complaint. The first was to enforce an oral lease for a term longer than one year. This is clearly barred by the Statute of Frauds. The third cause of action is premised on the theory that the parties contracted by exchanging promises that plaintiff would perform certain work in his building and defendant would enter into a lease for a term longer than one year. This is nothing more than a contract to enter into a lease; it is also subject to the Statute of Frauds. Hence, the third cause of action was properly dismissed.

"Plaintiff's second cause of action, however, is not barred by the Statute of Frauds. It merely seeks to recover for the value of the work performed by plaintiff in reliance on statements by and at the request of defendant. This is not an attempt to enforce an oral lease or an oral agreement to enter a lease, but is in disaffirmance of the void contract and so may be maintained. That defendant did not benefit from plaintiff's efforts does not require dismissal; plaintiff may recover for those efforts that were to his detriment and that thereby placed him in a worse position. * * *

"We should not be distracted by the manner in which a theory of recovery is titled. On careful consideration, it becomes clear that the commentators do not disagree in result, but only in nomenclature. Whether denominated 'acting in reliance' or 'restitution,' all concur that a promisee who partially performs (e.g., by doing work in a building or at an accelerated pace) at a promisor's request should be allowed to recover the fair and reasonable value of the performance rendered, regardless of the enforceability of the original agreement."

RESTATEMENT, SECOND, CONTRACTS § 370:

Illustration:

2. A contracts to sell B a machine for $100,000. After A has spent $40,000 on the manufacture of the machine but before its completion, B repudiates the contract. A cannot get restitution of the $40,000 because no benefit was conferred on B.

RESTATEMENT, SECOND, CONTRACTS § 371:

Illustration:

1. A, a carpenter, contracts to repair B's roof for $3,000. A does part of the work at a cost of $2,000, increasing the market price of B's house by $1,200. The market price to have a similar carpenter do the work done by A is $1,800. A's restitution interest is equal to the benefit conferred on B. That benefit may be measured either by the addition to B's wealth from A's services in terms of the $1,200 increase in the market price of B's house or the reasonable value to B of A's services in terms of the $1,800 that it would have cost B to engage a similar carpenter to do the same work. If the work was not completed because of a breach by A and restitution is based on the rule stated in § 374 [infra page 154], $1,200 is appropriate. If the work was not completed because of a breach by B and restitution is based on the rule stated in § 373 [supra page 95], $1,800 is appropriate.

SECTION 2: SPECIFIC PERFORMANCE

VAN WAGNER ADVERTISING CORP. v. S & M ENTERPRISES

Court of Appeals of New York, 1986.
67 N.Y.2d 186, 501 N.Y.S.2d 628, 492 N.E.2d 756.

KAYE, JUDGE. * * * By agreement dated December 16, 1981, Barbara Michaels leased to plaintiff, Van Wagner Advertising, for an initial period of three years plus option periods totaling seven additional years space on the eastern exterior wall of a building on East 36th Street in Manhattan. Van Wagner was in the business of erecting and leasing billboards, and the parties anticipated that Van Wagner would erect a sign on the leased space, which faced an exit ramp of the Midtown Tunnel and was therefore visible to vehicles entering Manhattan from that tunnel.

In early 1982 Van Wagner erected an illuminated sign and leased it to Asch Advertising, Inc. for a three-year period commencing March 1, 1982. However, by agreement dated January 22, 1982, Michaels sold the building to defendant S & M Enterprises. Michaels informed Van Wagner of the sale in early August 1982, and on August 19, 1982 S & M sent Van Wagner a letter purporting to cancel the lease as of October 18 pursuant to section 1.05, which provided

> "Notwithstanding anything contained in the foregoing provisions to the contrary, Lessor (or its successor) may terminate and cancel this lease on not less than 60 days prior written notice in the event and only in the event of:

>> "a) a bona fide sale of the building to a third party unrelated to Lessor".

Van Wagner abandoned the space under protest and in November 1982 commenced this action for declarations that the purported cancellation was ineffective and the lease still in existence, and for specific performance and damages.

In the litigation the parties differed sharply on the meaning of section 1.05 of the lease. Van Wagner contended that the lease granted a right to cancel only to the owner as it was about to sell the building— not to the new purchaser—so that the building could be conveyed without the encumbrance of the lease. S & M in contrast, contended that the provision clearly gave it, as Michaels' successor by virtue of a bona fide sale, the right to cancel the lease on 60 days' notice. * * *

Trial Term concluded that Van Wagner's position on the issue of contract interpretation was correct, either because the lease provision unambiguously so provided or, if the provision were ambiguous, because the parol evidence showed that the "parties to the lease intended that only an owner making a bona fide sale could terminate the lease." * * * However, the court declined to order specific performance in light of its finding that Van Wagner "has an adequate remedy at law for damages". Moreover, the court noted that specific performance "would be inequitable in that its effect would be disproportionate in its harm to the defendant and its assistance to plaintiff." Concluding that "[t]he value of the unique qualities of the demised space has been fixed by the contract Van Wagner has with its advertising client, Asch for the period of the contract", the court awarded Van Wagner the lost revenues on the Asch sublease for the period through trial, without prejudice to a new action by Van Wagner for subsequent damages if S & M did not permit Van Wagner to reoccupy the space. On Van Wagner's motion to resettle the judgment to provide for specific performance, the court adhered to its judgment.

On cross appeals the Appellate Division affirmed, without opinion. We granted both parties leave to appeal.   *   *   *

Whether or not to award specific performance is a decision that rests in the sound discretion of the trial court, and here that discretion was not abused. Considering first the nature of the transaction, specific performance has been imposed as the remedy for breach of contracts for the sale of real property, but the contract here is to lease rather than sell an interest in real property. While specific performance is available, in appropriate circumstances, for breach of a commercial or residential lease, specific performance of real property leases is not in this State awarded as a matter of course.

Van Wagner argues that specific performance must be granted in light of the trial court's finding that the "demised space is unique as to location for the particular advertising purpose intended". The word "uniqueness" is not, however, a magic door to specific performance. A distinction must be drawn between physical difference and economic interchangeability. The trial court found that the leased property is physically unique, but so is every parcel of real property and so are many consumer goods. Putting aside contracts for the sale of real property, where specific performance has traditionally been the remedy for breach, uniqueness in the sense of physical difference does not itself dictate the propriety of equitable relief.

By the same token, at some level all property may be interchangeable with money. Economic theory is concerned with the degree to which consumers are willing to substitute the use of one good for another (*see*, Kronman, *Specific Performance*, 45 U.Chi.L.Rev. 351, 359), the underlying assumption being that "every good has substitutes, even if only very poor ones", and that "all goods are ultimately commensurable" (*id.*). Such a view, however, could strip all meaning from uniqueness, for if all goods are ultimately exchangeable for a price, then all goods may be valued. Even a rare manuscript has an economic substitute in that there is a price for which any purchaser would likely agree to give up a right to buy it, but a court would in all probability order specific performance of such a contract on the ground that the subject matter of the contract is unique.

The point at which breach of a contract will be redressable by specific performance thus must lie not in any inherent physical uniqueness of the property but instead in the uncertainty of valuing it: "What matters, in measuring money damages, is the volume, refinement, and reliability of the available information about substitutes for the subject matter of the breached contract. When the relevant information is thin and unreliable, there is a substantial risk that an award of money damages will either exceed or fall short of the promisee's actual loss. Of course this risk can always be reduced—but only at great cost when reliable information is difficult to obtain. Conversely, when there is a great deal of consumer behavior generating abundant and highly dependable information about substitutes, the risk of error in measuring the promisee's loss may be reduced at much smaller cost. In asserting that the subject matter of a particular contract is unique and has no established market value, a court is really saying that it cannot obtain, at reasonable cost, enough information about substitutes to permit it to calculate an award of money damages without imposing an unacceptably high risk of undercompensation on the injured promisee. Conceived in this way, the uniqueness test seems economically sound." (45 UChiLRev, at 362.) This principle is reflected in the case law and is essentially the position of the Restatement (Second) of Contracts, which lists "the difficulty of proving damages with reasonable certainty" as the first factor affecting adequacy of damages (Restatement [Second] of Contracts § 360[a]).

Thus, the fact that the subject of the contract may be "unique as to location for the particular advertising purpose intended" by the parties does not entitle a plaintiff to the remedy of specific performance.

Here, the trial court correctly concluded that the value of the "unique qualities" of the demised space could be fixed with reasonable certainty and without imposing an unacceptably high risk of undercompensating the injured tenant. Both parties complain: Van Wagner asserts that while lost revenues on the Asch contract may be adequate compensation, that contract expired February 28, 1985, its lease with S & M continues until 1992, and the value of the demised space cannot reasonably be fixed for the balance of the term. S & M urges that future rents and continuing damages are necessarily conjectural, both during and after the Asch contract, and that Van Wagner's damages must be limited to 60 days—the period during which Van Wagner could cancel Asch's contract without consequence in the event Van Wagner lost the demised space. S & M points out that Van Wagner's lease could remain in effect for the full 10-year term, or it could legitimately be extinguished immediately, either in conjunction with a bona fide sale of the property by S & M, or by a reletting of the building if the new tenant required use of the billboard space for its own purposes. Both parties' contentions were properly rejected.

First, it is hardly novel in the law for damages to be projected into the future. Particularly where the value of commercial billboard space can be readily determined by comparisons with similar uses—Van Wagner itself has more than 400 leases—the value of this property between 1985 and 1992 cannot be regarded as speculative. Second, S & M having successfully resisted specific performance on the ground that there is an adequate remedy at law, cannot at the same time be heard to contend that damages beyond 60 days must be denied because they are conjectural. If damages for breach of this lease are indeed conjectural, and cannot be calculated with reasonable certainty, then S & M should be compelled to perform its contractual obligation by restoring Van Wagner to the premises. Moreover, the contingencies to which S & M points do not, as a practical matter, render the calculation of damages speculative. While S & M could terminate the Van Wagner lease in the event of a sale of the building, this building has been sold only once in 40 years; S & M paid several million dollars, and purchased the building in connection with its plan for major development of the block. The theoretical termination right of a future tenant of the existing building also must be viewed in light of these circumstances. If any uncertainty is generated by the two contingencies, then the benefit of that doubt must go to Van Wagner and not the contract violator. * * *

The trial court, additionally, correctly concluded that specific performance should be denied on the ground that such relief "would be inequitable in that its effect would be disproportionate in its harm to defendant and its assistance to plaintiff." It is well settled that the imposition of an equitable remedy must not itself work an inequity, and that specific performance should not be an undue hardship. * * *

While specific performance was properly denied, the court erred in its assessment of damages. Our attention is drawn to two alleged errors.

First, both parties are dissatisfied with the award of lost profits on the Asch contracts. * * * Based on the Asch contract indicating revenues, and the lease indicating expenses, the trial court properly calculated Van Wagner's lost profits. Having found that the value of the space was fixed by the Asch contract for the entire period of that contract, however, the court erred in awarding the lost revenues only through November 23, 1983. Damages should have been awarded for the duration of the Asch contract.

Second, the court fashioned relief for S & M's breach of contract only to the time of trial, and expressly contemplated that "[i]f defendant continues to exclude plaintiff from the leased space action for continuing damages may be brought." In requiring Van Wagner to bring a multiplicity of suits to recover its damages the court erred. Damages should have been awarded through the expiration of Van Wagner's lease.

Accordingly, the order of the Appellate Division should be modified, with costs to plaintiff, and the case remitted to Supreme Court, New York County, for further proceedings in accordance with this opinion and, as so modified, affirmed.

———

In the note on "Efficient Breach," above at p. 14, the question is raised as to why the seller's profit from breaking a contract should not belong to the buyer. Cases dealing with the sale of land permit the aggrieved buyer to recover the profit resulting from breach of contract, but usually on the ground that after the contract for sale of land is made, the seller holds the land "in trust" for the buyer. See, Timko v. Useful Homes Corp., 114 N.J.Eq. 433, 168 A. 824 (N.J. Ch. 1933). There are scholars who favor making recapture of the contract-breaker's profits generally available as a remedy. See, Dawson, Restitution of Damages?, 20 Ohio St.L.J. 175, 186–187 (1959).

In land contract cases, specific performance is typically available as a remedy. Perhaps recapture of profits is more likely to be available when specific performance would have been a possible remedy but for the sale to an innocent purchaser. In some foreign legal systems, specific performance is more generally available than it is in the United States.

RESTATEMENT, SECOND, CONTRACTS § 360:

Comment:

e. *Contracts for the sale of land.* Contracts for the sale of land have traditionally been accorded a special place in the law of specific performance. A specific tract of land has long been regarded as unique and impossible of duplication by the use of any amount of money. Furthermore, the value of land is to some extent speculative. Damages have therefore been regarded as inadequate to enforce a duty to transfer an interest in land, even if it is less than a fee simple. Under this traditional view, the fact that the buyer has made a contract for the resale of the land to a third person does not deprive him of the right to specific performance. If he cannot convey the land to his purchaser, he will be held for damages for breach of the resale contract, and it is argued that these damages cannot be accurately determined without litigation. Granting him specific performance enables him to perform his own duty and to avoid litigation and damages.

Similarly, the seller who has not yet conveyed is generally granted specific performance on breach by the buyer. Here it is argued that, because the value of land is to some extent speculative, it may be difficult for him to prove with reasonable certainty the difference between the contract price and the market price of the land. Even if he can make this proof, the land may not be immediately convertible into money and he may be deprived of funds with which he could have made other investments. Furthermore, before the seller gets a judgment, the existence of the contract, even if broken by the buyer, operates as a clog on saleability, so that it may be difficult to find a purchaser at a fair price. The fact that specific performance is available to the buyer has sometimes been regarded as of some weight under the now discarded doctrine of "mutuality of remedy," but this is today of importance only because it enables a court to assure the vendee that he will receive the agreed performance if he is required to pay the price. The fact that legislation may have prohibited imprisonment as a means of enforcing a decree for the payment of money does not affect the seller's right to such a decree. After the seller has transferred the interest in the land to the buyer, however, and all that remains is for the buyer to pay the price, a money judgment for the amount of the price is an adequate remedy for the seller.

———

LACLEDE GAS CO. v. AMOCO OIL CO., 522 F.2d 33 (8th Cir.1975). The court held that a contract in which Amoco promised to supply Laclede with propane for sale to its customers should be specifically enforced against Amoco:

"Generally the determination of whether or not to order specific performance of a contract lies within the sound discretion of the trial court. However, this discretion is, in fact, quite limited; and it is said that when certain equitable rules have been met and the contract is fair and plain 'specific performance goes as a matter of right.'

"With this in mind we have carefully reviewed the very complete record on appeal and conclude that the trial court should grant the injunctive relief prayed. We are satisfied that this case falls within that category in which specific performance should be ordered as a matter of right.

"Amoco contends that four of the requirements for specific performance have not been met. Its claims are: (1) there is no mutuality of remedy in the contract; (2) the remedy of specific performance would be difficult for the court to administer without constant and long-continued supervision; (3) the contract is indefinite and uncertain; and (4) the remedy at law available to Laclede is adequate. The first three contentions have little or no merit and do not detain us for long.

"There is simply no requirement in the law that both parties be mutually entitled to the remedy of specific performance in order that one of them be given that remedy by the court.

"While a court may refuse to grant specific performance where such a decree would require constant and long-continued court supervision, there is merely a discretionary rule of decision which is frequently ignored when the public interest is involved.

"Here the public interest in providing propane to the retail customers is manifest, while any supervision required will be far from onerous.

"Section 370 of the Restatement of Contracts (1932) provides:

> 'Specific enforcement will not be decreed unless the terms of the contract are so expressed that the court can determine with reasonable certainty what is the duty of each party and the conditions under which performance is due.'

We believe these criteria have been satisfied here. As * * * to all developments for which a supplemental agreement has been signed, Amoco is to supply all the propane which is reasonably foreseeably required, while Laclede is to purchase the required propane from Amoco and pay the contract price therefor. The parties have disagreed over what is meant by 'Wood River Area Posted Price' in the agreement, but the district court can and should determine with reasonable certainty what the parties intended by this term and should mold its decree, if necessary accordingly. Likewise, the fact that the agreement does not have a definite time of duration is not fatal since the evidence established that the last subdivision should be converted to natural gas in 10 to 15 years. This sets a reasonable time limit on performance and the district court can and should mold the final decree to reflect this testimony.

"It is axiomatic that specific performance will not be ordered when the party claiming breach of contract has an adequate remedy at law. This is especially true when the contract involves personal property as distinguished from real estate.

"However, in Missouri, as elsewhere, specific performance may be ordered even though personalty is involved in the 'proper circumstances.' [UCC § 2–716(1)]. And a remedy at law adequate to defeat the grant of specific performance 'must be as certain, prompt, complete, and efficient to attain the ends of justice as a decree of specific performance.' National Marking Mach. Co. v. Triumph Mfg. Co., 13 F.2d 6, 9 (8th Cir.1926).

"One of the leading Missouri cases allowing specific performance of a contract relating to personalty because the remedy at law was inadequate is Boeving v. Vandover, 240 Mo.App. 117, 218 S.W.2d 175, 178 (1949). In that case the plaintiff sought specific performance of a contract in which the defendant had promised to sell him an automobile. At that time (near the end of and shortly after World War II) new cars were hard to come by, and the court held that specific performance was a proper remedy since a new car 'could not be obtained elsewhere except at considerable expense, trouble or loss, which cannot be estimated in advance.'

"We are satisfied that Laclede has brought itself within this practical approach taken by the Missouri courts. As Amoco points out, Laclede has propane immediately available to it under other contracts with other suppliers. And the evidence indicates that at the present time propane is readily available on the open market. However, this analysis ignores the fact that the contract involved in this lawsuit is for a long-term supply of propane to these subdivisions. The other two contracts under which Laclede obtains the gas will remain in force only until March 31, 1977, and April 1, 1981, respectively; and there is no assurance that Laclede will be able to receive any propane under them after that time. Also it is unclear as to whether or not Laclede can use the propane obtained under these contracts to supply the Jefferson County subdivisions, since they were originally entered into to provide Laclede with propane with which to 'shave' its natural gas supply during peak demand periods. Additionally, there was uncontradicted expert testimony that Laclede probably could not find another supplier of propane willing to enter into a long-term contract such as the Amoco agreement, given the uncertain future of worldwide energy supplies. And, even if Laclede could obtain supplies of propane for the affected developments through its present contracts or newly negotiated ones, it would still face considerable expense and trouble which cannot be estimated in advance in making arrangements for its distribution to the subdivisions.

"Specific performance is the proper remedy in this situation, and it should be granted by the district court."

RESTATEMENT, SECOND, CONTRACTS § 359:

Comment:

a. During the development of the jurisdiction of courts of equity, it came to be recognized that equitable relief would not be granted if the award of damages at law was adequate to protect the interests of the injured party. There is, however, a tendency to liberalize the granting of equitable relief by enlarging the classes of cases in which damages are not regarded as an adequate remedy. This tendency has been encouraged by the adoption of the Uniform Commercial Code, which "seeks to further a more liberal attitude than some courts have shown in connection with the specific performance of contracts of sale." Comment 1 to Uniform Commercial Code [§ 2–716]. In accordance with this tendency, if the adequacy of the damage remedy is uncertain, the combined effect of such other factors as uncertainty of terms (§ 362), insecurity as to the agreed exchange (§ 363) and difficulty of enforcement (§ 366) should be considered. Adequacy is to some extent relative, and the modern approach is to compare remedies to determine which is more effective in serving the ends of justice. Such a comparison will often lead to the granting of equitable relief. Doubts should be resolved in favor of the granting of specific performance or injunction.

———

See UCC §§ 2–716; 2–306(1). Is the seller entitled to specific performance under UCC Article 2? See UCC §§ 1–103; 1–109; 2–703; 2–709. For an example of a seller of goods obtaining specific performance when remedies are not controlled by the UCC, see Foley v. Classique Coaches, Ltd., [1934] 2 K.B. 1 (C.A.) (buyer promised to buy all its gasoline from seller).

———

For the view that specific performance should be routinely available to promisees who request it, see Schwartz, The Case for Specific Performance, 89 Yale L.J. 271 (1979). Professor Schwartz argues that damage awards are likely to be undercompensatory and that promisees have economic incentives not to seek specific performance unless necessary to protect their interests.

———

THE UNITED NATIONS CONVENTION ON CONTRACTS FOR THE INTERNATIONAL SALE OF GOODS:

Article 28

If, in accordance with the provisions of this Convention, one party is entitled to require performance of any obligation by the other party, a court is not bound to enter a judgment for specific performance unless the court would do so under its own law in respect of similar contracts of sale not governed by this Convention.

Article 46

(1) The buyer may require performance by the seller of his obligations unless the buyer has resorted to a remedy which is inconsistent with this requirement.

Article 62

The seller may require the buyer to pay the price, take delivery or perform his other obligations, unless the seller has resorted to a remedy which is inconsistent with this requirement.

AMERICAN BROADCASTING CO. v. WOLF

New York Court of Appeals, 1981.
52 N.Y.2d 394, 438 N.Y.S.2d 482, 420 N.E.2d 363.

COOKE, CHIEF JUDGE.

This case provides an interesting insight into the fierce competition in the television industry for popular performers and favorable ratings. It requires legal resolution of a rather novel employment imbroglio.

The issue is whether plaintiff American Broadcasting Companies, Incorporated (ABC), is entitled to equitable relief against defendant Warner Wolf, a New York City sportscaster, because of Wolf's breach of a good faith negotiation provision of a now expired broadcasting contract with ABC. In the present circumstances, it is concluded that the equitable relief sought by plaintiff—which would have the effect of forcing Wolf off the air—may not be granted.

I.

Warner Wolf, a sportscaster who has developed a rather colorful and unique on-the-air personality, had been employed by ABC since 1976. In February, 1978, ABC and Wolf entered into an employment agreement which, following exercise of renewal option, was to terminate on March 5, 1980. The contract contained a clause, known as a good-faith negotiation and first-refusal provision, that is at the crux of this litigation: "You agree, if we so elect, during the last ninety (90) days prior to the expiration of the extended term of this agreement, to enter into good faith negotiations with us for the extension of this agreement on mutually agreeable terms. You further agree that for the first forty-five (45) days of this renegotiation period, you will not negotiate for your services with any other person or company other than WABC–TV or ABC. In the event we are unable to reach an agreement for an extension by the expiration of the extended term hereof, you agree that you will not accept, in any market for a period of three (3) months following expiration of the extended term of this agreement, any offer of employment as a sportscaster, sports news reporter, commentator, program host, or analyst in broadcasting (including television, cable television, pay television and radio) without first giving us, in writing, an opportunity to employ you on substantially similar terms and you agree to enter into an agreement with us on such terms." Under this provision, Wolf was bound to negotiate in good faith with ABC for the 90-day period from December 6, 1979 through March 4, 1980. For the first 45 days, December 6 through January 19, the negotiation with ABC was to be exclusive. Following expiration of the 90-day negotiating period and the contract on March 5, 1980, Wolf was required, before *accepting* any other offer, to afford ABC a right of first refusal; he could comply with this provision either by refraining from accepting another offer or by first tendering the offer to ABC. The first-refusal period expired on June 3, 1980 and on June 4 Wolf was free to accept any job opportunity, without obligation to ABC.

Wolf first met with ABC executives in September, 1979 to discuss the terms of a renewal contract. Counterproposals were exchanged, and the parties agreed to finalize the matter by October 15. Meanwhile, unbeknownst to ABC, Wolf met with representatives of CBS in early October. Wolf related his employment requirements and also discussed the first refusal-good faith negotiation clause of his ABC contract. Wolf furnished CBS a copy of that portion of the ABC agreement. On October 12, ABC officials and Wolf met, but were unable to reach agreement on a renewal contract. A few days later, on October 16 Wolf again discussed employment possibilities with CBS.

Not until January 2, 1980 did ABC again contact Wolf. At that time, ABC expressed its willingness to meet substantially all of his demands. Wolf rejected the offer, however, citing ABC's delay in communicating with him and his desire to explore his options in light of the impending expiration of the 45-day exclusive negotiation period.

On February 1, 1980, after termination of that exclusive period, Wolf and CBS orally agreed on the terms of Wolf's employment as sportscaster for WCBS–TV, a CBS-owned affiliate in New York. During the next two days, CBS informed Wolf that it had prepared two agreements and divided his annual compensation between the two: one covered his services as an on-the-air sportscaster, and the other was an off-the-air production agreement for sports specials Wolf was to produce. The production agreement contained an exclusivity clause which barred Wolf from performing "services of any nature for" or permitting the use of his "name, likeness, voice or endorsement by, any person, firm or corporation" during the term of the agreement, unless CBS consented. The contract had an effective date of March 6, 1980.

Wolf signed the CBS production agreement on February 4, 1980. At the same time, CBS agreed in writing, in consideration of $100 received from Wolf, to hold open an offer of employment to Wolf as sportscaster until June 4, 1980, the date on which Wolf became free from ABC's right of first refusal. The next day, February 5, Wolf submitted a letter of resignation to ABC.

Representatives of ABC met with Wolf on February 6 and made various offers and promises that Wolf rejected. Wolf informed ABC that they had delayed negotiations with him and downgraded his worth. He stated he had no future with the company. He told the officials he had made a "gentlemen's agreement" and would leave ABC on March 5. Later in February, Wolf and ABC agreed that Wolf would continue to appear on the air during a portion of the first-refusal period, from March 6 until May 28.[1]

ABC commenced this action on May 6, 1980, by which time Wolf's move to CBS had become public knowledge. The complaint alleged that Wolf, induced by CBS breached both the good-faith negotiation and first-refusal provisions of his contract with ABC. ABC sought specific enforcement of its right of first refusal and an injunction against Wolf's employment as a sportscaster with CBS.

After a trial, Supreme Court found no breach of the contract, and went on to note that, in any event, equitable relief would be inappropriate. A divided Appellate Division, while concluding that Wolf had breached both the good-faith negotiation and first-refusal provisions, nonetheless affirmed on the ground that equitable intervention was unwarranted. There should be an affirmance.

II.

Initially, we agree with the Appellate Division that defendant Wolf breached his obligation to negotiate in good faith with ABC from December, 1979 through March, 1980. When Wolf signed the production agreement with CBS on February 4, 1980, he obligated himself not to render services "of any nature" to any person, firm or corporation on and after March 6, 1980. Quite simply, then, beginning on February 4 Wolf was unable to extend his contract with ABC; his contract with CBS precluded him from legally serving ABC in any capacity after March 5. Given Wolf's existing obligation to CBS, any negotiations he engaged in with ABC, without the consent of CBS, after February 4 were meaningless and could not have been in good faith.

At the same time, there is no basis in the record for the Appellate Division's conclusion that Wolf violated the first-refusal provision by

---

1. The agreement also provided that on or after June 4, 1980 Wolf was free to "accept an offer of employment with anyone of [his] choosing and immediately begin performing on-air services." The par- ties agreed that their rights and obligations under the original employment contract were in no way affected by the extension of employment.

entering into an oral sportscasting contract with CBS on February 4. The first-refusal provision required Wolf, for a period of 90 days after termination of the ABC agreement, either to refrain from accepting an offer of employment or to first submit the offer to ABC for its consideration. By its own terms, the right of first refusal did not apply to offers accepted by Wolf prior to the March 5 termination of the ABC employment contract. It is apparent, therefore, that Wolf could not have breached the right of first refusal by accepting an offer during the term of his employment with ABC.[2] Rather, his conduct violates only the good-faith negotiation clause of the contract. The question is whether this breach entitled ABC to injunctive relief that would bar Wolf from continued employment at CBS.[3] To resolve this issue, it is necessary to trace the principles of specific performance applicable to personal service contracts.

III.

–A–

Courts of equity historically have refused to order an individual to perform a contract for personal services. Originally this rule evolved because of the inherent difficulties courts would encounter in supervising the performance of uniquely personal efforts.[4] During the Civil War era, there emerged a more compelling reason for not directing the performance of personal services: the Thirteenth Amendment's prohibition of involuntary servitude. It has been strongly suggested that judicial compulsion of services would violate the express command of that amendment. For practical, policy and constitutional reasons,

2. In any event, the carefully tailored written agreement between Wolf and CBS consisted only of an option prior to June 4, 1979. Acceptance of CBS's offer of employment as a sportscaster did not occur until after the expiration of the first-refusal period on June 4, 1979.

3. In its complaint, ABC originally sought specific enforcement of the right of first refusal. ABC now suggests that Wolf be enjoined from performing services for CBS for a two-year period. Alternatively, ABC requests this court to "turn the clock back to February 1, 1980" by: (1) setting aside Wolf's agreement with CBS and enjoining CBS from enforcing the agreement; (2) ordering Wolf to enter into good-faith negotiations with ABC for at least the period remaining under the negotiation clause when Wolf breached it; (3) ordering Wolf to honor the 90-day first-refusal period should the parties fail to reach agreement; and (4) enjoining CBS from negotiating with Wolf "for a period sufficient to render meaningful the above-described relief".

4. The New York Court of Chancery in De Rivafinoli v. Corsetti (4 Paige Chs. 264, 270) eloquently articulated the traditional rationale for refusing affirmative enforcement of personal service contracts: "I am not aware that any officer of this court has that perfect knowledge of the Italian language, or possesses that exquisite sensibility in the auricular nerve which is necessary to understand, and to enjoy with a proper zest, the peculiar beauties of the Italian opera, so fascinating to the fashionable world. There might be some difficulty, therefore, even if the defendant was compelled to sing under the direction and in the presence of a master in chancery, in ascertaining whether he performed his engagement according to its spirit and intent. It would also be very difficult for the master to determine what effect coercion might produce upon the defendant's singing, especially in the livelier airs; although the fear of imprisonment would unquestionably deepen his seriousness in the graver parts of the drama. But one thing at least is certain; his songs will be neither comic, or even semi-serious, while he remains confined in that dismal cage, the debtor's prison of New York."

therefore, courts continue to decline to affirmatively enforce employment contracts.

Over the years, however, in certain narrowly tailored situations, the law fashioned other remedies for failure to perform an employment agreement. Thus, where an employee refuses to render services to an employer in violation of an existing contract, and the services are unique or extraordinary, an injunction may issue to prevent the employee from furnishing those services to another person for the duration of the contract. Such "negative enforcement" was initially available only when the employee had expressly stipulated not to compete with the employer for the term of the engagement (see, e.g., Lumley v. Wagner, 1 De G.M. & G. 604, 42 Eng.Rep. 687; Shubert Theatrical Co. v. Rath, 271 F. 827, 830–833; 4 Pomeroy, Equity Jurisprudence [5th ed.], § 1343, at p. 944). Later cases permitted injunctive relief where the circumstances justified implication of a negative covenant. In these situations, an injunction is warranted because the employee either expressly or by clear implication agreed not to work elsewhere for the period of his contract. And, since the services must be unique before negative enforcement will be granted, irreparable harm will befall the employer should the employee be permitted to labor for a competitor.

–B–

After a personal service contract terminates, the availability of equitable relief against the former employee diminishes appreciably. Since the period of service has expired, it is impossible to decree affirmative or negative specific performance. Only if the employee has expressly agreed not to compete with the employer following the term of the contract, or is threatening to disclose trade secrets or commit another tortious act, is injunctive relief generally available at the behest of the employer. Even where there is an express anticompetitive covenant, however, it will be rigorously examined and specifically enforced only if it satisfies certain established requirements. There is, in short, general judicial disfavor of anticompetitive covenants contained in employment contracts.

Underlying the strict approach to enforcement of these covenants is the notion that, once the term of an employment agreement has expired, the general public policy favoring robust and uninhibited competition should not give way merely because a particular employer wishes to insulate himself from competition. Important, too, are the "powerful considerations of public policy which militate against sanctioning the loss of a man's livelihood" (Purchasing Assoc. v. Weitz, 13 N.Y.2d at p. 272, 246 N.Y.S.2d 600, 196 N.E.2d 245). At the same time, the employer is entitled to protection from unfair or illegal conduct that causes economic injury. The rules governing enforcement of anticompetitive covenants and the availability of equitable relief after termination of employment are designed to foster these interests of the employer without impairing the employee's ability to earn a living or the general competitive mold of society. * * *

IV.

Applying these principles, it is apparent that ABC's request for injunctive relief must fail. There is no existing employment agreement between the parties; the original contract terminated in March, 1980. Thus, the negative enforcement that might be appropriate during the term of employment is unwarranted here. Nor is there an express anticompetitive covenant that defendant Wolf is violating, or any claim of special injury from tortious conduct such as exploitation of trade secrets. In short, ABC seeks to premise equitable relief after termination of the employment upon a simple, albeit serious, breach of a general contract negotiation clause.[7] To grant an injunction in that situation would be to unduly interfere with an individual's livelihood and to inhibit free competition where there is no corresponding injury to the employer other than the loss of a competitive edge. Indeed, if relief were granted here, any breach of an employment contract provision relating to renewal negotiations logically would serve as the basis for an open-ended restraint upon the employee's ability to earn a living should he ultimately choose not extend his employment.[8] Our public policy, which favors the free exchange of goods and services through established market mechanisms, dictates otherwise.

Equally unavailing is ABC's request that the court create a noncompetitive covenant by implication. Although in a proper case an implied-in-fact covenant not to compete for the term of employment may be found to exist, anticompetitive covenants covering the postemployment period will not be implied. Indeed, even an express covenant will be scrutinized and enforced only in accordance with established principles.

This is not to say that ABC has not been damaged in some fashion or that Wolf should escape responsibility for the breach of his good-faith negotiation obligation.[10] Rather, we merely conclude that ABC is

---

7. Even if Wolf had breached the first-refusal provision, it does not necessarily follow that injunctive relief would be available. Outside the personal service area, the usual equitable remedy for breach of a first-refusal clause is to order the breaching party to perform the contract with the person possessing the first-refusal right (e.g., 5A Corbin, Contracts, § 1197, at pp. 377–378). When personal services are involved, this would result in an affirmative injunction ordering the employee to perform services for plaintiff. Such relief, as discussed, cannot be granted.

8. Interestingly, the negative enforcement ABC seeks—an injunction barring Wolf from broadcasting for CBS—is for a two-year period. ABC's request is premised upon the fact that Wolf and CBS entered into a two-year agreement. Had the agreement been for 10 years, presumably ABC would have requested a 10-year restraint. In short, since it lacks an express anticompetitive clause to enforce, plaintiff seeks to measure its relief in a manner unrelated to the breach or the injury. This well illustrates one of the reasons why the law requires an express anticompetitive clause before it will restrain an employee from competing after termination of the employment.

10. It should be noted that the dissenter would ground relief upon the first-refusal clause, a provision of the contract that defendant did not breach. The dissenting opinion fails to specify why the first-refusal clause—or for that matter any other provision of the contract that defendant did not

not entitled to equitable relief. Because of the unique circumstances presented, however, this decision is without prejudice to ABC's right to pursue relief in the form of monetary damages, if it be so advised.

Accordingly, the order of the Appellate Division should be affirmed.

FUCHSBERG, JUDGE (dissenting).

I agree with all the members of this court, as had all the Justices at the Appellate Division, that the defendant Wolf breached his undisputed obligation to negotiate in good faith for renewal of his contract with ABC. Where we part company is in the majority's unwillingness to mold an equitable decree, even one more limited than the harsh one the plaintiff proposed, to right the wrong.

Central to the disposition of this case is the first-refusal provision. Its terms are worth recounting. They plainly provide that, in the 90-day period immediately succeeding the termination of his ABC contract, before Wolf could accept a position as sportscaster with another company, he first had to afford ABC the opportunity to engage him on like terms. True, he was not required to entertain offers, whether from ABC or anyone else, during that period. In that event he, of course, would be off the air for that 90 days, during which ABC could attempt to orient its listeners from Wolf to his successor. On the other hand, if Wolf wished to continue to broadcast actively during the 90 days, ABC's right of first refusal put it in a position to make sure that Wolf was not doing so for a competitor. One way or the other, however labeled, the total effect of the first refusal agreement was that of an express conditional covenant under which Wolf could be restricted from appearing on the air other than for ABC for the 90-day posttermination period. * * *

In the face of these considerations, the majority rationalizes its position of powerlessness to grant equitable relief by choosing to interpret the contract as though there were no restrictive covenant, express or implied. However, as demonstrated, there is, in fact, an express three-month negative covenant which, because of Wolf's misconduct, ABC was effectively denied the opportunity to exercise. Enforcement of this covenant, by enjoining Wolf from broadcasting for a three-month period, would depart from no entrenched legal precedent. Rather, it would accord with equity's boasted flexibility.

breach—is relevant in determining the availability of equitable relief. And, while the dissent correctly noted the flexibility of equitable remedies, this does not mean that courts of equity totally dispense with governing rules. Our analysis of the relevant principles, guided by important underlying policy considerations, reveals that this case falls well beyond the realm where equitable intervention would be permissible.

The dissenting opinion would now create a new agreement for the parties, and apply the first-refusal clause backwards into the period of the ABC employment, under the guise of equitable interpretation. Although the reach of equity may be broad, so far as we are aware equitable principles have never sanctioned the creation of a new and different contract between sophisticated parties merely to condemn conduct which was permissible under an actual written agreement.

That said, a few words are in order regarding the majority's insistence that Wolf did not breach the first-refusal clause. It is remarkable that, to this end, it has to ignore its own crediting of the Appellate Division's express finding that, as far back as February 1, 1980, fully a month before the ABC contract was to terminate, "Wolf and CBS orally agreed on the terms of Wolf's employment as sportscaster for WCBS–TV". It follows that the overt written CBS–Wolf option contract, which permitted Wolf to formally accept the CBS sportscasting offer at the end of the first-refusal period, was nothing but a charade. * * *

JASEN, GABRIELLI, JONES, WACHTLER and MEYER, JJ., concur with COOKE, C.J.

FUCHSBERG, J., dissents in part and votes to modify in a separate opinion.

Order affirmed, with costs.

SECTION 3: AGREED REMEDIES

LAKE RIVER CORP. v. CARBORUNDUM CO.

United States Court of Appeals, Seventh Circuit, 1985.
769 F.2d 1284.

POSNER, CIRCUIT JUDGE:

This diversity suit between Lake River Corporation and Carborundum Company requires us to consider questions of Illinois commercial law, and in particular to explore the fuzzy line between penalty clauses and liquidated-damages clauses.

Carborundum manufactures "Ferro Carbo," an abrasive powder used in making steel. To serve its midwestern customers better, Carborundum made a contract with Lake River by which the latter agreed to provide distribution services in its warehouse in Illinois. Lake River would receive Ferro Carbo in bulk from Carborundum, "bag" it, and ship the bagged product to Carborundum's customers. The Ferro Carbo would remain Carborundum's property until delivered to the customers.

Carborundum insisted that Lake River install a new bagging system to handle the contract. In order to be sure of being able to recover the cost of the new system ($89,000) and make a profit of 20 percent of the contract price, Lake River insisted on the following minimum-quantity guarantee:

> In consideration of the special equipment [i.e., the new bagging system] to be acquired and furnished by LAKE–RIVER for handling the product, CARBORUNDUM shall, during the initial three-year term of this Agreement, ship to LAKE–RIVER for bagging a minimum quantity of [22,500 tons]. If, at the end of the three-year

term, this minimum quantity shall not have been shipped, LAKE–RIVER shall invoice CARBORUNDUM at the then prevailing rates for the difference between the quantity bagged and the minimum guaranteed.

If Carborundum had shipped the full minimum quantity that it guaranteed, it would have owed Lake River roughly $533,000 under the contract.

After the contract was signed in 1979, the demand for domestic steel, and with it the demand for Ferro Carbo, plummeted, and Carborundum failed to ship the guaranteed amount. When the contract expired late in 1982, Carborundum had shipped only 12,000 of the 22,500 tons it had guaranteed. Lake River had bagged the 12,000 tons and had billed Carborundum for this bagging, and Carborundum had paid, but by virtue of the formula in the minimum-guarantee clause Carborundum still owed Lake River $241,000—the contract price of $533,000 if the full amount of Ferro Carbo had been shipped, minus what Carborundum had paid for the bagging of the quantity it had shipped.

When Lake River demanded payment of this amount, Carborundum refused, on the ground that the formula imposed a penalty.

*   *   *

Lake River brought this suit for $241,000, which it claims as liquidated damages. [The district judge, after a non-jury trial, awarded this amount to Lake River as liquidated damages.]

The hardest issue in the case is whether the formula in the minimum-guarantee clause imposes a penalty for breach of contract or is merely an effort to liquidate damages. Deep as the hostility to penalty clauses runs in the common law, see Loyd, *Penalties and Forfeitures,* 29 Harv.L.Rev. 117 (1915), we still might be inclined to question, if we thought ourselves free to do so, whether a modern court should refuse to enforce a penalty clause where the signator is a substantial corporation, well able to avoid improvident commitments. Penalty clauses provide an earnest of performance. The clause here enhanced Carborundum's credibility in promising to ship the minimum amount guaranteed by showing that it was willing to pay the full contract price even if it failed to ship anything. On the other side it can be pointed out that by raising the cost of a breach of contract to the contract breaker, a penalty clause increases the risk to his other creditors; increases (what is the same thing and more, because bankruptcy imposes "deadweight" social costs) the risk of bankruptcy; and could amplify the business cycle by increasing the number of bankruptcies in bad times, which is when contracts are most likely to be broken. But since little effort is made to prevent businessmen from assuming risks, these reasons are no better than makeweights.

A better argument is that a penalty clause may discourage efficient as well as inefficient breaches of contract. Suppose a breach would cost the promisee $12,000 in actual damages but would yield the promisor

$20,000 in additional profits. Then there would be a net social gain from breach. After being fully compensated for his loss the promisee would be no worse off than if the contract had been performed, while the promisor would be better off by $8,000. But now suppose the contract contains a penalty clause under which the promisor if he breaks his promise must pay the promisee $25,000. The promisor will be discouraged from breaking the contract, since $25,000, the penalty, is greater than $20,000, the profits of the breach; and a transaction that would have increased value will be forgone.

On this view, since compensatory damages should be sufficient to deter inefficient breaches (that is, breaches that cost the victim more than the gain to the contract breaker), penal damages could have no effect other than to deter some efficient breaches. But this overlooks the earlier point that the willingness to agree to a penalty clause is a way of making the promisor and his promise credible and may therefore be essential to inducing some value-maximizing contracts to be made. It also overlooks the more important point that the parties (always assuming they are fully competent) will, in deciding whether to include a penalty clause in their contract, weigh the gains against the costs—costs that include the possibility of discouraging an efficient breach somewhere down the road—and will include the clause only if the benefits exceed those costs as well as all other costs.

On this view the refusal to enforce penalty clauses is (at best) paternalistic—and it seems odd that courts should display parental solicitude for large corporations. But however this may be, we must be on guard to avoid importing our own ideas of sound public policy into an area where our proper judicial role is more than usually deferential. The responsibility for making innovations in the common law of Illinois rests with the courts of Illinois, and not with the federal courts in Illinois. And like every other state, Illinois, untroubled by academic skepticism of the wisdom of refusing to enforce penalty clauses against sophisticated promisors, see, e.g., Goetz & Scott, *Liquidated Damages, Penalties and the Just Compensation Principle*, 77 Colum.L.Rev. 554 (1977), continues steadfastly to insist on the distinction between penalties and liquidated damages. To be valid under Illinois law a liquidation of damages must be a reasonable estimate at the time of contracting of the likely damages from breach, and the need for estimation at that time must be shown by reference to the likely difficulty of measuring the actual damages from a breach of contract after the breach occurs. If damages would be easy to determine then, or if the estimate greatly exceeds a reasonable upper estimate of what the damages are likely to be, it is a penalty.

The distinction between a penalty and liquidated damages is not an easy one to draw in practice but we are required to draw it and can give only limited weight to the district court's determination. Whether a provision for damages is a penalty clause or a liquidated-damages clause is a question of law rather than fact, and unlike some courts of appeals we do not treat a determination by a federal district judge of an issue of state law as if it were a finding of fact, and reverse only if persuaded that clear error has occurred, though we give his determination respectful consideration.

Mindful that Illinois courts resolve doubtful cases in favor of classification as a penalty, we conclude that the damage formula in this case is a penalty and not a liquidation of damages, because it is designed always to assure Lake River more than its actual damages. The formula—full contract price minus the amount already invoiced to Carborundum—is invariant to the gravity of the breach. When a contract specifies a single sum in damages for any and all breaches even though it is apparent that all are not of the same gravity, the specification is not a reasonable effort to estimate damages; and when in addition the fixed sum greatly exceeds the actual damages likely to be inflicted by a minor breach, its character as a penalty becomes unmistakable. This case is within the gravitational field of these principles even though the minimum-guarantee clause does not fix a single sum as damages.

Suppose to begin with that the breach occurs the day after Lake River buys its new bagging system for $89,000 and before Carborundum ships any Ferro Carbo. Carborundum would owe Lake River $533,000. Since Lake River would have incurred at that point a total cost of only $89,000, its net gain from the breach would be $444,000. This is more than four times the profit of $107,000 (20 percent of the contract price of $533,000) that Lake River expected to make from the contract if it had been performed: a huge windfall.

Next suppose (as actually happened here) that breach occurs when 55 percent of the Ferro Carbo has been shipped. Lake River would already have received $293,000 from Carborundum. To see what its costs then would have been (as estimated at the time of contracting), first subtract Lake River's anticipated profit on the contract of $107,000 from the total contract price of $533,000. The difference—Lake River's total cost of performance—is $426,000. Of this, $89,000 is the cost of the new bagging system, a fixed cost. The rest ($426,000 − $89,000 = $337,000) presumably consists of variable costs that are roughly proportional to the amount of Ferro Carbo bagged; there is no indication of any other fixed costs. Assume, therefore, that if Lake River bagged 55 percent of the contractually agreed quantity, it incurred in doing so 55 percent of its variable costs, or $185,000. When this is added to the cost of the new bagging system, assumed for the moment to be worthless except in connection with the contract, the total cost of performance to Lake River is $274,000. Hence a breach that occurred after 55 percent of contractual performance was complete would be expected to yield Lake River a modest profit of $19,000 ($293,000–$274,000). But now add the "liquidated damages" of $241,000 that Lake River claims, and the result is a total gain from the breach of $260,000, which is almost two and a half times the profit that

Lake River expected to gain if there was no breach. And this ignores any use value or salvage value of the new bagging system, which is the property of Lake River—though admittedly it also ignores the time value of money; Lake River paid $89,000 for that system before receiving any revenue from the contract.

To complete the picture, assume that the breach had not occurred till performance was 90 percent complete. Then the "liquidated damages" clause would not be so one-sided, but it would be one-sided. Carborundum would have paid $480,000 for bagging. Against this, Lake River would have incurred its fixed cost of $89,000 plus 90 percent of its variable costs of $337,000, or $303,000. Its total costs would thus be $392,000, and its net profit $88,000. But on top of this it would be entitled to "liquidated damages" of $53,000, for a total profit of $141,000—more than 30 percent more than its expected profit of $107,000 if there was no breach.

The reason for these results is that most of the costs to Lake River of performing the contract are saved if the contract is broken, and this saving is not reflected in the damage formula. As a result, at whatever point in the life of the contract a breach occurs, the damage formula gives Lake River more than its lost profits from the breach—dramatically more if the breach occurs at the beginning of the contract; tapering off at the end, it is true. Still, over the interval between the beginning of Lake River's performance and nearly the end, the clause could be expected to generate profits ranging from 400 percent of the expected contract profits to 130 percent of those profits. And this is on the assumption that the bagging system has no value apart from the contract. If it were worth only $20,000 to Lake River, the range would be 434 percent to 150 percent.

Lake River argues that it would never get as much as the formula suggests, because it would be requird to mitigate its damages. This is a dubious argument on several grounds. First, mitigation of damages is a doctrine of the law of court-assessed damages, while the point of a liquidated-damages clause is to substitute party assessment; and that point is blunted, and the certainty that liquidated-damages clauses are designed to give the process of assessing damages impaired, if a defendant can force the plaintiff to take less than the damages specified in the clause, on the ground that the plaintiff could have avoided some of them. It would seem therefore that the clause in this case should be read to eliminate any duty of mitigation, that what Lake River is doing is attempting to rewrite the clause to make it more reasonable, and that since actually the clause is designed to give Lake River the full damages it would incur from breach (and more) even if it made no effort to find a substitute use for the equipment that it bought to perform the contract, this is just one more piece of evidence that it is a penalty clause rather than a liquidated-damages clause.

But in any event mitigation would not mitigate the penal character of this clause. If Carborundum did not ship the guaranteed minimum quantity, the reason was likely to be—the reason was—that the steel industry had fallen on hard times and the demand for Ferro Carbo was therefore down. In these circumstances Lake River would have little prospect of finding a substitute contract that would yield it significant profits to set off against the full contract price, which is the method by which it proposes to take account of mitigation. At argument Lake River suggested that it might at least have been able to sell the new bagging equipment to someone for something, and the figure $40,000 was proposed. If the breach occurred on the first day when performance under the contract was due and Lake River promptly sold the bagging equipment for $40,000, its liquidated damages would fall to $493,000. But by the same token its costs would fall to $49,000. Its profit would still be $444,000, which as we said was more than 400 percent of its expected profit on the contract. The penal component would be unaffected.

With the penalty clause in this case compare the liquidated-damages clause in *Arduini v. Board of Education,* [93 Ill.App.3d 925, 49 Ill.Dec. 460, 418 N.E.2d 104, rev'd on other grounds, 92 Ill.2d 197, 65 Ill.Dec. 281, 441 N.E.2d 73 (1982).] which is representative of such clauses upheld in Illinois. The plaintiff was a public school teacher whose contract provided that if he resigned before the end of the school year he would be docked 4 percent of his salary. This was a modest fraction of the contract price. And the cost to the school of an untimely resignation would be difficult to measure. Since that cost would be greater the more senior and experienced the teacher was, the fact that the liquidated damages would be greater the higher the teacher's salary did not make the clause arbitrary. Even the fact that the liquidated damages were the same whether the teacher resigned at the beginning, the middle, or the end of the school year was not arbitrary, for it was unclear how the amount of actual damages would vary with the time of resignation. Although one might think that the earlier the teacher resigned the greater the damage to the school would be, the school might find it easier to hire a replacement for the whole year or a great part of it than to bring in a replacement at the last minute to grade the exams left behind by the resigning teacher. Here, in contrast, it is apparent from the face of the contract that the damages provided for by the "liquidated damages" clause are grossly disproportionate to any probable loss and penalize some breaches much more heavily than others regardless of relative cost.

We do not mean by this discussion to cast a cloud of doubt over the "take or pay" clauses that are a common feature of contracts between natural gas pipeline companies and their customers. Such clauses require the customer, in consideration of the pipeline's extending its line to his premises, to take a certain amount of gas at a specified price—and if he fails to take it to pay the full price anyway. The resemblance to the minimum-guarantee clause in the present case is obvious, but perhaps quite superficial. Neither party has mentioned take-or-pay clauses, and we can find no case where such a clause was

even challenged as a penalty clause—though in one case it was argued
that such a clause made the damages unreasonably low. See *National
Fuel Gas Distribution Corp. v. Pennsylvania Public Utility Comm'n*, 76
Pa.Commw. 102, 126–27 n. 8, 464 A.2d 546, 558 n. 8 (1983). If, as
appears not to be the case here but would often be the case in supplying
natural gas, a supplier's fixed costs were a very large fraction of his
total costs, a take-or-pay clause might well be a reasonable liquidation
of damages. In the limit, if *all* the supplier's costs were incurred before
he began supplying the customer, the contract revenues would be an
excellent measure of the damages from breach. But in this case, the
supplier (Lake River, viewed as a supplier of bagging services to
Carborundum) incurred only a fraction of its costs before performance
began, and the interruption of performance generated a considerable
cost saving that is not reflected in the damage formula.

The fact that the damage formula is invalid does not deprive Lake
River of a remedy. The parties did not contract explicitly with reference to the measure of damages if the agreed-on damage formula was
invalidated, but all this means is that the victim of the breach is
entitled to his common law damages. See, e.g., Restatement, Second,
Contracts § 356, comment a (1981). In this case that would be the
unpaid contract price of $241,000 minus the costs that Lake River saved
by not having to complete the contract (the variable costs on the other
45 percent of the Ferro Carbo that it never had to bag). The case must
be remanded to the district judge to fix these damages. * * *

Arguments Against Invalidating Penalty Clauses

In addition to the arguments stated in *Lake River* by Judge Posner,
economic analysis has been used to urge, (1) that the rule invalidating
penalty clauses does not take account of the fact that the promisor will
insist on a price sufficient to cover the increased risk, (2) that what
appears to the court to be a penalty may be the result of the parties'
different perceptions of the risk of breach, and (3) that if, as many
argue, expectancy damages are undercompensatory, permitting the
parties to stipulate damages makes efficient breach more, not less,
likely, and permits the parties to divide the gains resulting from an
efficient breach. See, e.g., Kornhhauser, An Introduction to the Economic Analysis of Contract Remedies, 57 U.Colo.L.Rev. 683, 720–721
(1986).

Are these arguments convincing? If they are accepted, would it be
necessary for courts to police against bargain distortion by fraud and
abuse of bargaining power? Might the promisee have an incentive to
cause a breach in ways that would be difficult to trace to the promisee?
Are the benefits of permitting unlimited freedom in stipulating damages greater than the costs of detecting bargain distortion and induced
breach?

CALIFORNIA AND HAWAIIAN SUGAR CO. v. SUN SHIP, INC.

United States Court of Appeals, Ninth Circuit, 1986.
794 F.2d 1433, amended, 811 F.2d 1264 (1986), cert. denied, 484 U.S. 871, 108
S.Ct. 200, 98 L.Ed.2d 151 (1987).

NOONAN, CIRCUIT JUDGE. * * *

BACKGROUND

C and H is an agricultural cooperative owned by fourteen sugar plantations in Hawaii. Its business consists in transporting raw sugar—the crushed cane in the form of coarse brown crystal—to its refinery in Crockett, California. Roughly one million tons a year of sugar are harvested in Hawaii. A small portion is refined there; the bulk goes to Crockett. The refined sugar—the white stuff—is sold by C and H to groceries for home consumption and to the soft drink and cereal companies that are its industrial customers.

To conduct its business, C and H has an imperative need for assured carriage for the raw sugar from the islands. Sugar is a seasonal crop, with 70 percent of the harvest occurring between April and October, while almost nothing is harvestable during December and January. Consequently, transportation must not only be available, but seasonably available. Storage capacity in Hawaii accommodates not more than a quarter of the crop. Left stored on the ground or left unharvested, sugar suffers the loss of sucrose and goes to waste. Shipping ready and able to carry the raw sugar is a priority for C and H.

In 1979 C and H was notified that Matson Navigation Company, which had been supplying the bulk of the necessary shipping, was withdrawing its services as of January 1981. While C and H had some ships at its disposal, it found a pressing need for a large new vessel, to be in service at the height of the sugar season in 1981. It decided to commission the building of a kind of hybrid—a tug of catamaran design with two hulls and, joined to the tug, a barge with a wedge which would lock between the two pontoons of the tug, producing an "integrated tug barge." In Hawaiian, the barge and the entire vessel were each described as a Mocababoo or push boat.

C and H relied on the architectural advice of the New York firm, J.J. Henry. It solicited bids from shipyards, indicating as an essential term a "preferred delivery date" of June 1981. It decided to accept Sun's offer to build the barge and Halter's offer to build the tug.

In the fall of 1979 C and H entered into negotiations with Sun on the precise terms of the contract. Each company was represented by a vice-president with managerial responsibility in the area of negotiation; each company had a team of negotiators; each company had the advice of counsel in drafting the agreement that was signed on November 14, 1979. * * *

Under Article I of the agreement, Sun was entitled to an extension of the delivery date for the usual types of force majeure and for "unavailability of the Tug to Contractor for joining to the Vessel, where it is determined that Contractor has complied with all obligations under the Interface Agreement." (The Interface Agreement, executed the same day between C and H, Sun, and Halter provided that Sun would connect the barge with the tug.) Article 17 "Delivery" provided that "the Vessel shall be offered for delivery fully and completely connected with the Tug." Article 8, "Liquidated Damages for Delay in Delivery" provided that if "Delivery of the Vessel" was not made on "the Delivery Date" of June 30, 1981, Sun would pay C and H "as per-day liquidated damages, and not as a penalty" a sum described as "a reasonable measure of the damages"—$17,000 per day.

On the same date C and H entered into an agreement with Halter to purchase "one oceangoing catamaran tug boat" for $20,350,000. The tug (the "Vessel" of that contract) was to be delivered on April 30, 1981 at Sun's shipyard. Liquidated damages of $10,000 per day were provided for Halter's failure to deliver.

Halter did not complete the tug until July 15, 1982. Sun did not complete the barge until March 16, 1982. Tug and barge were finally connected under C and H's direction in mid-July 1982 and christened the Moku Pahu. C and H settled its claim against Halter. Although Sun paid C and H $17,000 per day from June 30, 1981 until January 10, 1982, it ultimately denied liability for any damages, and this lawsuit resulted.

ANALYSIS

Sun contends that its obligation was to deliver the barge connected to the tug on the delivery date of June 30, 1981 and that only the failure to deliver the integrated hybrid would have triggered the liquidated damage clause. It is true that Article 17 creates some ambiguity by specifying that the Vessel is to be "offered for delivery completely connected with the Tug." The case of the barge being ready while the tug was not, is not explicitly considered. Nonetheless, the meaning of "Vessel" is completely unambiguous. From the "Whereas" clause to the articles of the agreement dealing with insurance, liens, and title, "the Vessel" is the barge. It would require the court to rewrite the contract to find that "the Vessel" in Article 8 on liquidated damages does not mean the barge. The article takes effect on failure to deliver "the Vessel"—that is, the barge.

Sun contends, however, that on such a reading of the contract, the $17,000 per day is a penalty, not to be enforced by the court. The barge, Sun points out, was useless to C and H without the tug. Unconnected, the barge was worse than useless—it was an expensive liability. C and H did not want the barge by itself. To get $17,000 per day as "damages" for failure to provide an unwanted and unusable craft is, Sun says, to exact a penalty. C and H seeks to be "paid according to the tenour of the bond"; it "craves the law." And if C and

H sticks to the letter of the bond, it must like Shylock end by losing; a court of justice will not be so vindictive. Breach of contract entitles the wronged party only to fair compensation.

Seductive as Sun's argument is, it does not carry the day. Represented by sophisticated representatives, C and H and Sun reached the agreement that $17,000 a day was the reasonable measure of the loss C and H would suffer if the barge was not ready. Of course they assumed that the tug would be ready. But in reasonable anticipation of the damages that would occur if the tug was ready and the barge was not, Article 8 was adopted. As the parties foresaw the situation, C and H would have a tug waiting connection but no barge and so no shipping. The anticipated damages were what might be expected if C and H could not transport the Hawaiian sugar crop at the height of the season. Those damages were clearly before both parties. As Joe Kleschick, Sun's chief negotiator, testified, he had "a vision" of a "mountain of sugar piling up in Hawaii"—a vision that C and H conjured up in negotiating the damage clause. Given the anticipated impact on C and H's raw sugar and on C and H's ability to meet the demands of its grocery and industrial customers if the sugar could not be transported, liquidated damages of $17,000 a day were completely reasonable.

The situation as it developed was different from the anticipation. The barge was not ready but neither was the tug. C and H was in fact able to find other shipping. The crop did not rot. The customers were not left sugarless. Sun argues that, measured by the actual damages suffered, the liquidated damages were penal.

We look to Pennsylvania law for guidance. Although no Pennsylvania case is squarely on point, it is probable that Pennsylvania would interpret the contract as a sale of goods governed by the Uniform Commercial Code. The governing statute provides that liquidated damages are considered reasonable "in the light of anticipated or actual harm." 2–718(1) [UCC].

The choice of the disjunctive appears to be deliberate. The language chosen is in harmony with the Restatement (Second) of Contracts § 356 (1979), which permits liquidated damages in the light of the anticipated or actual loss caused by the breach and the difficulties of proof of loss. Section 356, Comment b declares explicitly: "Furthermore, the amount fixed is reasonable to the extent that it approximates the loss anticipated at the time of the making of the contract, even though it may not approximate the actual loss."

Despite the statutory disjunctive and the Restatement's apparent blessing of it, the question is not settled by these authorities which must be read in the light of common law principles already established and accepted in Pennsylvania. Prior to the adoption of the Uniform Commercial Code, Pennsylvania enforced liquidated damage clauses that its courts labeled as nonpenal, but equitable considerations relating to the actual harm incurred were taken into account along with the difficulty of proving damages if a liquidated damage clause was rejected. We do not believe that the *UCC* overrode this line of reasoning. Indeed, in a lower court case, decided after the *UCC*'s enactment, it was stated that if liquidated damages appear unreasonable in light of the harm suffered, "the contractual provision will be voided as a penalty." *Unit Vending Corp. v. Tobin Enterprises,* 194 Pa.Super. 470, 473, 168 A.2d 750, 751 (1961). That case, however, is not on all fours with our case: *Unit Vending* involved an adhesion contract between parties of unequal bargaining power, the unfair contract was characterized by the court as "a clever attempt to secure both the penny and the cake" by the party with superior strength. *Id.* at 476, 168 A.2d at 753. Mechanically to read it as Pennsylvania law governing this case would be a mistake. The case, however, does show that Pennsylvania courts, like courts elsewhere, attempt to interpret the governing statute humanely and equitably.

The Restatement § 356 Comment b, after accepting anticipated damages as a measure, goes on to say that if the difficulty of proof of loss is slight, then actual damage may be the measure of reasonableness: "If, to take an extreme case, it is clear that no loss at all has occurred, a provision fixing a substantial sum as damages is unenforceable. See Illustration 4." Illustration 4 is a case of a contractor, A, agreeing to build B's race track by a specific date and to pay B $1,000 a day for every day's delay. A delays a month, but B does not get permission to operate the track for that month, so B suffers no loss. In that event, the Restatement characterizes the $1,000 per day as an unenforceable penalty. Sun contends that it is in the position of A: no actual loss was suffered by C and H because C and H had no tug to mate with the barge.

This argument restates in a new form Sun's basic contention that the liquidated damage clause was meant to operate only if the integrated tug barge was not delivered. The argument has been rejected by us as a misinterpretation of the contract. But in its new guise it gains appeal. If Illustration 4 is the present case, Sun is home scot-free. The Restatement, however, deals with a case where the defaulting contractor was alone in his default. We deal with a case of concurrent defaults. If we were to be so literal-minded as to follow the Restatement here, we would have to conclude that because both parties were in default, C and H suffered no damage until one party performed. Not until the barge was ready in March 1982 could C and H hold Halter for damages, and then only for the period after that date. The continued default of both parties would operate to take each of them off the hook. That cannot be the law.

Sun objects that Halter had a more absolute obligation to deliver than Sun did. Halter did not have to deliver the integrated tug, only the tug itself; it was not excused by Sun's default. Hence the spectacle of two defaulting contractors causing no damages would not be presented here. But Sun's objection does not meet the point that Halter's unexcused delivery would, on Sun's theory, have generated no damages. The tug by itself would have been no use to C and H.

We conclude, therefore, that in this case of concurrent causation each defaulting contractor is liable for the breach and for the substantial damages which the joint breach occasions. Sun is a substantial cause of the damages flowing from the lack of the integrated tug; Sun cannot be absolved by the absence of the tug.

Sun has a final argument. Even on the assumption that it is liable as a substantial cause of the breach of contract, Sun contends that the actual damages suffered by C and H for lack of the integrated tug boat were slight. Actual damages were found by the district court to consist of "interest on progress payments, unfavorable terms of conversion to long-term financing, and additional labor expense." No dollar amount was determined by the district court in finding that these damages "bore a reasonable relationship to the amount liquidated in the Barge Contract."

The dollar value of the damages found by the district judge is, to judge from C and H's own computation, as follows:

Additional Construction Interest	$1,486,000
Added Payments to J.J. Henry	161,000
Added Vessel Operating Expenses	73,000
C and H Employee Costs	109,000
	$1,829,000

But "actual damages" have no meaning if the actual savings of C and H due to the nondelivery of the integrated tug barge are not subtracted. It was clearly erroneous for the district judge to exclude these savings from his finding. These savings, again according to C and H's own computation, were:

Transportation savings	$525,000
Lay-up Costs	$936,000
	$1,461,000

The net actual damages suffered by C and H were $368,000. As a matter of law, Sun contends that the liquidated damages are unreasonably disproportionate to the net actual damages.

* * * Promising to pay damages of a fixed amount, the parties normally have a much better sense of what damages can occur. Courts must be reluctant to override their judgment. Where damages are real but difficult to prove, injustice will be done the injured party if the court substitutes the requirements of judicial proof for the parties' own informed agreement as to what is a reasonable measure of damages. Pennsylvania acknowledges that a seller is bound to pay consequential damages if the seller had reason to know of the buyer's special circumstances. The liquidated damage clause here functions in lieu of a court's determination of the consequential damages suffered by C and H.

These principles inform a leading common law case in the field, *Clydebank Engineering & Shipbuilding Co. v. Yzquierdo y Castaneda,*

1905 A.C. 6. The defendant shipyard had agreed to pay 500 pounds per week per vessel for delay in the delivery of four torpedo boat destroyers to the Spanish Navy in 1897. The shipyard pointed out that had the destroyers been delivered on schedule they would have been sunk with the rest of the Spanish Navy by the Americans in 1898. The House of Lords found the defense unpersuasive. To prove damages the whole administration of the Spanish Navy would have had to have been investigated. The House of Lords refused to undertake such a difficult investigation when the parties had made an honest effort in advance to set in monetary terms what the lack of the destroyers would mean to Spain.

C and H is not the Spanish Navy, but the exact damages caused its manifold operations by lack of the integrated tug boat are equally difficult of ascertainment * * *. Proof of it's loss is difficult—as difficult, perhaps, as proof of loss would have been if the sugar crop had been delivered late because shipping was missing. Whatever the loss, the parties had promised each other that $17,000 per day was a reasonable measure. The court must decline to substitute the requirements of judicial proof for the parties' own conclusion. The Moku Pahu, available on June 30, 1981, was a great prize, capable of multiple employments and enlarging the uses of the entire C and H fleet. When sophisticated parties with bargaining parity have agreed what lack of this prize would mean, and it is now difficult to measure what the lack did mean, the court will uphold the parties' bargain. C and H is entitled to keep the liquidated damages of $3,298,000 it has already received and to receive additional liquidated damages of $1,105,000 with interest thereon, less setoffs determined by the district court.

* * *

SOUTHWEST ENGINEERING CO. v. UNITED STATES, 341 F.2d 998 (8th Cir.1965).* Southwest Engineering entered into four contracts to install navigational aids at four airfields. Each contract stipulated a completion date and provided for damages ($100 per day in one contract, $50 per day in the others) for each day's delay beyond that date. The parties stipulated that although all of the projects were completed late, the United States "suffered no actual damage on any project." The Government nevertheless withheld the full stipulated amounts from payment, amounting to a total of $8,300. Southwest sued to recovery this amount. A judgment for the United States was affirmed:

"We believe that the cases holding that the situation existing at the time of the contract is controlling in determining the reasonableness of liquidated damages are based upon sound reasoning and represent the weight of authority. Where parties have by their contract agreed upon a liquidated damage provision as a reasonable forecast of just compensation for breach of contract and

* Cert. denied, 382 U.S. 819, 86 S.Ct. 45,
15 L.Ed.2d 66 (1965).

damages are difficult to estimate accurately, such provision should be enforced. If in the course of subsequent developments, damages prove to be greater than those stipulated, the party entitled to damages is bound by the liquidated damage agreement. It is not unfair to hold the contractor performing the work to such agreement if by reason of later developments damages prove to be less or nonexistent. Each party by entering into such contractual provision took a calculated risk and is bound by reasonable contractual provisions pertaining to liquidated damages."

MAHONEY v. TINGLEY

Supreme Court of Washington, en Banc, 1975.
85 Wash.2d 95, 529 P.2d 1068.

BRACHTENBACH, JUSTICE.

Plaintiff seeks against defendants damages arising out of the breach of an earnest money agreement, those damages being in excess of an amount stipulated in a liquidated damages clause.

The parties entered into an earnest money agreement in which the plaintiff agreed to sell residential property to the defendants. The price, originally fixed in the agreement at $21,500, was later reduced to $20,250 in order to conform to a Veterans Administration appraisal. Defendants deposited $50 as earnest money with the real estate broker and, subsequently, deposited $150 as additional earnest money. The agreement contained the following clause:

> If title is so insurable and purchaser fails or refuses to complete purchase, the earnest money shall be forfeited as liquidated damages unless seller elects to enforce this agreement.

At defendants' request, the plaintiff moved from the premises, but the defendants did not move in. Instead, upon being notified that the transaction was ready for closing, the defendants indicated that they did not intend to complete the purchase. Defendants' attorney wrote to the plaintiff's realtor and stated that the defendants wished to cancel the agreement. Plaintiff's attorney responded that cancellation was not justified and demanded that defendants complete the transaction. Defendants did not respond to that letter, and the plaintiff sold the property to a third party for $19,000.

On the basis of the defendants' breach, plaintiff sued, alleging damages totaling $3,141.44. The defendants answered the complaint with a general denial and prayed for dismissal of the suit. On the day set for trial, the trial judge met with counsel in chambers. During that conference, the trial judge determined that the case turned upon the effect to be given the liquidated damages clause. Accordingly, the judge decided to treat the matter as one in which summary judgment was appropriate. After hearing argument relating to the liquidated damages clause, the court ruled that plaintiff was entitled only to the stipulated amount and entered an order for summary judgment in favor of defendants.

The Court of Appeals reversed the summary judgment. ∗ ∗ ∗

The liquidated damages clause at issue here provided an option to the plaintiff once there was failure or refusal by defendants to complete the purchase. Plaintiff could elect to sue for specific performance of the earnest money agreement, or she could retain the earnest money as liquidated damages. The potential remedy of specific performance was, of course, foreclosed upon sale of the property to a third party. Plaintiff now seeks to avoid the limitation imposed by the provision for stipulated damages.

Plaintiff first argues that the alternative remedies provided by the earnest money agreement are not exclusive, and cites Reiter v. Bailey, 180 Wash. 230, 39 P.2d 370 (1934), for the proposition that a vendor may forego declaring a forfeiture of earnest money and elect, instead, to sue for actual damages. *Reiter* involved a real estate contract in which it was provided that, upon failure of the purchaser to make any payment:

> "[T]he seller *may elect* to declare a forfeiture and cancellation of this contract and upon such election being made, ∗ ∗ ∗ any payments theretofore made hereunder by the purchaser shall be retained by the seller in liquidation of all damages sustained by reason of such failure."

(Italics ours.) Reiter v. Bailey, supra at 231, 39 P.2d at 370. This court interpreted the clause to mean that the seller had reserved the options of seeking specific performance, liquidated damages or actual damages upon the buyer's default. Where parties expressly provide for such alternatives, there can be no objection to the seller's choice of one remedy from among those contemplated in the agreement. However, where an earnest money agreement provides that, upon the purchaser's failure or refusal to complete the transaction, the earnest money *shall be forfeited* as liquidated damages unless the seller chooses specific performance (as does the clause in the present case), we have clearly held that the seller cannot pursue a third remedy of unliquidated damages which is not written into the agreement. In this case the liquidated damages clause, if enforceable, will limit plaintiff's recovery to that amount stipulated in the earnest money agreement.

Plaintiff's principal contention is that the liquidated damages clause constitutes a penalty and is, therefore, unenforceable. However, no penalty is involved here. A penalty exists where there is an attempt to enforce an obligation to pay a sum fixed by agreement of the parties as a *punishment* for the failure to fulfill some primary contractual obligation. In this case, it is not the party in default who seeks relief from an excessively high liquidated damages provision. Rather, the provision operates to limit the recovery of the party who incurred a loss as a result of the other parties' breach. There being no element of punishment involved, it cannot be said that plaintiff is being penalized in any sense.

There is some authority to support the view that where a stipulated amount of damages is substantially below the actual damage, the limitation will be found to be unenforceable. There is, however, contrary authority. For example, the City of Kinston v. Suddreth, 266 N.C. 618, 146 S.E.2d 660 (1966), the argument was made that a liquidated damages clause, which stipulated an amount less than actual damages, was a penalty and unenforceable. The court refused even to consider the nature of the clause at issue, holding that an injured party cannot recover damages beyond the amount stipulated in a liquidated damages clause. We believe that the view expressed by the North Carolina court is the better one. * * *

Also, in addition to a background of case law which suggests that provisions for liquidated damages will ordinarily be upheld by the courts, there are practical considerations which lend further support to our decision that such provisions under these circumstances are binding upon the seller. We must assume that the seller considered the certainty of a liquidated damages clause to be preferable to the risk of seeking actual damages in the event of the purchasers' breach. We must also assume that the purchasers understood and relied upon the liability limitation stipulated in the agreement. Furthermore, it cannot be ignored that the seller, in making an earnest money agreement, can simply demand more protection—a larger deposit of earnest money—or even dispense with a liquidated damages provision altogether. Except where extraordinary circumstances are involved such as fraud or serious overreaching by the purchaser, a seller who chooses to utilize the device of liquidated damages in an earnest money agreement, with its attendant features of certainty and reliance upon the limitation, cannot avoid the effect of that agreement. * * *

We reverse the Court of Appeals and order the reinstatement of summary judgment for defendants.

Is UCC § 2–718(3) consistent with the principal case? See also UCC § 2–719.

LEFEMINE v. BARON, 573 So.2d 326 (Fla.1991). Mr. and Mrs. Lefemine contracted to purchase a house from Baron. The contract provided that upon a breach by buyer, "the deposit(s) [$38,500] made * * * by Buyer may be retained * * * as liquidated damages, consideration for the execution of the Contract and in full settlement of any claims; whereupon all parties shall be relieved of all obligations under the Contract; or Seller, at his option, may proceed at law or in equity to enforce his rights under the Contract." The Lefemines defaulted and, when Baron refused to return their deposit, they sued for its recovery. The trial and intermediate appellate courts held that

Baron could keep the deposit as liquidated damages. The Supreme Court of Florida, however, reversed on the ground that the stipulated damages clause "was an unenforceable penalty clause":

"We agree with the court below that the forfeiture of the $38,500 deposit was not unconscionable. The deposit represented only ten percent of the purchase price and half of this had to be paid to the broker. The $38,500 was not so grossly disproportionate to any damages that might reasonably be expected to follow from a breach of the contract so as to show that the parties intended only to induce full performance. * * *

"The reason why the forfeiture clause must fail in this case is that the option granted to Baron either to choose liquidated damages or to sue for actual damages indicates an intent to penalize the defaulting buyer and negates the intent to liquidate damages in the event of a breach. The buyer under a liquidated damages provision with such an option is always at risk for damages greater than the liquidated sum. On the other hand, if the actual damages are less than the liquidated sum, the buyer is nevertheless obligated by the liquidated damages clause because the seller will take the deposit under that clause. Because neither party intends the stipulated sum to be the agreed-upon measure of damages, the provision cannot be a valid liquidated damages clause."

KEARNEY & TRECKER CORP. v. MASTER ENGRAVING CO., INC.

Supreme Court of New Jersey, 1987.
107 N.J. 584, 527 A.2d 429.

STEIN, J.

The critical issue posed by this appeal is whether the Uniform Commercial Code, (UCC or Code), permits the enforcement of a contractual exclusion of consequential damages where the buyer's limited remedy authorized in the contract of sale has failed to achieve its essential purpose. Despite a specific exclusion of consequential damages in the contract between these parties, the trial court instructed the jury that it could award consequential damages if the seller, acting under its repair and replacement warranty, did not "make the machine as warranted." The Appellate Division affirmed the judgment entered on the jury verdict assessing damages against the seller, concluding that "the allocation of risk through exclusion of consequential damages was inextricably tied to the limitation of remedies." Our analysis of the UCC persuades us, however, that the enforceability of an exclusion of consequential damages does not necessarily depend on the effectiveness of the limited remedies afforded by the contract of sale, and that in this case the exclusion should have been enforced, even though the jury may have determined that the repair and replacement warranty failed of its essential purpose. Accordingly, we reverse the judgment below and remand the matter to the Law Division for a new trial.

I

Kearney & Trecker Corporation (K & T) is the manufacturer of the Milwaukee–Matic 180 (MM–180), a computer-controlled machine tool capable of performing automatically a series of machining operations on metal parts. At the time of trial K & T had sold approximately 700 of these machines throughout the world. Master Engraving Company, Inc. (Master) is engaged in the manufacture and engraving of component parts for industrial application. Organized in 1955, Master operated 22 machines at the time of trial, six of which were computer controlled.

In the fall of 1978, the parties began discussions about Master's purchase of an MM–180. K & T furnished Master with a sales brochure describing the MM–180: "The new Milwaukee–Matic 180 combines simplicity with efficiency. It was designed using fewer parts. It is this simplicity of design that does much to explain the MM 180's amazing low maintenance requirements."

In response to a proposal from K & T, Master issued its purchase order for the MM–180 in December 1978, and the order was promptly acknowledged and accepted by K & T. The purchase price was $167,000. The written proposal included the following provision:

WARRANTY, DISCLAIMER, LIMITATION OF LIABILITY AND REMEDY: Seller warrants the products furnished hereunder to be free from defects in material and workmanship for the shorter of (i) twelve (12) months from the date of delivery ∗ ∗ ∗ or (ii) four thousand (4,000) operating hours ∗ ∗ ∗.

THE WARRANTY EXPRESSED HEREIN IS IN LIEU OF ANY OTHER WARRANTIES EXPRESS OR IMPLIED INCLUDING, WITHOUT LIMITATION, ANY IMPLIED WARRANTY OF MERCHANTABILITY OR FITNESS FOR A PARTICULAR PURPOSE AND IS IN LIEU OF ANY AND ALL OTHER OBLIGATIONS OR LIABILITY ON SELLER'S PART. UNDER NO CIRCUMSTANCES WILL SELLER BE LIABLE FOR ANY INCIDENTAL OR CONSEQUENTIAL DAMAGES, OR FOR ANY OTHER LOSS, DAMAGE OR EXPENSE OF ANY KIND, INCLUDING LOSS OF PROFITS ARISING IN CONNECTION WITH THIS CONTRACT OR WITH THE USE OF OR INABILITY TO USE SELLER'S PRODUCTS FURNISHED UNDER THIS CONTRACT. SELLER'S MAXIMUM LIABILITY SHALL NOT EXCEED AND BUYER'S REMEDY IS LIMITED TO EITHER (i) REPAIR OR REPLACEMENT OF THE DEFECTIVE PART OF PRODUCT, OR AT SELLER'S OPTION, (ii) RETURN OF THE PRODUCT AND REFUND OF THE PURCHASE PRICE, AND SUCH REMEDY SHALL BE BUYER'S ENTIRE AND EXCLUSIVE REMEDY.

The MM–180 was delivered in March 1980. According to Master's witnesses, the machine malfunctioned frequently during the first year of operation, and was inoperable from 25% to 50% of the time available for its use, substantially more than the industry average of five percent "down-time" for comparable machines. No specific defect was predominant, according to Master's witnesses. Problems with tool changing, control, alignment and spindles were among Master's complaints. Over K & T's objection, testimony was introduced estimating lost profits on customer orders allegedly unfilled because of the inoperability of the machine. It was conceded that the machine's performance improved after the first year and that the machine was still in use at the time of trial, in September and October 1984. Master did not attempt to return the machine to K & T and obtain a refund of the purchase price.

K & T's witnesses disputed Master's account of the machine's first year of operation. Although conceding a substantial number of service calls, K & T's area service manager testified that only four or five of thirteen service calls were "valid." K & T's service personnel contended that Master had programmed the machine improperly and that the programs were extensively edited, thereby impairing the efficiency of the MM–180. K & T's witnesses testified that Master did not have adequate testing equipment or spare parts for the machine, and that Master's employees lacked the ability to "troubleshoot" and perform regular maintenance. The testimony about "downtime" during the first year was also disputed; the K & T witnesses testified that the MM–180 was not inoperative on most occasions that K & T service personnel visited the Master's plant. K & T's manager of technical services testified that no service calls were requested from May 1981 to March 1982, and that during the second year of operation the MM–180 was operable approximately 98% of the time available for its use.

Suit was instituted by K & T in July 1981 to recover the cost of two service calls made after the one-year warranty had expired; Master counterclaimed, seeking the damages that are the subject of this appeal.

At the conclusion of the trial, the trial court instructed the jury that it could award consequential damages notwithstanding the contractual exclusion if it found that K & T failed "to make the machine as warranted." The jury was not instructed concerning the proof necessary to demonstrate that the repair or replacement warranty had failed of its essential purpose. * * *

The jury returned a verdict in favor of Master for $57,000. In answer to written questions on the verdict sheet, the jury found that although K & T had not sold a defectively-designed product, it had nevertheless breached its contract with Master. In affirming, the Appellate Division interpreted the jury verdict to mean that the limited remedy of repair and replacement had failed of its essential purpose. [2–719(2)]. The Appellate Division concluded that under the circumstance of this case "the failure adequately to repair the machine rendered ineffective the exclusion of consequential damages." * * *

Under the Code, consequential losses constitute a recoverable item of damages in the event of a breach by the seller. [2–714(3)]. However, the potential significance of liability for consequential damages in commercial transactions undoubtedly prompted the Code's drafters, notwithstanding the Code's endorsement of the principle of freedom of contract, to make express provision for the limitation or exclusion of such damages. [2–719]. For certain sellers, exposure to liability for consequential damages could drastically affect the conduct of their business, causing them to increase their prices or limit their markets. * * * In a commercial setting, the seller's right to exclusion of consequential damages is recognized as a beneficial risk-allocation device that reduces the seller's exposure in the event of breach.

An equally fundamental principle of the Code, comparable in importance to the right of parties to limit or exclude consequential damages, is the Code's insistence that for a party aggrieved by breach of a sales contract, "at least minimum adequate remedies be available." Comment 1, [2–719]. To this end, the Code provides that

> [w]here circumstances cause an exclusive or limited remedy to fail of its essential purpose, remedy may be had as provided in this Act. [2–719(2)]. * * *

These competing policies—freedom of contract, including the right to exclude liability for consequential damages, and the insistence upon minimum adequate remedies to redress a breach of contract—frame the issue before us. If a limitation or exclusion of consequential damages is not unconscionable when the contract is made, must it be held unenforceable if the limited remedies provided in the contract do not achieve their intended purpose?

To the extent that the U.C.C. addresses this issue, its response is inconclusive. The Code provides merely that when a limited remedy fails of its essential purpose, "remedy may be had as provided in this Act." [2–719(2)]. As noted, consequential damages is a buyer's remedy "provided in this Act" [2–714(3)], but the Code is silent as to whether that remedy survives if the sales contract excludes it.

A related question concerns the extent of the remedies other than consequential damages that are available to a buyer relegated to a limited remedy that has failed to achieve its essential purpose. Typically, the limited remedy most often offered by sellers is the repair and replacement warranty found in the sales contract in this case. * * *

Courts that have considered the validity of an exclusion of consequential damages in the context of a repair or replacement warranty that has not fulfilled its purpose have reached significantly different results. A substantial number of courts seem to have adopted the view that there is an integral relationship between the exclusion of consequential damages and the limited remedy of repair or replacement, so that the failure of the limited remedy necessarily causes the invalidation of the exclusion of consequential damages. * * *

In sharp contrast, a number of other courts have concluded that an exclusion of consequential damages is to be viewed independently of a limited warranty of repair or replacement, so that if the warranty fails to fulfill its purpose, the validity of the consequential damages exclusion depends upon the specific circumstances and the probable intention of the parties.

* * * We are also persuaded that many routine business transactions would be dislocated by a rule requiring the invalidation of a consequential damage exclusion whenever the prescribed contractual remedy fails to operate as intended. Concededly, well-counseled businesses could avoid the problem posed by better draftsmanship of their sales contracts. *See* White & Summers, [Handbook of the Law Under the Uniform Commercial Code] § 12–11, at 470–71 [2d ed. 1980]. But the commercial reality is that for many sellers, immunity from liability for their customers' consequential damages may be indispensable to their pricing structure and, in extreme cases, to their solvency.

Nor do we find that enforcement of a consequential damages limitation when a limited remedy has failed of its essential purpose is necessarily inequitable to the buyer. As noted earlier, the Code affords remedies other than consequential damages when a warranty is breached. * * *

Accordingly, we conclude that [2–719] does not require the invalidation of an exclusion of consequential damages when limited contractual remedies fail of their essential purpose. It is only when the circumstances of the transaction, including the seller's breach, cause the consequential damage exclusion to be inconsistent with the intent and reasonable commercial expectations of the parties that invalidation of the exclusionary clause would be appropriate under the Code. For example, although a buyer may agree to the exclusion of consequential damages, a seller's wrongful repudiation of a repair warranty may expose a buyer to consequential damages not contemplated by the contract, and other Code remedies may be inadequate. In such circumstances, a court might appropriately decline to enforce the exclusion. * * *

III

In this case, a sophisticated buyer purchased for $167,000 a complex, computer-controlled machine tool. The sales agreement allocated to Master the risk of consequential damages. K & T's responsibility was to repair or replace the machine or any defective parts in order that the machine would be "free from defects in material and workmanship" for the shorter of twelve months or four thousand operating hours. The testimony at trial demonstrated that the MM–180 was a complex piece of equipment and that its normal operation could be adversely affected by a wide variety of factors, including deficiencies in maintenance or in computer-programming for which Master's employees were responsible. * * *

Furthermore, although the sales contract provided for the alternative remedy of return of the machine and refund of the purchase price with K & T's consent, there was no evidence indicating that Master ever attempted to invoke this relief. To the contrary, the evidence indicated that the machine's performance continued to improve and that it was in use at the time of trial, four-and-one-half years after delivery.

Nor was there any contention by Master that K & T did not make service calls when requested. The evidence at trial verified that K & T made at least thirteen service calls during the first twelve months of operation, at times sending several service personnel to work on the Master's machine. What was sharply disputed was Master's claim that the machine was defective during the first year, since K & T's witnesses testified that most of the problems encountered during this period were the fault of Master's employees.

Under these factual circumstances, the trial court's instruction to the jury was inappropriate. The jury was charged that it could award consequential damages "despite the language of the contract" if it found that K & T failed "to make the machine as warranted." In our view, the facts in this record do not justify invalidation of the consequential damage exclusion, a risk allocation agreed to by both parties. We do not agree with the Appellate Division's conclusion that "the allocation of risk through exclusion of consequential damages was inextricably tied to the limitation of remedies."

Master could have offered evidence, although it did not, that the value of the MM–180 was less than the contract price because of the erratic performance during the first year. In such event Master would have been entitled to a jury instruction as to the measure of damages for breach of the repair and replacement warranty. We are fully satisfied that the availability of damages for breach of the repair and replacement warranty under [2–714(2)], combined with the return and refund provision in the contract of sale not invoked by Master, adequately fulfills the U.C.C.'s mandate that "at least minimum adequate remedies be available" when a limited remedy fails to achieve its purpose.

For the reasons stated, the judgment of the Appellate Division is reversed and the matter is remanded to the Law Division for a new trial.

————

The court says that "well-counseled businesses could avoid the problem posed by better draftsmanship of their sales contracts." How?

BRITTON v. TURNER

Supreme Court of New Hampshire, 1834.
6 N.H. 481.

By Court, PARKER, J. It may be assumed that the labor performed by the plaintiff, and for which he seeks to recover a compensation in this action, was commenced under a special contract to labor for the defendant the term of one year, for the sum of one hundred and twenty dollars, and that the plaintiff has labored but a portion of that time, and has voluntarily failed to complete the entire contract.

It is clear, then, that he is not entitled to recover upon the contract itself, because the service, which was to entitle him to the sum agreed upon, has never been performed.

But the question arises, can the plaintiff, under these circumstances, recover a reasonable sum for the service he has actually performed, under the count in *quantum meruit?*

Upon this, and questions of a similar nature, the decisions to be found in the books are not easily reconciled.

It has been held, upon contracts of this kind for labor to be performed at a specified price, that the party who voluntarily fails to fulfill the contract, by performing the whole labor contracted for, is not entitled to recover anything for the labor actually performed, however much he may have done towards the performance, and this has been considered the settled rule of law upon this subject.

That such rule in its operation may be very unequal, not to say unjust, is apparent.

A party who contracts to perform certain specified labor, and who breaks his contract in the first instance, without any attempt to perform it, can only be made liable to pay the damages which the other party has sustained by reason of such non-performance, which in many instances may be trifling—whereas a party who, in good faith, has entered upon the performance of his contract, and nearly completed it, and then abandoned the further performance—although the other party has had the full benefit of all that has been done, and has perhaps sustained no actual damage—is in fact subjected to a loss of all which has been performed, in the nature of damages for the non-fulfillment of the remainder, upon the technical rule, that the contract must be fully performed, in order to a recovery of any part of the compensation.

By the operation of this rule, then, the party who attempts performance may be placed in a much worse situation than he who wholly disregards his contract, and the other party may receive much more, by the breach of the contract, than the injury which he has sustained by such breach, and more than he could be entitled to were he seeking to recover damages by an action.

The case before us presents an illustration. Had the plaintiff in this case never entered upon the performance of his contract, the damage could not probably have been greater than some small expense and trouble incurred in procuring another to do the labor which he had contracted to perform. But having entered upon the performance, and labored nine and a half months, the value of which labor to the defendant, as found by the jury, is ninety-five dollars, if the defendant can succeed in this defense, he in fact receives nearly five sixths of the value of a whole year's labor, by reason of the breach of contract by the plaintiff, a sum not only utterly disproportionate to any probable, not to say possible damage, which could have resulted from the neglect of the plaintiff to continue the remaining two and a half months, but altogether beyond any damage which could have been recovered by the defendant, had the plaintiff done nothing towards the fulfillment of his contract.

Another illustration is furnished in Lantry v. Parks, 8 Cow. 63. There the defendant hired the plaintiff for a year, at ten dollars per month. The plaintiff worked ten and a half months, and then left, saying he would work no more for him. This was on Saturday; on Monday the plaintiff returned, and offered to resume his work, but the defendant said he would employ him no longer. The court held that the refusal of the defendant on Saturday was a violation of his contract, and that he could recover nothing for the labor performed.

There are other cases, however, in which principles have been adopted leading to a different result.

It is said, that where a party contracts to perform certain work, and to furnish materials, as, for instance, to build a house, and the work is done, but with some variations from the mode prescribed by the contract, yet if the other party has the benefit of the labor and materials, he should be bound to pay so much as they are reasonably worth. * * *

It is, in truth, virtually conceded in such cases that the work has not been done, for if it had been, the party performing it would be entitled to recover upon the contract itself, which, it is held, he can not do.

Those cases are not to be distinguished, in principle, from the present, unless it be in the circumstance that where the party has contracted to furnish materials, and do certain labor, as to build a house in a specified manner, if it is not done according to the contract, the party for whom it is built may refuse to receive it—elect to take no benefit from what has been performed—and therefore if he does receive, he shall be bound to pay the value—whereas, in a contract for labor merely, from day to day, the party is continually receiving the benefit of the contract under an expectation that it will be fulfilled, and can not, upon the breach of it, have an election to refuse to receive what has been done, and thus discharge himself from payment.

But we think this difference in the nature of the contracts does not justify the application of a different rule in relation to them. The party who contracts for labor merely, for a certain period, does so with full knowledge that he must, from the nature of the case, be accepting part performance from day to day, if the other party commences the performance, and with knowledge also that the other may eventually fail of completing the entire term. * * *

If, under such circumstances, he actually receives a benefit from the labor performed, over and above the damage occasioned by the failure to complete, there is as much reason why he should pay the reasonable worth of what has thus been done for his benefit, as there is when he enters and occupies the house which has been built for him, but not according to the stipulations of the contract, and which he perhaps enters, not because he is satisfied with what has been done, but because circumstances compel him to accept it such as it is, that he should pay for the value of the house. * * *

If, on such failure to perform the whole, the nature of the contract be such that the employer can reject what has been done, and refuse to receive any benefit from the part performance, he is entitled so to do, and in such case is not liable to be charged, unless he has before assented to and accepted of what has been done, however much the other party may have done towards the performance. He has in such case received nothing, and having contracted to receive nothing but the entire matter contracted for, he is not bound to pay, because his express promise was only to pay on receiving the whole, and having actually received nothing, the law can not and ought not to raise an implied promise to pay. But where the party receives value, takes and uses the materials, or has advantage from the labor, he is liable to pay the reasonable worth of what he has received. And the rule is the same, whether it was received and accepted by the assent of the party prior to the breach, under a contract by which, from its nature, he was to receive labor, from time to time, until the completion of the whole contract; or whether it was received and accepted by an assent subsequent to the performance of all which was in fact done. If he received it under such circumstances as precluded him from rejecting it afterwards, that does not alter the case; it has still been received by his assent.

In fact, we think the technical reasoning that the performance of the whole labor is a condition precedent, and the right to recover anything dependent upon it—that the contract being entire, there can be no apportionment—and that there being an express contract no other can be implied, even upon the subsequent performance of service—is not properly applicable to this species of contract, where a beneficial service has been actually performed; for we have abundant reason to believe, that the general understanding of the community is, that the hired laborer shall be entitled to compensation for the service actually performed, though he do not continue the entire term contracted for, and such contracts must be presumed to be made with reference to that understanding, unless an express stipulation shows the contrary.

Where a beneficial service has been performed and received, therefore, under contracts of this kind, the mutual agreements can not be considered as going to the whole of the consideration, so as to make them mutual conditions, the one precedent to the other, without a specific proviso to that effect. It is easy, if parties so choose, to provide by an express agreement that nothing shall be earned, if the laborer leaves his employer without having performed the whole service contemplated, and then there can be no pretense for a recovery if he voluntarily deserts the service before the expiration of the time.

The amount, however, for which the employer ought to be charged, where the laborer abandons his contract, is only the reasonable worth, or the amount of advantage he receives upon the whole transaction, and in estimating the value of the labor, the contract price for the service can not be exceeded. * * *

The benefit and advantage which the party takes by the labor therefore, is the amount of value which he receives, if any, after deducting the amount of damage; and if he elects to put this in defense he is entitled to do so, and the implied promise which the law will raise, in such a case, is to pay such amount of the stipulated price for the whole labor, as remains after deducting what it would cost to procure a completion of the residue of the service, and also any damage which has been sustained by reason of the non-fulfillment of the contract.

If, in such case, it be found that the damages are equal to, or greater than the amount of the labor performed, so that the employer, having a right to the full performance of the contract, has not upon the whole case received a beneficial service, the plaintiff can not recover.

This rule, by binding the employer to pay the value of the service he actually receives, and the laborer to answer in damages where he does not complete the entire contract, will leave no temptation to the former to drive the laborer from his service near the close of his term, by ill-treatment, in order to escape from payment; nor to the latter to desert his service before the stipulated time, without a sufficient reason; and it will, in most instances, settle the whole controversy in one action, and prevent a multiplicity of suits and cross actions. * * *

Applying the principles thus laid down to this case, the plaintiff is entitled to judgment on the verdict.

The defendant sets up a mere breach of the contract in defense of the action, but this can not avail him. He does not appear to have offered evidence to show that he was damnified by such breach, or to have asked that a deduction should be made upon that account. The direction to the jury was therefore correct, that the plaintiff was entitled to recover as much as the labor performed was reasonably worth; and the jury appear to have allowed a *pro rata* compensation for the time which the plaintiff labored in the defendant's service. * * *

Judgment on the verdict.

RESTATEMENT, SECOND, CONTRACTS § 374:

(1) Subject to the rule stated in Subsection (2), if a party justifiably refuses to perform on the ground that his remaining duties of performance have been discharged by the other party's breach, the party in breach is entitled to restitution for any benefit that he has conferred by way of part performance or reliance in excess of the loss that he has caused by his own breach.

(2) To the extent that, under the manifested assent of the parties, a party's performance is to be retained in the case of breach, that party is not entitled to restitution if the value of the performance as liquidated damages is reasonable in the light of the anticipated or actual loss caused by the breach and the difficulties of proof of loss.

Comment:

b. * * * A party who intentionally furnishes services or builds a building that is materially different from what he promised is properly regarded as having acted officiously and not in part performance of his promise and will be denied recovery on that ground even if his performance was of some benefit to the other party. This is not the case, however, if the other party has accepted or agreed to accept the substitute performance.

Illustration:

2. A contracts to make repairs to B's building in return for B's promise to pay $10,000 on completion of the work. After spending $8,000 on the job, A fails to complete it because of insolvency. B has the work completed by another builder for $4,000, increasing the value of the building to him by a total of $9,000, but he loses $500 in rent because of the delay. A can recover $5,000 from B in restitution less $500 in damages for the loss caused by the breach, or $4,500.

RESTATEMENT [FIRST] OF CONTRACTS § 357:

Illustration:

3. A contracts to erect a building for B, who promises to pay $10,000 on completion. After spending $8000 on the work, A becomes insolvent and cannot complete it. The uncompleted building is worth $7000 as an addition to B's property. It costs B $4000 to complete the building, and he loses $500 in rent because of delay. A can get judgment against B for $5500—this being the value of the part performance less the harm caused by the breach. A's judgment will always be the unpaid contract price less the cost of completion and other addition-

al harm to B, except that it must never exceed the benefit actually received by B.

———

FREEDMAN v. RECTOR, WARDENS, & VESTRYMEN OF ST. MA-THIAS PARISH, 37 Cal.2d 16, 230 P.2d 629 (1951). Buyer paid $2,000 into escrow as a deposit for the purchase of real estate. After buyer repudiated the contract, seller sold the land to another for $2,000 more than buyer had agreed to pay. Seller was paid the money in the escrow account. Buyer then sued for the return of his deposit. The court, in an opinion by Judge Traynor, reversed a judgment for seller and stated that buyer was entitled to return of the $2,000 less escrow expenses and a commission deducted from the deposit by seller's broker. The court said that allowing seller to retain the entire deposit would "permit what are in effect punitive damages merely because a party has partially performed his contract before his breach."

Is UCC § 2–718(2) consistent with Freedman v. Rector? What form of agreement would permit seller to retain the money paid despite Freedman v. Rector?

Chapter 2

KINDS OF PROMISES THE LAW WILL ENFORCE

SECTION 1: REASONS FOR ENFORCING PROMISES: AN INTRODUCTION

FARNSWORTH, THE PAST OF PROMISE: AN HISTORICAL INTRODUCTION TO CONTRACT

69 Colum.L.Rev. 576, 591–92, 598 (1969).*

No legal system devised by man has eve[r] been reckless enough to make all promises enforceable. In Morris Cohen's words: "It is indeed very doubtful whether there are many who would prefer to live in an entirely rigid world in which one would be obliged to keep *all* one's promises instead of the present more viable system, in which a vaguely fair proportion is sufficient. Many of us indeed would shudder at the idea of being bound by every promise, no matter how foolish, without any chance of letting increased wisdom undo past foolishness. Certainly, some freedom to change one's mind is necessary for free intercourse between those who lack omniscience." But in framing a general theory for the enforcement of promises, this goal can be approached from two extremes. One can begin with the premise that promises are generally enforceable and then create exceptions for promises which it is thought undesirable to enforce. Or one can begin with the premise that promises are generally unenforceable and then create exceptions for promises which it is thought desirable to enforce. In the centuries following the Conquest in England, both views had substantial support.

The former view, which laid emphasis on the force of the promise itself, was held by the canon law, the law merchant, and equity. As for the canon law, already in the twelfth century the Church allowed a Christian to pawn his salvation, regarded a promise made with a pledge of faith as enforceable and its breach as a mortal sin, and was moving toward the view that even a simple promise, without a pledge of faith, was sacred and therefore enforceable. As for the law merchant, the fair and market courts entertained numerous actions, as commerce required, upon simple promises made by merchants. And as for equity, the Chancellor held the view that the law of man must accord with the law of God and, in his own words in the fifteenth century, because a man was "damaged by the non-performance of the promise, he shall have a remedy."

The view that promises are not generally enforceable, which started from the premise of Roman law that a mere agreement did not beget an action, was held by the common law. Its choice was scarcely surprising. It accorded well with the procedural niceties of common law courts, where recovery was not to be had unless the claim could be fitted within one of the established forms of action; and it suited the status-oriented society of the Middle Ages, which was anything but conducive to the flowering of promise. Furthermore, there was no great pressure for enforceability as contracts were not a significant part of the business of the common law courts. * * *

Nonetheless, it was the common law view that was ultimately to prevail. It achieved its success less on its intrinsic merits than as a by-product of the victories of the common law courts in their jurisdictional struggles with their competitors. * * *

Over the course of the fifteenth and sixteenth centuries the common law courts had succeeded in evolving a general basis for the enforceability of promises through the action of assumpsit. During the sixteenth century the word "consideration," which had earlier been used without technical significance, came to be used as a word of art to express the sum of the conditions necessary for an action in assumpsit to lie. It was therefore a tautology that a promise, if not under seal, was enforceable only where there was "consideration," for this was to say no more than that it was enforceable only under those circumstances in which the action of assumpsit was allowed. In this fashion, however, the word "consideration" came to be applied to the test of enforceability of a simple promise and to be used to distinguish those promises that in the eyes of the common law were of sufficient significance to society to justify the legal sanctions of assumpsit for their enforcement.

It was, to be sure, neither a simple nor a logical test. Bound up in it were several elements. Most important, from the *quid pro quo* of debt by way of *indebitatus assumpsit,* had come the idea that there must have been an exchange arrived at by way of bargain. This precept has remained at the core of the concept of consideration down to today. * * * The doctrine of consideration provided no ground for the enforceability of gratuitous promises, for which nothing is given in exchange, but it took good care of the bulk of economically vital commercial agreements.

A. ENFORCEABILITY AND FORM

FULLER, CONSIDERATION AND FORM

41 Colum.L.Rev. 799, 800–02, 806 (1941).*

I. THE FUNCTIONS PERFORMED BY LEGAL FORMALITIES

§ 2. *The Evidentiary Function.*—The most obvious function of a legal formality is, to use Austin's words, that of providing "evidence of the existence and purport of the contract, in case of controversy." The need for evidentiary security may be satisfied in a variety of ways: by requiring a writing, or attestation, or the certification of a notary. It may even be satisfied, to some extent, by such a device as the Roman *stipulatio,* which compelled an oral spelling out of the promise in a manner sufficiently ceremonious to impress its terms on participants and possible bystanders.

§ 3. *The Cautionary Function.*—A formality may also perform a cautionary or deterrent function by acting as a check against inconsiderate action. The seal in its original form fulfilled this purpose remarkably well. The affixing and impressing of a wax wafer—symbol in the popular mind of legalism and weightiness—was an excellent device for inducing the circumspective frame of mind appropriate in one pledging his future. To a less extent any requirement of a writing, of course, serves the same purpose, as do requirements of attestation, notarization, etc.

§ 4. *The Channeling Function.*—Though most discussions of the purposes served by formalities go no further than the analysis just presented, this analysis stops short of recognizing one of the most important functions of form. That a legal formality may perform a function not yet described can be shown by the seal. The seal not only insures a satisfactory memorial of the promise and induces deliberation in the making of it. It serves also to mark or signalize the enforceable promise; it furnishes a simple and external test of enforceability. This function of form Ihering described as "the facilitation of judicial diagnosis," and he employed the analogy of coinage in explaining it.

> Form is for a legal transaction what the stamp is for a coin. Just as the stamp of the coin relieves us from the necessity of testing the metallic content and weight—in short, the value of the coin (a test which we could not avoid if uncoined metal were offered to us in payment), in the same way legal formalities relieve the judge of an inquiry *whether* a legal transaction was intended, and—in case different forms are fixed for different legal transactions—*which* was intended.

In this passage it is apparent that Ihering has placed an undue emphasis on the utility of form for the judge, to the neglect of its significance for those transacting business out of court. If we look at the matter purely from the standpoint of the convenience of the judge, there is nothing to distinguish the forms used in legal transactions from the "formal" element which to some degree permeates all legal thinking. Even in the field of criminal law "judicial diagnosis" is "facilitated" by formal definitions, presumptions, and artificial constructions of fact. The thing which characterizes the law of contracts and conveyances is that in this field forms are deliberately used, and are intended to be so used, by the parties whose acts are to be judged by the law. To the business man who wishes to make his own or another's promise binding, the seal was at common law available as a device for the accomplishment of his objective. In this aspect form offers a legal framework into which the party may fit his actions, or, to change the figure, it offers channels for the legally effective expression of intention. It is with this aspect of form in mind that I have described the third function of legal formalities as "the channeling function."

In seeking to understand this channeling function of form, perhaps the most useful analogy is that of language, which illustrates both the advantages and dangers of form in the aspect we are now considering. One who wishes to communicate his thoughts to others must force the raw material of meaning into defined and recognizable channels; he must reduce the fleeting entities of wordless thought to the patterns of conventional speech. One planning to enter a legal transaction faces a similar problem. His mind first conceives an economic or sentimental objective, or, more usually, a set of overlapping objectives. He must then, with or without the aid of a lawyer, cast about for the legal transaction (written memorandum, sealed contract, lease, conveyance of the fee, etc.) which will most nearly accomplish these objectives. Just as the use of language contains dangers for the uninitiated, so legal forms are safe only in the hands of those who are familiar with their effects. Ihering explains that the extreme formalism of Roman law was supportable in practice only because of the constant availability of legal advice, *gratis*. * * *

So far as the channeling function of a formality is concerned it has no place where men's activities are already divided into definite, clear-cut business categories. Where life has already organized itself effectively, there is no need for the law to intervene. It is for this reason that important transactions on the stock and produce markets can safely be carried on in the most "informal" manner. At the other extreme we may cite the negotiations between a house-to-house book salesman and the housewife. Here the situation may be such that the housewife is not certain whether she is being presented with a set of books as a gift, whether she is being asked to trade her letter of recommendation for the books, whether the books are being offered to her on approval, or whether—what is, alas, the fact—a simple sale of the books is being proposed. The ambiguity of the situation is, of course, carefully cultivated and exploited by the canvasser. Some "channeling" here would be highly desirable, though whether a legal form is the most practicable means of bringing it about is, of course, another question.

LEAGE, ROMAN PRIVATE LAW 332–34
(1906, 3d ed. 1961).

[The Stipulation] was probably the single most important institution developed by Roman law. It permeated the whole law of contract and was of vast importance in the law of procedure, as well as greatly affecting the whole law of property. It was a formal act, yet the simplest of forms, and as such it could be used to effect any legal transaction. * * * A stipulation was a contract which imposed an obligation upon a person because he had answered in set terms a formal question put to him by the promisee, that question containing a statement of the subject matter of the promise. * * * An example makes this clearer. Titius means to promise to give Maevius his slave Stichus. If he merely says to Maevius, "I promise to give you Stichus", there is no contract. For a proper stipulation Maevius must ask Titius, "*Spondesne mihi hominem Stichum dari?*" and Titius must answer "*Spondeo*". Besides the form *spondesne? spondeo* ("do you pledge your word?" "I do pledge it") Gaius mentions the following: *dabisne? dabo* ("will you give?" "I will give"); *promittisne? promitto* (promise); *fidepromittisne? fidepromitto* (give one's word); *fideiubesne? fideiubeo* (guarantee); *faciesne? faciam* ("will you do?").

R. IHERING, 3 L'ESPRIT DU DROIT ROMAIN (THE SPIRIT OF THE LAW)
190 (de Meulenaere trans., 3d ed. 1887).

[T]he beneficial effect of formalities * * * comes * * * from the form itself, from the impression it makes on the minds of the parties, in warning them that they are obligating themselves, that they are making *a deal.* As soon as the little word "spondesne" was heard in the course of a conversation, it announced to the Roman that what had been until then a non-legal, a friendly talk, was about to take on the nature of a business transaction; it was the signal of a legal act. One who had given assurances, in the course of a casual conversation, must have been dumbfounded as soon as the other party began to take him at his word and wanted to settle the matter legally (for such is the meaning of the Latin word, *stipulari.*) With the word "spondesne" he was called upon to explain himself concerning the nature of his assurances, and to picture to himself the purport, the scope, the consequences of the stipulation that one was asking from him. This simple little word thus had the inestimable value of a *wakening of legal consciousness.*

Contracts Under Seal

In medieval England the action of covenant was, with debt, the most important common-law remedy for breach of an agreement. See p. 93 supra. Covenant was a general remedy for the enforcement of executory contracts: "[T]he action of covenant came to be regarded primarily as an action for compensation (assessed by a jury) for the tort or wrong of breach of covenant, in sharp contrast to the recuperatory nature of the action of debt." A. Simpson, A History of the Common Law of Contract 18 (1975).

By the middle of the 14th century it had become settled that to successfully sue in covenant the plaintiff must produce a written instrument "under seal." Under the circumstances of the time the seal was a powerful formality: an instrument was "sealed" when wax, softened by heat, was attached to the document and impressed with some personal insignia, often a signet ring. In addition, the instrument would usually be signed and, to be effective, had to be personally delivered to the promisee: hence the phrase—"signed, sealed and delivered"—which has passed into the collective memory of the race as a byword for ceremonious legal finality.

The "mystical solemnity" of heated wax and signet ring could not be expected to long survive changing social conditions. "In the United States the history of the seal has been one of erosion of the formality until it can be met by a printed form." (Restatement, Second, Contracts, Chapter 4, Topic 3, Introductory Note). Over the centuries, it came to be recognized that a "seal" could take the form of an impression directly onto the paper of the document, or of a red gummed wafer affixed to it. From there it was an easy step, by statute or judicial decision, to give effect to the printed word "Seal" or to the mysterious letters "L.S." ("locus sigilli," "place of the seal") after the space for signature, or to a promisor's scrawl made with his pen. In one celebrated case a testator had made a dash between $1/16$ and $1/8$ inch long, after her signature and the words, "in witness whereof I have hereunto set my hand and seal"; this was held sufficient to constitute a seal. Appeal of Hacker, 121 Pa.St. 192, 15 A. 500 (1888). And in several states the mere recital in the text of a document that it is "sealed" or "intended to take effect as a sealed instrument" is enough— without even "any semblance of a seal by scroll, impression or otherwise." Mass.Gen.Laws Ann. ch. 4, § 9A.

Use of the seal would make a promise binding by virtue of its form alone. But with the decay of the seal as a meaningful formality, pressure built up to eliminate the legal effects of a device which no longer served to impress upon a promisor the nature and importance of what he was about to do. "If language sometimes loses valuable distinctions by being too tolerant, the law has lost valuable institutions, like the seal, by being too liberal in interpreting them." Fuller, Consideration and Form, 41 Colum.L.Rev. 799, 803 (1941). In most states statutes have now changed the status of contracts under seal. The situation in a number of jurisdictions is obscure; however, we may attempt the following generalization (see the tabulation in Restatement, Second, Contracts, Chapter 4, Topic 3, Introductory Note):

(a) In more than a third of the states the seal seems to have retained much of its common law effect, although there are few modern decisions and dicta in some cases leave the question open and difficult to predict.

(b) Several states (including New Jersey, Michigan and Wisconsin) have made the seal "only ＊ ＊ ＊ presumptive evidence of a sufficient consideration." This betrays some historical misunderstanding: the seal long antedated the development in assumpsit of the requirement of consideration, and there is little connection between the two. But the evident purpose of such statutes is to permit a promisor, despite the presence of a seal, to allege and prove lack of consideration as an affirmative defense. In some cases the statute provides that this defense is available only for "executory instruments"; for "executed" transactions, such as a release purporting to surrender immediately existing rights, the seal would still be conclusive.

(c) Half of the states go still further. Some statutes provide that "all distinctions between sealed and unsealed instruments are abolished," e.g., Cal.Civ.Code § 1629 (West 1973); while the drafting is not ideal, the intention was presumably to require that sealed instruments be treated as if unsealed. Others (perhaps 15) provide forthrightly that the seal itself is "abolished," e.g., Ohio Rev.Code Ann. § 5.11 (Page 1978).

––––––––

For the position of the Uniform Commercial Code with respect to the seal, see UCC § 2–203.

––––––––

LINDER v. COMMISSIONER, 68 T.C. 792 (1977). Mr. Linder lived with his two sisters in a residence he owned in Bayonne, New Jersey. One sister, Rose, had responsibility for the day-to-day operation of the house, and used her own income to pay for groceries, cleaning and other household expenses. Mr. Linder desired to make a substantial gift to Rose but lacked sufficient liquid assets to make a cash gift. Instead, he gave her several "bonds" executed and sealed by him, and secured by mortgages on the Bayonne home. Each bond also obligated him to pay interest. Mr. Linder duly made these interest payments each year and deducted them from his Federal income tax return; in 1974 Mr. Linder paid Rose $52,000 and cancelled the outstanding bonds and mortgages. The Commissioner successfully challenged Mr. Linder's deductions of the "interest" paid to Rose while the "bonds" were outstanding. The test of whether interest is deductible is whether the bonds constituted "an unconditional and legally enforceable obligation for the payment of money" under the law of New Jersey. The Tax

Court held that they were not, relying upon N.J.Stat.Ann. § 2A:82–3 which provides: "In any claim upon a sealed instrument, a party may plead and set up, in defense thereto, fraud in the consideration of the contract upon which recovery is sought, or want or failure of consideration, as if the instrument were not sealed. In such cases the seal shall be only presumptive evidence of sufficient consideration, which presumption may be rebutted as if the instrument were not sealed."

The court stated:

"On its face, this statute, enacted in substantially its present form in 1900, appears to modify the common law rule and to make lack of consideration a defense to a sealed instrument. This would scarely be surprising, for the magic of the seal has long since been legislatively exorcised in most American jurisdictions. * * *

"We are of the opinion that if faced with the issue today, the highest court of New Jersey would more probably than not refuse to * * * enforce the gratuitous promise under seal. This conclusion is supported by the trend of modern cases. Research has disclosed no recent instance in which any court in the United States has enforced a gratuitous promise under seal. Since petitioner's bonds were not in our view legally enforceable in New Jersey, interest paid thereon is nondeductible."

Alternatives to the Seal

With the decline of the seal, does there remain any means for assuring the enforceability of a promise without consideration, such as Mr. Linder's promise to pay a gift?

Many of the states that have diminished or eliminated the legal effects of the seal provide that a simple written agreement alone creates a rebuttable presumption of consideration, e.g., Cal.Civ.Code §§ 1614, 1615 (West 1982): "A written instrument is presumptive evidence of a consideration. The burden of showing a want of consideration sufficient to support an instrument lies with the party seeking to invalidate or avoid it." In a few states, a written agreement is conclusive to make a promise binding without consideration. For example, the Model Written Obligations Act, in force only in Pennsylvania, provides: "A written release or promise, hereafter made and signed by the person releasing or promising, shall not be invalid or unenforceable for lack of consideration, if the writing also contains an additional express statement, in any form of language, that the signer intends to be legally bound." Pa.Stat.Ann. tit. 33, § 6 (Purdon 1967). (Is such a "statement," possibly hidden in a printed form, likely to fulfill the appropriate functions of legal formalities?)

The search for devices to assure the enforceability of gift promises need not be closely confined within the borders of "contract law." If Mr. Linder had handed over a diamond ring or $5000 in cash to his sister, we would have no difficulty in saying that the gift was effective, because "executed"; under the rules applied by the law of "property" the sister would have become the owner of the ring or the cash. The requirement that the property actually be delivered to the donee for the gift to be effective serves as a formality furnishing evidence of the donor's intent to part with his property, and making "vivid and concrete" to him the significance of what he is doing. ("The *wrench* of delivery, ＊ ＊ ＊ the little mental twinge at seeing his property pass from his hands into those of another, is an important element to the protection of the donor." See Mechem, The Requirement of Delivery in Gifts of Chattels, 21 Ill.L.Rev. 341, 348 (1926)).

There are many modern decisions holding that present ownership of property can also be transferred merely by the alternate formality of a signed unsealed writing. Consider Faith Lutheran Retirement Home v. Veis, 156 Mont. 38, 473 P.2d 503 (1970). A retired farmer, 81 years old, unmarried and with no children, entered the Retirement Home. Shortly thereafter he signed a formal agreement with the usual provisions for payment for room, board, and services; at the same time—and apparently after some prodding by the Home's administrator and chaplain—he dictated the following: "The Church through Faith Lutheran Home has been doing a wonderful piece of work among my old friends. For the comfort, care, happiness I have while I am here be it short or long I wish to pay for these values the sum of $10,000.00 on demand. This may however be collectable against my estate if not demanded sooner, or paid by me." After his death, it was held that he had made a valid gift of $10,000 to the Home.

(Might this instrument also have been upheld as a will? Writings indicating that a *present* gift is being made are often held to lack the requisite "testamentary intent"; admission to probate is reserved for bequests that become effective only upon death and which are until then, entirely revocable. Atkinson, Handbook of the Law of Wills 207–10 (2d ed. 1953). And in *Faith Lutheran*, testimony indicated that the "donor" had "rejected lawyers, a will, or a note and he stated directly that he 'wanted to give a gift' ＊ ＊ ＊.")

The "property" transferred as a gift can also consist of the donor's rights to performance under a contract. See Restatement, Second, Contracts § 332:

(1) Unless a contrary intention is manifested, a gratuitous assignment is irrevocable if

(a) the assignment is in a writing either signed or under seal that is delivered by the assignor; or

(b) the assignment is accompanied by delivery of a writing of a type customarily accepted as a symbol or as evidence of the right assigned.

For example, in Speelman v. Pascal, 10 N.Y.2d 313, 222 N.Y.S.2d 324, 178 N.E.2d 723 (1961), a theatrical producer wrote plaintiff that "I give you" certain percentages "from my shares of profits of the Pygmalion Musical stage version * * *. This participation * * * is a present to you, in recognition for your loyal work for me as my Executive Secretary." Four months later the producer died; the musical, at that time not yet written, was to become "My Fair Lady." The letter was held to be a "valid, complete, present gift to plaintiff by way of assignment of a share in future royalties * * *."

Another possibility is the "declaration of trust." A donor can declare himself, even orally, to be a "trustee" of specified property; he then holds it under a fiduciary duty to deal with it for the benefit of the "real," the "equitable" owner, the donee (or "beneficiary.") See Restatement, Trusts, Second, § 28, illustration 2 (1959): "A deposits $1000 of his own money in a savings bank in his own name. Later he gratuitously declares himself trustee of the deposit for B. A is trustee for B of his claim against the bank."

There is at least a theoretical distinction between these present transfers of property interests (even where the donee is to enjoy the fruits only at a later time), and a mere promise to make a *future* transfer. But an individual's behavior rarely fits neatly into one, and only one, legal category, and the line is difficult to draw with confidence. It should be obvious that through these "property" devices, results can be reached which in practice are very similar to those obtained by enforcement of a gratuitous promise.

Gratuitous Promises in the Civil Law

In the "civil law" systems exemplified by France and Germany, gift promises may be made binding, but only after compliance with strict formalities. (In this country the state of Louisiana, a "civil law" jurisdiction, closely follows the French treatment of gift promises.) Typically, the requirement is that the promise be executed before a notary (in France, before two notaries, or a notary and two witnesses). And the European "notary" has little to do with our "notary public": he is both public official and member of the legal profession, a specialist in land conveyancing and family matters such as wills and the administration of estates, and "occupies a place of great dignity and [honor] in French life." Brown, "The Office of the Notary in France," 2 Int. & Comp.L.Q. 60, 69 (1953). In a gift transaction, "[t]he donor and normally the donee would also be present. After the terms of the transaction had all been written down, one of the notaries must read the whole document 'aloud' to the group and all were required to sign. The only thing missing [from the Civil Code] was an indication whether the meeting must open and close with prayer." J.P. Dawson, Gifts and Promises 69 (1980).

While the notarial requirement seems to have been largely circumvented in France, it remains an important aspect of the German regulation of gratuitous promises.

VON MEHREN, CIVIL LAW ANALOGUES TO CONSIDERATION: AN EXERCISE IN COMPARATIVE ANALYSIS

72 Harv. L.Rev. 1009, 1077–78 (1959).

The hesitations of the common law are probably justified; it may well be that not all gift promises made with due formality should be effective. Indeed, French and German law provide techniques by which many questionable gift promises can be undone, but the approach is not in terms of contract formation. Their *ex post facto* technique may well be more appropriate for handling the gift problem than is the common law's prophylactic treatment.

Under article 955 of the [French] Code Civil, a promise to give (or completed gift) can be revoked on several grounds: that the donee attempted to kill the donor; that the donee abused the donor, wronged him, or committed a delict against him; and that the donee has refused needed support to the donor. A gift made by a person who has no children is automatically revoked by the subsequent birth to him of a child. * * *†

Comparable provisions are found in German law. A donor can revoke a promise to give (or a completed gift) on the ground that the donee has committed an act of grave ingratitude against the donor or one of his close relatives. The donor also has the right to reclaim a gift or revoke a promise to give if, subsequent to its making, he has suffered reverses such that he is no longer able to maintain a standard of living appropriate to his station in life and can no longer fulfill his statutory duty to furnish maintenance to certain relatives, his wife, or former wife. * * *

Lacking any developed body of law through which, in appropriate cases, gifts can be undone, the common law is understandably hesitant to hold enforceable all gift promises provided with an appropriate formality. Common-law courts have no good doctrinal basis for handling attempted revocations of gift promises on their particular facts. * * *

UNIFORM FRAUDULENT TRANSFER ACT, § 4(a):

A transfer made or obligation incurred by a debtor is fraudulent as to a creditor, whether the creditor's claim arose before or after the transfer was made or the obligation was incurred, if the debtor made the transfer or incurred the obligation:

† French law also reserves a substantial share of all property owned by an individual at death, *or given away during his lifetime,* to his heirs. In the interest of preserving resources within the family, even completed gifts can later be set aside if they exceed this guaranteed share of inheritance.—Ed.

(1) with actual intent to hinder, delay, or defraud any creditor of the debtor; or

(2) without receiving a reasonably equivalent value in exchange for the transfer or obligation, and the debtor:

    (i) was engaged or was about to engage in a business or a transaction for which the remaining assets of the debtor were unreasonably small in relation to the business or transaction; or

    (ii) intended to incur, or believed or reasonably should have believed that he would incur, debts beyond his ability to pay as they become due.

[In such circumstances a creditor may have the transfer or obligation set aside. The Uniform Fraudulent Transfer Act is in force in about half the states, and similar statutes may be found in most other states.]

B. THE BARGAIN PRINCIPLE

AUSTIN, FRAGMENTS ON CONTRACTS, FROM 2 LECTURES ON JURISPRUDENCE 907
(5th ed. 1885).

"In [contracts where nothing is given in exchange for the defendant's promise, like contracts under seal,] inconsiderateness is prevented by the unusual solemnity of the evidentiary incident annexed:—e.g., the sealing of a bond or covenant, the interrogation and answer in a Stipulation.

"[On the other hand, in contracts where some exchange of values has taken place between the parties, inconsiderateness] is supposed to be prevented by the mutuality: each party contracting for his own pecuniary advantage; contemplating a *quid pro quo;* and therefore, being in that circumspective frame of mind which a man who is only thinking of such advantage naturally assumes."

———

DAVIS & CO. v. MORGAN, 117 Ga. 504, 507–08, 43 S.E. 732, 733 (1903):

"When one receives a naked promise, and such promise is broken, he is no worse off than he was. He gave nothing for it, he has lost nothing by it, and on its breach he has suffered no damage cognizable by courts. * * * Such promises are not made within the scope of transactions intended to confer rights enforceable at law. They are lightly made, dictated by generosity, curtesy, or impulse, often by ruinous prodigality. To enforce them by a judgment in favor of those who gave nothing therefor would often bring such imperfect obligations into competition with the absolute duties to wife and children, or into competition with debts for property actually received, and make the law an instrument by which a man could be forced to be generous before he was just. * * *"

RESTATEMENT, SECOND, CONTRACTS § 72:

Comment:

b. Bargains are widely believed to be beneficial to the community in the provision of opportunities for freedom of individual action and exercise of judgment and as a means by which productive energy and product are apportioned in the economy. The enforcement of bargains rests in part on the common belief that enforcement enhances that utility. Where one party has performed, there are additional grounds for enforcement. Where, for example, one party has received goods from the other and has broken his promise to pay for them, enforcement of the promise not only encourages the making of socially useful bargains; it also reimburses the seller for a loss incurred in reliance on the promise and prevents the unjust enrichment of the buyer at the seller's expense. Each of these three grounds of enforcement, bargain, reliance and unjust enrichment, has independent force, but the bargain element alone satisfies the requirement of consideration * * *.

A. LEFF, SWINDLING AND SELLING
13–14 (1976).*

When Ahmed and Kevin contemplate exchange with each other, they bargain, each trying to get as much of the other's wealth as he can in exchange for as little as possible of his own. They each bargain toward *getting* a bargain, that is, toward maximizing their own utility *at the expense* of the other's. Ready-made pictures of that very familiar kind of human interaction abound, from the frantic gesticulations of the Casbah market to the cold mutual malice of telephone calls between sales managers and purchasing agents in a competitive industry.

Despite appearances, however, not all exchanges are exploitative. In fact, few are. When two people make a deal over things of value it is not necessarily the case that one or the other of them come out of it worse off than he went in. You don't have to have one of the traders dumber or weaker than the other in order for there to be a trade. Even in a situation of trading perfection (where both parties are equally free to trade or not, and where whatever one knows the other does also) there would still be trades. For it is frequently the case that what one has is worth less to oneself than to someone else, and, most important, vice versa too. In such cases, a trade will enrich both parties.

Within any "competitive" trading situation, then, there is almost always hidden a cooperative partnership: each party does try to maximize his utility at the expense of the other, but it is only *together* that they can increase the total utility in their joint system. It is over their

* Reprinted with permission of Macmillan Publishing Company from A. Leff, Swindling and Selling, Copyright © 1976 by The Free Press, a Division of Macmillan Publishing Company.

respective shares of this newly created potential value that the parties really contend.

This mechanism, trading items of differing personal utility so as to produce more of value for both parties jointly to gobble up, appears in two different guises, both of which can be, and are, adapted to selling and swindling. The first involves what is essentially a two-party universe and hence shows up early in most elementary-economics textbooks. It almost always goes something like this (right down to the gustatory setting). If I have two large pizzas and no beer, and you have two large beers and no pizza, it is most likely sensible for us to trade. For it is likely that your second beer will give you less satisfaction than it will give me, and the same (though in reverse) is true with respect to my second pizza. Let us assume that there was a standard unit of comparative happiness-from-things; call it a "util." My first pizza is worth, say, three utils to me, and my second is worth one. Your first beer is worth four utils to you, and your second is worth two. Thus there are ten utils between us if we both stand pat; my pizzas, if consumed by me, give me four utils, while your beers, if you drink them, give you six. Now let us assume that your second beer is worth four utils to me, while my second pizza is worth six to you. If we trade, there will be seventeen utils of satisfaction in the system. That is, there will have been an exchange after which both parties are, in their own perception, better off. They will thus have created value out of "thin air." ("Where's the bundle coming from?" "Out of thin air.")

P.S. ATIYAH, ESSAYS ON CONTRACT
28, 31–37 (1986).*

[In his essay entitled "Contracts, Promises, Obligations," the author asks why the law should recognize the binding nature of purely executory contracts, where the plaintiff has "done nothing whatever under the contract" and has not relied in any way on the defendant's promise. "Upon what, then, does liability rest in such circumstances? Wherein is the source of the obligation?"]

The modern, and perhaps even, by now, the traditional legal view would probably be that promises and executory contracts give rise to reasonable expectations and that it is the function of the law to protect reasonable expectations. But this is itself a somewhat circular justification. We all have a large number of expectations, many of which are perfectly reasonable, but only a few of them are protected by the law. Besides, the reasonableness of an expectation is itself something which turns largely upon whether it is in fact protected. If the law did not protect expectations arising from a wholly executory arrangement, then it would be less reasonable to entertain such expectations, or at any rate to entertain them as entitlements. * * * Another puzzling feature of the law's willingness to protect bare expectations is that a disappointed expectation is a psychological rather than a pecuniary injury, and the law is generally sparing in its willingness to award compensation for injuries or losses which are neither physical nor pecuniary. * * *

The second possible argument for upholding executory contracts is the argument from principle. Executory contracts are made so that the parties can rely upon each other and take the necessary preliminary steps to performance. The whole point of such contracts is that they invite reliance. Therefore, it may be urged, even if there *has in fact been no reliance yet,* it is desirable that the principle of upholding the sanctity of contracts should be maintained. Supporters of this argument, however, must explain why a shift in the onus of proof would not meet the case. Certainly, it may be justifiable to throw upon the promisor the burden of showing that the promisee has not yet acted upon the promise; but if in fact he can show this, or if it is conceded, can the argument on principle be maintained? What principle is it that requires contracts to be held binding because they may be relied upon where in fact it is conclusively demonstrated that the particular contract has not been relied upon? * * *

The third possible argument in support of the executory contract concerns the case where the contract is a deliberate exercise in risk allocation. Where the primary purpose of a contract is to shift a risk of some future possibility from one party to another, and where, in particular, the risk is thereby shifted to a party who in a commercial sense is better able to take the risk, or to take avoiding action against the risk eventuating, there appears to be a strong economic case for the executory contract. I believe that this argument lies at the heart of the historical development of the binding executory contract in English law, but it is imperative to note the limits upon its application. It is very far from being true that all contracts, even all executory contracts, are exercises in risk allocation. Frequently, it is the interpretation of the law which converts a simple postponed exchange into a risk-allocation exercise, rather than any deliberate intent of the parties. * * * It is also far from being always the case that the purpose of an executory contract is to shift a risk to a party whose business it is to handle such risks and who can, therefore, be assumed to be generally more efficient at handling them. Indeed, the clearest and most widespread example of a contract of a risk-allocation character is the simple bet, which involves no such economically efficient transfer of risk. * * *

[I]f the primary justification for the enforcement of executory contracts is that they are risk-allocation devices, then it follows that the enforcement of such contracts raises profoundly value-laden questions. The justification for the executory contract becomes, in effect, an economic justification, an argument for greater economic efficiency. The purpose of enforcing such contracts is that of facilitating the use of greater skill, intelligence, foresight, knowledge, and perhaps even resources by those who possess these advantages. To the extent that the law refuses to recognize the binding force of executory transactions in order to protect the weak, the foolish, the improvident or those who lack bargaining power, it must necessarily weaken the incentives and indeed the power of those not suffering these disadvantages.

One of the editors recently conducted a survey of corporate general counsel, in which a number of general counsel were asked questions based on hypothetical contract disputes and were told that "your answer should reflect your view of what the law should be, rather than your view of current law." One of the hypotheticals concerns a promptly repudiated promise:

"For a week, two companies, A and B, have been negotiating a contract. It is understood that either party is free to terminate negotiations and that neither is bound unless a final agreement is signed. Finally agreement is reached and the contract is signed. The next day, company A receives a notice from company B that B has decided not to perform the contract. A has not yet relied on the contract in any way, but will lose the profit it expected to make on the contract. Should A be able to recover this profit from B?"

Of the responses to this question, 67.5% were "yes" and 31.3% were "no." Weintraub, A Survey of Contract Practice and Policy, 1992 Wis.L.Rev. 1.

FULLER & PERDUE, THE RELIANCE INTEREST IN CONTRACT DAMAGES
46 Yale L.J. 52, 61–63 (1936).*

[In attempting to answer the question, "Why should the law ever protect the expectation interest?" the authors point out that granting expectancy damages may be viewed as the most efficient way to compensate for the changes in position—"very numerous and very difficult to prove"—which make up the promisee's reliance on a contract, and which may include the passing up of opportunities to enter into other deals. They continue:]

A justification can be developed from a less negative point of view. It may be said that there is not only a policy in favor of preventing and undoing the harms resulting from reliance, but also a policy in favor of promoting and facilitating reliance on business agreements. * * * Agreements can accomplish little, either for their makers or for society, unless they are made the basis for action. When business agreements are not only made but are also acted on, the division of labor is facilitated, goods find their way to the places where they are most needed, and economic activity is generally stimulated. These advantages would be threatened by any rule which limited legal protection to

* Reprinted by permission of The Yale Law Journal Company and Fred B. Roth-   man & Company from The Yale Law Journal, Vol. 46, pp. 52, 61–63.

the reliance interest. Such a rule would in practice tend to discourage reliance. The difficulties in proving reliance and subjecting it to pecuniary measurement are such that the business man knowing, or sensing, that these obstacles stood in the way of judicial relief would hesitate to rely on a promise in any case where the legal sanction was of significance to him. To encourage reliance we must therefore dispense with its proof. For this reason it has been found wise to make recovery on a promise independent of reliance, both in the sense that in some cases the promise is enforced though not relied on (as in the bilateral business agreement) and in the sense that recovery is not limited to the detriment incurred in reliance.

* * * In general our courts and our economic institutions attribute special significance to the same types of promises. The bilateral business agreement is, generally speaking, the only type of informal contract our courts are willing to enforce without proof that reliance has occurred—simply for the sake of facilitating reliance. This is, by no accident, precisely the kind of contract (the "exchange", "bargain", "trade", "deal") which furnishes the indispensable and pervasive framework for the "unmanaged" portions of our economic activity.

C. SOCIAL AND FAMILY RELATIONS

P. BLAU, EXCHANGE AND POWER IN SOCIAL LIFE
93–96 (1964).*

Social exchange differs in important ways from strictly economic exchange. The basic and most crucial distinction is that social exchange entails *unspecified* obligations. * * *

[I]t involves favors that create diffuse future obligations, not precisely specified ones, and the nature of the return cannot be bargained about but must be left to the discretion of the one who makes it. Thus, if a person gives a dinner party, he expects his guests to reciprocate at some future date. But he can hardly bargain with them about the kind of party to which they should invite him, although he expects them not simply to ask him for a quick lunch if he had invited them to a formal dinner. Similarly, if a person goes to some trouble in behalf of an acquaintance, he expects *some* expression of gratitude, but he can neither bargain with the other over how to reciprocate nor force him to reciprocate at all. * * *

In contrast to economic commodities, the benefits involved in social exchange do not have an exact price in terms of a single quantitative medium of exchange, which is another reason why social obligations are unspecific. It is essential to realize that this is a substantive fact, not simply a methodological problem. It is not just the social scientist who cannot exactly measure how much approval a given helpful action is worth; the actors themselves cannot precisely specify the worth of approval or of help in the absence of a money price. The obligations individuals incur in social exchange, therefore, are defined only in general, somewhat diffuse terms. Furthermore, the specific benefits exchanged are sometimes primarily valued as symbols of the supportiveness and friendliness they express, and it is the exchange of the underlying mutual support that is the main concern of the participants. Occasionally, a time-consuming service of great material benefit to the recipient might be properly repaid by mere verbal expressions of deep appreciation, since these are taken to signify as much supportiveness as the material benefits. In the long run, however, the explicit efforts the associates in a peer relation make in one another's behalf tend to be in balance, if only because a persistent imbalance in these manifestations of good will raise questions about the reciprocity in the underlying orientations of support and congeniality.   *   *   *

Since social benefits have no exact price, and since the utility of a given benefit cannot be clearly separated from that of other rewards derived from a social association, it seems difficult to apply the economic principles of maximizing utilities to social exchange. The impersonal economic market is designed to strip specific commodities of these entangling alliances with other benefits, so to speak, and thus to make possible rational choices between distinct alternatives with a fixed price. Even in economic exchange, however, the significance of each alternative is rarely confined to a single factor, which confounds rational decision-making; people's job choices are affected by working conditions as well as salaries, and their choices of merchants, by the atmosphere in a store as well as the quality of the merchandise. Although the systematic study of social exchange poses distinctive problems, the assumptions it makes about the maximization of utilities implicit in choice behavior are little different from those made by the economist in the study of consumption.

R. POSNER, GRATUITOUS PROMISES IN ECONOMICS AND LAW

6 J. Legal Stud. 411, 416–17 (1977).*

The general rule is that gratuitous promises are not enforceable. A good example of the rule and its economic logic would be a case where a man promised to take a woman to dinner but later reneged. The man presumably derived some utility from making the promise, and his utility might be greater if the promise were legally binding on him. But the increment in utility, if any, is probably small, both compared to that of the dinner itself and absolutely given the small size of the promised transfer. Moreover, the legal-error costs of enforcing such promises would be high because of the difficulty of distinguishing in casual social relations between a mere present intention, subject to change at will and a promise intended to be binding on the promisor.

* * * [This] analysis would not be materially altered if the dinner promise had been bilateral—if, that is, in return for the man's promise to take her out the woman had promised to accompany him. Where the utility of the promises being exchanged is small, the gains from legal enforcement are likely to be swamped by the costs of enforcement. The law recognizes this and refuses to enforce trivial social promises, especially within the family—where an additional factor pointing in the same direction, is the existence of an inexpensive alternative to legal enforcement refusal to engage in promissory transactions in the future. If the husband reneges on his promise, the wife will refuse in the future to perform services in exchange for his promises.[14]

RESTATEMENT, SECOND, CONTRACTS § 21:

Illustration:

5. A invites his friend B to dinner in his home, and B accepts. There is no contract. If A promised B a fee for attending and entertaining other guests, and B did so, there would be a contract to pay the fee.

BALFOUR v. BALFOUR [1919] 2 K.B. 571 (C.A.). Husband and wife lived in Ceylon, where the husband had a government post. They visited England in 1915; nine months later he had to return to his job, but the wife, who was ill, remained behind on her doctor's advice. Before his departure the husband promised to pay 30 per month to his wife until she returned. The court held the agreement to be unenforceable, Atkin, L.J., saying:

"All I can say is that the small Courts of this country would have to be multiplied one hundredfold if these arrangements were held to result in legal obligations. They are not sued upon, not because the parties are reluctant to enforce their legal rights when the agreement is broken, but because the parties, in the inception of the arrangement, never intended that they should be sued upon. Agreements such as these are outside the realm of contracts altogether. The common law does not regulate the form of agreements between spouses. Their promises are not sealed with seals and sealing wax. The consideration that really obtains for them is that natural love and affection which counts for so little in these cold Courts. The terms may be repudiated, varied or renewed as performance proceeds or as disagreements develop, and the principles of the common law as to exoneration and discharge and accord

14. This is part of the more general point that legal remedies for breach of contract are less important where the par- ties have a continuing relationship * * *.

and satisfaction are such as find no place in the domestic code. The parties themselves are advocates, judges, Courts, sheriff's officer and reporter. In respect of these promises each house is a domain into which the King's writ does not seek to run, and to which his officers do not seek to be admitted. * * *"

———

JONES v. PADAVATTON, [1969] 2 All E.R. 616 (C.A.). This was a suit, which one of the judges characterized as "really deplorable," by a mother against her daughter. In 1962, the daughter was living in Washington, D.C. with her son. Her mother, a resident of Trinidad, suggested she go to England and study to become a lawyer, and offered to send her $200 a month to allow her to do so. That year the daughter went to England and began her studies. In 1964, the mother bought a house in London so that her daughter and grandson could have a place to live; part of the house was to be rented out to cover expenses and the daughter's maintenance. Differences arose between the parties, and the mother brought suit to eject her daughter. Held, for the mother. Danckwerts, L.J., concluded that this "is one of those family arrangements which depend on the good faith of the promises which are made and are not intended to be rigid, binding agreements." On the other hand, Salmon, L.J. thought this was "entirely different from the ordinary case of a mother promising her daughter an allowance whilst the daughter read for the Bar, or a father promising his son an allowance at university if the son passed the necessary examinations to gain admission * * *. I cannot think that either intended that if, after the daughter had been in London, say, for six months, the mother dishonoured her promise and left her daughter destitute, the daughter would have no legal redress." But he too held for the mother, on the ground that the arrangement could not have been intended to last more than a "reasonable time," which had elapsed after five years.

———

MARVIN v. MARVIN, 18 Cal.3d 660, 134 Cal.Rptr. 815, 557 P.2d 106 (1976). Michelle Triola Marvin claimed that she had given up "her lucrative career as an entertainer [and] singer" in order to devote herself full time to actor Lee Marvin, "as a companion, homemaker, housekeeper, and cook." The two lived together, and held themselves out to the public as husband and wife, between 1964 and 1970; according to Michelle, they agreed that they would "combine their efforts and earnings and would share equally and any and all property accumulated." In 1970 Lee Marvin asked Michelle to move out; he stopped making support payments to her shortly thereafter, and she brought suit.

The trial court granted defendant's motion for judgment on the pleadings; held, reversed. Defendant had argued that enforcement of the express contract between the parties would violate public policy, because it was so closely related to the "immoral" character of their relationship. But the Supreme Court of California, citing "the prevalence of nonmarital relationships in modern society and the social acceptance of them," disagreed: "The fact that a man and woman live together without marriage, and engage in a sexual relationship, does not in itself invalidate agreements between them relating to their earnings, property, or expenses. Neither is such an agreement invalid merely because the parties may have contemplated the creation or continuation of a nonmarital relationship when they entered into it. Agreements between nonmarital partners fail only to the extent that they rest upon a consideration of meretricious sexual services."

The court also suggested that the plaintiff might pursue a cause of action based, not on an express contract, but on "an implied contract or implied agreement of partnership or joint venture or some other tacit understanding between the parties." In addition, it suggested that "a nonmarital partner may recover in quantum meruit for the reasonable value of household services rendered less the reasonable value of support received if he can show that he rendered services with the expectation of monetary reward. * * * There is no more reason to presume that services are contributed as a gift than to presume that funds are contributed as a gift; in any event the better approach is to presume * * * 'that the parties intend to deal fairly with each other.' " And the court held open the further possibility of "additional equitable remedies to protect the expectations of the parties * * * in cases in which existing remedies prove inadequate."

On remand, the trial court could find neither an express nor an implied contract to share the defendant's property ("There was no pooling of earnings, no property was purchased in joint names, and no joint income tax returns were executed.") And it felt that any services plaintiff may have rendered were more than compensated by the money spent on her by defendant, and by her having "acquired whatever clothes, furs and cars she wished and engaged in a social life amongst screen and state luminaries."

However, noting that the plaintiff was receiving unemployment benefits and that the value of Lee Marvin's property at the time of separation exceeded $1 million, the court nevertheless awarded plaintiff $104,000 "for rehabilitation purposes so that she may have the economic means to re-educate herself and to learn new, employable skills * * * so that she may return from her status as companion of a motion picture star to a separate, independent but perhaps more prosaic existence." (5 Fam.L.Rep. 3077, April 24, 1979).

This award was overturned on appeal, the Court of Appeal remarking that while a "court of equity admittedly has broad powers, * * * it may not create totally new substantive rights under the guise of doing equity." 122 Cal.App.3d 871, 876, 176 Cal.Rptr. 555, 559 (1981).

MORONE v. MORONE, 50 N.Y.2d 481, 429 N.Y.S.2d 592, 413 N.E.2d 1154 (1980). Plaintiff and defendant, although unmarried, had lived together since 1952; two children were born of the relationship. Plaintiff brought suit for $250,000, alleging, in a first cause of action, that she had "performed domestic duties and business services at the request of defendant with the expectation that she would receive full compensation for them." The lower court dismissed the complaint on the grounds that it sought recovery for " 'housewifely' duties within a marital-type arrangement for which no recovery could be had."

The Court of Appeals affirmed as to this cause of action: "Finding an implied contract such as was recognized in Marvin v. Marvin to be conceptually so amorphous as practically to defy equitable enforcement, * * * we decline to follow the *Marvin* lead. * * * Historically, we have required the explicit and structured understanding of an express contract and have declined to recognize a contract which is implied from the rendition and acceptance of services. The major difficulty with implying a contract from the rendition of services for one another by persons living together is that it is not reasonable to infer an agreement to pay for the services rendered when the relationship of the parties makes it natural that the services were rendered gratuitously. As a matter of human experience personal services will frequently be rendered by two people living together because they value each other's company or because they find it a convenient or rewarding thing to do. For courts to attempt through hindsight to sort out the intentions of the parties and affix jural significance to conduct carried out within an essentially private and generally noncontractual relationship runs too great a risk of error. Absent an express agreement, there is no frame of reference against which to compare the testimony presented and the character of the evidence that can be presented becomes more evanescent. There is, therefore, substantially greater risk of emotion-laden afterthought, not to mention fraud, in attempting to ascertain by implication what services, if any, were rendered gratuitously and what compensation, if any, the parties intended to be paid." However, since the plaintiff had also alleged an express oral "partnership agreement" in a second cause of action, the court held it was error to dismiss the case on the pleadings.

IN THE MATTER OF BABY M, 109 N.J. 396, 537 A.2d 1227 (1988). William Stern and Mary Beth Whitehead entered into a "surrogacy contract" in which Whitehead agreed, for a fee of $10,000, to be artificially inseminated with Stern's semen and to bear his child; after the child's birth, she was to surrender it to Stern and his wife, renounce all her maternal rights, and not "form or attempt to form a parent-child relationship" with the child. However, Whitehead refused to give up the baby after it was born, and Stern filed suit seeking enforcement of the surrogacy contract. The trial court held that the surrogacy contract was valid and enforceable: "The male gave his sperm; the female gave her egg in their pre-planned effort to create a child—thus, a contract." The court granted specific performance of the contract, and ordered that sole custody of the child be granted to Stern and that Whitehead's parental rights be terminated.

The Supreme Court of New Jersey upheld the trial court's award of custody to Stern on the ground that this was in the best interests of the child; it did so, however, "without regard to the provisions of the surrogacy contract," which it found to be unenforceable. The payment of money to a surrogate mother was "illegal, perhaps criminal, and potentially degrading to women"; the contract conflicted with laws prohibiting the use of money in connection with adoptions and with laws requiring proof of parental unfitness before termination of parental rights, and in addition, "violates the policy of the State that the rights of natural parents are equal concerning the child, the father's right no greater than the mother's":

"In the scheme contemplated by the surrogacy contract in this case, a middle man, propelled by profit, promotes the sale. Whatever idealism may have motivated any of the participants, the profit motive predominates, permeates, and ultimately governs the transaction. The demand for children is great and the supply small. * * * The situation is ripe for the entry of the middleman who will bring some equilibrium into the market by increasing the supply through the use of money. * * *

"The point is made that Mrs. Whitehead *agreed* to the surrogacy arrangement, supposedly fully understanding the consequences. Putting aside the issue of how compelling her need for money may have been, and how significant her understanding of the consequences, we suggest that her consent is irrelevant. There are, in a civilized society, some things that money cannot buy. * * * There are, in short, values that society deems more important than granting to wealth whatever it can buy, be it labor, love, or life. * * * "

SECTION 2: CONTRACT AS BARGAIN: THE REQUIREMENT OF CONSIDERATION

HAMER v. SIDWAY

New York Court of Appeals, 1891.
124 N.Y. 538, 27 N.E. 256.

Appeal from order of the General Term of the Supreme Court in the fourth judicial department, made July 1, 1890, which reversed a judgment in favor of plaintiff entered upon a decision of the court on trial at Special Term and granted a new trial.

This action was brought upon an alleged contract.

The plaintiff presented a claim to the executor of William E. Story, Sr., for $5,000 and interest from the 6th day of February, 1875. She acquired it through several mesne assignments from William E. Story,

2d. The claim being rejected by the executor, this action was brought. It appears that William E. Story, Sr., was the uncle of William E. Story, 2d; that at the celebration of the golden wedding of Samuel Story and wife, father and mother of William E. Story, Sr., on the 20th day of March, 1869, in the presence of the family and invited guests he promised his nephew that if he would refrain from drinking, using tobacco, swearing and playing cards or billiards for money until he became twenty-one years of age he would pay him a sum of $5,000. The nephew assented thereto and fully performed the conditions inducing the promise. When the nephew arrived at the age of twenty-one years and on the 31st day of January, 1875, he wrote to his uncle informing him that he had performed his part of the agreement and had thereby become entitled to the sum of $5,000. The uncle received the letter and a few days later and on the sixth of February, he wrote and mailed to his nephew the following letter:

"Buffalo, Feb. 6, 1875.

"W. E. STORY, JR.:

"DEAR NEPHEW—Your letter of the 31st ult. came to hand all right, saying that you had lived up to the promise made to me several years ago. I have no doubt but you have, for which you shall have five thousand dollars as I promised you. I had the money in the bank the day you was 21 years old that I intend for you, and you shall have the money certain. Now, Willie I do not intend to interfere with this money in any way till I think you are capable of taking care of it and the sooner that time comes the better it will please me. I would hate very much to have you start out in some adventure that you thought all right and lose this money in one year. The first five thousand dollars that I got together cost me a heap of hard work. You would hardly believe me when I tell you that to obtain this I shoved a jackplane many a day, butchered three or four years, then came to this city, and after three months' perseverence I obtained a situation in a grocery store. I opened this store early, closed late, slept in the fourth story of the building in a room 30 by 40 feet and not a human being in the building but myself. All this I done to live as cheap as I could to save something. I don't want you to take up with this kind of fare. I was here in the cholera season '49 and '52 and the deaths averaged 80 to 125 daily and plenty of smallpox. I wanted to go home, but Mr. Fisk, the gentleman I was working for, told me if I left then, after it got healthy he probably would not want me. I stayed. All the money I have saved I know just how I got it. It did not come to me in any mysterious way, and the reason I speak of this is that money got in this way stops longer with a fellow that gets it with hard knocks than it does when he finds it. Willie, you are 21 and you have many a thing to learn yet. This money you have earned much easier than I did besides acquiring good habits at the same time and you are quite welcome to the money; hope you will make good use of it. I was ten long years getting this together after I was your age. * * *

Truly Yours,
"W. E. STORY.

"P.S.—You can consider this money on interest."

The nephew received the letter and thereafter consented that the money should remain with his uncle in accordance with the terms and conditions of the letters. The uncle died on the 29th day of January, 1887, without having paid over to his nephew any portion of the said $5,000 and interest. * * *

PARKER, J. * * * The defendant contends that the contract was without consideration to support it, and, therefore, invalid. He asserts that the promisee by refraining from the use of liquor and tobacco was not harmed but benefited; that that which he did was best for him to do independently of his uncle's promise, and insists that it follows that unless the promisor was benefited, the contract was without consideration. A contention, which if well founded, would seem to leave open for controversy in many cases whether that which the promisee did or omitted to do was, in fact, of such benefit to him as to leave no consideration to support the enforcement of the promisor's agreement. Such a rule could not be tolerated, and is without foundation in the law. The Exchequer Chamber, in 1875, defined consideration as follows: "A valuable consideration in the sense of the law may consist either in some right, interest, profit or benefit accruing to the one party, or some forbearance, detriment, loss or responsibility given, suffered or undertaken by the other." Courts "will not ask whether the thing which forms the consideration does in fact benefit the promisee or a third party, or is of any substantial value to anyone. It is enough that something is promised, done, forborne or suffered by the party to whom the promise is made as consideration for the promise made to him." (Anson's Prin. of Con. 63.)

"In general a waiver of any legal right at the request of another party is a sufficient consideration for a promise." (Parsons on Contracts, 444.)

"Any damage, or suspension, or forbearance of a right will be sufficient to sustain a promise." (Kent, vol. 2, 465, 12th ed.)

Pollock, in his work on contracts, page 166, after citing the definition given by the Exchequer Chamber already quoted, says: "The second branch of this judicial description is really the most important one. Consideration means not so much that one party is profiting as that the other abandons some legal right in the present or limits his legal freedom of action in the future as an inducement for the promise of the first."

Now, applying this rule to the facts before us, the promisee used tobacco, occasionally drank liquor, and he had a legal right to do so. That right he abandoned for a period of years upon the strength of the promise of the testator that for such forbearance he would give him $5,000. We need not speculate on the effort which may have been required to give up the use of those stimulants. It is sufficient that he restricted his lawful freedom of action within certain prescribed limits upon the faith of his uncle's agreement, and now having fully performed the conditions imposed, it is of no moment whether such performance actually proved a benefit to the promisor, and the court will not inquire into it, but were it a proper subject of inquiry, we see nothing in this record that would permit a determination that the uncle was not benefited in a legal sense. Few cases have been found which may be said to be precisely in point, but such as have been support the position we have taken. * * *

The order appealed from should be reversed and the judgment of the Special Term affirmed, with costs payable out of the estate.

WHITE v. BLUETT, [1854] 23 L.J. Ex. (N.S.) 36 (1853). A son had given his now-deceased father a promissory note. In a suit on the note, the son alleged that he had complained to his father that he "had not received at his hands so much money or so many advantages as the other children," and the father had agreed that if the son "should for ever cease to make such complaints," the father would discharge him from all liability on the note. The court held that despite this agreement the son was still liable, Pollock, C.B., saying, "By the argument a principle is pressed to an absurdity, as a bubble is blown until it bursts. * * * The son had no right to complain, for the father might make what distribution of his property he liked; and the son's abstaining from doing what he had no right to do can be no consideration."

During the argument Parke, B., had asked, "Is an agreement by a father, in consideration that his son will not bore him, a binding contract?"

KIRKSEY v. KIRKSEY

Supreme Court of Alabama, 1845.
8 Ala. 131.

Assumpsit by the defendant, against the plaintiff in error. The question is presented in this Court, upon a case agreed, which shows the following facts:

The plaintiff was the wife of defendant's brother, but had for some time been a widow, and had several children. In 1840, the plaintiff resided on public land, under a contract of lease, she had held over, and was comfortably settled, and would have attempted to secure the land she lived on. The defendant resided in Talladega county, some sixty, or seventy miles off. On the 10th October, 1840, he wrote to her the following letter:

"Dear sister Antillico—Much to my mortification, I heard, that brother Henry was dead, and one of his children. I know that your situation is one of grief, and difficulty. You had a bad chance before, but a great deal worse now. I should like to come and see you, but cannot with convenience at present. * * * I do not know whether you have a preference on the place you live on, or not. If you had, I would advise you to obtain your preference, and sell the land and quit the country, as I understand it is very unhealthy, and I know society is very bad. If you will come down and see me, I will let you have a place to raise your family, and I have more open land than I can tend; and on the account of your situation, and that of your family, I feel like I want you and the children to do well."

Within a month or two after the receipt of this letter, the plaintiff abandoned her possession, without disposing of it, and removed with her family, to the residence of the defendant, who put her in comfortable houses, and gave her land to cultivate for two years, at the end of which time he notified her to remove, and put her in a house, not comfortable, in the woods, which he afterwards required her to leave.

A verdict being found for the plaintiff, for two hundred dollars, the above facts were agreed, and if they will sustain the action, the judgment is to be affirmed, otherwise it is to be reversed.

Ormond, J.—The inclination of my mind, is, that the loss and inconvenience, which the plaintiff sustained in breaking up, and moving to the defendant's, a distance of sixty miles, is a sufficient consideration to support the promise, to furnish her with a house and land to cultivate, until she could raise her family. My brothers, however think, that the promise on the part of the defendant, was a mere gratuity, and that an action will not lie for its breach. The judgment of the Court below must therefore be reversed, pursuant to the agreement of the parties.

O. W. HOLMES, THE COMMON LAW
292–94 (1881, 1923 ed.).

It appears to me that it has not always been sufficiently borne in mind that the same thing may be a consideration or not, as it is dealt with by the parties. * * * It is hard to see the propriety of erecting any detriment which an instrument may disclose or provide for, into a consideration, unless the parties have dealt with it on that footing. In many cases a promisee may incur a detriment without thereby furnishing a consideration. * * * The detriment may be nothing but a condition precedent to performance of the promise, as where a man promises another to pay him five hundred dollars if he breaks his leg.

* * *

It is said that consideration must not be confounded with motive. It is true that it must not be confounded with what may be the prevailing or chief motive in actual fact. A man may promise to paint a picture for five hundred dollars, while his chief motive may be a desire for fame. A consideration may be given and accepted, in fact, solely for the purpose of making a promise binding. But, nevertheless, it is the essence of a consideration, that, by the terms of the agreement, it is given and accepted as the motive or inducement of the promise. Conversely, the promise must be made and accepted as the conventional motive or inducement for furnishing the consideration. The root of the whole matter is the relation of reciprocal conventional inducement, each for the other, between consideration and promise.

The Restatement of Contracts divides all enforceable promises not under seal into two categories: (1) contracts supported by consideration, that is, a "bargained for" performance or return promise (§§ 71–81), and (2) "contracts without consideration," which are "exceptions to the general requirement of a bargain" (§§ 82–94). Even if we accept the characterization of the defendant's promise in Kirksey v. Kirksey as a "mere gratuity" and thus not supported by a "bargained for" consideration, it does not follow that under the Restatement all enforcement of the promise is necessarily precluded. Mrs. Kirksey's change of position in reliance on the promise might constitute an alternative basis for enforcement. See generally section 3, infra.

DUNCAN v. BLACK

Missouri Court of Appeals, 1959.
324 S.W.2d 483.

RUARK, JUDGE.

This is a suit on a note, but the tentacles of the question reach into the mysteries of cotton acreage allotments. The plaintiff, now appellant, sued the defendants-respondents on a $1,500 note. The note was pleaded in conventional form. The answer was admission of execution but denial of consideration. At trial, which was without jury, the plaintiff offered his note and rested. The defendants, as was their burden, since the note imports a valid consideration, then went forward with the evidence, and on the uncontradicted evidence the following facts were established.

Defendant William Black, who appears to have inherited considerable land from his father, sold some 359 acres of this land to the plaintiff. The contract, after referring to the description, consideration, and items not here concerned, announced in a separate paragraph, *"Party of the second part is to receive a 65 acre cotton allotment with the land he is purchasing from the party of the first part."* Deed was executed on December 29, 1954.

Now the land so sold did not "carry" a 65-acre cotton allotment. When and as fixed by the county committee, the allotment was only 49.6 acres, and the parties undertook to make up the 15-plus-acre difference by using a part of the allotment allowed to Black's unsold land. The first crop year defendants "made up that difference" out of their own cotton allotment.[2] The following year plaintiff came to defendants and requested that they "do that again" (make up the difference). Defendant Black first assented, but later decided that he didn't cotton to this idea, backed out, and did not do it. Sometime prior to September 13, 1956, the date of the note, plaintiff came to Black and told him that he (plaintiff) had been or would be penalized for planting more cotton than his allotment called for. He said he had been advised by a lawyer that defendant owed him damages "on the contract." Black asked if the matter couldn't be "settled," and the transaction was settled by the giving of the note in question.

* * * The court rendered judgment for the defendants, and plaintiff has appealed. His contentions are premised upon the proposition that the giving of the note was a compromise of a disputed claim; that because plaintiff did not receive the complete consideration for which he bargained (the complete 65-acre cotton allotment), he was entitled to rescind; that in the new agreement (the acceptance of the note) he forbore this right of rescission, and this was sufficient consideration.

Among the respondents' contentions are (1) the contract for a 65-acre allotment was complied with by "making it up" for the one year; (2) there was no consideration because plaintiff's claim for damages had no basis; and (3) if there was a consideration it was illegal.

It is necessary that we first understand the nature of the thing the parties were attempting to bargain:

In the Agricultural Adjustment Act, Title 7 U.S.C.A. § 1282, there is a declaration of policy, and in section 1341 there is a legislative finding and declaration that fluctuations in supplies of cotton disrupt orderly marketing, with consequent destruction of commerce; that without federal assistance farmers cannot prevent recurrence of excessive supplies and provide for orderly marketing; that it is in the interest of general welfare that the soil be not wasted by production of excessive supplies of cotton.

Accordingly it is provided that the Secretary of Agriculture shall fix and proclaim a national quota of cotton "for such marketing year," this to be submitted to a referendum, and if the required majority of the farmers vote to surrender a portion of their liberty in this respect, then the Secretary shall impose a national allotment for cotton "to be produced in the next calendar year." This allotment is thereafter apportioned among the states, and the state allotment is in turn apportioned among the counties, and the county allotment is in turn (by local committee) apportioned among the individual farms. The law provides * * * that any allotment acreage which is voluntarily surrendered shall be reapportioned to other farms; and it further provides a penalty against the farmer for planting more than the allotment which has been established for his land. * * *

2. How this was done we do not know.

The purpose and general scheme of the Act is to accomplish a national public benefit in controlling surplus and consequent abnormal prices by limiting production, which purpose and benefit will fail unless the plan is carried out at farm level. Under the Act and its administration, the individual farm acreage allotment is fixed by the county committee, whose finding of facts is final. The allotment runs with the land. It is not the separate "property" of the individual and is not subject to be sold, bartered or removed to other land. * * *

Our conclusion is that the attempt to buy and sell acreage of an allotment and move it from one farm to the other is not only invalid and contrary to the regulations governing operation of the Act, but also contrary to and destructive of the basic purpose of the Act.

The law favors compromise of doubtful claims, and forbearance may be a sufficient consideration for such compromise, even though the claim upon which it is based should develop to be ill-founded. The fact that, had the parties proceeded to litigate the claim, one of them would certainly have won, does not destroy the consideration for the compromise, for the consideration is said to be the settlement of the dispute.

But there are certain essentials to the validity of such consideration. For one thing, and by all authority, the claim upon which the settlement is based must be one made in good faith. Of that there is no dispute in this case. Secondly, the claim must have *some* foundation. As to this second consideration we find the courts using varying language. The claim cannot be "utterly baseless." It has been said that it must have a "tenable ground" or a "reasonable, tenable ground." It must be based on a "colorable right," or on some "legal foundation." It must have at least an appearance of right sufficient to raise a "possible doubt" in favor of the party asserting it. This is the Missouri rule.[13]

It is difficult to reconcile the antinomous rules and statements which are applied to the "doubtful claims" and to find the words which will exactly draw the line between the compromise (on the one hand) of an honestly disputed claim which has some fair element of doubt and is therefore to be regarded as consideration and (on the other hand) a claim, though honestly made, which is so lacking in substance and virility as to be entirely baseless. The Missouri courts have struggled and not yet found apt language. We think we had best leave definitions alone, confident that, as applied to each individual case, the facts will make the thing apparent. But if we should make further effort to

---

13. Although the law writers seem to make good faith alone the preponderant consideration. 11 Am.Jur., Compromise and Settlement, secs. 6 and 7, pp. 252, 253, says that the words "colorable," "plausible," et cetera, are mere catchwords underneath which lies the idea that the courts will not countenance extortion. 15 C.J.S. Compromise and Settlement § 11b, p. 732, states that the reality of the claim must be measured, not by the state of the law as it is ultimately discovered to be, but by the state of the knowledge of the person who at the time has to judge and make the concession. Professor Corbin (Corbin on Contracts, vol. 1, sec. 140, p. 436) states that the absence of reasonable ground for belief in validity is evidence of bad faith, but not conclusive.

distinguish we would say that if the claimant, *in good faith*, makes a mountain out of a mole hill the claim is "doubtful." But if there is no discernible mole hill in the beginning, then the claim has no substance.

The very nature of a cotton acreage allotment is such that it has no existence except for the one specific year. It expires with the crop year. It is not continuous. The fact there may (or may not) be another allotment fixed for the next year carries no certainty that a successive allotment will be in the same amount or acreage. The cotton allotment acreage is not like an oak tree which continues in existence through the years and sends forth new leaves on the same branches with each successive spring. Rather it is like the bindweed which springs from seed, a new life with the coming of a new life-giving season—from seed which may or may not sprout, dependent upon conditions of sun, moisture, and a charitable soil, and which produces a plant only to die by the icy sword of frost when the season ends. So in this case the only possible allotment of a definite acreage applicable to the situation was that in existence for the contemplated crop year. None other existed. And there was no way under heaven the parties could be assured that any future allotment, if there was to be such, would be of the same acreage, any more than the proposed purchaser of public welfare relief checks could be assured by the recipient of such benefits that his welfare check would be in the same amount through the next year and from there on.

It would therefore appear that the only thing the parties were contracting for, or could have contracted for, was the amount of acres (65) allotted for the ensuing crop year. The uncontradicted evidence is that Black "made up" that acreage out of the acreage on his own (retained) land. Hence plaintiff got all he could possibly have bargained for, and his claim of the purchase of some nonexistent, ethereal future allotment stretching perhaps into eternity was baseless and did not rise to the dignity of consideration. It falls into the same category as a claim of purchase of the green cheese monopoly on the moon. Whether the parties actually knew they could not sell a future unfixed cotton allotment acreage off one farm and on to the other is not shown. No one testified that either of them knew, or did not know. But, be that as it may, the age-old legal fiction is that they did know the law, and this rule has been applied to the workings of the Agricultural Adjustment Act in relation to cotton allotments.

But there is another and perhaps more potent reason why plaintiff cannot recover. The settlement of a claim based on a contract which is against public morals or public policy, or which is inherently illegal, or which is in direct violation of the statutes, cannot form the basis of consideration for a valid compromise settlement, for the reason that " 'the wrong done is against the state, and the state only can forgive it. To permit the subsequent ratification of such contract, or to consider it the sufficient and legal basis of a subsequent promise, would be a manifest inconsistency. It would be to annul the rule and enable the parties, by an easy expedient, to evade laws based upon considerations of public policy.' " The attempt here to transfer the allotment was the attempt to do that which was clearly contrary to and destructive of the Act and its workings. And, being illegal as such, it did not constitute a consideration which the law can recognize. The court must leave the parties where it found them.

* * * The decision of the trial court is obviously based upon the fact there was no valid consideration for the note. It being so, we must affirm the judgment. It is so ordered.

STONE, P.J., and McDOWELL, J. concur.

RESTATEMENT, SECOND, CONTRACTS § 74:

(1) Forbearance to assert or the surrender of a claim or defense which proves to be invalid is not consideration unless

(a) the claim or defense is in fact doubtful because of uncertainty as to the facts or the law, or

(b) the forbearing or surrendering party believes that the claim or defense may be fairly determined to be valid.

(2) The execution of a written instrument surrendering a claim or defense by one who is under no duty to execute it is consideration if the execution of the written instrument is bargained for even though he is not asserting the claim or defense and believes that no valid claim or defense exists.

Comment:

d. Forbearance without surrender. Forbearance to assert a valid claim or a doubtful or honestly-asserted claim may be consideration for a promise, just as surrender of the claim would be. Where the forbearance is temporary and it is contemplated that the claim will be asserted later, there is sometimes a question whether the forbearance is bargained for and given in exchange for the promise. * * * Forbearance which is not bargained for may in some cases be reliance sufficient to bring § 90 into play. [§ 90 is quoted at p. 226 infra.]

Illustrations:

8. A owes B $120. Without requesting B to forbear suit, C promises B in April that if A does not pay by October 1 C will pay $100. B's forbearance to sue until October is not consideration for C's promise.

10. A owns land and desires to mortgage it. He is informed that his title may be defective by reason of a possible interest in B. B says that he has no claim and has previously given a deed to the land to A's grantor. A promises to pay $50 for a new quit-claim deed. B's execution and delivery of such a deed is consideration for A's promise.

Reporter's Note:

Former § 76(b) [of the First Restatement] required "an honest and reasonable belief" in the "possible validity" of an invalid claim or defense. This Section substitutes an alternative requirement of doubtfulness in fact or law or of honest belief.

———

PALMER v. DEHN, 29 Tenn.App. 597, 198 S.W.2d 827 (1946). The plaintiff was a skilled mechanic and traveling representative of Transit Bus Sales Company. While he was working on a bus sold by the Company to defendant, defendant's driver started the motor, cutting off two of plaintiff's fingers. While rushing plaintiff to the hospital, defendant said, "I am awful sorry this happened, but don't worry a minute. I will see you are compensated for the loss of your finger, take care of your expenses * * *." Plaintiff later brought suit in two counts, for personal injuries due to negligence, and for breach of the defendant's promise. The court held that a jury verdict for plaintiff should be sustained. The jury "was justified in inferring" that plaintiff's "foregoing his right of action for a reasonable time was a good consideration" to defendant, "that the basis of the promise of [defendant] was for forbearance in bringing suit."

BATSAKIS v. DEMOTSIS
Texas Court of Civil Appeals, 1949.
226 S.W.2d 673.

McGill, Justice.

This is an appeal from a judgment of the 57th judicial District Court of Bexar County. Appellant was plaintiff and appellee was defendant in the trial court. The parties will be so designated.

Plaintiff sued defendant to recover $2,000 with interest at the rate of 8% per annum from April 2, 1942, alleged to be due on the following instrument, being a translation from the original, which is written in the Greek language:

"Peiraeus
April 2, 1942

"Mr. George Batsakis
Konstantinou Diadohou #7
Peiraeus

"Mr. Batsakis:

"I state by my present (letter) that I received today from you the amount of two thousand dollars ($2,000.00) of United States of America money, which I borrowed from you for the support of my family during these difficult days and because it is impossible for me to transfer dollars of my own from America.

"The above amount I accept with the expressed promise that I will return to you again in American dollars either at the end of the present war or even before in the event that you might be able to find a way to collect them (dollars) from my representative in America to whom I shall write and give him an order relative to this. You understand until the final execution (payment) to the above amount an eight per cent interest will be added and paid together with the principal.

"I thank you and I remain yours with respects.

"The recipient,

(Signed) Eugenia The. Demotsis."

Trial to the court without the intervention of a jury resulted in a judgment in favor of plaintiff for $750.00 principal, and interest at the rate of 8% per annum from April 2, 1942 to the date of judgment, totaling $1163.83, with interest thereon at the rate of 8% per annum until paid. Plaintiff has perfected his appeal.

The court sustained certain special exceptions of plaintiff to defendant's first amended original answer on which the case was tried, and struck therefrom paragraphs II, III and V. Defendant excepted to such action of the court, but has not cross-assigned error here. The answer, stripped of such paragraphs, consisted of a general denial contained in paragraph I thereof, and of paragraph IV, which is as follows:

"IV. That under the circumstances alleged in Paragraph II of this answer, the consideration upon which said written instrument sued upon by plaintiff herein is founded, is wanting and has failed to the extent of $1975.00, and defendant pleads specially under the verification hereinafter made the want and failure of consideration stated, and now tenders, as defendant has heretofore tendered to plaintiff, $25.00 as the value of the loan of money received by defendant from plaintiff, together with interest thereon.

"Further, in connection with this plea of want and failure of consideration defendant alleges that she at no time received from plaintiff himself or from anyone for plaintiff any money or thing of value other than, as hereinbefore alleged, the original loan of 500,000 drachmae. That at the time of the loan by plaintiff to defendant of said 500,000 drachmae the value of 500,000 drachmae in the Kingdom of Greece in dollars of money of the United States of America, was $25.00, and also at said time the value of 500,000 drachmae of Greek money in the United States of America in dollars was $25.00 of money of the United States of America. The plea of want and failure of consideration is verified by defendant as follows."

The allegations in paragraph II which were stricken, referred to in paragraph IV, were that the instrument sued on was signed and delivered in the Kingdom of Greece on or about April 2, 1942, at which time both plaintiff and defendant were residents of and residing in the Kingdom of Greece, and

"Plaintiff (emphasis ours) avers that on or about April 2, 1942 she owned money and property and had credit in the United States of America, but was then and there in the Kingdom of Greece in straitened financial circumstances due to the conditions produced by World War II and could not make use of her money and property and credit existing in the United States of America. That in the circumstances the plaintiff agreed to and did lend to defendant the sum of 500,000 drachmae, which at that time, on or about April 2, 1942, had the value of $25.00 in money of the United States of America. That the said plaintiff, knowing defendant's financial distress and desire to return to the United States of America, exacted of her the written instrument plaintiff sues upon, which was a promise by her to pay to him the sum of $2,000.00 of United States of America money."

Plaintiff specially excepted to paragraph IV because the allegations thereof were insufficient to allege either want of consideration or failure of consideration, in that it affirmatively appears therefrom that defendant received what was agreed to be delivered to her, and that plaintiff breached no agreement. The court overruled this exception, and such action is assigned as error. Error is also assigned because of the court's failure to enter judgment for the whole unpaid balance of the principal of the instrument with interest as therein provided.

Defendant testified that she did receive 500,000 drachmas from plaintiff. It is not clear whether she received all the 500,000 drachmas or only a portion of them before she signed the instrument in question. Her testimony clearly shows that the understanding of the parties was that plaintiff would give her the 500,000 drachmas if she would sign the instrument. She testified:

"Q. * * * who suggested the figure of $2,000.00?

"A. That was how he asked me from the beginning. He said he will give me five hundred thousand drachmas provided I signed that I would pay him $2,000.00 American money."

The transaction amounted to a sale by plaintiff of the 500,000 drachmas in consideration of the execution of the instrument sued on, by defendant. It is not contended that the drachmas had no value. Indeed, the judgment indicates that the trial court placed a value of $750.00 on them or on the other consideration which plaintiff gave defendant for the instrument if he believed plaintiff's testimony. Therefore the plea of want of consideration was unavailing. A plea of want of consideration amounts to a contention that the instrument never became a valid obligation in the first place.

Mere inadequacy of consideration will not void a contract.

Nor was the plea of failure of consideration availing. Defendant got exactly what she contracted for according to her own testimony. The court should have rendered judgment in favor of plaintiff against defendant for the principal sum of $2,000.00 evidenced by the instrument sued on, with interest as therein provided. We construe the provision relating to interest as providing for interest at the rate of 8% per annum. The judgment is reformed so as to award appellant a recovery against appellee of $2,000.00 with interest thereon at the rate of 8% per annum from April 2, 1942. Such judgment will bear interest at the rate of 8% per annum until paid on $2,000.00 thereof and on the balance interest at the rate of 6% per annum. As so reformed, the judgment is affirmed.

Reformed and affirmed.

SWEET–ESCOTT, GREECE: A POLITICAL AND ECONOMIC SURVEY, 1939–1953

93 (1954).

It has been said that Greece suffered more heavily during the war than any other Allied country except Soviet Russia. From 1941 to 1944 the country was visited by famine, destruction, and inflation. * * * Even if the Axis had been determined to maintain the existing standard of nutrition in Greece, it would have been a difficult task. As things were, the standard fell disastrously. It is estimated that the average daily diet in 1941, the worst of the three war winters, fell to 900 calories per person, and that it never exceeded 1,400 calories during the occupation. As the daily diet of a healthy man should be in the region of 3,000 calories, it is hardly surprising that Greece fell a prey to famine, especially in the towns. At one period in the winter of 1941–2 people were dying daily in the streets of Athens by the score. It will probably never be known how many perished of malnutrition and the diseases occasioned thereby, but the figure may well run into hundreds of thousands. * * *

———

The trial transcript in the principal case reveals that in 1942 Mrs. Demotsis was a widow with two children, aged 16 and 20, living with her. She testified that with the 500,000 drachmas given her by Batsakis, she was able to purchase five five-gallon cans of olive oil, and had enough left over to buy "a little something for a couple of days" on the black market to feed her family.

HOBBES, LEVIATHAN

78 (1651, 1928 ed.).

The value of all things contracted for, is measured in the Appetite of the Contractors: and therefore the just value, is that which they be contented to give.

VON MISES, HUMAN ACTION: A TREATISE ON ECONOMICS
204–05 (1949, 3d ed. 1966).

The basis of modern economics is the cognition that it is precisely the disparity in the value attached to the objects exchanged that results in their being exchanged. People buy and sell only because they appraise the things given up less than those received. Thus the notion of a measurement of value is vain. An act of exchange is neither preceded nor accompanied by any process which could be called a measuring of value. An individual may attach the same value to two things; but then no exchange can result. But if there is a diversity in valuation, all that can be asserted with regard to it is that one *a* is valued higher, that it is preferred to one *b*.   *   *   *

It does not matter whether a lover prefers one girl to other girls, a man one friend to other people, an amateur one painting to other paintings, or a consumer a loaf of bread to a piece of candy. Preferring always means to love or to desire *a* more than *b*. Just as there is no standard and no measurement of sexual love, of friendship and sympathy, and of aesthetic enjoyment, so there is no measurement of the value of commodities. If a man exchanges two pounds of butter for a shirt, all that we can assert with regard to this transaction is that he— at the instant of the transaction and under the conditions which this instant offers to him—prefers one shirt to two pounds of butter. It is certain that every act of preferring is characterized by a definite psychic intensity of the feelings it implies. There are grades in the intensity of the desire to attain a definite goal and this intensity determines the psychic profit which the successful action brings to the acting individual. But psychic quantities can only be felt. They are entirely personal, and there is no semantic means to express their intensity and to convey information about them to other people.

BENNET v. BENNET, 43 L.T.(N.S.) 246 (Ch.1876). A claim was made against the estate of Major Bennet, based on promissory notes he had given for money lent to him, with interest to be paid at the rate of 60% per year. Held, for the plaintiff. Jessel, M.R. wrote that unless the executors of the estate could set the transaction aside on the ground of fraud or insanity, "the thing is not arguable":

> "A man may agree to pay 100 per cent. if he chooses. There is no reason why a man should not be a fool. A man is allowed by law to be a fool if he likes. Suppose Major Bennet had gambled on the Stock Exchange, or at a gaming table, or had spent his substance in debauchery. A man may be a foolish man to do that, but still the law does not prevent him from being a fool."

P. ATIYAH, THE RISE AND FALL OF FREEDOM OF CONTRACT
402–04 (1979).

This emphasis on contract law as the law of the market was, in England at least, well established by 1870, although in America it may have been a later development. * * *

In general terms, this equation of general principles of contract law with the free market economy led to an emphasis on the framework within which individuals bargained with each other, and a retreat from interest in substantive justice or fairness. The model of contract theory which implicitly underlay the classical law of contract—for such we may now call it—was thus the model of the market. Essentially this model is based on the following principal features. First, the parties deal with each other "at arm's length" in the legal phrase; this carries the notion that each relies on his own skill and judgment, and that neither owes any fiduciary obligation to the other. In the market place, no man is his brother's keeper. Secondly, the parties bargain or negotiate, they higgle over the price and terms of the deal. Offers are made, accepted, rejected, or met by counter-offers. Prior to acceptance, offers can be revoked, even though relied upon. Neither party owes any duty to the other until a deal is struck * * *. Third, neither party owes any duty to volunteer information to the other, nor is he entitled to rely on the other except within the narrowest possible limits. Each party must study the situation, examine the subject-matter of the contract, and the general market situation, assess the future probabilities, and rely on his own sources of information. He may take advice, consult experts, buy information from third parties; but if he does not do so, he relies on his own judgment and acts at his peril. The only limitation to this market bargaining is that there must be no fraud or misrepresentation, but even these concepts are narrowly construed. Prima facie a man must rely on his own judgment, and not on what the other party says in the normal process of negotiation. * * * The agreement must be made "freely" and without "pressure" but these concepts are very narrowly interpreted, for they must not conflict with the rule of the market place; and in the market place pressures are themselves a normal part of the scene. It is not these pressures, but only abnormal pressures, wholly exceptional pressures, which can be said to affect a party's free consent or free will and hence relieve him of his obligations. Fifthly, the content of the contract, the terms and the price and the subject-matter, are entirely for the parties to settle. It is assumed that the parties know their own minds, that they are the best judges of their own needs and circumstances, that they will calculate the risks and future contingencies that are relevant, and that all these enter into the bargain. It follows that unfairness of the bargain—gross inadequacy or excess of price—is irrelevant, and that once made, the contract is binding. * * *

The Court's function in all this is to ensure procedural fair play: the Court is the umpire to be appealed to when a foul is alleged, but the Court has no substantive function beyond this. It is not the Court's business to ensure that the bargain is fair, or to see that one party does not take undue advantage of another, or impose unreasonable terms by virtue of superior bargaining position. Any superiority in bargaining power is itself a matter for the market to rectify. If there is free competition in the market, mere size or skill should not in any case confer an undue advantage, since the forces of competition will ensure fairness in terms and prices. * * *

FRENCH CIVIL CODE Art. 1674

(1804).

If a seller of real property has been harmed by receiving less than $5/12$ of its value, he has a right to have the sale rescinded, even if he has expressly renounced this right in the contract and has stated that he was making a gift of the additional value.

VON MEHREN, THE FRENCH DOCTRINE OF *LÉSION* IN THE SALE OF IMMOVABLE PROPERTY

49 Tul.L.Rev. 321, 323–26 (1975).

Where a *lésion* [harm] has been established under articles 1674–80 of the *Code civil*, the purchaser can either return the immovable— recovering from the seller the price paid—or retain the property— paying such sum as is required to give the seller nine-tenths of the "just price." * * *

Under the doctrine of *laesio enormis,* Roman law in a few situations refused enforcement to contracts in which the disparity of values in a bargained-for exchange was objectively very great. In the Middle Ages, *laesio enormis* was expanded into a fundamental principle of contract law. The *laesio* doctrine rested on ethical views which required a fair exchange of values and on the proposition that values, including economic values, were not inherently individualistic and subjective. A relatively static economic system, a stratified social structure, and the regulatory role of the guilds made the concept plausible. For the Middle Ages, the doctrine of *lésion* recognized an objective standard that was morally binding on all members of society.

As economic life became more active and varied, as guilds lost their power, and as social mobility increased, perceptions of value became increasingly individualistic and subjective. "Market price," as understood by modern economic analysis, emerged and supplanted "just price." Once price is seen as a function of marginal utilities, price terms are unfair only if the contracting process is flawed: there is no longer room for an objective theory of *lésion.* * * *

The decline of an objective theory of value and price coincided with—and doubtless encouraged—the rise of the view that an adult is responsible for his own well-being and must, for his own and society's good, bear the consequences of his decisions.   This view provided Berlier with a further basis for criticising the *lésion* provisions:

> [I]s it not repugnant to reason that an adult who does not allege either fraud as to himself personally, or force, can have his own contract rescinded on the sole ground that he sold too cheaply? An adult's duty is to contract with prudence, and the law does not owe him any protection against his own acts, when there is neither a delict nor a quasi-delict imputable to the party with whom he contracted.

In spite of these arguments attacking the doctrine's foundations, the *lésion* provisions were retained in the *Code civil.*   *   *   *

———

STATE v. MAJOR, 243 Ga. 255, 253 S.E.2d 724 (1979).   The defendants sold four tickets to a football game between the Atlanta Falcons and the Minnesota Vikings; they charged $20 each for two $9 tickets and two $15 tickets.   They were later convicted under a Georgia statute making it a misdemeanor to "scalp" tickets to sporting events "for a price in excess of the price printed on the ticket," with the exception of a $1 service charge.   The convictions were upheld, the court commenting that the "statute puts all sports fans on an equal footing in the race to the ticket window."

———

POST v. JONES, 60 U.S. (19 How.) 150, 15 L.Ed.2d 618 (1856).   The *Richmond* had been on a whaling voyage for three years when she ran aground near the Bering Straits.   Winter was approaching, and the nearest port of safety was 5000 miles away.   Three days later the whalers *Elizabeth Frith, Panama,* and *Junior* came near the spot where the *Richmond* was stranded.   None of these ships had completed their cargoes, and there was more whale oil in the *Richmond* than they could all take.   The captain of the *Junior* proposed that the *Richmond*'s oil be auctioned off, and "the forms of an auction sale were enacted; the master of the *Frith* bidding one dollar per barrel for as much as he needed, and the others seventy-five cents."   The three vessels took enough to complete their cargoes, as well as the *Richmond*'s crew, and proceeded on their voyage.

The owners of the *Richmond* later brought suit against the owners of the *Elizabeth Frith* and the *Panama,* seeking the recovery of the oil or the proceeds of its resale, "subject to 'salvage and freight.'"   ("Salvage" is a doctrine of maritime law by which those who save property at sea are entitled to a reward; the amount is at the court's discretion and takes into account the value of the property saved, the risks incurred, the labor expended, and the "promptitude, skill and energy displayed" by the salvors.   The Blackwall, 77 U.S. (10 Wall.) 1, 14, 19 L.Ed. 870 (1869).)   Held, the auction sale was invalid; however, the owners of the *Elizabeth Frith* and the *Panama* were entitled to half the value of the oil at the nearest port of safety as salvage, as well as to a freight charge for carrying the *Richmond*'s share to its home port:

"The contrivance of an auction sale, under such circumstances, where the master of the *Richmond* was hopeless, helpless, and passive—where there was no market, no money, no competition—where one party had absolute power, and the other no choice but submission—where the vendor must take what is offered or get nothing—is a transaction which has no characteristic of a valid contract. * * *

"It has been contended * * * that the sale was justifiable and valid, because it was better for the interests of all concerned to accept what was offered, than suffer a total loss. But this argument proves too much, as it would justify every sale to a salvor. Courts of admiralty will enforce contracts made for salvage service and salvage compensation, where the salvor has not taken advantage of his power to make an unreasonable bargain; but they will not tolerate the doctrine that a salvor can take the advantage of his situation, and avail himself of the calamities of others to drive a bargain; nor will they permit the performance of a public duty to be turned into a traffic of profit. The general interests of commerce will be much better promoted by requiring the salvor to trust for compensation to the liberal recompense usually awarded by courts for such services. * * *"

FEDERAL TRADE COMMISSION, OFFICE OF POLICY PLANNING AND EVALUATION, 1976 BUDGET OVERVIEW: "IMBALANCE–OF–BARGAINING–POWER PROGRAMS."

Before programs that seek to reallocate bargaining power between buyers and sellers are undertaken, consideration should be given to the question of whether or not such a reallocation is possible. It will be argued here that in fact it is impossible to reallocate bargaining power, at least where sellers compete with sellers and buyers compete with buyers. Any attempt by the Commission to do so will, in most cases, reduce consumer welfare and lead to perverse redistributions of wealth among buyers that will usually injure the socially disadvantaged.

Suppose that a landlord owns a building of apartments that he rents for $200 a month each. It is not out of magnanimity that he charges no more than $200. One can safely assume that he would charge more if he could do so. He does not charge more, because his losses from the vacancies that would be generated by any increased rent would outweigh his gains from the increased revenues that would derive from the increment paid by those who would choose to rent at the increased price. Similarly, the renters do not conceive the $200 rent payments, or any part of these payments, as a gesture of charity. They pay $200 and not less than $200 because, all else equal, they believe that no other landlord would give them a better deal.

Now assume that as a part of the rental agreement that the landlord "requires" tenants to deposit three months' rent to be held as security against damages during the course of the tenancy. It is true that $600 is a lot of money to set down as security for a $200 apartment, but it cannot be said that the tenants are coerced to pay this amount. They are coerced in the same way that the purchaser of any commodity is coerced to pay the selling price. Moreover, tenants are not likely to be victimized under this kind of system. If renters commonly find $600 too high, they have the option of renting elsewhere. If a $600 security deposit plus $200 a month rent is generally inferior to other rental opportunities, renters *will* live elsewhere, at least until their departure induces the diminished profits or increased losses that will convince the landlord to lower his security deposit *or* his rent or both. Clearly, it is not the $600 security deposit that tenants would regard as exorbitant; instead, it is the $600 security deposit in connection with rent of $200 a month that they would be unwilling to pay. There certainly would be many takers if rent were $10 a month and the security deposit were higher than $600.

Therefore, one should not be alarmed if one were to discover that all landlords require (by a form contract) that tenants put down three months' rent as security. There would still be ample opportunity to compete on the basis of the magnitude of rent. And so long as landlords compete for tenants—and they will compete even if apartments are scarce [38]—there is no reason to suppose that rents and security deposits are too high. The very concept is meaningless without reference to the market. * * *

If landlords were barred from making the security arrangements that they now make, it could confidently be predicted that rents will rise, if there is to be no net exit from the industry over time. However unfair some may believe these terms, it is clear that these security arrangements reduce costs to landlords. If they reduce costs and if the market for leaseholds is competitive, and there is every evidence that it is, then rents must increase if some security arrangements were barred. It might be suspected that the poor will lose most from increased rents.

MITCHELL v. C.C. SANITATION CO.

Texas Court of Civil Appeals, 1968.
430 S.W.2d 933.

[Mitchell was injured in a collision with a truck driven by Crane, and brought an action for damages against Crane and Crane's employ-

---

38. A scarcity or "shortage" of apartments does not confer any "monopoly power" on landlords. Although the general price of apartments would be higher than if there were more apartments—and this is always true—no landlord can charge above the market price, assuming that there are no impediments on the dissemination of information. If one asserts that this price is too high, one must first postulate what the right price is. Moral theory provides no answer to this question; only the market can. If there is free entry, the price cannot be too high—by market standards— over any considerable length of time. By any standards, the price could not be lower without (increased) government subsidies.

er, C.C. Sanitation Company. After the accident Mitchell signed two releases in favor of the defendants. The defendants moved for summary judgment on the ground that the releases barred any recovery, and the trial court granted this motion.]

SAM D. JOHNSON, JUSTICE. * * *

Appellant alleged that at the time of the occurrence in question, he was driving a truck in the course and scope of his employment for Herrin Transportation Company. As he was in the process of passing another truck driven by the defendant, Crane, who was in the course and scope of his employment for the defendant C.C. Sanitation Company, the defendant's truck suddenly and without warning was negligently steered to the left by defendant, Crane, thus proximately causing the accident which resulted in serious and permanent injuries to him, the appellant. Numerous specific acts of negligence were alleged against the driver, Crane. The appellant alleged his damages to be in the sum of $40,000.00, which included damages for pain and suffering, lost wages, loss of earning capacity, and past and future medical expenses.

As to the releases, Mitchell alleged that they were signed by him because of duress and fraud imposed upon him by his employer, Herrin Transportation Company. Herrin handled its own claim service through one Ross C. Hall, under the name of Southwestern Claims Adjustment Company. After the accident, Hall advised C.C. Sanitation of the damages to Herrin's truck and to Mitchell, and placed C.C. Sanitation on notice of "Herrin's subrogation interest for all property damage inflicted upon its equipment and all workmen's compensation payments to or on behalf of its driver, Mr. Mitchell." By letter, Hall advised C.C. Sanitation and its insurance company, Maryland Casualty Company, of Herrin's truck damage of $281.65, that Herrin had paid Mitchell's physician, Dr. Cobb, $107.00, and that Herrin was therefore due $388.65. Thereafter Hall advised one Patrick Gorski, an adjuster for Maryland Casualty Company, that Mitchell was expecting to be paid $62.12 which he, Mitchell, had paid for his doctor out of his own pocket.

Maryland Casualty, acting by and through Gorski, prepared the proposed releases. The first was in the sum of $388.65 to be executed by Herrin and Mitchell, and the second was in the sum of $62.12 to be executed only by Mitchell. These were then transmitted from Gorski to Hall so that they might be signed by Herrin and by Mitchell. Hall apparently undertook the responsibility of obtaining Mitchell's signature on both releases. After the two releases were signed they were returned to Maryland Casualty Company who then issued the two checks. The first was mailed directly to Herrin and the second directly to Mitchell. At no time during the negotiations outlined did Maryland Casualty Company or its adjuster Gorski have any personal conversation with, or see Mitchell.

The allegations of duress and fraud find their primary support in the deposition and affidavit of the appellant, Mitchell. According to

Mitchell, he was called to Hall's office and when he went there Hall had the two previously prepared releases in hand. Hall threatened that if Mitchell did not settle for the amounts stated in the releases and sign them that he, Mitchell, would be "through," that is that he would lose his job. Further, that "Ross Hall just told me that it was a release so they could get their money for the truck and I could keep my job." When asked if anyone for Herrin Transportation Company talked to him about the execution of the releases, Mitchell responded, "Well, before I signed them Ross Hall blew his stack because I refused to sign them. He had Eldon Brown call me and put pressure on me." He then testified that Eldon Brown was "second in command" for Herrin Transportation Company. He further testified, "Well, I was informed that I would either sign these releases or I wouldn't have a job." He was asked, "Now, were you told anything else that may have caused you to sign the releases?" He responded, "Nothing except if *they* didn't get *their* money I didn't have no job." (Emphasis added).

Mitchell stated that during this conversation and prior to signing the releases, Hall telephoned someone representing C.C. Sanitation and Crane and "What Mr. Hall said over the telephone was that he had finally convinced me that it would be better to sign it. In other words, it was either sign the release or not have a job." * * * By affidavit, Mitchell identified Patrick Gorski, the adjuster for Maryland Casualty Company, as the person with whom Hall was speaking on the telephone. Mitchell also testified to Hall's statements that he, Hall, was handling the matter for C.C. Sanitation and William Crane, was working on behalf of them, was "taking care" of it for them, and was getting the releases signed for them.

Mitchell testified that he would not have signed the releases had Hall not told him that he was going to lose his job if he didn't sign, that he did not feel that he was being adequately compensated for the injuries he sustained in the accident and that the only reason he would sign releases like those that he did sign would be to keep his job. By affidavit Mitchell stated, "I told Mr. Hall nothing was being paid me for the pain and suffering I had experienced or for my future doctor's bills," but, "he was insistent that I sign the releases so that Herrin Transportation could get the money for their truck." Mitchell stated, "Had he not threatened me with my job I would not have signed the releases. His threat caused me to do something (sign the releases) which was against my own free will and accord."

Mitchell further alleged that at the time Hall made the threats against his job, he did so with the knowledge, consent and acquiescence of the insurance company for the appellees, Maryland Casualty Company, who was acting by and through Gorski, their insurance adjuster. Mitchell alleged that not only did Gorski know of the threats but after such threats were made, Maryland Casualty Company accepted the benefits arising therefrom by accepting the releases and attempting to enforce them. Mitchell alleged that Hall, at the time he procured the execution of releases, was acting as the agent of Maryland Casualty Company. Appellant alleged further, as the basis of the fraud and/or inadequate consideration, that the amount of the releases went solely to compensate Herrin Transportation Company for its expenses, and the appellant and Herrin Transportation, for the amount of the doctor bills to date; that no cash was paid to the appellant in addition to the above mentioned amounts. * * *

It is a general rule that contracts obtained through duress or coercion are voidable and this rule is applicable to releases. * * * Appellee contends that duress cannot exist because Herrin Transportation Company was at liberty to discharge the appellant at any time and for any reason they so desired for he was not shown to be more than an employee at will. Stated another way, that the employer Herrin had the right to discharge the appellant at any time and the threat to do what they had the legal right to do cannot constitute duress or fraud.

As the disposition of the instant case was made on appellee's motion for summary judgment, * * * the following conclusions find support in the record and may be validly and helpfully made: (1) the employer Herrin had the right to discharge appellant at any time it desired; (2) there was a very real compulsion, economic and otherwise, here brought to bear on the appellant by his employer; (3) it was the force of this constraint alone, that caused appellant to do what he otherwise would not have considered doing; (4) this compulsion was brought to bear by the employer Herrin, working in concert with the defendant, C.C. Sanitation; (5) the employer Herrin did what it here did for its own economic benefit and advantage, and (6) the effect of such action was to effectively terminate and destroy a valid claim and otherwise good cause of action possessed by the appellant.

"Although an employer, acting singly, has the undoubted right to discharge an employee or one of his family, the coercion arising from a threat to do so, when employed as a means to force the employee to sign a release of an action which he has instituted against him or another employer is unlawful, and, under circumstances showing that such means in fact overcame the employee's resistance and will, may constitute duress." 20 A.L.R.2d 743, 751. We believe this reasoning is applicable to the instant case, and though no Texas cases directly in point are found, believe that substantial authority is otherwise available. * * *

In Holmes v. Industrial Cotton Mills Co., D.C., 64 F.Supp. 20, there had been an investigation by a representative of the wage and hour division of the defendant company. The employee was told by the company superintendent it looked as if he would lose his job if it had to pay overtime for over forty hours. The company president then called the employee into his office, read to him a previously prepared release, and told the employee that if he would sign the release it would clear the company and that he could then hold his job. It was there held as a matter of law that the employer had used duress in inducing the employee to sign the release of overtime pay. * * *

In Perkins Oil Co. of Delaware v. Fitzgerald, 197 Ark. 14, 121 S.W. 2d 877, an employee who was an oiler at a cotton seed oil mill lost both arms in a machine accident at the mill. To induce the employee to release the company, the mill superintendent told him that if he consulted an attorney, or tried to sue the company, his step-father, the sole support of plaintiff's invalid mother, would be discharged, and the company would prevent his re-employment in any other like business. Such evidence was held sufficient to warrant submission to the jury on the question of whether the employee signed the release under duress or coercion.

In the case at bar there was obvious opportunity for employer oppression to be brought against the employee. The parties stood on no equal footing, there was great economic disparity between them, and there was no equality of bargaining positions. The appellant undoubtedly was the weaker party, the threat to discharge him was very real and he was fully justified in expecting that he would be immediately discharged.

In addition, the employer, Herrin Transportation Company, had a direct economic interest in their employee signing the releases, and this was the reason for doing what the company did. Absent the releases being signed by Mitchell, Herrin would not be paid the damages to its truck ($281.65) or the doctor's bills it had previously paid ($107.00). The major portion of the money received for signing the releases went to Herrin Transportation Company, with only $62.12 being paid to appellant. Even this sum was for doctor's bills the appellant had previously paid out of his own pocket as a result of the accident in question. There was no consideration of, nor compensation for, the most important elements of damages allegedly suffered by appellant, these being mental and physical pain and suffering and reduced capacity to work. * * *

It is the opinion of the majority of this court that even where the right of an employer to discharge an employee is unquestioned, duress and coercion may be exercised by the employer by threats to discharge the employee, where circumstances such as are here presented appear. We cannot conclude that an employer with the opportunity for oppression on an employee that here appears, may use such power for his own economic interest, and yet conclude that no question of duress or coercion arises. Where there is such an inequality in the terms, sacrifice of benefits, and rights on the part of the employee, inadequacy of consideration, and advantage taken of the weaker party, we cannot conclude that no fact situation of duress or coercion exists.

It is the opinion of the majority of this court that under the circumstances here presented the existence of duress and coercion sufficient for the avoidance of the releases was a genuine issue of fact, which was raised by the record. There being such issue of fact, under the law applicable to summary judgment, this cause must be reversed and remanded.

Reversed and remanded.

TUNKS, CHIEF JUSTICE.

I respectfully dissent. * * *

The majority seems to place emphasis on the fact that it was to the financial interest of Herrin Transportation Company to get the plaintiff to release his claim. I would emphasize that fact as sustaining the validity and propriety of Herrin's conduct, rather than tainting it. It is uncontroverted that Herrin had a lawful right to terminate Mitchell's employment without any cause. It should follow, a fortiori, that they had a right to terminate his employment unless he would take such action as would permit them to recover on their claim. In my opinion their conduct would be more subject to attack if they, having no financial interest in the matter, had threatened to fire Mitchell because of personal spite or ill will or simply because they were permitting Maryland Casualty Company to avail itself of a lawful right to discharge which they, as employers at will, had. * * *

Nor is the appellant's contention that his settlement was involuntary because it was made under economic compulsion sound. In McKee, General Contractor v. Patterson, 153 Tex. 517, 271 S.W.2d 391, it was held that a workmen's acceptance or retaining employment in the face of known and appreciated dangers was voluntary though done under the economic necessity of earning a livelihood. Thus, Mitchell's settlement of his claim to avoid losing his job was nevertheless, voluntary.

I would affirm the judgment of the trial court.

RESTATEMENT, SECOND, CONTRACTS § 79:

If the requirement of consideration is met, there is no additional requirement of

(a) a gain, advantage, or benefit to the promisor or a loss, disadvantage, or detriment to the promisee; or

(b) equivalence in the values exchanged. * * *

Comment:

e. Effects of gross inadequacy. Although the requirement of consideration may be met despite a great difference in the values exchanged, gross inadequacy of consideration may be relevant in the application of other rules. Inadequacy "such as shocks the conscience" is often said to be a "badge of fraud," justifying a denial of specific performance. See § 364(1)(c). Inadequacy may also help to justify rescission or cancellation on the ground of lack of capacity, mistake, misrepresentation, duress or undue influence. Unequal bargains are also limited by the statutory law of usury, by regulation of the rates of public utilities and some other enterprises, and by special rules developed for the sale of an expectation of inheritance, for contractual penalties and forfeitures * * *.

RESTATEMENT, SECOND, CONTRACTS § 175:

(1) If a party's manifestation of assent is induced by an improper threat by the other party that leaves the victim no reasonable alternative, the contract is voidable by the victim.

RESTATEMENT, SECOND, CONTRACTS § 176:

(1) A threat is improper if

(a) what is threatened is a crime or a tort, or the threat itself would be a crime or a tort if it resulted in obtaining property,

(b) what is threatened is a criminal prosecution,

(c) what is threatened is the use of civil process and the threat is made in bad faith, or

(d) the threat is a breach of the duty of good faith and fair dealing under a contract with the recipient.

(2) A threat is improper if the resulting exchange is not on fair terms, and

(a) the threatened act would harm the recipient and would not significantly benefit the party making the threat,

(b) the effectiveness of the threat in inducing the manifestation of assent is significantly increased by prior unfair dealing by the party making the threat, or

(c) what is threatened is otherwise a use of power for illegitimate ends.

Illustrations:

13. A, who has sold goods to B on several previous occasions, intentionally misleads B into thinking that he will supply the goods at the usual price and thereby causes B to delay in attempting to buy them elsewhere until it is too late to do so. A then threatens not to sell the goods to B unless he agrees to pay a price greatly in excess of that charged previously. B, being in urgent need of the goods, makes the contract. If the court concludes that the effectiveness of A's threat in inducing B to make the contract was significantly increased by A's prior unfair dealing, A's threat is improper and the contract is voidable by B.

14. The facts being otherwise as stated in Illustration 13, A merely discovers that B is in great need of the goods and that they are in short supply but does not mislead B into thinking that he will supply them. A's threat is not improper, and the contract is not voidable by B.

16. A, a municipal water company, seeking to induce B, a developer, to make a contract for the extension of water mains to his develop-

ment at a price greatly in excess of that charged to those similarly situated, threatens to refuse to supply to B unless B makes the contract. B, having no reasonable alternative, makes the contract. Because the threat amounts to a use for illegitimate ends of A's power not to supply water, the contract is voidable by B.

RESTATEMENT, SECOND, CONTRACTS § 208:

If a contract or term thereof is unconscionable at the time the contract is made a court may refuse to enforce the contract, or may enforce the remainder of the contract without the unconscionable term, or may so limit the application of any unconscionable term as to avoid any unconscionable result.

Comments:

b. Historic standards. Traditionally, a bargain was said to be unconscionable in an action at law if it was "such as no man in his senses and not under delusion would make on the one hand, and as no honest and fair man would accept on the other;" damages were then limited to those to which the aggrieved party was "equitably" entitled. Hume v. United States, 132 U.S. 406 (1889), quoting Earl of Chesterfield v. Janssen, 2 Ves.Sen. 125, 155, 28 Eng.Rep. 82, 100 (Ch. 1750). Even though a contract was fully enforceable in an action for damages, equitable remedies such as specific performance were refused where "the sum total of its provisions drives too hard a bargain for a court of conscience to assist." Campbell Soup Co. v. Wentz, 172 F.2d 80, 84 (3d Cir.1948). Modern procedural reforms have blurred the distinction between remedies at law and in equity. For contracts for the sale of goods, Uniform Commercial Code § 2–302 states the rule of this Section without distinction between law and equity. Comment 1 to that section adds, "The principle is one of the prevention of oppression and unfair surprise (Cf. Campbell Soup Co. v. Wentz, * * *) and not of disturbance of allocation of risks because of superior bargaining power."

d. Weakness in the bargaining process. A bargain is not unconscionable merely because the parties to it are unequal in bargaining position, nor even because the inequality results in an allocation of risks to the weaker party. But gross inequality of bargaining power, together with terms unreasonably favorable to the stronger party, may confirm indications that the transaction involved elements of deception or compulsion, or may show that the weaker party had no meaningful choice, no real alternative, nor did not in fact assent or appear to assent to the unfair terms. * * *

SELMER v. BLAKESLEE–MIDWEST CO., 704 F.2d 924 (7th Cir.1983). Under a construction contract Subcontractor was to erect prestressed concrete materials supplied to it by the General Contractor. General failed to fulfill its obligations, among other things by being late in supplying Subcontractor with the concrete. Instead of terminating the contract, Subcontractor agreed to complete the work provided General would compensate it for its extra costs due to General's default. When the job was completed, Subcontractor demanded payment of $120,000. General offered $67,000 and refused to budge from this offer. Subcontractor, "because it was in desperate financial straits," accepted the offer.

Subcontractor later brought suit against General claiming that its extra costs had amounted to $150,000, and asking for that amount minus the $67,000 it had already received. The trial court held that the suit was barred by the settlement agreement; held (in an opinion by Posner, J.), affirmed:

"Since [General] did not acknowledge that it owed [Subcontractor] $120,000, and since the settlement exceeded 50 percent of [Subcontractor's] demand, the terms of the settlement are not unreasonable on their face. Thus the question is starkly posed whether financial difficulty can by itself justify setting aside a settlement on grounds of duress. It cannot. 'The mere stress of business conditions will not constitute duress where the defendant was not responsible for the conditions.' The adverse effect on the finality of settlements and hence on the willingness of parties to settle their contract disputes without litigation would be great if the cash needs of one party were alone enough to entitle him to a trial on the validity of the settlement. In particular, people who desperately wanted to settle for cash—who simply could not afford to litigate—would be unable to settle, because they could not enter into a *binding* settlement; being desperate, they could always get it set aside later on grounds of duress. It is a detriment, not a benefit to one's long-run interests not to be able to make a binding commitment.

"Matters stand differently when the complaining party's financial distress is due to the other party's conduct. Although [Subcontractor] claims that it was the extra expense caused by [General's] breaches of the original contract that put it in a financial vise, it could have walked away from the contract without loss or penalty when [General] broke the contract. [Subcontractor] was not forced by its contract to remain on the job, and was not prevented by circumstances from walking away from the contract * * *; it stayed on the job for extra pay. We do not know why [Subcontractor] was unable to weather the crisis that arose when [General] refused to pay $120,000 for [Subcontractor's] extra expenses—whether [Subcontractor] was undercapitalized or overborrowed or what—but [General] cannot be held responsible for whatever it was that made [Subcontractor] so necessitous, when, as we have said, [Subcontractor] need not have embarked on the extended contract."

FEDERAL DEPOSIT INSURANCE CORP. v. LINN, 671 F.Supp. 547 (N.D.Ill.1987). The Linns were actively involved in exploring for oil and natural gas. In order to finance such exploration, they borrowed extensively from a number of banks. When oil and gas prices collapsed, the Linns began negotiations with the banks on restructuring their debt. In 1985 these negotiations resulted in a consolidated loan agreement with new repayment terms. The Linns agreed to waive any potential defenses to the renegotiated debt and to pledge additional collateral. The Linns had earlier agreed to personally guarantee other loans to companies controlled by them; as part of the 1985 agreement they were also required to recognize the validity of these guarantees and to waive any defenses to their enforcement.

The Linns failed to make the payments required by the agreement, and the banks accelerated the indebtedness due and later brought suit. The Linns claimed that the 1985 agreement was unenforceable "because executed under economic duress imposed by" the banks. Held, the defense of duress "fails as a matter of law":

"Defendants insist Banks' threat to initiate 'wholesale litigation' on their debts unless defendants waived their defenses to the * * * [g]uaranties compelled defendants to cave in to those demands. They claim their alternative was bankruptcy. This Court does not doubt defendants were between a rock and a hard place when they negotiated the Agreement, but what defendants blithely ignore is their own responsibility for their financial predicament.

"Defendants borrowed large amounts of money * * * to explore for oil and gas, a highly speculative business venture in the best of economic times. Defendants cannot deflect their full responsibility for the consequences of such risks—their inability to repay those debts on time—by pointing out [the Banks] were eager to make such loans and profited from them. Banks did not coerce defendants into borrowing money. Defendants cannot blame Banks for the pressures caused by defendants' own business decisions and by general economic conditions. *Banks* were not responsible for the downturn in the oil industry.

"Threatened bankruptcy is insufficient to create economic duress. Quite the contrary is true on defendants' own version of things: Bankruptcy proceedings would appear to have been their opportunity for legal escape from oppressive demands by Banks. Any resulting financial embarrassment from declaring bankruptcy is not sufficient to explain why such legal redress would be inadequate. * * * [D]efendants' ability to declare bankruptcy was a two-edged sword: It posed an obvious threat to Banks' interests, just as defendants say *they* preferred to avoid that consequence."

————

BERGER v. BERGER, 466 So.2d 1149 (Fla.App.1985). Husband threatened that if his Wife did not sign a property settlement agreement, he would turn her and her partners in to the Internal Revenue Service. "Apparently the wife had been failing to report substantial cash receipts from the operation of her beauty salon business." Under the proposed settlement agreement the Wife gave up her interest in the marital residence and furnishings, a truck, and primary custody of the couple's two children. The Wife signed the settlement agreement against the advice of her attorney. The trial court found that the settlement had been voluntarily entered into; held, reversed. The Husband had committed "the crime of extortion" under a Florida statute making it a felony to threaten to expose another for the commission of any crime for one's own pecuniary advantage; "[i]n our view, the completed crime of extortion must inevitably involve coercion and duress":

"We certainly agree that the husband had a legal right to actually turn her in to the I.R.S. and that a claim of coercion cannot be predicated on a threat to do an act which the person has a lawful right to do. However * * * the husband does not have the right to threaten to do it *for his own pecuniary advantage.*"

A considerable body of legal literature has recently developed dealing with the theoretical paradox of blackmail: "Why can't you threaten to do what you have a legal right to do?" See Lindgren, Blackmail: On Waste, Morals, and Ronald Coase, 36 U.C.L.A. L.Rev. 597 (1989). See also Epstein, Blackmail, Inc., 50 U.Chi.L.Rev. 553, 557–8, 561 (1983):

"In the ordinary commercial negotiation individuals are allowed, indeed encouraged, to make explicit threats to their trading partners. Thus a seller of widgets can threaten not to sell them at all or to sell them to a competitor of the prospective purchaser unless he is paid a certain price, since the universal prohibition against force and fraud does not reach this transaction. By the same token the buyer can threaten the seller by saying that unless his price is met, he will close up shop or take his business to a competitor of the seller. To ban commercial threats outright is to insist that there is no place for commerce, for without the process of threat and counter-threat—offer and counteroffer—it would be quite impossible in the ordinary course of business to reach any voluntary agreement * * *

" * * * [W]here a person *has* the right to do a certain act—for example, not to sell goods at a particular price—he has the right to threaten to do that act. * * * There is nothing in the current law of crime or tort that prohibits [a defendant] from voluntarily disclosing to [a third party] true information about [a victim.] So too nothing prohibits [a defendant] from selling that information to [a third party], or indeed from becoming a private eye in the employ of anyone who wishes to learn about [the victim.]"

SCHNELL v. NELL

Supreme Court of Indiana, 1861.
17 Ind. 29, 79 Am.Dec. 453.

PERKINS, J.—Action by *J.B. Nell* against *Zacharias Schnell*, upon the following instrument:

"This agreement, entered into this 13th day of *February*, 1856, between *Zach. Schnell*, of *Indianapolis, Marion* county, State of *Indiana*, as party of the first part, and *J.B. Nell*, of the same place, *Wendelin Lorenz*, of *Stilesville, Hendricks* county, State of *Indiana*, and *Donata Lorenz*, of *Frickinger, Grand Duchy of Baden, Germany*, as parties of the second part, witnesseth: The said *Zacharias Schnell* agrees as follows: whereas his wife, *Theresa Schnell*, now deceased, has made a last will and testament, in which, among other provisions, it was ordained that every one of the above named second parties, should receive the sum of $200; and whereas the said provisions of the will must remain a nullity, for the reason that no property, real or personal, was in the possession of the said *Theresa Schnell*, deceased, in her own name, at the time of her death, and all property held by *Zacharias* and *Theresa Schnell* jointly, therefore reverts to her husband; and whereas the said *Theresa Schnell* has also been a dutiful and loving wife to the said *Zach. Schnell*, and has materially aided him in the acquisition of all property, real and personal, now possessed by him; for, and in consideration of all this, and the love and respect he bears to his wife; and, furthermore, in consideration of one cent, received by him of the second parties, he, the said *Zach. Schnell*, agrees to pay the above named sums of money to the parties of the second part, to wit: $200 to the said *J.B. Nell;* $200 to the said *Wendelin Lorenz;* and $200 to the said *Donata Lorenz*, in the following installments, viz., $200 in one year from the date of these presents; $200 in two years, and $200 in three years; to be divided between the parties in equal portions of $66⅔ each year, or as they may agree, till each one has received his full sum of $200.

"And the said parties of the second part, for, and in consideration of this, agree to pay the above named sum of money [one cent], and to deliver up to said *Schnell*, and abstain from collecting any real or supposed claims upon him or his estate, arising from the said last will and testament of the said *Theresa Schnell*, deceased.

"In witness whereof, the said parties have, on this 13th day of *February*, 1856, set hereunto their hands and seals.

"Zacharias Schnell, [Seal.]
"J.B. Nell, [Seal.]
"Wen. Lorenz. [Seal.]"

The complaint contained no averment of a consideration for the instrument, outside of those expressed in it; and did not aver that the one cent agreed to be paid, had been paid or tendered.

A demurrer to the complaint was overruled.

The defendant answered, that the instrument sued on was given for no consideration whatever.

He further answered, that it was given for no consideration, because his said wife, *Theresa*, at the time she made the will mentioned, and at the time of her death, owned, neither separately, nor jointly with her husband, or any one else (except so far as the law gave her an interest in her husband's property), any property, real or personal, &c.

* * *

The Court sustained a demurrer to these answers, evidently on the ground that they were regarded as contradicting the instrument sued on, which particularly set out the considerations upon which it was executed. But the instrument is latently ambiguous on this point.

The case turned below, and must turn here, upon the question whether the instrument sued on does express a consideration sufficient to give it legal obligation, as against *Zacharias Schnell*. It specifies three distinct considerations for his promise to pay $600:

1. A promise, on the part of the plaintiffs, to pay him one cent.

2. The love and affection he bore his deceased wife, and the fact that she had done her part, as his wife, in the acquisition of property.

3. The fact that she had expressed her desire, in the form of an inoperative will, that the persons named therein should have the sums of money specified.

The consideration of one cent will not support the promise of *Schnell*. It is true, that as a general proposition, inadequacy of consideration will not vitiate an agreement. Baker v. Roberts, 14 Ind. 552. But this doctrine does not apply to a mere exchange of sums of money, of coin, whose value is exactly fixed, but to the exchange of something of, in itself, indeterminate value, for money, or, perhaps, for some other thing of indeterminate value. In this case, had the one cent mentioned, been some particular one cent, a family piece, or ancient, remarkable coin, possessing an indeterminate value, extrinsic from its simple money value, a different view might be taken. As it is, the mere promise to pay six hundred dollars for one cent, even had the portion of that cent due from the plaintiff been tendered, is an unconscionable contract, void, at first blush, upon its face, if it be regarded as an earnest one. Hardesty v. Smith, 3 Ind. 39. The consideration of one cent is, plainly, in this case, merely nominal, and intended to be so. As the will and testament of *Schnell's* wife imposed no legal obligation upon him to discharge her bequests out of his property, and as she had none of her own, his promise to discharge them was not legally binding upon him, on that ground. A moral consideration, only, will not support a promise. And for the same reason, a valid consideration for his promise can not be found in the fact of a compromise of a disputed claim; for where such claim is legally groundless, a promise upon a compromise of it, or of a suit upon it, is not legally binding. Spahr v. Hollingshead, 8 Blackf. 415. There was no mistake of law or fact in this case, as the agreement admits the will inoperative and void. The promise was simply one to make a gift. The past services of his wife, and the love and affection he had borne her, are objectionable as legal considerations for *Schnell's* promise, on two grounds: 1. They are past considerations. 2. The fact that *Schnell* loved his wife, and that she had been industrious, constituted no consideration for his promise to pay *J.B. Nell,* and the *Lorenzes,* a sum of money. Whether, if his wife, in her lifetime, had made a bargain with *Schnell,* that, in consideration of his promising to pay, after her death, to the persons named, a sum of money, she would be industrious, and worthy of his affection, such a promise would have been valid and consistent with public policy, we need not decide. Nor is the fact that *Schnell* now venerates the memory of his deceased wife, a legal consideration for a promise to pay any third person money.

The instrument sued on, interpreted in the light of the facts alleged in the second paragraph of the answer, will not support an action. The demurrer to the answer should have been overruled.

Per Curiam.—The judgment is reversed, with costs.

RESTATEMENT [FIRST] OF CONTRACTS § 84:

Illustration:

1. A wishes to make a binding promise to his son B to convey to B Blackacre, which is worth $5000. Being advised that a gratuitous promise is not binding, A writes to B an offer to sell Blackacre for $1. B accepts. B's promise to pay $1 is sufficient consideration.

RESTATEMENT, SECOND, CONTRACTS § 71:

Illustrations:

4. A desires to make a binding promise to give $1000 to his son B. Being advised that a gratuitous promise is not binding, A writes out and signs a false recital that B has sold him a car for $1000 and a promise to pay that amount. There is no consideration for A's promise.

5. A desires to make a binding promise to give $1000 to his son B. Being advised that a gratuitous promise is not binding, A offers to buy from B for $1000 a book worth less than $1. B accepts the offer knowing that the purchase of the book is a mere pretense. There is no consideration for A's promise to pay $1000.

NEWMAN AND SNELL'S STATE BANK v. HUNTER

Supreme Court of Michigan, 1928.
243 Mich. 331, 220 N.W. 665.

Assumpsit by Newman and Snell's State Bank against Zennetta H. Hunter on a promissory note. Judgment for plaintiff on a directed verdict. Defendant appeals. Reversed, and no new trial ordered.
* * *

FELLOWS, J. Defendant is the widow of Lee C. Hunter, who died intestate January 25, 1926. His estate was insufficient to pay his funeral expenses and the widow's allowance. At the time of his death plaintiff bank held his note for $3,700, with 50 shares of the capital stock of the Hunter Company as collateral. This company was insolvent but was still doing business when the note was given; afterwards it was placed in the hands of a receiver and its assets were insufficient to pay its debts. The facts were agreed upon on the trial in the court below. We quote from the agreed statement of facts:

"On March 1, 1926, the defendant gave the plaintiff the note described in the plaintiff's declaration in this cause and the plaintiff surrendered to her therefor, and in consideration thereof, the note of said Lee C. Hunter. The defendant also paid the plaintiff the earned interest due on the deceased's note."

Defendant pleaded want of consideration. We shall presently consider the effect of what was done about the stock of the Hunter Company, and for the present will consider whether the surrender of the note of her deceased husband who left no estate was a sufficient consideration for the note sued upon. Counsel for both parties have furnished able briefs and their arguments have been helpful. They have doubtless brought to our attention all the cases which would be of assistance to us in reaching a conclusion. While all the authorities cited have been examined, we shall not take up each one of them and discuss them nor shall we cite them all, nor shall we attempt a reconciliation of the decisions of those States whose own decisions are claimed to be out of accord with each other. There is a definite conflict in the decisions from other States, and it is possible there is a conflict between cases from the same court. * * *

Doubtless plaintiff's strongest case is Judy v. Louderman, 48 Ohio St. 562, 29 N.E. 181. The father of an insolvent decedent took up decedent's note with his own. Although the note taken up was worthless, it was held that the consideration was adequate. The opinion largely rests on the desire of the father to acquire his son's note, and in part on the question of moral obligation. * * *

In Home State Bank v. DeWitt, 121 Kan. 29, 245 P. 1036, that court pointed out that while the note of a living person who was presently without means would furnish a consideration, one of a deceased insolvent would not. * * *

This court in one case (Taylor v. Weeks, 129 Mich. 233, 88 N.W. 466) has held that the widow's note given for the discharge of an unenforceable claim against the estate of her deceased husband, one outlawed under the statute of limitations, was one that was unenforceable as without sufficient consideration, and in two cases (Cawthorpe v. Clark, 173 Mich. 267, 138 N.W. 1075, and Steep v. Harpham, 241 Mich. 652, 217 N.W. 787), this court has held that the widow's note given for the discharge of obligations of her husband were enforceable in the absence of any testimony showing that the estate was insolvent. In the more recent of these cases it was stressed that there was no evidence of insolvency of the estate, and that while the duty of showing consideration rested on the plaintiff through the case, the recitals in the note made a *prima facie* case and the duty of going forward with the testimony rested on the defendant. Here we have the widow's note given to take up the note of her insolvent husband, a worthless piece of paper. When plaintiff surrendered this worthless piece of paper to the defendant, it parted with nothing of value and defendant received nothing of value, the plaintiff suffered no loss or inconvenience and defendant received no benefit. The weight of authority sustains defendant's contention, but going back to fundamentals it seems clear to me that the transaction was without consideration. It is urged that plaintiff's right as a creditor to administer the estate was valuable and was waived. Had there been assets or prospective undisclosed assets there might be some force to this contention. But the agreed statements of facts negative any such situation. Under the agreement of facts there was not enough in the estate to pay the funeral expenses or the widow's support.

We have now reached the question of whether the manner of handling the stock of the Hunter Company furnished a consideration. So far as the record discloses this stock was retained by the bank and was treated as collateral to defendant's note, and it was so stated in that instrument. The bank, so far as the record discloses, never surrendered it to the defendant but kept it and has it today. But plaintiff's counsel insist that as matter of law it was transferred to defendant. They insist that whatever interest the bank had in the stock passed to defendant when her husband's note was surrendered to her, even though it was not as matter of fact given to her. But if we accept this theory and thus create a legal fiction, we must have in mind that she at once and in the same transaction re-hypothecated the stock to the bank. Stripped of all legal fiction, the cold facts are that when the negotiations opened plaintiff had this stock and the worthless note of defendant's husband. When they ended the bank still had the stock and defendant's note. Defendant had her husband's worthless note and she had nothing more. But this discussion is largely academic. The agreed statement of facts shows that the company was insolvent. The stock then had no book value. There is no statement that it had a market value, and in the absence of anything showing or tending to show a market value, we cannot assume it had such value or what it was. It was suggested on the argument that even though the company was insolvent, it might have been revived by the infusion of new money in the enterprise. But no one has come along with any infusion of such new blood, and value based on such a possibility is altogether too problematical to form a fixed basis of property rights. The record shows the affairs of the company have been wound up, and that creditors were not paid in full. Upon this record the stock was worthless.

HARRIS v. TIME, INC., 191 Cal.App.3d 449, 237 Cal.Rptr. 584 (1987). The three-year old son of "a prominent Bay Area public interest attorney" received an offer in the mail from Time. The front of the envelope contained a see-through window revealing a picture of a calculator watch and the statement, "JOSHUA A. GNAIZDA, I'LL GIVE YOU THIS VERSATILE NEW CALCULATOR WATCH FREE Just for Opening this Envelope Before Feb. 15, 1985." When the child's mother opened the envelope, she realized that she had been deceived by a ploy to get her to open a piece of junk mail: The see-through window had not revealed the full text of Time's offer; not viewable through the window were the additional words: " * * * AND MAILING THIS CERTIFICATE TODAY!" The certificate itself required that Joshua purchase a subscription to Fortune Magazine in order to receive the free watch. "Time not only refused to give a watch, it did not even give Joshua or his father the time of day."

Joshua's father filed suit asking for a declaration that all recipients of Time's offer were entitled to recover compensatory damages equal to the value of the watch, and $15,000,000 punitive damages to be awarded to a consumer fund to be used for education and advocacy on behalf of consumer protection. Held, judgment of dismissal affirmed:

"Time * * * argues that there was no contract because the mere act of opening the envelope was valueless and therefore did not constitute adequate consideration. Technically, this is incorrect. It is basic modern contract law that * * * *any* bargained-for act or forbearance will constitute adequate consideration for a unilateral contract. Courts will not require equivalence in the values exchanged or otherwise question the adequacy of the consideration. * * * Moreover, the act at issue here—the opening of the envelope, with consequent exposure to Time's sales pitch—may have been relatively insignificant to the plaintiffs, but it was of great value to Time. At a time when our homes are bombarded daily by direct mail advertisements and solicitations, the name of the game for the advertiser or solicitor is to *get the recipient to open the envelope.* * * * From Time's perspective, the opening of the envelope was 'valuable consideration' in every sense of that phrase."

The court nevertheless upheld the dismissal of the suit based on the legal maxim "de minimis non curat lex," or "the law disregards trifles": "This lawsuit is an absurd waste of the resources of this court, the superior court, the public interest law firm handling the case and the citizens of California whose taxes fund our judicial system. * * * The law may permit junk mail to be delivered for a lower cost than the individual citizen must pay. It does not require that the public subsidize junk litigation."

SOULE v. BON AMI CO., 201 App.Div. 794, 195 N.Y.S. 574 (1922), aff'd per curiam, 235 N.Y. 609, 139 N.E. 754 (1923). Soule claimed that he had a plan which would enable the Bon Ami Company to increase its profits, and he agreed to reveal it in exchange for the company's promise to pay him one-half of the profits resulting from its use of his suggestion. Soule's plan was to increase the wholesale price at which the company sold its products to grocers, from $10 to $10.50 or $10.80 per gross. "The plaintiff explained that he had satisfied himself that this could be done by actual experience in relation to a similar, but not competing product; * * * and that the increase in price did not affect the sales." Bon Ami did shortly thereafter increase its price $1 per gross, and Soule brought suit for half of the increased profits. The court held that there was no consideration for Bon Ami's promise: "The central idea here, * * * was an obvious one. * * * This was not new, it was not original, and I am at a loss to understand how it could be deemed valuable."

SEYFERTH v. GROVES & SAND RIDGE RAILROAD CO.

Supreme Court of Illinois, 1905.
217 Ill. 483, 75 N.E. 522.

RICKS, J. The only question presented upon the record in this case is one of law, and is whether or not the written option set out in the opinion was binding upon [plaintiff] to the end of the time stated therein.

[Plaintiff, "in consideration of $1.00," signed an agreement on October 20, 1902, granting the railroad an option to purchase a strip of land for a right of way. The agreement stated that "if said railroad company shall, within four months from the date hereof, pay or tender to the [plaintiff] the further sum of $45 per acre, then the [plaintiff] agrees that he will make, execute, and deliver to the said railroad company a good and sufficient deed, with general warranty, conveying to the said railroad company a fee-simple title." The agreement allowed the railroad to immediately take possession of the land and to begin construction. The plaintiff later filed suit to enjoin the railroad "from going upon or doing any act preparatory to or in construction of its railroad" on the plaintiff's land. The trial court dismissed the suit.]

The Appellate Court, in stating and disposing of the case, made the following remarks, in which we concur and adopt the same as our views: * * *

"The consideration, $1.00, recited in the contract, was not in fact paid; and for this reason [plaintiff] contends that the contract or option agreement is void and without effect. Nothing was said about the $1.00 consideration by either the [plaintiff] or the agent of [the railroad] at the time the writing was drawn up and signed; but on the 5th day of November, when the agent returned with the notary public to [plaintiff's] house to take the acknowledgment of [plaintiff] and his wife, [plaintiff] called attention to the fact that he had not received the $1.00 consideration, and thereupon the agent took from his pocket $1.00 and tendered it to the [plaintiff]. He did not take it, saying, 'If I want anything, I will take it all at once.' On February 7, 1903, [plaintiff] served notice on [the railroad] that he withdrew the option and revoked the contract. The next day [the railroad], by its agent, tendered [plaintiff] the sum required by the contract and demanded a deed, which was refused. On the 12th day of May, 1903, according to the bill, which was filed on the 18th day of the same month, [the railroad] went upon the strip of land in controversy and took possession preparatory to the construction of its railroad thereon.

"* * * We are of the opinion that the conclusion reached by the chancellor who heard the case was justified, and that the decree was right. No question is made of the validity of this contract in all of its essential features, unless it may be held void for want of a consideration. This is a proceeding in a court of equity, and under the circumstances shown the complainant in the bill is not in a position to avoid an obligation for want of payment of a purely nominal consideration, which was tendered and declined for the stated and only reason that, if he wanted anything (meaning the $1.00 nominal consideration), 'I will take it all at once'; that is, when the defendant shall have exercised his option and paid for the land. It was equivalent to saying to [the railroad] that he waived the payment, or that he preferred postponement of the payment, or that, as between the parties, it should be considered as paid, though the money was not to be received until a later adjustment. From the evidence it clearly appears that, when the contract was acknowledged, and thereafter until the notice of his withdrawal, his understanding, no less than that of [the railroad], was that the contract was valid and binding. At any rate, from aught he said or did, no other conclusion can be drawn. He may not be heard to say that his undisclosed reason for refusing the tendered consideration was other than stated or reasonably to be inferred from what he did and said. That would be contrary to equity and conscience, and may not prevail in a proceeding of this kind. In this case the tender of the payment of the consideration at the time the contract was completed by the signature of the wife, formally acknowledged and delivered to the [railroad's] agent, must be held as effective, as though the money had been received. If [plaintiff] refused to receive the money when tendered, in order to secure the advantage now claimed, and concealed his purpose, as he did, then he was acting in bad faith, and therefore is not entitled to a hearing in the court of equity."

We might further add that it is now universally held that a written agreement to convey land, at the option of the proposed vendee, within a given time and at a certain price, if made upon a sufficient consideration, with full knowledge on the part of the person extending the option that he is bound and the other is not, is such a contract, though lacking mutuality, as will be enforced in equity, where the party holding the option signifies his acceptance within the time limited upon the terms as stated; and as is said in Guyer v. Warren, 175 Ill. 328, 51 N.E. 580, "where the one holding a buyer's option makes his election to purchase, and tenders the amount agreed to according to the terms of the contract, it is the duty of the seller to accept the price and execute a deed to the purchaser for the property. * * * Such contracts are perfectly valid, and it is now well settled that a court of equity may decree a specific performance of them."

We are of the opinion that the judgment of the Appellee Court, affirming the decree of the circuit court, is right, and it is accordingly affirmed.

Judgment affirmed.

––––––––––

MARSH v. LOTT, 8 Cal.App. 384, 97 P. 163 (1908). "For and in consideration of the sum of twenty-five cents * * * in hand paid," the defendant gave to the plaintiff an option to buy certain real estate at a price of $100,000; the option was to be exercised within four months. Before the expiration of this time, the defendant gave notice that she "withdrew" the property from sale. The court held that this purported revocation by defendant "was ineffectual for the purpose of terminating plaintiff's right" to exercise the option:

"From the very nature of the case no standard exists whereby to determine the adequate value of an option to purchase specific real estate. The land has a market value susceptible of ascertainment, but the value of an option upon a piece of real estate might, and oftentimes does, depend upon proposed or possible improvements in the particular vicinity. * * * In our judgment any money consideration, however small, paid and received for an option to purchase property at its adequate value is binding upon the seller thereof for the time specified therein, and is irrevocable for want of its adequacy."

RESTATEMENT, SECOND, CONTRACTS § 87:

(1) An offer is binding as an option contract if it

    (a) is in writing and signed by the offeror, recites a purported consideration for the making of the offer, and proposes an exchange on fair terms within a reasonable time; or

    (b) is made irrevocable by statute.

Comments:

b. Nominal consideration. Offers made in consideration of one dollar paid or promised are often irrevocable under Subsection (1)(a). The irrevocability of an offer may be worth much or little to the offeree, and the courts do not ordinarily inquire into the adequacy of the consideration bargained for. Hence a comparatively small payment may furnish consideration for the irrevocability of an offer proposing a transaction involving much larger sums. But gross disproportion between the payment and the value of the option commonly indicates that the payment was not in fact bargained for but was a mere formality or pretense. In such a case there is no consideration.
* * *

Nevertheless, such a nominal consideration is regularly held sufficient to support a short-time option proposing an exchange on fair terms. The fact that the option is an appropriate preliminary step in the conclusion of a socially useful transaction provides a sufficient substantive basis for enforcement, and a signed writing taking a form appropriate to a bargain satisfies the desiderata of form. In the absence of statute, however, the bargaining form is essential: a payment of one dollar by each party to the other is so obviously not a bargaining transaction that it does not provide even the form of an exchange.

c. False recital of nominal consideration. A recital in a written agreement that a stated consideration has been given is evidence of that fact as against a party to the agreement, but such a recital may ordinarily be contradicted by evidence that no such consideration was given or expected. In cases within Subsection (1)(a), however, the giving and recital of nominal consideration performs a formal function only. The signed writing has vital significance as a formality, while the ceremonial manual delivery of a dollar or a peppercorn is an inconsequential formality. In view of the dangers of permitting a solemn written agreement to be invalidated by oral testimony which is easily fabricated, therefore, the option agreement is not invalidated by proof that the recited consideration was not in fact given. A fictitious rationalization has sometimes been used for this rule: acceptance of delivery of the written instrument conclusively imports a promise to make good the recital, it is said, and that promise furnishes consideration. But the sound basis for the rule is that stated above.

———

See also UCC § 2–205.

———

LEWIS v. FLETCHER, 101 Idaho 530, 617 P.2d 834 (1980). In March 1971 defendant granted plaintiffs an option to purchase a 40–acre parcel of land; by its terms the option could be exercised in May 1976 "or earlier if the parties agreed." The option contract recited a consideration of $20, but the trial court found that the $20 had never been paid. Before the plaintiffs attempted to exercise the option, the defendant informed the plaintiffs "that he did not intend to go through with the option." The plaintiffs' suit for breach of contract was dismissed by the trial court on the ground of want of consideration; held, affirmed:

"The majority of jurisdictions hold that where the recited consideration has not been paid and no other consideration was given, the contract fails for want of consideration. A minority of jurisdictions have held otherwise, either on the theory that the parties are estopped from contradicting their written recital and acknowledgment, or on the theory that the recital of the consideration gives rise to an implied promise to pay it. The Restatement of Contracts takes the minority position that an option in writing and signed by the offeror which recites consideration is binding notwithstanding the fact that no such consideration was given or expected. However, we choose to adhere to the majority position.

"An option contract not supported by consideration is merely a revocable offer to sell. [Since the defendant had withdrawn his offer before the plaintiffs attempted to exercise the option,] plaintiffs do not have an enforceable contract to purchase the forty acres."

SECTION 3: RELIANCE ON A PROMISE AS A BASIS FOR ENFORCEMENT

DEVECMON v. SHAW

Maryland Court of Appeals, 1888.
69 Md. 199, 14 A. 464.

BRYAN, J. John Semmes Devecmon brought suit against the executors of John S. Combs, deceased. He declared on the common counts, and also filed a bill of particulars. After judgment by default, a jury was sworn to assess the damages sustained by the plaintiff. The evidence consisted of certain accounts taken from the books of the deceased, and testimony that the plaintiff was a nephew of the deceased, and lived for several years in his family, and was in his service as clerk for several years. The plaintiff then made an offer of testimony which is thus stated in the bill of exceptions: "That the plaintiff took a trip to Europe in 1878, and that said trip was taken by said plaintiff, and the money spent on said trip was spent by the said plaintiff, at the instance and request of said Combs, and upon a promise from him that he would reimburse and repay to the plaintiff all money expended by him in said trip; and that the trip was so taken, and the money so expended, by the said plaintiff, but that the said trip had no connection with the business of said Combs; and that said Combs spoke to the witness of his conduct, in being thus willing to pay his nephew's expenses, as liberal and generous on his part." On objection the court refused to permit the evidence to be given, and the plaintiff excepted.

It might very well be, and probably was the case, that the plaintiff would not have taken a trip to Europe at his own expense. But, whether this be so or not, the testimony would have tended to show that the plaintiff incurred expense at the instance and request of the deceased, and upon an express promise by him that he would repay the money spent. It was a burden incurred at the request of the other party, and was certainly a sufficient consideration for a promise to pay. Great injury might be done by inducing persons to make expenditures beyond their means, on express promise of repayment, if the law were otherwise. It is an entirely different case from a promise to make another a present, or render him a gratuitous service. It is nothing to the purpose that the plaintiff was benefited by the expenditure of his own money. He was induced by this promise to spend it in this way, instead of some other mode. If it is not fulfilled, the expenditure will have been procured by a false pretense.

The evidence ought to have been admitted. * * * Judgment reversed, and new trial ordered.

———

RICKETTS v. SCOTHORN, 57 Neb. 51, 77 N.W. 365 (1898). Plaintiff's grandfather gave her a promissory note for $2000, saying, "I have fixed out something that you have not got to work any more. None of my grandchildren work and you don't have to." Immediately thereafter plaintiff quit her job, at which she was earning $10 per week. Plaintiff's grandfather died after paying one year's interest on the note, and plaintiff brought suit against his executor. The court conceded that the grandfather had given the note "as a gratuity and looked for nothing in return." Nevertheless a judgment for plaintiff was upheld, on the ground that the executor was "estopped" by plaintiff's change of position to claim the absence of consideration: "[The grandfather], doubtless, desired that she should give up her occupation, but whether he did or not, it is entirely certain that he contemplated such action on her part as a reasonable and probable consequence of his gift. Having intentionally influenced the plaintiff to alter her position for the worse on the faith of the note being paid when due, it would be grossly inequitable to permit the maker, or his executor, to resist payment on the ground that the promise was given without consideration."

RESTATEMENT, SECOND, TORTS § 323 (1965):

One who undertakes, gratuitously or for consideration, to render services to another which he should recognize as necessary for the protection of the other's person or things, is subject to liability to the other for physical harm resulting from his failure to exercise reasonable care to perform his undertaking, if

(a) his failure to exercise such care increases the risk of such harm, or

(b) the harm is suffered because of the other's reliance upon the undertaking.

Caveat:

The Institute expresses no opinion as to whether:

(1) the making of a contract, or a gratuitous promise, without in any way entering upon performance, is a sufficient undertaking to result in liability under the rule stated in this Section * * *.

Comment on Caveat:

The early development of the law, and particularly of the forms of action of case and assumpsit, led to a distinction, as to tort liability, between "misfeasance" and "non-feasance." A defendant who actually entered upon the performance of his undertaking became liable, in an action on the case, for harm to the plaintiff which resulted from his negligent performance, whereas one who never commenced performance at all was not liable in such an action for his failure to do so. The mere breach of a promise, without more, was regarded as "non-feasance," for which any action must be in assumpsit, upon the contract and upon proof of a consideration for the promise, rather than on the case under any theory of tort liability. * * *

Where the plaintiff's reliance has led to his harm, the courts have tended to seize upon almost any trivial and technical conduct of the defendant, to find that he has commenced performance of his promise, and so has "entered upon" his undertaking. Thus the defendant is held liable where he has merely received a document, written a letter, appeared on the first day of a long employment, or accepted a general agency, although such acts themselves have played no part in inducing the plaintiff's reliance or in causing the harm to him.

There is no essential reason why the breach of a promise which has induced reliance and so caused harm should not be actionable in tort. This is true particularly where the harm is physical harm, to the person, land, or chattels of the plaintiff. The technicalities to which the courts have resorted in finding some commencement of performance indicate a development of the law toward such liability. In the absence of sufficient decisions, however, the question is left open.

COLONIAL SAVINGS ASSOCIATION v. TAYLOR, 544 S.W.2d 116 (Tex.1976). Taylor bought a lot containing both a larger, older house and a smaller garage apartment at the back of the lot. He was told by the seller that Colonial, which held a mortgage on the property, had purchased fire insurance and was charging for the premium along with the mortgage payments. After about a year Colonial wrote Taylor that "the insurance coverage * * * expired today and we have bound $8700.00 coverage with our agent on this property." Taylor received the fire insurance policy; three years later, the smaller house was damaged by fire. Only then did Taylor learn that this house was uninsured and that the policy covered only the larger house on the lot. Taylor brought suit against Colonial. The jury found that Colonial had undertaken to provide fire insurance coverage on the premises, and that it was negligent in failing to inform the insurance agent that there were two buildings on the lot. The trial court entered judgment n.o.v. for Colonial. On appeal, the Supreme Court agreed with Taylor that while "Colonial was not an insurance agent or insurer issuing a policy to Taylor for consideration," its liability could be established under § 323 of the Restatement of Torts. The case was remanded to the trial court for a finding of fact as to whether "Taylor forbore from obtaining his own insurance in reliance upon Colonial's undertaking to obtain it for him."

RESTATEMENT [FIRST] OF CONTRACTS § 75:

(1) Consideration for a promise is

(a) an act other than a promise, or

(b) a forbearance, or

(c) the creation, modification or destruction of a legal relation, or

(d) a return promise, bargained for and given in exchange for the promise.

Illustration:

2. A promises B $500 when B goes to college. If the promise is not made as an agreed exchange for B's going to college but is reasonably to be understood as a gratuity, payable on the stated contingency, B's going to college is not consideration for A's promise.

RESTATEMENT [FIRST] OF CONTRACTS § 90:

A promise which the promisor should reasonably expect to induce action or forbearance of a definite and substantial character on the part of the promisee and which does induce such action or forbearance is binding if injustice can be avoided only by enforcement of the promise.

Illustration:

3. A promises B that if B will go to college and complete his course he will give him $5000. B goes to college and has nearly completed his course when A notifies him of an intention to revoke the promise. A's promise is binding.

G. GILMORE, THE DEATH OF CONTRACT
61–65 (1974).*

And what is that all about? We have become accustomed to the idea, without in the least understanding it, that the universe includes both matter and anti-matter. Perhaps what we have here is Restatement and anti-Restatement or Contract and anti-Contract. We can be sure that Holmes, who relished a good paradox, would have laughed aloud at the sequence of § 75 and § 90. The one thing that is clear is that these two contradictory propositions cannot live comfortably together: in the end one must swallow the other up.

A good many years ago Professor Corbin gave me his version of how this unlikely combination came about. When the Restaters and their advisors came to the definition of consideration, Williston proposed in substance what became § 75. Corbin submitted a quite different proposal. To understand what the Corbin proposal was about, it is necessary to backtrack somewhat. Even after the Holmesian or bargain theory of consideration had won all but universal acceptance, the New York Court of Appeals had, during the Cardozo period, pursued a line of its own. There is a long series of Cardozo contract opinions, scattered over his long tenure on that court. Taken all in all, they express what might be called an expansive theory of contract. Courts should make contracts wherever possible, rather than the other way around. Missing terms can be supplied. If an express promise is lacking, an implied promise can easily be found. In particular Cardozo delighted in weaving gossamer spider webs of consideration. * * * Corbin, who had been deeply influenced by Cardozo, proposed to the Restaters what might be called a Cardozoean definition of consideration—broad, vague and, essentially, meaningless—a common law equivalent of causa, or cause. In the debate Corbin and the Cardozoeans lost out to Williston and the Holmesians. In Williston's view, that should have been the end of the matter.

Instead, Corbin returned to the attack. At the next meeting of the Restatement group, he addressed them more or less in the following manner: Gentlemen, you are engaged in restating the common law of contracts. You have recently adopted a definition of consideration. I now submit to you a list of cases—hundreds, perhaps or thousands?—in which courts have imposed contractual liability under circumstances in which, according to your definition, there would be no consideration and therefore no liability. Gentlemen, what do you intend to do about these cases? * * *

Going back into the past, there was an indefinite number of cases which had imposed liability, in the name of consideration, where nothing like Holmes's "reciprocal conventional inducement" was anywhere in sight. * * * [U]nlike Holmes, many judges, it appeared,

* Law Forum Series of the College of Law of the Ohio State University, No. 8.

were not prepared to look with stony-eyed indifference on the plight of a plaintiff who had, to his detriment, relied on a defendant's assurances without the protection of a formal contract. * * * In such a situation the word that comes instinctively to the mind of any judge is, of course, "estoppel" —which is simply a way of saying that, for reasons which the court does not care to discuss, there must be judgment for plaintiff. And in the contract cases after 1900 the word "estoppel," modulating into such phrases as "equitable estoppel" and "promissory estoppel," began to appear with increasing frequency. Thus Corbin, in his submission to the Restaters, was plentifully supplied with new, as well as with old, case material.

The Restaters, honorable men, evidently found Corbin's argument unanswerable. However, instead of reopening the debate on the consideration definition, they elected to stand by § 75 but to add a new section—§ 90—incorporating the estoppel idea although without using the word "estoppel." The extent to which the new section § 90 was to be allowed to undercut the underlying principle of § 75 was left entirely unresolved. * * * Section 90 is almost the only section of the Restatement of Contracts which has no Comment at all. Four hypothetical cases, none of them, so far as I know, based on a real case, are offered as "illustrations," presumably to indicate the range which the section was meant to have. An attentive study of the four illustrations will lead any analyst to the despairing conclusion, which is of course reinforced by the mysterious text of § 90 itself, that no one had any idea what the damn thing meant.

"Estoppel"

" 'Estoppe,' " wrote Lord Coke, "commeth of the French word *estoupe,* from whence the English word *stopped:* and it is called an estoppel or conclusion, because a man's own act or acceptance stoppeth or closeth up his mouth to alleage or plead the truth * * *." 2 Coke on Littleton § 667. In its time-honored form of "equitable estoppel" or "estoppel in pais," * estoppel rests on the generally shared moral intuition that a party who through some misrepresentation had induced another to change his position, should be precluded (estopped) in a later action from claiming that the truth is different from what he had represented it to be. "It only prevents a party from insisting on

---

* "In the country," that is, (in contrast to "estoppel by deed" or "estoppel by record") estoppel "arising from an open act, or a verbal representation or declaration upon which another has acted." J. Kinney, A Law Dictionary and Glossary 290 (1893). The expression originally referred to acts "(1) in transactions relating to land, and title thereto, (2) taking place on the very land the subject of the transaction, * * * and (3) of such notoriety, ceremony and solemnity as to render them equivalent to a declaration of title under seal." Spencer Bower on Estoppel by Representation 5 (1923). Eventually estoppel in pais came to prevent a party from denying the truth of *any* statement of fact which had induced reliance. This traditional use should be distinguished from the principle embodied in § 90 of the Restatement, baptized "promissory estoppel" by analogy.

his strict legal rights where it would be unjust to allow him to do so, having regard to the dealings which have taken place between the parties." Combe v. Combe, [1951] 1 All E.R. 767, 769 (C.A.).

A textbook example is illustration 2 to § 894 of the Restatement, Second, Torts: "A owns a tract of land adjacent to another tract owned by B. The descriptions in the deeds are such that before B sells his land to C, C for the purpose of being sure of the boundaries, asks A concerning them. Although A knows the boundaries, his description of them to C is such that C reasonably believes that they are located along a line that in fact is entirely on A's land. C enters and erects a fence at the supposed boundary. C is not liable to A for this act."

It was often said that an estoppel could arise only from a misrepresentation of "fact" as opposed to a promise or assurance relating to future conduct. For example, in Prescott v. Jones, 69 N.H. 305, 41 A. 352 (1898), insurance agents wrote the plaintiff that they would renew a fire insurance policy on his property unless he notified them to the contrary. Plaintiff believed that his policy would be renewed and gave no notice to the agents; however, no insurance was obtained before the plaintiff's buildings were destroyed by fire. The court held that the agents' demurrer to the complaint should have been sustained, quoting from an earlier case: "The intent of a party, however positive or fixed, concerning his future action, is necessarily uncertain as to its fulfillment * * *. [W]hen the representation relates only to a present intention or purpose of a party, * * * being in its nature uncertain, and liable to change, it could not properly form a basis or inducement upon which a party could reasonably adopt any fixed and permanent course of action."

Any distinction between "statements of fact" and "promises" or "statements of intention" is easily manipulated, and sometimes becomes little more than a semantic quibble. In Hetchler v. American Life Insurance Co., 266 Mich. 608, 254 N.W. 221 (1934), for example, Hetchler failed to pay one annual premium on a life insurance policy, and the company advised him that the policy had lapsed. The company wrote that despite the lapse, in accordance with the policy's terms, the cash value "has been used to buy insurance to May 13, 1932, until which date you are protected under the extended insurance provision of the policy." In response to a later inquiry, the company confirmed that "this is the present condition of your policy and you will notice that you will be protected for the full amount of the policy to that date [May 13, 1932]." Hetchler died on April 13, 1932. The company then discovered, after checking its records, that it had made a mistake in computing the period of the extended insurance and that the policy had actually expired on March 15. The trial court held that the company was "estopped from denying liability on the policy, on the ground that the insured had relied upon the statements of the company to his detriment," and this was upheld on appeal: "The fact that his failure to [secure some other protection or make other provision for his widow] was induced by reliance upon the representations of the defendant need not be proved by direct evidence, but may be inferred from the circumstances."

AMERICAN LAW INSTITUTE, 4 PROCEEDINGS, 4TH ANNUAL MEETING
98–99, 103–04 (1926).

MR. COUDERT: * * * Please let me see if I understand it rightly. Would you say, Mr. Reporter, in your case of Johnny and the uncle, the uncle promising the $1000 and Johnny buying the car—say, he goes out and buys the car for $500—that uncle would be liable for $1000 or would he be liable for $500?

MR. WILLISTON: If Johnny had done what he was expected to do, or is acting within the limits of his uncle's expectation, I think the uncle would be liable for $1000; but not otherwise.

MR. COUDERT: In other words, substantial justice would require that uncle should be penalized in the sum of $500.

MR. WILLISTON: Why do you say "penalized"? * * *

MR. COUDERT: Because substantial justice there would require, it seems to me, that Johnny get his money for his car, but should he get his car and $500 more? I don't see. * * *

MR. WILLISTON: Either the promise is binding or it is not. If the promise is binding it has to be enforced as it is made. * * * I could leave this whole thing to the subject of quasi contracts so that the promisee under those circumstances shall never recover on the promise but he shall recover such an amount as will fairly compensate him for any injury incurred; but it seems to me you have to take one leg or the other. You have either to say the promise is binding or you have to go on the theory of restoring the *status quo*. * * *

RESTATEMENT, SECOND, CONTRACTS § 90:

(1) A promise which the promisor should reasonably expect to induce action or forbearance on the part of the promisee or a third person and which does induce such action or forbearance is binding if injustice can be avoided only by enforcement of the promise. The remedy granted for breach may be limited as justice requires.

(2) A charitable subscription or a marriage settlement is binding under Subsection (1) without proof that the promise induced action or forbearance.

Comment:

d. Partial enforcement. A promise binding under this section is a contract, and full-scale enforcement by normal remedies is often appropriate. But the same factors which bear on whether any relief should be granted also bear on the character and extent of the remedy. In particular, relief may sometimes be limited to restitution or to damages or specific relief measured by the extent of the promisee's reliance rather than by the terms of the promise. ＊ ＊ ＊

Illustrations:

8. A applies to B, a distributor of radios manufactured by C, for a "dealer franchise" to sell C's products. Such franchises are revocable at will. B erroneously informs A that C has accepted the application and will soon award the franchise, that A can proceed to employ salesmen and solicit orders, and that A will receive an initial delivery of at least 30 radios. A expends $1,150 in preparing to do business, but does not receive the franchise or any radios. B is liable to A for the $1,150 but not for the lost profit on 30 radios. ＊ ＊ ＊

9. The facts being otherwise as stated in Illustration 8, B gives A the erroneous information deliberately and with C's approval and requires A to buy the assets of a deceased former dealer and thus discharge C's "moral obligation" to the widow. C is liable to A not only for A's expenses but also for the lost profit on 30 radios.

WALTERS v. MARATHON OIL CO., 642 F.2d 1098 (7th Cir.1981). Plaintiffs (husband and wife) contacted Marathon Oil about the possibility of locating a combination foodstore and service station on a vacant gasoline service station site. "In reliance on [Marathon's] promise to supply gasoline supplies to them," plaintiffs purchased the station and made improvements upon it; however, Marathon later refused to proceed with the transaction. The trial court found for plaintiffs on the theory of promissory estoppel; it also found that plaintiffs had lost anticipated profits of six cents per gallon for the 370,000 gallons they were entitled to receive under their allocation for the first year's gasoline sales, and awarded the resulting $22,200 in damages. Held, affirmed; "an award of damages based upon lost profits was appropriate in order to do complete justice":

"The [defendant] insists that since [plaintiffs] succeeded at trial solely on a promissory estoppel theory ＊ ＊ ＊ loss of profits is not a proper measure of damages. It contends that [plaintiffs'] damages should have been the amount of their expenditures in reliance on the promise, measured by the difference between their expenditures and the present value of the property. Using this measure of damages, [plaintiffs] would have received no award, for the present value of the real estate and its improvements is slightly more than the amount expended by [plaintiffs] in reliance upon the promise. As a consequence, [defendant] says that because [plaintiffs] can recoup all they spent in reliance on [defendant's] promise, they would be in the same position they would have been in had the promise not been made.

"However ＊ ＊ ＊ [i]t is unreasonable to assume that [plaintiffs] did not anticipate a return of profits from [their] investment of time and funds, [since] in reliance upon [defendant's] promise, they had foregone the opportunity to make the investment elsewhere. As indicated, the record reflects that had [defendant] performed according to its promise, [plaintiffs] would have received the anticipated net profit of $22,200.00. * * *

"Since promissory estoppel is an equitable matter, the trial court has broad power in its choice of a remedy. * * * [I]t is apparent that the [plaintiffs] suffered a loss of profits as a direct result of their reliance upon the promise made by [defendant], and the amount of the lost profits was ascertained with reasonable certainty. * * * "

FEINMAN, PROMISSORY ESTOPPEL AND JUDICIAL METHOD

97 Harv.L.Rev. 678, 687–88 (1984).

As damage theories have developed, the relation between the underlying basis of promissory enforcement and the type of remedy granted has in fact blurred. In bargain cases, reliance damages are often used as an alternative to expectation damages. More significantly, the current case law demonstrates that the remedial flexibility once attributed to promissory estoppel, if it ever existed, has been replaced by the application of remedies similar to those available in bargain cases. Specific performance (or occasionally other injunctive relief) is awarded in promissory estoppel cases when it would be available in a comparable cause of action involving bargained-for reliance. And the typical damage remedy applied in promissory estoppel cases is measured by the expectation interest. One explanation for the prevalence of expectation damages is a shift in the nature of the cases that constitute the bulk of promissory estoppel litigation, a shift from cases of donative promise to cases involving business exchanges. Courts perhaps recognize that, in business cases, expectation recovery may better reflect opportunity losses than would reliance recovery.

FEINBERG v. PFEIFFER CO.

Missouri Court of Appeals, 1959.
322 S.W.2d 163.

DOERNER, COMMISSIONER.

This is a suit brought in the Circuit Court of the City of St. Louis by plaintiff, a former employee of the defendant corporation, on an alleged contract whereby defendant agreed to pay plaintiff the sum of $200 per month for life upon her retirement. A jury being waived, the case was tried by the court alone. Judgment below was for plaintiff for $5,100, the amount of the pension claimed to be due as of the date of the trial, together with interest thereon, and defendant duly appealed.

The parties are in substantial agreement on the essential facts. Plaintiff began working for the defendant, a manufacturer of pharmaceuticals, in 1910, when she was but 17 years of age. By 1947 she had attained the position of bookkeeper, office manager, and assistant treasurer of the defendant, and owned 70 shares of its stock out of a total of 6,503 shares issued and outstanding. Twenty shares had been given to her by the defendant or its then president, she had purchased 20, and the remaining 30 she had acquired by a stock split or stock dividend. Over the years she received substantial dividends on the stock she owned, as did all of the other stockholders. Also, in addition to her salary, plaintiff from 1937 to 1949, inclusive, received each year a bonus varying in amount from $300 in the beginning to $2,000 in the later years.

On December 27, 1947, the annual meeting of the defendant's Board of Directors was held at the Company's offices in St. Louis, presided over by Max Lippman, its then president and largest individual stockholder. The other directors present were George L. Marcus, Sidney Harris, Sol Flammer, and Walter Weinstock, who, with Max Lippman, owned 5,007 of the 6,503 shares then issued and outstanding. At that meeting the Board of Directors adopted the following resolution, which, because it is the crux of the case, we quote in full:

"The Chairman thereupon pointed out that the Assistant Treasurer, Mrs. Anna Sacks Feinberg, has given the corporation many years of long and faithful service. Not only has she served the corporation devotedly, but with exceptional ability and skill. The President pointed out that although all of the officers and directors sincerely hoped and desired that Mrs. Feinberg would continue in her present position for as long as she felt able, nevertheless, in view of the length of service which she has contributed provision should be made to afford her retirement privileges and benefits which should become a firm obligation of the corporation to be available to her whenever she should see fit to retire from active duty, however many years in the future such retirement may become effective. It was, accordingly, proposed that Mrs. Feinberg's salary which is presently $350.00 per month, be increased to $400.00 per month, and that Mrs. Feinberg would be given the privilege of retiring from active duty at any time she may elect to see fit so to do upon a retirement pay of $200.00 per month for life, with the distinct understanding that the retirement plan is merely being adopted at the present time in order to afford Mrs. Feinberg security for the future and in the hope that her active services will continue with the corporation for many years to come. After due discussion and consideration, and upon motion duly made and seconded, it was—

"Resolved, that the salary of Anna Sacks Feinberg be increased from $350.00 to $400.00 per month and that she be afforded the privilege of retiring from active duty in the corporation at any time she may elect to see fit so to do upon retirement pay of $200.00 per month, for the remainder of her life."

At the request of Mr. Lippman his sons-in-law, Messrs. Harris and Flammer, called upon the plaintiff at her apartment on the same day to advise her of the passage of the resolution. Plaintiff testified on cross-examination that she had no prior information that such a pension plan was contemplated, that it came as a surprise to her, and that she would have continued in her employment whether or not such a resolution had been adopted. It is clear from the evidence that there was no contract, oral or written, as to plaintiff's length of employment, and that she was free to quit, and the defendant to discharge her, at any time.

Plaintiff did continue to work for the defendant through June 30, 1949, on which date she retired. In accordance with the foregoing resolution, the defendant began paying her the sum of $200 on the first of each month. Mr. Lippman died on November 18, 1949, and was succeeded as president of the company by his widow. Because of an illness, she retired from that office and was succeeded in October, 1953, by her son-in-law, Sidney M. Harris. Mr. Harris testified that while Mrs. Lippman had been president she signed the monthly pension check paid plaintiff, but fussed about doing so, and considered the payments as gifts. After his election, he stated, a new accounting firm employed by the defendant questioned the validity of the payments to plaintiff on several occasions, and in the Spring of 1956, upon its recommendation, he consulted the Company's then attorney, Mr. Ralph Kalish. Harris testified that both Ernst and Ernst, the accounting firm, and Kalish told him there was no need of giving plaintiff the money. He also stated that he had concurred in the view that the payments to plaintiff were mere gratuities rather than amounts due under a contractual obligation, and that following his discussion with the Company's attorney plaintiff was sent a check for $100 on April 1, 1956. Plaintiff declined to accept the reduced amount, and this action followed. Additional facts will be referred to later in this opinion.

Appellant's first assignment of error relates to the admission in evidence of plaintiff's testimony over its objection, that at the time of trial she was sixty-five and a half years old, and that she was no longer able to engage in gainful employment because of the removal of a cancer and the performance of a colocholecystostomy operation on November 25, 1957. Its complaint is not so much that such evidence was irrelevant and immaterial, as it is that the trial court erroneously made it one basis for its decision in favor of plaintiff. * * * However, in fairness to the trial court it should be stated that while he briefly referred to the state of plaintiff's health as of the time of the trial in his amended findings of fact, it is obvious from his amended grounds for decision and judgment that it was not, as will be seen, the basis for his decision.

Appellant's next complaint is that there was insufficient evidence to support the court's findings that plaintiff would not have quit defendant's employ had she not known and relied upon the promise of defendant to pay her $200 a month for life, and the finding that, from her voluntary retirement until April 1, 1956, plaintiff relied upon the continued receipt of the pension installments. The trial court so found, and, in our opinion, justifiably so. Plaintiff testified, and was corroborated by Harris, defendant's witness, that knowledge of the passage of the resolution was communicated to her on December 27, 1947, the very day it was adopted. She was told at that time by Harris and Flammer, she stated, that she could take the pension as of that day, if she wished. She testified further that she continued to work for another year and a half, through June 30, 1949; that at that time her health was good and she could have continued to work, but that after working for almost forty years she thought she would take a rest. Her testimony continued:

"Q. Now, what was the reason—I'm sorry. Did you then quit the employment of the company after you—after this year and a half? A. Yes.

"Q. What was the reason that you left? A. Well, I thought almost forty years, it was a long time and I thought I would take a little rest.

"Q. Yes. A. And with the pension and what earnings my husband had, we figured we could get along.

"Q. Did you rely upon this pension? A. We certainly did.

"Q. Being paid? A. Very much so. We relied upon it because I was positive that I was going to get it as long as I lived.

"Q. Would you have left the employment of the company at that time had it not been for this pension? A. No. * * *

"Q. You would not have. Did you ever seek employment while this pension was being paid to you—A. (interrupting): No.

"Q. Wait a minute, at any time prior—at any other place? A. No, sir.

"Q. Were you able to hold any other employment during that time? A. Yes, I think so.

"Q. Was your health good? A. My health was good."

It is obvious from the foregoing that there was ample evidence to support the findings of fact made by the court below.

We come, then, to the basic issue in the case. While otherwise defined in defendant's third and fourth assignments of error, it is thus succinctly stated in the argument in its brief: "* * * whether plaintiff has proved that she has a right to recover from defendant based upon a legally binding contractual obligation to pay her $200 per month for life."

It is defendant's contention, in essence, that the resolution adopted by its Board of Directors was a mere promise to make a gift, and that no contract resulted either thereby, or when plaintiff retired, because there was no consideration given or paid by the plaintiff. It urges that a promise to make a gift is not binding unless supported by a legal consideration; that the only apparent consideration for the adoption of the foregoing resolution was the "many years of long and faithful service" expressed therein; and that past services are not a valid consideration for a promise. Defendant argues further that there is nothing in the resolution which made its effectiveness conditional upon plaintiff's continued employment, that she was not under contract to work for any length of time but was free to quit whenever she wished, and that she had no contractual right to her position and could have been discharged at any time.

Plaintiff concedes that a promise based upon past services would be without consideration, but contends that there were two other elements which supplied the required element: First, the continuation by plaintiff in the employ of the defendant for the period from December 27, 1947, the date when the resolution was adopted, until the date of her retirement on June 30, 1949. And, second, her change of position, i.e., her retirement, and the abandonment by her of her opportunity to continue in gainful employment, made in reliance on defendant's promise to pay her $200 per month for life.

We must agree with the defendant that the evidence does not support the first of these contentions. There is no language in the resolution predicating plaintiff's right to a pension upon her continued employment. She was not required to work for the defendant for any period of time as a condition to gaining such retirement benefits. She was told that she could quit the day upon which the resolution was adopted, as she herself testified, and it is clear from her own testimony that she made no promise or agreement to continue in the employ of the defendant in return for its promise to pay her a pension. Hence there was lacking that mutuality of obligation which is essential to the validity of a contract.

But as to the second of these contentions we must agree with plaintiff. [The court here quoted § 90 of the Restatement of Contracts.]

This doctrine has been described as that of "promissory estoppel," as distinguished from that of equitable estoppel or estoppel in pais, the reason for the differentiation being stated as follows:

> "It is generally true that one who has led another to act in reasonable reliance on his representations of fact cannot afterwards in litigation between the two deny the truth of the representations, and some courts have sought to apply this principle to the formation of contracts, where, relying on a gratuitous promise, the promisee has suffered detriment. It is to be noticed, however, that such a case does not come within the ordinary definition of estoppel. If there is any representation of an existing fact, it is only that the promisor at the time of making the promise intends to fulfill it. As to such intention there is usually no misrepresentation and if there is, it is not that which has injured the promisee. In other words, he relies on a promise and not on a misstatement of

fact; and the term 'promissory' estoppel or something equivalent should be used to make the distinction." Williston on Contracts, Rev. Ed., Sec. 139, Vol. 1.

In speaking of this doctrine, Judge Learned Hand said in Porter v. Commissioner of Internal Revenue, 2 Cir., 60 F.2d 673, 675, that "* * * 'promissory estoppel' is now a recognized species of consideration." * * *

Was there such an act on the part of plaintiff, in reliance upon the promise contained in the resolution, as will estop the defendant, and therefore create an enforceable contract under the doctrine of promissory estoppel? We think there was. One of the illustrations cited under Section 90 of the Restatement is: "2. A promises B to pay him an annuity during B's life. B thereupon resigns a profitable employment, as A expected that he might. B receives the annuity for some years, in the meantime becoming disqualified from again obtaining good employment. A's promise is binding." This illustration is objected to by defendant as not being applicable to the case at hand. The reason advanced by it is that in the illustration B became "disqualified" from obtaining other employment *before* A discontinued the payments, whereas in this case the plaintiff did not discover that she had cancer and thereby became unemployable until *after* the defendant had discontinued the payments of $200 per month. We think the distinction is immaterial. The only reason for the reference in the illustration to the disqualification of A is in connection with that part of Section 90 regarding the prevention of injustice. The injustice would occur regardless of when the disability occurred. Would defendant contend that the contract would be enforceable if the plaintiff's illness had been discovered on March 31, 1956, the day before it discontinued the payment of the $200 a month, but not if it occurred on April 2nd, the day after? Furthermore, there are more ways to become disqualified for work, or unemployable, than as the result of illness. At the time she retired plaintiff was 57 years of age. At the time the payments were discontinued she was over 63 years of age. It is a matter of common knowledge that it is virtually impossible for a woman of that age to find satisfactory employment, much less a position comparable to that which plaintiff enjoyed at the time of her retirement.

The fact of the matter is that plaintiff's subsequent illness was not the "action or forbearance" which was induced by the promise contained in the resolution. As the trial court correctly decided, such action on plaintiff's part was her retirement from a lucrative position in reliance upon defendant's promise to pay her an annuity or pension. * * *

The Commissioner therefore recommends, for the reasons stated, that the judgment be affirmed.

PER CURIAM.

The foregoing opinion by Doerner, C., is adopted as the opinion of the court. The judgment is, accordingly, affirmed.

WOLFE, P.J., and ANDERSON and RUDDY, JJ., concur.

KATZ v. DANNY DARE, INC., 610 S.W.2d 121 (Mo.App.1980). Katz began work for Dare in 1950, and worked in a variety of positions including executive vice president and sales manager. In 1973, he was injured when attempting to prevent a robbery from a company store; although he returned to work, he was not able to function as he had before. Shopmaker (the company's president, and Katz's brother-in-law) decided that he could no longer carry Katz as an employee and began discussions with him concerning retirement. Katz insisted that he did not want to retire, but Shopmaker "persisted in his assessment that Katz was more of a liability than an asset" and for 13 months continued negotiations in an effort to reach an agreement by which Katz would retire with a pension. Katz, who was then earning $23,000 per year, finally agreed to take a pension of $13,000 per year for life; in 1975 the Board of Directors voted him such a pension, and Katz retired at age 67. "Shopmaker testified that * * * the board intended for Katz to rely on the resolution and to retire, but he said Katz would have been fired had he not elected to retire."

Three years later, Dare stopped sending Katz any checks, and Katz brought suit. The trial court found against Katz, distinguishing the *Feinberg* case "because Katz faced the prospect of being fired if he did not accept the pension offer. * * * Katz did not give up anything to which he was legally entitled when he elected to retire." Held, reversed. "Had Shopmaker desired to terminate Katz without any promise of a pension he could have done so and Katz would have had no recourse. However, the fact is that Shopmaker did not discharge Katz but actually made every effort to induce Katz to retire voluntarily on the promise of a pension of $13,000 per year."

HAYES v. PLANTATIONS STEEL COMPANY, 438 A.2d 1091 (R.I.1982). Hayes had been an employee of Plantations since 1947; he began as an "estimator and draftsman" and became the company's general manager. Early in 1972, at the age of 65, he announced his intention to retire in July of that year. One week before his retirement he spoke with an officer of the company, who told him that the company "would take care of him." There was no mention of any sum of money that Hayes would receive, and no formal authorization for payments by the company's board of directors. Beginning in 1973, Plantations paid Hayes $5000 each year. These payments were discontinued in 1976 after a change in control of the company, and Hayes brought suit. The trial court held for Hayes; its ruling "implied that barring bankruptcy or the cessation of business for any other reason, Hayes had a right to expect continued annual payments."

Held, reversed. Hayes's intention to retire "was arrived at without regard to any promise by Plantations. * * * In deciding to retire, Hayes acted on his own initiative." While in *Feinberg* the employer's promise "definitely shaped the thinking of the plaintiff," "[i]n this case the promise did not." Nor could it be said that Hayes's refraining from other employment after retirement constituted reliance within § 90 of the Restatement. "The underlying assumption of Hayes's initial decision to retire was that upon leaving the defendant's employ, he would no longer work."

————

BAGGS v. ANDERSON, 528 P.2d 141 (Utah 1974). Plaintiff and defendant were divorced, plaintiff being awarded custody of three minor children and $200 per month for their support. A later agreement between them provided that if defendant were to make certain payments which were then due, he would be relieved from the payment of any further support money. The court held that despite this agreement the plaintiff was not estopped from collecting support payments for later periods. Defendant had not shown that he had substantially changed his position in reliance on the plaintiff's promise: "This requirement is not satisfied by the mere fact that he indulged in the pleasant and euphoric assumption that he would not have to meet his obligations and that he bought a more expensive car and moved to a more expensive apartment."

SECTION 4: PROMISES AS CONSIDERATION: THE PROBLEM OF MUTUALITY

GREAT NORTHERN RAILWAY CO. v. WITHAM

Court of Common Pleas, 1873.
L.R. 9 C.P. 16.

The cause was tried before Brett, J., at the sittings at Westminster after the last term. The facts were as follows:—In October, 1871, the plaintiffs advertised for tenders for the supply of goods (amongst other things iron) to be delivered at their station at Doncaster, according to a certain specification. The defendant sent in a tender, as follows:—

"I, the undersigned, hereby undertake to supply the Great Northern Railway Company, for twelve months from the 1st of November, 1871, to 31st of October, 1872, with such quantities of each or any of the several articles named in the attached specification as the company's store-keeper may order from time to time, at the price set opposite each article respectively, and agree to abide by the conditions stated on the other side.

(Signed) "Samuel Witham."

The company's officer wrote in reply, as follows:—

"Mr. S. Witham.

"Sir,—I am instructed to inform you that my directors have accepted your tender, dated, &c., to supply this company at Doncaster station any quantity they may order during the period ending 31st of October, 1872, of the descriptions of iron mentioned on the inclosed list, at the prices specified therein. The terms of the contract must be strictly adhered to. Requesting an acknowledgment of the receipt of this letter,

> (Signed) "S. Fitch, Assistant Secretary."

To this the defendant replied,—"I beg to own receipt of your favor of 20th instant, accepting my tender for bars, for which I am obliged. Your specifications shall receive my best attention. S. Witham."

Several orders for iron were given by the company, which were from time to time duly executed by the defendant; but ultimately the defendant refused to supply any more, whereupon this action was brought.

A verdict having been found for the plaintiffs,

Nov. 5. *Digby Seymour, Q.C.,* moved to enter a nonsuit, on the ground that the contract was void for want of mutuality. He contended that, as the company did not bind themselves to take any iron whatever from the defendant, his promise to supply them with iron was a promise without consideration. * * *

Cur. adv. vult.

Nov. 6. Keating, J. * * * Some orders were given by the company, which were duly executed. But the order now in question was not executed; the defendant seeking to excuse himself from the performance of his agreement, because it was unilateral, the company not being bound to give the order. The ground upon which it was put by Mr. Seymour was, that there was no consideration for the defendant's promise to supply the goods; in other words, that, inasmuch as there was no obligation on the company to give an order, there was no consideration moving from the company, and therefore no obligation on the defendant to supply the goods. The case mainly relied on in support of that contention was Burton v. Great Northern Railway Co. [9 Ex. 507 (1854)]. But that is not an authority in the defendant's favor. It was the converse case. The Court there held that no action would lie against the company for not giving an order. If before the order was given the defendant had given notice to the company that he would not perform the agreement, it might be that he would have been justified in so doing. But here the company had given the order, and had consequently done something which amounted to a consideration for the defendant's promise. I see no ground for doubting that the verdict for the plaintiffs ought to stand.

Brett, J. The company advertised for tenders for the supply of stores, such as they might think fit to order, for one year. The defendant made a tender offering to supply them for that period at certain fixed prices; and the company accepted his tender. If there were no other objection, the contract between the parties would be found in the tender and the letter accepting it. This action is brought for the defendant's refusal to deliver goods ordered by the company; and the objection to the plaintiffs' right to recover is, that the contract is unilateral. I do not, however, understand what objection that is to a contract. Many contracts are obnoxious to the same complaint. If I say to another, "If you will go to York, I will give you 100*l.,*" that is in a certain sense a unilateral contract. He has not promised to go to York. But, if he goes, it cannot be doubted that he will be entitled to receive the 100*l.* His going to York at my request is a sufficient consideration for my promise. So, if one says to another, "If you will give me an order for iron, or other goods, I will supply it at a given price;" if the order is given, there is a complete contract which the seller is bound to perform. There is in such a case ample consideration for the promise. So, here, the company having given the defendant an order at his request, his acceptance of the order would bind them. * * * This is matter of every day's practice; and I think it would be wrong to countenance the notion that a man who tenders for the supply of goods in this way is not bound to deliver them when an order is given. I agree that this judgment does not decide the question whether the defendant might have absolved himself from the further performance of the contract by giving notice.

Rule refused.

———

DE LOS SANTOS v. GREAT WESTERN SUGAR CO., 217 Neb. 282, 348 N.W.2d 842 (1984). A hauling contract provided that the "Contractor [plaintiff] shall transport in the Contractor's trucks such tonnage of beets as may be loaded by the Company [defendant] from piles at the beet receiving stations of the Company, and unload said beets at such factory or factories as may be designated by the Company. The term of this contract shall be from October 1, 1980 until February 15, 1981." Plaintiff was required to furnish insurance and suitable trucks and equipment, and to obtain all necessary licenses; he was to be paid solely on the basis of the amount of beets that he transported. When he signed the contract plaintiff knew that defendant had executed identical contracts with other independent truckers who would also be hauling defendant's beets. After transporting beets under the contract for two months, plaintiff was informed by defendant that his services were no longer needed. "The plaintiff does not claim that he was entitled to transport all of the beets, but he does contend that he was entitled to continue to haul until all of the beets had been transported to the factory," and that the defendant's termination caused him to lose profits. Held, summary judgment for defendant affirmed:

"[T]he defendant made no promises at all other than the promise to pay for the transportation of those beets which were in fact loaded by the defendant onto the trucks of the plaintiff during that period. An agreement which depends upon the wish, will, or pleasure of one of the parties is unenforceable. * * * [I]t is apparent that the right of the defendant to control the amount of beets loaded onto the plaintiff's trucks was in effect a right to terminate the contract at any time, and this rendered the contract as to its unexecuted portions void for want of mutuality. * * *"

CORBIN, THE EFFECT OF OPTIONS ON CONSIDERATION
34 Yale L.J. 571, 574 (1925). *

[T]he chief feature of contract law is that by an expression of his will to-day the promisor limits his freedom of voluntary choice in the future. * * * [I]f A asks B to promise some future performance and B makes no answer, B has made no promise. This is true, even though when the future time arrives B may then be willing to perform as requested and may actually so perform. If, under these circumstances, A thinks that B has made a promise, he is under an illusion. The same is true if instead of making no answer B had replied, "I predict that when the time comes I shall be willing to do what you ask." A prediction of future willingness is not an expression of present willingness and is not a promise. To see a promise in it is to be under an illusion. We reach the same result if B's reply to A is, "I promise to do as you ask if I please to do so when the time arrives." In form this is a conditional promise, but the condition is the pleasure or future will of the promisor himself. The words used do not purport to effect any limitation upon the promisor's future freedom of choice. They do not lead the promisee to have an expectation of performance because of a present expression of will. He may hope that a future willingness will exist; but he has no more reasonable basis for such a hope than if B had merely made a prediction or had said nothing at all. As a promise, B's words are mere illusion. Such an illusory promise is neither enforceable against the one making it, nor is it operative as a consideration for a return promise.

When an agreement has been formed by an exchange of promises, it may be that one party will have a defense to liability that is not available to the other: A may be the victim of B's fraud or of B's wrongful threats, which induced him to enter into the contract. A may have lacked the capacity to contract, being a minor, or not mentally competent, or having been intoxicated at the time. (These are all examples of contractual obligations which are "voidable.") Or A may not have signed an agreement falling within the Statute of Frauds,

* Reprinted by permission of The Yale Law Journal Company and Fred B. Roth- man & Company from The Yale Law Journal, Vol. 34, pp. 571, 574.

while B has signed. If A nevertheless wishes to enforce the agreement, can B defend on the ground that the requisite "mutuality" is lacking? In a word, the answer is "no." "The fact that a rule of law renders a promise voidable or unenforceable does not prevent it from being consideration." Restatement, Second, Contracts § 78.

Professor Williston has, with his usual concern for doctrinal neatness, written that such a rule "must be regarded as an exception to the general principles of consideration": Suppose, he writes, that the terms of a voidable contract, such as that entered into by a minor, "be put in words and then made as a promise by an adult under no disability. It will be obvious that the promise is insufficient to support a counterpromise. Whether the infant's promise be translated as meaning—I promise to perform if I choose, or * * * I promise to perform unless I choose to avoid the whole agreement on both sides, in any event it is clear that the promise is illusory since its performance is by its very terms at the option of the promisor, and he can exercise this option without depriving himself of anything to which he was entitled before the formation of the agreement." Williston on Contracts, § 105 (3d ed. 1957).

————

LINDNER v. MID–CONTINENT PETROLEUM CORP., 221 Ark. 241, 252 S.W.2d 631 (1952). Mrs. Lindner leased a filling station to Mid-Continent; the lease was to be for three years, with an option in Mid-Continent to extend the term for two more years. Mid-Continent also had the right to terminate the lease at any time upon ten-days notice. Mid-Continent in turn sublet the property to Mr. Lindner on a month-to-month basis, and Mr. Lindner undertook the actual operation of the station. After two years, Mr. Lindner began buying gas and oil from a competing company. Mid-Continent then terminated its sublease with Mr. Lindner; in retaliation, Mrs. Lindner gave notice that she was cancelling her lease with Mid-Continent. Mid-Continent brought suit to recover possession of the station; a jury verdict awarding possession to it was affirmed:

"It is argued by [defendants] that the lease from Mrs. Lindner to Mid-Continent is lacking in mutuality in that the lessee can terminate the contract upon ten days notice, while no similar privilege is granted to the lessor. This contention is without merit. * * * [T]he requirement of mutuality does not mean that the promisor's obligation must be exactly co-extensive with that of the promisee. It is enough that the duty unconditionally undertaken by each party be regarded by the law as a sufficient consideration for the other's promise. * * * If * * * each party's binding duty of performance amounts to a valuable consideration the courts do not insist that the bargain be precisely as favorable to one side as to the other. * * * This is not an option by which the lessee may terminate the lease at pleasure and without notice; at the very least the lessee bound itself to pay rent for ten days."

————

GURFEIN v. WERBELOVSKY, 97 Conn. 703, 118 A. 32 (1922). Seller wrote Buyer that it had "accepted and entered your order for 5 cases of plate glass * * *. The above cases are to be shipped within 3 months from date. You have the option to cancel the above order before shipment." Buyer frequently demanded delivery of the goods during this three-month period, and, faced with Seller's continued refusal to ship, brought suit for breach of contract. Seller claimed that since the Buyer had the unconditional right to cancel, there was no consideration for the Seller's own promise to sell. The lower court gave judgment for the Seller on this ground, but it was reversed on appeal. If the Seller had any right to enforce the Buyer's promise to buy, that would constitute consideration, the Supreme Court said, "and if that right existed, even for the shortest space of time, it is enough to bring the contract into existence." The court added:

"On the face of this contract the buyer must exercise his option 'before shipment,' otherwise he is bound to take and pay for the goods. No time of shipment is specified otherwise than by the words 'to be shipped within three months.' Hence the seller had a right to ship at any time within the three months, and a shipment made before receiving notice of cancellation would put an end to the buyer's option. [Since seller] might have shipped at the same time that he accepted, there was one clear opportunity to enforce the entire contract, which the buyer could not have prevented or nullified by any attempted exercise of his option. * * * If the defendant voluntarily limited his absolute opportunity of enforcing the contract to the shortest possible time, the contract may have been improvident, but it was not void for want of consideration."

Problem

Before beginning publication in May 1973, Playgirl Magazine actively solicited advertising from established companies; as an unknown quantity, it may have found it difficult to do so successfully. In January 1973, Playgirl entered into a contract with American Tobacco in which American agreed to place ads on the back cover of the magazine for the first eight monthly issues. The form contract contained one typed-in sentence providing, "We [American] have the right to cancel the subsequent issues without penalty if the premiere issue is unsatisfactory to us"; another typed-in sentence provided that "we have the continuing and irrevocable right, at our option, to buy the back cover of Playgirl each and every twelve month period, for each issue of Playgirl within that period, for as long a time as Playgirl shall continue to be published."

Playgirl turned out to be extremely successful, increasing its circulation from the initial 600,000 to about 2 million in less than a year. In September 1973 the magazine informed American Tobacco that effective June 1974, it would no longer publish American's advertising on the desirable back cover. In American's suit for breach of contract, what result? Cf. American Brands, Inc. v. Playgirl, Inc., 498 F.2d 947 (2d Cir.1974); Restatement, Second, Contracts § 77, Illustration 3: "A offers to deliver to B at $2 a bushel as many bushels of wheat, not exceeding 5,000, as B may choose to order within the next 30 days, if B will promise to order at least 1,000 bushels within that time. B accepts. B's promise is consideration * * *."

SCOTT v. MORAGUES LUMBER CO.

Supreme Court of Alabama, 1918.
202 Ala. 312, 80 So. 394.

Suit by the Moragues Lumber Company, a corporation, against J. M. Scott, for damages for breach of an agreement of charter party. Judgment for plaintiff, and defendant appeals. Affirmed.

Count 2 of the complaint as amended is as follows:

The plaintiff claims of the defendant $13,000 as damages from breach of an agreement entered into between the plaintiff and the defendant on the 27th day of June, 1917, consisting of an offer by the defendant that, subject to his buying a certain American vessel, 15 years old, which he was then figuring on and which was of about 1,050 tons and then due in Chile he would charter said vessel to the plaintiff for the transportation of a cargo of lumber from any port in the Gulf of Mexico to Montevideo or Buenos Aires, for the freight of $65 per thousand feet of lumber, freight to be prepaid, free of discount and of insurance, and the vessel to be furnished to the plaintiff within a reasonable time after its purchase by the defendant, which said offer was accepted by the plaintiff, and the plaintiff avers that although the defendant purchased said vessel, and although the plaintiff was at all times ready, willing, and able to comply with all the provisions of said contract on its part, the defendant without notifying the plaintiff of said purchase, and before said vessel was delivered to him, chartered said vessel to a third person, and thereby rendered himself unable to comply with the said contract. * * *

SAYRE, J. * * * Appellant, against whom judgment was rendered in the trial court, insists that various of its grounds of demurrer to the complaint * * * should have been sustained.

It is said, in the first place, that the alleged contract between the parties was conditioned upon the will of appellant, defendant, and was therefore void for want of consideration or mutuality of obligation. A valid contract may be conditioned upon the happening of an event, even though the event may depend upon the will of the party who afterwards seeks to avoid its obligation. * * * Appellant was not bound to purchase the vessel; but, when he did, the offer—or the contract, if the offer had been accepted—thereafter remained as if this condition had never been stipulated, its mutuality or other necessary incidents of obligation depending upon its other provisions and the action of the parties thereunder. * * *

In substance, it is alleged in the complaint that appellant's offer was accepted; that appellant purchased the vessel; that appellee was able, ready, and willing to perform the contract on its part; but that appellant disabled himself, or failed and refused to perform on his part. From the order in which the facts are alleged it is to be inferred that appellee accepted appellant's offer before the latter purchased the vessel, and there is no ground of demurrer questioning the sufficiency of the complaint to that effect. Thereupon the offer was converted into a binding contract to be performed, if not otherwise stipulated, within a reasonable time; the promise on either hand constituting the consideration of the promise on the other. Appellant's purchase of the vessel was a condition precedent to the existence of a binding contract, it is true; but that was alleged, as it was necessary that it should be. And so with respect to appellee's acceptance of the offer. It was necessary that appellee communicate its acceptance to appellant. But this communication was a part of the acceptance and was covered by the general allegation of acceptance.

The defendant in the principal case did not unqualifiedly promise to acquire the vessel, or to charter it to the plaintiff; he merely promised that he would charter it in case he chose to buy it. His duty was therefore subject to a "condition." Restatement, Second, Contracts § 224 defines this term in a way that does not stray very far from its use in ordinary speech, as "an event, not certain to occur, which must occur * * * before performance under a contract becomes due." The subject of conditions is treated in some detail in Chapters 8 and 9 infra.

RESTATEMENT, SECOND, CONTRACTS § 76(2):

A promise conditional on a performance by the promisor is a promise of alternative performances within § 77 unless occurrence of the condition is also promised.

RESTATEMENT, SECOND, CONTRACTS § 77:

A promise or apparent promise is not consideration if by its terms the promisor or purported promisor preserves a choice of alternative performances unless

(a) each of the alternative performances would have been consideration if it alone had been bargained for * * *.

PAUL v. ROSEN, 3 Ill.App.2d 423, 122 N.E.2d 603 (1954). Plaintiff agreed to buy, and defendant agreed to sell, defendant's retail liquor business. The contract provided: "This agreement is conditioned upon the Buyer obtaining a new lease * * * from the owner * * * for a period of five years * * *."

An inventory was to be taken of defendant's merchandise before plaintiff paid the full purchase price and took possession of the business. However, defendant refused to permit the taking of the inventory, and later returned plaintiff's deposit. Plaintiff never obtained a lease, and brought suit for breach of contract arguing that defendant's repudiation had excused him from further performance. Held, judgment for defendant:

"It will be noted that there is no compulsion placed on plaintiff to obtain the lease. Plaintiff was free to get the lease or not as he willed. If plaintiff did get the lease defendant was under obligation to perform his part of the agreement. * * *

"The obtaining of the lease was * * * the condition precedent to the effectiveness of the agreement and to each and every other provision. Under these circumstances we think the entire contract was void for lack of mutuality."

SORENSON v. CONNELLY, 36 Colo.App. 168, 536 P.2d 328 (1975). Buyer agreed to buy Seller's home for $49,500; the contract was "contingent upon" Buyer's obtaining a loan in the amount of $39,600. One month later Buyer wrote Seller that "we have made other arrangements regarding a house"; Seller resold the house for $47,000 and brought suit against Buyer to recover $2500. Held, judgment for Seller affirmed. Buyer cannot rely on the contract condition to avoid liability on the contract; "such provisions imply a promise that the purchaser will make reasonable efforts to secure the loan, and a suit upon the contract lies if the purchaser fails to make such reasonable efforts. The trial court found, upon evidence, that [Buyer] made no attempt to secure the loan."

BLEECHER v. CONTE, 29 Cal.3d 345, 213 Cal.Rptr. 852, 698 P.2d 1154 (1981). Buyers brought suit seeking specific performance of a land sale agreement. The agreement obligated Buyers to "do everything in their power to expedite the recordation of the final map and [to] proceed with diligence." Buyers' obligation to pay was contingent upon their approval of the title report, plat map, and soil, zoning, and engineering reports; however, approval could not be unreasonably withheld. The agreement also included a clause by which "Seller's sole remedy in the event of any material breach by Buyer" would be possession of the reports and plans created for Buyers. Held, judgment for Buyers affirmed. The court rejected Seller's contention that "the buyers' promise was illusory since they assumed no real obligations under the agreement":

"The buyers do not have an unfettered right to cancel their contract or ignore their contractual obligations. * * * This land sale contract does not lack mutuality of obligation. The buyers are under an express duty to proceed diligently and to refrain from unreasonably denying approval. They have an implied duty to proceed in good faith and to act fairly."

Buyers were not prevented from obtaining specific performance merely because under the contract Seller had waived that remedy if Buyers failed to perform their duties.

———

A common form of business transaction allows a buyer to return goods if they fail to meet with his "approval," even though they may be wholly as warranted by the seller. Is there any consideration in such an arrangement for the seller's promise to deliver the goods? See UCC § 2–326, Comment 1.

———

LOUDENBACK FERTILIZER CO. v. TENNESSEE PHOSPHATE CO., 121 Fed. 298 (6th Cir.1903). Buyer, a manufacturer of fertilizer, informed Seller that it planned to increase its production of "acidulated phosphate," a fertilizer made by treating crushed phosphate rock with sulphuric acid. Buyer then agreed to buy, and Seller to sell, Buyer's entire "consumption of phosphate rock" for five years at a stipulated price per ton. Buyer was to have the right to demand as much as 3000 tons per year, although the contract recited that Buyer's "present annual consumption is estimated at something like 1,500 tons under normal conditions."

For about 1½ years Buyer ordered no rock at all from Seller or from any other producer. Increases in the price of sulphuric acid had made it cheaper for Buyer to buy acidulated phosphate directly, both for resale and for use in making a higher grade of fertilizer, and Buyer therefore ceased production of acidulated phosphate. Later, however, a decline in the price of sulphuric acid and an increase in the price of rock caused Buyer to enlarge its capacity for the production of acidulated phosphate. Buyer then ordered from Seller the maximum of 3000 tons permitted under the contract and, on Seller's refusal to fill the order, brought suit. The trial court sustained seller's demurrer to the complaint; held, affirmed:

"A contract to buy all that one shall require for one's own use in a particular manufacturing business is a very different thing from a promise to by all that one may desire, or all that one may order. The promise to take all that one can consume would be broken by buying from another, and it is this obligation to take the entire supply of an established business which saves the mutual character of the promise.
* * *

"The only consideration for the promise of the defendant to sell is the obligation of the plaintiff to take its entire consumption of rock, and if the plaintiff is in fact at liberty to carry on its business by buying its acidulated rock when its price was less than the cost of making it, and thereby avoiding any actual consumption of crude rock, the contract is one which it may perform or not, as it pleases. * * * But we do not accept the plaintiff's interpretation of the agreement as correct. From all the surrounding circumstances it was intended to make the amount of rock which the plaintiff was bound to take as definite as possible by the statement of the average or normal consumption in the manner in which the factory was operated and by the agreement to take the entire consumption for a definite time at a stipulated price. Undoubtedly, there is a margin of allowance to be made for the contraction or expansion of the business incident to the varfying conditions to which it is ordinarily subject. * * * This contract gave the plaintiff liberty to use more or less, so long as it did not reduce or increase its consumption beyond the requirements of the usual fluctuations incident to the character of manufacturing carried on by it. This diminution or increase according to the reasonable fluctuations of such a business, if the result of the carrying on of the business with good faith in view of the obligations of the plaintiff to the defendant, constitutes the limit of the liberty allowed by the contract * * *."

The plaintiff therefore committed the first substantial breach of the contract. "If there is anything well settled it is that the party who commits the first breach of the contract cannot maintain an action against the other for a subsequent failure to perform."

OSCAR SCHLEGEL MANUFACTURING CO. v. PETER COOPER'S GLUE FACTORY, 231 N.Y. 459, 132 N.E. 148 (1921). Defendant agreed with plaintiff to supply "your requirements of 'special BB' glue for the year 1916, price to be 9 cents per pound * * *. Deliveries, to be made to you as per your orders during the year, and quality same as heretofore." Plaintiff was a "jobber," sending salesmen out to solicit orders for wax, paints, and chemicals as well as glues. The parties had been dealing with each other for several years; between 1911 and 1915 plaintiff had ordered from defendant a total of 133,500 pounds of glue. The price of glue rose dramatically at the end of 1916, and by December prices were quoted as high as 21 to 25 cents per pound. For the first nine months of 1916 plaintiff ordered 43,700 pounds of glue; in October, November, and December, however, plaintiff ordered 126,100 pounds. Defendant refused to deliver approximately 80,000 pounds ordered by plaintiff, and plaintiff brought suit for damages. Held, for defendant; "the contract was invalid since a consideration was lacking":

"[T]he plaintiff * * * did not agree to do or refrain from doing anything. It was not obligated to sell a pound of defendant's glue or to make any effort in that direction. It did not agree not to sell other glue in competition with defendant's. The only obligation assumed by it was to pay nine cents a pound for such glue as it might order. Whether it should order any at all rested entirely with it. * * *

"There are certain contracts in which mutual promises are implied: Thus where the purchaser, to the knowledge of the seller, has entered into a contract for the resale of the article purchased; where the purchaser contracts for his requirements of an article necessary to be used in the business carried on by him; or for all the cans needed in a canning factory * * *; all the coal needed for a foundry during a specified time; all the iron required during a certain period in a furnace; and all the ice required in a hotel during a certain season (Great Northern Railway Co. v. Witham, L.R. 9 C.P. 16). In cases of this character, while the quantity of the article contracted to be sold is indefinite, nevertheless there is a certain standard mentioned in the agreement by which such quantity can be determined by an approximately accurate forecast. In the contract here under consideration there is no standard mentioned by which the quantity of glue to be furnished can be determined with any approximate degree of accuracy."

EMPIRE GAS CORPORATION v. AMERICAN BAKERIES COMPANY

United States Court of Appeals, Seventh Circuit, 1988.
840 F.2d 1333.

POSNER, CIRCUIT JUDGE.

This appeal in a diversity contract case presents a fundamental question—surprisingly little discussed by either courts or commentators—in the law of requirements contracts. Is such a contract essentially a buyer's option, entitling him to purchase all he needs of the good in question on the terms set forth in the contract, but leaving him free to purchase none if he wishes provided that he does not purchase the good from anyone else and is not acting out of ill will toward the seller?

Empire Gas Corporation is a retail distributor of liquefied petroleum gas, better known as "propane." It also sells converters that enable gasoline-powered motor vehicles to operate on propane. The sharp rise in gasoline prices in 1979 and 1980 made American Bakeries Company, which operated a fleet of more than 3,000 motor vehicles to serve its processing plants and bakeries, interested in the possibility of converting its fleet to propane, which was now one-third to one-half less expensive than gasoline. [The contract between the two companies, executed on April 17, 1980, was] "for approximately three thousand (3,000) [conversion] units, more or less depending upon requirements of Buyer, consisting of Fuel Tank, Fuel Lock Off Switch, Converter & appropriate Carburetor & Small Parts Kit," at a price of $750 per unit. American Bakeries agreed "to purchase propane motor fuel solely from EMPIRE GAS CORPORATION at all locations where EMPIRE GAS has supplied carburetion and dispensing equipment as long as EMPIRE GAS CORPORATION remains in a reasonably competitive price posture with other major suppliers." The contract was to last for four years.

American Bakeries never ordered any equipment or propane from Empire Gas. Apparently within days after the signing of the contract American Bakeries decided not to convert its fleet to propane. No reason has been given for the decision.

Empire Gas brought suit against American Bakeries for breach of contract and won a jury verdict for $3,254,963, representing lost profits on 2,242 conversion units (the jury's estimate of American Bakeries' requirements) and on the propane fuel that the converted vehicles would have consumed during the contract period. The judge added $581,916 in prejudgment interest. * * *

[The parties agree that the contract is a "requirements contract" governed by UCC § 2–306(1).] Over American Bakeries' objection the judge decided to read the statute to the jury verbatim and without amplification, remarking to the lawyers,

> Now, I have nothing to do with the fact that there may be some ambiguity in [§ 2–306]. If there is ambiguity, well, that is too bad. This is the law that the legislature has adopted. With due respect to all these great judges that [American Bakeries' counsel] has cited and these great academic lawyers he has called to my attention, well, good, they have a lot of time to mull over these problems.

> But I have the problem of telling this jury what the law is, and the law is right here, right here in this statute, and I have a good deal of faith in this jury's ability to apply this statute to the facts of this case.

It is not true that the law is what a jury might make out of statutory language. The law is the statute as interpreted. The duty of interpretation is the judge's. Having interpreted the statute he must then convey the statute's meaning, as interpreted, in words the jury can understand. If [§ 2–306] means something different from what it seems to say, the instruction was erroneous.

The interpretive question involves the proviso dealing with "quantity unreasonably disproportionate to any stated estimate." This limitation is fairly easy to understand when the disproportion takes the form of the buyer's demanding more than the amount estimated. If there were no ceiling, and if the price happened to be advantageous to the buyer, he might increase his "requirements" so that he could resell the good at a profit. This would place him in competition with the seller—a result the parties would not have wanted when they signed the contract. So the "unreasonably disproportionate" proviso carries out the likely intent of the parties. The only problem is that the same result could easily be reached by interpretation of the words "good faith" in the preceding clause of [§ 2–306(1)], thus making the proviso redundant. But redundancies designed to clarify or emphasize are common in legal drafting; and anyway the Uniform Commercial Code has its share of ambiguities.

The proviso does not distinguish between the buyer who demands more than the stated estimate and the buyer who demands less, and therefore if read literally it would forbid a buyer to take (much) less than the stated estimate. Since the judge did not attempt to interpret the statute, the jury may have read it literally, and if so the judge in effect directed a verdict for Empire Gas. The stated estimate was for 3,000 units; American Bakeries took none; if this was not unreasonably disproportionate to the stated estimate, what buyer shortfall could be?

So we must decide whether the proviso should be read literally when the buyer is demanding less rather than more than the stated estimate. There are no cases on the question in Illinois, and authority elsewhere is sparse, considering how often (one might think) the question must have arisen. But the clearly dominant approach is not to construe the proviso literally, but instead to treat the overdemanding and underdemanding cases differently. We think this is right. We also note that it was the common law approach: "the seller assumes the risk of all good faith variations in the buyer's requirements even to the extent of a determination to liquidate or discontinue the business."

* * *

[T]he entire proviso is in a sense redundant given the words "good faith" in the main clause of the statute. The proviso thus seems to have been designed to explicate the term "good faith" rather than to establish an independent legal standard. And the aspect of good faith that required explication had only to do with disproportionately *large* demands. If the buyer saw an opportunity to increase his profits by reselling the seller's goods because the market price had risen above the contract price, the exploitation of that opportunity might not *clearly* spell bad faith; the proviso was added to close off the opportunity. There is no indication that the draftsmen were equally, if at all, concerned about the case where the buyer takes less than his estimated requirements, provided, of course, that he does not buy from anyone else. We conclude that the Illinois courts would allow a buyer to reduce his requirements to zero if he was acting in good faith, even though the contract contained an estimate of those requirements.

This conclusion would be greatly strengthened—too much so, as we shall see—if the only purpose of a requirements contract were to give the seller a reasonably assured market for his product *by forbidding the buyer to satisfy any of his needs by buying from another supplier.* * * * The buyer's undertaking to deal exclusively with a particular seller gives the seller some, although far from complete, assurance of having a market for his goods; and of course he must compensate the buyer for giving up the opportunity to shop around for a better deal from competing sellers.

There was no breach of *this* obligation, or, at most, a trivial one. (American Bakeries did convert 229 of its vehicles to propane, using equipment bought from another company; but the record is silent on how many, if any, of these purchases occurred while the contract with Empire Gas was in force.) If the obligation were not just to refrain from buying a competitor's goods but to buy approximately the stated estimate (or, in the absence of any estimate, the buyer's "normal" requirements), the contract would be altogether more burdensome to the buyer. Instead of just committing himself not to buy from a competitor even if the competitor offered a better product or terms of sale, he would be committing himself to go through with whatever project generated the estimate of required quantity, no matter what happened over the life of the project save those exceptional events that would excuse performance under the related excuses of *force majeure,* impossibility, impracticability, or frustration. This would be a big commitment to infer from the inclusion in the contract of an estimated quantity, at least once the parties concede as they do here that their contract really is a requirements contract and not a contract for the estimate itself—not, in other words, a fixed-quantity contract.

Both extreme interpretations—that the buyer need only refrain from dealing with a competitor of the seller, and that the buyer cannot go significantly beneath the estimated quantity except in dire circumstances—must be rejected, as we shall see. Nevertheless the judge should not have read the "unreasonably disproportionate" proviso in [§ 2–306(1)] to the jury. The proviso does not apply, though the requirement of good faith does, where the buyer takes less rather than more of the stated estimate in a requirements contract.

This error in instructions requires reversal and a new trial on liability unless it is clear either that American Bakeries acted in good faith or that it acted in bad faith, since the statute requires the buyer to take his "good faith" requirements from the seller, irrespective of proportionality. The Uniform Commercial Code does not contain a definition of "good faith" that seems applicable to the buyer under a requirements contract. Compare [§ 2–104(1)] with [§ 2–103(1)(b)]. Nor has the term a settled meaning in law generally; it is a chameleon. Clearly, American Bakeries was acting in bad faith if during the contract period it bought propane conversion units from anyone other than Empire Gas, or made its own units, or reduced its purchases because it wanted to hurt Empire Gas (for example because they were competitors in some other market). Equally clearly, it was not acting in bad faith if it had a business reason for deciding not to convert that was independent of the terms of the contract or any other aspect of its relationship with Empire Gas, such as a drop in the demand for its bakery products that led it to reduce or abandon its fleet of delivery trucks. A harder question is whether it was acting in bad faith if it changed its mind about conversion for no (disclosed) reason. There is no evidence in the record on why it changed its mind beyond vague references to "budget problems" that, so far as appears, may have been nothing more than a euphemism for a decision by American Bakeries not to allocate funds for conversion to propane.

If no reason at all need be given for scaling back one's requirements even to zero, then a requirements contract is from the buyer's standpoint just an option to purchase up to (or slightly beyond, i.e., within the limits of reasonable proportionality) the stated estimate on the terms specified in the contract, except that the buyer cannot refuse to exercise the option because someone offers him better terms. This is not an unreasonable position, but it is not the law. * * *

The statement of an estimate invites the seller to begin making preparations to satisfy the contract, and although no reliance expense was incurred by the seller in this case, a seller is entitled to expect that the buyer will buy something like the estimated requirements unless it has a valid business reason for buying less. More important than the estimate * * * is the fact that ordinarily a requirements contract is terminated after performance has begun, rather than before as in the present case. Whether or not the seller can prove reliance damages, the sudden termination of the contract midway through performance is bound to disrupt his operations somewhat. The Illinois courts interpret a requirements contract as a sharing of risk between seller and buyer. The seller assumes the risk of a change in the buyer's business that makes continuation of the contract unduly costly, but the buyer assumes the risk of a less urgent change in his circumstances, perhaps illustrated by the facts of this case where so far as one can tell the buyer's change of mind reflected no more than a reassessment of the balance of advantages and disadvantages under the contract. American Bakeries did not agree to buy conversion units and propane for trucks that it got rid of, but neither did Empire Gas agree to forgo sales merely because new management at American Bakeries decided that its capital would be better employed in some other investment than conversion to propane.

The general distinction that we are trying to make is well illustrated by Southwest Natural Gas Co. v. Oklahoma Portland Cement Co., 102 F.2d 630 (10th Cir.1939), which to the drafters of the Uniform Commercial Code exemplified "reasonable variation of an extreme sort" * * *. [UCC § 2–306, comment 2]. A cement company agreed to buy all of its requirements of gas from the seller for 15 years. Seven years later, the cement company replaced its boiler, which had worn out, with more modern equipment; as a result its need for gas fell by 80 percent. The court deemed this a bona fide change in the cement company's requirements. It would have been unreasonable to make the company replace its worn-out plant with an obsolete facility.

It is a nice question how exigent the buyer's change of circumstances must be to allow him to scale down his requirements from either the estimated level or, in the absence of estimate, the "normal" level. Obviously it need not be so great as to give him a defense under the doctrines of impossibility, impracticability, or frustration, or under a *force majeure* clause. Yet, although more than whim is required, how much more is unclear. There is remarkably little authority on the question. This is a good sign; it suggests that, while we might think it unsatisfactory for the law to be unclear on so fundamental a question, the people affected by the law are able to live with the lack of certainty. The reason may be that parties linked in an ongoing relationship—the usual situation under a requirements contract—have a strong incentive to work out disagreements amicably rather than see the relationship destroyed by litigation.

The essential ingredient of good faith in the case of the buyer's reducing his estimated requirements is that he not merely have had second thoughts about the terms of the contract and want to get out of it. Whether the buyer has any greater obligation is unclear, but need not be decided here. Once it is decided (as we have) that a buyer cannot arbitrarily declare his requirements to be zero, this becomes an easy case, because American Bakeries has never given any reason for its change of heart.   *   *   *

Even though Empire Gas had the burden of proving breach of contract and therefore (we may assume) of proving that American Bakeries acted in bad faith in reducing its requirements from 3,000 conversion units to zero, no reasonable jury could have failed to find bad faith, and therefore the error in instructing the jury on proportionality was harmless. Empire Gas put in evidence, uncontested and incontestable, showing that American Bakeries had not got rid of its fleet of trucks and did have the financial wherewithal to go through with the conversion process. After this evidence came in, American Bakeries could avoid a directed verdict only by introducing some evidence concerning its reasons for reducing its requirements. It not only introduced no evidence, but * * * it has no evidence that it would care to put before the jury—no reasons that it would care to share with either the district court or this court. * * * It does not suggest that it has a case under the standard we have adopted, which requires at a minimum that the reduction of requirements not have been motivated solely by a reassessment of the balance of advantages and disadvantages under the contract to the buyer.

[The court then held that there was no error in the assessment of the plaintiff's damages. However, it held that the trial judge erred in awarding prejudgment interest.]

Modified and Affirmed.

[The dissenting opinion of Judge Kanne is omitted.]

TORNCELLO v. UNITED STATES, 231 Ct.Cl. 20, 681 F.2d 756 (1982). Plaintiff was awarded a government contract to do pest control work at a Navy housing project. His bid had specified a per call charge of $500. However, it turned out that the only work needed at the project was gopher control; since this work was customarily much cheaper than $500, the Navy gave no work to plaintiff at all but instead called a competitor who had submitted a lower bid. Plaintiff brought suit for breach of contract. The contract contained a standard "termination for convenience" clause by which the government "by written notice, may terminate this contract, in whole or in part, when it is in the best interest of the Government"; under the clause, where the government terminated the contract it would be liable only for prior services rendered by the contractor but not for any anticipated profits.

The Armed Services Board of Contract Appeals held against plaintiff on the ground that the Government had "constructively" resorted to the convenience for termination clause by refusing to accept plaintiff's performance. Held, plaintiff's motion for summary judgment granted. The ASBCA's reading of the termination clause "would destroy the contract":

> "The effect of the ASBCA's decision * * * was to allow the government not to give [plaintiff] any of its needs, to walk away from its cardinal contractual obligation. It is hornbook law * * * that a route of complete escape vitiates any other consideration furnished and is incompatible with the existence of a contract. * * * The contract bound the Navy to give to [plaintiff] all of its pest control needs at the six housing projects covered. The Navy could not just walk away from this promise without making a mockery of the contract."

The obligation on the government to give notice of termination could not serve as consideration, since notice was not given here, and "even if given * * * we would question whether it is sufficient to support a contract merely that one party promise to the other to tell him that he is walking away before he does so." Nor was it an adequate limitation on the government that the contracting officer was required to determine in good faith that termination would be in the government's best interest: "[T]he government, unlike private parties, is assumed always to act in good faith, subject only to an extremely difficult showing by the plaintiff to the contrary"; therefore any obligation to act in good faith "hardly functions as the meaningful obligation that it may for private persons."

The court held that the convenience for termination clause must not be construed so broadly that it "would make the government's promises only illusory." Accordingly, the court read the clause to require the government to show that since the date of the contract there had been "some kind of change from the circumstances of the bargain or in the expectations of the parties" so that the clause served only as an "allocation of the risk of changed conditions."

WOOD v. LUCY, LADY DUFF–GORDON

New York Court of Appeals, 1917.
222 N.Y. 88, 118 N.E. 214.

CARDOZO, J. The defendant styles herself "a creator of fashions." Her favor helps a sale. Manufacturers of dresses, millinery, and like articles are glad to pay for a certificate of her approval. The things which she designs, fabrics, parasols, and what not, have a new value in the public mind when issued in her name. She employed the plaintiff to help her to turn this vogue into money. He was to have the exclusive right, subject always to her approval, to place her indorsements on the designs of others. He was also to have the exclusive right to place her own designs on sale, or to license others to market them. In return she was to have one-half of "all profits and revenues" derived from any contracts he might make. The exclusive right was to last at least one year from April 1, 1915, and thereafter from year to year unless terminated by notice of 90 days. The plaintiff says that he kept the contract on his part, and that the defendant broke it. She placed her indorsement on fabrics, dresses, and millinery without his knowledge, and withheld the profits. He sues her for the damages, and the case comes here on demurrer.

The agreement of employment is signed by both parties. It has a wealth of recitals. The defendant insists, however, that it lacks the elements of a contract. She says that the plaintiff does not bind himself to anything. It is true that he does not promise in so many words that he will use reasonable efforts to place the defendant's indorsements and market her designs. We think, however, that such a promise is fairly to be implied. The law has outgrown its primitive stage of formalism when the precise word was the sovereign talisman, and every slip was fatal. It takes a broader view today. A promise may be lacking, and yet the whole writing may be "instinct with an obligation," imperfectly expressed (Scott, J., in McCall Co. v. Wright, 133 App.Div. 62, 117 N.Y.Supp. 775). If that is so, there is a contract.

The implication of a promise here finds support in many circumstances. The defendant gave an exclusive privilege. She was to have no right for at least a year to place her own indorsements or market her own designs except through the agency of the plaintiff. The acceptance of the exclusive agency was an assumption of its duties. We are not to suppose that one party was to be placed at the mercy of the other. Many other terms of the agreement point the same way. We are told at the outset by way of recital that:

> "The said Otis F. Wood possesses a business organization adapted to the placing of such indorsements as the said Lucy, Lady Duff-Gordon, has approved."

The implication is that the plaintiff's business organization will be used for the purpose for which it is adapted. But the terms of the defendant's compensation are even more significant. Her sole compensation for the grant of an exclusive agency is to be one-half of all the profits resulting from the plaintiff's efforts. Unless he gave his efforts, she could never get anything. Without an implied promise, the transaction cannot have such business "efficacy, as both parties must have intended that at all events it should have." Bowen, L.J., in The Moorcock, 14 P.D. 64, 68. But the contract does not stop there. The plaintiff goes on to promise that he will account monthly for all moneys received by him, and that he will take out all such patents and copyrights and trade-marks as may in his judgment be necessary to protect the rights and articles affected by the agreement. It is true, of course, as the Appellate Division has said, that if he was under no duty to try to market designs or to place certificates of indorsement, his promise to account for profits or take out copyrights would be valueless. But in determining the intention of the parties the promise has a value. It helps to enforce the conclusion that the plaintiff had some duties. His promise to pay the defendant one-half of the profits and revenues resulting from the exclusive agency and to render accounts monthly was a promise to use reasonable efforts to bring profits and revenues into existence. For this conclusion the authorities are ample.

The judgment of the Appellate Division should be reversed, and the order of the Special Term affirmed, with costs in the Appellate Division and in this court.

CUDDEBACK, MCLAUGHLIN, and ANDREWS, JJ., concur. HISCOCK, C.J., and CHASE and CRANE, JJ., dissent.

———

See UCC §§ 1–203, 2–306(2).

LLEWELLYN, A LECTURE ON APPELLATE ADVOCACY

29 U.Chi.L.Rev. 627, 637–38 (1962).

Cardozo was a truly great advocate, and the fact that he became a great judge didn't at all change the fact that he was a great advocate. [In the very process of reading Cardozo's statement of the facts in *Wood*,] you will find two things happening. The one is that * * * you arrive at the conclusion that the case has to come out one way. And the other is, that it fits into a legal frame that says, "How comfortable it will be, to bring it out that way. No trouble at all. No trouble at all." [How then might the facts of the *Wood* case have been stated in such as way as to lead instead to a decision for the defendant?]

All right, now try this: "The plaintiff in this action rests his case upon his own carefully prepared form agreement, which has as its first essence his own omission of any expression whatsoever of any obligation of any kind on the part of this same plaintiff. We thus have the familiar situation of a venture in which one party, here the defendant, has an asset, with what is, in advance, of purely speculative value. The other party, the present plaintiff, who drew the agreement, is a marketer eager for profit, but chary of risk. The legal question presented is whether the plaintiff, while carefully avoiding all risk in the event of failure, can nevertheless claim full profit in the event that the market may prove favorable in its response. The law of consideration joins with the principles of business decency in giving the answer. And the answer is no."

BLOOR v. FALSTAFF BREWING CORP.

United States Court of Appeals, Second Circuit, 1979.
601 F.2d 609.

FRIENDLY, CIRCUIT JUDGE:

This action, wherein federal jurisdiction is predicated on diversity of citizenship, 28 U.S.C. § 1332, was brought in the District Court for the Southern District of New York, by James Bloor, Reorganization Trustee of Balco Properties Corporation, formerly named P. Ballantine & Sons (Ballantine), a venerable and once successful brewery based in Newark, N.J. He sought to recover from Falstaff Brewing Corporation (Falstaff) for breach of a contract dated March 31, 1972, wherein Falstaff bought the Ballantine brewing labels, trademarks, accounts receivable, distribution systems and other property except the brewery. The price was $4,000,000 plus a royalty of fifty cents on each barrel of the Ballantine brands sold between April 1, 1972 and March 31, 1978.

Although other issues were tried, the appeals concern only two provisions of the contract. These are:

8. *Certain Other Covenants of Buyer.*

(a) After the Closing Date the [Buyer] will use its best efforts to promote and maintain a high volume of sales under the Proprietary Rights.

2(a)(v) [The Buyer will pay a royalty of $.50 per barrel for a period of 6 years], provided, however, that if during the Royalty Period the Buyer substantially discontinues the distribution of beer under the brand name "Ballantine" (except as the result of a restraining order in effect for 30 days issued by a court of competent jurisdiction at the request of a governmental authority), it will pay to the Seller a cash sum equal to the years and fraction thereof remaining in the Royalty Period times $1,100,000 payable in equal monthly installments on the first day of each month commencing with the first month following the month in which such discontinuation occurs * * *.

Bloor claimed that Falstaff had breached the best efforts clause, 8(a), and indeed that its default amounted to the substantial discontinuance that would trigger the liquidated damage clause, 2(a)(v). In an opinion that interestingly traces the history of beer back to Domesday Book and beyond, Judge Brieant upheld the first claim and awarded damages but dismissed the second. Falstaff appeals from the former ruling, Bloor from the latter. Both sides also dispute the court's measurement of damages for breach of the best efforts clause.

We shall assume familiarity with Judge Brieant's excellent opinion, 454 F.Supp. 258 (S.D.N.Y.1978), from which we have drawn heavily, and will state only the essentials. Ballantine had been a family owned business, producing low-priced beers primarily for the northeast market, particularly New York, New Jersey, Connecticut and Pennsylvania. Its sales began to decline in 1961, and it lost money from 1965 on. On June 1, 1969, Investors Funding Corporation (IFC), a real estate conglomerate with no experience in brewing, acquired substantially all the stock of Ballantine for $16,290,000. IFC increased advertising expenditures, levelling off in 1971 at $1 million a year. This and other promotional practices, some of dubious legality, led to steady growth in Ballantine's sales despite the increased activities in the northeast of the "nationals" [1] which have greatly augmented their market shares at the expense of smaller brewers. However, this was a profitless prosperity; there was no month in which Ballantine had earnings and the total loss was $15,500,000 for the 33 months of IFC ownership.

After its acquisition of Ballantine, Falstaff continued the $1 million a year advertising program, IFC's pricing policies, and also its policy of serving smaller accounts not solely through sales to independent distributors, the usual practice in the industry, but by use of its own warehouses and trucks—the only change being a shift of the retail distribution system from Newark to North Bergen, N.J., when brewing

---

1. Miller's, Schlitz, Anheuser-Busch, Coors and Pabst.

was concentrated at Falstaff's Rhode Island brewery. However, sales declined and Falstaff claims to have lost $22 million in its Ballantine brand operations from March 31, 1972 to June 1975. Its other activities were also performing indifferently, although with no such losses as were being incurred in the sale of Ballantine products, and it was facing inability to meet payrolls and other debts. In March and April 1975 control of Falstaff passed to Paul Kalmanovitz, a businessman with 40 years experience in the brewing industry. * * *

Mr. Kalmanovitz determined to concentrate on making beer and cutting sales costs. He decreased advertising, with the result that the Ballantine advertising budget shrank from $1 million to $115,000 a year. In late 1975 he closed four of Falstaff's six retail distribution centers, including the North Bergen, N.J. depot, which was ultimately replaced by two distributors servicing substantially fewer accounts. He also discontinued various illegal practices that had been used in selling Ballantine products. What happened in terms of sales volume is shown in plaintiff's exhibit 114 J, a chart which we reproduce in the margin.[4] With 1974 as a base, Ballantine declined 29.72% in 1975 and 45.81% in 1976 as compared with a 1975 gain of 2.24% and a 1976 loss of 13.08% for all brewers excluding the top 15. Other comparisons are similarly devastating, at least for 1976. Despite the decline in the sale of its own labels as well as Ballantine's, Falstaff, however, made a substantial financial recovery. In 1976 it had net income of $8.7 million and its year-end working capital had increased from $8.6 million to $20.2 million and its cash and certificates of deposit from $2.2 million to $12.1 million.

Seizing upon remarks made by the judge during the trial that Falstaff's financial standing in 1975 and thereafter "is probably not relevant" and a footnote in the opinion, 454 F.Supp. at 267 n. 7,[6] appellate counsel for Falstaff contend that the judge read the best

4.

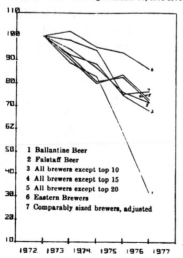

Percentage Increase or Decline in Sales Volume of Ballantine Beer, Falstaff Beer and Comparable Brewers for Years Ending December 31, 1972 1976

1 Ballantine Beer
2 Falstaff Beer
3 All brewers except top 10
4 All brewers except top 15
5 All brewers except top 20
6 Eastern Brewers
7 Comparably sized brewers, adjusted

6. "Even if Falstaff's financial position had been worse in mid-1975 than it actually was, and even if Falstaff had continued in that state of impecuniosity during the term of the contract, performance of the contract is not excused where the difficulty of performance arises from financial difficulty or economic hardship. As the New York Court of Appeals stated in 407 E. 61st St. Garage, Inc. v. Savoy Corp., 23 N.Y.2d 275, 281, 296 N.Y.S.2d 338, 344, 244 N.E.2d 37, 41 (1968):

'[W]here impossibility or difficulty of performance is occasioned only by financial difficulty or economic hardship, even to the extent of insolvency or bankruptcy, performance of a contract is not excused.' (Citations omitted.)"

efforts clause as requiring Falstaff to maintain Ballantine's volume by any sales methods having a good prospect of increasing or maintaining sales or, at least, to continue lawful methods in use at the time of purchase, no matter what losses they would cause. Starting from this premise, counsel reason that the judge's conclusion was at odds with New York law, stipulated by the contract to be controlling, as last expressed by the Court of Appeals in Feld v. Henry S. Levy & Sons, Inc., 37 N.Y.2d 466, 373 N.Y.S.2d 102, 335 N.E.2d 320 (1975). The court was there dealing with a contract whereby defendant agreed to sell and plaintiff to purchase all bread crumbs produced by defendant at a certain factory. During the term of the agreement defendant ceased producing bread crumbs because production with existing facilities was "very uneconomical", and the plaintiff sued for breach. The case was governed by § 2–306 of the Uniform Commercial Code * * *. Affirming the denial of cross-motions for summary judgment, the court said that, absent a cancellation on six months' notice for which the contract provided:

> defendant was expected to continue to perform in good faith and could cease production of the bread crumbs, a single facet of its operation, only in good faith. Obviously, a bankruptcy or genuine imperiling of the very existence of its entire business caused by the production of the crumbs would warrant cessation of production of that item; the yield of less profit from its sale than expected would not. Since bread crumbs were but a part of defendant's enterprise and since there was a contractual right of cancellation, good faith required continued production until cancellation, even if there be no profit. In circumstances such as these and without more, defendant would be justified, in good faith, in ceasing production of the single item prior to cancellation only if its losses from continuance would be more than trivial, which, overall, is a question of fact.

37 N.Y.2d 471–72, 373 N.Y.S.2d 106, 335 N.E.2d 323. Falstaff argues from this that it was not bound to do anything to market Ballantine products that would cause "more than trivial" losses.

We do not think the judge imposed on Falstaff a standard as demanding as its appellate counsel argues that he did. Despite his footnote 7, see note 6 supra, he did not in fact proceed on the basis that the best efforts clause required Falstaff to bankrupt itself in promoting Ballantine products or even to sell those products at a substantial loss. He relied rather on the fact that Falstaff's obligation to "use its best efforts to promote and maintain a high volume of sales" of Ballantine products was not fulfilled by a policy summarized by Mr. Kalmanovitz as being:

> We sell beer and you pay for it * * *. We sell beer, F.O.B. the brewery. You come and get it.

—however sensible such a policy may have been with respect to Falstaff's other products. Once the peril of insolvency had been averted, the drastic percentage reductions in Ballantine sales as related to any possible basis of comparison, required Falstaff at least to explore whether steps not involving substantial losses could have been taken to stop or at least lessen the rate of decline. The judge found that, instead of doing this, Falstaff had engaged in a number of misfeasances and nonfeasances which could have accounted in substantial measure for the catastrophic drop in Ballantine sales shown in the chart, see 454 F.Supp. at 267–72. These included the closing of the North Bergen depot which had serviced "Mom and Pop" stores and bars in the New York metropolitan area; Falstaff's choices of distributors for Ballantine products in the New Jersey and particularly the New York areas, where the chosen distributor was the owner of a competing brand; its failure to take advantage of a proffer from Guinness-Harp Corporation to distribute Ballantine products in New York City through its Metrobeer Division; Falstaff's incentive to put more effort into sales of its own brands which sold at higher prices despite identity of the ingredients and were free from the $.50 a barrel royalty burden; its failure to treat Ballantine products evenhandedly with Falstaff's; its discontinuing the practice of setting goals for salesmen; and the general Kalmanovitz policy of stressing profit at the expense of volume. In the court's judgment, these misfeasances and nonfeasances warranted a conclusion that, even taking account of Falstaff's right to give reasonable consideration to its own interests, Falstaff had breached its duty to use best efforts * * *.

Falstaff levels a barrage on these findings. The only attack which merits discussion is its criticism of the judge's conclusion that Falstaff did not treat its Ballantine brands evenhandedly with those under the Falstaff name. We agree that the subsidiary findings "that Falstaff but not Ballantine had been advertised extensively in Texas and Missouri" and that "[i]n these same areas Falstaff, although a 'premium' beer, was sold for extended periods below the price of Ballantine," while literally true, did not warrant the inference drawn from them. Texas was Falstaff territory and, with advertising on a cooperative basis, it was natural that advertising expenditures on Falstaff would exceed those on Ballantine. The lower price for Falstaff was a particular promotion of a bicentennial can in Texas, intended to meet a particular competitor.

However, we do not regard this error as undermining the judge's ultimate conclusion of breach of the best efforts clause. While that clause clearly required Falstaff to treat the Ballantine brands as well as its own, it does not follow that it required no more. With respect to its own brands, management was entirely free to exercise its business judgment as to how to maximize profit even if this meant serious loss in volume. Because of the obligation it had assumed under the sales contract, its situation with respect to the Ballantine brands was quite different. The royalty of $.50 a barrel on sales was an essential part of the purchase price. Even without the best efforts clause Falstaff would have been bound to make a good faith effort to see that substantial sales of Ballantine products were made, unless it discontinued under clause 2(a)(v) with consequent liability for liquidated damages. Cf. Wood v. Duff-Gordon, 222 N.Y. 88, 118 N.E. 214 (1917) (Cardozo, J.). Clause 8 imposed an added obligation to use "best efforts to promote and maintain a *high* volume of sales ＊ ＊ ＊." (emphasis supplied). Although we agree that even this did not require Falstaff to spend itself into bankruptcy to promote the sales of Ballantine products, it did prevent the application to them of Kalmanovitz' philosophy of emphasizing profit *über alles* without fair consideration of the effect on Ballantine volume. Plaintiff was not obliged to show just what steps Falstaff could reasonably have taken to maintain a high volume for Ballantine products. It was sufficient to show that Falstaff simply didn't care about Ballantine's volume and was content to allow this to plummet so long as that course was best for Falstaff's overall profit picture, an inference which the judge permissibly drew. The burden then shifted to Falstaff to prove there was nothing significant it could have done to promote Ballantine sales that would not have been financially disastrous.

Having correctly concluded that Falstaff had breached its best efforts covenant, the judge was faced with a difficult problem in computing what the royalties on the lost sales would have been. There is no need to rehearse the many decisions that, in a situation like this, certainty is not required; "[t]he plaintiff need only show a 'stable foundation for a reasonable estimate of royalties he would have earned had defendant not breached' ". Contemporary Mission, Inc. v. Famous Music Corp., 557 F.2d 918, 926 (2 Cir. 1977), quoting Freund v. Washington Square Press, Inc., 34 N.Y.2d 379, 383, 357 N.Y.S.2d 857, 861, 314 N.E.2d 419, 421 (1974). After carefully considering other possible bases, the court arrived at the seemingly sensible conclusion that the most nearly accurate comparison was with the combined sales of Rheingold and Schaefer beers, both, like Ballantine, being "price" beers sold primarily in the northeast, and computed what Ballantine sales would have been if its brands had suffered only the same decline as a composite of Rheingold and Schaefer. ＊ ＊ ＊

It is true, more generally, that the award may overcompensate the plaintiff since Falstaff was not necessarily required to do whatever Rheingold and Schaefer did. But that is the kind of uncertainty which is permissible in favor of a plaintiff who has established liability in a case like this. ＊ ＊ ＊

[The court rejected the plaintiff's contention that Falstaff's actions had amounted to a "substantial discontinuance of 'distribution' " and thus that the liquidated damages clause had been triggered.]

The judgment is affirmed. Plaintiff may recover two-thirds of his costs.

————

ZILG v. PRENTICE–HALL, INC., 717 F.2d 671 (2d Cir.1983). Plaintiff was the author of "DuPont: Behind the Nylon Curtain," a "harshly critical" portrait of the DuPont family and its role in American history. He entered into a contract with defendant Prentice–Hall in which defendant agreed to publish the book; defendant reserved the right "to determine the method and means of advertising, publicizing, and selling the work, * * * and all other publishing details, including the number of copies to be printed * * *." Defendant paid plaintiff an advance of $6500. Defendant initially decided on a first printing of 15,000 copies and an advertising budget for the book of $15,000. After protests from the DuPont family, however, the Fortune Book Club reversed its earlier decision to distribute the book; after further review of the manuscript, defendant cut the first printing to 10,000 copies and slashed the advertising budget to $5500. Plaintiff brought suit for breach of contract. The trial court held that defendant had had no "sound" or "valid" business reason for reducing the first printing and the advertising budget; defendant had therefore breached its obligation to use "its best efforts * * * to promote the Book fully and fairly." The court awarded damages to plaintiff on the basis of a finding that the book would have sold 25,000 copies had defendant not breached this obligation.

Held, reversed: "[W]e note that [plaintiff] neither bargained for nor acquired an explicit 'best efforts' or 'promote fully' promise, much less an agreement to make certain specific promotional efforts. * * * Working as we must in the context of a surprising absence of caselaw on the meaning of this not uncommon agreement, we believe that the contract in question establishes a relationship between the publisher and author which implies an obligation upon the former to make certain efforts in publishing a book it has accepted notwithstanding the clause which leaves the number of volumes to be printed and the advertising budget to the publisher's discretion. This obligation is derived both from the common expectations of parties to such agreements and from the relationship of those parties as structured by the contract. * * *

"Were the clause empowering the publisher to determine promotional expenses read literally, the contract would allow a publisher to refuse to print or distribute any copies of a book while having exclusive rights to it. In effect, authors would be guaranteed nothing but whatever up-front money had been negotiated, and the promise to publish would be meaningless. We think the promise to publish must be given some content and that it implies a good faith effort to promote the book including a first printing and an advertising budget adequate to give the book a reasonable chance of achieving market success in light of the subject matter and likely audience. * * *

"However, the clause empowering the publisher to decide in its discretion upon the number of volumes printed and the level of promotional expenditures must also be given some content. * * * We believe that once the obligation to undertake reasonable initial promotional activities has been fulfilled, the contractual language dictates that a business decision by the publisher to limit the size of a printing or advertising budget is not subject to second guessing by a trier of fact as to whether it is sound or valid. * * *

"Once the initial obligation is fulfilled, all that is required is a good faith business judgment. * * * Were courts to impose rigorous requirements as to promotional efforts, publishers would of necessity undertake to publish fewer books with unpredictable futures. * * * [W]e think the contract * * * left the decisions in question to the business judgment of the publisher, the author's protection being in the publisher's experience, judgment and quest for profits." The plaintiff had not shown that the defendant's initial efforts were so inadequate "as not to give the book a reasonable chance to catch on with the reading public"; nor had he shown that the failure to undertake even greater promotional efforts was attributable to any reason "other than a good faith business judgment."

CORENSWET, INC. v. AMANA REFRIGERATION, INC., 594 F.2d 129 (5th Cir. 1979). Between 1969 and 1976 Corenswet was the exclusive distributor in southern Louisiana of Amana refrigerators, freezers, room air conditioners and other products. (Amana products were sold to wholesale distributors such as Corenswet, who then resold the merchandise to retail dealers for sale to the public.) Corenswet invested over $1.5 million in developing the market for Amana products in its territory; it hired salesmen and specially-trained repairmen for the line and expanded its physical plant. Annual sales of Amana products in the area increased from $200,000 in 1969 to over $2.5 million in 1976, when they represented 26% of Corenswet's total sales of all products.

The agreement between Amana and Corenswet allowed termination by either party "at any time for any reason" on ten days' notice. Amana gave such notice of termination in 1976. The district court found that Amana had acted "arbitrarily"—whatever the reasons given, the "real factor" motivating the decision was personal animosity—and enjoined Amana from terminating the relationship. Held, reversed:

"[A]rbitrary termination is possible under both the contract and the law of Iowa * * * Amana's past conduct, with regard both to Corenswet and to its other distributors, may have created a reasonable expectation that Amana would not terminate a distributor arbitrarily, yet the contract expressly gives Amana the right to do so. We can find no justification, except in cases of conduct of the sort giving rise to promissory estoppel, for holding that a contractually reserved power, however distasteful, may be lost through nonuse. The express contract term cannot be construed as Corenswet would constitute it, and it therefore controls over any allegedly conflicting usage or course of dealing. [UCC §§ 1–205, 2–208(2)]."

The Court of Appeals noted a "division in the authorities" between those courts holding that the UCC's general good faith obligation in § 1–203 overrides "the specific rule of § 2–309(2) as applied to distributorship and franchise agreements," and those giving precedence to § 2–309(2). Iowa law, the court found, "follows the common law rule which is essentially the rule of § 2–309 as applied to distributorship contracts":

"We do not agree with Corenswet that the § 1–203 good faith obligation, like the Code's unconscionability provision, can properly be used to override or strike express contract terms. According to Professor Farnsworth, '[T]he chief utility of the concept of good faith performance has always been as a rationale in a process * * * of implying contract terms * * *.' Farnsworth, Good Faith Performance and Commercial Reasonableness under the Uniform Commercial Code, 30 U.Chi.L.Rev. 666, 672 (1963). He defines the Code's good faith obligation as 'an implied term of the contract requiring cooperation on the part of one party to the contract so that another party will not be deprived of his reasonable expectations'. Id. at 666. When a contract contains a provision expressly sanctioning termination without cause there is no room for implying a term that bars such a termination. In the face of such a term there can be, at best, an expectation that a party will decline to exercise his rights. * * *

"The better approach * * * is to test the disputed contract clause for unconscionability under § 2–302 of the Code. * * * We seriously doubt, however, that public policy frowns on any and all contract clauses permitting termination without cause. Such clauses can have the salutary effect of permitting parties to end a soured relationship without consequent litigation. Indeed when, as here, the power of unilateral termination without cause is granted to both parties, the clause gives the distributor an easy way to cut the knot should he be presented with an opportunity to secure a better distributorship from another manufacturer. What public policy does abhor is economic overreaching—the use of superior bargaining power to secure grossly unfair advantage. That is the precise focus of the Code's unconscionability doctrine; it is not at all the concern of the Code's good faith performance provision. * * *"

Since Corenswet had "never pressed" the issue of unconscionability, it was held the district court should not have granted a preliminary injunction.

––––––

See also UCC §§ 1–102(3), 1–208.

––––––

Terminating Dealerships

Attempts by dealers to invoke the notion of unconscionability in order to prevent termination of their dealerships have generally been rebuffed. See, e.g., Smith v. Price's Creameries, 98 N.M. 541, 650 P.2d 825 (1982), in which summary judgment for defendant was affirmed over plaintiff's objection that a clause allowing termination "for any reason" was "unconscionable and void as a matter of law." The court stressed that the plaintiff-distributor, who had worked both as an insurance salesman and a police officer, "also had three and one-half years of college education. Under the circumstances no material disputed factual issue has been shown to exist concerning lack of adequate opportunity to fairly review the contract, inability to understand the provisions of the document, or lack of opportunity to seek independent professional advice regarding the terms and provisions of the agreement." See also Blalock Machinery & Equipment Co. v. Iowa Mfg. Co. of Cedar Rapids, 576 F.Supp. 774 (N.D.Ga.1983) (the franchisor's preprinted standardized contract made the termination clause "basically non-negotiable," but the dealer "did not have to enter into the contract").

Some courts have inferred—in the absence of any express provision in the agreement—that the dealership was intended to last long enough to give the dealer an opportunity to "recoup his investment" in the business. See, e.g., Schultz v. Onan Corp., 737 F.2d 339 (3d Cir.1984) (terminated dealer may recover his unrecouped expenditures, but he may not recover damages for the lost value of his business or for lost future profits). For greater protection, however, the franchised dealer has had to look to the legislative branch.

A number of state statutes now restrict a franchisor's right to terminate ongoing dealership arrangements. The Wisconsin Fair Dealership Law is typical in that it prevents a franchisor from cancelling, failing to renew, or "substantially chang[ing] the competitive circumstances" of a dealership agreement "without good cause." "Good cause" is in turn defined as the dealer's failure substantially to comply with "essential and reasonable requirements" of the franchisor which are not "discriminatory as compared with requirements imposed on other similarly situated dealers." The burden of proving such "good cause" is on the franchisor, and any agreement by which the dealer gives up any of his statutory rights is expressly made "void and unenforceable." Wis.Stats. §§ 135.02, 135.025, 135.03. Query: Would statutes like this prohibit termination by a franchisor who for business reasons wishes to withdraw completely from a particular market? See Lee Beverage Co. v. I.S.C. Wines of California, Inc., 623 F.Supp. 867 (E.D.Wis.1985) (no; the decision to sell the defendant's product lines "was based on sound financial considerations" and was therefore "done for good cause").

At the federal level, the "Automobile Dealers' Day in Court Act," 15 U.S.C.A. § 1221, was enacted in 1956 in response to what was described as "abuse by the manufacturers [of automobiles] of their dominant position with respect to their dealers," made possible by "the unilateral nature of the franchise agreements," H.Rep. No. 2850, 84th

Cong., 2d Sess., reprinted in U.S.Code Cong. & Adm.News 4596, 4597, 4599 (1956). It gives a cause of action to dealers for their damages sustained "by reason of the failure of said automobile manufacturer * * * to act in good faith * * * in terminating, cancelling, or not renewing the franchise with said dealer." But the potential reach of the statute has been substantially limited by the restrictive statutory definition of "good faith":

> "The term 'good faith' shall mean the duty of each party to any franchise * * * to act in a fair and equitable manner toward each other so as to guarantee the one party freedom from coercion, intimidation, or threats of coercion or intimidation from the other party: *Provided,* That recommendation, endorsement, exposition, persuasion, urging or argument shall not be deemed to constitute a lack of good faith." 15 U.S.C.A. § 1221(e).

The cases uniformly hold that in order to show the necessary lack of "good faith," "it will not suffice to show that a dealership's termination was arbitrary, or even unfair. It must be shown that defendant coerced or intimidated plaintiff, and that the coercion was designed to achieve some objective which was improper or wrongful." Quarles v. General Motors Corp., 597 F.Supp. 1037 (W.D.N.Y.1984), aff'd, 758 F.2d 839 (2d Cir.1985). Suits brought by automobile dealers have therefore rarely been successful. However, it has been suggested that in practice passage of the statute led to the creation by automobile manufacturers of elaborate internal procedures for termination, making "capricious judgments to cancel a dealer rather unlikely." See S. Macaulay, Law and the Balance of Power 76 (1966).

In the Petroleum Marketing Practices Act of 1978, 15 U.S.C.A. § 2801, Congress extended protection to franchised distributors and retailers of gasoline, typically service station operators. The statute prohibits termination or failure to renew for any grounds other than those set out in the statute, including the "occurrence of an event which is relevant to the franchise relationship" and as a result of which termination or nonrenewal is "reasonable." (This is in turn defined in terms of a lengthy list, such as the franchisee's misconduct or his "continuing severe physical or mental disability" which renders him "unable to provide for the continued proper operation of the marketing premises.") The franchisor may, however, refuse to renew a franchise if the franchisee does not agree to changes or additions to the agreement suggested by the franchisor "in good faith and in the normal course of business," or if the franchisor determines in good faith that renewal "is likely to be uneconomical [to him] despite any reasonable changes [in the agreement] which may be acceptable to the franchisee."

In a recent study of dealer protection legislation, Professor Stewart Macaulay has concluded that "[a]ll the statutes may do is influence choices when there is something to say for the dealer. The chance of legal challenge may prompt superiors to review more carefully recommendations to cancel by field people who supervise dealers. * * *

[T]he costs and uncertainty of the outcome of litigation may prompt the franchisor to give the dealer another chance to cure the problem, buy out the dealer or arrange a sale of the business to another person." S. Macaulay, Long–Term Continuing Relations: The American Experience Regulating Dealerships and Franchises 55–56 (1990).

MABLEY & CAREW CO. v. BORDEN

Supreme Court of Ohio, 1935.
129 Ohio St. 375, 195 N.E. 697.

Ida C. Borden brought an action in the court of common pleas of Hamilton county against the Mabley & Carew Company, alleging in her petition that Anna Work, her sister, now deceased, was and had been for some years an employee of such company and that it promised and agreed in writing to pay to such person as was designated by Anna Work on the back of a certificate issued to her a sum equal to the wages received by her from the company for the year next preceding the date of her death. The plaintiff in error further alleges that she is the person designated on the back of the certificate; that Anna Work continued in the employ of the company until the date of her death; that her wages for the year preceding were $780, and she prays judgment for this amount with interest from the date of the death of Anna Work.

The Mabley & Carew Company in effect denies these allegations and states affirmatively that if the certificate was issued as claimed, it was issued voluntarily and gratuitously and without consideration, and was issued to Anna Work and accepted by her with the express understanding that it carried no legal obligation.

* * * The case came on for trial in the court of common pleas and at the conclusion of the plaintiff's evidence the trial court sustained a motion directing a verdict for the Mabley & Carew Company.

Motion for new trial was overruled, judgment was entered and error was prosecuted to the Court of Appeals of Hamilton county, which court reversed, set aside and held for naught the judgment of the court of common pleas. * * *

The following is a copy of the certificate upon which the action was predicated:

"The Mabley & Carew Co.

"To Mrs. Anna Work.

"In appreciation of the duration and faithful character of your services heretofore rendered as an employee of this Company, there will be paid in the event of your death, if still an employee of this Company, * * * to the party or parties designated by you on the back of this certificate a sum equal to the wages you have received from this Company for the year next preceding the day of your death, but in no event to exceed the sum of Two Thousand Dollars.

"The issue and delivery of this certificate is understood to be purely voluntary and gratuitous on the part of this Company and is accepted with the express understanding that it carries no legal obligation whatsoever or assurance or promise of future employment, and may be withdrawn or discontinued at any time by this Company.

"The Mabley & Carew Co.

"Adolph C. Weiss, Secy.

"Cincinnati, Ohio, Dec. 24, 1919."

Indorsement:

"The Mabley & Carew Co.   Date, _____

"Gentlemen:—It is my desire that you make all benefits payable under this Certificate to the following and in the proportions here indicated:

Name	Relation to Beneficiary	Address	Proportion
Mrs. Ida Borden	Sister"		

STEPHENSON, JUDGE. * * *

There is just one question in this case, and that is the consideration for the issuance of this certificate. It is true that Anna Work could not maintain an action on this certificate in her lifetime, as no right of action existed in her favor; but that fact did not prevent it from being enforceable, after her death, in the hands of Ida C. Borden.

This certificate was not a pure gratuity on the part of the Mabley & Carew Company, as there was a provision in the certificate to the effect that the payment would not be made in the event of death unless Anna Work was still an employee of the company. This was an inducement to Anna Work to continue in the employ of the company. That is not the only consideration, as it is expressed at the outset that the company appreciates the duration and faithful character of the services of the employee theretofore rendered. The employee, by virtue of the issuance of the certificate, had a right to expect that the person nominated by her would, in the event of her death, receive the amount designated by the certificate. This was certainly an incentive to remain in the service of the company.

It is not a tenable proposition that, because Anna Work had no enforceable right during her life, her beneficiary could take no more than she had. We think the learned Court of Appeals was right in holding that Anna Work, by continuing in the service of the company until her death, created a binding obligation upon the company to pay to her designated beneficiary the sum mentioned in the certificate.

It is stated in the certificate: "The issue and delivery of this certificate is understood to be purely voluntary and gratuitous on the part of this Company." That was a part of the contract so far as Anna Work was concerned. She had no right that she could possibly assert, as she had to die before the right would ripen in any one.

The case of Zwolanek v. Baker Mfg. Co., 150 Wis. 517, 137 N.W. 769 [1912] pronounces the law relative to certificates of this character in its true light as we see it. The court there said: "While the practice initiated by the defendant is beneficial to its employees, it is not difficult to see wherein it is also beneficial to the employer. It tends to induce employees to remain continuously in the employ of the same master, and to render efficient services, so as to minimize the possibility of discharge. It also tends to relieve the employer of the annoyance of hiring and breaking in new men to take the place of those who might otherwise voluntarily quit, and to insure a full working force at times when jobs are plentiful and labor is scarce."

True, Anna Work, by reason of this certificate, was under no obligation to continue in the service of the Mabley & Carew Company if she did not see fit so to do; neither was the company, by reason of the certificate, obligated to give her continuous or definite employment. But neither of these facts in any wise affected the right of the beneficiary, so far as Anna Work was concerned after this contract was executed. * * *

The judgment of the Court of Appeals is hereby affirmed.

Judgment affirmed.

What if the Mabley & Carew Co. tried to sell its wares on the same "empty" terms that it promised its bonuses—say, by making claims for its goods and then purporting to deny these promises any legal force? See UCC §§ 2–316(1), 2–719 Comment 1.

BELLINE v. K–MART CORPORATION

United States Court of Appeals, Seventh Circuit, 1991.
940 F.2d 184.

CUDAHY, J.

Our task in this diversity case is to divine the contours of the rather amorphous Illinois common law tort of retaliatory discharge. Frank Belline brought suit against his former employer, K–Mart Corporation, claiming that he was fired from his job in retaliation for reporting to K–Mart management suspicious behavior on the part of his supervisor. K–Mart assumes the truth of Belline's allegations for the purpose of its summary judgment motion but responds that Belline's termination for his internal report regarding his supervisor's irregular conduct is not actionable as retaliatory discharge because it implicates no public policy. The district court entered summary judgment in favor of K–Mart, concluding that the type of disclosure Belline made does not warrant protection because it falls outside "the heart of a citizen's social rights, duties, and responsibilities." Because, by our reading, Illinois law encourages all citizens to ferret out and expose possible criminal activity in the workplace, we reverse.

Frank Belline was employed as resident assistant manager of the K–Mart store in Wheeling, Illinois from February 1984 until May 1988. On November 15, 1987, while Belline was on duty, a Rotary Club representative entered the store to retrieve goods that he claimed had been set aside for him by the store manager, Dennis Dobberke. After telephoning Dobberke at home to verify the transaction, Belline released the merchandise. Dobberke explained that an itemized list of the goods and a payment check were locked in his desk and assured Belline that he would record the transaction later that evening. Belline mentioned the unusual incident to two of his co-workers—Scott Timmons, store security manager, and Pamela Bryan, assistant manager. As a result, when Dobberke returned to the store, all three employees kept a vigilant eye upon him. None of the three, however, spotted Dobberke running a check through the cash register. To Belline's knowledge, moreover, no such check was ever processed.

Timmons relayed word of Dobberke's suspicious behavior to Larry Clark, regional security manager. When Clark summoned Belline to his office, Belline himself recounted the precise course of events. He also notified Clark of his discovery that Dobberke had been improperly authorizing payment to an employee for days that the employee did not work. Although Belline pursued the Dobberke inquiry through the appropriate professional channels, he never reported the matter to the police. After an internal investigation, Dobberke was ultimately demoted and transferred to Ames, Iowa.

Belline charges K–Mart with penalizing all three employees who played a role in exposing Dobberke's suspect activities—Timmons, Bryan and himself. In February 1988, shortly after the close of the Dobberke investigation, Timmons was demoted from security manager to stockperson, a job that entails unloading trucks and hauling shopping carts from the parking lot. Shortly thereafter, Timmons was transferred to Elgin, Illinois. In March 1988, Belline himself was put on probation and on May 11, 1988, he was discharged, allegedly for unsatisfactory performance. Belline claims that Dobberke's replacement, the new store manager Tim Rommel, inadvertently let slip the reasons for his dismissal, bluntly stating: "You got Dobberke, I got you." Finally, Belline maintains that Pam Bryan, the third participant in the investigation, was also demoted: in June 1988, Bryan was transferred from her position as resident assistant manager of the K–Mart Wheeling store to a post as a merchandise assistant at a much smaller store 330 miles away in Madison, Indiana.

Belline filed suit charging K–Mart with retaliatory discharge and breach of his employment contract. The district court granted summary judgment in favor of K–Mart on both claims. Dismissing Belline's disclosure as just an internal report divulging a possible violation of company procedure or a crime, the district court concluded that it raised no issue of public policy. *   *   *

As a general rule, an employment contract of unspecified duration may be terminated at any time with or without cause. Because unfettered employer power may threaten the public welfare, however, Illinois law recognizes an exception to the general rule of at-will employment: it permits an employee who is dismissed in violation of a clearly mandated public policy to bring a cause of action for retaliatory discharge. Recognition of this tort strikes an appropriate balance among competing interests—the employer's interest in efficient operation of a business, the employee's interest in earning a livelihood and society's interest in the well-being of its citizens.

The tort of retaliatory discharge comprises three distinct elements: first, an employee must establish that she has been discharged; second, she must demonstrate that her discharge was in retaliation for her activities; and, finally, she must show that the discharge violates a clear mandate of public policy. But, as the Illinois Supreme Court has observed, the "Achilles heel of the principle lies in the definition of public policy." [Palmateer v. Int'l Harvester Co., 421 N.E.2d 876, 878 (Ill.1981)]. Struggling to articulate some formulation of the term, the *Palmateer* court declared that "public policy concerns what is right and just and what affects the citizens of the State collectively * * *. [A] matter must strike at the heart of a citizen's social rights, duties, and responsibilities before the tort will be allowed."

Although no law compels an individual to step forward and communicate his suspicions regarding criminal activity, public policy clearly favors the exposure of crime. A society's fundamental concern for the lives and property of its citizens is embodied in the criminal code. But the risk of discharge may deter employees who reasonably believe that crimes have been committed from acting on the information. To encourage citizen crime-fighters, Illinois law thus shields employees who volunteer such information from retaliatory discharge. In *Palmateer,* for example, the Illinois Supreme Court held that an employee who alleged that he had been fired because he notified the local law-enforcement agency of his co-worker's possible violation of the state criminal code had stated a cause of action for retaliatory discharge. "There is no public policy more basic, nothing more implicit in the concept of ordered liberty * * * than the enforcement of a State's criminal code," the court pronounced. * * *

But K–Mart contends that Belline's report regarding Dobberke's activities is merely a matter of private concern, not a matter of public policy. This argument relies upon two points. First, K–Mart seizes upon the fact that Belline reported his suspicions only to K–Mart management, not to the police. Second, K–Mart insists that the trifling magnitude of the crime involved removes it from the public realm.

K–Mart's emphasis on the private character of the parties to whom Belline voiced his suspicions, however, is misplaced. The great majority of courts interpreting Illinois law hold that an employee who reports unlawful conduct to an employer is protected under the tort of retaliatory discharge. To hold otherwise would be to create perverse incentives by inviting concerned employees to bypass internal channels altogether and immediately summon the police. Thus public policy, as well as state law, favors an approach that would allow dutiful employees who report wrongdoing to their employers to bring retaliatory discharge claims. As Judge Aspen observed in Parr v. Triplett, [727 F.Supp. 1163, 1166 (N.D.Ill.1989)]: " * * * A report to an employer does not transform a violation of the Illinois Criminal Code from a matter of public concern into a private dispute. The employee who chooses to approach his employer should not be denied a remedy simply because a direct report to law enforcement agencies might effectuate the exposure of crime more quickly. This would be a nonsensical distinction. * * * " In fact, as K–Mart conceded at oral argument, Belline would have violated store policy had he failed to pursue the incident through the proper commercial chain of command and instead taken his suspicions directly to the authorities. * * *

K–Mart's second argument fares no better. K–Mart contends that the nature and magnitude of the claim involved here transforms it from a public matter into a private dispute. But although there is no sharp line of demarcation dividing matters of public policy from those of purely private concern, one who exposes what appears to be a crime furthers public policy. Belline reported what he reasonably believed to be a crime—unauthorized removal of merchandise from the store without proper payment. That the illegal act may have involved only a paltry sum makes no difference, for public policy favors the reporting of crimes regardless of their magnitude. * * *

Focusing upon its policy regarding the donation of goods to charitable organizations, K–Mart also contends that Dobberke's activities may not have been illegal. Yet an employee's retaliatory discharge claim should not turn on the happenstance of whether the irregular conduct she reports is actually criminal. Public policy favors the exposure of apparently criminal activity. That the questionable conduct may later prove to be authorized and therefore legitimate is not dispositive. Admittedly, this is a close case since Dobberke's removal of the goods might actually prove to be an authorized contribution to a charitable organization. We think the apparent illegality of the acts Belline reported, however, is sufficient for him to survive summary judgment. * * *

The dissent raises several issues which are, of course, worthy of consideration under the circumstances of this close case. The facts here, however, do not suggest that K–Mart in any way condoned Dobberke's offense. In fact, Dobberke was ultimately demoted. There are hints in the record, moreover, that Belline was fired by a mid-level manager who was merely a friend of Dobberke. * * * In any event, the dissent's argument creates an ex ante/ex post problem by encouraging companies to redefine the crime of theft after the fact to insulate themselves from liability for retaliatory discharge. By the dissent's reasoning, an employee who is fired as a troublemaker for reporting what he reasonably believes to be a crime to the proper authority within the company could never bring suit for retaliatory discharge because the company could always define the apparent crime out of existence. Perhaps (as is suggested by the facts of this case) the company disavows the occurrence of any crime only to cut its losses and avoid liability after a mid-level manager has already fired the vigilant employee. Or, to pose another hypothetical, what if a store manager brazenly backs his truck up to the loading dock and drives off with enough furniture and appliances to completely equip his new home? His employer may choose to overlook the whole thing simply because the manager is the boss' nephew, or a fishing companion, or even because he is too good a merchandiser to lose. The dissent apparently believes that an employer's willingness to turn a blind eye to otherwise criminal activity should legitimate the filing of an employee who reports what he perceives to be illegal conduct. Yet such a stance hardly furthers Illinois' acute interest in the enforcement of its criminal laws. * * *

[The court held against the plaintiff on his breach of contract claim, "because he can point to no clear promise modifying his at-will employment status."] Belline also alleges, however, that he was discharged because he warned K–Mart management of what he reasonably believed to be a crime—removal of merchandise without proper payment. Assuming the truth of his allegations (as K–Mart does for the purpose of summary judgment), K–Mart is not entitled to judgment as a matter of law on Belline's retaliatory discharge claim. Illinois public policy protects vigilant employees who alert their employees to apparently criminal activity in the workplace. The district court's grant of summary judgment in favor of K–Mart is therefore AFFIRMED IN PART, REVERSED IN PART, and REMANDED for further proceedings consistent with this opinion.

EASTERBROOK, CIRCUIT JUDGE, dissenting.

* * * It is easy for a jury to mistake a pest, a busybody, for a champion of the law. Firms need to prune their work forces of persons who create more trouble than they are worth; time diverted from business means lower efficiency and higher prices for consumers, undermining still another public policy. Employers fearing litigation with high legal fees and the risk of punitive damages will keep troublesome and inefficient employees on the payroll. Everyone loses when that happens.

* * * What Belline reported is that the manager of one of K–Mart's stores let a local Rotary Club obtain some merchandise without filling in the proper forms. On one reading this is an offense against the sanctity of K–Mart's record-keeping system. (Retailers need to know what became of the inventory, and K–Mart also may want to keep tabs on the total volume of charitable gifts. It is unsurprising that K–Mart demoted the manager.) On another reading this is

"theft"—because theft is an unconsented taking, and K–Mart allowed managers to donate merchandise to charity only after using the right forms. But no matter which characterization we use, Illinois has no interest in the outcome independent of K–Mart's. Illinois has not tried to induce retailers to cleave to a particular path on gifts; K–Mart therefore is not using discharge to undermine any policy of Illinois. Whether there was a crime depends entirely on K–Mart's rule; there is no state policy beyond willingness to enforce K–Mart's decisions. If Belline was right in taking the manager's donation unauthorized, the victim is K–Mart itself. No state case I could find says that Illinois wants to crack down on firms that do not pay adequate attention to their interest in curtailing pilfering by their own employees. * * *

Because theft is an unconsented taking, putting the identification of the crime in the hands of the person with authority to give or withhold consent, Belline's claim fails. * * * Deployment of the state's power, through the tort law, is important only if there is some risk that the firm is using a discharge to undermine a legislative decision. Belline's discharge presents no such risk, and there is accordingly no reason to override the contract between Belline and K–Mart that leaves employment decisions to K–Mart.

———

Employment at Will

As the court notes in *Belline,* the dominant common-law rule was that an employment contract of indefinite duration is considered "terminable at will," so that employers may discharge employees "for good cause, for no cause or even for cause morally wrong, without being thereby guilty of legal wrong." Payne v. Western & Atlantic R.R. Co., 81 Tenn. 507 (1884). This doctrine has been considerably eroded in recent years. A large number of state and federal statutes now prohibit an employer from discharging an employee for certain reasons—for example, on the ground of an employee's race, age, gender, handicap, or union membership. See also Vernon's Ann.Tex. Health & Safety Code § 242.133 (nursing home employee has cause of action if terminated for reporting abuse or neglect of a resident of institution); Vernon's Ann.Tex. Health & Safety Code § 502.013 (employer who uses hazardous chemicals may not discharge employee who reports a violation of Hazard Communication Act). In addition, collective bargaining agreements negotiated between employers and labor unions commonly limit the employer's ability to fire workers: Approximately 94% of collective bargaining agreements contain provisions allowing dismissal only for "cause," "just cause," or for specific offenses. However, fewer than 20% of the nation's nonagricultural workers are now represented by unions and work under such collective bargaining agreements; employers in any event have no obligation under the National Labor Relations Act to bargain with "supervisors" or "managerial" employees. See Note, Employer Opportunism and the Need for a Just Cause

Standard, 103 Harv.L.Rev. 510 (1989). Finally, courts have also played an active role in limiting the "employment at will" doctrine. One management attorney has noted that "[w]e have entered a new era of employer-employee relationships, one marked by new court-created worker rights and employer obligations." Kramer, "The Hazards of Firing at Will," Wall St. J., March 9, 1987.

Courts have used various doctrinal tools to chip away at the "employment at will" doctrine:

(1) Perhaps the most widely accepted of these is the "public policy" exception involved in *Belline*. There is, of course, nothing new in the idea that courts may impose limits on a party's exercise of a contract right even though under the contract itself the right appears to be entirely unfettered. For example, an insurance company that writes a medical malpractice policy allowing it to cancel on ten days' notice may not be able to cancel the policy in retaliation for the insured's testifying for the plaintiff in a malpractice suit. L'Orange v. Medical Protective Co., 394 F.2d 57 (6th Cir.1968). The argument that a discharge of an employee is against "public policy" is perhaps strongest where an employee has been fired for refusing to violate the law. See, e.g., White v. American Airlines, Inc., 915 F.2d 1414 (10th Cir.1990) (employer should be held liable if its discharge of employee "was significantly motivated by [employee's] refusal to commit perjury" in employer's interest). But compare Herbster v. North American Co., 150 Ill.App.3d 21, 103 Ill.Dec. 322, 501 N.E.2d 343 (1986) (chief legal officer of corporation was fired for refusing to destroy or remove from the files documents that had been requested in discovery in pending lawsuits; held, no cause of action; "[a]ttorneys are governed by different rules and have different duties and responsibilities than the employees in recent retaliatory discharge cases").

In other cases, courts may impose liability where an employee has been fired for insisting on a right granted by statute—for example, for filing a worker's compensation claim, or for refusing to seek exemption from jury duty. Another category of public policy cases involves the "whistleblowing" employee like Belline, who typically is fired for bringing illegal or unsafe practices to the attention of a superior or the public. However, courts often distinguish between protected public policy concerns that "strike at the heart of a citizen's social rights, duties, and responsibilities" and mere "private and individual grievances." See Price v. Carmack Datsun, Inc., 109 Ill.2d 65, 92 Ill.Dec. 548, 485 N.E.2d 359 (1985) (employee was fired for filing a claim with company group health insurance plan; held, no cause of action); Pierce v. Ortho Pharmaceutical Corp., 84 N.J. 58, 417 A.2d 505 (1980) (physician employed by drug company opposed continued research on a controversial drug; held, summary judgment for defendant; an "employee does not have a right to continued employment when he or she refuses to conduct research simply because it would contravene his or her personal morals").

(2) Courts have also increasingly resorted to a "contract" analysis. In many cases—sometimes only after work has begun—the employer has distributed to employees a personnel manual or "handbook"; statements of policy made in these documents are frequently interpreted in such a way as to impose contractual limits on the employer's right to fire. One rather extreme example is Jeski v. American Express Co., 147 Ariz. 19, 708 P.2d 110 (App.1985). An employee was summarily discharged solely because of an accusation (later shown to be false) that he had sent obscene materials through the mail. While the "Employee Information Kit" distributed to all employees stated that "your employment * * * can be terminated at any time," it also promised "fair treatment and the personal respect which is rightfully yours * * * [W]e will constantly strive to maintain your respect for our individual treatment of your welfare and job security." The court held that this was sufficient to allow the plaintiff's complaint to survive the employer's motion for summary judgment: "The manual purports to make a number of assurances of fair treatment, personal respect, and significantly, job security, a concept completely at odds with the traditional at-will employment relationship."

Courts have also applied a "contract" analysis without relying on any express representations such as these. In some cases the employee's long service, "the commendations and promotions he received, the apparent lack of any direct criticism of his work," the employer's past practices and the "totality of the parties' relationship," are enough to permit an inference that the employer had impliedly agreed not to "act arbitrarily in dealing with its employees." Pugh v. See's Candies, Inc., 116 Cal.App.3d 311, 171 Cal.Rptr. 917 (1981) (employee had begun as a dishwasher and when fired 32 years later had risen to vice-president and member of the board of directors). Where company policy is to hire new employees for a "probationary period" during which they may be fired for any reason, a court may readily infer that any employee who survives such a period has in fact been promised job security. See Wiskotoni v. Michigan National Bank West, 716 F.2d 378 (6th Cir.1983). Of course, liability on grounds of breach of contract can readily be avoided through adequate planning, and in recent years many employers have been busily revising employee manuals to make it quite clear that employment may be terminated at any time without cause.

(3) A third device that courts have used is to imply a "covenant of good faith and fair dealing" in all contracts of employment. Cf. UCC § 1–203. The most common use of such a covenant is as a rule of construction; it is often implied, for example, to prevent the employer from exercising his right to fire in such a way as to deprive an employee of promised benefits "attributable to past service." The classic illustration is Fortune v. National Cash Register Co., 373 Mass. 96, 364 N.E.2d 1251 (1977). The plaintiff was a salesman who had worked for the defendant for almost 25 years. In addition to a salary, he was to receive a commission for sales made within his "territory"; the full commission was to be paid only if the territory was assigned to

him both when the order was placed and also when the equipment was delivered and installed. The plaintiff was fired three days after a large customer had placed a $5 million order. The employer had promised the customer that the services of a systems and installation person would be available, and the remainder of the commission was paid to this person rather than to the plaintiff. Although "according to a literal reading of the contract" the plaintiff had received all the commissions to which he was entitled," the court held that termination "motivated by a desire to pay [him] as little of the bonus credit as it could" would be a violation of the covenant of good faith and fair dealing. The "covenant of good faith and fair dealing" is, however, rarely if ever actually used to prevent an employer from firing an employee "without cause."

Courts that limit an employer's discretion by finding a violation of "public policy" most often impose liability on the ground of "tort," thereby leaving the door open to the recovery of punitive damages and damages for emotional distress. Where the plaintiff wins by invoking a "covenant of good faith and fair dealing," however, the tendency is otherwise. The California Supreme Court has held that for breach of the implied covenant in employment cases, courts should award "the generally predictable and circumscribed damages available for breach of contract." See Foley v. Interactive Data Corp., page 69 supra. Contra, K Mart Corp. v. Ponsock, 103 Nev. 39, 732 P.2d 1364 (1987) ("Merely giving to [plaintiff] that to which he is contractually entitled does not make him whole, does not compensate him for the injury, the insult, the wrong [he] suffered").

A "Model Termination of Employment Act" was approved by the National Conference of Commissioners on Uniform State Laws in 1991. Under this Act, an employee who has worked for the same employer for one year or more may not be fired without "good cause"; "good cause" is defined to include both the employee's misconduct and job performance, and the employer's good faith "exercise of business judgment" concerning the goals and organization of his operations and the size and composition of his work force. This right to job security cannot be waived except by an individually executed agreement guaranteeing the employee a minimum schedule of severance payments depending on length of service. Claims for wrongful termination are to be heard by an arbitrator, who may order reinstatement of the employee or may award up to three years' worth of severance pay; the employee may also recover attorneys' fees, but with those exceptions may not recover "punitive damages, compensatory damages, or any other monetary award."

EPSTEIN, IN DEFENSE OF THE CONTRACT AT WILL
51 U.Chi.L.Rev. 947, 951, 955, 969–70, 973 (1984).

The persistent tension between private ordering and government regulation exists in virtually every area known to the law, and in none has that tension been more pronounced than in the law of employer and employee relations. During the last fifty years, the balance of power has shifted heavily in favor of direct public regulation, which has been thought strictly necessary to redress the perceived imbalance between the individual and the firm. * * *

There is thus today a widely held view that the contract at will has outlived its usefulness. But this view is mistaken. * * *

First, the parties should be permitted as of right to adopt this term of contract if they so desire. The principle behind this conclusion is that freedom of contract tends both to advance individual autonomy and to promote the efficient operation of labor markets. * * *

An employee who knows that he can quit at will understands what it means to be fired at will, even though he may not like it after the fact. So long as it is accepted that the employer is the full owner of his capital and the employee is the full owner of his labor, the two are free to exchange on whatever terms and conditions they see fit * * *. If the arrangement turns out to be disastrous to one side, that is his problem; and once cautioned, he probably will not make the same mistake a second time. More to the point, employers and employees are unlikely to make the same mistake once. It is hardly plausible that contracts at will could be so pervasive in all businesses and at all levels if they did not serve the interests of employees as well as employers. * * *

[In addition, Professor Epstein argues that as a rule of construction "the contract at will represents the most efficient solution to the employment relation." For one thing, the contract at will "contains powerful limitations on employers' abuse of power"; should an employer engage in opportunistic behavior by making increased demands, "the worker can quit whenever the net value of the employment contract turns negative." And even under a contract-at-will rule there are "powerful correctives against capricious discharge by employers," who may face "powerful adverse economic consequences" if they are perceived as acting arbitrarily: "At the margin some workers will look elsewhere, and typically the best workers will have the greatest opportunities."]

The contract at will is also a sensible private adaptation to the problem of imperfect information over time. In sharp contrast to the purchase of standard goods, an inspection of the job before acceptance is far less likely to guarantee its quality thereafter. The future is not clearly known. More important, employees, employers, *know what they do not know.* They are not faced with a bolt from the blue, with an "unknown unknown." Rather, they face a known unknown for which they can plan. The at-will contract is an essential part of that planning because it allows both sides to take a wait-and-see attitude to their relationship so that new and more accurate choices can be made on the strength of improved information. ("You can start Tuesday and we'll see how the job works out" is a highly intelligent response to uncertainty.) * * *

[Finally, the contract at will has "an enormous advantage over its rivals" in that it is "cheap to administer." A "for-cause rule," by contrast, may generate considerable litigation. And the inquiry into whether the employer has erred in firing an employee may not even be worth conducting: "The chances of finding an innocent employee wronged by a firm vendetta are quite remote. By the same token, jury sympathy with aggrieved plaintiffs may result in a very large number of erroneous verdicts for employees."] * * *

The account thus far given of the contract at will in no way depends upon any notion of an inherent inequality of bargaining power that pervades all employment contracts. Indeed, if such an inequality did govern the employment relationship, we should expect to see conditions that exist in no labor market. Wages should be driven to zero, for no matter what their previous level, the employer could use his (inexhaustible) bargaining power to reduce them further, until the zero level was reached. Similarly, inequality of bargaining power implies that the employee will be bound for a term while the employer * * * retains the power to terminate at will. Yet in practice we observe both positive wages and employees with the right to quit at will.

COHEN & CO. v. MESSINA, 24 Ohio App.3d 22, 492 N.E.2d 867 (1985). Defendant was hired by plaintiff as an accountant. Sixteen months later plaintiff issued a company personnel manual that included a section on termination of employment; this section contained a "client ownership provision" providing that for one year following termination of employment, the employee was to remit to the firm 50% of all fees received from his "personal clients" and 100% of fees received from any other clients of the firm. After four years defendant left the firm; soon afterwards several clients left also and hired defendant. The firm then brought suit pursuant to the "client ownership" agreement for the fees paid by these former clients. The trial court held that "no adequate legal consideration" supported the enforcement of the agreement. Held, affirmed: "[Defendant's] position, duties, and the nature of the business remained exactly the same as before the manual was distributed; the employment relationship was 'at will,' and the company assumed no obligation it did not already have."

GROUSE v. GROUP HEALTH PLAN, INC., 306 N.W.2d 114 (Minn. 1981). Grouse, a retail pharmacist, was offered a job by defendant's Chief Pharmacist. After accepting, he gave the necessary two weeks notice of resignation to his current employer and declined another job offer. In the meantime defendant's General Manager informed the Chief Pharmacist that company policy required favorable written references before hiring could be final. The Chief Pharmacist could not obtain references for Grouse and so Grouse was told, when he reported for work, that another pharmacist had been hired in his place. Grouse's action for damages was dismissed by the trial court; held, reversed: "In our view the principle of contract law applicable here is promissory estoppel. Its effect is to imply a contract in law where none exists in fact. On these facts no contract exists because due to the bilateral power of termination neither party is committed to performance and the promises are, therefore, illusory."

Nevertheless, the court wrote, in these circumstances "it would be unjust not to hold Group Health to its promise":

"Group Health contends that recognition of a cause of action on these facts would result in the anomalous rule that an employee who is told not to report to work the day before he is scheduled to begin has a remedy while an employee who is discharged after the first day does not. We cannot agree since under appropriate circumstances we believe section 90 would apply even after employment has begun.

* * *

"The conclusion we reach does not imply that an employer will be liable whenever he discharges an employee whose term of employment is at will. What we do hold is that under the facts of this case the appellant had a right to assume he would be given a good faith opportunity to perform his duties to the satisfaction of respondent once he was on the job. He was not only denied that opportunity but resigned the position he already held in reliance on the firm offer which respondent tendered him. Since, as respondent points out, the prospective employment might have been terminated at any time, the measure of damages is not so much what he would have earned from respondent as what he lost in quitting the job he held and in declining at least one other offer of employment elsewhere."

SECTION 5: PRE–EXISTING DUTY AS CONSIDERATION; MODIFICATION AND DISCHARGE OF CONTRACTUAL DUTIES

STILK v. MYRICK

Common Pleas, 1809.
2 Camp. 317, 170 Eng.Rep. 1168.

This was an action for seaman's wages, on a voyage from London to the Baltic and back.

By the ship's articles, executed before the commencement of the voyage, the plaintiff was to be paid at the rate of £5 a month; and the principal question in the cause was, whether he was entitled to a higher rate of wages?—In the course of the voyage two of the seamen deserted; and the captain having in vain attempted to supply their places at Cronstadt, there entered into an agreement with the rest of the crew, that they should have the wages of the two who had deserted equally divided among them, if he could not procure two other hands at Gottenburgh. This was found impossible; and the ship was worked back to London by the plaintiff and eight more of the original crew, with whom the agreement had been made at Cronstadt.

Garrow for the defendant insisted, that this agreement was contrary to public policy, and utterly void. In West India voyages, crews are often thinned greatly by death and desertion; and if a promise of advanced wages were valid, exorbitant claims would be set up on all such occasions. This ground was strongly taken by Lord Kenyon in Harris v. Watson, Peak.Cas. 72 [1791], where that learned Judge held, that no action would lie at the suit of a sailor on a promise of a captain to pay him extra wages, in consideration of his doing more than the ordinary share of duty in navigating the ship; and his Lordship said, that if such a promise could be enforced, sailors would in many cases suffer a ship to sink unless the captain would accede to any extravagant demand they might think proper to make.

The Attorney–General, *contra*, distinguished this case from Harris v. Watson, as the agreement here was made on shore, when there was no danger or pressing emergency, and when the captain could not be supposed to be under any constraint or apprehension. The mariners were not to be permitted on any sudden danger to force concessions from the captain—but why should they be deprived of the compensation he voluntarily offers them in perfect security for their extra labour during the remainder of the voyage?

Lord Ellenborough.—I think Harris v. Watson was rightly decided; but I doubt whether the ground of public policy, upon which Lord Kenyon is stated to have proceeded, be the true principle on which the decision is to be supported. Here, I say, the agreement is void for want of consideration. There was no consideration for the ulterior pay promised to the mariners who remained with the ship. Before they sailed from London they had undertaken to do all that they could under all the emergencies of the voyage. They had sold all their services till the voyage should be completed. If they had been at liberty to quit the vessel at Cronstadt, the case would have been quite different; or if the captain had capriciously discharged the two men who were wanting, the others might not have been compellable to take the whole duty upon themselves, and their agreeing to do so might have been a sufficient consideration for the promise of an advance of wages. But the desertion of a part of the crew is to be considered an emergency of the voyage as much as their death; and those who remain are bound by the terms of their original contract to exert themselves to the utmost to bring the ship in safety to her destined port. Therefore, without looking to the policy of this agreement, I think it is void for want of consideration, and that the plaintiff can only recover at the rate of £5 a month.

Verdict accordingly.

ALASKA PACKERS' ASS'N v. DOMENICO

United States Court of Appeals, Ninth Circuit, 1902.
117 Fed. 99.

Ross, Circuit Judge. The libel in this case was based upon a contract alleged to have been entered into between the libelants and the appellant corporation on the 22d day of May, 1900, at Pyramid Harbor, Alaska, by which it is claimed the appellant promised to pay each of the libelants, among other things, the sum of $100 for services rendered and to be rendered. In its answer the respondent denied the execution, on its part, of the contract sued upon, averred that it was without consideration, and for a third defense alleged that the work performed by the libelants for it was performed under other and different contracts than that sued on, and that, prior to the filing of the libel, each of the libelants was paid by the respondent the full amount due him thereunder, in consideration of which each of them executed a full release of all his claims and demands against the respondent.

The evidence shows without conflict that on March 26, 1900, at the city and county of San Francisco, the libelants entered into a written contract with the appellants, whereby they agreed to go from San Francisco to Pyramid Harbor, Alaska, and return, on board such vessel as might be designated by the appellant, and to work for the appellant during the fishing season of 1900, at Pyramid Harbor, as sailors and fishermen, agreeing to do "regular ship's duty, both up and down, discharging and loading; and to do any other work whatsoever when requested to do so by the captain or agent of the Alaska Packers' Association." By the terms of this agreement, the appellant was to pay each of the libelants $50 for the season, and two cents for each red salmon in the catching of which he took part.

On the 15th day of April, 1900, 21 of the libelants signed shipping articles by which they shipped as seamen on the Two Brothers, a vessel chartered by the appellant for the voyage between San Francisco and Pyramid Harbor, and also bound themselves to perform the same work for the appellant provided for by the previous contract of March 26th; the appellant agreeing to pay them therefor the sum of $60 for the season, and two cents each for each red salmon in the catching of which they should respectively take part. Under these contracts, the libelants sailed on board the Two Brothers for Pyramid Harbor, where the appellants had about $150,000 invested in a salmon cannery. The libelants arrived there early in April of the year mentioned, and began to unload the vessel and fit up the cannery. A few days thereafter, to wit, May 19th, they stopped work in a body, and demanded of the company's superintendent there in charge $100 for services in operating the vessel to and from Pyramid Harbor, instead of the sums stipulated for in and by the contracts; stating that unless they were paid this additional wage they would stop work entirely, and return to San Francisco. The evidence showed, and the court below found, that it was impossible for the appellant to get other men to take the places of the libelants, the place being remote, the season short and just opening; so that, after endeavoring for several days without success to induce the libelants to proceed with their work in accordance with their contracts, the company's superintendent, on the 22d day of May, so far yielded to their demands as to instruct his clerk to copy the contracts executed in San Francisco, including the words 'Alaska Packers' Association' at the end, substituting, for the $50 and $60 payments, respectively, of those contracts, the sum of $100, which document, so prepared, was signed by the libelants before a shipping commissioner whom they had requested to be brought from Northeast Point; the superintendent, however, testifying that he at the time told the libelants that he was without authority to enter into any such contract, or to in any way alter the contracts made between them and the company in San Francisco. Upon the return of the libelants to San Francisco at the close of the fishing season, they demanded pay in accordance with the terms of the alleged contract of May 22d, when the company denied its validity, and refused to pay other than as provided for by the contracts of March 26th and April 5th, respectively. Some of the libelants, at least, consulted counsel, and, after receiving his advice, those of them who had signed the shipping articles before the shipping commissioner at San Francisco went before that officer, and received the amount due them thereunder, executing in consideration thereof a release in full, and the others being paid at the office of the company, also receipting in full for their demands.

On the trial in the court below, the libelants undertook to show that the fishing nets provided by the respondent were defective, and that it was on that account that they demanded increased wages. On that point, the evidence was substantially conflicting, and the finding of the court was against the libelants the court saying:

> "The contention of libelants that the nets provided them were rotten and unserviceable is not sustained by the evidence. The defendants' interest required that libelants should be provided with every facility necessary to their success as fishermen, for on such success depended the profits defendant would be able to realize that season from its packing plant, and the large capital invested therein. In view of this self-evident fact, it is highly improbable that the defendant gave libelants rotten and unserviceable nets with which to fish. It follows from this finding that libelants were not justified in refusing performance of their original contract."

The evidence being sharply conflicting in respect to these facts, the conclusions of the court, who heard and saw the witnesses, will not be disturbed.

The real questions in the case as brought here are questions of law, and, in the view that we take of the case, it will be necessary to consider but one of those. Assuming that the appellant's superintendent at Pyramid Harbor was authorized to make the alleged contract of

May 22d, and that he executed it on behalf of the appellant, was it supported by a sufficient consideration? From the foregoing statement of the case, it will have been seen that the libelants agreed in writing, for certain stated compensation, to render their services to the appellant in remote waters where the season for conducting fishing operations is extremely short, and in which enterprise the appellant had a large amount of money invested; and, after having entered upon the discharge of their contract, and at a time when it was impossible for the appellant to secure other men in their places, the libelants, without any valid cause, absolutely refused to continue the services they were under contract to perform unless the appellant would consent to pay them more money. Consent to such a demand, under such circumstances, if given, was, in our opinion, without consideration, for the reason that it was based solely upon the libelants' agreement to render the exact services, and none other, that they were already under contract to render. The case shows that they willfully and arbitrarily broke that obligation. As a matter of course, they were liable to the appellant in damages, and it is quite probable, as suggested by the court below in its opinion, that they may have been unable to respond in damages. But we are unable to agree with the conclusions there drawn, from these facts, in these words:

> "Under such circumstances, it would be strange, indeed, if the law would not permit the defendant to waive the damages caused by the libelants' breach, and enter into the contract sued upon,—a contract mutually beneficial to all the parties thereto, in that it gave to the libelants reasonable compensation for their labor, and enabled the defendant to employ to advantage the large capital it had invested in its canning and fishing plant."

Certainly, it cannot be justly held, upon the record in this case, that there was any voluntary waiver on the part of the appellant of the breach of the original contract. The company itself knew nothing of such breach until the expedition returned to San Francisco, and the testimony is uncontradicted that its superintendent at Pyramid Harbor, who, it is claimed, made on its behalf the contract sued on, distinctly informed the libelants that he had no power to alter the original or to make a new contract, and it would, of course, follow that, if he had no power to change the original, he would have no authority to waive any rights thereunder. The circumstances of the present case bring it, we think, directly within the sound and just observations of the supreme court of Minnesota in the case of King v. Railway Co., 61 Minn. 482, 63 N.W. 1105:

> "No astute reasoning can change the plain fact that the party who refuses to perform, and thereby coerces a promise from the other party to the contract to pay him an increased compensation for doing that which he is legally bound to do, takes an unjustifiable advantage of the necessities of the other party. Surely it would be a travesty on justice to hold that the party so making the promise

for extra pay was estopped from asserting that the promise was without consideration. A party cannot lay the foundation of an estoppel by his own wrong, where the promise is simply a repetition of a subsisting legal promise. There can be no consideration for the promise of the other party, and there is no warrant for inferring that the parties have voluntarily rescinded or modified their contract. The promise cannot be legally enforced, although the other party has completed his contract in reliance upon it."

[The court then discussed and quoted from Lingenfelder v. Brewing Co., 103 Mo. 578, 15 S.W. 844 (1891). In this case Jungenfeld, an architect, had entered into an agreement with Wainwright to design and supervise the construction of a new brewery. Jungenfeld was also the president of a refrigerating company, and he had hoped to get for his company the contract for putting the refrigeration plant into the brewery. When the brewery was "in process of erection," Jungenfeld learned that the refrigeration contract had been awarded to a competitor: He then "took away his plans, called off his superintendant * * * and notified Mr. Wainwright that he would have nothing more to do with the brewery. [Wainwright] was in great haste to have its new brewery completed for divers reasons. It would be hard to find an architect to fill Mr. Jungenfeld's place, and the making of new plans and arrangements when another architect was found would involve much loss of time." So Wainwright promised Jungenfeld additional compensation of five percent of the cost of the refrigerating equipment if he would resume work. The Supreme Court of Missouri held that Wainwright's promise was unenforceable]:

"It is urged upon us by respondents that this was a new contract. New in what? Jungenfeld was bound by his contract to design and supervise this building. Under the new promise, he was not to do anything more or anything different. What benefit was to accrue to Wainwright? He was to receive the same service from Jungenfeld under the new, that Jungenfeld was bound to tender under the original, contract. What loss, trouble, or inconvenience could result to Jungenfeld that he had not already assumed? No amount of metaphysical reasoning can change the plain fact that Jungenfeld took advantage of Wainwright's necessities, and extorted the promise of five per cent. on the refrigerator plant as the condition of his complying with his contract already entered into. Nor had he even the flimsy pretext that Wainwright had violated any of the conditions of the contract on his part. Jungenfeld himself put it upon the simple proposition that 'if he, as an architect, put up the brewery, and another company put up the refrigerating machinery, it would be a detriment to the Empire Refrigerating Company,' of which Jungenfeld was president. To permit plaintiff to recover under such circumstances would be to offer a premium upon bad faith, and invite men to violate their most sacred contracts that they may profit by their own wrong. That a promise to pay a man for doing that which he is already under contract to do is without consideration is conceded by respondents. The rule has been so long imbedded in the common law and decisions of the highest courts of the various states that nothing but the most cogent reasons ought to shake it. But it is 'carrying coals to Newcastle' to add authorities on a proposition so universally accepted, and so inherently just and right in itself. The learned counsel for respondents do not controvert the general proposition. Their contention is, and the circuit court agreed with them, that, when Jungenfeld declined to go further on his contract, the defendant then had the right to sue for damages, and not having elected to sue Jungenfeld, but having acceded to his demand for the additional compensation defendant cannot now be heard to say his promise is without consideration. While it is true Jungenfeld became liable in damages for the obvious breach of his contract, we do not think it follows that defendant is estopped from showing its promise was made without consideration. It is true that as eminent a jurist as Judge Cooley, in Goebel v. Linn, 47 Mich. 489, 11 N.W. 284, 41 Am.Rep. 723, held that an ice company which had agreed to furnish a brewery with all the ice they might need for their business from November 8, 1879, until January 1, 1881, at $1.75 per ton, and afterwards in May, 1880, declined to deliver any more ice unless the brewery would give it $3 per ton, could recover on a promissory note given for the increased price. Profound as is our respect for the distinguished judge who delivered the opinion, we are still of the opinion that his decision is not in accord with the almost universally accepted doctrine, and is not convincing. * * * What we hold is that, when a party merely does what he has already obligated himself to do, he cannot demand an additional compensation therefor; and although, by taking advantage of the necessities of his adversary, he obtains a promise for more, the law will regard it as nudum pactum, and will not lend its process to aid in the wrong." * * *

It results from the views above expressed that the judgment must be reversed, and the cause remanded, with directions to the court below to enter judgment for the respondent, with costs. It is so ordered.

———

AUSTIN INSTRUMENT, INC. v. LORAL CORP., 29 N.Y.2d 124, 324 N.Y.S.2d 22, 272 N.E.2d 533 (1971). In July 1965 Loral was awarded a contract by the Navy for the production of radar sets. The contract contained a schedule of deliveries and a liquidated damages clause for late deliveries. Loral awarded Austin a subcontract for 23 precision gear components needed to produce the sets. In May 1966 Loral was awarded a second Navy contract; Austin bid on the subcontract for 40 components, but was told that its bid would be accepted only for those items on which it was the low bidder. Austin then informed Loral that it would cease delivery of all parts due under the first subcontract unless Loral agreed to substantial increases in the price, even for parts already delivered, and awarded Austin the order for all 40 parts needed under the second contract. Loral contacted several other manufacturers but found none that could produce the parts in time to meet its commitments to the Navy. It therefore consented to the price increases and awarded Austin the second subcontract for all 40 gear parts.

Loral later brought suit to recover the amount of the price increases it had paid, on the ground of "economic duress." The Court of Appeals held that "the evidence makes out a classic case, as a matter of law, of such duress." The "ordinary remedy of an action for breach of contract" would not have been adequate for Loral, since it did a substantial amount of its business with the Government and feared that a failure to deliver as agreed would jeopardize its chances for future contracts. "In other words, Loral actually had no choice, when the prices were raised by Austin, except to take the gears at the 'coerced' price and then sue to get the excess back."

RESTATEMENT, SECOND, CONTRACTS § 73:

Performance of a legal duty owed to a promisor which is neither doubtful nor the subject of honest dispute is not consideration; but a similar performance is consideration if it differs from what was required by the duty in a way which reflects more than a pretense of bargain.

Comment:

a. *Rationale.* A claim that the performance of a legal duty furnished consideration for a promise often raises a suspicion that the transaction was gratuitous or mistaken or unconscionable. * * * Mistake, misrepresentation, duress, undue influence, or public policy may invalidate the transaction even though there is consideration. But the rule of this Section renders unnecessary any inquiry into the existence of such an invalidating cause, and denies enforcement to some promises which would otherwise be valid. Because of the likelihood that the promise was obtained by an express or implied threat to withhold performance of a legal duty, the promise does not have the presumptive social utility normally found in a bargain. Enforcement must therefore rest on some substantive or formal basis other than the mere fact of bargain.

Illustration:

1. A offers a reward to whoever produces evidence leading to the arrest and conviction of the murderer of B. C produces such evidence in the performance of his duty as a police officer. C's performance is not consideration for A's promise.

GLAMORGAN COUNTY COUNCIL v. GLASBROOK BROTHERS, [1924] 1 K.B. 879 (C.A.), affirmed [1925] A.C. 270 (House of Lords). After the settlement of a national coal strike, some of the miners at defendant's mines refused to return to work. The "safety men" operating the pumps were willing to work, but the striking miners put pressure on them to stay away and there were threats of violence. The absence of the "safety men" for three or four days would have resulted in serious damage to the mines through flooding. Defendant asked the local police for a garrison on the premises. The police thought that adequate protection could be provided by a mobile force, but at defendant's insistence agreed to station a garrison of 70 officers at the mines if defendant would agree to pay for the force provided. The "safety men," who had been staying away out of fear, returned to work, and the police garrison remained at defendant's mines until the dispute with the miners was resolved. A suit was brought by the local government authority to enforce defendant's promise to pay for the police services. In the Court of Appeal a judgment for plaintiff was upheld; Bankes, L.J. put the case "of an extremely nervous person who was unable to sleep for fear of burglars and who therefore applied for a constable to be stationed on point duty in the street all night opposite his house," and whose request was granted on condition that a payment would be made for the special service. He said, "unless it is shown that the granting of the request deprives other people of a reasonable amount of police protection, I can see nothing objectionable * * * about the transaction."

The House of Lords, divided 3–2, affirmed. Lord Blanesburgh in dissent suggested that "unless demands of payment for police services are jealously safeguarded the power to make them may readily become oppressive to the individual and injurious to the general interest. * * * In many cases it would become * * * a mere sale of the police discretion, * * * calculated, on the one hand, to lead to the withdrawal or refusal of proper protection from or to an individual unable to pay for it and, on the other, to a too ready compliance with the requisition of an individual ready and willing to defray the total cost of the protection he receives * * *."

FOAKES v. BEER

House of Lords, 1884.
L.R. 9 A.C. 605.

[Mrs. Beer had obtained a judgment against Dr. Foakes for £2090.19s. Dr. Foakes requested time to pay the judgment, and the parties agreed in writing that if Dr. Foakes would pay £500 immediately and further sums in installments over about five years, "until the whole of the said sum of £2090.19s shall have been fully paid and satisfied," then Mrs. Beer would not enforce the judgment. As interpreted by most of the judges who passed on the case, this meant that Mrs. Beer was giving up her right to interest on the debt. Dr. Foakes did pay the £2090.19s as agreed, but Mrs. Beer later claimed the interest as well. The Court of Appeal gave judgment for Mrs. Beer for the interest, saying, "[t]he defendant was bound to pay the judgment debt immediately, and it was a debt bearing interest. * * *

[A]lthough the plaintiff agreed to give time, she might at any time have changed her mind, and was not bound by the agreement for there was no consideration for it." This judgment was affirmed by the House of Lords.]

LORD BLACKBURN:—

* * * This is a question, I think, of difficulty.

In Coke, Littleton 212b, Lord Coke says: "where the condition is for payment of £ 20, the obligor * * * cannot at the time appointed pay a lesser sum in satisfaction of the whole, because *it is apparent* that a lesser sum of money *cannot* be a satisfaction of a greater." * * * For this he cites *Pinnel's Case* [5 Co.Rep. 117a (1602)] [in which] it was resolved by the Court of Common Pleas that "payment of a lesser sum on the day in satisfaction of a greater cannot be any satisfaction for the whole, because it appears to the judges that by no possibility a lesser sum can be a satisfaction to the plaintiff for a greater sum: but the gift of a horse, hawk, or robe, &c., in satisfaction is good, for it shall be intended that a horse, hawk, or robe, &c., might be more beneficial to the plaintiff than the money, in respect of some circumstance, or otherwise the plaintiff would not have accepted of it in satisfaction."

* * *

[I]n Sibree v. Tripp [15 M. & W. 23, 33 (Ex.1846)], Parke, B. says, "It is clear if the claim be a liquidated and ascertained sum, payment of part cannot be satisfaction of the whole, although it may, under certain circumstances, be evidence of a gift of the remainder." And Alderson, B. in the same case says, "It is undoubtedly true that payment of a portion of a liquidated demand, in the same manner as the whole liquidated demand which ought to be paid, is payment only in part, because it is not one bargain, but two; viz. payment of part, and an agreement without consideration to give up the residue. The Courts might very well have held the contrary, and have left the matter to the agreement of the parties, but undoubtedly the law is so settled."

* * *

What principally weighs with me in thinking that Lord Coke made a mistake of fact is my conviction that all men of business, whether merchants or tradesmen, do every day recognise and act on the ground that prompt payment of a part of their demand may be more beneficial to them than it would be to insist on their rights and enforce payment of the whole. Even where the debtor is perfectly solvent, and sure to pay at last, this often is so. Where the credit of the debtor is doubtful it must be more so. I had persuaded myself that there was no such long-continued action on this dictum as to render it improper in this House to reconsider the question. I had written my reasons for so thinking; but as they were not satisfactory to the other noble and learned Lords who heard the case, I do not now repeat them nor persist in them.

I assent to the judgment proposed, though it is not that which I had originally thought proper.

[The Earl of Selborne L.C. and Lords Watson and Fitzgerald concurred, in opinions which are omitted.]

FRYE v. HUBBELL, 74 N.H. 358, 68 A. 325 (1907).

"[The rule in Foakes v. Beer] is almost universally regarded with disfavor, although followed, and the extension of the exceptions has been carried so far by the discovery of sufficient consideration in trivial and apparently immaterial circumstances that the rule itself might more logically be abandoned * * *. * * *

"[T]he number of cases in which the rule has been applied and judgment rendered for the plaintiff, despite the agreement to discharge, is small in comparison with those in which the courts have been able to discover some circumstance, however trifling, which could be construed a technical legal consideration. * * *

"In Jaffray v. Davis [124 N.Y. 164, 26 N.E. 351 (1891)], notes for one-half the debt, secured by a chattel mortgage, were given in discharge of the claim. The discharge was held good, although it appears to be conceded that the payment of one-half in money at the time the notes were given, upon the same agreement, would not constitute a valid discharge. Under the doctrine of this case a one-day note for one-half the debt, secured by the pledge of an equal amount in gold coin, would constitute a valid discharge, while the direct payment of the same amount in gold coin could not. * * *

"The damages the law awards for the nonpayment of money is interest, and for the expense of obtaining judgment and execution, costs. If costs always equal the expense of litigation, if interest is always full recompense for delayed payment, and if an execution is always equivalent to money in hand, then a present part payment of a debt in cash is in fact never beneficial to the creditor or detrimental to the debtor, and can never be a consideration for a discharge of the balance. Whatever the conclusions of scholastic logic, as men having some acquaintance with affairs, judges are bound to know that none of these propositions are always, if ever, true; and, as they are not always all true, it cannot be matter of law that in a particular case a part payment was not such a benefit to the creditor or detriment to the debtor as to furnish a consideration for the creditor's agreement of discharge."

SUGARHOUSE FINANCE CO. v. ANDERSON, 610 P.2d 1369 (Utah 1980). Plaintiff obtained a judgment against defendant in the amount of $2423.86 plus interest, costs, and attorney's fees. When plaintiff began legal action to enforce the judgment, defendant asserted that because of his numerous financial obligations he was contemplating bankruptcy, which would result in a discharge of plaintiff's judgment. The parties then settled on a figure of $2200 in full satisfaction. Defendant gave plaintiff a check for that amount, asking him not to cash it until he could arrange a loan at his bank to cover it. Plaintiff later returned the check and disavowed the settlement. The court, noting "the modern trend * * * to uphold such agreements wherever possible," held the settlement to be supported by consideration. Defendant's negotiation of a loan to enable him to pay off the substitute obligation "was something defendant had no legal obligation to do; by law, plaintiff could only move by levy of execution against property already owned by the defendant—plaintiff could not legally require defendant to incur additional obligations to satisfy the judgment. By so doing, defendant deliberately incurred the detriment of surrendering his right to limit plaintiff's ability to obtain satisfaction of the underlying judgment."

RESTATEMENT, SECOND, CONTRACTS § 73:

Illustration:

8. A owes B a matured liquidated debt bearing interest. Mutual promises to extend the debt for a year even at a lower rate of interest are binding. By such an agreement A gives up the right to terminate the running of interest by paying the debt.

CAL.CIV.CODE § 1524 (West 1982):

Part performance of an obligation, either before or after a breach thereof, when expressly accepted by the creditor in writing, in satisfaction, or rendered in pursuance of an agreement in writing for that purpose, though without any new consideration, extinguishes the obligation.

N.Y.GEN.OBLIG.LAW § 5–1103 (McKinney 1989):

An agreement, promise or undertaking to change or modify, or to discharge in whole or in part, any contract, obligation, or lease, or any mortgage or other security interest in personal or real property, shall not be invalid because of the absence of consideration, provided that the agreement, promise or undertaking changing, modifying, or discharging such contract, obligation, lease, mortgage or security interest, shall be in writing and signed by the party against whom it is sought to enforce the change, modification or discharge, or by his agent.

See UCC §§ 1–107, 3–604, 3–303 and Comment 1.

FULLER, CONSIDERATION AND FORM
41 Colum.L.Rev. 799, 821 (1941).

[I]f we look at the problem now under discussion from the standpoint of the cautionary function of form it will be apparent that there is a difference between releasing a claim and creating a claim by a promise. The release of a claim, even if made orally, carries with it normally a sense of deprivation which is lacking in the case of a promise. Where words have this effect, where they tend to produce a psychological wrench on the speaker, they satisfy the desideratum of inducing deliberation as well as a writing or a seal. On the side of "substance," it may be observed that releases are normally transactions ancillary to a relationship of exchange.

BLAKESLEE v. BOARD OF WATER COMMISSIONERS OF CITY OF HARTFORD

Supreme Court of Errors of Connecticut, 1927.
106 Conn. 642, 139 A. 106.

MALTBIE, J. This action comes before us upon a demurrer to the complaint. The first count of the complaint states the following facts: On August 23, 1915, the plaintiffs entered into a contract with the defendant for the construction of a large dam, the price therefor being fixed in the contract at certain named sums for the various items of work to be performed. The contract provided that the work was to be completed in 33 months, and, unless this was done, the plaintiffs were to pay the defendant as liquidated damages $100 for each day thereafter required. Both parties understood when the contract was made that the plaintiffs had to move a great amount of earth and rock, necessitating the use, in large quantities, of high explosives, of coal for the operation of steam shovels and other apparatus, of lumber, cement, iron, steel, and vitrified pipe, and of small tools and equipment; and that the plaintiffs had to employ a great number of skilled and unskilled laborers. The parties did not contemplate that this country was to become involved in the war then ranging in Europe.

The complaint then proceeds to allege, in considerable detail, these further facts: Early in 1916, rumors became prevalent that this country might become embroiled in the war. Thereafter steps taken in this country in preparation for its becoming a participant therein, and in the conduct of it after war was declared, resulted in the practical impossibility of the plaintiffs procuring the laborers necessary to carry on the work under the contract, in embargoes upon the transportation of materials and supplies, in the diversion of materials and supplies for the use of the government, and in interference with the progress of the work. As a result of these conditions, "the contract became impossible of performance according to its terms." Thereupon the plaintiffs and the defendant discussed the situation, and the plaintiffs notified the defendant that because of the conditions confronting them due to the war, "it would be impossible for the plaintiffs to continue performance of said work at the prices specified in said contract." The defendant then stated that it recognized the conditions, and that the dam under construction was for the purpose of forming a compensating reservoir from which to supply water it was under contract to furnish to various milling concerns then engaged in the production of war materials. It is then alleged that (paragraph 8):

"Said defendant then and there agreed to and with the plaintiffs that if the plaintiffs would proceed with the work called for under said contract, it, the defendant, would waive the penalty provided for in said contract on account of its noncompletion within the 33 months' period specified in said contract, and that it would extend the time necessary for the completion of said work. The defendant informed the plaintiffs that under legislation as it then existed defendant was powerless to change the compensation provided for in said contract, but defendant then and there promised and agreed to and with the plaintiffs, if legislation could be effected permitting defendant to change the compensation called for under said contract, defendant would do all in its power to so change the compensation called for under said contract as to prevent the plaintiffs from suffering any actual loss which might be occasioned through its performance. The plaintiffs, relying upon [these promises and assurances] of defendant * * * continued to perform the work and furnish the material and supplies called for under said contract, and prosecuted said work expeditiously until the entire work called for under said contract had been completed. * * * (Paragraph 9.) The said contract theretofore existing between the plaintiffs and defendant was rescinded by waiving of the penalties already incurred, * * * and a new contract entered into whereby the time limit was to be extended and the compensation to be paid the contractor was to be the actual cost of the work, labor, and materials to be furnished by the plaintiffs, if legislation could be effected permitting defendant to alter the compensation so as to permit it to pay the actual cost."

The complaint then goes on to allege that the plaintiffs caused a bill to be presented in the General Assembly authorizing municipal corporations, boards and departments thereof, to change the terms of contracts, the cost of performance of which had been increased by war interference, so as to make the compensation therefor sufficient to prevent the contractor from suffering any actual loss due to performance of his contract, and that thereafter this bill was duly passed and approved by the Governor. The complaint then continues with an allegation that the plaintiffs have fully completed the contract and have presented to the defendant a bill for $159,000, representing the actual cost of the work above the amount paid to them under the terms of the contract, and that the defendant has refused to pay it.

The defendant demurred to this count of the complaint upon [the following grounds:] * * * (2) it does not appear that there was any consideration for any alleged agreement to increase the compensation provided by the original contract, and that it does appear that the plaintiffs performed no services or furnished no material except those required under that contract; (3) it appears that when the contract was made war was already being waged in Europe and the possibility of this country becoming involved then existed, that the contract had no provision for such a contingency, and that it was not impossible of performance * * *.

The second and third grounds of demurrer may be considered together. They raise the question which has been much discussed by legal scholars, whether a promise to pay additional compensation for the continued performance of work which the promisee is already obligated to the promisor to do by the terms of an existing contract is supported by a sufficient consideration. * * * In Connelly v. Devoe, 37 Conn. 570 [1871], it was held that there was a good consideration for an agreement by the promisor to extend the time of performance fixed by the terms of the contract, though the contract was otherwise unchanged. That decision rested in part upon the theory that there was, by the agreement for the extension of time, an abandonment of the original contract and the substitution of a new one. While the decision was correct, as we shall show, in the light of subsequent criticisms, we cannot now hold that theory to be sound. See 1 Williston on Contracts, § 130a.* * * *

[T]he rule supported by the great weight of authority [is] that a promise to do that which one is already bound by his contract to do is not a sufficient consideration to support an additional promise by the other party to the contract.

The basis of the rule is generally made to rest upon the proposition that in such a situation he who promises the additional compensation receives nothing more than that to which he is already entitled, and he to whom the promise is made gives nothing that he was not already under legal obligation to give. Where the promisee has abandoned or is about to abandon his undertaking, there is often in such a situation a substantial benefit in fact conferred upon the promisor in securing the continued performance of the contract, and an actual detriment to the promisee in proceeding with an undertaking which he has resolved to be too onerous. This fact we noted in Connelly v. Devoe, 37 Conn. 570, 576, where we said:

"And further, it was for the interest of the defendant that the work should be completed. He had doubtless made a good contract. Should the work stop where it was he would lose the benefit of it. * * * The

* [In this section Professor Williston had argued as follows:

"It must be conceded that the original agreement if still in part at least unperformed on each side, may be rescinded by mutual consent; and, if the original agreement is rescinded, a new agreement made thereafter on any terms to which the parties assent will be binding. * * * But calling an agreement an agreement for rescission does not do away with the necessity of consideration, and when the agreement for rescission is coupled with a further agreement that the work provided for in the earlier agreement shall be completed and that the other party shall give more than he originally promised, the total effect of the second agreement is that one party promises to do exactly what he had previously bound himself to do, and the other party promises to give an additional compensation therefor. If for a single moment the parties were free from the earlier contract so that each of them could refuse to enter into any bargain whatever relating to the same subject-matter, a subsequent agreement on any terms would be good."—Eds.]

plaintiff could do it as quickly as anyone. By so doing the defendant would reap the fruits of the contract. Surely it was for his interest to make the agreement."

The basis of the rule holding such agreement for additional compensation to be invalid must be, not that there is no consideration in fact, but that, to use Street's expression, "the consideration is deemed by the law to be incompetent." It is no doubt inaccurate to say that the promisee has the right to elect to pay those damages for which the law would make him liable if he did not perform, rather than to proceed with the performance of the contract, for the promisor bargained for that performance, not for that one of these two alternatives which the promisee might choose. But it is true that, except in a small class of cases, the law would not enforce performance of the contract * * *. The right that the promisor of the additional compensation has to exact performance as the sole obligation of him to whom the promise is made, is not one behind which the law puts the sanction of its compelling force. * * *

If the contractor has no right to elect to pay damages, it is not because the law will attempt to hold him to performance, but because it is not right, that is, morally justifiable that, lacking legal excuse, he should fail to keep his contract. * * * But if the contractor cannot be allowed to say that the prior legal obligation was not his determining motive, by the same token of honesty and good faith, how can the promisor of the additional compensation, who by the offered inducement of that compensation has caused the contractor to do to his detriment that which he had resolved not to do, be heard to say that he will not keep his promise. Judged from the standpoint of ordinary business morality, the situation of the promisor may well be less defensible than that of the contractor. This aspect of the situation we noted in Connelly v. Devoe, supra:

> "And besides, the defendant suffered the plaintiff to go on with the work after the agreement was made, under the expectation of being allowed the extended time for the completion of the work."
>
> * * *

The rule which holds that a promise of additional compensation is without consideration, if the promisee does or promises to do only that which he is already under a contract obligation to do, cannot be satisfactorily rested upon the ground that the promisee has suffered no detriment and the promisor received no benefit, nor upon the ground that the promisee has no right to take any other course than to perform. * * * [T]he circumstances of the particular case, or at least of the class of cases under consideration, must be considered. It may well be that there is in fact no appreciable detriment to the promisee or benefit to the promisor in many cases where a promise is made to induce the performance of that which the promisee is already under a contract obligation to do * * *. So, too, considerations of public policy may enter into the situation. And it may well be that broadly to admit the power of a contractor to exact additional compensation by refusing to continue performance would afford too many opportunities for exactions approaching very near to extortion. Lingenfelder v. Wainwright Brewing Co., 103 Mo. 578, 593, 15 S.W. 844.

Here the way is open for a distinction which commends itself at once to good sense and good morals. Where the contractor can justify his refusal to proceed with the contract by showing that he is confronted with circumstances not contemplated when the contract was made which render its performance impossible or unduly onerous and the promisor, being informed of the situation, induces him by a promise of additional compensation to proceed with it, the contractor's right to that compensation ought justly to be recognized. * * * Of such a situation, involving a contract to deliver ice, Cooley, Jr., said, in Goebel v. Linn, 47 Mich. 489, 493, 11 N.W. 2184, 285 [1882]:

> "Unexpected and extraordinary circumstances have rendered the contract worthless; and they must either make a new arrangement, or, in insisting on holding the ice company to the existing contract, they would ruin the ice company and thereby at the same time ruin themselves. It would be very strange if under such a condition of things the existing contract, which unexpected events had rendered of no value, could stand in the way of a new arrangement, and constitute a bar to any new contract which should provide for a price which would enable both parties to save their interests."

Within this class of cases falls our own case of Connelly v. Devoe, supra. There the contract was that the plaintiff would dig a well to such a depth that there would be three feet of water in it after it was stoned, and of a diameter of three feet; the work to be done within a limited time. The plaintiff met with unexpected difficulties in the caving in of the sides, the sand near the bottom proving to be unusually bad for the purpose of well digging, and this necessitated shoring and special equipment. The plaintiff's inability to perform the contract within the time set was thus due to circumstances not within the contemplation of the parties when the contract was made, and the circumstances were such as to bring the case within the principle we have been discussing.

Of the test to be applied in such a situation the Supreme Court of Minnesota said in King v. Duluth Missabe & Northern Ry. Co. [61 Minn. 482, 63 N.W. 1105 (1895)]:

> "What unforeseen difficulties and burdens will make a party's refusal to go forward with his contract equitable, so as to take the case out of the general rule and bring it within the exception, must depend upon the facts of each particular case. They must be substantial, unforeseen, and not within the contemplation of the parties when the contract was made. They need not be such as would legally justify the party in his refusal to perform his contract, unless promised extra pay, or to justify a court of equity in

relieving him from the contract; for they are sufficient if they are of such a character as to render the party's demand for extra pay manifestly fair, so as to rebut all inference that he is seeking to be relieved from an unsatisfactory contract, or to take advantage of the necessities of the opposite party to coerce from him a promise for further compensation. Inadequacy of the contract price which is the result of an error of judgment, and not of some excusable mistake of fact, is not sufficient."

Under the allegations of the complaint, the plaintiffs may be able to prove such a situation as would bring them within the scope of this principle. There is, however, a narrower ground upon which the facts which they may be able to prove under that complaint may justify the court in holding the promise for additional compensation to be upon a sufficient consideration. It will be noticed that while in the eighth paragraph the promise of the defendant there recited is that it would do all in its power to change the compensation so as to prevent the plaintiffs from suffering actual loss through performance of the contract, in the ninth paragraph the allegation is that a new contract was entered into whereby the compensation to be paid the plaintiffs was to be the actual cost of the work, labor, and material to be furnished by them. Any difficulties due to the somewhat contradictory nature of these allegations are not before us upon this demurrer, and all we have to ask is: Under them could the plaintiffs prove such a situation as would entitle them to recover? If they succeed in proving a new contract such as they allege in the ninth paragraph of the complaint, we would have a situation where there could be no doubt of its validity, for, as there alleged, the plaintiffs clearly surrendered any rights they might have to recover the contract price and agreed to accept the actual cost of the work, labor, and materials to be furnished. Of course, they were abundantly satisfied that that cost would exceed the contract price, but if through some unforeseen circumstances the actual cost had fallen below the contract price, under this allegation of their complaint, they would have been bound to accept the lesser sum. There would, in such a situation, be a clear surrender of rights on the part of the plaintiffs which would amply meet the requirements of a good consideration. * * *

The demurrer to the first count should have been overruled.

* * *

There is error; the judgment is set aside, and the cause remanded to be proceeded with according to law.

The other Judges concurred.

———

LEVINE v. BLUMENTHAL, 117 N.J.L. 23, 186 A. 457 (1936), aff'd per curiam, 117 N.J.L. 426, 189 A. 54 (1937). In April 1931 plaintiff leased premises to defendants for use as a women's clothing store. The rent was to be $175 per month for the first year of the lease, and $200 per month for the second year. At the end of the first year, defendants informed plaintiff that "it was absolutely impossible for them to pay any increase in rent; that their business had so fallen down that they had great difficulty in meeting the present rent of $175 per month; that if the plaintiff insisted upon the increase called for in the lease, they would be forced to remove from the premises or perhaps go out of business altogether."

The parties then orally agreed to change the lease so that during the second year defendants continued to pay the same rent of $175 per month. At the end of the two-year term defendants surrendered the premises, without paying the last month's rent, and plaintiff sued to recover that amount plus the full rental originally stipulated in the lease. Held, for plaintiff: "The rule was laid down in very early times that even though a part of a matured liquidated debt or demand has been given and received in full satisfaction thereof, the creditor may yet recover the remainder. * * * General economic adversity, however disastrous it may be in its individual consequences, is never a warrant for judicial abrogation of this primary principle of the law of contracts."

NASH v. ATLANTIC WHITE TOWER SYSTEM, INC., 404 Pa. 83, 170 A.2d 341 (1961).

"A contract is not to be regarded as a Kamikaze plane in which the parties seal themselves for mutual destruction."

WILLIAMS v. ROFFEY BROS. & NICHOLLS (CONTRACTORS) LTD., [1990] 1 All E.R. 512 (C.A.1989). Defendants (general contractors) entered into a sub-contract with plaintiff for the carpentry work on 27 apartment units. After six months, plaintiff had been paid 80% of the contract price but had completed work on only nine of the units. At that time he was in "financial difficulty," both because the contract price "was too low to enable [him] to operate satisfactorily and at a profit," and because he had failed to supervise his workmen adequately. Defendants were concerned that plaintiff might not finish the carpentry work on time; the carpentry work to be done by plaintiff was on "the critical path of the defendants' global operations," and the defendants wished "to retain the services of the plaintiff so that the work could be completed without the need to employ another sub-contractor." They therefore agreed to pay him an additional amount of £575 for each completed unit. Plaintiff "substantially completed" eight more units but defendant failed to make the promised payments, and plaintiff stopped work and brought suit for breach of contract. The trial judge found that the defendants' promise to pay additional compensation was "in the interests of both parties" and awarded plaintiff, in addition to amounts outstanding from the original sub-contract, £4600 less a small deduction for defective and incomplete items. Held, affirmed. Russell, L.J. wrote that it would be "unconscionable" if the defendants could escape liability "on the ground that the plaintiff undertook to do no more than he had originally contracted to do although, quite clearly, the defendants * * * were prepared to make the payment and only declined to do so at a later stage." "There is no hint * * * that the defendants were subjected to any duress to make the agreement * * *."

"In the * * * twentieth century I do not believe that the rigid approach to the concept of consideration to be found in Stilk v. Myrick is either necessary or desirable. * * * A gratuitous promise, pure and simple, remains unenforceable unless given under seal. But where, as in this case, a party undertakes to make a payment because by so doing it will gain an advantage arising out of the continuing relationship with the promisee the new bargain will not fail for want of consideration."

———

JE MAINTIENDRAI PTY. LTD. v. QUAGLIA & QUAGLIA, 26 S.A.S.R. 101 (Sup.Ct. South Australia, 1980). A tenant had operated a hairdresser's shop in a shopping center since the center opened in 1973. Under the lease, the rental was to increase with increases in the consumer price index. In 1976 the tenant found the rent "a little bit too much" and the lessor agreed to a reduction in rent for an indefinite period; at that time "there was no great demand for the shops in the shopping center" and a number of shops were empty. The lessor accepted the reduced rent for a period of eighteen months, during which the difference between the rent paid and the rent originally fixed by the lease increased considerably. After eighteen months the lessor demanded the accumulated arrears in rent under the original lease, and the tenant refused to pay. The trial judge found that the lessor was estopped from claiming the arrears: "That it is often easier for people to make small periodical payments than to find a lump sum is obvious * * * In the present case, instead of having to find a comparatively small sum of money every month, which the defendants were, though not without difficulty, able to do, they were in fact, after almost eighteen months of being lulled to sleep, suddenly faced with a demand to pay a large sum of accumulated 'arrears' * * *." Held, affirmed; King, C.J., wrote that:

"The evidence as to detriment is sparse. The [tenant's] case would be stronger if there were evidence of financial hardship or embarrassment as a result of the debt accumulating or that the money had been spent in other ways and that the [tenants] were unable to pay, at any rate without difficulty or inconvenience. It would be stronger if there were evidence that they had conducted their affairs differently as a result of the reduction, for example that they had refrained from exploring the possibility of selling the business and assigning the lease."

Nevertheless, the trial judge's conclusion would not be disturbed since he "was in a better position than is this Court to judge whether the accumulation of arrears of this magnitude would be a detriment to the [tenants]."

RESTATEMENT, SECOND, CONTRACTS § 89:

A promise modifying a duty under a contract not fully performed on either side is binding

(a) if the modification is fair and equitable in view of circumstances not anticipated by the parties when the contract was made; or

(b) to the extent provided by statute; or

(c) to the extent that justice requires enforcement in view of material change of position in reliance on the promise.

Comment:

a. *Rationale.* This Section relates primarily to adjustments in on-going transactions. Like offers and guaranties, such adjustments are ancillary to exchanges and have some of the same presumptive utility. Indeed, paragraph (a) deals with bargains which are without consideration only because of the rule that performance of a legal duty to the promisor is not consideration. See § 73 [supra page 285]. * * * [R]elation to a bargain tends to satisfy the cautionary and chanelling functions of legal formalities. * * *

RESTATEMENT, SECOND, CONTRACTS § 275:

If a party, before he has fully performed his duty under a contract, manifests to the other party his assent to discharge the other party's duty to render part or all of the agreed exchange, the duty is to that extent discharged without consideration.

Comment:

a. *Rationale.* A gift of tangible property may be made by delivery of possession. If, therefore, one party is under a duty to transfer such property to another who is under a duty to pay for it, the former can manifest his assent when he transfers it to do so as a gift, thereby discharging the other party's duty to pay for it. The rule stated in this Section extends this principle to performances other than the transfer of tangible property such as, for example, the furnishing of services. * * * The assent must be manifested before the completion of performance, by analogy to the rule as to a donor of tangible property, who must manifest his assent at the time of transfer. It may be manifested before performance, as long as it continues to the time of performance, but assent manifested after performance is completed does not come within the rule. * * *

Illustration:

2. A and B make a contract under which A promises to build a fence and B promises to pay A $1,000. As A begins to build the fence, he says to B, "The price we agreed on was too high, and you need pay only $900 for the fence." A then builds the fence. B's duty to pay A to the extent of $100 is discharged and B owes A only $900. See also § 89.

RESTATEMENT, SECOND, CONTRACTS § 273:

Illustration:

1. A, whom B owes $1,000 for goods delivered, gives B a signed writing that states, "I hereby irrevocably give, transfer, assign and release my right to the $1,000 that you owe me." B's debt is not discharged.

———

Cf. pp. 164–166 supra. Would the result in Illustration 1 to § 273 be affected by UCC § 2–209(1)?

UNITED STATES For the Use and Benefit of CRANE COMPANY v. PROGRESSIVE ENTERPRISES, INC.

United States District Court, Eastern District Virginia, 1976.
418 F.Supp. 662.

CLARKE, DISTRICT JUDGE.

This action was brought to recover the unpaid balance allegedly due for the purchase of a cast iron deaerator supplied by the plaintiff, Crane Company [hereinafter referred to as "Crane"], to the defendant, Progressive Enterprises, Inc. [hereinafter referred to as "Progressive"] to be installed as part of the defendant's contract with the United States. * * *

The material facts of the case are not in serious dispute. Plaintiff, on May 3, 1974, submitted a written proposal to furnish the machine to defendant for $5238.00, the price quoted as firm for acceptance within fifteen days. After the expiration of the fifteen-day period, Progressive submitted its bid dated June 7, 1974, for the government contract without arranging for an extension of the fifteen-day period. Progressive was awarded the government contract on June 14, 1974. Shortly thereafter, on June 17, 1974, Progressive verified the continued effectiveness of the quoted price for a thirty-day period. On July 1, 1974, Progressive accepted the offer to sell by submission of a purchase order. * * *

Crane, through its authorized selling agent, Hawkins-Hamilton Co., advised Progressive that "[b]ecause of rapidly escalating material costs, your purchase order can only be accepted subject to current price in effect at time of shipment." This communication went on to quote a current price of $7350.00.

The parties agree that the July 1, 1974 purchase order was an effective acceptance of Crane's offer to sell. However, apparently without protest to or discussion with Crane or its agent, Progressive agreed to the higher price and, on August 7, 1974, submitted a second purchase order for the machine, this time at $7350.00. Thereafter, the machine was delivered and Progressive paid $5,550.88 and asserted the balance not to be due because the increased price was not a valid modification of the contract. Crane then instituted this suit to recover $2,218.32 plus interest from March 2, 1975, representing the difference between the higher agreed price with interest and the amount paid by the defendant.

Crane contends that Progressive acquiesced in the increased price and that the August 7, 1974, purchase order effectively modified the existing contract.

[The court quoted from UCC § 2–209, and Comment 2.] This change from the common law of contracts supports the common business practice of adjusting the terms of agreements as conditions change.

* * *

The letters of May 3 and July 11, 1974, from Crane's agent support a finding that the seller's costs had increased, justifying a request for modification of the price to Progressive. Although Progressive possessed the contractual right to refuse to modify and to demand performance on the original terms, it failed to do so and gave objective assent to the higher price.

Notwithstanding this objective assent and apparent modification, it is the contention of Progressive that the modification of the contract price was the result of economic duress and, hence, unenforceable. This claim is based upon its obligation under its contract with the United States Government to supply the ordered machine within a specific time and the fact that Crane was the only supplier of the exact machine required to fulfill the Government contract.

The evidence reveals, however, that in making its bid to the Government, Progressive was not relying on the lower price quoted because the time period for acceptance had expired. Thus, Progressive is not in the position of a contractor who justifiably relied on a price quotation only to find itself squeezed by repudiation of the quoted price.

The evidence shows further that Progressive at no time protested the increased price, or in any way attempted to enforce the terms of the earlier, lower price contract.

* * * [I]n Rose v. Vulcan Materials Co., 282 N.C. 643, 194 S.E.2d 521 (1973), cited by Progressive, the buyer expressly reserved the right to sue for the overcharges. Such situations, where the inability to obtain alternative sources of supply is communicated, are more analogous to the seeking of cover from the only available source, the original seller. Where no such protest or notice is given, the seller has no idea that anything other than a new contract has been made. If the buyer wishes not to accede to the increased demand, the seller must be dealt with honestly to be able to consider other possibilities.

In the context of a lengthy, on-going business relationship, seeking modification of a sales price is not uncommon and, given increased costs, is a fair method of doing business in order to preserve the desirability of the relationship for both parties. In such a situation, the parties must be able to rely on objective, unequivocal manifestations of assent. The secret intention of Progressive never to pay the higher price (as admitted by its president) is hardly in keeping with the good faith requirement of the UCC of honesty in fact. If a seller in this situation cannot enforce such a modification, sought in good faith and objectively agreed to, the provisions of UCC § 2–209(1) would be hollow indeed. To avoid this predicament, the buyer must at least display some protest against the higher price in order to put the seller on notice that the modification is not freely entered into.

The availability of equitable relief belies Progressive's claim that it had no available remedies if it desired to enforce the original terms. Also, notification to Crane of the possible damages because of the threatened breach could have led to withdrawal of the requested increase. In any case, Progressive did nothing to alert Crane to the possibility that it did not mean what it said. Accordingly, it must be held to its agreement.

STATE DEPARTMENT OF FISHERIES v. J–Z SALES CORP.

Washington Court of Appeals, 1980.
25 Wash.App. 671, 610 P.2d 390.

PEARSON, JUDGE.

Washington's Department of Fisheries appeals from a summary judgment in favor of J–Z Sales, Inc., granted by the Thurston County Superior Court in a breach of contract action brought by the Department against J–Z Sales.

At issue is whether a check tendered by J–Z Sales "as payment in full" for surplus fish and fish eggs was accepted by the Department in such a manner as to establish an accord and satisfaction of the amount due the state for the fish products under the parties' contract. The pivotal issue is whether the amount of the contractual obligation was unliquidated or in dispute at the time payment was tendered. We affirm the judgment for the reasons set forth below.

The parties entered into a contract in 1974 whereby J–Z Sales agreed to buy surplus salmon carcasses and eggs from the Department. The Department had advertised for bids on the products and had estimated that the products available in the districts where J–Z Sales was the successful bidder would amount to 1,355,000 pounds of both edible and inedible fish and 39,000 pounds of eggs. The invitation to bid cautioned that

[t]he estimated pounds of fish in each district and category have been inserted in the bid form for the purpose of bidding on a per pound basis and are not to be regarded as being the actual pounds of fish to be taken under the contract.

The bid specifications went on to state that the "[s]uccessful bidder (or bidders) must take all fish or eggs offered in any category or district."

A problem arose, however. By letter of November 27, 1974, Mr. Kjell Dahl of J–Z Sales informed the Department that the amount of fish and eggs it was receiving under the contract had far exceeded the estimates provided on the bid sheet and that the market was flooded with cheaper fish caught by Indians. J–Z Sales suggested that the Department consider reducing the contract price to $.50/lb. for salmon eggs and $.10/lb. for fish, in contrast to the contractual prices of $1.75/lb. and $.21/lb., respectively. Thor Tollefson, then Director of the Department of Fisheries, replied by letter of December 5, 1974. He acknowledged the poor market conditions and the fact that J–Z Sales would receive at least twice the quantity of fish estimated for bid purposes. The letter then stated:

> Your request for reduction in prices from $.21/pound to $.10/pound, and from $1.75/pound to $.50/pound for salmon eggs will have to await my review of the statutes, the contract, and legal precedents with the State Auditor's Office and the Attorney General's Office. We assume you are referring to a price reduction for some reasonable portion of the surplus above the "Invitation to Bid Estimated Weight."

After all surplus fish and eggs had been accepted, J–Z Sales had received 843,630 pounds of fish above the bid sheet estimate and 94,480½ pounds of eggs above the estimate. Pursuant to the contract prices, J–Z Sales then owed $418,493.10 to the Department, excluding any interest or penalties.

By letter dated June 10, 1975, Craig Hayes of Bellingham, attorney for J–Z Sales, transmitted to the Department a check for $205,036.06 as "payment in full" of its contractual obligation. The letter explained that the unexpected surplus of fish and eggs had combined with the poor market to cause economic hardship to the buyer. J–Z Sales, the letter claimed, had agreed to continue to buy the excess "upon being told by Fisheries Department representatives that adjustments would be made to the original purchase contract." The letter quoted [UCC § 2–306(1)] and contended that J–Z Sales was not, under that statute, obligated to accept the excess products. The amount of the check was calculated as representing payment for the poundage in excess of the Department's bid estimates, multiplied by J–Z Sales' earlier suggested revised prices of $.10/pound for salmon and $.50/pound for eggs.

[The Department unsuccessfully attempted to return this check; in August, it brought suit for breach of contract and endorsed the check to the order of the clerk of the Superior Court "[i]n order to assist the Court in a determination of all claims of the parties [and] to prevent the loss and destruction of said check in further transmittals between Olympia and Bellingham, Washington * * *.″]

Defendants' motion for summary judgment was based upon the contention that an accord and satisfaction of the debt had been established by the conduct of the parties. The trial court granted the motion and the Department's appeal followed. The familiar rule is that the trial court can grant a motion for summary judgment when, construing the evidence in the record in favor of the nonmoving party, no genuine issue of fact exists and the moving party is entitled to judgment as a matter of law.

An accord is a contract between debtor and creditor to settle a claim by some performance other than that which is due. Satisfaction occurs when the accord is performed. * * * The parties agree, moreover, that in the factual context of this case the following statement of law applies:

> Where the amount of a debt or obligation is unliquidated or in dispute, then the tender by the debtor of a certain sum in full payment of the debt, followed by acceptance and retention of the amount tendered, establishes an accord and satisfaction.

For purposes of accord and satisfaction, the underlying dispute over the debt must be in good faith, i.e., the parties must have a bona fide belief in the validity of their positions with respect to the claim.

The Department's first challenge is to the trial court's reliance on [UCC § 2–306(1)] * * *. The trial court ruled that the quantity of fish and eggs acquired by J–Z Sales was, as a matter of law, "unreasonably disproportionate" under that statute, and that, even though J–Z Sales continued to accept the products, a "dispute" arose as to the fair price for the excess products.

The Department argues that the court had an obligation to assess the commercial background and intent of the parties and the industry practice as a whole before it could declare that the actual output of fish in this case was unreasonable to J–Z Sales, and that the record was completely devoid of any evidence on this point. Furthermore, the Department argues that as J–Z Sales did not rely on [§ 2–306(1)] to reject the tender of excess fish products, but took them anyway, it has effectively waived the argument that the excess products were unreasonably disproportionate.

We think that there was a dispute for purposes of accord and satisfaction, for the following reasons. We agree with the trial court that the Department's pre-bid estimate of the fish products to be supplied under the contract is the source of the dispute. The estimates of quantities were designed to allow "bidding on a per pound basis and are not to be regarded as being the actual pounds of fish to be taken under the contract." So, admittedly, J–Z Sales was alerted to the possibility of an output in excess of the estimates. Equally obvious is the fact that J–Z Sales relied on the estimates for purposes of bidding.

It is true J–Z Sales did not reject the excess fish products, as [§ 2–306(1)] might have allowed it to do. That does not, however, preclude a finding that the surplus of goods created a genuine dispute which could be resolved by an accord and satisfaction. * * *

A debt can be both disputed and liquidated, so the terms "unliquidated" and "in dispute" are not synonymous. In this case, however, we believe the debt was both in dispute and unliquidated.

The dispute was created by the great extent by which the Department's pre-bid estimates fell below the actual output of fish J–Z Sales was required to take. * * * It has been held as a matter of law that a demand for goods in excess of 20 percent over the offeree's estimate is "unreasonably disproportionate" and a breach of contract, and so is a demand of more than double the estimate. Similarly, we are convinced in this case that the output of more than three times the estimated amount of salmon eggs, and of nearly two-thirds more than the estimate for salmon carcasses, in the falling market conditions then prevalent, created for J–Z Sales a genuine concern about the price it was being asked to pay and a genuine dispute over whether it should have to pay the bid prices premised on the much smaller estimates. To be sure, J–Z Sales could not have decided unilaterally to modify the contract to allow payment of lower prices for the excess output. But it could and did genuinely dispute whether it should have to pay the contract price and it did tender the lesser sum in hopes of settling the obligation.

Moreover, we believe the debt was unliquidated. In First Nat'l Bank v. White-Dulaney Co., 123 Wash. 220, 212 P. 262 (1923), the court discussed the effect of an offset claimed by the debtor against the contract amount. In that case, the amount claimed by the creditor was definite and fixed, but the debtor claimed an offset, which rendered the debt unliquidated for purposes of accord and satisfaction. The Supreme Court employed the following language, at p. 224, 212 P. at p. 264:

> By the weight of authority, where the debtor has an offset or claim for damages against the creditor which the latter does not concede, his claim against the debtor, although not disputed, except in respect of the offset or damages claimed, will nevertheless be considered unliquidated, the view being taken that there is no material difference between a dispute directly involving the claim itself and a dispute involving an offset against the claim; that whatever may be the ground of the dispute the fact remains that there is one. [Quoting 1 C.J. 556 (1914).]

* * * The analogy to the facts of this case is strong. Here, the amount claimed by the Department is definite and fixed, but the debtor, J–Z Sales, contends it is entitled to a price reduction due to the excessive quantities of fish and eggs tendered and the poor market conditions. There is a genuine dispute as to which of the two sums (the

contractual sum or the amount tendered) is due, and the demand is unliquidated according to the above discussion.

The next question is whether the Department ever accepted the check tendered in full payment of the debt, so that it will be deemed to have entered into an accord and satisfaction. We hold that the Department's endorsement and deposit of the check with the county clerk was acceptance of it, despite the Department's earlier attempt to return it. True, the Department did not get the benefit or use of the funds; but the real test in such a case is whether the creditor has removed the funds from the control of the debtor. The check was endorsed to the clerk, cashed, and the proceeds were held beyond the reach of J–Z Sales absent a court order. As far as J–Z Sales was concerned, the situation was no different than if the Department had deposited the funds in its own bank account. The Department was trying to lodge the funds with a neutral third party, but it did so without advance notice to J–Z Sales, which might have preferred to take the check back had it known the funds were about to be deposited with a third party. In the circumstances, we subscribe to Professor Corbin's view:

> There is no accord, either executory or executed, unless there is an offer either by the debtor to give or by the creditor to receive a substituted performance in full settlement, and an acceptance by the other party of the offer so made. Usually the offer is made by the debtor, and the problem of acceptance involves the action of the creditor. *Where the amount due is in dispute, and the debtor sends cash or check for less than the amount claimed, clearly expressing his intention that it is sent as a settlement in full, and not on account or in part payment, the retention and use of the money or the cashing of the check is almost always held to be an acceptance of the offer operating as full satisfaction, even though the creditor may assert or send word to the debtor that the sum is received only in part payment.* The fact that the creditor scratches out the words "in full payment," or other similar words indicating that the payment is tendered in full satisfaction, does not prevent his retention of the money from operating as an assent to the discharge. The creditor's action in such case is quite inconsistent with his words. * * *

(Italics ours. Footnotes omitted.) 6 A. Corbin, Corbin on Contracts § 1279, at 126, 130 (1962).

Finally, the Department has raised for the first time on appeal the applicability of [UCC § 1–207].

The Department argues that its actions in this case are tantamount to a reservation of rights while negotiating the check, and negate the creation of an accord and satisfaction. This argument would allow the Department to accept a check as partial payment only, even when it is tendered on the express condition that it constitutes full payment. Thus applied, the statute would contravene the common law of accord and satisfaction.

Elsewhere in the Uniform Commercial Code, [§ 1–103] and Official Comment 1 thereto require that the principles of law and equity are not to be displaced by particular provisions of the Code unless done so explicitly by the Code. ✴ ✴ ✴ [§ 1–207] is completely inconsonant with accord and satisfaction, which contemplates that one party's assent to performance by the second party in a manner other than that spelled out in the contract will create a new contract, rather than permitting the first to accept part performance and still invoke remedies to enforce the original contract. The statute does not explicitly supersede the law pertaining to accord and satisfaction, and it should not be inferred as doing so.

We agree with the trial court that the parties had a genuine dispute over the amount to be paid in this case, that the debt was unliquidated, and that the Department of Fisheries by its conduct should be deemed to have assented to an accord and satisfaction of the debt, despite its subsequent protests to the contrary. The summary judgment is affirmed.

REED, C. J., and PETRIE, J., concur.

———

TANNER v. MERRILL, 108 Mich. 58, 65 N.W. 664 (1895). Plaintiff worked for the defendants, who were lumbermen, at Georgian Bay. His transportation expenses there from Saginaw had been advanced by defendants. When plaintiff quit, defendants' superintendent proposed to deduct the transportation from the wages due, saying "he did not pay any man's fare." Plaintiff, who claimed that he needed the money due him to go home because of his mother's illness, asserted that defendants should pay for the transportation; he nevertheless signed a "receipt in full" for his wages, less a deduction for railroad fares. Plaintiff later brought suit for the amounts which had been deducted, claiming that there was no consideration for this receipt. Held, for defendants. Plaintiff's contention "would seriously derange business affairs if it should be sustained." If plaintiff's claim were an unliquidated claim, the "authorities are in substantial accord that part payment of the claim may discharge the debt, if it is so received. Upon the undisputed facts, the claim of the plaintiff, *as made,* was not liquidated. It was not even admitted, but, on the contrary, was denied, because the defendants claimed that it had been partially paid by a valid offset. While the controversy was over the offset, it is plain that the amount due the plaintiff was in dispute. If so, it is difficult to understand how it could be treated as a liquidated claim, unless it is to be said that a claim may be liquidated piecemeal, and that, so far as the items are agreed upon, it is liquidated, and to that extent is not subject to adjustment on a basis of part payment." ✴ ✴ ✴

"[I]n calling a claim unliquidated, the courts have alluded to the whole claim, and have considered that, where the amount is not agreed upon, the claim as a whole is unliquidated, and therefore subject to adjustment. If this is not true, no man can pay an amount that he admits to be due without being subject to action whenever and so often as his creditor may choose to claim that he was not fully paid, no matter how solemn may have been his acknowledgment of satisfaction * * *."

Two judges dissented on the ground that "payment of an admitted indebtedness is no consideration for a discharge of a further claim by the creditor."

RESTATEMENT, SECOND, CONTRACTS § 74:

Illustrations:

6. A contracts to sell and deliver a lot of goods to B. On delivery B accepts a commercial unit priced at $30 and rejects the rest, priced at $50. See Uniform Commercial Code § 2–601. B claims in good faith but erroneously that the rejected goods are defective. A promises to surrender any claim based on the rejection if B pays the $30. B's payment is consideration for A's promise.

7. A stops payment on a check for $200 drawn on his account in the B bank, but the bank pays the check and charges his account, leaving a balance of $800. There is an honest dispute as to the propriety of the charge, and the bank refuses to pay any part of the $800 until the dispute is settled. To obtain the money, A promises to make no further claim. Payment of the $800 by the bank is not consideration for the promise.

_____

See UCC § 3–311.

_____

The "Full Payment" Check

Washington Fisheries illustrates the common dilemma faced by a claimant who is presented with a check stated to be "in full satisfaction" of his claim—although in an amount far less than he believes to be due. The 1990 addition of § 1–207(2) to the official text of the Code now makes it clear (as the court held) that the Code provides no way out from what has been called "this exquisite form of commercial torture." (White & Summers, Uniform Commercial Code 544 (2d ed. 1980)). The claimant may of course refuse or return the check. But if he cashes it, even after striking out any notation that the check is "payment in full" or after endorsing it "under protest," he has given up the balance of his claim. See Rosenthal, Discord and Dissatisfaction: Section 1–207 of the Uniform Commercial Code, 78 Colum.L.Rev. 48, 57–58 (1978) (the "full payment" check "offers an easy, inexpensive and convenient method for effecting settlements in a wide range of types of disagreement between businessmen").

Professors White and Summers are "inclined to [the] view" that the typical drawer of a full-payment check is likely to be a "chiseler" who "knows that he owes $10,000 and hopes to get away with $9,000." White & Summers, Uniform Commercial Code 610 (3d ed. 1988). Under UCC § 3–311, could such a "chiseler" be successful? Whether a debtor happens to be a "chiseler" or not, creditors often attempt to minimize the risks of an "accord and satisfaction" by contractual provisions in form documents. It is customary, for example, for banks to add language like the following to their agreements with credit card customers: "We can accept payments that are marked with restrictive endorsements such as 'payment in full' without losing any of our rights under this agreement." (FCC National Bank, "FirstCard Cardmember Agreement and Disclosure Statement"). Might this agreement itself be trumped by a subsequent "offer" of settlement accompanying a full-payment check? See also UCC § 3–311 Comment 5.

The "Executory Accord"

Reilly v. Barrett, 220 N.Y. 170, 115 N.E. 453 (1917), was a tort action brought to recover damages for personal injuries. Defendant answered that after the suit had been filed the parties had entered into a compromise by which defendant agreed to pay, and plaintiff to accept, $200 in full settlement of the claim. Defendant alleged that he had tendered the $200 but that plaintiff refused it in order to press the original action. The Court of Appeals held that this answer was insufficient to state a defense. There may indeed have been an "accord" which, when followed by "satisfaction"—actual payment of the money by defendant and acceptance of it by plaintiff—would have discharged plaintiff's claim. But until satisfaction, said the court, the agreement "has no effect." The plaintiff was free to disregard any settlement agreement until full performance had taken place.

An agreement such as that in *Reilly*, not followed by "satisfaction," is called an "executory accord." The explanation for the frequent assumption that such accords are ineffective until performed is somewhat obscure. It has been suggested that many cases purporting to so hold can be explained on the ground of a lack of consideration, since the agreement in question was to receive a lesser amount in satisfaction of a pre-existing liquidated debt. 6 Corbin, Contracts, § 1271. In other cases cited for the "rule," the parties may never actually have entered into a settlement agreement in the first place: Perhaps the creditor had merely made an offer, not intended to be binding on him until actually performed by the debtor. ("Your promise is of no concern to me at all, but if you do pay me $200 by Monday your debt will be discharged.") In such a case, on ordinary principles of contract formation either side would be free to change his mind before performance is tendered by the debtor—or even perhaps until it is actually accepted by the creditor. Cf. Petterson v. Pattberg, infra page 489. However,

Reilly v. Barrett itself cannot readily be explained away in either of these convenient ways.

The court in Reilly v. Barrett noted one traditional qualification to the general proposition that unperformed settlement agreements are unenforceable. The "accord" *itself*, rather than the performance of the accord, may have been *intended* as a "satisfaction"; the parties may have intended immediately to replace the debtor's obligation with "a new and superior contract superseding and extinguishing" the original claim. See Moers v. Moers, 229 N.Y. 294, 300, 128 N.E. 202, 203 (1920). If they so intend, the debtor will be discharged even before his promised performance has been rendered. The Restatement, Second, § 279 refers to this as a case of a "substituted contract." (Courts sometimes use the term "novation," although the Restatement in § 280 restricts the use of this word to substituted contracts that bring in a *new party*. See p. 866 infra.)

One critical problem, then, has been to decipher the "intention" of the parties. It is safe to say that debtor and creditor will rarely have arranged their dealings so as to make them fit neatly into one of these legal categories: They are unlikely to have distinguished clearly between a settlement agreement intended to discharge the debtor immediately, and one intended to discharge him only when performed. A court that has been called upon to characterize an agreement as one or the other may thus be forced to rely on certain presumptions. For example, a comment to § 279(c) of the Restatement predicts that a court will be "less likely to find a substituted contract and more likely to find an accord if the original duty was one to pay money, if it was undisputed, if it was liquidated and if it was matured." See also Rhea v. Marko Construction Co., 652 S.W.2d 332 (Tenn.1983) ("it is difficult for us to conceive that [plaintiff] would have accepted a promise of $10,000 in the indefinite future in exchange for an existing obligation found to exceed $17,000").

The decision is also likely to be responsive to factual elements affecting a court's judgment as to the relative equities of the parties. One can easily imagine a finding of a "substituted contract" if the debtor has changed his position in reliance on the settlement agreement, and if the creditor is himself in breach of the new agreement by refusing to accept the substitute performance. This is exemplified by Christie v. Craige, 20 Pa. 430 (1853), in which the court upheld a defense to the plaintiff's suit on a promissory note, saying: "The parties agreed that no money should be paid, but that yarn should be furnished instead of money. They had the right to do this; and, having done it, the bargain was for yarn, as much as if money had never been thought of. If a creditor consents to accept merchandise in satisfaction of his claim, and the debtor invests the money with which he would otherwise have paid it in the goods contracted for, and has those goods ready at the time and place agreed upon, it would be wrong to say that money might be claimed afterwards."

But where it suspects that the new agreement was made without full deliberation or under some bargaining pressure, by a creditor to whom it turns out to be disadvantageous, a court may more readily find that only the debtor's performance would discharge the original obligation. (See, e.g., Goldbard v. Empire State Mutual Life Insurance Co., 5 A.D.2d 230, 171 N.Y.S.2d 194 (1958)).

The Restatement, in line with many modern cases, gives some legal effect even to the purely executory accord. Section 281 provides that an accord "suspends" the creditor's right to enforce his original claim in order to give the debtor the chance to perform. Should the creditor breach by preventing the debtor's performance, the debtor may have a claim for damages or even obtain specific performance of the accord. (This would call for a different result on the facts of Reilly v. Barrett). However, if it is the *debtor* who has defaulted on the accord by failing to render the substitute performance, the accord does not restrict the creditor's rights: unlike the case of a "substituted contract," the debtor's original duty has not been discharged, and the creditor may at his option enforce his original claim. Restatement, Second, Contracts § 281(2); cf. § 279(2).

WHEELER v. WHEELER, 299 N.C. 633, 263 S.E.2d 763 (1980). In 1956 Husband and Wife entered into a separation agreement. Under this agreement Wife was to get custody of the couple's children and specified alimony and child support; in return she agreed to make no further financial claims, to allow Husband visitation rights, and to allow him to declare the children as deductions for income tax purposes. Husband's duty to pay alimony was to continue only "so long as [Wife] observes and performs the conditions of this contract." Husband met with resistance when he tried to assert his visitation rights and in 1964 he gave up trying to enforce them; however, he continued to pay child support until each child reached age 21. He also continued alimony payments, but stopped in 1975 on the ground that Wife had herself violated the agreement by denying him visitation. Wife brought an action seeking back alimony payments. The trial court instructed the jury that they were to find for Wife despite her breach of the agreement if Husband had waived his visitation rights by "intentionally surrendering" them. After a jury verdict in her favor, judgment was entered for Wife for back alimony. The Court of Appeals held the jury charge was erroneous and reversed, reasoning that "an agreement to alter the terms of a contract is treated as another contract" and must be supported either by additional consideration or detrimental reliance. Held, reversed and judgment for Wife reinstated; the jury charge was sufficient on the issue of waiver:

"While we agree that an agreement to alter the terms of a contract must be supported by new consideration, we note that continued performance or continued acceptance of performance by an innocent party after partial breach of a contract involves another legal principle entirely.   Such behavior constitutes a valid waiver of a contractual provision and does not need to be supported by additional consideration or estoppel to effect a binding agreement.

"* * * [T]his court [has] held that where a landlord received rent after full knowledge of tenant's breach of a lease condition, the landlord's behavior constituted a waiver of its contractual right to terminate the lease.   The reasoning of the Court was that where a party accepted continuing benefits under the contract, with full knowledge of a prior breach, he waived his right to declare the contract terminated for the prior breach.   * * * [A] party may waive the breach of a contractual provision or condition without consideration or estoppel if [he] is the innocent, or non-breaching party, and the breach does not involve total repudiation of the contract so that the nonbreaching party continues to receive some of the bargained-for consideration.   Generally this means either that the contract involved is a continuing one * * * or it means that the breach of the contractual provision did not go to the totality of the contract.   * * * "

RESTATEMENT, SECOND, CONTRACTS § 84:

(1) Except as stated in Subsection (2), a promise to perform all or part of a conditional duty under an antecedent contract in spite of the non-occurrence of the condition is binding, whether the promise is made before or after the time for the condition to occur, unless

(a) occurrence of the condition was a material part of the agreed exchange for the performance of the duty and the promisee was under no duty that it occur; or

(b) uncertainty of the occurrence of the condition was an element of the risk assumed by the promisor.

(2) If such a promise is made before the time for the occurrence of the condition has expired and the condition is within the control of the promisee or a beneficiary, the promisor can make his duty again subject to the condition by notifying the promisee or beneficiary of his intention to do so if

(a) the notification is received while there is still a reasonable time to cause the condition to occur under the antecedent terms or an extension given by the promisor; and

(b) reinstatement of the requirement of the condition is not unjust because of a material change of position by the promisee or beneficiary; and

(c) the promise is not binding apart from the rule stated in Subsection (1).

Illustration:

3.   A employs B to build a house, promising to pay therefor $10,000 on the production of a certificate from A's architect, C, stating that the work has been satisfactorily completed.   B builds the house

but the work is defective in certain trivial particulars. C refuses to give B a certificate. A says to B, "My architect rightfully refuses to give you a certificate but the defects are not serious; I will pay you the full price which I promised." A is bound to do so, and has no power to restore the requirement of the condition.

RESTATEMENT, SECOND, CONTRACTS § 246:

Illustration:

2. A contracts to sell and B to buy a machine for $10,000, delivery to be on March 1 and payment to be within 30 days thereafter. A does not deliver the machine until March 10, in such circumstances that the delay is a material breach. B accepts the machine but refuses to pay the price. A has a claim against B for the price of $10,000 under UCC § 2–709, subject to a claim by B against A for damages for partial breach because of the delay under UCC §§ 2–607(2) and 2–714.

———

DE CICCO v. SCHWEIZER, 221 N.Y. 431, 117 N.E. 807 (1917). In 1902 defendant and Count Oberto Gulinelli signed these "articles of agreement":

"Whereas, Miss Blanche Josephine Schweizer, daughter of said Mr. Joseph Schweizer and of said Mrs. Ernestine Teresa Schweizer, is now affianced to and is to be married to the above said Count Oberto Giacomo Giovanni Francesco Maria Gulinelli, Now, in consideration of all that is herein set forth the said Mr. Joseph Schweizer promises and expressly agrees by the present contract to pay annually to his said daughter Blanche, during his own life and to send her, during her lifetime, the sum of Two Thousand Five Hundred dollars." * * *

Defendant made the first payment when the marriage took place in 1902, and made annual payments thereafter until 1912. An assignee of Blanche and of her husband brought suit for the 1912 installment. The trial court directed a verdict for plaintiff; held, affirmed.

The defendant argued that there was no consideration for his promise since the Count was already engaged to Blanche, and the marriage "was merely the fulfillment of an existing legal duty." Judge Cardozo wrote for the Court:

"The courts of this state are committed to the view that a promise by A to B to induce him not to *break* his contract with C is void. If that is the true nature of this promise, there was no consideration. We have never held, however, that a like infirmity attaches to a promise by A, not merely to B, but to B and C jointly, to induce them not to *rescind* or *modify* a contract which they are free to abandon."

That, Judge Cardozo concluded, was "in substance the promise before us."

"From all [the] circumstances, we may infer that at the time of the marriage the promise was known to the bride as well as the husband, and that both acted upon the faith of it.

"The situation, therefore, is the same in substance as if the promise had run to husband and wife alike, and had been intended to induce performance by both. They were free by common consent to terminate their engagement or to postpone the marriage. If they forebore from exercising that right and assumed the responsibilities of marriage in reliance on the defendant's promise, he may not now retract it."

Nor was it necessary, wrote Judge Cardozo, that there be any evidence that one of the parties was in fact ready to terminate the engagement: "It is not to be expected that they should lay bare all the motives and promptings, some avowed and conscious, others perhaps half-conscious and inarticulate, which swayed their conduct. It is enough that the natural consequences of the defendant's promise was to induce them to put the thought of rescission or delay aside. From that moment, there was no longer a real alternative. There was no longer what philosophers call a 'living' option. This in itself permits the inference of detriment * * *. If the tendency of the promise is to induce them to persevere, reliance and detriment may be inferred from the mere fact of performance. The springs of conduct are subtle and varied. One who meddles with them must not insist upon too nice a measure of proof that the spring which he released was effective to the exclusion of all others."

RESTATEMENT, SECOND, CONTRACTS § 73:

Illustrations:

11. A contracts with B to install heating units in houses being built by B for C. B becomes insolvent and discontinues work, and C promises to pay A if A completes the installation in accordance with the contract between A and B. A's performance is consideration for C's promise.

12. A is employed to drive B's horse in a race. C owns the dam of B's horse and is entitled to a prize if B's horse wins the race. C promises A a bonus if he wins the race. A's driving in the race is consideration for C's promise, but B may be entitled to the bonus. See Restatement, Second, Agency § * * * 388. [Restatement, Second, Agency § 388 provides that "Unless otherwise agreed, an agent who makes a profit in connection with transactions conducted by him on behalf of the principal is under a duty to give such profit to the principal."]

SECTION 6: "PAST" CONSIDERATION AND MORAL OBLIGATION

MILLS v. WYMAN

Supreme Judicial Court of Massachusetts, 1825.
20 Mass. (3 Pick.) 207.

This was an action of *assumpsit* brought to recover a compensation for the board, nursing, &c., of Levi Wyman, son of the defendant, from the 5th to the 20th of February, 1821. The plaintiff then lived at Hartford, in Connecticut; the defendant, at Shrewsbury, in this county. Levi Wyman, at the time when the services were rendered, was about 25 years of age, and had long ceased to be a member of his father's family. He was on his return from a voyage at sea, and being suddenly taken sick at Hartford, and being poor and in distress, was relieved by the plaintiff in the manner and to the extent above stated. On the 24th of February, after all the expenses had been incurred, the defendant wrote a letter to the plaintiff promising to pay him such expenses. There was no consideration for this promise, except what grew out of the relation which subsisted between Levi Wyman and the defendant, and *Howe* J., before whom the cause was tried in the Court of Common Pleas, thinking this not sufficient to support the action, directed a nonsuit. To this direction the plaintiff filed exceptions. * * *

Parker C.J. General rules of law established for the protection and security of honest and fair-minded men, who may inconsiderately make promises without any equivalent, will sometimes screen men of a different character from engagements which they are bound in *foro conscientiae* to perform. This is a defect inherent in all human systems of legislation. The rule that a mere verbal promise, without any consideration, cannot be enforced by action, is universal in its application, and cannot be departed from to suit particular cases in which a refusal to perform such a promise may be disgraceful.

The promise declared on in this case appears to have been made without any legal consideration. The kindness and services towards the sick son of the defendant were not bestowed at his request. The son was in no respect under the care of the defendant. He was twenty-five years old, and had long left his father's family. On his return from a foreign country, he fell sick among strangers, and the plaintiff acted the part of the good Samaritan, giving him shelter and comfort until he died. The defendant, his father, on being informed of this event, influenced by a transient feeling of gratitude, promises in writing to pay the plaintiff for the expenses he had incurred. But he has determined to break this promise, and is willing to have his case appear on record as a strong example of particular injustice sometimes necessarily resulting from the operation of general rules.

It is said a moral obligation is a sufficient consideration to support an express promise; and some authorities lay down the rule thus broadly; but upon examination of the cases we are satisfied that the universality of the rule cannot be supported, and that there must have been some preëxisting obligation, which has become inoperative by positive law, to form a basis for an effective promise. The cases of debts barred by the statute of limitations, of debts incurred by infants, of debts of bankrupts, are generally put for illustration of the rule. Express promises founded on such preëxisting equitable obligations may be enforced; there is a good consideration for them; they merely remove an impediment created by law to the recovery of debts honestly due, but which public policy protects the debtors from being compelled to pay. In all these cases there was originally a *quid pro quo;* and according to the principles of natural justice the party receiving ought to pay; but the legislature has said he shall not be coerced; then comes the promise to pay the debt that is barred, the promise of the man to pay the debt of the infant, of the discharged bankrupt to restore to his creditor what by the law he had lost. In all these cases there is a moral obligation founded upon an antecedent valuable consideration. These promises therefore have a sound legal basis. They are not promises to pay something for nothing; not naked pacts; but the voluntary revival or creation of obligation which before existed in natural law, but which had been dispensed with, not for the benefit of the party obliged solely, but principally for the public convenience. If moral obligation, in its fullest sense, is a good substratum for an express promise, it is not easy to perceive why it is not equally good to support an implied promise. What a man ought to do, generally he ought to be made to do, whether he promise or refuse. But the law of society has left most of such obligations to the *interior* forum, as the tribunal of conscience has been aptly called. Is there not a moral obligation upon every son who has become affluent by means of the education and advantages bestowed upon him by his father, to relieve that father from pecuniary embarrassment, to promote his comfort and happiness, and even to share with him his riches, if thereby he will be made happy? And yet such a son may, with impunity, leave such a father in any degree of penury above that which will expose the community in which he dwells, to the danger of being obliged to preserve him from absolute want. Is not a wealthy father under strong moral obligation to advance the interest of an obedient, well disposed son, to furnish him with the means of acquiring and maintaining a becoming rank in life, to rescue him from the horrors of debt incurred by misfortune? Yet the law will uphold him in any degree of parsimony, short of that which would reduce his son to the necessity of seeking public charity.

Without doubt there are great interests of society which justify withholding the coercive arm of the law from these duties of imperfect obligation, as they are called; imperfect, not because they are less binding upon the conscience than those which are called perfect, but because the wisdom of the social law does not impose sanctions upon them.

A deliberate promise, in writing, made freely and without any mistake, one which may lead the party to whom it is made into contracts and expenses, cannot be broken without a violation of moral duty. But if there was nothing paid or promised for it, the law, perhaps wisely, leaves the execution of it to the conscience of him who makes it. It is only when the party making the promise gains something, or he to whom it is made loses something, that the law gives the promise validity. And in the case of the promise of the adult to pay the debt of the infant, of the debtor discharged by the statute of limitations or bankruptcy, the principle is preserved by looking back to the origin of the transaction, where an equivalent is to be found. An exact equivalent is not required by the law; for there being a consideration, the parties are left to estimate its value: though here the courts of equity will step in to relieve from gross inadequacy between the consideration and the promise.

These principles are deduced from the general current of decided cases upon the subject, as well as from the known maxims of the common law. The general position, that moral obligation is a sufficient consideration for an express promise, is to be limited in its application, to cases where at some time or other a good or valuable consideration has existed.

A legal obligation is always a sufficient consideration to support either an express or an implied promise; such as an infant's debt for necessaries, or a father's promise to pay for the support and education of his minor children. But when the child shall have attained to manhood, and shall have become his own agent in the world's business, the debts he incurs, whatever may be their nature, create no obligation upon the father; and it seems to follow, that his promise founded upon such a debt has no legally binding force.

The cases of instruments under seal and certain mercantile contracts, in which considerations need not be proved, do not contradict the principles above suggested. They first import a consideration in themselves, and the second belong to a branch of the mercantile law, which has found it necessary to disregard the point of consideration in respect to instruments negotiable in their nature and essential to the interests of commerce.   *   *   *

It has been attempted to show a legal obligation on the part of the defendant by virtue of our statute, which compels lineal kindred in the ascending or descending line to support such of their poor relations as are likely to become chargeable to the town where they have their settlement. But it is a sufficient answer to this position, that such legal obligation does not exist except in the very cases provided for in the statute, and never until the party charged has been adjudged to be of sufficient ability thereto. We do not know from the report any of the facts which are necessary to create such an obligation. Whether the deceased had a legal settlement in this commonwealth at the time of his death, whether he was likely to become chargeable had he lived, whether the defendant was of sufficient ability, are essential facts to be adjudicated by the court to which is given jurisdiction on this subject. The legal liability does not arise until these facts have all been ascertained by judgment, after hearing the party intended to be charged.

For the foregoing reasons we are all of opinion that the nonsuit directed by the Court of Common Pleas was right, and that judgment be entered thereon for costs for the defendant.

RESTATEMENT, SECOND, CONTRACTS § 82:

(1) A promise to pay all or part of an antecedent contractual or quasi-contractual indebtedness owed by the promisor is binding if the indebtedness is still enforceable or would be except for the effect of a statute of limitations.

(2) The following facts operate as such a promise unless other facts indicate a different intention:

(a) A voluntary acknowledgment to the obligee, admitting the present existence of the antecedent indebtedness; or

(b) A voluntary transfer of money, a negotiable instrument, or other thing by the obligor to the obligee, made as interest on or part payment of or collateral security for the antecedent indebtedness; or

(c) A statement to the obligee that the statute of limitations will not be pleaded as a defense.

Comment:

b. Historical note: types of indebtedness. The rule of Subsection (1) was established in the action of general or indebitatus assumpsit, based on a fictitious promise to pay an antecedent debt. * * * The rule was the same whether the new promise was made before or after the statute of limitations had run on the original debt; it was enough that the new promise was made within the statutory period before the bringing of the action. General assumpsit was extended to unliquidated contractual obligations and later to quasi-contractual obligations; it was not available for claims to damages for breach of a promissory bargain not performed on either side or for tort claims not involving unjust enrichment. The word "indebtedness" is intended to carry forward the distinction; a promise to pay damages for a tort or breach of contract may be made binding by consideration or reliance, but it is not within the rule stated in Subsection (1).

Illustrations:

2. A owes B three debts of $500 each. All of the debts are barred by the statute of limitations. A writes to B. "I promise to pay you one of those $500 debts which I owe; the other two I shall not pay." A's promise of $500 is binding.

3. A owes B a debt for some work which B has done but the amount due is in dispute. A writes to B, "I will pay you whatever I owe." The promise is binding during the statutory period of limitation from the time when it was made, and subjects A to a duty to pay whatever amount B can prove was due him.

Most states require by statute that the subsequent promise or acknowledgment be in writing and signed, although the possibility of the debt's being revived by part payment alone is commonly preserved. However, in most jurisdictions any acknowledgment or part payment must be made "under circumstances from which a new promise to pay the balance could be inferred." Zabella v. Pakel, 242 F.2d 452, 455 (7th Cir.1957). Therefore, much litigation has turned on delicate questions of judgment as to whether the particular circumstances of a case are sufficient to give rise to such an inference. A close comparison of cases holding that soothing statements by debtors are sufficient (e.g., "Now that I have got the ball rolling, am in hopes to do good business in the future. * * *," Wright v. Parmenter, 23 Misc. 629, 52 N.Y.S. 99 (1898)) or insufficient (e.g., "I think a little later as soon as things start up I may be able to do something for you," Gill v. Gibson, 225 Mass. 226, 114 N.E. 198 (1916)) to revive a debt is not greatly illuminating.

The Restatement also provides that "[a]n express promise to pay all or part of an indebtedness of the promisor, discharged or dischargeable in bankruptcy proceedings begun before the promise is made, is binding." Restatement, Second, Contracts § 83. In practice, giving effect to such promises often interfered with the purpose of the bankruptcy laws to give a "fresh start" to the discharged debtor. Debtors were often badgered into reaffirming discharged debts by creditors eager to remind them of their "moral obligation" to pay. The Federal Bankruptcy Act of 1978, 11 U.S.C.A. § 524, significantly altered this rule and now provides:

"(c) An agreement between a holder of a claim and the debtor, the consideration for which, in whole or in part, is based on a debt that is dischargeable in a case under this title is enforceable only to any extent enforceable under applicable nonbankruptcy law, whether or not discharge of such debt is waived, only if—

(1) such agreement was made before the granting of the discharge * * *;

(2) such agreement contains a clear and conspicuous statement which advises the debtor that the agreement may be rescinded at any time prior to discharge or within sixty days after such agreement is filed with the court, whichever occurs later * * * [and if the debtor has not in fact rescinded the agreement within that time];

(3) such agreement has been filed with the court and, if applicable, accompanied by a declaration or an affidavit of the attorney that represented the debtor during the course of negotiating an agreement under this subsection, which states that such agreement—

(A) represents a fully informed and voluntary agreement by the debtor; and

(B) does not impose an undue hardship on the debtor or a dependent of the debtor; * * * and

(6)(A) in a case concerning an individual who was not represented by an attorney during the course of negotiating an agreement under this subsection, [and where the debt is a consumer debt not secured by real property], the court approves such agreement as—

(i) not imposing an undue hardship on the debtor or a dependent of the debtor; and

(ii) in the best interest of the debtor. * * *

(d) In a case concerning an individual, when the court has determined whether to grant or not to grant a discharge * * *, the court may hold a hearing at which the debtor shall appear in person. * * * If a discharge has been granted and if the debtor desires to make an agreement of the kind specified in subsection (c) of this section, then the court shall hold a hearing at which the debtor shall appear in person and at such hearing the court shall—

(1) inform the debtor—

(A) that such an agreement is not required under this title, under nonbankruptcy law, or under any agreement not made in accordance with the provisions of subsection (c) of this section; and

(B) of the legal effect and consequences of [the reaffirmation agreement, and of any default under such an agreement] * * *.

(f) Nothing contained in subsection (c) or (d) of this section prevents a debtor from voluntarily repaying any debt."

––––––––

An agreement entered into by a minor (in the eyes of the law, an "infant") is "voidable" at his option; unlike the case of the statute-barred or discharged debt, the agreement was never originally enforceable against him. Nevertheless it is commonly assumed that the minor's later promise to honor the contract, made after reaching the age of majority, would be enforceable. This result is often expressed in terms of the minor's "affirmance" or "ratification" of the original transaction. In a few jurisdictions statutes require that the later promise be in writing, e.g., N.J.Stat.Ann. 25:1–6 (West 1940).

WEBB v. McGOWIN

Alabama Court of Appeals, 1935.
27 Ala.App. 82, 168 So. 196.

BRICKEN, PRESIDING JUDGE.

This action is in assumpsit. The complaint as originally filed was amended. The demurrers to the complaint as amended were sustained, and because of this adverse ruling by the court the plaintiff took a nonsuit, and the assignment of errors on this appeal are predicated upon said action or ruling of the court.

A fair statement of the case presenting the questions for decision is set out in appellant's brief which we adopt.

"On the 3d day of August, 1925, appellant while in the employ of the W.T. Smith Lumber Company, a corporation, and acting within the scope of his employment, was engaged in clearing the upper floor of mill No. 2 of the company. While so engaged he was in the act of dropping a pine block from the upper floor of the mill to the ground below; this being the usual and ordinary way of clearing the floor, and it being the duty of the plaintiff in the course of his employment to so drop it. The block weighed about 75 pounds.

"As appellant was in the act of dropping the block to the ground below, he was on the edge of the upper floor of the mill. As he started to turn the block loose so that it would drop to the ground, he saw J. Greeley McGowin, testator of the defendants, on the ground below and directly under where the block would have fallen had appellant turned it loose. Had he turned it loose it would have struck McGowin with such force as to have caused him serious bodily harm or death. Appellant could have remained safely on the upper floor of the mill by turning the block loose and allowing it to drop, but had he done this the block would have fallen on McGowin and caused him serious injuries or death. The only safe and reasonable way to prevent this was for appellant to hold to the block and divert its direction in falling from the place where McGowin was standing and the only safe way to divert it so as to prevent its coming into contact with McGowin was for appellant to fall with it to the ground below. Appellant did this, and by holding to the block and falling with it to the ground below, he diverted the course of its fall in such way that McGowin was not injured. In thus preventing the injuries to McGowin appellant himself received serious bodily injuries, resulting in his right leg being broken, the heel of his right foot torn off and his right arm broken. He was badly crippled for life and rendered unable to do physical or mental labor.

"On September 1, 1925, in consideration of appellant having prevented him from sustaining death or serious bodily harm and in consideration of the injuries appellant had received, McGowin agreed with him to care for and maintain him for the remainder of appellant's life at the rate of $15 every two weeks from the time he sustained his injuries to and during the remainder of appellant's life; it being agreed that McGowin would pay this sum to appellant for his maintenance. Under the agreement McGowin paid or caused to be paid to appellant the sum so agreed on up until McGowin's death on January 1, 1934. After his death the payments were continued to and including January 27, 1934, at which time they were discontinued. Thereupon plaintiff brought suit to recover the unpaid installments accruing up to the time of the bringing of the suit. * * *

The action was for the unpaid installments accruing after January 27, 1934, to the time of the suit.

The principal grounds of demurrer to the original and amended complaint are: (1) It states no cause of action; (2) its averments show the contract was without consideration; (3) it fails to allege that McGowin had, at or before the services were rendered, agreed to pay appellant for them; (4) the contract declared on is void under the statute of frauds.

1. The averments of the complaint show that appellant saved McGowin from death or grievous bodily harm. This was a material benefit to him of infinitely more value than any financial aid he could have received. Receiving this benefit, McGowin became morally bound to compensate appellant for the services rendered. Recognizing his moral obligation, he expressly agreed to pay appellant as alleged in the complaint and complied with this agreement up to the time of his death; a period of more than 8 years.

Had McGowin been accidentally poisoned and a physician, without his knowledge or request, had administered an antidote, thus saving his life, a subsequent promise by McGowin to pay the physician would have been valid. Likewise, McGowin's agreement as disclosed by the complaint to compensate appellant for saving him from death or grievous bodily injury is valid and enforceable.

Where the promisee cares for, improves, and preserves the property of the promisor, though done without his request, it is sufficient consideration for the promisor's subsequent agreement to pay for the service, because of the material benefit received.

In Boothe v. Fitzpatrick, 36 Vt. 681, the court held that a promise by defendant to pay for the past keeping of a bull which had escaped from defendant's premises and been cared for by plaintiff was valid, although there was no previous request, because the subsequent promise obviated that objection; it being equivalent to a previous request. On the same principle, had the promisee saved the promisor's life or his body from grievous harm, his subsequent promise to pay for the services rendered would have been valid. Such service would have been far more material than caring for his bull. Any holding that saving a man from death or grievous bodily harm is not a material benefit sufficient to uphold a subsequent promise to pay for the service, necessarily rests on the assumption that saving life and preservation of the body from harm have only a sentimental value. The converse of this is true. Life and preservation of the body have material, pecuniary values, measurable in dollars and cents. Because of this, physicians practice their profession charging for services rendered in saving life and curing the body of its ills, and surgeons perform operations. The same is true as to the law of negligence, authorizing the assessment of damages in personal injury cases based upon the extent of the injuries, earnings, and life expectancies of those injured.

In the business of life insurance, the value of a man's life is measured in dollars and cents according to his expectancy, the soundness of his body, and his ability to pay premiums. The same is true as to health and accident insurance.

It follows that if, as alleged in the complaint, appellant saved J. Greeley McGowin from death or grievous bodily harm, and McGowin subsequently agreed to pay him for the service rendered, it became a valid and enforceable contract.

2. It is well settled that a moral obligation is a sufficient consideration to support a subsequent promise to pay where the promisor has received a material benefit, although there was no original duty or liability resting on the promisor. * * *

The case at bar is clearly distinguishable from that class of cases where the consideration is a mere moral obligation or conscientious duty unconnected with receipt by promisor of benefits of a material or pecuniary nature. Here the promisor received a material benefit constituting a valid consideration for his promise.

3. Some authorities hold that, for a moral obligation to support a subsequent promise to pay, there must have existed a prior legal or equitable obligation, which for some reason had become unenforceable, but for which the promisor was still morally bound. This rule, however, is subject to qualification in those cases where the promisor, having received a material benefit from the promisee, is morally bound to compensate him for the services rendered and in consideration of this obligation promises to pay. In such cases the subsequent promise to pay is an affirmance or ratification of the services rendered carrying with it the presumption that a previous request for the service was made. * * *

McGowin's express promise to pay appellant for the services rendered was an affirmance or ratification of what appellant had done raising the presumption that the services had been rendered at McGowin's request.

4. The averments of the complaint show that in saving McGowin from death or grievous bodily harm, appellant was crippled for life. This was part of the consideration of the contract declared on. McGowin was benefited. Appellant was injured. Benefit to the promisor or injury to the promisee is a sufficient legal consideration for the promisor's agreement to pay.

5. Under the averments of the complaint the services rendered by appellant were not gratuitous. The agreement of McGowin to pay and

the acceptance of payment by appellant conclusively shows the contrary.

6. The contract declared on was not void under the statute of frauds (Code 1923, § 8034). The demurrer on this ground was not well taken. * * *

From what has been said, we are of the opinion that the court below erred in the ruling complained of; that is to say, in sustaining the demurrer, and for this error the case is reversed and remanded.

Reversed and remanded.

SAMFORD, Judge (concurring).

The questions involved in this case are not free from doubt, and perhaps the strict letter of the rule, as stated by judges, though not always in accord, would bar a recovery by plaintiff, but following the principle announced by Chief Justice Marshall in Hoffman v. Porter, Fed.Cas. No. 6,577, 2 Brock. 156, 159, where he says, "I do not think that law ought to be separated from justice, where it is at most doubtful," I concur in the conclusions reached by the court.

HARRINGTON v. TAYLOR, 225 N.C. 690, 36 S.E.2d 227 (1945).

"The defendant had assaulted his wife, who took refuge in plaintiff's house. The next day the defendant gained access to the house and began another assault upon his wife. The defendant's wife knocked him down with an axe, and was on the point of cutting his head open or decapitating him while he was laying on the floor, and the plaintiff intervened, caught the axe as it was descending, and the blow intended for defendant fell upon her hand, mutilating it badly, but saving defendant's life.

"Subsequently, defendant orally promised to pay the plaintiff her damages; but, after paying a small sum, failed to pay anything more."

* * *

The trial court sustained defendant's demurrer to the complaint, and this judgment was affirmed:

"The question presented is whether there was a consideration recognized by our law as sufficient to support the promise. The Court is of the opinion that however much the defendant should be impelled by common gratitude to alleviate the plaintiff's misfortune, a humanitarian act of this kind, voluntarily performed, is not such consideration as would entitle her to recover at law."

RESTATEMENT, SECOND, CONTRACTS § 86:

Illustration:

6. A finds B's escaped bull and feeds and cares for it. B's subsequent promise to pay reasonable compensation to A is binding.

N.Y.GEN.OBLIG. LAW § 5–1105 (McKinney 1989): A promise in writing and signed by the promisor or by his agent shall not be denied effect as a valid contractual obligation on the ground that consideration for the promise is past or executed, if the consideration is expressed in the writing and is proved to have been given or performed and would be a valid consideration but for the time when it was given or performed.

TALBERT v. TALBERT, 22 Misc.2d 782, 199 N.Y.S.2d 212 (1960). Defendant attempted to commit suicide by locking himself in his garage with the car motor running. His son, who was visiting at the time, managed to rescue defendant by breaking a window but in doing so was himself injured. The court held that the son's complaint alleging these facts stated a cause of action in tort for negligence; it quoted from Bohlen, Studies in the Law of Torts (1926):

"The rescuer's right of action * * * must rest upon the view that one who imperils another, at a place where there may be bystanders, must take into account the chance that some bystander will yield to the meritorious impulse to save life or even property from destruction, and attempt to rescue. If this is so, the right of action depends not upon the wrongfulness of the defendant's conduct in its tendency to imperil the person whose rescue is attempted, but upon its tendency to cause the rescuer to take the risk involved in the attempted rescue. And it would seem that a person who carelessly exposes himself to danger or who attempts to take his life in a place where others may be expected to be, does commit a wrongful act towards them in that it exposes them to a recognizable risk of injury."

Plaintiff, a housewife, wrote an unsolicited letter to Procter and Gamble, suggesting it produce "a new kind of laundry soap that would be a sensation and a great god-send to many housewives on washday! A soap I would call Blue. A new kind of soap with blue added into it." Procter and Gamble later put out a combination of soap and bluing called "Blue Cheer," and plaintiff brought suit for $1 million in damages, alleging that the company had adopted her idea. Held, that defendant's motion for summary judgment should be denied; a "defendant may be held liable in quantum meruit on the theory of unjust enrichment where defendant utilized a concrete and novel idea submitted by plaintiff." However, the court expressed "considerable doubt" whether plaintiff would be able to sustain her burden of proof at trial. Galanis v. Procter & Gamble Corp., 153 F.Supp. 34 (S.D.N.Y.1957).

One author has written, of the many cases like this "arising from the unsolicited disclosure of a business idea allegedly put to use by the transferee," that "[t]here is little doubt that the claimant's tender is made with economics in mind. But because of difficulties in identifying and valuing plaintiff's idea in defendant's business operation, the recognition of obligation poses real dangers of imposition. Hence, unless the claimant carries the burden of argument that his claim is plausible, the fear of overreaching is good reason for a court to reject leverage unilaterally acquired. The significance of a subsequent promise of compensation in such cases is that it effectively performs a variety of functions: it is conclusive on the imposition question, removes the objection that the claimant is both a volunteer and a self-seeker, and explicitly identifies an operative moral obligation resting in unjust enrichment." Henderson, Promises Grounded in the Past: The Idea of Unjust Enrichment and the Law of Contracts, 57 Va.L.Rev. 1115, 1172–1173 (1971).

REECE v. REECE, 239 Md. 649, 212 A.2d 468 (1965). Plaintiff filed a claim against the estate of his aunt, alleging that he had rendered personal services for her and for the corporation which she owned. A statute, one of a type popularly known as "dead man's statutes," prohibited a party from testifying "concerning any transaction with or statement made by [a] dead or incompetent person". Defendant, the administrator of the estate, argued that this statute prohibited plaintiff from testifying that he had made any contract with his aunt or that he had performed any services for her.

Held, judgment for plaintiff affirmed. In 1949 the aunt had signed "agreements" in which she acknowledged that plaintiff had since 1930 rendered services "to me and the company for my financial and personal benefit" for which he had not been paid; she promised to pay plaintiff $150 per month for such services for the period between 1930 and 1949. It was therefore not necessary for plaintiff to testify directly as to the services he performed during this period, in possible violation of the "dead man's statute": "[A] recital of facts which may constitute consideration in an unsealed written agreement, is prima facie evidence of those facts." The defendant argued that in any event the services referred to in these agreements were all "past services," and thus could not be consideration for the promise. The court disagreed:

"[A] present promise to pay in consideration of an act previously done at the request of the promisor will be enforceable as supported by sufficient consideration even though that consideration consists of an act previously done. * * * [T]he question arises as to whether a request by [the aunt] to the plaintiff Reece to perform the services may be implied. We are of the opinion that such a request may be implied. The services rendered were of a business nature. In the second document [the aunt] states that the services were rendered *'for me* at the office of the company *I own'* (emphasis supplied). * * * As Professor Williston states in Williston, Contracts § 146:

" 'Where * * * services are rendered because requested as a matter of business and where consequently there is a contemporaneous promise implied in fact to pay for them, the weight of authority supports the validity of a subsequent promise defining the extent of the promisor's undertaking.' * * *

"There is no evidence that [plaintiff] was living in the household of his aunt or that the services performed, or to be performed, by him were household services of such a character as to be presumed to have been gratuitously rendered. On the contrary, it appears that they were business services in regard to which the presumption of gratuitous service does not apply."

Chapter 3

INTENTION, INTERPRETATION, IMPLICATION AND RELATED MYSTERIES

The Restatement, Second, of Contracts provides that "the formation of a contract requires a bargain in which there is a manifestation of mutual assent to the exchange and a consideration." § 17(1). A manifestation of assent may be made "wholly or partly by written or spoken words or by other acts or by a failure to act." § 19(1).

RESTATEMENT, SECOND, CONTRACTS
§§ 19(2), (3):

(2) The conduct of a party is not effective as a manifestation of his assent unless he intends to engage in the conduct and knows or has reason to know that the other party may infer from his conduct that he assents.

(3) The conduct of a party may manifest assent even though he does not in fact assent. * * *

RESTATEMENT, SECOND, CONTRACTS § 21:

Neither real nor apparent intention that a promise be legally binding is essential to the formation of a contract, but a manifestation of intention that a promise shall not affect legal relations may prevent the formation of a contract.

Illustrations:

1. A draws a check for $300 payable to B and delivers it to B in return for an old silver watch worth about $15. Both A and B understand the transaction as a frolic and a banter, but each believes that he would be legally bound if the other dishonestly so asserted. There is no contract.

2. A orally promises to sell B a book in return for B's promise to pay $5. A and B both think such promises are not binding unless in writing. Nevertheless there is a contract, unless one of them intends

not to be legally bound and the other knows or has reason to know of that intention.

4.   A and B, two business corporations, have a contract by which B is the exclusive distributor in a certain territory of goods made by A. By a detailed written agreement they agree to continue the distributorship for three years.   The writing provides that it is not to be a legal agreement or subject to legal jurisdiction in the law courts.   The written agreement may be read and given effect to terminate the prior contract and to prevent any legal duty arising from the making of the agreement or from the acceptance of orders under it; but it does not excuse B from paying for goods delivered under it.

HOMAN v. EARLE, 53 N.Y. 267 (1873).   In an action for damages for breach of a promise of marriage, Church, Ch.J., rather delicately described the facts as follows:

"The parties are highly respectable, belonging to the same church of which the defendant is an elder.   Except in pecuniary resources they seem to have been equals.   The plaintiff was about thirty and the defendant fifty.   He had lost his wife, to whom he was affectionately devoted.   The plaintiff was the intimate personal friend of his wife during her life, and the two families were upon friendly if not intimate terms.   Soon after the death of his wife, the defendant commenced visiting the family of the plaintiff.   There was no significance in this circumstance other than what we might expect from a desire for sympathy and consolation for the great affliction which the defendant had suffered; but the evidence shows that these visits became more and more frequent, during which the defendant evinced marked and significant personal attentions to and apparent affection for the plaintiff; and these attentions were of a character which, it is claimed, could proceed from no honorable motive except an intention to marry.   It is not claimed by the plaintiff that the engagement was made in express words.   She stated that he never asked her in so many words to be his wife, but thought she had a right to expect that he meant it.   It is claimed that during their intercourse, his language and acts assured her of his desire to marry her; that she evinced a willingness, and that both regarded themselves as engaged.   There are many facts and circumstances from which it is claimed that the jury were justified in drawing this inference.   The force and weight to be given to these circumstances are matters of fact and not of law, and a few of them only will be referred to for the purpose of establishing this proposition. There were rides and walks and frequent visits, extending sometimes until late in the evening; there was language of endearment and such caressing as might be expected between lovers, accompanied with expressions by the defendant indicative, to say the least, of a desire that the plaintiff would become his wife.   *   *   * After this had continued about two months, upon an occasion when the defendant expected to leave home for a few days, the subject of their relations was alluded to, when the plaintiff told him that he had said many things which she thought meant a great deal, but he need not feel under any obligation from what he had said, and that he was free and had his liberty.   He only answered at the moment that he regretted that she had misunderstood him, without explaining in what respect she had misunderstood him; but he drew his chair nearer, put his arm around her, and told her that he thought a great deal of her; he remained until quite late, and said he did not want to go home. * * * The parties were then separated for six weeks, one or both being absent from the city. Immediately upon their return in September, the defendant commenced and continued his visits as before, three or four times a week, sometimes twice a day, both in the daytime and evening, often staying quite late.   These visits were apparently of the same cordial and affectionate character, and at one of them the defendant informed the plaintiff that he intended to marry when the year was up; that he supposed it would make a great talk, but he should not care, and asked plaintiff if she should care, and what she thought about it.   The jury may have thought this was strongly confirmatory of the plaintiff's right to expect marriage, and that the defendant intended she should so regard it.   On the 20th of October the defendant requested a note from the plaintiff as to the character of his visits.   Upon being asked his reasons for it, he told her it was as much for her good as his; that he didn't want her folks to know (or think) there was an understanding between them so soon.   He drafted the note and she copied it, retaining the draft.   It was in substance that she regarded his visits as evidence of his friendship "and nothing more." * * * The fact is that sometime prior to this the defendant had become acquainted with the lady whom he afterward married, and was probably engaged to her at that time, and the jury doubtless believed that his object in procuring the letter was not for the reason assigned, but to relieve himself from an obligation which he felt that he had incurred, and that the transaction viewed in this light was not quite in accordance with the code of morals which an elder of the church should practice. * * *"

The Court affirmed a judgment for the plaintiff based on a favorable jury verdict:

"Acts and even declarations which between some persons and under some circumstances might be unimportant would be significant and decisive between other persons and under other circumstances. A mutual pledge of love might be of insignificant import, or it might be indicative of an engagement depending upon a variety of surrounding circumstances evincing the intent of the parties.   So of caresses. They may indicate trivial flirtation or the sealing of the delicate contract of marriage.   The defendant was marriageable and openly avowed his intention to marry at a certain time, and although he did not in words ask the plaintiff, he said and did everything else indicating such a purpose, and received her assent, and was warned by her that his continuance would be so regarded by her, and after all that he declared to her that she was all the world to him, and after a six weeks' absence renewed his suit with the same apparent ardor as before. The defendant testified that he did not intend to marry the plaintiff. This may be so; yet if his acts and language were such as to induce her to believe that there was an engagement, and she acted upon that belief, and he knew that she so regarded them, and so acted and still continued, he cannot deny that the engagement existed. She has a right to enforce the obligation which he professed to incur."

EMBRY v. HARGADINE, McKITTRICK DRY GOODS CO.

Missouri Court of Appeals, 1907.
127 Mo.App. 383, 105 S.W. 777.

Action by Charles R. Embry against the Hargadine, McKittrick Dry Goods Company. From a judgment for defendant, plaintiff appeals. Reversed and remanded.

GOODE, J. We dealt with this case on a former appeal (115 Mo.App. 130, 91 S.W. 170). It has been retried, and is again before us for the determination of questions not then reviewed. The appellant was an employé of the respondent company under a written contract to expire December 15, 1903, at a salary of $2,000 per annum. His duties were to attend to the sample department of respondent, of which he was given complete charge. It was his business to select samples for the traveling salesmen of the company, which is a wholesale dry goods concern, to use in selling goods to retail merchants. Appellant contends that on December 23, 1903, he was re-engaged by respondent, through its president, Thos. H. McKittrick, for another year at the same compensation and for the same duties stipulated in his previous written contract. On March 1, 1904, he was discharged, having been notified in February that, on account of the necessity of retrenching expenses, his services and that of some other employés would no longer be required. The respondent company contends that its president never re-employed appellant after the termination of his written contract, and hence that it had a right to discharge him when it chose. The point with which we are concerned requires an epitome of the testimony of appellant and the counter testimony of McKittrick, the president of the company, in reference to the alleged re-employment. Appellant testified: That several times prior to the termination of his written contract on December 15, 1903, he had endeavored to get an understanding with McKittrick for another year, but had been put off from time to time. That on December 23d, eight days after the expiration of said contract, he called on McKittrick, in the latter's office, and said to him that as appellant's written employment had lapsed eight days before, and as there were only a few days between then and the 1st of January in which to seek employment with other firms, if respondent wished to retain his services longer he must have a contract for another year, or he would quit respondent's service then and there. That he had been put off twice before and wanted an understanding or contract at once so that he could go ahead without worry. That McKittrick asked him how he was getting along in his department, and appellant said he was very busy, as they were in the height of the season getting men out—had about 110 salesmen on the line and others in preparation. That McKittrick then said: "Go ahead, you're all right. Get your men out and don't let that worry you." That appellant took McKittrick at his word and worked until February 15th without any question in his mind. It was on February 15th that he was notified his services would be discontinued on March 1st. McKittrick denied this conversation as related by appellant, and said that, when accosted by the latter on December 23d, he (McKittrick) was working on his books in order to get out a report for a stockholders' meeting, and, when appellant said if he did not get a contract he would leave, that he (McKittrick) said: "Mr. Embry, I am just getting ready for the stockholders' meeting tomorrow. I have no time to take it up now. I have told you before I would not take it up until I had these matters out of the way. You will have to see me at a later time. I said: 'Go back upstairs and get your men out on the road.' I may have asked him one or two other questions relative to the department, I don't remember. The whole conversation did not take more than a minute."

Embry also swore that, when he was notified he would be discharged, he complained to McKittrick about it, as being a violation of their contract, and McKittrick said it was due to the action of the board of directors, and not to any personal action of his, and that others would suffer by what the board had done as well as Embry. Appellant requested an instruction to the jury setting out, in substance, the conversation between him and McKittrick according to his version, and declaring that those facts, if found to be true, constituted a contract between the parties that defendant would pay plaintiff the sum of $2,000 for another year, provided the jury believed from the evidence that plaintiff commenced said work believing he was to have $2,000 for the year's work. This instruction was refused, but the court gave another embodying in substance appellant's version of the conversation, and declaring it made a contract "if you (the jury) find both parties thereby intended and did contract with each other for plaintiff's employment for one year from and including December 23, 1903, at a salary of $2,000 per annum." Embry swore that, on several occasions when he spoke to McKittrick about employment for the ensuing year, he asked for a renewal of his former contract, and that on December 23d, the date of the alleged renewal, he went into Mr. McKittrick's office and told him his contract had expired, and he wanted to renew it for a year, having always worked under year contracts. Neither the refused instruction nor the one given by the court embodied facts quite as strong as appellant's testimony, because neither referred to appellant's alleged statement to McKittrick that unless he was re-employed he would stop work for respondent then and there.

It is assigned for error that the court required the jury, in order to return a verdict for appellant, not only to find the conversation occurred as appellant swore, but that both parties intended by such conversation to contract with each other for plaintiff's employment for the year from December, 1903, at a salary of $2,000. If it appeared from the record that there was a dispute between the parties as to the terms on which appellant wanted re-employment, there might have been sound reason for inserting this clause in the instruction; but no issue was made that they split on terms; the testimony of McKittrick tending to prove only that he refused to enter into a contract with appellant regarding another year's employment until the annual meeting of stockholders was out of the way. Indeed, as to the proposed terms McKittrick agrees with Embry, for the former swore as follows: "Mr. Embry said he wanted to know about the renewal of his contract. Said if he did not have the contract made he would leave." As the two witnesses coincided as to the terms of the proposed re-employment, there was no reason for inserting the above-mentioned clause in the instruction in order that it might be settled by the jury whether or not plaintiff, if employed for one year from December 23, 1903, was to be paid $2,000 a year. Therefore it remains to determine whether or not this part of the instruction was a correct statement of the law in regard to what was necessary to constitute a contract between the parties; that is to say, whether the formation of a contract by what, according to Embry, was said, depended on the intention of both Embry and McKittrick. Or, to put the question more precisely: Did what was said constitute a contract of re-employment on the previous terms irrespective of the intention or purpose of McKittrick?

Judicial opinion and elementary treatises abound in statements of the rule that to constitute a contract there must be a meeting of the minds of the parties, and both must agree to the same thing in the same sense. Generally speaking, this may be true; but it is not literally or universally true. That is to say, the inner intention of parties to a conversation subsequently alleged to create a contract cannot either make a contract of what transpired, or prevent one from arising, if the words used were sufficient to constitute a contract. In so far as their intention is an influential element, it is only such intention as the words or acts of the parties indicate; not one secretly cherished which is inconsistent with those words or acts. The rule is thus stated by a text-writer, and many decisions are cited in support of his text: "The primary object of construction in contract law is to discover the intention of the parties. This intention in express contracts is, in the first instance, embodied in the words which the parties have used and is to be deduced therefrom. This rule applies to oral contracts, as well as to contracts in writing, and is the rule recognized by courts of equity." 2 Paige, Contracts, § 1104. So it is said in another work: "Now this measure of the contents of the promise will be found to coincide in the usual dealings of men of good faith and ordinary competence, both with the actual intention of the promisor and with the actual expectation of the promisee. But this is not a constant or a necessary coincidence. In exceptional cases a promisor may be bound to perform something which he did not intend to promise, or a promisee may not be entitled to require that performance which he understood to be promised to him." Walds-Pollock, Contracts (3d Ed.) 309. In Brewington v. Mesker, 51 Mo.App. 348, 356, it is said that the meeting of minds, which is essential to the formation of a contract, is not determined by the secret intention of the parties, but by their expressed intention, which may be wholly at variance with the former. * * * In Smith v. Hughes, L.R. 6 Q.B. 597, 607, it was said: "If, whatever a man's real intention may be, he so conducts himself that a reasonable man would believe that he was assenting to the terms proposed by the other party, and that other party upon that belief enters into the contract with him, the man thus conducting himself would be equally bound as if he had intended to agree to the other party's terms." * * * Even more pointed was the language of Baron Bramwell in Brown v. Hare, 3 Hurlst. & N. *484, *495: "Intention is immaterial till it manifests itself in an act. If a man intends to buy, and says so to the intended seller, and he intends to sell, and says so to the intended buyer, there is a contract of sale; and so there would be if neither had the intention." In view of those authorities, we hold that, though McKittrick may not have intended to employ Embry by what transpired between them according to the latter's testimony, yet if what McKittrick said would have been taken by a reasonable man to be an employment, and Embry so understood it, it constituted a valid contract of employment for the ensuing year.

The next question is whether or not the language used was of that character, namely, was such that Embry, as a reasonable man, might consider he was re-employed for the ensuing year on the previous terms, and act accordingly. We do not say that in every instance it would be for the court to pronounce on this question, because, peradventure, instances might arise in which there would be such an ambiguity in the language relied on to show an assent by the obligor to the proposal of the obligee that it would be for the jury to say whether a reasonable mind would take it to signify acceptance of the proposal. Belt v. Goode, 31 Mo. 128. In Lancaster v. Elliott, 28 Mo.App. 86, 92, the opinion, as to the immediate point, reads: "The interpretation of a contract in writing is always a matter of law for determination by the court, and equally so, upon like principles, is the question what acts and words, in nearly every case, will suffice to constitute an acceptance by one party, of a proposal submitted by the other, so that a contract or agreement thereby becomes matured." The general rule is that it is for the court to construe the effect of writings relied on to make a contract, and also the effect of unambiguous oral words. Belt v. Goode, supra. However, if the words are in dispute, the question of whether they were used or not is for the jury. Belt v. Goode, supra. With these rules of law in mind, let us recur to the conversation of December 23d between Embry and McKittrick as related by the former. Embry was demanding a renewal of his contract, saying he had been put off from time to time, and that he had only a few days before the end of the year in which to seek employment from other houses, and that he would quit then and there unless he was re-employed. McKittrick inquired how he was getting along with the department, and Embry said they, i.e., the employés of the department, were very busy getting out salesmen. Whereupon McKittrick said: "Go ahead, you are all right. Get your men out, and do not let that worry you." We think no reasonable man would construe that answer to Embry's demand that he be employed for another year, otherwise than as an assent to the demand, and that Embry had the right to rely on it as an assent. The natural inference is, though we do not find it testified to, that Embry was at work getting samples ready for the salesmen to use during the ensuing season. Now, when he was complaining of the worry and mental distress he was under because of his uncertainty about the future, and his urgent need, either of an immediate contract with respondent, or a refusal by it to make one, leaving him free to seek employment elsewhere, McKittrick must have answered as he did for the purpose of assuring appellant that any apprehension was needless, as appellant's services would be retained by the respondent. The answer was unambiguous, and we rule that if the conversation was according to appellant's version, and he understood he was employed, it constituted in law a valid contract of re-employment, and the court erred in making the formation of a contract depend on a finding that both parties intended to make one. It was only necessary that Embry, as a reasonable man, had a right to and did so understand.

Some other rulings are assigned for error by the appellant, but we will not discuss them because we think they are devoid of merit.

The judgment is reversed, and the cause remanded. All concur.

———

Embry testified that at the critical conversation with McKittrick he requested to be employed "for this year," "for the ensuing year" or "for another year." Based on this testimony the defendant sought to interpose the statute of frauds as a defense, an issue that was resolved in Embry's favor in the prior appeal. What argument did the defendant make about the statute of frauds?

———

TOLMIE v. UNITED PARCEL SERVICE, INC., 930 F.2d 579 (7th Cir. 1991):

"When William Tolmie first came to work for United Parcel Service the terms of his employment were governed by a collective bargaining agreement that allowed dismissal only for cause. Two years later, while considering an offer of promotion to a management position, Tolmie realized that this 'good cause' protection would not follow him. When he voiced this concern to his supervisor, the supervisor assured him that he would have nothing to worry about, insofar as job security was concerned, because 'it is harder to fire management than other employees' of UPS. Tolmie then accepted the promotion, relying upon the assurance, and was thereafter terminated for reasons that ostensibly would not constitute good cause."

After his discharge, Tolmie brought suit alleging breach of an employment contract. Applying Illinois law, the Court of Appeals affirmed a dismissal of the complaint on the ground that no claim was stated:

"[E]mployment contracts are presumed to be 'at will' and are therefore terminable by either party for good reason, bad reason, or no reason at all. *See Duldulao v. Saint Mary of Nazareth Hosp. Center,* 115 Ill.2d 482, 489, 106 Ill.Dec. 8, 11–12, 505 N.E.2d 314 (1987). The 'at will' presumption is not unassailable, however. An employee may rebut it by a showing that the parties contracted otherwise, *id.* at 489, 106 Ill.Dec. at 12, 505 N.E.2d at 318, and Tolmie argues that his employment contract falls within that category.

"Any attempt to 'contract otherwise,' however, was not in writing. The only evidence that Tolmie was not an at-will employee derives exclusively from the statement by his supervisor. And oral employment contracts, at least under Illinois law, are viewed with more skepticism than their formal, written counterparts. * * * In particular, not just any offer will support an oral employment contract. On the contrary, the offer must encompass terms that are 'clear and definite.'

"In addition to saving the judiciary from the very difficult task of reconstructing ex post facto the uncertain terms of an uncertain agreement, the requirement of a clear and definite offer prevents employers from incurring contractual liability for informal statements that were never intended to be anything more than expressions of ' "long continuing good will and hope for eternal association." ' And as one might expect, the analysis is objective, not subjective; Illinois law seeks to determine whether the alleged promise is 'clear enough that an employee would reasonably believe that an offer has been made.' * * *

"Applying the test articulated by the Illinois courts, we conclude that the supervisor's response cannot support Tolmie's cause of action. By his own account, Tolmie voiced a very pointed question about job security and the 'good cause' provision that applied to union employees. The answer he received, however, was hardly pointed. Indeed, its general nature allows any number of interpretations,[3] only one of which would create a 'good cause' provision. The statement was vague, not clear and definite, and would not cause a reasonable employee to believe that an offer had been made. *See Titchener v. Avery Coonley School,* 39 Ill.App.3d 871, 874, 350 N.E.2d 502, 506 (1976) (rejecting as

---

3. For example, the supervisor's statement could mean that higher levels of supervisors had to be involved in the decision. It could mean that UPS was reluctant to terminate upper-level employees for whom there had been a substantial investment in training. It could also be a reference to the phenomenon, although less frequent today, that layoffs are less common among management than among salaried employees.

too vague the following statement: 'Your future is here * * * and I hope it will be for many years to come.')."

"Tolmie walked out of his supervisor's office with a vague and informal assurance, not an offer. * * * Tolmie was an at-will employee who could be discharged for any reason, and his claim was therefore susceptible to dismissal under rule 12(b)(6) of the Federal Rules of Civil Procedure. The decision of the district court is Affirmed."

COHEN, THE BASIS OF CONTRACT
46 Harv.L.Rev. 553, 575–77 (1933).

According to the classical view, the law of contract gives expression to and protects the will of the parties, for the will is something inherently worthy of respect. Hence such authorities as Savigny, Windsheid, Pothier, Planiol, Pollock, Salmond, and Langdell hold that the first essential of a contract is the agreement of wills, or the meeting of minds.

The metaphysical difficulties of this view have often been pointed out. Minds or wills are not in themselves existing things that we can look at and recognize. We are restricted in our earthly experience to the observation of the changes or actions of more or less animated bodies in time and space; and disembodied minds or wills are beyond the scope and reach of earthly law. But while this objection has become familiar, it has not been very effective. The force of the old ideas, embodied in the traditional language, has not always been overcome even by those who like Langdell and Salmond profess to recognize the fictional element in the will theory.

Another line of objection can be found in the incompatibility of the classical theory with the consequences that the law attaches to an offer. Suppose that I offer to buy certain goods from *A* at a given price, and, following his refusal, give him a week's time to reconsider it. If I change my mind the next day but fail to notify him, a contractual obligation will none the less arise if five days later he notifies me that he has accepted my terms. Here obviously there is never a moment of time when the two parties are actually in agreement or of one mind. Yet no one denies that the resulting rights and duties are identical with those called contractual. It does not help the classical theory to say that I am under a legal duty to notify *A* (the offeree) and that if I fail to perform this duty in the proper way, the law will treat my change of mind as a nullity, *as if* it had never happened. The phrase italicized indicates that we are moving in the realm of fiction (or better, rights and duties imposed by law) and not in the realm of fact. No one denies that the contractual obligation should attach in this case; but there is in point of fact no actual agreement or meeting of minds. The latter, then, is not always necessary for a legal contract.

The logical inconsistency of the classical theory is not cured if we say that the law protects not the will but the expression or declaration of the will. Suppose that in the case mentioned I make a solemn declaration of the revocation of my offer, or write a letter but fail to communicate it. The law, in refusing to give effect to my declared revocation, is not protecting my expressed will, but is enforcing a duty on me in the interest of the general security of business transactions.

A more important objection to the theory that every contract expresses the consensus or agreed wills of the two parties is the fact that most litigation in this field arises precisely because of the advent of conditions that the two parties did not foresee when they entered into the transaction. Litigation usually reveals the absence of genuine agreement between the parties *ab initio.* If both parties had foreseen the difficulty, provision would have been made for it in the beginning when the contract was drawn up. When courts thus proceed to interpret* the terms of the contract they are generally not merely seeking to discover the actual past meanings (though these may sometimes be investigated), but more generally they decide the "equities," the rights and obligations of the parties, in such circumstances; and these legal relations are determined by the courts and the jural system and not by the agreed will of the contesting parties.

WHITTIER, THE RESTATEMENT OF CONTRACTS AND MUTUAL ASSENT

17 Cal.L.Rev. 441 (1929).**

It will probably be admitted by everybody that in the making of most contracts there is actual assent communicated by each party to the other. Professor Williston himself says: [1] "An outward manifestation of assent to the express terms of a contract almost invariably connotes mental assent." It is only in the very exceptional case, therefore, that any doctrine other than that of mutual assent communicated is made necessary by the decisions.

As Professor Williston pointed out in his strong article on Mutual Assent in the Formation of Contracts,[2] no new doctrine for exceptional cases appeared until about 1850 and then chiefly as a misapplication of the principle of estoppel. The substance of the new doctrine which was adopted seems to have been that one who did not actually assent to the contract may be held to it if he carelessly led the other party to reasonably think that there was assent.

As an original proposition the wisdom of the innovation may well be doubted. It would have simplified our law of contracts if actual meeting of the minds mutually communicated had remained essential. The liability for carelessly misleading the other party into the reasonable belief that there was assent might well have been held to be in tort. * * * Under the present law the non-consenting party is liable on the

---

* In modern usage, this process is more likely to be described as "construction" rather than "interpretation." See Weiner, infra, page 413.

1. 2 Williston, Contracts (1920) § 659.

2. (1919) 14 Illinois L.Rev. 85.

contract itself if careless. The chief unfortunate result of this state of the law is that he is bound to the contract though the other party is notified of the mistake before the latter has changed his position or suffered any damage. To hold one for a merely careless use of language which causes no damage whatever to the party to whom the language is addressed is certainly inconsistent with principles generally applied. If D drives down Michigan Avenue, Chicago, in a careless manner but no one is hurt, can any of those who might have been hurt sue D?

But taking the law as settled that one is liable on the contract where he carelessly misleads the other party to reasonably believe there was assent, is it wise to state the entire law of mutual assent in terms of these admittedly exceptional cases? Why not say that actual assent communicated is the basis of "mutual assent" except where there is careless misleading which induces a reasonable belief in assent? The writer thinks that this approach to the problems involved is more likely to lead one to just conclusions.

———

HOTCHKISS v. NATIONAL CITY BANK OF NEW YORK, 200 Fed. 287, 293 (S.D.N.Y.1911). (L. Hand, J.):

"A contract has, strictly speaking, nothing to do with the personal, or individual, intent of the parties. A contract is an obligation attached by the mere force of law to certain acts of the parties, usually words, which ordinarily accompany and represent a known intent. If, however, it were proved by twenty bishops that either party, when he used the words, intended something else than the usual meaning which the law imposes upon them, he would still be held, unless there were some mutual mistake, or something else of the sort. Of course, if it appear by other words, or acts, of the parties, that they attribute a peculiar meaning to such words as they use in the contract, that meaning will prevail, but only by virtue of the other words, and not because of their unexpressed intent."

———

RICKETTS v. PENNSYLVANIA R. CO., 153 F.2d 757, 760–64 (2d Cir. 1946). This case involved a suit for injuries suffered by a railroad dining car waiter; the defense was that the plaintiff had executed a release. The release was for $750, one-tenth of the amount later awarded by a jury. The plaintiff was unable to read as a result of the accident; he testified that he signed the release after his attorney incorrectly advised him that it was merely a receipt for payments representing his lost wages and tips. He further testified that he had hired the attorney solely to help him collect his lost wages and tips and not to bring suit against his employer. The court affirmed a judgment against the defendant based on the jury verdict. Frank, J., concurred:

"In the early days of this century a struggle went on between the respective proponents of two theories of contracts, (a) the 'actual intent' theory—or 'meeting of the minds' or 'will' theory—and (b) the so-called 'objective' theory.[2] Without doubt, the first theory had been carried too far: Once a contract has been validly made, the courts attach legal consequences to the relation created by the contract, consequences of which the parties usually never dreamed—as, for instance, where situations arise which the parties had not contemplated. As to such matters, the 'actual intent' theory induced much fictional discourse which imputed to the parties intentions they plainly did not have.

"But the objectivists also went too far. They tried (1) to treat virtually all the varieties of contractual arrangements in the same way, and (2) as to all contracts in all their phases, to exclude, as legally irrelevant, consideration of the actual intention of the parties or either of them, as distinguished from the outward manifestation of that intention. The objectivists transferred from the field of torts that stubborn anti-subjectivist, the 'reasonable man'; so that, in part at least, advocacy of the 'objective' standard in contracts appears to have represented a desire for legal symmetry, legal uniformity, a desire seemingly prompted by aesthetic impulses. Whether (thanks to the 'subjectivity' of the jurymen's reactions and other factors) the objectivists' formula, in its practical workings, could yield much actual objectivity, certainty, and uniformity may well be doubted.[6] * * * At any rate, the sponsors of complete 'objectivity' in contracts largely won out in the wider generalizations of the Restatement of Contracts and in some judicial pronouncements.[9]

"Influenced by their passion for excessive simplicity and uniformity, many objectivists have failed to give adequate special consideration

2. Some adherents of the objective theory have suggested that the "actual intent" theory was undesirably transplanted into the common law, in the 19th century from Roman-law dominated continental sources. See, e.g., Williston, Contracts (Rev.ed.1936) §§ 20, 21, 94; The historical accuracy of that suggestion seems somewhat questionable to one who reads a 16th century English decision like Thoroughgood's Case, 1582, 2 Co.Rep. 9a, 76 Eng.Reprint 408, relating to a unilateral mistake. Sponsors of the "objective" theory did not, however, rest their case primarily on chauvinistic common law distaste for continental attitudes. Nor could they consistently have done so. For the "reasonable man," dear to the objectivists, seems to have been imported into the common law.

The "actual intent" theory, said the objectivists, being "subjective" and putting too much stress on unique individual motivations, would destroy that legal certainty and stability which a modern commercial society demands. They depicted the "objective" standard as a necessary adjunct of a "free enterprise" economic system. In passing, it should be noted that they ar-

rived at a sort of paradox. For a "free enterprise" system is, theoretically, founded on "individualism"; but, in the name of economic individualism, the objectivists refused to consider those reactions of actual specific individuals which sponsors of the "meeting-of-the-minds" test purported to cherish. "Economic individualism" thus shows up as hostile to real individualism. This is nothing new: The "economic man" is of course an abstraction, a "fiction." * * *

6. Perhaps the most fatuous of all notions solemnly voiced by learned men who ought to know better is that when legal rules are "clear and complete" litigation is unlikely to occur.

Such writers surely cannot be unaware that thousands of decisions yearly turn on disputes concerning the facts, i.e., as to whether clear-cut legal rules were in fact violated. It is the uncertainty about the "facts" that creates most of the unpredictability of decisions.

9. See, e.g., Hotchkiss v. National City Bank, 200 F. 287, 293 (S.D.N.Y.1911).

to releases of claims for personal injuries, and especially to such releases by employees to their employers. Williston, the leader of the objectivists, insists that, as to all contracts, without differentiation, the objective theory is essential because 'founded upon the fundamental principle of the security of business transactions'. [10] * * *

"It is little wonder that a considerable number of competent legal scholars have criticized the extent to which the objective theory, under Williston's influence, was carried in the Restatement of Contracts. * * *

"[One] critic [21] suggests that, in general, Williston, because he did not searchingly inquire into the practical results of many of his formulations, assumed, unwarrantably, without proof, that those results must invariably have a general social value, although (as Williston admits as to the objective theory) they are 'frequently harsh.' * * *

"Fortunately, most judges are too common-sensible to allow, for long, a passion for aesthetic elegance, or for the appearance of an abstract consistency, to bring about obviously unjust results. Accordingly, courts not infrequently have departed from the objective theory when necessary to avoid what they have considered an unfair decision against a person who, for a small sum, signed a release without understanding either the seriousness of his injury or the import of the words of the release, provided (1) he was not 'negligent' and (2) the other party (the releasee) had not, in reliance on the release, importantly 'changed his position.' Some courts, in some of the mistake cases, frankly abandon the 'objective' test, saying boldly that a non-negligent unilateral mistake justifies cancellation or rescission of a contract. As New York, a lively center of commerce, at least to some extent allows relief for such unilateral mistakes, it should be obvious that, contrary to Williston & Co., any deviation from the objective theory is not fatal to the functioning of business."

The enforceability of releases from liability, particularly in circumstances where claims for serious injury were released for modest

----

10. Williston, Contracts (Rev.ed.) § 23. * * *

21. F.S. Cohen says that Williston, "a master of classical jurisprudence," in many of his formulations "has in mind neither the question of * * * prediction which the practical lawyer faces nor the question of values which the conscientious judge faces. If he had in mind the former question, his studies would no doubt reveal the extent to which courts actually enforce various types of contractual obligation. His conclusions would be in terms of probability and statistics. On the other hand, if Professor Williston were interested in the ethical aspects of contractual liability, he would undoubtedly offer a sig-

nificant account of human values, and social costs involved in different types of agreement and in the means of their enforcement. In fact, however, the discussions of a Williston oscillate between a theory of what courts actually do and a theory of what courts ought to do, without coming to rest either on the plane of social realities or on the plane of values long enough to come to grips with significant problems. This confused wandering between the world of fact and the world of justice vitiates every argument and every analysis." Cohen, Transcendental Nonsense and The Functional Approach, 25 Col.L.Rev. (1935) 809, 840, 841.

payments before the full extent of the injury was known, has been considered in a large number of cases. Plaintiffs in such cases have a considerable amount of judicial sympathy, particularly where there has been no apparent reliance by the defendant other than the amount paid in settlement. Depending on the circumstances, releases may be attacked frontally on theories of mistake, fraud, duress, breach of fiduciary duty, and unconscionability, or indirectly by arguing for a narrow construction of the language of the release. These and related issues are considered in chapters 5, 6, and 7.

KABIL DEVELOPMENTS CORP. v. MIGNOT, 279 Or. 151, 566 P.2d 505 (1977). The plaintiff brought suit on an alleged oral contract under which defendant agreed to provide helicopter services for a construction project. In attempting to establish that a contract existed, the plaintiff's president was permitted to testify that he felt in his own mind at the time that his corporation had a binding agreement with the defendant. (Linde, J.):

"These opposing contentions echo debates that occupied the jurisprudence of contracts a half-century and more ago. * * * But accepting the test of manifested assent regardless of subjective intent does not dispose of the present question. It need not follow that the test also compels keeping a party from testifying whether he thought at the time of the events that he was in fact entering into an agreement. Here the witness was permitted to testify that he did, indeed, act in the belief that he was making a contract. More often, no doubt, the subjective testimony seeks to deny or vary the objectively manifested agreement asserted by the opposing party, which is what concerns the objective theorists. It is not clear from Judge Hand's words in *Hotchkiss*, supra, whether he would have admitted the testimony of the twenty bishops at all.

"Usually, however, probative testimony is admissible unless some rule compels its exclusion, and it is difficult to deny that a person's own view of his position in a negotiation can bear on his behavior as perceived by other parties. That perception is, of course, the crux of the objective theory, despite an occasional statement that the parties' manifestations are to be judged by the standards of a 'reasonable man;' the staunchest 'objectivist' would not let a jury hold two parties to an apparently manifested agreement if neither thought the other meant to assent. When the dispute concerns an unwritten agreement, the conclusion that the parties manifested mutual assent must be constructed from evidence of their negotiations or other past conduct. It must be constructed from their 'communications and overt acts,' not their 'undisclosed intents and ideas,' but in face-to-face negotiations, words are not everything, and a factfinder might well believe that what a party thought he was doing would show in what he did. Thus it was not error to permit Munroe to testify to his own sense of the state of negotiations, as long as the jury was not misled into treating this testimony, in its context, as something more than evidence bearing on the behavior and the perceptions of the parties to the negotiation."

KONIC INTERNATIONAL v. SPOKANE COMPUTER SERVICES, INC.

Idaho Court of Appeals, 1985.
109 Idaho 527, 708 P.2d 932.

WALTERS, CHIEF JUDGE.

Konic International Corporation sued Spokane Computer Services, Inc., to collect the price of an electrical device allegedly sold by Konic to Spokane Computer. The suit was tried before a magistrate sitting without a jury. The magistrate entered judgment for Spokane Computer, concluding there was no contract between the parties because of lack of apparent authority of an employee of Spokane Computer to purchase the device from Konic. The district court, on appeal, upheld the magistrate's judgment. On further appeal by Konic, we also affirm the magistrate's judgment but base our result on reasoning different from that of the lower court.

The magistrate found the following facts. David Young, an employee of Spokane Computer, was instructed by his employer to investigate the possibility of purchasing a surge protector, a device which protects computers from damaging surges of electrical current. Young's investigation turned up several units priced from $50 to $200, none of which, however, were appropriate for his employer's needs. Young then contacted Konic. After discussing Spokane Computer's needs with a Konic engineer, Young was referred to one of Konic's salesmen. Later, after deciding on a certain unit, Young inquired as to the price of the selected item. The salesman responded, "fifty-six twenty." The salesman meant $5,620. Young in turn thought $56.20.

The salesman for Konic asked about Young's authority to order the equipment and was told that Young would have to get approval from one of his superiors. Young in turn prepared a purchase order for $56.20 and had it approved by the appropriate authority. Young telephoned the order and purchase order number to Konic who then shipped the equipment to Spokane Computer. However, because of internal processing procedures of both parties the discrepancy in prices was not discovered immediately. Spokane Computer received the surge protector and installed it in its office. The receipt and installation of the equipment occurred while the president of Spokane Computer was on vacation. Although the president's father, who was also chairman of the board of Spokane Computer, knew of the installation, he only inquired as to what the item was and who had ordered it. The president came back from vacation the day after the surge protector had been installed and placed in operation and was told of the purchase. He immediately ordered that power to the equipment be turned off because he realized that the equipment contained parts which alone were worth more than $56 in value. Although the president then told

Young to verify the price of the surge protector, Young failed to do so. Two weeks later, when Spokane Computer was processing its purchase order and Konic's invoice, the discrepancy between the amount on the invoice and the amount on the purchase order was discovered. The president of Spokane Computer then contacted Konic, told Konic that Young had no authority to order such equipment, that Spokane Computer did not want the equipment, and that Konic should remove it. Konic responded that Spokane Computer now owned the equipment and if the equipment was not paid for, Konic would sue for the price. Spokane Computer refused to pay and this litigation ensued. * * *

Basically what is involved here is a failure of communication between the parties. A similar failure to communicate arose over 100 years ago in the celebrated case of *Raffles v. Wichelhaus,* 2 Hurl. 906, 159 Eng.Rep. 375 (1864) which has become better known as the case of the good ship "Peerless". In *Peerless,* the parties agreed on a sale of cotton which was to be delivered from Bombay by the ship "Peerless". In fact, there were two ships named "Peerless" and each party, in agreeing to the sale, was referring to a different ship. Because the sailing time of the two ships was materially different, neither party was willing to agree to shipment by the "other" Peerless. The court ruled that, because each party had a different ship in mind at the time of the contract, there was in fact no binding contract. The *Peerless* rule later was incorporated into section 71 of the Restatement of Contracts and has now evolved into section 20 of Restatement (Second) of Contracts (1981). Section 20 states in part:

(1) There is no manifestation of mutual assent to an exchange if the parties attach materially different meanings to their manifestations and

(a) neither knows or has reason to know the meaning attached by the other.

Comment (c) to section 20 further explains that "even though the parties manifest mutual assent to the same words of agreement, there may be no contract because of a material difference of understanding as to the terms of the exchange." Another authority, Williston, discussing situations where a mistake will prevent formation of a contract, agrees that "where a phrase of contract * * * is reasonably capable of different interpretations * * * there is no contract." 1 S. Williston, Contracts § 95 (3d ed. 1957).

One commentator on the *Peerless* case, maintaining that the doctrine should be cautiously applied, indicates three principles about the case doctrine that are generally in agreement: (1) "the doctrine applies only when the parties have different understandings of their expression of agreement"; (2) the doctrine does not apply when one party's understanding, because of that party's fault, is less reasonable than the other party's understanding; and (3) parol evidence is admissible to establish the facts necessary to apply the rule. Young, *Equivocation in the Making of Agreements,* 64 COLUM.L.REV. 619 (1964).

The second principle indicates that the doctrine may be applicable to this case because, arguably, both parties' understandings were reasonable. Also, as pointed out by the district court, both parties were equally at fault in contributing to the resulting problems. The third principle is not relevant to the present case. * * *

In the present case, both parties attributed different meanings to the same term, "fifty-six twenty." Thus, there was no meeting of the minds of the parties. With a hundred fold difference in the two prices, obviously price was a material term. Because the "fifty-six twenty" designation was a material term expressed in an ambiguous form to which two meanings were obviously applied, we conclude that no contract between the parties was ever formed. Accordingly, we do not reach the issue of whether Young had authority to order the equipment.

Konic asserts that the conduct of the parties reflects the formation of a contract and, this being a "transaction in goods," the provisions of the Uniform Commercial Code should apply. Konic also raises issues based on implied-in-law contract, estoppel, and mistake—all arguments which have as their basis some form of contract. We conclude that the foregoing analysis is equally applicable to these arguments. The mutual misunderstanding of the parties was so basic and so material that any agreement the parties thought they had reached was merely an illusion.

Although Konic asserts that Spokane Computer was unjustly enriched, the magistrate found no evidence establishing unjust enrichment of Spokane Computer which would support any restitution to Konic. We have held that restitution may sometimes be required even though no contract has materialized. *Dursteler v. Dursteler,* 108 Idaho 230, 697 P.2d 1244 (Ct.App.1985). However, our review of the record in this case discloses no evidence warranting such a remedy. Therefore, Konic's other theories of recovery are equally unpersuasive.

* * * The decision of the district court is affirmed. Costs and attorney fees to respondent, Spokane Computer.

SWANSTROM and BURNETT, JJ., concur.

RESTATEMENT, SECOND, CONTRACTS § 20:

(1) There is no manifestation of mutual assent to an exchange if the parties attach materially different meanings to their manifestations and

    (a) neither party knows or has reason to know the meaning attached by the other; or

    (b) each party knows or each party has reason to know the meaning attached by the other.

(2) The manifestations of the parties are operative in accordance with the meaning attached to them by one of the parties if

(a) that party does not know of any different meaning attached by the other, and the other knows the meaning attached by the first party; or

(b) that party has no reason to know of any different meaning attached by the other, and the other has reason to know the meaning attached by the first party.

Illustrations:

1. A offers to sell B goods shipped from Bombay ex steamer "Peerless". B accepts. There are two steamers of the name "Peerless", sailing from Bombay at materially different times. If both parties intend the same Peerless, there is a contract, and it is immaterial whether they know or have reason to know that two ships are named Peerless.

2. The facts being otherwise as stated in Illustration 1, A means Peerless No. 1 and B means Peerless No. 2. If neither A nor B knows or has reason to know that they mean different ships, or if they both know or if they both have reason to know, there is no contract.

3. The facts being otherwise as stated in Illustration 1, A knows that B means Peerless No. 2 and B does not know that there are two ships named Peerless. There is a contract for the sale of the goods from Peerless No. 2, and it is immaterial whether B has reason to know that A means Peerless No. 1. If A makes the contract with the undisclosed intention of not performing it, it is voidable by B for misrepresentation. Conversely, if B knows that A means Peerless No. 1 and A does not know that there are two ships named Peerless, there is a contract for the sale of the goods from Peerless No. 1, and it is immaterial whether A has reason to know that B means Peerless No. 2, but the contract may be voidable by A for misrepresentation.

4. The facts being otherwise as stated in Illustration 1, neither party knows that there are two ships Peerless. A has reason to know that B means Peerless No. 2 and B has no reason to know that A means Peerless No. 1. There is a contract for the sale of goods from Peerless No. 2. In the converse case, where B has reason to know and A does not, there is a contract for sale from Peerless No. 1. In either case * * * the contract [may be] voidable for mistake * * *.

LONDON COUNTY COUNCIL v. HENRY BOOT & SONS LTD., [1959] 1 W.L.R. 1069 (House of Lords). Plaintiffs were building contractors who entered into a standard form contract with the London County Council for the construction of apartment buildings. This contract contained an escalator clause (called a "rise-and-fall clause") under which the Council would increase its payments to the plaintiffs in the event of increases in the "rates of wages" paid by them. Plaintiffs were parties to an arrangement in the construction industry under which employers would make weekly payments towards the cost of an employee's annual holiday by buying "holiday stamps" for him. Plaintiffs contended that increases in the costs of the holiday stamps fell within the escalator clause as increases in "rates of wages". The House of Lords agreed with the Council that they did not; Lord Denning wrote:

"I may add, perhaps, a word on the correspondence which took place before the contract was executed. The London County Council there made it clear that they did not regard holiday credits as coming within the rise-and-fall clause; but the builders' association took a different view. Neither side inserted any words in the contract so as to clear up the difference between them. They left the rise-and-fall clause as it was. It was suggested that on this account there was no consensus ad idem: Your Lordships rejected this suggestion without wishing to hear further argument upon it. There was, to all outward appearances, agreement by the parties on the one thing that really mattered—on the terms that should bind them. In case of difference as to the meaning of those terms, it was for the court to determine it. It does not matter what the parties, in their inmost states of mind, thought the terms meant. They may each have meant different things. But still the contract is binding according to its terms—as interpreted by the court."

RESTATEMENT [FIRST] OF CONTRACTS § 71:

Illustration:

2. A says to B, "I offer to sell you my horse for $100." B, knowing that A intends to offer to sell his cow, not his horse for that price, and that the use of the word "horse" is a slip of the tongue, replies, "I accept." There is no contract for the sale of either the horse or the cow.

RESTATEMENT [FIRST] OF CONTRACTS § 231:

Illustrations:

1. A, a stock speculator, and B, a stock broker, agree orally for the purpose of concealing the nature of A's dealings, that in any transactions between them the word "abracadabra" shall mean "Northern Pacific." A sends a signed written order to B directing him to buy 100 shares "abracadabra." B buys 100 shares of Northern Pacific stock and tenders the certificate, and on A's refusal to accept, brings an action against him. B can recover. * * * [T]he meaning of "abracadabra" [is] uncertain and hence the oral definition of the parties can be shown * * *.

2. A and B are engaged in buying and selling shares of stock from one another and agree orally for the purpose of concealing the nature of their dealings that in transactions between them the word "buy" shall be used to mean "sell," and that the word "sell" shall be used to mean "buy." A sends a written offer to B to "sell" certain shares of

stock. B, having in mind the oral agreement, accepts the offer and tenders the shares to A. On A's refusal to accept the tender, B brings an action against him. B cannot recover, unless reformation is had of the writings. The private oral agreement cannot make "buy" mean "sell," though a private agreement may give to a word which has no inconsistent meaning, a meaning in accordance with the agreement.

RESTATEMENT, SECOND, CONTRACTS § 20:

Illustration:

5. A says to B, "I offer to sell you my horse for $100." B, knowing that A intends to offer to sell his cow for that price, not his horse, and that the word "horse" is a slip of the tongue, replies, "I accept." The price is a fair one for either the horse or the cow. There is a contract for the sale of the cow and not of the horse. If B makes the contract with the undisclosed intention of not performing it, it is voidable by A for misrepresentation.

RESTATEMENT, SECOND, CONTRACTS § 212:

Illustrations:

3. A agrees orally with B, a stockbroker, that in transactions between them "abracadabra" shall mean X Company. A sends a signed written order to B to buy 100 shares "abracadabra," and B buys 100 shares of X Company. The parties are bound in accordance with the oral agreement.

4. A and B are engaged in buying and selling shares of stock from each other, and agree orally to conceal the nature of their dealings by using the word "sell" to mean "buy" and using the word "buy" to mean "sell." A sends a written offer to B to "sell" certain shares, and B accepts. The parties are bound in accordance with the oral agreement.

FRIGALIMENT IMPORTING CO. v. B.N.S. INTERNATIONAL SALES CORP.

United States District Court, Southern District of New York, 1960.
190 F.Supp. 116.

FRIENDLY, CIRCUIT JUDGE.

The issue is, what is chicken? Plaintiff says "chicken" means a young chicken, suitable for broiling and frying. Defendant says "chicken" means any bird of that genus that meets contract specifications on weight and quality, including what it calls "stewing chicken" and plaintiff pejoratively terms "fowl". Dictionaries give both meanings, as well as some others not relevant here. To support it plaintiff sends a number of volleys over the net; defendant essays to return them and adds a few serves of its own. Assuming that both parties were acting in good faith, the case nicely illustrates Holmes' remark "that the making of a contract depends not on the agreement of two minds in one intention, but on the agreement of two sets of external signs—not on the parties' having *meant* the same thing but on their having *said* the same thing." The Path of the Law, in Collected Legal Papers, p. 178. I have concluded that plaintiff has not sustained its burden of persuasion that the contract used "chicken" in the narrower sense.

The action is for breach of the warranty that goods sold shall correspond to the description. Two contracts are in suit. In the first, dated May 2, 1957, defendant, a New York sales corporation, confirmed the sale to plaintiff, a Swiss corporation of

> "US Fresh Frozen Chicken, Grade A, Government Inspected, Eviscerated
>
> 2½–3 lbs. and 1½–2 lbs. each all chicken individually wrapped in cryovac, packed in secured fiber cartons or wooden boxes, suitable for export
>
> > 75,000 lbs. 2½–3 lbs.............................. @ $33.00
> > 25,000 lbs. 1½–2 lbs.............................. @ $36.50
> > per 100 lbs. FAS New York
>
> scheduled May 10, 1957 pursuant to instructions from Penson & Co., New York."

The second contract, also dated May 2, 1957, was identical save that only 50,000 lbs. of the heavier "chicken" were called for, the price of the smaller birds was $37 per 100 lbs., and shipment was scheduled for May 30. The initial shipment under the first contract was short but the balance was shipped on May 17. When the initial shipment arrived in Switzerland, plaintiff found, on May 28, that the 2½–3 lbs. birds were not young chicken suitable for broiling and frying but stewing chicken or "fowl"; indeed, many of the cartons and bags plainly so indicated. Protests ensued. Nevertheless, shipment under the second contract was made on May 29, the 2½–3 lbs. birds again being stewing chicken. Defendant stopped the transportation of these at Rotterdam.

This action followed. ＊ ＊ ＊

Since the word "chicken" standing alone is ambiguous, I turn first to see whether the contract itself offers any aid to its interpretation. Plaintiff says the 1½–2 lbs. birds necessarily had to be young chicken since the older birds do not come in that size, hence the 2½–3 lbs. birds must likewise be young. This is unpersuasive—a contract for "apples" of two different sizes could be filled with different kinds of apples even though only one species came in both sizes. Defendant notes that the contract called not simply for chicken but for "US Fresh Frozen Chicken, Grade A, Government Inspected." It says the contract thereby incorporated by reference the Department of Agriculture's regulations, which favor its interpretation; I shall return to this after reviewing plaintiff's other contentions.

The first hinges on an exchange of cablegrams which preceded execution of the formal contracts. The negotiations leading up to the contracts were conducted in New York between defendant's secretary,

Ernest R. Bauer, and a Mr. Stovicek, who was in New York for the Czechoslovak government at the World Trade Fair. A few days after meeting Bauer at the fair, Stovicek telephoned and inquired whether defendant would be interested in exporting poultry to Switzerland. Bauer then met with Stovicek, who showed him a cable from plaintiff dated April 26, 1957, announcing that they "are buyer" of 25,000 lbs. of chicken 2½–3 lbs. weight, Cryovac packed, grade A Government inspected, at a price up to 33¢ per pound, for shipment on May 10 to be confirmed by the following morning, and were interested in further offerings. After testing the market for price, Bauer accepted, and Stovicek sent a confirmation that evening. Plaintiff stresses that, although these and subsequent cables between plaintiff and defendant, which laid the basis for the additional quantities under the first and for all of the second contract, were predominantly in German, they used the English word "chicken"; it claims this was done because it understood "chicken" meant young chicken whereas the German word, "Huhn," included both "Brathuhn" (broilers) and "Suppenhuhn" (stewing chicken), and that defendant, whose officers were thoroughly conversant with German, should have realized this. Whatever force this argument might otherwise have is largely drained away by Bauer's testimony that he asked Stovicek what kind of chickens were wanted, received the answer "any kind of chickens," and then, in German, asked whether the cable meant "Huhn" and received an affirmative response. * * *

Plaintiff's next contention is that there was a definite trade usage that "chicken" meant "young chicken." Defendant showed that it was only beginning in the poultry trade in 1957, thereby bringing itself within the principle that "when one of the parties is not a member of the trade or other circle, his acceptance of the standard must be made to appear" by proving either that he had actual knowledge of the usage or that the usage is "so generally known in the community that his actual individual knowledge of it may be inferred." 9 Wigmore, Evidence (3d ed. 1940) § 2464. Here there was no proof of actual knowledge of the alleged usage; indeed, it is quite plain that defendant's belief was to the contrary. In order to meet the alternative requirement, the law of New York demands a showing that "the usage is of so long continuance, so well established, so notorious, so universal and so reasonable in itself, as that the presumption is violent that the parties contracted with reference to it, and made it a part of their agreement." Walls v. Bailey, 1872, 49 N.Y. 464, 472–473.

Plaintiff endeavored to establish such a usage by the testimony of three witnesses and certain other evidence. Strasser, resident buyer in New York for a large chain of Swiss cooperatives, testified that "on chicken I would definitely understand a broiler." However, the force of this testimony was considerably weakened by the fact that in his own transactions the witness, a careful businessman, protected himself by using "broiler" when that was what he wanted and "fowl" when he wished older birds. Indeed, there are some indications, dating back to a remark of Lord Mansfield, Edie v. East India Co., 2 Burr. 1216, 1222 (1761), that no credit should be given "witnesses to usage, who could not adduce instances in verification." 7 Wigmore, Evidence (3d ed. 1940), § 1954. While Wigmore thinks this goes too far, a witness' consistent failure to rely on the alleged usage deprives his opinion testimony of much of its effect. Niesielowski, an officer of one of the companies that had furnished the stewing chicken to defendant, testified that "chicken" meant "the male species of the poultry industry. That could be a broiler, a fryer or a roaster", but not a stewing chicken; however, he also testified that upon receiving defendant's inquiry for "chickens", he asked whether the desire was for "fowl or frying chickens" and, in fact, supplied fowl, although taking the precaution of asking defendant, a day or two after plaintiff's acceptance of the contracts in suit, to change its confirmation of its order from "chickens," as defendant had originally prepared it, to "stewing chickens." Dates, an employee of Urner-Barry Company, which publishes a daily market report on the poultry trade, gave it as his view that the trade meaning of "chicken" was "broilers and fryers." In addition to this opinion testimony, plaintiff relied on the fact that the Urner-Barry service, the Journal of Commerce, and Weinberg Bros. & Co. of Chicago, a large supplier of poultry, published quotations in a manner which, in one way or another, distinguish between "chicken," comprising broilers, fryers and certain other categories, and "fowl," which, Bauer acknowledged, included stewing chickens. This material would be impressive if there were nothing to the contrary. However, there was, as will now be seen.

Defendant's witness Weininger, who operates a chicken eviscerating plant in New Jersey, testified "Chicken is everything except a goose, a duck, and a turkey. Everything is a chicken, but then you have to say, you have to specify which category you want or that you are talking about." Its witness Fox said that in the trade "chicken" would encompass all the various classifications. Sadina, who conducts a food inspection service, testified that he would consider any bird coming within the classes of "chicken" in the Department of Agriculture's regulations to be a chicken. The specifications approved by the General Services Administration include fowl as well as broilers and fryers under the classification "chickens." Statistics of the Institute of American Poultry Industries use the phrases "Young chickens" and "Mature chickens," under the general heading "Total chickens." and the Department of Agriculture's daily and weekly price reports avoid use of the word "chicken" without specification.

Defendant advances several other points which it claims affirmatively support its construction. Primary among these is the regulation of the Department of Agriculture, 7 C.F.R. § 70.300–70.370, entitled, "Grading and Inspection of Poultry and Edible Products Thereof." and in particular § 70.301 which recited:

"*Chickens.* The following are the various classes of chickens:

(a) Broiler or fryer * * *

(b) Roaster * * *

(c) Capon * * *

(d) Stag * * *

(e) Hen or stewing chicken or fowl * * *

(f) Cock or old rooster * * *"

Defendant argues, as previously noted, that the contract incorporated these regulations by reference. Plaintiff answers that the contract provision related simply to grade and Government inspection and did not incorporate the Government definition of "chicken," and also that the definition in the Regulations is ignored in the trade. However, the latter contention was contradicted by Weininger and Sadina; and there is force in defendant's argument that the contract made the regulations a dictionary, particularly since the reference to Government grading was already in plaintiff's initial cable to Stovicek.

Defendant makes a further argument based on the impossibility of its obtaining broilers and fryers at the 33¢ price offered by plaintiff for the 2½–3 lbs. birds. There is no substantial dispute that, in late April, 1957, the price for 2½–3 lbs. broilers was between 35 and 37¢ per pound, and that when defendant entered into the contracts, it was well aware of this and intended to fill them by supplying fowl in these weights. It claims that plaintiff must likewise have known the market since plaintiff had reserved shipping space on April 23, three days before plaintiff's cable to Stovicek, or, at least, that Stovicek was chargeable with such knowledge. It is scarcely an answer to say, as plaintiff does in its brief, that the 33¢ price offered by the 2½–3 lbs. "chickens" was closer to the prevailing 35¢ price for broilers than to the 30¢ at which defendant procured fowl. Plaintiff must have expected defendant to make some profit—certainly it could not have expected defendant deliberately to incur a loss.

Finally, defendant relies on conduct by the plaintiff after the first shipment had been received. On May 28 plaintiff sent two cables complaining that the larger birds in the first shipment constituted "fowl." Defendant answered with a cable refusing to recognize plaintiff's objection and announcing. "We have today ready for shipment 50,000 lbs. chicken 2½–3 lbs. 25,000 lbs. broilers 1½–2 lbs.," these being the goods procured for shipment under the second contract, and asked immediate answer "whether we are to ship this merchandise to you and whether you will accept the merchandise." After several other cable exchanges, plaintiff replied on May 29 "Confirm again that merchandise is to be shipped since resold by us if not enough pursuant to contract chickens are shipped the missing quantity is to be shipped within ten days stop we resold to our customers pursuant to your contract chickens grade A you have to deliver us said merchandise we again state that we shall make you fully responsible for all resulting costs." [2] Defendant argues that if plaintiff was sincere in thinking it was entitled to young chickens, plaintiff would not have allowed the shipment under the second contract to go forward, since the distinction between broilers and chickens drawn in defendant's cablegram must have made it clear that the larger birds would not be broilers. However, plaintiff answers that the cables show plaintiff was insisting on delivery of young chickens and that defendant shipped old ones at its peril. Defendant's point would be highly relevant on another disputed issue—whether if liability were established, the measure of damages should be the difference in market value of broilers and stewing chicken in New York or the larger difference in Europe, but I cannot give it weight on the issue of interpretation. Defendant points out also that plaintiff proceeded to deliver some of the larger birds in Europe, describing them as "poulets"; defendant argues that it was only when plaintiff's customers complained about this that plaintiff developed the idea that "chicken" meant "young chicken." There is little force in this in view of plaintiff's immediate and consistent protests.

When all the evidence is reviewed, it is clear that defendant believed it could comply with the contracts by delivering stewing chicken in the 2½–3 lbs. size. Defendant's subjective intent would not be significant if this did not coincide with an objective meaning of "chicken." Here it did coincide with one of the dictionary meanings, with the definition in the Department of Agriculture Regulations to which the contract made at least oblique reference, with at least some usage in the trade, with the realities of the market, and with what plaintiff's spokesman had said. Plaintiff asserts it to be equally plain that plaintiff's own subjective intent was to obtain broilers and fryers; the only evidence against this is the material as to market prices and this may not have been sufficiently brought home. In any event it is unnecessary to determine that issue. For plaintiff has the burden of showing that "chicken" was used in the narrower rather than in the broader sense, and this it has not sustained.

This opinion constitutes the Court's findings of fact and conclusions of law. Judgment shall be entered dismissing the complaint with costs.

———

DADOURIAN EXPORT CORP. v. UNITED STATES, 291 F.2d 178, 187 (2d Cir.1961). Friendly, J., dissenting, refers to "a failure of the minds to meet, bringing into play a principle akin to that of Raffles v. Wichelhaus." He also appends the following footnote: "It may be that Frigaliment Importing Co. v. B.N.S. International Sales Corp., D.C.S.D. N.Y.1961, 190 F.Supp. 116, decided by the writer, might better have been placed on that ground, with the loss still left on the plaintiff because of defendant's not unjustifiable change of position, 5 Williston,

_____

2. These cables were in German; "chicken", "broilers" and, on some occasions, "fowl," were in English.

Contracts (2d ed.), § 1595; American Law Institute, Restatement of Restitution, § 178."

RESTATEMENT, SECOND, CONTRACTS § 201:

Illustration:

4. A agrees to sell and B to buy a quantity of eviscerated "chicken." A tenders "stewing chicken" or "fowl"; B rejects on the ground that the contract calls for "broilers" or "fryers." Each party makes a claim for damages against the other. It is found that each acted in good faith and that neither had reason to know of the difference in meaning. Both claims fail.

U.S. NAVAL INSTITUTE v. CHARTER COMMUNICATIONS

United States District Court, Southern District of New York, 1988.
687 F.Supp. 115, rev'd 875 F.2d 1044 (2d Cir.1989).

LEVAL, DISTRICT JUDGE.

This is an action alleging breach of contract and copyright infringement arising from the paperback reprint publication of the best-selling novel, *The Hunt for the Red October* by Thomas L. Clancy. The plaintiff, United States Naval Institute, published the hardcover edition in October 1984 and licensed the defendant[1] to "publish the * * * Work in a paperback edition not sooner than October 1985." Plaintiff contends this term of the license was violated when defendant shipped the book to booksellers prior to October 1985. It contends furthermore that pre-October sales were unauthorized by the license and therefore constituted infringements of the plaintiff's copyright. Defendant does not dispute that it shipped the book to domestic outlets before October. It contends, however, that pre-October shipment is contemplated in the industry by the term "October publication" and that its actions were entirely consistent with the rights conferred to it under the license agreement.

Trial was conducted before the court without a jury. I find the defendant has proved its case beyond dispute. There is no basis for plaintiff's contentions. The action is dismissed. * * *

United States Naval Institute is a small specialized publisher whose list is limited to books of naval interest. Before *Red October*, it had no experience in the publication of best sellers.

As assignee of the author's copyright, plaintiff planned to publish the hardcover edition in October 1984 and to license a paperback reprint edition. Plaintiff showed the manuscript to a number of paperback publishers and received a bid from defendant. Plaintiff then

---

1. The license was in favor of Charter Communications Inc., a member of the defendant Berkley Group. When the book became a leading seller in hardcover, the defendants planned to publish the paperback edition under their flagship Berkley imprint, instead of Charter.

decided it would conduct an auction using the defendant's bid as a "floor" and granting defendant the right to top the auction's highest bid by ten percent. Plaintiff had never before conducted an auction of paperback rights and was unfamiliar with industry practices, customs and procedures. It sought advice from various knowledgeable people in the publishing industry as to how such auctions were conducted. It distributed a packet of materials to invited bidders, including a notice which set forth the terms of the auction. The materials made no mention of the date on which publication of the paperback edition would be permitted. There was no need to specify this date because, according to the conventions and business practices of the publishing industry, the paperback publication right would begin one year after the month of the hardcover publication.

Bids were received by telephone on the date specified. At the conclusion, Berkley exercised its option to top the highest bid by ten percent. Berkley then prepared the license agreement on its own form, as is the industry practice, and sent it to plaintiff. Berkley filled in the blank on the printed form pertaining to the date of hardcover publication as "October 1984" and filled in "October 1985" as the earliest permitted paperback publication date. This was in accordance with industry practice and the understanding on which its bid was predicated. The parties negotiated a few minor changes, including an obligation on the licensee to print the book in its entirety. The license was executed on September 14, 1984.

Plaintiff published its hardcover edition in October as anticipated. Shortly after its appearance, it became a leading best seller and continued on the best-seller lists throughout the event in dispute.

Berkley, which publishes hundreds of paperback titles each year, included *Red October* in its October 1985 catalogue list and proceeded with its plans and preparations for October publication in a manner consistent with its regular practices and with the practices and understandings of the industry. For *Red October,* as with its other October publication titles, it scheduled the various production tasks leading up to what is referred to in the industry as the "pub date." Solicitation of orders and to-the-trade advertising was to begin in April 1985, printing in early August, and shipping to domestic outlets in early September.

When plaintiff learned in August of defendant's plans to ship, it protested. Plaintiff was concerned that the appearance of the paperback in book outlets would cut into hardcover sales. Plaintiff asserted that the license forbade pre-October shipment; it demanded that the defendant delay shipment to October. The defendant responded that its shipment plans were customary for October publication. Plaintiff sought a preliminary injunction which this court denied.

Defendant proved conclusively at trial (without any contrary evidence being offered) that "publication date" is uniformly understood in the industry to refer to the time when the concentrated selling effort begins, and not the time of shipment to outlets. The "publication date" refers usually to a month and presupposes that nationwide distribution has already been accomplished by the start of that month. Industry leaders representing both hardcover and paperback establishments testified to the industry's understanding and practice that books are shipped three to six weeks prior to the start of the month of "publication." [2] This interval between shipping and publication is necessary to insure that the distribution process has been accomplished nationwide before the concentrated selling effort begins on the "pub date."

The process of nationwide distribution is complex and uses different channels. Some of the channels are simple and relatively quick, consuming only a few days. Others (generally involving larger volumes of books) are complicated and slow, relying on warehouses, break-up agents, wholesalers and truckers, none of whom are under the publisher's control. Cost control is an important factor. Shipment through these channels to more distant points often consumes substantially more than a minimum of two weeks. Publishers generally attempt to follow a distribution plan that ships first by the more time consuming routes to more distant points and later by the quicker routes. An effort is made in this fashion to schedule shipment so as to avoid wide disparities in the time the book goes on sale in different parts of the country. The principal objective is to be sure that, by the start of the month of publication when the concentrated selling effort begins, the book has reached and is offered by retail outlets throughout the country.

The shipping dates of the Berkley group in relation to its publication dates were entirely consistent with the practices of the publishing industry. Its scheduled dates varied as between its different imprint labels primarily to allow for access to the printer's press schedules and to permit aggregation of titles so as to qualify by bulk for minimum freight rates. Titles under the Berkley imprint were shipped on the 8th day of the month preceding the month of "publication" (or nearest working day), Jove titles were shipped on the 30th of the second preceding month, and Ace titles on the 20th of the second preceding month, with press runs beginning in each case 30 days prior to shipment date. This schedule was in conformity with the industry practice of shipping between 3 to 6 weeks prior to the month of publication.

Berkley began shipment of *Red October* to domestic outlets on September 3 and 4. Because this was a huge shipment (approximately 1.3 million copies) of a certain best seller, Berkley shipped it separately from its other October titles. In order to economize on freight rates, a month's various titles are generally packed together for shipment. When the shipment volume for a single title is sufficiently large, the lower rates can be achieved without group packing. The title is likely to benefit from more efficient and prompt handling on reaching the

---

2. The variation between three and six weeks is attributable largely to the fact that printing facilities are in limited supply.

bookstore if the boxes are exclusively devoted to a single best-selling title, as compared with boxes containing numerous different titles that need to be separated. Although the book was designated for "special" treatment in the sense that it was shipped alone, beginning September 3, rather than in combined shipments on September 8, this treatment was entirely consistent with "October publication." This was "special handling" in the sense that *Red October* was separated from the shipment of the other October titles, but such handling was conventional for leading titles shipped in large volume.

Because the hardcover edition had an unusually long best-selling run and was still high on the best-seller lists in September 1985, the paperback was shipped into extraordinarily favorable market conditions and achieved best-seller status before nationwide distribution had been completed. This is illustrated by the reports made weekly by the leading bookselling chains to the publishers. For the week ending September 20, the Waldenbook and B. Dalton chains reported to Berkley that *Red October* was their second and third largest volume paperback seller respectively, based on the aggregate sales of 836 Walden stores and 679 B. Dalton stores. (There is no evidence how early in the week the shipments reached their various stores.) During the following week the book reached an additional 57 Walden stores and 48 Dalton stores; and sales increased substantially. * * *

Plaintiff contends that the contractual language authorizing the defendant to publish "not sooner than October 1985" implicitly prohibited defendant from shipping before October. Plaintiff contends that the meaning of the contract is so clear and unambiguous that the court should not have received evidence of industry custom. Plaintiff relies on authority to the effect that industry custom may not be received to contradict explicit contractual obligations. *See Croce v. Kurnit,* 737 F.2d 229 (2d Cir.1984).

Those authorities have no bearing on the problem. The evidence was received not to contradict an explicit contract but to help interpret an ambiguous one. Without the help of industry understandings, the meaning of this contract would be unclear. A prohibition on "publishing" sooner than October might mean many different things. It might be understood on its face to bar a publisher from taking any steps that are part of the "publication" process prior to October, including printing and advertising to the trade; it might imply the technical copyright sense of "publish," thus prohibiting any public revelation of the content before October. (Under such an understanding, any act that would constitute an infringement if done by an unlicensed interloper would be similarly unauthorized if done by the licensee before the first permitted publication date.) It might be understood to bar any shipment prior to October, or it might permit pre-October shipments only if done in a manner to preclude pre-October retail selling. At another extreme, it might have no bearing whatever on date of shipment since what is limited by contract is not "shipment" but "publication." In fact, one cannot understand the relationship between the contractual term "publication" and the fact of shipping without some understanding of how the industry functions. A judge or jury called upon to interpret this contract without the benefit of evidence of industry understanding of the terminology would be engaging in guesswork. Defendant's evidence showed beyond dispute that the contractual term is used in the industry with a clearly understood meaning, that the understood meaning is regularly observed, and that defendant's conduct was wholly consistent with that understanding. When understood in the light of industry terminology, the license did not forbid shipment prior to October; it provided for October publication, which called for shipment three to six weeks earlier.[3]

It is the law in New York that evidence of trade usage may be used to "give particular meaning to and supplement or qualify terms of an agreement." N.Y.U.C.C. § 1–205(3) (McKinney's 1964); *see Tannenbaum v. Zeller,* 552 F.2d 402, 414 (2d Cir.), *cert. denied,* 434 U.S. 934, 98 S.Ct. 421, 54 L.Ed.2d 293 (1977). Evidence of trade usage is admissible to explain or supplement a contractual term. *See Walk–In Medical Centers, Inc. v. Breuer Capital Corp.,* 818 F.2d 260, 264 (2d Cir.1987) (trade usage used to explain phrase "adverse market conditions" in firm commitment underwriting agreement); *Seven Star Shoe Co. v. Strictly Goodies, Inc.,* 657 F.Supp. 917, 921 (S.D.N.Y.1987) (trade usage admissible on meaning of term sales "representative"); *East Europe Domestic International Sales Corp. v. Island Creek Coal Sales Co.,* 572 F.Supp. 702, 708–09 (S.D.N.Y.1983) (evidence of course of dealing admissible on issue whether "metric tons of coal" in contract meant dry coking coal); *Joyce Beverages of New York, Inc. v. Royal Crown Cola Co.,* 555 F.Supp. 271, 277 (S.D.N.Y.1983) (trade usage admissible to read "best efforts" clause in franchise agreement to require exclusive efforts of distributor). In *Trans World Metals Inc. v. Southwire Co.,* 769 F.2d 902 (2d Cir.1985), for example, the court considered whether a manufacturer of aluminum had breached its agreement to ship 1,000 metric tons of aluminum per month to the defendant by shipping one-fourth of that amount in the following month. The Court held evidence of trade usage properly admissible on the issue whether some part of each month's shipment could be delivered in the following month.

Similarly, in *Edison v. Viva International, Ltd.,* 70 A.D.2d 379, 421 N.Y.S.2d 203 (1st Dept.1979), where an author brought a breach of contract action against his publisher for materially altering his article, the court denied the defendant's motion to dismiss premised on the defendant's contractual "right to edit or otherwise change the Work." The Court held that "a contract must be construed according to the

---

3. Plaintiff argues that this reading is inconsistent with defendant's interpretation of the term "publication" as used elsewhere in the contract in the provisions calling for royalty payments on, and six months after "publication," which defendant observed by paying on, and six months after October 1. Plaintiff is mistaken. There is no inconsistency. In each case, defendant and the court construe the contractual term "publish" to refer to the "pub date" of October 1, not to the earlier date of shipment.

custom and usage prevailing in a particular trade," and that evidence of the meaning of the words "edit" and "change" should be ascertained from their usage in the publishing industry to determine whether the editor had exceeded its contractual right. *Id.* 421 N.Y.S.2d at 205.

Naval Institute contends it should not be bound by publishing industry practices of which it was unaware. A party is bound by trade usage if it knows *or has reason to know* of the usage. *See Flower City Painting Contractors, Inc. v. Gumina Constr. Co.*, 591 F.2d 162, 165 (2d Cir.1979). Where a party is engaged in a particular trade, it is presumed to have knowledge of the trade usages in that trade. *See* [UCC § 1–205(3)]; *Du Pont de Nemours International S.A. v. S.S. Mormacvega*, 367 F.Supp. 793, 797 (S.D.N.Y.1972) ("Trade usages sanctioned by the passage of time, are presumed to be within the knowledge of parties regularly engaged in the business"), *aff'd*, 493 F.2d 97 (2d Cir. 1974).

Thus, whether plaintiff did or did not in fact know of the industry practice is irrelevant. It engaged in business in the publishing industry and entered into contracts with other publishers utilizing the conventional terminology of the industry. If Naval Institute was ignorant of publishing terminology and custom, Berkley had no way of knowing it. Plaintiff had engaged in the business of publishing for nearly a century and had previously contracted with Berkley and other houses for paperback licenses. It conducted an auction according to the conventions of the industry (notwithstanding the fact undisclosed to bidders that it needed outside advice as to how such auctions are conducted). Berkley had the right to assume that this conventional everyday contractual reprint license would have the same meaning that it holds for all other participants in the publishing industry. Plaintiff cannot obtain special interpretations of its contracts by afterwards claiming it was unaware of the meaning of industry terminology. * * *

I find that plaintiff has failed to prove its contentions. The defendant has convincingly shown that it acted in accordance with its contractual entitlement. There was no breach of contract and no infringement of copyright. The action is dismissed.

SO ORDERED.

———

The Second Circuit accepted Judge Leval's conclusions that the interpretation of the phrase "publish * * * not sooner than" was a question of fact rather than a question of law, that that term was ambiguous and subject to several plausible interpretations, and that the agreement permitted Berkley to ship large volumes of the book before October. The court, however, reversed and remanded for entry of judgment in favor of the Naval Institute on the following ground:

"There remains the question of whether the Agreement prohibited substantial pre-October 1985 retail sales. The trial court implicitly arrived at a negative answer, apparently viewing that answer as inferable from its finding that the Agreement permitted pre-October 1985 shipping. It does not follow from Naval's constructive knowledge of industry custom permitting early shipping, however, that Naval intended to permit voluminous pre-October sales, and we conclude that in drawing its inference, the court failed to give appropriate effect to pertinent legal principles.

"The court should interpret a contract in a way that ascribes meaning, if possible, to all of its terms, *see, e.g., Spaulding v. Benenati,* 57 N.Y.2d 418, 425, 456 N.Y.S.2d 733, 736, 442 N.E.2d 1244, 1247 (1982); *Restatement (Second) of Contracts* § 203(a) (1981), giving due consideration to the purpose to be accomplished and the object to be advanced, *see M. O'Neil Supply Co. v. Petroleum Heat & Power Co.,* 280 N.Y. at 55, 19 N.E.2d at 679. Where the parties ascribed different meanings to a term, the court must determine whether there was a meeting of the minds, *i.e.,* 'whether either one of them knew, or had reason to know, that the other gave a particular meaning to the quoted words and assented in reliance thereon.' 3 *Corbin on Contracts* § 537, at 45. If neither party knew or had reason to know of the other's interpretation, the court may be forced to conclude that there was no meeting of the minds and that hence there was no contract. *Id.* at 50. Finally, if, after all of the other guides to interpretation have been exhausted and the court concludes that there remain two reasonable interpretations of the contract, with each party knowing or having reason to know of the other party's understanding of the term, the court should as a policy matter, assuming it is clear that the parties have indeed attempted to enter into a contract, choose the interpretation that is adverse to the party that drafted the contract. 3 *Corbin on Contracts* § 559, at 262. The district court's decision did not apply these principles to the question of whether the term 'publish the * * * paperback edition not sooner than October 1985' forbade substantial retail sales of that edition prior to that date.

"In ruling that Naval had no valid claim against Berkley, the court inferred that Berkley was permitted to cause voluminous paperback sales well in advance of the earliest permitted date of publication. Yet it is plain that the words 'publish * * * not sooner than' are words of limitation. The trial court should have sought an interpretation of the 'not sooner than' phrase that would have given that limitation some meaning.

"Naval contended, *inter alia,* that 'publish * * * not sooner than' was intended to prohibit at least pre-October 1985 retail sales. Berkley's position was that license to ship prior to October exonerated it from liability for all ensuing pre-October sales. Thus, Berkley's view, like that ultimately adopted by the district court, was that the "not sooner than" phrase did not require Berkley to withhold the paperback from retail sale prior to October 1985. However, in order to determine whether that phrase did impose such a limitation, the court should have explored whether Berkley knew or had reason to know of Naval's understanding of the phrase. The record here makes clear that Berkley had ample reason to know that Naval intended a prohibition against voluminous pre-October sales. It was the custom in the industry to delay paperback publication until one year after the month of the hardcover edition; it was on this basis that Berkley filled in the October 1985 date on its form. Berkley's three industry witnesses stated that the reason for this 12–month delay was to provide a period in which the paperback edition would not compete with the hardcover edition. One such witness repeatedly referred to this period as the hardcover edition's 'window of opportunity.' Berkley cannot have been unaware that the reason for a softcover licensing agreement's provision for the publication of a paperback edition 'not sooner than' a given date is that sales of the hardcover edition of any book diminish sharply after a less expensive softcover edition becomes available. * * *

"* * * Berkley must be deemed to have had constructive knowledge that Naval intended that there not be sales of the paperback edition of *Red October* during the one-year period in which the hardcover edition would normally be the only edition. And if the Agreement's prohibition on 'publish[ing]' sooner than October 1985 did not at least forbid voluminous paperback retail sales during that period, we would be at a loss to see that the term 'not sooner than' had any meaning whatever. Thus, proper application of principles of contract interpretation requires the conclusion that at the very least, the Agreement's ban on pre-October 1985 publication meant that Berkley was not permitted to cause a sufficient volume of sales of its edition of the Book to allow that edition to become a bestseller weeks in advance of the earliest permissible date of publication.

"Given this view of the Agreement, it is clear that Naval established Berkley's liability. Approximately 400,000 copies of the paperback version were sold at retail prior to October 1. By mid-September Berkley's paperback edition of the Book was already near the top of the bestseller lists of major national bookstore chains. Ranking second or third in paperback sales volume at a total of more than 1,500 Waldenbook and B. Dalton stores for the week ending September 20, the Berkley edition arrived at 100 more stores in these chains alone the following week, and 'sales increased substantially.' 687 F.Supp. at 118. * * *

"We recognize that in most instances, breach of a contractual limitation on publication of the paperback 'not sooner than' one year after the month of publication of the hardcover edition is unlikely to be material. The evidence at trial was that even a successful hardcover edition normally remains popular for no more than three or four months. Thus, the publisher of that edition is usually unconcerned and uninjured by an early release of the paperback edition. But the fact that early publication of the paperback edition is usually uncontested cannot deprive an injured hardcover publisher of the right to enforce the agreed-upon limitation.

"In sum, we conclude that the trial court erred in not concluding that Berkley's paperback edition of *Red October* was 'publish[ed]' within the meaning of the Agreement when significant retail sales of that edition were made to the public. Naval is entitled to judgment against Berkley, and we remand to the district court for further proceedings not inconsistent with this opinion and for the fashioning of appropriate relief. * * *"

———

DE KALB BANK v. PURDY, 166 Ill.App.3d 709, 715–16, 117 Ill.Dec. 606, 520 N.E.2d 957, 963–64 (1988). Plaintiff bank had lent money to the Purdys and as security had taken assignments to the right to receive the rents on several farms owned by the Purdys that had been leased to others. One farm was leased to Myrom Kinzler, a friend and the farm manager for the Purdys. It provided for a rental of $25,000, payable upon the execution of the lease plus "35 bushels of corn per tillable acre, payable in kind at the time of harvest." The Purdys defaulted on the loan and agreed that the bank might collect the rentals on the leases to apply against the loan. Kinzler delivered 62,895 bushels of harvested corn, reflecting the rentals on the 1797 acres he leased, but the trial court held that he did not meet his contractual obligation, and this was affirmed on appeal:

"The trial court found the lease ambiguous or silent on several issues involved in computing the amount of rent due. First, the term 'corn' was found to be ambiguous because the industry custom concerning the type of lease implied corn meant No. 2 corn as opposed to wet corn, the difference being that No. 2 corn is the standard in which corn as a commodity is traded or business transacted. Wet corn has a higher moisture content, and thus a bushel of wet corn is approximately 15% heavier than No. 2 corn with the consequence that before being sold, a bushel of wet corn must be processed into No. 2 quality corn before it is marketable or wet corn would be discounted by the costs incurred to process it into No. 2 corn. In addition, the drying of wet corn to No. 2 corn results in shrinkage so that in practice a bushel of wet corn contains less than a bushel of No. 2 corn. In the instant case, the difference between the wet corn delivered under the lease by Kinzler and the No. 2 corn found by the court to be due under the lease, was 7,849.25 bushels. This represented the difference between the 62,895 bushels of wet corn Kinzler delivered under the lease and the 55,045.75 bushels which resulted after processing to No. 2 corn. At $2.61 per bushel the difference in rent amounted to $20,486.54.
* * *

"Defendants argue that the trial court reformed the contract under the guise of interpreting the contract. Their argument is without merit. The trial court properly found latent ambiguities to exist.
* * *

"In the instant case, all of the experts, and even defendants, testified to the customary and standard usage of No. 2 corn in the industry. The experts testified that unless a landlord was in the feed or cattle business, he would have no reason to want wet corn. All the testimony of the experts indicated that the value of corn was determined relative to the No. 2 standard. Defendants testified they meant wet corn. The trial court was in the best position to assess the credibility of the testimony. In light of the overwhelming testimony as to the standard reference of corn to mean No. 2 corn and not wet corn, the trial court's finding was not against the manifest weight of the evidence."

RESTATEMENT, SECOND, CONTRACTS § 202:

Illustration:

11. A contract for the sale of horsemeat scraps calls for "minimum 50% protein." As both parties know, by a usage of the business in which they are engaged, 49.5 per cent is treated as the equivalent of 50 per cent. The contract is to be interpreted in accordance with the usage.

RESTATEMENT, SECOND, CONTRACTS § 220:

Illustration:

8. A leases a rabbit warren to B. The written lease contains a covenant that at the end of the term A will buy and B will sell the rabbits at "60£ per thousand." The parties contract with reference to a local usage that 1,000 rabbits means 100 dozen. The usage is part of the contract.

RESTATEMENT, SECOND, CONTRACTS § 202:

(1) Words and other conduct are interpreted in the light of all the circumstances, and if the principal purpose of the parties is ascertainable it is given great weight.

(2) A writing is interpreted as a whole, and all writings that are part of the same transaction are interpreted together.

(3) Unless a different intention is manifested,

(a) where language has a generally prevailing meaning, it is interpreted in accordance with that meaning;

(b) technical terms and words of art are given their technical meaning when used in a transaction within their technical field.

(4) Where an agreement involves repeated occasions for performance by either party with knowledge of the nature of the performance and opportunity for objection to it by the other, any course of performance accepted or acquiesced in without objection is given great weight in the interpretation of the agreement.

(5) Wherever reasonable, the manifestations of intention of the parties to a promise or agreement are interpreted as consistent with

each other and with any relevant course of performance, course of dealing, or usage of trade.

Illustrations:

9. A leases restaurant premises to B. The lease provides that A will pay for electricity and that B will "pay for gas or fuel used in the preparation of food." In the absence of contrary indication, "fuel" should be read not to include electricity.

10. The facts being otherwise as stated in Illustration 9, there is a local usage in the restaurant trade that "fuel" includes electricity used in cooking. In the absence of contrary indication, "fuel" may be read in accordance with the usage. But a provision in the lease that if B installs a new electric range he will also install a special meter and pay for electricity used by the range would show that the parties did not adopt the local usage.

RESTATEMENT, SECOND, CONTRACTS § 203:

In the interpretation of a promise or agreement or a term thereof, the following standards of preference are generally applicable:

(a) an interpretation which gives a reasonable, lawful, and effective meaning to all the terms is preferred to an interpretation which leaves a part unreasonable, unlawful, or of no effect;

(b) express terms are given greater weight than course of performance, course of dealing, and usage of trade, course of performance is given greater weight than course of dealing or usage of trade, and course of dealing is given greater weight than usage of trade;

(c) specific terms and exact terms are given greater weight than general language;

(d) separately negotiated or added terms are given greater weight than standardized terms or other terms not separately negotiated.

RESTATEMENT, SECOND, CONTRACTS § 205:

Every contract imposes upon each party a duty of good faith and fair dealing in its performance and its enforcement.

RESTATEMENT, SECOND, CONTRACTS § 206:

In choosing among the reasonable meanings of a promise or agreement or a term thereof, that meaning is generally preferred which operates against the party who supplies the words or from whom a writing otherwise proceeds.

―――――――

With regard to the Uniform Commercial Code's standards of "course of dealing," "usage of trade" and "course of performance," see UCC §§ 1–205, 2–208. See also UCC § 2–202, comment 2.

Ambiguity and Vagueness in Drafting Contracts

This note considers the situation where a contractual document is being negotiated between two parties, each represented by counsel and each with a fair degree of bargaining power. This is a very common situation but probably not as common as (1) contracts in which one party effectively drafts all provisions of the contract (e.g., new car warranties, life or casualty insurance policies), or (2) contracts in which each party uses his own form and no attempt is made to reconcile the numerous differences between the forms (e.g., most routine purchases by and between large commercial entities).

Every lawyer with experience negotiating and drafting contracts quickly realizes that it is not possible to create, and indeed it is not desirable to try to create, a document that covers all possible contingencies in a way that effectively precludes controversy or litigation. Thus, no matter how good or bad the draftsman, courts will continue to have to resolve disputes over the interpretation or meaning of contracts.* The disputes over the meaning of the "ship Peerless" or "chicken" are illustrative of one class or kind of interpretive difficulty. Problems arising out of the "ambiguity" of language, as in Raffles v. Wichelhaus, may be distinguished from problems caused by simple "vagueness," arising from imprecise terms such as "pink," "heap," or "thoroughly dry," see Young, Equivocation in the Making of Agreements, 64 Colum. L.Rev. 619 (1964). However, problems of interpretation may well arise even if both parties had precisely the same understanding as to the "meaning" of a word or phrase. In the classification of problems below it is important to recognize that the classification is to some extent arbitrary and the categories shade together.

A. *Blind spots.* A very common problem in drafting a contract is concentration on one problem to the point that no attention is paid to other potential problems. While blind spots are most often found in contracts drafted by lay persons without the benefit of legal assistance, they also regularly appear in litigation involving lawyer-drafted documents. A good example is Spaulding v. Morse, 322 Mass. 149, 76 N.E.2d 137 (1947), where in a support agreement for his minor children executed in 1937, a father agreed to pay "for his said minor son Richard the sum of twelve hundred dollars ($1,200) per year * * * until the entrance of Richard D. Morse into some college, university or higher institution of learning beyond the completion of the high school grades, and thereupon, instead of said payments, amounting to twelve hundred dollars ($1,200) yearly, he shall and will then pay * * * payments in the sum of twenty-two hundred dollars ($2,200) per year for a period of said higher education but not more than four years. * * * "

* The basic goal of drafting contracts is, of course, to protect the client's interest without requiring resort to expensive litigation to vindicate one's drafting skill. Thus, clarity and lack of ambiguity are the goals when drafting clauses dealing squarely with specific issues or problems. The basic point of the comments in the text is that the goal of total clarity is, as a practical matter, never fully attainable.

Clear enough, one might say. However the blind spot is the assumption that young Richard will finish high school and then immediately go to college. In fact, Richard finished high school in 1946 and was inducted into the army. With the benefit of hindsight, it is easy to criticize the draftsman for overlooking such an obvious possibility. However, the draftsman's assumption was probably reasonable in depression-ridden 1937 with World War II four years in the future; certainly the oversight is understandable. The court held, incidentally, that the father did not have to keep making the $100 per month payments while Richard was in the army.

The attorney representing the other side may or may not share the draftsman's blind spot. Even if he does not, however, he is unlikely to raise the question since the provision is apt to be more favorable to his client as it is drafted.

B. *Unpredictable future events.* Even if a draftsman wanted to, he could not draft a document that covers all possible contingencies, remote or probable. No matter how vivid one's imagination, in real life unpredictable and unplanned contingencies occur with surprising frequency. New technology may make accustomed ways of doing things obsolete overnight. During the 1970's, two unexpected and very large increases in energy costs made many long-term fixed price contracts ruinous to one party and created unexpected windfalls for the other. Fixed price contracts for future delivery are of course a method of allocating the risk of price fluctuations; before the 1970's, however, energy costs were low and prices stable and many fixed priced contracts were entered into on the assumption that these trends would continue. Should the legal system let people out of such disastrous commitments when the assumptions turn out to be incorrect? Should not the answer to that be "no, that is what free enterprise is all about"? See however, UCC § 2–615, which is discussed at greater length in chapter 5. The occurrence of unexpected events or changes in circumstances usually places great strain on language that was drafted with an entirely different (and often more modest) problem in mind, and they may lead to unavoidable litigation over contract construction. For example, in 1899 the publishers of a popular novel (Ben-Hur) granted the defendants the exclusive right to "perform" or "produce" a "dramatic version" of the novel. Do the defendants later have the right to make a *movie* based on Ben-Hur? (See Harper Bros. v. Klaw, 232 F. 609 (S.D. N.Y.1916)).

C. *Failure to handle remote but predictable contingencies.* Even if a remote contingency is accurately foreseen and the problem is discussed by the attorneys and/or their clients, it is quite possible that the agreement will not attempt to resolve the issue, or may refer to it in a summary and nonexplicit way, such as a "reasonable reduction in price" or an "equitable adjustment," or some other similar phrase. Basically, the hammering out of a clause involves real costs (often called "transaction costs") to the clients; excessive spinning out of remote scenarios that may never occur is therefore expensive and often unproductive. There is, furthermore, the consequence that the contract becomes longer, less manageable, more complex and verbose, and more open to misconstruction. Further, there is always the outside possibility that the parties will not be able to agree on how a remote contingency should be resolved if it actually comes up. It seems sort of silly to give up a mutually advantageous deal because of inability to work out the way to handle a problem that may never arise. Hence, the parties may agree to remain silent on the issue and "handle it in some way if it should arise."

D. *The need for flexibility.* Particularly in periods of inflation, long-term contracts cannot be very specific. Either one party or both parties will usually feel it necessary to provide for some kind of renegotiation or readjustment. The most common kind of provision is that the price will not be fixed but will "be agreed upon from time to time." Similar open-ended provisions may also relate to quantity, quality, shipping times, and other business terms. As described below, the common law courts tended to treat such arrangements as mere "agreements to agree" and no contract at all. This common law "no contract" solution often leads to horrendous injustice (e.g., because that might allow a supplier to cut off your client entirely during periods of scarcity), and attorneys have long striven to draft clauses that contain needed business flexibility on the one hand, and yet are enforceable under common law concepts on the other. In an effort to avoid the nonenforceability problem (and also to put some limits on the possible range of negotiation in the future) a wide variety of drafting devices have evolved: for example, compulsory arbitration in the event of a failure to agree, or "price escalation" clauses based on the consumer price index. Another type of solution is to attempt to formulate general standards: e.g., a "reasonable price" or a "price taking due account of increases in fuel costs." Still another solution is to say nothing at all or expressly leave matters entirely open, e.g., "a price to be agreed upon." *

In considering the attitude of courts to the problems of construction and interpretation, one must separate the rhetoric from reality. As described in the cases which follow, courts state that they are only seeking to find the parties' "intention," that they do not "make agreements for the parties," that an agreement to be enforceable must be "definite," and that, as indicated above, an "agreement to agree" is not enforceable. Every experienced lawyer realizes that the process is more complicated than these statements indicate, that the problem often is that there is no "intention" one way or the other, and that

---

* While the discussion in the text deals only with price clauses, the same problems arise under other clauses as well. Every real estate attorney, for example, regularly deals with the conflict between a tenant, desiring unlimited freedom to assign or sublet, and the landlord, desiring control over who occupies the premises and what type of business he engages in.

courts in a sense "make" contracts for the parties almost every time they resolve an issue of contract interpretation or construction.

CONSUMERS ICE CO. v. UNITED STATES
United States Court of Claims, 1973.
475 F.2d 1161.

Before COWEN, CHIEF JUDGE, DURFEE, SENIOR JUDGE, and DAVIS, SKELTON, NICHOLS, KUNZIG, and BENNETT, JUDGES.

BENNETT, JUDGE:

The uncontested facts of this case present the court with the problem of interpreting, on cross-motions for summary judgment, the language in a written lease in which the plaintiff, Consumers Ice Company, is the lessor and the defendant, the United States, is the lessee. For reasons to be stated, the court grants the plaintiff's motion for summary judgment on the issue of liability alone and remands the case, pursuant to Rule 131(c), to the Trial Division for further proceedings on the issue of damages. The defendant's cross-motion for summary judgment is denied. * * *

The lease in question was executed on October 29, 1954, between the Consumers Ice Company and the Army Corps of Engineers for a parcel of land located in San Mateo County, California. The land covered by the original lease is 8.55 acres near the center of a larger undeveloped tract of approximately 1100 acres owned by the plaintiff. The Army wished to use the property as part of the anti-aircraft facilities protecting the San Francisco Bay area with the Nike–Hercules missile. A radar installation was constructed on the land covered by the lease, which installation is still in operation.

The lease required the Government to pay a nominal rent of one dollar per year, which is all the defendant paid for the use of this property up to 1969 when the plaintiff stopped accepting the checks. The apparent motivation on the part of the plaintiff for entering into this agreement was the fact that the Government had been prepared to condemn the property in 1954 and the plaintiff felt that a lease at a dollar per year was preferable to the loss of the fee interest in the property at that time.

The focus of the problem in this case is the interpretation to be given clause No. 3 of the lease, which reads as follows:

> 3. To have and to hold the said premises for the term beginning July 1, 1954, through June 30, 1955, provided that unless and until the Government shall give notice of termination in accordance with provision 6 hereof, this lease shall remain in force thereafter from year to year without further notice; provided further that adequate appropriations are available from year to year for the payment of rentals and *provided further that this lease shall in no event extend beyond June 30, 1964, or as long as required for Anti-aircraft purposes.* [Emphasis added.]

The problem comes in determining how long the parties intended this lease to run. The plaintiff served notice on the Government in a letter dated May 22, 1969, to vacate the property covered by the lease before July 1, 1969. The defendant responded by a letter dated June 9, 1969, in which it asserted its right under the lease to continue to occupy the premises. Each party interprets the emphasized passage, *supra,* in a different way, which requires this court to sort out the various interpretations and come up with the reading that is most reasonable under the total circumstances involved.

The plaintiff contends the lease expired no later than June 30, 1964. Thereafter, the Government was a mere tenant at will who could stay only as long as the lessor did not voice objection by giving a 30–day notice to vacate. Thus, the Government occupied the premises from July 1, 1964 through June 30, 1969, as a tenant at will and has stayed in possession of the property after that time against the will of the plaintiff for which the plaintiff now seeks a reasonable rental value from June 30, 1969 until the date of judgment. The Government's interpretation of the lease emphasizes the language "or as long as required for Anti-aircraft purposes." It feels the lease is still in full force and effect and will continue to be so until it is determined by the appropriate military authorities that the property is no longer needed for the anti-aircraft defenses of the San Francisco Bay area.

Clearly, the interpretations given the identical language by the two parties are entirely at odds. The language of clause No. 3 of the lease is certainly not a model of legal drafting, and as a result, the court finds itself in the position of determining, if possible, which of the two competing alternative phrases ["this lease shall in no event extend beyond June 30, 1964" or "or as long as required for Anti-aircraft purposes"] controls the duration of the lease. * * *

While it might be like placing the cart before the horse to discuss the matter at this point since no analysis has as yet been made of the possible interpretations this lease might be given, it should be noted that the pertinent language contained in clause No. 3 of the lease was typed into a standard form Government lease, and was apparently the product of negotiations between the parties in 1954. As a result, the *contra proferentem* rule has no application to these facts. Kaiser Aluminum & Chem. Corp. v. United States, 388 F.2d 317, 181 Ct.Cl. 902 (1967). It seems likewise clear that since the contract language was the product of negotiation, neither party may be called to task for failing to seek clarification of what seems to be language that is ambiguous on its face. The duty described in Blount Bros. Constr. Co. v. United States, 346 F.2d 962, 171 Ct.Cl. 478 (1965), and Beacon Constr. Co. v. United States, 314 F.2d 501, 161 Ct.Cl. 1 (1963), to seek clarification of obviously ambiguous contract language is nothing more than the other side of the coin from the *contra proferentem* rule.

The court then is left with the alternative possibilities of either enforcing the contract between the parties by finding, if possible, a reasonable means of assigning a definite interpretation to the language in clause No. 3 without undertaking to write provisions into the contracts when the record fails to show what the parties actually intended, 3 Corbin, Contracts § 541 (1960), or finding that the ambiguity went to the heart of the contract while both parties held reasonable, but different views of what the contract meant, so that it can be said that no contract existed at all because there was no "meeting of minds." Courts will generally not follow the latter course, typified by the "Peerless" case,[4] if there is any reasonable means of giving effect to the contract at issue. The rule of the "Peerless" case has been dealt with more recently by other federal courts in Oswald v. Allen, 417 F.2d 43 (2d Cir.1969), and Julius Kayser & Co. v. Textron, Inc., 228 F.2d 783 (4th Cir.1956), but in neither of these situations had the parties acted for any appreciable period under the terms of the disputed contract. In the case at hand, the lease clearly governed the parties' actions through 1969, a period of 15 years. Such a document should not be lightly found to be without effect at this late date. This court has said before that where there is a gap in an agreement due to the fact that there was clearly no meeting of the minds with respect to a certain issue, that gap will not be "permitted to swallow the whole contract except perhaps where the gulf is far closer to the bounds of the entire consensual perimeter than here." WPC Enterprises, Inc. v. United States, 323 F.2d 874, 879, 163 Ct.Cl. 1, 11 (1963). For these reasons and because this case does not involve an "equivocal" term in the contract, but instead turns on simply deciding which of two competing phrases in a clause should be given priority, the court feels that adoption of the "Peerless" rule would be improper in this case since the contract language can be given a reasonable interpretation by using other devices for interpreting the agreement.

It may reasonably be inferred from the conduct of the parties in agreeing to the language of clause No. 3 in the first place, that each party assumed that the other held its view of what the lease actually meant, but in the face of the almost painful ambiguity of the clause they each kept quite still in order not to make waves or find out for sure how the other party viewed the agreement. It could be said that both parties seemed to be keeping their cards close to their chests throughout the period from 1954 to 1969. The court's problem is to decide which of the interpretations is most reasonable under the total circumstances.

In order to do this, it seems necessary for the court to read one of two additional phrases into the pertinent portion of clause No. 3 by implication if it is to be given a valid meaning. The clause must read: " * * * and provided further that this lease shall in no event extend beyond June 30, 1964, or as long as required for Anti-aircraft purposes," adding *whichever occurs first or whichever comes later*. To read

4. Raffles v. Wichelhaus, 2 Hurl. & C. 906, 159 Eng.Rep. 375 (Ex. 1864).

the clause as the Government would desire [whichever comes later] places the termination of the lease strictly within the discretion of the appropriate military authorities to determine when, in fact, the land is no longer "required for Anti-aircraft purposes." Such a need has obviously existed for some 19 years now and it seems unlikely that such a need would diminish in the near future. The plaintiff argues that whether or not the defendant requires the property for the specified purpose should be a justiciable issue. The court does not agree that it has a role in determining what the military's needs might be in this or any other situation in which informed discretion is so important to making a decision concerning tactical military requirements. In the alternative, the plaintiff would then like to classify the lease, assuming the defendant's view is adopted, as a lease in perpetuity and unenforceable as such. The defendant, of course, does not agree that this lease grants rights to the Government in perpetuity, but it is obvious that if the defendant's view is adopted, the lease is certainly for an indefinite term with the ultimate decision as to the precise duration controlled solely by the defendant.

While it is clear that the terms of the lease do not specifically define a period in perpetuity, it is also clear that the lease could continue for such a long period of time as to constitute, for all practical purposes, a perpetual right to occupation, should the Government feel there was a continuing need for the land for the designated purpose. The fact that a contract leaves indefinite the period for performance will not usually invalidate it or make it unenforceable, but the longer the period for performance the heavier the burden on the enforcing party to prove that the extended duration was intended. Thus, contracts for performance in perpetuity may be valid, but under certain conditions are considered unreasonable and contrary to public policy. 3 Corbin, Contracts § 553 (1960). There is, therefore, an apparent judicial reluctance to interpret any contract to require performance in perpetuity, and some of this reluctance should carry over to situations in which there exists a visible possibility that a contract might extend in practical perpetuity. Such a possibility is a relevant factor in determining which of two competing interpretations is the most reasonable. * * *

The defendant's interpretation of this lease has at least one other difficulty, and that is if the lease was to run so long as the Government "required for Anti-aircraft purposes," why was the June 30, 1964 date placed in the lease at all? The only possible explanation is that if the defendant were to find it no longer needed the property for the designated purpose prior to June 30, 1964, it could use it for some other purposes until that date. Such an explanation seems unlikely and outside the general purpose for which the defendant sought the particular piece of property in the first place.

The plaintiff's interpretation does not seem to suffer from the difficulties inherent in the defendant's view. Plaintiff's view clearly leaves no room for a lease in perpetuity at the defendant's discretion. Under this interpretation the lease would terminate on June 30, 1964, or sooner should the Government cease to have a further need for the property for anti-aircraft purposes. This view is also far more in line with what a reasonable businessman might do in exchanging valuable property rights for a nominal consideration. The Government asserts, however, that while it might be said the plaintiff made a bad bargain back in 1954, which it came to realize in 1969, when it tried to force the Government to vacate the property, the court should not look behind the consideration for the agreement when asked to enforce the terms of the contract. This, as a general proposition, is certainly true where the contract is clear or should be clear to the party against whom the agreement is being enforced; but where the contract terms are as ambiguous as these terms, the court is free to examine the reasonableness of the business transaction in order to determine which of several competing interpretations is most reasonable and likely under the total circumstances including the business realities of the case. *See* 3 Corbin, Contracts § 553 (1960). * * *

For all of the reasons discussed, the court feels the plaintiff's interpretation of this lease is the most reasonable under the total circumstances. * * * It should * * * be noted that in reaching the conclusion urged by the plaintiff, these parties will be left in roughly the same position they were in 1954. The defendant, if it still has a need for the property in question, can try to negotiate a new and, hopefully, clearer lease with the plaintiff at a reasonable rental for the future, or it can proceed to condemn the property and pay the plaintiff a reasonable amount for the rights received. In neither event can it be said that the nation's defense has been threatened or the Government's interests prejudiced since the Army did make use of the property for some 15 years while paying only $15 for the privilege.

———

HAINES v. CITY OF NEW YORK, 41 N.Y.2d 769, 396 N.Y.S.2d 155, 364 N.E.2d 820 (1977). In 1924 the City of New York entered into a contract with the Town of Hunter and Village of Tannersville to construct a sewage system to serve the village and a portion of the town. The purpose of the contract was to prevent the discharge of untreated sewage by residents of the area into Gooseberry Creek, a stream which fed a reservoir of the City's water supply system in the Schoharie watershed. Under this contract, the City of New York assumed the obligation of constructing a sewage system consisting of a sewage disposal plant and sewer mains and laterals, and agreed that "all costs of construction and subsequent operation, maintenance and repair of said sewerage system with the house connections thereof and said disposal works shall be at the expense of" the City. The contract also required the City to extend the sewer lines when "necessitated by future growth and building constructions of the respective communities." The village and town were obligated to and did obtain the

necessary easements for the construction of the system and sewage
lines. In 1958 the City expended $193,000 to rehabilitate and expand
the treatment plant and facilities. By 1975, the average flow of the
plant had increased from an initial figure of 118,000 gallons per day to
over 600,000 gallons daily and the plant was "operating substantially in
excess of design capacity." Haines, the owner of 50 undeveloped
residential lots applied to the City for permission to connect houses
which he intended to construct on the lots to the existing sewer lines.
The City refused permission on the ground that the system would not
bear any significant additional "loadings," which might result in inadequate treatment of all the sewage and consequently harm the City's
water supply. The City also argued that it had no obligation to further
expand the plant to accommodate new construction. Haines then
brought suit for declaratory and injunctive relief arguing that the 1924
agreement was perpetual in duration and obligated the city to expend
additional capital funds to accommodate the present and future needs
of the municipalities, which intervened in the law suit and were joined
as plaintiffs. The court held for the City of New York:

"We conclude that the city is presently obligated to maintain the
existing plant but is not required to expand that plant or construct any
new facilities to accommodate plaintiff's substantial, or any other,
increased demands on the sewage system. The initial problem encountered in ascertaining the nature and extent of the city's obligation
pursuant to the 1924 agreement, is its duration. We reject, as did the
courts below, the plaintiff's contention that the city is perpetually
bound under the agreement. The contract did not expressly provide for
perpetual performance and both the trial court and the Appellate
Division found that the parties did not so intend. Under these circumstances, the law will not imply that a contract calling for continuing
performance is perpetual in duration. Town of Readsboro v. Hoosac
Tunnel & Wilmington R. R. Co., 2 Cir., 6 F.2d 733 [L. Hand, J.]; 1
Williston, Contracts [3d ed.], § 38, p. 113. On the other hand, the city's
contention that the contract is terminable at will because it provides
for no express duration should also be rejected. In the absence of an
express term fixing the duration of a contract, the courts may inquire
into the intent of the parties and supply the missing term if a duration
may be fairly and reasonably fixed by the surrounding circumstances
and the parties' intent. It is generally agreed that where a duration
may be fairly and reasonably supplied by implication, a contract is not
terminable at will (1 Williston, *op. cit.*, p. 112; see, also, Restatement,
Contracts 2d [§ 204]). While we have not previously had occasion to
apply it, the weight of authority supports the related rule that where
the parties have not clearly expressed the duration of a contract, the
courts will imply that they intended performance to continue for a
reasonable time.

"For compelling policy reasons, this rule has not been, and should
not be, applied to contracts of employment or exclusive agency, distributorship, or requirements contracts which have been analogized to

employment contracts (see, e.g., Clark Paper & Mfg. Co. v. Stenacher, 236 N.Y. 312, 140 N.E. 316). The considerations relevant to such contracts do not obtain here. Thus, we hold that it is reasonable to infer from the circumstances of the 1924 agreement that the parties intended the city to maintain the sewage disposal facility until such time as the city no longer needed or desired the water, the purity of which the plant was designed to insure. The city argues that it is no longer obligated to maintain the plant because State law now prohibits persons from discharging raw sewage into streams such as Gooseberry Creek. However, the parties did not contemplate the passage of environmental control laws which would prohibit individuals or municipalities from discharging raw, untreated sewage into certain streams. Thus, the city agreed to assume the obligation of assuring that its water supply remained unpolluted and it may not now avoid that obligation for reasons not contemplated by the parties when the agreement was executed, and not within the purview of their intent, expressed or implied.

"Having determined the duration of the city's obligation, the scope of its duty remains to be defined. By the agreement, the city obligated itself to build a specifically described disposal facility and to extend the lines of that facility to meet future increased demand. At the present time, the extension of those lines would result in the overloading of the system. Plaintiff claims that the city is required to build a new plant or expand the existing facility to overcome the problem. We disagree. The city should not be required to extend the lines to plaintiffs' property if to do so would overload the system and result in its inability to properly treat sewage. In providing for the extension of sewer lines, the contract does not obligate the city to provide sewage disposal services for properties in areas of the municipalities not presently served or even to new properties in areas which are presently served where to do so could reasonably be expected to significantly increase the demand on present plant facilities.

"Thus, those paragraphs of the judgment which provide that the city is obligated to construct any additional facilities required to meet increased demand and that plaintiff is entitled to full use of the sewer lines should be stricken. * * * "

ACTION ADS, INC. v. JUDES

Supreme Court of Wyoming, 1983.
671 P.2d 309.

Before ROONEY, C.J., and RAPER, THOMAS, ROSE and BROWN, JJ.

ROSE, JUSTICE.

Appellee Kenneth Judes brought this action against his employer, appellant Action Ads, Inc., to enforce a term of the employment contract which required appellant to provide a medical insurance program for appellee. The determinative question on appeal is whether the agreement by Action Ads, Inc. to provide insurance coverage was sufficiently definite and certain to constitute an enforceable contract. We hold that it was not and will reverse.

FACTS

Action Ads, Inc. is a Wyoming corporation with its principal place of business in Cheyenne, Wyoming. On April 23, 1981, the corporation hired Kenneth Judes as a salesman for the Sheridan area. The contract of employment contained the following term:

"In addition, sixty days from your date of hire, Action Ads Inc. will provide a medical insurance program for you and your dependents."

Action Ads failed to provide any insurance coverage, and on November 14, 1981, Mr. Judes was seriously burned in a gas explosion in a mobile home. He brought this action against his employer to recover his medical expenses on the ground that Action Ads breached the employment contract by failing to maintain a medical insurance program for him. The trial court determined that Mr. Judes was entitled to recover the total amount of his medical expenses, $18,824.86, plus costs.

* * *

We perceive the initial question to be whether the contract, as established by plaintiff-appellee, is sufficiently definite to permit the court to determine with reasonable certainty the extent of the promissor's contractual duties. Where the terms of a contract are not sufficiently definite to permit this initial determination, the court lacks the information necessary to rule on the issues of breach of contract, damages, or duty to mitigate damages.

CONTRACT TO PROCURE INSURANCE

It is a general principle of contract law that the plaintiff bears the burden of proving the terms of a contract. *Madrid v. Norton,* Wyo., 596 P.2d 1108 (1979). Where the plaintiff seeks to recover for breach of a contract to procure insurance, the general elements of the promised insurance policy are an essential part of the plaintiff's case.[1] 18 Couch on Insurance 2d, § 74:61, pp. 293–294. The following rule was set out in *Howarth v. First National Bank of Anchorage, Alaska,* 596 P.2d 1164, 1167–1168 (1979):

" * * * In a contract for the procurement of insurance, the party proving the contract has the burden of showing the subject matter of the contract, the risk insured against, the amount of coverage, the duration of the coverage, and the premiums to be paid."

---

1. The instant case and the cases cited in this opinion are concerned with the obligation of one who is not an insurance agent or broker to procure insurance for the benefit of another. A different rule may apply where an insurance broker or agent is involved, since such persons hold themselves out as experts in the field and generally are committed to obtaining insurance on terms favorable to the purchaser. In those cases, an enforceable contract to procure insurance may arise even though it remains to the broker to supply some of the terms essential to the formation of the ultimate insurance policy. See *Maryland Casualty Company v. Clean–Rite Maintenance Co.,* 380 F.2d 166, 167 (9th Cir.1967).

A similar rule was applied in *Forster–Davis Motor Co. v. Slaterbeck,* 186 Okl. 395, 98 P.2d 17 (1939), a case comparable on its facts to the case at bar. There, the employee, following a job-related injury, sued his employer for damages on the theory that the employer had agreed, as additional compensation, to furnish the plaintiff with insurance that would provide the same protection as workmen's compensation would provide. The jury decided that since the defendant had not procured any such insurance, the plaintiff was entitled to damages.

On appeal, the Oklahoma Supreme Court reversed, concluding that the verdict violated the well-established rule that a valid contract must be sufficiently definite to lead to a clear conclusion as to the full duties required to constitute compliance, or to permit the accurate measurement of damages for its breach. 98 P.2d at 18. The court found that the employment contract, as proven by the plaintiff, provided no details concerning the promised insurance policy:

"* * * There was no agreement or statement as to when the defendant was to procure such an insurance policy, or when or whether such a policy was to be delivered to the plaintiff, nor any designation as to the insurance company or the character of the insurance company from which any such policy was to be procured. There was no suggestion as to the length of time any such policy should continue in force or operate, or the term for which it was to be procured in the first instance; nor was anything said as to the details, amounts or provisions to be included in any such insurance policy to be furnished by the defendant.

"In fact, if this contract was made as the plaintiff contends it was, we regard it as a practical impossibility to state what acts on the part of the defendant would constitute a clear or complete compliance therewith; nor can we see any sound or logical rule by which the damage for the breach thereof could be logically and reasonably measured. * * * If the plaintiff thought he was protected by a statement of his employer placing him in the status of an employee covered by the Workmen's Compensation Act, it is * * * unfortunate, for any such promise, if it existed, must be measured by this court for sufficient certainty to justify compensation for its breach. When tested by the applicable rules this promise or contract is wholly indefinite and uncertain and cannot be relied upon to compensate plaintiff for his physical injuries upon plaintiff's theory of a valid contract breached to his damage." 98 P.2d at 19.

The same conclusion was reached by the Ninth Circuit Court of Appeals in *Maryland Casualty Company v. Clean–Rite Maintenance Co.,* 380 F.2d 166 (9th Cir.1967). There, the casualty company, claiming to be subrogated to the rights of the building owners, sought to enforce an agreement by the maintenance company

"'to provide insurance protection' which would have indemnified the building owners against 'any and all claims of any kind and

nature arising out of the window washing operations,' * * *."
380 F.2d at 167.

The appellate court applied Oregon law and concluded that "no promise
of reasonable certainty" existed. The court said further:

> "The only real thrust of any promise, as such can be seen from the
> testimony of [the representative of the building owners], is that the
> insurance coverage provided by Clean–Rite was 'extra heavy' or
> 'complete.' These descriptions are so vague that only speculation
> could support a determination of the precise terms and extent of
> that coverage and resolution of the question of whether or not it
> would afford indemnity against many different types of loss, includ-
> ing that which was sustained here. We therefore hold that the
> alleged contract is, for lack of certainty in its terms, unenforceable,
> and that the district judge properly granted the appellee's motion
> for a directed verdict." 380 F.2d at 168–169.

These cases stand for the principle that in a suit on a contract to
procure insurance, the plaintiff has the burden of proving the elements
of the insurance policy with sufficient certainty to enable the court to
establish damages in the event of breach. The corollary to that
principle is a well-known rule: The measure of damages for breach of a
contract to obtain insurance is that amount which would have been
recovered had the insurance been furnished as agreed. *Mid–America
Corporation v. Roach*, Okl., 412 P.2d 188, 191 (1966).

In the present case, * * * [t]he appellee offered no evidence as to
the risks insured against, the amount of coverage, or any other details
of the "insurance program" that Action Ads, Inc. was obligated to
provide. There was no proof of the insurance carrier contemplated by
the parties. Most important, there was no showing that the injury
actually sustained by Mr. Judes would have been covered by the
insurance program had Action Ads fully complied with the employment
contract.

It is apparent that the pertinent contract term is not sufficiently
definite and certain to permit this court to determine the extent of the
promised performance. Without that information, we are unable to
measure the damages to which the promisee might reasonably be
entitled in the event of a breach. The indefiniteness of the agreement
is due to the absence of any evidence whatsoever concerning the
elements of the insurance coverage that Action Ads was obligated to
provide. Since the plaintiff failed to show to what extent, if any, the
promised insurance program would have compensated him for his
injury, we hold that the agreement to provide insurance was too
uncertain and indefinite to be enforceable.

Reversed.

RAPER, JUSTICE, Retired, concurring.

I am in concurrence with the majority opinion. The only purpose
of this opinion is to enlarge upon that of the majority.

* * * As pointed out in footnote 1 of the majority, we do not apply the same rules applicable to one in the business of selling insurance to one in the position of Action Ads, Inc. carrying on a business other than selling insurance.

In such case the ordinary rules of contract law would apply and are controlling. 1 Restatement of the Law, Second, Contracts 2d § 33 (1979) provides:

"(1) Even though a manifestation of intention is intended to be understood as an offer, it cannot be accepted so as to form a contract unless the terms of the contract are reasonably certain.

"(2) The terms of a contract are reasonably certain if they provide a basis for determining the existence of a breach and for giving an appropriate remedy.

"(3) The fact that one or more terms of a proposed bargain are left open or uncertain may show that a manifestation of intention is not intended to be understood as an offer or as an acceptance."

While the parties appear to agree that there was an agreement that appellant would furnish to appellee a policy of health insurance from an objective point of view by a judiciary called upon to furnish a remedy, the "agreement" was too nebulous, too vague and too uncertain to be a contract. * * * While courts do their best to award damages whenever possible, the impossible is not required. Though contracts are construed most strongly against the drafter, *McGinnis v. General Petroleum Corporation*, Wyo., 385 P.2d 198, 201 (1963), courts will not permit parties to strain construction to bring the contract within that rule, *Reed v. Wadsworth*, Wyo., 553 P.2d 1024 (1976). Courts cannot write a contract which the parties have not made. *Quin Blair Enterprises, Inc. v. Julien Construction Company*, Wyo., 597 P.2d 945 (1979). There must be some reasonable basis for computation in the evidence if not in the contract.

The rule of definiteness is applied to all types of contracts and, contrary to the views of the dissent in this case, the court must find something to hang its hat on before damages can be determined. There is nothing of that sort here. Under the Restatement rule, supra, some employment contracts which are analogous have been decided. In *Douglass v. Panama, Inc.*, Tex.Civ.App., 487 S.W.2d 228 (1972), aff'd 504 S.W.2d 776 (1974), it was held that a statement by the company president when he hired various employees that there would be a salary and a bonus is too indefinite to be enforceable as to the bonus. The corporation paid bonuses when it had profitable years but did not when it had a year of loss. The promise was not considered sufficiently definite to require payment of a bonus in a year of loss but was too vague and indefinite to result in a legally enforceable contract even in the event of a profit. It was held in *Petersen v. Pilgrim Village*, 256 Wis. 621, 42 N.W.2d 273, 274, 18 A.L.R.2d 206 (1950), that an agreement that the plaintiff would be paid a stated salary and that he "would share in the profits of the corporation" was too indefinite as to compensation to establish a valid and enforceable contractual obligation in that there is no basis for computation.   *   *   *

I concur.

BROWN, JUSTICE, dissenting, joined by THOMAS, JUSTICE.

I cannot agree with the majority. Appellant promised to provide appellee a "medical insurance program." However, appellant failed to carry out this promise. The majority allows appellant to use this dereliction to defeat appellee's claim. As a result, appellee gets no recovery for the $18,824.86 he incurred in medical expenses.

The majority talks a great deal about the indefiniteness of the contract. The contract was to provide medical insurance. Medical insurance is not some new and mysterious phenomenon. It should be an unnecessary statement of the obvious that medical insurance provides coverage for medical expenses. The majority seems to say that the agreement between the parties was indefinite because it did not spell out: 1) The elements of an insurance policy, 2) the amount to be received had the insurance been furnished, 3) the risks covered, 4) the contemplated insurance carrier, and 5) the specific injuries covered by the insurance appellant was to provide.

The majority concludes that there was a failure of proof in these indefinite areas of the contract of the parties. It is no wonder that there was a "failure of proof." The majority wants appellee to conjure up an insurance policy where none existed. But, what did exist was a contract between appellant and appellee. There is no indefiniteness regarding appellant's obligation to provide "medical insurance" under the contract.

A contract is construed most strongly against the party who drafted it. *McGinnis v. General Petroleum Corporation,* Wyo., 385 P.2d 198 (1963). Here the agreement was produced by appellant and on its letterhead. Appellee had nothing to do with the language of the agreement. Appellant caused all the indefiniteness referred to in the majority opinion.

Appellee did prove the terms of the contract between appellant and appellee by introducing the letter agreement of April 23, 1981, which was clear on its face: "In addition, sixty days from your date of hire, Action Ads *will provide a medical insurance program for you and your dependents.*" (Emphasis added.) The contract does not state the type of program which was to be provided, only that a coverage would be provided. Appellant, in effect, became the insurer, since the term of the contract was that coverage would be provided. The only uncertainty in this contract concerns the amount of coverage.

In essence then, appellant breached its contract with appellee. As a result, appellant was damaged because he had no insurance coverage. The only question left was the amount of the damage.

———

See UCC §§ 2–204(3); 2–305. Would these sections, if applicable to *Action Ads,* change the result in that case?

WILLISTON, THE LAW OF SALES IN THE PROPOSED UNIFORM COMMERCIAL CODE

63 Harv.L.Rev. 561, 576 (1950).

[After quoting UCC § 2–204(3), the author continues] If a contract does not "fail for indefiniteness," as the section provides, it *is* a contract and there is necessarily an appropriate remedy for breach of it. I should like to insert the word "minor" before "terms" and end the clause with the second word "contract." If parties choose to leave important terms open and nevertheless intend a contract, I think their only reliance should be on business "honor."

RESTATEMENT, SECOND, CONTRACTS § 204:

When the parties to a bargain sufficiently defined to be a contract have not agreed with respect to a term which is essential to a determination of their rights and duties, a term which is reasonable in the circumstances is supplied by the court.

OGLEBAY NORTON CO. v. ARMCO, INC.

Supreme Court of Ohio, 1990.
520 Ohio St.3d 232, 556 N.E.2d 515.

On January 9, 1957, Armco Steel Corporation, n.k.a. Armco, Inc., appellant, entered into a long-term contract with Columbia Transportation Company, which later became a division of Oglebay Norton Company, appellee. The principal term of this contract required Oglebay to have adequate shipping capacity available and Armco to utilize such shipping capacity if Armco wished to transport iron ore on the Great Lakes from mines in the Lake Superior district to Armco's plants in the lower Great Lakes region.

In the 1957 contract, Armco and Oglebay established a primary and a secondary price rate mechanism which stated:

"*Armco agrees to pay* * * * for all iron ore transported hereunder *the regular net contract rates for the season* in which the ore is transported, *as recognized by the leading iron ore shippers* in such season for the transportation of iron ore * * *. *If,* in any season of navigation hereunder, *there is no regular net contract rate recognized by the leading iron ore shippers* for such transportation, *the parties shall mutually agree upon a rate* for such transportation, *taking into consideration the contract rate being charged for similar transportation* by the leading independent vessel operators engaged in transportation of iron ore from The Lake Superior District." (Emphasis added.)

During the next twenty-three years, Armco and Oglebay modified the 1957 contract four times. With each modification Armco agreed to extend the time span of the contracts beyond the original date. Both parties acknowledged that the ever-increasing requirements capacity Armco sought from Oglebay would require a substantial capital investment from Oglebay to maintain, upgrade, and purchase iron ore carrier vessels.

The fourth amendment, signed in 1980, required Oglebay to modify and upgrade its fleet to give each Oglebay vessel that Armco utilized a self-unloading capability.[1] It is undisputed that Oglebay began a $95 million capital improvement program at least in part to accommodate Armco's new shipping needs. For its part, Armco agreed to pay an additional twenty-five cents per ton for ore shipped in Oglebay's self-unloading vessels[2] and agreed to extend the running of the contract until December 31, 2010.

During trial, the court recognized Armco's and Oglebay's close and long-standing business relationship, which included a seat for Armco on Oglebay's Board of Directors, Armco's owning Oglebay Norton stock, and a partnership in another venture. In fact, one of Oglebay's vessels was named "The Armco."

This relationship is perhaps best characterized by the language contained in the 1962 amendment, wherein the parties provided:

" * * * Armco has a vital and unique interest in the continued dedication of * * * [Oglebay's] bulk vessel fleet * * * since such service is a necessary prerequisite to Armco's operation as a major steel producer. * * * Armco's right to require the dedication of * * * [Oglebay's] bulk vessels to Armco's service * * * is the essence of this Agreement[.] * * *."

The amendment also granted to Armco the right to seek a court order for specific performance of the terms of the contract.

From 1957 through 1983 the parties established the contract shipping rate that Oglebay charged Armco by referring to a specified rate published in "Skillings Mining Review," in accordance with the 1957 contract's primary price mechanism. The published rate usually represented the price that Innerlake Steamship Company, a leading independent iron ore shipper, charged its customers for a similar service. Oglebay would quote this rate to Armco, which would then pay it to Oglebay.

Unfortunately, in 1983 the iron and steel industry suffered a serious downturn in business. Thus, in late 1983, when Oglebay quoted Armco the shipping rate for the 1984 season, Armco challenged that

---

1. A self-unloading vessel has the capability to unload without the assistance of cranes and crews standing by on dockside. This capability somewhat lessens cargo capacity but allows the vessel more freedom from docking restraints.

2. The twenty-five cents per gross ton differential was a standard rate charged by Columbia and Oglebay Norton to its shipping customers for use of its self-unloading vessels.

rate. Due to its weakened economic position, Armco requested that Oglebay reduce the rate Oglebay was going to charge Armco. The parties then negotiated a mutually satisfactory rate for the 1984 season.

In late 1984 the parties were unable to establish a mutually satisfactory shipping rate for the 1985 season. Oglebay billed Armco $7.66 ($.25 self-unloading vessel surcharge included) per gross ton, and Armco reduced the invoice amount to $5 per gross ton. Armco then paid the $5 per ton figure, indicating payment in full language on the check to Oglebay, and explaining its position in an accompanying letter. In late 1985, the parties again attempted to negotiate a rate, this time for the 1986 season. Again they failed to reach a mutually satisfactory rate.

On April 11, 1986, Oglebay filed a declaratory judgment action requesting the court to declare the rate set forth in the contract to be the correct rate, or in the absence of such a rate, to declare a reasonable rate for Oglebay's services. Armco's answer denied that the $7.41 rate sought by Oglebay was the "contract rate," and denied that the trial court had jurisdiction to declare this rate of its own accord, as a "reasonable rate" or otherwise.

During the 1986 season, Oglebay continued to ship iron ore for Armco. Armco paid Oglebay $4.22 per gross ton for ore shipped prior to August 1, 1986 and $3.85 per gross ton for ore shipped after August 1, 1986.

On August 12, 1987, Armco filed a supplemental counterclaim seeking a declaration that the contract was no longer enforceable, because the contract had failed of its purpose due to the complete breakdown of the rate pricing mechanisms.

After a lengthy bench trial, the trial court on November 20, 1987 issued its declaratory judgment, which made four basic findings of fact and law. First, the court held that it was apparent from the evidence presented that Oglebay and Armco intended to be bound by the 1957 contract, even though the rate or price provisions in the contract were not settled.

Second, the court held that where the parties intended to be bound, but where a service contract pricing mechanism based upon the mutual agreement of the parties fails, " * * * then the price shall be the price that is 'reasonable' under all the circumstances at the time the service is rendered."

Third, the trial court held that the parties must continue to comply with the alternative pricing provision contained within paragraph two of the 1957 contract. That alternative pricing provision mandates that the parties consider rates charged for similar services by leading independent iron ore vessel operators.

Fourth, the trial court held that if the parties were unable to agree upon a rate for the upcoming seasons, then the parties must notify the court immediately. Upon such notification, the court, through its equitable jurisdiction, would appoint a mediator and require the parties' chief executive officers " * * * to meet for the purpose of mediating and determining the rate for such season, *i.e.,* that they 'mutually agree upon a rate.' "

The court of appeals affirmed the judgment of the trial court. * * *

PER CURIAM.

This case presents three mixed questions of fact and law. First, did the parties intend to be bound by the terms of this contract despite the failure of its primary and secondary pricing mechanisms? Second, if the parties did intend to be bound, may the trial court establish $6.25 per gross ton as a reasonable rate for Armco to pay Oglebay for shipping Armco ore during the 1986 shipping season? Third, may the trial court continue to exercise its equitable jurisdiction over the parties, and may it order the parties to utilize a mediator if they are unable to mutually agree on a shipping rate for each annual shipping season? We answer each of these questions in the affirmative and for the reasons set forth below affirm the decision of the court of appeals.

I

Appellant Armco argues that the complete breakdown of the primary and secondary contract pricing mechanisms renders the 1957 contract unenforceable, because the parties never manifested an intent to be bound in the event of the breakdown of the primary and secondary pricing mechanisms. Armco asserts that it became impossible after 1985 to utilize the first pricing mechanism in the 1957 contract, *i.e.,* examining the published rate for a leading shipper in the "Skillings Mining Review," because after 1985 a new rate was no longer published. Armco asserts as well that it also became impossible to obtain the information necessary to determine and take into consideration the rates charged by leading independent vessel operators in accordance with the secondary pricing mechanism. This is because that information was no longer publicly available after 1985 * * * Armco argues that since the parties never consented to be bound by a contract whose specific pricing mechanisms had failed, the trial court should have declared the contract to be void and unenforceable.

The trial court recognized the failure of the 1957 contract pricing mechanisms. Yet the trial court had competent, credible evidence before it to conclude that the parties intended to be bound despite the failure of the pricing mechanisms. The evidence demonstrated the long-standing and close business relationship of the parties, including joint ventures, interlocking directorates and Armco's ownership of Oglebay stock. As the trial court pointed out, the parties themselves contractually recognized Armco's vital and unique interest in the combined dedication of Oglebay's bulk vessel fleet, and the parties recognized that Oglebay could be required to ship up to 7.1 million gross tons of Armco iron ore per year.

Whether the parties intended to be bound, even upon the failure of the pricing mechanisms, is a question of fact properly resolved by the trier of fact. *Normandy Place Assoc. v. Beyer* (1982), 2 Ohio St.3d 102, 106, 2 OBR 653, 656, 443 N.E.2d 161, 164. Since the trial court had ample evidence before it to conclude that the parties did so intend, the court of appeals correctly affirmed the trial court regarding the parties' intent. We thus affirm the court of appeals on this question.

II

Armco also argues that the trial court lacked jurisdiction to impose a shipping rate of $6.25 per gross ton when that rate did not conform to the 1957 contract pricing mechanisms. The trial court held that it had the authority to determine a reasonable rate for Oglebay's services, even though the price mechanism of the contract had failed, since the parties intended to be bound by the contract. The court cited 1 Restatement of the Law 2d, Contracts (1981) 92, Section 33, and its relevant comments to support this proposition. Comment *e* to Section 33 explains in part:

> "* * * Where * * * [the parties] * * * intend to conclude a contract for the sale of goods * * * and the price is not settled, the price is a reasonable price at the time of delivery if * * * (c) the price is to be fixed in terms of some agreed market or other standard as set or recorded by a third person or agency and it is not so set or recorded. Uniform Commercial Code § 2–305(1)." *Id.* at 94–95. * * *

The court therefore determined that a reasonable rate for Armco to pay to Oglebay for transporting Armco's iron ore during the 1986 shipping season was $6.00 per gross ton with an additional rate of twenty-five cents per gross ton when self-unloading vessels were used. The court based this determination upon the parties' extensive course of dealing, "* * * the detriment to the parties respectively, and valid comparisons of market price which reflect [the] economic reality of current depressed conditions in the American steel industry."

The court of appeals concluded that the trial court was justified in setting $6.25 per gross ton as a "reasonable rate" for Armco to pay Oglebay for the 1986 season, given the evidence presented to the trial court concerning various rates charged in the industry and given the intent of the parties to be bound by the agreement.

The court of appeals also held that an open price term could be filled by a trial court, which has the authority to review evidence and establish a "reasonable price," when the parties clearly intended to be bound by the contract. To support this holding, the court cited Restatement of the Law 2d, Contracts, *supra,* at 92, Section 33, and its comments, and 179, Section 362, and its comments.

Section 33, Comment *a* provides in part:

" * * * [T]he actions of the parties may show conclusively that they have intended to conclude a binding agreement, even though one or more terms are missing or are left to be agreed upon. In such cases courts endeavor, if possible, to attach a sufficiently definite meaning to the bargain.

"An offer which appears to be indefinite may be given precision by usage of trade or by course of dealing between the parties. Terms may be supplied by factual implication, and in recurring situations the law often supplies a term in the absence of agreement to the contrary. * * *" *Id.* at 92.

As the court of appeals noted, we have held that "agreements to agree," such as the pricing mechanisms in the 1957 contract, are enforceable when the parties have manifested an intention to be bound by their terms and when these intentions are sufficiently definite to be specifically enforced. *Normandy Place Assoc., supra,* 2 Ohio St.3d at 105–106, 443 N.E.2d at 164. We have also held that "[i]f it is found that the parties intended to be bound, the court should not frustrate this intention, if it is reasonably possible to fill in some gaps that the parties have left, and reach a fair and just result." *Litsinger Sign Co. v. American Sign Co.* (1967), 11 Ohio St.2d 1, 14, 40 O.O.2d 30, 37, 227 N.E.2d 609, 619.

The court of appeals conducted an extensive review of the evidence presented to the trial court and concluded that the $6.25 per gross ton figure was a "reasonable rate" in this situation. The court of appeals noted that Oglebay presented evidence from Jesse J. Friedman, an economic and financial expert, who testified that $7.44 per gross ton was a reasonable rate for such services. Further evidence showed that Armco paid $5.00 per gross ton to Oglebay for the 1985 season, even though the published rate for that season was $7.41 per gross ton.

There was also testimony that Oglebay quoted Armco $5.66 per gross ton as the rate for the 1987 season. The evidence also showed that LTV Steel, prior to its bankruptcy renegotiations with Oglebay, had paid Oglebay the published rate of $7.41 per gross ton. Evidence also indicated that American Steamship Co. had quoted Armco a $5.90 per gross ton rate for the 1986 season.

The court of appeals concluded that the $6.25 per gross ton figure fell acceptably between the rate range extremes proven at trial. The court found this to be a reasonable figure. We find there was competent, credible evidence in the record to support this holding and affirm the court of appeals on this question.

III

Armco also argues that the trial court lacks equitable jurisdiction to order the parties to negotiate or in the failure of negotiations, to mediate, during each annual shipping season through the year 2010.

The court of appeals ruled that the trial court did not exceed its jurisdiction in issuing such an order.

3 Restatement of the Law 2d, Contracts (1981) 179, Section 362, entitled "Effect of Uncertainty of Terms," is similar in effect to Section 33 and states:

> "Specific performance or an injunction will not be granted unless the terms of the contract are sufficiently certain to provide a basis for an appropriate order."

Comment *b* to Section 362 explains:

> " * * * Before concluding that the required certainty is lacking, however, a court will avail itself of all of the usual aids in determining the scope of the agreement. * * * Expressions that at first appear incomplete may not appear so after resort to usage * * * or the addition of a term supplied by law * * *." *Id.* at 179.

Ordering specific performance of this contract was necessary, since, as the court of appeals pointed out, " * * * the undisputed dramatic changes in the market prices of great lakes shipping rates and the length of the contract would make it impossible for a court to award Oglebay accurate damages due to Armco's breach of the contract." We agree with the court of appeals that the appointment of a mediator upon the breakdown of court-ordered contract negotiations neither added to nor detracted from the parties' significant obligations under the contract.

It is well-settled that a trial court may exercise its equitable jurisdiction and order specific performance if the parties intend to be bound by a contract, where determination of long-term damages would be too speculative. See 3 Restatement of the Law 2d, Contracts, *supra,* at 171–172, Section 360(a), Comment *b; Columbus Packing Co. v. State, ex rel. Schlesinger* (1919), 100 Ohio St. 285, 294, 126 N.E. 291, 293–294. Indeed, the court of appeals pointed out that under the 1962 amendment, Armco itself had the contractual right to seek a court order compelling Oglebay to specifically perform its contractual duties.

The court of appeals was correct in concluding that ordering the parties to negotiate and mediate during each shipping season for the duration of the contract was proper, given the unique and long-lasting business relationship between the parties, and given their intent to be bound and the difficulty of properly ascertaining damages in this case. The court of appeals was also correct in concluding that ordering the parties to negotiate and mediate with each shipping season would neither add to nor detract from the parties' significant contractual obligations. This is because the order would merely facilitate in the most practical manner the parties' own ability to interact under the contract. Thus we affirm the court of appeals on this question.

* * *

Judgment affirmed.

MOYER, C.J. and SWEENEY, HOLMES, DOUGLAS, WRIGHT, HERBERT R. BROWN and RESNICK, JJ., concur.

RESTATEMENT, SECOND, CONTRACTS § 223:

(1) A course of dealing is a sequence of previous conduct between the parties to an agreement which is fairly to be regarded as establishing a common basis of understanding for interpreting their expressions and other conduct.

(2) Unless otherwise agreed, a course of dealing between the parties gives meaning to or supplements or qualifies their agreement.

JOSEPH MARTIN, JR., DELICATESSEN, INC. v. SCHUMACHER, 52 N.Y.2d 105, 436 N.Y.S.2d 247, 417 N.E.2d 541 (1981). A five-year lease of a retail store at an annual rental varying from $500 per month for the first year to $650 per month for the fifth year contained the following renewal term: "The Tenant may renew this lease for an additional period of five years at annual rentals to be agreed upon; Tenant shall give Landlord thirty (30) days written notice, to be mailed certified mail, return receipt requested, of the intention to exercise such right." The tenant gave timely notice of its desire to renew but the landlord insisted that he would do so only if the tenant agreed to increase the rental to $900 per month for the first year of the renewal term. The tenant engaged an appraiser who opined that a fair market rental value for the store would be $545.41 per month. The tenant thereupon brought suit to compel the landlord to extend the lease for the additional term at the appraiser's figure (or such other figure established by the court). The trial court held that the renewal term was unenforceable as a matter of law for uncertainty; the Appellate Division reversed, holding that a renewal clause providing for a future agreement on the rent was enforceable if the parties did not intend to terminate in the event of a failure to agree, and it remanded the case to the trial court to establish the amount of the rental. On further appeal, held, Appellate Division reversed and opinion of trial court reinstated:

"We begin our analysis with the basic observation that, unless otherwise mandated by law (e.g., residential emergency rent control statutes), a contract is a private 'ordering' in which a party binds himself to do, or not to do, a particular thing (Fletcher v. Peck, 6 Cranch [10 U.S.] 87, 136; 3 L.Ed. 162. Hart and [Sachs], Legal Process, 147–148 [1958]). This liberty is no right at all if it is not accompanied by freedom not to contract. The corollary is that, before one may secure redress in our courts because another has failed to honor a promise, it must appear that the promisee assented to the obligation in question.

"It also follows that, before the power of law can be invoked to enforce a promise, it must be sufficiently certain and specific so that what was promised can be ascertained. Otherwise, a court, in intervening, would be imposing its own conception of what the parties should or might have undertaken, rather than confining itself to the implementation of a bargain to which they have mutually committed themselves. Thus, definiteness as to material matters is of the very essence in contract law. Impenetrable vagueness and uncertainty will not do (1 Corbin, Contracts, § 95, Contracts, § 301; Restatement, Contracts 2d, [§ 33] Comment a).

"Dictated by these principles, it is rightfully well settled in the common law of contracts in this State that a mere agreement to agree, in which a material term is left for future negotiations, is unenforceable. * * *

"This is not to say that the requirement for definiteness in the case before us now could only have been met by explicit expression of the rent to be paid. The concern is with substance, not form. It certainly would have sufficed, for instance, if a methodology for determining the rent was to be found within the four corners of the lease, for a rent so arrived at would have been the end product of agreement between the parties themselves. Nor would the agreement have failed for indefiniteness because it invited recourse to an objective extrinsic event, condition or standard on which the amount was made to depend. All of these, *inter alia*, would have come within the embrace of the maxim that what can be made certain is certain (9 Coke, 47a). (Cf. Backer Mgt. Corp. v. Acme Quilting Co., 46 N.Y.2d 211, 219, 413 N.Y.S.2d 135, 385 N.E.2d 1062 [escalation of rent keyed to building employees' future wage increases]; City of Hope v. Fisk Bldg. Assoc., 63 A.D.2d 946, 406 N.Y.S.2d 472 [rental increase to be adjusted for upward movement in US Consumer Price Index]; see, generally, 87 A.L.R.3d 986; Lease Provisions Providing for Rent Adjustment Based on Event or Formula Outside Control of Parties.)

"But the renewal clause here in fact contains no such ingredients. Its unrevealing, unamplified language speaks to no more than 'annual rentals to be agreed upon'. Its simple words leave no room for legal construction or resolution of ambiguity. Neither tenant nor landlord is bound to any formula. There is not so much as a hint at a commitment to be bound by the 'fair market rental value' which the tenant's expert reported or the 'reasonable rent' the Appellate Division would impose, much less any definition of either. Nowhere is there an inkling that either of the parties directly or indirectly assented, upon accepting the clause, to subordinate the figure on which it ultimately would insist, to one fixed judicially, as the Appellate Division decreed be done, or, for that matter, by an arbitrator or other third party.

"Finally, in this context, we note that the tenant's reliance on May Metropolitan Corp. v. May Oil Burner Corp., 290 N.Y. 260, 49 N.E.2d 13 is misplaced. There the parties had executed a franchise agreement for the sale of oil burners. The contract provided for annual renewal, at which time each year's sales quota was 'to be mutually agreed upon'. In holding that the defendant's motion for summary judgment should have been denied, the court indicated that the plaintiff should be given an opportunity to establish that a series of annual renewals had ripened into a course of dealing from which it might be possible to give meaning to an otherwise uncertain term. This decision, in the more fluid sales setting in which it occurred, may be seen as a precursor to the subsequently enacted Uniform Commercial Code's treatment of open terms in contracts for the sale of goods (see Uniform Commercial Code, [§ 1–205, subd. [1]; § 2–204, subd. [3]]; see, also, Restatement, Contracts 2d, [§ 223]). As the tenant candidly concedes, the code, by its very terms, is limited to the sale of goods. The *May* case is therefore not applicable to real estate contracts. Stability is a hallmark of the law controlling such transactions."

––––––––

STANCROFF v. BROWN, 76 Mich.App. 589, 257 N.W.2d 179 (1977). The tenant sought specific enforcement of the following clause: "Lessee shall have the option to renew this lease for a further term of Ten (10) years from October 18, 1975 to September 30, 1985, or any other period of time to be agreed upon by lessee and lessor, for such terms and rentals agreeable to both parties ninety days (90) prior to initial lease expiration. Lessee shall have first refusal to purchase said premises of first parties, in the event that the property becomes available for sale."

In the negotiation the principal point of disagreement was not the amount of rent but the term of years. The tenant offered $400 per month and the landlord responded that $300 or $350 was enough, that he had never "held any other tenant up as far as price." However, the landlord was adamant that ten years was too long. Held, the landlord was obliged to accept a reasonable rental for a term of 10 years, no shorter period having been agreed to. The court stated:

"Anno: Validity and enforceability of provision for renewal of lease at rental to be fixed by subsequent agreement of parties, 58 A.L.R.3d 500–517, refers to a majority and minority view:

" '* * * the modern trend seemed to be in favor of relaxation of the strictness of the rule, particularly when only the amount of rental was left to future agreement. Emphasizing that like all other branches of the law, the rules as to uncertainty in interpreting contracts were developing along with changing conditions in business and human affairs, the court stated that at an earlier time in California, a lease of real property providing for renewal upon rental to be agreed upon at the time of the renewal was considered to be void for uncertainty, the court indicating that California no longer adhered to this view.'

"If no standards can be gleaned from the instrument and no mechanics are provided, some jurisdictions hold the contract void for ambiguity and indefiniteness; however, even in those jurisdictions, when the landlord has lulled tenant into a false sense of security by permitting tenant to make substantial improvements to the real estate, the landlord has been held to be estopped to deny that the term 'reasonable' is implicit in the lease. When the Court has a basis for implying a standard, it then proceeds to judicially determine what is a reasonable rental." The court remanded to the trial court to establish a reasonable rental.

———

GENEST v. JOHN GLENN CORPORATION, 298 Or. 723, 696 P.2d 1058, 1067–1068, 1070, 1072–1073, 1081 (1985). The Wilburs owned a restaurant called the "Keg and Platter" which they wished to sell. They employed Crain, a business broker to assist them in the sale. Genest was interested in purchasing the restaurant and extensive negotiations and close bargaining ensued. An integral part of "the deal" was that Genest was to have a ten year lease on the restaurant building with an option to purchase. The terms of the lease and option to purchase were at the center of the negotiation. At the final stage of the negotiation, an "Earnest Money Receipt" was prepared to reflect the terms of the sale of the business and the lease while a "supplement" was prepared to reflect the terms of the option to purchase. This Supplement provided:

> " 'Purchaser is hereby granted the option to purchase the real property on the following terms and conditions: Purchase price to be $425,000 with credit of 10% of total lease payments during the life of the lease being allowed as a credit against the purchase price. Option to purchase may not be exercised for a period of five years. Down payment and principal payment may not exceed 29% in year option is exercised.' "

On February 29, 1972, the Wilburs signed the Receipt and signed the supplement for the Keg & Platter Corporation. The court then describes what followed:

"Crain then took the Receipt and supplement to plaintiff, who would not agree without further change. Crain prepared another supplement that, among other things, specified, 'Credit on lease fees paid to be increased from 10% to 15%.' That supplement was dated March 1, 1972, and was signed as 'Approved' by the Wilburs and plaintiff. By their terms, the supplements were to be attached to and become a part of the Receipt.

"The Wilburs undertook to have their lawyer prepare a lease and a contract of sale. John Wilbur, without any discussion of the matter with plaintiff or securing his prior approval, told the lawyer to change the option price to 'not less than $425,000.' That part of the lease was drawn to read as follows:

> " '(23) *Option to Purchase Real Property.* Lessee submits to Lessor its option to purchase the real property upon which the Keg

& Platter is located and adjacent property which presently is owned by the Lessor. Said option proposed by Lessee shall be not less than $425,000.00 and said option may be exercised by Lessee at any time after five years from the date of this agreement, and while this lease is in force and effect. The terms of Lessee's option to purchase said real property provide in part, that no more than twenty-nine percent (29%) of the total purchase price shall be paid as a down payment during the year the option is exercised; also, under the terms of this lease, Lessee shall have as a credit for the purchase of said real property an amount of fifteen percent (15%) of the total lease payments made to the date of Lessee's purchase of the real property, to apply to the purchase price.'

"When Crain presented the lease to plaintiff, plaintiff drew Crain's attention to the words 'not less than $425,000.00' and inquired as to the "significance" of that language. Crain told him that it was not significant 'because the purchase price was specifically spelled out in the sales agreement and the exhibits attached thereto as $425,000.' " * * *

"Approximately four years later plaintiff orally told the Wilburs that he desired to exercise the option in accordance with the Sale Agreement. * * *"

The Wilburs insisted on a right to renegotiate upward the option price. After negotiations broke down, Genest brought suit for specific performance. The Court held that the "Supplement" controlled and the option price was therefore $425,000, and not subject to negotiation, but that the option agreement as set forth in the "Supplement" was too indefinite to be specifically enforced:

"What we have is an option to purchase real property for $425,000, of which no more than 29% could be paid 'in year option is exercised,' and against which the optionee would have credit for 15% of the lease payments. Obviously, the parties had not reached agreement on the following items that we have concluded are material and important rather than being minor or mere details:

"(1) What did the parties intend to be the 'year' to which the 29% limitation applies? More than one possibility comes to mind. It could have been intended to be the twelve-month period commencing on the date of first payment on the purchase price. It could have been intended to be the number of the calendar year in which the first payment was made. Obviously, plaintiff chose, after the fact, so to interpret it when he tendered 29% in 1978 and expressed his intention to pay the balance in 1979 on a date less than a month after the tender. On the other hand, at the time of making the contract, the corporation that owned the real property may have intended to fix the year for purposes of its taxable or fiscal year. (There is evidence that in connection with the sale of the business the corporation that owned the business did intend to establish a fiscal year for business and tax purposes that would hinge on the date of sale of the business and payment of the 29%.) [13]

"(2) What did the parties intend at the time of making the contract as to the right or obligation to finance the balance of the purchase price? Their contract is silent in this respect.

"(3) What did the parties intend at the time of making the contract would be the form of the sale? Land sale contract? Deed with note and mortgage back? Trust deed? The contract is silent.

"(4) What did the parties intend at the time of making the contract to govern the fixing of the interest rate on the unpaid balance after an initial payment in any amount up to 29% in the year the option would be exercised? The contract is silent.

"(5) What did the parties intend at the time of making the contract concerning the subordination of existing liens? There is some, albeit puzzling, evidence in the record indicating that the property was encumbered by a mortgage.

"With those unanswered questions in mind, we now turn to a review of the decisions on which the plaintiff, the Court of Appeals and the dissent in this court rely to support the remedy of specific performance. * * *

"In *Southworth v. Oliver,* 284 Or. 361, 587 P.2d 994 (1978), the purchaser sought specific performance of a claimed contract for the sale of real property. A writing sent by defendants to plaintiff fixed the asking price and provided for 29% of that price as down payment, with the balance to be paid 'over 5 years at 8% interest.' Plaintiff wrote to defendants that plaintiff accepted the offer. Later when defendants refused to proceed with sale of the property to plaintiff, plaintiff brought his suit. The primary defense was that there was no contract because the writing fixing the price and terms of payment of the balance was not an offer. The fall-back position of defendants was that if there was a contract, it would not permit of a decree of specific performance because of uncertainty 'with the terms' of the security rights of defendants.

"We first held that there was an offer and acceptance for an installment sale. We found that the defendants' real reason for failure to perform was not because of the claimed uncertainty as to the security for performance of the contract. We then affirmed the trial court's decree that the parties would be required to sign a 'standard printed form document * * * in the form of a printed land sale

---

13. I.R.C. § 453(b) made it important to fix the taxpayer's "taxable year" for the purposes of reporting gains on installment sales, which was the most obvious reason for the insertion of the 29% limit. Of course, there would be other important income tax effects turning on the period of time over which the principal balance would be paid. The option did not fix that period. The negotiations, to which reference is made in the text, that occurred between November 30, 1977, and June, 1978, show that the parties were keenly aware of the fiscal importance of fixing that period.

contract on installment payments, with standard form security provisions.' 284 Or. at 380, 587 P.2d 994.

"The only material term supplied by the court was the form of security. We believe it important to note that in *Southworth* we were convinced that the claim of uncertainty was a sham and a pretext for refusing to perform. Even in those circumstances, we now believe that the court went as far as ever it could go in filling in the gaps for the purposes of decreeing specific performance in equity. * * *

"It is true that in *Southworth v. Oliver, supra,* we directed the parties to employ a 'printed land sale contract on installment payments, with standard form security provisions.' 284 Or. at 380, 587 P.2d 994. It is true that in *Howard v. Thomas,* [270 Or. 6, 526 P.2d 552 (1974)], this court affirmed the decree of the trial court requiring the seller to accept as his security 'a first mortgage prepared on Stevens–Ness [a purveyor of legal forms in the State of Oregon] form No. 105A.' A majority of this court believes those portions of those decisions to have been at least unfortunate.

"If a contractual obligation is sufficiently definite in its material terms to support a judgment in equity for specific performance, the court should be able to draw the judgment so as to set forth specifically those terms. The directive to the parties to employ the 'standard provisions' of a 'printed land sale contract' appears to be a confession that the court has not discovered the material terms of the agreement that the court is ordering to be enforced. The court's directive itself is hardly specific. There are many printed land sale, installment payment contracts with divers forms of security provisions. Just to mention a few places in which such contracts may be found, we note: 16 Am. Jur. Legal Forms 2d (rev.) (containing some 400 pages concerned with Real Estate Sales Contract forms); Modern Legal Forms (West Publishing Company 1969) (containing almost 300 pages of forms concerning Sale and Purchase of Land); 8 Nichols, Cyclopedia of Legal Forms, Annotated (1980) (containing approximately 200 pages of forms dealing with Sales and Exchanges of Real Estate); and Stevens–Ness forms found in many stationery and book stores in Oregon. A directive to enter into a form contract or mortgage without specifying which one may well result in simply sending the parties off to a new area of disagreement as they each weigh the advantages and disadvantages to themselves of the various printed forms.

"In *Howard v. Thomas, supra,* the decree did direct the parties to a specific form. One immediately perceives a danger in doing that. The court has placed its imprimatur on that form, but it may well be that future litigation will arise, even among the same parties, in which the meaning, indeed the very legality, of those printed provisions may be in issue. What does the court that has approved that form then do?

"We conclude that judgments for specific performance should themselves spell out what a party is being ordered to do. That would ensure the attention of the court to whether the pleadings and the evidence support any particular text in the judgment."

Four justices concurred in this opinion. Three justices dissented on the ground that the omitted terms cited by the majority were either not material or could be inferred from the prior negotiations of the parties. With respect to the possible differences of various forms, the dissent stated:

"I would hold that in this case the parties be required to execute a standard land sale contract. If there is any dispute as to the form of land sale contract, I would allow the trial judge to make that choice on remand." [8]

———

In Southworth v. Oliver, 284 Or. 361, 587 P.2d 994 (1978), discussed and limited in *Genest,* Oliver and Southworth were ranchers in Bear Valley, Oregon. Oliver decided to sell his Bear Valley ranch and, on May 20, 1976, stopped by Southworth's ranch to see if Southworth was interested in buying it. Southworth replied that he was "very interested" in the land. No price or terms were discussed, and the conversation terminated with the understanding, in the words of Southworth, "[t]hat he would develop and determine value and price and I would make an investigation to determine whether or not I could find the money and get everything arranged for a purchase. In other words, he was going to do A and then I would do B." Oliver recalled the conversation as concluding that "whenever we got this information together we were going to send it to him [Southworth] and some of my neighbors and give them first chance at it." On June 13, 1976, Southworth called Oliver and asked if he was still planning on selling; Oliver replied that he was still interested but had been delayed in getting information together.

On June 17, 1976, Oliver sent to Southworth and to three other neighbors the following letter and attachment:

"Enclosed please find the information about the ranch sales that I had discussed with you previously.

"These prices are the market value according to the records of the Grant County Assessor.

"Please contact me if there are any questions."

8. I agree with the majority that this court should not put its stamp of approval on any particular form of sales contract. That should be left for the trial court to determine under the particular circumstances of each individual case. The briefs in Howard v. Thomas, 270 Or. 6, 526 P.2d 552 (1974), disclose that the trial court ordered the defendants to accept a "first mortgage prepared on Stevens–Ness Form No. 105A" because the plaintiff buyer had tendered a mortgage on that particular form and it was not objected to by sellers.

There were two enclosures with that letter. The first was as follows:

"JOSEPH C. and ARLENE G. OLIVER
200 Ford Road
John Day, OR 97845

"Selling approximately 2933 Acres in Grant County in T. 16 S., R. 81 E., W./M. near Seneca, Oregon at the assessed market value of:

LAND	$806,409
IMPROVEMENTS	18,010
Total	$824,419

"Terms available—29% down—balance over 5 years at 8% interest. Negotiate sale date for December 1, 1976 or January 1, 1977.

"Available after hay is harvested and arrangements made for removal of hay, equipment and supplies.

"ALSO: Selling

"Little Bear Creek allotment permit 100   head @ $225
"Big Bear Creek allotment permit 200   head @ $250"

On June 21, after receiving the letter, Southworth responded, "I accept your offer." Oliver responded on June 24, "You have misconstrued our prior negotiations * * *. That was not made as or intended to be a firm offer of sale. * * * The memorandum of ours was for informational purposes only and as a starting point for further negotiation between us and you and the others also interested in the properties. It is also impossible to tell from the attachment to our letter * * * as to the legal description of the lands to be sold, and would not in any event constitute an enforceable contract." On these facts the court held the letter of June 17 was an offer to sell the Bear Creek ranch, Southworth's letter of June 17 was an acceptance, and Southworth was entitled to specific performance, the court to designate a "standard printed form contract."

Can an argument be made that the Supreme Court of Oregon got both of these cases wrong on their facts?

INTERWAY, INC. v. ALAGNA

Illinois Court of Appeals, First District, 1980.
85 Ill.App.3d 1094, 41 Ill.Dec. 117, 407 N.E.2d 615.

PERLIN, PRESIDING JUSTICE:

Plaintiff filed a contract action against defendants seeking damages, specific performance and injunctive relief. Defendants filed a motion to dismiss the complaint for failure to state a cause of action * * *. The trial court granted defendant's motion * * *. For the reasons hereinafter set forth, we affirm the action of the circuit court of Cook County.

The facts, as pleaded, are not disputed. Defendant, Matthew J. Alagna, Sr., is the President and principal shareholder of Trailer Leasing Corporation, Inc., (TLC) a Delaware Corporation engaged in the business of leasing trailers. Prior to March 1978, Alagna engaged the services of the brokerage firm of Clements, Garvey and Dole "to seek out prospective purchasers and otherwise assist in the negotiation and consummation of" a sale of the assets of TLC. Pursuant thereto, Clements, Garvey and Dole informed plaintiff, Interway, Inc., that the stock of TLC owned by Alagna was "available for purchase." Interway responded that they were interested in acquiring Alagna's stock and subsequently conducted an extensive analysis of TLC. Thereafter, the Board of Directors of Interway authorized officers of that corporation "to negotiate and consummate the purchase of Alagna's stock." On July 27, 1978, after various negotiations between the parties, a draft of a letter setting forth the terms and conditions of the proposed sale was reviewed at a meeting of Alagna, his attorney Donald Gillis, Interway's vice-president and general counsel, Dennis Kenney and the brokers, Clements, Garvey and Dole. On July 28, 1978, the parties met again and discussed changes in their agreement. A "Letter of Intent" was prepared and was signed by Dennis Kenney as an agent of Interway and accepted by Matthew Alagna, Sr. This letter was set forth as Exhibit A of the Complaint and substantively provides that Interway would transfer $1,618,157.13 worth of Interway stock to Alagna in exchange for Alagna's interest in TLC. The document also contained provisions concerning bonuses, brokerage fees, warranties, insurance, non-competition clauses and discharge of a note. Plaintiff's amended complaint alleges that Dennis Kenney, Interway's representative in the negotiations, indicated on July 28, 1978 that "it was his understanding and intent that the letter agreement be contractually binding on the parties," and that neither Alagna nor his attorney indicated a contrary intention prior to the execution of the Letter. On oral argument counsel for Alagna stated that he (Alagna) did not indicate an intent to be bound by the document. This is the sole discrepancy enunciated by the parties. However, the Letter specifically states that:

"Our purchase is subject to a definitive Purchase and Sale Contract to be executed by the parties."

On the following business day, July 31, 1978, Alagna informed Interway that he would not proceed with the execution of the formal contract.

* * *

Initially, we must determine whether a document that embodies the essential terms of a contract, yet recites that a more formal agreement will be executed by the parties, is enforceable in Illinois. Commonly referred to as "Letters of Intent," these documents present the issue of whether the provisions agreed upon in the letter are contractually binding or are mere articulations of the parties' present state of negotiation.

The fact that parties contemplate that a formal agreement will eventually be executed does not necessarily render prior agreements "mere negotiations, where it is clear that the ultimate contract will be substantially" based upon the same terms as the previous document. *Evans, Inc. v. Tiffany & Co.* (N.D.Ill.1976), 416 F.Supp. 224; *Borg–Warner Corp. v. Anchor Coupling Co.* (1959), 16 Ill.2d 234, 156 N.E.2d 513. If the parties in the instant case intended that the Letter be contractually binding, that intention would not be defeated by the mere recitation in the writing that a more formal agreement was yet to be drawn. However, parties may specifically provide that negotiations are not binding until a formal agreement is, in fact, executed. (*Terracom Dev. Grp. v. Coleman Cable & Wire* (1st Dist.1977), 50 Ill.App.3d 739, 8 Ill.Dec. 642, 365 N.E.2d 1028. If the parties construe the execution of a formal agreement as a condition precedent, then no contract arises unless and until that formal agreement is executed. (*Brunette v. Vulcan Materials Co.* (1st Dist.1970), 119 Ill.App.2d 390, 256 N.E.2d 44; *S.N. Nielsen Co. v. National Heat and Power Co.* (1st Dist.1975), 32 Ill. App.3d 941, 946, 337 N.E.2d 387.) Consequently, it appears that although Letters of Intent may generally be enforceable in Illinois, such letters are not necessarily enforceable unless the parties intend them to be contractually obligatory.

The determination of the intent of the parties to a contract may be a question of law or a question of fact, depending on the documents presented. Our resolution of this issue in the instant case ultimately depends upon the characterization of the "subject to" language in the Letter of Intent. If this language is ambiguous, then the determination of its meaning is a question of fact (*Borg–Warner; Itek v. Chicago Aerial Industries Inc.* (Del.Supr.1968), 248 A.2d 625, applying Illinois law) and not properly resolved by a Section 45 motion to dismiss. However, if the language is unambiguous, then the construction of the alleged contract is a question of law (*Nitrin, Inc. v. Bethlehem Steel Corp.* (1st Dist.1976), 35 Ill.App.3d 577, 342 N.E.2d 65) and therefore properly determined by the trial court pursuant to Section 45 of the Civil Practice Act. * * *

In the case at bar, the trial court determined that the "subject to" language in the Letter of Intent was unambiguous and held, as a matter of law, that this language indicated that a formal, written agreement was a condition precedent to the formation of a binding contract. In appealing from the court's order, plaintiff argues that the term "subject to" is ambiguous and that the intention of the parties should therefore be subject to proof at a full trial. "Subject to" may have more than one meaning depending on the circumstances of its use; however, when used in connection with contracts, these words usually indicate a condition on a party's duty of performance and suggest that mere negotiation is contemplated by the parties. * * * We agree with the trial court that the "subject to" language used in this contractual situation was unambiguous and consequently the parties' intent could be discerned from the writing itself.

Interway additionally argues that inconsistencies exist on the face of the document which render the letter ambiguous. In support of this contention, Interway argues that in contrast to the futurity of the "subject to" language, the letter contains other, definitive statements such as "[T]his will confirm our agreement" and "we have agreed." Thus, Interway argues, even if the "subject to" language itself is clear, the letter, taken as a whole, reveals internal inconsistencies and the document is therefore ambiguous on its face. We do not agree. We think that a review of the letter exhibits the tentative nature of any agreement between the parties. In addition to the express disclaimer that the purchase of Alagna's business was "subject to a definitive Purchase and Sale Contract," the Letter contains various provisions which indicate the inconclusive state of the negotiations between the parties at the time the letter was signed. These provisions may more aptly be characterized as "subject headings" than a description of binding obligations. The following provisions demonstrate this lack of specificity:

"(d) Usual warranties including financial warranties on June 30, 1978, financials and bring down warranties.

(e) Opinion of Counsel for Seller.

(f) Non-compete clause of seller and wife. Seller will not directly or indirectly assist his son to compete with TLC."

It is obvious from the foregoing that questions concerning satisfactory warranties, discussions and/or disagreements involving the opinion of Seller's Counsel, and the extent, in both temporal and geographical terms of the non-competition clause, could arise and would require either clarification or additional agreements before the terms would have contractual finality. We also note that the letter requires Alagna to bear the risk of loss until closing and additionally to "cause any minority shareholders to transfer their shares." This latter statement is not amplified, and there is no provision which explains the obligation, if any, in the event that Alagna would be unable to secure the minority shareholders' compliance with the proposed sale. These provisions read in conjunction with the "subject to" language clearly impart an incomplete state of agreement, and the letter on its face gives rise to no ambiguity. Contrary to Interway's contention, the clause, "This will confirm our agreement" when read in the context of the total letter is not inconsistent because the parties had, in fact, preliminarily agreed to some aspects of the potential transaction. However, the clause in question does not establish that the process of negotiation had been completed.

Finally, we will comment on Interway's reliance upon the cases of *Borg–Warner, Itek* and *Evans* to persuade this court that the parties' intention is a question of fact, and that its complaint should not have been dismissed for failure to state a cause of action. In each of those cases the parties had disagreed about the facts surrounding their negotiations and their intentions regarding the writings. Additionally, each case evidences some substantial acts or expenditures on the part of at least one party in reliance upon the fact that they had a binding contract. We are aware of the principle set forth in 17 *Am.Jur.2d, Contracts* § 28 at 366 (1964), where it is stated that:

> "If the parties act under the preliminary agreement or receive benefits thereunder, they will be held to be bound notwithstanding a formal contract has never been executed."

It seems, therefore, that where substantial action has been taken by one party in reliance upon the expressed intentions of the parties, a contractually binding agreement may exist. However, no such "detrimental reliance" as evidenced by the *Borg–Warner, Itek* and *Evans* cases are present here. On the contrary, Alagna's intention to halt the negotiations was communicated to Interway on the first business day following the acceptance of the Letter. Alagna does not dispute the facts as alleged by Interway. The pleadings, taken in the light most favorable to plaintiff, at best indicate that only one party (Interway) was of the opinion that the Letter of Intent was binding on all parties. This does not appear to be sufficient to contradict the plain, unambiguous meaning of the sentence that "Our purchase is subject to a definitive Purchase and Sale Contract to be executed by the parties." Since the intention of the parties must be determined from the face of the writing when such writing is unambiguous, we conclude that the trial court did not err in finding, as a matter of law, that the Letter of Intent in this instance evidenced mere negotiations and was not contractually binding on the parties.

For the foregoing reasons we affirm the order of the circuit court of Cook County dismissing plaintiff's complaint.

Affirmed.

STAMOS and HARTMAN, JJ., concur.

TEXACO, INC. v. PENNZOIL CO.

Texas Court of Appeals, First District, 1987.
729 S.W.2d 768, error ref'd, n.r.e., cert. denied, 485 U.S. 994, 108 S.Ct. 1305,
99 L.Ed.2d 686 (1988).

Before WARREN, JACK SMITH and SAM BASS, JJ.

WARREN, JUSTICE.

This is an appeal from a judgment awarding Pennzoil damages for Texaco's tortious interference with a contract between Pennzoil and the "Getty entities" (Getty Oil Company, the Sarah C. Getty Trust, and the J. Paul Getty Museum).

The jury found, among other things, that:

(1) At the end of a board meeting on January 3, 1984, the Getty entities intended to bind themselves to an agreement providing for the purchase of Getty Oil stock, whereby the Sarah C. Getty Trust would own $\frac{4}{7}$th of the stock and Pennzoil the remaining $\frac{3}{7}$th; and providing for a division of Getty Oil's assets, according to their respective owner-

ship if the Trust and Pennzoil were unable to agree on a restructuring of Getty Oil by December 31, 1984;

(2) Texaco knowingly interfered with the agreement between Pennzoil and the Getty entities;

(3) As a result of Texaco's interference, Pennzoil suffered damages of $7.53 billion;

(4) Texaco's actions were intentional, willful, and in wanton disregard of Pennzoil's rights; and,

(5) Pennzoil was entitled to punitive damages of $3 billion.

The main questions for our determination are: (1) whether the evidence supports the jury's finding that there was a binding contract between the Getty entities and Pennzoil, and that Texaco knowingly induced a breach of such contract; * * *

Though many facts are disputed, the parties' main conflicts are over the inferences to be drawn from, and the legal significance of, these facts. There is evidence that for several months in late 1983, Pennzoil had followed with interest the well-publicized dissension between the board of directors of Getty Oil Company and Gordon Getty, who was a director of Getty Oil and also the owner, as trustee, of approximately 40.2% of the outstanding shares of Getty Oil. On December 28, 1983, Pennzoil announced an unsolicited, public tender offer for 16 million shares of Getty Oil at $100 each.

Soon afterwards, Pennzoil contacted both Gordon Getty and a representative of the J. Paul Getty Museum, which held approximately 11.8% of the shares of Getty Oil, to discuss the tender offer and the possible purchase of Getty Oil. In the first two days of January 1984, a "Memorandum of Agreement" was drafted to reflect the terms that had been reached in conversations between representatives of Pennzoil, Gordon Getty, and the Museum.

Under the plan set out in the Memorandum of Agreement, Pennzoil and the Trust (with Gordon Getty as trustee) were to become partners on a 3/7ths to 4/7ths basis respectively, in owning and operating Getty Oil. Gordon Getty was to become chairman of the board, and Hugh Liedtke, the chief executive officer of Pennzoil, was to become chief executive officer of the new company.

The Memorandum of Agreement further provided that the Museum was to receive $110 per share for its 11.8% ownership, and that all other outstanding public shares were to be cashed in by the company at $110 per share. Pennzoil was given an option to buy an additional 8 million shares to achieve the desired ownership ratio. The plan also provided that Pennzoil and the Trust were to try in good faith to agree upon a plan to restructure Getty Oil within a year, but if they could not reach an agreement, the assets of Getty Oil were to be divided between them, 3/7ths to Pennzoil and 4/7ths to the Trust.

The Memorandum of Agreement stated that it was subject to approval of the board of Getty Oil, and it was to expire by its own terms if not approved at the board meeting that was to begin on January 2. Pennzoil's CEO, Liedtke, and Gordon Getty, for the Trust, signed the Memorandum of Agreement before the Getty Oil board meeting on January 2, and Harold Williams, the president of the Museum, signed it shortly after the board meeting began. Thus, before it was submitted to the Getty Oil board, the Memorandum of Agreement had been executed by parties who together controlled a majority of the outstanding shares of Getty Oil.

The Memorandum of Agreement was then presented to the Getty Oil board, which had previously held discussions on how the company should respond to Pennzoil's public tender offer. A self-tender by the company to shareholders at $110 per share had been proposed to defeat Pennzoil's tender offer at $100 per share, but no consensus was reached.

The board voted to reject recommending Pennzoil's tender offer to Getty's shareholders, then later also rejected the Memorandum of Agreement price of $110 per share as too low. Before recessing at 3 a.m., the board decided to make a counter-proposal to Pennzoil of $110 per share plus a $10 debenture. Pennzoil's investment banker reacted to this price negatively. In the morning of January 3, Getty Oil's investment banker, Geoffrey Boisi, began calling other companies, seeking a higher bid than Pennzoil's for the Getty Oil shares.

When the board reconvened at 3 p.m. on January 3, a revised Pennzoil proposal was presented, offering $110 per share plus a $3 "stub" that was to be paid after the sale of a Getty Oil subsidiary ("ERC"), from the excess proceeds over $1 billion. Each shareholder was to receive a pro rata share of these excess proceeds, but in any case, a minimum of $3 per share at the end of five years. During the meeting, Boisi briefly informed the board of the status of his inquiries of other companies that might be interested in bidding for the company. He reported some preliminary indications of interest, but no definite bid yet.

The Museum's lawyer told the board that, based on his discussions with Pennzoil, he believed that if the board went back "firm" with an offer of $110 plus a $5 stub, Pennzoil would accept it. After a recess, the Museum's president (also a director of Getty Oil) moved that the Getty board should accept Pennzoil's proposal provided that the stub be raised to $5, and the board voted 15 to 1 to approve this counter-proposal to Pennzoil. The board then voted themselves and Getty's officers and advisors indemnity for any liability arising from the events of the past few months. Additionally, the board authorized its executive compensation committee to give "golden parachutes" (generous termination benefits) to the top executives whose positions "were likely to be affected" by the change in management. There was evidence that during another brief recess of the board meeting, the counter-offer of $110 plus a $5 stub was presented to and accepted by Pennzoil. After Pennzoil's acceptance was conveyed to the Getty board, the meeting was adjourned, and most board members left town for their respective homes.

That evening, the lawyers and public relations staff of Getty Oil and the Museum drafted a press release describing the transaction between Pennzoil and the Getty entities. The press release, announcing an agreement in principle on the terms of the Memorandum of Agreement but with a price of $110 plus a $5 stub, was issued on Getty Oil letterhead the next morning, January 4, and later that day, Pennzoil issued an identical press release. * * *

This press release * * * stated:

"Getty Oil Company, The J. Paul Getty Museum and Gordon Getty, as Trustee of the Sarah C. Getty Trust, announced today that they have agreed in principle with Pennzoil Company to a merger of Getty Oil and a newly formed entity owned by Pennzoil and the Trustee.

"In connection with the transaction, the shareholders of Getty Oil * * * *will* receive $110 per share cash plus the right to receive a deferred cash consideration in a formula amount. The deferred consideration *will* be equal to a pro rata share of the * * * proceeds, in excess of $1 billion, * * * of ERC Corporation, * * * and *will* be paid upon the disposition. In any event, under the formula, each shareholder *will* receive at least $5 per share within five years.

"Prior to the merger, Pennzoil *will* contribute approximately $2.6 billion in cash and the Trustee and Pennzoil *will* contribute the Getty Oil shares owned by them to the new entity. Upon execution of a definitive merger agreement, the * * * tender offer by a Pennzoil subsidiary for shares of Getty Oil stock *will* be withdrawn.

"The agreement in principle also provides that Getty Oil *will* grant to Pennzoil an option to purchase eight million treasury shares for $110 per share.

"The transaction is *subject to* execution of a definitive merger agreement, approval by the stockholders of Getty Oil and completion of various governmental filing and waiting period requirements.

"Following consummation of the merger, the Trust *will* own 4/7ths of the * * * stock of Getty Oil and Pennzoil *will* own 3/7ths. The Trust and Pennzoil have also agreed in principle that following consummation of the merger they *will* endeavor in good faith to agree upon a plan for restructuring Getty Oil [within a year] and that if they are unable to reach such an agreement then they *will* cause a division of assets of the company." (Emphasis added.)

On January 4, Boisi continued to contact other companies, looking for a higher price than Pennzoil had offered. After talking briefly with Boisi, Texaco management called several meetings with its in-house financial planning group, which over the course of the day studied and reported to management on the value of Getty Oil, the Pennzoil offer terms, and a feasible price range at which Getty might be acquired. Later in the day, Texaco hired an investment banker, First Boston, to represent it with respect to a possible acquisition of Getty Oil. Meanwhile, also on January 4, Pennzoil's lawyers were working on a draft of a formal "transaction agreement" that described the transaction in more detail than the outline of terms contained in the Memorandum of Agreement and press release.

On January 5, the Wall Street Journal reported on an agreement reached between Pennzoil and the Getty entities, describing essentially the terms contained in the Memorandum of Agreement. The Pennzoil board met to ratify the actions of its officers in negotiating an agreement with the Getty entities, and Pennzoil's attorneys periodically attempted to contact the other parties' advisors and attorneys to continue work on the transaction agreement.

The board of Texaco also met on January 5, authorizing its officers to make an offer for 100% of Getty Oil and to take any necessary action in connection therewith. Texaco first contacted the Museum's lawyer, Lipton, and arranged a meeting to discuss the sale of the Museum's shares of Getty Oil to Texaco. Lipton instructed his associate, on her way to the meeting in progress of the lawyers drafting merger documents for the Pennzoil/Getty transaction, to not attend that meeting, because he needed her at his meeting with Texaco. At the meeting with Texaco, the Museum outlined various issues it wanted resolved in any transaction with Texaco, and then agreed to sell its 11.8% ownership in Getty Oil.

That evening, Texaco met with Gordon Getty to discuss the sale of the Trust's shares. He was informed that the Museum had agreed to sell its shares to Texaco. Gordon Getty's advisors had previously warned him that the Trust shares might be "locked out" in a minority position if Texaco bought, in addition to the Museum's shares, enough of the public shares to achieve over 50% ownership of the company. Gordon Getty accepted Texaco's offer of $125 per share and signed a letter of his intent to sell his stock to Texaco, as soon as a California temporary restraining order against his actions as trustee was lifted.

At noon on January 6, Getty Oil held a telephone board meeting to discuss the Texaco offer. The board voted to withdraw its previous counter-proposal to Pennzoil and unanimously voted to accept Texaco's offer. Texaco immediately issued a press release announcing that Getty Oil and Texaco would merge.

Soon after the Texaco press release appeared, Pennzoil telexed the Getty entities, demanding that they honor their agreement with Pennzoil. Later that day, prompted by the telex, Getty Oil filed a suit in Delaware for declaratory judgment that it was not bound to any contract with Pennzoil. The merger agreement between Texaco and Getty Oil was signed on January 6; the stock purchase agreement with the Museum was signed on January 6; and the stock exchange agreement with the Trust was signed on January 8, 1984.   *   *   *

Texaco argues first that there was no evidence or there was insufficient evidence to support the jury's answers to Special Issue No. 1. The jury found that the Trust, the Museum, and Getty Oil Company intended to bind themselves to an agreement with Pennzoil containing certain enumerated terms at the end of the Getty Oil Company board meeting on January 3, 1984.   *   *   *

Texaco contends that under controlling principles of New York law, there was insufficient evidence to support the jury's finding that at the end of the Getty Oil board meeting on January 3, the Getty entities intended to bind themselves to an agreement with Pennzoil.

Pennzoil responds that the question of the parties' intent is a fact question, and the jury was free to accept or reject Texaco's after-the-fact testimony of subjective intent. Pennzoil contends that the evidence showed that the parties intended to be bound to the terms in the Memorandum of Agreement plus a price terms of $110 plus a $5 stub, even though the parties may have contemplated a later, more formal document to memorialize the agreement already reached. Pennzoil also argues that the binding effect of the Memorandum of Agreement was conditioned only upon approval of the board, not also upon execution of the agreement by a Getty signator.

Under New York law, if parties do not intend to be bound to an agreement until it is reduced to writing and signed by both parties, then there is no contract until that event occurs. *Scheck v. Francis*, 26 N.Y.2d 466, 311 N.Y.S.2d 841, 260 N.E.2d 493 (1970). If there is no understanding that a signed writing is necessary before the parties will be bound, and the parties have agreed upon all substantial terms, then an informal agreement can be binding, even though the parties contemplate evidencing their agreement in a formal document later. *Municipal Consultants & Publishers, Inc. v. Town of Ramapo*, 47 N.Y.2d 144, 417 N.Y.S.2d 218, 220, 390 N.E.2d 1143, 1145 (1979); *R.G. Group, Inc. v. Horn & Hardart Co.*, 751 F.2d 69, 74 (2d Cir.1984).

If the parties do intend to contract orally, the mere intention to commit the agreement to writing does not prevent contract formation before execution of that writing, *Winston v. Mediafare Entertainment Corp.*, 777 F.2d 78, 80 (2d Cir.1985), and even a failure to reduce their promises to writing is immaterial to whether they are bound. *Schwartz v. Greenberg*, 304 N.Y. 250, 107 N.E.2d 65 (1952).

However, if either party communicates the intent not to be bound before a final formal document is executed, then no oral expression of agreement to specific terms will constitute a binding contract. *Winston*, 777 F.2d at 80; *R.G. Group*, 751 F.2d at 74.

Thus, under New York law, the parties are given the power to obligate themselves informally or only by a formal signed writing, as they wish. *R.G. Group*, 751 F.2d at 74. The emphasis in deciding when a binding contract exists is on intent rather than on form. *Reprosystem, B.V. v. SCM Corp.*, 727 F.2d 257, 261 (2d Cir.), *cert. denied*, 469 U.S. 828, 105 S.Ct. 110, 83 L.Ed.2d 54 (1984).

It is the parties' expressed intent that controls which rule of contract formation applies. To determine intent, a court must examine the words and deeds of the parties, because these constitute the objective signs of such intent. *Winston*, 777 F.2d at 80; *R.G. Group*, 751 F.2d at 74. Only the outward expressions of intent are considered—secret or subjective intent is immaterial to the question of whether the parties were bound. *Porter v. Commercial Casualty Insurance Co.*, 292 N.Y. 176, 54 N.E.2d 353 (1944).

Several factors have been articulated to help determine whether the parties intended to be bound only by a formal, signed writing: (1) whether a party expressly reserved the right to be bound only when a written agreement is signed; (2) whether there was any partial performance by one party that the party disclaiming the contract accepted; (3) whether all essential terms of the alleged contract had been agreed upon; and (4) whether the complexity or magnitude of the transaction was such that a formal, executed writing would normally be expected. *Winston*, 777 F.2d at 80; *R.G. Group*, 751 F.2d at 76.

Evaluating the first factor, Texaco contends that the evidence of expressed intent not to be bound establishes conclusively that there was no contract at the time of Texaco's alleged inducement of breach. Texaco argues that this expressed intent is contained in (1) the press releases issued by the Getty entities and Pennzoil, which stated that "the transaction is subject to execution of a definitive merger agreement"; (2) the phrasing of drafts of the transaction agreement, which Texaco alleges "carefully stated that the parties' obligations would become binding only 'after the execution and delivery of this Agreement'"; and (3) the deliberate reference by the press releases to the parties' understanding as an "agreement in principle."

In its brief, Texaco asserts that, as a matter of black letter New York law, the "subject to" language in the press release established that the parties were not then bound and intended to be bound only after signing a definitive agreement, citing *Banking & Trading Corp. v. Reconstruction Finance Corp.*, 147 F.Supp. 193, 204 (S.D.N.Y.1956), *aff'd*, 257 F.2d 765 (2d Cir.1958). The court in that case stated that "if the agreement is expressly subject to the execution of a formal contract, this intent must be respected and no contract found until then." However, the court went on to say that where intent is less sharply expressed, the trier of fact must determine it as best he can. *Id.* at 204–05. Although the intent to formalize an agreement is some evidence of an intent not to be bound before signing such a writing, it is not conclusive. *Id.* at 204. The issue of when the parties intended to be bound is a fact question to be decided from the parties' acts and communications. *See Chromalloy American Corp. v. Universal Housing*

Systems of America, Inc., 495 F.Supp. 544, 550 (S.D.N.Y.1980), *aff'd,* 697 F.2d 289 (2d Cir.1982). * * *

[Nor does the press release] establish, as a matter of law, that there was no contract at that time. The press release does refer to an agreement "in principle" and states that the "transaction" is subject to execution of a definitive merger agreement. But the release as a whole is worded in indicative terms, not in subjunctive or hypothetical ones. The press release describes what shareholders *will* receive, what Pennzoil *will* contribute, that Pennzoil *will* be granted an option, etc.

The description of the transaction as subject to a definitive merger agreement also includes the need for stockholder approval and the completion of various governmental filing and waiting requirements. There was evidence that this was a paragraph of routine details, that the referred to merger agreement was a standard formal document required in such a transaction under Delaware law, and that the parties considered these technical requirements of little consequence.

There is also an arguable difference between a "transaction" being subject to various requirements and the formation of the agreement itself being dependent upon completion of these matters. In *F. W. Berk & Co. v. Derecktor,* 301 N.Y. 110, 92 N.E.2d 914 (1950), cited in Texaco's brief, the defendant's very acceptance of the plaintiff's order was made subject to the occurrence of certain events. The court defined the phrase "subject to" as being the equivalent of "conditional upon or depending on" and held that making the acceptance of an offer subject to a condition was not the kind of assent required to make it a binding promise. However, making the acceptance of an offer conditional, or expressly making an agreement itself conditional, is a much clearer expression of an intent not to be bound than the use of the more ambiguous word "transaction."

Other cases cited by Texaco involved writings that specifically stated that no party would be committed until a written contract was executed. *See, e.g., Reprosystem, B.V.,* 727 F.2d at 260 (draft agreements clearly stated that formal execution was required before the contract would have any binding effect); *Chromalloy American Corp.,* 495 F.Supp. at 547–48 (letter of intent stated that neither party would be committed until a contract was executed). Yet, despite the clear language of reservation in those cases, the parties' intent to be bound was still evaluated as a question of fact to be determined from all the circumstances of the case. *Reprosystem, B.V.,* 727 F.2d at 261–62; *Chromalloy American Corp.,* 495 F.Supp. at 550.

So it is here. Regardless of what interpretation we give to the conditional language in the press release, we conclude that it did not so clearly express the intent of the parties not to be bound to conclusively resolve that issue, as Texaco asserts.

Texaco also contends that explicit language of reservation in drafts of Pennzoil's transaction agreement indicates the parties' expressed intent not to be bound without a signed writing. Texaco asserts that

"Pennzoil's lawyers carefully stated that the parties' obligations would become binding only 'after the execution and delivery of this Agreement.' "

That assertion is not accurate. In fact, "after the execution and delivery of this Agreement" was merely used as an introductory phrase before each party's obligations were described, e.g., after the execution and delivery of this Agreement, Pennzoil shall terminate the tender offer; * * * Pennzoil and the Company shall terminate all legal proceedings; * * * the Company shall purchase all shares held by the Museum; etc. Other clauses in the transaction agreement did not contain that phrase, e.g., the Company *hereby* grants to Pennzoil the option to purchase up to 8 million shares of treasury stock; *on or prior to the effective date*, Pennzoil and the Trustee shall form the merging company; etc.

A reasonable conclusion from reading the entire drafts is that the phrase "after the execution and delivery of this Agreement" was used chiefly to indicate the timing of various acts that were to occur, and not to impose an express precondition to the formation of a contract. *Compare Reprosystem, B.V.*, 727 F.2d at 262 ("when executed and delivered," the agreement would become "a valid and binding agreement"). Again, the language upon which Texaco relies does not so clearly express an intent not to be bound to resolve that issue or to remove the question from the ambit of the trier of fact.

Next, Texaco states that the use of the term "agreement in principle" in the press release was a conscious and deliberate choice of words to convey that there was not yet any binding agreement. Texaco refers to defense testimony that lawyers for Getty Oil and the Museum changed the initial wording of the press release from "agreement" to "agreement in principle" because they understood and intended that phrase to mean that there was no binding contract with Pennzoil.

Texaco cites *Mine Safety Appliance Co. v. Energetics Science, Inc.*, No. 75 Civ. 4925, slip op. at 3, n. 2 (S.D.N.Y., Feb. 5, 1980), an unreported case where the court in dicta characterized an agreement in principle as "a far cry from a final contract." However, the court in that case acknowledged that intent to be bound was a fact issue. A motion to declare an alleged agreement binding and enforceable was denied, because the court found that a question of material fact had been raised on whether the non-movants intended to be bound. In another of Texaco's cited cases, *Debreceni v. Outlet Co.*, 784 F.2d 13, 18 (1st Cir.1986), an *offer* was subject to the execution of definitive agreements of sale, and the agreement itself provided that it would become a binding obligation only after execution. Applying New York law, the court stated that the parties would not be bound until a written agreement was executed *if that was their intention.*

Pennzoil and Texaco presented conflicting evidence at trial on the common business usage and understanding of the term "agreement in principle." Texaco's witnesses testified that the term is used to convey an invitation to bid or that there is no binding contract. Pennzoil's witnesses testified that when business people use "agreement in principle," it means that the parties have reached a meeting of the minds with only details left to be resolved. There was testimony by Sidney Petersen, Getty Oil's chief executive officer, that an "agreement in principle" requires the parties to proceed to try to implement the details of the agreement in good faith, and that that was the case with the agreement in principle with Pennzoil.

The jury was the sole judge of the credibility of the witnesses and was entitled to accept or reject any testimony it wished, as well as to decide what weight to give the testimony. *Rego Co. v. Brannon*, 682 S.W.2d 677, 680 (Tex.App.—Houston [1st Dist] 1984, writ ref'd n.r.e.). There was sufficient evidence at trial on the common business usage of the expression "agreement in principle" and on its meaning in this case for the jury reasonably to decide that its use in the press release did not necessarily establish that the parties did not intend to be bound before signing a formal document.

A second factor that may indicate whether the parties intended to be bound only by a signed, formal writing is whether there was partial performance by one party that the party disclaiming the contract accepted. *Winston*, 777 F.2d at 80; *R.G. Group*, 751 F.2d at 76.

Texaco asserts that there was no partial performance that would indicate an intent to be bound, but conversely, that the conduct of the parties here was inconsistent with the existence of a binding contract.

* * *

Pennzoil points out that Texaco's alleged interference with Pennzoil's agreement occurred scarcely 48 hours after the agreement came into existence, and there was very little time for any performance under the agreement to have occurred. * * *

Other than the preliminary financial arrangements made by Pennzoil, we find little relevant partial performance in this case that might show that the parties believed that they were bound by a contract. However, the absence of relevant part performance in this short period of time does not compel the conclusion that no contract existed. Texaco has pointed out that there was some conduct inconsistent with the existence of an intent to be bound to a contract. But partial performance, and on the other hand, conduct that is inconsistent with an intent to be bound, are again merely circumstances that the finder of fact could consider in reaching a decision on whether the parties intended to be bound. The evidence on the parties' conduct was presented to the jury, which could either accept or reject the inferences the parties asked it to draw from these facts.

The next factor showing intent to be bound is whether there was agreement on all essential terms of the alleged agreement. Texaco contends that numerous items of "obvious importance" were still being negotiated at the time Pennzoil claims a contract had been formed.

* * *

There was sufficient evidence for the jury to conclude that the parties had reached agreement on all essential terms of the transaction with only the mechanics and details left to be supplied by the parties' attorneys. Although there may have been many specific items relating to the transaction agreement draft that had yet to be put in final form, there is sufficient evidence to support a conclusion by the jury that the parties did not consider any of Texaco's asserted "open items" significant obstacles precluding an intent to be bound.

The fourth factor that Texaco discusses as showing that the parties did not intend to be bound before executing a formal contract is the magnitude and complexity of the transaction. There is little question that the transaction by which Getty Oil was to be taken private by the Trust and Pennzoil involved an extremely large amount of money. It is unlikely that parties to such a transaction would not have expected a detailed written document, specifically setting out the parties' obligations and the exact mechanics of the transaction, whether it was to be executed before the parties intended to be bound or only to memorialize an agreement already reached.

We agree with Texaco that this factor tends to support its position that the transaction was such that a signed contract would ordinarily be expected before the parties would consider themselves bound. However, we cannot say, as a matter of law, that this factor alone is determinative of the question of the parties' intent.

The trial of this case lasted many weeks, with witnesses for both sides testifying extensively about the events of those first days of January 1984. Eyewitnesses and expert witnesses interpreted and explained various aspects of the negotiations and the alleged agreement, and the jury was repeatedly made aware of the value of Getty Oil's assets and how much money would be involved in the company's sale. There was testimony on how the sale of the company could be structured and on the considerations involved in buying and restructuring, or later liquidating, the company. But there was also testimony that there were companies that in the past had bound themselves to short two-page acquisition agreements involving a lot of money, and Getty's involvement banker testified that the Texaco transaction included "one page back-of-the-envelope kinds of agreements" that were formalized. The Memorandum of Agreement containing the essential terms of the Pennzoil/Getty agreement was only four pages long.

Although the magnitude of the transaction here was such that normally a signed writing would be expected, there was sufficient evidence to support an inference by the jury that that expectation was satisfied here initially by the Memorandum of Agreement, signed by a majority of shareholders of Getty Oil and approved by the board with a higher price, and by the transaction agreement in progress that had

been intended to memorialize the agreement previously reached.
* * *

Affirmed.

––––––

Texas jurisprudence generally has a strong predilection toward reliance on jury determinations on all controverted issues. Texas also has a "special issues" submission practice that is somewhat similar to special verdicts in other jurisdictions. Following the eighteen week trial in the *Pennzoil* case, the jury was requested to respond to Special Issue No. 1, which asked whether Pennzoil and the Getty interests "intended to bind themselves to an agreement" at the end of the Getty Oil board meeting on January 3, 1984. The following "instructions" accompanied this special issue:

"2. In answering Issue No. 1, you should look to the intent of Pennzoil and the Getty entities as outwardly or objectively demonstrated to each other by their words and deeds. The question is not determined by the parties' secret, inward, or subjective intentions.

"3. Persons may intend to be bound to an agreement even though they plan to sign a more formal and detailed document at a later time. On the other hand, parties may intend not to be bound until such a document is signed.

"4. There is no legal requirement that parties agree on all the matters incidental to their agreement before they can intend to be bound. Thus, even if certain matters were left for future negotiations, those matters may not have been regarded by Pennzoil and the Getty entities as essential to their agreement, if any, on January 3. On the other hand, you may find that the parties did not intend to be bound until each and every term of their transaction was resolved.

"5. Every binding agreement carries with it a duty of good faith performance. If Pennzoil and the Getty entities intended to be bound at the end of the Getty Oil board meeting of January 3, they were obliged to negotiate in good faith the terms of the definitive merger agreement and to carry out the transaction."

––––––

Should the proper interpretation of an "agreement in principle" be a matter of law to be resolved by a judge (presumably on a motion to dismiss, as in *Interway,* or on a motion for summary judgment) or an issue of fact to be submitted to and resolved by a jury (as in *Pennzoil*)? Should it depend on whether the "agreement in principle" may be viewed as "ambiguous"?

––––––

EASTERBROOK, C.J., in EMPRO MFG. CO., INC. v. BALL–CO MFG., INC., 870 F.2d 423, 424 (7th Cir.1989):

"We have a pattern common in commercial life. Two firms reach concord on the general terms of their transaction. They sign a document, captioned 'agreement in principle' or 'letter of intent,' memorializing these terms but anticipating further negotiations and decisions— an appraisal of the assets, clearing of a title, the list is endless. One of these terms proves divisive, and the deal collapses. The party that perceives itself the loser then claims that the preliminary document has legal force independent of the definitive contract. Ours is such a dispute. * * *

"Empro insists on appeal that the binding effect of a document depends on the parties' intent, which means that the case may not be dismissed—for Empro says that the parties intended to be bound, a factual issue. Empro treats 'intent to be bound' as a matter of the parties' states of mind, but if intent were wholly subjective * * * no contract case could be decided without a jury trial, and no one could know the effect of a commercial transaction until years after the documents were inked. That would be a devastating blow to business. Put differently, 'intent' in contract law is objective rather than subjective—a point *Interway* makes by holding that as a matter of law parties who make their pact 'subject to' a later definitive agreement have manifested an (objective) intent not to be bound * * *

"Because letters of intent are written without the care that will be lavished on the definitive agreement, it may be a bit much to put dispositive weight on 'subject to' in every case, and we do not read *Interway* as giving these the status of magic words. They might have been used carelessly, and if the full agreement showed that the formal contract was to be nothing but a memorial of an agreement already reached the letter of intent would be enforceable. * * * "

––––––––

CITY STORES CO. v. AMMERMAN, 266 F.Supp. 766 (D.D.C.1967), aff'd per curiam, 394 F.2d 950 (D.C.Cir.1968). The plaintiff, owner of Lansburgh's Department Store, a major retailer in the District of Columbia, was desirous of obtaining a large store in the Tyson's Corner Shopping Center project proposed to be constructed by the defendants. The Tyson's Corner shopping center was involved in zoning hearings, the outcome of which was uncertain. The defendants offered plaintiff an opportunity to become a major tenant in Tyson's Corner if Lansburgh's would write a letter to the Fairfax county zoning authorities expressing a desire to participate in the Tyson's Corner project. (Similar letters had been solicited from other Washington, D.C. department stores, but those stores refused to express a preference between the Tyson's Corner project and a competing project proposed by another developer.) Such a letter was written, as evidenced by the following acknowledgment from the defendants:

"Dear Mr. Jagels:

We very much appreciate the efforts which you have expended in endeavoring to assist Mr. Gudelsky and me in our application for zoning at Tyson's Corner for a Regional Shopping Center.

You have our assurance that in the event we are successful with our application, that we will give you the opportunity to become one of our contemplated center's major tenants with rental and terms at least equal to that of any other major department store in the center.

> Sincerely yours,
> /s/
> Isadore M. Gudelsky
> /s/
> Theodore N. Lerner"

After the defendants obtained the necessary zoning, they entered into leases with two major Washington D.C. department stores (Hecht's and Woodward & Lothrop) and then decided that it would be more profitable to lease the remaining department store site to Sears rather than to Lansburgh's. In a suit for specific performance, the court held (a) that the parties had entered "an option for an opportunity to accept or reject a lease," (b) the services performed by plaintiff in sending the requested letter "constituted adequate consideration for a valid unilateral contract," and (c) that the option contract so secured by plaintiff was sufficiently definite to be the subject of a decree of specific performance:

"It is not contested by the plaintiff that if it were to accept a lease tendered by defendants in accordance with the contract, there would be numerous complex details left to be worked out. The crucial elements of rate of rental and the amount of space can readily be determined from the Hecht and Woodward & Lothrop leases. But some details of design, construction and price of the building to be occupied by plaintiff at Tyson's Corner would have to be agreed to by the parties, subject to further negotiation and tempered only by the promise of equal terms with other tenants. The question is whether a court of equity will grant specific performance of a contract which has left such substantial terms open for future negotiation."

After concluding that the court may order specific performance despite the lack of specificity in the agreement, it continued:

"The defendants contend that the granting of specific performance in this case will confront the court with insuperable difficulties of supervision, but after reviewing the evidence, I am satisfied that the standards to be observed in construction of the plaintiff's store are set out in the Hecht and Woodward & Lothrop leases with sufficient particularity (Plaintiff's Ex. F) as to make design and approval of plaintiff's store a fairly simple matter, if the parties deal with each other in good faith and expeditiously, as I shall hereafter order.

"For example, Article VIII, Sec. 8.1, Paragraph (G) of the Hecht lease (the Woodward & Lothrop lease contains a similar provision) says:

'The quality of (i) the construction, (ii) the construction components, (iii) the decorative elements (including landscaping irrigation systems for the landscaping) and (iv) the furnishings; and the general architectural character and general design, the materials selection, the decor and the treatment values, approach and standards of the Enclosed Mall shall be comparable, at minimum, to the qualities, values, approaches and standards as of the date hereof of the enclosed mall at Topanga Plaza Shopping Center, Los Angeles, California. * * * '

"The existing leases contain further detailed specifications which will be identical to those in the lease granted to plaintiff. The site for plaintiff's store has already been settled by the design of the center. Although the exact design of plaintiff's store will not be identical to the design of any other store, it must be remembered that all of the stores are to be part of the same center and subject to its overall design requirements. If the parties are not in good faith able to reach an agreement on certain details, the court will appoint a special master to help settle their differences, unless they prefer voluntarily to submit their disagreements to arbitration."

MEYERS v. SELZNICK CO., 373 F.2d 218, 221–23 (2d Cir.1966) (Friendly, J.):

The books are indeed studded with statements that "The construction of all *written instruments* belongs to the court." 9 Wigmore, Evidence § 2556 at 522 (3d ed. 1940); 4 Williston, Contracts § 616 at 649 (3d ed. 1961). If this really were an unvarying rule, there would seem to be no sound reason why it should not also apply to contracts that are partly written and partly oral or wholly oral, except for the possible impracticability in some cases of severing the jury's task in ascertaining what was said from the judge's in interpreting what was meant, see 3 Corbin on Contracts § 554 at 223 (2d ed. 1960)—although such a distinction has been drawn. However, the traditional formulation goes considerably beyond the authorities, at least for the federal courts.[1] In a case often cited in support of the orthodox view, Hamilton v. Liverpool & London and Globe Ins. Co., 136 U.S. 242, 255, 10 S.Ct. 945, 950, 34 L.Ed. 419 (1890), Mr. Justice Gray, in holding that in that case the question was solely for the court, was careful to point out that there the answer "did not depend in any degree * * * on oral testimony or extrinsic facts". And in Rankin v. Fidelity Insurance, Trust & Safe Deposit Co., 189 U.S. 242, 252–253, 23 S.Ct. 553, 557, 47 L.Ed. 792 (1903), the Court ruled that "Although the construction of written instruments is one for the court, where the case turns upon the proper conclusions to be drawn from a series of letters, particularly of a commercial character, taken in connection with other facts and circumstances, it is one which is properly referred to a jury." The Court there

---

1. The relative function of judge and jury in contract interpretation in a suit in the federal courts is an issue of federal "procedural" law and is not governed by *Erie* considerations. Cf. Byrd v. Blue Ridge Rural Elec. Co-op, 356 U.S. 525, 78 S.Ct. 893, 2 L.Ed.2d 953 (1958).

quoted language of Mr. Justice Story in William & James Brown & Co. v. McGran, 14 Pet. (39 U.S.) 479, 493, 10 L.Ed. 550 (1840), which remains illuminating:

> "But there certainly are cases, in which, from the different senses of the words used, or their obscure and indeterminate reference to unexplained circumstances, the true interpretation of the language may be left to the consideration of the jury, for the purpose of carrying into effect the real intention of the parties. This is especially applicable to cases of commercial correspondence, where the real objects, and intentions, and agreements of the parties, are often to be arrived at only by allusions to circumstances which are but imperfectly developed."

With the courts' growing appreciation of Professor Corbin's lesson that words are seldom so "plain and clear" as to exclude proof of surrounding circumstances and other extrinsic aids to interpretation, see 3 Corbin on Contracts § 542, the exception bids fair largely to swallow the supposed general rule. About all that is left of the latter, at least where parol evidence has been properly admitted, is that, save for contracts so technical or complex as to lie beyond a jury's comprehension, "If the meaning after taking the parol evidence, if any, into account is so clear that no reasonable man could reach more than one conclusion as to the meaning of the writing under the circumstances," 4 Williston, supra, § 616 at 661–62, the court will instruct the jury as to the proper interpretation in the light of its findings with respect to the parol evidence or, where the parol evidence is undisputed, will direct a verdict—just as it would do on any other question where the evidence would warrant only one result.

Whether determination of meaning be regarded as a question of fact, a question of law, or just itself, reliance on the jury to resolve ambiguities in the light of extrinsic evidence seems quite as it should be, save where the form or subject-matter of a particular contract outruns a jury's competence; indeed, the old formulation may have rested to some extent on the jurors' then illiteracy and inability to understand more than exceedingly simple terms.

WEINER, THE CIVIL JURY TRIAL AND THE LAW–FACT DISTINCTION

54 Calif.L.Rev. 1867, 1930–32 (1966): *

Another doctrine requiring re-examination is the frequently repeated maxim that, unless parol evidence is admitted, interpretation of the provisions of a contract presents a question of law for the court. Analytically, determination of the meaning of a document may entail no more than an inquiry into actual states of mind. The trier may attempt to reconstruct the thought processes of the contracting parties at the time that the bargain was struck to learn what they intended their words to mean. Such an inquiry will be truly "factual"; it will require the ascertainment of mental events as they have occurred in the past. If the trier concludes that the understanding of both contracting parties was in fact the same, or that one party knew what the other's understanding in fact was, this conclusion by itself will determine the meaning to be given their agreement.

If it is concluded that the subjective intent of the contracting parties was not the same when the agreement was consummated, and that neither party knew the actual understanding of the other, then, as Professor Corbin analyzes the problem, the question to be determined is whether one of the contracting parties had reason to know the other's understanding. This inquiry is more commonly phrased in terms of what a reasonable man in the position of the contracting parties would have thought was meant by the use of certain language. Under either of these approaches, the trier must perform the familiar task of applying a standard of reasonableness. More specifically, he must determine how a hypothetical person would have reacted in a given situation. In this case the reaction would be a mental one, rather than one consisting of observable acts.

In other cases said to present a question of contract interpretation, the trier may be confronted with an issue which neither of the parties considered at the time that the agreement was reached, presumably because they failed to foresee the event which created the dispute. Under these circumstances, the agreement will have to be supplemented to fill the gaps left by the contracting parties. Corbin describes this process as one of "construction" rather than "interpretation." In performing such a task, the trier will seek a result consistent with "fairness and justice," and may draw upon sources such as trade usage.

Regardless of which of these problems is posed, one may question why the decision-maker should be the court rather than the jury.

F.D.I.C. v. W.R. GRACE & CO., 877 F.2d 614, 620–621 (7th Cir.1989). (Posner, J.):

" * * * [T]wo types of ambiguity can usefully be distinguished. One is internal ('intrinsic'), and is present when the agreement itself is unclear. The other is external ('extrinsic') and is present when, although the agreement itself is a perfectly lucid and apparently complete specimen of English prose, anyone familiar with the real-world context of the agreement would wonder what it meant with reference to the particular question that has arisen. See, e.g., Amoco Oil Co. v. Ashcraft, 791 F.2d 519, 521 (7th Cir.1986). So parol and other extrinsic evidence is [always] admissible * * * to demonstrate that the contract is ambiguous. Admissible, that is to say, even if the contract has no intrinsic ambiguity—even if it would seem perfectly clear to a normal reader of English, although to persons knowledgeable about the circumstances in which the contract had been intended to apply the 'normal' reading might be nonsense. See Lucie v. Kleen–Leen, Inc., 499 F.2d 220 (7th Cir.1974) (per curiam). That is what it means to say that extrinsic evidence is admissible to demonstrate an ambiguity. There is no ambiguity on the surface of the document; the ambiguity appears only when extrinsic evidence is considered.

"The Illinois cases provide firmer support for allowing extrinsic evidence when the contract is patently ambiguous than for allowing such evidence to establish that an otherwise clear contract is (to those in the know) ambiguous. * * * The older view, sometimes called the 'four corners' rule, which excludes extrinsic evidence if the contract is clear 'on its face,' is not ridiculous. (There is ancient wisdom as well as ancient prejudice.) The rule tends to cut down on the amount of litigation, in part by reducing the role of the jury; for it is the jury that interprets contracts when interpretation requires consideration of extrinsic evidence. Parties to contracts may prefer, ex ante (that is, when negotiating the contract, and therefore before an interpretive dispute has arisen), to avoid the expense and uncertainty of having a jury resolve a dispute between them, even at the cost of some inflexibility in interpretation."

Chapter 4

OFFER AND ACCEPTANCE

SECTION 1: THE OFFER

NEBRASKA SEED CO. v. HARSH, 98 Neb. 89, 152 N.W. 310 (1915). The defendant, a farmer, mailed the following letter to plaintiff, a corporation engaged in buying and selling seed in Omaha, Nebraska:

> " 'Lowell, Nebraska, 4–24–1912.

> " 'Neb. Seed Co., Omaha, Neb.—Gentlemen: I have about 1800 bu. or thereabouts of millet seed of which I am mailing you a sample. This millet is recleaned and was grown on sod and is good seed. I want $2.25 per cwt. for this seed f.o.b. Lowell.

> " 'Yours truly,
> H.F. Harsh'

The plaintiff received this letter on April 26, and on the same day telegraphed to the defendant the following message:

> " '4–26–12.

> " 'H.F. Harsh, Lowell, Nebr. Sample and letter received. Accept your offer. Millet like sample two twenty-five per hundred. Wire how soon can load.

> The Nebraska Seed Co.'

The same day the plaintiff wrote confirming the telegram and adding, "please be so kind as to load this seed at once and ship to us at Omaha." The defendant refused to deliver the seed. Held, no contract existed:

"In our opinion the letter of defendant cannot be fairly construed into an offer to sell to the plaintiff. After describing the seed, the writer says, 'I want $2.25 per cwt. for this seed f.o.b. Lowell.' He does not say, 'I offer to sell to you.' The language used is general, and such as may be used in an advertisement, or circular addressed generally to those engaged in the seed business, and is not an offer by which he may be bound, if accepted, by any or all of the persons addressed. * * *

"The letter as a whole shows that it was not intended as a final proposition, but as a request for bids. It did not fix a time for delivery, and this seems to have been regarded as one of the essentials by plaintiff, for in his telegram he requests defendant to 'wire how soon can load.' * * *

"We do not think the correspondence made a complete contract. To so hold where a party sends out letters to a number of dealers would subject him to a suit by each one receiving a letter, or invitations to bid, even though his supply of seed were exhausted."

MOULTON v. KERSHAW, 59 Wis. 316, 18 N.W. 172 (1884). Defendants, dealers in salt in the city of Milwaukee, sent the following letter to plaintiff, also a dealer in salt:

"Milwaukee, September 19, 1882.

"*J.H. Moulton, Esq., La Crosse, Wis.*—Dear Sir: In consequence of a rupture in the salt trade, we are authorized to offer Michigan fine salt, in full car-load lots of 80 to 95 bbls., delivered at your city, at 85c. per bbl., to be shipped per C. & N.W.R.R. Co. only. At this price it is a bargain, as the price in general remains unchanged. Shall be pleased to receive your order.

"Yours truly,
C.J. Kershaw & Son."

The day this letter was received, plaintiff sent the following telegraph to defendant:

"La Crosse, September 20, 1882.

"*To C.J. Kershaw & Son, Milwaukee, Wis.*: Your letter of yesterday, received and noted. You may ship me two thousand (2,000) barrels Michigan fine salt, as offered in your letter. Answer.

J.H. Moulton."

After defendant declined to ship the salt and "withdrew the offer," plaintiff brought suit alleging "that two thousand barrels of said salt was a reasonable quantity for this plaintiff to order in response to said offer, and not in excess of the amount which the defendants, from their knowledge of the business of the plaintiff, might reasonably expect him to order in response thereto." Held, no contract exists:

"We * * * place our opinion upon the language of the letter of the [defendants], and hold that it cannot be fairly construed into an offer to sell to the [plaintiff] any quantity of salt he might order, nor any reasonable amount he might see fit to order. The language is not such as a business man would use in making an offer to sell to an individual a definite amount of property. The word 'sell' is not used. They say, 'we are authorized to offer Michigan fine salt,' etc., and volunteer an opinion that at the terms stated it is a bargain. They do not say, we offer to sell to you. They use general language proper to be addressed generally to those who were interested in the salt trade. It is clearly in the nature of an advertisement or business circular, to attract the attention of those interested in that business to the fact that good bargains in salt could be had by applying to them, and not as an offer by which they were to be bound, if accepted, for any amount the persons to whom it was addressed might see fit to order."

In the course of its discussion, the court distinguished Keller v. Ybarru, 3 Cal. 147 (1853). The defendant in that case had a crop of growing grapes; he offered to pick from the vines and deliver to the plaintiff at the defendant's vineyard "so many grapes then growing in said vineyard as the plaintiff should wish to take during the present year" at "10 cents per pound on delivery." The plaintiff specified 1,900 pounds, and a contract for that amount was found to exist. The court pointed out while "the fixing of the quantity was left to the person to whom the offer was made, * * * the amount which the defendant offered, beyond which he could not be bound, was also fixed by the amount of grapes he might have in his vineyard in that year."

FAIRMOUNT GLASS WORKS v. GRUNDEN–MARTIN WOODEN-WARE CO., 106 Ky. 659, 51 S.W. 196 (1899). On April 20, 1895, plaintiff wrote defendant the following letter:

"St. Louis, Mo., April 20, 1895. Gentlemen: Please advise us the lowest price you can make us on our order for ten car loads of Mason green jars, complete, with caps, packed one dozen in a case, either delivered here, or f.o.b. cars your place, as you prefer. State terms and cash discount. Very truly, Grunden-Martin W.W. Co."

To this letter defendant replied:

"Fairmount, Ind., April 23, 1895. Grunden-Martin Wooden Ware Co., St. Louis, Mo.—Gentlemen: Replying to your favor of April 20, we quote you Mason fruit jars, complete, in one-dozen boxes, delivered in East St. Louis, Ill.: Pints $4.50, quarts $5.00, half gallons $6.50, per gross, for immediate acceptance, and shipment not later than May 15, 1895; sixty days' acceptance, or 2 off, cash in ten days. Yours truly, Fairmount Glass Works.

"Please note that we make all quotations and contracts subject to the contingencies of agencies or transportation, delays or accidents beyond our control."

Plaintiff then sent the following telegram on April 24, 1895:

"Fairmount Glass Works, Fairmount, Ind.: Your letter twenty-third received. Enter order ten car loads as per your quotation. Specifications mailed. Grunden-Martin W.W. Co."

On the same day plaintiff sent a confirming letter quoting the above exchange and adding,

"The jars and caps to be strictly first-quality goods. You may ship the first car to us here assorted: Five gross pint, fifty-five gross quart, forty gross one-half gallon. Specifications for the remaining 9 cars we will send later."

On receipt of plaintiff's April 24 telegram, defendant responded, "Impossible to book your order. Output all sold." Plaintiff then brought suit for breach of contract. Held, judgment for plaintiff affirmed:

"We are referred to a number of authorities holding that a quotation of prices is not an offer to sell, in the sense that a completed contract will arise out of the giving of an order for merchandise in accordance with the proposed terms. * * * But each case must turn largely upon the language there used. In this case we think there was more than a quotation of prices, although [defendant's] letter uses the word 'quote' in stating the prices given. The true meaning of the correspondence must be determined by reading it as a whole. [Plaintiff's] letter of April 20th, which began the transaction, did not ask for a quotation of prices. It reads: 'Please advise us the lowest price you can make us on our order for ten car loads of Mason green jars. * * * State terms and cash discount.' From this [defendant] could not fail to understand that [plaintiff] wanted to know at what price it would sell it ten car loads of these jars; so when, in answer it wrote: 'We quote you Mason fruit jars * * * pints $4.50, quarts $5.00, half gallons $6.50, per gross, for immediate acceptance; * * * 2 off, cash in ten days,'—it must be deemed as intending to give [plaintiff] the information it had asked for. We can hardly understand what was meant by the words 'for immediate acceptance,' unless the latter was intended as a proposition to sell at these prices if accepted immediately. In construing every contract, the aim of the court is to arrive at the intention of the parties. In none of the cases to which we have been referred on behalf of [defendant] was there on the face of the correspondence any such expression of intention to make an offer to sell on the terms indicated. * * * The expression in [defendant's] letter, 'for immediate acceptance,' taken in connection with [plaintiff's] letter, in effect, at what price it would sell it the goods, is, it seems to us, * * * evidence of a present offer, which, when accepted immediately, closed the contract. [Plaintiff's] letter was plainly an inquiry for the price and terms on which [defendant] would sell it the goods, and [defendant's] answer to it was not a quotation of prices, but a definite offer to sell on the terms indicated, and could not be withdrawn after the terms had been accepted. * * * "

In many cases that conclude that the language used did not constitute an offer, the court has stressed the indefiniteness or incompleteness of the communication. For example, in Nebraska Seed Co. v. Harsh the court argued that: "The letter of acceptance is not in the terms of the offer. Defendant stated that he had 1,800 bushels or thereabouts. He did not fix a definite and certain amount. It might be

1,800 bushels; it might be more; it might be less; but plaintiff under-took to make an acceptance for 1,800 bushels—no more, no less. Defendant might not have this amount, and therefore be unable to deliver, or he might have a greater amount, and, after filling plaintiff's order, have a quantity of seed left for which he might find no market. We may assume that when he wrote the letter he did not contemplate the sale of more seed than he had, and that he fixed the price on the whole lot whether it was more or less than 1,800 bushels."

In the preceding chapter we have seen the willingness of many courts to supply missing terms in existing contracts by "gap filling" or finding an obligation to bargain in good faith. Why should not the court apply similar principles to fill omissions in communications when the issue is whether specific language amounts to an offer?

LEFKOWITZ v. GREAT MINNEAPOLIS SURPLUS STORE, INC.

Supreme Court of Minnesota, 1957.
251 Minn. 188, 86 N.W.2d 689.

MURPHY, JUSTICE.

This is an appeal from an order of the Municipal Court of Minneap-olis denying the motion of the defendant for amended findings of fact, or, in the alternative, for a new trial. The order for judgment awarded the plaintiff the sum of $138.50 as damages for breach of contract.

This case grows out of the alleged refusal of the defendant to sell to the plaintiff a certain fur piece which it had offered for sale in a newspaper advertisement. It appears from the record that on April 6, 1956, the defendant published the following advertisement in a Minne-apolis newspaper:

> "Saturday 9 A.M. Sharp
> 3 Brand New
> Fur
> Coats
> Worth to $100.00
> First Come
> First Served
> $1
> Each"

On April 13, the defendant again published an advertisement in the same newspaper as follows:

> "Saturday 9 A.M.
> 2 Brand New Pastel
> Mink 3-Skin Scarfs
> Selling for $89.50
> Out they go
> Saturday. Each $1.00
> 1 Black Lapin Stole

> Beautiful,
> worth $139.50 .... $1.00
> First Come
> First Served"

The record supports the findings of the court that on each of the Saturdays following the publication of the above-described ads the plaintiff was the first to present himself at the appropriate counter in the defendant's store and on each occasion demanded the coat and the stole so advertised and indicated his readiness to pay the sale price of $1. On both occasions, the defendant refused to sell the merchandise to the plaintiff, stating on the first occasion that by a "house rule" the offer was intended for women only and sales would not be made to men, and on the second visit that plaintiff knew defendant's house rules.

The trial court properly disallowed plaintiff's claim for the value of the fur coats since the value of these articles were speculative and uncertain. The only evidence of value was the advertisement itself to the effect that the coats were "Worth to $100.00," how much less being speculative especially in view of the price for which they were offered for sale. With reference to the offer of the defendant on April 13, 1956, to sell the "1 Black Lapin Stole * * * worth $139.50 * * *" the trial court held that the value of this article was established and granted judgment in favor of the plaintiff for that amount less the $1 quoted purchase price.

1. The defendant contends that a newspaper advertisement offering items of merchandise for sale at a named price is a "unilateral offer" which may be withdrawn without notice. He relies upon authorities which hold that, where an advertiser publishes in a newspaper that he has a certain quantity or quality of goods which he wants to dispose of at certain prices and on certain terms, such advertisements are not offers which become contracts as soon as any person to whose notice they may come signifies his acceptance by notifying the other that he will take a certain quantity of them. Such advertisements have been construed as an invitation for an offer of sale on the terms stated, which offer, when received, may be accepted or rejected and which therefore does not become a contract of sale until accepted by the seller; and until a contract has been so made, the seller may modify or revoke such prices or terms.

The defendant relies principally on Craft v. Elder & Johnston Co., [38 N.E.2d 416, 34 Ohio L.A. 603 (Ohio Ct.App.1941)]. In that case, the court discussed the legal effect of an advertisement offering for sale, as a one-day special, an electric sewing machine at a named price. The view was expressed that the advertisement was (38 N.E.2d 417, 34 Ohio L.A. 605) "not an offer made to any specific person but was made to the public generally. Thereby it would be properly designated as a unilateral offer and not being supported by any consideration could be withdrawn at will and without notice." It is true that such an offer may be withdrawn before acceptance. Since all offers are by their nature unilateral because they are necessarily made by one party or on one side in the negotiation of a contract, the distinction made in that decision between a unilateral offer and a unilateral contract is not clear. On the facts before us we are concerned with whether the advertisement constituted an offer, and, if so, whether the plaintiff's conduct constituted an acceptance.

There are numerous authorities which hold that a particular advertisement in a newspaper or circular letter relating to a sale of articles may be construed by the court as constituting an offer, acceptance of which would complete a contract.

The test of whether a binding obligation may originate in advertisements addressed to the general public is "whether the facts show that some performance was promised in positive terms in return for something requested." 1 Williston, Contracts (Rev. ed.) § 27.

The authorities above cited emphasize that, where the offer is clear, definite, and explicit, and leaves nothing open for negotiation, it constitutes an offer, acceptance of which will complete the contract. The most recent case on the subject is Johnson v. Capital City Ford Co., La.App., 85 So.2d 75, in which the court pointed out that a newspaper advertisement relating to the purchase and sale of automobiles may constitute an offer, acceptance of which will consummate a contract and create an obligation in the offeror to perform according to the terms of the published offer.

Whether in any individual instance a newspaper advertisement is an offer rather than an invitation to make an offer depends on the legal intention of the parties and the surrounding circumstances. Annotation, 157 A.L.R. 744, 751. We are of the view on the facts before us that the offer by the defendant of the sale of the Lapin fur was clear, definite, and explicit, and left nothing open for negotiation. The plaintiff having successfully managed to be the first one to appear at the seller's place of business to be served, as requested by the advertisement, and having offered the stated purchase price of the article, he was entitled to performance on the part of the defendant. We think the trial court was correct in holding that there was in the conduct of the parties a sufficient mutuality of obligation to constitute a contract of sale.

The defendant contends that the offer was modified by a "house rule" to the effect that only women were qualified to receive the bargains advertised. The advertisement contained no such restriction. This objection may be disposed of briefly by stating that, while an advertiser has the right at any time before acceptance to modify his offer, he does not have the right, after acceptance, to impose new or arbitrary conditions not contained in the published offer.

Affirmed.

IZADI v. MACHADO (GUS) FORD, INC., 550 So.2d 1135 (Fla.App. 1989). Machado Ford placed the following advertisement in the February 21, 1988 edition of the *Miami Herald:*

Izadi attempted to purchase a 1988 Ford Ranger Pick–Up—the vehicle referred to at the foot of the ad—by tendering Gus Machado Ford $3,595 in cash[1] and an unspecified trade-in. The proposal was made on the basis of Izadi's belief that the ad offered $3,000 as a "minimum trade-in allowance" for any vehicle, regardless of its actual value. This understanding was based on the belief that the $3,000 trade-in figure was prominently referred to at the top of the ad apparently as a portion of the consideration needed to "buy a new Ford" and that it was also designated as the projected deduction from the $7,095 gross cost for the Ranger Pick–Up. Machado, however, refused to accept this interpretation of its advertisement and turned Izadi down. In doing so, it apparently relied instead on "the infinitesimally small print under the $3,000 figure which indicated it applied only toward the purchase of 'any New '88 Eddie Bauer Aerostar or Turbo T–Bird in stock'—neither of which was mentioned in the remainder of the ad—and the statements in the individual vehicle portions that the offer was based on a trade-in that was 'worth $3,000.' "

Izadi then brought suit for breach of contract and misleading advertising; the court held that his complaint stated a cause of action:

"1. *Breach of Contract.* We first hold, on two somewhat distinct but closely related grounds, that the complaint states a cause of action for breach of an alleged contract which arose when Izadi accepted an offer contained in the advertisement, which was essentially to allow $3,000 toward the purchase of the Ranger for any vehicle the reader-offeree would produce, or, to put the same proposed deal in different words, to sell the Ranger for $3,595, plus any vehicle.

"(a) It is of course well settled that a completed contract or, as here, an allegedly binding offer must be viewed as a whole, with due emphasis placed upon each of what may be inconsistent or conflicting provisions. *NLRB v. Federbush Co.,* 121 F.2d 954, 957 (2d Cir.1941) ('Words are not pebbles in alien juxtaposition; they have only a communal existence; and not only does the meaning of each interpenetrate the other, but all in their aggregate take their purport from the setting in which they are used * * *.'); *Transport Rental Systems, Inc. v. Hertz Corp.,* 129 So.2d 454, 456 (Fla. 3d DCA 1961) ('The real intention, as disclosed by a fair consideration of all parts of a contract, should control the meaning given to mere words or particular provisions when they have reference to the main purpose.'). In this case, that process might well involve disregarding both the superfine print and apparent qualification as to the value of the trade-in, as contradictory to the far more prominent thrust of the advertisement to the effect that $3,000 will be allowed for any trade-in on any Ford. *Transport Rental Systems, Inc. v. Hertz Corp.,* 129 So.2d at 456 ('If a contract contains clauses which are apparently repugnant to each other, they must be given such an interpretation as will reconcile them.'). * * * We therefore believe that the complaint appropriately alleges that,

1. Plus a $500 factory rebate allowance.

objectively considered, the advertisement indeed contained just the unqualified $3,000 offer which was accepted by the plaintiff.[6] On the face of the pleadings, the case thus is like many previous ones in which it has been held, contrary to what is perhaps the usual rule, see 1 Williston on Contracts § 27 (W. Jaeger 3d ed. 1957); 1 Corbin on Contracts § 25 (1963), that an enforceable contract arises from an offer contained in an advertisement. *Lefkowitz v. Great Minneapolis Surplus Store*, 251 Minn. 188, 86 N.W.2d 689 (1957).

"Of course, if an offer were indeed conveyed by an objective reading of the ad, it does not matter that the car dealer may subjectively have not intended for its chosen language to constitute a binding offer.

* * *

"(b) As a somewhat different, and perhaps more significant basis for upholding the breach of contract claim, we point to the surely permissible conclusion from the carefully chosen language and arrangement of the advertisement itself that Machado—although it did not intend to adhere to the $3,000 trade-in representation—affirmatively, but wrongly sought to make the public believe that it would be honored; that, in other words, the offer was to be used as the 'bait' to be followed by a 'switch' to another deal when the acceptance of that offer was refused.[8] Indeed, it is difficult to offer any other explanation for the blanket representation of a $3,000 trade-in for *any* vehicle—which is then hedged in sub-microscopic print to apply only to two models which were not otherwise referred to in the ad—or the obvious non-coincidence that the only example of the trade-in for the three vehicles which was set out in the ad was the very same $3,000. This situation invokes the applicability of a line of persuasive authority that a binding offer may be implied from the very fact that deliberately misleading advertising intentionally leads the reader to the conclusion that one exists. See Corbin on Contracts § 64, at 139 (Supp.1989) (where 'bait and switch' advertising suspected, public policy 'ought to justify a court in holding deceptive advertising to be an offer despite the seller's * * * intent not to make any such offer'). In short, the dealer can hardly deny that it did not mean what it purposely misled its customer into believing. This doctrine is expressed in the [Restatement (Second) of Contracts § 20.] * * * Restatement (Second) of Contracts § 20(2)(a)

6. It goes almost without saying that the plaintiff's ability eventually to recover on the theories suggested in this opinion depends on the showing that he was, in fact, led or misled into a genuine—even if unjustified—belief that such an offer had indeed been made. If he were merely attempting to take a knowing advantage of imprecise language in the advertisement and did not, in fact, rely upon it, he may not recover. See *Vance v. Indian Hammock Hunt & Riding Club, Ltd.*, 403 So.2d 1367 (Fla. 4th DCA 1981); Restatement (Second) of Contracts § 167 comment a

(1981) ("A misrepresentation is not a cause of a party's making a contract unless he relied on the misrepresentation in manifesting his assent.").

8. " 'Bait and switch' describes an offer which is made not in order to sell the advertised product at the advertised price, but rather to draw the customer to the store to sell him another similar product which is more profitable to the advertiser." *Tashof v. Federal Trade Commission*, 437 F.2d 707, 709 n. 3 (D.C.Cir.1970).

comment d ('[I]f one party knows the other's meaning and manifests assent intending to insist on a different meaning, he may be guilty of misrepresentation. Whether or not there is such misrepresentation as would give the other party the power of avoidance, there is a *contract* under Subsection (2)(a), and the mere negligence of the other party is immaterial.'). In *Johnson v. Capital City Ford Co.*, 85 So.2d 75 (La.App. 1955), the court dealt with a case very like this one, in which the issue was whether a newspaper advertisement stating that any purchaser who bought a 1954 automobile before a certain date could exchange it for a newer model without an extra charge constituted a binding offer. The dealership argued that, despite the plain wording of the advertisement, it had no intention of making an offer, but merely sought to lure customers to the sales lot; it claimed also that, because of the small print at the bottom of the contract, any promises by the purchaser to exchange the vehicle for a later model were not binding. The court rejected these contentions on the holding that a contract had been formed even though the dealership 'had an erroneous belief as to what the advertisement, as written, meant, or what it would legally convey.' *Johnson*, 85 So.2d at 80. As the court said:

"There is entirely too much disregard of law and truth in the business, social, and political world of to-day. * * * It is time to hold men to their primary engagements to tell the truth and observe the law of common honesty and fair dealing. *Johnson*, 85 So.2d at 82. We entirely agree. * * *

"3. *Statutory Violation.* It follows from what we have said concerning the allegedly misleading nature of the advertisement in making an offer which the advertiser did not intend to keep, that the complaint properly alleged claims for violations of the Florida Deceptive and Unfair Trade Practices Act, sections 501.201–501.213, Florida Statutes (1987),[9] and the statutory prohibition against misleading advertising, section 817.41, Florida Statutes (1987)." [10]

STEINBERG v. CHICAGO MEDICAL SCHOOL, 69 Ill.2d 320, 13 Ill. Dec. 699, 371 N.E.2d 634 (1977). The 1974–75 bulletin of the Chicago Medical School (an institution that is not connected with the University of Chicago) contained the following statement: "Students are selected on the basis of scholarship, character, and motivation without regard to race, creed, or sex. The student's potential for the study and practice

9. 501.204 Unlawful acts and practices.—

(1) Unfair methods of competition and unfair or deceptive acts or practices in the conduct of any trade or commerce are hereby declared unlawful.

10. 817.41 Misleading advertising prohibited.—

(1) It shall be unlawful for any person to make or disseminate or cause to be made or disseminated before the general public of the state, or any portion thereof, any misleading advertisement. Such making or dissemination of misleading advertising shall constitute and is hereby declared to be fraudulent and unlawful, designed and intended for obtaining money or property under false pretenses.

of medicine will be evaluated on the basis of academic achievement, Medical College Admission Test results, personal appraisals by a pre-professional advisory committee or individual instructors, and the personal interview, if requested by the Committee on Admissions." Robert Steinberg received a catalog and applied for admission, paying a $15 filing fee, but was rejected. He then filed a class action against the school claiming that the school used nonacademic criteria in rejecting his application, "primarily the ability of the applicant or his family to pledge or make payment of large sums of money to the school." 371 N.E.2d at 638. Steinberg's prayer for relief included an injunction against continuation of such admission practices and an accounting of all application fees, donations, and contributions collected from applicants during the previous ten years. Steinberg did not request that the court direct his admission, review his application or return his application fee. The court held that a cause of action was stated on a theory of breach of contract:

"Steinberg alleges that [the] * * * brochure describing the criteria that defendant would employ in evaluating applications * * * constituted an invitation for an offer to apply, that the filing of the applications constituted an offer to have their credentials appraised under the terms described by defendant, and that defendant's voluntary reception of the application and fee constituted an acceptance, the final act necessary for the creation of a binding contract.

"This situation is similar to that wherein a merchant advertises goods for sale at a fixed price. While the advertisement itself is not an offer to contract, it constitutes an invitation to deal on the terms described in the advertisement. (1 A. Corbin, Contracts sec. 25 (1950)).

"Although in some cases the advertisement itself may be an offer (see Lefkowitz v. Great Minneapolis Surplus Store, Inc. (1957), 251 Minn. 188, 86 N.W.2d 689), usually it constitutes only an invitation to deal on the advertised terms. Only when the merchant takes the money is there an acceptance of the offer to purchase.

"Here the description in the brochure containing the terms under which an application will be appraised constituted an invitation for an offer. The tender of the application, as well as the payment of the fee pursuant to the terms of the brochure, was an offer to apply. Acceptance of the application and fee constituted acceptance of an offer to apply under the criteria defendant had established."

The court also held that the complaint stated a cause of action for fraud but that no cause of action was stated under the Illinois Consumer Fraud and Deceptive Practices Act (because the plaintiff was not a "consumer") or the Illinois Uniform Deceptive Trade Practices Act (because that Act is limited only to "goods or services"). In the discussion of fraud, the court referred to testimony in an earlier case involving the defendant in which it was shown that "in 1970, at least 64 out of 83 entering students had pledges made in their behalves totalling $1,927,900. The pledges varied in amounts from $1400 to $100,000 and averaged $30,123. In 1971, at least 55 out of 83 students had pledges made in their behalves totalling $1,893,000. The pledges varied in amounts from $3000 to $100,000 and averaged $34,418." Similar patterns of gifts were shown for students enrolling in 1972 and 1973.

SECTION 2: REVOCATION, REJECTION, AND COUNTEROFFER

DICKINSON v. DODDS

Chancery Division, Court of Appeals, 1876.
2 Ch.D. 463.

On Wednesday, the 10th of June, 1874, the Defendant *John Dodds* signed and delivered to the Plaintiff, *George Dickinson*, a memorandum, of which the material part was as follows:—

"I hereby agree to sell to Mr. *George Dickinson* the whole of the dwelling-houses, garden ground, stabling, and outbuildings thereto belonging, situate at *Croft*, belonging to me, for the sum of £800. As witness my hand this tenth day of June, 1874.

"£800.   (Signed)   *John Dodds.*"

"P.S.—This offer to be left over until Friday, 9 o'clock, A.M. *J.D.* (the twelfth), 12th June, 1874.

"(Signed)   *J. Dodds.*"

The bill alleged that *Dodds* understood and intended that the Plaintiff should have until Friday 9 A.M. within which to determine whether he would or would not purchase, and that he should absolutely have until that time the refusal of the property at the price of £800, and that the Plaintiff in fact determined to accept the offer on the morning of Thursday, the 11th of June, but did not at once signify his acceptance to *Dodds*, believing that he had the power to accept it until 9 A.M. on the Friday.

In the afternoon of the Thursday the Plaintiff was informed by a Mr. *Berry* that *Dodds* had been offering or agreeing to sell the property to *Thomas Allan*, the other Defendant. Thereupon the Plaintiff, at about half-past seven in the evening, went to the house of Mrs. *Burgess*, the mother-in-law of *Dodds*, where he was then staying, and left with her a formal acceptance in writing, of the offer to sell the property. According to the evidence of Mrs. *Burgess* this document never in fact reached *Dodds*, she having forgotten to give it to him.

On the following (Friday) morning, at about seven o'clock, *Berry*, who was acting as agent for *Dickinson*, found *Dodds* at the *Darlington* railway station, and handed to him a duplicate of the acceptance by *Dickinson*, and explained to *Dodds* its purport. He replied that it was too late, as he had sold the property. A few minutes later *Dickinson* himself found *Dodds* entering a railway carriage, and handed him another duplicate of the notice of acceptance, but *Dodds* declined to receive it, saying, "You are too late. I have sold the property."

It appeared that on the day before, Thursday, the 11th of June, *Dodds* had signed a formal contract for the sale of the property to the Defendant *Allan* for £800, and had received from him a deposit of £40.

The bill in this suit prayed that the Defendant *Dodds* might be decreed specifically to perform the contract of the 10th of June, 1874; that he might be restrained from conveying the property to *Allan;* that *Allan* might be restrained from taking any such conveyance; that, if any such conveyance had been or should be made, *Allan* might be declared a trustee of the property for, and might be directed to convey the property to, the Plaintiff; and for damages.

The cause came on for hearing beforce Vice-Chancellor *Bacon* on the 25th of January, 1876, [who entered a decree for specific performance with a declaration that *Allan* has no interest in the property. The defendants appealed]. * * *

JAMES, L.J., after referring to the document of the 10th of June, 1874, continued:—

The document, though beginning "I hereby agree to sell," was nothing but an offer, and was only intended to be an offer, for the Plaintiff himself tells us that he required time to consider whether he would enter into an agreement or not. Unless both parties had then agreed there was no concluded agreement then made; it was in effect and substance only an offer to sell. The Plaintiff, being minded not to complete the bargain at that time, added this memorandum—"This offer to be left over until Friday, 9 o'clock A.M., 12th June, 1874." That shews it was only an offer. There was no consideration given for the undertaking or promise, to whatever extent it may be considered binding, to keep the property unsold until 9 o'clock on Friday morning; but apparently *Dickinson* was of opinion, and probably *Dodds* was of the same opinion, that he (*Dodds*) was bound by that promise, and could not in any way withdraw from it, or retract it, until 9 o'clock on Friday morning, and this probably explains a good deal of what afterwards took place. But it is clear settled law, on one of the clearest principles of law, that this promise, being a mere *nudum pactum*, was not binding, and that at any moment before a complete acceptance by *Dickinson* of the offer, *Dodds* was as free as *Dickinson* himself. Well, that being the state of things, it is said that the only mode in which *Dodds* could assert that freedom was by actually and distinctly saying to *Dickinson,* "Now I withdraw my offer." It appears to me that there is neither principle nor authority for the proposition that there must be an express and actual withdrawal of the offer, or what is called a retractation. It must, to constitute a contract, appear that the two minds were at one, at the same moment of time, that is, that there was an offer continuing up to the time of the acceptance. If there was not such a continuing offer, then the acceptance comes to nothing. Of course it may well be that the one man is bound in some way or other to let the other man know that his mind with regard to the offer has been changed; but in this case, beyond all question, the Plaintiff knew that *Dodds* was no longer minded to sell the property to him as plainly and clearly as if *Dodds* had told him in so many words, "I withdraw the offer." This is evident from the Plaintiff's own statements in the bill.

The Plaintiff says in effect that, having heard and knowing that *Dodds* was no longer minded to sell to him, and that he was selling or had sold to some one else, thinking that he could not in point of law withdraw his offer, meaning to fix him to it, and endeavouring to bind him, "I went to the house where he was lodging, and saw his mother-in-law, and left with her an acceptance of the offer, knowing all the while that he had entirely changed his mind. I got an agent to watch for him at 7 o'clock the next morning, and I went to the train just before 9 o'clock, in order that I might catch him and give him my notice of acceptance just before 9 o'clock, and when that occurred he told my agent, and he told me, you are too late, and he then threw back the paper." It is to my mind quite clear that before there was any attempt at acceptance by the Plaintiff, he was perfectly well aware that *Dodds* had changed his mind, and that he had in fact agreed to sell the property to *Allan*. It is impossible, therefore, to say there was ever that existence of the same mind between the two parties which is essential in point of law to the making of an agreement. I am of opinion, therefore, that the Plaintiff has failed to prove that there was any binding contract between *Dodds* and himself.

MELLISH, L.J.:—

I am of the same opinion. ＊ ＊ ＊ [T]his being only an offer, the law says—and it is a perfectly clear rule of law—that, although it is said that the offer is to be left open until Friday morning at 9 o'clock, that did not bind *Dodds*. He was not in point of law bound to hold the offer over until 9 o'clock on Friday morning. He was not so bound either in law or in equity. Well, that being so, when on the next day he made an agreement with *Allan* to sell the property to him, I am not aware of any ground on which it can be said that that contract with *Allan* was not as good and binding a contract as ever was made. Assuming *Allan* to have known (there is some dispute about it, and *Allan* does not admit that he knew of it, but I will assume that he did) that *Dodds* had made the offer to *Dickinson*, and had given him till Friday morning at 9 o'clock to accept it, still in point of law that could not prevent *Allan* from making a more favourable offer than *Dickinson*, and entering at once into a binding agreement with *Dodds*.

Then *Dickinson* is informed by *Berry* that the property has been sold by *Dodds* to *Allan*. *Berry* does not tell us from whom he heard it, but he says that he did hear it, that he knew it, and that he informed *Dickinson* of it. Now, stopping there, the question which arises is this—If an offer has been made for the sale of property, and before that offer is accepted, the person who has made the offer enters into a binding agreement to sell the property to somebody else, and the person to whom the offer was first made receives notice in some way that the property has been sold to another person, can he after that make a binding contract by the acceptance of the offer? I am of opinion that he cannot. The law may be right or wrong in saying that a person who has given to another a certain time within which to accept an offer is not bound by his promise to give that time; but, if he is not bound by that promise and may still sell the property to some one else, and if it be the law that, in order to make a contract, the two minds must be in agreement at some one time, that is, at the time of the acceptance, how is it possible that when the person to whom the offer has been made knows that the person who has made the offer has sold the property to someone else, and that, in fact, he has not remained in the same mind to sell it to him, he can be at liberty to accept the offer and thereby make a binding contract? It seems to me that would be simply absurd. If a man makes an offer to sell a particular horse in his stable, and says, "I will give you until the day after to-morrow to accept the offer," and the next day goes and sells the horse to somebody else, and receives the purchase-money from him, can the person to whom the offer was originally made then come and say, "I accept," so as to make a binding contract, and so as to be entitled to recover damages for the non-delivery of the horse? If the rule of law is that a mere offer to sell property, which can be withdrawn at any time, and which is made dependent on the acceptance of the person to whom it is made, is a mere *nudum pactum,* how is it possible that the person to whom the offer has been made can by acceptance make a binding contract after he knows that the person who has made the offer has sold the property to some one else? It is admitted law that, if a man who makes an offer dies, the offer cannot be accepted after he is dead, and parting with the property has very much the same effect as the death of the owner, for it makes the performance of the offer impossible. I am clearly of opinion that, just as when a man who has made an offer dies before it is accepted it is impossible that it can then be accepted, so when once the person to whom the offer was made knows that the property has been sold to some one else, it is too late for him to accept the offer, and on that ground I am clearly of opinion that there was no binding contract for the sale of this property by *Dodds* to *Dickinson,* and even if there had been, it seems to me that the sale of the property to *Allan* was first in point of time. However, it is not necessary to consider, if there had been two binding contracts, which of them would be entitled to priority in equity, because there is no binding contract between *Dodds* and *Dickinson.*

THE LAW OF OFFER AND ACCEPTANCE

Dickinson v. Dodds is a classic example of the 19th century model of contract formation, which was largely based on the rules of offer and acceptance. These rules are usually favorites of law students: they are easily stated and tend to be rather mechanical in their operation. They also involve situations that are relatively easy to grasp and in which various policy considerations are close to the surface. However, one should not assume that one has mastered the law of contracts simply because one is conversant with the rules of offer and acceptance. While these rules doubtless form a structure within which many negotiations occur, and may even determine the results reached in some cases, most modern contract litigation involves problems other than the principles of offer and acceptance. Relatively few modern cases turn on the application of these principles, and, as a result, modern contracts scholars tend to deprecate their importance. See generally G. Gilmore, The Death of Contract (1974); L. Friedman, Contract Law in America (1965).

A. TERMINOLOGY

The person making the offer is referred to as the *offeror* and the person to whom the offer is addressed is the *offeree*. The rules of offer and acceptance typically deal with an executory contract in which consideration for the promise is a return promise by the offeree. The person making the promise in question is the *promisor*; the person receiving the promise is the *promisee*. (While the rules of offer and acceptance also deal with situations in which the offeree performs rather than promises to perform, such situations create additional problems that are discussed in the following section.) Thus, if the offeror states, "I offer to sell you my car for $500," the offeree, when he says "I accept" has formed a binding bilateral contract. The offeree has in effect made a return promise to pay $500 when the car is delivered.

If the offeror withdraws his offer before it is accepted (as in Dickinson v. Dodds), he is said to *revoke* his offer. In contrast, if the offeree refuses to enter into the deal (as by saying, "no, $500 is too much") he has *rejected* the offer. A *counteroffer* is a statement by the offeree suggesting substitute terms (e.g., "I'll pay you $450 for it"), which usually has the effect of rejecting the original offer and making the former offeree an offeror of a different promise.

B. DURATION OF AN OFFER

Colloquially, an offer is said "to remain open" during the period the offeree has a power of acceptance, i.e., the power to complete the formation of a contract by an unqualified acceptance or assent to the terms. An offer may terminate in several different ways:

(1) Rejection

The "black letter" rule is that an unequivocal rejection terminates the power of acceptance. This rule can readily be justified on the basis of the probable effect of a rejection on the offeror. After making an offer, the offeror usually makes plans or takes steps to assure that he or she will be able to perform if the offer is accepted. Upon receipt of a rejection, the offeror will likely suspend planning or preparations if they have begun, or will not begin them at all. At this point, it is unfair to the offeror to allow the offeree to first blow cold and then blow hot by changing his mind and unexpectedly accepting the offer. Further, it is always possible that the offeror has mentally resolved to revoke the offer; when a rejection is received, the offeror will naturally conclude that it is unnecessary to communicate his revocation. Again, there is a liklihood of reliance in a negative way that will usually be difficult or impossible to prove.

The rule that a rejection normally terminates an offer may also protect the offeree, who may thereafter reopen negotiations with the offeror without concern that his or her renewed expression of interest might be viewed as an acceptance of the original offer.

RESTATEMENT, SECOND, CONTRACTS § 38:

Illustrations:

1. A makes an offer to B and adds: "This offer will remain open for a week." B rejects the offer the following day, but later in the week purports to accept it. There is no contract unless the offer was itself a contract. B's purported acceptance is itself a new offer.

2. A makes an offer to sell water rights to B, and states, "You may accept this offer by applying to the appropriate authority for a permit to use the water." B rejects the offer, obtains water rights elsewhere, and later applies for the permit contemplated by the offer. There is no contract. Even if A's offer was a binding option, B has not exercised it.

The rule that a rejection terminates the power of acceptance is designed to give effect to the probable intention of the parties. Either party may signify a different intention, and that expressed intention will normally control. For example, the offeree may reject an offer for the present, but add that he will reconsider it in the near future; such a rejection should not of itself terminate the power of acceptance. Or, the offeror may state in his or her offer that the offer will remain open for a specified period despite a rejection, and such a statement probably means that the offer survives despite the "black letter" rule to the contrary.

If an offer has been rejected with the effect of terminating the power of acceptance, and the offeror then states that he or she will disregard the rejection, the offeror has made a new offer on the same terms.

(2) Counteroffers and Conditional Acceptances

The "black letter" rule is that a counteroffer is a rejection of the offer, and thus has the same effect as a rejection on the duration of the offer. There is an important difference between an outright rejection and a counteroffer: the first is a statement of lack of interest on the part of the offeree while the second indicates an interest in the transaction but on different terms. A counteroffer is itself an offer that is capable of being accepted by the original offeror; it therefore carries on negotiations rather than breaking them off. The black letter rule that a counteroffer terminates the power of acceptance may be justified on the theory that it reflects the normal understanding that putting forth a new proposal for consideration indicates that the prior proposal is unacceptable.

RESTATEMENT, SECOND, CONTRACTS § 39:

Illustration:

1. A offers B to sell him a parcel of land for $5,000, stating that the offer will remain open for thirty days. B replies, "I will pay $4,800 for the parcel," and on A's declining that, B writes, within the thirty day period, "I accept your offer to sell for $5,000." There is no contract unless A's offer was itself a contract * * * or unless A's reply to the counter-offer manifested an intention to renew his original offer.

———

A communication that is intended to be an acceptance but adds qualifications or conditions is a counteroffer and a rejection rather than an acceptance. It doesn't matter whether the qualification or condition changes the substantive terms of the proposal or simply imposes additional procedural requirements; in either event it is a counteroffer if it imposes new terms.

RESTATEMENT, SECOND, CONTRACTS § 59:

Illustration:

1. A makes an offer to B, and B in terms accepts but adds, "This acceptance is not effective unless prompt acknowledgement is made of receipt of this letter." There is no contract, but a counter-offer.

———

On the other hand, many communications that appear at first blush to impose new conditions may be acceptances rather than counteroffers; it depends on whether a condition adds a new term.

RESTATEMENT, SECOND, CONTRACTS § 61:

Illustrations:

1. A offers to sell B 100 tons of steel at a certain price. B replies, "I accept your offer. I hope that if you can arrange to deliver the steel in weekly installments of 25 tons you will do so." There is a contract, but A is not bound to deliver in installments.

2. A offers to sell specified hardware to B on stated terms. B replies: "I accept your offer; ship in accordance with your statement.

Please send me also one No. 5 hand saw at your list price." The request for the saw is a separate offer, not a counter-offer.

———

Similarly, communications that suggest the offer be modified or that inquire whether different terms might be acceptable may not terminate the power of acceptance. They may have no contractual significance, they may be proposals for new contracts, or they may by their own terms make clear that the offeree still is actively considering the initial offer while proposing a different set of terms for the offerors' immediate attention. Whether or not such communications terminate the power of acceptance depends on what is a reasonable interpretation of the language used under the circumstances. Compare the discussion of the effect of a rejection, pp. 432–3 supra.

RESTATEMENT, SECOND, CONTRACTS § 39:

Illustrations:

2. * * * [A offers B to sell him a parcel of land for $5,000, stating that the offer will remain open for thirty days. B] replies, "Won't you take less?" A answers, "No." An acceptance thereafter by B within the thirty-day period is effective. B's inquiry was not a counter-offer, and A's original offer stands.

3. A makes the same offer to B as that stated in Illustration [2]. B replies, "I am keeping your offer under advisement, but if you wish to close the matter at once I will give you $4,800." A does not reply, and within the thirty-day period B accepts the original offer. B's acceptance is effective.

RESTATEMENT, SECOND, CONTRACTS § 59:

Illustrations:

2. A makes a written offer to sell B a patent in exchange for B's promise to pay $10,000 if B's adviser X approves the purchase. B signs the writing in a space labelled "Accepted" and returns the writing to A. B has made a conditional promise and an unconditional acceptance. There is a contract, but B's duty to pay the price is conditional on X's approval.

3. A makes a written offer to B to sell him Blackacre. By usage the offer is understood as promising a marketable title. B replies, "I accept your offer if you can convey me a marketable title." There is a contract.

———

Despite these various qualifications, an acceptance, to be effective, must be unequivocal; the offeror is entitled to know unambiguously whether or not his offer has been accepted. A "wishy-washy," ambiguous, or verbose communication that does not address the offeree's intention squarely is unlikely to be an effective acceptance.

RESTATEMENT, SECOND, CONTRACTS § 57:

Illustrations:

1. A gives an order for goods to B's traveling salesman, subject to approval by B at his home office. B sends a letter to A stating that the order has been received and will receive B's attention. A promptly sends a letter of revocation to B, which B receives before doing anything further. There is no contract.

3. Pursuant to the terms of a lease from A to B, A writes to B that he is about to sell the premises and that B may have the option to purchase by meeting an offer of $37,000. B replies, "I tender you $37,000 in exercise of my option rights. I demand that I be notified concerning your acceptance or rejection of my offer within ten days." Within ten days, A notifies B that A has decided not to sell. There is no contract.

4. A writes to B offering to extend a lease for two years. B replies, "I accept your offer, but I am assigning my interest to C, and have had a lease drawn up from you to C. C has signed it in duplicate, and when you sign it will be complete. Keep one copy and mail the other to me for C. If this is not satisfactory let me know." A's letter of revocation crosses B's letter in the mail. There is no contract.

––––––

CULTON v. GILCHRIST, 92 Iowa 718, 61 N.W. 384 (1894). In the course of several written communications between a landowner and his tenant, the owner offered the tenant either a three-year or five-year lease "as you prefer, for $200 per year, in two payments, first by September second; payment first February each year." The tenant responded, saying that he accepted the five-year term and adding: "Mr. Culton, the reason I ask for the place for five years is I would like to put a small cookroom at the south side, so we could have some place to cook, wash, as it is very hard for my wife to only have one room. We have stood it quite a while through hot weather. I would like to do this myself if in the lease you will give me the privilege of taking the same, providing I do not buy." Six months later the owner regretted the transaction and sued to dispossess the tenant. The court held that "it seems to us that all that is said about the cookroom and the taking it away is a mere request, which plaintiff might comply with or not at his election. The acceptance was complete and absolute, and depended in no way upon the matter relating to this cookroom." Do you agree?

––––––

These rules with respect to counteroffers are qualified in significant respects by UCC § 2–207, discussed below (see infra page 565).

––––––

(3) Lapse of Time

As illustrated by Dickinson v. Dodds, an offer may itself establish the period during which it is open; to be effective an acceptance must occur within the specified time. Thus, if there had been no sale to Allan, Dodds' offer would have expired by its own terms on June 12, 1874, at 9 a.m. With such a precise lifespan for the offer, there is more likely to be a dispute about precisely when an acceptance becomes effective, a subject discussed below at some length.

Where the offer does not specify a time period for its existence, the "black letter" rule is that the offer expires at the end of a "reasonable time." Restatement, Second, Contracts § 41(1). What is reasonable depends on the circumstances: the nature of the proposed contract, the communications of the parties as to their goals or purposes, their prior course of dealing, if any, and applicable usages of trade. The test is similar to the tests described in Chapter 3: what time period would be thought satisfactory to the offeror by a reasonable person in the position of the offeree? The offeror, however, may extend the period by indicating that the time taken was acceptable to him.

RESTATEMENT, SECOND, CONTRACTS § 23:

Illustration:

> A offers by letter to sell goods to B, stating no definite time limit for acceptance. B accepts by letter after what might or might not be more than a reasonable time. The acceptance crosses a letter from A stating that he has not heard from B and that A's offer will terminate if B does not reply by return mail. There is a contract.

———

The test of what is a "reasonable time" can best be addressed by consideration of specific circumstances.

(a) *Direct negotiations.* Where the parties bargain face to face or through instantaneous electronic means such as the telephone or electronic mail, a reasonable time usually does not extend beyond the termination of the discussion or communication. A longer period, of course, is implied if the parties agree to use a slower means of communication, such as the United States mail, private overnight delivery services, or telefax communication, to complete the transaction.

RESTATEMENT, SECOND, CONTRACTS § 41:

Illustration:

> 4. While A and B are engaged in conversation, A makes B an offer to which B then makes no reply, but on meeting A again a few hours later B states that he accepts the offer. There is no contract unless the

offer or the circumstances indicate that the offer is intended to continue beyond the immediate conversation.

5. A makes B an offer by mail to sell goods. B receives the offer at the close of business hours and accepts it by letter promptly the next morning. The acceptance is timely.

————

(b) *Speculative transactions.* Where contracts involve the purchase or sale of commodities, securities, or goods that fluctuate rapidly in price, a reasonable time is normally very short, particularly when the contemplated transaction involves a fixed price. The offeror normally does not expect to give the offeree an opportunity to speculate at his or her expense while deciding whether or not to enter into the transaction. Indeed, with the most volatile products that are widely traded, such as securities, commodities, foreign currencies, indexes, options, or futures, virtually instantaneous response is expected. Where values tend to be relatively stable over short periods of time, as is usually true with land, many consumer goods, and the like, the likelihood of speculation is usually not great, and the period during which an offer is open is longer.

RESTATEMENT, SECOND, CONTRACTS § 41:

Illustrations:

6. A sends B an offer by mail to sell a piece of farm land. B does not reply for three days and then mails an acceptance. It is a question of fact under the circumstances of the particular case whether the delay is unreasonable.

8. A sends B an offer by mail to sell at a fixed price corporate stock not listed on an exchange. B waits two days after receiving the offer and then sends a telegraphic acceptance after learning of a sharp rise in the price bid over-the-counter. The acceptance may be too late even though it arrives before a prompt acceptance by mail would have arrived.

————

Where an offeree in fact uses the time made available for communication to take advantage of price movements favorable to him, there may be a lack of good faith that permits the offeror to refuse to complete the transaction. See UCC §§ 1–105, 2–103(1)(b).

RESTATEMENT, SECOND, CONTRACTS § 41:

Illustration:

7. A sends B a telegraphic offer to sell oil which at the time is subject to rapid fluctuations in price. The offer is received near the close of business hours, and a telegraphic acceptance is sent the next day, after the offeree has learned of a sharp price rise. The acceptance

is too late if a fixed price was offered, but may be timely if the price is market price at time of delivery.

———

(4) Death or incapacity of offeror

The "black letter" rule is that the offeree's power of acceptance is terminated upon the death or incapacity of the offeror. Restatement, Second, Contracts § 48. This rule, originally based on the subjective "meeting of the minds" theory, has been criticized on the ground that it creates unnecessary potential injustice to offerees who are unaware of the death or incapacity. This rule seems anachronistic in a modern society in which air travel permits persons to be in remote parts of the country or the world, so that death may occur in distant locations with the result that the offeree is unlikely to be immediately aware of it. It would obviously be possible to hold the estate of the decedent or incompetent liable for breach of contract for offers accepted after the death or incompetence of the offeror as well as offers accepted prior to that event. On the other hand, this black letter rule simplifies the problems often faced by personal representatives who may have great difficulty locating (and revoking) outstanding offers.

While this rule is generally accepted, there are a few precedents rejecting it; there also has been some chipping away at it by statute. See, e.g., UCC § 4–405, Restatement, Second, Agency, § 120, which states the common law rule and then adds the following exceptions:

"(2) Until notice of a depositor's death, a bank has authority to pay checks drawn by him or by agents authorized by him before death.

"(3) Until notice of the death of the holder of a check deposited for collection, the bank in which it is deposited and those to which the check is sent for collection have authority to go forward with the process of collection."

C. TO WHOM AN OFFER IS ADDRESSED

The "black letter" rule is that an offeror may exclusively determine the person or persons in whom a power of acceptance is created.

RESTATEMENT, SECOND, CONTRACTS § 52:

Illustrations:

1. A makes an offer to B, who dies after receiving it. His executor, though acting within the permitted time, cannot accept.

2. A offers to guarantee payment for goods delivered to B by C. D cannot accept by delivering goods to B.

3. A promises B that A will sell and deliver a set of books to B if B's father C will promise to pay $150 for the set. B is the promisee of

A's promise; C is the offeree of A's offer. Only C can accept the offer by making the return promise invited by A.

4. A sends B an order for goods. C, from whom A has previously refused to buy such goods, has purchased B's business. Without notifying A of the change of proprietorship, C ships the goods as ordered. Neither B nor C has accepted A's offer.

5. A, in Illustration 4, before using the goods, discovers that they have come from C. A's retention or use of them is an acceptance of an offer from C, and a contract arises.

As illustrated by *Minneapolis Surplus Store*, however, an offeror may make an offer to the world in general; in that case, of course, the offer provided a method of selection so that the first acceptance extinguished the power of all other persons to form a contract. Many rewards are of this character, but they need not be. See, for example, Carlill v. Carbolic Smoke Ball Co. [1892] 2 Q.B. 484 (C.A.) discussed at page 535, infra.

D. WHAT CONSTITUTES A REVOCATION

A revocation must be a clear manifestation of unwillingness to enter into the proposed bargain. Magic words are not required; for example an unequivocal statement that property previously offered for sale to the offeree has been disposed of to a third person is an effective revocation of the offer to sell the property to the offeree. On the other hand equivocal language does not necessarily destroy the power of acceptance. The question again is one of the reasonable interpretation of the language used in the specific circumstances.

RESTATEMENT, SECOND, CONTRACTS § 42:

Illustration:

4. A makes an offer to buy goods from B, and later requests B not to deliver the goods until A is in a better condition to handle them. The request does not revoke the offer.

5. A makes an offer to B, and later says to B, "Well, I don't know if we are ready. We have not decided, we might not want to go through with it." The offer is revoked.

E. INDIRECT REVOCATIONS

Offers, acceptances, and other related communications generally must be communicated to the person to be effective. The possible inference from the subjective "meeting of the minds" concept that an unexpressed revocation may be effective is, of course, universally rejected. Dickinson v. Dodds involves a somewhat different problem: Dickinson learned through Berry that Dodds had apparently changed his mind about selling the property to him. It was, in other words, an indirect revocation.

RESTATEMENT [FIRST] OF CONTRACTS § 42:

Where an offer is for the sale of an interest in land or in other things, if the offeror, after making the offer, sells or contracts to sell the interest to another person, and the offeree acquires reliable information of that fact, before he has exercised his power of creating a contract by acceptance of the offer, the offer is revoked.

RESTATEMENT, SECOND, CONTRACTS § 43:

An offeree's power of acceptance is terminated when the offeror takes definite action inconsistent with an intention to enter into the proposed contract and the offeree acquires reliable information to that effect.

Illustrations:

2. A offers to employ B to replace C, an employee of A who has given A a month's notice of intention to quit. A gives B a week to consider the proposal. C changes his mind and makes a contract with A for continued employment for a year. B asks C about his duties, and C informs B of the new contract. B immediately mails a letter of acceptance to A, which arrives within the week allowed for acceptance. There is no contract between A and B.

3. A offers to sell B a hundred shares of stock at a fixed price, and states that the offer will not be revoked for a week. Within the week C offers A a higher price for the same stock, and B learns of the higher offer. B's power of acceptance is not terminated, since he is entitled to assume that A will honor his commitment regardless of its legal effect.

———

These two illustrations were included despite the fact that the reporter's notes to § 43 indicate that no case involving the application of this section outside of land transactions was discovered. Are not these two illustrations basically inconsistent?

F. COMMUNICATION TO THIRD PERSONS

In Dickinson v. Dodds, Dickinson delivered an acceptance to Mrs. Burgess, Mr. Dodds' mother-in-law, who promptly forgot to give it to him. Should such a communication be given legal effect (absent the fact that Mr. Dickinson had already learned indirectly that Mr. Dodds had changed his mind)?

The Restatement of Contracts, Second, § 68, states that a written revocation, rejection or acceptance is received when it "comes into the possession of the person addressed, or of some person authorized by him to receive it for him, or when it is deposited in some place which he has authorized as the place for this or similar communications to be deposited for him." Under this section it seems clear that a written communication may be given legal effect even though it never comes to the attention of the person to whom it is addressed. Does it resolve the question whether delivery to Mrs. Burgess bound Mr. Dodds? Compare UCC §§ 1–201(26), 1–201(27).

RESTATEMENT, SECOND, CONTRACTS § 68:

Illustrations:

1. A sends B by mail an offer dated from A's house and states as a condition of the offer that an acceptance must be received within three days. B mails an acceptance which reaches A's house and is delivered to a servant or is deposited in a mail box at the door within three days; but A has been called away from home and does not personally receive the letter for a week. There is a contract.

2. A sends B by mail an offer, but later, desiring to revoke the offer, telegraphs B to that effect. The messenger boy carrying the telegram from the receiving office meets C, B's neighbor, who volunteers to carry the telegram to B, and accordingly is given it by the messenger boy. C forgets to deliver it to B until the following morning. An acceptance by B mailed prior to this time creates a contract.

G. MANNER OF SIGNIFYING ACCEPTANCE

The "black letter" rule is that an acceptance must comply with the precise requirements of the offer, since the offeror is the "master of his offer" and can specify what actions constitute an effective acceptance. A related problem of considerably greater complexity and dealt with separately (see infra page 489), occurs when the offeror does *not* specify precisely what actions constitute an effective acceptance.

RESTATEMENT, SECOND, CONTRACTS § 30:

Illustration:

1. A sends a letter to B stating the terms of a proposed contract. At the end he writes, "You can accept this offer only by signing on the dotted line below my own signature." A replies by telegram, "I accept your offer." There is no contract.

RESTATEMENT, SECOND, CONTRACTS § 58:

Illustrations:

1. A offers to sell a book to B for $5 and states that no other acceptance will be honored but the mailing of B's personal check for exactly $5. B personally tenders $5 in legal tender, or mails a personal check for $10. There is no contract.

2. A offers to pay B $100 for plowing Flodden field, and states that acceptance is to be made only by posting a letter before beginning work and before the next Monday noon. Before Monday noon B

completes the requested plowing and mails to A a letter stating that the work is complete. There is no contract.

These are primarily "classroom hypotheticals." In the real world, an offeror is probably little concerned with the formal aspects of an acceptance; it is unlikely, for example, that a person would prefer a personal check by mail to a payment of cash or that he wants a written promise to plow and not the plowing itself. Much more likely are disputes that involve business or economic matters that are unfavorable to the offeror; e.g., the offeror specifies a cash payment in exchange for property and the offeree tenders a personal check. Such a response by an offeree is a counteroffer, not a deviant type of acceptance, since the offeror did not offer to extend credit even for the brief time that it would take for the check to clear, and certainly did not contemplate giving up his property for a piece of paper that might "bounce."

RESTATEMENT, SECOND, CONTRACTS § 60:

Illustrations:

2. A makes an offer to B and adds, "Send your office boy around with an answer to this by twelve o'clock." The offeree comes himself before twelve o'clock and accepts. There is a contract.

3. A offers to sell his land to B on certain terms, also saying: "You must accept this, if at all, in person at my office at ten o'clock tomorrow." B's power is strictly limited to one method of acceptance.

4. A offers to sell his land to B on certain terms, also saying: "You may accept by leaving word at my house." This indicates one operative mode of acceptance; but B's power is not limited to that mode alone. A personal statement to A would serve just as well.

5. A makes an offer to B and adds, "my address is 53 State Street." This is a business address. B sends an acceptance to A's home which A receives promptly. Unless the circumstances indicate that A has made a positive requirement of the place where the acceptance must be sent, there is a contract.

A formal requirement of an acceptance being in a particular form may be ignored by the offeror; the result is an acceptance by conduct of the parties despite the restrictive language of the offer. In many situations, actions speak louder than words:

RESTATEMENT, SECOND, CONTRACTS § 22:

Illustration:

1. A, a general contractor preparing a bid on a government construction contract, receives a bid by a proposed subcontractor, B, in a given amount. A names B as a subcontractor in A's bid, but after A

receives the government contract, A unsuccessfully asks B to reduce its bid, and also unsuccessfully seeks permission from the Government to replace B as a subcontractor. Pursuant to A's instructions, B proceeds with the work, but refuses to accept a work order from A which recites that A is still seeking permission to replace B. No new work order is issued. A does issue "change orders" using B's bid as the base "contract amount." B completes the job, but A refuses to pay the full amount, contending that B is entitled only to restitutionary damages because there never was a contract. There is an enforceable contract based upon A's assent to B's bid, as manifested by A's conduct, and B is entitled to the amount it bid, as modified by the change orders.

H. WHEN IS A COMMUNICATION EFFECTIVE? HEREIN OF THE "MAILBOX RULE" AND OTHER MYSTERIES

The "black letter" rule is that in the absence of an express specification by the offeror, an acceptance is effective when it is put into the mail (or put out of the offeree's possession) while all other communications—offers, counteroffers, revocations, etc.—are effective only when received. The rule about acceptances is often colloquially referred to as "the mail box rule" though the principle is usually applied to other means of communication as well. See UCC § 2–206(1)(a) and comment 1 thereto. These counter-intuitive rules have a long history and are not fully accepted in all states.

The problem of when communications become effective is most acute when the parties are physically distant and there are no available means of instant communication. It is not surprising, therefore, that the great bulk of the cases involving these rules arose before the twentieth century and the widespread use of the modern telephone. However, it should not be assumed that these rules are obsolete: problems continue to arise from time to time which involve the application of these rules. See for example Morrison v. Thoelke, 155 So.2d 889 (Fla.App.1963), where potential purchasers of real estate received a signed formal contract through the mails from the owners; they signed the contract and mailed it back, but then had second thoughts and called the sellers' attorney to cancel the deal before the contract was received. Following the black letter rules described above, the court held that the purchasers were bound to the purchase because the acceptance became effective when it was mailed and the telephoned rejection was too late even though it was received before the acceptance was received. The correctness of such a result is certainly not self-evident.

---

(1) Historical Development

In considering the common law rules described above, one has to start with history. The case usually cited as the leading case in the development of the mail box rule is Adams v. Lindsell, 1 B. & Ald. 680,

106 Eng.Rep. 250 (K.B.1818). This case involved an offer to sell wool that was mailed on September 2, 1817, with the stipulation, "receiving your answer in the course of post." The letter was "misdirected" and as a result did not reach the plaintiffs until late on September 5. An answer accepting the offer was posted the same evening and received by the defendants on September 9; however, expecting an answer by September 7 they had sold the wool on September 8. Reasoning from the subjective theory, the defendants argued that until the plaintiff's letter was actually received there could be no binding contract, and by the time the letter was received the defendants had revoked their offer by selling the wool elsewhere. This argument was rejected:

> "The Court said, that if that were so, no contract could ever be completed by the post. For if the defendants were not bound by their offer when accepted by the plaintiffs till the answer was received, then the plaintiffs ought not to be bound till after they had received the notification that the defendants had received their answer and assented to it. And so it might go on ad infinitum. The defendants must be considered in law as making, during every instant of the time their letter was travelling, the same identical offer to the plaintiffs; and then the contract is completed by the acceptance of it by the latter. Then as to the delay in notifying the acceptance, that arises entirely from the mistake of the defendants, and it therefore must be taken as against them, that the plaintiffs' answer was received in course of post."

It should be apparent that this explanation, resting on a fiction, is not an adequate justification for the rule that acceptances are generally deemed to be effective when they are mailed. A new explanation of the "rule" was evolved: when an offeror sends his offer by mail, he makes the post office his agent to receive and carry the acceptance. The receipt by the post office is therefore receipt by the offeror himself. In some cases it was argued that the post office was the agent of both parties. See, e.g., Household Fire and Carriage Accident Insurance Co. v. Grant, 4 Ex.D. 216 (1879). However, as Professor Corbin pointed out, this argument also contains fundamental defects:

> "The term 'agent' is generally used to refer only to some human person with power to act on his principal's behalf. The 'post' is not a person, although there are many persons in the postal service; and it is by no act of any such person that the making of the contract is consummated. A letter box on the corner is neither a person nor an agent; and yet the acceptance is effective when the letter of acceptance is dropped into that box. It is the offeree himself (or some person authorized by him) who drops the letter in the box. It is he who has the power and who exercises it by his action. The 'box' has no power and does no act. It is true that a postman may thereafter remove the letter from the box; but the contract has already been made and the removal has no legal

operation. All this is equally true in case the letter is mailed by dropping it through the proper slit inside of a post office building."

1 A. Corbin, Contracts, 335–36 (1963). The agency argument has sometimes been buttressed by the further argument that by posting the letter the acceptance has been irrevocably placed out of the offeree's hands. Dickey v. Hurd, 33 F.2d 415 (1st Cir.1929). The problem with these arguments is that for nearly a century the United States postal regulations have provided that a mailer can reclaim a letter after it has been posted. A few courts have stated or intimated that this change in postal regulations must dictate abandonment of the mail box rule for acceptances, Rhode Island Tool Co. v. United States, 130 Ct.Cl. 698, 128 F.Supp. 417 (1955); Dick v. United States, 113 Ct.Cl. 94, 82 F.Supp. 326 (1949). However, these arguments have generally been rejected. In Soldau v. Organon Inc., 860 F.2d 355 (9th Cir.1988), for example, John Soldau, an employee of Organon, was discharged; he received a letter from Organon offering to pay him double the normal severance pay if Soldau would sign a release of all claims against Organon. The letter contained the proposed release, which Soldau immediately signed and dated, and deposited in a mailbox outside the post office. When Soldau returned home he found another envelope from Organon containing a check for the amount of the increased severance pay without any reference to a release. He returned to the post office, persuaded a postal employee to open the mailbox and retrieved the release. He then cashed Organon's check, and later brought suit against Organon alleging violation of state law and of the federal Age Discrimination in Employment Act. The Court held that, under both federal law and under California law, Soldau's acceptance was effective when it was mailed, and that his subsequent retrieval of the release did not affect that result. Accordingly Soldau's suit was dismissed on the ground that it was barred by the release of all claims.

The mail box rule must rest on more fundamental grounds than these rationalizations:

"A better explanation of the existing rule seems to be that in such cases the mailing of a letter has long been a customary and expected way of accepting the offer. It is ordinary business usage. More than this, however, is needed to explain why the letter is operative on mailing rather than on receipt by the offeror. Even though it is business usage to send an offer by mail, it creates no power of acceptance until it is received. Indeed, most notices sent by mail are not operative unless actually received.

"The additional reasons for holding that a different rule applies to an acceptance and that it is operative on mailing may be suggested as follows: When an offer is by mail and the acceptance also is by mail, the contract must date either from the mailing of the acceptance or from its receipt. In either case, one of the parties will be bound by the contract without being actually aware of that fact. If we hold the offeror bound on the mailing of the acceptance, he may change his position in ignorance of the acceptance; even though he waits a reasonable time before acting, he may still remain unaware that he is bound by contract because the letter of acceptance is delayed, or is actually lost or destroyed in the mails. Therefore this rule is going to cause loss and inconvenience to the offeror in some cases. But if we adopt the alternative rule that the letter of acceptance is not operative until receipt, it is the offeree who is subjected to the danger of loss and inconvenience. He can not know that his letter has been received and that he is bound by contract until a new communication is received by him. His letter of acceptance may never have been received and so no letter of notification is sent to him; or it may have been received, and the letter of notification may be delayed or entirely lost in the mails. One of the parties must carry the risk of loss and inconvenience. We need a definite and uniform rule as to this. We can choose either rule; but we must choose one. We can put the risk on either party; but we must not leave it in doubt. The party not carrying the risk can then act promptly and with confidence in reliance on the contract; the party carrying the risk can insure against it if he so desires. The business community could no doubt adjust itself to either rule; but the rule throwing the risk on the offeror has the merit of closing the deal more quickly and enabling performance more promptly. It must be remembered that in the vast majority of cases the acceptance is neither lost nor delayed; and promptness of action is of importance in all of them. Also it is the offeror who has invited the acceptance."

1 A. Corbin, Contracts, 336–37 (1950).

————

The "mail box rule" has potential application in a variety of different contexts. It should not be surprising that a broad unitary principle such as "acceptances are effective when mailed while other communications are effective on receipt" does not always lead to reasonable or plausible conclusions.

————

(2) A Revocation Crossing an Acceptance
RESTATEMENT, SECOND, CONTRACTS § 63:

Illustration:

1. A makes B an offer, inviting acceptance by telegram, and B duly telegraphs an acceptance. A purports to revoke the offer in person or by telephone or telegraph, but the attempted revocation is received by B after the telegram of acceptance is dispatched. There is no effective revocation. As demonstrated by this illustration, the mail

box rule is not limited to the postal service but applies generally to all forms of non-instantaneous communication.

The application of the mail box rule to the situation where a revocation crosses the mailed acceptance seems justified. After mailing the acceptance the offeree is likely to change position in reliance on the existence of a contract since he or she will assume the offeror still desires the transaction; the mail box rule protects this reliance. If the offeror in fact does change his mind and wishes to be sure that the revocation is effective, he must use an instantaneous means of communication to verify that the offeree has not accepted in the meantime. Since the offeree may unexpectedly be exposed while the offeror may readily protect himself, it seems reasonable to conclude that a revocation should be ineffective if it is communicated after an acceptance has been mailed.

Assume that the offeree mails an acceptance and the next day receives an unexpected revocation. What should the offeree do? He certainly may advise the offeror that the revocation is too late and he proposes to hold the offeror to the contract. May he also treat the revocation as an anticipatory repudiation? As an offer to modify or rescind the contract?

RESTATEMENT, SECOND, CONTRACTS § 42:

Illustration:

3. A sends B an offer by mail to buy a piece of land. The next day A sends B a letter stating that A has changed his mind and will not buy the land even if B has already accepted the offer. B receives A's second letter after he has duly mailed a letter of acceptance, but promptly sells the land to C. B's duty of performance is discharged.

---

(3) The Lost or Delayed Acceptance

The early case of Adams v. Lindsell involved a delayed acceptance because of a misaddressed offer. Essentially the same problem arises if the offer is received on a timely basis, but the acceptance is lost or delayed, even though properly addressed. The justification for applying the mail box rule to these situations is less clear than it is for the acceptance that is crossed by a revocation. Nevertheless some rule must be established for these situations, and the decision in Adams v. Lindsell seems to have been generally followed.

In many instances of lost or delayed acceptances, the language of the offer itself may specify the time and manner of acceptance in terms that are sufficiently precise to bring into play the general principle that an offeror is the master of his own offer, thus making Adams v. Lindsell inapplicable.

RESTATEMENT, SECOND, CONTRACTS § 63:

Illustrations:

2.   A offers to buy cotton from B, the operator of a cotton gin, B to accept by specifying the number of bales in a telegram sent before 8 p.m. the same day.   B duly sends a telegram of acceptance and ships the cotton, but the telegram is not delivered.   There is a contract, and A is bound to take and pay for the cotton.

3.   A mails to B an offer to lease land, stating, "Telegraph me Yes or No.   If I do not hear from you by noon on Friday, I shall conclude No."   B duly telegraphs "Yes," but the telegram is not delivered until after noon on Friday.   Any contract formed by the telegraphic acceptance is discharged.

4.   A offers to buy cattle for B, on an understanding that if B telegraphs "Yes" A will notify B of the amount of money needed and B will supply it.   B's "Yes" telegram is duly dispatched but does not arrive within a reasonable time.   Any contract formed by the dispatch of the telegram is discharged.

――――

The lost or delayed acceptance cases may be further justified on the theory that the offeror, having instituted communication, should normally expect a reply one way or the other; if one fails to arrive he may normally use an instantaneous method of communication to ask, "what did you decide to do?"   In contrast, an offeree would normally not know of the delay or misadventure of his communication and hence may rely on the existence of a contract.   This kind of practical justification, of course, may not be present in every case.

――――

(4) The Overtaking Rejection

The Florida case of Morrison v. Thoelke (see page 444 supra) is an example of this sequence.   When the offeror learns of the rejection before he learns that an acceptance was earlier put into the mail, Corbin's justification for the mailbox rule has little force and at first blush there seems to be no reason to insist on the literal application of the mailbox rule.   On the other hand, to permit overtaking rejections or attempted revocations of acceptance to be given effect might encourage an offeree, after mailing an acceptance, to speculate at the expense of the offeror by sending a rejection by instantaneous communication when the market moves favorably to him and remaining silent in other situations.   As indicated in *Morrison*, the case law has generally applied the mailbox rule in this situation so that the acceptance is effective even though the offeror learns of the rejection before he or she learns of the acceptance.

Since the acceptance is effective when it is mailed, an overtaking rejection is referred to in the Second Restatement as a "revocation of acceptance" rather than as a "rejection." Depending on the circumstances, a revocation of acceptance may be an anticipatory repudiation, an offer to rescind, or may permit the offeror to exercise rights of stoppage in transit or to demand additional assurance of performance. See UCC §§ 2–609, 2–702, 2–705.

RESTATEMENT, SECOND, CONTRACTS § 63:

Illustrations:

7. A mails an offer to B to appoint B A's exclusive distributor in a specified area. B duly mails an acceptance. Thereafter B mails a letter which is received by A before the acceptance is received and which rejects the offer and makes a counter-offer. On receiving the rejection and before receiving the acceptance, A executes a contract appointing C as exclusive distributor instead of B. B is estopped to enforce the contract.

8. The Government mails to A an offer to pay the amount quoted by him for the manufacture of two sets of ship propellers, and A mails an acceptance. A then discovers that by mistake he has quoted the price for a single set, and so informs the Government by a telegram which arrives before the acceptance. A's mailing the acceptance created a contract. The question whether the contract is voidable for mistake is governed by [other] rules. * * *

---

(5) A Rejection Followed by the Mailing of an Acceptance

Unlike an acceptance, a rejection is effective only when it is received. This rule may be justified by the following argument: Since the legal effect of a rejection is to terminate the offeree's power of acceptance, the rule protects the offeror's probable negative reliance upon the rejection. See the discussion at page 432 supra. However, if the offeree first mails a rejection and then mails an acceptance, a straight forward application of the mail box rule would result in a contract being formed whenever the acceptance is put into the mail before the rejection is received. This makes little sense. Not only may it encourage the offeree to take advantage of price movements at the expense of the offeror, but also, if the rejection arrives first, the offeror may rely in a negative way on there being no contract. In this situation, the Second Restatement of Contracts abandons the mail box rule and provides that a contract exists only if the offeror receives the acceptance before he receives the rejection.

RESTATEMENT, SECOND, CONTRACTS § 40:

Illustration:

1.   A makes B an offer by mail. B immediately after receiving the offer mails a letter of rejection. Within the time permitted by the offer B accepts. This acceptance creates a contract only if received before the rejection * * *. Apparently there is no modern case involving the problem of a rejection followed by the mailing of an acceptance.

In Soldau v. Organon Inc. (see p. 446 supra), the offeree successfully retrieved his acceptance from the postal service and yet was held to be bound by it. Presumably the offeror in this case was unaware of the acceptance until after the litigation was commenced when it learned through discovery that an acceptance had been mailed and subsequently retrieved. In the normal case where an acceptance is mailed and then retrieved, the offeror would presumably assume that no contract had been formed and that his offer had lapsed after the expiration of a reasonable time. Should not the withdrawn acceptance problem therefore be treated the same way as the rejection followed by an acceptance problem? Does not the rule applied in *Soldau* mean that the offeror has the choice of deciding whether or not the acceptance is effective in these situations if the offeree both accepts and rejects?

The result reached in *Soldau* is a vivid example of the principle that an executory contract is enforceable despite the absence of reliance. See The Bargain Principle, Chapter 2, Section 1, supra, at 170.

---

(6) Other Situations

The mailbox rule has potential application in a variety of issues that tangentially involve the time or place of making a contract—for example, the application of tax or regulatory laws, the choice of governing law, venue of litigation, or the date on which the statute of limitations began to run. It is customary for attorneys involved in litigation over such issues to cite and rely on the mailbox rule when it is favorable to them, and to argue that it is limited to issues of contract formation when it is unfavorable to them. While the mailbox rule may be relied on to some extent in those situations, the outcome of such situations often turns on policies broader than or different from the policies discussed in this note.

RESTATEMENT, SECOND, CONTRACTS § 63:

Illustrations:

9.   A mails to B an offer to buy goods, and B mails an acceptance. The application of a new tax statute depends on when title to the goods passes to A, and under Uniform Commercial Code § 2–401(3)(b) title

passes at the time of contracting. The time of contracting is the time when B's acceptance is mailed.

10. A offers to insure B's house against fire, the insurance to take effect upon actual payment of the premium, and invites B to reply by mailing his check for a specified amount. B duly mails the check. While B's letter is in transit, the house burns. The loss is within the period of insurance coverage.

I. WHEN IS A COMMUNICATION EFFECTIVE (Continued)

In considering the mailbox rule for acceptances, it is important to recognize when the rule is, or may not be applicable.

(1) Specification by the Offeror

The mailbox rule may be varied or rejected by the offeror's specification of the manner of acceptance. The offeror is the "master of his offer" and may specify how and when assent must be communicated.

Example. A telegraphs an offer to sell to B 100 bushels of wheat for a specified price, concluding "I must hear from you by noon tomorrow, the sixteenth, if you want this wheat." An acceptance mailed before noon on the sixteenth should not be effective unless it is received by noon on the sixteenth.

One should compare this conclusion carefully with the language used in Restatement, Second, Contracts § 63, illustration 3 (supra page 449). Are the late telegrams in these illustrations not effective as acceptances at all, or are they effective when dispatched but the contracts "discharged" when they are received after the times specified in the offers? The Restatement draws the latter inference, saying that "the language of the offer is often properly interpreted as making the offeror's duty of performance conditional upon receipt of the acceptance." Restatement, Second, Contracts, § 63, comment b. That may be true of language such as "your acceptance must be received by noon on Friday" (though even that is open to some question); however, what about an offer that states "your acceptance is not effective until received and it must be received by noon on Friday"? The issue is of importance in situations in which revocations are dispatched after the acceptances are dispatched but before they are received.

———

(2) Use of an Improper Medium of Transmission

While there is not much case law on the question, it is usually assumed that the mailbox rule is applicable only if a reasonable means of communication is adopted by the offeree. This usually means adopting at least as rapid and reliable a means of communication as that chosen by the offeror—a mail response to a mailed offer, a telegraph response to a telegraphed offer, and so forth. But cf. UCC § 2–206(1)(a), and Comment 1 thereto. Section 67 of Restatement, Second, Contracts takes the position that a communication sent by an improper medium of transmission is nevertheless effective on dispatch if it is received no later than the time transmission by a proper medium would have been received.

RESTATEMENT, SECOND, CONTRACTS § 67:

Illustration:

A makes an offer to B by telegram on Monday, requesting a reply by telegram to be sent no later than Thursday noon. B mails an acceptance on Monday which A receives on Thursday morning. Even if the mail is an unreasonable medium of acceptance under the circumstances, a revocation of the offer by A by telephone on Tuesday, or a revocation of the acceptance by B by telephone, is ineffective.

RESTATEMENT, SECOND, CONTRACTS § 60:

Illustration:

1. A mails an offer to B in which A says, "I must receive your acceptance by return mail." An acceptance sent within a reasonable time by any other means, which reaches A as soon as a letter sent by return mail would normally arrive, creates a contract on arrival. As to what is a reasonable time, see Illustration 8 to § 41 [supra page 438].

———

(3) *Messages That are not "Properly Dispatched"*

The Restatement, Second, Contracts § 66 states that the mailbox rule is not applicable to acceptances that are not properly addressed, on which proper postage is not affixed, and so forth.

———

(4) *Messages Delivered by an Agent of the Sender*

RESTATEMENT, SECOND, CONTRACTS § 63:

Illustration:

11. A makes B an offer by mail, or messenger, and B promptly sends an acceptance by his own employee. There is no contract until the acceptance is received by the offeror.

———

(5) *Alternative rules*

The mailbox rule for acceptances provides a plausible set of principles for situations in which the two parties are at a distance and communicate by mail, telegraph, or other less than instantaneous forms of communication. As Corbin demonstrates, it is possible to establish other rules which might be equally workable, and indeed some states and countries have done so. These alternative rules, of course, are neither right nor wrong; the issue is which are preferable from policy or social standpoints.

(a) Field Code States. Several western states, the most important of which is California, adopt the rule that both acceptances and revocations are effective on dispatch. S. Williston, A Treatise on the Law of Contracts § 56 (3rd ed. 1957).

(b) Civil Law Countries. The rule in civil law countries generally is that both acceptances and revocations are effective on receipt; however, the potential consequences of this rule to offerees are largely mitigated by the further rule that offers, when made, are irrevocable for a limited period.

J. CROSSING COMMUNICATIONS

A largely theoretical issue arises when identical offers cross in the mail. The law of offer and acceptance is interactive and one can argue that neither offer was intended to manifest assent to the offer of the other. As a result no contract is formed.

RESTATEMENT, SECOND, CONTRACTS § 23:

Illustration:

4. A sends B an offer through the mail to sell A's horse for $500. While this offer is in the mail, B in ignorance thereof, mails to A an offer to pay $500 for the horse. There is no contract.

———————

A more realistic example arises when negotiations are underway and the parties exchange crossing communications which, taken together, indicate agreement on all terms.

RESTATEMENT, SECOND, CONTRACTS § 23:

Illustration:

5. After negotiations through a broker, A writes B a letter purporting to confirm a contract for the sale of cloth. A's letter crosses in the mail a similar letter from B, which differs as to quantity and time of payment. A replies insisting on the quantity stated in his first letter but otherwise agreeing, B replies insisting on the time of payment stated in his first letter but otherwise agreeing. The two replies cross in the mail. There is a contract.

———————

Is this consistent with Illustration 4?

———————

K. THE EFFECT OF TECHNOLOGICAL INNOVATION

The "mail box rule", of course, was a product of the early nineteenth century. The development of the telegraph and then the telephone later that century did not affect the vitality of this rule. The decades since 1970 have seen the development of additional important electronic means of virtually instantaneous communication. Telecopiers (more popularly known as "facsimile" or "fax" machines) permit the transmission of copies of documents nearly as quickly as oral telephone conversations. Electronic data interchange (usually referred to as "EDI" or "E-mail") permits the interchange of text between computers, with the text thereafter being printed out on a printer attached to the recipient computer. Should these developments cause a reconsideration of the "mail box" rule?

The American Bar Association has developed a "Model Electronic Data Interchange Trading Partner Agreement" dealing with the increasingly common use of EDI for the transmission of contract documents between businesses that deal regularly with each other. 45 Bus. Law. 1717 (1990). Section 2.1 of this Model Agreement provides that "no document shall give rise to any obligation, until accessible to the receiving party at such party's Receipt Computer." Does that reverse the "mail box rule"? Section 2.2 adds that "upon proper receipt of any document, the receiving party shall promptly and properly transmit a functional acknowledgment in return * * *. A functional acknowledgment shall constitute conclusive evidence a document has been properly received."

Given this rapidly improving and widely used technology of document and data transmission, should other aspects of the law of contracts, e.g. UCC § 2–201, be reconsidered? Consult Report of the Electronic Messaging Services Task Force, The Commercial Use of Electronic Data Interchange—A Report and Model Trading Partner Agreement, 45 Bus.Law. 1645 (1990).

Problem

Seller sends the following offer to Buyer: "I offer to sell you one hundred gross of men's polo shirts, all sizes, assorted colors. Price $85,000. If you wish these shirts, you must let me know by November 1." The price is an attractive one, and Buyer wishes to accept. However, he would like to order only shirts that are in the season's fashionable colors of fig, cinnamon, and sage. He would particularly wish to avoid purple shirts, although he is willing to take a few purple shirts if necessary. Buyer is unable to reach Seller by telephone, and the time for acceptance will soon expire. Which of the following replies should Buyer send?

(1) "Accept your offer; fig, cinnamon, and sage only."

(2) "Accept your offer. We assume you do not send purple, which we cannot use."

(3) "Accept your offer; please send shirts in fig, cinnamon, and sage; would prefer no purple shirts in shipment."

Are there still better alternatives that you might suggest to Buyer?

———

Cf. UCC § 2–311. See also pp. 565–572, infra.

HUMBLE OIL & REFINING CO. v. WESTSIDE INVESTMENT CORP.

Supreme Court of Texas, 1968.
428 S.W.2d 92.

SMITH, JUSTICE.

Petitioner, Humble Oil & Refining Company, filed this suit on February 10, 1965, against Westside Investment Corporation seeking a judgment commanding specific performance based on a written option and contract for the sale of real estate. * * * Westside [and] Humble * * * each filed a motion for summary judgment. The court granted Westside's motion and overruled * * * [Humble's motion]. The court of civil appeals affirmed. 419 S.W.2d 448. We reverse the judgments of the courts below. We hold that Humble is entitled to specific performance of the option contract and render judgment for Humble. * * *

The facts, most of which are either stipulated or established by affidavits, are these:

On April 5, 1963, Westside as seller and Humble as buyer agreed and entered into a written contract whereby Westside gave and granted to Humble an exclusive and irrevocable option to purchase for a consideration of $35,000.00 a tract of land situated outside of the city limits of San Antonio, Bexar County, Texas, being all of lots 19, 20, 21, 22 and 23 of Block 2, Lackland Heights Subdivision.

The option contract was supported by a consideration. The contract provided that Humble might exercise the option by giving notice at any time prior to 9:00 p.m. on the 4th day of June, 1963, and by paying to Westside at the time of such notice or within ten (10) days following such notice the sum of $1750.00 as earnest money. This sum of money, together with the sum of Fifty Dollars ($50.00) as consideration paid at the time of the execution of the option contract, made a total of $1800.00 paid by Humble, leaving a balance of $33,200.00 yet to be paid as purchase money in accordance with the option contract.

On May 14, 1963, within the time period provided for in the option contract, Humble paid the above mentioned sum of $1750.00 to the designated escrow agent, Commercial Abstract & Title Company.

Westside admits in its pleadings that it entered into the option contract with Humble, but contends that the option agreement was "rejected, repudiated, and terminated by Humble." Westside contends that summary judgment proof of rejection of the option contract is contained in letters written by Humble to Westside on May 2, 1963, and May 14, 1963. The pertinent portion of the May 2nd letter reads:

"Humble Oil & Refining Company hereby exercises its option to purchase Lots 19, 20, 21, 22 and 23, Block 2, Lackland Heights Subdivision, in or near the City of San Antonio, Bexar County, Texas, granted in Option and Purchase Contract dated April 5, 1963. As additional inducement for Humble to exercise its option to purchase, you have agreed that all utilities (gas, water, sewer and electricity) will be extended to the property prior to the closing of the transaction. The contract of sale is hereby amended to provide that Seller shall extend all utility lines to the property before the date of closing.

"Please sign and return one copy of this letter in the space indicated below to signify your agreement to the amendment to the purchase contract."

The May 14th communication provided, in part, as follows:

"Humble ＊ ＊ ＊ hereby notifies you of its intention to exercise the option granted in option and purchase contract dated April 5, 1963, covering Lots 19, 20, 21, 22 and 23, Block 2, Lackland Heights Subdivision in or near the City of San Antonio, Bexar County, Texas. *The exercise of said option is not qualified and you may disregard the proposed amendment to the contract suggested in letter of May 2, 1963.* ＊ ＊ ＊ " (Emphasis added.)

We conclude from this record that the parties are in agreement that Humble's letter of May 14, 1963, and the payment of earnest money within 10 days thereof was in law a timely exercise of the option to purchase *unless* Humble's letter of May 2, 1963, terminated and rendered unenforceable the option contract. The narrow question to be determined is whether or not the letter of May 2, 1963, constitutes a rejection of the option contract. If it does, the trial court properly granted Westside's motion for summary judgment and the court of civil appeals correctly affirmed such judgment.

Westside contends that Humble's letter of May 2nd was a conditional acceptance which amounted in law to a rejection of the option contract. Westside argues that the letter of May 2nd "clearly evidences Humble's intent to accept the offer *only if* Westside would agree to an amendment to the terms of its original offer." (Emphasis added.) It further argues that Humble's letter of May 14, 1963, reflects that Humble itself understood that its letter of May 2, 1963, contained a qualified acceptance, and did not form a contract. The basis for this conclusion is the sentence in the May 14 letter which reads: "The exercise of said option is not qualified and you may disregard the proposed amendment to the contract suggested in letter dated May 2, 1963, from the undersigned. ＊ ＊ ＊ " We cannot agree with Westside's contentions.

The mere fact that the parties may choose to negotiate before accepting an option does not mean that the option contract is repudiated. As stated in James on Option Contracts § 838:

"It is laid down in the law of offers that a qualified or conditional acceptance is a rejection of the offer. It is clearly established by the decisions that a qualified or conditional acceptance of an offer does not raise a contract because the minds of the parties do not meet in agreement upon the same terms. It is said that such an acceptance is a counter-proposal for a new contract, to give legal life to which requires the assent or acceptance of the other party. It is in this sense that a qualified or conditional acceptance is a rejection of the offer first made because the original negotiations are dropped and negotiations for a new and different contract begun.

"An option is a contract, the negotiations for the making of which are concluded by the execution and delivery of the option. The minds of the parties have met in agreement, the distinctive feature of which is that the optionor, for a consideration, binds himself to keep the option open for election by the optionee, for and during the time stipulated, or implied by law.

"Under an option, the act necessary to raise a binding promise to sell, is not, therefore, an acceptance of the offer, but rather the performance of the condition of the option contract. If this is true, then the rule peculiar to offers to the effect that a conditional acceptance is, in itself, in every case, a rejection of the offer, is not applicable to an option contract, supported by a consideration and fixing a time limit for election."

The case of Cerbo v. Carabello, 376 Pa. 571, 103 A.2d 908 (1954), is to the same effect. It involved an option contract supported by a consideration wherein a lessor granted a lessee an option to purchase real estate for $11,500.00 during a stated term. Before the expiration of the term, the lessee sought unsuccessfully to obtain a reduction of the proposed sale price to $11,000.00; however, prior to the expiration date, the lessee exercised the option. The Court, in overruling lessor's contention that the negotiations instituted by lessee resulted in a termination of the option, said:

"It is true that parties to a written contract may abandon, modify or change it by words or conduct, Elliott v. Linquist, 356 Pa. 385, 388, 52 A.2d 180, 169 A.L.R. 1369. But the difficulty with defendants' position is that neither the words nor conduct establish an intention to rescind or abandon the rights under the option. * * * At most it was a non-acceptance of an offer to enter into a new contract on the same terms except for a reduction in price. * * * Nowhere does it appear that the lessee waived his rights under the option to purchase." Supra at 909.

We hold that Humble's letter of May 2, 1963, did not terminate the option contract. Humble, for a valuable consideration, purchased the right to keep the option contract open for the time specified, and the right to create a contract of purchase. Although Humble did have the right to *accept* or *reject* the option in the sense that it was free to take the action required to close the transaction, Humble was not foreclosed from negotiating relative to the contract of sale as distinguished from the option. The option, considered as an independent completed agreement, gave the optionee the right to purchase the property within the time specified. The option contract bound Humble to do nothing but granted it the right to accept or reject the option in accordance with its terms within the time and in the manner specified in the option. Westside was bound to keep the option open and could not act in derogation of the terms of the option. By the letter of May 2, 1963, Humble did not surrender or reject the option. The option to purchase was still a binding obligation between the parties when Humble exercised it on May 14, 1963.

Our holding falls within the rule stated in 1 Corbin on Contracts § 91. According to Corbin:

"If the original offer is an irrevocable offer, creating in the offeree a 'binding option,' the rule that a counter offer terminates the power of acceptance does not apply. Even if it is reasonable to hold that it terminates a revocable power, it should not be held to terminate rights and powers created by a contract. A 'binding option' is such a contract (usually unilateral); and an offer in writing, that allows a time for acceptance (either definite or reasonable) and that is irrevocable by virtue of a statute, is itself a unilateral contract. A counter offer by such an offeree, or other negotiation not resulting in a contract, does not terminate the power of acceptance."

Westside relies upon * * * cases [that] * * * are distinguishable in that they are factually different. They either show a mere offer, no stated term for the option to remain open, or no consideration for the option.

On the basis of the undisputed facts herein discussed, we hold that Humble's motion for summary judgment praying for specific performance of the contract should have been granted. * * *

———

Assume that an option may be exercised "by the optionee by giving notice to the optionor at any time prior to 9:00 p.m. on the 4th day of June, 1991." Assume further that the optionee prepares an unequivocal notice of exercise on the afternoon of June 4, 1991 and mails it at 4:00 p.m. on that date. It is received by the optionor on the morning of June 5, 1991. Is the notice of exercise timely? Restatement of Contracts, Second, § 63, comment f states that "the usual understanding is that the notification that the option has been exercised must be received by the offeror before that time."

Assume that the person granting an option for a consideration is an individual. Does her death terminate the option? Restatement, Second, Contracts § 37 states that it does not.

RESTATEMENT, SECOND, CONTRACTS § 37:

Illustrations:

1. A leases land to B, giving B an option to purchase the land for $10,000 in cash during the term of the lease. Misinterpreting the lease, B attempts to exercise the option by tendering a mortgage for $10,000. A refuses to accept the mortgage. B retains power to exercise the option by a tender conforming to the terms of the lease.

2. A gives B the same option as that stated in Illustration 1. A receives an offer from C to purchase the land and so informs B. B states that he will not exercise the option and A conveys the land to C. B's power to exercise the option is terminated.

WELL v. SCHOENEWEIS

Illinois Court of Appeals, Fourth District, 1981.
101 Ill.App.3d 254, 56 Ill.Dec. 797, 427 N.E.2d 1343.

WEBBER, JUSTICE:

Plaintiffs, buyers at a public auction of farm land, brought this action for specific performance against the defendant sellers. The circuit court of Macoupin County, sitting without a jury, entered judgment in favor of the plaintiffs and the defendants appeal. We affirm.

The evidence and exhibits at trial disclose that the defendants determined to sell their interests in 98 acres of farm land and to that end employed Homer Henke, a real estate salesman and broker as well as an auctioneer. Under their direction Henke prepared the sale bills and advertising on a budget set by defendants. He was to be compensated by a commission predicated on the sale price which he obtained.

The sale bills which were distributed prior to the sale contained the following:

"TERMS:

Buyer to enter into written real estate contract. Purchase price 98 acres × per acre bid price, unless buyer elects to have survey made at buyers expense. In which case, acreage determined by survey will be used. Buyer to pay ten per cent [10%] of purchase price day of sale and balance within 30 days or upon delivery of warranty deed conveying merchantable title. Buyer to have possession of tillable acreage after 1979 crops have been harvested. Buyer to have possession of remainder upon completion of Real Estate contract. Seller to pay 1979 taxes due in 1980. Buyer to pay 1980 taxes due in 1981. Sale held subject to owners approval."

At some time after the printing of the sale bills the defendants agreed with the auctioneer that they would offer the farm on an option as well as under the terms of the sale bill. The option was to allow the highest bidder to purchase the farm with a 10 percent down payment on the day of the sale, then quarterly payments for ten years under a contract for deed. The defendants also decided to allow the purchaser the option of taking a landlord's share of the crops and pay the 1979 taxes due in 1980 or to leave the landlord's share of the crops with the defendants requiring them to pay those taxes.

The sale was held on Saturday, July 14, 1979, and was cried by Henke as previously arranged. There is no dispute that the alternative terms concerning installment payments were announced at the sale by Henke. Plaintiffs were the successful bidders and tendered to Henke their check in the amount of 10% of the purchase price. They and Henke then signed a printed form which bore Henke's advertising and picture at the top and then is read in pertinent part as follows:

"PURCHASE OFFER

I certify that I am Ready, Willing and Able to pay $118,090 for the 98 Acre Farm—Schoeneweis and Evans Property   Property in Macoupin County, in the state of Illinois and to Immediately Execute a SALES–PURCHASE CONTRACT, Subject to the Terms and Conditions as Publicly Announced, this date:

July 14   , 1979

Don Well Lloyd Well Brighton, Ill.

Buyer

Olen Leonard   Buyer

Address: Brighton   ; Phone 372–3630

Witness: Homer Henke

[Underscoring indicates blank lines on the form; material inserted is handwritten on original.]

The purchase offer form, as set forth above, was admitted at trial without objection. Henke testified that the check was tendered and the purchase order form executed immediately after the property was struck off to plaintiffs, but then a dispute erupted concerning the meaning of "quarterly payments". Plaintiffs asked if such payments could be made in smaller amounts from the beginning with a "balloon" payment at the end. Henke and defendants insisted that equal payments were meant. * * *

[The plaintiffs and defendants held several meetings to discuss the terms of the sale. They were unable to reach agreement largely because defendants proposed that the interest rate be lowered and the purchase price increased to affect the reduced interest payments. Defendants finally broke off negotiations, directing Henke to return plaintiffs' funds, which had been placed in an escrow account. Henke, however, did not do so, awaiting the outcome of the litigation.]

Plaintiffs filed suit for specific performance and alternatively for damages on November 5, 1979. The trial court * * * ordered the defendants to perform the terms of the contract, which it found to be: 98 acres at $1,205 per acre, the balance of the purchase price to be paid at the option of the plaintiffs either within 30 days or by contract for deed with equal quarterly payments over a ten-year period with interest at 10%.

A central fact in this litigation is the existence of the public auction sale of the real estate. While such procedure is not unknown in private transactions, the great majority of reported authorities concern auctions of personal property in such circumstances. The public auction of real estate appears most often in the context of judicial or execution sales. However, it is our opinion that the basic rules governing an auction are the same, whether it be for chattels or judicial sales or private sales of real estate.

The sale at auction of chattel property is now governed by [§ 2–328] of the Uniform Commercial Code. Defendants claim that the trial court improperly applied this section to the instant case in that it does not apply to real estate. The record discloses that the trial court did make reference to the Uniform Commercial Code in its letter opinion, but there is no indication that it relied on it in making its final judgment. * * *

The fundamental rule at common law, and now incorporated into statute insofar as chattels are concerned, is that a bid at an auction constitutes an offer to buy, the fall of the hammer or any other customary means constitutes the acceptance, and a contract is then made. In the case of judicial sales at auction, there is a variation because of the necessity of court supervision of the sale which it has ordered. The final acceptance is made by the court, not the crier of the sale, and the bid remains an offer only until confirmation of the crier's acceptance by the court. *Guettel v. Hillebrecht* (1952), 347 Ill.App. 104, 106 N.E.2d 146.

At the private auction of real estate, as has been said, the contract is made upon the fall of the hammer: the bidder agrees to buy and to pay the amount of his bid; the owners agree to sell and convey at that price. The only remaining question is the terms of sale. The rule for real estate is the same as for chattels. The publicly proclaimed terms of sale are binding upon both parties. In Restatement (Second) of Contracts sec. 28(2) (1981) it is said:

> "Unless a contrary intention is manifested, bids at an auction embody terms made known by advertisement, posting or other publication of which bidders are or should be aware, as modified by any announcement made by the auctioneer when the goods are put up".

In applying these principles to the instant case, it is clear that the contract was made when Henke struck off the property to the plaintiffs. The terms of sale were clearly set forth in the sale bills and the public announcement at the time of the auction. Defendants argue that the language in the sale bills, "Buyer to enter into written real estate contract," makes the written contract a precondition to the acceptance of the bid. We do not agree. Any written contract would be nothing more than a memorialization of what had taken place at the auction. Defendants' efforts to alter the terms of sale *ex post facto,* * * * were necessarily futile. There is nothing in either the sale bills or the public pronouncement to indicate that other and different terms were to be incorporated in the written contract. Defendants elected the auction method of disposing of their property and they are bound by the rules governing auctions. After the hammer falls, there is no further room for negotiation, and any misgivings on the part of the sellers come too late.

Defendants argue that the contract was too indefinite to be susceptible of specific performance and cite a long list of specific performance cases where such was the holding of the courts. We have no quarrel with the doctrine which is well established in the law, but it has no application here. None of the cases cited involved an auction sale, but were concerned with oral contracts to convey, negotiations which had not yet been completed, ambiguous terms (what is a "standard mortgage"), and the like. Specific performance cases, like will construction cases, have very little precedential value, since each must be determined on its own facts. It has been truly said that no will has a brother. The same is equally applicable to contracts. * * *

Two further contentions of defendants merit short mention. First, they argue that plaintiffs have abandoned the contract and the trial court's finding in this regard, that they had not, is contrary to the manifest weight of the evidence. We do not agree. The source of all the difficulty was the attempt by defendants to substitute a new contract for that made at the auction. Such action would be sufficient to excuse plaintiffs if they so desired. They have not so indicated, but on the contrary stand ready to perform under the terms of the auction agreement. Defendants' contention has no merit.

Defendants' final argument relates to the Statute of Frauds. They cite the familiar rule that partial payment without more is insufficient to take the case out from under the statute. However, equity will not permit one to take advantage of his own wrong. Defendants' actions described above made further performance by plaintiffs impossible. Furthermore, when one authorizes another to make a parol contract for him, he cannot insist on the Statute of Frauds as a defense. *Doty v. Wilder* (1854), 15 Ill. 407.

Here the purchase offer might be considered a sufficient memorandum to satisfy the statute except that it omits the alternative method of payment, *i.e.*, 40 equal quarterly payments, which must be proved by parol. However, we need not deal with such a problem since Henke had authority to make such a contract.

The order of the circuit court of Macoupin County directing specific performance by the defendants is affirmed.

Affirmed.

MILLS and LONDRIGAN, JJ., concur.

SPECIALTY MAINTENANCE AND CONSTRUCTION, INC. v. ROSEN SYSTEMS, INC.

Texas Court of Appeals, First District, 1990.
790 S.W.2d 835.

Before COHEN, WARREN and DUNN, JJ.

COHEN, JUSTICE.

Specialty Maintenance & Construction, Inc. ("Specialty") sued Rosen Systems, Inc. ("Rosen"), alleging Rosen violated the Deceptive Trade Practices Act by advertising goods for auction with intent not to sell them as advertised. The trial court rendered a take-nothing judgment, based on the jury verdict that Rosen did not advertise deceptively. * * *

Rosen conducted an auction of new and used heavy machinery in Houston on October 30, 1984. Rosen mailed an advertisement about the auction to appellant in Florida. The advertisement stated:

SPECIAL NOTICE

Certain machines have **minimum opening bids** which are set out in this brochure. [All emphasis here and below is in the original advertisement, except as stated.]

All other machinery will be sold **without minimum** to the highest bidder.

TERMS:

Everything offered on as-is, where-is basis without warranty or guarantee. Payment in full sale day. 25% deposit when bid struck down. Balance at conclusion of sale. Nothing can be removed until sale is over. Payment shall be in cash or cashier's check. Company or personal check accepted only if accompanied by letter from Payor's bank guaranteeing payment. No exceptions. Sale subject to local sales tax. **Complete terms will be printed in catalog of sale.** [Not emphasized in the advertisement].

The following appeared in red print:

NOTICE TO AUCTION BUYERS: The new machines listed on this page will be sold with a **minimum opening bid.** The minimums are listed with the machinery. We know that most auctions you attend have reserves on some of the major pieces of equipment. These reserves are not revealed to the buyers and they sometimes feel deceived when they do attend and find out there were unreasonable reserves placed on items of interest to them.

We have strived in our 67 years of operation to be straight forward and honest with our customers. It is for this reason that we have implemented this method at this auction. Further we believe these minimums are at such a level that it will entice you to come and bid rather than discourage you from coming.

All other items in the sale except the real estate will be **sold without minimums** to the highest bidder.

Lester Garringer, appellant's production manager, saw an 84–inch vertical boring mill he wanted to buy. The brochure did not state a minimum bid for this equipment.

Garringer came to Houston primarily to purchase the mill and brought a letter of credit for $20,000. When he registered at the auction, he received a bidder's card that contained the terms and conditions of sale below the highlighted words, "Note well." Garringer signed the card, but did not read it that day.

The terms of sale included the following:

13. **ADDITION TO OR WITHDRAWAL FROM SALE:** The auctioneer reserves the right to withdraw from sale any of the property listed or to sell at this sale property not listed, and also reserves the right to group one or more lots into one or more selling lots or to subdivide into two or more selling lots. Whenever the best interest of the seller will be served, the auctioneer reserves the right to sell all the property listed in bulk. * * *

16. **RESERVE:** The Auctioneer reserves the right to reject any and all bids. On lots upon which there is a reserve, the auctioneer shall have the right to bid on behalf of the seller which in the opinion of the auctioneer is merely a nominal or fractional advance and might prove injurious to the sale.

Upon arriving at the auction, Garringer also received a catalog listing the items for sale. The vertical boring mill was listed in the catalog without a minimum bid specified. Minimum bids were listed for other items in the catalog. The inside cover of the catalog also listed general terms and conditions of sale in language similar to the bidding card. Garringer first saw the bidding card and catalog of sale at the auction.

Before the auction began, the auctioneer, Mike Rosen, read the rules of sale, including paragraphs 13 and 16, above. Bidding on the vertical boring mill began with the auctioneer requesting a bid of $10,000. There was no response, and Rosen then asked for a beginning bid. Garringer bid $2,000, and Rosen looked at him, identifying him as the bidder. Garringer testified that Rosen looked at him after he made the same bid once or twice more, and shook his head, "no." Then, Rosen passed the piece of equipment, "no sale," and turned over the auction to another auctioneer. No one else bid on the mill. Garringer purchased two other pieces of equipment at the auction that day.

Mike Rosen testified that he rejected Garringer's bid because it was too low. Rosen testified the auction was "with reserve," and thus, he could reject any bids. [The Court quotes UCC § 2–328(c) and the first sentence of Comment 2.]

Thus, if a sale is "without reserve," the auctioneer must sell to the highest bidder. If it is "with reserve," the auctioneer may reject the highest bid and refuse to sell. *Intertex, Inc. v. Cowden*, 728 S.W.2d 813, 818 (Tex.App.—Houston [1st Dist.] 1986, no writ). Statements in advertisements that goods will be offered "to the highest bidder," do not mean that the auction will be conducted without reserve. *See Drew v. John Deere Co. of Syracuse*, 19 A.D.2d 308, 241 N.Y.S.2d 267, 270 (1963). Such statements are considered preliminary negotiation, not creating legal relations; thus, sellers may still reject bids, and bidders may still withdraw them.

Rosen testified that in the auction trade in Harris County and in Texas, the concepts "reserve" and "without minimum" have different meanings. He testified that "reserve" means the auctioneer may reject all bids and refuse to sell, while in an auction "without reserve," the auctioneer must sell at any price. Thus, in an auction without reserve, if someone bid 50 cents on an 84–inch vertical mill, he would sell for 50 cents.

Rosen also explained the terms "with minimum" and "without minimum." He stated that "with minimum" meant a starting bid was advertised, but it was not necessarily an acceptable bid, just a minimum starting point. Thus, in a sale with reserve, even though the advertised minimum was $10,000, the auctioneer could still reject it. He testified that "without minimum" meant only that no minimum bid was set. He stated:

> Any bid offered would be entered. And if there is reserve on the sale, then the reserve is still in place and could be exercised * * *. If it is without minimum and without reserve, no matter what the sale price, it sells. But if it is without minimum and with reserve, then the auctioneer still reserves his rights to bid on behalf of the owner.

Rosen testified that if, as here, he advertised "without minimum," he could nevertheless reject any bid and refuse to sell to the highest bidder. He testified that when he mailed the brochure, he intended, despite its language, to conduct the sale "with reserve," in accordance with the rules of the catalog, the bidder's card, the industry custom, and his company's practice. He admitted that nothing in the brochure stated Rosen reserved the right to reject bids, but testified it was the industry custom not to include the auction rules in mailed advertisements.

Rosen admitted the brochure stated that the goods would be sold to the highest bidder; that he knew when he sent the brochure that the goods would not necessarily be sold to the highest bidder because this and all Rosen auctions were with reserve and the highest bid could therefore be rejected; that the brochure said exactly what Rosen intended it to say; and that its purpose was to entice buyers to attend.

Rosen testified his intent in listing some machinery without a minimum bid was:

> to let people know that there were no minimums in the rest of the machinery other than the new pieces. The intent was that we wanted to let people know that on those new pieces of equipment just exactly what the minimums would be. We felt like the buyers out there would think that they were not going to be able to buy them at a reasonable price, so we wanted to let them know that they could.

Garringer testified the term "reserve" meant to him that the auctioneer could refuse to sell for any reason. To him, selling "without minimum" was the same as selling "without reserve." On the day of the auction, he did not know that under Texas law, all auctions were with reserve unless otherwise stated.

We note that the evidence here would have supported the opposite verdict, i.e., that Rosen Systems, Inc. intended not to sell its goods as advertised. In particular, Rosen's flattering comparison of itself to other auctioneers used the terms "reserves" and "minimums" interchangeably, so that a jury could have easily found that Rosen intended to convey the false impression that "reserves" and "minimums" were the same thing. Although this language may invite lawsuits like this one, the issue before us is whether there was overwhelming evidence that Rosen intended not to sell as advertised.

The evidence showed that:

1) The brochure did not advertise the sale as being without reserve;

2) The brochure disclosed that there were other terms of sale, and Rosen disclosed those terms to Garringer at least twice before the sale, orally and in writing;

3) The term "without minimum" had a specific meaning in the auction industry, and Garringer made his living, at least in part, by buying industrial goods worth tens of thousands of dollars at auctions; and

4) The brochure advertised industrial goods only and was a targeted mailing to an experienced auction purchaser; there was no evidence of advertising on television, radio, or in general circulation print media that reached, or was intended to reach, an unsophisticated plaintiff.

We deem the foregoing to be probative of Rosen's intent, an element of appellant's claim. Giving great deference, as we must, to the jury's discretion, we find that it could have inferred that Rosen did not intend to sell other than as advertised because Rosen could have reasonably assumed that an experienced auction buyer, like Garringer's employer, would know the law and customs of the trade and thus would assume the auction was with reserve. We may not set aside a jury verdict just because we may disagree with it.

We conclude that although the brochure was potentially highly misleading, the jury could have found it was not intended to mislead this particular plaintiff. Therefore, the verdict was not against the great weight of the evidence.

The point of error is overruled.

The judgment is affirmed.

PITCHFORK RANCH CO. v. BAR TL, 615 P.2d 541 (1980). Bar TL (a Wyoming corporation) announced that it planned to sell its entire ranch valued at approximately $4,000,000 at "an absolute auction with no reserves and no minimum." Kennedy, the auctioneer, announced that bids would be confined to $25,000 minimum increments before the bidding began. Pitchfork made a bid of $1,600,000 and the bidding stalled. Ronald Florance, who had come into the room after the $25,000 minimum increment policy was announced, then made a bid of $1,610,000. This bid was ignored (whether because it was not heard by Kennedy or because it violated Kennedy's minimum increment announcement, or both, was unclear) and Kennedy announced that the properties had been sold to Pitchfork for $1,600,000. In an action by Pitchfork for specific performance, judgment was entered for the defendant. Under an auction without reserve, the auctioneer was obligated to sell the property to the highest lawful bidder. The announced minimum increment policy was invalid since it had not been approved by BAR TL, and Pitchfork was not the highest lawful bidder. Pitchfork had also obtained an assignment of any rights that Florance may have had arising from the auction. Should that have made any difference?

---

1. Amy Smith is in financial difficulty and must sell jewels and heirlooms that have been in her family for generations. She has decided on a public sale by auction. However, she wants to be sure that individual items sell for not less than specific amounts. How should she proceed? Does she have to announce these minimum prices before the sale?

2. May Amy Smith secretly station two of her grandchildren in the audience to put in bids if the auction seems to be lagging in order to increase bidding interest? This is sometimes referred to as "salting" the audience.

3. May the four antique collectors most likely to bid on the largest items agree that they will put in a single joint bid?

RESTATEMENT, SECOND, CONTRACTS § 28:

Illustrations:

3. A advertises, "I offer my farm Blackacre for sale to the highest cash bidder and undertake to make conveyance to the person submitting the highest bid received at the address below within the next thirty

days." This is an offer, and each bid operates as an acceptance creating rights and duties conditional on no higher bid being received within thirty days.

5. A advertises a sale of his household furniture without reserve. An article is put up for sale without contrary announcement and B is the highest bidder; but A, dissatisfied with the bidding, either accepts a higher fictitious bid from an agent employed for the purpose, or openly withdraws the article from sale. A is bound by contract to sell the article to B. Neither B nor the others attending the auction have legal ground for complaint if A withdraws the remaining furniture from sale before it is actually put up.

JAMES BAIRD CO. v. GIMBEL BROTHERS, INC.

United States Court of Appeals, Second Circuit, 1933.
64 F.2d 344.

Before MANTON, L. HAND, and SWAN, CIRCUIT JUDGES.

L. HAND, CIRCUIT JUDGE.

The plaintiff sued the defendant for breach of a contract to deliver linoleum under a contract of sale; the defendant denied the making of the contract; the parties tried the case to the judge under a written stipulation and he directed judgment for the defendant. The facts as found, bearing on the making of the contract, the only issue necessary to discuss, were as follows: The defendant, a New York merchant, knew that the Department of Highways in Pennsylvania had asked for bids for the construction of a public building. It sent an employee to the office of a contractor in Philadelphia, who had possession of the specifications, and the employee there computed the amount of the linoleum which would be required on the job, underestimating the total yardage by about one-half the proper amount. In ignorance of this mistake, on December twenty-fourth the defendant sent to some twenty or thirty contractors, likely to bid on the job, an offer to supply all the linoleum required by the specifications at two different lump sums, depending upon the quality used. These offers concluded as follows: "If successful in being awarded this contract, it will be absolutely guaranteed, * * * and * * * we are offering these prices for reasonable" (sic), "prompt acceptance after the general contract has been awarded." The plaintiff, a contractor in Washington, got one of these on the twenty-eighth, and on the same day the defendant learned its mistake and telegraphed all the contractors to whom it had sent the offer, that it withdrew it and would substitute a new one at about double the amount of the old. This withdrawal reached the plaintiff at Washington on the afternoon of the same day, but not until after it had put in a bid at Harrisburg at a lump sum, based as to linoleum upon the prices quoted by the defendant. The public authorities accepted the plaintiff's bid on December thirtieth, the defendant having meanwhile written a letter of confirmation of its withdrawal, received on the thirty-first. The plaintiff formally accepted the offer on January second, and, as the defendant persisted in declining to recognize the existence of a contract, sued it for damages on a breach.

Unless there are circumstances to take it out of the ordinary doctrine, since the offer was withdrawn before it was accepted, the acceptance was too late. Restatement of Contracts § 35. To meet this the plaintiff argues as follows: It was a reasonable implication from the defendant's offer that it should be irrevocable in case the plaintiff acted upon it, that is to say, used the prices quoted in making its bid, thus putting itself in a position from which it could not withdraw without great loss. While it might have withdrawn its bid after receiving the revocation, the time had passed to submit another, and as the item of linoleum was a very trifling part of the cost of the whole building, it would have been an unreasonable hardship to expect it to lose the contract on that account, and probably forfeit its deposit. While it is true that the plaintiff might in advance have secured a contract conditional upon the success of its bid, this was not what the defendant suggested. It understood that the contractors would use its offer in their bids, and would thus in fact commit themselves to supplying the linoleum at the proposed prices. The inevitable implication from all this was that when the contractors acted upon it, they accepted the offer and promised to pay for the linoleum, in case their bid were accepted.

It was of course possible for the parties to make such a contract, and the question is merely as to what they meant; that is, what is to be imputed to the words they used. Whatever plausibility there is in the argument, is in the fact that the defendant must have known the predicament in which the contractors would be put if it withdrew its offer after the bids went in. However, it seems entirely clear that the contractors did not suppose that they accepted the offer merely by putting in their bids. If, for example, the successful one had repudiated the contract with the public authorities after it had been awarded to him, certainly the defendant could not have sued him for a breach. If he had become bankrupt, the defendant could not prove against his estate. It seems plain therefore that there was no contract between them. And if there be any doubt as to this, the language of the offer sets it at rest. The phrase, "if successful in being awarded this contract," is scarcely met by the mere use of the prices in the bids. Surely such a use was not an "award" of the contract to the defendant. Again, the phrase, "we are offering these prices for * * * prompt acceptance after the general contract has been awarded," looks to the usual communication of an acceptance, and precludes the idea that the use of the offer in the bidding shall be the equivalent. It may indeed be argued that this last language contemplated no more than an early notice that the offer had been accepted, the actual acceptance being the bid, but that would wrench its natural meaning too far, especially in the light of the preceding phrase. The contractors had a ready escape from their difficulty by insisting upon a contract before they used the figures; and in commercial transactions it does not in the end promote justice to seek strained interpretations in aid of those who do not protect themselves.

But the plaintiff says that even though no bilateral contract was made, the defendant should be held under the doctrine of "promissory estoppel." This is to be chiefly found in those cases where persons subscribe to a venture, usually charitable, and are held to their promises after it has been completed. It has been applied much more broadly, however, and has now been generalized in section 90, of the Restatement of Contracts. We may arguendo accept it as it there reads, for it does not apply to the case at bar. Offers are ordinarily made in exchange for a consideration, either a counter-promise or some other act which the promisor wishes to secure. In such cases they propose bargains; they presuppose that each promise or performance is an inducement to the other.

But a man may make a promise without expecting an equivalent; a donative promise, conditional or absolute. The common law provided for such by sealed instruments, and it is unfortunate that these are no longer generally available. The doctrine of "promissory estoppel" is to avoid the harsh results of allowing the promisor in such a case to repudiate, when the promisee has acted in reliance upon the promise. Siegel v. Spear & Co., 234 N.Y. 479, 138 N.E. 414, 26 A.L.R. 1205. Cf. Allegheny College v. National Bank, 246 N.Y. 369, 159 N.E. 173, 57 L.R.A. 980. But an offer for an exchange is not meant to become a promise until a consideration has been received, either a counter-promise or whatever else is stipulated. To extend it would be to hold the offeror regardless of the stipulated condition of his offer. In the case at bar the defendant offered to deliver the linoleum in exchange for the plaintiff's acceptance, not for its bid, which was a matter of indifference to it. That offer could become a promise to deliver only when the equivalent was received; that is, when the plaintiff promised to take and pay for it. There is no room in such a situation for the doctrine of "promissory estoppel."

Nor can the offer be regarded as of an option, giving the plaintiff the right seasonably to accept the linoleum at the quoted prices if its bid was accepted, but not binding it to take and pay, if it could get a better bargain elsewhere. There is not the least reason to suppose that the defendant meant to subject itself to such a one-sided obligation. True, if so construed, the doctrine of "promissory estoppel" might apply, the plaintiff having acted in reliance upon it, though, so far as we have found, the decisions are otherwise. As to that, however, we need not declare ourselves.

Judgment affirmed.

DRENNAN v. STAR PAVING CO.

Supreme Court of California, 1958.
51 Cal.2d 409, 333 P.2d 757.

TRAYNOR, JUSTICE.

Defendant appeals from a judgment for plaintiff in an action to recover damages caused by defendant's refusal to perform certain paving work according to a bid it submitted to plaintiff.

On July 28, 1955, plaintiff, a licensed general contractor, was preparing a bid on the "Monte Vista School Job" in the Lancaster school district. Bids had to be submitted before 8:00 p.m. Plaintiff testified that it was customary in that area for general contractors to receive the bids of subcontractors by telephone on the day set for bidding and to rely on them in computing their own bids. Thus on that day plaintiff's secretary, Mrs. Johnson, received by telephone between fifty and seventy-five subcontractors' bids for various parts of the school job. As each bid came in, she wrote it on a special form, which she brought into plaintiff's office. He then posted it on a master cost sheet setting forth the names and bids of all subcontractors. His own bid had to include the names of subcontractors who were to perform one-half of one per cent or more of the construction work, and he had also to provide a bidder's bond of ten per cent of his total bid of $317,385 as a guarantee that he would enter the contract if awarded the work.

Late in the afternoon, Mrs. Johnson had a telephone conversation with Kenneth R. Hoon, an estimator for defendant. He gave his name and telephone number and stated that he was bidding for defendant for the paving work at the Monte Vista School according to plans and specifications and that his bid was $7,131.60. At Mrs. Johnson's request he repeated his bid. Plaintiff listened to the bid over an extension telephone in his office and posted it on the master sheet after receiving the bid form from Mrs. Johnson. Defendant's was the lowest bid for the paving. Plaintiff computed his own bid accordingly and submitted it with the name of defendant as the subcontractor for the paving. When the bids were opened on July 28th, plaintiff's proved to be the lowest, and he was awarded the contract.

On his way to Los Angeles the next morning plaintiff stopped at defendant's office. The first person he met was defendant's construction engineer, Mr. Oppenheimer. Plaintiff testified: "I introduced myself and he immediately told me that they had made a mistake in their bid to me the night before, they couldn't do it for the price they had bid, and I told him I would expect him to carry through with their original bid because I had used it in compiling my bid and the job was being awarded them. And I would have to go and do the job according to my bid and I would expect them to do the same."

Defendant refused to do the paving work for less than $15,000. Plaintiff testified that he "got figures from other people" and after trying for several months to get as low a bid as possible engaged L & H Paving Company, a firm in Lancaster, to do the work for $10,948.60.

The trial court found on substantial evidence that defendant made a definite offer to do the paving on the Monte Vista job according to the plans and specifications for $7,131.60, and that plaintiff relied on defendant's bid in computing his own bid for the school job and naming defendant therein as the subcontractor for the paving work. Accordingly, it entered judgment for plaintiff in the amount of $3,817.00 (the difference between defendant's bid and the cost of the paving to plaintiff) plus costs.

Defendant contends that there was no enforceable contract between the parties on the ground that it made a revocable offer and revoked it before plaintiff communicated his acceptance to defendant.

There is no evidence that defendant offered to make its bid irrevocable in exchange for plaintiff's use of its figures in computing his bid. Nor is there evidence that would warrant interpreting plaintiff's use of defendant's bid as the acceptance thereof, binding plaintiff, on condition he received the main contract, to award the subcontract to defendant. In sum, there was neither an option supported by consideration nor a bilateral contract binding on both parties.

Plaintiff contends, however, that he relied to his detriment on defendant's offer and that defendant must therefore answer in damages for its refusal to perform. Thus the question is squarely presented: Did plaintiff's reliance make defendant's offer irrevocable?

[The court here quoted from § 90 of the Restatement of Contracts.] This rule applies in this state.

Defendant's offer constituted a promise to perform on such conditions as were stated expressly or by implication therein or annexed thereto by operation of law. (See 1 Williston, Contracts [3rd ed.], § 24A, p. 56, § 61, p. 196.) Defendant had reason to expect that if its bid proved the lowest it would be used by plaintiff. It induced "action * * * of a definite and substantial character on the part of the promisee."

Had defendant's bid expressly stated or clearly implied that it was revocable at any time before acceptance we would treat it accordingly. It was silent on revocation, however, and we must therefore determine whether there are conditions to the right of revocation imposed by law or reasonably inferable in fact. In the analogous problem of an offer for a unilateral contract, the theory is now obsolete that the offer is revocable at any time before complete performance. Thus section 45 of the Restatement of Contracts provides: "If an offer for a unilateral contract is made, and part of the consideration requested in the offer is given or tendered by the offeree in response thereto, the offeror is bound by a contract, the duty of immediate performance of which is conditional on the full consideration being given or tendered within the time stated in the offer, or, if no time is stated therein, within a reasonable time." In explanation, comment *b* states that the "main offer includes as a subsidiary promise, necessarily implied, that if part of the requested performance is given, the offeror will not revoke his offer, and that if tender is made it will be accepted. Part performance or tender may thus furnish consideration for the subsidiary promise. Moreover, merely acting in justifiable reliance on an offer may in some cases serve as sufficient reason for making a promise binding (see § 90)."

Whether implied in fact or law, the subsidiary promise serves to preclude the injustice that would result if the offer could be revoked after the offeree had acted in detrimental reliance thereon. Reasonable reliance resulting in a foreseeable prejudicial change in position affords a compelling basis also for implying a subsidiary promise not to revoke an offer for a bilateral contract.

The absence of consideration is not fatal to the enforcement of such a promise. It is true that in the case of unilateral contracts the Restatement finds consideration for the implied subsidiary promise in the part performance of the bargained-for exchange, but its reference to section 90 makes clear that consideration for such a promise is not always necessary. The very purpose of section 90 is to make a promise binding even though there was no consideration "in the sense of something that is bargained for and given in exchange." (See 1 Corbin, Contracts 634 et seq.) Reasonable reliance serves to hold the offeror in lieu of the consideration ordinarily required to make the offer binding. In a case involving similar facts the Supreme Court of South Dakota stated that "we believe that reason and justice demand that the doctrine [of section 90] be applied to the present facts. We cannot believe that by accepting this doctrine as controlling in the state of facts before us we will abolish the requirement of a consideration in contract cases, in any different sense than an ordinary estoppel abolishes some legal requirement in its application. We are of the opinion, therefore, that the defendants in executing the agreement [which was not supported by consideration] made a promise which they should have reasonably expected would induce the plaintiff to submit a bid based thereon to the Government, that such promise did induce this action, and that injustice can be avoided only by enforcement of the promise." Northwestern Engineering Co. v. Ellerman, 69 S.D. 397, 408, 10 N.W.2d 879, 884; see also, Robert Gordon, Inc., v. Ingersoll-Rand Co., 7 Cir., 117 F.2d 654, 661; cf. James Baird Co. v. Gimbel Bros., 2 Cir., 64 F.2d 344.

When plaintiff used defendant's offer in computing his own bid, he bound himself to perform in reliance on defendant's terms. Though defendant did not bargain for this use of its bid neither did defendant make it idly, indifferent to whether it would be used or not. On the contrary it is reasonable to suppose that defendant submitted its bid to obtain the subcontract. It was bound to realize the substantial possibility that its bid would be the lowest, and that it would be included by plaintiff in his bid. It was to its own interest that the contractor be awarded the general contract; the lower the subcontract bid, the lower the general contractor's bid was likely to be and the greater its chance of acceptance and hence the greater defendant's chance of getting the paving subcontract. Defendant had reason not only to expect plaintiff to rely on its bid but to want him to. Clearly defendant had a stake in plaintiff's reliance on its bid. Given this interest and the fact that plaintiff is bound by his own bid, it is only fair that plaintiff should have at least an opportunity to accept defendant's bid after the general contract has been awarded to him.

It bears noting that a general contractor is not free to delay acceptance after he has been awarded the general contract in the hope of getting a better price. Nor can he reopen bargaining with the subcontractor and at the same time claim a continuing right to accept the original offer. See, R. J. Daum Const. Co. v. Child, Utah, 247 P.2d 817, 823. In the present case plaintiff promptly informed defendant that plaintiff was being awarded the job and that the subcontract was being awarded to defendant.

Defendant contends, however, that its bid was the result of mistake and that it was therefore entitled to revoke it. It relies on the rescission cases of M. F. Kemper Const. Co. v. City of Los Angeles, 37 Cal.2d 696, 235 P.2d 7, and Brunzell Const. Co. v. G. J. Weisbrod, Inc., 134 Cal.App.2d 278, 285 P.2d 989. In those cases, however, the bidder's mistake was known or should have been known to the offeree, and the offeree could be placed in status quo. Of course, if plaintiff had reason to believe that defendant's bid was in error, he could not justifiably rely on it, and section 90 would afford no basis for enforcing it. Robert Gordon, Inc., v. Ingersoll-Rand, Inc., 7 Cir., 117 F.2d 654, 660. Plaintiff, however, had no reason to know that defendant had made a mistake in submitting its bid, since there was usually a variance of 160 per cent between the highest and lowest bids for paving in the desert around Lancaster. He committed himself to performing the main contract in reliance on defendant's figures. Under these circumstances defendant's mistake, far from relieving it of its obligation, constitutes an additional reason for enforcing it, for it misled plaintiff as to the cost of doing the paving. Even had it been clearly understood that defendant's offer was revocable until accepted, it would not necessarily follow that defendant had no duty to exercise reasonable care in preparing its bid. It presented its bid with knowledge of the substantial possibility that it would be used by plaintiff; it could foresee the harm that would ensue from an erroneous underestimate of the cost. Moreover, it was motivated by its own business interest. Whether or not these considerations alone would justify recovery for negligence had the case been tried on that theory (see Biakanja v. Irving, 49 Cal.2d 647, 650, 320 P.2d 16), they are persuasive that defendant's mistake should not defeat recovery under the rule of section 90 of the Restatement of Contracts. As between the subcontractor who made the bid and the general contractor who reasonably relied on it, the loss resulting from the mistake should fall on the party who caused it.

Leo F. Piazza Paving Co. v. Bebek & Brkich, 141 Cal.App.2d 226, 296 P.2d 368, 371, and Bard v. Kent, 19 Cal.2d 449, 122 P.2d 8, 139 A.L.R. 1032, are not to the contrary. In the Piazza case the court sustained a finding that defendants intended, not to make a firm bid, but only to give the plaintiff "some kind of an idea to use" in making its bid; there was evidence that the defendants had told plaintiff they were unsure of the significance of the specifications. There was thus no offer, promise, or representation on which the defendants should reasonably have expected the plaintiff to rely. The Bard case held that an option not supported by consideration was revoked by the death of the optionor. The issue of recovery under the rule of section 90 was not pleaded at the trial, and it does not appear that the offeree's reliance was "of a definite and substantial character" so that injustice could be avoided "only by the enforcement of the promise."

There is no merit in defendant's contention that plaintiff failed to state a cause of action, on the ground that the complaint failed to allege that plaintiff attempted to mitigate the damages or that they could not have been mitigated. Plaintiff alleged that after defendant's default, "plaintiff had to procure the services of the L & H Co. to perform said asphaltic paving for the sum of $10,948.60." Plaintiff's uncontradicted evidence showed that he spent several months trying to get bids from other subcontractors and that he took the lowest bid. Clearly he acted reasonably to mitigate damages. * * *

The judgment is affirmed.

GIBSON C. J., and SHENK, SCHAUER, SPENCE and McCOMB, JJ., concur.

RESTATEMENT, SECOND, CONTRACTS § 87(2):

(2) An offer which the offeror should reasonably expect to induce action or forbearance of a substantial character on the part of the offeree before acceptance and which does induce such action or forbearance is binding as an option contract to the extent necessary to avoid injustice.

NOTE, ANOTHER LOOK AT CONSTRUCTION BIDDING AND CONTRACTS AT FORMATION
53 Va.L.Rev. 1720, 1724, 1732–44, 1746–47 (1967).

But even when the promissory estoppel doctrine is properly applied, its value and adequacy are limited because it protects only the general contractor. Although the sub is bound once the general uses the bid, the general has the choice of reopening negotiations with other subs. This allows him to use the low bid as a lever to deflate bids from other subs (bid shopping) and encourages other subs to undercut the low bidder after the prime contract has been awarded (bid peddling). The general can thus enforce the bid against the sub or, at his option, give up the bid made firm by promissory estoppel and shop for lower bids. The sub has no equivalent power.

As bid shopping becomes widespread in a given area, subs puff their initial bids to leave room for later negotiations, thus fictionalizing the bidding process. Moreover, when a sub accepts a lower price to avoid losing a contract, he may be tempted to cut corners, producing a less satisfactory job. Additionally, the awarding authority receives no benefit since it has already agreed to pay the general a fixed sum. In short, only the general benefits in this situation.

Although extrajudicial methods have been formulated to meet these evils,[26] the common law has largely ignored them. Ever since James Baird Co. v. Gimbel Brothers the courts have uniformly refused to treat the general's use of the sub's bid as acceptance which would bind the general. Instead, the sub's bid is treated as an offer to form a bilateral contract, and the general is bound only if he accepts by a return promise. * * *

[The principal portion of this note consists of the results of a questionnaire sent to 100 general contractors and 94 subcontractors active in Virginia. Replies were received from 67 generals and 53 subs. Some of the results of this questionnaire are set forth below.]

SUBCONTRACTOR SURVEY

(1) *When do you submit your bid to the general?*

The answers given by the subs to this question fall into three groups: twenty-four hours or more before the general makes his bid (4), twelve to twenty-four hours before the general makes his bid (4), one to four hours before the general makes his bid (42). Of those in the last category, 26 stated that they withheld their bids until the last one or two hours.

The reason for this late bidding is to minimize bid shopping by the general. Several subs stated that the time of bid submission varied according to the general with whom they were dealing. Eleven subs indicated that their bids were submitted "immediately prior to the time the general is to bid" or "at the last possible minute so the general will have a minimum amount of time to do his bid shopping." The clear conclusion is that most subs exert time pressure on the general by last-minute bidding. * * *

---

26. For example, some states and the federal government require generals to submit a list of proposed subs; this list can only be altered for good cause. E.g., Cal. Gov't Code § 4104 (West 1966). While this requirement protects the awarding authority from substandard work by untrustworthy subs, it has been held to confer no rights on the sub. Klose v. School Dist., 118 Cal.App.2d 636, 258 P.2d 515 (1953).

Subs have formed "bid depositories" as a form of self-regulation, but these depositories arguably violate the antitrust laws.

Furthermore, the depository cannot control nonmembers and has not proven completely satisfactory. See generally Schueller, Bid Depositories, 58 Mich.L.Rev. 497 (1960).

(4) *If you learn that the general has used your bid in his own bid but you also discover that you made a mistake in your bid, do you feel*

    [53] a. bound to go ahead and perform the work at your original bid price?

    [0] b. free to withdraw? * * *

(6) *Would you feel compelled to do the job if*

    a. you knew the general relied on your bid and you felt morally or legally bound to him?

        Yes: [51] No: [0] Sometimes: [1].

    b. you feared loss of business reputation that would endanger future business?

        Yes: [17] No: [7] Sometimes: [4]

    c. Some other reason (please comment): [3]. * * *

(9) *Do you ever have any difficulty with a general who bid shops (in other words, uses the low bid he has received to bargain with other subs to get them to lower their own bids) before awarding the subcontract?*

    Yes: [44] No: [8].

(10) *In your opinion is it unethical for the general contractor to bid shop before the award of the prime contract?*

    Yes: [47] No: [6];

    after the award of the prime contract?

    Yes: [47] No: [3]. * * *

(11) *Have you ever felt compelled to take any measures to counteract bid shopping?*

    Yes: [45] No: [5].

    If so, please describe.

    * * * By far the largest number (31) indicated they would stop submitting bids to a bid-shopping general. Seven reported they had tried a bid depository, and 6 indicated they would "puff" their bids to that general. Four subs said they would publicize the general's actions to other subs. Strangely, only 3 listed late bidding as a weapon, although the vast majority in fact follow this procedure, as is indicated by the response to question one. Other methods to counteract bid shopping included "trapping" the general by first quoting a low price and then withdrawing. One sub said only that he would "get griped"; another said he would "do nothing." At the other extreme, one sub listed an arsenal of weapons he employed: "Refuse to bid, quote higher price, quote late, quote only with commitment at time of quoting." Another reported that the best method to counteract bid shopping was to submit bids only to honest and competent generals since "bid shoppers are most always the poorest contractors and credit risks." One harried sub said, "Sorry, don't have time to write a book on this subject. Believe me, I could do just that." Significantly, no sub mentioned the possibility of taking the general to court. * * *

GENERAL CONTRACTOR SURVEY

(1) *When do you normally receive bids from the subcontractor in preparing your own bids?*

As with the subs, answers to this question fell into three categories. For 62 responses, the breakdown was as follows:

[41] One to two hours before the general must submit his bid.

[14] Within twelve hours before the general must submit his bid.

[7] Twenty-four hours or more.

The response to this question coincides with the answers given by the subs and dramatizes the pressure under which generals operate. As one general observed, there is "insufficient time to enter sub price and submit bids. Subs generally hold out until the last minute to minimize bid shopping." Another noted: "The whole chain of supply is suspicious of someone 'leaking' bid information to his competitors." This same general described preparation of bids in the following terms:

> Preparation of bids is a *thoroughly hectic affair* when it comes to receipt of subbids. In our office three in-coming telephones are in continuous use for two or three hours before the bids are due with three people answering and scribbling down abbreviated notes representing subbids as fast as they can. It is *remarkable* that errors and misunderstandings are rare. * * *

(3) *Do you always use the low bid from among those submitted by the subs?*

Yes: [31] No: [35].

If not, please comment.

The Yes-No tabulation has little significance by itself. The question calls for an absolute answer, and the responses fortunately tempered the question with business-world qualifications. Twenty of the 31 answering "Yes" volunteered that they used the low bid unless the low bidder had a poor reputation or had performed unsatisfactorily on previous jobs. Three others qualified a "Yes" answer by stating that they used the lowest solicited bid. Since bids are only solicited from trustworthy subs, these three answers can also be placed in the last category. Twenty-six of the 35 answering "No" qualified their answers by volunteering that they would not use a low bid from a sub with a poor reputation or from one who was in financial trouble. Thus 49 of 66 responding generals volunteered that they would use the lowest bid unless the sub was considered untrustworthy.

The answers to this question yielded an unexpected premium. The number of unsolicited responses indicating a serious concern with untrustworthy subs gives added credence to the responses to the key question, number twelve, which will be discussed at a later point.

* * *

(5) *After using a sub's bid in computing the amount of your own bid price, do you consider that*

[15]   a. he is committed to performing the work at the bidded price?

[46]   b. that both of you are bound to each other as of the time you used his bid?

[5]   c. that neither of you is bound until there are further negotiations or a formal contract is completed?   * * *

(7) *If the sub withdraws his bid after you have been awarded the prime contract, would you feel that he has been unjust?*

Yes: [65] No: [2].   * * *

(8) *Is it ever your practice to use a sub's bid as an estimate of what that portion of the job should cost with an eye perhaps to doing that part of the work yourself, finding a better price or accepting a lower bid from another sub?*

Yes: [11]   No: [54].

Please comment.

The wording of this question may have been unfortunate since a "Yes" answer without qualification would have included two distinct practices—using bids as estimates and shopping for bids. The "Yes" answers all included comments, and none reveals a general who admitted bid shopping. Several generals answering "Yes" agreed with the following comment:

> Only in the case where one sub-bid is received on a particular portion of the work and the bid when compared with our estimate seems to be completely out of reason do we feel justified in soliciting additional bids after the contract award. In this case we would use our estimated price in preparing the bid.

As one general, agreeing with the above, stated:

> By doing so, we commit ourselves to the responsibility for getting this work done for the price we used. It is normally our custom to then attempt to negotiate a contract with the subcontractor by pointing out the reasons why we feel the work should only cost so much. If we are unable to negotiate a contract with this man, we then proceed to negotiate with another subcontractor.

Several answering "No" stated that it would be unfair to request a sub to expend the time and money to compute a bid, only to have the general do the work himself. Many reminded the writer that such practices were unethical under the AGC Code of Ethics.   * * *

(12) *What objections, if any, would you have if a law court found that a contract was formed as of the time you used the sub's bid in your bid? This contract would only take effect on the condition that you receive the prime contract.*

Objections: [28] No objection: [35].

This was the key question submitted to the general contractors. That a majority of the generals did not object seems remarkable in view of the fact that the change in the law posited by the question would bind the general at an earlier time than is the case under present law. Unreserved acceptance of the proposal was voiced by 21 generals. Comments ranged from "All for it," "Excellent law" and "No objections whatever" to the following statement by one general: "None. We consider we have a contract under those conditions. If such a law were in effect it might serve to eliminate bid shopping." However, it must be noted that 1 nonobjector added that half his work was performed as a sub.

As in question number three, many generals, both objecting and nonobjecting, commented that the reliability of the sub was all important. Thus one objector stated that "a sub's ability to perform is a bid cost factor to the general contractor." Likewise, a nonobjector said that he had no objection "so long as we have the right to use the second low bid if for some reason we do not wish to work with the low bidder." Fourteen nonobjectors qualified their answers along these same lines. Fifteen objectors listed this as their primary reason. Thus if this single objection can be satisfied, and if the votes are realigned accordingly, the result would be 13 objecting and 50 not objecting—certainly an overwhelming response. * * *

The principal concern of most objecting generals is the spectre of being forced to deal with the "unknown" bidder. One general described his objections to the bid-use proposal as follows:

> In a few cases I do not think this would be satisfactory because we have had certain subcontractors bid on work who were not registered and could not qualify to do the work. Also, we have had subcontractors bid on work who do not have a sufficient labor force nor sufficient office personnel to handle a job of this size, and in some cases where there is only a couple hundred dollars difference between the two bids, we will then select the one who is the most capable and who will do the best job. In bidding jobs, over the State there are many times when we receive bids from people we do not know or have never heard of before, and we feel like they should be investigated before awarding them the work. So generally, we would object to this procedure.

This problem is dramatically illustrated by the comments of a general who reported receiving a bid ten minutes before his own bid was due which was 85,000 dollars lower than the next lowest bid. There simply was not sufficient time to investigate the bid or the bidder, yet since his competitors most likely had received the same bid, he was torn between using it or discarding it.

Because of competitive pressures, a general cannot be criticized for using a low bid from an unknown sub. Yet it would not be sound to force him to deal with the sub if he is later found to be unreliable. This so troubled one general that he drafted a model provision which provided that a contract should be found "unless later investigation revealed financial or technical incompetence on the part of the subcontractor, said opinion registered by an impartial panel of five or more persons qualified to make the decision."

A possible solution was suggested by the generals themselves. Although no question dealt with this possibility, 12 generals volunteered that they treated solicited bids differently than unsolicited bids. If a general solicits bids, he should know in advance the financial position and reliability of the sub. Thus if a sub's bid is solicited and is responsive to the specifications, it is likely a trade usage exists that at the time a bid is used, a contract is formed. It is also likely that this usage exists if the general knows the sub's qualifications in advance. This necessarily introduces the problem of proving the general's prior knowledge, a task which would not seem overly burdensome.

The California Experience

As indicated in the footnote to the Virginia Law Review note, the California statute applicable in the *Drennan* case may have the effect of limiting bid shopping. That this was the principal goal of this statute was made clear by amendments to the statute made in 1963. 1963 Cal. Stat. 4411. A statement of policy was added to § 4101:

> "The Legislature finds that the practices of bid shopping and bid peddling in connection with the construction, alteration, and repair of public improvements often result in poor quality of material and workmanship to the detriment of the public, deprive the public of the full benefits of fair competition among prime contractors and subcontractors, and lead to insolvencies, loss of wages to employees, and other evils."

In 1963, § 4107 of the California statute was revised to read in part as follows:

"No prime contractor whose bid is accepted shall: (a) Substitute any person as subcontractor in place of the subcontractor listed in the original bid, except that the awarding authority may consent to the substitution of another person as a subcontractor, when the subcontractor listed in the bid after having had a reasonable opportunity to do so fails or refuses to execute a written contract, when such written contract, based upon the general terms, conditions, plans and specifications for the project involved or the terms of such subcontractor's written bid, is presented to him by the prime contractor, or becomes insolvent or fails or refuses to perform a written contract for the work or fails or refuses to meet the bond requirements of the prime contractor as set forth in Section 4108. Prior to approval of any such substitution the awarding authority shall give notice in writing of at least three working days to the listed subcontractor of the prime contractor's request to substitute another subcontractor. * * *"

Southern California Acoustics Co. v. C.V. Holder, Inc., 71 Cal.2d 719, 79 Cal.Rptr. 319, 456 P.2d 975 (1969) arose under this revised statute. Holder (the general contractor) had listed the plaintiff in his bid as the acoustical tile subcontractor, but had later substituted another contractor to do the work with the permission of the contracting authority, on the ground that the plaintiff's name had been listed inadvertently. The court held that the plaintiff could not recover under contract law but could recover "for breach of a statutory duty":

"There was no contract between plaintiff and Holder, for Holder did not accept plaintiff's offer. Silence in the face of an offer is not an acceptance, unless there is a relationship between the parties or a previous course of dealing pursuant to which silence would be understood as acceptance. No such relationship or course of dealing is alleged. Nor did Holder accept the bid by using it in presenting its own bid. In the absence of an agreement to the contrary, listing of the subcontractor in the prime bid is not an implied acceptance of the subcontractor's bid by the general contractor. The listing by the general contractor of the subcontractors he intends to retain is in response to statutory command (Gov.Code, § 4104) and cannot reasonably be construed as an expression of acceptance.

"Plaintiff contends, however, that its reliance on Holder's use of its bid and Holder's failure to reject its offer promptly after Holder's bid was accepted constitute acceptance of plaintiff's bid by operation of law under the doctrine of promissory estoppel. * * * This rule applies in this state. (Drennan v. Star Paving Co. (1958) 51 Cal.2d 409, 413, 333 P.2d 757.) Before it can be invoked, however, there must be a promise that was relied upon.

"In *Drennan*, we held that implicit in the subcontractor's bid was a subsidiary promise to keep his bid open for a reasonable time after award of the prime contract to give the general contractor an opportunity to accept the offer on which he relied in computing the prime bid. The subsidiary promise was implied 'to preclude the injustice that would result if the offer could be revoked after the offeree had acted in detrimental reliance thereon.' (51 Cal.2d at p. 414, 333 P.2d at p. 760.)

"Plaintiff urges us to find an analogous subsidiary promise not to reject its bid in this case, but it fails to allege facts showing the existence of any promise by Holder to it upon which it detrimentally relied. * * *

"Plaintiff contends, however, that the Subletting and Subcontracting Fair Practices Act confers rights on listed subcontractors that arise when the prime contract is awarded and that these rights may be enforced by an action for damages. * * *

"Since the purpose of the statute is to protect both the public and subcontractors from the evils of the proscribed unfair bid peddling and bid shopping we hold that it confers the right on the listed subcontractor to perform the subcontract unless statutory grounds for a valid substitution exist. Moreover, that right may be enforced by an action for damages against the prime contractor to recover the benefit of the bargain the listed subcontractor would have realized had he not wrongfully been deprived of the subcontract. * * * " [9]

The court held, further, that while the general contractor was liable for damages under § 4107, the contracting authority was not:

"The question remains whether plaintiff has stated a cause of action against the school district. Since there is no statutory provision for the recovery of damages against a public entity for its consenting to a substitution of subcontractors in violation of section 4107, the school district is not liable for such violation. Plaintiff contends, however, that it was a third-party beneficiary of the contract between Holder and the school district and that therefore it may recover against the school district for breach of contract. (See Gov.Code, § 814.) There is no merit in this contention. Plaintiff was listed in response to statutory command and not because the contracting parties' purpose was expressly to benefit it. Accordingly, plaintiff was at most an incidental beneficiary and therefore cannot recover as a third-party beneficiary of the contract between Holder and the school district."

While the *Holder* case was in litigation, the California legislature again amended this statute by adding as a new ground for the substitution of subcontractors: "(5) When the prime contractor demonstrates to the awarding authority, or its duly authorized officer, subject to the further provisions set forth in Section 4107.5, that the name of the subcontractor was listed as the result of an inadvertent clerical error. * * * " 1969 Cal.Stat. 705.

The new section of the Government Code, § 4107.5, referred to in § 4107(a)(5) of the session laws, grants procedural protections for a subcontractor with respect to whom it is claimed that his name was included by "inadvertent clerical error." These protections include the right to a "public hearing" before the awarding authority, the submission of evidence by affidavit, and where appropriate, the taking of testimony under oath and with the right of cross-examination.

FOUR NINES GOLD, INC. v. 71 CONST., INC., 809 P.2d 236 (Wyo. 1991). Four Nines Gold bid on a street construction project in Riverton, Wyoming, incorporating in its bid a subbid of $88,316 for aggregate

---

9. In addition to seeking recovery of its anticipated profits of $15,000, plaintiff in a separate cause of action, seeks to recover his expenses of $500 "in preparation and planning to perform the contract" on the theory that its incurring of those expenses was caused by Holder's negligence in listing plaintiff as a subcontractor. We find no basis under the facts pleaded for a separate cause of action for negligence. After plaintiff learned, however, that it had been listed as a subcontractor in a prime contract awarded to Holder, it was entitled to assume that it would be offered the subcontract as required by section 4107 until Holder notified it of the intended substitution. Expenses reasonably incurred during this period may be recovered in addition to plaintiff's anticipated profits in order to give it the benefit of the bargain to which it was entitled.

bituminous surfacing from 71 Construction. The Riverton City Engineer informally notified Four Nines Gold that it was the low bidder. However, before the City Council met to award the contract, 71 Construction realized it had made a mistake of about $30,000 in its subbid. Its President tried unsuccessfully to contact Four Nines Gold, and then contacted the City Engineer, the City Attorney, and the Project Engineer. As a result, the City Engineer recommended that the City reject all bids and put out the project for new bids. The City did so and Four Nines Gold bid, but was not the low bidder and did not receive the contract. Four Nines Gold then sued 71 Construction for wrongful interference with contractual relationship and breach of an implied covenant of good faith and fair dealing. Summary Judgment for 71 Construction was affirmed: 71 Construction's actions were not improper since the statements made were truthful and the actions were taken in good faith to protect an economic interest of 71 Construction. Further, Four Nines Gold's use of the subbid did not create a contract between Four Nines Gold and 71 Construction under a theory of promissory estoppel since no binding obligation is created until the prime contractor's bid was accepted. For the same reason no implied covenant of good faith and fair dealing could arise. One judge dissented:

"We create by this decision a new way for a subcontractor-bidder to escape from an inopportunely priced street construction bid. The way now *paved* is for the subcontractor to go to the owner to get the general contractor's bid cancelled—no general contract and no subcontract responsibility to meet the terms of its bid. * * * "

ALLEN M. CAMPBELL CO. v. VIRGINIA METAL INDUSTRIES, INC., 708 F.2d 930, 932–934 (4th Cir.1983). Campbell was the successful bidder on a Navy contract to construct enlisted personnel housing at Camp LeJeune, North Carolina. Shortly before bids were due, Virginia Metal telephoned Campbell and offered to supply all hollow metal doors and frames required by the plans and specifications for $193,121. Campbell used this quotation in its bid. When Virginia Metal thereafter refused to enter into a contract to supply the doors and frames, Campbell was forced to purchase them from another supplier for $238,683. Virginia Metal argued unsuccessfully that § 2–201 prevented enforcement of its promise to supply the doors and frames:

"In the case as pleaded by Campbell, the elements of a promissory estoppel are clearly present. Under the well-pleaded allegations of fact, even in the absence of consideration, there was a sufficiently binding promise by Virginia Metal.

"Having come so far, we must next deal with the contention of Virginia Metal that, nevertheless, it cannot be held liable since its promise was not in writing. The Uniform Commercial Code has been adopted in North Carolina and [§ 2–201] requires that a contract for the sale of goods involving more than $500 must be in writing. The answer, however, lies in the language of [§ 1–103]:

> Unless displaced by the particular provisions of this chapter, the principles of law and equity, including * * * the law relevant to * * * estoppel * * * or other validating or invalidating cause shall supplement its provisions.

"The question then becomes whether North Carolina's doctrine of promissory estoppel creates an exception to or is displaced by the statute of frauds. There is a split of authority in decisions from states other than North Carolina on the question of whether promissory estoppel is to be deemed an exception to the statute of frauds. *See Ralston Purina Co. v. McCollum*, 271 Ark. 840, 844, 611 S.W.2d 201, 203 (1981) ('The [Uniform Commercial] Code states that the principles of law and equity, including estoppel, supplement the UCC unless displaced by a particular provision * * *. Thus the doctrine of promissory estoppel may be asserted by one party to an oral contract for the sale of goods, to prevent the other party from asserting the defense of the statute of frauds.'); *R.S. Bennett & Co., Inc. v. Economy Mechanical Industries, Inc.*, 606 F.2d 182 (7th Cir.1979) (Illinois law interpreted as applying the statute of frauds to bar recovery on a breach of contract theory in the absence of a writing, yet permitting a promissory estoppel approach to succeed notwithstanding the lack of a writing containing the promise); *Warder & Lee Elevator, Inc. v. Briten*, 274 N.W.2d 339, 342 (Iowa 1979) ('We have long recognized promissory estoppel as a means of defeating the general statute of frauds * * *. We hold that the provisions of § 554.2201 do not displace the doctrine of estoppel in relation to the sale of goods in Iowa.'); *Decatur Cooperative Association v. Urban*, 219 Kan. 171, 547 P.2d 323 (1976); *Jamestown Terminal Elevator, Inc. v. Hieb*, 246 N.W.2d 736 (N.D.1976).

"*Contra: Edward Joy Co. v. Noise Control Products, Inc.*, 111 Misc. 2d 64, 443 N.Y.S.2d 361, 362 (N.Y.Sup.Ct. Onondaga Cty.1981) (The subcontractor's bid was based on a substantial calculating mistake. 'It is clear that the possibility of error was sufficiently strong so as to prompt an inquiry by plaintiff and * * * that if Reid had brought plaintiff's inquiry to the attention of Noise Control, most likely the error would have been ascertained before plaintiff relied upon it in submitting its bid.'); [5] *Lige Dickson Co. v. Union Oil Co. of California*, 96 Wash. 291, 635 P.2d 103 (1981) (The court refused to adopt as Washington law the concepts of Restatement (Second) of Contracts § 139 (§ 217A in the Tentative Drafts), advancing the rather surprising reason that the Restatement rule would defeat rather than promote uniformity among the several states. A principal purpose of the Restatement has been to promote reasoned uniformity); *Anderson*

---

5. Such a human error may substantially affect the answer to the question of where, as between the parties, injustice lies. It may, without regard to the statute of frauds, excuse compliance with a written bid, even though the mistake was unilateral, not mutual. *City of Baltimore v. DeLuca–Davis Construction Co.*, 210 Md. 518, 124 A.2d 557 (1956).

Construction Co., Inc. v. Lyon Metal Products, Inc., 370 So.2d 935 (Miss. 1979) (another case where the subcontractor's computation error made its bid glaringly low); *C.G. Campbell & Son, Inc. v. Comdeq Corp.*, 586 S.W.2d 40 (Ky.App.1979) (Only § 2–201 of the UCC is cited; there is no reference to the ameliorating provisions of [§ 1–103] nor to the Restatement); *Wilkie v. Holdrege Cooperative Equity Exchange*, 200 Neb. 803, 265 N.W.2d 672 (1978); *C.R. Fedrick, Inc. v. Borg–Warner Corp.*, 552 F.2d 852 (9th Cir.1977); *Tiffany, Inc. v. W.M.K. Transit Mix, Inc.*, 16 Ariz.App. 415, 493 P.2d 1220 (1972) (Subcontractor's bid mistakenly calculated on wrong type of highway chip).

"While North Carolina has not explicitly committed itself as to the availability *vel non* of promissory estoppel as a means for overcoming the UCC statute of frauds, it has expressed approval of the position taken in Restatement (Second) of Contracts § 139, the cornerstone of the rationale adopted by the courts which have held that promissory estoppel will, in circumstances like those here presented, render inapplicable the UCC statute of frauds. * * *

"In light of the status of what we perceive to be the law that North Carolina courts would apply to the facts of this case, the fact that the promise was entirely oral would not bar recovery.[7] Consequently, the grant to Virginia Metal of judgment on the pleadings or for failure to state a claim upon which relief can be granted was erroneous. * * *"

MONTGOMERY INDUSTRIES, INTERNATIONAL, INC. v. THOMAS CONSTRUCTION CO., 620 F.2d 91 (5th Cir.1980). Montgomery, acting under the trade name "Trans Vac" submitted a bid to Thomas, the prime contractor, under the following circumstances:

"Thomas, in preparing for its bid to the University, solicited bids from many suppliers including Trans Vac. The University had set December 18, 1973, at 2:00 P.M. as the deadline for submission of bids and on that morning Trans Vac telephoned Thomas and submitted its initial bid in the amount of $355,650.00 for the trash conveying system. Trans Vac also informed Thomas that detailed plans of the system would not be provided.[1] Later that day, Trans Vac called and submitted a lower bid to Thomas in the amount of $319,650.00. Within less than an hour of Thomas' bidding deadline, Trans Vac called and

7. Plaintiff also offered an alternative theory stronger perhaps in linguistics than in logic for avoidance of the statute of frauds. Campbell argued that the technical lack of consideration here (the very predicate for the application of promissory estoppel) necessarily implies that no contract existed, and concluded that the statute of frauds, by its terms applicable only to contracts for the sale of goods, is therefore not a bar to enforcement of Virginia Metal's promise.

Since we find that the avoidance of injustice commands the broader conclusion that promissory estoppel renders a promise like the one here enforceable notwithstanding the statute of frauds, we do not determine the merits of such a fine spun construction of the relevant terms.

1. The trial court found that Trans Vac's general policy was to refrain from submitting detailed plans prior to being awarded a contract in order to prevent disclosure of trade secrets.

submitted an even lower bid in the amount of $287,000.00.[2] Trans Vac also submitted identical bids to several other general contractors bidding on the project. The bid given to Thomas contained no conditions or reservations nor did it indicate any deviation from the specifications issued by the University. Thomas estimated its own costs in connection with the Trans Vac alternative and submitted its entire bid to the University along with a $1,500,000.00 bid bond, with Travelers as the surety, to assure prompt and proper performance in the event the contract was awarded to it.

"* * * Thomas was * * * the lowest bidder. The University did not immediately award the contract to Thomas but Thomas telephoned Trans Vac that their bids had been the low ones. On January 7, 1974, Thomas received a letter from Trans Vac which indicated that there existed a deviation from the system bid by Trans Vac and the system called for by the plans. This was the first indication to Thomas that Trans Vac's bid deviated from the plans. On January 10, 1974, the University officially awarded Thomas the general contract which included the Trans Vac alternative trash conveying system.

"On January 14, 1974, Trans Vac notified Thomas that certain 'concessions' would be required in order for Trans Vac to sign its subcontract. On January 15, 1974, Thomas was informed by Trans Vac that a 'mistake'[3] in the approximate amount of $50,000.00, had been made in Trans Vac's bid. Prior to this time, Thomas had no indication that Trans Vac would require either concessions or more money to perform their subcontract. In an attempt to resolve the problems, both Thomas and Trans Vac met with University representatives which resulted in University approval of all of Trans Vac's building concessions. The result of these concessions was to make Trans Vac's construction easier and less costly. However, Trans Vac's demands for more money were not resolved and Trans Vac refused to sign and perform its subcontract without an additional amount of $32,500.00 for a subcontract price of $321,000.00. It was clear that Thomas could not increase its contract amount in order to accommodate Trans Vac's increase. At this point, Thomas had three alternatives: (1) refuse the increased price, pursue its legal remedies, and face possible forfeiture of its bid bond due to delays in construction, (2) enter a contract for the next closest alternative trash disposal system at an increased cost in excess of $500,000.00 over Trans Vac's $287,000.00 bid and attempt to persuade the University to accept that alternative, or (3) enter into a contract with Trans Vac at the increased price.

"Viewing the latter as the only realistic alternative, Thomas entered into a contract with Trans Vac on February 26, 1974, for the

2. The trial produced evidence that the practice of initially submitting high bids and then submitting lower bids in the final minutes before deadline is common among subcontractors in a competitive bidding situation and is done to confuse the competition in the event the subcontractor's bid amounts become known to other bidding subcontractors.

3. The testimony and briefs are silent as to what "mistake", if any, was made.

increased amount. The evidence is undisputed that Thomas received nothing for the increased price nor was Trans Vac required to perform differently or give up anything in exchange for the price increase.

"All work was performed by Trans Vac to the satisfaction of all concerned, but Thomas refused to pay Trans Vac $32,500.00—the amount of the increase. * * *"

Montgomery sued for this amount and won in the lower court but lost on appeal. The court relied on promissory estoppel, citing *Drennan*, and held that Montgomery was bound by its original, lowest offer. Furthermore, the argument that the subsequent February 26, 1974 agreement was a novation binding on Thomas was also rejected on the ground of "duress and lack of consideration."

SECTION 3: ACCEPTANCE BY PERFORMANCE OR PROMISE

PETTERSON v. PATTBERG

New York Court of Appeals, 1928.
248 N.Y. 86, 161 N.E. 428.

KELLOGG, J. The evidence given upon the trial sanctions the following statement of facts: John Petterson, of whose last will and testament the plaintiff is the executrix, was the owner of a parcel of real estate in Brooklyn, known as 5301 Sixth Avenue. The defendant was the owner of a bond executed by Petterson, which was secured by a third mortgage upon the parcel. On April 4, 1924, there remained unpaid upon the principal the sum of $5,450. This amount was payable in installments of $250 on April 25, 1924, and upon a like monthly date every three months thereafter. Thus the bond and mortgage had more than five years to run before the entire sum became due. Under date of the 4th of April, 1924, the defendant wrote Petterson as follows:

"I hereby agree to accept cash for the mortgage which I hold against premises 5301 6th Ave., Brooklyn, N.Y. It is understood and agreed as a consideration I will allow you $780 providing said mortgage is paid on or before May 31, 1924, and the regular quarterly payment due April 25, 1924, is paid when due."

On April 25, 1924, Petterson paid the defendant the installment of principal due on that date. Subsequently, on a day in the latter part of May, 1924, Petterson presented himself at the defendant's home, and knocked at the door. The defendant demanded the name of his caller. Petterson replied: "It is Mr. Petterson. I have come to pay off the mortgage." The defendant answered that he had sold the mortgage. Petterson stated that he would like to talk with the defendant, so the defendant partly opened the door. Thereupon Petterson exhibited the cash, and said he was ready to pay off the mortgage according to the agreement. The defendant refused to take the money. Prior to this conversation, Petterson had made a contract to sell the land to a third person free and clear of the mortgage to the defendant. Meanwhile, also, the defendant had sold the bond and mortgage to a third party. It therefore became necessary for Petterson to pay to such person the full amount of the bond and mortgage. It is claimed that he thereby sustained a loss of $780, the sum which the defendant agreed to allow upon the bond and mortgage, if payment in full of principal, less that sum, was made on or before May 31, 1924. The plaintiff has had a recovery for the sum thus claimed, with interest.

Clearly the defendant's letter proposed to Petterson the making of a unilateral contract, the gift of a promise in exchange for the performance of an act. The thing conditionally promised by the defendant was the reduction of the mortgage debt. The act requested to be done, in consideration of the offered promise, was payment in full of the reduced principal of the debt prior to the due date thereof. "If an act is requested, that very act, and no other, must be given." Williston on Contracts, § 73. "In case of offers for a consideration, the performance of the consideration is always deemed a condition." Langdell's Summary of the Law of Contracts, § 4. It is elementary that any offer to enter into a unilateral contract may be withdrawn before the act requested to be done has been performed. Williston on Contracts, § 60; Langdell's Summary, § 4; Offord v. Davies, 12 O.B. (N.S.) 748. A bidder at a sheriff's sale may revoke his bid at any time before the property is struck down to him. Fisher v. Seltzer, 23 Pa. 308, 62 Am.Dec. 335. The offer of a reward in consideration of an act to be performed is revocable before the very act requested has been done. Shuey v. United States, 92 U.S. 73, 23 L.Ed. 697. So, also, an offer to pay a broker commissions, upon a sale of land for the offeror, is revocable at any time before the land is sold, although prior to revocation the broker performs services in an effort to effectuate a sale. Stensgaard v. Smith, 43 Minn. 11, 44 N.W. 669, 19 Am.St.Rep. 205.

An interesting question arises when, as here, the offeree approaches the offeror with the intention of proffering performance and, before actual tender is made, the offer is withdrawn. Of such a case Williston says:

> "The offeror may see the approach of the offeree and know that an acceptance is contemplated. If the offeror can say 'I revoke' before the offeree accepts, however brief the interval of time between the two acts, there is no escape from the conclusion that the offer is terminated." Williston on Contracts, § 60b.

In this instance Petterson, standing at the door of the defendant's house, stated to the defendant that he had come to pay off the mortgage. Before a tender of the necessary moneys had been made, the defendant informed Petterson that he had sold the mortgage. That was a definite notice to Petterson that the defendant could not perform his offered promise, and that a tender to the defendant, who was no longer the creditor, would be ineffective to satisfy the debt. "An offer to sell property may be withdrawn before acceptance without any formal notice to the person to whom the offer is made. It is sufficient if that person has actual knowledge that the person who made the offer has done some act inconsistent with the continuance of the offer, such as selling the property to a third person." Dickinson v. Dodds, 2 Ch.Div. 463 ∗ ∗ ∗ Thus it clearly appears that the defendant's offer was withdrawn before its acceptance had been tendered. It is unnecessary to determine, therefore, what the legal situation might have been had tender been made before withdrawal. It is the individual view of the writer that the same result would follow. This would be so, for the act requested to be performed was the completed act of payment, a thing incapable of performance, unless assented to by the person to be paid. Williston on Contracts, § 60b. Clearly an offering party has the right to name the precise act performance of which would convert his offer into a binding promise. Whatever the act may be until it is performed, the offer must be revocable. However, the supposed case is not before us for decision. We think that in this particular instance the offer of the defendant was withdrawn before it became a binding promise, and therefore that no contract was ever made for the breach of which the plaintiff may claim damages.

The judgment of the Appellate Division and that of the Trial Term should be reversed, and the complaint dismissed, with costs in all courts.

LEHMAN, J. (dissenting). The defendant's letter to Petterson constituted a promise on his part to accept payment at a discount of the mortgage he held, provided the mortgage is paid on or before May 31, 1924. Doubtless, by the terms of the promise itself, the defendant made payment of the mortgage by the plaintiff, before the stipulated time, a condition precedent to performance by the defendant of his promise to accept payment at a discount. If the condition precedent has not been performed, it is because the defendant made performance impossible by refusing to accept payment, when the plaintiff came with an offer of immediate performance. "It is a principle of fundamental justice that if a promisor is himself the cause of the failure of performance either of an obligation due him or of a condition upon which his own liability depends, he cannot take advantage of the failure." Williston on Contracts, § 677. The question in this case is not whether payment of the mortgage is a condition precedent to the performance of a promise made by the defendant, but, rather, whether, at the time the defendant refused the offer of payment, he had assumed any binding obligation, even though subject to condition.

The promise made by the defendant lacked consideration at the time it was made. Nevertheless, the promise was not made as a gift or mere gratuity to the plaintiff. It was made for the purpose of obtaining from the defendant something which the plaintiff desired. It constituted an offer which was to become binding whenever the plaintiff should give, in return for the defendant's promise, exactly the consideration which the defendant requested.

Here the defendant requested no counter promise from the plaintiff. The consideration requested by the defendant for his promise to accept payment was, I agree, some act to be performed by the plaintiff. Until the act requested was performed, the defendant might undoubtedly revoke his offer. Our problem is to determine from the words of the letter, read in the light of surrounding circumstances, what act the defendant requested as consideration for his promise.

The defendant undoubtedly made his offer as an inducement to the plaintiff to "pay" the mortgage before it was due. Therefore, it is said, that "the act requested to be performed was the completed act of payment, a thing incapable of performance, unless assented to by the person to be paid." In unmistakable terms the defendant agreed to accept payment, yet we are told that the defendant intended, and the plaintiff should have understood, that the act requested by the defendant, as consideration for his promise to accept payment, included performance by the defendant himself of the very promise for which the act was to be consideration. The defendant's promise was to become binding only when fully performed; and part of the consideration to be furnished by the plaintiff for the defendant's promise was to be the performance of that promise by the defendant. So construed, the defendant's promise or offer, though intended to induce action by the plaintiff, is but a snare and delusion. The plaintiff could not reasonably suppose that the defendant was asking him to procure the performance by the defendant of the very act which the defendant promised to do, yet we are told that, even after the plaintiff had done all else which the defendant requested, the defendant's promise was still not binding because the defendant chose not to perform.

I cannot believe that a result so extraordinary could have been intended when the defendant wrote the letter. "The thought behind the phrase proclaims itself misread when the outcome of the reading is injustice or absurdity." See opinion of Cardozo, C. J., in Surace v. Danna, 248 N.Y. 18, 161 N.E. 315. If the defendant intended to induce payment by the plaintiff and yet reserve the right to refuse payment when offered he should have used a phrase better calculated to express his meaning than the words: "I agree to accept." A promise to accept payment, by its very terms, must necessarily become binding, if at all, not later than when a present offer to pay is made.

I recognize that in this case only an offer of payment, and not a formal tender of payment, was made before the defendant withdrew his offer to accept payment. Even the plaintiff's part in the act of payment was then not technically complete. Even so, under a fair construction of the words of the letter, I think the plaintiff had done the act which the defendant requested as consideration for his promise. The plaintiff offered to pay, with present intention and ability to make that payment. A formal tender is seldom made in business transactions, except to lay the foundation for subsequent assertion in a court of justice of rights which spring from refusal of the tender. If the defendant acted in good faith in making his offer to accept payment, he could not well have intended to draw a distinction in the act requested of the plaintiff in return, between an offer which, unless refused, would ripen into completed payment, and a formal tender. Certainly the defendant could not have expected or intended that the plaintiff would make a formal tender of payment without first stating that he had come to make payment. We should not read into the language of the defendant's offer a meaning which would prevent enforcement of the defendant's promise after it had been accepted by the plaintiff in the very way which the defendant must have intended it should be accepted, if he acted in good faith.

The judgment should be affirmed.

CARDOZO, C. J., and POUND, CRANE, and O'BRIEN, JJ., concur with KELLOGG, J.

LEHMAN, J., dissents in opinion, in which ANDREWS, J., concurs.

NOTE, CONTRACTS: ACCEPTANCE OF AN OFFER FOR UNILATERAL CONTRACT: EFFECT OF TENDER 14 Cornell L.Q. 81, 83–84 (1928).*

After discussing Petterson v. Pattberg, this Note continues:

"Granting, however, that there was no formal tender in the principal case, it does not seem unreasonable to say that the presence of the offeree on the doorstep with the money, while the offer was still unrevoked, was part performance of the act requested. He had expended time and labor in getting the money at the proper place within the specified period, and had gone as far as he could go without the cooperation of the offeror. He was not merely willing, but ready and able to perform; it was more than mere preparation for beginning performance. * * * It seems that the demands of good faith in business dealings would require a more liberal decision in cases of this kind." [18]

WORMSER, THE TRUE CONCEPTION OF UNILATERAL CONTRACTS
26 Yale L.J. 136 (1916).**

Suppose A says to B, "I will give you $100 if you walk across the Brooklyn Bridge," and B walks—is there a contract? It is clear that A

18. Other facts in the case, not appearing in the opinion, may have influenced the court. The record of the trial (folios 95–97) reveals that the defendant was prevented from testifying as to a letter, sent to the plaintiff's testator, revoking the offer because such testimony was inadmissible under § 347 of the Civil Practice Act, which excludes the testimony of one of the interested parties, to a transaction, where the other is dead and so unable to contradict the evidence. The record (folio 59) also seems to suggest that the mortgagor knew of the previous sale of the mortgage, since he brought $4,000 in cash with him, and was accompanied by his wife and a notary public as witnesses; anticipation of the defendant's refusal by seeking to get evidence on which to base this action seems to be a plausible explanation. There was no actual proof of knowledge of the defendant's inability to carry out his offer but the situation was suspicious.

** Reprinted by permission of The Yale Law Journal Company and Fred B. Roth-is not asking B for B's *promise* to walk across the Brooklyn Bridge. What A wants from B is the *act* of walking across the bridge. When B has walked across the bridge there is a contract, and A is then bound to pay to B $100. At that moment there arises a unilateral contract. A has bartered away his volition for B's act of walking across the Brooklyn Bridge.

When an act is thus wanted in return for a promise, a unilateral contract is created when the act is done. It is clear that only one party is bound. B is not bound to walk across the Brooklyn Bridge, but A is bound to pay B $100 if B does so. Thus, in unilateral contracts, on one side we find merely an act, on the other side a promise. On the other hand, in bilateral contracts, A barters away his volition in return for another promise; that is to say, there is an exchange of promises or assurances. In the case of the bilateral contract both parties, A and B, are bound from the moment that their promises are exchanged. Thus, if A says to B, "I will give you $100 if you will promise to walk across the Brooklyn Bridge," and B then promises to walk across the bridge, a bilateral contract is created at the moment when B promises, and both parties are thereafter bound. The conception of the bilateral contract, while presenting various theoretical difficulties, has in the main been developed by the courts with a reasonable degree of precision; but the unilateral contract has proven a stumbling block to nearly every court which has had occasion to consider the question. In no domain of the law are the opinions marked by such lack of clear thinking.

It is plain that in the Brooklyn Bridge case as first put, what A wants from B is the act of walking across the Brooklyn Bridge. A does not ask for B's promise to walk across the bridge and B has never given it. B has never bound himself to walk across the bridge. A, however, has bound himself to pay $100 to B, if B does so. Let us suppose that B starts to walk across the Brooklyn Bridge and has gone about one-half of the way across. At that moment A overtakes B and says to him, "I withdraw my offer." Has B then any rights against A? Again, let us suppose that after A has said "I withdraw my offer," B continues to walk across the Brooklyn Bridge and completes the act of crossing. Under these circumstances, has B any rights against A?

In the first of the cases just suggested, A withdrew his offer before B had walked across the bridge. What A wanted from B, what A asked for, was the act of walking across the bridge. Until that was done, B had not given to A what A had requested. The acceptance by B of A's offer could be nothing but the act on B's part of crossing the bridge. It is elementary that an offeror may withdraw his offer until it has been accepted. It follows logically that A is perfectly within his rights in withdrawing his offer before B has accepted it by walking across the bridge—the act contemplated by the offeror and the offeree as the acceptance of the offer. A did not want B to walk half-way across or

man & Company from The Yale Law Journal, Vol. 26, pp. 136–40, 142.

three-quarters of the way across the bridge. What A wanted from B, and what A asked for from B, was a certain and entire act. B understood this. It was for that act that A was willing to barter his volition with regard to $100. B understood this also. Until this act is done, therefore, A is not bound, since no contract arises until the completion of the act called for. Then, and not before, would a unilateral contract arise. Then, and not before, would A be bound.

The objection is made, however, that it is very "hard" upon B that he should have walked half-way across the Brooklyn Bridge and should get no compensation. This suggestion, invariably advanced, might be dismissed with the remark that "hard" cases should not make bad law. But going a step further, by way of reply, the pertinent inquiry at once suggests itself, "Was B bound to walk across the Brooklyn Bridge?" The answer to this is obvious. By hypothesis, B was not bound to walk across the Brooklyn Bridge. * * * It follows that at the moment when A overtook B, after B had walked half-way across the bridge, that B was not then bound to complete the crossing of the bridge. B, on his side, could have refused at that time, or at any other time, to continue to cross the bridge without making himself in any way legally liable to A. If B is not bound to continue across the bridge, if B is will-free, why should not A also be will-free? * * * If B has a *locus poenitentiae*, so has A. * * * Critics of the doctrine of unilateral contract on the ground that the rule is "hard" on B, forget the primary need for mutuality of withdrawal and in lamenting the alleged hardships of B, they completely lose sight of the fact that B has the same right of withdrawal that A has. To the writer's mind, the doctrine of unilateral contract is thus as just and equitable as it is logical. So long as there is freedom of contract and parties see fit to integrate their understanding in the form of a unilateral contract, the courts should not interfere with their evident understanding and intention simply because of alleged fanciful hardship. * * *

It will be noted that in the Brooklyn Bridge cases there is no unjust enrichment of A and consequently no occasion for quasi-contractual recovery by B. Let us assume a different set of facts. Suppose A says to B "If you build a garage on my land, I will give you $1,000." There is no interchange of promises, and it is clear that a unilateral contract is contemplated by the parties. Suppose B starts to build the garage on A's land and after it is one-half completed, A then says to B, "I withdraw my offer." It is clear that B had not yet accepted the offer of A at the time of its revocation and, therefore, that B is not entitled to recover in an action of contract. B could have ceased building the garage at any time, since he had never agreed to complete it; therefore, A has, and should have, the same privilege to draw back on his side. This conclusion cannot be considered as unjust, for B is not deprived thereby of any right in respect of the unfinished garage. *Prima facie,* that has become part of A's realty. * * * Yet, in a case like this, it seems that A is unjustly enriched by an improvement to his land, consisting of one-half a garage, if no return therefor is made to B. If the law will permit A, without B's consent, to retain this improvement to the land, it is only just that the law should afford B compensation for the improvement he made, even against A's express dissent. * * *

The writer can see no injustice whatever in the operation of the doctrine of unilateral contract. *It is logical in theory, simple in application, and just in result.* * * * True unilateral contracts are not infrequently met with in the practice of the law. Properly understood, and logically applied, the conception presents few difficulties.

WORMSER, REVIEW OF CASES ON CONTRACTS BY PATTERSON & GOBLE (3rd ed. 1949) 3 J.L.Ed. 145, 146 (1950).

I note that * * * the authors quote at length from my article written thirty-four years ago, "The True Conception of Unilateral Contracts." Since that time I have repented, so that now, clad in sackcloth, I state frankly, that my point of view has changed. I agree, at this time, with the rule set forth in the Restatement of the Law of Contracts of the American Law Institute, Section 45.

BRACKENBURY v. HODGKIN

Supreme Judicial Court of Maine, 1917.
116 Me. 399, 102 A. 106.

CORNISH, C. J. The defendant Mrs. Sarah D. P. Hodgkin on the 8th day of February, 1915, was the owner of certain real estate—her home farm, situated in the outskirts of Lewiston. She was a widow and was living alone. She was the mother of six adult children, five sons, one of whom, Walter, is the codefendant, and one daughter, who is the coplaintiff. The plaintiffs were then residing in Independence, Mo. Many letters had passed between mother and daughter concerning the daughter and her husband returning to the old home and taking care of the mother, and finally on February 8, 1915, the mother sent a letter to the daughter and her husband which is the foundation of this bill in equity. In this letter she made a definite proposal, the substance of which was that if the Brackenburys would move to Lewiston, and maintain and care for Mrs. Hodgkin on the home place during her life, and pay the moving expenses, they were to have the use and income of the premises, together with the use of the household goods, with certain exceptions, Mrs. Hodgkin to have what rooms she might need. The letter closed, by way of postscript, with the words, "you to have the place when I have passed away."

Relying upon this offer, which was neither withdrawn nor modified, and in acceptance thereof, the plaintiffs moved from Missouri to Maine late in April, 1915, went upon the premises described and entered upon the performance of the contract. Trouble developed after a few weeks, and the relations between the parties grew most disagreeable. The mother brought two suits against her son-in-law on trifling matters, and finally ordered the plaintiffs from the place, but they refused to leave. Then on November 7, 1916, she executed and delivered to her son, Walter C. Hodgkin, a deed of the premises, reserving a life estate in herself. Walter, however, was not a bona fide purchaser for value without notice, but took the deed with full knowledge of the agreement between the parties and for the sole purpose of evicting the plaintiffs. On the very day the deed was executed he served a notice to quit upon Mr. Brackenbury, as preliminary to an action of forcible entry and detainer which was brought on November 13, 1916. This bill in equity was brought by the plaintiffs to secure a reconveyance of the farm from Walter to his mother, to restrain and enjoin Walter from further prosecuting his action of forcible entry and detainer, and to obtain an adjudication that the mother holds the legal title impressed with a trust in favor of the plaintiffs in accordance with their contract.

The sitting justice made an elaborate and carefully considered finding of facts and signed a decree, sustaining the bill with costs against Walter C. Hodgkin, and granting the relief prayed for. The case is before the law court on the defendants' appeal from this decree.

Four main issues are raised.

1. As to the completion and existence of a valid contract.

A legal and binding contract is clearly proven. The offer on the part of the mother was in writing, and its terms cannot successfully be disputed. There was no need that it be accepted in words, nor that a counter promise on the part of the plaintiffs be made. The offer was the basis, not of a bilateral contract, requiring a reciprocal promise, a promise for a promise, but of a unilateral contract requiring an act for a promise. "In the latter case the only acceptance of the offer that is necessary is the performance of the act. In other words, the promise becomes binding when the act is performed." 6 R.C.L. 607. This is elementary law.

The plaintiffs here accepted the offer by moving from Missouri to the mother's farm in Lewiston and entering upon the performance of the specified acts, and they have continued performance since that time so far as they have been permitted by the mother to do so. The existence of a completed and valid contract is clear.

2. The creation of an equitable interest.

This contract between the parties, the performance of which was entered upon by the plaintiffs, created an equitable interest in the land described in the bill in favor of the plaintiffs. * * *

3. Alleged breach of duty on the part of the plaintiffs.

The defendants contend that, granting an equitable estate has been established, the plaintiffs have failed of performance because of their improper and unkind treatment of Mrs. Hodgkin, and therefore have forfeited the right to equitable relief which they might otherwise be entitled to. The sitting justice decided this question of fact in favor of the plaintiffs, and his finding is fully warranted by the evidence. Mrs. Hodgkin's temperament and disposition, not only as described in the testimony of others, but as revealed in her own attitude, conduct, and testimony as a witness, as they stand out on the printed record, mark her as the provoking cause in the various family difficulties. She was "the one primarily at fault." * * *

The plaintiffs are entitled to the remedy here sought and the entry must be:

Appeal dismissed.

Decree of sitting justice affirmed, with costs against Walter C. Hodgkin.

———

DAWSON, HARVEY AND HENDERSON, CASES AND COMMENTS ON CONTRACTS 335 (4th ed. 1982):

"We are informed that, after the decree in the principal case, the Brackenburys and Mrs. Hodgkin continued to live together until the death of Mrs. Hodgkin in January, 1921, and that 'the relations were unpleasant to the end.' Our informant learned from Mr. Brackenbury that the latter secured a transcript of the record in the equity case and 'would, from time to time, read from it to the old lady.'"

———

DAWSON, HARVEY, AND HENDERSON, TEACHER'S MANUAL TO CASES AND COMMENTS ON CONTRACTS, at 66:

A statement privately communicated in 1959 by a younger brother of Mrs. Brackenbury, who sided with his mother, Mrs. Hodgkin, provides some additional information: "Conditions got to be unbearable for my mother chiefly from Brackenbury. I have been in when they were eating and food was not passed to her, but rather thrown to her by Brackenbury. I never did hear my sister in any argument with mother, but apparently approving what her husband did. The fork which she always had to use was an old iron one with two tines broken off, fit only for the waste cart. I went into the house once when he followed with a gun and threatened to shoot me. But I did not budge."

We do not know how long the unhappy relationship lasted, but apparently the Brackenburys continued to provide 'care' for Mrs. Hodgkin until she died of pneumonia. The Brackenburys immediately sold the property and returned to Missouri. After her husband's death, Mrs. Brackenbury went to California to live with her son and his family. We know nothing about how that worked out. Our last report indicates that in late 1958, Mrs. Brackenbury, at the age of 94 or 95, had returned to Missouri and entered a home for elderly people.

———

Despite the logical nature of the arguments in favor of the revocability of offers for unilateral contracts, several early courts, like the Maine court in *Brackenbury*, refused to allow the offeror to revoke after the offeree began substantial and expensive performance. See, e.g., Los

Angeles Traction Co. v. Wilshire, 135 Cal. 654, 67 P. 1086 (1902), where, in an apparently pure unilateral contract situation, the court said that "[t]he contract at the date of its making was unilateral, a mere offer that if subsequently accepted and acted upon by the other party to it would ripen into a binding enforceable obligation. When the respondent purchased and paid upwards of $1,500 for a franchise it had acted upon the contract, and it would be manifestly unjust thereafter to permit the offer that had been made to be withdrawn. The promised consideration had been partly performed, and the contract had taken on a bilateral character." (In considering these early cases it is important to recognize that they long antedate section 90 of the first Restatement of Contracts.) Academic commentary, however, suggested a solution.

McGOVNEY, IRREVOCABLE OFFERS
27 Harv.L.Rev. 644, 659–60 (1914).

Let us assume a concrete case: A. says to B., "I have had enough of your promises in the past and want no promise from you, but if you will put my sugar-house machinery in good repair I will pay you $100 for the job, and if you will begin immediately I will give you a reasonable time to complete the work."

Are there not two offers here—one, the principal offer of $100 for the repair of the machinery; another, or collateral, offer to keep the principal offer open for a reasonable time if the offeree begins work at once? The principal offer contemplates acceptance by the act of repairing the machinery, and no contract will result from it until the machinery is full repaired. The collateral offer also contemplates a unilateral contract, the acceptance to be beginning the work at once. If the work is begun at once there is a contract to keep the principal offer open for a reasonable time. By beginning immediately the offeree has "paid-for" the offer. So if the principal offer had fixed a definite time for completing the work, the commencement of the work would be the acceptance of, and consideration for, the implied promise to keep the principal offer open for the time so fixed in it.

The offeree is thus protected by a contract to keep the offer open. Should the offerer thereafter attempt to withdraw the offer, this repudiation of his contractual obligation would give the offeree an action for damages, and it may be that in exceptional cases the offeree may ignore the repudiation, complete the performance and hold the offerer to the resulting contract.

The analysis above suggested fully accords with the intentions of the parties * * * The offerer incurs no liability on his principal offer until the work is done, not because it is a condition in a contract already made that the doing of the work is to precede payment—a bilateral contract could be made to serve equally well for that—but because the principal offer, *viz.*, to pay for the work, will not ripen into a contract at all until the whole work is done: the offerer has only given the offeree an option to reject the principal offer or accept it by completing the act or acts called for, within the time limit. * * *

On the other hand, the offeree is secured the intended position. By commencing the work he is not bound to complete it. The principal offer contemplates a unilateral contract. By commencing the work the offeree has only accepted the collateral offer and paid for the option of accepting or rejecting the principal offer. He is secured the very opportunity which in such cases it is normally expected he shall have, i.e., an opportunity to see whether he can accomplish the work within the allotted time and entitle himself to the contemplated compensation. * * *

RESTATEMENT [FIRST] OF CONTRACTS § 45:

If an offer for a unilateral contract is made, and part of the consideration requested in the offer is given or tendered by the offeree in response thereto, the offeror is bound by a contract, the duty of immediate performance of which is conditional on the full consideration being given or tendered within the time stated in the offer, or, if no time is stated therein, within a reasonable time.

Comment:

 a. What is tendered must be part of the actual performance requested in order to preclude revocation under this Section. Beginning preparations though they may be essential to carrying out the contract or to accepting the offer, is not enough.

Illustrations:

 1. A says to B, "I will not ask you to promise to instal an intramural telephone system which will work perfectly in my building, but if you care to try to do it, I will pay you $1000 if you succeed." B begins the work. When it is partly finished, A revokes his offer. If B can prove that he would have complied with the terms of the offer, he has a right to damages—the contract price less the cost of completing the installation. If B cannot prove that he would have fulfilled the conditions of the offer he cannot recover.

 2. A promises B to sell him a specified chattel for $5. B tenders $5 within a reasonable time. A refuses to accept the tender. There is a breach of contract.

RESTATEMENT, SECOND, CONTRACTS § 45:

(1) Where an offer invites an offeree to accept by rendering a performance and does not invite a promissory acceptance, an option contract is created when the offeree tenders or begins the invited performance or tenders a beginning of it.

(2) The offeror's duty of performance under any option contract so created is conditional on completion or tender of the invited performance in accordance with the terms of the offer.

RESTATEMENT, SECOND, CONTRACTS § 47:

An offer contemplating a series of independent contracts by separate acceptances may be effectively revoked so as to terminate the power to create future contracts, though one or more of the proposed contracts have already been formed by the offeree's acceptance.

Illustrations:

1. A offers to guarantee the payment of all bills of exchange drawn by B and discounted by C. C discounts one such bill. A is bound to pay it. A then notifies C that the guaranty is withdrawn. A is not bound to pay bills subsequently discounted.

2. A offers B to sell him five tons of steel daily, and tenders five tons at once. B accepts the tender. The same amount is furnished daily for a number of days. A then states to B that he revokes the offer. A contract is formed each day that steel is furnished, but the revocation prevents the formation of any contracts thereafter.

3. A offers to buy from B at the market price 100 tons of steel per month for the next 12 months, promising that in consideration of the delivery of the first installment B is to have an option to sell any or all of the other eleven installments. B delivers the first 100 tons as requested. There is an irrevocable offer to buy the eleven undelivered installments.

"Preparing to Perform" and "Beginning to Perform"

The original section 45 of the first Restatement of Contracts was apparently devised primarily to protect the reliance of an offeree who had begun to perform from a premature revocation by the offeror. As stated by Wormser, "the objection is made, however, that it is very 'hard' upon B that he should have walked half-way across the Brooklyn Bridge and should get no compensation." (Wormser, The True Conception of Unilateral Contracts, 26 Yale L.J. 136 (1916)). Section 45 provides B a remedy in this type of situation by binding the offeror when B gives or tenders part of the consideration. In the first Restatement the concept of protection of reliance was not well developed; it is therefore not surprising that a separate principle for reliance on an offer for a unilateral contract was developed despite the addition of section 90, dealing with the protection of reliance in some other situations. Restatement, Second, Contracts, on the other hand, contains not only section 90 (reliance on promises) (see supra page 226), but also section 87(2) (reliance on offers) (see supra page 476) and section 139 (reliance as a means of avoidance of the statute of frauds) (see infra page 894). Given this infusion of reliance-protection provisions, and the now almost-universal recognition of reliance as an alternative basis for the enforcement of promises, is section 45 necessary under the new Restatement? If a person begins performance (so as to come under section 45) could not those acts be viewed as foreseeable reliance on a promise under section 90 or on an offer under section 87(2)? If so, is not section 45 unnecessary? The reporters apparently believed that section 45 contributed something that the reliance-protection sections did not, since they retained section 45 (with the same section number and with only minor changes in wording).

Consider the following hypothetical: A says to B: "If you will build me a porch on my summer house by next June, I will pay you for the materials and your going rate for your time, plus $1,000 profit in addition." In response, B makes up a list of things he will need and arranges for other people to do the projects he had planned to work on but will give up to do A's work. (B does not subcontract out work but does all work with his own hands). He also goes down to the lumber yard and places an order for needed supplies. At this point, and before B goes any further, A revokes his offer. Under both Restatements, B's conduct would not trigger section 45, since that section requires the *beginning of performance*, not *preparation to perform*. Comment f to section 45, Restatement, Second, Contracts makes this explicit: "What is begun or tendered must be part of the actual performance invited in order to preclude revocation under this section. Beginning preparations, though they may be essential to carrying out the contract or to accepting the offer, is not enough. Preparations to perform may, however, constitute justifiable reliance sufficient to make the offeror's promise binding under section 87(2)." Thus, in the above situation, B must look to section 87(2) for relief. On the other hand, if B also takes the lumber out to A's summer house and begins to lay forms for the porch's foundations, that is probably the beginning of performance, and if A revokes at that point, B should look to section 45 rather than section 87(2).

There are at least three problems with this line between sections 45 and 87(2). In the first place, the line between *beginning to perform* and *preparing to perform* is often a slippery one. Comment f to section 45 of the Second Restatement states that this line often requires the exercise of delicate judgment: "The distinction between preparing for performance and beginning performance * * * may turn on many factors: the extent to which the offeree's conduct is clearly referable to the offer, the definite and substantial character of that conduct, and the extent to which it is of actual or prospective benefit to the offeror rather than the offeree, as well as the terms of the communications between the parties, their prior course of dealing, and any relevant usages of trade." Two examples from a different section of the Restatement (Section 62) also illustrate the difficulty of this distinction:

"1. A, a merchant, mails B, a carpenter in the same city, an offer to employ B to fit up A's office in accordance with A's specifications and

B's estimate previously submitted, the work to be completed in two weeks. The offer says, 'You may begin at once,' and B immediately buys lumber and begins to work on it in his own shop. The next day, before B has sent a notice of acceptance or begun work at A's office or rendered the lumber unfit for other jobs, A revokes the offer. The revocation is timely, since B has not begun to perform. [This illustration is based on White v. Corlies, 46 N.Y. 467 (1871), but with some differences in factual nuances.]

"2. A, a regular customer of B, orders fragile goods from B which B carries in stock and ships in his own trucks. Following his usual practice, B selects the goods ordered, tags them as A's, crates them and loads them on a truck at substantial expense. Performance has begun, and A's offer is irrevocable. See Uniform Commercial Code § 2–206 and Comment 2."

Second, the line between beginning to perform and preparing to perform is often arbitrary and does not reflect a significant increase in the economic commitment by the offeree. In the porch hypothetical, for example, the cost to B of preparing to perform may be quite substantial while the actual beginning of performance may involve no additional meaningful investment.

Third, the retention of the line increases the complexity of the Restatement's internal structure. That should be evident from the numerous citations to the Restatement's provisions dealing with acceptance in this subsection.

On the other hand, the distinction between beginning to perform and preparing to perform is important if significantly different legal consequences flow from the category in which a particular situation is placed. If the offeree is viewed as having begun to perform when the offeror revokes, the offeree's rights are determined under section 45 and "an option contract is created," but the offeror's "duty of performance * * * is conditional on completion or tender of the invited performance in accordance with the terms of the offer." Section 45(2). This does not speak to the rights of the offeree if the offeror directs him to stop work after this "option contract" is created. Presumably, the offeree must stop work, see *Luten Bridge*, supra page 16, and damages for the breach are measured in accordance with normal principles of expectancy damages, including the recovery of lost profits, salvage of purchased materials, mitigation, and similar limitations on the expectancy measure. On the other hand, if the offeror revokes his offer before the offeree has begun to perform but after he has relied on the offer by preparing to perform, the offeree's rights are determined under section 87(2) of the second Restatement; such an offer "is binding as an option contract to the extent necessary to avoid injustice." Comment e to this section contains the following description of how damages should be measured in the event of the breach of this type of "option contract":

"e. Full-scale enforcement of the offered contract is not necessarily appropriate * * * Restitution of benefits conferred may be enough, or partial or full reimbursement of losses may be proper. Various factors may influence the remedy: the formality of the offer, its commercial or social context, the extent to which the offeree's reliance was understood to be at his own risk, the relative competence and the bargaining position of the parties, the degree of fault on the part of the offeror, the ease and certainty of proof of particular items of damage and the likelihood that unprovable damages have been suffered."

In other words, the only difference between sections 45 and 87(2) appears to involve the measure of damages: section 45 leads to the normal expectancy recovery while 87(2) may lead to an expectancy recovery or something less. In the porch hypothetical, for example, if the offeree has begun to perform and is therefore under section 45, he is probably entitled to recover the promised $1,000 profit; the recovery of this amount is much more doubtful under section 87(2). On the other hand, in real life, such differences seldom appear so neatly: consider the discussion of the recovery of the commission in the *Sunshine* case, infra. Was the recovery in *Drennan* (supra page 472) consistent with the recovery contemplated in § 45 or in § 87? Of course, recovery under § 87(2) may lead to a full expectancy recovery, in which case there may be no difference at all between the two sections. Other differences in damage measurement may also arise. Consider, for example, the question whether B in the porch hypothetical can recover the profit he would have made on the other jobs he gave up to do A's porch; he may probably recover for this loss under section 87(2) since the reimbursement of such losses fits comfortably within the concept of protection of reliance. But it is unlikely that such amounts may be recovered under the expectancy theory of section 45: since B is hiring out only his own services, he could not both construct A's porch and do the other work. Whether B would prefer a recovery under § 45 or under § 87 may depend on the amounts of the respective profits on A's job and the other jobs he gave up, and possibly on the difficulty of proof of the amount of the profit actually lost.

On the other hand, if B **were** the typical contractor who could expand his work force to handle both A's porch and the other work, he would presumably not give up the other work while he was working on A's porch. If A countermands after B has begun performance, under section 45, B should recover both his reliance expenses and the $1,000 profit without offset for the profit on the other work. If A countermands at an earlier time, after B has made preparations to perform but before he has begun performance, B may recover under section 87 on a reliance theory, and B might well be limited to a recovery of his out-of-pocket expenses but not the $1,000 profit. There thus appears to be at least a theoretical difference in recovery between the cases in which the contractor began performance and the cases in which he or she only made preparations to perform. Do you think this difference is significant as a practical matter?

Short term option contracts may be created without consideration (in the formal sense) for the sale of goods under [UCC § 2–205], or, presumably, by the recitation of nominal consideration in a firm offer for an arms-length transaction at a fair price. See p. 217, supra. In both of these situations, the expectancy is the normal measure of recovery, as it is under § 45. If the expectancy is the normal measure in such cases, why should it not also be for preparations to perform that clearly evidence an intention to accept the offer? Or should the court reach the "right" result by viewing conduct that clearly evidences an intention to accept as the actual beginning of performance?

As discussed earlier, promissory estoppel had its roots in gratuitous, non-commercial promises but quickly became applicable to promises made in a commercial context as well. In the Second Restatement, explicit recognition is given to the possibility of partial enforcement, a concept which clearly contemplates that recovery may be based on the expectancy interest in appropriate section 90 cases.

Do you agree with the decision made in the second Restatement to retain section 45?

SUNSHINE v. MANOS
Texas Court of Civil Appeals, 1973.
496 S.W.2d 195.

MOORE, JUSTICE.

This is an appeal from a summary judgment. Plaintiff, Howard A. Sunshine, dba Sunshine Exploration Company, sued defendants, Peter N. Manos and James A. Muncey dba Manos & Muncey Architects, a partnership, for breach of a loan brokerage contract alleging that on April 12, 1972, the parties entered into a letter agreement by the terms of which defendants offered to pay plaintiff a 1% commission provided he could obtain and deliver to defendants a loan within thirty days of between $560,000.00 and $575,000.00, at a rate of interest of "9.67% constant or better (equivalent to 8¾%—25 year)." * * *

After a hearing the trial court denied plaintiff's motion for summary judgment but granted defendants' motion and entered a summary judgment in favor of defendants. From this judgment plaintiff duly perfected this appeal. * * *

The pertinent parts of the letter agreement are as follows:

"This is your authorization to proceed to secure for our benefit a mortgage loan secured by the above project and property. The terms and conditions of said loan can be: Loan Amount: $560,000.00 to $575,000.00—Rate: 9.67% (constant, or better, (equivalent to 8¾%—25 yr.).

"From the above date you are authorized to work in our behalf exclusively for a period of not less than thirty (30) calendar days. If at the end of the thirty day period, you have in progress the processing of said loan, there will be an automatic extension of fifteen calendar days.

"In consideration of your efforts in our behalf, and upon delivery of a commitment in accordance with the terms above stated, or terms as modified and agreed to by us, we agree to accept the commitment and to pay Sunshine Exploration Company, or assigns, a fee equivalent to one (1%) per cent of the loan amount for services rendered.

"If you are successful in placing this loan, we shall consider that lender your exclusive lender for a period of two (2) years from the date the loan commitment was issued, and we shall not seek to obtain a loan from him without going through you, or your assigns, as broker for us."

Both parties signed the agreement on April 12, 1972. On the day the agreement was executed plaintiff commenced performance by contacting the Oak Cliff Savings and Loan Association and requesting a loan on behalf of the defendants for $575,000.00 at $8\frac{1}{4}\%$ to $8\frac{5}{8}\%$ interest amortized over twenty-five years. The company later advised plaintiff that it would make a $550,000.00 loan at the rate of $8\frac{3}{4}\%$. After further negotiations with plaintiff, the company agreed to a $560,000.00 loan at 9% amortized over twenty-eight years. On April 18, 1972, plaintiff called defendant Peter N. Manos and told Manos that he could procure a loan in the amount of $560,000.00 at 9% interest amortized over a period of twenty-eight years. Mr. Manos construed this statement as an attempt on the part of plaintiff to vary the terms of the letter of agreement. In the course of the conversation, Mr. Manos then requested that plaintiff cease efforts to procure the loan and on April 19, 1972, defendants wrote a letter to plaintiff advising him to cease work on the loan. Thereafter, on or about April 21 or 22, 1972, defendants received a letter from plaintiff dated April 20, 1972, enclosing a real estate loan application from the Oak Cliff Savings and Loan Association. The loan application reads, in part, as follows:

"We hereby apply to Oak Cliff Savings and Loan Association * * * for a loan of $560,000.00 for 25 years, with 28 years amortization, with 9% interest per annum. This loan is to be repaid in 299 monthly installments of $5,388.00 including interest at the rate of 9% * * * and is to be secured by a first lien on the property * * *. With a baloon-payment [sic] at the time of the 300th installment. * * * the Sponsors will endorse the top 25% of the loan amount ($560,000.00), and for the balance the Lender shall look to the real estate and improvements thereon."

According to the affidavit of Donald L. Hanson, Vice President of Oak Cliff Savings and Loan Association, the loan which his company proposed was a loan for $560,000.00 at 9% for a twenty-five-year term on the note but was to be amortized on a twenty-eight-year term to keep the rate constant at 9.80%. Other provisions of the proposed loan required the borrower to pay a 1% initial loan fee. Defendants did not sign or return the application and plaintiff does not contend that they agreed to the terms proposed. There is nothing in the record showing that plaintiff made any effort to secure another loan within the thirty-day period allowed by the contract, or that defendants ever secured a loan from other sources.

     *   *   * [P]laintiff contends that the trial court erred in rendering summary judgment in favor of defendants. In reply defendants argue first that the judgment must be sustained because the record conclusively shows that plaintiff failed to comply with the agreement in that he failed to obtain a loan and secondly, that the agreement being unilateral, defendants had a right to rescind it at any time and therefore no breach of contract was shown. We have concluded that the defendants failed to discharge their burden of demonstrating that no genuine issue of fact existed on any element of plaintiff's cause of action and therefore the trial court erred in granting a summary judgment in favor of defendants.

The letter agreement, as we view it, amounted to an offer to make a unilateral contract. There was no exchange of promises, no mutuality and no consideration at the time defendants signed the letter. Yet defendants appointed plaintiff as their exclusive agent for thirty days and promised to pay plaintiff the commission, provided he could get a loan commitment within that time. Plaintiff made no promise, did not agree to try to get a loan commitment, but was free to either pursue the matter or not. The writing itself was not binding as a contract. It was only an offer to make a unilateral contract—an offer to pay for an act to be performed, a commitment for a loan.

Where a contract is unilateral on its face, it does not come into existence as a binding contract until the broker has performed, or at least partly performed, his duties under the agreement. Prior to that time, it is nudum pactum and may be revoked by the offeror at any time.

The principal may of course revoke a unilateral offer but there is a distinction between his power to revoke and his right to revoke. He may at any time before full performance revoke the authority of an agent so the agent will lose his authority to bring the principal into legal relations with a third party. However, if he has no right to revoke it, he will be liable for damages suffered by the agent by reason of the wrongful revocation. There is nothing in the contract giving defendants a right of rescission.

The promise which the defendants made in this instance was such that they should have expected to induce action of a substantial nature on the part of the plaintiff. It is without dispute that plaintiff did subsequently enter upon performance and expended at least some time and effort in attempting to negotiate the loan before defendants rescinded.

This brings us to the question of whether partial performance of the consideration will ripen into a contract so as to make such unilateral offer irrevocable. The question has sharply divided judicial opinion. In some jurisdictions it is held that there must have been a complete performance of the unilateral contract by the agent before there would be a binding contract. 28 A.L.R. 894. The decisions in this state, however, seem to indicate that partial performance of a unilateral contract is sufficient to make the same a binding contract. Park v. Swartz, 110 Tex. 564, 222 S.W. 156 (Tex.1920).

The specific question to be resolved in this case is whether the acts and conduct of plaintiff constituted part performance amounting to an acceptance of the offer and a sufficient consideration to make the offer irrevocable, or turn it into a bilateral contract. It has been held that in order to prove partial performance, it must be shown that there was an expenditure of time and money. Park v. Swartz, supra. On the other hand it has been held that a mere making of a local telephone call does not amount to a sufficient part performance so as to cause a unilateral offer to ripen into a binding contract. Strother v. Ryon, 239 S.W.2d 858 (Tex.Civ.App., Ft. Worth, 1951, n.w.h.). Practically all of the cases in other jurisdictions hold that the expenditure of time and effort is sufficient. 12 Am.Jur.2d Brokers, sec. 32. Also see 64 A.L.R. 404, 416–420. While most of the authorities on the subject deal with real estate brokerage contracts, we think the same legal principles are applicable here. We hold that the expenditure of time and effort is sufficient consideration to make a unilateral contract binding and irrevocable. It is undisputed that plaintiff expended at least some time and effort in attempting to obtain the loan prior to the time defendants rescinded the offer. For this reason we believe that under the foregoing authorities the unilateral offer in this instance ripened into a binding contract.

Having failed to establish a right of revocation or that the offer was rescinded prior to the time plaintiff expended time and effort to perform, defendants thereby breached their contract and became liable to plaintiff for such damages as he could prove were sustained by him, as a result of the breach. A summary judgment is proper only if the record establishes a right thereto as a matter of law. It follows, therefore, that since the record shows plaintiff had a cause of action for damages for breach of contract, defendants, as the moving parties, were not entitled to a summary judgment.

We turn now to the question of whether the plaintiff was entitled to a summary judgment. We have concluded that he was not and that the action of the trial court in denying the plaintiff's motion for summary judgment must be sustained. While we believe that the summary judgment evidence was sufficient to establish a breach of contract, we are of the opinion that plaintiff failed to conclusively establish the amount of his damages, if any, and therefore a fact question with regard to damages remains to be determined.

In cases involving a breach of a brokerage contract, the courts generally support the principle that a broker whose employment or authority is wrongfully revoked may consider his contract of employment as rescinded and sue for damages, in which event he is entitled to have his recovery include the value of the services he has already rendered, his disbursements, and such prospective profits as he can establish would have been his but for such revocation; or he may refuse to consider his contract as rescinded, and if he proceeds and succeeds in performing that which his contract requires him to perform, his employer is liable for the agreed compensation. If, upon wrongful revocation, however, a loan broker considers his contract of employment revoked, and sues for damages for wrongful revocation without finding a lender, then he may recover only such damages as proximately result from the termination of the employment contract. 12 Am.Jur.2d Brokers, sec. 64.

In the case at bar, plaintiff urges he should be permitted to recover his 1% commission because he argues that he succeeded in fully performing the contract in that he obtained a loan in accordance with the contract which was refused by the defendants. Therefore, he insists as a matter of law he was entitled to the fee stipulated in the contract and was entitled to liquidated damages in the amount of $5,600.00.

As we view the record the proposed loan which plaintiff obtained from Oak Cliff Savings and Loan did not constitute full performance of the agreement because it did not constitute an unqualified agreement to make the loan on the terms proposed by defendants. In addition to the fact that the rate of interest on the loan proffered by plaintiff was greater than the rate stipulated by defendants, the lender also attached two additional conditions: (1) that the defendants would be personally liable and (2) that they would agree to pay a 1% initial lending fee to the lender. The proffered loan was thus conditioned and defendants had a right to accept it or not at their option. Since defendants refused to accept the conditional loan, plaintiff did not obtain a loan as contemplated by the agreement and therefore failed to perform the contract. Keystone Mortgage Co. v. McDonald, 254 Cal.App.2d 808, 62 Cal.Rptr. 562 (1967). It follows that plaintiff would not be entitled to the fee stipulated in the contract.

Plaintiff presented no evidence showing that he probably could and would have performed the contract but for the revocation, nor did he present any evidence showing that he probably could and would have performed by showing that the contract was subsequently performed by defendants or their agents. The only evidence of damages presented by plaintiff was that he expended some time and effort before revocation. Such evidence does nothing more than raise a fact question of the issue of damages and consequently would not entitle plaintiff to a summary judgment.

Inasmuch as the case must be reversed for a new trial, we think it proper to discuss the measure of damages in the case. Since plaintiff failed to obtain a loan in accordance with the terms of the contract, and since he apparently made no attempt to find another lender after the revocation, his cause of action would be for damages rather than a suit on the contract. Therefore, his measure of recovery would be for the value of his services already rendered, if any; his disbursements and expenses, if any; and such prospective profits as he can establish that he would have earned but for the wrongful revocation. In connection with the loss of prospective profits, he can recover only to the extent that the evidence he produces affords a sufficient basis for estimating with reasonable certainty the amount of profits prevented by the wrongful breach of the contract. Thus, if he can show that he could and would have probably obtained a loan in accordance with the contract, or if he can show that during the contract period, defendants or their agents actually obtained a loan as contemplated by the terms of the contract, such evidence would be sufficient to raise an issue of fact with respect to the loss of prospective profits. Restatement, Second, Agency, sec. 455, Comment (e); Alderson v. Houston, 154 Cal. 1, 96 P. 884 (1908). The case of Park v. Swartz, supra, involved a situation where the principal wrongfully revoked a real estate broker-age contract and subsequently sold the property through another agent. There, the trial court impliedly found that the plaintiff in that case could and would have sold the property but for the wrongful revocation and awarded the agent damages in the amount of the prospective loss of profits as stipulated in the contract. The * * * Supreme Court affirmed the judgment of the trial court holding that since the evidence showed that the property was subsequently sold, that such evidence was sufficient to sustain the trial court's implied finding that the plaintiff could have probably performed the contract and that the plaintiff was entitled to recover prospective damages in the amount of the stipulated commission. The court went on to point out, however, that the defendant had a right to plead and prove that the plaintiff could not and would not have performed the contract. * * *

For the reasons stated, the judgment is reversed and the cause is remanded.

REAL ESTATE BROKERS

Real estate owners, desiring to sell their property, typically enlist the services of a real estate broker to find a buyer. Persons acting as real estate brokers must be licensed under state law. The broker earns a commission when he or she produces a buyer "ready, willing, and able" to complete the purchase. The commission is a significant cost normally born solely by the seller: typically between 5 and 10 per cent of the aggregate sales price, depending on the tradition in the area (and the state of the local real estate market). A listing may be "open" (in which case the property is listed with several brokers, and the one who finds the buyer is entitled to the commission) or "exclusive" (in which case one broker is entitled to the commission exclusively if the property is sold during a specified period). Exclusive listings are much more common than open ones; brokers naturally prefer them, and owners usually find that a broker working on an exclusive contract is much more likely to advertise the availability of the property and use greater efforts to sell it than one working on an open contract. The almost universal use of multiple listing services (MLS) in metropolitan areas (by which every broker receives information about most listings in the area) has doubtless also increased the use of exclusive listings, since multiple-listing services assure that all potential buyers being shown properties in the area by other brokers are aware of the availability of the property.

What is the relationship between the broker and owner of real property who have entered into an "exclusive" listing agreement? Most listing agreements involve the use of preprinted forms prepared by a trade association representing real estate brokers. As a result, their terms strongly favor the broker: a listing agreement sets forth the seller's minimum price, the amount of the commission, and the period the agreement is in effect; the owner usually promises to pay the commission on a sale to any person during this period (including buyers located by the seller other than through the broker's efforts) and, after the period has expired, to any person who was shown the property by the broker. What does the broker promise? Typically, not very much. The contract may involve a promise by the broker to use "reasonable" efforts to find a buyer but more likely it requires the broker only to use such efforts as he or she may feel to be reasonable. But that may be enough to avoid the mutuality problem and assure that a bargained for exchange exists. If the buyer attempts to revoke such a listing, and the court concludes that a bilateral contract exists, the broker is entitled to his or her commission upon proof that the broker has or would have found a buyer ready, willing, and able to buy the property.

What is the relationship between the broker who lists a property in the MLS (the "listing broker") and the broker who shows the property to a potential buyer (the "selling broker")? The traditional analysis is that the selling broker, when he or she shows the property to a prospective purchaser, becomes a subagent *of the listing broker,* agreeing to share the commission on a predetermined basis, and, as such, is within a chain of agency to the seller. Stortroen v. Beneficial Co., 736 P.2d 391 (1987).

At first blush, it may seem that the selling broker has a serious conflict of interest, owing duties to the seller as a subagent of the listing broker and also, presumably, duties to the potential purchaser. This conflict, however, is more apparent than real in normal circumstances, because most courts hold that the selling broker does not automatically owe a fiduciary duty to the potential purchaser. Jim Royer Realty, Inc. v. Moreira, 184 Ga.App. 848, 363 S.E.2d 10 (1987). The selling broker's duty, in short, is to the seller and not to the buyer. Of course, by special agreement, a selling broker may assume fiduciary duties to the seller, in which case the broker owes duties to both purchaser and seller. All of this points up the fact that purchasers of real estate live dangerously unless they obtain legal advice prior to the time they enter a binding sales contract.

There are some cases in which real estate brokers, like Howard Sunshine, accept brokerage contracts which appear to be true unilateral contracts rather than bilateral exclusive listing contracts. Presumably the revocability of these contracts is controlled by sections 45 or 87. Is there any practical difference between such a contract and a bilateral contract in which finding a buyer is a condition to the obligation to pay the commission?

In Shear v. National Rifle Ass'n of America, 606 F.2d 1251 (D.C.Cir. 1979), the National Rifle Association decided to sell its Washington, D.C. national headquarters building and move to Colorado Springs, Colorado. It requested Shear, a licensed real estate broker, to seek to find possible purchasers. No listing agreement was signed, but Shear was successful: he found two potential purchasers. Three other potential purchasers also surfaced. The NRA decided to establish a sealed bid process to obtain the best price. The successful bidder was one of the persons found by Shear; the successful bidder entered into a purchase contract "subject to the approval of the Board of Directors of the NRA" (a requirement of which the bidders had been advised). In addition, Shear and the NRA entered into a separate brokerage commission agreement by which the NRA agreed to pay Shear a $150,000 commission "contingent on settlement." Unexpectedly there was a change in personnel on the NRA board of directors, and the new board decided to retain its Washington headquarters and not move to Colorado Springs. The property was withdrawn from the market. Shear then brought suit for his commission. The court held for Shear, finding that performance of the condition that settlement occur was excused because the other party to the contract, the NRA, wrongfully or unjustly prevented it from occurring.

DAVIS v. JACOBY

Supreme Court of California, 1934.
1 Cal.2d 370, 34 P.2d 1026.

PER CURIAM.

Plaintiffs appeal from a judgment refusing to grant specific performance of an alleged contract to make a will. The facts are not in dispute and are as follows:

The plaintiff Caro M. Davis was the niece of Blanche Whitehead, who was married to Rupert Whitehead. Prior to her marriage in 1913 to her coplaintiff Frank M. Davis, Caro lived for a considerable time at the home of the Whiteheads, in Piedmont, Cal. The Whiteheads were childless and extremely fond of Caro. The record is replete with uncontradicted testimony of the close and loving relationship that existed between Caro and her aunt and uncle. During the period that Caro lived with the Whiteheads, she was treated as and often referred to by the Whiteheads as their daughter. In 1913, when Caro was married to Frank Davis, the marriage was arranged at the Whitehead home and a reception held there. After the marriage Mr. and Mrs. Davis went to Mr. Davis' home in Canada, where they have resided ever since. During the period 1913 to 1931 Caro made many visits to the Whiteheads, several of them being of long duration. The Whiteheads visited Mr. and Mrs. Davis in Canada on several occasions. After the marriage and continuing down to 1931 the closest and most friendly relationship at all times existed between these two families. They corresponded frequently, the record being replete with letters showing the loving relationship.

By the year 1930 Mrs. Whitehead had become seriously ill. She had suffered several strokes and her mind was failing. Early in 1931 Mr. Whitehead had her removed to a private hospital. The doctors in attendance had informed him that she might die at any time or she might linger for many months. Mr. Whitehead had suffered severe financial reverses. He had had several sieges of sickness and was in poor health. The record shows that during the early part of 1931 he was desperately in need of assistance with his wife, and in his business affairs, and that he did not trust his friends in Piedmont. On March 18, 1931, he wrote to Mrs. Davis telling her of Mrs. Whitehead's condition and added that Mrs. Whitehead was very wistful. "Today I endeavored to find out what she wanted. I finally asked her if she wanted to see you. She burst out crying and we had great difficulty in getting her to stop. Evidently, that is what is on her mind. It is a very difficult matter to decide. If you come it will mean that you will have to leave again, and then things may be serious. I am going to see the doctor, and get his candid opinion and will then write you again. * * * Since writing the above, I have seen the doctor, and he thinks it will help considerably if you come." Shortly thereafter, Mr. Whitehead wrote to Caro Davis further explaining the physical condition of Mrs. Whitehead and himself. On March 24, 1931, Mr. Davis, at the request of his wife, telegraphed to Mr. Whitehead as follows: "Your letter received. Sorry to hear Blanche not so well. Hope you are feeling better yourself. If you wish Caro to go to you can arrange for her to leave in about two weeks. Please wire me if you think it advisable for her to go." On March 30, 1931, Mr. Whitehead wrote a long letter to Mr. Davis, in which he explained in detail the condition of Mrs. Whitehead's health and also referred to his own health. He pointed out that he had lost a considerable portion of his cash assets but still owned considerable realty, that he needed some one to help him with his wife and some friend he could trust to help him with his business affairs and suggested that perhaps Mr. Davis might come to California. He then pointed out that all his property was community property; that under his will all the property was to go to Mrs. Whitehead; that he believed that under Mrs. Whitehead's will practically everything was to go to Caro. Mr. Whitehead again wrote to Mr. Davis under date of April 9, 1931, pointing out how badly he needed some one he could trust to assist him, and giving it as his belief that if properly handled he could still save about $150,000. He then stated: "Having you [Mr. Davis] here to depend on and to help me regain my mind and courage would be a big thing." Three days later, on April 12, 1931, Mr. Whitehead again wrote, addressing his letter to "Dear Frank and Caro," and in this letter made the definite offer, which offer it is claimed was accepted and is the basis of this action. In this letter he first pointed out that Blanche, his wife, was in a private hospital and that "she cannot last much longer * * * my affairs are not as bad as I supposed at first. Cutting everything down I figure 150,000 can be saved from the wreck." He then enumerated the values placed upon his various properties and then continued:

"My trouble was caused by my friends taking advantage of my illness and my position to skin me.

"Now if Frank could come out here and be with me, and look after my affairs, we could easily save the balance I mention, provided I dont get into another panic and do some more foolish things.

"The next attack will be my end, I am 65 and my health has been bad for years, so, the Drs. dont give me much longer to live. So if you can come, Caro will inherit everything and you will make our lives happier and see Blanche is provided for to the end.

"My eyesight has gone back on me, I cant read only for a few lines at a time. I am at the house alone with Stanley [the chauffeur] who does everything for me and is a fine fellow. Now, what I want is some one who will take charge of my affairs and see I don't lose any more. Frank can do it, if he will and cut out the booze.

"Will you let me hear from you as soon as possible, I know it will be a sacrifice but times are still bad and likely to be, so by settling down you can help me and Blanche and gain in the end. If I had you here my mind would get better and my courage return, and we could work things out."

This letter was received by Mr. Davis at his office in Windsor, Canada, about 9:30 a.m. April 14, 1931. After reading the letter to Mrs. Davis over the telephone, and after getting her belief that they must go to California, Mr. Davis immediately wrote Mr. Whitehead a letter, which, after reading it to his wife, he sent by air mail. This letter was lost, but there is no doubt that it was sent by Davis and received by Whitehead; in fact, the trial court expressly so found. Mr. Davis testified in substance as to the contents of this letter. After acknowledging receipt of the letter of April 12, 1931, Mr. Davis unequivocally stated that he and Mrs. Davis accepted the proposition of Mr. Whitehead and both would leave Windsor to go to him on April 25. This letter of acceptance also contained the information that the reason they could not leave prior to April 25 was that Mr. Davis had to appear in court on April 22 as one of the executors of his mother's estate. The testimony is uncontradicted and ample to support the trial court's finding that this letter was sent by Davis and received by Whitehead. In fact, under date of April 15, 1931, Mr. Whitehead again wrote to Mr. Davis and stated:

> "Your letter by air mail received this a.m. Now, I am wondering if I have put you to unnecessary trouble and expense, if you are making any money dont leave it, as things are bad here. * * * You know your business and I dont and I am half crazy in the bargain, but I dont want to hurt you or Caro.

> "Then on the other hand if I could get some one to trust and keep me straight I can save a good deal, about what I told you in my former letter."

This letter was received by Mr. Davis on April 17, 1931, and the same day Mr. Davis telegraphed to Mr. Whitehead: "Cheer up—we will soon be there, we will wire you from the train."

Between April 14, 1931, the date the letter of acceptance was sent by Mr. Davis, and April 22, Mr. Davis was engaged in closing out his business affairs, and Mrs. Davis in closing up their home and in making other arrangements to leave. On April 22, 1931, Mr. Whitehead committed suicide. Mr. and Mrs. Davis were immediately notified and they at once came to California. From almost the moment of her arrival Mrs. Davis devoted herself to the care and comfort of her aunt, and gave her aunt constant attention and care until Mrs. Whitehead's death on May 30, 1931. On this point the trial court found: "From the time of their arrival in Piedmont, Caro M. Davis administered in every way to the comforts of Blanche Whitehead and saw that she was cared for and provided for down to the time of the death of Blanche Whitehead on May 30, 1931; during said time Caro M. Davis nursed Blanche Whitehead, cared for her and administered to her wants as a natural daughter would have done toward and for her mother."

This finding is supported by uncontradicted evidence and in fact is conceded by respondents to be correct. In fact, the record shows that after their arrival in California Mr. and Mrs. Davis fully performed their side of the agreement.

After the death of Mrs. Whitehead, for the first time it was discovered that the information contained in Mr. Whitehead's letter of March 30, 1931, in reference to the contents of his and Mrs. Whitehead's wills was incorrect. By a duly witnessed will dated February 28, 1931, Mr. Whitehead, after making several specific bequests, had bequeathed all of the balance of his estate to his wife for life, and upon her death to respondents Geoff Doubble and Rupert Ross Whitehead, his nephews. Neither appellant was mentioned in his will. It was also discovered that Mrs. Whitehead by a will dated December 17, 1927, had devised all of her estate to her husband. The evidence is clear and uncontradicted that the relationship existing between Whitehead and his two nephews, respondents herein, was not nearly as close and confidential as that existing between Whitehead and appellants.

After the discovery of the manner in which the property had been devised was made this action was commenced upon the theory that Rupert Whitehead had assumed a contractual obligation to make a will whereby "Caro Davis would inherit everything"; that he had failed to do so; that plaintiffs had fully performed their part of the contract; that damages being insufficient, quasi specific performance should be granted in order to remedy the alleged wrong, upon the equitable principle that equity regards that done which ought to have been done. The requested relief is that the beneficiaries under the will of Rupert Whitehead, respondents herein, be declared to be involuntary trustees for plaintiffs of Whitehead's estate.

It should also be added that the evidence shows that as a result of Frank Davis leaving his business in Canada he forfeited not only all insurance business he might have written if he had remained, but also forfeited all renewal commissions earned on past business. According to his testimony this loss was over $8,000.

The trial court found * * * that the offer of April 12 was not accepted. As already stated, the court found that plaintiffs sent a letter to Rupert Whitehead on April 14 purporting to accept the offer of April 12, and also found that this letter was received by the Whiteheads, but finds that in fact such letter was not a legal acceptance. The court also found that the offer of April 12 was "fair and just and reasonable, and the consideration therefor, namely, the performance by plaintiffs of the terms and conditions thereof, if the same had been performed, would have been an adequate consideration for said offer and for the agreement that would have resulted from such performance; said offer was not, and said agreement would not have been, either harsh or oppressive or unjust to the heirs at law, or devisees, or legatees, of Rupert Whitehead, or to each or any of them, or otherwise."

The court also found that plaintiffs did not know that the statements made by Whitehead in reference to the wills were not correct until after Mrs. Whitehead's death, that after plaintiffs arrived in Piedmont they cared for Mrs. Whitehead until her death and "Blanche Whitehead was greatly comforted by the presence, companionship and association of Caro M. Davis, and by her administering to her wants."

The theory of the trial court and of respondents on this appeal is that the letter of April 12 was an offer to contract, but that such offer could only be accepted by performance and could not be accepted by a promise to perform, and that said offer was revoked by the death of Mr. Whitehead before performance. In other words, it is contended that the offer was an offer to enter into a unilateral contract, and that the purported acceptance of April 14 was of no legal effect.

The distinction between unilateral and bilateral contracts is well settled in the law. It is well stated in section 12 of the American Institute's Restatement of the Law of Contracts as follows: "A unilateral contract is one in which no promisor receives a promise as consideration for his promise. A bilateral contract is one in which there are mutual promises between two parties to the contract; each party being both a promisor and a promisee." This definition is in accord with the law of California.

In the case of unilateral contracts no notice of acceptance by performance is required. Section 1584 of the Civil Code provides: "Performance of the conditions of a proposal * * * is an acceptance of the proposal." See Los Angeles Traction Co. v. Wilshire, 135 Cal. 654, 67 P. 1086.

Although the legal distinction between unilateral and bilateral contracts is thus well settled, the difficulty in any particular case is to determine whether the particular offer is one to enter into a bilateral or unilateral contract. Some cases are quite clear cut. Thus an offer to sell which is accepted is clearly a bilateral contract, while an offer of a reward is a clear-cut offer of a unilateral contract which cannot be accepted by a promise to perform, but only by performance. Berthiaume v. Doe, 22 Cal.App. 78, 133 P. 515. Between these two extremes is a vague field where the particular contract may be unilateral or bilateral depending upon the intent of the offer and the facts and circumstances of each case. The offer to contract involved in this case falls within this category. By the provisions of the Restatement of the Law of Contracts it is expressly provided that there is a *presumption* that the offer is to enter into a bilateral contract. Section 31 provides: "In case of doubt it is presumed that an offer invites the formation of a bilateral contract by an acceptance amounting in effect to a promise by the offeree to perform what the offer requests, rather than the formation of one or more unilateral contracts by actual performance on the part of the offeree."

Professor Williston, in his Treatise on Contracts, volume 1, § 60, also takes the position that a presumption in favor of bilateral contracts exists.

In the comment following section 31 of the Restatement the reason for such presumption is stated as follows: "It is not always easy to determine whether an offerer requests an act or a promise to do the act. As a bilateral contract immediately and fully protects both parties, the interpretation is favored that a bilateral contract is proposed."

While the California cases have never expressly held that a presumption in favor of bilateral contracts exists, the cases clearly indicate a tendency to treat offers as offers of bilateral rather than of unilateral contracts. Roth v. Moeller, 185 Cal. 415, 197 P. 62; see, also, Wood v. Lucy, Lady Duff-Gordon, 222 N.Y. 88, 118 N.E. 214.

Keeping these principles in mind, we are of the opinion that the offer of April 12 was an offer to enter into a bilateral as distinguished from a unilateral contract. Respondents argue that Mr. Whitehead had the right as offerer to designate his offer as either unilateral or bilateral. That is undoubtedly the law. It is then argued that from all the facts and circumstances it must be implied that what Whitehead wanted was performance and not a mere promise to perform. We think this is a non sequitur, in fact the surrounding circumstances lead to just the opposite conclusion. These parties were not dealing at arm's length. Not only were they related, but a very close and intimate friendship existed between them. The record indisputably demonstrates that Mr. Whitehead had confidence in Mr. and Mrs. Davis, in fact that he had lost all confidence in every one else. The record amply shows that by an accumulation of occurrences Mr. Whitehead had become desperate, and that what he wanted was the promise of appellants that he could look to them for assistance. He knew from his past relationship with appellants that if they gave their promise to perform he could rely upon them. The correspondence between them indicates how desperately he desired this assurance. Under these circumstances he wrote his offer of April 12, above quoted, in which he stated, after disclosing his desperate mental and physical condition, and after setting forth the terms of his offer: *"Will you let me hear from you as soon as possible*—I know it will be a sacrifice but times are still bad and likely to be, so by settling down you can help me and Blanche and gain in the end." By thus specifically requesting an immediate reply Whitehead expressly indicated the nature of the acceptance desired by him, namely, appellants' promise that they would come to California and do the things requested by him. This promise was immediately sent by appellants upon receipt of the offer, and was received by Whitehead. It is elementary that when an offer has indicated the mode and means of acceptance, an acceptance in accordance with that mode or means is binding on the offerer.

Another factor which indicates that Whitehead must have contemplated a bilateral rather than an unilateral contract, is that the contract required Mr. and Mrs. Davis to perform services until the death of both Mr. and Mrs. Whitehead. It is obvious that if Mr. Whitehead died first some of these services were to be performed after his death, so that he would have to rely on the promise of appellants to perform these services. It is also of some evidentiary force that Whitehead received the letter of acceptance and acquiesced in that means of acceptance.

Shaw v. King, 63 Cal.App. 18, 218 P. 50, relied on by respondents, is clearly not in point. In that case there was no written acceptance, nor was there an acceptance by partial or total performance.

For the foregoing reasons we are of the opinion that the offer of April 12, 1931, was an offer to enter into a bilateral contract which was accepted by the letter of April 14, 1931. Subsequently appellants fully performed their part of the contract. Under such circumstances it is well settled that damages are insufficient and specific performance will be granted. Wolf v. Donahue, 206 Cal. 213, 273 P. 547. Since the consideration has been fully rendered by appellants the question as to mutuality of remedy becomes of no importance.

Respondents also contend the complaint definitely binds appellants to the theory of a unilateral contract. This contention is without merit.

The complaint expressly alleges the parties entered into a contract. It is true that the complaint also alleged that the contract became effective by performance. However, this is an action in equity. Respondents were not misled. No objection was made to the testimony offered to show the acceptance of April 14. A fair reading of the record clearly indicates the case was tried by the parties on the theory that the sole question was whether there was a contract—unilateral or bilateral.

For the foregoing reasons the judgment appealed from is reversed.

———

California is a community property state and it is therefore probable that one-half of the Whitehead property belonged to Blanche. How can Rupert's letter affect the title of property he does not own? [The trial court found that Rupert only promised "that by last will and testament Rupert Whitehead would devise and bequeath to Caro M. Davis all property and estate owned by him at the time of his death, *other than the property constituting the community interest of Blanche Whitehead.* * * *"] What then did happen to Blanche's interest in the community property?

WHITTIER, THE RESTATEMENT OF CONTRACTS AND MUTUAL ASSENT
17 Calif.L.Rev. 441, 453 (1929).*

In Section 31 it is provided that an offer, in case of doubt, is to be taken as one seeking a bilateral contract. There is certainly scant authority for this. It would appear to be much better to presume that it was indifferently for either a bilateral or unilateral contract. Then either form of acceptance, a promise or an act, would suffice. This solution permits people to make contracts as they will. * * * The argument for the presumption advanced in the Restatement is that bilateral contracts protect both parties better and so should be favored. But persons who are *sui juris* may well be allowed to choose what kind of contracts they will make. If an offeror is indifferent as to which kind he gets, the offeree should be able to accept the offer in either manner.

RESTATEMENT, SECOND, CONTRACTS § 32:

In case of doubt an offer is interpreted as inviting the offeree to accept either by promising to perform what the offer requests or by rendering the performance, as the offeree chooses.

Comment:

a. *Promise or performance.* In the ordinary commercial bargain a party expects to be bound only if the other party either renders the return performance or binds himself to do so either by express words or by part performance or other conduct. Unless the language or the circumstances indicate that one party is to have an option, therefore, the usual offer invites an acceptance which either amounts to performance or constitutes a promise. The act of acceptance may be merely symbolic of assent and promise, or it may also be part or all of the performance bargained for. In either case notification of the offeror may be necessary. * * *

The offeror is often indifferent as to whether acceptance takes the form of words of promise or acts of performance, and his words literally referring to one are often intended and understood to refer to either. Where performance takes time, however, the beginning of performance may constitute a promise to complete it. See § 62 [reprinted below].

Illustrations:

1. A writes B: "If you will mow my lawn next week, I will pay you $10." B can accept A's offer either by promptly promising to mow the lawn or by mowing it as requested.

2. A says to B: "If you finish that table you are making and deliver it to my house today, I will give you $100 for it." B replies, "I'll do it." There is a contract. B could also accept by delivering the table as requested.

Comment:

b. Offer limited to acceptance by performance only. Language or circumstances sometimes make it clear that the offeree is not to bind himself in advance of performance. * * *

It is a separate question whether the offeree undertakes any responsibility to complete performance once begun, or whether he takes any responsibility for the quality of the performance when completed.

Illustrations:

3. A publishes the following offer: "I will pay $50 for the return of my diamond bracelet lost yesterday on State Street." B sees this advertisement and at once sends a letter to A, saying "I accept your offer and will search for this bracelet." There is no acceptance.

4. A writes to B, his nephew aged 16, that if B will refrain from drinking, using tobacco, swearing, and playing cards or billiards for money until he becomes 21 years of age, A will pay B $5,000. B makes a written reply promising so to refrain. There is probably no contract. But if B begins to refrain, A may be bound by an option contract under § 45; and if B refrains until he becomes 21, A is bound to pay him $5,000.

RESTATEMENT, SECOND, CONTRACTS § 62:

(1) Where an offer invites an offeree to choose between acceptance by promise and acceptance by performance, the tender or beginning of the invited performance or a tender of a beginning of it is an acceptance by performance.

(2) Such an acceptance operates as a promise to render complete performance.

Comments:

b. *Part performance or tender.* Where acceptance by performance is invited and no promise is invited, the beginning of performance or the tender of part performance creates an option contract and renders the offer irrevocable. See §§ 37, 45. Under Subsection (1) of this Section the offer is similarly rendered irrevocable where it invites the offeree to choose between acceptance by promise and acceptance by performance. In both types of cases, if the invited performance takes time, the invitation to perform necessarily includes an invitation to begin performance; if performance requires cooperation by the offeror, there is an offer only if acceptance can be completed by tender of performance. But unless an option contract is contemplated, the offeree is expected to be bound as well as the offeror, and Subsection (2) of this Section states the implication of promise which results from that expectation. In such standard cases as the shipment of goods in response to an order, the acceptance will come to the offeror's attention in normal course; in other cases, the rule of § 54(2) [see page 531, infra] ordinarily requires notification.

c. *Manifestation of contrary intention.* The rule of Subsection (1), like the rule of § 45, is designed to protect the offeree in justifiable reliance on the offeror's promise; both rules yield to a manifestation of intention which makes such reliance unjustified. * * * [T]he rule of Subsection (2) is designed to preclude the offeree from speculating at the offeror's expense where no option contract is contemplated by the offer, and to protect the offeror in justifiable reliance on the offeree's implied promise * * *.

d. *Preparations for performance.* As under § 45, what is begun or tendered must be part of the actual performance invited, rather than preparation for performance, in order to make the rule of this Section applicable.

————

See also UCC § 2–206.

RESTATEMENT, SECOND, CONTRACTS § 50:

Illustrations:

1. A, who is about to leave on a month's vacation, tells B that A will pay B $50 if B will paint A's porch while A is away. B says he may

not have time, and A says B may decide after A leaves. If B begins the painting, there is an acceptance by performance which operates as a promise to complete the job. See §§ 32, 62.

2. In Illustration 1, B also expresses doubt whether he will be able to finish the job, and it is agreed that B may quit at any time but will be paid only if he finishes the job during A's vacation. If B begins the painting, there is an acceptance by performance creating an option contract. See § 45.

3. A sends to B plans for a summer cottage to be built on A's land in a remote wilderness area, and writes, "If you will undertake to build a cottage in accordance with the enclosed plans, I will pay you $5,000." B cannot accept by beginning or completing performance, since A's letter calls for acceptance by promise. * * *

4. A mails a written order to B, offering to buy on specified terms a machine of a type which B regularly sells from stock. The order provides. "Ship at once." B immediately mails a letter of acceptance. This is an acceptance by promise, even though under § 32 B might have accepted by performance.

5. A gives an order to B Company's traveling salesman which provides, "This proposal becomes a contract without further notification when approval by an executive officer of B Company is noted hereon at its home office." The notation of approval is an acceptance by promise. * * *

EMPIRE MACHINERY CO. v. LITTON BUSINESS TELEPHONE SYSTEMS

Arizona Court of Appeals, 1979.
115 Ariz. 568, 566 P.2d 1044.

JACOBSON, PRESIDING JUDGE.

This is a contract action in which we are called upon to determine whether execution of a "home office acceptance" clause is the exclusive means by which a contract can be made binding.

This action was instituted by Empire Machinery Co. (Empire) against Litton Systems Co. and various divisions and subsidiary companies of Litton Systems Co. (collectively referred to as Litton) seeking damages for breach of a contract to install and "interconnect" telephone system for Empire's use. On cross-motions for summary judgment, the trial court granted judgment in favor of Litton, in essence finding, as a matter of law, that a binding contract was never consummated between the parties. Empire has appealed.

The facts are not in material dispute between the parties.

Empire is the dealer for Caterpillar Tractor Company in Arizona. In the summer of 1973, Empire became interested in acquiring an "interconnect" telephone system. An "interconnect" system is one in which the telephone customer owns the "in-house" switching equipment, telephones and wiring, as compared to this equipment being owned by the telephone company, in this case, Mountain Bell. Litton is a manufacturer and seller of interconnect systems and on April 2, 1973, Russell R. Murphy, National Accounts Manager for Litton wrote Empire a letter extolling the virtues of the Litton system and enclosing a card to be returned to Litton if Empire was interested in its system. Empire returned the card and on April 17, 1973 Murphy personally contacted Empire.

During this visit, Murphy explained that Litton was developing a "Superplex" switching system which would be available in approximately a year. Mr. Ronald E. Mathis, Jr., communications coordinator for Empire, expressed interest in Litton's system which embraced the "Superplex" switch.

On June 5, 1973, Litton, through Murphy, submitted a proposal to Empire which was rejected. Negotiations continued between Murphy and Mathis until July 30, 1973. On that date, Murphy submitted a letter to Empire which stated in pertinent part that:

> "To confirm our previous discussions, upon receipt of a signed order and deposit, Litton BTS will install a Common Control Crossbar Telephone System on your premises. This system will be replaced upon your request and in accordance with our normal delivery schedule with our computer-controlled electronic solid state TDM system ["Superplex"] at no further expense to your company."

Following receipt of this letter from Murphy, Mr. Jack W. Whitman, president of Empire, signed an "Equipment Sales Agreement" and delivered to Murphy a check in the sum of $8,546.00, as the down payment. Murphy, on the Equipment Sales Agreement, acknowledged receipt of this amount.

This Equipment Sales Agreement contained on its face a clause which read:

> "6. This agreement shall become effective and binding upon the Purchaser and BTS [Litton] only upon approval, acceptance, and execution hereof by BTS and its home office."

At the right hand bottom of the front page, the following appeared:

> "Approved and Accepted by Litton Business Telephone, Division of Litton Systems, Inc. (Seller)

> "By:

> _____

> "(Signature)

> _____

> "(Type Name and Title)

> _____

> "(Date)"

It is acknowledged that Murphy did not sign this portion of the contract. It is also acknowledged that Empire's President, Mr. Whitman, read and understood paragraph 6 quoted above. The estimated date for installation of the Litton system was set at November 15, 1973.

On August 9, 1973, Mathis, on behalf of Empire, was requested by Murphy to send a form letter to Mountain Bell designating Litton as Empire's representative with authority to act in connection with the installation of the interconnect system. The form letter supplied by Litton contained the following lead paragraph:

> "We have this date entered into a contractual agreement with LITTON BTS Division, Litton Systems, Inc. for the installation of an 'interconnect telephone system'."

On August 30, 1973, John Parlett, National Systems Representative for Litton, wrote Mountain Bell advising that company of the details of the installation of the interconnect system. The letter contained the following lead paragraph:

> "We have this date entered into a contractual agreement with Empire Machinery Company for the installation of an 'interconnect' telephone system."

Empire, at Litton's request, purchased approximately $12,000 worth of electrical equipment to facilitate Litton's equipment.

On December 3, 1973, W. P. Scott, service manager of Litton, requested that Mountain Bell supply a new telephone number for Empire to be put in service as of December 21, 1973. Nothing further was done by either party in furtherance of the contract. Litton never shipped nor prepared the interconnect system.

Apparently Litton encountered difficulties in perfecting its "Superplex" system and on January 10, 1974, Mr. E. E. Bolles, then Mountain Area Manager for Litton, met with Murphy and Mathis and advised Mathis that Litton would be unable to supply Empire with a "Superplex" interconnect telephone system. At that time Bolles tendered back Empire's down payment. This oral tender was verified by a letter the following day.

Subsequently, Empire purchased a Stromborg-Carlson interconnect telephone system in lieu of the Litton system. The electrical equipment purchased by Empire was substantially adaptable to the Stromborg-Carlson system. This litigation then ensued.

The parties have presented several issues for our determination, which may be summarized into two issues as follows:

> 1. Did Murphy's letter of July 30, 1973 constitute an offer to sell which was accepted by Empire executing the Equipment Sales Agreement so as to constitute a binding agreement?

> 2. If not, did the Equipment Sales Agreement constitute an offer by Empire to purchase which could only be accepted and made binding by Litton at its home office in accordance with paragraph 6 of that agreement?

Empire first contends that the letter from Litton dated July 30, 1973, signed by Murphy which stated "upon receipt of a signed order and deposit, Litton BTS will install an ['interconnect system'] on your premises", constituted an offer to sell. They further argue that having complied with that offer by signing the Equipment Sales Agreement and giving Murphy a check in the sum of $8,546.00, they accepted that offer and a binding contract was created. The problem with this reasoning is that it ignores the express language of the Equipment Sales Agreement, stating that the agreement would become effective and binding "only upon approval, acceptance, and execution hereof by BTS and its home office." Because of this language, we believe the correct rule is that stated in 1 Corbin, Contracts § 88 (1963):

> "When one party solicits and receives an order or other expression of agreement from another, clearly specifying that there is to be no contract until ratification or assent by some officer or representative of the solicitor, the solicitation is not itself an offer; it is a request for an offer. The order that is given upon such a request is an offer, not an acceptance."

We therefore hold that Murphy's letter of July 30, 1973 constituted a request for an offer from Empire, and that the Equipment Sales Agreement was in compliance with that request and therefore an offer which required Litton's acceptance.

This brings us to the second issue presented, that is, the offer having designated the manner in which it would be accepted, is this the exclusive means by which that acceptance can occur? * * * We therefore assume, for the purposes of this appeal, that there was no formal execution of the Equipment Sales Agreement by "BTS and its home office."

The crux of the problem is thus presented. Litton argues that because of clause 6 in the contract, Empire's offer was never accepted in the manner designated and therefore a binding contractual relationship never existed between the parties. Empire argues that clause number 6 can be waived by it and assented to by Litton and the conduct of Litton subsequent to the submission of the Equipment Sales Agreement shows such an assent or at least a fact issue which would preclude summary judgment. Litton counters this argument by contending that in any event, the conduct relied upon by Empire to show assent was performed by agents who had no authority to bind Litton.

As the ground floor for both Litton's and Empire's positions, both cite [§ 2–206], Uniform Commercial Code. * * *

Empire points to the language contained under paragraph 1 of this statute and contends the conduct of Litton constitutes, as a matter of law, an acceptance of its offer under the Equipment Sales Agreement. Litton, on the other hand, points to the lead paragraph of this statute and argues that paragraph 6 of the Equipment Sales Agreement, as a matter of law, "otherwise unambiguously indicated" that only home office acceptance shall constitute an acceptance of the contract. In our opinion, both arguments miss the mark.

As the official comment to [§ 2–206] of the Uniform Commercial Code makes clear, this section was an attempt to simplify the common law rule that an acceptance of a contract could only be made in the manner and medium of the offer, that is, a written offer could only be accepted by an acceptance in writing. Litton is correct that this statute did not intend to change the common law rule that if an offer by its terms indicated that acceptance would only be made in a particular manner, one must comply with the particular manner. See UCC [§ 2–206], Comment 1 (1969). Nor is such an acceptance clause contrary to the Uniform Commercial Code. West Penn Power Co. v. Bethlehem Steel Corp., 236 Pa.Super. 413, 348 A.2d 144 (1975) (holding that UCC [§ 2–206(1)(a)] envisions "home office" acceptance clauses.)

However, even under the common law, a contract containing a clause that acceptance can only be made by approval of officers at the home office could be accepted in a manner other than by such written approval. See Pratt-Gilbert Co. v. Renaud, 25 Ariz. 79, 213 P. 400 (1923) (holding that complete performance of contract constituted acceptance).

At this point, it is important to clarify the respective positions of the parties to this contract. We have previously held that insofar as the Equipment Sales Agreement was concerned, Empire was the offeror and Litton the offeree. This is important for it is the offeror who creates the power of acceptance. While normally, in transactions such as this where the offer to purchase is made on forms supplied by the seller, the buyer may adopt the manner of acceptance suggested by the seller. However, it is clear under such circumstances that the offeror who has the power to control the manner of acceptance may waive that requirement, 1 Corbin, Contracts § 88 (1963). It is equally clear that the offeree can rely upon that manner of acceptance specified in the contract and the offeror's "waiver" of the manner of acceptance cannot create a contract without the assent of the offeree. See Power Service Corp. v. Joslin, 175 F.2d 698 (9th Cir.1949). This assent may be sufficiently expressed by the conduct of the soliciting offeree so as to bring into being a binding contract. Dunkel Oil Corp. v. Independent Oil & Gas Co., 70 F.2d 967 (7th Cir.1934); 1 Corbin, Contracts § 88 (1963).

The conduct on the part of the offeree which will constitute assent under these circumstances must be directed towards fulfilling the contractual obligation (that is, beginning performance) and that conduct must be conveyed by the offeree to the offeror. Albright v. Stegeman Motorcar Co., supra. Moreover, the conduct must be by persons who have at least apparent authority to bind the offeree. See O'Daniel Motors, Inc. v. Handy, 390 S.W.2d 453 (Ky.Ct.App.1965) (holding that sales contract for used car which required approval of dealer was not made binding on dealer by delivery of car by salesman who had no authority to bind dealer.)

With these principles in mind, the resolution of this appeal requires a determination of (1) whether the conduct of Litton in this matter was directed toward the fulfilling of its obligations so as to sufficiently express its assent to the Equipment Sales Agreement and (2) if so, whether such conduct was performed by individuals who had authority to bind Litton.

The conduct of Litton contended by Empire to constitute assent is as follows:

(1) Murphy's request to Empire that Empire inform Mountain Bell that Litton was Empire's representative to install the "interconnect" system and the existence of a contractual relationship between Litton and Empire.

(2) Parlett's letter of August 30, 1973, on behalf of Litton to Mountain Bell advising Mountain Bell of the contractual relationship existing between Litton and Empire and advising of the details of the installation of the "interconnect" system.

(3) The purchase by Empire of $12,000 worth of equipment in reliance upon the installation of the Litton "interconnect" system.

(4) The cashing of Empire's down payment check and the retention of the proceeds of that check.

(5) The request by Scott, Litton's Service Manager, to Mountain Bell for a new telephone number for Empire's business.

We will analyze each of these to determine whether the conduct, (1) constituted beginning performance of the contractual obligation and, (2) whether the conduct was performed by individuals who could bind Litton by its conduct.

As to Murphy's request that Empire inform Mountain States that a contractual obligation existed between Litton and Empire, we would agree that such conduct could be considered by a trier of fact as constituting assent to the formation of a binding contractual relationship between the parties, if performed by an individual having authority to bind Litton. However, we also agree upon the record presented here that Murphy had no authority expressed or apparent to bind Litton. Here Empire was put on notice by paragraph 6 of the contract that Murphy had no authority to bind Litton by his actions. While it might be argued that this lack of authority only went to Murphy's ability to execute binding contracts and not subsequent conduct, we can see no logical difference between Murphy's conduct after receiving the order and the conduct of the used car salesman in O'Daniel Motors, Inc. v. Handy, supra, in delivering possession to the buyer of the used car. We therefore conclude upon the record presented here that Murphy had no apparent authority to bind Litton by his letter.

The same cannot be said of Parlett, National Systems Representative, and his letter of August 30, 1973, advising Mountain Bell of the contractual relationship existing between Litton and Empire. While Parlett may, in fact, have no actual authority to bind Litton, there is nothing in the record to indicate his buyer was aware of that defect. Moreover, we note that Parlett apparently represents a different division of Litton BTS than Murphy, his headquarters are in a different city than Murphy and on the face of his letter he appears to speak with the authority to bind Litton. In short, we are of the opinion that a question of fact exists as to whether Parlett's letter of August 30, 1973 constituted an assent by Litton to be bound by the Equipment Sales Agreement and whether Parlett had apparent authority to so bind Litton. The same can be said of Scott's letter to Mountain Bell concerning change of telephone numbers. In this regard, Empire's purchase of equipment in reliance on this authority, if this be the fact, can be considered by the trier of fact.

Likewise, in our opinion the cashing of Empire's down payment check raises an issue of fact as to whether Litton assented to the contract. We view this conduct not in the context of ratification of an agent's acts, but as evidence that Litton assented to the contractual relationship by converting the negotiable instrument. See Restatement of Contracts, § 72(2) (1932). We agree with Litton that the mere acceptance of the check in accordance with the terms of the offer does not constitute any evidence of binding conduct on Litton's part. It is the cashing of that check and the retention of the proceeds over a period of several months that gives rise to the factual inferences as to Litton's intent to enter into a binding contractual relationship with Empire. Since the record is silent as to who in the Litton organization negotiated the instrument, that individual's authority to do so must abide the trial of this matter.

Litton argues that in any event all of the conduct referred to by Litton does not amount to "substantial performance" of the Equipment Sales Agreement and therefore as a matter of law cannot constitute an assent of that contract. In this regard, Litton equates substantial performance to conduct dealing with the actual installing, assembling or shipping of the "interconnect" system—conduct Litton did not embark upon. Admittedly, the cases relied upon by Empire have these elements. However, in our opinion, the rule should be that if the offeree takes steps in furtherance of its contractual obligations which would lead a reasonable businessman to believe that the contract had been accepted, such conduct may, under the circumstances, constitute acceptance of the contract.

We therefore hold that factual issues were presented, both as to whether the conduct shown here was in furtherance of Litton's contractual obligations and whether the persons engaging in that conduct had authority, actual or apparent to do so. Such material, factual issues preclude the granting of summary judgment to either party.

Judgment reversed and the matter remanded for proceedings consistent with this opinion.

HAIRE and OGG, JJ., concur.

BISHOP v. EATON

Supreme Judicial Court of Massachusetts, 1894.
161 Mass. 496, 37 N.E. 665.

Evidence was offered tending to show that in 1886, and for some time prior to 1886, the plaintiff and Harry H. Eaton, a brother of the defendant, lived in the county of De Kalb, Ill., for the most of said time in Sycamore, and were together socially, and, to some extent, were engaged in business and in political matters. Some time near the last of December, 1886, defendant wrote to plaintiff, "If Harry needs more money, let him have it, or assist him to get it, and I will see that it is paid." Thereupon said Harry, needing more money, on January 7, 1887, made a promissory note for $200 on one year's time, with interest at the rate of 8 per centum per annum. To assist said Harry to get the money, plaintiff signed this note as surety. Without the suretyship of plaintiff, the note would not have been accepted by the payee. Plaintiff signed the note relying on said letter, and looked to defendant, solely, for reimbursement, if called on to pay the note. Shortly after signing the note, plaintiff deposited in the mail at Sycamore a letter, properly addressed (and stamped) to defendant at the latter's home in Nova Scotia, in which letter plaintiff set forth the giving of the note and the particulars thereof. Defendant testified that he never received said letter. When said note became due, the time of payment was extended for a year, whether with or without the knowledge or consent of defendant was in dispute. In August, 1889, there was an interview between the parties about the note, in which plaintiff asked defendant to take up the note still outstanding, and pay it. Defendant replied, in substance: "Try to get Harry to pay it. If he don't, I will. It shall not cost you anything." * * *

KNOWLTON, J. * * * The judge found that the plaintiff signed the note relying upon the letter, "and looked to the defendant, solely, for reimbursement, if called upon to pay the note." The promise contained in the letter was in these words: "If Harry needs more money, let him have it, or assist him to get it, and I will see that it is paid." On a reasonable interpretation of this promise the plaintiff was authorized to adopt * * * the second alternative, and assist him to get money from some one else in such a way as to create a debt from Harry to the person furnishing the money, and, if Harry failed to pay, to look to the defendant to relieve him from the liability. The words fairly imply that Harry was to be primarily liable for the debt, either to the plaintiff or such other person as should furnish the money, and that the defendant was to guaranty the payment of it. We are therefore of opinion that, if the plaintiff relied solely upon the defendant, he was authorized by the letter to rely upon him only as a guarantor.

* * * The language relied on was an offer to guaranty which the plaintiff might or might not accept. Without acceptance of it, there was no contract, because the offer was conditional, and there was no

consideration for the promise. But this was not a proposition which was to become a contract only upon the giving of a promise for the promise, and it was not necessary that the plaintiff should accept it in words, or promise to do anything before acting upon it. It was an offer which was to become effective as a contract upon the doing of the act referred to. It was an offer to be bound in consideration of an act to be done, and in such a case the doing of the act constitutes the acceptance of the offer, and furnishes the consideration. Ordinarily, there is no occasion to notify the offeror of the acceptance of such an offer, for the doing of the act is a sufficient acceptance, and the promisor knows that he is bound when he sees that action has been taken on the faith of his offer. But, if the act is of such a kind that knowledge of it will not quickly come to the promisor, the promisee is bound to give him notice of his acceptance within a reasonable time after doing that which constitutes the acceptance. In such a case it is implied in the offer that, to complete the contract, notice shall be given with due diligence, so that the promisor may know that a contract has been made. * * * In the present case the plaintiff seasonably mailed a letter to the defendant, informing him of what he had done, in compliance with the defendant's request, but the defendant testified that he never received it, and there is no finding that it ever reached him. The judge ruled as a matter of law that, upon the facts found, the plaintiff was entitled to recover, and the question is thus presented whether the defendant was bound by the acceptance when the letter was properly mailed, although he never received it. When an offer of guaranty of this kind is made, the implication is that notice of the act which constitutes an acceptance of it shall be given in a reasonable way. What kind of a notice is required depends upon the nature of the transaction, the situation of the parties, and the inferences fairly to be drawn from their previous dealings, if any, in regard to the matter. If they are so situated that communication by letter is naturally to be expected, then the deposit of a letter in the mail is all that is necessary. If that is done which is fairly to be contemplated from their relations to the subject-matter, and from their course of dealing, the rights of the parties are fixed, and a failure actually to receive the notice will not affect the obligation of the guarantor.

The plaintiff in the case now before us resided in Illinois, and the defendant in Nova Scotia. The offer was made by letter, and the defendant must have contemplated that information in regard to the plaintiff's acceptance or rejection of it would be by letter. It would be a harsh rule which would subject the plaintiff to the risk of the defendant's failure to receive the letter giving notice of his action on the faith of the offer. We are of opinion that the plaintiff, after assisting Harry to get the money, did all that he was required to do when he seasonably sent the defendant the letter by mail informing him of what had been done. * * *

We find one error in the rulings which requires us to grant a new trial. It appears from the bill of exceptions that, when the note became due, the time for the payment of it was extended without the consent of the defendant. The defendant is thereby discharged from his liability, unless he subsequently assented to the extension, and ratified it. The court should * * * [not have found] for the plaintiff as a matter of law on the facts reported. Whether the judge would have found a ratification on the evidence, if he had considered it, we have no means of knowing. Exceptions sustained.

RESTATEMENT, SECOND, CONTRACTS § 54:

Illustrations:

1. A mails a written order to B for goods to be manufactured specially for A, and requests B to begin at once since manufacture will take several weeks. Under § 62 acceptance is complete when B begins, but A's contractual duty is discharged and he may treat the offer as having lapsed before acceptance unless within a reasonable time B sends notification of acceptance or unless the offer or a prior course of dealing indicates that notification is not required.

2. A, the proprietor of a medical preparation, offers $100 to anyone who contracts a certain disease after using the preparation as directed. B uses it as directed. B has accepted the offer, and is entitled to the $100 if she later contracts the disease. No notification to A is required until after B has contracted the disease.

4. A, the president of a corporation, agrees to guarantee payment for goods to be sold to the corporation by B. B sells and delivers the goods. B has accepted A's offer, and no notification of acceptance is necessary.

———

Compare UCC § 2–206(2).

NEWMAN v. SCHIFF
778 F.2d 460 (8th Cir.1985).

Before HEANEY, CIRCUIT JUDGE, BRIGHT, SENIOR CIRCUIT JUDGE, and ARNOLD, CIRCUIT JUDGE.

BRIGHT, SENIOR CIRCUIT JUDGE.

John A. Newman, an attorney practicing law in St. Louis, Missouri, brought this action against Irwin Schiff of Hamden, Connecticut, alleging breach of contract. Newman claimed that Schiff had made a public offer of reward to anyone who could cite any section of the Internal Revenue Code that says an individual is required to file an income tax return. Newman asserted that he accepted Schiff's offer, and that Schiff breached the contract by failing to pay him the reward. The district court ruled in favor of Schiff by finding that Newman's acceptance was not timely, and Newman appeals. We affirm the judgment of the district court.

I. BACKGROUND

Irwin Schiff is a self-styled "tax rebel", who has made a career and substantial profits out of his tax protest activities.[2] Schiff's basic contention is that the federal income tax is a voluntary tax which no one is required to pay.[3] Schiff has prepared various books and materials espousing his point of view, including *The Tax Rebel's Guide to the Constitution and Declaration of Independence, The Freedom Kit* ("For those wanting the original work that ignited the tax rebellion * * *"), *The Biggest Con: How the Government is Fleecing You,* and *How Anyone Can Stop Paying Income Taxes* ("The amazing new best seller that exposes the fraud and deception by which the IRS extracts income taxes from uninformed Americans . . . and shows you how you can PUT A STOP TO IT—NOW!"). He has promoted his books by appearing on over five hundred radio and television programs, including Larry King's national radio talk show, Tom Snyder's "Tomorrow" show, and "The David Susskind Show," and by giving lectures in over sixty cities. Schiff claims that his activities have caused over 100,000 people to no longer file or pay income taxes.

On February 7, 1983, Irwin Schiff appeared live on CBS News Nightwatch (Nightwatch), a nighttime television program with a viewer participation format. Schiff was interviewed by host Karen Stone from approximately 3:00 a.m. to 4:00 a.m. Eastern Time. The words "Nightwatch Phone–In" and the telephone number (212) 955–9555 were flashed on the screen periodically during Schiff's appearance. In addition, Ms. Stone repeated the telephone number and encouraged viewers to call and speak directly with Schiff on the air.

During the course of the Nightwatch program, Schiff repeated his long-standing position that, "there is nothing in the Internal Revenue Code which I have here, which says anybody is legally required to pay the tax." Following a discussion of his rationale for that conclusion, Schiff stated: "If anybody calls this show—I have the Code—and cites any section of this Code that says an individual is required to file a tax return, I will pay them $100,000."

Newman did not see Schiff's live appearance on Nightwatch. He did, however, see a two-minute taped segment of the original Nightwatch interview that was rebroadcast several hours later on the CBS Morning News. The CBS Morning News rebroadcast included Schiff's reward proposal.[4]

2. Schiff refers to himself as an "economist and constitutionalist", and as "America's leading untax expert." He recently served four months in prison for failing to file federal income tax returns.

3. This position is meritless. p. [537].

4. The following is a partial transcript of the CBS Morning News rebroadcast of Schiff's Nightwatch appearance:

DIANE SAWYER [Morning News commentator]: Benjamin Franklin said nothing is certain in this world but death and taxes. Irwin Schiff has gone a long way to try to disprove the second part of that certainty, because Schiff says no one really has to pay taxes, and he talked about that this morning with Karen Stone on the CBS News broadcast NIGHTWATCH.

Newman felt certain that Schiff's statements regarding the Internal Revenue Code were incorrect. Upon arriving at work that day, he researched the issue and located several sections of the Code that to his satisfaction demonstrated the mandatory nature of the federal income tax system. The next day Newman telephoned CBS Morning News and cited the following provisions of the Internal Revenue Code as authority for his position that individuals are required to pay federal income tax: 26 U.S.C. §§ 1, 6012, 6151, 6153, 7201, 7202 and 7203. Newman placed his call to (212) 975–4321, the number given him by the long distance operator for CBS in New York. He then reduced this conversation to writing and sent it to the CBS Morning News.[5] Newman's letter stated

[Thereafter, the following was replayed in part]:

KAREN STONE: Why do you object to the federal income tax?

IRWIN SCHIFF: Well, first of all, there's two reasons I object to it, on legal grounds, and I object to it on economic grounds. But first of all—legally, the income tax is a voluntary tax. There's nothing in the Internal Revenue Code, which I have here, which says anybody's legally required to pay the tax. It's a voluntary tax, and if it were mandatory, it would be unconstitutional. Now, the question is why—

STONE: But you went to jail for four months and paid a $10,000 fine. So in essence, haven't you really paid your federal income taxes for those years that you didn't file?

SCHIFF: No. No. No, no. That was a fine, and I'm going to be getting that back. We'll be suing the government

* * *

STONE: Now—okay—Every year—you know, we all get our 1040s in the mail or go pick them up, and you're saying that—that we are tricked into believing that we—

SCHIFF: You're required to file.

STONE: That we're required to file.

SCHIFF: Absolutely. *If anybody calls this show—I have the Code—and cites any section of this Code that says an individual is required to file a tax return, I'll pay them $100,000.* The fact of the matter is that you're not required to file. The income tax is voluntary, and it's not that I say it—(emphasis added).

5. The text of Newman's letter to the CBS Morning News, dated February 8, 1983, reads as follows:

This letter is in response to a statement made by Mr. Erwin [sic] Schiff, who was a guest on the CBS Morning

News on Monday, February 7, 1983. During the interview, Mr. Schiff, who regards himself as a tax protestor, stated that the Internal Revenue Code did not mandate the payment of tax. Mr. Schiff presented a copy of the Code, declaring that if anyone could find any provision in the Code making the payment of tax mandatory, he would pay that person $100,000.

In response to Mr. Schiff's offer, I have located the pertinent portions of the Internal Revenue Code mandating the payment of tax. Code section 1 "imposes" tax on individuals according to their respective income levels and filing status. Code section 6012 provides that individuals meeting certain income threshholds [sic] "shall" file a return. Webster's New Collegiate Dictionary states that "shall," when used in laws or regulations, constitutes a directive "to express what is mandatory." Code section 6151 provides that persons required to make returns "shall * * * pay such tax * * * at the time and place for filing the return." Section 6653 imposes various civil penalties for "failure to pay tax," the severity of which depends on the taxpayer's degree of culpability. Finally, Code sections 7201, 7202 and 7203 impose criminal sanctions, including fines and imprisonment, for failure to pay tax imposed by the Code.

In light of the foregoing, it is clear that our system of taxation is indeed mandatory and that we are required to pay tax. This letter is intended to constitute performance of the consideration requested by Mr. Schiff in exchange for his promise to pay $100,000.

I am communicating directly with CBS in this matter because the offer was extended over the CBS network and your staff was unable to provide Mr. Schiff's own address. I will, of course, look solely to Mr. Schiff for performance of his

that it represented "performance of the consideration requested by Mr. Schiff in exchange for his promise to pay $100,000."

CBS responded to Newman's letter on March 3, 1983, informing him that a copy of it had been forwarded to Schiff at Freedom Press. On April 13, 1983, after not hearing from Schiff for over a month, Newman wrote to him at Freedom Press. Newman repeated the portion of his previous letter which discussed Internal Revenue Code provisions that stand for the mandatory nature of the federal tax system. He then reiterated his claim for the $100,000 reward.

On April 20, 1983, Schiff wrote to Newman and stated that: "[y]our letter to Mr. O'Regan at CBS Morning News was forwarded to me. I did make an offer on the February 7, 1983 news (which was actually part of an interview conducted earlier in the week)." Schiff said, however, that Newman had not properly accepted his offer for both substantive and procedural reasons.[6]

Newman then sued Schiff in federal district court for breach of contract. The district court decided that: (1) Schiff intended for his offer to remain open only until the conclusion of the live Nightwatch broadcast; (2) the rebroadcast on CBS Morning News did not renew or extend Schiff's offer; and therefore (3) Newman's acceptance of the offer was untimely. The district court went on to state that Schiff's argument that there is no requirement for individuals to file a tax return is "blatant nonsense."

Newman moved for additional findings of fact and an amendment of judgment. The district court did not alter its judgment, but did make additional conclusions. The district court decided that Schiff ratified the CBS Morning News rebroadcast of his original Nightwatch offer by failing to object after learning of the rebroadcast, by accepting the benefits of the added publicity, and expressly by his letter dated April 20, 1983. The district court said that the ratification constituted a renewal of Schiff's original offer. Nevertheless, it decided that Newman's failure to respond on the morning of the rebroadcast meant that his acceptance was still untimely. This appeal followed.

promise. Meanwhile, could you please send me a copy of the relevant portions of the program transcript, and Mr. Schiff's address if it can be located?

6. The text of Schiff's letter to Newman, dated April 20, 1983, reads as follows:

Your letter to Mr. O'Regan at CBS Morning News was forwarded to me. I did make an offer on the February 7, 1983 news (which was actually part of an interview conducted earlier in the week). That offer was to pay $100,000 to the *first* person who could produce a section of the code that states anyone is *required* to file.

You did not produce a section that states an individual is *required* to file a return. Section 6012 *does not* state anyone is required to file as explained in my book (see attachment). In addition, my offer was extended beginning last October and I had received numerous letters claiming that same section of the code as proof prior to the February 8 date of your letter (which obviously had to be mailed after February 8). Since that letter was dated after receipt of others naming the same code you did, you would not, in any case, be eligible even if that section proved that individuals were required to file.

II. DISCUSSION

Newman contends that the district court applied the wrong standard in judging the timeliness of his response to the rebroadcast. We do not reach the issue of timeliness, however, because we conclude that the district court erred by ruling that Schiff renewed his Nightwatch offer through ratifying the CBS Morning News rebroadcast. Consequently, we affirm the judgment of the district court on grounds that Newman did not accept Schiff's initial and only offer that had been made on the Nightwatch program.

A. *The Requirement of Mutual Assent*

It is a basic legal principle that mutual assent is necessary for the formation of a contract. A significant doctrinal struggle in the development of contract law revolved around whether it was a party's actual or apparent assent that was necessary. This was a struggle between subjective and objective theorists. * * *

By the end of the nineteenth century the objective approach to the mutual assent requirement had become predominant, and courts continue to use it today. * * *

B. *The Mechanics of Mutual Assent: Offer and Acceptance*

Courts determine whether the parties expressed their assent to a contract by analyzing their agreement process in terms of offer and acceptance. An offer is the "manifestation of willingness to enter into a bargain, so made as to justify another person in understanding that his assent to that bargain is invited and will conclude it." *Restatement (Second) of Contracts* § 24 (1981). *Coffman Industries, Inc. v. Gorman–Taber Co.,* 521 S.W.2d 763, 768 (Mo.Ct.App.1975).

The present case concerns a special type of offer: an offer for a reward. At least since the time of Lilli Carlill's unfortunate experience with the Carbolic Smoke Ball, courts have enforced public offers to pay rewards. *Carlill v. Carbolic Smoke Ball Co.,* (1892), 2 Q.B. 484, *aff'd,* (1893) 1 Q.B. 256 (C.A.1892). In that case, frequently excerpted and discussed in student lawbooks, the Carbolic Smoke Ball Company advertised that it would pay a "100£ reward" to anyone who contracted "the increasing epidemic influenza, colds, or any disease caused by taking cold, after having used the Carbolic Smoke Ball three times daily for two weeks according to the printed directions supplied with each ball." *Id.* Ms. Carlill, relying upon this promise, purchased and used a Carbolic Smoke Ball. It did not, however, prevent her from catching the flu. The court held that the advertised reward constituted a valid offer which Ms. Carlill had accepted, thereby entitling her to recovery.

The Missouri courts enforced a public reward offer in a case concerning the notorious desperado Jesse James. Rudy Turilli, operator of the "Jesse James Museum," appeared before a nationwide televised audience and offered $10,000 to anyone who could disprove his contention that Jesse James was not murdered in 1882, but in fact lived for many years thereafter under the alias J. Frank Dalton and last resided with Turilli at his museum into the 1950's. Stella James, a relative of Jesse James, accepted the challenge and produced affidavits of persons who had identified Jesse James' body after the shooting in 1882. Turilli denied that the evidence satisfied the requisite degree of proof and refused to pay the $10,000. The trial court ruled that Ms. James was entitled to the reward, and the Missouri Court of Appeals upheld this judgment. *James v. Turilli,* 473 S.W.2d 757, 763 (Mo.Ct. App.1971).

1. *The Nightwatch Offer*

In the present case, Schiff's statement on Nightwatch that he would pay $100,000 to anyone who called the show and cited any section of the Internal Revenue Code "that says an individual is required to file a tax return" constituted a valid offer for a reward. In our view, if anyone had called the show and cited the code sections that Newman produced, a contract would have been formed and Schiff would have been obligated to pay the $100,000 reward, for his bluff would have been properly called.

2. *The CBS Morning News Rebroadcast*

Newman, however, never saw the live CBS Nightwatch program upon which Schiff appeared and this lawsuit is not predicated on Schiff's Nightwatch offer. Newman saw the CBS Morning News rebroadcast of Schiff's Nightwatch appearance. This rebroadcast served not to renew or extend Schiff's offer, but rather only to inform viewers that Schiff had made an offer on Nightwatch. The rebroadcast constituted a newsreport and not a renewal of the original offer. An offeror is the master of his offer and it is clear that Schiff by his words, "If anybody calls this show * * *", limited his offer in time to remain open only until the conclusion of the live Nightwatch broadcast. A reasonable person listening to the news rebroadcast could not conclude that the above language—"calls this show"—constituted a new offer; rather than what it actually was, a newsreport of the offer previously made, which had already expired.

The district court further concluded, however, that Schiff's conduct subsequent to the rebroadcast and his letter of April 20, 1983 were a ratification of the CBS Morning News rebroadcast and constituted a renewal of the Nightwatch offer. We disagree.

Schiff's conduct and letter should not be analyzed under the rubric of ratification. Instead they are pertinent to the initial question of whether the CBS Morning News rebroadcast was an offer. As we discussed above, this question is to be decided using an objective approach without completely disregarding the actual and proven assent of either of the parties. Here, in Schiff's letter, we have a statement indicating that the rebroadcast may have been an offer. If Schiff believed that the rebroadcast was an offer, then that belief would tend to make it appear more reasonable for Newman to have reached the same conclusion. We note, however, that both Schiff's conduct and his letter are indefinite. He still denied the obligation. Schiff's conduct and correspondence do not change the facts that the rebroadcast was merely a newsreport and that it was not reasonable for the hearer to construe the newsreport as a new offer. * * *

D. *Mandatory Nature of the Federal Income Tax System*

Schiff's claim that there is nothing in the Internal Revenue Code that requires an individual to file a federal income tax return demands comment. The kindest thing that can be said about Schiff's promotion of this idea is that he is grossly mistaken or a mere pretender to knowledge in income taxation. We have nothing but praise for Mr. Newman's efforts which have helped bring this to light.

Section 6012 of the Internal Revenue Code is entitled "Persons required to make returns of income," and provides that individuals having a gross income in excess of a certain amount "shall" file tax returns for the taxable year. 26 U.S.C. § 6012. Thus, section 6012 requires certain individuals to file tax returns. *United States v. Drefke,* 707 F.2d 978, 981 (8th Cir.), *cert. denied,* 464 U.S. 942, 104 S.Ct. 359, 78 L.Ed.2d 321 (1983).

The district court stated that Schiff's argument is "blatant nonsense." Schiff did not challenge this ruling in his cross-appeal.

III. CONCLUSION

We affirm the judgment of the district court for the reasons discussed above.

Although Newman has not "won" his lawsuit in the traditional sense of recovering a reward that he sought, he has accomplished an important goal in the public interest of unmasking the "blatant nonsense" dispensed by Schiff. For that he deserves great commendation from the public. Perhaps now CBS and other communication media who have given Schiff's mistaken views widespread publicity will give John Newman equal time in the public interest.

Affirmed but without any costs against John Newman.

THE LAW OF REWARDS

As indicated in Newman v. Schiff, the law of rewards is generally viewed as an application of the principles of offer and acceptance. Of course, the offer in a reward is made publicly, usually by an advertisement, and the acceptance must be the performance of the act that is called for (a promise will not suffice). These two features raise unique problems that are not likely to be found in other types of contracts. These problems include the following:

A. Must the person claiming the reward have been aware of it when he performed the act in question?

The "black letter" law of contracts clearly requires an offeree to be aware of the offer if the performance of the act called for is to be an acceptance of the offer. In the case of rewards, the requirement that the offeree know of the offer may be justified on the theory that an offer of a reward is intended to induce action by people. A person who acts without knowledge of the reward is not induced thereby and arguably is therefore not within the class or group of persons to whom the offer was addressed. On this theory, it makes no difference if the person claiming the reward was not acting gratuitously and intended to claim the reward, if there was one. His action was not induced by **this** offer of a reward. While other noncontractual hypotheses about the motivation of the offeror of a reward may be put forth, private offers of rewards are enforceable only to the extent they are contracts. A well recognized exception exists for offers of rewards by governmental bodies, which arguably are not contractual at all but a governmental act that is designed to encourage all citizens to assist in the performance of some generally desirable action. On this theory, a person may recover on an offer for a reward by the government even if ignorant of the existence of the offer.

RESTATEMENT, SECOND, CONTRACTS § 23:

Illustrations:

2. A advertises that he will give a specified reward for certain information, or writes B a similar proposal. B gives the information in ignorance of the advertisement, or without having received the letter. There is no contract enforceable as a bargain.

3. A city ordinance provides that a standing reward of $1000 will be paid for information leading to the arrest and conviction of anyone guilty of arson within the city limits. A furnishes such information. A is entitled to the reward whether or not he knew of the reward or was motivated by hope of reward.

B. *Lapse of Reward Offer.* The "black letter" rule is that an offer lapses after a reasonable time. See supra page 437. How is that standard to be applied in the case of published rewards?

RESTATEMENT, SECOND, CONTRACTS § 41:

Illustrations:

1. A publishes an offer of reward for information leading to the arrest and conviction of the person guilty of a specified murder. B, intending to obtain the reward, gives the requested information a year after the publication of the offer. The acceptance is timely.

2. After a series of incendiary attempts, a city publishes each day for a week an offer of reward for information leading to the arrest and conviction of any person who shall set fire to any building within the city. The responsible city officials serve for one year terms. A fire set three years after the last publication is not within the terms of the offer.

3. A bank posts in its office an offer of reward for information leading to the arrest and conviction of any person who robs any bank which is a member of an association of banks in the same county. After several years the poster is removed. A robbery three years after the removal may be found to be within the terms of the offer.

C. Revocation of Reward.

RESTATEMENT, SECOND, CONTRACTS § 46:

Where an offer is made by advertisement in a newspaper or other general notification to the public or to a number of persons whose identity is unknown to the offeror, the offeree's power of acceptance is terminated when a notice of termination is given publicity by advertisement or other general notification equal to that given to the offer and no better means of notification is reasonably available.

Illustrations:

1. A, a newspaper, publishes an offer of prizes to the persons who procure the largest number of subscriptions as evidenced by cash or checks received by a specified time. B completes and mails an entry blank giving his name and address, which is received by A. Thereafter, during the contest, A publishes a notice that personal checks will not be counted; B does not see the notice. Unless the original offer provided otherwise, B is not bound by the later notice, since A could have given B personal notice.

2. The United States Government publishes an offer of reward for the arrest of a named fugitive. Seven months later the President publishes a proclamation revoking the offer, which is given the same publicity as the offer. Five months after the proclamation, A, who has been in Italy continuously and who learned indirectly of the offer but not of the revocation, arrests the fugitive in Italy. There is no contract.

Since rewards are usually publicly proclaimed, it is impossible, as a practical matter, to notify every person who may be aware of the offer that it has been revoked. The manner of revocation suggested by § 46 of the Restatement of Contracts, Second, seems justified by a principle of necessity: one cannot normally expect to do better than publish the revocation in the same manner as the offer was published. As a result, persons aware of the offer but unaware of the revocation are nevertheless bound by the revocation. On the other hand, section 46 is applicable only if "no better means of notification is reasonably available." If A has published an offer of a reward for a lost dog and knows that B is actively looking for it, does A, if she wishes to revoke the offer, have to seek B out and tell him that the offer is revoked?

Assume that A has posted a notice of the offer of a reward for the lost dog on several telephone poles in the vicinity. In order to revoke this offer, does A have to place notices on each of the telephone poles? If A sees B approaching with the lost dog safely in tow, may A revoke by calling out to B, "I hereby revoke my offer of a reward"?

RESTATEMENT, SECOND, CONTRACTS § 29:

Illustrations:

1. A publishes an offer of reward to whoever will give him certain information. There is no indication that A intends to pay more than once. Any person learning of the offer has power to accept * * * but the giving of the information by one terminates the power of every other person.

3. A, the proprietor of a medical preparation, offers $100 to anyone who contracts a certain disease after using the preparation as directed. B, C and D use it as directed. Each has made a contract independent of the others, and is entitled to the $100 if he later contracts the disease.

———

D. *Whether performance is acceptance.* Reward offers may also give rise to unique problems in the area of acceptance which, of course, must be the performance of the act or acts requested.

———

(1) Some Part of Acts Performed Before Learning of the Reward

The first Restatement of Contracts took the position that in order to earn a reward, a person must have been aware of the offer at the time he or she commenced the performance requested by the offer. Restatement of Contracts, First, § 53 (1932). Even though there was apparently no intervening case, the Restatement of Contracts, Second, § 51, reverses this position and states that an offeree who learns of a reward offer after he or she has rendered a part of the performance requested, may accept by completing the requested performance. This is based on the theory that reward offers are usually motivated by a desire for the completed act, e.g. returning a lost dog, and that completion of performance is as valuable to the maker of such an offer as the entire performance. Recognizing that this change is based on an assumed intention of the offeror, § 51 recognizes that a manifested intention by the offeror to the contrary should be given effect.

RESTATEMENT, SECOND, CONTRACTS § 51:

Illustrations:

1. A offers a reward for the apprehension and delivery into police custody of a criminal. Before learning of the reward, B arrests the criminal. After learning of the reward, B delivers the criminal into police custody. B is entitled to the reward.

2. A posts a notice on his bulletin board offering a specified bonus to any employee who remains in A's employment for four months. B, one of the employees, continues to work for one month before learning of the offer. Thereafter, B completes the four-month period of employment. B is entitled to the bonus.

---

(2) Actions Taken Pursuant to a Legal Duty

The "black letter" rule is that a public official who is under a legal duty to perform an act may not claim a reward that has been offered for the performance of that act. Restatement of Contracts, Second, § 73, comment b. This illustrates the policy aspects of the preexisting duty rule. See p. 285 supra. What are the potential dangers if peace officers, for example, were permitted to claim rewards?

---

(3) Actions Not Motivated by Reward

WILLIAMS v. CARWARDINE, 4 B. & Ad. 621, 110 Eng.Rep. 590 (K.B. 1833), involved an offer of reward for information leading to the discovery of the murderer of one Walter Carwardine. The plaintiff gave this information knowing of the offer; however, she did so because she had been "severely beaten and bruised [by the murderer], and * * * believing she had not long to live, and to ease her conscience." The plaintiff survived, however, and was held to be entitled to the reward. There are some American cases that look in the opposite direction, e.g., Vitty v. Eley, 51 A.D. 44, 64 N.Y.S. 397 (1900); Taft v. Hyatt, 105 Kan. 35, 180 P. 213 (1919).

RESTATEMENT, SECOND, CONTRACTS § 53:

Illustrations:

1. A offers a reward for information leading to the conviction of a criminal. B, a friend of the criminal, knows of the reward and gives the information voluntarily. B is entitled to the reward even though he acts because he thinks he is about to die and wants both to ease his conscience and to revenge himself for a beating received from the criminal.

2. The facts being otherwise as stated in Illustration 1, B is interrogated by the police and threatened with arrest as an accomplice

of the criminal. During the interrogation, without any mention of the reward, B is tricked into giving the information to clear himself. B is not entitled to the reward.

3. The facts being otherwise as stated in Illustration 1, B states after giving the information that he does not claim the reward. B is not entitled to the reward.

————

(4) Actions Different From the Requested Acceptance

SMITH v. STATE, 38 Nev. 477, 479, 151 P. 512 (1915). In a true wild West scenario, the governor of Nevada, pursuant to a statute adopted by the state legislature, offered a reward of $1,000 for the "arrest and conviction of the person or persons guilty of the murder of Harry Cambron and three associates." Plaintiffs were part of a possee trying to run down the murderers, who included "Indian Squaw Jennie," "Shoshone Mike," "Buck Desenda," "Buck Kinnan" and "Buck Cupena." The Indians were surrounded but refused to surrender and were killed while resisting arrest. The court held that the plaintiffs were entitled to the reward even though no one was arrested or convicted of anything, quoting a statement that "courts have been inclined to look with disfavor on a too technical interpretation of the word 'conviction.'" Incidentally, in this case, it appeared that the posse was unaware of the act of the Nevada legislature or of the governor and yet were held to be entitled to the reward. Is that consistent with settled law?

————

(5) Apportionment of Rewards

What should be done about the not uncommon situation where several persons contribute toward the action called for by the reward? For example, A offers a reward of $1,000 for the "arrest and conviction of X for arson." B catches X in B's home apparently with arsonous intentions, disarms him, and holds him for police to arrive. X is subsequently tried for arson and is convicted largely on the basis of testimony of C and D. B is not called as a witness. Has B earned the reward? Have C and D?

————

E. *Reliance on a Reward Offer.* Assume that A makes an offer to B, "if you will find my lost dog, I will pay you a reward of $50." B agrees to do so, and begins a systematic search for the dog, but A revokes three days later before B has found the dog. May B argue that he should be entitled to reimbursement of his reliance expenditures? How does that differ from Manos' offer to Sunshine to pay him a commission if Sunshine can find a loan that meets specified terms (page 505, supra)? If the offer is not made directly to B but to the world in general through a public advertisement, may anyone claim a right to reimbursement of reliance expenditures?

SECTION 4: ACCEPTANCE BY SILENCE OR BY ACCEPTANCE OF BENEFITS

HOBBS v. MASSASOIT WHIP CO.

Supreme Judicial Court of Massachusetts, 1893.
158 Mass. 194, 33 N.E. 495.

HOLMES, J. This is an action for the price of eel skins sent by the plaintiff to the defendant, and kept by the defendant some months, until they were destroyed. It must be taken that the plaintiff received no notice that the defendants declined to accept the skins. The case comes before us on exceptions to an instruction to the jury that, whether there was any prior contract or not, if skins are sent to the defendant, and it sees fit, whether it has agreed to take them or not, to lie back, and to say nothing, having reason to suppose that the man who has sent them believes that it is taking them, since it says nothing about it, then, if it fails to notify, the jury would be warranted in finding for the plaintiff.

Standing alone, and unexplained, this proposition might seem to imply that one stranger may impose a duty upon another, and make him a purchaser, in spite of himself, by sending goods to him, unless he will take the trouble, and bear the expense, of notifying the sender that he will not buy. The case was argued for the defendant on that interpretation. But, in view of the evidence, we do not understand that to have been the meaning of the judge, and we do not think that the jury can have understood that to have been his meaning. The plaintiff was not a stranger to the defendant, even if there was no contract between them. He had sent eel skins in the same way four or five times before, and they had been accepted and paid for. On the defendant's testimony, it was fair to assume that if it had admitted the eel skins to be over 22 inches in length, and fit for its business, as the plaintiff testified and the jury found that they were, it would have accepted them; that this was understood by the plaintiff; and, indeed, that there was a standing offer to him for such skins.

In such a condition of things, the plaintiff was warranted in sending the defendant skins conforming to the requirements, and even if the offer was not such that the contract was made as soon as skins corresponding to its terms were sent, sending them did impose on the defendant a duty to act about them; and silence on its part, coupled with a retention of the skins for an unreasonable time, might be found by the jury to warrant the plaintiff in assuming that they were accepted, and thus to amount to an acceptance.

The proposition stands on the general principle that conduct which imports acceptance or assent is acceptance or assent, in the view of the law, whatever may have been the actual state of mind of the party,—a principle sometimes lost sight of in the cases. O'Donnell v. Clinton, 145

Mass. 461, 463, 14 N.E.Rep. 747; McCarthy v. Railroad Corp., 148 Mass. 550, 552, 20 N.E.Rep. 182.

Exceptions overruled.

———

ROBERTS v. BUSKE, 12 Ill.App.3d 630, 298 N.E.2d 795 (1973):

"In September, 1969, plaintiff, an insurance agent, sent defendant [an automobile liability] policy which was a renewal of one defendant's father had previously held. Defendant had not ordered or requested issuance of this policy, but he accepted it and paid the premium. In September, 1970, just prior to the expiration date of the policy, a second unsolicited renewal was sent to defendant and attached to it was a printed notice stating that if defendant did not wish to accept it he must return it or be liable for the premium. Defendant made no response either to this notice or to two subsequent bills mailed to him. Finally, in December, the agent telephoned defendant personally to inquire about the premium. Defendant informed him that he had purchased a policy from another company in August and that since he had not ordered the renewal he felt no obligation to pay for it. The policy was then returned to the company and cancelled, resulting in a loss to the agent for the pro-rated portion of the premium which he had advanced, [and for which he sought recovery. Held, for defendant.]

"In his brief plaintiff * * * argues that because defendant had previously accepted a renewal policy and thereafter paid the premium his silence in replying to the second renewal constituted an implied acceptance thereof and obligated him to pay the premium. * * *

"We recognize that the practice of sending renewals oftentimes serves the best interests of an insured; but, likewise, it serves the best business interests of the insurance agent. And it is the agent, as the offeror, who must assure himself that his offer has been accepted. Under ordinary circumstances silence cannot be relied upon to establish an acceptance of an offer to enter into a contract. (Corbin on Contracts, Vol. 1, Sec. 72.) We do not preclude the possibility of an implied acceptance being established under certain circumstances. However, * * * we cannot find that acceptance of a single previous renewal in itself is sufficient to constitute an implied acceptance of a second renewal based solely on the silence of the offeree. Not only is the mailing of a first renewal policy insufficient to show a previous course of dealing between the parties, the plaintiff presented no evidence regarding the customary trade practice, if any, in situations similar to that presented here. It is obvious that plaintiff feels abused in that defendant did not inform him that he had bought another policy, but a simple telephone call would have revealed this fact and there would have been no reason for plaintiff to have incurred the loss caused by his unwarranted assumption."

———

KUKUSKA v. HOME MUTUAL HAIL–TORNADO INSURANCE CO., 204 Wis. 166, 235 N.W. 403 (1931).

Plaintiff, "a farmer of very limited understanding and experience," applied for hail insurance for his crop with defendant on July 2, 1928. The application form stated that no contract was formed until the application was approved by the company. Defendant's agent in River Falls, Wisconsin forwarded the application and the premium of $14.70 to defendant the same day. Defendant did not finally act on the application for internal reasons until July 27, 1928, when it instructed its agent to advise Kukuska that his application had been rejected. Kukuska received a notice to this effect at 11:00 a.m. on August 1, 1928; at 4:00 p.m. that afternoon a violent hailstorm swept over Kukuska's farm. Held, the insurance company is liable for Kukuska's loss:

"By the soliciting, making and receiving of the application, the parties had entered into some kind of a consensual relationship. By the terms of the application it was not to ripen into a contract until the application was approved. But for this language in the application, it might be held that the failure to act within a reasonable time resulted in approval. * * *

"Under such circumstances, having in view the nature of the risk against which the insurer seeks protection, is there not a duty upon the insurer to act upon the application within a reasonable time? Can the insurer, having pre-empted the field, retain control of the situation and the applicant's funds indefinitely? Does not the very nature of the transaction impose upon the insurer a duty to act? It is considered that there is a duty. If the insurer is under such a duty and fails to perform the duty within a reasonable time and, as a consequence, the applicant sustains damage, it is not vastly important that the legal relationship be placed in a particular category. If we say it is contractual, that is, there is an implied agreement under the circumstances on the part of the insurer to act within a reasonable time, or, having a duty to act, the insurer negligently fails in the performance of that duty, or that the duty springs out of a consensual relationship, and is therefore in the nature of a quasi contractual liability, is not vitally important. Each view finds some support in the cases. It seems to be more in accord with ordinary legal concepts to say that it is a quasi contractual duty. * * *"

RANSOM v. THE PENN MUTUAL LIFE INSURANCE CO.

Supreme Court of California, en banc, 1954.
43 Cal.2d 420, 274 P.2d 633.

GIBSON, CHIEF JUSTICE.

The jury impliedly found that defendant refused to perform a contract in which it agreed with plaintiff's deceased husband, Ralph W. Ransom, to insure his life. Defendant has appealed from the judgment against it, contending that no contract of insurance was in force at the time of Ransom's death and that if any contract existed it was vitiated by fraud.

In September 1949 Ransom, who was twenty-eight years old, was solicited for insurance by an agent of defendant. A doctor selected by defendant examined Ransom and found nothing wrong with his physical condition. Ransom made a written application for insurance on a form provided by defendant and paid the first premium in full. In the application he stated that he had previously been examined by a Dr. Long, and, in response to inquiries made by defendant, Dr. Long replied that Ransom visited him in 1947 complaining of a "heavy feeling" in the chest. Dr. Long stated that his examination of Ransom revealed a "moderately obese patient with no important clinical findings," that laboratory studies included an electrocardiogram which was "essentially normal," that the first blood pressure reading was above normal and that the second reading taken about a week later under less tension was normal as to the systolic pressure and a little above normal as to the diastolic pressure. Dr. Long advised Ransom to lose weight and "reassured" him as to his physical status.

After receiving Dr. Long's report, defendant requested Ransom, to submit to further medical examination, but before this could be arranged Ransom was killed in an automobile accident. An autopsy was performed which disclosed no evidence of disease and showed that Ransom's death resulted from external violence. Several days after the accident defendant, having received information of Ransom's death, tendered plaintiff the full amount of the first premium payment and informed her that, in view of Dr. Long's report, Ransom's application could not be approved.

The first question presented is whether an insurance agreement was in effect at the time of Ransom's death. The application contained the following clause: "If the first premium is paid in full in exchange for the attached receipt signed by the Company's agent when this application is signed the insurance shall be in force, subject to the terms and conditions of the policy applied for, from the date of Part I or Part II of this application, whichever is the later, provided the Company shall be satisfied that the Proposed Insured was at that date acceptable under the Company's rules for insurance upon the plan at the rate of premium and for the amount applied for, but that if such first premium is not so paid or if the Company is not satisfied as to such acceptability, no insurance shall be in force until both the first premium is paid in full and the policy is delivered while the health, habits, occupation and other facts relating to the Proposed Insured are the same as described in Part I and Part II of this application and in any amendments thereto."

We must determine whether a contract of insurance arose immediately upon receipt by defendant of the completed application with the premium payment, subject to the right of defendant to terminate the agreement if it subsequently concluded that Ransom was not acceptable, or whether, as defendant contends, its satisfaction as to Ransom's acceptability for insurance was a condition precedent to the existence of any contract.

The courts in several jurisdictions have construed clauses similar to the one involved here. A number of decisions have held, in accordance with defendant's view, that no contract of insurance exists until the insurer has been satisfied as to an applicant's acceptability, and that the provision that the insurance shall be in force from the date of the application means that, if and when the company is satisfied, the contract shall be considered to relate back and take effect as of that date. Mofrad v. New York Life Ins. Co., 10 Cir., 206 F.2d 491.

On the other hand, a number of courts have held that the provision to the effect that the insurance shall be in force from the date of the application if the premium is paid gives rise to a contract of insurance immediately upon receipt of the application and payment of the premium, and that the proviso that the company shall be satisfied that the insured was acceptable at the date of the application creates only a right to terminate the contract if the company becomes dissatisfied with the risk before a policy is issued. Gaunt v. John Hancock Mut. Life Ins. Co., 2 Cir., 160 F.2d 599, 601–602; cf. Stonsz v. Equitable Life Assur. Soc., 324 Pa. 97, 187 A. 403, 405–406, 107 A.L.R. 178 [stating that this view represents a trend to construe the conditions liberally].

In the Gaunt case Judge Learned Hand stressed the fact that an application must be construed as it would be taken by the ordinary applicant, and that such a person would assume that he was getting immediate insurance for his money and would not understand that he was left uncovered until the insurer at its leisure approved the risk. 160 F.2d at pages 601–602. In Albers v. Security Mut. Life Ins. Co., 41 S.D. 270, 170 N.W. 159, 160, it was said that if the company did not intend that the insurance should be effective from the date of the application it would be obtaining a premium for a period during which there was no insurance, and this would not be dealing honestly with the insured. In Duncan v. John Hancock Mut. Life Ins. Co., 137 Ohio St. 441, 31 N.E.2d 88, 91, the court said that the provisions of the clause are obviously ambiguous and susceptible of two different constructions, that the insurer could have used clear language and that the ambiguity must be resolved against the company.

We are of the view that a contract of insurance arose upon defendant's receipt of the completed application and the first premium payment. The clause quoted above is subject to the interpretation that the applicant is offered a choice of either paying his first premium when he signs the application, in which event "the insurance shall be in force * * * from the date * * * of the application," or of "paying upon receipt of the policy," in which event "no insurance shall be in force until * * * the policy is delivered." The understanding of an ordinary person is the standard which must be used in construing the contract, and such a person upon reading the application would believe that he would secure the benefit of immediate coverage by paying the premium in advance of delivery of the policy. There is an obvious advantage to the company in obtaining payment of the premium when the application is made, and it would be unconscionable to permit the company, after using language to induce payment of the premium at that time, to escape the obligation which an ordinary applicant would reasonably believe had been undertaken by the insurer. Moreover, defendant drafted the clause, and had it wished to make clear that its satisfaction was a condition precedent to a contract, it could easily have done so by using unequivocal terms. While some of the language tends to support the company's position, it does no more than produce an ambiguity, and the ambiguity must be resolved against defendant. * * *

The judgment is affirmed.

SHENK, CARTER, TRAYNOR, SCHAUER and SPENCE, JJ., and PEEK, J. PRO TEM, concur.

Rehearing denied; SPENCE, J., dissenting. EDMONDS, J., not participating.

INSURANCE BINDERS

When a person applies for life insurance coverage and pays a premium pending a medical examination, he may be making only an offer if one reads literally the application form. However, such a person is likely to assume that he is covered immediately; certainly he is not likely to try to arrange alternative insurance while the first insurance company decides whether or not to accept his offer. Courts have generally protected insureds against interim losses unless the absence of such interim protection is clearly stated in the application form or brought to the attention of the insured. Indeed, insurance companies today generally recognize that their agents in effect issue temporary insurance or "binders" when they accept applications for insurance and the initial premiums. As a result, numerous possible problems about the precise date an insurance application is accepted or whether the insurance company delayed unreasonably in acting on the application (as in Kukuska's case) have been eliminated. Where the death of the insured occurs shortly after the application is received, courts have permitted insurers to reject the application if they can establish that the application would not have been accepted according to the insurer's usual standards. On the other hand, numerous cases hold that an insurer cannot welsh on a promise of binder coverage simply by rejecting an application when there has been a loss while the application is pending. These insurance cases are discussed in the context of contract principles generally in Gergen, Liability for Mistake in Contract Formation, 64 S.Cal.L.Rev. 1, 8–9, 13–15, 25–26 (1990).

FELTON v. FINLEY

Supreme Court of Idaho, 1949.
69 Idaho 381, 209 P.2d 899.

GIVENS, JUSTICE.

In March 1944, Seigle Finley and W.E. or William Finley, two of the three surviving nephews of Seigle Coleman, who died testate December 4, 1943, employed respondent to contest the deceased Coleman's will, which was successfully done. In re Coleman's Estate, 66 Idaho 567, 163 P.2d 847. At that time respondent told Seigle and William Finley that he would accept the employment only on condition that the other nephew and brother, Orval Finley, and the three sisters, Ida Davis, Nan Holder, and Rose Finley Nichles, likewise employ respondent as their attorney and that all six of the heirs participate in the contest.

Respondent requested Seigle and William Finley to contact their brother and sisters and secure signed contracts of employment similar to the ones which Seigle and William signed; namely, on a 50% contingent basis. Respondent likewise wrote the other four heirs requesting their execution of such contracts. Such heirs never replied to respondent's initial letter or to subsequent letters written by him continuing to request their execution of such contracts of employment and advising them as to the course of the litigation.

Seigle and William Finley contacted two sisters, Nan Holder and Ida Davis in Pilot Rock, Oregon, with reference to their joining in the employment of respondent and related that:

> "＊ ＊ ＊ they said they would have nothing to do with it. My oldest sister, Ida Davis, is very religious and she said she didn't feel like protesting. She said, 'What you boys do is your business, but I will have nothing to do with it.'"

> "Q. Did they, the two sisters, make any statement that they would not oppose the contest? A. The only statement they made was they would have nothing to do with it one way or the other."

Testifying further that they (Seigle and William Finley) attempted to get the three sisters and the other brother to join with them—that is, in the employment of respondent in the prosecution of the contest, stating further:

> "A. I had quite a time contacting my brother (Orval). He was in Alaska part of the time and I called him in St. Paul, Minnesota, that's his home, and he said, 'I am having nothing whatever to do with a dead man's money.'"

and that he (Orval),

> "＊ ＊ ＊ would have nothing to do one way or the other, what I did was my business, to forget about him."

and about the same as to Rose Finley Nichles:

> "She said she would have nothing to do with the estate. She said, 'If you and Bill sign, that's your business. I am not going to. There is no use sending the contract.' I read it to her over the phone and she said, 'No.'"

Respondent testified he understood from Seigle and William, that while the other brother and sisters said they would have nothing to do with it, they would leave the further handling of the matter to Seigle and William and he prosecuted the action on that basis, though Seigle testified he told respondent:

> "I told him I couldn't get in touch with them and they wouldn't sign and would have nothing to do with it."

William Finley testified with regard to the conference with the two sisters as follows:

> "A. * * * When they came we talked about the contract and breaking the will and my sisters were very much opposed to breaking the will or having anything to do with it, and we talked quite a while and I finally asked them if they would not fight us if we went ahead.

> "Q. Not fight you? A. That's right, and they said they wouldn't oppose us, but would have nothing to do with breaking the will. One of my sisters thinks it is a terrible sin.

> "Q. Did you have copies of the contract for the signature of Nan Holder and Ida Davis? A. We did.

> "Q. Were you able to get them to sign them? A. They would not.

> "Q. You advised Mr. Felton that you were unable to get those contracts signed? A. Yes, sir."

Mrs. Holder testified that when she was in Missouri she followed the case in the Moscow newspapers and knew respondent was representing Seigle and William and admitted she had received one letter from respondent, but not the others. The other sisters and brother did not testify.

At the conclusion of the contest action, distributive checks were made out to each one of the six heirs jointly with respondent for their respective shares, which the three sisters and Orval refused to accept, taking the position they had never employed respondent and were not obligated to pay him any fee and subsequent conferences between respondent and Mrs. Holder were unavailing.

The present suit to establish the implied contract and to enforce the attorney's lien, resulted with findings, conclusions and decree there was an implied contract of employment, from which decree the present appeal was taken.

By stipulation, the appellants have been paid their distributive shares less the portion thereof claimed by respondent and decreed to him as his fee from them. * * *

It is an elementary rule that, whenever services are rendered and received, a contract of hiring or an obligation to pay what they are reasonably worth will generally be presumed. 28 R.C.L. 668, § 3. Hartley v. Bohrer, 52 Idaho 72, at page 75, 11 P.2d 616, 617.

The rule applicable to the above situation has been recently declared in a Washington case to be as follows:

"The rule is well established that the acceptance of the services rendered by an attorney may raise an implied promise to pay therefor, which will supply the place of a contract of employment. If an attorney renders valuable services, as in the case at bar, to one who has received the benefit thereof, a promise to pay the reasonable value of such services is presumed unless the circumstances establish the fact that such services were intended to be gratuitous." (Citing authorities.) McKevitt v. Golden Age Breweries, 14 Wash.2d 50, 126 P.2d 1077, at page 1081.

The record herein affirmatively and positively shows the respondent was not undertaking the services herein for anyone gratuitously. It is also held the acceptance of benefits must be voluntary. The acceptance and receipt by appellants of their share of their enhanced inheritance were entirely voluntary, because there is no law which required them to accept the greater amount; they could have taken only the $500.00 which the will initially gave them and refused the additional sum. Whatever scruples or feelings they had about not signing contracts, taking a dead man's money or interfering with his will, had thus evidently disappeared when the money was made available to them, even though without their active participation. Nevertheless, it was solely through respondent's efforts and successful prosecution of the contest case which procured this additional money for them and which, when thus secured to them by respondent's services, they promptly demanded and have pocketed.

Such course of conduct on their part amounts to such ratification and recognition of respondent's actions as to create in law an implied contract of employment and fully justified the decree in respondent's favor. * * *

The decree is, therefore, affirmed. Costs awarded to respondent.

FEATHERSTONE and TAYLOR, DISTRICT JUDGES, concur.

HOLDEN, CHIEF JUSTICE (dissenting). * * *

It is urged in the case at bar that where one permits another to perform services for him, the law raises an implied promise to pay the reasonable value of the services. But respondent does not bring himself within the rule. Here, appellants, notwithstanding several efforts were made to induce them to employ respondent, refused to do so. It is true respondent performed services in contesting the will, but the services were performed for "S.P. Finley [Seigle]" and William Finley under the terms of a written contract. He was thus obligated to perform all the services he performed. He could not repudiate his solemn contract without committing a breach. Nor was respondent expected by those who thus employed him to perform such or any services gratuitously. The contract which respondent himself drew provided for the payment of the compensation which he thought his services were worth. The benefits which came to appellants were the result of the performance of the terms of the written contract entered into by respondent with Seigle and William Finley, not the result of any contract with appellants, because they refused to employ him. And, further, the services respondent performed in contesting the will were performed with knowledge appellants would not employ him. In fact, appellants were opposed to the contest and would not and did not, have anything to do with it. No case has been cited and none can be found holding an implied promise or implied contract to pay for services under such facts and circumstances. Nor does Morning Star Mining Co. v. Williams, 171 Ark. 187, 283 S.W. 354, hold that a set of facts such as above stated creates an implied contract of employment. It is true that was a case to recover attorney fees on an implied contract to pay. But in that case it appears Williams, an attorney, accepted employment in good faith to prosecute a suit to remove a cloud upon the title to certain real property, believing that one Chase was authorized to employ him. Chase had previously employed him for the Morning Star Mining Company and the company had regularly paid the fees.

*   *   *

But it is argued the acceptance of accruing benefits created an implied contract to pay respondent. In resolving that question the above stated facts of this case should be kept in mind. The courts are unanimous in holding an acceptance of benefits does not create an implied contract to pay.   *   *   *

SUTPHEN, DISTRICT JUDGE, concurs in this dissenting opinion.

ON REHEARING

HOLDEN, CHIEF JUSTICE.

A rehearing was had at Lewiston at our May, 1949, term. Since such rehearing the various contentions of the respective parties have been fully and carefully re-examined. We conclude, as a result of such re-examination, that the decree appealed from in the case at bar should be, and it is hereby, reversed and the cause remanded with directions to dismiss the action, in accordance with the views expressed in the foregoing dissenting opinion of Chief Justice Holden. Costs awarded to appellants.

TAYLOR, J., and FEATHERSTONE and SUTPHEN, DISTRICT JUDGES, concur.

GIVENS, JUSTICE (dissenting on rehearing). [opinion omitted]

———

VINCENT v. HUGHES AIR WEST, INC., 557 F.2d 759, 769–770 (9th Cir.1977). This case involved an award of attorneys fees in consolidated cases arising out of a 1971 air crash disaster. The court permitted plaintiffs' lead counsel to recover from awards to plaintiffs who had not retained them on the following theory:

"The common fund doctrine provides that a private plaintiff, or his attorney, whose efforts create, discover, increase or preserve a fund to which others also have a claim is entitled to recover from the fund the costs of his litigation, including attorneys' fees. The doctrine is 'employed to realize the broadly defined purpose of recapturing unjust enrichment.' [Dawson, Lawyers and Involuntary Clients: Attorney Fees From Funds, 87 Harv.L.Rev. 1597 (1974).] That is, the doctrine is designed to spread litigation costs proportionately among all the beneficiaries so that the active beneficiary does not bear the entire burden alone and the 'stranger' beneficiaries do not receive their benefits at no cost to themselves.

"The doctrine is exemplified by the fountainhead case, *Trustees v. Greenough,* 105 U.S. 527, 26 L.Ed. 1157 (1881). Vose held bonds of the Florida Railroad Company. A fund, consisting of ten or eleven million acres of state-owned land, had been pledged for the payment of the interest accruing on the bonds and installments of the sinking fund for meeting the principal. The fund's trustees, however, through various fraudulent conveyances, wasted a portion of the fund and failed to pay the interest on the bonds or the sinking fund installments. Vose, 'with great vigor and at much expense,' pursued litigation that secured and saved a large amount of the fund. Other bondholders thereupon 'came in and took the benefit of the litigation.' When Vose sought reimbursement for his expenditure of attorneys' fees, the Supreme Court permitted it. In the Court's view, the most equitable way to reimburse Vose for his expenses was by making them a charge upon the fund, which at that time was still being administered by a receiver under the trial court's direction. 105 U.S. at 532.

"A significant expansion of *Greenough,* relevant to this case, occurred four years later in *Central Railroad & Banking Co. v. Pettus,* 113 U.S. 116, 5 S.Ct. 387, 28 L.Ed. 915 (1885). Attorney Pettus' client successfully brought a creditors' bill to reach the assets of a debtor-railroad, and the client paid Pettus the amount set in their contract. Pettus thereupon attempted to recover for the services he had 'provided' to creditors named as class members in the creditors' bill. The Supreme Court allowed the *extra* fee and even gave Pettus a lien on the railroad's assets that had been preserved by the original decree and made available to satisfy the creditors' claims. As Professor Dawson has noted:

"The *Pettus* case totally transformed [the claim of a *client* for contribution to the litigation costs that he had incurred, as recognized in *Greenough,*] into an independent right of the *lawyer,* reinforced by lien, to an extra reward so that he might share the wealth of strangers. The lawyer was suddenly thought of as producer of this wealth, though he did nothing more than perform his contract with his own client, and furthermore had been paid by his client in full the sum he had agreed to accept."

[Dawson,] 1603–04 (emphasis in original).

"Certain elements of the common fund doctrine, either as developed in these two cases or as fashioned in the many cases applying the doctrine since, are relevant to the present case. First, the original client's attorney's fees are not shifted to—or the attorney's personal claim for an extra fee is not lodged against—the adversary-losing party; rather, fees are shifted to third parties, people viewed as beneficiaries of the fund in some way. Second, no contractual relationship exists between the original attorney and the third parties. Rather, the common fund doctrine is rooted in concepts of quasi-contract and restitution. Third, the beneficiaries are expected to pay litigation costs in proportion to the benefits that the litigation produced for them. Fourth, as a general rule, if the third parties hire their own attorneys and appear in the litigation, the original claimant cannot shift to them his attorney's fees. Some cases stand as an exception to this element, however. *E.g., Doherty v. Bress,* 104 U.S.App.D.C. 308, 262 F.2d 20 (1958), *cert. denied,* 359 U.S. 934, 79 S.Ct. 649, 3 L.Ed.2d 636 (1959). Fifth, the third parties are not personally liable for the litigation costs. Any claim must be satisfied out of the fund. A concomitant element of the doctrine, indeed one of its foundation stones, is that there must exist some identifiable assets on which a court can impose a charge. Nevertheless, the concept of 'fund' is flexible, and it is now settled that a money judgment or even a settlement can serve as a fund. What is crucial is that the court can legitimately exercise authority or control over the asset."

LOUISVILLE TIN & STOVE v. LAY, 251 Ky. 584, 65 S.W.2d 1002 (1933). Mrs. May Lay was engaged in business under the firm name Lay's Variety Store. She was solvent and had good credit. Her husband was engaged in an independent business under the firm name Lay's Electric Shop. He was insolvent and had no credit. The Louisville Tin & Stove Company consigned a lot of heaters, gas ranges, and similar goods to Lay's Variety Store—goods which she did not carry and which she had not ordered. Mrs. Lay was advised that these goods were at the freight station. Mrs. Lay became angry and announced, "that was some of Mr. Lay's doings, and that she knew nothing about the shipments at all and had nothing to do with them, but that she would find out about them." Later that day she directed the deliveryman to deliver the shipment to Lay's Electric Shop; Mr. Lay accepted them and gave the deliveryman a check for the freight and drayage. When the goods were not paid for, suit was brought against Mrs. Lay who was held liable for them:

"The testimony　*　*　* shows that although the merchandise was billed and shipped to Lay's Variety Store without the knowledge or consent of Mrs. Lay, she, after its arrival, assumed control of its disposition, knowing full well that it had been so billed and shipped by the Louisville Tin & Stove Company. It was entirely optional with her to reject it unqualifiedly, or to accept it or direct it to be delivered to her husband.　*　*　* After so doing on his failure to pay the balance due thereon, she cannot escape her liability therefor to the consignor, the Louisville Tin & Stove Company. It was at her direction and by her authority that the merchandise reached the possession of her husband at his place of business.

"*　*　* [She] failed to exercise her right to repudiate the shipment, but exercised the authority of authorizing the drayman to see her husband for directions over it. Her acts constitute an acceptance of the shipment.　*　*　*"

What should a person in Mrs. Lay's position do with respect to unordered goods? See UCC §§ 2–601, 2–602, 2–603, 2–604, 2–606(1)(c), 2–711(3). Are these sections applicable to the precise facts of this case?

AUSTIN v. BURGE, 156 Mo.App. 286, 137 S.W. 618 (1911). Plaintiff was publisher of a newspaper in Butler, Missouri; defendant's father-in-law subscribed to the paper to be sent to defendant for two years, and he paid for it for that time. The paper continued to be sent to defendant through the mail for several years more. The paper apparently was delivered to a post office box and defendant took it from the post office to his home. On two occasions defendant paid a bill presented for the subscription price but each time directed it to be stopped. However, notwithstanding the order to stop it, the paper continued to be sent to defendant who continued to receive and read it until finally he removed to another state. Held, for plaintiff:

"There are　*　*　* certain well-understood principles in the law of contracts that ought to solve the question. It is certain that one cannot be forced into contractual relations with another and that therefore he cannot, against his will, be made the debtor of a newspaper publisher. But it is equally certain that he may cause contractual relations to arise by necessary implication from his conduct. The law in respect to contractual indebtedness for a newspaper is not different from that relating to other things which have not been made the subject of an express agreement. Thus one may not have ordered supplies for his table, or other household necessities, yet if he continue to receive and use them, under circumstances where he had no right to suppose they were a gratuity, he will be held to have agreed by implication, to pay their value. In this case defendant admits that, notwithstanding he ordered the paper discontinued at the time when he paid a bill for it, yet plaintiff continued to send it, and he continued to take it from the post office to his home. This was an acceptance and use of the property, and, there being no pretense that a gratuity was intended, an obligation arose to pay for it. * * *

"The preparation and publication of a newspaper involves much mental and physical labor, as well as an outlay of money. One who accepts the paper, by continuously taking it from the post office, receives a benefit and pleasure arising from such labor and expenditure as fully as if he had appropriated any other product of another's labor, and by such act he must be held liable for the subscription price. On the defendant's own evidence, plaintiff should have recovered."

MAILING OF UNORDERED MERCHANDISE

39 U.S.C.A. § 3009 (1980)

(a) Except for (1) free samples clearly and conspicuously marked as such, and (2) merchandise mailed by a charitable organization soliciting contributions, the mailing of unordered merchandise or of communications prohibited by subsection (c) of this section constitutes an unfair method of competition and an unfair trade practice * * *.

(b) Any merchandise mailed in violation of subsection (a) of this section, or within the exceptions contained therein, may be treated as a gift by the recipient, who shall have the right to retain, use, discard, or dispose of it in any manner he sees fit without any obligation whatsoever to the sender. All such merchandise shall have attached to it a clear and conspicuous statement informing the recipient that he may treat the merchandise as a gift to him and has the right to retain, use, discard, or dispose of it in any manner he sees fit without any obligation whatsoever to the sender.

(c) No mailer of any merchandise mailed in violation of subsection (a) of this section, or within the exceptions contained therein, shall mail to any recipient of such merchandise a bill for such merchandise or any dunning communications.

(d) For the purposes of this section, "unordered merchandise" means merchandise mailed without the prior expressed request or consent of the recipient.

Many record and book clubs involve "negative option plans." Under these plans, a person joins the "club," often receiving a "bonus" for doing so, and commits to purchase a limited number of records or books over the following year. A member is not obligated to take any specific record or book, but a monthly selection is automatically sent unless the member mails in a form in advance declining to accept the selection. The details of these plans are regulated by the Federal Trade Commission. See 16 C.F.R. 425.1, et seq. (1991). Is there any possibility of applying 39 U.S.C.A. § 3009 to such plans?

RESTATEMENT, SECOND, CONTRACTS § 69:

(1) Where an offeree fails to reply to an offer, his silence and inaction operate as an acceptance in the following cases only:

(a) Where an offeree takes the benefit of offered services with reasonable opportunity to reject them and reason to know that they were offered with the expectation of compensation.

(b) Where the offeror has stated or given the offeree reason to understand that assent may be manifested by silence or inaction, and the offeree in remaining silent and inactive intends to accept the offer.

(c) Where because of previous dealings or otherwise, it is reasonable that the offeree should notify the offeror if he does not intend to accept.

(2) An offeree who does any act inconsistent with the offeror's ownership of offered property is bound in accordance with the offered terms unless they are manifestly unreasonable. But if the act is wrongful as against the offeror it is an acceptance only if ratified by him.

———

HOUSTON DAIRY, INC. v. JOHN HANCOCK MUTUAL LIFE INSURANCE CO., 643 F.2d 1185 (5th Cir.1981). John Hancock mailed a commitment letter to Houston Dairy on December 30, 1977, in which it agreed to lend Houston Dairy $800,000 at 9¼ per cent interest provided that within seven days Houston Dairy return the commitment letter with a written acceptance and the payment of $16,000 as a "good faith deposit"; the commitment letter also provided that forfeiture of the deposit was the appropriate measure of liquidated damages in the event Houston Dairy defaulted. Houston Dairy did not execute the commitment letter until January 17, 1978, and Hancock's agent did not receive the commitment letter and a cashier's check for $16,000 until January 23. The cashier's check was deposited by Hancock. Houston Dairy requested that its attorney meet with the Hancock attorney to arrange for the closing and determine closing fees, and one such meeting occurred. On January 30, however, Houston Dairy learned that it could borrow $800,000 from another source at 9 per cent interest; Houston Dairy then "revoked its counter-offer" and demanded a return of its deposit. The district court found that a contract existed and upheld the forfeiture provision as a valid liquidated damages clause. Held, reversed since no contract existed:

"It is fundamental that a contract is formed only upon acceptance of an offer. Just as basic is the principle that an offeror is free to limit acceptance to a fixed time period. 1 A Corbin, Contracts § 35 (1963). Once the time period has expired, a belated attempt to accept would be ineffective. However, such an untimely attempt to accept normally constitutes a counter offer which would shift the power of acceptance to

(H.,R.&W.) Contracts, 2d Ed. ACB—20

the original offeror. 1 Corbin § 74. Additionally, acceptance of a counter offer is established only by conforming to the rules governing acceptance, not a separate theory of 'waiver and ratification.' Kurio v. United States, 429 F.Supp. 42, 64 (S.D.Tex.1970).[1]

"It is therefore clear in the instant case that upon expiration of the seven-day time period, John Hancock's offer terminated. Thus the action taken by Houston Dairy in signing and returning the commitment letter subsequent to the termination of the offer constituted a counter offer which John Hancock could accept within a reasonable time.

"In Mississippi, the courts have long recognized that for acceptance to have effect, it must be communicated to the proposer of the offer. John Hancock contends it did accept Houston Dairy's counter offer and that the acceptance was communicated to Houston Dairy.

"According to John Hancock, depositing Houston Dairy's check was itself sufficient to operate as communication of its acceptance of the counter offer. John Hancock argues that its silence plus retention of Houston Dairy's money constituted acceptance and notification. Indeed, Mississippi has specifically recognized the validity of acceptance by silence within the guidelines laid down in Restatement [of Contracts] § 72 (1932). However, the present facts do not fit within these guidelines. Houston Dairy neither had previous dealings nor had otherwise been led to understand that John Hancock's silence and temporary retention of its deposit would operate as acceptance. In addition, Houston Dairy had no knowledge that its check had been deposited in John Hancock's depository. Since Houston Dairy sent a cashier's check, it could not have known the check had even been deposited unless notified by John Hancock or its bank. No such notice arrived from John Hancock and none is required from the bank. * * *

"John Hancock also contends that Houston Dairy was notified of its acceptance in the conversation between the attorneys for both parties on January 28. However, a review of the testimony concerning that conversation shows no communication of acceptance. Indeed, John Hancock's closing attorney testified that at the time of his conversation with Houston Dairy's attorney, he had not received the executed commitment letter and had no knowledge a counter offer had even been made. His conversation only concerned the method to be used to close the loan and the distribution of the fee to be charged, not

---

1. In *Kurio*, the court considered an issue in contract law similar to the instant case. An offer had been terminated by lapse of time and a belated attempt to accept the offer was construed as a counter offer. As in the present case, an argument was made that the original offeror could waive the untimeliness of the acceptance. After outlining the basic requirements for formation of a contract and acceptance of a counter offer, the court dismissed the "waiver" argument stating that the original offer cannot be revived once it is terminated. The original offeror may only renew the original offer or accept the counter offer implicit in the defective acceptance. Consequently, once an offer's time period has terminated, a contract may be formed only by formal acceptance of the counter offer and not by a theory of waiver of the expired time limitation. 429 F.Supp. at 63–65.

acceptance of the counter offer. Houston Dairy cannot be deemed to have knowledge of John Hancock's acceptance simply by requesting and receiving information on the procedures for closing a loan should an agreement be reached."

SECTION 5: OFFER AND ACCEPTANCE IN FORM CONTRACTS

The "black letter" rule set forth earlier (see page 434) is that any communication in response to an offer that attempts to accept the offer must conform precisely to the terms of the offer; any purported acceptance that varies any term of the offer is not an acceptance but a counteroffer. This rule is universally called the "mirror image rule". This section discusses the problems created by the mirror image rule and the widespread use of standardized forms by buyers and sellers of goods. The "solution" to these problems appears in § 2–207 of the Uniform Commercial Code, perhaps the most controversial single section in the entire Uniform Commercial Code.

DAVENPORT, HOW TO HANDLE SALES OF GOODS: THE PROBLEM OF CONFLICTING PURCHASE ORDERS AND ACCEPTANCES AND NEW CONCEPTS IN CONTRACT LAW

19 Bus.Law. 75, 77–78 (1963).*

The "mirror image" rule understandably produced many commercial disappointments at common law. While both parties to an exchange of communications in a commercial transaction undoubtedly intended a contract at the time of the exchange, intentions change with a change in fortune or with a rapid rise or fall in the market. The safest way for an offeree to make a contract "stick" was to indorse the single word "accepted" and his signature on a copy of the offer or to write simply, "I accept your offer."

The practical problem presented, however, was that businessmen do not have forms so tersely worded. The forms used by businessmen are much more elaborate. Also they are understandably slanted in favor of the drafting party. In both the buyer's and the seller's forms the quantity description, price, payment and delivery terms are usually contained on the front side. The front side of the form is generally free of other printed matter except the billhead (containing the name, address and similar information identifying the drafting party) and a line, generally in conspicuous type, incorporating the printed terms on the reverse side as part of the agreement. The most likely point of difference on the front side of the buyer's and seller's forms is the payment or credit term. The seller's form probably provides for payment at a short date; the buyer's form, at a more remote date. The quantity, description, price and shipment terms are the most likely to coincide. The principal difference between the buyer's and seller's forms is found in the terms on the reverse side which are incorporated by the conspicuous legend on the front side. Frequently the seller's form contains a clause making some kind of express warranty and disclaiming all other warranties, express or implied. It may also contain a provision that overshipment or undershipment by a small percentage will fill the order. It may also have a paragraph that the buyer will inspect the goods and give notice of all claimed defects within a short period of time. The buyer's form probably has clauses on the same subjects but slanted in the opposite direction. These forms, whether they be labeled "Sales Order", "Purchase Order", "Acknowledgment", "Acceptance", or "Confirmation", are frequently exchanged almost without reference to each other. An unceasing conflict in offer and acceptance forms has been the necessary result of this practice of businessmen. The conflict has become known as the "battle of the forms". In addition to problems of contract formation, the "battle" has raised problems of contract content where the parties (or either of them) have begun performance before completion of the exchange of all forms.

This, then, was the commercial reality with which the common law of offer and acceptance had not kept pace. An updating of the law to bring it into alignment with commercial practice was in order.

Businesses apparently began using printed forms to conduct their transactions at about the beginning of the Twentieth Century. The sophistication of these forms has increased enormously over the years. They may be packaged in the form of pads or in multiple copies fixed together already interleaved with carbon paper or the equivalent. Their use provides tangible benefits to the user in the form of increased efficiency: (1) they simplify decision-making since only a limited number of blanks need to be filled in to describe any specific transaction and it is unnecessary to consider other terms; (2) they permit a business to seek to establish favorable, standardized terms on which they purchase or sell goods; (3) they limit the discretion of lower level personnel; (4) and they enable large, bureaucratic businesses to systematically keep track of their transactions through the use of multiple copies of each form, usually coded by different colors for each department or office that needs information about the transaction.

Consider an average transaction that involves the purchase of a standard component by an automobile manufacturer, the buyer, from one of several regular suppliers, the seller. The transaction may be initiated by a purchasing agent for the buyer telephoning potential sellers to ascertain prices and product availability. Based on this information, the buyer selects a seller, and sends a purchase order on the manufacturer's standard form. The front of the form sets forth the component, the number of units, the price, the delivery date, possibly the manner of delivery, and other specially negotiated "dickered" terms as well. The back contains the buyer's standard purchase terms, carefully crafted by the buyer's attorney to maximize the buyer's legal position in the event a problem arises. The back may be titled "Conditions," and the front may contain language such as "the conditions set forth on the reverse side of this purchase order are part of this contract." The purchase order may be sent by mail, overnight mail, telefax, or by other means of communication. When the seller receives the purchase order, the terms on the front are reviewed, and if acceptable, an "acknowledgement" may be sent to the buyer of the order. This "acknowledgement" is on the seller's standard form. The front contains blanks that reflect the information about the order taken from the buyer's purchase order form; the back contains printed terms crafted by the seller's attorney to maximize the seller's legal position in the event a problem arises. Of course, the probability that these standardized terms are identical is zero. Typically, purchasing and sales agents are instructed to use their own forms exclusively and not sign or acknowledge the other party's form. Thereafter, typically, the goods are shipped by the seller, accompanied by (or in some cases shortly followed by) an invoice that repeats the terms set forth on the back of the seller's acknowledgement. The goods are received by the buyer and in due course used by it. If this transaction were subject to the mirror image rule, whose terms would control on such questions as whether the goods were sold subject to a "full warranty" (the buyer's form) or an exclusion of all implied warranties and a limited responsibility to replace any goods that do not conform to express warranties (the seller's form)?

The transaction described in the last paragraph is the subject of much of the discussion that follows. It should be emphasized, however, that all sorts of variants may readily be envisioned, and given the immense volume of form-oriented transactions that occur every day, it is likely that every conceivable variant will occur sometime, someplace. For example, the purchasing agent for the buyer may orally place an order with the sales agent and send a "confirmation" rather than a "purchase order;" the seller may respond with an "acknowledgement." Or the oral order may be placed and the seller responds with an "acknowledgement" without a purchase order being sent. Or the first communication may be a "notice of intent to issue a purchase order" that is in the form of a letter rather than a printed form. The seller may send an "acknowledgement" and the buyer may thereafter send its purchase order. The sales agent may initial the buyer's form, staple it to the seller's form and send it to the buyer. The parties may initial each other's form. Each form may contain language of varying degrees of specificity seeking to establish that in the case of a conflict of terms, the terms of the particular form are to prevail.

BAIRD AND WEISBERG, RULES, STANDARDS, AND THE BATTLE OF THE FORMS: A REASSESSMENT OF § 2–207

68 Va.L.Rev. 1217, 1219–1220 (1982).

These disputes arise only when the parties do not explicitly dicker over the terms at issue. Thus, the law cannot resolve the battle of the forms with a simple inquiry into the parties' intent.[4] It is useless to ask what terms the parties intended to govern this transaction.[5] The buyer and seller were content to leave their mutual rights uncertain, because greater certainty would have come only with negotiations, the cost of which probably would have exceeded the expected cost of leaving things open to dispute.

The law cannot avoid choosing among terms that the parties never explicitly agreed on; any approach to the battle of the forms that allows each party to insist on its own contract terms is doomed to failure. If, for example, the buyer wants a warranty on the goods and the seller does not, the lawmaker has several choices. A rule could say that the buyer wins, that the seller wins, that the first party to send its form wins, or that the last party to send its form wins. No rule of law, however, can allow both parties to prevail. Likewise, a rule that purports to enforce one party's clause saying "My terms govern or there is no deal" cannot resolve the many cases where both parties have such a clause and the deal has already gone through.

4. Dean Murray forcefully argues that battle of the forms disputes can and should be determined by referring to the "bargain-in-fact" of the parties. See Murray, Section 2–207 of the Uniform Commercial Code: Another Word About Incipient Unconscionability, 39 U.Pitt.L.Rev. 597, 601–02 (1978). Our point of difference with Dean Murray is not that the inquiry he thinks courts should engage in is necessarily the wrong one, but rather that it is a necessarily imprecise one. ∗ ∗ ∗.

5. It is also of limited value even to have a legal rule that determines whether a contract exists by focusing exclusively on the parties' intent. The intent of the parties may not be independent of the legal rule. As is true in many areas of the law, when parties do reflect on the legal consequences of their acts, their expectations depend in some measure on what they assume the legal rule to be. If, for exam-ple, as a matter of common knowledge, courts enforced only those contracts executed under a seal, parties would never think they had formed binding contracts unless they had used a seal. Where the rules of contract formation are less certain, the intent of the parties may be no more than their rough prediction of how the court will treat their exchange.

This, of course, is not to say that noncontractual elements are not of great importance. See Macaulay, Non–Contractual Relations in Business: A Preliminary Study, 28 Am.Soc.Rev. 55 (1963). More recent empirical work, however, suggests that parties are aware of the legal consequences of documents that differ. See Beale & Dugdale, Contracts Between Businessmen: Planning and the Use of Contractual Remedies, 2 Brit.J.L. & Soc'y 45, 50 (1975).

ROTO–LITH, LTD. v. F.P. BARTLETT & CO., INC.

United States Court of Appeals, First Circuit, 1962.
297 F.2d 497.

ALDRICH, CIRCUIT JUDGE.

Plaintiff-appellant Roto-Lith, Ltd., is a New York corporation engaged *inter alia* in manufacturing, or "converting," cellophane bags for packaging vegetables. Defendant-appellee is a Massachusetts corporation which makes emulsion for use as a cellophane adhesive. This is a field of some difficulty, and various emulsions are employed, depending upon the intended purpose of the bags. In May and October 1959 plaintiff purchased emulsion from the defendant. Subsequently bags produced with this emulsion failed to adhere, and this action was instituted in the district court for the District of Massachusetts. At the conclusion of the evidence the court directed a verdict for the defendant. This appeal followed.

Defendant asks us to review the October transaction first because of certain special considerations applicable to the May order. The defense in each instance, however, is primarily the same, namely, defendant contends that the sales contract expressly negatived any warranties. We will deal first with the October order.

On October 23, 1959, plaintiff, in New York, mailed a written order to defendant in Massachusetts for a drum of "N–132–C" emulsion stating "End use: wet pack spinach bags." Defendant on October 26 prepared simultaneously an acknowledgment and an invoice. The printed forms were exactly the same, except that one was headed "Acknowledgment" and the other "Invoice," and the former contemplated insertion of the proposed, and the latter of the actual, shipment date. Defendant testified that in accordance with its regular practice the acknowledgment was prepared and mailed the same day. The plaintiff's principal liability witness testified that he did not know whether this acknowledgment "was received, or what happened to it." On this state of the evidence there is an unrebutted presumption of receipt. Johnston v. Cassidy, 1932, 279 Mass. 593, 181 N.E. 748. The goods were shipped to New York on October 27. On the evidence it must be found that the acknowledgment was received at least no later than the goods. The invoice was received presumably a day or two after the goods.

The acknowledgment and the invoice bore in conspicuous type on their face the following legend, "All goods sold without warranties, express or implied, and subject to the terms on reverse side." In somewhat smaller, but still conspicuous, type there were printed on the back certain terms of sale, of which the following are relevant:

> "1. Due to the variable conditions under which these goods may be transported, stored, handled, or used, Seller hereby expressly excludes any and all warranties, guaranties, or representations whatsoever. Buyer assumes risk for results obtained from use of

these goods, whether used alone or in combination with other products. Seller's liability hereunder shall be limited to the replacement of any goods that materially differ from the Seller's sample order on the basis of which the order for such goods was made.

"7. This acknowledgment contains all of the terms of this purchase and sale. No one except a duly authorized officer of Seller may execute or modify contracts. Payment may be made only at the offices of the Seller. *If these terms are not acceptable, Buyer must so notify Seller at once."* (Ital. suppl.)

It is conceded that plaintiff did not protest defendant's attempt so to limit its liability, and in due course paid for the emulsion and used it. It is also conceded that adequate notice was given of breach of warranty, if there were warranties. The only issue which we will consider is whether all warranties were excluded by defendant's acknowledgment.[3]

The first question is what law the Massachusetts court would look to in order to determine the terms of the contract. Under Massachusetts law this is the place where the last material act occurs. Under the Uniform Commercial Code, [§ 2–206], mailing the acknowledgment would clearly have completed the contract in Massachusetts by acceptance had the acknowledgment not sought to introduce new terms. [The Court here quoted [§ 2–207].]

Plaintiff exaggerates the freedom which this section affords an offeror to ignore a reply from an offeree that does not in terms coincide with the original offer. According to plaintiff defendant's condition that there should be no warranties constituted a proposal which "materially altered" the agreement. As to this we concur. See Uniform Commercial Code comment to this section, paragraph 4. Plaintiff goes on to say that by virtue of the statute the acknowledgment effected a completed agreement without this condition, and that as a further proposal the condition never became part of the agreement because plaintiff did not express assent. We agree that [§ 2–207] changed the existing law, but not to this extent. Its purpose was to modify the strict principle that a response not precisely in accordance with the offer was a rejection and a counteroffer. Kehlor Flour Mills Co. v. Linden, 1918, 230 Mass. 119, 123, 119 N.E. 698. Now, within stated limits, a response that does not in all respects correspond with the offer constitutes an acceptance of the offer, and a counteroffer only as to the differences. If plaintiff's contention is correct that a reply to an offer stating additional conditions unilaterally burdensome upon the offeror is a binding acceptance of the original offer plus simply a proposal for the additional conditions, the statute would lead to an absurdity. Obviously no offeror will subsequently assent to such conditions.

---

3. Defendant also relies upon the terms of the invoice in view of the fact that it was admittedly received before plaintiff *used* the goods. Whether an invoice not re- ceived until after the goods can modify the contract raises some possible matters which we do not reach.

The statute is not too happily drafted. Perhaps it would be wiser in all cases for an offeree to say in so many words, "I will not accept your offer until you assent to the following: * * *" But businessmen cannot be expected to act by rubric. It would be unrealistic to suppose that when an offeree replies setting out conditions that would be burdensome only to the offeror he intended to make an unconditional acceptance of the original offer, leaving it simply to the offeror's good nature whether he would assume the additional restrictions. To give the statute a practical construction we must hold that a response which states a condition materially altering the obligation solely to the disadvantage of the offeror is an "acceptance * * * expressly * * * conditional on assent to the additional * * * terms."

Plaintiff accepted the goods with knowledge of the conditions specified in the acknowledgment. It became bound.[4] Garst v. Harris, 1900, 177 Mass. 72, 58 N.E. 174; Doerr v. Woolsey, 1889, 5 N.Y.S. 447 (Com.Pl.Gen.Term); cf. Joseph v. Atlantic Basin Iron Works, Inc., Sup., 1954, 132 N.Y.S.2d 671, aff'd Sup., 143 N.Y.S.2d 601 (App.Div.). * * *

Judgment will be entered affirming the judgment of the District Court.

See UCC § 2–314 for a description of the implied warranty made by every seller who is a merchant of the goods in question. This implied warranty may be excluded or modified by specific contractual provision, and this is what the seller attempted to do in *Rotolith*. See UCC § 2–316; Overstreet v. Norden Laboratories, Inc., p. 43 supra; Chapters 5 and 6, infra.

C. ITOH & CO. (AMERICA) INC. v. JORDAN INTERNATIONAL CO.

United States Court of Appeals, Seventh Circuit, 1977.
552 F.2d 1228.

Before FAIRCHILD, CHIEF JUDGE, and SPRECHER and WOOD, CIRCUIT JUDGES.

SPRECHER, CIRCUIT JUDGE.

The sole issue on this appeal is whether the district court properly denied a stay of the proceedings pending arbitration under Section 3 of the Federal Arbitration Act, 9 U.S.C. § 3.

I

C. Itoh & Co. (America) Inc. ("Itoh") submitted a purchase order dated August 15, 1974 for a certain quantity of steel coils to the Jordan

---

4. It does not follow that if the acknowledgment had miscarried plaintiff's receipt of the goods would have completed a contract which did not include the terms of the acknowledgment. We are not faced with the question of how the statute may affect the common law under such circumstances.

International Company ("Jordan"). In response, Jordan sent its acknowledgment form dated August 19, 1974. On the face of Jordan's form, the following statement appears:

> Seller's acceptance is, however, expressly conditional on Buyer's assent to the additional or different terms and conditions set forth below and printed on the reverse side. If these terms and conditions are not acceptable, Buyer should notify seller at once.

One of the terms on the reverse side of Jordan's form was a broad provision for arbitration.[1] Itoh neither expressly assented nor objected to the additional arbitration term in Jordan's form until the instant litigation. * * *

[After the steel was delivered by Jordan and paid for by Itoh, a dispute arose between Itoh and the Riverview Steel Corporation, Inc., the corporation that had repurchased the steel coils from Itoh, as to whether the steel coils were defective. Itoh simultaneously brought suit against Riverview for refusing to pay for the steel coils and against Jordan for selling defective steel. Jordan interposed the arbitration clause and moved for a stay pending arbitration, which the district court denied. Jordan appealed.]

III.

* * * The pertinent facts may be briefly restated. Itoh sent its purchase order for steel coils to Jordan which contained no provision for arbitration. Subsequently, Jordan sent Itoh its acknowledgment form which included, *inter alia*, a broad arbitration term on the reverse side of the form.[3] * * * After the exchange of documents, Jordan delivered and Itoh paid for the steel coils. Itoh never expressly assented or objected to the additional arbitration term in Jordan's form.

In support of its contention that there exists an agreement in writing to arbitrate, Jordan places some reliance on certain New York decisions interpreting [§ 2–201] of the Uniform Commercial Code, the UCC Statute of Frauds provision. That section provides in pertinent part: * * * [the Court quotes from 2–201(1) and (2)].

Several New York lower court decisions have apparently held that under [§ 2–201], where there has been an oral offer or agreement followed by a written confirmation containing an additional arbitration term and where the merchant recipient of the confirmation has reason to expect that a provision for arbitration would be included in any

---

1. The arbitration clause provides:

Any controversy arising under or in connection with the contract shall be submitted to arbitration in New York City in accordance with the rules then obtaining of the American Arbitration Association. Judgment on any award may be entered in any court having jurisdiction. The parties hereto submit to the jurisdiction of the Federal and State Courts in New York City and notice of process in connection with arbitral or judicial proceedings may be served upon the parties by registered or certified mail, with the same effect as if personally served.

3. See note 1 supra. There is apparently no dispute that, if the arbitration provision is part of a written agreement between the parties, it is sufficiently broad to encompass the instant dispute.

written confirmation of an oral offer or agreement, the arbitration provision becomes a part of the parties' agreement unless notice of objection is given within the prescribed period. See e.g., Trafalgar Square, Ltd. v. Reeves Brothers, Ltd., 35 A.D.2d 194, 315 N.Y.S.2d 239 (1970).

These decisions are premised on a fundamental misconception of the purpose and effect of [§ 2–201]. See generally Duesenberg & King, Sales and Bulk Transfers Under the Uniform Commercial Code [§ 308[1] at 97–99 (1976)]. The *only* effect of a failure to object to a written confirmation of an oral offer or agreement under [§ 2–201] is to take away from the receiving merchant the defense of the Statute of Frauds. See Official Comment 3 to [§ 2–201]. Although [§ 2–201] may make *enforceable* an oral agreement which was in fact reached by the parties, it does not relieve the party seeking enforcement of the alleged oral agreement of the obligation to prove its existence. Official Comment 3 to [§ 2–201]. [2–201] obviously cannot be relied on to make a particular term, such as a provision for arbitration, binding on a party if that section does not even serve to establish the *existence* of an agreement.

The Official Comments make clear that, while under [§ 2–201] the failure to object to a written confirmation of an oral agreement has the limited effect of removing the Statute of Frauds as a bar to the enforceability of an oral agreement, under [§ 2–207] a failure to object to a term in a written confirmation may, *under the circumstances specified by that section,* have the effect of making that term a part of whatever agreement is proved to have been reached by the parties. Official Comment 3 to [§ 2–201]. Hence, once the existence and terms of an alleged oral agreement have been established, it is necessary to refer to [§ 2–207], Additional Terms in Acceptance *or Confirmation,* not [§ 2–201], to ascertain whether a term included in a written confirmation but not in the parties' oral agreement is binding on the recipient of the written confirmation. See, e.g., Dorton v. Collins & Aikman Corp., 453 F.2d 1161 (6th Cir.1972). * * *

The instant case, therefore, involves the classic "battle of the forms," and [§ 2–207], not [§ 2–201], furnishes the rules for resolving such a controversy. Hence, it is to [§ 2–207] that we must look to determine whether a contract has been formed by the exchange of forms between Jordan and Itoh and, if so, whether the additional arbitration term in Jordan's form is to be included in that contract. See, e.g., Application of Doughboy Industries, Inc., 17 A.D.2d 216, 233 N.Y.S.2d 488 (1962).

[The Court quotes § 2–207 in its entirety.] Under [§ 2–207] it is necessary to first determine whether a contract has been formed under [§ 2–207(1)] as a result of the *exchange of forms* between Jordan and Itoh.

At common law, "an acceptance * * * which contained terms additional to * * * those of the offer * * * constituted a rejection of the offer * * * and thus became a counter-offer." *Dorton*, supra, at 1166. Thus, the mere presence of the additional arbitration term in Jordan's acknowledgment form would, at common law, have prevented the exchange of documents between Jordan and Itoh from creating a contract, and Jordan's form would have automatically become a counter-offer.

Section [2–207(1)] was intended to alter this inflexible common law approach to offer and acceptance:

> This section of the Code recognizes that in current commercial transactions, the terms of the offer and those of the acceptance will seldom be identical. Rather, under the current "battle of the forms," each party typically has a printed form drafted by his attorney and containing as many terms as could be envisioned to favor that party in his sales transactions. Whereas under common law the disparity between the fine-print terms in the parties' forms would have prevented the consummation of a contract when these forms are exchanged, [§ 2–207] recognizes that in many, but not all, cases the parties do not impart such significance to the terms on the printed forms. * * * Thus, under Subsection (1), a contract * * * [may be] recognized notwithstanding the fact that an acceptance * * * contains terms additional to * * * those of the offer * * *.

Id. at 1166. See also Comment 2 to [§ 2–207]. And it is now well-settled that the *mere presence* of an additional term, such as a provision for arbitration, in one of the parties' forms will not prevent the formation of a contract under [§ 2–207(1)]. See, e.g., *Dorton*, supra.[5]

However, while [§ 2–207(1)] constitutes a sharp departure from the common law "mirror image" rule, there remain situations where the inclusion of an additional term in one of the forms exchanged by the parties will prevent the consummation of a contract *under that section*. Section [2–207(1)] contains a proviso which operates to prevent an exchange of forms from creating a contract where "acceptance is expressly made conditional on assent to the additional * * * terms." In the instant case, Jordan's acknowledgment form contained the following statement:

> Seller's acceptance is * * * *expressly conditional* on Buyer's *assent* to the additional or different terms and conditions set forth below and printed on the reverse side. If these terms and conditions are not acceptable, Buyer should notify Seller at once.

---

5. But see Roto-Lith, Ltd. v. F. P. Bartlett & Co., 297 F.2d 497 (1st Cir.1962) (holding that inclusion of warranty disclaimer in seller's acknowledgment form prevented the formation of a contract under [§ 2–207(1)]). The *Roto-Lith* decision has been subjected to severe criticism by the commentators.

And, more importantly, *Roto-Lith* has not been followed in numerous decisions involving the "battle of the forms" under [§ 2–207]. * * *

The arbitration provision at issue on this appeal is printed on the reverse side of Jordan's acknowledgment, and there is no dispute that Itoh never expressly assented to the challenged arbitration term.

The Court of Appeals for the Sixth Circuit has held that the proviso must be construed narrowly:

> Although * * * [seller's] use of the words "subject to" suggests that the acceptances were conditional to some extent, we do not believe the acceptances were "expressly made conditional on [the buyer's] assent to the additional or different terms," as specifically required under the Subsection [2–207(1)] proviso. In order to fall within this proviso, it is not enough that an acceptance is expressly conditional on additional or different terms; rather, an acceptance must be expressly conditional on the offeror's *assent* to those terms (emphasis in original).

Dorton, supra, at 1168. In Construction Aggregates Corp. v. Hewitt-Robins, Inc., 404 F.2d 505 (7th Cir.1968), this court found that an acceptance came within the ambit of the [§ 2–207(1)] proviso even though the language employed in the acceptance did not precisely track that of the proviso. Under either *Construction Aggregates* or *Dorton*, however, it is clear that the statement contained in Jordan's acknowledgment form comes within the [§ 2–207(1)] proviso.

Hence, the exchange of forms between Jordan and Itoh did not result in the formation of a contract under [§ 2–207(1)], and Jordan's form became a counteroffer. "[T]he consequence of a clause conditioning acceptance on assent to the additional or different terms is that *as of the exchanged writings, there is no contract.* Either party may at this point in their dealings walk away from the transaction." Duesenberg & King, *supra*, § 3.06[3] at 73. However, neither Jordan nor Itoh elected to follow that course; instead, both parties proceeded to performance—Jordan by delivering and Itoh by paying for the steel coils.

At common law, the "terms of the counter-offer were said to have been accepted by the original offeror, when he proceeded to perform under the contract without objecting to the counter-offer." *Dorton*, supra, at 1166. Thus, under pre-Code law, Itoh's performance (i.e., payment for the steel coils) probably constituted acceptance of the Jordan counter-offer, including its provision for arbitration. However, a different approach is required under the Code.

[The court here quotes UCC § 2–207(3).] * * * As the court noted in *Dorton*, supra, at 1166:

> [W]hen no contract is recognized under Subsection 2–207(1) * * * the entire transaction aborts at this point. If, however, the subsequent conduct of the parties—particularly, performance by both parties under what they apparently believe to be a contract—recognizes the existence of a contract, under Subsection 2–207(3) such conduct by both parties is sufficient to establish a

contract, notwithstanding the fact that no contract would have been recognized on the basis of their writings alone.

Thus, "[s]ince * * * [Itoh's] purchase order and * * * [Jordan's] counter-offer did not in themselves create a contract. Section [2–207(3)] would operate to create one because the subsequent performance by both parties constituted 'conduct by both parties which recognizes the existence of a contract.'"

What are the terms of a contract created by conduct under [§ 2–207(3)] rather than by an exchange of forms under [§ 2–207(1)]? [7] As noted above, at common law the terms of the contract between Jordan and Itoh would be the terms of the Jordan counter-offer. However, the Code has effectuated a radical departure from the common law rule. [8] The second sentence of [§ 2–207(3)] provides that where, as here, a contract has been consummated by the conduct of the parties, "the terms of the particular contract consist of those terms on which the writings of the parties agree, together with any supplementary terms incorporated under any other provisions of this Act." Since it is clear that the Jordan and Itoh forms do not "agree" on arbitration, the only question which remains *under the Code* is whether arbitration may be considered a supplementary term incorporated under some other provision of the Code.

We have been unable to find any case authority shedding light on the question of what constitutes "supplementary terms" within the meaning of [§ 2–207(3)] and the Official Comments to [§ 2–207] provide no guidance in this regard. We are persuaded, however, that the disputed, additional terms (i.e., those terms on which the writings of the parties do not agree) which are necessarily excluded from a Subsection (3) contract by the language, "terms on which the writings of the parties agree," cannot be brought back into the contract under the guise of "supplementary terms." This conclusion has substantial support among the commentators who have addressed themselves to the issue. As two noted authorities on Article two of the Code have stated:

> It will usually happen that an offeree-seller who returns an acknowledgment form will also concurrently or shortly thereafter ship the goods. If the responsive document [sent by the seller] contains a printed assent clause, and the goods are shipped and accepted, Subsection (3) of [§ 2–207] comes into play. * * * [T]he terms on which the exchanged communications do not agree drop out of the transaction, and reference to the Code is made to

---

7. If a contract had been formed by the exchange of forms between Jordan and Itoh, it would have been necessary to look to [§ 2–207(2)] to ascertain the terms of that contract.

8. Jordan relies on *Roto-Lith*, supra, in support of its contention that Itoh's payment for the steel coils constituted acceptance of all the terms in Jordan's counter-offer. In *Roto-Lith* the court ignored [§ 2–207(3)] and simply applied the common law rule. * * * [B]eing faced with the issue, we adopt the consensus of the courts and commentators that *Roto-Lith*, in reading [§ 2–207(3)] out of the Code, evidences an incorrect interpretation and application of [§ 2–207]. See note 5 *supra*.

supply necessary terms. * * * Rather than choosing the terms of one party over those of the other * * * it compels supplying missing terms by reference to the Code. * * *

Duesenberg & King, supra, § 3.06[4] at 73–74. * * *

Accordingly, we find that the "supplementary terms" contemplated by [§ 2–207(3)] are limited to those supplied by the standardized "gap-filler" provisions of Article Two. See, e.g., [§ 2–308(a)] ("Unless otherwise agreed * * * the place for delivery of goods is the seller's place of business or if he has none his residence"); [§ 2–309(1)] ("The time for shipment or delivery or any other action under a contract if not * * * agreed upon shall be a reasonable time"); [§ 2–310(a)] ("Unless otherwise agreed * * * payment is due at the time and place at which the buyer is to receive the goods even though the place of shipment is the place of delivery"). Since provision for arbitration is not a necessary or missing term which would be supplied by one of the Code's "gap-filler" provisions unless agreed upon by the contracting parties, there is no arbitration term in the [§ 2–207(3)] contract which was created by the conduct of Jordan and Itoh in proceeding to perform even though no contract had been established by their exchange of writings.

We are convinced that this conclusion does not result in any unfair prejudice to a seller who elects to insert in his standard sales acknowledgment form the statement that acceptance is expressly conditional on buyer's assent to additional terms contained therein. Such a seller obtains a substantial benefit *under* [§ 2–207(1)] through the inclusion of an "expressly conditional" clause. If he decides after the exchange of forms that the particular transaction is not in his best interest, Subsection (1) permits him to walk away from the transaction without incurring any liability so long as the buyer has not in the interim expressly assented to the additional terms. Moreover, whether or not a seller will be disadvantaged *under Subsection (3)* as a consequence of inserting an "expressly conditional" clause in his standard form is within his control. If the seller in fact does not intend to close a particular deal unless the additional terms are assented to, he can protect himself by not delivering the goods until such assent is forthcoming. If the seller does intend to close a deal irrespective of whether or not the buyer assents to the additional terms, he can hardly complain when the contract formed under Subsection (3) as a result of the parties' conduct is held not to include those terms. Although a seller who employs such an "expressly conditional" clause in his acknowledgment form would undoubtedly appreciate the dual advantage of not being bound to a contract under Subsection (1) if he elects not to perform and of having his additional terms imposed on the buyer under Subsection (3) in the event that performance is in his best interest, we do not believe such a result is contemplated by [§ 2–207]. Rather, while a seller may take advantage of an "expressly conditional" clause under Subsection (1) when he elects not to perform, he must accept the potential risk under Subsection (3) of not getting his additional terms when he elects to proceed with performance without first obtaining buyer's assent to those terms. Since the seller injected ambiguity into the transaction by inserting the "expressly conditional" clause in his form, he, and not the buyer, should bear the consequence of that ambiguity under Subsection (3). * * *

Accordingly, for the reasons stated in this opinion, the decision of the district court is affirmed.

Affirmed.

————

The foregoing case law should make it clear that the forms used by both buyers and sellers should be carefully tailored to the precise language of § 2–207. Most large business enterprises have long ago had their forms reviewed by legal counsel to ensure maximum protection is obtained under that section, but the same may not be true of smaller businesses. If your client has used the same forms since 1960, what language would you recommend be inserted?

Section 2–206(1)(b) of the Uniform Commercial Code deals with the situation where a seller ships non-conforming goods to a buyer as an "accommodation." The section states that such a shipment "does not constitute an acceptance if the seller reasonably notifies the buyer" that the shipment is offered "only as an accommodation." Might it be sensible to draft sellers' acknowledgment and invoice forms so that *all* goods shipped are offered "only as an accommodation"?

————

DAITOM, INC. v. PENNWALT CORP., 741 F.2d 1569, 1578–1579 (10th Cir.1984). Daitom purchased from Pennwalt two rotary vacuum dryers with dust filters and heating systems to dry dextro calcium pantothenate. The dryers did not work as warranted and the suit involved claims for breach of warranty. Pennwalt's form (a "proposal" to supply the dryers) provided that all claims for breaches of warranties had to be brought within one year after the dryers were delivered while Daitom's form (a "purchase order" for the dryers) expressly reserved "all rights and remedies available at law." Claims were actually asserted by Daitom more than one year after delivery but within four years. The trial court held that a contract was formed on the documents under UCC § 2–207(1), and that Pennwalt's form controlled since it was the "offer." The court of appeals agreed that a contract was formed on the documents, and then addressed the problem created when the two forms contained different terms dealing with the same matter:

"Section [2–207(2)] is silent on the treatment of terms stated in the acceptance that are *different*, rather than merely additional, from those stated in the offer. It is unclear whether 'different' terms in the acceptance are intended to be included under the aegis of 'additional' terms in [§ 2–207(2)] and, therefore, fail to become part of the agreement if they materially alter the contract. Comment 3 suggests just such an inclusion. However, Comment 6 suggests that different terms in exchanged writings must be assumed to constitute mutual objections by each party to the other's conflicting terms and result in a mutual 'knock-out' of both parties' conflicting terms; the missing terms to be supplied by the UCC's 'gap-filler' provisions. At least one commentator, in support of this view, has suggested that the drafting history of the provision indicates that the word 'different' was intentionally deleted from the final draft of [§ 2–207(2)] to preclude its treatment under that subsection. The plain language, comments, and drafting history of the provision, therefore, provide little helpful guidance in resolving the disagreement over the treatment of different terms pursuant to [§ 2–207].

"Despite all this, the cases and commentators have suggested three possible approaches. The first of these is to treat 'different' terms as included under the aegis of 'additional' terms in [§ 2–207(2)]. Consequently, different terms in the acceptance would never become part of the contract, because, by definition, they would materially alter the contract (i.e., the offeror's terms). Several courts have adopted this approach.

"The second approach, which leads to the same result as the first, is that the offeror's terms control because the offeree's different terms merely fall out; [§ 2–207(2)] cannot rescue the different terms since that subsection applies only to *additional* terms. Under this approach, Comment 6 (apparently supporting a mutual rather than a single term knockout) is not applicable because it refers only to conflicting terms in confirmation forms following *oral* agreement, not conflicting terms in the *writings* that form the agreement. This approach is supported by Professor Summers. J.J. White & R.S. Summers, *Uniform Commercial Code,* § 1–2, at 29 (2d ed. 1980).

"The third, and preferable approach, which is commonly called the 'knock-out' rule, is that the conflicting terms cancel one another. Under this view the offeree's form is treated only as an acceptance of the terms in the offeror's form which did not conflict. The ultimate contract, then, includes those non-conflicting terms and any other terms supplied by the UCC, including terms incorporated by course of performance [§ 2–208], course of dealing [§ 1–205], usage of trade [§ 1–205], and other 'gap-fillers' or 'off-the-rack' terms (e.g., implied warranty of fitness for particular purpose, [§ 2–315]). As stated previously, this approach finds some support in Comment 6. Professor White supports this approach as the most fair and consistent with the purposes of [§ 2–207]. *White & Summers, supra,* at 29. Further, several courts have adopted or recognized the approach. *E.g., Idaho Power Company v. Westinghouse Electric Corporation,* 596 F.2d 924 (9th Cir. 1979) (applying Idaho law, although incorrectly, applying [§ 2–207(3)] after finding a contract under [§ 2–207(1)]); *Hartwig Farms, Inc. v. Pacific Gamble Robinson Company,* 28 Wash.App. 539, 625 P.2d 171

(1981); *S.C. Gray, Inc. v. Ford Motor Company,* 92 Mich.App. 789, 286 N.W.2d 34 (1979).

"We are of the opinion that this is the more reasonable approach, particularly when dealing with a case such as this where from the beginning the offeror's specified period of limitations would expire before the equipment was even installed. The approaches other than the 'knock-out' approach would be inequitable and unjust because they invited the very kind of treatment which the defendant attempted to provide."

J. WHITE & R. SUMMERS, UNIFORM COMMERCIAL CODE
29–31 (3d Ed. 1988).

Unfortunately, * * * 2–207 is in one respect like the amphibious tank that was originally designed to fight in the swamps, but was ultimately sent to fight in the desert. The original draftsman of § 2–207 designed it (though not exclusively) to keep the welsher in the contract. * * *

But unfortunately the courts have had to press 2–207 into service not just to hold the welsher in. Parties to sales much more often call on courts to use 2–207 to decide the terms of their contract after they exchange documents, perform, or start to perform and then fall into dispute. Here the courts are not deciding whether there is a contract. They are answering a different question: What are its terms? This is not only a different but also a more difficult problem for the law than that of keeping the welsher in.

Not only does 2–207 suffer from being designed for the swamps yet called on to fight in the desert, it also suffers because the desert terrain has proved to be so varied. We discuss eight significantly different types of cases with which 2–207 must deal and these are not all. We believe each type arises often in real life; 2–207 deals with several well, with others not so well. (We number these cases with some trepidation, for we realize that those who can analyze do, and that those who cannot, number.) The eight are:

(1) Cases in which the parties send printed forms to one another, and a crucial term is covered one way in one form and the other way in the other form. (Assume, for example, that buyer's form states that disputes must be arbitrated, whereas the seller's form says "no arbitration").

(2) Cases in which a crucial term is found in the first form sent (the offer), but no term on that question appears in the second.

(3) Cases in which a crucial term is found in the second form (the acceptance), but there is no consistent or conflicting term in the first.

(4) Cases in which a crucial term is found in the second form but not in the first, and the second form is a counter-offer (because "expressly conditional").

(5) Cases in which at least one form contains a term that provides that no contract will be formed unless the other party accedes to all of the terms on that form and offers no others.

(6) Cases in which there is a prior oral agreement. (In cases, (1) through (5) we have assumed that there may be prior oral negotiations but that no oral agreement was reached before parties sent their forms.)

(7) Cases in which the parties do not use forms but send a variety of messages and letters and conduct intermittent oral negotiations that ultimately produce an agreement.

(8) Cases in which the second form differs so radically from the first that it does not constitute an "acceptance."

In our discussion of the foregoing types of cases, one central problem will be this: how may 2–207 be interpreted so as not to give an unearned and unfair advantage to the contracting party who by pure happenstance sends the first or in other cases the second form? When the parties to the contract send their forms blindly and after no, or only cursory examination of the bargained terms file the forms they receive, it makes no sense to give one an advantage over the other with respect to unbargained terms *simply* because he mailed the first form. Yet avoiding apparent favoritism under 2–207 is a difficult task.

———

In the detailed discussion of each of the eight situations that follow, there are numerous instances in which the authors expressly disagree between themselves as to how § 2–207 and its comments should be applied.

UNITED NATIONS CONVENTION ON CONTRACTS FOR THE INTERNATIONAL SALE OF GOODS

ARTICLE 19

(1) A reply to an offer which purports to be an acceptance but contains additions, limitations or other modifications is a rejection of the offer and constitutes a counter-offer.

(2) However, a reply to an offer which purports to be an acceptance but contains additional or different terms which do not materially alter the terms of the offer constitutes an acceptance, unless the offeror, without undue delay, objects orally to the discrepancy or dispatches a notice to that effect. If he does not so object, the terms of the contract are the terms of the offer with the modifications contained in the acceptance.

(3) Additional or different terms relating, among other things, to the price, payment, quality and quantity of the goods, place and time of delivery, extent of one party's liability to the other or the settlement of disputes are considered to alter the terms of the offer materially.

LEGAL ANALYSIS OF THE UNITED NATIONS CONVENTION ON CONTRACTS FOR THE INTERNATIONAL SALE OF GOODS (1980)

15 U.S.C.A.App.

ARTICLE 19. "ACCEPTANCE WITH MODIFICATIONS"

Article 19 faces the situation in which a reply to an offer purports to be an acceptance but contains modifications of the offer. This situation most commonly results from the routine exchange of the buyer's printed purchase order and the seller's printed acknowledgement of sale form. Under the Convention, no contract results from such an exchange if the purported acceptance contains additional or different terms that materially alter the offer. A list of examples of material alterations makes it clear that most alterations are material. However, an acceptance with an immaterial modification will be effective unless the offeror objects.

The Convention's approach to this difficult problem differs from that of the Uniform Commercial Code, under which even a material alteration may not prevent the purported acceptance from creating a contract (UCC § 2–207). The Convention would thus avoid many of the problems that have arisen under and resulted in criticism of the Code provision.

SECTION 6: PRECONTRACTUAL LIABILITY

KEARNS v. ANDREE

Supreme Court of Errors of Connecticut, 1928.
107 Conn. 181, 139 A. 695.

Argued before WHEELER, C. J., and MALTBIE, HAINES, HINMAN, and BANKS, JJ.

MALTBIE, J. The plaintiff was the owner of a lot of land at the corner of Prospect and Edwards streets in the town of East Hartford, on which stood a dwelling house then in the process of construction, but practically finished. In the rear of the land upon which this house stood, he owned other land upon which another house was located. He and the defendant entered into an oral contract, whereby, as it is stated in the finding, "the defendant agreed to purchase the house and lot at the corner of Prospect and Edwards streets at a price of $8,500; it being agreed the defendant should assume a first mortgage of $4,500, a bank mortgage, and pay $4,000 in cash." This mortgage was not then in existence, but the plaintiff promised to obtain it; there being no agreement, however, as to the identity of the mortgagee or as to its terms.

The defendant thereafter became dissatisfied with his purchase, but finally agreed to stand by the bargain, if certain alterations were made in the house, if it was finished in a certain way, and if certain trees standing upon the lot were cut down. The plaintiff proceeded to make the changes and finish the house as desired by the defendant, and to cut down the trees, and he also secured a bank mortgage upon the premises in the sum of $4,500. The defendant, however, refused to complete the purchase. The way in which the house had been finished at the defendant's request made the premises less salable, but the plaintiff finally secured a purchaser for the price of $8,250, after, to meet this purchaser's desires, he had repainted the house a different color and repapered certain rooms. The plaintiff brings this action to recover for the expenses to which he was put in order to finish the house to meet the defendant's wishes, and thereafter, to adapt it to the desires of the purchaser, and also to recover the difference between the price agreed to be paid by the defendant and that for which the house was finally sold.

The trial court reached the conclusion that the acts of the plaintiff in finishing the house were sufficient to take the case out of the statute of frauds, but that the agreement between the plaintiff and defendant was too indefinite to be enforceable, because the land sold was not sufficiently identified, and because the agreement as to the mortgage to be secured and assumed by the defendant did not specify either the identity of the mortgagee or the terms it was to contain, and it gave judgment for the plaintiff to recover the value of the trees cut and the cost of repainting and repapering to meet the desires of the ultimate purchaser.

If the trial court was right in its conclusion that the agreement was too indefinite to be enforced, it becomes of no moment whether the acts done by the plaintiff were sufficient part performance to take the case out of the statute of frauds. The finding, particularly when read in the light of the memorandum of decision made a part of it, does not present the situation with reference to the land and houses owned by the plaintiff in such a way as to afford any satisfactory basis for a review of its conclusion that the premises sold were not sufficiently described so as to make the agreement definite enough to be enforceable. But its conclusion as to the indefiniteness of the provison concerning the mortgage which the plaintiff was to secure is clearly sound. In Griffin v. Smith, 101 Conn. 219, 125 A. 465, we had before us an oral agreement for the sale of land, in which it was provided that the price was to be $2,850, of which $850 was to be paid in cash, and the balance secured by mortgage; and we there said:

"The defendants claim that the parol contract * * * is too indefinite to be enforced, in that the contract did not provide when the $2,000 to be left on mortgage was to become due. This claim we sustain."

In Platt v. Stonington Savings Banks, 46 Conn. 476, we had before us an agreement between a savings bank which was foreclosing a mortgage upon certain premises and a second mortgagee that, on failure of redemption, the bank would convey the land to him, and that he would pay the accrued interest on the debt, and secure the principal by a mortgage upon the real estate conveyed, without any specification of the length of time the mortgage was to run; and we said:

"How long is it to remain? No time is mentioned. How shall the court decree as to the time the loan should remain when the contract is silent on the subject? The court can make no contract for the parties; they must stand or fall upon the contract they have made, and this contract is clearly void for uncertainty in this particular."

The case is then one where the plaintiff seeks to recover the expense and loss which he has incurred in reliance upon the performance by the defendant of an agreement unenforceable because too indefinite in its terms. That in such a case recovery may often be had admits of no doubt. But the work done and the expenditures made by the plaintiff to adapt it to meet the wishes of the defendant in the instant case have been of no benefit to the latter, and his main contention is that the basis of a recovery in such cases is the benefit conferred. Several decisions might be cited in which it has been so held. No doubt there are cases where, to support a recovery, it must appear that benefit has accrued to the defendant. For instance, such is the rule where a vendee of real estate has made improvements upon the land in reliance upon an oral agreement of sale and upon his own initiative, but the vendor refuses thereafter to carry out the agreement (Wainwright v. Talcott, 60 Conn. 43, 52, 22 A. 484) so, where one, in the honest belief that he is the absolute owner of property, makes improvements thereon, he is entitled to an allowance of their fair value in a suit to foreclose a mortgage on the premises (Ensign v. Batterson, 68 Conn. 298, 307, 36 A. 51). Within the same category fall, perhaps, those actions wherein a plaintiff who has substantially but not fully performed a contract is yet in certain circumstances permitted to recover for the work he has done. We have stated the rule applicable in such a case in this way:

"The plaintiff, not being found to have been in willful default, had a cause of action for the reasonable value of the work and materials so furnished, estimated with reference to the contract price, and to the resulting benefit to the defendant, provided she appropriated that benefit under circumstances sufficient to raise an implied promise to pay for it." Jones & Hotchkiss Co. v. Davenport, 74 Conn. 418, 420, 50 A. 1028.

But there are other cases wherein a plaintiff, who cannot bring an action upon a special contract for some reason other than his own fault, is permitted a recovery for the reasonable value of the services which he has performed, without regard to the extent of the benefit conferred upon the other party to the contract. Examples are those where the defendant has himself prevented full performance of the contract (Valente v. Weinberg, 80 Conn. 134, 67 A. 369, 13 L.R.A.[N.S.] 448); or where there has been a rescission of the contract during the course of performance; (Young v. Shetucket Coal & Wood Co., 97 Conn. 92, 94, 115 A. 672); or where a building which is in the course of construction under a contract is destroyed by fire (Goldfarb v. Cohen, 92 Conn. 277, 284, 102 A. 649); or where one has agreed to perform personal services for another during the latter's life upon a promise of compensation by will, and dies before that other (Leahy v. Cheney, 90 Conn. 611, 98 A. 132, L.R.A.1917D, 809); or where services have been performed by one who has been promised compensation by will or by an heir, who has been promised that no will would be made (Grant v. Grant, 63 Conn. 530, 29 A. 15, 38 Am.St.Rep. 379.

The rationale of these decisions is best seen in the latter class of cases, where a special promise to make compensation by will is unenforceable by reason of the statute of frauds. In such a case the services have been performed at the request of him for whom they were done, and in the expectation that compensation would be made for them, to his knowledge, and with his acquiescence. In the absence of any special contract, the law would in such a situation imply an agreement that reasonable compensation should be made. The basis of that implication is that the services have been requested and have been performed by the plaintiff in the known expectation that he would receive compensation, and neither the extent nor the presence of benefit to the defendant from their performance is of controlling significance. If there were a valid and subsisting special contract, that would control; but where, though an attempt has been made to bring about such a contract, it has proved unavailing, the attempted contract is ordinarily of no consequence save as it shows the expectation of the parties that compensation for the services was to be made. It therefore leaves unimpaired the legal implication arising out of the rendition of the services upon request and in the known expectation of receiving compensation therefor. The measure of recovery is the reasonable value of the services performed, and not the amount of benefit which actually accrued from them to him for whom they were performed.

The same principles apply where the parties have attempted to make a contract which is void because its terms are too indefinite, but where one party has, in good faith, and believing that a valid contract existed, performed part of the services which he had promised in reliance upon it. He has performed those services at the request of the other party to the contract, and in the expectation, known to the other, that he would be compensated therefor. Here is a sufficient basis for an implication in law that reasonable compensation would be made.

The attempted special contract being void, there is nothing to overcome that implication. Vickery v. Ritchie, 202 Mass. 247, 88 N.E. 835, 26 L.R.A. (N.S.) 810. The situation is therefore one recognized by the law as falling within the underlying principle of implied contracts, which, in the various situations we have noted, and no doubt others, places a legal obligation upon one to do that which in equity and good conscience he ought to do.

The sums allowed to the plaintiff for the repapering and repainting, which was done after the defendant refused to purchase, do not fall within the principles applicable to the case; to allow them in this action would be, in effect, to permit a recovery upon an unenforceable contract, which may not be done. But, if the work done on the property to adapt it to the desires of the defendant was done under the terms of an oral agreement for the sale of the premises, in good faith, and in the honest belief that the agreement was sufficiently definite to be enforced, the plaintiff is entitled to recover reasonable compensation therefor. In fixing the amount of that compensation, however, a proper deduction must be made for any benefit that has accrued to the plaintiff himself by reason of the work he did upon the premises at the defendant's request.

There is error, the judgment is set aside, and a new trial ordered.

All concur.

———

WHEELER v. WHITE, 398 S.W.2d 93 (Tex.1965). Wheeler owned a three-lot tract of land in Port Arthur, Texas on which he desired to build a commercial building or a shopping center. The property presently had an older building on it with a rental value of $400 per month. Wheeler entered into a formal written "contract" with White to pay a commission (partially based on future rentals) to White if White arranged for a construction loan "in the sum of SEVENTY THOUSAND AND 00/100 ($70,000) DOLLARS and to be payable in monthly installments over a term of fifteen (15) years and bear interest at a rate of not more than six (6%) per cent per annum." After the "contract" had been signed, White urged Wheeler to proceed with the task of demolishing the building presently on the site; he assured Wheeler that the money would be available, and that if it were not, "he would make the loan himself." Wheeler razed the older building, but no loan was forthcoming. Held, the "contract" was not sufficiently definite to be enforced, but a claim was stated based on promissory estoppel. The "contract" did not contain essential elements to its enforceability in that it failed to provide "the amount of monthly installments, the amount of interest due upon the obligation, how such interest would be computed, [and] when such interest would be paid." So far as promissory estoppel was concerned:

"Where a promisee acts to his detriment in reasonable reliance upon an otherwise unenforceable promise, courts in other jurisdictions have recognized that the disappointed party may have a substantial and compelling claim for relief. * * * The function of the doctrine of promissory estoppel is, under our view, defensive in that it estops a promisor from denying the enforceability of the promise. * * *

"Under this theory, losses of expected profits will not be allowed even if expected profits are provable with certainty. The rule thus announced should be followed in the present case. We agree with the reasoning announced in those jurisdictions that, in cases such as we have before us, where there is actually no contract the promissory estoppel theory may be invoked, thereby supplying a remedy which will enable the injured party to be compensated for his foreseeable, definite and substantial reliance. Where the promisee has failed to bind the promisor to a legally sufficient contract, but where the promisee has acted in reliance upon a promise to his detriment, the promisee is to be allowed to recover no more than reliance damages measured by the detriment sustained. Since the promisee in such cases is partially responsible for his failure to bind the promisor to a legally sufficient contract, it is reasonable to conclude that all that is required to achieve justice is to put the promisee in the position he would have been in had he not acted in reliance upon the promise."

HOFFMAN v. RED OWL STORES, INC.

Supreme Court of Wisconsin, 1965.
26 Wis.2d 683, 133 N.W.2d 267.

Action by Joseph Hoffman (hereinafter "Hoffman") and wife, plaintiffs, against defendants Red Owl Stores, Inc. (hereinafter "Red Owl") and Edward Lukowitz.

The complaint alleged that Lukowitz, as agent for Red Owl, represented to and agreed with plaintiffs that Red Owl would build a store building in Chilton and stock it with merchandise for Hoffman to operate in return for which plaintiffs were to put up and invest a total sum of $18,000; that in reliance upon the above mentioned agreement and representations plaintiffs sold their bakery building and business and their grocery store and business; also in reliance on the agreement and representations Hoffman purchased the building site in Chilton and rented a residence for himself and his family in Chilton; plaintiffs' actions in reliance on the representations and agreement disrupted their personal and business life; plaintiffs lost substantial amounts of income and expended large sums of money as expenses. Plaintiffs demanded recovery of damages for the breach of defendants' representations and agreements.

The action was tried to a court and jury. The facts hereafter stated are taken from the evidence adduced at the trial. Where there was a conflict in the evidence the version favorable to plaintiffs has been accepted since the verdict rendered was in favor of plaintiffs.

Hoffman assisted by his wife operated a bakery at Wautoma from 1956 until sale of the building late in 1961. The building was owned in joint tenancy by him and his wife. Red Owl is a Minnesota corporation having its home office at Hopkins, Minnesota. It owns and operates a number of grocery supermarket stores and also extends franchises to agency stores which are owned by individuals, partnerships and corporations. Lukowitz resides at Green Bay and since September, 1960, has been divisional manager for Red Owl in a territory comprising Upper Michigan and most of Wisconsin in charge of 84 stores. Prior to September, 1960, he was district manager having charge of approximately 20 stores.

In November, 1959, Hoffman was desirous of expanding his operations by establishing a grocery store and contacted a Red Owl representative by the name of Jansen, now deceased. Numerous conversations were had in 1960 with the idea of establishing a Red Owl franchise store in Wautoma. In September, 1960, Lukowitz succeeded Jansen as Red Owl's representative in the negotiations. Hoffman mentioned that $18,000 was all the capital he had available to invest and he was repeatedly assured that this would be sufficient to set him up in business as a Red Owl store. About Christmastime, 1960, Hoffman thought it would be a good idea if he bought a small grocery store in Wautoma and operated it in order that he gain experience in the grocery business prior to operating a Red Owl store in some larger community. On February 6, 1961, on the advice of Lukowitz and Sykes, who had succeeded Lukowitz as Red Owl's district manager, Hoffman bought the inventory and fixtures of a small grocery store in Wautoma and leased the building in which it was operated.

After three months of operating this Wautoma store, the Red Owl representatives came in and took inventory and checked the operations and found the store was operating at a profit. Lukowitz advised Hoffman to sell the store to his manager, and assured him that Red Owl would find a larger store for him elsewhere. Acting on this advice and assurance, Hoffman sold the fixtures and inventory to his manager on June 6, 1961. Hoffman was reluctant to sell at that time because it meant losing the summer tourist business, but he sold on the assurance that he would be operating in a new location by fall and that he must sell this store if he wanted a bigger one. Before selling, Hoffman told the Red Owl representatives that he had $18,000 for "getting set up in business" and they assured him that there would be no problems in establishing him in a bigger operation. The makeup of the $18,000 was not discussed; it was understood plaintiff's father-in-law would furnish part of it. By June, 1961, the towns for the new grocery store had been narrowed down to two, Kewaunee and Chilton. In Kewaunee, Red Owl had an option on a building site. In Chilton, Red Owl had nothing under option, but it did select a site to which plaintiff obtained an option at Red Owl's suggestion. The option stipulated a purchase price of $6,000 with $1,000 to be paid on election to purchase and the balance to be paid within 30 days. On Lukowitz's assurance that everything was all set plaintiff paid $1,000 down on the lot on September 15th.

On September 27, 1961, plaintiff met at Chilton with Lukowitz and Mr. Reymund and Mr. Carlson from the home office who prepared a projected financial statement. Part of the funds plaintiffs were to supply as their investment in the venture were to be obtained by sale of their Wautoma bakery building.

On the basis of this meeting Lukowitz assured Hoffman: " * * * [E]verything is ready to go. Get your money together and we are set." Shortly after this meeting Lukowitz told plaintiffs that they would have to sell their bakery business and bakery building, and that their retaining this property was the only "hitch" in the entire plan. On November 6, 1961, plaintiffs sold their bakery building for $10,000. Hoffman was to retain the bakery equipment as he contemplated using it to operate a bakery in connection with his Red Owl store. After sale of the bakery Hoffman obtained employment on the night shift at an Appleton bakery.

The record contains different exhibits which were prepared in September and October, some of which were projections of the fiscal operation of the business and others were proposed building and floor plans. Red Owl was to procure some third party to buy the Chilton lot from Hoffman, construct the building, and then lease it to Hoffman. No final plans were ever made, nor were bids let or a construction contract entered. Some time prior to November 20, 1961, certain of the terms of the lease under which the building was to be rented by Hoffman were understood between him and Lukowitz. The lease was to be for 10 years with a rental approximating $550 a month calculated on the basis of 1 percent per month on the building cost, plus 6 percent of the land cost divided on a monthly basis. At the end of the 10-year term he was to have an option to renew the lease for an additional 10-year period or to buy the property at cost on an instalment basis. There was no discussion as to what the instalments would be or with respect to repairs and maintenance.

On November 22nd or 23rd, Lukowitz and plaintiffs met in Minneapolis with Red Owl's credit manager to confer on Hoffman's financial standing and on financing the agency. Another projected financial statement was there drawn up entitled, "Proposed Financing For An Agency Store." This showed Hoffman contributing $24,100 of cash capital of which only $4,600 was to be cash possessed by plaintiffs. Eight thousand was to be procured as a loan from a Chilton bank secured by a mortgage on the bakery fixtures, $7,500 was to be obtained on a 5 percent loan from the father-in-law, and $4,000 was to be obtained by sale of the lot to the lessor at a profit.

A week or two after the Minneapolis meeting Lukowitz showed Hoffman a telegram from the home office to the effect that if plaintiff could get another $2,000 for promotional purposes the deal could go through for $26,000. Hoffman stated he would have to find out if he could get another $2,000. He met with his father-in-law, who agreed to put $13,000 into the business provided he could come into the business as a partner. Lukowitz told Hoffman the partnership arrangement "sounds fine" and that Hoffman should not go into the partnership arrangement with the "front office." On January 16, 1962, the Red Owl credit manager teletyped Lukowitz that the father-in-law would have to sign an agreement that the $13,000 was either a gift or a loan subordinate to all general creditors and that he would prepare the agreement. On January 31, 1962, Lukowitz teletyped the home office that the father-in-law would sign one or other of the agreements. However, Hoffman testified that it was not until the final meeting some time between January 26th and Feburary 2nd, 1962, that he was told that his father-in-law was expected to sign an agreement that the $13,000 he was advancing was to be an outright gift. No mention was then made by the Red Owl representatives of the alternative of the father-in-law signing a subordination agreement. At this meeting the Red Owl agents presented Hoffman with the following projected financial statement:

"Capital required in operation:

"Cash	$ 5,000.00	
"Merchandise	20,000.00	
"Bakery	18,000.00	
"Fixtures	17,500.00	
"Promotional Funds	1,500.00	
"TOTAL:		$62,000.00

"Source of funds:

"Red Owl 7-day terms	$ 5,000.00	
"Red Owl Fixture contract (Term 5 years)	14,000.00	
"Bank loans (Term 9 years) Union State Bank of Chilton (Secured by Bakery Equipment)	8,000.00	
"Other loans (Term No-pay) No interest "Father-in-law "(Secured by None)	13,000.00	
"(Secured by Mortgage on Wautoma Bakery Bldg.)	2,000.00	
"Resale of land	6,000.00	
"Equity Capital: $ 5,000.00-Cash 17,500.00-Bakery Equip.		
"Amount owner has to invest:	22,500.00	
"TOTAL:		$70,500.00"

Hoffman interpreted the above statement to require of plaintiffs a total of $34,000 cash made up of $13,000 gift from his father-in-law, $2,000 on mortgage, $8,000 on Chilton bank loan, $5,000 in cash from plaintiff, and $6,000 on the resale of the Chilton lot. Red Owl claims $18,000 is the total of the unborrowed or unencumbered cash, that is, $13,000 from the father-in-law and $5,000 cash from Hoffman himself. Hoffman informed Red Owl he could not go along with this proposal, and particularly objected to the requirement that his father-in-law sign an agreement that his $13,000 advancement was an absolute gift. This terminated the negotiations between the parties.

The case was submitted to the jury on a special verdict with the first two questions answered by the court. This verdict, as returned by the jury, was as follows:

"Question No. 1: Did the Red Owl Stores, Inc. and Joseph Hoffman on or about mid-May of 1961 initiate negotiations looking to the establishment of Joseph Hoffman as a franchise operator of a Red Owl Store in Chilton? Answer: Yes. (Answered by the Court.)

"Question No. 2: Did the parties mutually agree on all of the details of the proposal so as to reach a final agreement thereon? Answer: No. (Answered by the Court.)

"Question No. 3: Did the Red Owl Stores, Inc., in the course of said negotiations, make representations to Joseph Hoffman that if he fulfilled certain conditions that they would establish him as a franchise operator of a Red Owl Store in Chilton? Answer: Yes.

"Question No. 4: If you have answered Question No. 3 'Yes,' then answer this question: Did Joseph Hoffman rely on said representations and was he induced to act thereon? Answer: Yes.

"Question No. 5: If you have answered Question No. 4 'Yes,' then answer this question: Ought Joseph Hoffman, in the exercise of ordinary care, to have relied on said representations? Answer: Yes.

"Question No. 6: If you have answered Question No. 3 "Yes" then answer this question: Did Joseph Hoffman fulfill all the conditions he was required to fulfill by the terms of the negotiations between the parties up to January 26, 1962? Answer: Yes.

"Question No. 7: What sum of money will reasonably compensate the plaintiffs for such damages as they sustained by reason of:

"(a) The sale of the Wautoma store fixtures and inventory?

"Answer: $16,735.00.

"(b) The sale of the bakery building?

"Answer: $2,000.00.

"(c) Taking up the option on the Chilton lot?

"Answer: $1,000.00.

"(d) Expenses of moving his family to Neenah?

"Answer: $140.00.

"(e) House rental in Chilton?

"Answer: $125.00."

Plaintiffs moved for judgment on the verdict while defendants moved to change the answers to Questions 3, 4, 5, and 6 from "Yes" to "No", and in the alternative for relief from the answers to the subdivisions of Question 7 or a new trial. On March 31, 1964, the circuit court entered the following order:

"IT IS ORDERED in accordance with said decision on motions after verdict hereby incorporated herein by reference:

"1. That the answer of the jury to Question No. 7(a) be and the same is hereby vacated and set aside and that a new trial be had on the sole issue of the damages for loss, if any, on the sale of the Wautoma store, fixtures and inventory.

"2. That all other portions of the verdict of the jury be and hereby are approved and confirmed and all after-verdict motions of the parties inconsistent with this order are hereby denied."

Defendants have appealed from this order and plaintiffs have cross-appealed from paragraph 1. thereof. ＊ ＊ ＊

CURRIE, CHIEF JUSTICE.

The instant appeal and cross-appeal present these questions:

(1) Whether this court should recognize causes of action grounded on promissory estoppel as exemplified by sec. 90 of Restatement, 1 Contracts?

(2) Do the facts in this case make out a cause of action for promissory estoppel?

(3) Are the jury's findings with respect to damages sustained by the evidence?

RECOGNITION OF A CAUSE OF ACTION GROUNDED
ON PROMISSORY ESTOPPEL

[The court quotes and discusses at length section 90 of the first Restatement of Contracts. It points out that it has not been applied before in Wisconsin.]

[W]e are squarely faced in the instant case with that issue. Not only did the trial court frame the special verdict on the theory of sec. 90 of Restatement, 1 Contracts, but no other possible theory has been presented to or discovered by this court which would permit plaintiffs to recover. Of other remedies considered that of an action for fraud and deceit seemed to be the most comparable. An action at law for fraud, however, cannot be predicated on unfulfilled promises unless the promisor possessed the present intent not to perform. Suskey v. Davidoff (1958), 2 Wis.2d 503, 507, 87 N.W.2d 306, and cases cited. Here, there is no evidence that would support a finding that Lukowitz made any of the promises, upon which plaintiffs' complaint is predicated, in bad faith with any present intent that they would not be fulfilled by Red Owl. ＊ ＊ ＊

Because we deem the doctrine of promissory estoppel, as stated in sec. 90 of Restatement, 1 Contracts, is one which supplies a needed tool which courts may employ in a proper case to prevent injustice, we endorse and adopt it.

Applicability of Doctrine to Facts of this Case

The record here discloses a number of promises and assurances given to Hoffman by Lukowitz in behalf of Red Owl upon which plaintiffs relied and acted upon to their detriment.

Foremost were the promises that for the sum of $18,000 Red Owl would establish Hoffman in a store. After Hoffman had sold his grocery store and paid the $1,000 on the Chilton lot, the $18,000 figure was changed to $24,100. Then in November, 1961, Hoffman was assured that if the $24,100 figure were increased by $2,000 the deal would go through. Hoffman was induced to sell his grocery store fixtures and inventory in June, 1961, on the promise that he would be in his new store by fall. In November, plaintiffs sold their bakery building on the urging of defendants and on the assurance that this was the last step necessary to have the deal with Red Owl go through.

We determine that there was ample evidence to sustain the answers of the jury to the questions of the verdict with respect to the promissory representations made by Red Owl, Hoffman's reliance thereon in the exercise of ordinary care, and his fulfillment of the conditions required of him by the terms of the negotiations had with Red Owl.

There remains for consideration the question of law raised by defendants that agreement was never reached on essential factors necessary to establish a contract between Hoffman and Red Owl. Among these were the size, cost, design, and layout of the store building; and the terms of the lease with respect to rent, maintenance, renewal, and purchase options. This poses the question of whether the promise necessary to sustain a cause of action for promissory estoppel must embrace all essential details of a proposed transaction between promisor and promisee so as to be the equivalent of an offer that would result in a binding contract between the parties if the promisee were to accept the same.

Originally the doctrine of promissory estoppel was invoked as a substitute for consideration rendering a gratuitous promise enforceable as a contract. See Williston, Contracts (1st ed.), p. 307, sec. 139. In other words, the acts of reliance by the promisee to his detriment provided a substitute for consideration. If promissory estoppel were to be limited to only those situations where the promise giving rise to the cause of action must be so definite with respect to all details that a contract would result were the promise supported by consideration, then the defendants' instant promises to Hoffman would not meet this test. However, sec. 90 of Restatement, 1 Contracts, does not impose the requirement that the promise giving rise to the cause of action must be so comprehensive in scope as to meet the requirements of an offer that would ripen into a contract if accepted by the promisee. Rather the conditions imposed are:

(1) Was the promise one which the promisor should reasonably expect to induce action or forbearance of a definite and substantial character on the part of the promisee?

(2) Did the promise induce such action or forbearance?

(3) Can injustice be avoided only by enforcement of the promise? [2]

We deem it would be a mistake to regard an action grounded on promissory estoppel as the equivalent of a breach of contract action. As Dean Boyer points out, it is desirable that fluidity in the application of the concept be maintained. 98 University of Pennsylvania Law Review (1950), 459, at page 497. While the first two of the above listed three requirements of promissory estoppel present issues of fact which ordinarily will be resolved by a jury, the third requirement, that the remedy can only be invoked where necessary to avoid injustice, is one that involves a policy decision by the court. Such a policy decision necessarily embraces an element of discretion.

We conclude that injustice would result here if plaintiffs were not granted some relief because of the failure of defendants to keep their promises which induced plaintiffs to act to their detriment.

DAMAGES

Defendants attack all the items of damages awarded by the jury.

The bakery building at Wautoma was sold at defendants' instigation in order that Hoffman might have the net proceeds available as part of the cash capital he was to invest in the Chilton store venture. The evidence clearly establishes that it was sold at a loss of $2,000. Defendants contend that half of this loss was sustained by Mrs. Hoffman because title stood in joint tenancy. They point out that no dealings took place between her and defendants as all negotiations were had with her husband. Ordinarily only the promisee and not third persons are entitled to enforce the remedy of promissory estoppel against the promisor. However, if the promisor actually foresees, or has reason to foresee, action by a third person in reliance on the promise, it may be quite unjust to refuse to perform the promise. 1A Corbin, Contracts, p. 220, sec. 200. Here not only did defendants foresee that it would be necessary for Mrs. Hoffman to sell her joint interest in the bakery building, but defendants actually requested that this be done. We approve the jury's award of $2,000 damages for the loss incurred by both plaintiffs in this sale.

Defendants attack on two grounds the $1,000 awarded because of Hoffman's payment of that amount on the purchase price of the Chilton lot. The first is that this $1,000 had already been lost at the time the final negotiations with Red Owl fell through in January, 1962, because the remaining $5,000 of purchase price had been due on October 15, 1961. The record does not disclose that the lot owner had foreclosed

---

2. See Boyer, 98 University of Pennsylvania Law Review (1950), 459, 460. "Enforcement" of the promise embraces an award of damages for breach as well as decreeing specific performance.

Hoffman's interest in the lot for failure to pay this $5,000. The $1,000 was not paid for the option, but had been paid as part of the purchase price at the time Hoffman elected to exercise the option. This gave him an equity in the lot which could not be legally foreclosed without affording Hoffman an opportunity to pay the balance. The second ground of attack is that the lot may have had a fair market value of $6,000, and Hoffman should have paid the remaining $5,000 of purchase price. We determine that it would be unreasonable to require Hoffman to have invested an additional $5,000 in order to protect the $1,000 he had paid. Therefore, we find no merit to defendants' attack upon this item of damages.

We also determine it was reasonable for Hoffman to have paid $125 for one month's rent of a home in Chilton after defendants assured him everything would be set when plaintiff sold the bakery building. This was a proper item of damage.

Plaintiffs never moved to Chilton because defendants suggested that Hoffman get some experience by working in a Red Owl store in the Fox River Valley. Plaintiffs, therefore, moved to Neenah instead of Chilton. After moving, Hoffman worked at night in an Appleton bakery but held himself available for work in a Red Owl store. The $140 moving expense would not have been incurred if plaintiffs had not sold their bakery building in Wautoma in reliance upon defendants' promises. We consider the $140 moving expense to be a proper item of damage.

We turn now to the damage item with respect to which the trial court granted a new trial, i.e., that arising from the sale of the Wautoma grocery store fixtures and inventory for which the jury awarded $16,735. The trial court ruled that Hoffman could not recover for any loss of future profits for the summer months following the sale on June 6, 1961, but that damages would be limited to the difference between the sales price received and the fair market value of the assets sold, giving consideration to any goodwill attaching thereto by reason of the transfer of a going business. There was no direct evidence presented as to what this fair market value was on June 6, 1961. The evidence did disclose that Hoffman paid $9,000 for the inventory, added $1,500 to it and sold it for $10,000 or a loss of $500. His 1961 federal income tax return showed that the grocery equipment had been purchased for $7,000 and sold for $7,955.96. Plaintiffs introduced evidence of the buyer that during the first eleven weeks of operation of the grocery store his gross sales were $44,000 and his profit was $6,000 or roughly 15 percent. On cross-examination he admitted that this was gross and not net profit. Plaintiffs contend that in a breach of contract action damages may include loss of profits. However, this is not a breach of contract action.

The only relevancy of evidence relating to profits would be with respect to proving the element of goodwill in establishing the fair market value of the grocery inventory and fixtures sold. Therefore, evidence of profits would be admissible to afford a foundation for expert opinion as to fair market value.

Where damages are awarded in promissory estoppel instead of specifically enforcing the promisor's promise, they should be only such as in the opinion of the court are necessary to prevent injustice. Mechanical or rule of thumb approaches to the damage problem should be avoided. In discussing remedies to be applied by courts in promissory estoppel we quote the following views of writers on the subject:

"Enforcement of a promise does not necessarily mean Specific Performance.

It does not necessarily mean Damages for breach. Moreover the amount allowed as Damages may be determined by the plaintiff's expenditures or change of position in reliance as well as by the value to him of the promised performance. Restitution is also an 'enforcing' remedy, although it is often said to be based upon some kind of a rescission. In determining what justice requires, the court must remember all of its powers, derived from equity, law merchant, and other sources, as well as the common law. Its decrees should be molded accordingly." 1A Corbin, Contracts, p. 221, sec. 200.

"The wrong is not primarily in depriving the plaintiff of the promised reward but in causing the plaintiff to change position to his detriment. It would follow that the damages should not exceed the loss caused by the change of position, which would never be more in amount, but might be less, than the promised reward." Seavey, Reliance on Gratuitous Promises or Other Conduct, 64 Harvard Law Review (1951), 913, 926.

"There likewise seems to be no positive legal requirement, and certainly no legal policy, which dictates the allowance of contract damages in every case where the defendant's duty is consensual." Shattuck, Gratuitous Promises—A New Writ?, 35 Michigan Law Review (1936), 908, 912.[3]

At the time Hoffman bought the equipment and inventory of the small grocery store at Wautoma he did so in order to gain experience in the grocery store business. At that time discussion had already been had with Red Owl representatives that Wautoma might be too small for a Red Owl operation and that a larger city might be more desirable. Thus Hoffman made this purchase more or less as a temporary experiment. Justice does not require that the damages awarded him, because of selling these assets at the behest of defendants should exceed any actual loss sustained measured by the differences between the sales price and the fair market value.

3. For expression of the opposite view, that courts in promissory estoppel cases should treat them as ordinary breach of contract cases and allow the full amount of damages recoverable in the latter, see note, 13 Vanderbilt Law Review (1960), 705.

Since the evidence does not sustain the large award of damages arising from the sale of the Wautoma grocery business, the trial court properly ordered a new trial on this issue.

Order affirmed. Because of the cross-appeal, plaintiffs shall be limited to taxing but two-thirds of their costs.

———

Not all courts today might agree with the court in Kearns v. Andree that a promise to "assume a first mortgage of $4,500, a bank mortgage" is too indefinite to be enforced. However, if the court's premise is taken at face value, it is clear that the court was protecting reliance on a "near offer"—language that appears to involve a commitment but does not rise to the level of an "offer." Is this also true of Hoffman v. Red Owl Stores? If the language that is being relied upon in that case is not even close to constituting an "offer," what is the obligation being imposed on the speaker?

———

KNAPP, ENFORCING THE CONTRACT TO BARGAIN
44 N.Y.U. L.Rev. 673, 688–90 (1969).*

The importance of the *Hoffman* case ＊ ＊ ＊ lies as much in the way the decision is explained as in the decision itself. With commendable candor, the court makes no attempt to obscure the fact that the parties had not reached final agreement on all material terms when the deal fell through. The defendant thus could not be said to have made an offer so definite that plaintiff, simply by accepting, could cause a contract to come into being. The court compensated plaintiff for his reliance on defendant's assurance not that agreement had been reached, but only that it would be reached—and on terms satisfactory to the plaintiff.

It is thus reasonable to interpret *Hoffman* as furnishing authority for the proposition that one may in some circumstances come under a duty to bargain in good faith, breach of which duty may result in liability for damages, at least to the extent of compensating the detrimental reliance of the injured party. Certain questions do arise, however, in the course of attempting to fit the *Hoffman* case into the pattern of a contract to bargain, as previously defined. First, it is not clear from the opinion whether the principle of recovery there announced may be restricted to cases in which there is some kind of bargaining imbalance which gives the plaintiff a claim to extra indulgence from the court, beyond that to which a businessman bargaining as an equal would be entitled. Although the decision is not based expressly upon such factors, it is difficult to escape an initial impression that Hoffman appeared to the court as a sort of babe in the

* © 1969, N.Y.U.L.Rev. Reprinted with permission.

Wisconsin woods, dealing with a bunch of city slickers from the Red Owl gang.   *   *   *

A second problem in characterizing the *Hoffman* negotiations is the difficulty in evaluating the extent of actual agreement reached by the parties and the degree to which they manifested their commitment to the proposed exchange of performances. It is possible, for instance, that the court in *Hoffman* could have concluded that plaintiff really believed that the deal was finally agreed upon, or at least that the negotiations were so advanced as to amount to a contract fully binding in all respects. Even more likely, from the facts described by the court, is the possibility that the manifestations of "commitment," on which the decision largely depends, came principally from Red Owl rather than from Hoffman. If so, had the tables been turned and Hoffman been the one who backed out of the agreement, he would not have been liable to Red Owl.

Whatever its consequences in terms of legal recognition of rights and granting of remedies, the contract to bargain is basically a bilateral arrangement; its claim for legal recognition is principally based upon the contention that there are cases where a level of agreement has been reached, and manifested, which is sufficient in the eyes of the parties themselves to bind them, absent good faith justification for withdrawal. A fundamental characteristic of promissory estoppel is its one-sidedness—only one party having enforceable rights against the other.

CONSOLIDATED GRAIN AND BARGE CO. v. MADGETT

United States Court of Appeals, Eighth Circuit, 1991.
928 F.2d 816.

Before LAY, CHIEF JUDGE, MCMILLIAN and ARNOLD, CIRCUIT JUDGES.

PER CURIAM.

John Madgett appeals from the district court's order granting summary judgment for Consolidated Grain and Barge Co. (Consolidated) on his counter claim for enforcement of a contract clause requiring the parties to "negotiate in good faith." The district court held the clause too indefinite to be enforceable, citing *Ohio Calculating, Inc. v. CPT Corp.*, 846 F.2d 497, 501 (8th Cir.1988). We affirm.

BACKGROUND

Madgett and Consolidated each owned 50% of several companies involved in barge shipping on inland waterways. In 1982, Consolidated and Madgett were co-defendants in a class action suit brought by dissatisfied limited partners of one of the companies. In settlement of this suit, Consolidated and Madgett bought out the limited partners and reorganized the companies. As part of the reorganization, Consolidated obtained the right to profits from operation of the barges. The parties agreed that Madgett might be entitled to a share of those profits by virtue of his one-half interest in Wellspring Energy Corporation, the entity that procured the barge contracts that would be fulfilled by Consolidated after the reorganization. However, the parties could not agree on the amount of Madgett's share. Rather than hold up settlement of the class action, Madgett and Consolidated included the following stipulation in a letter agreement that resolved their other concerns:

> Consolidated has agreed that it will negotiate in good faith with Madgett concerning Madgett's share of any monies which Consolidated may be entitled to receive under the barge charter arrangement between Hutton and Consolidated which is part of the proposed settlement of the [class action].

Madgett claims that Consolidated refused to negotiate or discuss the matter except in the context of an overall severance of its contractual relations with Madgett. Consolidated has committed itself to paying Madgett $20,000 per year during the term of the present barge charter, apparently reflecting Consolidated's determination of Madgett's share of the charter commission earned by Wellspring Energy Corporation.

Consolidated sued Madgett for, among other things, dissolution of the businesses the parties jointly owned. Madgett counterclaimed for enforcement of the negotiation stipulation. The district court decided only the counterclaim, as all other issues were settled. The district court found the clause unenforceable because "it is impossible to determine what Madgett's share . . . should be, and it is likewise impossible to determine whether Consolidated negotiated in good faith."

DISCUSSION

In *Ohio Calculating*, a diversity case, we determined that a similar clause would be held unenforceable under Minnesota law because it provided "neither a basis for determining the existence of a breach nor for giving an appropriate remedy." 846 F.2d at 501. Although it is unclear whether the contract at issue is governed by Missouri or Minnesota law, the district court found no difference between the law of the two states on this point. The parties do not dispute this finding.

We find *Ohio Calculating* directly on point and dispositive in holding that an agreement to negotiate is unenforceable. See also Jenks v. Jenks, 385 S.W.2d 370, 376 (Mo.App.1964) (stating "since agreement cannot be compelled, equity will not indulge the futility of ordering the parties to 'meet together' to discuss 'in good faith' the very problem on which they have demonstrated their inability to agree"). The stipulation evidences nothing more than an intention to negotiate in the future.[2]

Madgett's main contention is that, unlike the plaintiff in *Ohio Calculating*, there is no question that Madgett is entitled to some share

---

2. We decline to accept Madgett's invitation to apply federal labor law precedents to a state law contract case. Labor law cases are clearly distinguishable. In labor law, the court can impose negative sanctions or other penalties; the court is not under an obligation to decide what the parties might agree upon.

of the profits held by Consolidated. Thus, Madgett argues, failure to enforce the agreement will result in Consolidated's unjust enrichment. However, even assuming that Madgett is entitled to a portion of the profits, we still have no basis for determining how much. Madgett's several suggested remedies all suffer from the same basic flaw; they would require the court to determine the substance of the agreement. Because the parties deferred this issue to negotiation, there is no objective basis for determining Madgett's share of the profits.

The judgment of the district court granting summary judgment for Consolidated is AFFIRMED.

BARNET AND BECKER, BEYOND RELIANCE: PROMISSORY ESTOPPEL, CONTRACT FORMALITIES, AND MISREPRESENTATIONS

15 Hofstra L.Rev. 443, 491–492 (1987).

Hoffman is the first of a small but continuing line of cases in which courts have used promissory estoppel to afford a remedy for negligent promissory misrepresentation, i.e., to afford relief when a promise is made to induce a promisee to rely in a desired way in circumstances such that the promisor knows (or should know) that the promise will appear to be more reliable than it is. In each of these cases, the plaintiff relied detrimentally on the defendant's promises.[221] Consistent with this explanation of liability—that it is based on misrepresentation of the reliability of the promise—courts have generally denied relief for losses sustained during preliminary negotiations no matter how reasonable the reliance.

The courts using promissory estoppel to impose liability for negligent promissory misrepresentation could reach the same result under

---

221. For a case quite similar to *Hoffman*, see Werner v. Xerox Corp., 732 F.2d 580 (7th Cir.1984) (applying Wisconsin law). Wolf, a Xerox agent, encouraged Werner to set up production of "off-load rollers" by assuring Werner that Xerox would buy them. When Wolf's supervisor visited the facility, he immediately told Werner that the facility would never make parts for Xerox. It seems likely that Wolf knew, or should have known, that his assurances would appear more reliable to Werner than they actually were. Liability might therefore be based on negligent promissory misrepresentation. Liability would not lie in contract because too few terms of the exchange were worked out for Werner to have reasonably thought that there was a binding contract. Xerox also produced these parts (on equipment built by Werner) and nothing had apparently been said about price, quantity, or duration of any supply contract.

In two cases, the measure of damages suggests that the courts used promissory estoppel to impose tort liability. In both cases, some lower measure of damages could have been imposed on the basis of contract principles, but punitive damages were appropriate because the defendants intentionally and deliberately led the plaintiffs to think that a promise was more reliable than the defendants intended it to be. *See* Greenstein v. Flatley, 19 Mass. App.Ct. 351, 474 N.E.2d 1130 (1985); Chrysler Corp. v. Quimby, 51 Del. 264, 144 A.2d 123 (1958).

In *Greenstein*, the court indicated that it was using promissory estoppel to remedy misrepresentation, and imposed punitive damages because the misrepresentation was intentional. Although the promissory misrepresentation was made intentionally to mislead the plaintiffs, it might not have been a lie when made under Massachusetts case law. *See* McCusker v. Geiger, 195 Mass. 46, 80 N.E. 648 (1907) (requiring the additional element of an "affirmative" intent not to perform for a promise to be a lie when made).

tort, by changing the standard for promissory misrepresentation from lie-when-made to negligent or reckless. For over a hundred years, however, common law courts have repeatedly held that tort liability for promissory misrepresentation requires that the promise be a lie when made. The tort standard has become fairly rigid, and promissory estoppel is a relatively new, and certainly more flexible basis for liability. * * *

———

GIANT FOOD, INC. v. ICE KING, INC., 74 Md.App. 183, 536 A.2d 1182, 1183, 1186–87, cert. denied, 313 Md. 7, 542 A.2d 844 (1988). Richard Epple was the owner of Ice King, Inc., a corporation that was planning and building a plant to manufacture ice. Epple entered into extensive discussions, extending over seven months, with Knippen and Hendricks, employees of Giant Food. While Epple was seeking a buyer for his corporation's ice, the Giant employees were seeking a new supplier of ice only in the event its own plant was not ready in time for the next heat wave. Unknown to Epple, Ice King was considered by Giant to be a safety valve, a fallback position, and not a permanent supplier. Epple had thirty to forty conversations with Hendricks, in which Epple sought guidance to ensure that Ice King's production conformed to Giant's requirements, including 1) the type, price, quality, and quantity of ice; 2) the delivery terms; 3) the location of Ice King's plant at a site most suitable to Giant; and, 4) the size of the storage facility needed to satisfy Giant's demand. Giant authorized Epple to make a statement on a loan application that Giant was going to buy ice from Ice King; Knippen also assured Epple that everything was "all right" when Epple expressed his concern over hearing about Giant's plans to build its own ice plant. Giant also inspected Ice King's plant and requested Ice King to supply further samples of ice and a certificate of insurance. Knippen and Hendricks knew that Epple was investing all his resources in the ice plant; Hendricks became so concerned about Epple's reliance on Giant that he communicated his concerns to his supervisor, Knippen. However, when Epple's son asked Knippen whether Epple should seek to develop other customers, Knippen answered, "no." Giant's ice plant was later found to be adequate for Giant's needs and no ice was bought from Ice King. Held, Giant was liable to Ice King in tort for negligent misrepresentation. As described by the Court:

> "The action for negligent misrepresentation was created to provide a tort remedy for the plaintiff who had acted in reliance upon the false [2] statement of a defendant whose conduct in uttering the statement was culpably careless, but not deliberately fraudulent, and who was aware that the plaintiff would reasonably act in reliance upon the statement."

2. It need not be proven that the defendant knew that the statement was false. "All that the plaintiff need show in that respect is that the statement was negligently made without regard to whether it was true or false." Gilbert, *Maryland Tort Law Handbook,* § 17.5.1 at 181 (1986).

Note, *Deceit and Negligent Misrepresentation in Maryland,* 35 Md.L. Rev. 651, 673 (1976).

The Court concluded,

*   *   * "[A]lthough no written contract existed between the parties, a fact repeatedly stressed by appellants, the evidence strongly suggested that a 'businessman in Epple's shoes' might have reasonably relied on the informal 'deal' or 'gentlemen's agreement' that is the custom of the trade. The evidence demonstrated that neither of Giant's previous ice suppliers had written contracts. It was clear that Giant's practice was *not* to issue written contracts. That a lending institution viewed the 'deal' between Giant and Ice King as reliable underscores why it was reasonable for Epple to rely upon the information supplied by the appellants.

"Significantly, Hendricks in May 1985 assured Epple that 'everything was all right.' We think that Epple was justified in relying upon that statement as an assertion of fact."

BREWER STREET INVESTMENTS LTD. v. BARCLAYS WOOLLEN CO. LD. [1954] 1 Q.B. 428 (C.A.). The defendants, prospective tenants of certain premises, were in negotiation with the plaintiffs, owners, for a lease. Both parties believed that a lease would be entered into. The plaintiffs began certain alterations in the premises desired by the defendants, who agreed, as part of the lease arrangement, to pay for their cost. As negotiations continued, it became apparent that no agreement could be reached, the defendants insisting on an option to purchase the premises and the plaintiffs willing to grant only a right of first refusal to purchase. When this impasse was discovered, the plaintiffs ordered the work on the alterations to be stopped before they were completed and sued the defendants for the amount expended on them. Held, for the plaintiffs. Lord Denning wrote:

"It is clear on the facts that the parties proceeded on a fundamental assumption—that the lease would be granted—which has turned out to be wrong. The work done has been wasted. The question is: on whom is the loss to fall? The parties themselves did not envisage the situation which has emerged and did not provide for it; and we do not know what they would have provided if they had envisaged it. Only the law can resolve their rights and liabilities in the new situation, either by means of implying terms or, more simply, by asking on whom should the risk fall. This is how the court approached a similar question in Jennings & Chapman Ld. v. Woodman, Matthews & Co., [1952] 2 T.L.R. 409 and I think that we should approach the question in the same way.

"Morris, L.J., gave a reserved judgment in which he put the matter in a way which appeals to me. He asked himself: what was the reason for the negotiations breaking down? If it was the landlords' fault, as, for instance, if they refused to go on with the lease for no reason at all, or because they demanded a higher rent than that which had been already agreed, then they should not be allowed to recover any part of the cost of the alterations. Even if the landlords derived no benefit from the work, they should not be allowed to recover the cost from the prospective tenants, seeing that it was by their fault that the prospective tenants were deprived of it.

"On the other hand, if it was the prospective tenants' fault that the negotiations broke down, as, for instance, if they sought a lower rent than that which had been agreed upon, then the prospective tenants ought to pay the cost of the alterations up to the time they were stopped. After all, they did promise to pay for the work, and they should not be able to get out of their promise by their own fault, even though the alterations were not completed. It is a very old principle laid down by Sir Edward Coke that a man shall not be allowed to take advantage of a condition brought about by himself.

"I do not think, however, that in the present case it can be said that either party was really at fault. Neither party sought to alter the rent or any other point which had been agreed upon. They fell out on a point which had not been agreed at all. From the very beginning the prospective tenants wanted an option to purchase, whereas the landlords were only ready to give them the first refusal. Each of them in the course of the negotiations sought on this point to get more favourable terms—the prospective tenants to get a firm option to purchase, the landlords to give a first refusal of little value—but their moves in the negotiations can hardly be considered a default by one or other.

"What, then, is the position when the negotiations go off without the default of either? On whom should the risk fall? In my opinion the prospective tenants ought to pay all the costs thrown away. The work was done to meet their special requirements and was prima facie for their benefit and not for the benefit of the landlords. If and in so far as the work is shown to have been of benefit to the landlords, credit should be given in such sum as may be just. Subject to such credit, the prospective tenants ought to pay the cost of the work, because they in the first place agreed to take responsibility for it; and when the matter goes off without the default of either side, they should pay the costs thrown away. There is no finding here that the work was of any benefit to the landlords, and in the circumstances the prospective tenants should, I think, pay the amount claimed."

CHILDRES & SPITZ, STATUS IN THE LAW OF CONTRACT

47 N.Y.U.L.Rev. 1, n. 1 (1972).*

The law of offer and acceptance has been slow to fall apart primarily because of its near irrelevance. It will continue to work mischief for a short while, but with the level of attack rising in legal

* © 1972, N.Y.U.L.Rev. Reprinted with permission.

literature, see, e.g., Knapp, Enforcing the Contract to Bargain, 44 N.Y. U.L.Rev. 673 (1969), and Summers, "Good Faith" in General Contract Law and the Sales Provisions of the Uniform Commercial Code, 54 Va. L.Rev. 195, 220–32 (1968), in legislation, see, e.g., Uniform Commercial Code §§ 2–206, 2–207 * * * and in the courts, see, e.g., Hoffman v. Red Owl Stores, Inc., 26 Wis.2d 683, 133 N.W.2d 267 (1965), we are not far from recognizing the law of offer and acceptance as an entirely irrelevant anachronism.

———

Chapter 5

MISTAKE, IMPOSSIBILITY, AND FRUSTRATION

SHERWOOD v. WALKER

Supreme Court of Michigan, 1887.
66 Mich. 568, 33 N.W. 919.

MORSE, J. Replevin for a cow. Suit commenced in justice's court. Judgment for plaintiff. Appealed to circuit court of Wayne county, and verdict and judgment for plaintiff in that court. The defendants bring error, and set out 25 assignments of the same. * * *

The defendants reside at Detroit, but are in business at Walkerville, Ontario, and have a farm at Greenfield, in Wayne county, upon which were some blooded cattle supposed to be barren as breeders. The Walkers are importers and breeders of polled Angus cattle.

The plaintiff is a banker living at Plymouth, in Wayne county. He called upon the defendants at Walkerville for the purchase of some of their stock, but found none there that suited him. Meeting one of the defendants afterwards, he was informed that they had a few head upon this Greenfield farm. He was asked to go out and look at them, with the statement at the time that they were probably barren, and would not breed.

May 5, 1886, plaintiff went out to Greenfield and saw the cattle. A few days thereafter, he called upon one of the defendants with the view of purchasing a cow, known as "Rose 2d of Aberlone." After considerable talk, it was agreed that defendants would telephone Sherwood at his home in Plymouth in reference to the price. The second morning after this talk he was called up by telephone, and the terms of the sale were finally agreed upon. He was to pay five and one-half cents per pound, live weight, fifty pounds shrinkage. He was asked how he intended to take the cow home, and replied that he might ship her from King's cattle-yard. He requested defendants to confirm the sale in writing, which they did by sending him the following letter:

"Walkerville, May 15, 1886.

"T. C. Sherwood,

"President, etc.,—

"*Dear Sir:* We confirm sale to you of the cow Rose 2d of Aberlone, lot 56 of our catalogue, at five and a half cents per pound, less fifty pounds shrink. We inclose herewith order on Mr. Graham for the cow. You might leave check with him, or mail to us here, as you prefer.

"Yours truly,
"Hiram Walker & Sons."

The order upon Graham inclosed in the letter read as follows:

"Walkerville, May 15, 1886.

"*George Graham:* You will please deliver at King's cattle-yard to Mr. T. C. Sherwood, Plymouth, the cow Rose 2d of Aberlone, lot 56 of our catalogue. Send halter with cow, and have her weighed.

"Yours truly,
"Hiram Walker & Sons."

On the twenty-first of the same month the plaintiff went to defendants' farm at Greenfield, and presented the order and letter to Graham, who informed him that the defendants had instructed him not to deliver the cow. Soon after, the plaintiff tendered to Hiram Walker, one of the defendants, $80, and demanded the cow. Walker refused to take the money or deliver the cow. The plaintiff then instituted this suit.

After he had secured possession of the cow under the writ of replevin, the plaintiff caused her to be weighed by the constable who served the writ, at a place other than King's cattle-yard. She weighed 1,420 pounds.

* * * The defendants then introduced evidence tending to show that at the time of the alleged sale it was believed by both the plaintiff and themselves that the cow was barren and would not breed; that she cost $850, and if not barren would be worth from $750 to $1,000; that after the date of the letter, and the order to Graham, the defendants were informed by said Graham that in his judgment the cow was with calf, and therefore they instructed him not to deliver her to plaintiff, and on the twentieth of May, 1886, telegraphed to the plaintiff what Graham thought about the cow being with calf, and that consequently they could not sell her. The cow had a calf in the month of October following.

On the nineteenth of May, the plaintiff wrote Graham as follows:

"Plymouth, May 19, 1886.

"Mr. George Graham,

"Greenfield,—

"*Dear Sir:* I have bought Rose or Lucy from Mr. Walker, and will be there for her Friday morning, nine or ten o'clock. Do not water her in the morning.

"Yours, etc.,
"T. C. Sherwood."

Plaintiff explained the mention of the two cows in this letter by testifying that, when he wrote this letter, the order and letter of defendants were at his house, and, writing in a hurry, and being uncertain as to the name of the cow, and not wishing his cow watered, he thought it would do no harm to name them both, as his bill of sale would show which one he had purchased. Plaintiff also testified that he asked defendants to give him a price on the balance of their herd at Greenfield, as a friend thought of buying some, and received a letter dated May 17, 1886, in which they named the price of five cattle, including Lucy at $90, and Rose 2d at $80. When he received the letter he called defendants up by telephone, and asked them why they put Rose 2d in the list, as he had already purchased her. They replied that they knew he had, but thought it would make no difference if plaintiff and his friend concluded to take the whole herd.

The foregoing is the substance of all the testimony in the case.

The circuit judge instructed the jury that if they believed the defendants, when they sent the order and letter to plaintiff, meant to pass the title to the cow, and that the cow was intended to be delivered to plaintiff, it did not matter whether the cow was weighed at any particular place, or by any particular person; and if the cow was weighed afterwards, as Sherwood testified, such weighing would be a sufficient compliance with the order; if they believed that defendants intended to pass the title by the writing, it did not matter whether the cow was weighed before or after suit brought, and the plaintiff would be entitled to recover. * * * The court also charged the jury that it was immaterial whether the cow was with calf or not. * * *

[The Supreme Court held that the trial court was correct in submitting to the jury the fact question "whether the parties intended the title [to the cow] should pass before delivery or not."]

It appears from the record that both parties supposed this cow was barren and would not breed, and she was sold by the pound for an insignificant sum as compared with her real value if a breeder. She was evidently sold and purchased on the relation of her value for beef, unless the plaintiff had learned of her true condition, and concealed such knowledge from the defendants. Before the plaintiff secured possession of the animal, the defendants learned that she was with calf, and therefore of great value, and undertook to rescind the sale by refusing to deliver her. The question arises whether they had a right to do so.

The circuit judge ruled that this fact did not avoid the sale, and it made no difference whether she was barren or not. I am of the opinion that the court erred in this holding. I know that this is a close question, and the dividing line between the adjudicated cases is not easily discerned. But it must be considered as well settled that a party who has given an apparent consent to a contract of sale may refuse to execute it, or he may avoid it after it has been completed, if the assent was founded, or the contract made, upon the mistake of a material fact,—such as the subject-matter of the sale, the price, or some collateral fact materially inducing the agreement; and this can be done when the mistake is mutual.

If there is a difference or misapprehension as to the substance of the thing bargained for, if the thing actually delivered or received is different in substance from the thing bargained for and intended to be sold, then there is no contract; but if it be only a difference in some quality or accident, even though the mistake may have been the actuating motive to the purchaser or seller, or both of them, yet the contract remains binding.

"The difficulty in every case is to determine whether the mistake or misapprehension is as to the substance of the whole contract, going, as it were, to the root of the matter, or only to some point, even though a material point, an error as to which does not affect the substance of the whole consideration." Kennedy v. Panama, etc., Mail Co., L. R. 2 Q. B. 580, 588.

It has been held, in accordance with the principles above stated, that where a horse is bought under the belief that he is sound, and both vendor and vendee honestly believe him to be sound, the purchaser must stand by his bargain, and pay the full price, unless there was a warranty.

It seems to me, however, in the case made by this record, that the mistake or misapprehension of the parties went to the whole substance of the agreement. If the cow was a breeder, she was worth at least $750; if barren, she was worth not over $80. The parties would not have made the contract of sale except upon the understanding and belief that she was incapable of breeding, and of no use as a cow. It is true she is now the identical animal that they thought her to be when the contract was made; there is no mistake as to the identity of the creature. Yet the mistake was not of the mere quality of the animal, but went to the very nature of the thing. A barren cow is substantially a different creature than a breeding one. There is as much difference between them for all purposes of use as there is between an ox and a cow that is capable of breeding and giving milk. If the mutual mistake had simply related to the fact whether she was with calf or not for one season, then it might have been a good sale; but the mistake affected the character of the animal for all time, and for her present and ultimate use. She was not in fact the animal, or the kind of animal, the defendants intended to sell or the plaintiff to buy. She was not a barren cow, and, if this fact had been known, there would have been no contract. The mistake affected the substance of the whole consideration, and it must be considered that there was no contract to sell or sale of the cow as she actually was. The thing sold and bought had in fact no existence. She was sold as a beef creature would be sold; she is in fact a breeding cow, and a valuable one.

The court should have instructed the jury that if they found that the cow was sold, or contracted to be sold, upon the understanding of both parties that she was barren, and useless for the purpose of breeding, and that in fact she was not barren, but capable of breeding, then the defendants had a right to rescind, and to refuse to deliver, and the verdict should be in their favor.

The judgment of the court below must be reversed, and a new trial granted, with costs of this Court to defendants.

CAMPBELL, C. J., and CHAMPLIN, J., concurred.

SHERWOOD, J. (dissenting). I do not concur in the opinion given by my brethren in this case. I think the judgments before the justice and at the circuit were right. * * *

As has already been stated by my brethren, the record shows that the plaintiff is a banker, and farmer as well, carrying on a farm, and raising the best breeds of stock, and lived in Plymouth, in the county of Wayne, 23 miles from Detroit; that the defendants lived in Detroit, and were also dealers in stock of the higher grades; that they had a farm at Walkerville, in Canada, and also one in Greenfield, in said county of Wayne, and upon these farms the defendants kept their stock. The Greenfield farm was about 15 miles from the plaintiff's.

In the spring of 1886 the plaintiff, learning that the defendants had some "polled Angus cattle" for sale, was desirous of purchasing some of that breed, and, meeting the defendants, or some of them, at Walkerville, inquired about them, and was informed that they had none at Walkerville, "but had a few head left on their farm in Greenfield, and they asked the plaintiff to go and see them, stating that in all probability they were sterile and would not breed." * * *

The record further shows that the defendants, when they sold the cow, believed the cow was not with calf, and barren; that from what the plaintiff had been told by defendants (for it does not appear he had any other knowledge or facts from which he could form an opinion) he believed the cow was farrow, but still thought she could be made to breed. The foregoing shows the entire interview and treaty between the parties as to the sterility and qualities of the cow sold to the plaintiff. The cow had a calf in the month of October.

There is no question but that the defendants sold the cow representing her of the breed and quality they believed the cow to be, and that the purchaser so understood it. And the buyer purchased her believing her to be of the breed represented by the sellers, and possessing all the qualities stated, and even more. He believed she would breed. There is no pretense that the plaintiff bought the cow for beef, and there is nothing in the record indicating that he would have bought her at all only that he thought she might be made to breed. Under the foregoing facts,—and these are all that are contained in the record material to the contract,—it is held that because it turned out that the plaintiff was more correct in his judgment as to one quality of the cow than the defendants, and a quality, too, which could not by any possibility be positively known at the time by either party to exist, the contract may be annulled by the defendants at their pleasure. I know of no law, and have not been referred to any, which will justify any such holding, and I think the circuit judge was right in his construction of the contract between the parties.

It is claimed that a mutual mistake of a material fact was made by the parties when the contract of sale was made. There was no warranty in the case of the quality of the animal. When a mistaken fact is relied upon as ground for rescinding, such fact must not only exist at the time the contract is made, but must have been known to one or both of the parties. Where there is no warranty, there can be no mistake of fact when no such fact exists, or, if in existence, neither party knew of it, or could know of it; and that is precisely this case. If the owner of a Hambletonian horse had speeded him, and was only able to make him go a mile in three minutes, and should sell him to another, believing that was his greatest speed, for $300, when the purchaser believed he could go much faster, and made the purchase for that sum, and a few days thereafter, under more favorable circumstances, the horse was driven a mile in 2 min. 16 sec., and was found to be worth $20,000, I hardly think it would be held, either at law or in equity, by any one, that the seller in such case could rescind the contract. The same legal principles apply in each case.

In this case neither party knew the actual quality and condition of this cow at the time of the sale. The defendants say, or rather said, to the plaintiff, "they had a few head left on their farm in Greenfield, and asked plaintiff to go and see them, stating to plaintiff that in all probability they were sterile and would not breed." Plaintiff did go as requested, and found there three cows, including the one purchased, with a bull. The cow had been exposed, but neither knew she was with calf or whether she would breed. The defendants thought she would not, but the plaintiff says that he thought she could be made to breed, but believed she was not with calf. The defendants sold the cow for what they believed her to be, and the plaintiff bought her as he believed she was, after the statements made by the defendants. No conditions whatever were attached to the terms of sale by either party. It was in fact as abolute as it could well be made, and I know of no precedent as authority by which this Court can alter the contract thus made by these parties in writing, and interpolate in it a condition by which, if the *defendants should be mistaken in their belief that the cow was barren,* she should be returned to them, and their contract should be annulled.

It is not the duty of courts to destroy contracts when called upon to enforce them, after they have been legally made. There was no mistake of any such material fact by either of the parties in the case as would license the vendors to rescind. There was no difference between the parties, nor misapprehension, as to the substance of the thing bargained for, which was a cow supposed to be barren by one party, and believed not to be by the other. As to the quality of the animal, subsequently developed, both parties were equally ignorant, and as to this each party took his chances. If this were not the law, there would be no safety in purchasing this kind of stock.

I entirely agree with my brethren that the right to rescind occurs whenever "the thing actually delivered or received is different in substance from the thing bargained for, and intended to be sold; but if it be only a difference in some quality or accident, even though the misapprehension may have been the actuating motive" of the parties in making the contract, yet it will remain binding. In this case the cow sold was the one delivered. What might or might not happen to her after the sale formed no element in the contract. * * *

Replevin

At common law the action of replevin was available to a plaintiff claiming to be the owner of personal property, and seeking its return from one who had wrongfully taken or who was wrongfully holding it. A Michigan statute in effect at the time of Sherwood v. Walker provided that when the plaintiff filed an affidavit stating that he was "then lawfully entitled to the possession of the property," the court would issue a writ óf replevin to the sheriff. The sheriff would then seize the goods and return them immediately to the plaintiff pending resolution of the dispute on the merits; for that purpose he could "break open any house, stable, out-house, or other building in which such property may be concealed * * *." Mich. Comp. Laws §§ 6732, 6733 (1871). Before the plaintiff could take advantage of this summary procedure he had to post a bond equal to double the value of the goods; this was intended to insure that he would prosecute his suit to final judgment and that he would return the goods to the defendant should the court ultimately find against him. Statutes commonly permitted a defendant to retain possession of the goods pending trial by posting his own bond, although the Michigan statute did not so provide.

Where as in Sherwood v. Walker the plaintiff was the buyer under a contract of sale, it was essential to his claim of ownership to demonstrate that "title" to the goods had passed to him. Where "title" had passed, the seller in default "is guilty of both a tort and a breach of contract. He is detaining or converting without just cause the property which belongs to the buyer * * *." Williston on Sales p. 986 (1909). The precise location of this "intangible something" called "title" was the focus of much litigation. However, the importance of the "title" concept has been severely diminished under the Uniform Commercial Code. See § 2–101, Official Comment and § 2–401. The purchaser's right to actual possession of the promised goods is now governed by § 2–716 (see also § 2–502). The requirement of 2–716(3)—that the buyer be "unable to effect cover"—is a limitation which seems to make replevin even less readily available than under earlier law. In addition, the usefulness of replevin as a summary procedure, providing a plaintiff with possession before any hearing on the merits of the case, has been restricted in response to constitutional concerns. See "Survey of Consumer Protection Issues," infra pp. 777–778.

In what circumstances, then, might a buyer prefer to seek replevin rather than the equitable remedy of specific performance? The paucity of cases arising under § 2–716(3) may itself be an answer to the question. See Putnam Ranches, Inc. v. Corkle, 189 Neb. 533, 203 N.W.2d 502 (1973) (replevin for possession of 30 Holstein milk cows; "[t]he evidence was insufficient to support a finding that any cow had been identified to the contract.")

————

Suppose that by the time it was discovered that Rose was not in fact barren, there had been a general increase in prices; the market price even of a "beef creature" such as Rose had been assumed to be was now $100. Would judgment for the buyer then be justified?

West's Ann.Cal.Civ.Code § 1692 provides:

> When a contract has been rescinded in whole or in part, any party to the contract may seek relief based upon such rescission by bringing an action to recover any money or thing owing to him * * * as a consequence of such rescission or for any other relief to which he may be entitled under the circumstances * * *.

> If in an action or proceeding a party seeks relief based upon rescission, the court may require the party to whom such relief is granted to make any compensation to the other which justice may require and may otherwise in its judgment adjust the equities between the parties.

————

LENAWEE COUNTY BOARD OF HEALTH v. MESSLERLY, 417 Mich. 17, 331 N.W.2d 203 (1982). Buyer agreed to purchase an apartment house. The contract provided that "[p]urchaser has examined this property and agrees to accept same in its present condition." Unknown to both Buyer and Seller, the sewage system was inadequate and it was not economically feasible to meet the requirements of the county sanitation code; after execution of the contract, the Board of Health obtained an injunction forbidding occupancy of the premises. The lower court granted rescission to the Buyer, concluding that the "mutual mistake" of the parties "went to a basic, as opposed to a collateral, element of the contract"; held, reversed:

"[Buyer] and [Seller] both mistakenly believed that the property which was the subject of their land contract would generate income as rental property. The fact that it could not be used for human habitation deprived the property of its income-earning potential and rendered it less valuable. [T]his mistake, while directly and dramatically affecting the property's value, cannot accurately be characterized as collateral because it also affects the very essence of the consideration. 'The thing sold and bought [income generating rental property] had in fact no existence.' Sherwood v. Walker, 66 Mich. 568, 33 N.W. 919 (1887).

"We find that the inexact and confusing distinction between contractual mistakes running to value and those touching the substance of the consideration serves only as an impediment to a clear and helpful analysis for the equitable resolution of cases in which mistake is alleged and proven. Accordingly, the [holding] of *Sherwood* with respect to the material or collateral nature of a mistake [is] limited to the facts of [the case].

"Instead, we think the better-reasoned approach is a case-by-case analysis whereby rescission is indicated when the mistaken belief relates to a basic assumption of the parties upon which the contract is made, and which materially affects the agreed performance of the parties. Restatement, Second, Contracts § 152. Rescission is not available, however, to relieve a party who has assumed the risk of loss in connection with the mistake. * * * If the 'as is' clause is to have any meaning at all, it must be interpreted to refer to those defects which were unknown at the time that the contract was executed. Thus, the parties themselves assigned the risk of loss to [the Buyer.]"

The Court indicated that if this "risk-of-loss analysis" had been applied in *Sherwood v. Walker*, "the result might have been different."

WEST COAST AIRLINES, INC. v. MINER'S AIRCRAFT & ENGINE SERVICE, INC., 66 Wash.2d 513, 403 P.2d 833 (1965). West Coast purchased two aircraft engines worth approximately $3500 each and sealed them in large metal storage containers. In the course of its operations West Coast accumulated scrap metal which it sold to junk dealers. The two sealed cans containing the engines were inadvertently included among empty cans sold at 2¢ per pound to Junk Traders. Junk Traders began to cut the cans into scrap and then discovered the engines inside. Shortly thereafter, Miner visited the Junk Traders yard and noticed the engines; knowing they were valuable and that they had originally belonged to West Coast, he nevertheless advised Junk Traders that the engines were of no use to anyone and were worth only scrap metal prices. Miner then purchased the two engines for $125. West Coast filed an action in replevin against Miner seeking the return of the engines; the trial court entered judgment for West Coast (Junk Traders was also given a judgment of $175 against West Coast). Held, affirmed:

"[T]he law of 'mutual mistake' is not applicable. The parties never made a contract for the sale of the engines. Thus, there was no contractual mistake, mutual or otherwise. * * *

"The 'cans' must be distinguished from their contents. West Coast intended to sell 'cans' and Junk Traders intended to buy them. Their title passed to Junk Traders. However, neither party was aware of the contents. Neither the vendor nor the vendee intended that title to the engines would pass with the 'cans'. * * *

"There was no meeting of the minds, no contract and thus no sale of the engines. Title to the two engines remained in West Coast."

WOOD v. BOYNTON, 64 Wis. 265, 25 N.W. 42 (1885). Plaintiff had found a small stone "the nature and value of which she was ignorant," and took it to the defendant, who was a jeweler. She told him "that I had been told it was a topaz, and he said it might be." Plaintiff then sold the stone to defendant for $1. Later it was discovered that the stone was really an uncut diamond, worth around $700, and plaintiff brought suit to recover it. Defendant testified that "at the time he bought this stone he had never seen an uncut diamond; * * * he had no idea this was a diamond, and it never entered his brain at the time." The court directed the jury to find a verdict for the defendant; held, affirmed:

"There is no pretense of any mistake as to the identify of the thing sold. It was produced by the plaintiff and exhibited to the vendee before the sale was made, and the thing sold was delivered to the vendee when the purchase price was paid. * * * When the sale was made the value of the thing sold was open to the investigation of both parties, neither knew its intrinsic value, and * * * both supposed that the price paid was adequate. * * * We can find nothing in the evidence from which it could be justly inferred that [the defendant], at the time he offered the plaintiff one dollar for the stone, had any knowledge of the real value of the stone, or that he entertained even a belief that the stone was a diamond. It cannot, therefore, be said that there was a suppression of knowledge on the part of the defendant as to the value of the stone which a court of equity might seize upon to avoid the sale."

KOWALKE v. MILWAUKEE ELECTRIC RAILWAY & LIGHT CO., 103 Wis. 472, 79 N.W. 762 (1899). Plaintiff was injured in jumping from defendant's streetcar in an emergency. On discovering a slight uterine hemorrhage defendant's physician suggested that she be examined for pregnancy, but plaintiff refused to submit to such an examination, "stating that she was sure * * * that nothing of the sort existed." Plaintiff later signed a full release of all claims against defendant. After suffering a miscarriage, plaintiff brought suit for damages for personal injury. The trial court found that at the time the release was signed both plaintiff and defendant's physician believed she was not pregnant and that her injury was slight; it set aside the release and entered judgment on a jury verdict for $2900. Held, reversed:

"Where a party enters into a contract, ignorant of a fact, but meaning to waive all inquiry into it, or waives an investigation after his attention has been called to it, he is not in mistake, in the legal sense.

These limitations are predicated upon common experience, that, if people contract under such circumstances, they usually intend to abide the resolution either way of the known uncertainty, and have insisted on and received consideration for taking that chance. * * *

"[The plaintiff] necessarily knew that the question of her condition was one of uncertainty."

J. SEARLE, INTENTIONALITY 155, 157 (1983):

Suppose as I go into my office, I suddenly discover a huge chasm on the other side of the door. My efforts to enter my office would certainly be frustrated and that is a failure to achieve the conditions of satisfaction of an Intentional state. But the reason for the failure has to do with a breakdown in my Background presuppositions. It is not that I have always had a belief—conscious or unconscious—that there would be no chasms on the other side of my door, or even that I always believed that my floor was 'normal'; rather, the set of habits, practices, and preintentional assumptions that I make about my office when I intentionally attempt to enter it have failed in this case, and for that reason my intention is frustrated. * * *

[S]ince the only vocabulary we have available is the vocabulary of first-order mental states, when we do reflect on the Background, the temptation is to represent its elements on the model of other mental phenomena * * * Eating lunch in a restaurant, I am surprised when I lift my mug of beer by its near weightlessness. Inspection reveals that the thick mug is not glass but plastic. We would naturally say I *believed* that the mug was made of glass, and I *expected* it to be heavy. But that is wrong. In the sense in which I really do believe without ever having explicitly thought about it that interest rates will go down and I really do expect a break in the current heat wave, I had no such expectations and beliefs about the mug; I simply acted.

G. TREITEL, THE LAW OF CONTRACT 218 (7th ed. 1987).*

A thing has many qualities. A car may be black, old, fast and so forth. For any particular purpose one or more of these qualities may be uppermost in the minds of the persons dealing with the thing. Some particular quality may be so important to them that they actually use it to *identify* the thing. If the thing lacks that quality, it is suggested that the parties have made a fundamental mistake, even though they have not mistaken one thing for another, or made a mistake as to the existence of the thing. The matter may be tested by imagining that one can ask the parties, immediately after they made the contract, what its subject-matter was. If, in spite of the mistake, they would give the right answer the contract is valid at law. * * *

* Reprinted by permission, Sweet & Maxwell Limited.

[Professor Treitel then proceeds to discuss two English cases. In Nicholson & Venn v. Smith-Marriott, 177 L.T.R. (n.s.) 189 (K.B.1947), the defendants auctioned off linen tablecloths and napkins "with the crest and arms of Charles I and which were the authentic property of that monarch." On the faith of that description the buyer bought the lot for £787 10s., but the linen turned out to be only Georgian and worth £105. In Scott v. Coulson, [1903] 2 Ch. 249, plaintiffs agreed to sell to defendants an insurance policy on the life of a man named Alfred Timothy Death. At the time of the contract both plaintiffs and defendants believed that Death was alive; the contract price was "determined by reference to, and was slightly in excess of, the surrender value of the policy." Death, however, was dead.]

In Nicholson & Venn v. Smith-Marriott they might have said, rightly, "We are contracting about antique table linen," in which case the contract would be valid; or they might have said, wrongly, "We are contracting about a Carolean relic," in which case the contract would be void. ＊ ＊ ＊

In Scott v. Coulson the subject-matter of the contract would no doubt have been described as "an insurance policy" so that the contract ought to have been valid at law. ＊ ＊ ＊

RESTATEMENT, SECOND, CONTRACTS § 152:

Illustration:

6. A pays B, an insurance company, $100,000 for an annuity contract under which B agrees to make quarterly payments to C, who is 50 years old, in a fixed amount for the rest of C's life. A and B believe that C is in good health and has a normal life expectancy, but in fact C is dead. The contract is voidable by A.

RESTATEMENT, SECOND, CONTRACTS § 154:

Illustration:

3. The facts being otherwise as stated in Illustration 6 to § 152, C is not dead but is afflicted with an incurable fatal disease and cannot live more than a year. The contract is not voidable by A, because the court will allocate to A the risk of the mistake.

———

GRIFFITH v. BRYMER, 19 T.L.R. 434 (K.B.1903). The Coronation procession of Edward VII was scheduled to take place on June 26, 1902. At 11 a.m. on June 24, the plaintiff entered into an agreement with the defendant's agents to take a room at 8, St. James's Street, for the purpose of viewing the procession; plaintiff gave his check for £100. "It was admitted that the decision to operate on the King, which rendered the procession impossible, had been reached at about 10 a.m. that morning. But neither party was aware of this fact when the agreement was entered into and the cheque given; and it was contended for the plaintiff that, as both parties were under a misconception with regard to the existing state of facts about which they were contracting, the plaintiff was entitled to the return of his money." The court held that the agreement was "void" and that the plaintiff was entitled to recover his £100:

"The agreement was made on the supposition by both parties that nothing had happened which made performance impossible. This was a missupposition of the state of facts which went to the whole root of the matter."

The Cancelled Coronation

During the month of June, Edward VII had cancelled a number of official engagements, giving rise to the circulation of "disquieting rumors" concerning his health; on Saturday June 21 his Private Secretary found it necessary to announce that there was "not a word of truth in the reports." Until Monday the 23rd, "no one doubted that the Coronation would take place as arranged." (The Times, June 25, 1902, p. 10.) There was however a worsening of the King's symptoms on Monday evening, and at 10 a.m. Tuesday the King's doctors agreed on a diagnosis of "perityphlitis" (we would now say "appendicitis.") A public announcement that an operation would be necessary was made at 11:15 a.m., and the operation was performed that afternoon.

The Times found it "impossible to estimate the loss and the inconvenience caused by this calamitous turn of events, the waste of time, of energy, of trouble, and of money that it implies, the intensity of the disappointment that it will create among all classes." A large number of private rooms along the route of the procession had been rented for the occasion, and a large number of tickets sold for seats on reviewing stands and for a Naval Review scheduled for June 28. Some sellers offered a refund of all or a portion of the money which had been paid in advance; one announced that while they were under no legal obligation to do so, "he thought personally stand-holders should deal with the public as generously as they could without landing themselves in the Bankruptcy Court." (The Times, June 26, 1902, p. 3; July 1, 1902, p. 8.) Some sellers were insured against the cancellation of the procession; doubt was expressed, however, whether they could collect if they returned money to their customers without being required to do so by the terms of their contracts. (The Times, July 3, 1902, p. 8; July 4, 1902, p. 8.)

The King eventually recovered and the Coronation procession, somewhat truncated and with considerably diminished splendor, took place on August 9.

PILOT LIFE INSURANCE CO. v. CUDD, 208 S.C. 6, 36 S.E.2d 860 (1945). In 1936 Pilot Life issued an insurance policy on the life of

Lewis Cudd; defendant (his aunt and adoptive mother) was named as beneficiary. Cudd served as a cook in the Merchant Marine and in November 1942 sailed from Ceylon. In January 1943 Cudd's wife was informed by the Navy that his vessel was overdue and that Cudd was missing and "presumed lost" as a result of enemy action. The Maritime War Emergency Board issued a "Certificate of Presumptive Death." This information was given to Pilot Life, which paid defendant the face value of the policy. However, in August the Coast Guard informed Cudd's wife that he was being held as a prisoner of war in Japan. At the time of trial Cudd was alive and back in the United States. On defendant's refusal to refund the money paid, Pilot brought suit. Defendant argued that "there was no mutual mistake but rather a mistake or error of judgment on the part of the insurer," and that "settlement was made under the realization of an uncertainty and that the settlement was a compromise of a doubtful liability." A directed verdict for plaintiff was affirmed: "To follow [defendant's] line of argument would be to allow the beneficiary to be enriched to the amount of $1,013.36 for which the essential prerequisite was the death of the insured when in fact he is still alive."

————

METROPOLITAN LIFE INSURANCE CO. v. KASE, 718 F.2d 306 (9th Cir.1983). Kase suffered a severe eye injury while working as a rigger at a naval shipyard. An ophthalmologist concluded that "there is no possibility of useful vision being restored" to his right eye; "in my opinion the loss is irrecoverable." A group disability policy issued by Metropolitan provided for a lump sum payment if an employee suffered "Total and Irrecoverable Loss of Sight of One Eye." Metropolitan accepted the doctor's report and paid Kase the appropriate amount. Three years later, "for reasons that neither party can explain," sight returned to Kase's right eye. When Metropolitan learned of the apparent miracle, it demanded return of its payment, and Kase refused. The trial court granted summary judgment for Metropolitan; held, reversed: "In recent years, the remarkable progress of medical science has upset many a doctor's opinion that was valid when given. * * * If, after an accident that causes an irreparable or irrecoverable loss, a new technique or treatment is devised that makes the injury reparable or recoverable, must the injured party repay the insurance money that he has received? We think not."

————

Releases of Personal Injury Claims

When settling a personal injury claim, a defendant or his insurer will usually insist on a release from the plaintiff of any claim that he may have, both for injuries known at the time and for those that will only become apparent in the future. For example:

"[The plaintiff acknowledges] that injuries * * * may not now be fully known and may be more numerous and more serious than now believed. * * * [This release] includes all injuries which are unknown * * * and includes all consequences of such injuries which may hereafter develop as well as consequences now developed. This settlement is intended to be final, the undersigned taking his or her chances that the injuries may prove to be more serious than now believed."

Attempts to avoid a release based on interpretation of the document's language—based on the argument that the release did not include within its scope the plaintiff's particular injury—are often made by plaintiffs and are occasionally successful. See, e.g., Rensink v. Wallenfang, 8 Wis.2d 206, 99 N.W.2d 196 (1959) (wife and husband were injured in automobile accident; wife's release of "all claims of any kind or character which I have or might have against [defendant] * * * whether developed or undeveloped, resulting or to result from accident" held not to cover her claim for wrongful death of husband who died subsequent to release). However, such attempts can usually be checkmated by competent drafting.

Where the plaintiff had been under a serious misapprehension when he signed the release as to the nature or extent of his injuries, there is naturally pressure on a court simply to ignore the drafting and to set aside the release on the ground of "mutual mistake." Even the language quoted above, for example, was not enough to save a release where both parties "had proceeded on the basis" that the plaintiff had suffered a "temporary, though painful" strain for which he had received only a "modest settlement," but where he was later diagnosed as suffering from a ruptured disc. Taylor v. Chesapeake & Ohio Railway Co., 518 F.2d 536 (1975). See also Williams v. Glash, 789 S.W.2d 261 (Tex.1990). In this case the plaintiff had been in an automobile accident; the cost of repairs to her car was estimated at $889.46 but "there were no observable injuries" to the plaintiff herself. A check for $889.46 was sent by the insurance company and deposited; on the back was language making the payment "in full settlement of all claims for damages to property and for bodily injury whether known or unknown." The plaintiff was later diagnosed as having "temporomandibular joint syndrome" and sued for this injury. The court held that it was improper to grant summary judgment for the defendant, remarking that "whether the parties to a release intended to cover an unknown injury cannot always be determined exclusively by reference to the language of the release itself. It may require consideration of the conduct of the parties and the information available to them at the time of signing." Three dissenters protested that the court had "render[ed] useless most releases. How is one to buy peace and settle a claim? If the release here can be avoided, then no release buys peace until the statute of limitations has run."

Cf. Rabin, A Proposed Black–Letter Rule Concerning Mistaken Assumptions in Bargain Transactions, 45 Tex.L.Rev. 1273, 1294–95

(1967): "[I]f one suffering personal injuries in an accident signs a release, he may sign it in the mistaken impression that his injuries are minor. If he knows that the full extent of his injuries are unknown one might assume that he has knowingly assumed this risk and cannot therefore complain if his injuries later prove more serious. Nevertheless social conditions may require that even a knowing assumption of risk may not be given effect since it may be necessary or desirable to protect this class of people from their own folly, or to erect certain safeguards around the signing of such releases."

———

McNAMARA CONSTRUCTION OF MANITOBA, LTD. v. UNITED STATES, 509 F.2d 1166, 206 Ct.Cl. (1975). By a fixed-price contract, McNamara undertook to construct a canal lock and related structures at Sault Ste. Marie for the Army Corps of Engineers. McNamara was plagued throughout the performance of the contract by "unusually severe labor problems—strikes, delays and harassment"—which resulted in additional labor costs; it sought to recover those additional costs "on a theory of reformation of contract due to an alleged mutual mistake of fact." McNamara argued that "neither the contractor nor the [Engineering] Corps was aware of or could possibly have anticipated the unreasonble and uncooperative attitude and conduct of the labor unions." Held, "[p]laintiff's claim must fail":

"There was, simply, no mutual mistake of fact by the parties of the type for which judicial relief may be given. Both parties, at the time of executing the contract, were fully aware of the potential for labor difficulties. * * * [W]e could take judicial notice of the risk of strikes and other labor problems inherent in the vast majority of construction contracts. This is a fact of modern commercial life. Neither the contractor nor the Government could be presumed ignorant of this risk. * * *"

The plaintiff had relied heavily on National Presto Industries v. United States, 338 F.2d 99, 167 Ct.Cl 749 (1964):

"In that case the contractor had agreed to produce 105-mm. shells by a new experimental method. Prior to contract, the parties had mutually agreed after discussion that the shells could be produced without the use of turning equipment. This belief proved incorrect. We held that the unanticipated need for turning equipment was a mutual mistake of fact. We also held that plaintiff should not assume the entire risk, because the parties were engaged in a 'joint enterprise' in which the Government was just as interested in the 'perfection of the new process' as in the end product. We further noted that because of the Government's interest in perfecting the process, it received a direct benefit from the costs expended in determining that turning machines were required. * * * Based on the peculiar facts of the case, we awarded the contractor one-half of the unanticipated cost."

However, the court noted that the result in *National Presto* "was reached on the unique facts there presented." In the present case, "[t]he Government received no benefit from the additional cost of the labor strikes and expressed no willingness to assume such costs. * * * McNamara's contract was a fixed-price agreement to build a lock, and defendant got only what it contracted for in that contract."

"However sympathetic we may be to plaintiff's hardship, we can find no basis for plaintiff's recovery as a matter of law or in equity through contract reformation. We cannot assume that had it known these increased labor costs were inevitable Congress would have agreed to pay for them. We cannot base an award by judgment upon speculation or inference as to congressional attitudes."

Judge Skelton wrote a lengthy dissenting opinion, detailing the "irresponsible conduct and outrageous misbehavior" and the "disruptive, arbitrary and capricious acts" of labor at the site, and arguing that the fixed price agreed on in the contract included only "an amount that the contractor would have to pay in performing the contract for responsible labor based on prevailing rates in the area." He urged that the contract be reformed to "require the parties to share equally the increased costs resulting from the unavailability of responsible labor in the project area."

SMITH v. ZIMBALIST, 2 Cal.App.2d 324, 38 P.2d 170 (1934), hearing denied by Supreme Court of California, 1935. Plaintiff, aged 86, was a collector of rare violins. He was visited at his home by defendant, "a violinist of great prominence, internationally known, and himself the owner and collector of rare and old violins made by the old masters," who asked to see plaintiff's collection. In the course of his visit defendant picked up two violins, calling one a "Stradivarius" and another a "Guarnerius," and asked plaintiff what he would take for them. Plaintiff replied that he would sell both violins for $8000, and the parties agreed that defendant would pay $2000 immediately and the balance of $6000 later. A "bill of sale" signed by plaintiff "certifie[d] that I have on this date sold to Mr. Efrem Zimbalist one Joseph Guarnerius violin and one Stradivarius violin dated 1717 * * *." Plaintiff later brought suit to recover the unpaid balance of the purchase price. The trial court found that at the time of the sale each party believed the violins were genuine, but that there was a preponderance of evidence to the effect that both were imitations worth not more than $300. Held, judgment for defendant affirmed; "the strict rule of *caveat emptor* may not be applied to the facts of the instant case. * * *"

"[T]he parties to the proposed contract are not bound where it appears that in its essence each of them is honestly mistaken or in error with reference to the identity of the subject-matter of such contract. In other words, in such circumstances, no enforceable sale has taken place. But if it may be said that a sale, with a voidable condition attached, was the outcome of the transaction in the instant case, * * * from a consideration of the language employed by the parties in each of the documents that was exchanged between them * * *, together with the general conduct of the parties, and particularly the acquiescence by plaintiff in the declaration made by defendant regarding each of the violins and by whom it was made,—it becomes apparent that, in law, a warranty was given by plaintiff that one of the violins was a Guarnerius and that the other was a Stradivarius."

"Mistake" and "Breach of Warranty" as Alternative Theories

(1) As a practical matter, might it make any difference to the defendant whether the court rules in his favor on grounds of "mutual mistake" or on grounds of "breach of warranty"?   See p. 50 supra.

(2) Zimbalist himself appears to have been something of an expert on the subject of old and valuable violins.   And he apparently had "a passion for bargains, and for collecting things, and for gambling," The New Yorker, Dec. 5, 1931, at 24.   If the court were convinced that Zimbalist had formed his own opinion as to the identity of these violins, and that he did not rely on Smith's judgment, might this affect the conclusion that there had been a breach of warranty?

This question was raised in Overstreet v. Norden Laboratories, Inc., supra p. 43.   See also Harlingdon & Leinster Enterprises Ltd. v. Christopher Hull Fine Art Ltd., [1990] 1 All E.R. 737 (C.A.1989) (invoice incorrectly described painting as by a particular artist; held, judgment for seller affirmed; buyers "relied on their own assessment"; "this may be powerful evidence that the parties did not contemplate that the authenticity of the description should constitute a term of the contract, in other words, that they contemplated that the purchaser would be buying the goods *as they were* ").

Cf. UCC § 2–313, Comments 3, 7, 8.   Do these comments indicate that the issue under § 2–313 is not whether the buyer has "relied" on the seller in entering the contract, but whether, under proper standards of interpretation, the buyer's understanding that the warranty is part of the deal can be imposed on the seller?   See Cipollone v. Liggett Group, Inc., 893 F.2d 541 (3d Cir.1990) (suit against manufacturer based on cigarette advertisements):

"[A] plaintiff effectuates the 'basis of the bargain' requirement of [§ 2–313] by proving that she read, heard, saw or knew of the advertisement containing the fact or promise. * * * [O]nce the buyer has become aware of the affirmation of fact or promise, the statements are presumed to be part of the 'basis of the bargain' unless the defendant, by 'clear affirmative proof,' shows that the buyer knew that the affirmation of fact or promise was untrue. * * * If the defendant proves that the buyer did not believe in the warranty, the plaintiff should then be given the opportunity to show that the buyer nonetheless relied on the warranty. It is possible to disbelieve, but still rely on, the existence of a warranty. In this sense, the buyer can 'buy' a lawsuit."

(3) See also N.Y. Arts & Cult. Aff. § 13.01 (McKinney 1984):

Any provision in any other law to the contrary notwithstanding: 1. Whenever an art merchant, in selling or exchanging a work of fine art, furnishes to the buyer of such work who is not an art merchant, a written instrument which, in describing the work, identifies it with any author or authorship, such description (i) shall be presumed to be part of the basis of the bargain and (ii) shall create an express warranty of the authenticity of such authorship as of the date of such sale or exchange. Such warranty shall not be negated or limited because the seller in the written instrument did not use formal words such as "warrant" or "guarantee" or because he did not have a specific intention or authorization to make a warranty or because any statement relevant to authorship is, or purports to be, or is capable of being merely the seller's opinion.

––––––––

SUMMIT TIMBER CO. v. UNITED STATES, 677 F.2d 852, 230 Ct.Cl. 434 (1982). The Forest Service offered for sale government-owned timber within a national forest and plaintiff, as the high bidder, agreed to purchase, cut and remove this timber from two clear-cutting areas. The Forest Service purported to mark on the ground the boundaries of these areas but in doing so, used a "false corner" as a reference point and marked "false blaze lines," so that a certain portion of plaintiff's own timber was included. Plaintiff relied on this purported boundary and paid the Forest Service for some of plaintiff's own timber.

Under the terms of the contract plaintiff could not export the sold timber; its own timber from the area erroneously included in the sale was therefore sold on the domestic market. Plaintiff contended that if it were not for the Service's erroneous marking of the sale area, plaintiff could have sold its timber on the export market at a higher price. The Forest Service paid back what it had erroneously collected for timber from the plaintiff's own land but rejected the rest of plaintiff's claim, and plaintiff successfully brought suit for damages for breach of contract. Defendant argued that plaintiff was not entitled to relief because the parties had made a "mutual mistake of fact," but the court was not persuaded:

"In a very real sense, both parties to a contract which contains a misrepresentation can, absent unusual circumstances, be described as having a mutual 'state of mind that is not in accord with the facts'. Restatement of the Law of Contracts, § 471, comment h (1932).
*   *   *

"The precise problem here is not that the contract was at variance with the intent of the parties to it, but that a material, and witting, representation contained in that contract and reasonably relied upon by plaintiff was erroneous. Although neither defendant nor plaintiff realized that the contract embodied that misrepresentation until long after it had been performed, that fact does not transform a claim to damages for breach by misrepresentation into one for purely equitable relief for mutual mistake."

———

HINSON v. JEFFERSON, 287 N.C. 422, 215 S.E.2d 102 (1975). Defendants conveyed to plaintiff a lot on which she planned to build a home. Deed restrictions limited use of the land to residential purposes, and in the absence of a municipal sewage system, a septic tank or on-site sewage disposal system was necessary. Before beginning to build, plaintiff was informed by the County Health Department that no such sewage disposal system could be installed because of severe drainage problems (the lot was only 2.6 feet above the water level of "Black Swamp"). Correction of the condition would require extensive improvements costing "several hundred thousand dollars." Plaintiff sued for rescission of the contract and for the return of the purchase price. The court of appeals granted relief on the ground that both parties had been mistaken as to a fact "which was of the essence of the agreement."

The Supreme Court affirmed, although it rejected the lower court's rationale. Because of "the uncertainty surrounding the law of mistake," its application to an executed transfer of real property "might well create an unwarranted instability with respect to North Carolina real estate transactions." The court observed that "many of the mutual mistake cases * * * were in fact embryo implied warranty cases":

> "In recent years the rule of *caveat emptor* has suffered severe inroads in sales of houses to be built or in the course of construction. Today, it appears that a majority of the states imply some form of warranty in the purchase of a new home by a first purchaser from a builder-vendor."

Judgment for plaintiff was based on the seller's breach of "an implied warranty arising out of [the] restrictive covenants," where for reasons "both unknown to and not reasonably discoverable by the grantee before or at the time of conveyance, the property cannot be used by the grantee * * * for the specific purpose to which its use is limited by the restrictive covenants."

———

See UCC §§ 2–314, 2–315.

LAIDLAW v. ORGAN

United States Supreme Court, 1817.
15 U.S. (2 Wheat.) 178, 4 L.Ed. 214.

[Plaintiff entered into a contract to buy 111 hogsheads of tobacco from defendant Laidlaw & Co., a commission merchant in New Orleans.

Defendant later refused to deliver the tobacco and plaintiff obtained a "writ of sequestration" by which the goods were seized pending trial. Evidence was introduced to show that:] on the night of the 18th of February, 1815, Messrs. Livingston, White, and Shepherd brought from the British fleet the news that a treaty of peace had been signed at Ghent by the American and British commissioners, ＊ ＊ ＊ and that Mr. White caused the same to be made public in a handbill on Sunday morning, 8 o'clock, the 19th of February, 1815, and that the brother of Mr. Shepherd, ＊ ＊ ＊ who was interested in one-third of the profits of the purchase set forth in said plaintiff's petition, had, on Sunday morning, the 19th of February, 1815, communicated said news to the plaintiff; that the said plaintiff, on receiving said news, called on Francis Girault, (with whom he had been bargaining for the tobacco mentioned in the petition, the evening previous,) said Francis Girault being one of the said house of trade of Peter Laidlaw & Co., soon after sunrise on the morning of Sunday, the 19th of February, 1815, before he had heard said news. Said Girault asked if there was any news which was calculated to enhance the price or value of the article about to be purchased; and that the said purchase was then and there made, and the bill of parcels annexed to the plaintiff's petition delivered to the plaintiff between 8 and 9 o'clock in the morning of that day; and that in consequence of said news the value of said article had risen from 30 to 50 per cent. ＊ ＊ ＊ [The trial court directed the jury to find for the plaintiff.]

Mr. *C.J. Ingersoll*, for [defendant-appellant]. ＊ ＊ ＊ Suppression of material circumstances within the knowledge of the vendee, and not accessible to the vendor, is equivalent to fraud, and vitiates the contract. ＊ ＊ ＊ The parties treated on an unequal footing, as the one party had received intelligence of the peace of Ghent, at the time of the contract, and the other had not. This news was unexpected, even at Washington, much more at New-Orleans, the recent scene of the most sanguinary operations of the war. In answer to the question, whether there was any news calculated to enhance the price of the article, the vendee was silent. This reserve, when such a question was asked, was equivalent to a false answer, and as much calculated to deceive as the communication of the most fabulous intelligence. Though the plaintiffs in error, after they heard the news of peace, still went on, in ignorance of their legal rights, to complete the contract, equity will protect them. ＊ ＊ ＊

Mr. *Key* contra. ＊ ＊ ＊ The only real question in the cause is, whether the sale was invalid because the vendee did not communicate information which he received precisely as the vendor *might* have got it had he been equally diligent or equally fortunate? And, surely, on this question there can be no doubt. Even if the vendor had been entitled to the disclosure, he waived it by not insisting on an answer to his question; and the silence of the vendee might as well have been interpreted into an *affirmative* as a *negative* answer. But, on principle, he was not bound to disclose. Even admitting that his conduct was unlawful, in *foro conscientiae,* does that prove that it was so in the civil forum? Human laws are imperfect in this respect, and the sphere of morality is more extensive than the limits of civil jurisdiction. The maxim of *caveat emptor* could never have crept into the law, if the province of ethics had been co-extensive with it. There was, in the present case, no circumvention or manoeuvre practised by the vendee, unless rising earlier in the morning, and obtaining by superior diligence and alertness that intelligence by which the price of commodities was regulated, be such. It is a romantic equality that is contended for on the other side. Parties never can be precisely equal in knowledge, either of facts or of the inferences from such facts, and both must concur in order to satisfy the rule contended for. The absence of all authority in England and the United States, both great commercial countries, speaks volumes against the reasonableness and practicability of such a rule.

Mr. *C. J. Ingersoll,* in reply. Though the record may not show that any thing tending to mislead by positive assertion was said by the vendee, in answer to the question proposed by Mr. Girault, yet it is a case of manoeuvre; of mental reservation; of circumvention. The information was monopolized by the messengers from the British fleet, and not imparted to the public at large until it was too late for the vendor to save himself. The rule of law and of ethics is the same. It is not a romantic, but a practical and legal rule of equality and good faith that is proposed to be applied. * * *

Mr. Chief Justice Marshall delivered the opinion of the court.

The question in this case is, whether the intelligence of extrinsic circumstances, which might influence the price of the commodity, and which was exclusively within the knowledge of the vendee, ought to have been communicated by him to the vendor? The court is of opinion that he was not bound to communicate it. It would be difficult to circumscribe the contrary doctrine within proper limits, where the means of intelligence are equally accessible to both parties. But at the same time, each party must take care not to say or do any thing tending to impose upon the other.

The court thinks that the absolute instruction of the judge was erroneous, and that the question, whether any imposition was practised by the vendee upon the vendor ought to have been submitted to the jury. For these reasons the judgment must be reversed, and the cause remanded to the district court of Louisiana, with directions to award a *venire facias de novo.*

Venire de novo awarded.

KRONMAN, MISTAKE, DISCLOSURE, INFORMATION, AND THE LAW OF CONTRACTS
7 J. Legal Stud. 1, 11–14 (1978).*

News of the treaty of Ghent affected the price of tobacco in New Orleans. Price measures the relative value of commodities: information regarding the treaty revealed a new state of affairs in which the value of tobacco—relative to other goods and to tobacco-substitutes in particular—had altered. An alteration of this sort is almost certain to affect the allocation of social resources.[34] If the price of tobacco to suppliers rises, for example, farmers will be encouraged to plant more tobacco and tobacco merchants may be prepared to pay more to get their goods to and from market. In this way, the proportion of society's (limited) resources devoted to the production and transportation of tobacco will be increased. Information revealing a change in circumstances which alters the relative value of a particular commodity will always have some (perhaps unmeasurable) allocative impact. * * *

From a social point of view, it is desirable that information which reveals a change in circumstances affecting the relative value of commodities reach the market as quickly as possible (or put differently, that the time between the change itself and its comprehension and assessment be minimized). If a farmer who would have planted tobacco had he known of the change plants peanuts instead, he will have to choose between either uprooting one crop and substituting another (which may be prohibitively expensive and will in any case be costly), or devoting his land to a nonoptimal use. In either case, both the individual farmer and society as a whole will be worse off than if he had planted tobacco to begin with. The sooner information of the change reaches the farmer, the less likely it is that social resources will be wasted. * * *

Allocative efficiency is promoted by getting information of changed circumstances to the market as quickly as possible. Of course, the information doesn't just "get" there. Like everything else, it is supplied by individuals * * *.

In some cases, the individuals who supply information have obtained it by a deliberate search; in other cases, their information has been acquired casually. A securities analyst, for example, acquires information about a particular corporation in a deliberate fashion—by carefully studying evidence of its economic performance. By contrast, a businessman who acquires a valuable piece of information when he

34. This will not be true in a regime of "pure exchange," that is, in a regime where goods are only exchanged and not produced (the pool of exchanged goods remaining constant). In "the more realistic regime in which production and exchange both take place," however, information of the sort involved in Laidlaw v. Organ will have allocative consequences.

accidentally overhears a conversation on a bus acquires the information casually. * * *

If information has been deliberately acquired * * * and its possessor is denied the benefits of having and using it, he will have an incentive to reduce (or curtail entirely) his production of such information in the future. * * * By being denied the same benefits, one who has casually acquired information will not be discouraged from doing what—for independent reasons—he would have done in any case.

FEIST v. ROESLER, 86 S.W.2d 787 (Tex.Civ.App.1935).   Defendant owned land leased to the Manhattan Oil Company near the town of Rowena.   Plaintiff lived in Rowena; "the families had been friends" for some years.   Plaintiff visited defendant's home 225 miles away "and spent the night with him, at which time defendant told him that he desired to sell the land, provided there was no immediate development for oil in the vicinity."   Two months later plaintiff learned that the oil company had placed a drilling rig on an adjoining tract and had begun to develop it for oil; he then telephoned defendant and offered to buy the land.   Defendant agreed to sell, but refused to carry out the contract when he later learned of the oil development.   In plaintiff's suit for damages, judgment for defendant was affirmed; plaintiff, "whose duty it was to speak under the circumstances, concealed this fact from defendant, thereby inducing him to contract for the sale of the land."

STAMBOVSKY v. ACKLEY, 169 A.D.2d 254, 572 N.Y.S.2d 672 (1991). Buyer, a Wall Street bond trader, agreed to pay $650,000 for the Seller's large Victorian house in Nyack, New York.   After the contract was signed but prior to the closing, Buyer learned that the house had a reputation for being haunted—a reputation apparently encouraged by the Seller, who had publicized in the Reader's Digest and in the local press her close encounters with the spirits inhabiting the house.   The trial court dismissed the Buyer's complaint; held, reversed: "[While] in his pursuit of a legal remedy for fraudulent misrepresentation against the seller, plaintiff hasn't a ghost of a chance, I am nevertheless moved by the spirit of equity to allow the buyer to seek rescission of the contract of sale and recovery of his downpayment."

"Applying the strict rule of caveat emptor to a contract involving a house possessed by poltergeists conjures up visions of a psychic or medium routinely accompanying the structural engineer and Terminix man on an inspection of every home subject to a contract of sale.   It portends that the prudent attorney will establish an escrow account lest the subject of the transaction come back to haunt him and his client. * * * [T]he most meticulous inspection * * * would not reveal the presence of poltergeists at the premises or unearth the property's ghoulish reputation in the community.   Therefore, there is no sound policy reason to deny plaintiff relief for failing to discover a state of affairs which the most prudent purchaser would not be expected to even contemplate. * * *

[Defendant contended that an "as is" clause in the contract barred recovery of the buyer's deposit. The court rejected this argument, noting that the clause "expressly disclaims only representations made with respect to the physical condition of the premises and merely makes general reference to representations concerning 'any other matter or things affecting or relating to the aforesaid premises.' "] "As broad as this language may be, a reasonable interpretation is that its effect is limited to tangible or physical matters and does not extend to paranormal phenomena. Finally, if the language of the contract is to be construed as broadly as defendant urges to encompass the presence of poltergeists in the house, it cannot be said that she has delivered the premises 'vacant' in accordance with her obligation under the provisions of the contract rider."

———

BROWN v. COUNTY OF GENESEE, 872 F.2d 169 (6th Cir.1989). The county had refused to hire the plaintiff as a security guard because of a diabetic condition. The threat of a lawsuit, however, ultimately led to settlement negotiations and to the county's offer of a position. The settlement agreement provided that the plaintiff would be paid at the "C"-step level; her attorney was under the impression that this would be the highest level she could have attained if she had been hired when she originally applied for a job. In reality, the higher-paying "D" grade was the highest level she could have obtained. The county's attorney knew this, and "believed it probable that Plaintiff and her counsel were under the mistaken impression" that the "C" step was the highest, but "felt no obligation" to advise them of their mistake. The trial court found the behavior of the county attorney "unethical" and overturned the settlement. Held, reversed: The plaintiff's mistake resulted from failing to examine public records which were available to all; since there was no misrepresentation or "fraudulent conduct," the defendant "had no duty to advise [plaintiff] of any factual error, whether unknown or suspected."

RESTATEMENT, SECOND, TORTS § 551:

(1) One who fails to disclose to another a fact that he knows may justifiably induce the other to act or refrain from acting in a business transaction is subject to the same liability to the other as though he had represented the nonexistence of the matter that he has failed to disclose, if, but only if, he is under a duty to the other to exercise reasonable care to disclose the matter in question.

(2) One party to a business transaction is under a duty to exercise reasonable care to disclose to the other before the transaction is consummated,

(a) matters known to him that the other is entitled to know because of a fiduciary or other similar relation of trust and confidence between them; and ＊ ＊ ＊

(e) facts basic to the transaction, if he knows that the other is about to enter into it under a mistake as to them, and that the other, because of the relationship between them, the customs of the trade or other objective circumstances, would reasonably expect a disclosure of those facts.

Illustrations:

6. A is a violin expert. He pays a casual visit to B's shop, where second-hand musical instruments are sold. He finds a violin which, by reason of his expert knowledge and experience, he immediately recognizes as a genuine Stradivarius, in good condition and worth at least $50,000. The violin is priced for sale at $100. Without disclosing his information or his identity, A buys the violin from B for $100 A is not liable to B.

8. B has a shop in which he sells second-hand musical instruments. In it he offers for sale for $100 a violin, which he knows to be an imitation Stradivarius and worth at most $50. A enters the shop, looks at the violin and is overheard by B to say to his companion that he is sure that the instrument is a genuine Stradivarius. B says nothing, and A buys the violin for $100. B is not liable to A.

Liability for Misrepresentation

(1) Under § 551 of the Restatement of Torts, a party to a business transaction who breaches a duty to disclose facts to the other party is liable as though he had actually *misrepresented* the facts he failed to disclose. The resulting liability is liability in the traditional tort action of "deceit." In most jurisdictions, where the misrepresentation was fraudulent, the damages awarded the innocent party are those necessary "to give him the benefit of his contract," Restatement, Second, Torts, § 549(2). See, for example, Powell v. Fletcher, 18 N.Y. 451 (Common Pleas 1892). In this case the seller of a violin had made "false and fraudulent" representations that the violin had been made by "Gaspard di Dniffoprugear, celebrated in the sixteenth century for his skill in the construction of such instruments," and that it was worth $1000. The court upheld a jury verdict in favor of the plaintiff, and noted that "the true rule of damages, in actions for deceit, is the difference between the real and the represented value."

The Restatement of Torts also contains a section on "negligent misrepresentation," imposing liability on one who "supplies false information for the guidance of others in their business transactions ＊ ＊ ＊ if he fails to exercise reasonable care or competence in obtaining or communicating the information." Restatement, Second, Torts, § 552.

Damages under § 552 "do not include the benefit of the plaintiff's contract with the defendant," but are limited to the plaintiff's "out-of-pocket" losses: the difference between what he has received and what he has paid, and other "pecuniary loss suffered * * * as a consequence of the recipient's reliance upon the misrepresentation." Section 552B. For one case imposing liability for "negligent misrepresentation" in the process of contract formation, see Giant Food, Inc. v. Ice King, Inc., supra p. 595.

Finally, in some cases the Restatement of Torts imposes liability for "innocent misrepresentation" as well: Where one party in a "sale, rental or exchange transaction" makes a "misrepresentation of a material fact for the purpose of inducing [another party] to act or to refrain from acting in reliance upon it," he is liable to the other "for pecuniary loss caused to him by his justifiable reliance upon the misrepresentation, even though it is not made fraudulently or negligently." Restatement, Second, Torts § 552C. Damages under § 552C are limited to the difference between the value of what the plaintiff has paid and what he has received, excluding not only the benefit of his bargain but consequential loss as well. Comment b. to § 552C notes that the remedy provided by the section "is very similar to that afforded under the law of restitution," although the plaintiff "is permitted to retain what he has received and recover damages, rather than rescind and seek restitution, in which case he must return what he received."

In cases involving the sale of goods, is liability for "innocent misrepresentation" under § 552C distinguishable in any significant way from liability for breach of warranty, supra pp. 43–51? Might it make a difference whether the claim is characterized as one in "contract" or in "tort"? See Hill, Breach of Contract as a Tort, 74 Colum.L. Rev. 40 (1974) ("If the buyer insists on keeping what he obtained under the contract, and sues for damages arising from the breach of what is essentially a term of the contract, it would seem that he is claiming a right under the contract, and that his claim ought to be controlled by contract law").

(2) Under contract law, even in the absence of a warranty that "is the basis of the bargain" a misrepresentation made by one party may at least allow the innocent party to *avoid* the contract. "[B]ecause tort law imposes liability in damages for misrepresentation, while contract law does not, the requirements imposed by contract law are in some instances less stringent." Restatement, Second, Contracts, Chapter 7, Introductory Note. Under tort law a misrepresentation does not give rise to liability in deceit unless it is both fraudulent and material; by contrast, under § 164 of the Restatement of Contracts, a contract is "voidable" if one party's agreement has been "induced by *either a fraudulent or a material misrepresentation* by the other party upon which the recipient is justified in relying." A misrepresentation is considered "fraudulent" if the maker "intends his assertion to induce a party to manifest his assent," and the maker:

"(a) knows or believes that the assertion is not in accord with the facts, or

"(b) does not have the confidence that he states or implies in the truth of the assertion, or

"(c) knows that he does not have the basis that he states or implies for the assertion."

It is considered "material" if "it would be likely to induce a reasonable person to manifest his assent, or if the maker knows that it would be likely to induce the recipient to do so." Restatement, Second, Contracts § 162.

Assume that an applicant for life insurance states falsely that he has never smoked cigarettes. In fact, he had been smoking for the past 13 years and was currently smoking 10 cigarettes a day. If the insurance company had known the true facts it would have issued the insurance policy anyway, but at a higher premium. Shortly after the policy is issued, the insured dies. May the insurance company refuse payment and avoid the contract completely? Even if the insured had in fact died after being hit by a bus? The Third Circuit held "yes" in New York Life Ins. Co. v. Johnson, 923 F.2d 279 (3d Cir.1991). (The trial court had held that in preference to this "draconian" remedy, either the proceeds of the policy should be reduced by the amount by which the insurance company would have increased the premium had it known the applicant's true smoking history, or the face amount of the policy should be reduced to that amount of insurance that could have been bought by the premiums that were in fact paid.)

(3) Under the Restatement of Contracts, as under the law of torts, *nondisclosure* of facts by one party may in some circumstances have the same effect as an actual misrepresentation of the facts. § 161 infra.

RESTATEMENT, SECOND, CONTRACTS § 161:

A person's non-disclosure of a fact known to him is equivalent to an assertion that the fact does not exist in the following cases only:
* * *

(b) where he knows that disclosure of the fact would correct a mistake of the other party as to a basic assumption on which that party is making the contract and if non-disclosure of the fact amounts to a failure to act in good faith and in accordance with reasonable standards of fair dealing. * * *

(d) where the other person is entitled to know the fact because of a relation of trust and confidence between them.

Illustrations:

4. A, seeking to induce B to make a contract to buy land, knows that B does not know that the land has been filled with debris and

covered but does not disclose this to B. B makes the contract. A's non-disclosure is equivalent to an assertion that the land has not been filled with debris and covered, and this assertion is a misrepresentation. Whether the contract is voidable by B is determined by the rule stated in § 164.

7. A, seeking to induce B to make a contract to sell land, knows that B does not know that the land has appreciably increased in value because of a proposed shopping center but does not disclose this to B. B makes the contract. Since B's mistake is not one as to a basic assumption A's non-disclosure is not equivalent to an assertion that the value of the land has not appreciably increased * * * The contract is not voidable by B.

RESTATEMENT OF RESTITUTION § 12 (1937):

Illustrations:

8. A, looking at cheap jewelry in a store which sells both very cheap and expensive jewelry, discovers what he at once recognizes as being a valuable jewel worth not less than $100 which he correctly believes to have been placed there by mistake. He asks the clerk for the jewel and gives 10c. for it. The clerk puts the 10c. in the cash drawer and hands the jewel to A. The shopkeeper is entitled to restitution because the shopkeeper did not, as A knew, intend to bargain except with reference to cheap jewelry.

9. A enters a second-hand bookstore where, among books offered for sale at one dollar each, he discovers a rare book having, as A knows, a market value of not less than $50. He hands this to the proprietor with one dollar. The proprietor, reading the name of the book and the price tag, keeps the dollar and hands the book to A. The bookdealer is not entitled to restitution since there was no mistake as to the identity of the book and both parties intended to bargain with reference to the ability of each to value the book.

HELENE CURTIS INDUSTRIES, INC. v. UNITED STATES, 312 F.2d 774, 160 Ct.Cl. 437 (1963). In 1951 plaintiff contracted with the Army to supply large quantities of a disinfectant powder to be used by troops in the field. Army specifications provided that the disinfectant was to be a "uniformly mixed powder or granular material" composed of chlormelamine and other ingredients. Chlormelamine was then a new and patented chemical whose properties were not widely known; the disinfectant based on it had never been mass produced. Plaintiff had assumed in preparing its bid that the disinfectant could be produced by simply mixing chlormelamine with the other ingredients without any grinding of the chlormelamine particles; after it began production, however, it discovered that simple mixing would not suffice and that it was necessary to grind the chlormelamine in order to meet the Army's solubility standard.

Plaintiff brought suit for the additional costs it had incurred in the production of the disinfectant. The court held that the Government's conduct amounted to a breach of contract:

"[T]he circumstances here gave rise to a duty to share information. The disinfectant was novel and had never been mass-produced; the Government had sponsored the research and knew much more about the product than the bidders did or could; it knew, in particular, that the main ingredient, chlormelamine, was a recent invention, uncertain in reaction, and requiring extreme care in handling; it also knew that the more costly process of grinding would be necessary to meet the requirements of the specification, but that in their understandable ignorance the bidders would consider simple mixing adequate; and the urgency for the disinfectant was such that potential contractors could not expend much time learning about it before bidding. In this situation the Government, possessing vital information which it was aware the bidders needed but would not have, could not properly let them flounder on their own. Although it is not a fiduciary toward its contractors, the Government—where the balance of knowledge is so clearly on its side—can no more betray a contractor into a ruinous course of action by silence than by the written or spoken word.

"On similar grounds, we hold the specification for the disinfectant to have been misleading with respect to grinding. This was not merely a specification for an end-product, without any implications at all as to method of manufacture. To reasonable bidders it erroneously implied, in its context, that grinding would not be necessary to make the desired item; and in the circumstances defendant should have known that this would be the inference. Specifications so susceptible of a misleading reading (or implication) subject the defendant to answer to a contractor who has actually been misled to his injury."

RESTATEMENT, SECOND, CONTRACTS § 159:

Illustration:

4. A, seeking to induce B to make a contract to buy an apartment house, tells B that the apartments are all rented to tenants at $200 a month. A knows that the rent of $200 has not been approved by the local rent control authorities and that without this approval it is illegal but does not tell this to B. B makes the contract. A's statement omits matter needed to prevent the implied assertion that the rent is legal, and this assertion is a misrepresentation. * * *

FIRST BAPTIST CHURCH OF MOULTRIE v. BARBER CONTRACTING COMPANY

Court of Appeals of Georgia, 1989.
189 Ga.App. 804, 377 S.E.2d 717.

McMurray, Presiding Judge.

The First Baptist Church of Moultrie, Georgia, invited bids for the construction of a music, education and recreation building. The bids were to be opened on May 15, 1986. They were to be accompanied by a bid bond in the amount of 5 percent of the base bid. The bidding instructions provided, in pertinent part: "Negligence on the part of the bidder in preparing the bid confers no right for the withdrawal of the bid after it has been opened."

Barber Contracting Company ("Barber") submitted a bid for the project in the amount of $1,860,000. The bid provided, in pertinent part: "For and in consideration of the sum of $1.00, the receipt of which is hereby acknowledged, the undersigned agrees that this proposal may not be revoked or withdrawn after the time set for the opening of bids but shall remain open for acceptance for a period of thirty-five (35) days following such time." The bid also provided that if it was accepted within 35 days of the opening of bids, Barber would execute a contract for the construction of the project within 10 days of the acceptance of the bid.

A bid bond in the amount of 5 percent of Barber's bid ($93,000) was issued by The American Insurance Company to cover Barber's bid. With regard to the bid bond, the bid submitted by Barber provided: "If this proposal is accepted within thirty-five (35) days after the date set for the opening of bids and the undersigned [Barber] fails to execute the contract within ten (10) days after written notice of such acceptance * * * the obligation of the bid bond will remain in full force and effect and the money payable thereon shall be paid into the funds of the Owner as liquidated damages for such failure * * *."

The bids were opened by the church on May 15, 1986, as planned. Barber submitted the lowest bid. The second lowest bid, in the amount of $1,975,000, was submitted by H & H Construction and Supply Company, Inc. ("H & H").

Barber's president, Albert W. Barber, was present when the bids were opened, and of course, he was informed that Barber was the low bidder. Members of the church building committee informally asked President Barber if changes could be made in the contract to reduce the amount of the bid. He replied that he was sure such changes could be made.

On May 16, 1986, Albert W. Barber informed the architect for the project, William Frank McCall, Jr., that the amount of the bid was in error—the bid should have been $143,120 higher. In Mr. Barber's words: "[T]he mistake in Barber's bid was caused by an error in totaling the material costs on page 3 of Barber's estimate work sheets. The subtotal of the material cost listed on that page is actually $137,990. The total listed on Barber's summary sheet for the material cost subtotal was $19,214. The net error in addition was $118,776. After adding in mark-ups for sales tax (4 percent), overhead and profit (15 percent), and bond procurement costs (.75 percent), the error was compounded to a total of $143,120 * * *." The architect immediately telephoned Billy G. Fallin, co-chairman of the church building committee, and relayed the information which he received from President Barber.

On May 20, 1986, Barber delivered letters to the architect and the church. In the letter to the architect, Barber enclosed copies of its estimate sheets and requested that it be permitted to withdraw its bid. In the letter to the church, Barber stated that it was withdrawing its bid on account of "an error in adding certain estimated material costs." In addition, Barber sought the return of the bid bond from the church.

On May 29, 1986, the church forwarded a construction contract, based upon Barber's bid, to Barber. The contract had been prepared by the architect and executed by the church. The next day, Barber returned the contract to the church without executing it. In so doing, Barber pointed out that its bid had been withdrawn previously.

On July 25, 1986, the church entered into a construction contract for the project with H & H, the second lowest bidder. Through deletions and design changes, the church was able to secure a contract with H & H for $1,919,272.

In the meantime, the church demanded that Barber and The American Insurance Company pay it $93,000 pursuant to the bid bond. The demand was refused.

On May 26, 1987, the church brought suit against Barber and The American Insurance Company seeking to recover the amount of the bid bond. Answering the complaint, defendants denied they were liable to plaintiff.

Thereafter, defendants moved for summary judgment and so did the plaintiff. In support of their summary judgment motions, defendants submitted the affidavit of Albert W. Barber. He averred that in preparing its bid, Barber exercised the level of care ordinarily exercised by contractors submitting sealed bids. In support of its summary judgment motion, the church submitted the affidavit of a building contractor who averred that he would never submit a bid of any magnitude without obtaining assistance in verification and computation.

The trial court denied the summary judgment motions, certified its rulings for immediate review and we granted these interlocutory appeals. *Held:*

The question for decision is whether Barber was entitled to rescind its bid upon discovering that it was based upon a miscalculation or whether Barber should forfeit its bond because it refused to execute the contract following the acceptance of its bid by the church. We hold that Barber was entitled to rescind its bid.

That equity will rescind a contract upon a unilateral mistake is a generally accepted principle. See Corbin on Contracts, § 609 (1960). As it is said: "Where a mistake of one party at the time a contract was made as to a basic assumption on which he made the contract has a material effect on the agreed exchange of performances that is adverse to him, the contract is voidable by him if he does not bear the risk of the mistake ＊ ＊ ＊ and (a) the effect of the mistake is such that enforcement of the contract would be unconscionable, or (b) the other party had reason to know of the mistake or his fault caused the mistake." Restatement, Second, Contracts § 153 (1979).

The following illustration demonstrates the rule: "In response to B's invitation for bids on the construction of a building according to stated specifications, A submits an offer to do the work for $150,000. A believes that this is the total of a column of figures, but he has made an error by inadvertently omitting a $50,000 item, and in fact the total is $200,000. B, having no reason to know of A's mistake, accepts A's bid. If A performs for $150,000, he will sustain a loss of $20,000 instead of making an expected profit of $30,000. If the court determines that enforcement of the contract would be unconscionable, it is voidable by A." Restatement, Second, Contracts § 153 (1979) (Illustration 1).

Corbin explains: "Suppose ＊ ＊ ＊ a bidding contractor makes an offer to supply specified goods or to do specified work for a definitely named price, and that he was caused to name this price by an antecedent error of computation. If, before acceptance, the offeree knows, or has reason to know, that a material error has been made, he is seldom mean enough to accept; and if he does accept, the courts have no difficulty in throwing him out. He is not permitted 'to snap up' such an offer and profit thereby. If, without knowledge of the mistake and before any revocation, he has accepted the offer, it is natural for him to feel a sense of disappointment at not getting a good bargain, when the offeror insists on withdrawal; but a just and reasonable man will not insist upon profiting by the other's mistake. There are now many decisions to the effect that if the error was a substantial one and notice is given before the other party has made such a change of position that he cannot be put substantially in status quo, the bargain is voidable and rescission will be decreed." Corbin on Contracts, § 609 (1960).

Georgia law is no different. It provides for rescission and cancellation "upon the ground of mistake of fact material to the contract of one party only." OCGA § 23–2–31. The mistake must be an "unintentional act, omission, or error arising from ignorance, surprise, imposition, or misplaced confidence." OCGA § 23–2–21(a).* But relief will be granted even in cases of negligence if the opposing party will not be prejudiced. OCGA § 23–2–32.

We can see these principles at work in M.J. McGough Co. v. Jane Lamb Memorial Hosp., 302 F.Supp. 482 (S.D.Iowa 1969). In that case, a bid of $1,957,000 was submitted for a hospital improvement by a

---

* [Section 23–2–21 of the Georgia Code provides:

"(a) A mistake relievable in equity is some unintentional act, omission, or error arising from ignorance, surprise, im-

position, or misplaced confidence. ＊ ＊ ＊

"(c) The power to relieve mistakes shall be exercised with caution; to justify it, the evidence shall be clear, unequivocal, and decisive as to the mistake."—Eds.]

contractor. A bond in the amount of $100,000 was given to secure the contractor's bid. The contractor submitted the lowest bid. After the bids were opened, but before its bid was accepted, the contractor informed the hospital that it erroneously transcribed numbers in computing the bid and that, therefore, it underbid the project by $199,800. Nevertheless, the hospital tried to hold the contractor to its bid. When the contractor refused to execute a contract, the hospital awarded the contract to the next lowest bidder. The contractor and surety sought rescission of the bid and the return of the bond. The hospital sued the contractor and surety for damages. The district court allowed the contractor to rescind. Its decision is noteworthy and illuminating. We quote it at length:

"By the overwhelming weight of authority a contractor may be relieved from a unilateral mistake in his bid by rescission under the proper circumstances. The prerequisites for obtaining such relief are: (1) the mistake is of such consequence that enforcement would be unconscionable; (2) the mistake must relate to the substance of the consideration; (3) the mistake must have occurred regardless of the exercise of ordinary care; (4) it must be possible to place the other party in status quo. It is also generally required that the bidder give prompt notification of the mistake and his intention to withdraw.

"Applying the criteria for rescission for a unilateral mistake to the circumstances in this case, it is clear that [the contractor] and his surety * * * are entitled to equitable relief. The notification of mistake was promptly made, and [the contractor] made every possible effort to explain the circumstances of the mistake to the authorities of [the hospital]. Although [the hospital] argues to the contrary, the Court finds that notification of the mistake was received before acceptance of the bid. The mere opening of the bids did not constitute the acceptance of the lowest bid. * * * Furthermore, it is generally held that acceptance prior to notification does not bar the right to equitable relief from a mistake in the bid. * * *

"The mistake here was a simple clerical error. To allow [the hospital] to take advantage of this mistake would be unconscionable. * * * Furthermore, [the hospital] has suffered no actual damage by the withdrawal of the bid of [the contractor]. The Hospital has lost only what it sought to gain by taking advantage of [the contractor's] mistake. Equitable considerations will not allow the recovery of the loss of bargain in this situation." M.J. McGough Co. v. Jane Lamb Memorial Hosp., 302 F.Supp. 482, 485, 486, supra.

In the case sub judice, Barber, the contractor, promptly notified the plaintiff that a mistake was made in calculating the amount of the bid. The plaintiff had actual knowledge of the mistake before it forwarded a contract to Barber. The mistake was a "simple clerical error." It did not amount to negligence preventing equitable relief. Furthermore, it was a mistake which was material to the contract—it went to the substance of the consideration. (The mistake amounted to approximately 7 percent of the bid.) To allow the plaintiff to take advantage of the mistake would not be just.

The contention is made that Barber's miscalculation constituted negligence sufficient to prevent relief in equity. * * *

Relief in equity "may be granted even in cases of negligence by the complainant if it appears that the other party has not been prejudiced thereby." OCGA § 23–2–32(b). It cannot be said that plaintiff was prejudiced by Barber's rescission. After all, plaintiff "lost only what it sought to gain by taking advantage of [the contractor's] mistake."

The plaintiff takes the position that rescission is improper since, pursuant to the language set forth in the bid, Barber agreed not to withdraw the bid for a period of 35 days after the bids were opened. It also asserts that the language set forth in the bidding instructions prohibited Barber from withdrawing the bid on the ground of "negligence." We disagree. "[P]rovisions such as these have been considered many times in similar cases, and have never been held effective when equitable considerations dictate otherwise."

The trial court properly denied the plaintiff's (the church's) motion for summary judgment. It erred in denying defendants' (Barber's and The American Insurance Company's) motions for summary judgment.

Bidding Errors in Construction Contracts

(1) In M.F. Kemper Construction Co. v. City of Los Angeles, 37 Cal. 2d 696, 235 P.2d 7 (1951), a contractor was preparing a bid to do certain construction work for the city. Three employees calculated the costs of different parts of the work, and the figures arrived at by each man were transcribed from his "work sheet" to a "final accumulation sheet" from which the total amount of the bid was taken. "[T]he men were exhausted after working long hours under pressure," and as a consequence one item estimated on a work sheet in the amount of $301,769 was inadvertently omitted from the accumulation sheet and was overlooked in computing the bid. The contractor was the low bidder at $780,305; several hours after the bids were opened, the company discovered its error and immediately notified the city of the mistake.

The Supreme Court of California found that it "would be unjust and unfair to permit the city to take advantage of the company's mistake," and the contractor was permitted to cancel its bid. The court drew a distinction "between mere mechanical or clerical errors made in tabulating or transcribing figures and errors of judgment, as, for example, underestimating the cost of labor or materials." It suggested that relief for mistaken contractors should be limited to the former category, explaining that "[w]here a person is denied relief because of an error in judgment, the agreement which is enforced is the one he intended to make, whereas if he is denied relief from a clerical error, he is forced to perform an agreement he had no intention of making."

How, then, should a court treat a contractor who failed to include in his bid the cost of certain equipment because of an error in interpreting the engineer's specifications? Was this a "mere" "clerical" error, or an "error in judgment"? See Balaban–Gordon Co., Inc. v. Brighton Sewer District No. 2, 41 A.D.2d 246, 342 N.Y.S.2d 435 (1973) (error "did not pertain to an evaluation of risks or estimation of requirements or costs by the bidder and the effect of the mistake was verifiable in much the same way" as a clerical or arithmetical error). In James Baird Co. v. Gimbel Brothers, Inc., supra p. 469, was the defendant held to the agreement it "intended to make"?

(2) Suppose that the amount of the error in Barber's bid had been only $110,000. In such a case, Barber would still have been the original low bidder even if it had not made any "mistake." Should this fact affect in any way the form of the relief granted to Barber? Should Barber be allowed to reform the agreement so that it could perform at the "real" price it had intended? See Department of Transportation v. Ronlee, Inc., 518 So.2d 1326 (Fla.App.1987) (no; "the remedy is rescission of the contract").

(3) Cf. Four Nines Gold, Inc., supra p. 484.

———

GENERAL ELECTRIC SUPPLY CORP. v. REPUBLIC CONSTRUCTION CORP., 201 Or. 690, 272 P.2d 201 (1954). Before being awarded a contract to build an apartment house, defendant received from plaintiff a bid of $126,531 for the installation of kitchen equipment in the apartments. After further negotiations and certain changes in the plans and specifications, plaintiff finally offered to furnish the equipment for $93,503, and a contract was entered into at that price. The kitchen equipment was delivered and installed. Some months later plaintiff discovered that a mathematical error in totalling its bid had been made in the amount of $30,150, and demanded rescission of the contract. "Since the equipment went into the building, which placed it beyond the power of defendant to return, the [trial] court, in addition to rescinding the contract, entered judgment against defendants for the amount of the discrepancy." Held, reversed. Plaintiff had argued that the disparity between its preliminary and its final bids was so great as to put the defendant on notice of the mistake, but the court was unwilling to draw this inference: "How the plaintiff could charge defendant with notice of the mistake from such circumstances, when it claims it did not know of the same, is beyond comprehension." A number of plaintiff's employees had checked the figures, and "with so many fingers in the pie someone should have plucked out the plum. Therefore, if defendant should have had knowledge of the mistake a fortiori plaintiff should have had knowledge."

———

REED'S PHOTO MART v. MONARCH MARKING SYSTEM CO., 475
S.W.2d 356 (Tex.Civ.App.1971), reversed, 485 S.W.2d 905 (Tex.1972).
Defendant, a small photography store, placed an order with the plaintiff for five different kinds of specially manufactured pricing labels; as
to four a quantity of "2M" was specified while the fifth, the subject of
the suit, called for "4MM" labels. Shipment was to be by parcel post.
Defendant had intended to order 4000 labels and his use of "4MM" was
a mistake. When to his surprise a truck drove up to unload "a
truckload of cartons" containing 4 million labels, he refused to accept
delivery or to pay for the labels.

Plaintiff brought suit for the price of the 4 million labels. A jury
finding was to the effect that in the label industry "MM" was used and
understood to mean one million. Defendant requested the court to
submit an issue to the jury inquiring whether, at the time defendant's
order was received, plaintiff ought to have known that the order was an
error. The Court of Civil Appeals held that such an issue should have
been submitted to the jury. It noted that defendant had been doing
business with plaintiff since the 1950's and "had never ordered any
quantity remotely near the figure of one million"; plaintiff's sales
representative had testified that he had never received an order as
large as 4 million for one catalogue number. The Texas Supreme Court
reversed:

" [R]elief from a unilateral mistake depends upon the ability of the
party mistaken to put the other party into the same situation as he was
prior to the transaction in question. * * * We have in this case a
fully executed contract on the part of Monarch and the record is devoid
of proof of any effort on the part of Reed's to restore Monarch to the
status quo even to the extent that circumstances would permit."

UPTON–ON–SEVERN RURAL DISTRICT
COUNCIL v. POWELL

Court of Appeal, England, 1942.
1 All E.R. 220.

LORD GREENE, M.R.: The appellant lives at Strensham, and in Nov.,
1939, a fire broke out in his Dutch barn; he thereupon telephoned to
the police inspector at the Upton police office and told him that there
was a fire and asked for the fire brigade to be sent. The police
inspector telephoned a garage near to the fire station at Upton, which
itself had no telephone, the Upton brigade was informed and immediately went to the fire, where it remained for a long time engaged in
putting it out. It so happens that, although the appellant's farm is in
the Upton police district, it is not in the Upton fire district. It is in the
Pershore fire district, and the appellant was entitled to have the
services of the Pershore fire brigade without payment. The Upton fire
brigade, on the other hand, was entitled to go to a fire outside its area
and, if it did so, quite apart from its statutory rights, it could make a
contract that it would be entitled to repayment of its expenses.

The sole question here is whether or not any contract was made by which the Upton fire brigade rendered services on an implied promise to pay for them made by or on behalf of the appellant. It appears that some 6 hours after the arrival of the Upton fire brigade, the officer of the Pershore brigade arrived on the scene, but without his brigade; he pointed out to the Upton officer that it was a Pershore fire, and not an Upton fire, but the Upton fire brigade continued rendering services until the next day when the Pershore fire brigade arrived and took over. In the view that I take in this case, what happened in relation to the arrival of the Pershore officer and his conversation with the Upton officer and the subsequent arrival of the Pershore fire brigade has nothing whatever to do with the issue which we have to decide. The county court judge held that the appellant when he rang up the police inspector, asked for "the fire brigade" to be sent. He also held that the inspector summoned the local Upton fire brigade, which was perfectly natural, and that he took the order as being one for the fire brigade with which he was connected. It appears that neither the appellant, nor the police officer, nor the Upton fire brigade, until it was so informed by the Pershore officer, knew that the appellant's farm was, in fact, not in the Upton area, but was in the Pershore area. The county court judge then goes on to find that the inspector passed on the order and sent his fire brigade, and that was the fire brigade, I have no doubt, which the appellant expected. The county court judge said:

> The defendant did not know that if he sent for the Pershore fire brigade what advantage he would have obtained. In my view, there is no escape from the legal liability the defendant has incurred. I think he gave the order for the fire brigade he wanted, and he got it.

[Counsel for defendant argued that " [i]n the circumstances of the present case, the judge was quite wrong in inferring that any contract had been entered into. There is no evidence of *animus contrahendi* in anybody at all. The fire brigade went intending to render a gratuitous service. It was only when it was discovered that the fire was in another area that it was decided that a charge should be made."]

Now ＊ ＊ ＊ it is said that, as the defendant did not know what fire brigade area he was in, what he really wanted was to get the fire brigade of his area, whatever it might be. It does not seem to me that there is any justification for attacking the finding of the judge on that basis. What the defendant wanted was somebody to put out his fire, and put it out as quickly as possible, and in ringing up the Upton police he must have intended that the inspector at Upton would get the Upton fire brigade; that is the brigade which he would naturally ask for when he rang up Upton. Even apart from that, it seems to me quite sufficient if the Upton inspector reasonably so construed the request made to him, and, indeed, I do not see what other construction the inspector could have put upon that request. It follows, therefore, that on any view the appellant must be treated as having asked for the

Upton fire brigade. That request having been made to the Upton fire brigade by a person who was asking for its services, does it prevent there being a contractual relationship merely because the Upton fire brigade, which responds to that request and renders the services, thinks, at the time it starts out and for a considerable time afterwards, that the farm in question is in its area, as the officer in charge appears to have thought? In my opinion, that can make no difference. The real truth of the matter is that the appellant wanted the services of Upton; he asked for the services of Upton—that is the request that he made—and Upton, in response to that request, provided those services. He cannot afterwards turn round and say: "Although I wanted Upton, although I did not concern myself when I asked for Upton as to whether I was entitled to get free services, or whether I would have to pay for them, nevertheless, when it turns out that Upton can demand payment, I am not going to pay them, because Upton were under the erroneous impression that they were rendering gratuitous services in their own area." That, it seems to me, would be quite wrong on principle. In my opinion, the county court judge's finding cannot be assailed and the appeal must be dismissed with costs.

LUXMOORE, L.J.: I agree.

GODDARD, L.J.: I agree.

––––––––

(1) Has anyone been "unjustly enriched" by the actions of the Upton fire brigade? Who? The defendant? Or Pershore? See County of Carleton v. City of Ottawa, 52 D.L.R.2d 220 (Sup.Ct. Canada 1965). In this case the County had for some time been responsible for the care of an institutionalized indigent woman who lived in the County, and it paid for her maintenance in a home. The town where the woman resided was later annexed by the City of Ottawa, which took over responsibility for the County's welfare cases; however, "through an oversight" the County continued to pay for the woman's care until the error was discovered. The court held that the County was entitled to recover from the City the payments it had made.

(2) Four orphan children were admitted to an orphanage, which cared for and educated them. The by-laws of the institution authorized it to enter into contracts for compensation with the guardians of orphans who had property, but in this case the orphanage assumed that the children were penniless. Only later did the orphanage discover that the children did in fact have some money, including a Government pension which came to them by virtue of their father's Army service. May it then recover for its services? See St. Joseph's Orphan Society v. Wolpert, 80 Ky. 86 (1882); cf. In re Agnew's Will, 132 Misc. 466, 230 N.Y.S. 519 (Surr.1928).

OPERA COMPANY OF BOSTON, INC. v. WOLF TRAP FOUNDATION FOR THE PERFORMING ARTS

United States Court of Appeals, Fourth Circuit, 1987.
817 F.2d 1094.

DONALD RUSSELL, CIRCUIT JUDGE: * * *

I.

The parties in this suit are The Opera Company of Boston, Inc., an operatic organization recognized both nationally and internationally. The defendant The Wolf Trap Foundation for the Performing Arts is an organization for the advancement of the performing arts [that] sponsors at the Filene Center in the Wolf Trap Park operatic performances and similar artistic programs. The Filene Center is located in the Wolf Trap National Park and is a part of the various facilities maintained and controlled by the National Park Service. It consists of a main stage tower, an auditorium and an open lawn. The main stage tower contains the stage, dressing rooms and space for the scenery and electrical effects. In front of the tower is a covered auditorium seating approximately 3,500 people. Beyond this is the uncovered lawn providing seating for an additional 3,000 people. The Park provides parking space. This parking area is separated from the Center itself. A number of pathways leading from the parking area to the Filene Center are available. The distance of the parking area from the Center varies from approximately 300 to 700 yards. Ordinarily, when there are any night performances at the Center, the roads in the park, the parking area and the pathways to the Center are lighted for the guidance of patrons at performances at the Center.

This suit between the parties arises under a contract between the plaintiff The Opera Company of Boston, Inc. (Opera Company) and the defendant The Wolf Trap Foundation for the Performing Arts (Wolf Trap) by which the Opera Company for its part agreed to give four "fully staged orchestrally accompanied [operatic] performances to the normally recognized standards" of the Opera Company on the nights of June 12, 13, 14, and 15, 1980 at the Filene Center. For this the Opera Company was to be paid by Wolf Trap $272,000 payable under a schedule providing for payment of $20,000 at the signing of the contract and a further $40,000 on April 1, 1980, with the balance payable in four equal installments before the rise of the curtain on each performance. Wolf Trap, in turn, for its part under the contract was obliged to make the above payments and also to furnish the place of performance including an undertaking "to provide lighting equipment as shall be specified by the Opera Company of Boston's lighting designer."

Both parties to the contract performed apparently all their obligations under the contract through the operatic performance on June 14. These performances had been fully sold as well as had the remaining performance on June 15. During this final day, the weather was described as hot and humid, with rain throughout the day. Sometime between 6:00 and 6:30 p.m. a severe thunderstorm arose causing an electrical power outage. As a result all electrical service in the Park, in its roadways, parking area, pathways and auditorium were out. Conferences were had among representatives of the Park Service and that of Wolf Trap. The public utility advised that it would be at least after eleven o'clock before any service by it could be resumed in the Park and that it was likely power might not be available before morning. Various alternatives for supplying power were considered but none was regarded as relieving the situation. Already some 3,000 people were in the Park for the performance; 3,500 more were expected before 8:00 p.m. when the performance was to begin. The Park Service recommended the immediate cancellation of the performance and advised Wolf Trap if the performance were not cancelled, it disclaimed any responsibility for the safety of the people who were to attend as well as those who were to perform. It was the Park Service's view that a prompt cancellation was necessary to enable the parties to leave the park safely and to prevent others from coming. Wolf Trap agreed and the performance was cancelled. While some of these discussions were being carried on a representative of the Opera Company was present but she took no part in the decision to cancel, though she voiced no objection. Since the performance was cancelled, Wolf Trap failed to make the final payment under the contract to the Opera Company. Five years after the cancellation, the Opera Company filed this suit to recover the balance due under the contract. Wolf Trap defended on the ground that performance by it of its obligation under the contract was excused under the doctrine of impossibility of performance. The basis for this defense was that the final performance by the Opera Company for which payment was claimed had been cancelled because a performance was impracticable as a result of the power outage.

II.

The district judge * * * found as a fact "that the Opera Company was there [at the Park] and was ready to go forward with the performance," but that "the only reason the performance did not go on was the fact that there wasn't adequate lighting." As he read the contract Wolf Trap was obligated to provide sufficient lighting "for the performance to go on," and that power outages were "reasonably foreseeable," as there had been some outages in the past and while "none had affected a performance prior to this occasion," it was "readily foreseeable that a power outage could affect a performance." He, therefore, held Wolf Trap had not made out its defense of impossibility of performance and granted judgment for the plaintiff.

The single question on appeal is whether this dismissal of Wolf Trap's defense of impossibility of performance was proper. The resolution of this issue requires a review of the doctrine of impossibility. We proceed first to that review.

III.

The doctrine of impossibility of performance as an excuse or defense for a breach of contract was for long smothered under a declared commitment to the principle of sanctity of contracts. This rationale for constrained application of the doctrine was expressed by the United States Supreme Court in Dermott v. Jones (2 Wall.), 69 U.S. 1, 8, 17 L.Ed. 762 (1864): ＊ ＊ ＊

> [The law] requires parties to do what they have agreed to do. If unexpected impediments lie in the way, and a loss must ensue, it leaves the loss where the contract places it. If the parties have made no provision for a dispensation, the rule of law gives none.
> ＊ ＊ ＊

The growth of commercial activity in the nineteenth century, however, made this rigidity of the doctrine of impossibility both "economically and socially unworkable," and in Taylor v. Caldwell ＊ the English courts recognized these changed conditions and, relying largely on civil law precedents, relaxed the constraints on the doctrine by the principle of sanctity of contracts ＊ ＊ ＊. It based such relaxation on the theory of an implied condition arising without express condition in the contract itself. In stating this new rule on impossibility of performance as a defense to a breach of contract suit, the court said:

> The principle seems to us to be that in contracts in which the performance depends on the continued existence of a given person or thing, a condition is implied that the impossibility arising from the perishing of the person or thing shall excuse the performance. ＊ ＊ ＊ [T]hat excuse is by law implied, because from the nature of the contract it is apparent that the parties contracted on the basis of the continued existence of the particular person or chattel.

＊ ＊ ＊ As we have indicated, *Taylor v. Caldwell,* the United States Supreme Court cases and the Virginia cases all relied in their statement of the doctrine on an implied, though unstated, condition in the contract. Increasingly, though, commentators and text writers were uncomfortable with the implied condition rationale for the new doctrine of impossibility of performance. ＊ ＊ ＊ 18 Williston on *Contracts,* § 1937, p. 33 (3d ed. Jaeger 1978) is ＊ ＊ ＊ forceful in its rejection of the implied condition theory:

> Any qualification of the promise is based on the unfairness or unreasonableness of giving it the absolute force which its words clearly state. In other words, because the court thinks it fair to qualify the promise, it does so and quite rightly; but clearness of thought would be increased if it were plainly recognized that the qualification of the promise or the defense to it is not based on any expression of intention by the parties.

＊ [See the note following the principal case.]

Moreover, in line with the "tendency of the law * * * towards an enlargement," modern authorities also abandoned any absolute definition of impossibility and, following the example of the Uniform Commercial Code,[7] have adopted impracticability or commercial impracticability as synonomous with impossibility in the application of the doctrine of impossibility of performance as an excuse for breach of contract.   Matter of Westinghouse Elec. Corp., Etc., 517 F.Supp. 440, 451 (E.D.Va.1981).[8] * * *

In its Introductory Note to Chapter 11 on Impossibility of Performance (pp. 309–10) Restatement (Second) on Contracts said:

Even where the obligor has not limited his obligation by agreement, a court may grant him relief.   An extraordinary circumstance may make performance so vitally different from what was reasonably to be expected as to alter the essential nature of that performance.   In such a case the court must determine whether justice requires a departure from the general rule that the obligor bear the risk that the contract may become more burdensome or less desirable.

This is but another way of declaring * * * that essentially the doctrine is an equitable one to be applied when fair and just.

The modern doctrine of impossibility or impracticability, deduced from these authorities, has been formulated in § 265, pp. 334–35 of the Restatement (Second) of Contracts in these words:

Where, after a contract is made, a party's principal purpose is substantially frustrated without his fault by the occurrence of an event the non-occurrence of which was a basic assumption on which the contract was made, his remaining duties to render performance are discharged, unless the language or the circumstances indicate the contrary. * * *

Probably, though, the fullest statement of the modern doctrine of impossibility or impracticability is that of Judge Wright, speaking for the Court, in Transatlantic Financing Corporation v. United States [**]:

The doctrine of impossibility of performance has gradually been freed from the earlier fictional and unrealistic strictures of such tests as the "implied term" and the parties' "contemplation." It is now recognized that "A thing is impossible in legal contemplation when it is not practicable; and a thing is impracticable when it can only be done at an excessive and unreasonable cost."   The

---

7. See UCC § 2–615(a) (1978).

8. Impossibility or impracticability may not be "subjective" but must be "objective," and the difference between the two concepts has been summarized in the phrases "the thing cannot be done" (this being objective impossibility or impracticability) and "I cannot do it" (classified as subjective impossibility or impracticability).   It is often necessary in this connection to consider when the performance, as stipulated, is objectively impossible, whether there is an alternative form of performance and, if there is, if it is not "so excessive [in cost of performance] as to make performance extremely impracticable," there is no objective impracticability so far as the obligor is concerned.

** [See the note following the principal case.]

doctrine ultimately represents the ever-shifting line, drawn by courts hopefully responsive to commercial practices and mores, at which the community's interest in having contracts enforced according to their terms is outweighed by the commercial senselessness of requiring performance. ✳ ✳ ✳

Manifestly the first fact to be established in making out this modern defense of impossibility or impracticability of performance is the existence of an "occurrence of an event, the non-occurrence of which was a basic assumption on which the contract was made." ✳ ✳ ✳ The occurrence, as *Transatlantic* puts it, must be unexpected but it does not necessarily have to have been unforeseeable. A requirement of absolute non-foreseeability as a condition to the application of the doctrine would be so logically inconsistent that in effect it would nullify the doctrine. This was recognized by Judge Clark in L.N. Jackson & Co. v. Royal Norwegian Government, 177 F.2d 694, 699 (2d Cir.1949), where he said that to require an absolute absence of foreseeability would, if accepted,

> practically destroy the doctrine of supervening impossibility, notwithstanding its present wide and apparently growing popularity. Certainly the death of a promisor, the burning of a ship, the requisitioning of a merchant marine on the outbreak of a war could, and perhaps should, be foreseen. In fact, the more common expression of the rule appears to be in terms which tend to state the burden the other way, e.g., that "the duty of the promisor is discharged, unless a contrary intention has been manifested" or "in the absence of circumstances showing either a contrary intention or contributing fault on the part of the person subject to the duty." ✳ ✳ ✳

In Comment c, § 261 of the Restatement (Second) on Contracts the drafters follow this reasoning in the requirement of foreseeability in the application of the doctrine. They said:

> If the supervening event was not reasonably foreseeable when the contract was made, the party claiming discharge can hardly be expected to have provided against its occurrence. However, if it was reasonably foreseeable, or even foreseen, the opposite conclusion does not necessarily follow. Factors such as the practical difficulty of reaching agreement on the myriad of conceivable terms of a complex agreement may excuse a failure to deal with improbable contingencies.

These statements ✳ ✳ ✳ were accepted and repeated by Judge Wright in the decision in *Transatlantic:*

> Foreseeability or even recognition of a risk does not necessarily prove its allocation. Parties to a contract are not always able to provide for all the possibilities of which they are aware, sometimes because they cannot agree, often simply because they are too busy. Moreover, that some abnormal risk was contemplated is probative

but does not necessarily establish an allocation of the risk of the contingency which actually occurs.

As the Court in Mishara Const. Co., Inc. v. Transit–Mixed Concrete Corp., [365 Mass. 122, 310 N.E.2d 363 (1974)] remarked this question is much broader than mere foreseeability and is, "Was the contingency which developed one which the parties could reasonably be thought to have foreseen as a *real possibility* which could affect performance?" * * * After all, as Williston has said, practically any occurrence can be foreseen but whether the foreseeability is sufficient to render unacceptable the defense of impossibility is "one of degree" of the foreseeability and whether the non-occurrence of the event was sufficiently unlikely or unreasonable to constitute a reason for refusing to apply the doctrine. And that is the rule which we think accords with modern reasoning of the doctrine as an equitable doctrine and is the one we approve.

The second fact to be determined in the proposed application of the doctrine is that the frustration of performance was substantial. To satisfy this requirement "[t]he frustration must be so severe that it is not fairly to be regarded as within the risks [the obligor] assumed under the contract." Restatement, Second, Contracts § 265, Comment a. And, finally, the defendant asserting the defense must establish that performance was impossible as that term has been defined in the refinements of the doctrine.

In summary, then, a party relying on the defense of impossibility of performance must establish (1) the unexpected occurrence of an intervening act, (2) such occurrence was of such a character that its non-occurrence was a basic assumption of the agreement of the parties, and (3) that occurrence made performance impracticable. When all those facts are established the defense is made out.

IV.

Applying the law as above stated to the facts of this case, we conclude, as did the district judge, that the existence of electric power was necessary for the satisfactory performance by the Opera Company on the night of June 15. While he seems to conclude that public safety was the main consideration on which the cancellation was based, he found that the power outage was the reason assigned for cancellation, and in that connection he found it to be questionable that "a generator could [have been] set up to provide additional light for the theater itself (when power from the utility company became unavailable) and still provide adequate light for the people who had to move backstage." Such findings meet the requirement of Restatement (Second) on Contracts § 263 for an event, the "non-occurrence of which was a basic assumption on which the contract was made" and accordingly satisfies the definition of an impracticability which will relieve the obligor of his duty to perform as declared in § 265 of such Restatement. * * * The district judge, however, refused to sustain the defense because he held that if the contingency that occurred was one that could have been foreseen reliance on the doctrine of impossibility as a defense to a breach of contract suit is absolutely barred. As we have said, this is not the modern rule and he found that the power outage was foreseeable. In this the district judge erred.

Foreseeability, as we have said, is at best but one fact to be considered in resolving first how likely the occurrence of the event in question was and, second whether its occurrence, based on past experience, was of such reasonable likelihood that the obligor should not merely foresee the risk but, because of the degree of its likelihood, the obligor should have guarded against it or provided for non-liability against the risk. This is a question to be resolved by the trial judge after a careful scrutiny of all the facts in the case. The trial judge in this case made no such findings. The cause must be remanded for such findings. In connection with that remand, the parties may be permitted to offer additional evidence on the matters in issue.

* * * [W]hile the lack of power may have interfered with the immediate commencement of the performance, that, as we have seen, was not the basic consideration which motivated the Park Service in pressing for the cancellation of the performance and it must be remembered that it was the Park Service which was the primary advocate of cancellation. There was, it is admitted, auxiliary power available for the stage and perhaps the dressing rooms furnished by the Park as a part of the Park's service. But to have made this auxiliary service operable would have delayed the commencement of the performance until ten or eleven o'clock. The Park Service's concern was for the safety of the thirty-five hundred people already in the Park and the additional three thousand who were due to come into the Park for the performance. The situation confronting the Park Service must be understood: Should the performance be delayed while the auxiliary services *for the Pavillion* were brought into operation? Even when the auxiliary service was brought into operation, it would not have provided lights for the roads and paths in the wooded park. To have sixty-five hundred people stranded in a wooded park during a lightning storm without any lights for a period of hours was a hazard to safety for which the Park Service was understandably unwilling to take the responsibility. * * * It may be that this situation would not have arisen if the Park had had auxiliary power services which, in the event of a power shortage on the part of the public utility, would have provided ample lighting for the roads and paths in the Park. But can it fairly be said that this was the obligation of Wolf Trap, the lessee of merely the Pavillion area, whatever may have been its obligation for the stage and dressing rooms at the Pavillion itself, or that the failure of Wolf Trap to provide auxiliary lighting for all the roads and paths in the Park was such action on its part as would preclude it from asserting the defense of impossibility of performance *on its part?* We think not.

CONCLUSION

The judgment herein must, therefore, be vacated and the action remanded to the district court to make findings, based on a statement of reasons, whether the possible foreseeability of the power failure in this case was of that degree of reasonable likelihood as to make improper the assertion by Wolf Trap of the defense of impossibility of performance.

The judgment of the district court is reversed, and the action is remanded with instructions.

VACATED and REMANDED WITH INSTRUCTIONS.

McMILLAN, DISTRICT JUDGE, dissenting in part and concurring in part:

* * * Evening opera on an indoor stage obviously requires power and lights. Supplying power and lights was a necessary part of Wolf Trap's undertaking, a cost figured into their charges for the facility.

The financing and the preparation for the delivery of the essential power required nothing esoteric, inspirational, unforeseeable or expensive. * * *

It would have taken only a few seconds to write into the contract a sentence which said, in effect, "If the electric power fails, Wolf Trap will not be responsible for any losses caused by the power failure."

If the parties had agreed to such a provision I would not raise my voice.

They did not so agree.

I do not think we should write for the defendant a defense it did not write for itself.

I would affirm the decision of the trial court.

———

See UCC §§ 2–614, 2–615, 2–616.

———

TAYLOR v. CALDWELL, 3 B. & S. 826, 122 Eng.Rep. 309, 6 R.C. 603 (Q.B.1863). The defendants contracted with the plaintiffs to let them have the use of a music hall for four days for the purpose of giving a series of concerts. Before the concerts were scheduled to begin, the music hall was destroyed by fire. The plaintiffs brought suit for breach of contract, seeking compensation for amounts that they had spent in advertising and preparing for the concerts. The court held for the defendants. Both parties "must have contemplated [the] continuing existence [of the music hall] as the foundation of what was to be done"; "the Music Hall having ceased to exist, without fault of either party, both parties are excused."

———

TRANSATLANTIC FINANCING CORP. v. UNITED STATES, 363 F.2d 312 (D.C.Cir.1966). Transatlantic agreed with the United States to carry a cargo of wheat from an American port to Iran. The agreement was signed in October 1956, in the midst of the international crisis that resulted from Egypt's nationalization of the Suez Canal. Several weeks later the ship sailed on a route that would have taken it through the Canal; within a week, however, Britain and France invaded the Suez Canal Zone and Egypt closed the canal. The ship changed course and went around the Cape of Good Hope. Transatlantic then made a claim against the United States in quantum meruit for the added expense of the longer voyage, which was allegedly $43,972 above the contract price of $305,842. The trial court denied relief; held, affirmed: "While it may be an overstatement to say that increased cost and difficulty of performance never constitute impracticability, to justify relief there must be more of a variation between expected cost and the cost of performing by an available alternative than is present in this case, where the promisor can legitimately be presumed to have accepted some degree of abnormal risk * * *

JOSKOW, COMMERCIAL IMPOSSIBILITY, THE URANIUM MARKET AND THE WESTINGHOUSE CASE

6 J. Legal Stud. 119, 157–158 (1977).*

The foreseeability doctrine appears to raise a number of difficulties. To some extent every occurrence is foreseeable. There is always some probability that a fire will destroy the anticipated source of supply, that a key person will die, that various acts of God—like floods—will occur, that there will be an embargo or war, etc. In an objective sense, virtually nothing is truly unforeseeable to the extent that theoretically every possible state of the world could be enumerated and some probability assigned to its occurrence.

The foreseeability requirement may only make sense if we introduce the concept of "bounded rationality." Following Simon and Williamson, the concept of bounded rationality recognizes that human beings cannot evaluate all possible states of the world or all available information that might affect a particular situation. One way of thinking about the foreseeability doctrine is as delineating the boundary between those contingencies that are reasonably part of the decision-making process and those that are not. This recognizes that most contracts are not complete contingent claims contracts, commonly including only some subset of all possible occurrences as a reasonable basis for decisionmaking and appropriately included either explicitly or implicitly in the terms of the contract.

The foreseeability doctrine is therefore more of a "contemplation" doctrine. What occurrences were or should have been included in the negotiations underlying the contract and what contingencies were not? [84] In recognizing such cognitive realities, the courts effectively enforce the contract only over that set of contingencies that was or should have been part of the decisionmaking process. Such a requirement makes good sense because it recognizes the realities of voluntary exchange. To require performance under contingencies that could not efficiently be part of the decisionmaking process would encourage the costly and difficult enumeration of a large number of contingencies, raising the costs of private exchange.

Under a "contemplation" test we would ask: "Did one of the parties to the contract contemplate or should one of the parties to the contract have contemplated a certain occurrence based on his superior economic ability to do so and make the probability of this occurrence one of the bases on which the terms of the contract (including the price) were negotiated?" If the answer is no, then an additional requirement for excuse has been satisfied, the occurrence not being covered by the contract. If the answer is yes, then the reverse is the case, and we would assume that the risk of the occurrence which has now occurred was covered in the contract.

Under the circumstances it would appear that the "foreseen" interpretation of this requirement would be sufficient. * * * However, a "foreseen, should have foreseen, or reason to know" test appears in principle to have certain advantages. It allows us to ask a normative question: whether one or more of the parties *should* have contemplated such occurrences and made them a basis of the terms of the contract. This stronger interpretation provides an incentive to both parties to carefully evaluate available information about uncertain occurrences involving supply and demand and make this information part of the dickered terms of the contract. * * * This stronger test should encourage more efficient use of available information and help to insure that contingencies are properly reflected in contract terms. This has the effect of not penalizing a shrewd buyer (or, alternatively, rewarding an incompetent seller) who recognizes that the possibility of certain occurrences which should increase the price of the contract even if the seller fails to. In the long run this will serve to eliminate those sellers from the market who do not utilize information about alternative states of the world efficiently, as would occur in a competitive market without transactions costs.

––––––––

JENSON v. HAYNES, 633 S.W.2d 154 (Mo.App.1982). Lessor and Lessees entered into a two-year lease of a 700-acre tract; the rent was to be in semi-annual installments of $22,000. Lessees paid only a portion of the second installment, and Lessor declared the lease forfeited and brought suit to recover the balance due. Lessees claimed that

84. The UCC has this "contemplation" or "reason to know" standard running through it. See for example UCC § 2–715.

their payment "was rendered impossible by the unusual, sudden, violent and extraordinary floods of the East Nishnabotna River, which inundated and covered the said farmland, rendering it impossible to adequately farm the same." Held, summary judgment for Lessor affirmed:

"Even were it to be assumed that inability of defendants to raise crops profitably on the leased land for a season or part of a season of the lease term constitutes impracticability of performance where cash rent is the only consideration due the lessor, the event is readily foreseeable. Crop failures from a multitude of causes, excess moisture or drought, insect infestation to name but a few, are widely experienced and are an inherent risk in any farming operation. The event is a calamity which occurs without the fault of the farmer and is usually dependent on the vagaries of nature. There is no basis to assume that this or any farmland is let on the condition that the lessee produce a successful crop. Indeed, were such a condition to be required, it is doubtful a lease could be negotiated at a rental any tenant would accept, if a lease could be arranged at all.

"Defendants here accepted the risk of crop failure because the lease contract did not provide otherwise."

———

DUNAVANT ENTERPRISES, INC. v. FORD, 294 So.2d 788, 792 (Miss. 1974):

"The rule is that if the parties contract for the purchase and sale of all or a part of a particular crop to be grown in the future from a particular tract or tracts of land and by reason of weather conditions or other forces of nature the seller is unable to plant all or part of the crop or if all or part of the crop fails or is destroyed by conditions beyond the control of the seller, nonperformance to the extent of the failure is excused in the absence of an expressed condition in the contract to the contrary. The reason for this rule is that the parties to the contract for the sale of a crop to be grown in the future are well aware of the fact that weather and other conditions of nature control to a large extent the ability of the seller to grow and harvest the crop contemplated. Therefore, the absence of an express condition in the contract to the contrary, the foregoing rule is an implied condition of the contract."

RESTATEMENT, SECOND, CONTRACTS § 263:

Illustrations:

3. A contracts with B to shingle the roof of B's house. When A has done part of the work, much of the house including the roof is destroyed by fire without his fault, so that he is unable to complete the work. A's duty to shingle the roof is discharged, and A is not liable to B for breach of contract.

4. A contracts with B to build a house for B. When A has done part of the work, much of the structure is destroyed by fire without his fault. A refuses to finish building the house. A's duty to build the house is not discharged, and A is liable to B for breach of contract.

7. A, a farmer, contracts with B in the spring to sell a large quantity of beans to B during the following season. Although the contract does not state where the beans are to be grown, A owns but one tract of land, on which he has in the past raised beans, and both parties understand that the beans will be raised on this tract. A properly plants and cultivates beans on the tract in sufficient quantity to perform the contract, but an extraordinary flood destroys the crop. A delivers no beans to B. A's duty to deliver beans is discharged, and A is not liable to B for breach of contract. Compare * * * Illustration 12 to § 261.

RESTATEMENT, SECOND, CONTRACTS § 261:

Illustration:

12. A, a milkman, and B, a dairy farmer, make a contract under which B is to sell and A to buy all of A's requirements of milk, but not less than 200 quarts a day, for one year. B may deliver milk from any source but expects to deliver milk from his own herd. B's herd is destroyed because of hoof and mouth disease and he fails to deliver any milk. B's duty to deliver milk is not discharged, and B is liable to A for breach of contract.

See UCC §§ 2–615 comment 9; 2–613; 2–509.

BARBAROSSA & SONS, INC. v. ITEN CHEVROLET, INC., 265 N.W.2d 655 (Minn.1978). Barbarossa, a general contractor, sought to purchase a large truck to replace an old, worn-out truck used in its business. It submitted specifications to three dealers for their bids, and in November 1973 ultimately accepted a bid submitted by Iten Chevrolet. Iten then ordered the truck from General Motors. In June 1974 General Motors canceled the order for Barbarossa's truck, allegedly because of shortages caused by suppliers of component parts. Barbarossa purchased a similar International truck elsewhere, and brought suit against Iten for damages. The trial court found Iten in breach of contract; held, affirmed:

"We need not decide whether * * * Iten's performance was made 'impracticable' under [UCC § 2–615] for we find that General Motors' cancellation of this order was not 'a contingency the non-occurrence of which was a basic assumption on which the contract was made.' * * * Under the evidence submitted, the possibility that Iten would be unable to procure the truck from General Motors was clearly a contingency foreseen by the seller before entering the contract. Iten's salesman testified that it was Iten's usual practice to use a standard form order which included an escape clause making the obligation to deliver contingent upon the seller's ability to obtain the vehicle from the manufacturer. The standard order form was not used in this case, however, and no escape clause was included in Iten's offer to Barbarossa, nor was General Motors mentioned as the source of supply. * * *

"[W]e conclude that General Motors' possible cancellation of this order was one of those varieties of foreseeable risks which the parties have tacitly allocated to the seller-promisor by its failure to provide against it in the contract. * * * Iten could have conditioned its offer on its ability to obtain the truck from General Motors. It failed to do so and therefore must be held to its bargained obligation."

SELLAND PONTIAC–GMC v. KING, 384 N.W.2d 490 (Minn.App.1986). In May 1983 Selland agreed to buy four school bus bodies from King. Under the contract, the bodies were to be built on top of chassis provided by Selland; the agreement specified that the bodies would be manufactured by Superior Manufacturing. In reliance on the contract, Selland ordered four bus chassis from General Motors and had them sent to Superior. In July, Superior went into receivership, and the company later went out of business. The bodies were never manufactured. In December, Selland's customer cancelled their order for the school buses, and Selland had to sell the chassis at a loss. In Selland's suit against King for breach of contract, the trial court granted judgment for King. Held, affirmed: "Supply of Superior bus bodies was a basic assumption on which the contract was made. These become impracticable to supply when Superior ceased manufacturing. * * * [B]oth parties testified that they had no knowledge of Superior's questionable financial circumstances when they contracted and King did not expressly assume the risk of Superior's ceasing production."

MINERAL PARK LAND CO. v. HOWARD, 172 Cal. 289, 156 P. 458 (1916). Defendants agreed to take from the plaintiff's land all the earth and gravel needed for the construction of a concrete bridge, and to pay 5¢ per cubic yard. Defendants used 101,000 cubic yards in all, but took from the plaintiff's land only 50,131 cubic yards—all that there was above water level. The trial court found that "[n]o greater quantity could have been taken 'by ordinary means,' or except by the use, at great expense, of a steam dredger," and that "any greater amount could have been taken only at a prohibitive cost, that is, at an expense 10 or 12 times as much as the usual cost per yard." Held, defendants were not liable for failing to take more earth and gravel from the plaintiff:

"The defendants were not binding themselves to take what was not there. And, in determining whether the earth and gravel were 'available,' we must view the conditions in a practical and reasonable way.

Although there was gravel on the land, it was so situated that the defendants could not take it by ordinary means, nor except at a prohibitive cost. To all fair intents then, it was impossible for defendants to take it. * * * We do not mean to intimate that the defendants could excuse themselves by showing the existence of conditions which would make the performance of their obligation more expensive than they had anticipated, or which would entail a loss upon them. But, where the difference in cost is so great as here, and has the effect, as found, of making performance impracticable, the situation is not different from that of a total absence of earth and gravel."

———

ASPHALT INTERNATIONAL, INC. v. ENTERPRISE SHIPPING CORP., S.A., 667 F.2d 261 (2d Cir. 1981). Enterprise leased a tanker to Asphalt; under the charter agreement Enterprise was required to repair and insure the vessel, and to "maintain [it] * * * in good order and condition * * *." Enterprise was absolved from responsibility for "any loss or damage arising or resulting from * * * collision"; it was also provided that "[s]hould the vessel be lost, hire shall cease * * *." While loading cargo, the tanker was rammed by another vessel and sustained extensive damage. Convinced that the cost of repair was prohibitive, Enterprise sold the vessel for scrap. The tanker was 33 years old and its fair market value before the collision was approximately $750,000; the cost of repair was estimated to be $1.5 million. Enterprise collected insurance proceeds amounting to $1,335,000. Asphalt brought suit for breach of contract to recover the profits from voyages it would have made had the tanker been repaired. Held, for Enterprise:

"Surely, imposing the repair obligation on Enterprise sought by Asphalt would require a type of performance essentially different from that for which Asphalt contracted. Indeed, Asphalt's repair request, which would, in effect, require Enterprise to rebuild its virtually demolished vessel, would alter the essential nature of the contract. The contract merely provided for leasing of the vessel to transport asphalt.

"Finally, we cannot agree with the argument advanced by Asphalt that Enterprise may not enjoy the defense of impracticability because it suffered no financial hardship, but rather received a windfall profit of $961,000 by virtue of the insurance proceeds it collected. The doctrine of commercial impracticability focuses on the reasonableness of the expenditure at issue, not upon the ability of a party to pay the commercially unreasonable expense. The existence of insurance coverage in excess of the fair market value of the ship bears no relationship to the controlling issue—the reasonableness of the requested repairs. Insurance coverage is like any other asset—it enhances a party's ability to bear a loss, but is not material to the question whether a party has a duty to bear the loss."

———

The Seller's Duty to Allocate "Fairly and Reasonably"

(1) In July 1988 Seller agreed to sell Buyer 3.2 million pounds of tomato paste; delivery of the paste was to be spread over the following year. Seller had forecast sales of approximately 53 million pounds of paste from the 1988 tomato crop, and it made contracts with growers to supply 170,000 tons of raw tomatoes; it planned to purchase additional tonnage on the spot market in order to acquire sufficient amounts to support its sales forecast. Weather conditions in the Southwest during the summer caused a shortage in the year's crop, and the growers with whom Seller had contracted delivered only 95–100,000 tons of tomatoes. As a result, Seller was able to deliver only 42 million pounds of tomato paste to its customers, and it delivered substantially less than one million pounds to Buyer. This amount was almost as much as Buyer had received from Seller during the previous year; however, while Buyer received only 31% of its original order, other customers of Seller received 85% or even 100% of their orders. In making allocations to its customers Seller considered such factors as customer loyalty and needs, Seller's past relationship with the customer, and its projection of potential future sales to that customer. Is Seller in breach of contract? See Cliffstar Corp. v. Riverbend Products, Inc., 750 F.Supp. 81 (W.D. N.Y.1990).

(2) Professor James White has made a study of allocation practices in the chemical industry at a time of widespread shortages. White found a considerable variation in company practices; most sellers admitted that they devoted more than a pro rata share of their supply to their own internal uses ("We sure as hell are not going to short our own plant"), and in a number of cases admitted also that they made sales to new customers at spot prices (times of shortage were when one "added to his market share"). White concluded that "rules of law cast only a pale light upon the landscape of commercial contract administration, and [that] light is insufficient to hold at bay a variety of wolves and harpies who threaten and beckon to the typical contract administrator." White, Contract Law in Modern Commercial Transactions, An Artifact of Twentieth Century Business Life?, 22 Washburn L.J. 1 (1982).

FLORIDA POWER & LIGHT CO. v. WESTINGHOUSE ELECTRIC CORP., 826 F.2d 239 (4th Cir.1987). In 1966 Westinghouse agreed to supply Florida Power & Light with a "pressurized water reactor"-type nuclear power plant. While Westinghouse was more expert in the field of nuclear energy, the trial court found that Florida was more expert in the drafting of agreements and that it had demonstrated this superior expertise by "out-negotiating" Westinghouse. The contract gave Florida an option either to require Westinghouse to dispose of the spent fuel discharged by the plant's reactors during the first ten years of operation, or to dispose of the fuel itself; Florida chose the first option in

1972. The two plants provided by Westinghouse became operational in 1973 and have since been operated "with considerable savings to Florida and its customers in energy costs." In 1975 Florida called on Westinghouse to comply with its obligation to dispose of the spent fuel, and when Westinghouse failed to do so, "Florida became concerned with the accumulation of spent fuel at the site." It filed suit against Westinghouse seeking specific performance or damages.

Electric utilities planning to operate nuclear power reactors had contemplated from the industry's earliest days that the spent fuel would be reprocessed to recover the remaining quantities of uranium and plutonium, and that the materials recovered would have "significant residual value" once recycled back into fresh reactor fuel. "Reprocessing was firmly accepted by the Government and the utility industry as the approved and proper method of disposing of spent fuel." The Government had given assurances to the nuclear power industry that it would provide reprocessing services for any commercial nuclear plants if commercial reprocessing were not available, and shortly after the Westinghouse contract was signed a number of companies had begun the construction of reprocessing facilities to dispose of spent fuel discharged by nuclear plants. "Reprocessing of spent fuel appeared both practical and available up to 1970." However, by the early 1970's, a "rising crescendo of environmental complaints" began to contest the safety of reprocessing; applications for construction of reprocessing facilities were tied up in "interminable dilatory proceedings." In 1975 the Government abandoned its policy of accepting spent fuel for reprocessing, and in 1977 the President announced that the processing of spent fuel would be "indefinitely deferred." In 1982 Congress provided for the development of permanent storage repositories for nuclear waste as an alternative to reprocessing; under this Act, nuclear power plants were required to enter into agreements with the Government for future removal and storage of the spent fuel. However, no such sites for storage have yet been located; "since 1972 there have been not only no available reprocessing facilities to dispose of spent fuel from the [Florida] plants but also there have been no available alternative off-site storage facilities for such disposal."

On these facts, the court held that "Westinghouse has made out its defense of impossibility of performance":

"It is important to emphasize at the outset that the doctrine of impossibility-impracticability does not depend on nor is it limited in its application by the specific language of the contract. * * * [T]he language of the contract itself is irrelevant in the application of the doctrine, since * * * the doctrine of impossibility or commercial impracticability of performance * * * is 'essentially an equitable defense,' without any basis in the specific language of the contract in question or 'any expression of intention by the parties,' but resting firmly 'on the unfairness [and] unreasonableness of giving [the contract] the absolute force which its words clearly state.' * * *

"[L]ong-term storage [of spent fuel] was not available in 1966 when the contract was executed, was not available when performance by Westinghouse was required under the contract, and is not now available for disposal of spent fuel from commercial nuclear power plants. Reprocessing [was therefore] the only, the 'exclusive,' means for disposing of spent fuel in the contemplation of the parties in 1966 * * *. [I]n 1975, when Florida called upon Westinghouse to dispose of the spent fuel the 'intended' means of disposal did not exist nor was there any reasonable alternative available. Such findings * * * make out a textbook illustration of the circumstances warranting the application of the doctrine of impracticability/impossibility of performance as a valid excuse for breach of a contract. * * *

"Florida's continued insistence on guaranteed fuel costs, for as long a period as possible, together with the extreme importance Westinghouse placed on obtaining the construction contracts, prompted Westinghouse's offer of a guaranteed ten year fuel cycle cost. This, of course, included the cost of uranium and the purchase and disposal of the spent fuel as a part of the fuel cycle. * * * It is difficult to imagine any scenario of negotiations and contracting that would establish more clearly and conclusively that not only Westinghouse but also Florida contemplated and contracted on the 'basic assumption' that the spent fuel would be reprocessed, whether done by Florida or Westinghouse, than that the price to be paid for performance under the contract was based on what the parties assumed to be the cost or profit realized from reprocessing the spent fuel discharged by the plants' reactors. After all, nothing in the contract was more important than the price bargained for. When the bargained-for price was understood to include as an integral part thereof the cost of reprocessing and the profit realized for the sale or use of the products resulting from the reprocessing, such reprocessing must be taken as a basic assumption of the contracting parties. * * *

[The trial court had found that the passage of legislation in 1982 had given Westinghouse "a means whereby it could remove all the fuel and dispose of it in government storage at what is not an impracticable cost."] "We do not, however, regard the promise of storage, as made by the Government under the Act of 1982, to represent a reasonable alternative to [reprocessing]. * * * Had reprocessing been available, Westinghouse would reasonably have realized a profit from disposing of the spent fuel. * * * What is now offered Westinghouse as an alternative is a method of disposal which neither existed nor was even planned or considered by the parties when the contract was executed or when performance was due in 1975. Assuming the storage is finally provided, it would not only fail to yield a profit of some $18,000,000 to $20,000,000 to Westinghouse, as contemplated by the parties when this contract was signed, but would * * * cost Westinghouse at least well over $80,000,000. * * * We know of no case where the use of the alternative not only wiped out the expected profit but resulted in a loss some four or five times greater than the expected profit and that was not found to be so excessive as to justify the application of the impossibility doctrine. ＊ ＊ ＊

[The trial court had also concluded that this extra cost of Government storage would not be "so extreme as to constitute commercial impracticability": It reasoned that Westinghouse's total revenues from its contracts with Florida were $224 million; Westinghouse had already spent $236 million in costs on the contracts, "and hence if it is found liable for the full amounts Florida seeks, its total losses will be just under 50% of contract revenues. While this expense is high, it is not beyond the normal range of risk that a promisor signing a fixed-price contract in a new high-risk field could have expected." However, the Court of Appeals found this method of calculation improper:] "The only thing to be considered is the cost or profit to be realized by Westinghouse if reprocessing had been available compared with the cost of storage as an alternative to that method of disposal of the spent fuel. Under this scenario, a method of performance under which Westinghouse would have netted just less than twenty million dollars is to be compared with an alternative which would have burdened Westinghouse with a loss of well over eighty million dollars. ＊ ＊ ＊ [I]t is obvious that the alleged alternative represents an unreasonable and excessive cost to Westinghouse. ＊ ＊ ＊

"[A]nother reason for concluding that the cost of this promised alternative is too different in character to qualify as damages reasonable in an action for breach of contract and too 'excessive' to [bar the defense of impossibility] is based on the long-established principle stated in Hadley v. Baxendale. ＊ ＊ ＊ [C]osts of long-term storage of the spent fuel were not damages that either party to this contract— either Westinghouse or Florida—had any reason 'to foresee as a probable result of the breach when the contract was made.' ＊ ＊ ＊ Neither party foresaw that reprocessing would be completely unavailable, that the Government's [commitment] to reprocess would be abandoned, and that, after years of waffling, the Government would impose on all nuclear power operators the requirement that they should pay the Government substantial storage fees for the storage of this spent fuel in a facility that at best will only be available so far in the future that by that time these plants will have completed their operating life. This certainly is not what the parties contemplated or intended when this contract was signed. ＊ ＊ ＊

"Accordingly, we hold that Florida is not entitled to recover from Westinghouse the cost of future storage in a Government storage facility, to be hereafter built, for the spent fuel discharged by the nuclear power plants ＊ ＊ ＊ In reaching this conclusion we are aware that in all probability Florida will be permitted to recover its costs from its ratepayers."

————

EASTERN AIR LINES, INC. v. McDONNELL DOUGLAS CORP., 532 F.2d 957 (5th Cir. 1976). McDonnell agreed to manufacture and sell to

Eastern almost 100 jet planes for approximately half a billion dollars. Eastern brought suit for damages alleging that 90 of these planes were delivered a total of 7,426 days late. A jury verdict resulted in a judgment for Eastern for over $24 million. The contract provided:

"EXCUSABLE DELAY

"Seller shall not be responsible nor deemed to be in default on account of delays in performance of this Agreement due to causes beyond Seller's control and not occasioned by its fault or negligence, including but not being limited to civil war, insurrections, strikes, riots, fires, floods, explosions, earthquakes, serious accidents, any act of government, governmental priorities, allocation regulations or orders affecting materials, equipment, facilities or completed aircraft, * * * acts of God or the public enemy, failure of transportation, epidemics, quarantine restrictions, failure of vendors (due to causes similar to those within the scope of this clause) to perform their contracts or labor troubles causing cessation, slow-down, or interruption of work, provided such cause is beyond Seller's control."

"[T]he heart of [McDonnell's] defense" was that the delivery delays were the result of informal Government pressure ('jawboning') on McDonnell and its suppliers, during the escalation of the Vietnam war, to give priority to military projects over civilian production. The trial court had limited the class of 'excusable delays' under the contract to delays resulting from events not 'reasonably foreseeable' when the contract was signed. This was held to be erroneous. The court quoted from Comment 8 to § 2–615 and noted:

"While this provision could have been drafted in less vague terms, we presume that Comment 8 establishes "mercantile sense and reason" as a general standard governing our construction of agreements enlarging upon the protections of § 2–615. As we understand Comment 8, where there is doubt concerning the parties' intention, exemption clauses should not be construed as broadening the excuses available under the Code's impracticability rule. Applying this standard to the excusable delay clause, we cannot, in the absence of evidence to the contrary, hold that McDonnell is exempt from liability for any delay, regardless of its foreseeability, that is due to causes beyond its control. Exculpatory provisions which are phrased merely in general terms have long been construed as excusing only unforeseen events which make performance impracticable. Courts have often held, therefore, that if a promisor desires to broaden the protections available under the excuse doctrine he should provide for the excusing contingencies with particularity and not in general language.

"We realize, of course, that this rule of construction developed in the pre-UCC era when the scope of the impossibility and frustration doctrines was unclear and varied from jurisdiction to jurisdiction. Because of the uncertainty surrounding the law of excuse, parties had good reason to resort to general contract provisions relieving the promisor of liability for breaches caused by events 'beyond his control.' Although the Uniform Commercial Code has ostensibly eliminated the need for such clauses, lawyers, either through an abundance of caution or by force of habit, continue to write them into contract. Thus, even though our interpretation would render the general terms of the excusable delay clause merely duplicative of § 2–615, we will adhere to the established rule of construction because it continues to reflect prevailing commercial practices.

"We reiterate, however, that we are applying only a canon of contract interpretation which generally reflects commercial standards of reasonableness. * * * Even in the absence of detailed wording, trade usage and the circumstances surrounding a particular agreement may indicate that the parties intended to accord the seller an exemption broader than is available under the UCC. * * * While we hold that the provision of the excusable delay clause exempting McDonnell from liability for delays beyond its control should be interpreted as incorporating the Code's commercial impracticability doctrine, we disagree with the trial judge's jury instruction on foreseeability insofar as it implies that the events specifically listed in the excusable delay clause in each contract must have been unforeseeable at the time the agreement was executed. The rationale for the doctrine of impracticability is that the circumstance causing the breach has made performance so vitally different from what was anticipated that the contract cannot reasonably be thought to govern. However, because the purpose of a contract is to place the reasonable risk of performance on the promisor, he is presumed, in the absence of evidence to the contrary, to have agreed to bear any loss occasioned by an event which was foreseeable at the time of contracting. Underlying this presumption is the view that a promisor can protect himself against foreseeable events by means of an express provision in the agreement. Therefore, when the promisor has anticipated a particular event by specifically providing for it in a contract, he should be relieved of liability for the occurrence of such event regardless of whether it was foreseeable. * * * In this case, it is clear that Eastern specifically 'contemplated and voluntarily assumed' the risk that deliveries would be delayed by governmental acts, priorities, regulations or orders."

Finally, it was held that the Government's "informal but nonetheless concerted priorities policy" came within the excusable delay clause, so that "as a matter of law McDonnell is not liable for any delivery delay proximately resulting from the informal procurement program." (The trial court had taken the position that only delays resulting from formal, written government orders were excusable.) The judgment was reversed and the case remanded for a new trial.

———

NORTHERN INDIANA PUBLIC SERVICE COMPANY v. CARBON COUNTY COAL COMPANY

United States Court of Appeals, Seventh Circuit, 1986.
799 F.2d 265.

POSNER, CIRCUIT JUDGE.

These appeals bring before us various facets of a dispute between Northern Indiana Public Service Company (NIPSCO), an electric utility in Indiana, and Carbon County Coal Company, a partnership that until recently owned and operated a coal mine in Wyoming. In 1978 NIPSCO and Carbon County signed a contract whereby Carbon County agreed to sell and NIPSCO to buy approximately 1.5 million tons of coal every year for 20 years, at a price of $24 a ton subject to various provisions for escalation which by 1985 had driven the price up to $44 a ton.

NIPSCO's rates are regulated by the Indiana Public Service Commission. In 1983 NIPSCO requested permission to raise its rates to reflect increased fuel charges. Some customers of NIPSCO opposed the increase on the ground that NIPSCO could reduce its overall costs by buying more electrical power from neighboring utilities for resale to its customers and producing less of its own power. Although the Commission granted the requested increase, it directed NIPSCO, in orders issued in December 1983 and February 1984 (the "economy purchase orders"), to make a good faith effort to find, and wherever possible buy from, utilities that would sell electricity to it at prices lower than its costs of internal generation. The Commission added ominously that "the adverse effects of entering into long-term coal supply contracts which do not allow for renegotiation and are not requirement contracts, is a burden which must rest squarely on the shoulders of NIPSCO management." Actually the contract with Carbon County did provide for renegotiation of the contract price—but one-way renegotiation in favor of Carbon County; the price fixed in the contract (as adjusted from time to time in accordance with the escalator provisions) was a floor. And the contract was indeed not a requirements contract: it specified the exact amount of coal that NIPSCO must take over the 20 years during which the contract was to remain in effect. NIPSCO was eager to have an assured supply of low-sulphur coal and was therefore willing to guarantee both price and quantity.

Unfortunately for NIPSCO, as things turned out it was indeed able to buy electricity at prices below the costs of generating electricity from coal bought under the contract with Carbon County; and because of the "economy purchase orders" * * * NIPSCO could not expect to be allowed by the Public Service Commission to recover in its electrical rates the costs of buying coal from Carbon County. NIPSCO therefore decided to stop accepting coal deliveries from Carbon County, [and] brought this diversity suit against Carbon County in a federal district court in Indiana, seeking a declaration that [its] * * * performance was excused or suspended—either under the contract's *force majeure* clause or under the doctrines of frustration or impossibility—by reason of the economy purchase orders.

[Carbon County counterclaimed for breach of contract. Trial resulted in a jury verdict for Carbon County of $181 million.] The judge entered judgment in accordance with the verdict, rejecting Carbon County's argument that in lieu of damages it should get an order of specific performance requiring NIPSCO to comply with the contract. * * * [S]hortly afterward the mine—whose only customer was NIPSCO—shut down. NIPSCO has appealed from the damage judgment, and Carbon County from the denial of specific performance. * * *

The contract permits NIPSCO to stop taking delivery of coal "for any cause beyond [its] reasonable control * * * including but not limited to * * * orders or acts of civil * * * authority * * * which wholly or partly prevent * * * the utilizing * * * of the coal." This is what is known as a *force majeure* clause. NIPSCO argues that the Indiana Public Service Commission's "economy purchase orders" prevented it, in whole or part, from using the coal that it had agreed to buy, and it complains that the district judge instructed the jury incorrectly on the meaning and application of the clause. The complaint about the instructions is immaterial. The judge should not have put the issue of *force majeure* to the jury. It is evident that the clause was not triggered by the orders.

All that those orders do is tell NIPSCO it will not be allowed to pass on fuel costs to its ratepayers in the form of higher rates if it can buy electricity cheaper than it can generate electricity internally using Carbon County's coal. Such an order does not "prevent," whether wholly or in part, NIPSCO from using the coal; it just prevents NIPSCO from shifting the burden of its improvidence or bad luck in having incorrectly forecasted its fuel needs to the backs of the hapless ratepayers. * * *

This is all the clearer when we consider that the contract price was actually fixed just on the downside; it put a floor under the price NIPSCO had to pay, but the escalator provisions allowed the actual contract prices to rise above the floor, and they did. This underscores the gamble NIPSCO took in signing the contract. It committed itself to paying a price at or above a fixed minimum and to taking a fixed quantity at that price. It was willing to make this commitment to secure an assured supply of low-sulphur coal, but the risk it took was that the market price of coal or substitute fuels would fall. A *force majeure* clause is not intended to buffer a party against the normal risks of a contract. The normal risk of a fixed-price contract is that the market price will change. If it rises, the buyer gains at the expense of the seller (except insofar as escalator provisions give the seller some protection); if it falls, as here, the seller gains at the expense of the buyer. The whole purpose of a fixed-price contract is to allocate risk in this way. A *force majeure* clause interpreted to excuse the buyer from the consequences of the risk he expressly assumed would nullify a central term of the contract.   *   *   *

If the Commission had ordered NIPSCO to close a plant because of a safety or pollution hazard, we would have a true case of *force majeure.* As a regulated firm NIPSCO is subject to more extensive controls than unregulated firms and it therefore wanted and got a broadly worded *force majeure* clause that would protect it fully (hence the reference to partial effects) against government actions that impeded its using the coal. But as the only thing the Commission did was prevent NIPSCO from using its monopoly position to make consumers bear the risk that NIPSCO assumed when it signed a long-term fixed-price fuel contract, NIPSCO cannot complain of *force majeure;* the risk that has come to pass was one that NIPSCO voluntarily assumed when it signed the contract.

The district judge refused to submit NIPSCO's defenses of impracticability and frustration to the jury, ruling that Indiana law does not allow a buyer to claim impracticability and does not recognize the defense of frustration. Some background may help make these rulings intelligible. In the early common law a contractual undertaking unconditional in terms was not excused merely because something had happened (such as an invasion, the passage of a law, or a natural disaster) that prevented the undertaking. Excuses had to be written into the contract; this is the origin of *force majeure* clauses. Later it came to be recognized that negotiating parties cannot anticipate all the contingencies that may arise in the performance of the contract; a legitimate judicial function in contract cases is to interpolate terms to govern remote contingencies—terms the parties would have agreed on explicitly if they had had the time and foresight to make advance provision for every possible contingency in performance. Later still, it was recognized that physical impossibility was irrelevant, or at least inconclusive; a promisor might want his promise to be unconditional, not because he thought he had superhuman powers but because he could insure against the risk of nonperformance better than the promisee, or obtain a substitute performance more easily than the promisee. Thus the proper question in an "impossibility" case is not whether the promisor could not have performed his undertaking but whether his nonperformance should be excused because the parties, if they had thought about the matter, would have wanted to assign the risk of the contingency that made performance impossible or uneconomical to the promisor or to the promisee; if to the latter, the promisor is excused.

Section 2–615 of the Uniform Commercial Code takes this approach.   *   *   * Notice, however, that the only type of promisor referred to is a seller; there is no suggestion that a buyer's performance might be excused by reason of impracticability. The reason is largely semantic. Ordinarily all the buyer has to do in order to perform his side of the bargain is pay, and while one can think of all sorts of reasons why, when the time came to pay, the buyer might not have the money, rarely would the seller have intended to assume the risk that the buyer might, whether through improvidence or bad luck, be unable to pay for the seller's goods or services. To deal with the rare case where the buyer or (more broadly) the paying party might have a good excuse based on some unforeseen change in circumstances, a new rubric was thought necessary, different from "impossibility" (the common law term) or "impracticability" (the Code term, picked up in Restatement (Second) of Contracts § 261 (1979)), and it received the name "frustration." Rarely is it impracticable or impossible for the payor to pay; but if something has happened to make the performance for which he would be paying worthless to him, an excuse for not paying, analogous to impracticability or impossibility, may be proper.

The leading case on frustration remains Krell v. Henry, [1903] 2 K.B. 740 (C.A.). Krell rented Henry a suite of rooms for watching the coronation of Edward VII, but Edward came down with appendicitis and the coronation had to be postponed. Henry refused to pay the balance of the rent and the court held that he was excused from doing so because his purpose in renting had been frustrated by the postponement, a contingency outside the knowledge, or power to influence, of either party. The question was, to which party did the contract (implicitly) allocate the risk? Surely Henry had not intended to insure Krell against the possibility of the coronation's being postponed, since Krell could always relet the room, at the premium rental, for the coronation's new date. So Henry was excused.

NIPSCO is the buyer in the present case, and its defense is more properly frustration than impracticability; but the judge held that frustration is not a contract defense under the law of Indiana. * * * At all events, the facts of the present case do not bring it within the scope of the frustration doctrine, so we need not decide whether the Indiana Supreme Court would embrace the doctrine in a suitable case.

For the same reason we need not decide whether * * * a buyer can urge impracticability under § 2–615 of the Uniform Commercial Code, which applies to this suit. * * * It may be * * * that buyers cannot use § 2–615 in Indiana. But it is not clear that this has substantive significance. Section 1–103 of the Uniform Commercial Code authorizes the courts to apply common law doctrines to the extent consistent with the Code—this is the basis on which NIPSCO is able to plead frustration as an alternative defense to [§ 2–615]; and the essential elements of frustration and of impracticability are the same. * * * NIPSCO gains nothing by pleading [§ 2–615] of the Uniform Commercial Code as well as common law frustration, and thus loses nothing by a ruling that buyers in Indiana cannot use [§ 2–615].

Whether or not Indiana recognizes the doctrine of frustration, and whether or not a buyer can ever assert the defense of impracticability under [§ 2–615] of the Uniform Commercial Code, these doctrines, so closely related to each other and to *force majeure* as well, cannot help NIPSCO. All are doctrines for shifting risk to the party better able to bear it, either because he is in a better position to prevent the risk from materializing or because he can better reduce the disutility of the risk (as by insuring) if the risk does occur. Suppose a grower agrees before the growing season to sell his crop to a grain elevator, and the crop is destroyed by blight and the grain elevator sues. Discharge is ordinarily allowed in such cases. The grower has every incentive to avoid the blight; so if it occurs, it probably could not have been prevented; and the grain elevator, which buys from a variety of growers not all of whom will be hit by blight in the same growing season, is in a better position to buffer the risk of blight than the grower is.

Since impossibility and related doctrines are devices for shifting risk in accordance with the parties' presumed intentions, which are to minimize the costs of contract performance, one of which is the disutility created by risk, they have no place when the contract explicitly assigns a particular risk to one party or the other. As we have already noted, a fixed-price contract is an explicit assignment of the risk of market price increases to the seller and the risk of market price decreases to the buyer, and the assignment of the latter risk to the buyer is even clearer where, as in this case, the contract places a floor under price but allows for escalation. If, as is also the case here, the buyer forecasts the market incorrectly and therefore finds himself locked into a disadvantageous contract, he has only himself to blame and so cannot shift the risk back to the seller by invoking impossibility or related doctrines. * * *

This completes our consideration of NIPSCO's attack on the damages judgment and we turn to Carbon County's cross-appeal, which seeks specific performance in lieu of the damages it got. * * * [T]he request for specific performance has no merit. Like other equitable remedies, specific performance is available only if damages are not an adequate remedy, and there is no reason to suppose them inadequate here. The loss to Carbon County from the breach of contract is simply the difference between (1) the contract price (as escalated over the life of the contract in accordance with the contract's escalator provisions) times quantity, and (2) the cost of mining the coal over the life of the contract. Carbon County does not even argue that $181 million is not a reasonable estimate of the present value of the difference. Its complaint is that although the money will make the owners of Carbon County whole it will do nothing for the miners who have lost their jobs because the mine is closed and the satellite businesses that have closed for the same reason. Only specific performance will help them.

But since they are not parties to the contract their losses are irrelevant. Indeed, specific performance would be improper as well as unnecessary here, because it would force the continuation of production that has become uneconomical. No one wants coal from Carbon County's mine. With the collapse of oil prices, which has depressed the price of substitute fuels as well, this coal costs far more to get out of the ground than it is worth in the market. Continuing to produce it, under compulsion of an order for specific performance, would impose costs on society greater than the benefits. NIPSCO's breach, though it gave Carbon County a right to damages, was an efficient breach in the sense that it brought to a halt a production process that was no longer cost-justified. The reason why NIPSCO must pay Carbon County's loss is not that it should have continued buying coal it didn't need but that the contract assigned to NIPSCO the risk of market changes that made continued deliveries uneconomical. The judgment for damages is the method by which that risk is being fixed on NIPSCO in accordance with its undertakings.

With continued production uneconomical, it is unlikely that an order of specific performance, if made, would ever actually be implemented. If, as a finding that the breach was efficient implies, the cost of a substitute supply (whether of coal, or of electricity) to NIPSCO is less than the cost of producing coal from Carbon County's mine, NIPSCO and Carbon County can both be made better off by negotiating a cancellation of the contract and with it a dissolution of the order of specific performance. * * *

As for possible hardships to workers and merchants in Hanna, Wyoming, where Carbon County's coal mine is located, we point out that none of these people were parties to the contract with NIPSCO or third-party beneficiaries. They have no legal interest in the contract.
* * *

[The] orders appealed from are affirmed. * * *

In The Opera Company of Boston, Inc. v. The Wolf Trap Foundation for the Performing Arts, supra p. 638, which party was "better able to bear" the risk of the power outage?

More on the Cancelled Coronation

(1) In Krell v. Henry (discussed in the principal case at p. 661), the defendant Henry agreed to pay £ 75 for the use of Krell's rooms from which he could view the Coronation procession; Krell's attorney conceded "that the price to be paid for the rooms was fixed with reference to the expected procession." The agreement was entered into on June 20, 1902. Compare Griffith v. Brymer, supra page 610.

(2) The court in *Krell* stressed that the parties' arrangement "was not a demise of the rooms * * *. It is a license to use rooms for a particular purpose and none other." Why should it matter that there had been no "demise of the rooms" but merely a "license"? Some common-law cases refuse to admit that a lessee can ever be excused on the ground of frustration, since a "lease is much more than a contract. It creates and vests in the lessee an estate or interest in the land." According to this notion, since a conveyance of the estate has already taken place, the "price" (the rent) remains due. Cricklewood Property & Investment Trust, Ltd. v. Leightons Investment Trust, Ltd., [1945] 1

All E.R. 252, 258 (H.L.) (Lord Russell). This rather formalistic view has been rejected by many modern courts, and it has frequently been altered by statute. Especially in long-term leases, however, the lessee will be excused only in "extremely rare" circumstances where the "frustration" of his purposes is "complete or nearly complete." Perry v. Champlain Oil Co., 101 N.H. 97, 134 A.2d 65 (1957); National Carriers Ltd. v. Panalpina (Northern) Ltd., 1981 1 All E.R. 161 (H.L.1980) ("It is the difference immortalised in HMS Pinafore between 'never' and 'hardly ever' ").

ALUMINUM CO. OF AMERICA v. ESSEX GROUP, INC.

United States District Court, Western District Pennsylvania, 1980.
499 F.Supp. 53.

TEITELBAUM, DISTRICT JUDGE.

Plaintiff, Aluminum Company of America (ALCOA), brought the instant action against defendant, Essex Group, Inc. (Essex), in three counts. The first count requests the Court to reform or equitably adjust an agreement entitled the Molten Metal Agreement entered into between ALCOA and Essex. * * *

In 1966 Essex made a policy decision to expand its participation in the manufacture of aluminum wire products. Thus, beginning in the spring of 1967, ALCOA and Essex negotiated with each other for the purpose of reaching an agreement whereby ALCOA would supply Essex with its long-term needs for aluminum that Essex could use in its manufacturing operations.

By December 26, 1967 the parties had entered into what they designated as a toll conversion service contract known as the Molten Metal Agreement under which Essex would supply ALCOA with alumina which ALCOA would convert by a smelting process into molten aluminum. Under the terms of the Molten Metal Agreement, Essex delivers alumina to ALCOA which ALCOA smelts (or toll converts) into molten aluminum at its Warrick, Indiana, smelting facility. Essex then picks up the molten aluminum for further processing.

The contract is to run until the end of 1983. Essex has the option to extend it until the end of 1988. The price for each pound of aluminum converted is calculated by a complex formula which includes three variable components based on specific indices. The initial contract price was set at fifteen cents per pound, computed as follows:

A.	Demand Charge	$0.05/lb.
B.	Production Charge	
	(i) Fixed component	.04/lb.
	(ii) Non-labor production cost component	.03/lb.
	(iii) Labor production cost component	.03/lb.
	Total initial charge	$0.15/lb.

The demand charge is to vary from its initial base in direct proportion to periodic changes in the Engineering News Record Construction Cost–20 Cities Average Index published in the Engineering News Record. The Non-labor Production Cost Component is to vary from its initial base in direct proportion to periodic changes in the Wholesale Price Index–Industrial Commodities (WPI–IC) published by the Bureau of Labor Statistics of the United States Department of Labor. The Labor Production Cost Component is to vary from its initial base in direct proportion to periodic changes in ALCOA's average hourly labor cost at the Warrick, Indiana works. The adjusted price is subject to an overall "cap" price of 65% of the price of a specified type of aluminum sold on specified terms, as published in a trade journal, American Metal Market.

The indexing system was evolved by ALCOA with the aid of the eminent economist Alan Greenspan. ALCOA examined the non-labor production cost component to assure that the WPI–IC had not tended to deviate markedly from their non-labor cost experience in the years before the contract was executed. Essex agreed to the contract including the index provisions after an examination of the past record of the indices revealed an acceptable pattern of stability.

ALCOA sought, by the indexed price agreement, to achieve a stable net income of about 4¢ per pound of aluminum converted. This net income represented ALCOA's return (i) on its substantial capital investment devoted to the performance of the contracted services, (ii) on its management, and (iii) on the risks of short-falls or losses it undertook over an extended period. The fact that the non-labor production cost component of ALCOA's costs was priced according to a surrogate, objective index opened the door to a foreseeable fluctuation of ALCOA's return due to deviations between ALCOA's costs and the performance of the WPI–IC. The range of foreseeable deviation was roughly three cents per pound. That is to say that in some years ALCOA's return might foreseeably (and did, in fact) rise to seven cents per pound, while in other years it might foreseeably (and did, in fact) fall to about one cent per pound.

Essex sought to assure itself of a long term supply of aluminum at a favorable price. Essex intended to and did manufacture a new line of aluminum wire products. The long term supply of aluminum was important to assure Essex of the steady use of its expensive machinery. A steady production stream was vital to preserve the market position it sought to establish. The favorable price was important to allow Essex to compete with firms like ALCOA which produced the aluminum and manufactured aluminum wire products in an efficient, integrated operation.

In the early years of the contract, the price formula yielded prices related, within the foreseeable range of deviation, to ALCOA's cost figures. Beginning in 1973, OPEC actions to increase oil prices and unanticipated pollution control costs greatly increased ALCOA's electricity costs. Electric power is the principal non-labor cost factor in aluminum conversion, and the electric power rates rose much more rapidly than did the WPI–IC. As a result, ALCOA's production costs rose greatly and unforeseeably beyond the indexed increase in the contract price. * * *

[After a period of declining profits under the contract, ALCOA lost over $3 million in 1977 and over $8 million in 1978 in converting alumina for Essex.]

During the most recent years, the market price of aluminum has increased even faster than the production costs. At the trial ALCOA introduced the deposition of Mr. Wilfred Jones, an Essex employee whose duties included the sale of surplus metal. Mr. Jones stated that Essex had resold some millions of pounds of aluminum which ALCOA had refined. The cost of the aluminum to Essex (including the purchase price of the alumina and its transportation) was 36.35 cents per pound around June of 1979. Mr. Jones further stated that the resale price in June 1979 at one cent per pound under the market, was 73.313 cents per pound, yielding Essex a gross profit of 37.043 cents per pound. This margin of profit shows the tremendous advantage Essex enjoys under the contract as it is written and as both parties have performed it. A significant fraction of Essex's advantage is directly attributable to the corresponding out of pocket losses ALCOA suffers. ALCOA has sufficiently shown that without judicial relief or economic changes which are not presently foreseeable, it stands to lose in excess of $75,000,000 out of pocket during the remaining term of the contract. [ALCOA sought relief "on the basis of mutual mistake of fact, unilateral mistake of fact, unconscionability, frustration of purpose, and commercial impracticability." It urged that the WPI–IC "was in fact incapable of reasonably reflecting changes in the non-labor costs" at ALCOA's plant and that the "actual costs incurred" by ALCOA should be substituted for it.

The court first held that the parties had made a mistake "of fact rather than one of simple prediction of future events":] Here the practical necessities of the very long term service contract demanded an agreed risk limiting device. Both parties understood this and adopted one. The capacity of their selected device to achieve the known purposes of the parties was not simply a matter of acknowledged uncertainty * * *. It was more in the nature of an actuarial prediction of the outside limits of variation in the relation between two variable figures—the WPI–IC and the non-labor production costs of ALCOA. Its capacity to work as the parties expected it to work was a matter of fact, existing at the time they made the contract.

This crucial fact was not known, and was scarcely knowable when the contract was made. But this does not alter its status as an existing fact. The law of mistake has not distinguished between facts which are unknown but presently knowable, and facts which presently exist but

are unknowable. Relief has been granted for mistakes of both kinds.
* * *

In *Sherwood* [*v. Walker*, supra p. 599], the buyer didn't know the highly pedigreed Rose was with calf. He probably could not have discovered it at the time of the sale with due diligence. Here the parties could not possibly have known of the sudden inability of the Wholesale Price Index to reflect ALCOA's non-labor costs. If, over the previous twenty years, the Wholesale Price Index had tracked, within a 5% variation, pertinent costs to ALCOA, a 500% variation of costs to Index must be deemed to be unforeseeable, within any meaningful sense of the word.

Essex has not seriously argued that the mistake does not relate to an assumption which is basic to the contract. The relation is clear. The assumed capacity of the price formula in a long term service contract to protect against vast windfall profits to one party and vast windfall losses to the other is so clearly basic to the agreement as to repel dispute. * * *

Essex concedes that the result of the mistake has a material effect on the contract and that it has produced a severe imbalance in the bargain. The most that Essex argues is this: ALCOA has not proved that enforcement of the contract would be *unconscionable*. Essex correctly points out that at the time of the trial ALCOA had shown a net profit of $9 million on the contract. Essex further argues that ALCOA has failed to prove that it ever will lose money on the contract, and that such proof would require expert testimony concerning future economic values and costs. These arguments are insufficient.

The evidence shows that during the last three years ALCOA has suffered increasingly large out of pocket losses. If the contract were to expire today that net profit of $9 million would raise doubts concerning the materiality of the parties' mistake. But even on that supposition, the court would find the mistake to be material because it would leave ALCOA dramatically short of the minimum return of one cent per pound which the parties had contemplated.

But the contract will not expire today. Essex has the power to keep it in force until 1988. * * * Where future predictions are necessary, the law commonly accepts and applies a prediction that the future economy will be much like the present (except that inflation will cease). Since some prediction of the future is inescapable in this case, that commonly accepted one will necessarily apply. On that prediction, ALCOA has proved that over the entire life of the contract it will lose, out of pocket, in excess of $60 million, and the whole of this loss will be matched by an equal windfall profit to Essex. This proof clearly establishes that the mistake had the required material effect on the agreed exchange. Indeed, if this case required a determination of the conscionability of enforcing this contract in the current circumstances, the Court would not hesitate to hold it unconscionable. * * *

Essex * * * asserts that ALCOA expressly or implicitly assumed the risk that the WPI–IC would not track ALCOA's non-labor production costs. Essex asserts that ALCOA drafted the index provision; that it did so on the basis of its superior knowledge of its cost experience at the Warrick Works; and that ALCOA's officials knew of the inherent risk that the index would not reflect cost changes. Essex emphasizes that, during the negotiation of the contract, it insisted on the inclusion of a protective "ceiling" on the indexed price of ALCOA's services at 65% of a specified published market price. Essex implies that ALCOA could have sought a corresponding "floor" provision to limit its risks.

* * * The question here is precisely this: By omitting a floor provision did ALCOA accept the risk of any and every deviation of the selected index from its costs, no matter how great or how highly improbable? The course of dealing between the parties repels the idea. Essex and ALCOA are huge industrial enterprises. The management of each is highly trained and highly responsible. The corporate officers have access to and use professional personnel including lawyers, accountants, economists and engineers. The contract was drafted by sophisticated, responsible businessmen who were intensely conscious of the risks inherent in long term contracts and who plainly sought to limit the risks of their undertaking. The parties' laudable attention to risk limitation appears in many ways: in the complex price formula, in the 65% ceiling, in the "most favored customer" clause which Essex wrote into the contract, and in the elaborate "force majeur" clause favoring ALCOA. It appears as well in the care and in the expense of the negotiations and drafting process. Essex negotiated with several aluminum producers, seeking a long term assured supply, before agreeing to the ALCOA contract. Its search for an assured long term supply for its aluminum product plants itself bespeaks a motive of limiting risks. * * * ALCOA's management was equally attentive to risk limitation. They went so far as to retain the noted economist Dr. Alan Greenspan as a consultant to advise them on the drafting of an objective pricing formula. They selected the WPI–IC as a pricing element for this long term contract only after they assured themselves that it had closely tracked ALCOA's non-labor production costs for many years in the past and was highly likely to continue to do so in the future. In the context of the formation of the contract, it is untenable to argue that ALCOA implicitly or expressly assumed a limitless, if highly improbable, risk. On this record, the absence of an express floor limitation can only be understood to imply that the parties deemed the risk too remote and their meaning too clear to trifle with additional negotiation and drafting. * * *

Once courts *recognize* that supposed specific values lie, and are commonly understood to lie, within a penumbra of uncertainty, and that the range of probability is subject to estimation, the principle of conscious uncertainty requires reformulation. The proper question is not simply whether the parties to a contract were conscious of uncertainty with respect to a vital fact, but whether they believed that uncertainty was effectively limited within a designated range so that they would deem outcomes beyond that range to be highly unlikely. In this case the answer is clear. Both parties knew that the use of an objective price index injected a limited range of uncertainty into their projected return on the contract. Both had every reason to predict that the likely range of variation would not exceed three cents per pound. That is to say both would have deemed deviations yielding ALCOA less of a return on its investment, work and risk of less than one cent a pound or of more than seven cents a pound to be highly unlikely. Both consciously undertook a closely calculated risk rather than a limitless one. Their mistake concerning its calculation is thus fundamentally unlike the limitless conscious undertaking of an unknown risk which Essex now posits.

What has been said to this point suffices to establish that ALCOA is entitled to some form of relief due to mutual mistake of fact. [The court then held that ALCOA was also entitled to relief "on the grounds of impracticability and frustration of purpose." The court noted that within the "substantial area of similarity" between those doctrines and ALCOA's mistake claim, its earlier discussion of mistake would apply here as well. "ALCOA's 'principal purpose' in making the contract was to earn money. This purpose has plainly been severely disappointed. The gravity of ALCOA's loss is undisputably sufficient to meet the stern standard for relief."]

[The court then turned to the question of framing a remedy for ALCOA.] To decree rescission in this case would be to grant ALCOA a windfall gain in the current aluminum market. It would at the same time deprive Essex of the assured long term aluminum supply which it obtained under the contract and of the gains it legitimately may enforce within the scope of the risk ALCOA bears under the contract. A remedy which merely shifts the windfall gains and losses is neither required nor permitted by Indiana law. * * *

A remedy modifying the price term of the contract in light of the circumstances which upset the price formula will better preserve the purposes and expectations of the parties than any other remedy. Such a remedy is essential to avoid injustice in this case.

During the trial the parties agreed that a modification of the price term to require Essex to pay ALCOA the ceiling price specified in the contract would be an appropriate remedy if the Court held for ALCOA. The Court understands from the parties that ALCOA will continue to suffer a substantial but smaller out of pocket loss at this price level. But ALCOA has not argued that the ceiling price term is subject to the same basic assumptions about risk limitation as is the indexed price term. Accordingly the Court adopts the ceiling price term as part of the remedy it grants to ALCOA.

The Court must recognize, though, that before the contract expires economic changes may make this remedy excessively favorable to ALCOA. To deal with that possibility, the Court must frame a remedy which is suitable to the expectations and to the original agreement of the parties. A price fixed at the contract ceiling could redound to ALCOA's great profit and to Essex's great loss in changed circumstances. Therefore the Court adopts the following remedial scheme. For the duration of the contract the price for each pound of aluminum converted by ALCOA shall be the lesser of the current Price A or Price B indicated below.

Price A shall be the contract ceiling price computed periodically as specified in the contract.

Price B shall be the greater of the current Price B1 or Price B2. *Price B1* shall be the price specified in the contract, computed according to the terms of the contract. *Price B2* shall be that price which yields ALCOA a profit of one cent per pound of aluminum converted. This will generally yield Essex the benefit of its favorable bargain, and it will reduce ALCOA's disappointment to the limit of risk the parties expected in making the contract. * * *

[The court acknowledged that the "attitude toward contract law and toward the work of the courts" reflected in its opinion would "disturb some people even at this late date."] It strains against half-remembered truths and remembered half-truths from the venerated first year course in Contract Law. The core of the trouble lies in the hoary maxim that the courts will not make a contract for the parties. The maxim requires three replies. First, courts today can indeed make contracts for the parties. Given certain minimal indicators of an intent to contract, the courts are today directed to impose on the parties the necessary specific provisions to complete the process. See UCC §§ 2–204, 2–207, 2–208.

Second, a distinction has long been noted between judicial imposition of initial terms and judicial interpretations and implications of terms to resolve disputes concerning contracts the parties have made for themselves. The maxim bears less weight when it is applied to dispute resolution than it does when it is applied to questions of contract formation. This case is plainly one of dispute resolution. * * * [W]hile the Court willingly concedes that the managements of ALCOA and Essex are better able to conduct their business than is the Court, in this dispute the Court has information from hindsight far superior to that which the parties had when they made their contract. The parties may both be better served by an informed judicial decision based on the known circumstances than by a decision wrenched from words of the contract which were not chosen with a prevision of today's circumstances. The Court gladly concedes that the parties might today evolve a better working arrangement by negotiation than the Court can impose. But they have not done so, and a rule that the Court may not act would have the perverse effect of discouraging the parties from resolving this dispute or future disputes on their own. Only a rule which permits judicial action of the kind the Court has taken in this case will provide a desirable practical incentive for businessmen to negotiate their own resolution to problems which arise in the life of long term contracts. * * *

The ALCOA Case

(1) Would it be relevant to inquire into the overall financial condition of Alcoa, or the profitability of its other operations due to the increased market price of aluminum? Cf. Missouri Public Service Co. v. Peabody Coal Co., 583 S.W.2d 721, 726 (Mo.App.1979) (seller claiming excuse "had experienced an approximate three-fold increase in the value of its coal reserves, presumably brought about by the same inflationary trend and other causes to which it ascribes its loss under the contract").

(2) "[T]he trial judge's decision never went into effect as the case was settled. * * * During the oral argument on appeal, a federal appellate court managed to convey to the parties its doubts about the innovative decision that favored ALCOA. After a huge investment in lawyers, expert witnesses, court costs and the like, the reaction of the appellate court prompted ALCOA to offer a settlement to Essex Group that was too good to refuse. What remains is an opinion by the district court for scholars to write about. * * * Many of these articles discuss judges imposing their views on the parties and rewriting contracts. That did not happen in the ALCOA case, and it probably would not happen in many cases even if *Aluminum Company of America v. Essex Group, Inc.* were recognized as the law everywhere. The District Judge's opinion and the uncertain result of the appeal changed the balance of bargaining power, but it did not impose a final result on the parties. The decision plus the appellate process worked as a form of coercive mediation. Faced with the situation, the parties worked out their own solution. The chance that a judge might rework a written contract after circumstances had changed also could affect bargaining situations. Perhaps this kind of coercion toward settlement is a good way to handle contracts that have gone on the rocks; perhaps it is a terrible way. Nevertheless, it is hard to evaluate a process without describing it accurately." Macaulay, An Empirical View of Contract, 1985 Wis.L.Rev. 465, 476.

CARROLL v. BOWERSOCK
Supreme Court of Kansas, 1917.
100 Kan. 270, 164 P. 143.

BURCH, J. The action was one to recover for part performance of a contract to construct a reinforced concrete floor in a warehouse, which was destroyed by fire before the floor was completed. The plaintiff recovered, and the defendant appeals.

The contract was formed by acceptance of the following proposal:

"We hereby propose to furnish all labor and material, and construct reinforced concrete floor in warehouse with necessary columns and column footings * * *.

"We propose to use the old floor now in place for forms for concrete, but will cut the old floor away from walls and remove all or part of the upper floor, the subfloor and joists to remain in place. We are to have the use for construction purposes of any of the old lumber removed. * * *

"Payment for this work to be made as follows:

"$600.00 when footings and reinforcing steel are in place.

"$600.00 when concrete of floor slab is poured.

"$375.00 when work is completed.

"The balance of $250.00 to be retained for sixty days, and to be due and payable at that time providing contract has been satisfactorily completed. * * *"

The plaintiff gave testimony abstracted as follows:

"That the first work to do under the contract was putting in concrete footings, then building pillars on these footings, then laying the concrete floor on top; that the columns are given form by building wooden boxes the desired height, putting in reinforcing rods connected at the bottom with dowels, and pouring the boxes full of concrete; that then the floor rods are so laid so that they come over into a bell on top of the column made by bending the column rods over horizontally in four directions at the top, and running the floor rods into the bell so formed; that when he last saw the building the footings were all in, the column rods set up and forms made, but no floor rods had been laid; that no cement had been poured in the columns at the time of the fire, and very few floor rods had then been put in place; that no lumber was used in the building, except in the temporary forms for columns intended to be later removed; * * * that the upright rods in the columns were wired together, but not fastened to the building; and that some spirals and some column rods were not yet in place."

[The trial court found that the] "plaintiff entered upon the performance of the work in harmony with said contract, and worked for about three weeks. * * * At the end of the third week, the building was totally destroyed by fire, without fault of either party to the contract. It was insured in the condition in which it was before the plaintiff commenced work, but there was no insurance upon the improvements made by the plaintiff. The defendant collected the insurance, and failed and refused to reconstruct the building upon demand of the plaintiff, so that it was impossible for the plaintiff to complete his contract."

[The trial court awarded the plaintiff $698.09; this included amounts for the steel, lumber, hardware, and cement used by the plaintiff; for "money paid for labor and miscellaneous items"; and for the "reasonable value of superintending the work and for use of tools."]

It is apparent that the court permitted recovery for substantially what the plaintiff had done by way of performance of the contract before the fire.

The contract was to place the floor in a specific warehouse. Destruction of the warehouse without fault of either party put an end to construction of a floor in that warehouse. No warehouse except the one destroyed having been contemplated or contracted about, the defendant could not be charged with delinquency for not building another. To do so would be to charge him with breach of an obligation which he did not assume. If continued existence of the particular warehouse to which the contract related were not taken for granted by both parties, the plaintiff would be bound by his contract and could not recover at all; no concrete floor having been constructed.

It was not material that the defendant collected insurance on the warehouse, purchased before the contract was made. The insurance covered nothing but property of the defendant. He paid for the insurance and was entitled to it, just as the plaintiff would have been entitled to insurance on his property had he seen fit to insure. If any part of the plaintiff's labor and material was incorporated into the insured building, so that the insurance covered it as substance of the structure, the plaintiff can recover, if at all, not because of the insurance, but because of the incorporation.

If a contractor should engage to furnish all labor and material and build a house, and the house should burn before completion, the loss falls on him. If a contractor should engage to refloor two rooms of a house already in existence, and should complete one room before the house burned, he ought to be paid something. So far the authorities are in substantial agreement.

The principle upon which the contractor may recover in a case of the character last instanced has been variously stated. Sometimes it is said that it was a material and substantive part of the contract on the owner's side that he would have the house in existence as long as might be necessary for the contractor to do the work. This statement of the principle arbitrarily attaches to the contract a warranty which the parties did not put there, and places the owner in default when he has been guilty of no wrong. * * *

The owner cannot be called on to reimburse the contractor merely because the contractor has been to expense in taking steps tending to performance. A contractor may have purchased special material to be used in repairing a house, and may have had much millwork done upon it. If the material remain in the mill, and the house burn, there can be no recovery. If the milled material be delivered at the house ready for use, and the house burn, there can be no recovery. It takes something more to make the owner liable for what the contractor has done toward performance. The owner must be benefited. He should not be enriched at the expense of the contractor. That would be unjust, and to the extent that the owner has been benefited, the law may properly consider him as resting under a duty to pay. The benefit which the owner has received may or may not be equivalent to the detriment which the contractor has suffered. The only basis on which the law can raise an obligation on the part of the owner is the consideration he has received by way of benefit, advantage, or value to him.

The question whether or not the owner has been benefited frequently presents difficulties. Sometimes the question is answered by the owner's own conduct, as when by taking possession, or by insuring as his own property, or by other act, he evinces a purpose to appropriate the contractor's material and labor. Sometimes the circumstances are such that the owner is precluded from rejecting the fruits of the contractor's efforts if he would, as when one room is finished under a contract to refloor two. In such cases it merely confuses the matter to bring in the terms "acceptance," "assent," and similar expressions indicative of the owner's attitude. If he should pay, it is not because assent or acceptance of benefit is "implied," or because he is "regarded as accepting benefit," but because of the fact that he has been benefited.

The test of benefit received has been variously stated. Sometimes it is said that benefit accrues whenever the contractor's material and labor, furnished and performed according to the contract, have become attached to the owner's realty. The facts of particular cases suggest different forms of expression. After considering all the authorities cited in the briefs, the court is inclined to approve, for the purposes of this case, the form adopted by the Supreme Court of Massachusetts, in the case of Young v. Chicopee, 186 Mass. 518, 72 N.E. 63, cited by the plaintiff. The action was one for labor and material furnished to repair a bridge destroyed by fire while the work was proceeding. The contract required at least half of the material to be "upon the job" before work commenced. The contractor complied with this condition, and distributed material "all along the bridge" and on the river bank. A portion of the material thus distributed but not wrought into the structure was destroyed by fire. Liability for work done upon and material wrought into the structure was not disputed, but the contractor sought to make good his entire loss. The court said:

> "In whatever way the principle may be stated, it would seem that the liability of the owner in a case like this should be measured by the amount of the contract work done which, at the time of the destruction of the structure, had become so far identified with it as that but for the destruction it would have inured to him as contemplated by the contract." 186 Mass. 520, 72 N.E. 64.

Applying the test stated to the facts of the present controversy, it is clear that the plaintiff should recover for the work done in cutting the old floor away from the wall and in removing such part of the old floor as was necessary. The warehouse was improved to that extent by labor, the benefit of which had inured to the defendant when the fire occurred. If the fire had not occurred, the undesirable floor would have been out of the way, precisely as the contract contemplated. Likewise, the contractor should recover for the completed concrete footings.

The contractor should not recover for material furnished or labor performed in the construction of either column or floor forms. They were temporary devices, employed to give form to the structure which was to be produced. They were not themselves wrought into the warehouse, were to be removed when the work was completed, and inured to nobody's benefit but that of the contractor.

The contractor should not recover for either upright or floor rods, or for the labor of putting them in place. While the rods were wired together, they were not attached to the building and would not have been wrought into the structure until the concrete was poured. If the fire had not occurred, the contractor could have removed the rods without dismembering or defacing the warehouse, and the defendant could not have held the rods as amalgamated into the fabric of his structure.

There should be no recovery for superintendence and use of tools, except as regards that part of the work done which had become identified with the warehouse itself. Other items sued for should be allowed or disallowed by application of the principle indicated.

The rule adopted and applied has been foreshadowed by utterances of the court in earlier cases. In the case of Duncan v. Baker, 21 Kan. 99, an entire contract for personal service was partially performed, when it was terminated by the fault of the employé. He was allowed to recover for what the work done was reasonably worth, less damages for his breach of the contract. In the course of the opinion it was said:

"Suppose a miller purchases a thousand bushels of wheat for a thousand dollars, the wheat to be delivered within one month; he receives the wheat as it is delivered, and grinds it into flour; when the vendor has delivered 500 bushels he refuses to deliver any more—what choice has the miller, except to retain what he has already received? This kind of supposition will also apply to the purchase and sale of all other kinds of articles, where the purchaser on receiving them changes their character so that he cannot return them. Or suppose that an owner of real estate employs a man to build or repair some structure thereon for a gross but definite sum, the owner of the real estate to furnish the materials or a portion thereof in case of building, and either to furnish them in case of repairing, and the job is only half finished; what choice has the owner of the real estate with reference to retaining or returning the proceeds of the workman's labor? This kind of supposition will also apply to all kinds of work done on real estate, and will often apply to work done on personal property. Of course, in all cases where the employer can refuse to accept the work and does refuse to accept it or returns it, he is not bound to pay for it unless it exactly corresponds with the contract; but where he receives it and retains it, whether he retains it from choice or from necessity, he is bound to pay for the same what it is reasonably worth, less any damage that he may sustain by reason of the partial nonfulfillment of the contract. * * *"

In this case nonperformance was not the result of the contractor's fault, and no damages can be deducted on that account. In other respects the doctrine stated applies.

The defendant says he had a right to a specific kind of completed floor which he could test and which would comply with a prescribed test, and that cutting away the old floor from the walls of the building, and concrete footings for a floor which was never laid, were of no value to him. The test is whether or not the work would have inured to his benefit as contemplated by the contract if the fire had not occurred. The cutting away of the old floor was done according to the contract, and the defendant had the benefit of that work as soon as it was finished. The evidence was that putting in the concrete footings was the next step in the construction of the concrete floor. Those footings would have inured to his benefit, in accordance with the contract, if the fire had not occurred. They became a part of his warehouse. Unless he could reject them for want of substantial compliance with the contract so far as they were concerned, he was benefited by them at the time of their incorporation into his structure. Test of a completed concrete floor was one of the things rendered impossible by the fire. * * *

The judgment of the district court is reversed, and the cause is remanded, with direction to take such additional evidence as may be necessary and determine the rights of the parties according to the views which have been expressed.

MASON, PORTER, WEST, and MARSHALL, JJ., concurring.

JOHNSTON, C.J. (dissenting in part). I am of opinion that the upright rods set up and tied together were a part of the building, and a recovery for them should be allowed.

DAWSON, J. I concur in this statement.

———

MORE v. LUTHER, 153 Mich. 206, 116 N.W. 986 (1908). Rueben, his wife, and son Andrew lived together on a farm from 1866 until Andrew's death in 1897. After his wife's death Rueben went to live with one of his two daughters, and he deeded the family farm to the daughters in exchange for their agreement to support him for the rest of his life. Rueben died in 1904. The administrator of Andrew's estate then presented a claim against Rueben's estate for Andrew's services on the farm. At trial defendant offered to prove that when Andrew died,

Rueben had had no property other than the farm and certain personal property connected with it; this testimony was excluded. The jury gave a verdict for plaintiff for the reasonable value of Andrew's services. Held, reversed. The court first held that "[t]he relation of father and son existing between Rueben and Andrew prevents the implication of any agreement that the latter should receive compensation for his services." There was testimony permitting the inference of an *express* agreement that Andrew would receive the farm in exchange for working on the property until the death of Rueben and his wife; however, the court noted that "[t]his agreement was clearly made upon the assumption that Andrew should outlive Rueben and his wife":

"Upon what principle then can he recover the reasonable worth of his services? He cannot recover upon the contract he made with his father, because he did not perform that contract. Neither can he recover upon the basis of an implied contract deducible from the rendition and acceptance of his services * * * because, as we have already shown, the law will permit no agreement to be implied from the rendition and acceptance of claimant's services. * * *

"[N]either Rueben nor Andrew intended that their agreement should apply in such a contingency, for the terms of that agreement clearly indicate that the right of Andrew in the farm should be subordinate to its use for the maintenance of his father and mother."

————

ALABAMA FOOTBALL, INC. v. WRIGHT, 452 F.Supp. 182 (N.D.Tex. 1977), aff'd 607 F.2d 1004 (5th Cir. 1979). In 1974 the parties entered into a contract by which Wright, then employed by the Dallas Cowboys, agreed to play professional football for Alabama, a member of the World Football League, in 1977, 1978, and 1979. Alabama paid Wright a $75,000 bonus at the time the agreement was signed. By 1975 both the team and the World Football League had ceased to operate. Alabama sued for the return of the $75,000, arguing that Wright would be unjustly enriched if allowed to keep the bonus. Held, for Wright:

"In considering the word 'bonus' in the context of the contract and the usage made of such word in professional football, the court finds that the parties intended Wright to be paid a $75,000 bonus upon his execution of a player's contract with Alabama and that no further services were contemplated by the parties as a condition to such payment or the retention of such payment by Wright. The bonus was not paid merely in anticipation of Wright's future services as a football player, but in exchange for a fully performed act, Wright's signing of the contract."

The court held against Wright on his counterclaim for breach of contract: "Alabama could not have reasonably foreseen such sudden demise of its team and the World Football League," and both parties were excused from further performance of the contract.

Problem

Employee agreed to work as a bookkeeper for Employer for 12 months, in exchange for which Employer promised to convey Blackacre to him. Employee worked faithfully for 9 months but then died. The reasonable value of Employee's work, measured by what other similarly skilled persons would have demanded for the work done, is $14,000. Blackacre at all times is worth only $12,000. After Employee's death Employer has to pay $7000 to another competent person to work out the remainder of the year. What, if anything, may the executor of Employee's estate recover against Employer?

Losses Following "Frustration"; The Frustrated Contracts Act

Lumsden v. Barton & Co., 19 T.L.R. 53 (K.B.Div.1902) was a "coronation case" in which the plaintiff had paid £42 in advance for eight "seats to view the procession." After the procession was cancelled she sought to recover her money back. The defendants gave evidence to the effect that their "expenses amounted to £291 9s., of which £85 was for decorations, £26 6s. 11d. printing cards, photographs of house, and postal expenses, £49 6s. advertising in newspapers, £118 9s. 6d. erecting stand, and £11 6s. hire of goods from Harrod's." The judge held for the defendants:

"He came to the conclusion that the defendants would not have agreed to return the whole of the money, as they would, for no fault of their own, have lost a large sum in getting the place ready. No English Court ever attempted to decide what kind of a bargain the parties would have made as to giving back part of the money on a partial failure of consideration."

The same result was reached in another coronation case, Chandler v. Webster, [1904] 1 K.B. 493 (C.A.). While there was no mention made of any expenses the defendant might have incurred, the court held that in the absence of any "condition express or implied in the contract," the plaintiff could not recover the £100 he had paid. The effect of the cancellation was not that the contract was "wiped out altogether"; although both parties are discharged from further performance, "it remains a perfectly good contract up to that point."

Chandler v. Webster was expressly overruled in Fibrosa Spolka Akcyjna v. Fairbairn Lawson Combe Barbour, Ltd., [1943] A.C. 32 (House of Lords 1942). An English manufacturer (Fairbairn) had agreed on July 12, 1939 to sell a Polish company (Fibrosa) certain "flax-hackling machines" for £4800. "The machines were of a special kind" and were to be delivered "c.i.f. Gdynia." Fibrosa made a down payment of £1000, but on September 1 Germany invaded Poland and it became clear that the delivery under the contract could not take place.

Fairbairn later refused Fibrosa's demands for the return of its £1000, stating that "considerable work has been done upon these machines and we cannot consent to the return of this payment." The House of Lords was of the unanimous opinion that the £1000 should be returned. Fibrosa's claim for restitution need not be "based on any provision contained in the contract, but arises because, in the circumstances that have happened, the law gives a remedy in quasi-contract to the party who has not got that for which he bargained." (Viscount Simon L.C.)

What, then, of the problem adumbrated by the *Lumsden* case, that of the defendant's expenditures prior to the "frustrating" event in preparing to perform the contract? The Law Lords were sympathetic, but could no more find a way of apportioning this loss themselves than could the judge in *Lumsden*: "He may have to repay the money, though he has executed almost the whole of the contractual work, which will be left on his hands. These results follow from the fact that the English common law does not undertake to apportion a prepaid sum in such circumstances * * *. It must be for the legislature to decide whether provision should be made for an equitable apportionment of prepaid moneys which have to be returned by the recipient in view of the frustration of the contract in respect of which they were paid." (Viscount Simon L.C.)

THE LAW REFORM (FRUSTRATED CONTRACTS) ACT
1943 6 & 7 Geo. 6, ch. 40.

1. Adjustment of rights and liabilities of parties to frustrated contracts.—(1) Where a contract governed by English law has become impossible of performance or been otherwise frustrated, and the parties thereto have for that reason been discharged from the further performance of the contract, the following provisions of this section shall, subject to the provisions of section two of this Act, have effect in relation thereto.

(2) All sums paid or payable to any party in pursuance of the contract before the time when the parties were so discharged (in this Act referred to as "the time of discharge") shall, in the case of sums so paid, be recoverable from him as money received by him for the use of the party by whom the sums were paid, and, in the case of sums so payable, cease to be so payable:

Provided that, if the party to whom the sums were so paid or payable incurred expenses before the time of discharge in, or for the purpose of, the performance of the contract, the court may, if it considers it just to do so having regard to all the circumstances of the case, allow him to retain or, as the case may be, recover the whole or any part of the sums so paid or payable, not being an amount in excess of the expenses so incurred.

(3) Where any party to the contract has, by reason of anything done by any other party thereto in, or for the purpose of, the perform-

ance of the contract, obtained a valuable benefit (other than a payment of money to which the last foregoing subsection applies) before the time of discharge, there shall be recoverable from him by the said other party such sum (if any), not exceeding the value of the said benefit to the party obtaining it, as the court considers just, having regard to all the circumstances of the case and, in particular,—

(a) the amount of any expenses incurred before the time of discharge by the benefited party in, or for the purpose of, the performance of the contract, including any sums paid or payable by him to any other party in pursuance of the contract and retained or recoverable by that party under the last foregoing subsection, and

(b) the effect, in relation to the said benefit, of the circumstances giving rise to the frustration of the contract. * * *

(5) In considering whether any sum ought to be recovered or retained under the foregoing provisions of this section by any party to the contract, the court shall not take into account any sums which have, by reason of the circumstances giving rise to the frustration of the contract, become payable to that party under any contract of insurance unless there was an obligation to insure imposed by an express term of the frustrated contract or by or under any enactment * * *

2. Provision as to application of this Act. * * * (3) Where any contract to which this Act applies contains any provision which, upon the true construction of the contract, is intended to have effect in the event of circumstances arising which operate, or would but for the said provision operate, to frustrate the contract, or is intended to have effect whether such circumstances arise or not, the court shall give effect to the said provision and shall only give effect to the foregoing section of this Act to such extent, if any, as appears to the court to be consistent with the said provision.

———

Almost forty years were to pass before a case was actually decided under the Act. B.P. Exploration Co. (Libya) Ltd. v. Hunt (No. 2) arose out of the expropriation by the Libyan Government of B.P.'s share of an oil concession which the company was developing under an agreement with Nelson Bunker Hunt. Under the agreement Hunt had transferred a one-half interest in the concession to B.P., and B.P. was to provide all the skill, resources, and capital for exploration and development until the field began to produce oil in commercial quantities. The Libyan expropriation was held to have frustrated the contractual arrangements by which B.P. was to be reimbursed out of the oil produced. Hunt was found to have received a "benefit" equal to the amount of oil he had received due to B.P.'s efforts, plus the compensation paid to him by the Libyan government. The trial judge then awarded B.P. a "just sum" under § 1(3) of the Act, consisting of "the costs and expenses incurred by B.P. for Mr. Hunt's account," less the market value of the oil already received by B.P. and credited to reimbursement under the contract. This came to the equivalent of over $30 million. The Court of Appeal, affirming, commented that it was not "the judge's task to draw up a balance sheet showing on one side how B.P. benefited from the joint venture, on the other how Mr. Hunt did, and making an award in favor of B.P. if Mr. Hunt had benefited more than it had done. The Act does not require the judge to perform such an accountancy exercise * * *. All the Act requires him to do is to fix a sum which he considers just."

[1982] 1 All E.R. at 983, aff'd, [1982] 1 All E.R. 986 [H.L.]

———

Cf. UCC § 2–615, comment 6.

Chapter 6

THE PAROL EVIDENCE RULE

MITCHILL v. LATH

New York Court of Appeals, 1928.
247 N.Y. 377, 160 N.E. 646.

Action by Catherine C. Mitchill against Charles Lath and another. Judgment of Special Term in plaintiff's favor, directing specific performance of an agreement to remove an icehouse, was affirmed by the Appellate Division and defendants appeal. * * *

ANDREWS, J. In the fall of 1923 the Laths owned a farm. This they wished to sell. Across the road, on land belonging to Lieutenant Governor Lunn, they had an icehouse which they might remove. Mrs. Mitchill looked over the land with a view to its purchase. She found the icehouse objectionable. Thereupon "the defendants orally promised and agreed, for and in consideration of the purchase of their farm by the plaintiff, to remove the said icehouse in the spring of 1924." Relying upon this promise, she made a written contract to buy the property for $8,400, for cash and a mortgage and containing various provisions usual in such papers. Later receiving a deed, she entered into possession, and has spent considerable sums in improving the property for use as a summer residence. The defendants have not fulfilled their promise as to the icehouse, and do not intend to do so. We are not dealing, however, with their moral delinquencies. The question before us is whether their oral agreement may be enforced in a court of equity.

This requires a discussion of the parol evidence rule—a rule of law which defines the limits of the contract to be construed. It is more than a rule of evidence, and oral testimony, even if admitted, will not control the written contract unless admitted without objection. It applies, however, to attempts to modify such a contract by parol. It does not affect a parol collateral contract distinct from and independent of the written agreement. It is, at times, troublesome to draw the line. Williston, in his work on Contracts (section 637) points out the difficulty. "Two entirely distinct contracts," he says, "each for a separate consideration, may be made at the same time, and will be distinct legally. Where, however, one agreement is entered into wholly or partly in consideration of the simultaneous agreement to enter into another, the transactions are necessarily bound together. * * * Then if one of the agreements is oral and the other in writing, the problem arises whether the bond is sufficiently close to prevent proof of the oral agreement." That is the situation here. It is claimed that the defendants are called upon to do more than is required by their written contract in connection with the sale as to which it deals.

The principle may be clear, but it can be given effect by no mechanical rule. As so often happens, it is a matter of degree, for, as Prof. Williston also says, where a contract contains several promises on each side it is not difficult to put any one of them in the form of a collateral agreement. If this were enough, written contracts might always be modified by parol. Not form, but substance, is the test.

In applying this test, the policy of our courts is to be considered. We have believed that the purpose behind the rule was a wise one, not easily to be abandoned. Notwithstanding injustice here and there, on the whole it works for good. Old precedents and principles are not to be lightly cast aside, unless it is certain that they are an obstruction under present conditions. New York has been less open to arguments that would modify this particular rule, than some jurisdictions elsewhere. Thus in Eighmie v. Taylor, 98 N.Y. 288, it was held that a parol warranty might not be shown, although no warranties were contained in the writing.

Under our decisions before such an oral agreement as the present is received to vary the written contract, at least three conditions must exist: (1) The agreement must in form be a collateral one; (2) it must not contradict express or implied provisions of the written contract; (3) it must be one that parties would not ordinarily be expected to embody in the writing, or, put in another way, an inspection of the written contract, read in the light of surrounding circumstances, must not indicate that the writing appears "to contain the engagements of the parties, and to define the object and measure the extent of such engagement." Or, again, it must not be so clearly connected with the principal transaction as to be part and parcel of it.

The respondent does not satisfy the third of these requirements. It may be, not the second. We have a written contract for the purchase and sale of land. The buyer is to pay $8,400 in the way described. She is also to pay her portion of any rents, interest on mortgages, insurance premiums, and water meter charges. She may have a survey made of the premises. On their part, the sellers are to give a full covenant deed of the premises as described, or as they may be described by the surveyor, if the survey is had, executed, and acknowledged at their own expense; they sell the personal property on the farm and represent they own it; they agree that all amounts paid them on the contract and the expense of examining the title shall be a lien on the property; they assume the risk of loss or damage by fire until the deed is delivered; and they agree to pay the broker his commissions. Are they to do

more? Or is such a claim inconsistent with these precise provisions?
It could not be shown that the plaintiff was to pay $500 additional. Is
it also implied that the defendants are not to do anything unexpressed
in the writing?

That we need not decide. At least, however, an inspection of this
contract shows a full and complete agreement, setting forth in detail
the obligations of each party. On reading it, one would conclude that
the reciprocal obligations of the parties were fully detailed. Nor would
his opinion alter if he knew the surrounding circumstances. The
presence of the icehouse, even the knowledge that Mrs. Mitchill
thought it objectionable, would not lead to the belief that a separate
agreement existed with regard to it. Were such an agreement made it
would seem most natural that the inquirer should find it in the
contract. Collateral in form it is found to be, but it is closely related to
the subject dealt with in the written agreement—so closely that we
hold it may not be proved. * * *

We do not ignore the fact that authorities may be found that would
seem to support the contention of the appellant. * * * A line of
cases in Massachusetts, of which Durkin v. Cobleigh, 156 Mass. 108, 30
N.E. 474, 17 L.R.A. 270, 32 Am.St.Rep. 436, is an example, have to do
with collateral contracts made before a deed is given. But the fixed
form of a deed makes it inappropriate to insert collateral agreements,
however closely connected with the sale. This may be cause for an
exception. Here we deal with the contract on the basis of which the
deed to Mrs. Mitchill was given subsequently, and we confine ourselves
to the question whether its terms may be modified. * * *

It is argued that what we have said is not applicable to the case as
presented. The collateral agreement was made with the plaintiff. The
contract of sale was with her husband, and no assignment of it from
him appears. Yet the deed was given to her. It is evident that here
was a transaction in which she was the principal from beginning to
end. We must treat the contract as if in form as it was in fact, made by
her.

Our conclusion is that the judgment of the Appellate Division and
that of the Special Term should be reversed and the complaint dismissed, with costs in all courts.

Lehman, J. (dissenting). I accept the general rule as formulated by
Judge Andrews. I differ with him only as to its application to the facts
shown in the record. * * *

Three conditions, at least, must exist before an oral agreement may
be proven to increase the obligation imposed by the written agreement.
I think we agree that the first condition that the agreement "must in
form be a collateral one" is met by the evidence. I concede that this
condition is met in most cases where the courts have nevertheless
excluded evidence of the collateral oral agreement. The difficulty here,
as in most cases, arises in connection with the two other conditions.

The second condition is that the "parol agreement must not contradict express or implied provisions of the written contract." Judge Andrews voices doubt whether this condition is satisfied. The written contract has been carried out. * * * By the oral agreement the plaintiff seeks to hold the defendants to other obligations to be performed by them thereafter upon land which was not conveyed to the plaintiff. The assertion of such further obligation is not inconsistent with the written contract, unless the written contract contains a provision, express or implied, that the defendants are not to do anything not expressed in the writing. Concededly there is no such express provision in the contract, and such a provision may be implied, if at all, only if the asserted additional obligation is "so clearly connected with the principal transaction as to be part and parcel of it," and is not "one that the parties would not ordinarily be expected to embody in the writing." The hypothesis so formulated for a conclusion that the asserted additional obligation is inconsistent with an implied term of the contract is that the alleged oral agreement does not comply with the third condition as formulated by Judge Andrews. In this case, therefore, the problem reduces itself to the one question whether or not the oral agreement meets the third condition.

* * * Exclusion of proof of the oral agreement on the ground that it varies the contract embodied in the writing may be based only upon a finding or presumption that the written contract was intended to cover the oral negotiations for the removal of the icehouse which led up to the contract of purchase and sale. To determine what the writing was intended to cover, "the document alone will not suffice. What it was intended to cover cannot be known till we know what there was to cover. The question being whether certain subjects of negotiation were intended to be covered, we must compare the writing and the negotiations before we can determine whether they were in fact covered." Wigmore on Evidence (2d Ed.) § 2430. * * *

The fact that in this case the parol agreement is established by the overwhelming weight of evidence is, of course, not a factor which may be considered in determining the competency or legal effect of the evidence. Hardship in the particular case would not justify the court in disregarding or emasculating the general rule. It merely accentuates the outlines of our problem. The assumption that the parol agreement was made is no longer obscured by any doubts. The problem, then, is clearly whether the parties are presumed to have intended to render that parol agreement legally ineffective and non-existent by failure to embody it in the writing. Though we are driven to say that nothing in the written contract which fixed the terms and conditions of the stipulated conveyance suggests the existence of any further parol agreement, an inspection of the contract, though it is complete on its face in regard to the subject of the conveyance, does not, I think, show that it was intended to embody negotiations or agreements, if any, in regard to a matter so loosely bound to the conveyance as the removal of an icehouse from land not conveyed.

The rule of integration undoubtedly frequently prevents the assertion of fraudulent claims. Parties who take the precaution of embodying their oral agreements in a writing should be protected against the assertion that other terms of the same agreement were not integrated in the writing. The limits of the integration are determined by the writing, read in the light of the surrounding circumstances. A written contract, however complete, yet covers only a limited field. I do not think that in the written contract for the conveyance of land here under consideration we can find an intention to cover a field so broad as to include prior agreements, if any such were made, to do other acts on other property after the stipulated conveyance was made. * * *

CARDOZO, C.J., and POUND, KELLOGG and O'BRIEN, JJ., concur with ANDREWS, J.

LEHMAN, J., dissents in opinion in which CRANE, J., concurs.

Judgment accordingly.

RESTATEMENT, SECOND, CONTRACTS § 213:

(1) A binding integrated agreement * discharges prior agreements to the extent that it is inconsistent with them.

(2) A binding completely integrated agreement ** discharges prior agreements to the extent that they are within its scope.

(3) An integrated agreement that is not binding or that is voidable and avoided does not discharge a prior agreement. But an integrated agreement, even though not binding, may be effective to render inoperative a term which would have been part of the agreement if it had not been integrated.

———

See UCC § 2–202.

———

"PAROL EVIDENCE RULE." From the preceding materials, the suspicion emerges that the title "parol evidence rule" is about as descriptive as "Holy Roman Empire," which was neither holy, nor Roman, nor an empire.

The rule includes not only "parol" (oral) agreements, but also prior written agreements.

It is not a rule of "evidence" but one of substantive law. There are two major indications of this. First, evidence of prior oral or written or contemporaneous oral agreements, if excluded under the rule, is excluded not, or at least not only, because it is untrustworthy, but because it

———

* An "integrated agreement" "is a writing or writings constituting a final expression of one or more terms of an agreement." Restatement, Second, Contracts § 209(1).

** A "completely integrated agreement" "is an integrated agreement adopted by the parties as a complete and exclusive statement of the terms of the agreement." Id. § 210(1).

is irrelevant. Those agreements have been superseded by the integration. Second, failure to object to evidence excludable under the rule does not waive the objection. An instruction that the agreements admitted into evidence are irrelevant and should be disregarded by the jury can be given at any time during trial.

Finally, it is not a "rule" but a complex collection of rules and doctrine.

––––––

DOYLE v. NORTHROP CORP., 455 F.Supp. 1318, 1333 (D.N.J.1978):

"The question whether a parol agreement entered into contemporaneously with a written agreement may be considered valid and enforceable or merely negotiations or a prior agreement which has been either modified or superseded by the subsequent written agreement, is one in which the authorities are in serious dispute. A distinction is made between final and complete writings, i.e. fully integrated, or final but incomplete writings, i.e. partially integrated. This has been a major area of conflict between Professor Williston and Professor Corbin. The two schools of thought are as follows: Williston argues that the normal test for determining intent, if applied in this context, would effectively emasculate the parol evidence rule. 4 Williston, Contracts § 673 (3d ed. 1957), (hereinafter Williston). This appears to be the position taken by the [first] Restatement. See Restatement, Contracts § 237 and comment (a) to that section. Corbin, on the other hand, takes the view that such expressions are prior or subsequent to the writing and thus, at the very least, superseded by the writing; however the writing itself does not control this determination. 3 Corbin § 577. This is also the position adopted by the Code. See UCC § 2–202.

"Thus Williston would have us exclude all evidence, relevant or not, except the written agreement [to determine whether the parties intended the writing as the complete and exclusive statement of their agreement]. Whereas Corbin would require a review of evidence extrinsic to the writing, i.e. what the parties have said and done, in order to determine their intent."

McCORMICK, THE PAROL EVIDENCE RULE AS A PROCEDURAL DEVICE FOR CONTROL OF THE JURY
41 Yale L.J. 365, 366–69 (1932) *.

When an issue arises involving choice between a writing and an alleged oral agreement, usually the one who sets up the spoken against the written word is economically the under-dog. He may be a person who has signed a note at the bank for himself or his neighbor and who asserts that it was agreed that the note or endorsement should not be enforced until certain funds should be realized by the debtor, or he may be a farmer who has purchased a tractor on credit and who resists

* Reprinted by permission of The Yale Law Journal Company and Fred B. Rothman & Company from The Yale Law Journal, Vol. 41, pp. 365, 366–69.

collection on the ground that the agent of the tractor company orally warranted the power-rating of the tractor in a way not specified in the written sales agreement. The types of transaction wherein is involved this kind of competition between claims based upon writings and those based upon alleged oral agreements dealing with the same affair, are infinitely various, but usually if there is a difference between the two parties in economic status, the one who relies upon the writing is likely to be among the "haves," and the one who seeks escape through the oral word will probably be ranged among the "have nots," in Sancho Panza's classification. The average jury will, other things being equal, lean strongly in favor of the side which is threatened with possible injustice and certain hardship by the enforcement of the writing.

* * *

The danger from allowing juries to do their worst with written transactions was doubtless sensed intuitively by the judges, but this was prevented from emerging into consciousness and expression by the prevailing idolatry, sincerely enough entertained by the judges themselves, of the jury as a symbol of political liberty. Otherwise, they might frankly have reserved for the judge's decision (as one of the exceptions to the general practice) the question of fact as to whether an alleged oral agreement set up in competition with a writing, was actually made, and, if so, whether it was intended to be abandoned or to survive, when the writing was signed. Forbidden this straight path by their own preconceptions, by a zig-zag route they came out near the same goal. The approach was made through doctrinal devices which gave no hint of any departure from the usual division of functions between judge and jury, but which were subtly convenient for jury control in cases where written transactions were threatened by claims of agreed oral variations not credited by the judge.

In the first place, they said, "Parol evidence is inadmissible to vary, contradict, or add to the terms of a written instrument." The phrase becomes a shibboleth, repeated in ten thousand cases. It obviously enables the judge to head off the difficulty at its source, not by professing to decide any question as to the credibility of the asserted oral variation, but by professing to exclude the evidence from the jury altogether because forbidden by a mysterious legal ban. * * *

Distinction Between Collateral Contract and Partial Integration

Mitchill v. Lath introduces not only the parol evidence rule, but also a classic "exception" to that rule—the collateral contract. The "collateral contract" exception to the parol evidence rule is based on the common-sense notion that although the parties have executed a "total" integration, they probably do not intend to supersede every other agreement that they have made in the past. If the party subject to suit on the total integration has a claim under this past and separate agreement, and under local procedure he may assert this claim, the parol evidence rule does not prevent doing so. A clear example would be a case in which the defendant is being sued on a written contract for the sale of coal, but has a claim against the plaintiff under a prior contract for the sale of aluminum. Even when there is the same consideration for both agreements, however, they may be collateral. The collateral contract argument in practice is that, although the contracts in litigation are not as "collateral" as the coal and aluminum contracts in this example, they are sufficiently collateral so that evidence of one may be admitted despite a complete integration of the other.

Another ground on which evidence of a prior oral agreement might be admitted is that although it is not collateral, the writing is only a partial, not complete, integration. It was not intended by the parties as the complete and exclusive statement of the agreement that includes the prior oral term. Evidence of a prior agreement that does not contradict the writing is admissible even if that prior agreement forms part of the same deal that is partially memorialized in the writing.

Thus in Mitchill v. Lath the opposite result could have been reached on either of these grounds. The agreement concerning the ice house might have been declared "collateral" (as the dissent maintained), or the written contract might have been held a partial, not complete, statement of the parties' agreement.

Is there any difference between deciding to admit evidence of a prior agreement on the ground that it is "collateral" and admitting it on the ground that the writing is not complete? Does it make a difference whether the jurisdiction takes Williston's or Corbin's view of proper evidence of the intent to integrate; whether there is a "merger clause," which declares that the writing constitutes the entire agreement? Might the answer turn on the wording of the parol evidence rule in the jurisdiction (see problem on explanation evidence under UCC § 2–202 infra page 708)?

Although of tactical importance when attempting to get in evidence despite a parol-evidence-rule objection, the distinction between collateral contract and partial integration may seem a semantic quibble. The two arguments are easy to confuse. For example, toward the end of Judge Andrews' opinion in Mitchill v. Lath, he writes "the fixed form of a deed makes it inappropriate to insert collateral agreements, however closely connected with the sale." A "closely connected collateral agreement" is a contradiction in terms. What Judge Andrews probably means is that because of its fixed form, a deed is a paradigmatic example of a partial integration.

HOBBS TRAILERS v. J.T. ARNETT GRAIN CO., INC., 560 S.W.2d 85 (Tex.1977). A contract purporting to be a lease of truck trailers recited that it was "a leasing and not a sale." It further provided that the lessee did not acquire any interest in the trailers except to possess them as long as the lessee was not in default. The lease also recited that it constituted "the entire agreement between the parties pertaining to the subject matter." The lessor's salesman testified that he and the lessee had orally agreed that the lessee would be able to purchase the trailers at the end of the lease for $1.00 each. The lessor sued for rental payments for a period after the expiration of the lease. The lessee defended on the ground that the trailers had become its property under the oral understanding. The court ruled for the lessor holding that the writing could not be contradicted by evidence of the oral agreement. Two judges dissented, arguing that the oral purchase agreement was a collateral contract.

————

MASTERSON v. SINE, 68 Cal.2d 222, 65 Cal.Rptr. 545, 436 P.2d 561 (1968). Owner sold his ranch to his sister and brother-in-law. The deed reserved an option in owner to repurchase the land. After owner was adjudged bankrupt, the trustee in bankruptcy sued to enforce the repurchase option for the benefit of creditors. Owner offered evidence that the parties wished that the land be kept in the family and that the option was therefore intended to be personal to owner and could not be exercised by the trustee. The trial court held that the parol evidence rule precluded the admission of this evidence, but the Supreme Court of California reversed in an opinion by Judge Traynor. The understanding that the option was personal to owner was admissible as a collateral agreement:

"Evidence of oral collateral agreements should be excluded only when the fact finder is likely to be misled. The rule must therefore be based on the credibility of the evidence. One such standard, adopted by section 240(1)(b) of the [first] Restatement of Contracts, permits proof of a collateral agreement if it 'is such an agreement as might *naturally* be made as a separate agreement by parties situated as were the parties to the written contract.' (Italics added). The draftsmen of the Uniform Commercial Code would exclude the evidence in still fewer instances: 'If the additional terms are such that, if agreed upon, they would *certainly* have been included in the document in the view of the court, then evidence of their alleged making must be kept from the trier of fact.' (Com. 3, § 2–202, italics added.)"

RESTATEMENT, SECOND, CONTRACTS § 214:

Agreements and negotiations prior to or contemporaneous with the adoption of a writing are admissible in evidence to establish

(a) that the writing is or is not an integrated agreement;

(b) that the integrated agreement, if any, is completely or partially integrated;

(c) the meaning of the writing, whether or not integrated;

(d) illegality, fraud, duress, mistake, lack of consideration, or other invalidating cause;

(e) ground for granting or denying rescission, reformation, specific performance, or other remedy.

3 A. CORBIN, CONTRACTS, § 575: STATUTE OF FRAUDS COMPARED WITH THE PAROL EVIDENCE RULE, at 831: *

The statute makes certain oral contracts unenforceable by action, if not evidenced by a signed memorandum; the "parol evidence rule" protects a completely integrated writing from being varied and contradicted by parol.

The statute does not exclude any parol evidence, such evidence always being admissible to show that the writing does not correctly represent the agreement actually made; the "parol evidence rule," as commonly stated, purports to exclude such evidence.

The statute does not require that the written memorandum shall be an "integration" of the agreement, although such an integration satisfies its requirements; the "parol evidence rule" does not purport to have any operation at all unless such an integration exists.

When the statute is applied because its requirements are not satisfied, an agreement that may actually have been made is not enforced; when the "parol evidence rule" is applied, the court finds that there is a complete integration in writing and enforces the contract thus evidenced.

The statute, when strictly applied, may prevent the enforcement of a contract that the parties in fact made; the application of the "parol evidence rule" results in the enforcement of a contract that the parties did not make, if in fact the written document was not agreed upon as a final and complete integration of terms.

JORDAN v. DOONAN TRUCK & EQUIPMENT, INC.

Supreme Court of Kansas, 1976.
220 Kan. 431, 552 P.2d 881.

OWSLEY, JUSTICE:

This is an action brought by plaintiff-appellant, Arthur N. Jordan, to recover damages from defendant-appellee, Doonan Truck & Equipment, Inc., for breach of oral express warranties and representations allegedly made by appellee during negotiations prior to the purchase of a truck. Appellant contends the trial court erred by refusing to instruct the jury that express warranties could not be excluded or disclaimed.

* Reprinted from Corbin on Contracts (1960) with permission of West Publishing Company.

On or about February 10, 1972, appellant and his brother, Charles Jordan, went to appellee's place of business in Great Bend, Kansas, to inquire about the purchase of a truck. The substance of the negotiations is subject to considerable dispute. According to testimony of appellant and his brother, when discussing the purchase of a 1962 Peterbilt truck, appellee's employees represented that the engine would run for three or four months without having any major repair work done, that the truck was basically in sound condition, and that the cab legs and kingpins were in good shape.

The employees of appellee denied making any such representations as to the condition of the truck, other than stating that it was generally sound. Jack Goldman, a used truck salesman for appellee, testified that the truck he showed appellant had been placed on the back lot since it still needed repair work. He testified that after showing appellant the Peterbilt truck they dickered on the price. He claimed he told appellant the price of the truck was $5,500 and that figure included additional work to get it ready for sale. Appellant told Goldman he would do the work himself and he would give $3,000 for it without any guarantee or warranties. When the deal was approved by appellee, appellant read and signed a "Purchaser's Retail Order Form." The contract listed the total sales price as $3,000 and in fine print on the lower corner of the document stated that it was "the complete and exclusive statement of the terms of the agreement relating to the subject matters covered thereby." Handwritten on the face of the form was the additional disclaimer that the used truck was "Sold as is, where is, no warranty." Appellant testified that he read the disclaimer and knew what it meant, but he still assumed the earlier representations were true.

Immediately after purchasing the truck appellant was forced to spend considerable money for repairs. The kingpins, air cleaner, and front wheel bearings had to be replaced. The right cab leg had broken off, the engine block had cracks in it, and the engine had to be replaced. In all, appellant claims he spent $7,246.08 to place the truck in working condition.

Suit was subsequently brought by appellant for the cost of repairs and loss of the use of the truck, as well as punitive damages. The jury returned a verdict for appellee and a timely appeal was filed to this court.

Appellant argues the trial court erred in refusing to instruct the jury that oral express warranties could not be disclaimed. Appellant's petition alleged appellee made false oral representations and warranties as to the condition of the truck, which he relied upon in entering into the written contract. Appellee answered by denying any such warranties were made and setting up the defense of warranty disclaimers in the purchase order contract. At trial, appellee objected to the introduction of any evidence of the alleged oral warranties on the ground evidence of prior oral agreements was inadmissible under the parol evidence rule, [UCC § 2–202]. The trial court overruled the objection and permitted testimony by appellant and his brother as to the substance of the representations made by appellee prior to entering into the contract. Throughout the trial appellee emphasized its position that regardless of any statements made by its employees, the written contract controlled and the truck was sold "as is, where is, no warranty."

Appellant requested the court to instruct the jury to "deny effect to disclaimer language which is inconsistent with an express warranty." It is the court's refusal to so instruct which forms the basis of appellant's argument on appeal.

It is appellant's position that under [UCC § 2–316(1)] oral express warranties by the seller cannot be excluded or modified by disclaimer clauses contained in a written contract. Because appellee relied principally upon the disclaimer language found in the "Purchaser's Retail Order Form," appellant contends the jury should have been instructed to disregard such language. Had this been done, appellant believes the jury would have awarded damages to him based on the breach of the oral express warranties.

Appellant's entire case rests upon the oral representations allegedly made by various employees of appellee prior to the signing of the contract. Rather than responding to appellant's argument on the effectiveness of the disclaimer language, appellee argues it is unnecessary to reach that question because the evidence of the oral warranties was inadmissible in the first place. If the evidence of the oral warranties was inadmissible, as appellee contends, then appellant's cause of action for breach of warranty must necessarily fail.

The Uniform Commercial Code provision controlling the exclusion or modification of warranties is [§ 2–316]. * * * Subsection (1) is expressly made subject to the provisions of the parol evidence rule found in [§ 2–202]. * * *

These two sections of the Code, [§§ 2–202 and 2–316(1)], create a conflict as to whether parol evidence is admissible to establish the existence of oral express warranties which are inconsistent with disclaimers in a written contract. On the one hand, [§ 2–316(1)], directs that when the oral warranty and the written disclaimer cannot reasonably be construed as consistent with each other, the disclaimer is ineffective and the warranty prevails. This result, however, is made subject to the parol evidence rule under [§ 2–202]. If the writing is intended to give final expression of the parties' agreement, then evidence of prior oral express warranties is inadmissible. Several jurisdictions have held that [§ 2–202] is not a bar to the admission of oral express warranties because the written contract was not intended as a "final expression" of the parties' agreement. In other cases the courts have refused to permit the introduction of similar parol evidence on the ground that [§ 2–202] prevails over the disclaimer provisions of [§ 2–316(1)]. * * *

From the Comments accompanying [§ 2–202] and case law construing that section, it is clear the Code is not meant to change the local parol evidence rule. Section [2–202] does not preclude the admission of parol evidence if the written agreement was not intended by the parties as a final expression of their agreement. It has also been held in many jurisdictions that, although not referred to in the statute, fraud is an exception to the parol evidence rule.

The purpose of the Code provisions with respect to warranty disclaimers and parol evidence is to protect the buyer from "unexpected and unbargained" language of disclaimer, while at the same time providing the seller with a defense against false allegations of sales representations.

Mindful of the policy behind the statutes we conclude that under the facts and circumstances of the instant case the trial court erred in admitting the parol evidence of the alleged express warranties. Although appellant's testimony, if believed, would be sufficient to create express warranties inconsistent with the disclaimer in the purchase order contract, the parol evidence rule operates to exclude the testimony relied on to prove the alleged representations. We are satisfied the purchase order contract was intended by the parties as a final expression of their agreement. Appellant has failed to adequately allege or prove such fraud as would bar the application of the parol evidence rule. It is undisputed that appellant read the contract, saw the handwritten disclaimer, understood what it meant, and signed the contract. This is clearly not the situation where a purchaser is surprised by "unexpected and unbargained" language of a disclaimer. We believe that appellant's right to rely on appellee's representations in the face of the unequivocal and conspicuous "as is" disclaimer is unsupported. Accordingly, we hold that under [§ 2–202] the testimony as to the alleged representations made by appellee's employees was inadmissible.

This being true, appellant's cause of action for breach of express warranty cannot stand and it is immaterial whether the trial court instructed the jury as to the effect of the disclaimer. Having reached the right decision, albeit for the wrong reason, the judgment of the trial court is affirmed.

Affirmed.

———

ZWIERZYCKI v. OWENS, 499 P.2d 996 (Wyo.1972). Buyer of a mobile home was permitted to testify that before the parties signed the sales contract, Seller orally promised to fix certain defects pointed out by the buyer. The contract stated that there were no representations or promises unless incorporated in the contract and that no modification of the contract would be valid unless made in writing. In affirming a judgment awarding Buyer damages for the defects, the court said: "The

Code was intended to liberalize the parol evidence rule and to eliminate the presumption that a written contract is a total integration."

GOODE v. RILEY

Supreme Judicial Court of Massachusetts, 1891.
153 Mass. 585, 28 N.E. 228.

HOLMES, J. This is a bill in equity for the reformation of a deed. The judge who tried the case found the following facts proved beyond a reasonable doubt.

The parties, just prior to the execution and delivery of the deed, made and completed an oral agreement, the plaintiff to sell and the defendant to buy a lot of land, situate on the southerly side of Summer Street in Lowell, bounded and described as testified to by the plaintiff, and a warranty deed thereof was to be executed and delivered. The parties were upon the land together, and then both saw and examined the same, and knew the location, description, and bounds thereof, and the rear line of the premises was then marked by a board fence five feet high, and other monuments, and both parties understood and knew its exact location and limits. The deed, when executed and delivered, described more land, to wit, about one thousand and thirty-one (1031) square feet to the rear and beyond said board fence, land not owned by the plaintiff, and so much more than was bargained for, and both parties then erroneously supposed and believed that said deed described the land orally agreed upon, and no more. This mutual mistake of the parties was not discovered until two months or more thereafter.

The court also found that the plaintiff had not been guilty of negligence or laches, and that he was entitled to the relief prayed for,—a decree to reform and rectify said deed.

The only question argued is raised by the defendant's exception to the refusal of a ruling that, if both parties intended that the description should be written as it was written, the plaintiff was not entitled to a reformation. It would be a sufficient answer that the contrary is settled in this Commonwealth. * * *

When both parties to a conveyance have intended to describe a certain parcel of land identified by their senses and by the words of their previous agreement, and have used words supposed by them to be apt for their purpose, but in fact describing that parcel and something more, the full purport of all their acts taken together is only to convey the parcel intended. And yet that result cannot be reached by way of construction merely. For you cannot prove a mere private convention between the two parties to give language a different meaning from its common one. It would open too great risks if evidence were admissible to show that when they said five hundred feet they agreed it should mean one hundred inches, or that Bunker Hill Monument should signify the Old South Church. As an artificial construction cannot be given to plain words by express agreement, the same rule is applied when there is a mutual mistake not apparent on the face of the instrument.

Since, then, the instrument must be construed to mean what the words would mean if there were no mistake, evidence of the mistake shows that neither party has purported or been understood to express assent to the conveyance as it stands. It is not necessarily fatal that the evidence is parol which is relied on to show that the contract was not made as it purports on the face of the document to have been made. There was a time when a man was bound if his seal was affixed to an instrument by a stranger, and against his will. But the notion that one who has gone through certain forms of this sort, even in his own person, is bound always and unconditionally, gave way long ago to more delicate conceptions.

So it is settled, at least in equity, that this particular kind of parol evidence, that is to say, evidence of mutual mistake as to the meaning of the words used, is admissible for the negative purpose we have mentioned. And this principle is entirely consistent with the rule that you cannot set up prior or contemporaneous oral dealings to modify or override what you knew was the effect of your writing.

But the effect of the evidence is not to show that no conveyance was made. It is only to show that no conveyance was made of part of the land embraced in the description. Obviously, therefore, it would be most unjust simply to rescind the whole transaction, and in order to do complete justice, the grantor who has used too extensive language should have a reconveyance, to set his title right on the face of the instruments. For, as things stand, a purchaser without notice could hold him to the words which he has used. If a purchaser were attempting to insert a parcel left out under similar circumstances, he would be met by the statute of frauds. But there is no such difficulty here.

The defendant's testimony, although ambiguous, looked toward the conclusion that the price was fixed by the number of feet; but this was denied by the plaintiff, and it does not appear what the judge found to be the fact, or what he did, and no question as to whether an allowance should be made to the defendant is before us.

Exceptions overruled.

––––––––

AMEND v. HURLEY, 293 N.Y. 587, 595, 59 N.E.2d 416, 419 (1944):

"Before [a party] can be granted reformation, *he must establish his right to such relief by clear, positive and convincing evidence.* Reformation may not be granted upon a probability nor even upon a mere preponderance of evidence, but only upon a certainty of error."

RESTATEMENT, SECOND, CONTRACTS § 166:

If a party's manifestation of assent is induced by the other party's fraudulent misrepresentation as to the contents or effect of a writing evidencing or embodying in whole or in part an agreement, the court at the request of the recipient may reform the writing to express the terms of the agreement as asserted,

(a) if the recipient was justified in relying on the misrepresentation, and

(b) except to the extent that rights of third parties such as good faith purchasers for value will be unfairly affected.

Illustration:

4. A, seeking to induce B to make a contract to sell a tract of land to A for $100,000, makes a written offer to B. A knows that B mistakenly thinks that the offer contains a provision under which A assumes an existing mortgage and that it does not contain such a provision, but does not disclose this to B for fear that B will not accept. B is induced by A's non-disclosure to sign the writing, which is an integrated agreement. A's non-disclosure is equivalent to an assertion that the writing contains such a provision * * * and amounts to a fraudulent misrepresentation. At the request of B, the court will reform the writing to add the provision for assumption.

———

SILK v. PHILLIPS PETROLEUM CO., 760 P.2d 174 (Okl.1988). A broker acting for Phillips asked Silk if she would lease her land to Phillips for oil and gas exploration. Silk told the broker the terms on which she would lease the land. These terms did not include an option to renew. Phillips had leased land in the county before, but none of these leases contained an option to renew. Several days after their conversation, Phillips' broker brought the lease to Silk at her place of work. The lease contained an option to renew in a separate clause, but the broker did not point this out. Silk testified that she signed the lease, including the option clause, hurriedly and without reading them because her employer objected to conducting personal business during working hours. Silk sued to rescind the lease and for damages. At trial, Silk was awarded actual and punitive damages, but rescission was not granted. Both parties appealed. The Supreme Court of Oklahoma reversed the judgment for damages and affirmed the denial of rescission stating that "there is no indication that [the broker] prevented Silk from reading the lease documents by insisting that she sign them at that time."

———

RESTATEMENT, SECOND, CONTRACTS § 155:

Illustration:

7. A agrees to sell and B to buy the American patent rights on an invention as to which A holds American, British and French patent rights. In reducing their agreement to writing, the parties use the term "all patent rights," meaning all American rights. A court will interpret the writing in the light of the circumstances to cover only the American and not the British or French patent rights, and it will not reform the writing.

RESTATEMENT, SECOND, CONTRACTS § 156:

Illustration:

4. A agrees to sell and B to buy a tract of land for $100,000. They prepare and sign a document that does not, as they both realize, contain the price, although neither party is aware of the legal consequences of this omission. Because, apart from the Statute of Frauds, reformation would not otherwise be appropriate, a court will not, at the request of either A or B, reform the writing to include the price.

LYONS v. KEITH, 316 S.W.2d 785 (Tex.Civ.App.1958). Plaintiff agreed to sell defendants a tract of land described as "[l]ying and situated in the County of Jefferson, * * * 164.325 acres" (with an identification of the property by field notes). The purchase price was stated to be $9859.50. Two years later defendants sold the tract to the Federal Land Corporation for $85,000. About this time, plaintiff learned that the tract contained an acreage greatly in excess of 164.325 and brought suit to recover the value of the excess acreage. The seller testified that the bargaining between the parties began with the buyer's offer of $30 per acre and culminated in an agreement of $60 per acre; "as I recall it [the buyer] and myself both grabbed a pencil and a piece of paper and started figuring out 164 acres against $60.00."

The trial court sitting without a jury found that both parties had been mistaken as to the true size of the tract, which was 303.950 acres, and that the sale was on a "per acre basis"; it held that plaintiff was entitled to $8355.90 (139.265 excess acres at $60 per acre). Held, affirmed. Under the testimony, whether this was a sale per acre or "in gross" was a question of fact for the trial court. Plaintiff had sought recovery for the excess acreage on the basis of the $60 per acre price which he alleged defendants had agreed to pay for the tract:

"[T]he appellants contend that it was error to render judgment for the excess upon the contract price of $60 per acre. They submit that the correct measure of recovery would be the actual value of the excess. In this connection, they call attention to the undisputed evidence that only 103 acres of the tract is above flood state; that much of the remainder is flooded several times a year and fit only for pasturage, and is, therefore, of much less value. This point is without merit. As hereinbefore observed, all of the parties to this transaction had for several years theretofore been intimately familiar with the tract in controversy. They had each been upon it, observed it and discussed it. All the evidence supports the conclusion that they agreed among themselves that each acre as a part of the undivided whole of the tract was of the value of $60. * * *"

LUSK CORP. v. BURGESS

Supreme Court of Arizona, 1958.
85 Ariz. 90, 332 P.2d 493.

PHELPS, JUSTICE.

This is an appeal by appellant, defendants below, from a judgment entered in favor of the appellee plaintiffs. * * * The cause was tried to the court sitting without a jury and findings of fact were requested by the defendants.

From the record it appears that plaintiffs, husband and wife, entered into a written contract with defendants for the construction and purchase of a certain house and lot in the Highland Vista subdivision of Pima County, Arizona. Prior to the execution of this contract agents for the defendants made oral representations to plaintiffs that the adjoining lot across the alley to the back of plaintiffs' residence would be used for the purpose of constructing a burnt adobe service station with a gravel-covered roof; that the plans had already been drawn up and that they could see them; that it would be the latest thing in the west; that Texaco had drawn the plans and were all for it. The agent also represented that a patio wall would be built on the service station lot between the service station and plaintiffs' proposed house, and that the service station would have a low roof and the architecture would conform to the architecture of the houses in the subdivision. After making these representations defendants conveyed this lot without restriction to third persons who erected upon the lot a service station constructed of red brick and painted white. This service station did not conform to the representations nor to the architecture of the houses in the Highland Vista subdivision. In addition to the service station, a square cement block building containing a barber shop and beauty shop was built on a portion of the service station lot immediately adjoining the lot sold to the plaintiffs by defendants. Plaintiffs were not informed that any buildings other than the service station building were to be constructed on the service station lot. On these facts the trial court entered a judgment in favor of the plaintiffs and against the defendants in the amount of $1,500, together with costs and disbursements incurred in the action.

Defendants essentially have made three assignments of error. First, defendants contend that the judgment is not supported by the evidence because defendants' promise was that a future act would be performed and plaintiffs have not proved by a preponderance of the evidence that at the time this promise was made the promisors in fact did not intend to carry out their promise. In the case of Waddell v. White, 56 Ariz. 420, 108 P.2d 565, 569 we said:

> " * * * Representations which give rise to an action of fraud must, of course, be of matters of fact which exist in the present, and not merely an agreement or promise to do something in the future, or an expression of opinion or judgment as to something which has happened or is expected to happen. To this there is one exception, that when a promise to perform a future act is made with the present intention on the part of the promisor that he will not perform it, it is such a representation as will give rise to an action of fraud."

The trial judge found that the representations made by the defendants or their agents were false and known to be false when made and relied upon by plaintiffs and that they had a right to rely upon them.

It appears from the evidence that the representations concerning the service station were made to plaintiffs between June 2, 1954 and June 9, 1954. Subsequently to these representations plaintiffs to wit: on June 9, 1954, entered into a written contract for construction and purchase of the house and lot from defendants. The testimony indicates that as early as the first part of May, 1954 the defendants were negotiating to sell the service station lot to third persons, the successful conclusion of which depended upon whether the purchasers could lease said property to the Texas company. Other evidence bearing upon this matter is that pursuant to these negotiations defendants thereafter on June 15, 1954, only six days after the execution of the contract of purchase with plaintiffs, conveyed by deed the service station lot to the person with whom they had been negotiating for its sale.

In the case of Law v. Sidney, 47 Ariz. 1, 53 P.2d 64, we said that the circumstances and conduct of the promisor has an important bearing in the determination of what the promisor's intention was when he made the promise. In the present case we believe the inference is clear that defendants divested themselves of control of the service station lot prior to the time the representations claimed by plaintiffs to be false were made to them. This inference is strengthened by the fact that within six days after conveying the lot to plaintiffs defendants conveyed the service station lot to the purchaser without incorporating in the deed restrictions in conformity with the representations made to plaintiffs. These two circumstances considered together, we believe, are sufficient evidence to support a finding by the court that defendants made said representations with the intent then formed to not perform them. This being true said representations constitute actionable fraud. The further fact that plaintiffs' agent represented as an existing fact that Texaco had already drawn the service station plans and were all for it when considered in connection with all of the other evidence, seems to us to make the representations actionable fraud. We find no merit in the first assignment.

The written contract dated June 9, 1954, entered into by plaintiffs and defendants contains a provision that it covers all agreements expressed or implied between the parties. Defendants urge as an assignment of error that when parties have integrated their agreement into a written contract, parol evidence is not admissible to vary the terms of the integrated writing. In answer to this assignment of error it is sufficient to say that the law has long been settled that whereas evidence of prior or contemporaneous oral agreements and negotiations is inadmissible, to vary terms of a written contract, nevertheless parol evidence is admissible to show fraud in the inducement of said contract. As a further answer to the above argument it is also a well-settled rule that a person can not free himself from fraud by incorporating a clause like the one above in a contract.

[The court also held that plaintiffs' evidence did not support the amount of damages awarded and remanded for a new trial on this issue.]

EDGINGTON v. FITZMAURICE, 29 Ch.D. 459 (1885). The court upheld an action for deceit against directors who issued a prospectus, which invited subscriptions for debentures but misstated the purposes for which the money would be used. The plaintiff had relied on the misstatement. Lord Bowen wrote concerning the requirements for an action for deceit: "There must be a misstatement of existing fact: but the state of a man's mind is as much of a fact as the state of his digestion." Id. at 483. For discussion of "Liability for Misrepresentation," see supra p. 624.

Sweet, Promissory Fraud and the Parol Evidence Rule, 49 Cal.L. Rev. 877, 889–90 (1961), states that "a sizeable number of cases" do not recognize fraud as an exception to the parol evidence rule, but warns of the "hazards of attempting to determine the position of any state in this area of the law." As an example of these "hazards," see Lovejoy Electronics, Inc. v. O'Berto, 873 F.2d 1001, 1004 (7th Cir.1989): "the [Illinois] cases often preface their discussion of the issue [whether there is a fraud exception to the parol evidence rule] by saying that 'Illinois does not allow a recovery for promissory fraud,' but then they explain that there is an exception 'if the promise is part of a scheme employed to accomplish the fraud,' and that the exception has swallowed the rule."

ASSOCIATED HARDWARE SUPPLY CO. v. BIG WHEEL DISTRIBUTING CO., 355 F.2d 114 (3d Cir.1965). Buyer bought goods at list price less 11%. Seller sued Buyer to recover the purchase price.

Buyer counterclaimed for fraud and sought to introduce evidence of Seller's prior oral representations that the prices charged were the equivalent of cost plus 10%. The evidence was held admissible to establish fraud:

"The Code parol evidence rule, UCC 2–202, contains no prefatory clause such as 'in the absence of fraud, accident or mistake.' Associated maintains that the absence of such a clause precludes the application of the exceptions found in the well settled law of Pennsylvania. Absent some overriding rule of interpretation, the position taken by appellee might well be correct since the parties have cited and our independent research has disclosed no case, either in Pennsylvania or in any other Code jurisdiction which has decided this issue. However, the Code itself contains a rule which compels a contrary result. UCC 1–103 states that '[u]nless displaced by the particular provisions of this Act, the principles of law and equity, including the law merchant and the law relative to * * * fraud [and] misrepresentation * * * shall supplement its provisions.' Thus, it is clear that the Pennsylvania exceptions would apply and testimony of prior oral agreements would be admissible."

RESTATEMENT, SECOND, CONTRACTS § 216:

Comment:

    e. *Written term excluding oral terms ("merger" clause).* Written agreements often contain clauses stating that there are no representations, promises or agreements between the parties except those found in the writing. Such a clause may negate the apparent authority of an agent to vary orally the written terms, and if agreed to is likely to conclude the issue whether the agreement is completely integrated. Consistent additional terms may then be excluded even though their omission would have been natural in the absence of such a clause. But such a clause does not control the question whether the writing was assented to as an integrated agreement, the scope of the writing if completely integrated, or the interpretation of the written terms.

RESTATEMENT, SECOND, AGENCY § 161:

    A general agent * for a disclosed or partially disclosed principal subjects his principal to liability for acts done on his account which usually accompany or are incidental to transactions which the agent is authorized to conduct if, although they are forbidden by the principal, the other party reasonably believes that the agent is authorized to do them and has no notice that he is not so authorized.

---

   * A "general agent" "is an agent authorized to conduct a series of transactions involving a continuity of service." Restatement, Second, Agency § 3(1). [Ed.]

Comment:

a. [Explaining the rationale for Section 161].   *   *   *   It is based primarily upon the theory that, if one appoints an agent to conduct a series of transactions over a period of time, it is fair that he should bear losses which are incurred when such an agent, although without authority to do so, does something which is usually done in connection with the transactions he is employed to conduct. Such agents can properly be regarded as part of the principal's organization in much the same way as a servant is normally part of the master's business enterprise. In fact most general agents are also servants, such as managers and other persons continuously employed and subject to physical supervision by the employer. The basis of the extended liability stated in this Section is comparable to the liability of a master for the torts of his servant. See Comment *a* on § 219. In the case of the master, it is thought fair that one who benefits from the enterprise and has a right to control the physical activities of those who make the enterprise profitable, should pay for the physical harm resulting from the errors and derelictions of the servants while doing the kind of thing which makes the enterprise successful. The rules imposing liability upon the principal for some of the contracts and conveyances of a general agent,   *   *   *   are based upon a similar public policy. Commercial convenience requires that the principal should not escape liability where there have been deviations from the usually granted authority by persons who are such essential parts of his business enterprise. In the long run it is of advantage to business, and hence to employers as a class, that third persons should not be required to scrutinize too carefully the mandates of permanent or semi-permanent agents who do no more than what is usually done by agents in similar positions.

RESTATEMENT, SECOND, AGENCY, § 166:

Illustration:

1. The P company employs A to sell its shares, instructing A not to make any representations except those contained in the prospectus. The prospectus states nothing as to the assets of the company, the number of shareholders, or the company affiliations. A knowingly makes untruthful statements concerning the assets of the company upon which T relies, and then contracts with T by a written contract in which it is stated that A is not authorized to make statements except those in the prospectus. It may be found that, from the known habit of stock salesmen and the necessity of making statements concerning the assets of the company, the P company intended that A should make such statements; if so, an action for deceit will lie against the principal.

DANANN REALTY CORP. v. HARRIS, 5 N.Y.2d 317, 184 N.Y.S.2d 599, 157 N.E.2d 597 (1959). Buyer claimed that he was fraudulently

704 THE PAROL EVIDENCE RULE Ch. 6

induced to buy Seller's building by Seller's oral representations as to the costs of operating the building. The representations were made before the sales contract was signed. The contract stated:

"The Seller has not made and does not make any representations as to the physical condition, rents, leases, *expenses, operation* or any other matter or thing affecting or related to the aforesaid premises, except as herein specifically set forth, and the Purchaser hereby *expressly acknowledges that no such representations have been made, and the Purchaser further acknowledges that it has inspected the premises and agrees to take the premises 'as is'* * * * It is understood and agreed that all understandings and agreements heretofore had between the parties hereto are merged in this contract, which alone fully and completely expresses their agreement, *and that the same is entered into after full investigation, neither party relying upon any statement or representation,* not embodied in this contract, made by the other. The Purchaser has inspected the buildings standing on said premises and is thoroughly acquainted with their condition." (Emphasis supplied.)

When the costs exceeded the representations, Buyer sued for damages. The court held that the disclaimer clause in the contract prevented Buyer from recovering:

"Were we dealing solely with a general and vague merger clause, our task would be simple. A reiteration of the fundamental principle that a general merger clause is ineffective to exclude parol evidence to show fraud in inducing the contract would then be dispositive of the issue. * * *

"Here, however, plaintiff has in the plainest language announced and stipulated that it is not relying on any representations as to the very matter as to which it now claims it was defrauded. Such a specific disclaimer destroys the allegations in plaintiff's complaint that the agreement was executed in reliance upon these contrary oral representations. * * *"

INTERNATIONAL MILLING CO. v. HACHMEISTER, INC., 380 Pa. 407, 110 A.2d 186 (1955). Buyer purchased flour from Seller. Before signing the contract, Buyer told Seller that the flour must be warranted to meet the standards for human consumption set by the American Institute of Baking and asked that these standards be inserted in the contract. Seller said that the contract was "uniform all over the country and they didn't want to violate the normal contract," but that Seller would include the standards in a separate letter sent to Buyer. Seller sent the letter to Buyer on the same day that Seller sent the form contract that did not refer to the Institute standards. The form contract stated that it "constitutes the complete agreement between the parties." Buyer rejected shipments of flour because they did not meet Institute standards. Seller sued for breach and prevailed, the court holding that the parol evidence rule prevented proof of the specifications not included in the form contract. Held, reversed:

"In none of the cases cited [by the seller] was it charged that a term was omitted from a contract at the insistence of one party who, although agreeing to incorporate the omitted term in a separate writing, nevertheless, employed a printed contract form which denominated itself the entire agreement of the parties. Contrary to the conception of the learned court below, this case is not merely an instance of a broken promise. Rather, if the jury believes the evidence adduced by the defendant, it is an illustration of deliberate misrepresentation. The presence of an integration clause cannot invest a writing with any greater sanctity than the writing merits where, as here, it assertedly does not fully express the essential elements of the parties' undertakings."

DAVE MARKLEY FORD, INC. v. LAIR, 565 P.2d 671 (Okl.1977). As part of the consideration for a new car, Buyer traded in her old car, which had body damage. Dealer alleged that before the sales contract was signed, Buyer orally agreed to pay Dealer for the cost of repairing the body damage. The contract, on a form supplied by Dealer, stated: "This contract constitutes the entire agreement between the parties and no modification hereof shall be valid in any event." The contract did not mention Buyer's promise to pay for repairing the old car. Buyer received a check from her insurance company for the damage to her old car, but refused to pay Dealer for repairing the body damage. Dealer sued for the amount of repairs. A judgment for Dealer was reversed on the ground that evidence of the prior oral agreement was not admissible.

DENNISON v. HARDEN

Supreme Court of Washington, 1947.
29 Wash.2d 243, 186 P.2d 908.

HILL, JUSTICE.

On May 12, 1943, the appellant and his wife and the respondents entered into an executory real estate contract whereby the respondents agreed to sell, and the appellant and his wife agreed to purchase, for twelve thousand dollars,

"＊ ＊ ＊ the following described lot, tract, or parcel of land situated in King County, State of Washington. ＊ ＊ ＊

"Purchase price to include property and fruit trees, all tools, tractor, truck, fertilizer, etc., fruit trees, berry bushes, and crops in ground." ＊ ＊ ＊

Appellant urges that there was a warranty that there were 276 Pacific Gold peach trees, that being the number of trees in the so-called "commercial orchard." Appellant expressly disclaims any fraud on the part of the respondents, but insists that there was a breach of the warranty in that the trees were of a scrub or worthless variety, and asks damages therefor. The evidence sustaining this claim of express warranty was that the respondents had represented, on two or three occasions during the preliminary negotiations, that there were 276 Pacific Gold peach trees in the commercial orchard, and had agreed to and did furnish documents from the nursery company which had supplied the trees substantiating the fact that they were Pacific Gold peach trees. These documents were offered and refused as exhibits.

The trial court ultimately became convinced that the parol evidence rule was applicable, and that the evidence which had been received and the exhibits which had been offered, varied and added to the terms of the written contract between the parties. It therefore granted a motion to strike the evidence which had already been admitted, and a judgment of dismissal necessarily followed. * * *

Appellant urges [as a reason] why the evidence concerning the warranty was admissible: * * *

It was within an exception to the rule permitting parol and extrinsic evidence to "clarify and properly identify the subject matter of the contract."

We assume that the recognized exception to the parol evidence rule that appellant has in mind is that parol evidence is admissible to explain an ambiguity. Appellant argues that because the contract said "fruit trees" and did not identify the kind, other evidence should have been admitted for that purpose. Appellant states in his reply brief:

"The very fact that under the terms of the contract as written by the respondents, the subject-matter is shrouded in mystery and confusion, demands the admission of parol or extrinsic evidence to clarify this patent ambiguity * * *."

No question is raised here concerning the meaning of "etc.," which is the only word that might call for clarification. We see nothing shrouded in mystery and confusion about "property and fruit trees" or "fruit trees, berry bushes, and crops in ground." The purchaser knew exactly what trees he was getting; the contract called for fruit trees, and he got fruit trees. There would be no patent ambiguity clarified by permitting appellant to add, after "fruit trees," the words "of which 276 are Pacific Gold peach trees." * * *

Finding no merit in any of the four arguments advanced by the appellant as to why the evidence stricken by the trial court should have been received, we are of the opinion that the trial court was correct, and the judgment of dismissal which necessarily followed that opinion is affirmed.

MALLERY, C. J., and MILLARD, ROBINSON, and SCHWELLENBACH, JJ., concur.

RESTATEMENT, SECOND, CONTRACTS § 212:

Illustration:

5. In an integrated agreement A promises B to insert B's "business card" in A's "advertising chart" for a price to be paid when the chart is "published." The quoted terms are to be read in the light of the circumstances known to the parties, including their oral statements as to their meaning.

———

PACIFIC GAS & ELECTRIC CO. v. G.W. THOMAS DRAYAGE & RIGGING CO., 69 Cal.2d 33, 69 Cal.Rptr. 561, 442 P.2d 641 (1968). (Traynor, C.J.) "The test of admissibility of extrinsic evidence to explain the meaning of a written instrument is not whether it appears to the court to be plain and unambiguous on its face, but whether the offered evidence is relevant to prove a meaning to which the language of the instrument is reasonably susceptible.

"A rule that would limit the determination of the meaning of a written instrument to its four-corners merely because it seems to the court to be clear and unambiguous, would either deny the relevance of the intention of the parties or presuppose a degree of verbal precision and stability our language has not attained. * * *

"If words had absolute and constant referents, it might be possible to discover contractual intention in the words themselves and in the manner in which they were arranged. Words, however, do not have absolute and constant referents. 'A word is a symbol of thought but has no arbitrary and fixed meaning like a symbol of algebra or chemistry, * * *.' (Pearson v. State Social Welfare Board, 54 Cal.2d 184, 195, 5 Cal.Rptr. 553, 559, 353 P.2d 33, 39 (1960).) The meaning of particular words or groups of words varies with the ' * * * verbal context and surrounding circumstances and purposes in view of the linguistic education and experience of their users and their hearers or readers (not excluding judges). * * * A word has no meaning apart from these factors; much less does it have an objective meaning, one true meaning.' (Corbin, The Interpretation of Words and the Parol Evidence Rule (1965) 50 Cornell L.Q. 161, 187.) Accordingly, the meaning of a writing ' * * * can only be found by interpretation in the light of all the circumstances that reveal the sense in which the writer used the words. The exclusion of parol evidence regarding such circumstances merely because the words do not appear ambiguous to the reader can easily lead to the attribution to a written instrument of a meaning that was never intended.'

"Although extrinsic evidence is not admissible to add to, detract from, or vary the terms of a written contract, these terms must first be determined before it can be decided whether or not extrinsic evidence is being offered for a prohibited purpose. The fact that the terms of an instrument appear clear to a judge does not preclude the possibility that the parties chose the language of the instrument to express different terms. That possibility is not limited to contracts whose terms have acquired a particular meaning by trade usage, but exists whenever the parties' understanding of the words used may have differed from the judge's understanding.

"Accordingly, rational interpretation requires at least a preliminary consideration of all credible evidence offered to prove the intention of the parties. Such evidence includes testimony as to the 'circumstances surrounding the making of the agreement * * * including the object, nature and subject matter of the writing * * *' so that the court can 'place itself in the same situation in which the parties found themselves at the time of contracting.' If the court decides, after considering this evidence, that the language of a contract, in the light of all the circumstances, is 'fairly susceptible of either one of the two interpretations contended for * * *.' extrinsic evidence relevant to prove either of such meanings is admissible."

See Restatement [First] of Contracts § 231, illustration 2, supra page 346; Restatement, Second, Contracts § 212, illustration 4, supra page 347; Goode v. Riley, supra page 695.

BEUC v. MORRISSEY, 463 S.W.2d 851 (Mo. 1971). An architect sued for his fee. The client introduced evidence that before the contract was signed, the architect had orally agreed to submit plans by March 1, 1965 and that he failed to do so. The architect contended that evidence about the oral agreement was not admissible under the parol evidence rule because it contradicted an implied term of the contract that the architect had a reasonable time for performance, the contract being silent as to the time. The court held the evidence admissible, quoting from Corbin on Contracts, § 593:

"* * * By the weight of authority, supported by the better reason, oral testimony is admissible to prove that a time or place was agreed on and to rebut the usual presumptions and inferences that would otherwise prevail. The contrary is held in a smaller number of cases. Oral testimony admitted for this purpose is not varying or contradicting the writing; it is merely enabling the court to fill a gap by adding something that is not expressed in the writing at all. Nor is it the contradiction of a meaning found by interpretation or implication in fact. * * *"

Problem

Buyer and Seller are negotiating the first transaction between them. Just before signing a written contract for the sale of bolts, they orally agree that "bolts" shall mean Seller's size 4 bolts and not bolts of 11 other sizes sold by Seller. Seller tenders bolts that are not size 4 and Buyer rejects them. In subsequent litigation Buyer offers proof of the oral agreement on size. What arguments may Seller make under § 2–202 in objecting to the introduction of the testimony and how should Buyer respond?

LUTHER WILLIAMS, JR., INC. v. JOHNSON

District of Columbia Court of Appeals, 1967.
229 A.2d 163.

QUINN, JUDGE:

Appellant (plaintiff below) sought to recover $670 as liquidated damages under a contract for improvements on appellees' home. Appellees' defense was that the contract never came into existence because of an unfulfilled condition precedent. This appeal raises the sole question of whether the parol evidence rule required exclusion of all testimony regarding the alleged condition.

At the trial, Luther Williams, Jr., president of appellant corporation, testified that prior to the signing of the contract, he offered to arrange any necessary financing for appellees, but was advised that they had their own. He was further informed that the down payment would be made in a few days when they received their funds. After drawing plans and contacting appellees several times, he was told that their financing had not been obtained and that they had procured another contractor to make certain improvements on the property.

Appellees testified that they signed the contract thinking it was merely an estimate; that they told Mr. Williams the improvements would depend upon approval of their financing by their bank; and that it was their understanding with him that they would not become obligated until they had procured the funds. Appellant objected to the introduction of all testimony concerning a parol agreement regarding financing, and later objected to jury instructions on that subject. The objections were overruled, and the jury returned a verdict for appellees.

As previously stated, the issue here is a narrow one, namely, whether the admission of testimony concerning the oral condition precedent violated the parol evidence rule. * * *

In this jurisdiction, * * * it is well settled that a written contract may be conditioned on an oral agreement that the contract shall not become binding until some condition precedent resting in parol shall have been performed. Furthermore, parol testimony to prove such a condition is admissible when the contract is silent on the matter, the testimony does not contradict nor is it inconsistent with the writing, and if under the circumstances it may properly be inferred that the parties did not intend the writing to be a complete statements of their transaction.

The contract in question contained the following clause:

"This contract embodies the entire understanding between the parties, and there are no verbal agreements or representations in connection therewith."

Two problems thus arise when applying the above rules to the instant case. First, in the light of an "integration clause," can evidence be admitted to show that the parties did not intend the writing to be a complete statement of their transaction? Second, can it be said that the testimony regarding the condition precedent does not contradict the writing when the contract states there are no agreements other than those contained in the writing?

As to the first question, it has always been presumed that a written contract is the final repository of the agreement of the parties. In this regard, an integration clause merely strengthens this presumption. However, intent is a question of fact, and to determine the intent of the parties, it is necessary to look not only to the written instrument, but to the circumstances surrounding its execution. * * *

As to the second question, we are aware that some courts have answered it in the negative. See, e.g., Rowe v. Shehyn, 192 F.Supp. 428 (D.D.C.1961); J & J Construction Co. v. Mayernik, 241 Or. 537, 407 P.2d 625 (1965). We believe, however, that this is an erroneous interpretation of Restatement, Contracts § 241 (1932) which provides as follows:

> "Where parties to a writing which purports to be an integration of a contract between them orally agree, before or contemporaneously with the making of the writing, that it shall not become binding until a future day or until the happening of a future event, the oral agreement is operative *if there is nothing in the writing inconsistent therewith.*" (Emphasis added.)

To explain this section, the following illustration is given:

> "A and B make and sign a writing in which A promises to sell and B promises to buy goods of a certain description at a stated price. The parties at the same time orally agree that the writing shall not take effect unless within ten days their local railroad has cars available for shipping the goods. The oral agreement is operative according to its terms. If, however, the writing provides 'delivery shall be made within thirty days' from the date of the writing, the oral agreement is inoperative."

In our opinion, it is clear from the example that what is intended is not the exclusion of evidence because of the existence of an "integration clause," 3 Corbin, op. cit. supra § 578 at 405–407, but an exclusion only if the alleged parol condition contradicts some other specific term of the written agreement.

In the instant case, no provision was made regarding financing. Therefore, the parol condition would not contradict the terms of the writing.

For the above-stated reasons, we hold that it was not error to admit testimony tending to show that the writing was not intended to be a complete statement of the agreement of the parties and to instruct the jury to find for appellees if they determined that the negotiations regarding the condition precedent had taken place and that the contract was not to become binding unless the financing was first obtained.

Affirmed.

———

PYM v. CAMPBELL, 6 El. & Bl. 370, 119 Eng.Rep. 903 (Q.B.1856). Defendants signed a contract agreeing to buy rights in plaintiff's invention. When defendants were sued for refusing to complete the purchase, they testified that before the contract was signed, all parties agreed that to save time, the contracts would be signed, but that defendants would thereafter submit the invention to Abernethie (an engineer who had left the meeting before all the principals had assembled) for his approval. It was also agreed that "if Abernethie approved of the invention, [the signed writing] should be the agreement, but if Abernethie did not approve, should not be one." Abernethie did not approve. The jury was instructed to find for the defendants "if they were satisfied that, before the paper was signed, it was agreed amongst them all that it would not operate as an agreement until Abernethie approved of the invention." The jury returned a verdict for the defendants, and a request for a new trial was denied on appeal:

"The point made is that this is a written agreement, absolute on the face of it; and that evidence was admitted to shew it was conditional: and if that had been so it would have been wrong. But I am of opinion that the evidence shewed that in fact there was never any agreement at all. The production of a paper purporting to be an agreement by a party, with his signature attached, affords a strong presumption that it is his written agreement; and, if in fact he did sign the paper animo contrahendi, the terms contained in it are conclusive, and cannot be varied by parol evidence: but in the present case the defence begins one step earlier: the parties met and expressly stated to each other that, though for convenience they would then sign the memorandum of the terms, yet they were not to sign it as an agreement until Abernethie was consulted. I grant the risk that such a defence may be set up without ground; and I agree that a jury should therefore always look on such a defence with suspicion: but, if it be proved that in fact the paper was signed with the express intention that it should not be an agreement, the other party cannot fix it as an agreement upon those so signing. The distinction in point of law is that evidence to vary the terms of an agreement in writing is not admissible, but evidence to shew that there is not an agreement at all is admissible."

———

PITCAIRN v. PHILIP HISS CO., 125 F. 110 (3d Cir.1903). Defendant signed a contract for remodeling his house. He refused to pay, testifying that shortly before the parties signed the contract, plaintiff agreed that there would be no charge if the defendant's wife was not satisfied with the work and that defendant's wife was not satisfied. The trial judge refused to instruct the jury that defendant was not liable if his wife "acting honestly and not capriciously, was not satisfied." Rather, he instructed the jury that the written contract could not be "contradicted or varied by evidence of an oral agreement before or at the time of the execution." Judgment for plaintiff was affirmed:

"Neither can the alleged undertaking of Mr. Hiss be regarded as a separate agreement resting in parol outside of the writings, and constituting a condition precedent, on fulfillment of which the obligation of the principal contract was to attach. It must stand, if at all, as an added term, by which the right of the plaintiff to final compensation is measured and concluded, entering into it vitally from the start."

HUNT FOODS & INDUSTRIES, INC. v. DOLINER, 26 A.D.2d 41, 270 N.Y.S.2d 937, aff'd without opinion, 26 A.D.2d 623, 272 N.Y.S.2d 686 (1966). The defendant signed an agreement giving plaintiff an option to buy defendant's stock in a corporation. When plaintiff sought to enforce the option, defendant testified that before signing, the parties agreed that the option would be exercised only if defendant solicited an outside offer. The trial judge granted plaintiff's motion for summary judgment on the ground that this evidence was barred by the parol evidence rule. On appeal the judgment was reversed, the court ruling that UCC § 2–202 applied to sales of securities under UCC Article 8 and that the evidence was admissible under § 2–202(b):

"The term (that the option was not to be exercised unless Doliner sought outside bids), admittedly discussed but whose operative effect is disputed, not being set out in the writing, is clearly 'additional' to what is in the writing. So the first question presented is whether that term is 'consistent' with the instrument. In a sense any oral provision which would prevent the ripening of the obligations of a writing is inconsistent with the writing. But that obviously is not the sense in which the word is used. To be inconsistent the term must contradict or negate a term of the writing. A term or condition which has a lesser effect is provable".

LURIA BROTHERS & CO., INC. v. PIELET BROTHERS SCRAP IRON & METAL, INC., 600 F.2d 103 (7th Cir.1979). Buyer sued Seller for failure to deliver scrap metal. Buyer was permitted to introduce evidence of oral agreements on delivery date and mode of shipment, and that discrepancies on these matters in the forms exchanged by the parties were due to a clerical error on the part of buyer. When Seller offered evidence of a conversation with Buyer during which the parties agreed that Seller was not bound unless he was able to obtain the metal from a particular source, the trial judge ruled that this evidence was not admissible under UCC § 2–202. Judgment for Buyer was affirmed:

"Allowing one party to use parol evidence to clarify a mistake in a writing, does not open the flood gates to any and all parol evidence bearing on the agreement.

"Having found § 2–202 applicable, the next question is whether the excluded evidence contradicts or is inconsistent with the terms of the writings. Pielet argues that the offered testimony did not 'contradict' but instead 'explained or supplemented' the writings with 'consistent additional terms.' For this contention, Pielet relies upon Hunt Foods & Industries, Inc. v. Doliner, 26 A.D.2d 41, 270 N.Y.S.2d 937 (1966).

*   *   *

"The narrow view of inconsistency espoused in [Hunt Foods] has been criticized. In Snyder v. Herbert Greenbaum & Associates, Inc., 38 Md.App. 144, 380 A.2d 618 (1977), the court held that parol evidence of a contractual right to unilateral rescission was inconsistent with a written agreement for the sale and installation of carpeting. The court defined 'inconsistency' as used in § 2–202(b) as 'the absence of reasonable harmony in terms of the language *and* respective obligations of the parties.' Id. at 623 (emphasis in original) (citing UCC § 1–205(4)).

"We adopt this latter view of inconsistency and reject the view expressed in *Hunt*. Where writings intended by the parties to be a final expression of their agreement call for an unconditional sale of goods, parol evidence that the seller's obligations are conditioned upon receiving the goods from a particular supplier is inconsistent and must be excluded.

"Had there been some additional reference such as 'per our conversation' on the written confirmation indicating that oral agreements were meant to be incorporated into the writing, the result might have been different.

"We also note that Comment 3 of the Official Comment to § 2–202 provides, among other things:

'If the additional terms are such that, if agreed upon, they would certainly have been included in the document in the view of the court, then evidence of their alleged making must be kept from the trier of fact.'

"Pielet makes much of the fact that this transaction was an unusual one due to the size and the amount of scrap involved. Surely a term relieving Pielet of its obligations under the contract in the event its supplier failed it would have been included in the Pielet sales confirmation."

WISCONSIN KNIFE WORKS v. NATIONAL
METAL CRAFTERS

United States Court of Appeals, Seventh Circuit, 1986.
781 F.2d 1280.

POSNER, CIRCUIT JUDGE. *   *   * Wisconsin Knife Works, having some unused manufacturing capacity, decided to try to manufacture spade bits for sale to its parent, Black & Decker, a large producer of tools, including drills. A spade bit is made out of a chunk of metal called a spade bit blank; and Wisconsin Knife Works had to find a source of supply for these blanks. National Metal Crafters was eager to be that source. After some negotiating, Wisconsin Knife Works sent National Metal Crafters a series of purchase orders on the back of each of which was printed, "Acceptance of this Order, either by acknowledgment or performance, constitutes an unqualified agreement to the following." A list of "Conditions of Purchase" follows, of which the first is, "No modification of this contract, shall be binding upon Buyer [Wisconsin Knife Works] unless made in writing and signed by Buyer's authorized representative. Buyer shall have the right to make changes in the Order by a notice, in writing, to Seller." There were six purchase orders in all, each with the identical conditions. National Metal Crafters acknowledged the first two orders (which had been placed on August 21, 1981) by letters that said, "Please accept this as our acknowledgment covering the above subject order," followed by a list of delivery dates. The purchase orders had left those dates blank. Wisconsin Knife Works filled them in, after receiving the acknowledgments, with the dates that National Metal Crafters had supplied in the acknowledgments. There were no written acknowledgments of the last four orders (placed several weeks later, on September 10, 1981). Wisconsin Knife Works wrote in the delivery dates that National Metal Crafters orally supplied after receiving purchase orders in which the space for the date of delivery had again been left blank.

Delivery was due in October and November 1981. National Metal Crafters missed the deadlines. But Wisconsin Knife Works did not immediately declare a breach, cancel the contract, or seek damages for late delivery. Indeed, on July 1, 1982, it issued a new batch of purchase orders (later rescinded). By December 1982 National Metal Crafters was producing spade bit blanks for Wisconsin Knife Works under the original set of purchase orders in adequate quantities, though this was more than a year after the delivery dates in the orders. But on January 13, 1983, Wisconsin Knife Works notified National Metal Crafters that the contract was terminated. By that date only 144,000 of the more than 281,000 spade bit blanks that Wisconsin Knife Works had ordered in the six purchase orders had been delivered.

Wisconsin Knife Works brought this breach of contract suit, charging that National Metal Crafters had violated the terms of delivery in the contract that was formed by the acceptance of the six purchase orders. National Metal Crafters replied that the delivery dates had not been intended as firm dates. * * *

The judge ruled that there had been a contract but left to the jury to decide whether the contract had been modified and, if so, whether the modified contract had been broken. The jury found that the contract had been modified and not broken. Judgment was entered dismissing Wisconsin Knife Works' suit. * * * Wisconsin Knife Works has appealed from the dismissal of its suit. * * *

The principal issue is the effect of the provision in the purchase orders that forbids the contract to be modified other than by a writing signed by an authorized representative of the buyer. The theory on which the judge sent the issue of modification to the jury was that the contract could be modified orally or by conduct as well as by a signed writing. National Metal Crafters had presented evidence that Wisconsin Knife Works had accepted late delivery of the spade bit blanks and had cancelled the contract not because of the delays in delivery but because it could not produce spade bits at a price acceptable to Black & Decker.

Section [2–209(2)] of the Uniform Commercial Code provides that "a signed agreement which excludes modification or rescission except by a signed writing cannot be otherwise modified or rescinded, but except as between merchants such a requirement on a form supplied by the merchant must be separately signed by the other party." * * * The meaning of this provision and its proviso is not crystalline and there is little pertinent case law. One might think that an agreement to exclude modification except by a signed writing must be signed in any event by the party against whom the requirement is sought to be enforced, that is, by National Metal Crafters, rather than by the party imposing the requirement. But if so the force of the proviso ("but except as between merchants * * * ") becomes unclear, for it contemplates that between merchants no separate signature by the party sought to be bound by the requirement is necessary. A possible reconciliation, though not one we need embrace in order to decide this case, is to read the statute to require a separate signing or initialing of the clause forbidding oral modifications, as well as of the contract in which the clause appears. There was no such signature here; but it doesn't matter, this was a contract "between merchants." * * *

Of course there must still be a "signed agreement" containing the clause forbidding modification other than by a signed writing, but there was that (see definition of "agreement" and of "signed" in [UCC §§ 1–201(3), (39)]). National Metal Crafters' signed acknowledgments of the first two purchase orders signified its assent to the printed conditions and naturally and reasonably led Wisconsin Knife Works to believe that National Metal Crafters meant also to assent to the same conditions should they appear in any subsequent purchase orders that it accepted. Those subsequent orders were accepted, forming new contracts on the same conditions as the old, by performance—that is, by National Metal Crafters' beginning the manufacture of the spade bit blanks called for by the orders. See [UCC § 2–207(3)]. So there was an agreement, signed by National Metal Crafters, covering all the purchase orders. The fact that the delivery dates were not on the purchase orders when received by National Metal Crafters is nothing of which it may complain; it was given *carte blanche* to set those dates.

When National Metal Crafters had difficulty complying with the original specifications for the spade bit blanks, Wisconsin Knife Works modified them; and National Metal Crafters argues that the engineering drawings containing those modifications are the written modification that [§ 2–209(2)], if applicable, calls for. In fact these particular modifications seem to fall within the clause of the contract that allows the buyer (Wisconsin Knife Works) to modify the specifications by notice. The context of this clause makes clear that such notice is not the written modification to which the previous sentence refers. But in any event there was no modification of the delivery dates. The "pert charts" which National Metal Crafters supplied Wisconsin Knife Works, and which showed new target dates for delivery, do not purport to modify the contract and were not signed by Wisconsin Knife Works.

We conclude that the clause forbidding modifications other than in writing was valid and applicable and that the jury should not have been allowed to consider whether the contract had been modified in some other way. This may, however, have been a harmless error. Section [2–209(4)] of the Uniform Commercial Code provides that an "attempt at modification" which does not satisfy a contractual requirement that modifications be in writing nevertheless "can operate as a waiver." Although in instructing the jury on modification the judge did not use the word "waiver," maybe he gave the substance of a waiver instruction and maybe therefore the jury found waiver but called it modification. Here is the relevant instruction:

> Did the parties modify the contract? The defendant bears the burden of proof on this one. You shall answer this question yes only if you are convinced to a reasonable certainty that the parties modified the contract.
>
> If you determine that the defendant had performed in a manner different from the strict obligations imposed on it by the contract, and the plaintiff by conduct or other means of expression induced a reasonable belief by the defendant that strict enforcement was not insisted upon, but that the modified performance was satisfactory and acceptable as equivalent, then you may conclude that the parties have assented to a modification of the original terms of the contract and that the parties have agreed that the different mode of performance will satisfy the obligations imposed on the parties by the contract.

To determine whether this was in substance an instruction on waiver we shall have to consider the background of [§ 2–209], the Code provision on modification and waiver.

Because the performance of the parties to a contract is typically not simultaneous, one party may find himself at the mercy of the other unless the law of contracts protects him. Indeed, the most important thing which that law does is to facilitate exchanges that are not simultaneous by preventing either party from taking advantage of the vulnerabilities to which sequential performance may give rise. If A contracts to build a highly idiosyncratic gazebo for B, payment due on completion, and when A completes the gazebo B refuses to pay, A may be in a bind—since the resale value of the gazebo may be much less than A's cost—except for his right to sue B for the price. Even then, a right to sue for breach of contract, being costly to enforce, is not a completely adequate remedy. B might therefore go to A and say, "If you don't reduce your price I'll refuse to pay and put you to the expense of suit"; and A might knuckle under. If such modifications are allowed, people in B's position will find it harder to make such contracts in the future, and everyone will be worse off.

The common law dealt with this problem by refusing to enforce modifications unsupported by fresh consideration. See, e.g., *Alaska Packers' Ass'n v. Domenico*, 117 Fed. 99 (9th Cir.1902), discussed in *Selmer Co. v. Blakeslee–Midwest Co.*, 704 F.2d 924, 927 (7th Cir.1983). Thus in the hypothetical case just put B could not have enforced A's promise to accept a lower price. But this solution is at once overinclusive and underinclusive—the former because most modifications are not coercive and should be enforceable whether or not there is fresh consideration, the latter because, since common law courts inquire only into the existence and not the adequacy of consideration, a requirement of fresh consideration has little bite. B might give A a peppercorn, a kitten, or a robe in exchange for A's agreeing to reduce the contract price, and then the modification would be enforceable and A could no longer sue for the original price.

The draftsmen of the Uniform Commercial Code took a fresh approach, by making modifications enforceable even if not supported by consideration (see [§ 2–209(1)]) and looking to the doctrines of duress and bad faith for the main protection against exploitive or opportunistic attempts at modification, as in our hypothetical case. See [UCC § 2–209, official comment 2]. But they did another thing as well. In [§ 2–209(2)] they allowed the parties to exclude oral modifications. National Metal Crafters argues that two subsections later they took back this grant of power by allowing an unwritten modification to operate as a waiver.

The common law did not enforce agreements such as [§ 2–209(2)] authorizes. The "reasoning" was that the parties were always free to agree orally to cancel their contract and the clause forbidding modifications not in writing would disappear with the rest of the contract when it was cancelled. "The most ironclad written contract can always be cut into by the acetylene torch of parol modification supported by adequate proof." *Wagner v. Graziano Construction Co.*, 390 Pa. 445, 448, 136 A.2d 82, 83–84 (1957). This is not reasoning; it is a conclusion disguised as a metaphor. It may have reflected a fear that such clauses, buried in the fine print of form contracts, were traps for the unwary; a sense that they were unnecessary because only modifications supported by consideration were enforceable; and a disinclination to allow parties in effect to extend the reach of the Statute of Frauds, which requires only some types of contract to be in writing. But the framers of the Uniform Commercial Code, as part and parcel of rejecting the requirement of consideration for modifications, must have rejected the traditional view; must have believed that the protection which the doctrines of duress and bad faith give against extortionate modifications might need reinforcement—if not from a requirement of consideration, which had proved ineffective, then from a grant of power to include a clause requiring modifications to be in writing and signed. An equally important point is that with consideration no longer required for modification, it was natural to give the parties some means of providing a substitute for the cautionary and evidentiary function that the requirement of consideration provides; and the means chosen was to allow them to exclude oral modifications.

If [§ 2–209(4)], which as we said provides that an attempted modification which does not comply with subsection (2) can nevertheless operate as a "waiver," is interpreted so broadly that *any* oral modification is effective as a waiver notwithstanding [§ 2–209(2)], both provisions become superfluous and we are back in the common law—only with not even a requirement of consideration to reduce the likelihood of fabricated or unintended oral modifications. A conceivable but unsatisfactory way around this result is to distinguish between a modification that substitutes a new term for an old, and a waiver, which merely removes an old term. On this interpretation National Metal Crafters could not enforce an oral term of the allegedly modified contract but could be excused from one of the written terms. This would take care of a case such as *Alaska Packers,* where seamen attempted to enforce a contract modification that raised their wages, but would not take care of the functionally identical case where seamen sought to collect the agreed-on wages without doing the agreed-on work. Whether the party claiming modification is seeking to impose an onerous new term on the other party or to wriggle out of an onerous term that the original contract imposed on it is a distinction without a difference. We can see that in this case. National Metal Crafters, while claiming that Wisconsin Knife Works broke their contract as orally modified to extend the delivery date, is not seeking damages for that breach. But this is small comfort to Wisconsin Knife Works, which thought it had a binding contract with fixed delivery dates. Whether called modification or waiver, what National Metal Crafters is seeking to do is to nullify a key term other than by a signed writing. If it can get away with this merely by testimony about an oral modification, [§ 2–209(2)] becomes very nearly a dead letter.

The path of reconciliation with subsection (4) is found by attending to the precise wording of (4). It does not say that an attempted modification "is" a waiver; it says that "it can operate as a waiver." It does not say in what circumstances it can operate as a waiver; but if an attempted modification is effective as a waiver only if there is reliance, then both [§§ 2–209(2) and 2–209(4)] can be given effect. Reliance, if reasonably induced and reasonable in extent, is a common substitute for consideration in making a promise legally enforceable, in part because it adds something in the way of credibility to the mere say-so of one party. The main purpose of forbidding oral modifications is to prevent the promisor from fabricating a modification that will let him escape his obligations under the contract; and the danger of successful fabrication is less if the promisor has actually incurred a cost, has relied. There is of course a danger of bootstrapping—of incurring a cost in order to make the case for a modification. But it is a risky course and is therefore less likely to be attempted than merely testifying to a conversation; it makes one put one's money where one's mouth is. * * *

Our approach is not inconsistent with [§ 2–209(5)], which allows a waiver to be withdrawn while the contract is executory, provided there is no "material change of position in reliance on the waiver." Granted, in (5) there can be no tincture of reliance; the whole point of the section is that a waiver may be withdrawn unless there is reliance. But the section has a different domain from [§ 2–209(4)]. It is not limited to attempted modifications invalid under subsections (2) or (3); it applies, for example, to an express written and signed waiver, provided only that the contract is still executory. Suppose that while the contract is still executory the buyer writes the seller a signed letter waiving some term in the contract and then, the next day, before the seller has relied, retracts it in writing; we have no reason to think that such a retraction would not satisfy [§ 2–209(5)], though this is not an issue we need definitively resolve today. In any event we are not suggesting that "waiver" means different things in (4) and (5); it means the same thing; but the *effect* of an attempted modification as a waiver under (4) depends in part on (2), which (4) (but not (5)) qualifies. Waiver and estoppel (which requires reliance to be effective) are frequently bracketed. * * *

Missing from the jury instruction on "modification" in this case is any reference to reliance, that is, to the incurring of costs by National Metal Crafters in reasonable reliance on assurances by Wisconsin Knife Works that late delivery would be acceptable. And although there is evidence of such reliance, it naturally was not a focus of the case, since the issue was cast as one of completed (not attempted) modification, which does not require reliance to be enforceable. National Metal Crafters must have incurred expenses in producing spade bit blanks after the original delivery dates, but whether these were *reliance* expenses is a separate question. Maybe National Metal Crafters would have continued to manufacture spade bit blanks anyway, in the hope of selling them to someone else. * * * The question of reliance cannot be considered so open and shut as to justify our concluding that the judge would have had to direct a verdict for National Metal Crafters, the party with the burden of proof on the issue. Nor, indeed, does National Metal Crafters argue that reliance was shown as a matter of law.

There is no need to discuss most of the other alleged errors in the conduct of the trial; they are unlikely to recur in a new trial. We do however point out that Wisconsin Knife Works' objections to the introduction of parol evidence have no merit once the issue is recast as one of waiver. The purpose of the parol evidence rule is to defeat efforts to vary by oral evidence the terms of a written instrument that the parties intended to be the fully integrated expression of their contract; it has no application when the issue is whether one of the parties later waived strict compliance with those terms. * * *

When a jury instruction is erroneous there must be a new trial unless the error is harmless. On the basis of the record before us we cannot say that the error in allowing the jury to find that the contract had been modified was harmless; but we do not want to exclude the possibility that it might be found to be so, on motion for summary judgment or otherwise, without the need for a new trial. Obviously National Metal Crafters has a strong case both that it relied on the waiver of the delivery deadlines and that there was no causal relationship between its late deliveries and the cancellation of the contract. We just are not prepared to say on the record before us that it is such a strong case as not to require submission to a jury. * * *

Reversed and Remanded.

EASTERBROOK, CIRCUIT JUDGE, dissenting. * * * I do not think that detrimental reliance is an essential element of waiver under [§ 2–209(4)].

"Waiver" is not a term the UCC defines. At common law "waiver" means an intentional relinquishment of a known right. A person may relinquish a right by engaging in conduct inconsistent with the right or by a verbal or written declaration. I do not know of any branch of the law—common, statutory, or constitutional—in which a renunciation of a legal entitlement is effective only if the other party relies to his detriment. * * *

Not all novel things are wrong, although legal novelties, like biological mutations, usually die out quickly. This novelty encounters an obstacle within [§ 2–209]. Section [2–209(5)] states that a person who "has made a waiver affecting an executory portion of the contract may retract the waiver" on reasonable notice "unless the retraction would be unjust in view of a material change of position in reliance on the waiver." Section [2–209] therefore treats "waiver" and "reliance" as different. Under [§ 2–209(4)] a waiver may be effective; under [§ 2–209(5)] a waiver may be effective *prospectively* only if there was also detrimental reliance.

The majority tries to reconcile the two subsections by stating that they have different domains. Section [2–209(4)] deals with oral waivers, while [§ 2–209(5)] "is not limited to attempted modifications invalid under subsections (2) or (3); it applies, for example, to express written waivers, provided only that the contract is executory." This distinction implies that subsection (4) applies to a subset of the subjects of subsection (5). Things are the other way around. Subsection (4) says that an attempt at modification may be a "waiver," and subsection (5) qualifies the effectiveness of "waivers" in the absence of reliance. See comment 4 to [§ 2–209]. The two have the same domain—all attempts at modification, be they oral, written, or implied from conduct, that do not satisfy the Statute of Frauds, [§ 2–209(3)], or a "signed writing" requirement of a clause permitted under [§ 2–209(2)]. The majority suggests that [§ 2–209(5)] also applies to signed waivers, but this gets things backward. A "signed writing" is binding as a modification under [§ 2–209(2)] without the need for "waiver." Section [2–209(1)] lifts the requirement of consideration, so a signed pledge not to enforce a term of a contract may not be revoked under [§ 2–209(5)] unless the pledge reserves the power of revocation. Because "waiver" is some subset of failed efforts to modify, it cannot be right to treat a successful effort to modify (a signed writing) as a "waiver" governed by subsection (5). * * *

The subsections read well together if waiver means "intentional relinquishment of a known right" in both. Section [2–209(4)] says that a failed attempt at modification may be a waiver and so relinquish a legal entitlement (such as the entitlement to timely delivery); [§ 2–209(5)] adds that a waiver cannot affect the executory portion of the contract (the time of future deliveries, for example) if the waiving party retracts, unless there is also detrimental reliance. But for [§ 2–209(2)] the oral waiver could affect the executory portion of the contract even without reliance. It is not necessary to vary the meaning of the word to make sense of each portion of the statute.

The majority makes reliance an ingredient of waiver not because the structure of the UCC demands this reading, but because it believes that otherwise the UCC would not deal adequately with the threat of opportunistic conduct. The drafters of the UCC chose to deal with opportunism not through a strict reading of waiver, however, but through a statutory requirement of commercial good faith. See [§ 2–103] and comment 2 to [§ 2–209]. The modification-only-in-writing clause has nothing to do with opportunism. A person who has his contracting partner over a barrel, and therefore is able to obtain a concession, can get the concession in writing. The writing will be the least of his worries. In almost all of the famous cases of modification the parties reduced the new agreement to writing. * * *

If National Metal Crafters were claiming damages for lost profits, it would be necessary to determine whether National Metal Crafters detrimentally relied on Wisconsin Knife Works's waiver. But National Metal Crafters does not want damages for work to be performed after January 1983. It simply wants to defeat Wisconsin Knife Works's claim for damages for belated delivery. * * * The jury, although improperly instructed, has found enough to support a judgment discharging National Metal Crafters from liability to Wisconsin Knife Works. This requires us to affirm the judgment.

A requirement of reliance will not make a difference very often—certainly not in this case. Any waiver that is more than a condonation of an existing default will induce some reliance. The buyer who asks a seller of fungible goods to defer delivery induces reliance even though the waiver of timely delivery will not affect the production of the goods. When the goods have a custom design, as the spade bit blanks do, some reliance is close to a certainty. I doubt that National Metal Crafters would have produced the same goods in the same quantity but for a belief that Wisconsin Knife Works wanted to have them. A change of position in reliance on the frequent discussions is all the majority requires. Summary judgment cannot be far away. Still, it is better not to ask unnecessary questions even when the questions have ready answers.

––––––––

UNITED NATIONS CONVENTION ON CONTRACTS FOR THE INTERNATIONAL SALE OF GOODS, ART. 29:

(1) A contract may be modified or terminated by the mere agreement of the parties.

(2) A contract in writing which contains a provision requiring any modification or termination by agreement to be in writing may not be otherwise modified or terminated by agreement. However, a party may be precluded by his conduct from asserting such a provision to the extent that the other party has relied on that conduct.

––––––––

Chapter 7

POLICING THE BARGAINING PROCESS

HAHN v. FORD MOTOR CO., INC.

Indiana Court of Appeals, 1982.
434 N.E.2d 943.

SHIELDS, JUDGE.

Appellants Michael and Judith Hahn initiated an action against Ford Motor Company (Ford) and Dick Lorey Ford, Inc. (Lorey) for breach of warranties on a 1977 Ford LTD II. Lorey counterclaimed for the balance due on the purchase price of the vehicle. At trial the jury rendered a verdict in favor of Ford and Lorey and against the Hahns on the breach of warranties action; the jury also held in favor of Lorey on its counterclaim, awarding damages of two thousand nine hundred dollars ($2,900). The Hahns present the following issues on appeal:

(1) Did the trial court err in admitting the Ford warranty facts booklet into evidence?

(2) Did the trial court err in admitting Lorey's warranty disclaimer into evidence? * * *

We affirm.

On June 27, 1977 Michael Hahn went to the Dick Lorey Ford dealership in Muncie to inquire about purchasing a new car. Hahn had observed advertisements on television and in magazines in which general statements were made concerning the quality of Ford cars. He indicated to the salesman he was interested in an auto which would be durable enough to haul a camper-trailer on family vacations. The next day Hahn, accompanied by his wife Judith, returned to the dealership and test-drove a 1977 Ford LTD II. On June 29 the Hahns once again returned to the agency and expressed a desire to purchase the same LTD II they had driven the previous day. That same date Michael Hahn executed a purchase agreement with Lorey and signed a dealers warranty disclaimer entitled "As Is Manufacturers Warranty Only." He and Mrs. Hahn executed a Merchants National Bank of Muncie retail installment sales agreement. The dealers warranty disclaimer represents dealer Lorey's attempt to disclaim all warranties, express and implied. It limits purchasers to recourse against the manufacturer and does not purport to affect warranties that may be provided by Ford.

The Hahns took delivery of the vehicle July 1, 1977. When Mr. Hahn arrived home with the new car he found a Ford warranty facts booklet in the glove box. According to Hahn, this was the first opportunity he had to read the pamphlet. He further claims the contents of the booklet were not discussed prior to the consummation of the sale.

Shortly after the date of purchase the Hahns began to experience persistent difficulties with the vehicle. According to service orders contained in the record, the car was taken to the dealership for repairs on numerous occasions. The Hahns also claim there were additional instances when the car was taken to the dealer and no formal service order prepared.

The most frequently reported defects included persistent oil and transmission leaks, difficulties with the electrical and heating systems, and a defective cruise control. Many of the problems ensued after the period of 12,000 mile and/or 12 months. However, Ford made repairs at no cost to purchaser even though this is not, necessarily the company's policy.

On January 20, 1979, nearly 18 months after the date of purchase, the Hahns attempted to permanently return the car to the dealership. The tender was refused by Lorey. When proceedings were initiated in April 1979 the Hahns placed the vehicle in storage alleging continual problems with the electrical system prevented the car from starting.

I

The Hahns contend the trial court erred when it admitted in evidence the Ford warranty facts booklet which limited the duration of implied warranties and disclaimed liability for incidental and consequential damages. They argue the booklet was inadmissible as a matter of law because the modification of implied warranties and the limitation of remedy were (A) inconspicuous, (B) not part of the bargain, (C) unconscionable, and (D) in violation of the Federal Magnuson-Moss Warranty Act.

A

Mr. Hahn claims to have found the booklet in the car's glove box after he had taken delivery of the vehicle and driven it home. The pertinent language of the booklet reads:

> "ANY IMPLIED WARRANTY OF MERCHANTABILITY OR FITNESS IS LIMITED TO THE 12–MONTH/12,000 MILE DURATION OF THIS WRITTEN WARRANTY.

> "TO THE EXTENT ALLOWED BY LAW, NEITHER FORD NOR THE SELLING DEALER SHALL HAVE ANY RESPONSIBILITY FOR LOSS OF USE OF THE VEHICLE, LOSS OF TIME, INCON-

VENIENCE, COMMERCIAL LOSS OR CONSEQUENTIAL DAMAGES.

"Some states do not allow limitations on how long an implied warranty lasts or the exclusion or limitation of incidental or consequential damages, so the above limitations may not apply to you.

"This warranty gives you specific legal rights, and you also may have other rights which vary from state to state."

The Hahns contend the modification of implied warranties and limitation of remedy contained in Ford's warranty facts manual were inconspicuous as a matter of law and should have been excluded from the jury.

[UCC § 2–316(2)] provides any attempt to exclude or modify an implied warranty of merchantability must mention merchantability and, *if written,* must be conspicuous, while any limitation of the implied warranty of fitness must be in writing *and* conspicuous. The term "conspicuous" is defined in [UCC § 1–201(10)]. * * *

The purpose behind the conspicuousness requirement is to protect the buyer from unfair surprise. In the present case the language modifying the implied warranties of merchantability and fitness is printed in bold face type on the front page of the booklet. It is sufficiently conspicuous so that a reasonable person ought to be placed on notice as to the terms of modification. We thus conclude that, as a matter of law, the modification of warranties complied with the requirements of [§§ 1–201(10) and 2–316(2)].[2]

B

The Hahns further note the modification of implied warranties and limitation of remedy contained in the Ford warranty facts booklet were given to them subsequent to the execution of the sales contract. They argue the pamphlet was therefore inadmissible as a matter of law because it was not part of the bargain.

The UCC is silent as to when disclaimers, modifications, and limitations must be made. However, modification of warranties and limitation of remedies are not favored in Indiana and are strictly construed against the seller and manufacturer on the basis of public policy. * * * Therefore, in instances where seller does not attempt a modification of warranty or limitation of remedy until after the contract for sale has been made even properly worded limitations or exclusions are ineffective. A modification of warranty or limitation of remedy contained in a manufacturers manual received by purchaser subsequent to sale has not been bargained for and thus does not limit recovery for implied or express warranties which arose prior to sale.

2. [UCC § 2–719] permits a contractual modification or limitation of remedies. This section, however, does not require the seller or manufacturer to conspicuously state such limitations. Therefore, Ford's limitation on remedy may not fail for want of conspicuousness.

In essence, the parties have not consented to and are not contractually bound by the modification or limitation. * * *

In the instant case, as we have noted, the Ford warranty manual contained both a modification on the duration of implied warranties and a limitation of remedy. We acknowledge the evidence clearly reveals Hahn was not aware of, and therefore never assented to, the limitation of remedy contained in the pamphlet. His attention was not directed to the specific limitations, nor was he afforded a reasonable opportunity to read the booklet. However, the trial court removed the issue of whether there was a valid limitation of remedy from the jury when it instructed the jury as to the standards to be used in measuring damages. These instructions charged the jury they were to consider the full panoply of damages available to a buyer in an action for breach of warranty.

Therefore, the lone question presented is whether there was evidence from which the trial court could conclude Ford made a prima facie showing Mr. Hahn assented to the limitation on the duration of implied warranties. Mr. Hahn, of course, testified he did not become aware of the warranty booklet until after he drove the new car home and searched the glove box. On the other hand, there is evidence which reveals Mr. Hahn was cognizant of a 12,000 mile/12 month limitation on the duration of any implied warranties. He testified:
* * *

"Q. Okay. So you're testifying in Court today that you proceeded to buy a car without any information whatsoever of the kind of warranty, the length of warranty of [sic] the things the warranty covered?

A. *Well the basic warranty on a car is twelve years, I mean twelve months or twelve thousand miles. I think everybody is aware of that.*"

(emphasis supplied) * * *

"Q. And I think you also testified that you knew there was a one year, twelve thousand mile, some type of warranty, at least in effect on the car, is that correct?

A. Yes, sir."

Q. And you were aware that that was also from Ford Motor Company?

A. Yes sir."

In addition, there was testimony the Lorey salesman discussed an extended warranty option program with Mr. Hahn. It was not specifically disclosed whether in the course of such conversation he was informed as to the 12,000 mile/12 month limitation on the duration of the standard warranty plan. The trial court, however, could have reasonably inferred such a discussion would, of necessity, entail an explanation of the duration of the basic warranty program in order to illustrate the benefits provided by the extended warranty option.

We thus hold there was evidence from which the trial court could conclude Ford made a prima facie showing the limitation on duration of implied warranties contained in the Ford warranty facts booklet was within the Hahns' knowledge at the time the parties entered into the bargain. The trial court therefore did not err in admitting into evidence the booklet which contained an identical limitation.

C

The Hahns next argue the modification of warranties and limitation of remedy were unconscionable as a matter of law and should have been excluded from the jury's consideration.

Pre-code Indiana cases recognized a clause or contract could be declared void on the basis of unconscionability.

> "An unconscionable contract has been defined to be such as no reasonable man not under delusion, duress or distress would make, and such as no honest and fair man would accept. There exists here an inequality so strong, gross, and manifest that it is impossible to state it to a man of common sense without producing an exclamation at the inequality of it."

Franklin Fire Insurance Co. v. Noll, (1945) 115 Ind.App. 289, 58 N.E.2d 947, 949. There are few Indiana cases explicitly applying [§ 2–302], the Code section governing unconscionability. * * * According to Uniform Commercial Code § 2–302, official comment 1:

> "The basic test is whether, in the light of the general commercial background and the commercial needs of the particular trade or case, the clauses involved are so one-sided as to be unconscionable under the circumstances existing at the time of the making of the contract * * * the principle is one of the prevention of oppression and unfair surprise (Cf. Campbell Soup Co. v. Wentz, 172 F.2d 80, 3d Cir. 1948) and not of disturbance of allocation of risks because of superior bargaining power."

The two evils addressed in [§ 2–302], "oppression" and "unfair surprise," suggest a framework for analysis heretofore not applied in this state but endorsed elsewhere. This analysis concentrates upon the two branches of unconscionability: substantive and procedural. Substantive unconscionability refers to oppressively one-sided and harsh terms of a contract, while procedural unconscionability involves the manner and process by which the terms become part of the contract.

Substantive unconscionability generally involves cases where courts have determined the price unduly excessive or where the terms of the contract unduly limit debtor remedies. White and Summers, Handbook of the Law Under the Uniform Commercial Code § 4–4 (2nd ed. 1980). Procedural unconscionability most frequently arises in cases characterized by consumer ignorance. For example, in one oft-cited case where a buyer who had a poor command of the English language signed a sales contract which waived implied warranties the court held the disclaimer invalid even though it otherwise complies with the code.

Jefferson Credit Corp. v. Marcano, (1969 Civ.Ct.) 60 Misc.2d 138, 302 N.Y.S.2d 390. Procedural unconscionability may also be found where "[s]eller's guile * * * takes the form of a clause difficult to understand and placed in fine print on the rear of the contract." White and Summers § 4–3, at 154.

Section [2–302(1)] assigns the question of unconscionability exclusively to the court. The party raising the issue bears the burden of proof. The Hahns must, therefore, establish as a matter of law the unconscionability of the modification of warranties and limitation of remedy.

Several commentators and cases have suggested that the terms of the modification of warranties and limitation of remedy are to be tested only against the precepts of [§§ 2–316 and 2–719] respectively. F.M.C. Finance Corp. v. Murphree, (1980 5th Cir.) 632 F.2d 413. They argue if the modification or limitation in question complies with [§ 2–316 or 2–719] it may not as a matter of law be deemed unconscionable unless there are procedural irregularities.[7] Tacoma Boatbuilding; Special Project, Article Two Warranties in Commercial Transactions, 64 Cornell L.Rev. 30. There is admittedly some merit to this argument, especially with regard to [§ 2–316] which has as its purpose the prevention of unfair surprise and oppression. Uniform Commercial Code [§ 2–316, offical comment 1]. Yet, [§ 2–302] expressly applies to "any clause of the contract," and neither section 2–316 nor 2–719 affirmatively states that limitations meeting its requirements are immune from [§ 2–302].

We are mindful, however, that parties to a contract are provided broad latitude within which to fashion their own liability and remedies. Modification of warranties and limitations of remedy are not *per se* unconscionable. In the present case the terms of the Ford modification of warranties and limitation of remedy are not so one-sided as to be unconscionable as a matter of law.

D

The Hahns also allege the Ford warranty facts booklet violates the Federal Magnuson-Moss Warranty Act. 15 U.S.C.A. § 2301 et seq.

In 1975 Congress enacted the Magnuson-Moss Act which establishes a Federal consumer warranty law. Section 2301 of the Act defines consumer goods to include "tangible personal property * * * distributed in commerce * * * [and] normally used for personal, family or household purposes * * *." The Act provides the types and methods of disclaimer and modification one may employ with

---

7. According to this view, the only occasion in which a modification of warranties or limitation of remedy would be held substantively unconscionable is when it limits the conssequential damages and runs afoul of [§ 2–719(3)]. We note that cases finding warranty disclaimers or modifications unconscionable frequently flow from a misapplication of [§ 2–719(3)]. This is the result of a misunderstanding of the differences between a warranty disclaimer or modification subject to [§ 2–316] and a limitation of remedies subject to [§ 2–719].

regard to implied warranties. It applies exclusively to disclaimers and modifications contained in written warranties. The statute relies, however, on state law in defining the contours of implied warranties.

According to the Hahns, the Ford warranty booklet violates 15 U.S.C. § 2308 because it limits the damages available to purchasers upon a breach of implied warranty.[8] Section 2308 provides:

"(a) No supplier may disclaim or modify (except as provided in subsection (b) of this section) any implied warranty to a consumer with respect to such consumer product if (1) such supplier makes any written warranty to the consumer with respect to such consumer product, or (2) at the time of sale, or within 90 days thereafter, such supplier enters into a service contract with the consumer which applies to such consumer product.

(b) For purposes of this chapter (other than section 2304(a)(2) of this title), implied warranties may be limited in duration to the duration of a written warranty of reasonable duration, if such limitation is conscionable and is set forth in clear and unmistakable language and prominently displayed on the face of the warranty.

(c) A disclaimer, modification, or limitation made in violation of this section shall be ineffective for purposes of this chapter and State law. Pub.L. 93–367, Title I, Sec. 108, Jan. 4, 1975, 88 Stat. 2189."

Ford's attempt to limit its liability for a breach of implied warranty, the Hahns contend, contravenes § 2308(a) and (b) which provides that warrantor may not limit an implied warranty except to the extent its duration is limited to the reasonable duration of the written warranty.

The Hahns' analysis, however, fails to adequately differentiate between a limitation of remedy and a disclaimer or modification of warranty. Although it is frequently difficult to appreciate the distinction between warranty disclaimers or modifications and limitations of remedy, these two devices in theory constitute two separate mechanisms for eliminating responsibility for product quality. A disclaimer or modification of warranty eliminates the quality commitment. It limits the circumstances in which the seller or manufacturer may be deemed to be in breach of warranty. A limitation of remedy, on the other hand, acknowledges the quality commitment but restricts the remedy available once a breach has been established.

The Magnuson-Moss Act provision cited above provides the warrantor may not "disclaim or modify * * * any implied warranty" except to the extent its duration is limited to that of the written

8. The booklet provides:

"*TO THE EXTENT ALLOWED BY LAW,* NEITHER FORD NOR THE SELLING DEALER SHALL HAVE ANY RESPONSIBILITY FOR LOSS OF USE OF THE VEHICLE, LOSS OF TIME, INCONVENIENCE, COMMERCIAL LOSS OR CONSEQUENTIAL DAMAGES. (emphasis supplied)"

warranty. It does not make reference to any attempt to limit or restrict available remedies for breach of an implied warranty. There is no indication the Act even contemplates limiting the ability of the warrantor to limit relief.[9] In the present case Ford limited the duration of any implied warranty to the duration of its written express warranty. The fact it restricted available relief for a breach of implied warranty did not violate the terms of section 2308.

For the aformentioned reasons, we thus conclude Hahn's claim that Ford's modification of warranties and limitation of remedy were inadmissible as a matter of law is without merit.

II

The Hahns similarly contend Dick Lorey Ford Inc.'s disclaimer of warranty was inadmissible as a matter of law. They rely on many of the same arguments advanced with regard to Ford's warranty booklet to support this contention. The Lorey disclaimer is entitled "As Is, Manufacturers Warranty Only." It represents dealer Lorey's attempt to disclaim all warranties, express and implied, and limit buyer to recourse against the manufacturer, Ford Motor Co.

As we noted earlier, the pertinent language disclaiming all warranties running from the dealer is printed in bold type and on its face complies with [§ 2–316]. Michael Hahn executed the document June 29, 1977, the date of purchase, and its terms thus became a part of the bargain.

The Hahns contend, however, they were not aware of the nature and contents of the instrument since the Lorey salesman allegedly informed Mr. Hahn its execution was a mere formality. Fraudulent practices in the bargaining setting may be an indicia of procedural unconscionability. Nonetheless, the alleged conduct of the Lorey salesman was not so overreaching or oppressive as to rise to the level of unconscionability. There is no evidence Mr. Hahn was misled or fraudulently induced as to the nature and contents of the disclaimer despite the salesman's alleged statement. Moreover, the terms of the disclaimer were so boldly displayed and the purpose of the document was so clearly manifest a consumer of ordinary sophistication ought to have been on notice as to its contents. * * *

Because the Magnuson-Moss Act applies only to written warranties, it has no applicability with regard to Lorey. The evidence discloses Lorey made no written warranties. To the contrary, its disclaimer clearly excluded all warranties, express and implied. Therefore, Hahns' allegation that the Lorey disclaimer violated the Magnuson-Moss Act is misplaced. * * *

9. Regulations promulgated by the Federal Trade Commission, the government agency charged with administering the Act, appear to support the conclusion that warrantors are not prohibited from limiting available relief for a breach of warranty. 16 C.F.R. 701.3(a)(8) states that warrantor should explicitly disclose to purchaser "[a]ny exclusions of or limitations on relief such as incidental or consequential damages * * *" Ford has complied with such regulation.

We therefore conclude the Hahns fail to establish the Lorey disclaimer was inadmissible as a matter of law. * * *

Judgment affirmed.

BUCHANAN, C. J., and SULLIVAN, J., concur.

"LEMON" LAWS

The Magnuson-Moss Warranty—Federal Trade Commission Improvement Act referred to in the principal case provides that when a consumer product is advertised as having a "full warranty," "if the product (or a component part thereof) contains a defect or malfunction after a reasonable number of attempts of the warrantor to remedy defects or malfunctions in such product, such warrantor must permit the consumer to elect either a refund for, or replacement without charge of, such product or part (as the case may be)." 15 U.S.C.A. § 2304(a)(4). This provision has had little effect because almost all warranties are now advertised to be "limited" rather than "full." A number of states, however, have passed so-called "lemon" laws with similar repair-within-a-reasonable time-or-replace provisions, but applicable to all express warranties of motor vehicles, even express warranties that would not be classified as "full" under the Magnuson-Moss Act. One of the first was passed in Connecticut in 1982. As amended (Conn.Gen.S.Ann. § 42–179), the Connecticut lemon law provides:

NEW AUTOMOBILE WARRANTIES

(d) If the manufacturer, or its agents or authorized dealers are unable to conform the motor vehicle to any applicable express warranty by repairing or correcting any defect or condition which substantially impairs the use, safety or value of the motor vehicle to the consumer after a reasonable number of attempts, the manufacturer shall replace the motor vehicle with a new motor vehicle acceptable to the consumer, or accept return of the vehicle from the consumer and refund to the consumer, lessor and lienholder, if any, as their interests may appear, the following: (1) The full contract price including, but not limited to charges for undercoating, dealer preparation and transportation and installed options, (2) all collateral charges, including, but not limited to, sales tax, license and registration fees, and similar government charges, (3) all finance charges incurred by the consumer after he first reports the nonconformity to the manufacturer, agent or dealer and during any subsequent period when the vehicle is out of service by reason of repair, and (4) all incidental damages as defined in [UCC § 2–715] less a reasonable allowance for the consumer's use of the vehicle. * * *

(e) It shall be presumed that a reasonable number of attempts have been undertaken to conform a motor vehicle to the applicable express warranties, if (1) the same nonconformity has been subject to repair four or more times by the manufacturer or its agents or authorized dealers during the period of two years following the date of original delivery of the motor vehicle to a consumer or during the period of the first eighteen thousand miles of operation, whichever period ends first, but such nonconformity continues to exist or (2) the vehicle is out of service by reason of repair for a cumulative total of thirty or more calendar days during the applicable period, determined pursuant to subdivision (1) of this subsection. * * *

(j) If a manufacturer has established an informal dispute settlement procedure which is certified by the attorney general as complying in all respects with the provisions of Title 16 Code of Federal Regulations * * * the provisions of subsection (d) of this section concerning refunds or replacement shall not apply to any consumer who has not first resorted to such procedure.

A & M PRODUCE CO. v. FMC CORP.

Court of Appeal, Fourth District, Division 1, 1982.
135 Cal.App.3d 473, 186 Cal.Rptr. 114.

[A & M Produce decided to grow tomatoes, and it purchased from FMC a machine to sort the tomatoes by weight and size for packing. The contract of sale disclaimed all warranties and provided that "Seller in no event shall be liable for consequential damages arising out of or in connection with this agreement." The machine failed to operate efficiently and damaged tomatoes. Except for a few tomatoes that were sold to a cannery, the crop could not be marketed. A & M sued FMC for damages resulting from breach of express warranties and the implied warranty of fitness for a particular purpose. (See UCC § 2–315). The trial judge ruled that the disclaimer of warranties and exclusion of consequential damages were unconscionable and unenforceable. Judgment for A & M in the amount of $255,000 was affirmed.]

WIENER, ASSOCIATE JUSTICE. * * *

The Uniform Commercial Code does not attempt to precisely define what is or is not "unconscionable." Nevertheless, "[u]nconscionability has generally been recognized to include an absence of meaningful choice on the part of one of the parties together with contract terms which are unreasonably favorable to the other party." (Williams v. Walker-Thomas Furniture Company (D.C.Cir. 1965) 350 F.2d 445, 449, fn. omitted.) Phrased another way, unconscionability has both a "procedural" and a "substantive" element. (Industralease Automated & Scientific Eq. Corp., Etc. (1977) 58 A.D.2d 482, 396 N.Y.S.2d 427, 431, fn. 4; see also Leff, [Unconscionability and the Code—The Emperor's New Clause,] 115 U.Pa.L.Rev. at p. 487; White and Summers, [Uniform Commercial Code (2d ed. 1980)] § 4–3 at p. 151.)

The procedural element focuses on two factors: "oppression" and "surprise." * * * "Oppression" arises from an inequality of bargaining power which results in no real negotiation and "an absence of meaningful choice." (Williams v. Walker-Thomas Furniture Company, supra, 350 F.2d at p. 449; see Spanogle, Analyzing Unconscionability

Problems (1969) 117 U.Pa.L.Rev. 931, 944–946). "Surprise" involves the extent to which the supposedly agreed-upon terms of the bargain are hidden in a prolix printed form drafted by the party seeking to enforce the disputed terms. (See Ellinghaus, In Defense of Unconscionability (1969) 78 Yale L.J. 757, 764–765; Eddy, On the "Essential" Purposes of Limited Remedies: The Metaphysics of UCC Section 2–719(2) (1977) 65 Cal.L.Rev. 28, 43; Spanogle, supra, 117 U.Pa.L.Rev. at pp. 934–935, 943.) Characteristically, the form contract is drafted by the party with the superior bargaining position. (See Calamari and Perillo, Contracts (2d ed. 1977) § 9–40, p. 325.)

Of course the mere fact that a contract term is not read or understood by the non-drafting party or that the drafting party occupies a superior bargaining position will not authorize a court to refuse to enforce the contract. Although an argument can be made that contract terms not actively negotiated between the parties fall outside the "circle of assent" which constitutes the actual agreement (see Eddy, supra, 65 Cal.L.Rev. at p. 43), commercial practicalities dictate that unbargained-for terms only be denied enforcement where they are also *substantively* unreasonable. (Ellinghaus, supra, 78 Yale L.J. at pp. 766–767; Murray on Contracts, [2d ed. 1974] at pp. 748–749.) No precise definition of substantive unconscionability can be proffered. Cases have talked in terms of "overly-harsh" or "one-sided" results. One commentator has pointed out, however, that "* * * unconscionability turns not only on a 'one-sided' result, but also on an absence of 'justification' for it." (Eddy, supra, 65 Cal.L.Rev. at p. 45), which is only to say that substantive unconscionability must be evaluated as of the time the contract was made. (See [UCC § 2–302].) The most detailed and specific commentaries observe that a contract is largely an allocation of risks between the parties, and therefore that a contractual term is substantively suspect if it reallocates the risks of the bargain in an objectively unreasonable or unexpected manner. (Murray, Unconscionability: Unconscionability (1969) 31 U.Pitt.L.Rev. 1, 12–23; But not all unreasonable risk reallocations are unconscionable; rather, enforceability of the clause is tied to the procedural aspects of unconscionability such that the greater the unfair surprise or inequality of bargaining power, the less unreasonable the risk reallocation which will be tolerated. (See Spanogle, supra, 117 U.Pa.L.Rev. at pp. 950, 968.) * * *

Turning first to the procedural aspects of unconscionability, we note at the outset that this contract arises in a commercial context between an enormous diversified corporation (FMC) and a relatively small but experienced farming company (A & M). Generally, "* * * courts have not been solicitous of businessmen in the name of unconscionability." (White and Summers, supra, § 4–9 at p. 170). This is probably because courts view businessmen as possessed of a greater degree of commercial understanding and substantially more economic muscle than the ordinary consumer. Hence, a businessman usually has a more difficult time establishing procedural unconscionability in the sense of either "unfair surprise" or "unequal bargaining power."

Nevertheless, generalizations are always subject to exceptions and categorization is rarely an adequate substitute for analysis. With increasing frequency, courts have begun to recognize that experienced but legally unsophisticated businessmen may be unfairly surprised by unconscionable contract terms and that even large business entities may have *relatively* little bargaining power, depending on the identity of the other contracting party and the commercial circumstances surrounding the agreement. This recognition rests on the conviction that the social benefits associated with freedom of contract are severally skewed where it appears that had the party actually been aware of the term to which he "agreed" or had he any real choice in the matter, he would never have assented to inclusion of the term.

Both aspects of procedural unconscionability appear to be present on the facts of this case. Although the printing used on the warranty disclaimer was conspicuous, the terms of the consequential damage exclusion are not particularly apparent, being only slightly larger than most of the other contract text. Both provisions appear in the middle of the back page of a long preprinted form contract which was only casually shown to Abatti [owner of A & M] . It was never suggested to him, either verbally or in writing, that he read the back of the form. Abatti testified he never read the reverse side terms. There was thus sufficient evidence before the trial court to conclude that Abatti was in fact surprised by the warranty disclaimer and the consequential damage exclusion. How "unfair" his surprise was is subject to some dispute. He certainly had the opportunity to read the back of the contract or to seek the advice of a lawyer. Yet as a factual matter, given the complexity of the terms and FMC's failure to direct his attention to them, Abatti's omission may not be totally unreasonable. In this regard, the comments of the Indiana Supreme Court in Weaver v. American Oil Company, supra, 276 N.E.2d at pp. 147–148 are apposite:

> "The burden should be on the party submitting [a standard contract] in printed form to show that the other party had knowledge of any unusual or unconscionable terms contained therein. The principle should be the same as that applicable to implied warranties, namely that a package of goods sold to a purchaser is fit for the purposes intended and contains no harmful materials other than that represented."

Here, FMC made no attempt to provide A & M with the requisite knowledge of the disclaimer or the exclusion. In fact, one suspects that the length, complexity and obtuseness of most form contracts may be due at least in part to the seller's preference that the buyer will be dissuaded from reading that to which he is supposedly agreeing. This process almost inevitably results in a one-sided "contract."

Even if we ignore any suggestion of unfair surprise, there is ample evidence of unequal bargaining power here and a lack of any real negotiation over the terms of the contract. Although it was conceded that A & M was a large-scale farming enterprise by Imperial Valley standards, employing five persons on a regular basis and up to fifty seasonal employees at harvest time, and that Abatti was farming some 8,000 acres in 1974, FMC Corporation is in an entirely different category. The 1974 gross sales of the Agriculture Machinery Division alone amounted to $40 million. More importantly, the terms on the FMC form contract were standard. FMC salesmen were not authorized to negotiate any of the terms appearing on the reverse side of the preprinted contract. Although FMC contends that in some special instances, individual contracts are negotiated, A & M was never made aware of that option. The sum total of these circumstances leads to the conclusion that this contract was a "bargain" only in the most general sense of the word.

Although the procedural aspects of unconscionability are present in this case, we suspect the substantive unconscionability of the disclaimer and exclusion provisions contributed equally to the trial court's ultimate conclusion. As to the disclaimer of warranties, the facts of this case support the trial court's conclusion that such disclaimer was commercially unreasonable. The warranty allegedly breached by FMC went to the basic performances characteristics of the product. In attempting to disclaim this and all other warranties, FMC was in essence guaranteeing nothing about what the product would do. Since a product's performance forms the fundamental basis for a sales contract, it is patently unreasonable to assume that a buyer would purchase a standardized mass-produced product from an industry seller without any enforceable performance standards. From a social perspective, risk of loss is most appropriately borne by the party best able to prevent its occurrence. Rarely would the buyer be in a better position than the manufacturer-seller to evaluate the performance characteristics of a machine.

In this case, moreover, the evidence establishes that A & M had no previous experience with weight-sizing machines and was forced to rely on the expertise of FMC in recommending the necessary equipment. FMC was abundantly aware of this fact. The jury here necessarily found that FMC either expressly or impliedly guaranteed a performance level which the machine was unable to meet. Especially where an inexperienced buyer is concerned, the seller's performance representations are absolutely necessary to allow the buyer to make an intelligent choice among the competitive options available. A seller's attempt, through the use of a disclaimer, to prevent the buyer from reasonably relying on such representations calls into question the commercial reasonableness of the agreement and may well be substantively unconscionable. The trial court's conclusion to that effect is amply supported by the record before us.

As to the exclusion of consequential damages, several factors combine to suggest that the exclusion was unreasonable on the facts of this case. Consequential damages are a commercially recognized type of damage actually suffered by A & M due to FMC's breach. A party "＊ ＊ ＊ should be able to rely on their existence in the absence of being informed to the contrary, ＊ ＊ ＊." (Schroeder v. Fagoel Motors, Inc., supra, 544 P.2d at p. 24.) This factor is particularly important given the commercial realities under which the contract was executed. If the seller's warranty was breached, consequential damages were not merely "reasonably foreseeable"; they were explicitly obvious. All parties were aware that once the tomatoes began to ripen, they all had to be harvested and packed within a relatively short period of time.

Another factor supporting the trial court's determination involves the avoidability of the damages and relates directly to the allocation of risks which lies at the foundation of the contractual bargain. It has been suggested that "[r]isk shifting is socially expensive and should not be undertaken in the absence of a good reason. An even better reason is required when to so shift is contrary to a contract freely negotiated." (S.M. Wilson & Co. v. Smith Intern., Inc. (9th Cir. 1978) 587 F.2d 1363, 1375.) But as we noted previously, FMC was the only party reasonably able to prevent this loss by not selling A & M a machine inadequate to meet its expressed needs. "If there is a type of risk allocation that should be subjected to special scrutiny, it is probably the shifting to one party of a risk that *only* the other party can avoid." (*Eddy,* supra, 65 Cal.L.Rev. at p. 47, italics in original.)

GEORGE MITCHELL (CHESTERHALL) LTD. v. FINNEY LOCK SEEDS LTD.

Court of Appeal, 1982.
[1983] 1 All E.R. 108, [1982] 3 W.L.R. 1036.＊

LORD DENNING MR.

IN OUTLINE

Many of you know Lewis Carroll's *Through the Looking–Glass.* In it there are these words (ch 4):

" 'The time has come,' the Walrus said,

'To talk of many things:

Of shoes—and ships—and sealing wax—

Of cabbages—and kings ＊ ＊ ＊' "

Today it is not "of cabbages and kings", but of cabbages and whatnots. Some farmers, called George Mitchell (Chesterhall) Ltd., ordered 30 lb of cabbage seed. It was supplied. It looked just like cabbage seed. No one could say it was not. The farmers planted it over 63 acres. Six months later there appeared out of the ground a lot of loose green leaves. They looked like cabbage leaves but they never turned in. They had no hearts. They were not "cabbages" in our common par-

＊ Appeal dismissed [1983] 2 All E.R. 737,
[1983] 3 W.L.R. 163 (House of Lords, 1983).

lance because they had no hearts. The crop was useless for human consumption. Sheep or cattle might eat it if hungry enough. It was commercially useless. The price of the seed was £192. The loss to the farmers was over £61,000. They claimed damages from the seed merchants, Finney Lock Seeds Ltd. The judge awarded them that sum with interest. The total comes to nearly £100,000.

The seed merchants appeal to this court. They say that they supplied the seed on a printed clause by which their liability was limited to the cost of the seed, that is £192. They rely much on two recent cases in the House of Lords: *Photo Production Ltd. v Securicor Transport Ltd* [1980] 1 All ER 556 [1980] AC 827 and *Ailsa Craig Fishing Co Ltd v Malvern Fishing Co Ltd* [1983] 1 All ER 101 (the two *Securicor* cases). * * *

ARE THE CONDITIONS PART OF THE CONTRACT?

The farmers were aware that the sale was subject to some conditions of sale. All seed merchants have conditions of sale. They were on the back of the catalogue. They were also on the back of the invoice each year. So it would seem that the farmers were bound at common law by the terms of them. The inference from the course of dealing would be that the farmers had accepted the conditions as printed, even though they had never read them and did not realize that they contained a limitation on liability.

But, in view of modern developments, it is to be noticed that the conditions were not negotiated at all between any representative bodies. They were not negotiated by the National Farmers' Union. They were introduced by the seed merchants by putting them in their catalogue and invoice, and never objected to by the farmers.

It is also to be noticed that the farmers never thought of insuring against any breach of contract by the seedsmen. It would be difficult to get any quotation. It might be possible for the seed merchants to insure themselves, something in the nature of a product liability insurance. Some seed merchants do so.

THE PRINTED CONDITION HERE

The limitation clause here is of long standing in the seed trade. It has been in use for many years. The material part of it is as follows:

"All Seeds, Bulbs, Corms, Tubers, Roots, Shrubs, Trees and Plants (hereinafter referred to as 'Seeds or Plants') offered for sale or sold by us to which the Seeds Act 1920 or the Plant Varieties and Seeds Act 1964 as the case may be and the Regulations thereunder apply have been tested in accordance with the provisions of the same. In the event of any seeds or plants sold or agreed to be sold by us not complying with the express terms of the contract of sale or with any representation made by us or by any duly authorised agent or representative on our behalf prior to, at the time of, or in any such contract, or any seeds or plants proving defective in varietal purity *we will, at our option, replace the defective seeds or plants, free of charge to the buyer or will refund all payments made to us by the buyer in respect of the defective seeds or plants and this shall be the limit of our obligation. We hereby exclude all liability for any loss or damage arising from the use of any seeds or plants supplied by us and for any consequential loss or damage arising out of such use* or any failure in the performance of or any defect in any seeds or plants supplied by us *or for any other loss or damage whatsoever save for, at our option, liability for any such replacement or refund as aforesaid.* In accordance with the established custom of the Seed Trade any express or implied condition, statement or warranty, statutory or otherwise, not stated in these Conditions is hereby excluded. *The price of any seeds or plants sold or offered for sale by us is based upon the foregoing limitations upon our liability. The price of such seeds or plants would be much greater if a more extensive liability were required to be undertaken by us.*" (My emphasis.)

The Natural Meaning

There was much discussion before us as to the construction of that condition. I am much impressed by the words I have emphasised. Taking the clause in its natural plain meaning, I think it is effective to limit the liability of the seed merchants to a return of the money or replacement of the seeds. The explanation they give seems fair enough. They say that it is so as to keep the price low, and that if they were to undertake any greater liability the price would be much greater.

After all, the seed merchants did supply seeds. True, they were the wrong kind altogether. But they were seeds. On the natural interpretation, I think the condition is sufficient to limit the seed merchants to a refund of the price paid or replacement of the seeds.

The Hostile Meaning

Before the decisions of the House of Lords in the two *Securicor* cases, I would have been inclined to decide the case as the judge did. I would have been "hostile" to the clause. I would have said that the goods supplied here were different *in kind* from those that were ordered, and that the seed merchants could not avail themselves of the limitation clause. But in the light of the House of Lords cases, I think that that approach is not available.

I am particularly impressed by the words of Lord Wilberforce in the *Ailsa Craig* case [1983] 1 All ER 101 at 102–103, where he said:

" * * * one must not strive to create ambiguities by strained construction, as I think the appellants have striven to do. The relevant words must be given, if possible, their natural, plain meaning. Clauses of limitation are not regarded by the courts with the same hostility as clauses of exclusion; this is because they must be related to other contractual terms, in particular to the risks to which the defending party may be exposed, the remuneration which he receives and possibly also the opportunity of the other party to insure."

To my mind these two cases have revolutionised our approach to exemption clauses. In order to explain their importance, I propose to take you through the story.

THE HEYDAY OF FREEDOM OF CONTRACT

None of you nowadays will remember the trouble we had, when I was called to the Bar, with exemption clauses. They were printed in small print on the back of tickets and order forms and invoices. They were contained in catalogues or timetables. They were held to be binding on any person who took them without objection. No one ever did object. He never read them or knew what was in them. No matter how unreasonable they were, he was bound. All this was done in the name of "freedom of contract". But the freedom was all on the side of the big concern which had the use of the printing press. No freedom for the little man who took the ticket or order form or invoice. The big concern said, "Take it or leave it." The little man had no option but to take it. The big concern could and did exempt itself from liability in its own interest without regard to the little man. It got away with it time after time. When the courts said to the big concern, "You must put it in clear words," the big concern had no hesitation in doing so. It knew well that the little man would never read the exemption clauses or understand them.

It was a bleak winter for our law of contract. * * *

THE SECRET WEAPON

Faced with this abuse of power, by the strong against the weak, by the use of the small print of the conditions, the judges did what they could to put a curb on it. They still had before them the idol, "freedom of contract". They still knelt down and worshipped it, but they concealed under their cloaks a secret weapon. They used it to stab the idol in the back. This weapon was called "the true construction of the contract". They used it with great skill and ingenuity. They used it so as to depart from the natural meaning of the words of the exemption clause and to put on them a strained and unnatural construction. In case after case, they said that the words were not strong enough to give the big concern exemption from liability, or that in the circumstances the big concern was not entitled to rely on the exemption clause. If a ship deviated from the contractual voyage, the owner could not rely on the exemption clause. If a warehouseman stored the goods in the wrong warehouse, he could not pray in aid the limitation clause. If the seller supplied goods different in kind from those contracted for, he could not rely on any exemption from liability. If a shipowner delivered goods to a person without production of the bill of lading, he could not escape responsibility by reference to an exemption clause. In short, whenever the wide words, in their natural meaning, would give rise to an unreasonable result, the judges either rejected them as repugnant to the main purpose of the contract or else cut them down to size in order to produce a reasonable result. * * * But when the clause was itself reasonable and gave rise to a reasonable result, the judges upheld it, at any rate when the clause did not exclude liability entirely but only limited it to a reasonable amount. So, where goods were deposited in a cloakroom or sent to a laundry for cleaning, it was quite reasonable for the company to limit their liability to a reasonable amount, having regard to the small charge made for the service. * * *

FUNDAMENTAL BREACH

No doubt had ever been cast thus far by anyone. But doubts arose when in this court, in a case called *Karsales (Harrow) Ltd v Wallis* [1956] 2 All ER 866, [1956] 1 WLR 936, we ventured to suggest that if the big concern was guilty of a breach which went to the "very root" of the contract, sometimes called a "fundamental breach", or at other times a "total failure" of its obligations, then it could not rely on the printed clause to exempt itself from liability. * * * But we did make a mistake, in the eyes of some, in elevating it, by inference, into a "rule of law". That was too rude an interference with the idol of "freedom of contract". We ought to have used the secret weapon. We ought to have said that in each case, on the "true construction of the contract" in that case, the exemption clause did not avail the party where he was guilty of a fundamental breach or a breach going to the root. * * *

THE CHANGE IN CLIMATE

In 1969 there was a change in climate. Out of winter into spring. It came with the first report of the Law Commission on Exemption Clauses in Contracts (Law Com no 24) which was implemented in the Supply of Goods (Implied Terms) Act 1973. In 1975 there was a further change. Out of spring into summer. It came with their second report on Exemption Clauses (Law Com no 69) which was implemented by the Unfair Contract Terms Act 1977. No longer was the big concern able to impose whatever terms and conditions it liked in a printed form, no matter how unreasonable they might be. These reports showed most convincingly that the courts could and should only enforce them if they were fair and reasonable in themselves and it was fair and reasonable to allow the big concern to rely on them. So the idol of "freedom of contract" was shattered. In cases of personal injury or death, it was not permissible to exclude or restrict liability at all. In consumer contracts any exemption clause was subject to the test of reasonableness. * * *

THE EFFECT OF THE CHANGES

What is the result of all this? To my mind it heralds a revolution in our approach to exemption clauses; not only where they exclude liability altogether and also where they limit liability; not only in the specific categories in the Unfair Contract Terms Act 1977, but in other contracts too. Just as in other fields of law we have done away with the multitude of cases on "common employment", "last opportunity", "invitees" and "licensees" and so forth, so also in this field we should do away with the multitude of cases on exemption clauses. We should no longer have to go through all kinds of gymnastic contortions to get round them. We should no longer have to harass our students with the study of them. We should set about meeting a new challenge. It is presented by the test of reasonableness.

THE TWO SECURICOR CASES

The revolution is exemplified by the recent two *Securicor* cases in the House of Lords (*Photo Production Ltd v. Securicor Transport Ltd* [1980] 1 All ER 556, [1980] AC 827 and *Ailsa Craig Fishing Co Ltd v. Malvern Fishing Co Ltd* [1983] 1 All ER 101). In each of them the Securicor company provided a patrolman to keep watch on premises so as to see that they were safe from intruders. They charged very little for the service. In the *Photo Production* case it was a factory with a lot of paper in it. The patrolman set light to it and burnt down the factory. In the *Ailsa Craig* case it was a quay at Aberdeen where ships were berthed. The patrolman went off for the celebrations on New Year's Eve. He left the ships unattended. The tide rose. A ship rose with it. Its bow got "snubbed" under the deck of the quay. It sank. In each case the owners were covered by insurance. The factory owners had their fire insurance. The shipowners had their hull insurance. In each case the Securicor company relied on a limitation clause. Under it they were protected from liability beyond a limit which was quite reasonable and their insurance cover was limited accordingly. The issue in practical terms was: which of the insurers should bear the loss? The question in legal terms in each case was whether Securicor could avail themselves of the limitation clause. In each case the House held that they could.

In the first case the House made it clear that the doctrine of "fundamental breach" was no longer applicable. They replaced it by the test of reasonableness. * * *

In the second case the House made a distinction between clauses which excluded liability altogether, and those which only limited liability to a certain sum. Exclusion clauses were to be construed strictly contra proferentem, whereas limitation clauses were to be construed naturally. This must be because a limitation clause is more likely to be reasonable than an exclusion clause. If you go by the plain, natural meaning of the words (as you should do) there is nothing to choose between them. * * *

If you read the speeches in the *Ailsa Craig* case, it does look as if the House of Lords were relying on the reasonableness of the limitation clause. They held it was applicable even though the failure of the Securicor company was a "total failure" to provide the service contracted for. They also said, obiter, that they would construe an exclusion clause much more strictly, just as was done in the old cases decided in the winter time. But I would suggest that the better reason is because it would not be fair or reasonable to allow the propounder of them to rely on them in the circumstances of the case.

THE SUPPLY OF GOODS (IMPLIED TERMS) ACT 1973

In any case the contract for these cabbage seeds was governed by s 4 of the Supply of Goods (Implied Terms) Act 1973: see now s 55(4) as set out in para 11 of Sch 1 to the Sale of Goods Act 1979. That section says that in the case of a contract of sale of goods any term "is ＊ ＊ ＊ not enforceable to the extent that it is shown that it would not be fair or reasonable to allow reliance on the term". That provision is exactly in accord with the principle which I have advocated above. So the ultimate question, to my mind, in this case is just this: to what extent would it be fair or reasonable to allow the seed merchants to rely on the limitation clause?

FAIR AND REASONABLE

There is only one case in the books so far on this point. It is *R W Green Ltd v Cade Bros Farm* [1978] 1 Lloyd's Rep 602. There Griffiths J held that it was fair and reasonable for seed potato merchants to rely on a limitation clause which limited their liability to the contract price of the potatoes. That case was very different from the present. The terms had been evolved over twenty years. The judge said (at 607): "They are therefore not conditions imposed by the strong upon the weak; but are rather a set of trading terms upon which both sides are apparently content to do business." The judge added (at 608): "No moral blame attaches to either party; neither of them knew, nor could be expected to know, that the potatoes were infected." In that case the judge held that the clause was fair and reasonable and that the seed merchants were entitled to rely on it.

Our present case is very much on the borderline. There is this to be said in favour of the seed merchants. The price of this cabbage seed was small: £192. The damages claimed are high: £61,000. But there is this to be said on the other side. The clause was not negotiated between persons of equal bargaining power. It was inserted by the seed merchants in their invoices without any negotiation with the farmers.

To this I would add that the seed merchants rarely, if ever, invoked the clause. Their very frank director said: "The trade does not stand on the strict letter of the clause ＊ ＊ ＊ Almost invariably when a customer justifiably complains, the trade pays something more than a refund." The papers contain many illustrations where the clause was not invoked and a settlement was reached.

Next, I would point out that the buyers had no opportunity at all of knowing or discovering that the seed was not cabbage seed, whereas the sellers could and should have known that it was the wrong seed altogether. The buyers were not covered by insurance against the risk. Nor could they insure. But, as to the seed merchants, the judge said [1981] 1 Lloyd's Rep 476 at 480):

"I am entirely satisfied that it is possible for seedsmen to insure against this risk. I am entirely satisfied that the cost of so doing would not materially raise the price of seeds on the market. I am entirely satisfied that the protection of this clause for the purposes of protecting against the very rare case indeed, such as the present, is not reasonably required. If and in so far as it may be necessary to consider the matter, I am also satisfied that it is possible for seedsmen to test seeds before putting them on the market."

To that I would add this further point. Such a mistake as this could not have happened without serious negligence on the part of the seed merchants themselves or their Dutch suppliers. So serious that it would not be fair to enable them to escape responsibility for it.

In all the circumstances I am of opinion that it would not be fair or reasonable to allow the seed merchants to rely on the clause to limit their liability.

I would dismiss the appeal accordingly.

———

HANSON v. FUNK SEEDS INTERNATIONAL, 373 N.W.2d 30 (S.D.1985). Farmer Hanson purchased seed corn from Funk Seeds. The delivery receipt, which was signed by Hanson's agent, warranted that "the seeds are as described on the tag attached to the bag," disclaimed all other warranties, and limited buyer's remedy for breach of warranty to return of the purchase price. An identical disclaimer and limitation of remedy was also contained on the tag attached to each of the 55 bags of seed corn. The corn that grew from Funk's seeds had only a few ears and these were defective. Hanson sued for breach of warranty. The trial judge held the disclaimer of warranty and limitation of remedy unconscionable under UCC § 2–302 and Hanson won a verdict and judgment for $23,253. The Supreme Court of South Dakota ruled in "Decision II" of its opinion on appeal that there was no error "in holding the warranty disclaimer and limitation of remedy provisions to be unconscionable." The court noted that Hanson was "not in a position to bargain for more favorable contract terms" and that enforcing the limitation of damages "would leave [Hanson] without any substantial recourse for his loss."

———

1986 S.D. Session Laws, Ch. 410: "The ruling in Decision II of Hanson v. Funk Seeds International is hereby abrogated."

———

MARTIN v. JOSEPH HARRIS CO., INC., 767 F.2d 296 (6th Cir.1985).*
Farmer Martin planted cabbage seed that he had purchased from

---

* Overruled on another issue, Salve Regina College v. Russell, ___ U.S. ___, 111 S.Ct. 1217, 113 L.Ed.2d 190 (1991) (courts of appeal must review *de novo* district courts' determinations of state law).

Harris. Much of the crop was infected with "black leg" and had to be destroyed. Black leg is a seed-borne fungus disease that can be prevented by treating the seed with hot water. Harris had used this hot water treatment for 25 years, but had discontinued its use. The court of appeals affirmed a judgment for Martin for the value of the lost crop and approved a finding that a clause in the order form disclaiming warranty and limiting damages was unconscionable under UCC § 2–302. One of the factors that the court listed as supporting the finding of unconscionability was: black leg is a latent defect that cannot be detected by the farmer before planting, but can be prevented by the seller, and the cost of prevention is small in comparison with damage caused by the fungus.

Several states' versions of the Uniform Commercial Code include non-uniform sections that limit the power to disclaim warranties in consumer transactions. One example is Massachusetts (M.G.L.A. c. 106):

§ 2–316A.　Limitation of Exclusion or Modification of Warranties

The provisions of [§ 2–316] shall not apply to sales of consumer goods, services or both. Any language, oral or written, used by a seller or manufacturer of consumer goods and services, which attempts to exclude or modify any implied warranties of merchantability and fitness for a particular purpose or to exclude or modify the consumer's remedies for breach of those warranties, shall be unenforceable.

Any language, oral or written, used by a manufacturer of consumer goods, which attempts to limit or modify a consumer's remedies for breach of such manufacturer's express warranties, shall be unenforceable, unless such manufacturer maintains facilities within the commonwealth sufficient to provide reasonable and expeditious performance of the warranty obligations.

The provisions of this section may not be disclaimed or waived by agreement.

RESTATEMENT, SECOND, TORTS § 402A:

(1) One who sells any product in a defective condition unreasonably dangerous to the user or consumer or to his property is subject to liability for physical harm thereby caused to the ultimate user or consumer, or to his property, if

　　(a) the seller is engaged in the business of selling such a product, and

　　(b) it is expected to and does reach the user or consumer without substantial change in the condition in which it is sold.

(2) The rule stated in Subsection (1) applies although

(a) the seller has exercised all possible care in the preparation and sale of his product, and

(b) the user or consumer has not bought the product from or entered into any contractual relation with the seller.

Comment:

m. * * * The rule stated in this Section does not require any reliance on the part of the consumer upon the reputation, skill, or judgment of the seller who is to be held liable, nor any representation or undertaking on the part of that seller. The seller is strictly liable although, as is frequently the case, the consumer does not even know who he is at the time of consumption. The rule stated in this Section is not governed by the provisions of the * * * Uniform Commercial Code, as to warranties; and it is not affected by limitations on the scope and content of warranties, or by limitation to "buyer" and "seller" in [that statute]. Nor is the consumer required to give notice to the seller of his injury within a reasonable time after it occurs, as is provided by the Uniform Act. The consumer's cause of action does not depend upon the validity of his contract with the person from whom he acquires the product, and it is not affected by any disclaimer or other agreement, whether it be between the seller and his immediate buyer, or attached to and accompanying the product into the consumer's hands. In short, "warranty" must be given a new and different meaning if it is used in connection with this Section. It is much simpler to regard the liability here stated as merely one of strict liability in tort.

EAST RIVER STEAMSHIP CORP. v. TRANSAMERICA DELAVAL, INC.

Supreme Court of the United States, 1986.
476 U.S. 858, 106 S.Ct. 2295, 90 L.Ed.2d 865.

[Delaval designed and manufactured the turbines for four supertankers. The owners of the tankers chartered them to East River and three other shipping companies for periods of 20 or 22 years. Under the charters, the shipping companies assumed responsibility for the cost of repairs. The turbines malfunctioned. The ship owners and the shipping companies sued Delaval on theories of breach of warranty and tort to recover the cost of repairs and the income lost while the ships were out of service for repair. Delaval moved to dismiss the breach of warranty claims on the grounds that the period of limitations had expired and that the contract provided only a limited warranty, which excluded consequential damages. The owners dropped their claims and the shipping companies filed an amended complaint based on strict liability in tort and negligence. The Supreme Court of the United States affirmed a summary judgment for Delaval.*]

* Some facts are taken from the briefs.

JUSTICE BLACKMUN delivered the opinion of the Court.

In this admiralty case, we must decide whether a cause of action in tort is stated when a defective product purchased in a commercial transaction malfunctions, injuring only the product itself and causing purely economic loss. The case requires us to consider preliminarily whether admiralty law, which already recognizes a general theory of liability for negligence, also incorporates principles of products liability, including strict liability. Then, charting a course between products liability and contract law, we must determine whether injury to a product itself is the kind of harm that should be protected by products liability or left entirely to the law of contracts. * * *

We join the Courts of Appeals in recognizing products liability, including strict liability, as part of the general maritime law. * * *

IV

Products liability grew out of a public policy judgment that people need more protection from dangerous products than is afforded by the law of warranty. See *Seely v. White Motor Co.,* 63 Cal.2d 9, 15, 45 Cal. Rptr. 17, 21, 403 P.2d 145, 149 (1965). It is clear, however, that if this development were allowed to progress too far, contract law would drown in a sea of tort. See G. Gilmore, The Death of Contract 87–94 (1974). We must determine whether a commercial product injuring itself is the kind of harm against which public policy requires manufacturers to protect, independent of any contractual obligation.

A

The paradigmatic products-liability action is one where a product "reasonably certain to place life and limb in peril," distributed without reinspection, causes bodily injury. See, *e.g., MacPherson v. Buick Motor Co.,* 217 N.Y. 382, 389, 111 N.E. 1050, 1051, 1053 (1916). The manufacturer is liable whether or not it is negligent because "public policy demands that responsibility be fixed wherever it will most effectively reduce the hazards to life and health inherent in defective products that reach the market." *Escola v. Coca Cola Bottling Co. of Fresno,* 24 Cal.2d, at 462, 150 P.2d, at 441 (opinion concurring in judgment).

For similar reasons of safety, the manufacturer's duty of care was broadened to include protection against property damage. Such damage is considered so akin to personal injury that the two are treated alike.

In the traditional "property damage" cases, the defective product damages other property. In this case, there was no damage to "other" property. Rather, the first, second, and third counts allege that each supertanker's defectively designed turbine components damaged only the turbine itself. Since each turbine was supplied by Delaval as an integrated package, each is properly regarded as a single unit. "Since all but the very simplest of machines have component parts, [a contrary] holding would require a finding of 'property damage' in virtually every case where a product damages itself. Such a holding would eliminate the distinction between warranty and strict products liability." *Northern Power & Engineering Corp. v. Caterpillar Tractor Co.,* 623 P.2d 324, 330 (Alaska 1981). The fifth count [based on negligence] also alleges injury to the product itself. * * * Obviously, damage to a product itself has certain attributes of a products-liability claim. But the injury suffered—the failure of the product to function properly—is the essence of a warranty action, through which a contracting party can seek to recoup the benefit of its bargain.

B

The intriguing question whether injury to a product itself may be brought in tort has spawned a variety of answers.[3] At one end of the spectrum, the case that created the majority land-based approach, *Seely v. White Motor Co.,* 63 Cal.2d 9, 45 Cal.Rptr. 17, 403 P.2d 145 (1965) (defective truck), held that preserving a proper role for the law of warranty precludes imposing tort liability if a defective product causes purely monetary harm.

At the other end of the spectrum is the minority land-based approach, whose progenitor, *Santor v. A & M Karagheusian, Inc.,* 44 N.J. 52, 66–67, 207 A.2d 305, 312–313 (1965) (marred carpeting), held that a manufacturer's duty to make nondefective products encompassed injury to the product itself whether or not the defect created an unreasonable risk of harm.[4] The courts adopting this approach, including the majority of the Courts of Appeals sitting in admiralty that have considered the issue, find that the safety and insurance rationales behind strict liability apply equally where the losses are purely economic. These courts reject the *Seely* approach because they find it arbitrary that economic losses are recoverable if a plaintiff suffers bodily injury or property damage, but not if a product injures itself. They also find no inherent difference between economic loss and personal injury or property damage, because all are proximately caused by the defendant's conduct. Further, they believe recovery for economic loss would not lead to unlimited liability because they think a manufacturer can predict and insure against product failure.

3. The question is not answered by the Restatement (Second) of Torts §§ 395 and 402A (1965), or by the Uniform Commercial Code, see Wade, Is Section 402A of the Second Restatement of Torts Preempted by the UCC and Therefore Unconstitutional?, 42 Tenn.L.Rev. 123 (1974).

Congress, which has considered adopting national products-liability legislation, also has been wrestling with the question whether economic loss should be recoverable under a products-liability theory. See 1 L. Frumer & M. Friedman, Products Liability § 4C (1986). When S. 100, 99th Cong., 1st Sess. (1985) (the Product Liability Act) was introduced, it excluded, § 2(6),

recovery for commercial loss. Suggestions have been made for revising this provision. * * *

4. Interestingly, the New Jersey and California Supreme Courts have each taken what appears to be a step in the direction of the other since *Santor* and *Seely.* In *Spring Motors Distributors, Inc. v. Ford Motor Co.,* 98 N.J., at 579, 489 A.2d, at 672, the New Jersey court rejected *Santor* in the commercial context. And in *J'Aire Corp. v. Gregory,* 24 Cal.3d 799, 157 Cal. Rptr. 407, 598 P.2d 60 (1979), the California court recognized a cause of action for negligent interference with prospective economic advantage.

Between the two poles fall a number of cases that would permit a products-liability action under certain circumstances when a product injures only itself. These cases attempt to differentiate between "the disappointed users * * * and the endangered ones," *Russell v. Ford Motor Co.*, 281 Or. 587, 595, 575 P.2d 1383, 1387 (1978), and permit only the latter to sue in tort. The determination has been said to turn on the nature of the defect, the type of risk, and the manner in which the injury arose. The Alaska Supreme Court allows a tort action if the defective product creates a situation potentially dangerous to persons or other property, and loss occurs as a proximate result of that danger and under dangerous circumstances. *Northern Power & Engineering Corp. v. Caterpillar Tractor Co.*, 623 P.2d 324, 329 (1981).

We find the intermediate and minority land-based positions unsatisfactory. The intermediate positions, which essentially turn on the degree of risk, are too indeterminate to enable manufacturers easily to structure their business behavior. Nor do we find persuasive a distinction that rests on the manner in which the product is injured. We realize that the damage may be qualitative, occurring through gradual deterioration or internal breakage. Or it may be calamitous. But either way, since by definition no person or other property is damaged, the resulting loss is purely economic. Even when the harm to the product itself occurs through an abrupt, accident-like event, the resulting loss due to repair costs, decreased value, and lost profits is essentially the failure of the purchaser to receive the benefit of its bargain—traditionally the core concern of contract law.

We also decline to adopt the minority land-based view espoused by *Santor* and *Emerson*. Such cases raise legitimate questions about the theories behind restricting products liability, but we believe that the countervailing arguments are more powerful. The minority view fails to account for the need to keep products liability and contract law in separate spheres and to maintain a realistic limitation on damages.

C

Exercising traditional discretion in admiralty, we adopt an approach similar to *Seely* and hold that a manufacturer in a commercial relationship has no duty under either a negligence or strict products-liability theory to prevent a product from injuring itself. * * *

The tort concern with safety is reduced when an injury is only to the product itself. When a person is injured, the "cost of an injury and the loss of time or health may be an overwhelming misfortune," and one the person is not prepared to meet. *Escola v. Coca Cola Bottling Co.*, 24 Cal.2d, at 462, 150 P.2d, at 441 (opinion concurring in judgment). In contrast, when a product injures itself, the commercial user stands to lose the value of the product, risks the displeasure of its customers who find that the product does not meet their needs, or, as in this case, experiences increased costs in performing a service. Losses like these can be insured. Society need not presume that a customer needs special protection. The increased cost to the public that would result from holding a manufacturer liable in tort for injury to the product itself is not justified.

Damage to a product itself is most naturally understood as a warranty claim. Such damage means simply that the product has not met the customer's expectations, or, in other words, that the customer has received "insufficient product value." See J. White and R. Summers, Uniform Commercial Code 406 (2d ed. 1980). The maintenance of product value and quality is precisely the purpose of express and implied warranties. See UCC § 2–313 (express warranty), § 2–314 (implied warranty of merchantability), and § 2–315 (warranty of fitness for a particular purpose). Therefore, a claim of a nonworking product can be brought as a breach-of-warranty action. Or, if the customer prefers, it can reject the product or revoke its acceptance and sue for breach of contract. See UCC §§ 2–601, 2–608, 2–612.

Contract law, and the law of warranty in particular, is well suited to commercial controversies of the sort involved in this case because the parties may set the terms of their own agreements.[8] The manufacturer can restrict its liability, within limits, by disclaiming warranties or limiting remedies. See UCC §§ 2–316, 2–719. In exchange, the purchaser pays less for the product. Since a commercial situation generally does not involve large disparities in bargaining power, we see no reason to intrude into the parties' allocation of the risk.

While giving recognition to the manufacturer's bargain, warranty law sufficiently protects the purchaser by allowing it to obtain the benefit of its bargain. See White & Summers, *supra,* ch. 10. The expectation damages available in warranty for purely economic loss give a plaintiff the full benefit of its bargain by compensating for forgone business opportunities. See Fuller & Perdue, The Reliance Interest in Contract Damages: I, 46 Yale L.J. 52, 60–63 (1936); R. Posner, Economic Analysis of Law § 4.8 (3d ed. 1986). Recovery on a warranty theory would give the charterers their repair costs and lost profits, and would place them in the position they would have been in had the turbines functioned properly.[9] See *Hawkins v. McGee,* 84 N.H. 114, 146 A. 641 (1929). Thus, both the nature of the injury and the

8. We recognize, of course, that warranty and products liability are not static bodies of law and may overlap. In certain situations, for example, the privity requirement of warranty has been discarded. *E.g., Henningsen v. Bloomfield Motors, Inc.,* 32 N.J. 358, 380–384, 161 A.2d 69, 81–84 (1960). In other circumstances, a manufacturer may be able to disclaim strict tort liability. See, *e.g., Keystone Aeronautics Corp. v. R.J. Enstrom Corp.,* 499 F.2d 146, 149 (CA3 1974). Nonetheless, the main currents of tort law run in different directions from those of contract and warranty, and the latter seem to us far more appropriate for commercial disputes of the kind involved here.

9. In contrast, tort damages generally compensate the plaintiff for loss and return him to the position he occupied before the injury. Cf. *Sullivan v. O'Connor,* 363 Mass. 579, 584–586, 588, n. 6, 296 N.E.2d 183, 187–188, 189, n. 6 (1973); Prosser, The Borderland of Tort and Contract, in Selected Topics on the Law of Torts 380, 424–427 (Thomas M. Cooley Lectures, Fourth Series 1953). Tort damages are analogous to reliance damages, which are awarded in contract when there is particular difficulty in measuring the expectation interest. See, *e.g., Security Store & Mfg. Co. v. American Railways Express Co.,* 227 Mo.App. 175, 51 S.W.2d 572 (1932).

resulting damages indicate it is more natural to think of injury to a product itself in terms of warranty.

A warranty action also has a built-in limitation on liability, whereas a tort action could subject the manufacturer to damages of an indefinite amount. The limitation in a contract action comes from the agreement of the parties and the requirement that consequential damages, such as lost profits, be a foreseeable result of the breach. See *Hadley v. Baxendale,* 9 Ex. 341, 156 Eng.Rep. 145 (1854). In a warranty action where the loss is purely economic, the limitation derives from the requirements of foreseeability and of privity, which is still generally enforced for such claims in a commercial setting. See UCC § 2–715; White & Summers, *supra,* at 389, 396, 406–410.

In products-liability law, where there is a duty to the public generally, foreseeability is an inadequate brake. Cf. *Kinsman Transit Co. v. City of Buffalo,* 388 F.2d 821 (CA2 1968). See also Periman, Interference with Contract and Other Economic Expectancies: A Clash of Tort and Contract Doctrine, 49 U.Chi.L.Rev. 61, 71–72 (1982). Permitting recovery for all foreseeable claims for purely economic loss could make a manufacturer liable for vast sums. It would be difficult for a manufacturer to take into account the expectations of persons downstream who may encounter its product. In this case, for example, if the charterers—already one step removed from the transaction— were permitted to recover their economic losses, then the companies that subchartered the ships might claim their economic losses from the delays, and the charterers' customers also might claim their economic losses, and so on. "The law does not spread its protection so far." *Robins Dry Dock & Repair Co. v. Flint,* 275 U.S. 303, 309, 48 S.Ct. 134, 135, 72 L.Ed. 290 (1927). * * *

———

Note 4 of the principal case refers to Spring Motors Distributors, Inc. v. Ford Motor Co., and to J'Aire Corp. v. Gregory. In *Spring Motors,* the Supreme Court of New Jersey held that a commercial buyer, seeking damages for economic loss resulting from defective goods, may recover for breach of UCC warranty, but not under theories of strict tort liability or negligence. The court commented that, because only commercial parties were involved, it "need not reconsider the *Santor* rule that an ultimate consumer may recover in strict liability for direct economic loss." *J'Aire Corp.* is a note case in chapter 10.

MUNICIPALITY OF ANCHORAGE v. LOCKER
Supreme Court of Alaska, 1986.
723 P.2d 1261.

BURKE, JUSTICE.

The Municipality of Anchorage, doing business as Anchorage Telephone Utility, and GTE Directories Corporation (ATU) petitioned for review of the superior court's grant of partial summary judgment to certain advertisers, whose Yellow Pages advertisements were allegedly omitted or erroneously published. At issue is whether limited liability provisions in ATU's tariff and its Yellow Pages advertising contract are valid. The superior court held that these provisions were unconscionable and, therefore, void. * * *

I. FACTUAL AND PROCEDURAL BACKGROUND

Phillip Locker, D.D.S. (advertiser) contracted with ATU for a listing in the Yellow Pages of the Anchorage telephone directory. The listing was allegedly either wholly or partially omitted, misclassified, or wrongly printed by ATU. Advertiser alleged substantial losses as a result of ATU's acts.

As a defense to advertisers' action, ATU claimed that its liability was limited by both a contractual provision and its tariff filed with the APUC. Advertiser moved for partial summary judgment to prohibit ATU from relying on these affirmative defenses. The superior court granted advertiser's motion. The court followed "the rationale and holdings" in *Allen v. Michigan Bell Telephone,* 18 Mich.App. 632, 171 N.W.2d 689 (1969) and *Discount Fabric House v. Wisconsin Telephone,* 117 Wis.2d 587, 345 N.W.2d 417 (1984). The court stated that advertisers were obligated to prove damages "with the requisite degree of specificity," and refused to express any further opinion on damages issues.

II. DISCUSSION

In addition to the Wisconsin Supreme Court decision in *Discount Fabric,* 345 N.W.2d 417, and the Michigan Appellate Court decision in *Allen,* 171 N.W.2d 689, the Alabama Supreme Court has also invalidated a telephone company exculpatory clause. *Morgan v. South Central Bell Telephone,* 466 So.2d 107 (Ala.1985). Virtually every other state court which has considered the issue has upheld exculpatory clauses as valid, because they are either part of a tariff on file with the appropriate public commission or a private contract. We nevertheless are persuaded by the reasoning in *Allen, Discount Fabric,* and *Morgan.*

A. *The Tariff Provision Filed by ATU Does Not Bar Recovery In Excess of Stated Liability for Yellow Pages Errors*

ATU, as a public utility, is regulated by the APUC. *See* AS 42.05.720(4)(B) and AS 42.05.720(8). ATU must file with the APUC a

complete tariff showing all rates, including joint rates, tolls, rentals and charges collected and all classifications, rules, regulations, and terms and conditions under which it furnishes its services and facilities * * * together with a copy of every special contract with customers which in any way affects or relates to the serving utility's rates, tolls, charges, rentals, classifications, services or facilities.

* * * Pursuant to these regulations, ATU filed a tariff with the APUC which states:

> No liability arising from errors or omission in the making up or printing of its directories shall be attached to the Municipality of Anchorage except in the case of charge listings; in connection with these its liability shall be limited to a refund at the monthly rate for each listing for the time an error or omission continues after a reasonable notice in writing to the Municipality of Anchorage.

Tariff Advice No. 182B.

ATU argues that once such tariff is filed with the APUC it has the effect of law. A number of courts have held that exculpatory provisions filed with a regulatory agency effectively limit liability for errors in Yellow Pages advertising. Other courts limit the application of the tariff to services which the agency may regulate. Those latter courts reason that since the regulatory agencies lack jurisdiction over private contracts, the tariff provisions apply only to the alphabetical directory required as part of the public service provided. Still other courts extend the tariff limitation to a single listing in the classified section where the listing is required and for which there is no advertising fee.

Advertiser argues that the tariff should not apply because the APUC does not regulate classified advertisements. We agree. Even though public utilities are regulated by the APUC, not all of their activities are proscribed. The APUC specifically regulates the "furnishing of telecommunications services and facilities to the public." 3 AAC 52.200(a): AS 42.05.361(a). Although the powers of the APUC are to be liberally construed, AS 42.05.141(1), its jurisdiction does not extend beyond regulation of required services or facilities. Yellow Pages advertisements are not a telecommunication service. To apply the tariff provision to such advertisements we would imply that APUC could regulate the Yellow Pages. We decline to imply such regulatory authority. The administrative regulations explicitly make publication of the Yellow Pages optional. *See* 3 AAC 52.250(a) & 52.340(22).

ATU also argues that the limited liability provision is necessarily part of its tariff because such limitation directly affects the rates it charges. Without such a limitation, it asserts, the overall rates for its service might increase. Therefore, ATU reasons, the APUC properly accepted the tariff limiting Yellow Pages liability under its authority to regulate overall rates. ATU relies on *Davidian v. Pacific Telephone and Telegraph,* 16 Cal.App.3d 750, 94 Cal.Rptr. 337 (1971) and *Garrison v. Pacific Northwest Bell,* 45 Or.App. 523, 608 P.2d 1206 (1980). Those courts do indeed hold that the limitation of liability is an inherent part of the overall rate. *Davidian,* 94 Cal.Rptr. at 339; *Garrison,* 608 P.2d at 1211.

Other courts, however, hold otherwise. The United States Court of Appeals for the District of Columbia has held that the District's regulatory body explicitly does not have jurisdiction to regulate the rates charged for Yellow Pages advertising. *Classified Directory Sub-*

scribers Association v. Public Services Commission, 383 F.2d 510 (D.C. Cir.1967) (defining "services and facilities" in enabling legislation). It reasoned that even if the Commission considers advertising revenues as part of gross revenues for rate making, advertising rates are not subject to comprehensive regulation. We agree. A mere tangential effect upon overall rates will not suffice to limit categorically ATU's liability for negligence. We, therefore, reject ATU's argument that its liability is limited by the tariff.

B. The Limited Liability Clause in the Advertising Contract Is Invalid

The courts in *Allen,* 171 N.W.2d 689, *Discount Fabric,* 345 N.W.2d 417, and *Morgan,* 466 So.2d 107, all determined that publication of the Yellow Pages was affected with the public interest, and that exculpatory clauses were unconscionable. ATU urges us to disregard the reasoning of these courts and to apply the majority position, thus validating its contractual exculpatory clause. ATU correctly asserts that publication of the Yellow Pages is not required by the APUC. However, such publication is affected with a public interest. ATU is in a unique position to publish the Yellow Pages only because it is authorized to operate the monopoly utility for the public.

In defining a contract affected with a public interest, the *Allen* and *Morgan* courts relied on *Tunkl v. Regents of the University of California,* 60 Cal.2d 92, 32 Cal.Rptr. 33, 383 P.2d 441 (1963). The California court described transactions in which exculpatory provisions will be invalidated on public policy grounds.

> It concerns a business of a type generally thought suitable for public regulation. The party seeking exculpation is engaged in performing a service of great importance to the public, which is often a matter of practical necessity for some members of the public. The party holds himself out as willing to perform this service for any member of the public who seeks it, or at least for any member coming within certain established standards. As a result of the essential nature of the service, in the economic setting of the transaction, the party invoking exculpation possesses a decisive advantage of bargaining strength against any member of the public who seeks his services. In exercising a superior bargaining power the party confronts the public with a standardized adhesion contract of exculpation whereby a purchaser may pay additional reasonable fees and obtain protection against negligence. Finally, as a result of the transaction, the person or property of the purchaser is placed under the control of the seller, subject to the risk of carelessness by the seller or his agents.

Id. 32 Cal.Rptr. at 37–8, 383 P.2d at 445–46 (footnotes omitted).

ATU fits squarely within this profile. ATU is a type of business suitable for regulation and is so regulated by the APUC. The publication of the telephone directory, in general, and the Yellow Pages, in particular, is a service of great importance to the public; Yellow Pages advertising is often the only affordable means of advertising for small businesses. ATU holds itself out as willing to perform this service, and indeed extols the benefits of Yellow Pages advertising in commercial advertising of its own. Thus, we conclude that publication of the Yellow Pages is affected with a public interest.

Since we have so determined we must more closely scrutinize the transaction between ATU and the advertisers to ascertain whether the exculpatory clause is unconscionable. Most recently in *Vochner v. Erickson*, 712 P.2d 379 (Alaska 1986), we considered all of the circumstances surrounding the making of the contract and held that unconscionability may exist where those circumstances indicate a vast disparity of bargaining power coupled with terms unreasonably favorable to the stronger party. *Id.* at 381–83. *See also Morrow v. New Moon Homes*, 548 P.2d 279, 292 n. 43 (Alaska 1976) (approving of the definition of unconscionability in *Williams v. Walker–Thomas Furniture*, 350 F.2d 445, 449 (D.C.Cir.1965) ("Unconscionability has generally been recognized to include an absence of meaningful choice on the part of one of the parties together with contract terms which are unreasonably favorable to the other party."); Restatement (Second) of Contracts § 208 comment d at 109 (1981).

ATU argues that there was insufficient evidence that ATU was "in an unfairly superior bargaining position vis-a-vis the plaintiff-advertisers." * * * ATU has presented no evidence that it would have negotiated individually with potential advertisers. The sales representatives' lack of authority to renegotiate terms would generally discourage, if not completely forestall potential advertisers from seeking more favorable terms.

In addressing the position held by many courts and advanced by the ATU here—that advertisers are free to advertise elsewhere if the terms with the telephone company are not advantageous—the Alabama court in *Morgan* stated:

> The issue, however, is not whether there are other forms of advertising available, but whether such other modes are tied directly to the telephone service enjoyed by almost every home and business in the state. *The telephone company has an exclusive private advertising business which is tied to its public utility service* * * * *and which reaches almost every home and office in the state.* Therefore, the telephone company can state to a customer that an ad will be published but name its own terms, including a limitation of its own liability for negligence. * * *

Morgan, 466 So.2d at 117–18 (emphasis added); *see also Discount Fabrics*, 345 N.W.2d 417. We are persuaded by such reasoning.

We, therefore, believe that ATU had a decided advantage in bargaining with advertiser. Advertiser was presented with a form contract by sales representatives who had no authority to alter the provisions of the contract. Additionally the terms of the contract were decidedly unreasonable to advertiser. Under the contract, it could only recover the amount paid for a service that was negligently performed. The *Discount Fabric* court aptly described the clause as "the non-bargaining, non-responsibility clause." 345 N.W.2d at 421. As a state-regulated monopoly, ATU cannot shield itself from its own negligence. Through its privileged position ATU has an exclusive private advertising business and has created a public interest in the Yellow Pages. The publication of the Yellow Pages is an inextricable and substantial benefit of the phone company's duty to provide service. Under such circumstances, we refuse to allow ATU to limit unilaterally its liability for negligence.

ATU also argues that limiting its liability was reasonable since ascertaining damages for errors or omissions in the Yellow Pages would be difficult. The courts are split on this issue. Those which uphold the limited liability clause maintain that the clause protects the company from speculative damages. *Gas House Inc. v. Southern Bell Telephone & Telegraph*, 289 N.C. 175, 221 S.E.2d 499, 505 (1976). Those which invalidate such clauses reason that a party is protected from speculative damages by the jury system, the instructions given the jury, and the trial judge's rulings during the trial and motions after verdict.

*   *   *

The potential difficulty in ascertaining damages does not inhibit us from invalidating the exculpatory clause. Advertiser will have to show a reasonable basis for recovery.

We therefore AFFIRM the trial court's grant of partial summary judgment to advertiser on the exculpatory issue. The limited liability clause in the advertising contract is unconscionable and void as against public policy.

———

SCHLOBOHM v. SPA PETITE, INC., 326 N.W.2d 920 (Minn.1982). Ms. Schlobohm joined Spa Petite, a health club. The membership contract contained a clause excusing Spa and its employees from liability for negligence. Schlobohm was injured after a Spa employee doubled the weights on an exercise machine that Schlobohm was using. In a 5–4 opinion, the Supreme Court of Minnesota reversed the trial court's invalidation of the exculpatory clause. The court used the same factors (taken from the California opinion, Tunkl v. Regents) used in Municipality of Anchorage v. Locker, and concluded: "that the exculpatory clause in Spa Petite's membership contract was unambiguous and limited to exoneration from negligence; that there was no disparity of bargaining power; and that the clause was not void as against public policy."

What result would have been reached under the United Kingdom's Unfair Contract Terms Act, referred to by Lord Denning in George

Mitchell (Chesterhall) Ltd. v. Finney Lock Seeds Ltd., supra in this chapter?

———

KUGLER v. ROMAIN, 58 N.J. 522, 279 A.2d 640 (1971). The Attorney General of New Jersey, acting under his state's Consumer Fraud Act, instituted an action against defendant who was engaged in "the house-to-house sale of certain so-called educational books." The Attorney General prayed for an injunction barring defendant from making misrepresentations. Matters misrepresented included sponsorship of the materials by well-known educational institutions, the total price, and that purchase would lead to a high school equivalency diploma. The suit also asked that all contracts with purchasers listed be rescinded and that civil penalties be imposed. Similar relief was also requested for those consumers not listed but similarly situated. There was expert testimony that the materials were not suited for the purposes for which they were sold and that the price charged was about two and one-half times the maximum retail value of the materials. The trial court granted the Attorney General the relief requested as to the consumers he listed. On appeal, the judgment was modified to include all consumers similarly situated and was affirmed:

"We have no doubt that an exorbitant price ostensibly agreed to by a purchaser of the type involved in this case—but in reality unilaterally fixed by the seller and not open to negotiation—constitutes an unconscionable bargain from which such a purchaser should be relieved * * *.

"Sale at an exorbitant price especially in the market described by the evidence in this case raises a strong inference of imposition. Here the facts reveal that the seller's price was not only roughly two and one half times a reasonable market price, assuming functional adequacy of the book package for the represented purpose, but they indicate also that most of the package was actually practically worthless for that purpose. Such price-value clearly constitutes unconscionability * * *.

"In other jurisdictions exorbitant prices for consumer goods sold in a marketing milieu similar to our case have been declared unconscionable. In State by Lefkowitz v. ITM, Inc., supra, 275 N.Y.S.2d 303, the seller marketed broilers, vacuum cleaners and color television sets using various types of deceptive sales practices. Among other things it appeared that the sales prices to the consumers for the various items ranged from two to six times the costs to the seller. The proof showed also that defendant represented that the goods were not obtainable elsewhere at its prices. But they were available and at much lower prices. The court said it was clear that 'these excessively high prices constituted 'unconscionable contractual provisions' within the meaning of section 63, subsection 12 of the Executive Law,' N.Y.Executive Law § 63(12) (McKinney, 1970–71 Supp.), and further that even if the prices were not unconscionable *per se*, 'they were unconscionable within the context of this case' under [§ 2–302] of the Uniform Commercial Code.

"In Jones v. Star Credit Corp., supra, 298 N.Y.S.2d 264, defendant sold a home freezer unit for $900 ($1439.69 with credit charges and sales tax) to plaintiffs who were welfare recipients at the time. The actual retail value was $300. The sale was held unconscionable as a matter of law under [§ 2–302] of the Uniform Commercial Code.

"The New Hampshire Supreme Court in American Home Improvement, Inc. v. MacIver, 105 N.H. 435, 201 A.2d 886 (1964) had for decision a home improvement contract where the materials to be furnished and the services to be rendered were valued at $959. The home owner agreed to pay $2568.60 therefor, the price including service charges and commissions. It was held that 'the contract should not be enforced because of its unconscionable features.' 201 A.2d at 889. In so holding the court referred to [UCC § 2–302(1)] and to the New Hampshire counterpart, R.S.A. 382–A:2–302(1). * * *

"As set forth above, we are satisfied that the price for the book package was unconscionable in relation to defendant's cost and the value to the consumers and was therefore a fraud within the contemplation of N.J.S.A. 56:8–2. Further, for the reasons stated we are convinced that a view that such price unconscionability gives rise only to a private remedy is an unreasonable limitation on the aim and scope of the Consumer Fraud Act, N.J.S.A. 56:8–1 et seq. The public purpose to be served thereby (and we see the legislative emphasis as being more on public than on private remedies) can be accomplished effectively only by recognizing the authority of the Attorney General to intervene in behalf of all consumers similarly affected by the broadly described fraudulent sales tactics of merchandise sellers."

Slum Stores and Redlining

Kugler v. Romain states that "an exorbitant price" may itself be an "unconscionable" term from which a consumer can obtain relief. The assertion is often made that excessive prices are charged to low income customers by slum stores. There are reasons why a person pays the higher prices charged by slum stores. First, a person with a low income has to buy durable goods on credit. He is not likely to qualify for credit in "general market" stores (as distinguished from "low-income market" stores). Moreover, low-income consumers are unlikely to be sophisticated in making price and quality comparisons. Does this mean that slum stores are taking advantage of a captive market by charging excessive prices? Perhaps, but to answer that question concerning any particular price, the store's costs must first be ascertained and compared with costs of a general market store. Some of the factors that prevent a low income consumer from shopping elsewhere also increase the costs of the slum store. The fact that slum dwellers are likely to be poor credit risks means that a store that extends credit to them experiences more collection costs, more bad debts, and generally has higher costs of extending credit. If state law does not permit charging sufficient interest to cover these costs, the "cash" price of the merchandise must be raised as an alternative means of meeting expenses. In such circumstances, the "cash" price is purely theoretical because the store's customers cannot pay cash. The higher price permits a greater return on credit sales when interest is figured as a percentage of the cash price. Moreover, a slum store is likely to experience greater risks of larceny and property damage. Insurance premiums to cover these risks are higher than those paid by general market stores.

There is even a possibility that insurance is not available because insurance companies are unwilling to underwrite the risks of slum stores at any reasonable premium. The same phenomenon is likely to occur concerning other institutions, such as mortgage lenders, asked to finance slum stores or residences. An insurer or mortgage lender's refusal to deal with slum property is sometimes referred to as "red lining" because it appears as if a red line were drawn around the slum district and a decision made not to deal with property within the marked area. Red lining greatly aggravates the already depressed economic conditions in slum areas. Solutions to this problem are difficult because red lining is allegedly based on actuarial necessity. Measures can be taken to require attention to the merits of each application rather than writing off an entire area of a city. Costs of lenders and insurers can be subsidized by government loans or guarantees.

For reports on empirical studies of the problems of low-income neighborhoods, see, e.g., D. Caplovitz, The Poor Pay More (1967); Federal Trade Commission, Economic Report on Installment Credit and Retail Sales Practices of District of Columbia Retailers (1968).

OWENS v. OWENS

Supreme Court of Virginia, 1955.
196 Va. 966, 86 S.E.2d 181.

[Plaintiff and defendant were brothers. Plaintiff, who was heavily indebted and had been indicted for forgery, left Virginia and did not communicate with his family. Defendant lived close to his parents and managed his father's affairs. The father died intestate. Plaintiff inherited one half of the realty and one third of the personalty in the estate. Defendant was the administrator of the estate. Plaintiff learned of his father's death, obtained a five-day leave from his employment in Indiana, and returned to Virginia—ten years after he had left. Plaintiff wished to secure a dismissal of the indictments against him, which the prosecutor was willing to arrange if plaintiff paid his debts. Plaintiff sold his interest in the estate to his brother for $5,000. When plaintiff learned that his interest in the estate was worth much more than this, he sued to obtain reconveyance of the land and an accounting of the proceeds of the personal property that plaintiff had sold to defendant. There was conflicting testimony as to whether plaintiff's conveyance to his brother was intended to be absolute or merely serve as security for the $5,000 that he had obtained from his brother. The trial court dismissed the suit and plaintiff appealed.]

In Rowland v. Kable, 174 Va. 343, 368, 6 S.E.2d 633, 643, Mr. Justice Spratley, speaking for the court, said: " 'In Waddy v. Grimes, 154 Va. 615, 647, 153 S.E. 807, 817, the majority rule is stated thus: "There is a distinction to be made between transactions occurring directly between a trustee and his *cestui que trust,* and those transactions in which the trustee deals with himself in respect to the trust estate. The latter class of transactions are voidable by the *cestui que trust* at his election without giving any reason or alleging any fraud, or any advantage or inadequacy of price. But where the trustee deals directly with the *cestui que trust,* the transaction is not *ipso facto* voidable at the election of the *cestui que trust;* but only *prima facie* presumed to be invalid, which presumption may be rebutted." ' "

Courts cannot relieve one of the consequences of a contract merely because it was unwise. " 'They are not guardians in general to the people at large, but where inadequacy of price is such as to shock their conscience equity is alert to seize upon the slightest circumstance indicative of fraud, either actual or constructive.' " Jackson v. Seymour, 193 Va. 735, 741, 71 S.E.2d 181, 185, quoting from Planters' Nat. Bank of Fredericksburg v. E. G. Heflin Co., 166 Va. 166, 173–174, 184 S.E. 216, 219. * * *

The defendant contends that plaintiff made the initial offer to sell and suggested the price of $5,000, that he knew or had the opportunity of knowing the value of the estate, and that he sold with full knowledge of what he was doing. Plaintiff contends, on the other hand, that the deed was made absolute on its face to facilitate settling the estate and that it was understood that there would be an accounting after the estate was settled. Regardless of whether the plaintiff made the initial offer to sell his interest in the estate for $5,000 or whether there was an understanding that there would be an accounting after the estate was settled, the defendant was administrator of the estate and as such his relationship to the plaintiff was that of trustee to beneficiary. It is true that the real property of an intestate descends to his heirs and does not pass through the hands of an administrator, but in view of the superior position held by the defendant under the circumstances of this case, he occupies a fiduciary relationship with respect both to the personalty and the realty. In any event the result is the same.

The transaction is *prima facie* presumed invalid, and in order to rebut the presumption, equity casts upon the defendant the burden of proving affirmatively that he made to the plaintiff an honest and complete disclosure of all the information concerning the property possessed by him and the price paid was fair and adequate and that he obtained no undue or inequitable advantage.

Whatever may be the conflict in the evidence on other points, there is none as to the fact that A. J. Owens, while acting as administrator of his father's estate, received a conveyance of the entire interest of his brother, an heir and distributee, in both the personal property and the real estate owned by their father for a consideration which was less than the interest of his brother in the personal property alone. As stated above, the evidence clearly shows that the property obtained by defendant was worth more than five times what he paid for it. * * *

For the reasons stated the decree of the trial court is reversed, the deed from W. C. Owens, to A. J. Owens set aside and annulled, and the case remanded with directions that A. J. Owens be required to account for W. C. Owens' interest in the personal property of H. S. Owens' estate.

Reversed and remanded.

BAL–FEL, INC. v. BOYD
Texas Court of Civil Appeals, 1973.
503 S.W.2d 673.

[Plaintiff had paid for dance lessons in Austin where she lived. She brought suit in Austin to recover damages for fraud. The defendants were the local dance studio, individuals connected with the operation of that studio, the Texas company that licensed the local studio, and a Florida company that franchised the studios nationally. The Texas licensing company was located in Dallas and moved to dismiss for improper venue, claiming that it had to be sued in Dallas. Resolution of this issue turned on whether plaintiff had proven a claim against the Austin defendants. The trial court held that a claim was proven and overruled the motion. The Dallas-based defendant appealed.]

Appellee was a widow, aged 56, when in March of 1970 as the guest of a friend she visited the Fred Astaire Dance Studios in Austin, where she was asked to enroll for an introductory course of five dance lessons at a charge of five dollars for the course. After completing three lessons appellee was asked to enroll in a larger program. During these early lessons appellee was "made over * * * [and] flattered" by the male personnel of the studio who told her that she "had the potential to be a great dancer." It was learned also in this period that appellee was a widow whose husband had been dead less than three years.

Appellee testified that she was lonely and "had not been out, at all, since * * *" her husband's death and "was wanting to meet friends and to be in a social climate." Appellee admitted that she "was real anxious for the flattery and involvement that * * * [she] would get there at the studio." In this brief period, appellee said, "* * * they flattered me and played upon my emotions as a lonely widow to take more dance lessons."

Responding to the coaxing and blandishments of the men at the studio, appellee on March 19, 1970, signed an agreement to take 45 dance lessons, for which she paid the Fred Astaire Studio $364.50 in advance. Fifteen of the lessons were to be private, fifteen were "class" lessons, and the remaining fifteen were to be "practice" lessons. This contract was but the first of a series of contracts, made in rapid succession over a period of months, with the numbers of the lessons increasing to a total approaching 2,500 and their costs ascending to an aggregate in excess of $27,000 before the end of the year.

After completing about ten of the first set of forty-five dance lessons, appellee was induced by the operators of the studio to contract, early in April, for 191 additional lessons at a cost of $1,750. This program was divided into 91 private lessons, 50 class lessons, and 50 practice lessons, which the studio called the "Amalgamated Program of Dancing." Appellee paid for this series in advance from her bank account which contained the life insurance money left appellee by her deceased husband.

Within less than two weeks after entering the "Amalgamated Program of Dancing," appellee was persuaded to enter another program at the studio, a program of 508 lessons costing $4,450. Appellee testified that after buying the "Amalgamated Program" she acquired a status at the studio in which, she said, "* * * they were very nice to me, flattering, and they would embrace me when I would come in. They were always glad to see me, and I felt like I was in a happy, lovable atmosphere, and they knew that I was lonely, and they would make me feel welcome."

The contract appellee made for the new program, dated April 23, was marked "Confidential" by the studio and designated the "Supreme Gold Dance Standard." Appellee testified that the term "Confidential" as applied to the contract "* * * meant that it was loaned to me by the studio, and I wasn't supposed to tell anyone that, but then I was asked right away to pay the money because they needed it, so I paid in one check."

Appellee did not have funds remaining in her bank account sufficient to pay the $4,450 and was obliged to borrow the money. Appellee, a school teacher, borrowed the $4,450 from the credit union in which she had membership as a teacher. Appellee borrowed the money on April 29, and paid the studio, six days after entering the "Supreme Gold Dance Standard" contract.

In the month of June appellee yielded to further persuasion by the men at the studio and entered into two contracts, on June 12 and on June 15, for a total of 1,068 dance lessons at an aggregate cost of $9,612. Appellee paid this contract in advance by two checks in amounts of $6,260 and $3,352, the first for dance lessons in the "Gold Cane Club" and the other in "Theater Arts Club."

Early in September appellee was induced to enter two additional clubs offered by the studio which were designated the "Single Mingle Club" and the "Fiesta Dance Clubs," at a total cost of $1,400. Initially, appellee agreed to pay $200 down and the balance of $1,200 in ten monthly payments of $120 each. This contract obligation was discharged subsequently in full.

Prior to making the September contracts, appellee in August sold her home, from which sale she realized about $17,000 above indebtedness, in order to buy stock in the dance studio. Appellee testified, "* * * I was told that the stock was very good, and that since I was dancing there that I would want to own stock in the Studio, and therefore, derive benefits from the other people who came to take dancing, so I was asked if I would buy some stock." The solicitations were confidential, appellee said, " * * * and we were taken into little offices to do that [buy stock] confidentially, and just two members of the staff are there, but no one else. They would tell me that, 'We are not going to sell it to just anybody, but you are one of our favorites, so we want to give you a chance to make some money.' "

Appellee wrote a check on August 31 in the sum of $10,000 to buy the stock. Later, in December, after being persuaded to join the "Executive Competition Club" at an additional cost of $9,418, appellee turned the stock "back over to them in exchange for the Executive Competition Club" in which she was scheduled to receive 626 additional hours of dance lessons. Appellee testified that she "* * * was told that the stock could be turned into the Executive Competition Club because * * * I would derive more benefits from it * * * than the stock, because the stock * * * wasn't paying any dividends. Nobody was getting anything from the stock, anyway."

When induced in December to join the "Executive Competition Club," appellee was told by an operator at the studio, she testified, "It was a club that just his very best dancers were to join, and we were to be in competition with dancers all over the United States, and even internationally; eventually in Japan, to go to Japan. It was a very elite club." Appellee was already at that time making short trips with other dancers from Austin to enter competition against clubs in other cities, for which she paid the studio $60 per trip plus expenses.

Appellee testified that between March 18, 1970, and the end of that year, in a series of five contracts, she bought 2,438 hours of dancing lessons, and that these purchases, together with cost of joining the "Single Mingle Club" and the "Fiesta Dance Clubs," she paid the Fred Astaire Dance Studios more than $27,000 in cash.

When asked * * * why she made these payments, appellee testified, "I was lonely. My husband had passed away. I had no social life, and when I went to this Studio, they were very friendly and loving, and in an intimate atmosphere, they would tell me, 'You want to be a great dancer? You are going to be the best * * *' and they would flatter me and play upon my emotional status as a lonely widow to induce me to buy more lessons, and I kept getting in deeper, and I thought, 'Well what is the use? I am just getting in where I can't get out, looks like,' so I decided I just had to stop."

It was with this decision that appellee sought legal advice, after which this lawsuit was filed when the studio refused to refund the money appellee had paid.

From examination of the record we conclude that appellee made proof of a *bona fide* claim against the resident individual defendants and against the resident corporate defendant acting through its officers and agents. * * *

Appellee as plaintiff below pleaded several theories of recovery in the alternative. We confine our decision to pleadings and proof pertaining to fraudulent conduct of the resident defendants. In the making of a contract if fraudulent representations or fraudulent concealment of material facts constitute the inducement to the making of the contract, a case of manifest fraud exists, and "fraud vitiates every contract, and may consist either in misrepresentation or in concealment." Wintz v. Morrison, 17 Tex. 372, 383–384 (1856). * * * In this case it was shown that defendants created and operated in a confidential relationship with appellee. * * * In representing to appellee, a woman 56 years old, that this school teacher could complete nearly 2,500 dancing lessons and thereby become "a great dancer," capable of professional performance in international competition, is conduct manifestly deceptive and fraudulent. It is obvious from the record that the purpose of such fantastic representations was to obtain substantial sums of money from appellee, a design that yielded more than $27,000 in less than nine months.

But for the fact that appellee was cautious and unpersuaded at one stage of the studied treatment she received from defendants, appellee perhaps would have lost her home and remained in debt to the credit union from which she had borrowed money to buy the first contracts with defendants. The defendants urged appellee to permit them to sell her home for her and to allow defendants to keep all proceeds above the debt on the home. Instead, appellee sold her home and, after paying her debt to the credit union, amounting to about $7,800, she bought $10,000 of stock in the Fred Astaire Dance Studio. The sale of the stock was a confidential transaction, by arrangement of the defendants.

Defendants insisted the stock was valuable. They told appellee, "We are not going to sell it to just anybody, but you are one of our favorites, so we want to give you a chance to make some money." A few weeks later the defendants induced appellee to turn the $10,000 in stock into membership in the "Executive Competition Club," offering some 628 additional dancing lessons, and explained to appellee that the stock was not paying dividends and that nobody was getting anything from the stock.

Our examination of decisions appearing in the national reporter system discloses that suits of this nature, in which dance studios have induced persons to buy hundreds of hours of dancing lessons for sums amounting to thousands of dollars, are not uncommon. In only one jurisdiction, California, have the courts held the studio operators under provisions of a statute. In the other states the conduct of the studio operators has been dealt with without the aid of statutory precepts and entirely upon rules of common law as applied under case law. * * *

Affirmed.

————

ORTELERE v. TEACHERS' RETIREMENT BOARD OF THE CITY OF NEW YORK, 25 N.Y.2d 196, 303 N.Y.S.2d 362, 250 N.E.2d 460 (1969). Mrs. Ortelere had been a teacher for 40 years. At the age of 60, she suffered a "nervous breakdown", went on a leave of absence, and came under the care a psychiatrist. The doctor administered tranquilizers and shock therapy, but suspended treatment when he began to suspect, as was later confirmed, that she suffered from cerebral arteriosclerosis. About a year after taking her leave of absence, Mrs. Ortelere decided not to return to work but to retire. Before she executed the retirement application, Mrs. Ortelere asked questions that indicated she had a detailed understanding of the various payment options and their effect. She then executed a retirement application selecting maximum retirement benefits during her life but providing no payments to her husband should he survive her. She died less than two months later of a cerebral thrombosis. Under the plan selected by Mrs. Ortelere, her retirement payments were $450 per month. If she had selected the option for payment during her life and her husband's life if he survived her, the monthly payments would have been $375. Her husband, as executor of her estate, sued to set aside her election of the retirement option on the ground that she was not mentally competent to make it. The trial court granted the relief, but the Appellate Division reversed on the ground that there was insufficient proof of mental incompetency. The husband appealed. Held, reversed and remanded for a new trial:

"While the psychiatrist used terms referring to 'rationality', it is quite evident that Mrs. Ortelere's psychopathology did not lend itself to a classification under the legal test of irrationality. It is undoubtedly, for this reason, that the Appellate Division was unable to accept his testimony and the trial court's finding of irrationality in the light of the prevailing rules as they have been formulated.

"The well-established rule is that contracts of a mentally incompetent person who has not been adjudicated insane are voidable. Even where the contract has been partly or fully performed it will still be avoided upon restoration of the *status quo*.

"Traditionally, in this State and elsewhere, contractual mental capacity has been measured by what is largely a cognitive test (Aldrich v. Bailey, 132 N.Y. 85, 30 N.E. 264). Under this standard the 'inquiry' is whether the mind was 'so affected as to render him wholly and absolutely incompetent to comprehend and understand the nature of the transaction' (Aldrich v. Bailey, supra, at p. 89, 30 N.E. at p. 265). A requirement that the party also be able to make a rational judgment concerning the particular transaction qualified the cognitive test. Conversely, it is also well recognized that contractual ability would be affected by insane delusions intimately related to the particular transaction.

"These traditional standards governing competency to contract were formulated when psychiatric knowledge was quite primitive. They fail to account for one who by reason of mental illness is unable to control his conduct even though his cognitive ability seems unimpaired. When these standards were evolving it was thought that all the mental faculties were simultaneously affected by mental illness.

"Of course, the greatest movement in revamping legal notions of mental responsibility has occurred in the criminal law. The nineteenth century cognitive test embraced in the *M'Naghten* rules has long been criticized and changed by statute and decision in many jurisdictions.

"While the policy considerations for the criminal law and the civil law are different, both share in common the premise that policy considerations must be based on a sound understanding of the human mind and, therefore, its illnesses. Hence, because the cognitive rules are, for the most part, too restrictive and rest on a false factual basis they must be re-examined. Once it is understood that, accepting plaintiff's proof, Mrs. Ortelere was psychotic and because of that psychosis could have been incapable of making a voluntary selection of her retirement system benefits, there is an issue that a modern jurisprudence should not exclude, merely because her mind could pass a 'cognition' test based on nineteenth century psychology.

"There has also been some movement on the civil law side to achieve a modern posture. For the most part, the movement has been glacial and has been disguised under traditional formulations. Various devices have been used to avoid unacceptable results under the old rules by finding unfairness or overreaching in order to avoid transactions. * * *

"It is quite significant that Restatement, 2d, Contracts, states the modern rule on competency to contract. This is in evident recognition, and the Reporter's Notes support this inference, that, regardless of how the cases formulated their reasoning, the old cognitive test no longer explains the results. Thus, the new Restatement section reads: '(1) A person incurs only voidable contractual duties by entering into a transaction if by reason of mental illness or defect * * * (b) he is unable to act in a reasonable manner in relation to the transaction and the other party has reason to know of his condition.' (Restatement, 2d, Contracts [§ 15]). * * *

"The avoidance of duties under an agreement entered into by those who have done so by reason of mental illness, but who have understanding, depends on balancing competing policy considerations. There must be stability in contractual relations and protection of the expectations of parties who bargain in good faith. On the other hand, it is also desirable to protect persons who may understand the nature of the transaction but who, due to mental illness, cannot control their conduct. Hence, there should be relief only if the other party knew or was put on notice as to the contractor's mental illness. Thus, the Restatement provision for avoidance contemplates that 'the other party has reason to know' of the mental illness (id.).

"When, however, the other party is without knowledge of the contractor's mental illness and the agreement is made on fair terms, the proposed Restatement rule is: 'The power of avoidance under subsection (1) terminates to the extent that the contract has been so performed in whole or in part or the circumstances have so changed that avoidance would be [unjust]. In such a case a court may grant relief on such equitable terms as [justice] requires.' (Restatement, 2d, Contracts, [§ 15(2)].

"The system was, or should have been, fully aware of Mrs. Ortelere's condition. They, or the Board of Education, knew of her leave of absence for medical reasons and the resort to staff psychiatrists by the Board of Education. Hence, the other of the conditions for avoidance is satisfied.

"Lastly, there are no significant changes of position by the system other than those that flow from the barest actuarial consequences of benefit selection.

"Nor should one ignore that in the relationship between retirement system and member, and especially in a public system, there is not involved a commercial, let alone an ordinary commercial, transaction. Instead the nature of the system and its announced goal is the protection of its members and those in whom its members have an interest. It is not a sound scheme which would permit 40 years of contribution and participation in the system to be nullified by a one-instant act committed by one known to be mentally ill. This is especially true if there would be no substantial harm to the system if the act were avoided. On the record none may gainsay that her selection of a 'no option' retirement while under psychiatric care, ill with cerebral arteriosclerosis, aged 60, and with a family in which she had always manifested concern, was so unwise and foolhardy that a factfinder might conclude that it was explainable only as a product of psychosis.

"On this analysis it is not difficult to see that plaintiff's evidence was sufficient to sustain a finding that, when she acted as she did on February 11, 1965, she did so solely as a result of serious mental illness, namely, psychosis. Of course, nothing less serious than medically classified psychosis should suffice or else few contracts would be invulnerable to some kind of psychological attack. Mrs. Ortelere's psychiatrist testified quite flatly that as an involutional melancholiac in depression she was incapable of making a voluntary 'rational' decision. Of course, as noted earlier, the trial court's finding and perhaps some of the testimony attempted to fit into the rubrics of the traditional rules.

For that reason rather than reinstatement of the judgment at Trial Term there should be a new trial under the proper standards frankly considered and applied."

BLOSSOM FARM PRODUCTS CO. v. KASSON CHEESE CO., INC.

Court of Appeals of Wisconsin, 1986.
133 Wis.2d 386, 395 N.W.2d 619, rev. denied, 134 Wis.2d 458,
401 N.W.2d 10 (1987).

SCOTT, CHIEF JUSTICE.

Blossom Farm Products Company (Blossom) appeals from a judgment dismissing its suit on an open-account contract for $138,306 owed by defendant Kasson Cheese Company, Inc. (Kasson) for its last purchase of Isokappacase.[1] Blossom contends that the trial court was in error when it concluded that the contract was illegal and unenforceable. Blossom argues that the contract for the sale of Isokappacase was not illegal because use of a yield-enhancing agent in cheese by Kasson was not illegal, even though Blossom knew Kasson was misbranding the product and selling it as real cheese. In its cross-appeal, Kasson contends that the contract between Blossom and Kasson was illegal because Blossom knew, not only that Kasson's product was labeled illegally, but it participated in and benefited from the illegality.

The trial court held that the contract was illegal and unenforceable because both parties knew and benefited from Kasson's "illegal use" of Isokappacase. Because we conclude that enforcement of the contract is against public policy, we affirm the trial court's refusal to enforce the contract.

The dispositive issues on appeal are:

(1) whether there is sufficient evidence in the record to support the trial court's findings of fact; and

(2) whether the contract between Blossom and Kasson regarding the sale and purchase of Isokappacase is unenforceable.

Julian Podell, a salesman at Blossom, was sole United States distributor for PTX Food Corporation's (PTX) production of Isokappacase. Blossom sold this product to Kasson from August 1981 until February 13, 1984. The label on Isokappacase indicated that the product was a "starter media, a bacteriophage preventive medium." In

---

1. A brief description of the properties and uses of Isokappacase will help clarify the legal issues regarding Kasson's use of the product. Isokappacase, manufactured by Marvin T. Silverman, president of PTX, was designed for two purposes: (1) as a starter medium; and (2) as a bacteriophage preventive. * * * A third use for Isokappacase was as a yield enhancer whereby the powder had to be put directly into the *cheese milk.* * * * When Isokappacase is used as a yield enhancer, however, the resulting product must: (1) be labeled a cheese "analog," an imitation cheese, or a name other than real cheese; and (2) list the ingredients in the end product to reflect the larger percentage of protein or caseins characteristic of imitation cheese.

fact, however, because Isokappacase contained more than 75% caseins or protein, its composition was characteristic primarily of a yield enhancer. Kasson introduced the Isokappacase directly into the cheese milk to enhance cheese yields from milk but did not label its final product as imitation cheese as required by federal standards.

Blossom was aware of the fact that Kasson's extremely large volume purchases of the product could only be accounted for by Kasson's use of Isokappacase as a yield enhancer. Both Kasson and Blossom benefited economically from this volume purchase and use. When Kasson stopped using Isokappacase as a yield enhancer, PTX stopped making the product. Further facts will be discussed as needed.

Generally, if a promisee has substantially performed its part of the contract, enforcement of a promise is not precluded on grounds of public policy because of some improper use that the promisor intends to make of what he obtains; however, if the promisee acts for the purpose of furthering the promisor's inmproper use, the promisee is barred from recovering. Restatement (Second) of Contracts § 182 (1981). Whether the promisee has acted for such purpose is a question of fact which may be evidenced by the promisee's "doing of specific acts to facilitate the promisor's improper use" and/or "a course of dealing with persons engaged in improper conduct." *Id.* at comment b. A court engages in a balancing process to determine factually if the improper use or conduct at issue is unenforceable on grounds of public policy. *Id.* at § 178 and § 182 comments a and b.

The trial court held the contract "illegal and unenforceable." We restrict our holding to whether the contract is unenforceable. Our position is in keeping with the Restatement at §§ 178 and 182, which deal with the issue in terms of "unenforceability" rather than "illegality."

We turn to the Restatement because the Wisconsin cases relied on by the parties do not distinguish between illegal contracts which are unenforceable and legal contracts which contravene public policy and are thus unenforceable. Despite some confusion in these cases regarding this distinction, we read these cases to be consistent with our decision and support our extension of this distinction, in keeping with the Restatement. ＊ ＊ ＊

Blossom, as promisee, performed its part of the contract; it delivered the $138,306 shipment of Isokappacase to Kasson. Blossom's contract to sell Isokappacase to Kasson was legal; use of a yield enhancer is legal as long as the end product is properly labeled as an imitation or analog cheese with the concomitant ingredient line listed. Only when a promisor, such as Kasson, intends to use Isokappacase as a yield enhancer and sell its end product as a real cheese that purportedly conforms to federal standards of identity does the use of Isokappacase become improper. ＊ ＊ ＊

A decision as to the enforceability of a contract can be reached after a careful balancing, in light of all the circumstances, of the interest in the enforcement of the particular promise against the policy against enforcement of such terms. Restatement (Second) of Contracts § 178 (1981). In weighing a public policy against enforcement of a term, account is taken of: (1) the strength of that policy as manifested by legislation or judicial decisions; (2) the likelihood that a refusal to enforce the term will further that policy; (3) the seriousness of any misconduct involved and the extent to which it was deliberate; and (4) the directness of the connection between that misconduct and the term. *Id.*

A promise may be unenforceable if it involves conduct offensive to public policy, even though the promise does not actually induce the conduct. *Id.* at comments b, c and d. If the conduct to be engaged in by the promisor is deemed improper conduct because it is against public policy, the promisee's doing of specific acts to facilitate the improper use is a bar to recovery. *Id.* at § 182 comment b.

State legislation which adopted federal standards of identity enforces the public policy of accurately distinguishing imitation or analog cheese from real cheese and labeling it accordingly. Sec. 97.09, Stats. Even though Vande Yacht of Kasson testified that neither Podell nor Silverman was directly told about the mislabeling, sufficient evidence reveals that Podell tacitly knew of Kasson's subsequent misbranding of its end product because of the economics of the situation. Furthermore, despite being aware of Kasson's improper conduct, Blossom chose to overlook it and continued to supply volume shipments to Kasson, thereby engaging in a course of dealing which facilitated Kasson in its improper conduct. This course of dealing benefited both Blossom and Kasson. Because mislabeling cheese involves conduct offensive to public policy, the trial court correctly concluded that the transaction which anticipated such improper conduct is unenforceable.

By the Court.—Judgment affirmed.

————

EISENBERG, THE BARGAIN PRINCIPLE AND ITS LIMITS

95 Harv.L.Rev. 741, 798–801 (1982).

The proposition that promises made as part of a bargain ought to be enforced is relatively straightforward; the real question is to what extent.

The traditional answer to this question is embodied in the paradigmatic bargain principle, namely, that damages for the unexcused breach of a bargain promise should invariably be measured by the value that the promised performance would have had to the plaintiff, regardless of the value for which the defendant's promise was exchanged.

This principle, which in the typical case is supported by considerations of both fairness and efficiency, finds its fullest justification in the exemplary case of a half-completed bargain made in a perfectly competitive market. Bargains made in other kinds of markets are not intrinsically suspect. Nevertheless, that a market is less than perfectly competitive does set the stage for transactions in which the bargain principle loses much or all of its force, because it is supported by neither fairness nor efficiency. For example, a market that involves a monopoly sets the stage for the exploitation of distress; a market in which transactions are complex and differentiated rather than simple and homogeneous sets the stage for the exploitation of transactional incapacity; a market in which actors do not simply take a price established by a general market and are susceptible to transient economic irrationality sets the stage for unfair persuasion; a market that involves imperfect price-information sets the stage for the exploitation of price-ignorance.

Until recently, courts have tended either to apply the bargain principle to cases raising such problems, despite the difficulties this application presents, or to deal with these difficulties in covert and unsystematic ways. Over the past thirty years, however, a new paradigmatic principle—unconscionability—has emerged. This principle explains and justifies the limits that should be placed upon the bargain principle on the basis of the quality of a bargain.

Looking backward, the new paradigm enables us to reconstruct prior theory and phenomena by providing a general explanation for a wide variety of contract concepts that heretofore seemed distinct. So, for example, duress may now be seen as simply a special case of the exploitation of distress; undue influence may now be seen as simply a special case of unfair persuasion; and the prohibition against exploiting palpable unilateral mistake may now be seen as a specific norm of unconscionability. Similarly, the apparent anomaly of review for fairness in courts of equity and admiralty can be explained by the new paradigm, while guidelines can now be set for that review; and the doctrine of general incapacity might be reformulated to apply only when exploitation is present.

Looking forward, the paradigm must be articulated and extended through the development of more specific norms to guide the resolution of specific cases, provide affirmative relief to exploited parties, and channel the discretion of administrators and legislators. In accomplishing this task, it now appears that the distinction between procedural and substantive unconscionability, which may have served a useful purpose at an earlier stage, does not provide much help once the relatively obvious norms of unconscionability, such as unfair surprise, have been articulated. For example, it is both difficult and unproductive to classify as exclusively either "substantive" or "procedural" the problems posed by the extraction of an unduly high price from a person who is in distress, lacks transactional capacity, or is price-ignorant. Development of more specific norms must instead proceed by the identification of classes of cases in which neither fairness nor efficiency supports the application of the bargain principle—an effort that can be guided in part by the reconstruction and extension of existing contract doctrines. * * *

Placing limits on the bargain principle is not cost-free. A major advantage of that principle, at least in theory, is its conceptual simplicity and the ease with which it can be administered. To apply the principle, it need only be determined whether a bargain was made, and if so, what remedy is required to put the innocent party in the position he would have been in had the bargain been performed. Development of specific unconscionability norms and limitations on the full reach of the bargain principle in certain types of executory contracts make doctrine more complex by singling out certain transaction-types for special treatment. Administration is also made more complex and problematical by requiring decisions on such issues as whether a given course of conduct was exploitive or whether a given price was unfairly high.

The simplicity of the bargain principle, however, is partly a mirage. Concepts of fairness were smuggled into contract law even when the principle seemed most secure, through doctrines such as the legal-duty rule and the principle of mutuality. Partly because these doctrines are allowed to achieve their ends only in a covert fashion, they operate in an extremely technical manner and are riddled with legalistic exceptions. Furthermore, an increase in the complexity of some areas of law may be desirable, if it accurately mirrors the increased complexity of social and economic life. Placing limits on the bargain principle involves costs of administration. Failure to place such limits, however, involves still greater costs to the system of justice.

UNGER, THE CRITICAL LEGAL STUDIES MOVEMENT
96 Harv.L.Rev. 563, 629 (1983).

According to this doctrine [economic duress] a contract may be voidable whenever a significant inequality of bargaining power exists between the parties. Gross inequalities of bargaining power, however, are all too common in the current forms of market economy, a fact shown not only by the dealings between individual consumers and large corporate enterprises, but also by the huge disparities of scale and market influence among enterprises themselves. Thus, the doctrine of economic duress must serve as a roving commission to correct the most egregious and overt forms of an omnipresent type of disparity. But the unproven assumption of the doctrine is that the amount of corrective intervention needed to keep a contractual regime from becoming a power order will not be so great that it destroys the vitality of decentralized decisionmaking through contract. If this assumption proved false, no compromise between correction and abstention could achieve its intended effect. The only solution would be the one that every such compromise is meant to avoid: the remaking of the institutional arrangements that define the market economy. The doctrinal manifestation of this problem is the vagueness of the concept of economic duress. The cost of preventing the revised duress doctrine from running wild and from correcting almost everything is to draw unstable, unjustified, and unjustifiable lines between the contracts that are voidable and those that are not. In the event, the law draws these lines by a strategy of studied indefinition, though it might just as well have done so—as it so often does elsewhere—through precise but makeshift distinctions.

Survey of Consumer Protection Issues

A. SCOPE OF SURVEY. Keeping up with developments in the area of consumer law is a full time job. There is a steady stream of consumer related legislation, court decisions, and proposals for new laws and regulations. This note discusses a few of the consumer protection issues that have generated continuing debate. In this context, a "consumer" is one who uses or buys for use goods or services "primarily for personal, family, or household purposes." Cf. UCC § 9–109(1) (definition of "consumer goods").

B. THE ECONOMIC PERSPECTIVE. Sellers of consumer goods and services understandably seek to make as much profit as possible. Any practice that they engage in is likely to be related to that central profit motive. Therefore any rule that prevents merchants from doing as they wish is likely to increase the cost and reduce the availability of consumer goods, services, and credit. Before advocating any particular consumer protection rule it would be helpful to have some reliable indication of how much that rule will affect cost. Consumer protection issues are likely to fall into three categories. In the first category are those practices that are so obviously undesirable that they should not be tolerated in any civilized community, even though permitting them might reduce the cost of goods, services, or credit. Use of physical force to collect debts is an example. Second are those practices that, at best, are of marginal importance in consumer protection and which should not be prevented or regulated if there is any substantial effect on cost. In a third group are practices that are the subject of reasonable disagreement concerning their desirability and information concerning the cost of regulation is important to intelligent debate.

Empirical data on the cost of consumer protection rules is collected in Consumer Credit in the United States (1972), a report to the President and Congress by The National Commission on Consumer Finance (hereafter referred to as "Commission Report"). This Commission was established by Title IV of the Consumer Credit Protection Act of 1968. (Title IV, §§ 401–07, Pub.L. No. 90–321). The Commission used cross-state econometric studies to determine how various regulations of consumer sales and financing affect the cost and availability of goods, services, and credit. The commission's economic findings have been verified in subsequent studies (See, e.g., Peterson & Frew, Creditor Remedy Restrictions and Interstate Differences in Personal Loan Rates and Availability, Working Paper No. 14, Credit Research Center, Purdue Univ. (1977)). Barth, Cordes, & Yezer, Benefits and Costs of Legal Restrictions on Personal Loan Markets, 29 J.L. & Econ. 357 (1986) presents the result of an empirical analysis of the effect on borrowers of restricting some creditors' remedies (late charges, garnishment of wages, confession of judgment, attorneys' fees, deficiency judgments), and of banning a security interest in real estate. The conclusion is that, with the exception of limiting deficiency judgments, these limitations on credit practices resulted in more costs than benefits for the typical borrower.

C. USURY. Debate has raged through the years over whether the amount of interest that can be charged for the use of money should be limited by law or set by market forces. Proponents of usury statutes argue that borrowers, especially low income consumer borrowers, need protection against extortionate interest rates; if a consumer is so great a credit risk that he cannot borrow at legal rates, he should not incur indebtedness. On the other hand, if legal interest rates do not permit a return on money that is reasonable in the light of economic conditions and the risk involved, credit will be very difficult to obtain except from "loan sharks" and similar sources. If interest rates are unrealistically low, cash prices are likely to be higher than they would be if more interest could be charged, high risk borrowers will be excluded entirely from borrowing, and other borrowers will be able to borrow less. Studies have shown that in Arkansas, a 10 percent state constitutional limit on interest, now removed, had a depressing effect on economic development, particularly in areas bordering other states, which had higher interest rates.

As the first step in dealing with excessive interest rates, the Commission Report recommends increasing competition in the loan industry. Two kinds of state legislation are necessary to increase competition. First, regulations that inhibit particular kinds of businesses from entering the field should be amended. For example, banks should be permitted to make loans under the same rates as finance companies. Second, if lack of competition is being caused in part by low statutory ceilings on interest, the permissible rates should be raised. When sufficient competition is present in a state, interest ceilings should be raised substantially or eliminated (Commission Report at xxii–xxiii, 147–49).

During periods of high inflation, statutory interest rates are especially likely to be unrealistically low. Title V of the Monetary Control Act of 1980 (Pub.L. No. 96–221) preempted state usury laws on loans for residential housing, business and agricultural. The Act pegged allowable interest to a rate that varied with the discount rate for ninety-day commercial paper in the local Federal Reserve district.

D. PROVISIONS IN CONSUMER CONTRACTS. Clauses disclaiming warranties or limiting remedies for breach of warranty are not the only clauses in consumer contracts that have spurred debate as to whether they should be held unconscionable under UCC § 2–302 or be otherwise forbidden or controlled.

(1) *Cutting Off Defenses Against an Assignee.* This kind of clause can best be described by an illustration. Buyer buys a television set from Seller for $1000, $100 down and the rest in monthly installments. A statute in the jurisdiction prevents Seller from disclaiming an implied warranty of merchantability or eliminating Buyer's remedy of revocation of acceptance if the set fails to function properly after a reasonable number of attempts at repair. Buyer's set is not usable after repeated attempts by Seller to repair it. Buyer revokes his acceptance of the set under UCC § 2–608. Buyer then receives a letter from assignee informing him that Seller has "assigned" to assignee the right to receive payments under the contract and that the next payment should be made to assignee. Assuming that Buyer's revocation of acceptance is proper, is Buyer obligated to continue making payments to assignee?

It is black letter law that the assignee stands in the shoes of the assignor and that any defense under the contract good against the assignor is good against the assignee. See UCC § 9–318(1)(a), infra page 879. Suppose, however, that the contract of sale contains the following clause: "If Seller assigns his rights to payments under this contract, Buyer promises not to assert against the assignee any defenses or claims he may have against Seller, but will look only to Seller for redress." If this clause is valid, Buyer must continue paying assignee. Buyer has a theoretical right of reimbursement against Seller, but it may be expensive to enforce this right, even if Seller is solvent and still servable with process in the locality. A similar device that might be used to cut off Buyer's defenses when the contract is assigned is to have Buyer sign a negotiable promissory note for the price and negotiate this note to assignee. If assignee qualifies as a "holder in due course," he will take the note free of Buyer's ordinary contract defenses. See UCC §§ 3–305(2), 3–302, infra page 884.

These methods of cutting off defenses of consumer-buyers were widely used. They have been substantially eliminated by the Federal Trade Commission Holder-In-Due-Course Regulations. 16 C.F.R. §§ 433.1–433.3. Under these regulations, it is "an unfair or deceptive act or practice" to fail to provide in any consumer credit contract that an assignee is subject to the buyer's defenses and to all claims up to the amounts paid by the buyer. The same protection is afforded the buyer if credit for the purchase is extended not by the seller but by a lender affiliated with the seller.

(2) *Compelling Defense in Inconvenient Forum; Cognovit Clause; Sewer Service.* One way to increase the already substantial likelihood that a consumer debtor will default when sued is to sue him far from home. This might be done by utilizing a long-arm statute or by including in the sales contract the consumer's "consent" to be sued there. An extreme example of these techniques is a "cognovit clause,"

by which the consumer consents to the creditor's obtaining judgment without giving the consumer notice and opportunity to be heard. In April, 1990, the Federal Trade Commission declared it an unfair trade practice to include a cognovit clause in consumer credit contracts. 16 C.F.R. § 444.2(a)(1).

Spiegel, Inc. v. Federal Trade Commission, 540 F.2d 287 (7th Cir. 1976), upheld an FTC order that a mail-order retailer cease and desist from suing nonresident customers in Illinois where the retailer was headquartered. The FTC charged that this was an "unfair business practice."

Whether the use of a cognovit clause violates due process depends upon whether the defendant's waiver of notice and opportunity to be heard is knowing and voluntary. This turns on the circumstances of each case. D.H. Overmyer Co., Inc. v. Frick Co., 405 U.S. 174, 92 S.Ct. 775, 31 L.Ed.2d 124 (1972), held a cognovit clause valid when bargained for in a transaction between companies, but noted that "where the contract is one of adhesion, where there is great disparity in bargaining power, and where the debtor receives nothing for the cognovit provision, other legal consequences may ensue." Swarb v. Lennox, 405 U.S. 191, 92 S.Ct. 767, 31 L.Ed.2d 138 (1972), refused to hold the Pennsylvania cognovit statute unconstitutional on its face but affirmed a three-judge court decision that the Pennsylvania act was unconstitutional as applied to any debtor with an income of less than $10,000 per year unless it is shown that the debtor "intentionally, understandingly and voluntarily" waived his rights.

Cognovit clauses in consumer transactions are permitted under the law of only a few states. The Commission Report found "that prohibition or restriction of confessions of judgment had no significant effect on the rate of charge for consumer credit or its availability" and recommended that cognovit clauses be prohibited in all consumer credit transactions. But see Peterson & Frew, supra page 772, disagreeing with the Commission Report on the economic impact of cognovit clauses.

The Commission Report refers to a "systematic practice" by process servers (usually private process servers) of filing an affidavit of service on the defendant-debtor when, in fact, the summons has never been served but stuffed in a " 'sewer' or elsewhere." When this occurs, the Commission recommends that "any judgment entered shall be voided and the claim reopened upon the debtor's motion" (Commission Report at 41).

(3) *Cross-Collateral Clauses.* A cross-collateral clause takes a security interest not only in the item sold, but also in other property of the debtor. Williams v. Walker-Thomas Furniture Co., 350 F.2d 445 (D.C.Cir.1965), is the classic case involving cross-collateralization. Ora Lee Williams, a person of limited education, was separated from her husband and maintained herself and seven children by means of public

assistance.* Over a period of five years, she had purchased furniture, curtains, mattresses, rugs, sheets, and a washing machine from Walker-Thomas. The total amount of these purchases was over $1200. When the balance owed was only $164, Mrs. Williams purchased a stereo set from Walker-Thomas for $514.95. She defaulted in her payments shortly thereafter and the furniture company brought suit to repossess all the items that she had purchased during the five years. Walker-Thomas claimed the right to do this because the price of each purchase was secured by a lien not only on the new acquisition but also on all items previously purchased. Each payment was credited to the goods in proportion to the outstanding indebtedness. This meant that no item would be "paid off" and its lien discharged until the last item purchased had been paid for. The case was remanded to determine whether this kind of cross-collateralization is unconscionable. The Commission Report declares that it is (Commission Report at 27). The Uniform Consumer Credit Code (U3C) provides that in cases like Williams, payments must be credited to the first item purchased until it is paid for. Then the security interest in that item terminates (1968 Act § 2.409; 1974 Act § 3.303). As of January 1, 1991, the Act was in force in 11 states and Guam. The Federal Trade Commission has declared it an unfair trade practice for a consumer credit contract to impose a security interest on household goods except to secure the purchase price of the goods on which the lien is imposed. 16 C.F.R. § 444.2(a)(4).

(4) *Balloon Payments.* Consumer debts are usually payable in approximately equal monthly installments of principal and interest. A "balloon payment" is an installment much larger than previous payments. For example, a consumer credit agreement may provide for 12 payments, 11 payments of $100 each and a final "balloon" payment of $500. The purchaser is unlikely to be able to make the balloon payment and will have to refinance the debt with the creditor, often at an interest rate higher than that charged on the original loan. The Commission Report recommends that if any scheduled payment is more than twice the amount of the average of earlier payments, the consumer shall have the right to refinance the payment on terms no less favorable than the original terms (Commission Report at 39). The U3C codifies this recommendation (1968 Act § 2.405; 1974 Act § 3.308).

(5) *Wage Assignment.* A wage assignment is a transfer from debtor to creditor of debtor's right to payment of all or part of debtor's future wages. The economic hardship that a wage assignment can create for the debtor is obvious, but the Commission Report indicates strong evidence that complete prohibition would substantially increase the cost and reduce the availability of credit, particularly for small loans. The Commission recommended prohibiting wage assignments for debts over $300 but permitting them for smaller debts. The

* Some of the facts are taken from the opinion of the District of Columbia Court of Appeals, 198 A.2d 914 (1964).

assignment would then be valid only for the portion of the weekly wage in excess of 40 times the federal minimum wage or exceeding 75% of take-home pay, whichever gives the debtor more disposable earnings. The U3C, however, bans wage assignments entirely. (1968 Act § 2.410; 1974 Act § 3.305). See also infra page 885.

E. COLLECTION PRACTICES. Another important issue is whether certain collection practices should be forbidden or controlled. Any restrictions on collection practices are likely to have a substantial effect on the cost of goods, services, and credit. Moreover, this added cost will be borne by all purchasers, including those who do not default. Harassment, intimidation, and threats of bodily harm cannot be tolerated, and the debtor's opportunity to contest the fact or amount of his indebtedness must be preserved. Further regulation of collection practices, however, requires balancing the social values being protected against the cost of the proposed rules, a fact not always recognized by persons who propose sharp restrictions on collection practices.

(1) *Garnishment of Wages.* Garnishment of wages occurs when the creditor obtains a court order that directs the debtor's employer to withhold all or part of the debtor's wages and pay them to the creditor. This is a very efficient collection device and the Commission Report finds that a complete prohibition of wage garnishment would substantially increase the cost and decrease the availability of credit (Commission Report at 34). But wage garnishment can also have a devastating impact on the wage earner and his family. The Consumer Credit Protection Act provides a compromise solution. Wage garnishment is limited to 25% of take-home pay or an amount by which take-home pay exceeds 30 times the federal minimum wage, whichever will leave the employee with more disposable earnings. (15 U.S.C.A. § 1673). In addition, an employer is prohibited from discharging any employee "by reason of the fact that his earnings have been subjected to garnishment for any one indebtedness." (15 U.S.C.A. § 1674.)

(2) *Prejudgment Remedies; Self-Help Repossession; Deficiency Judgments.* In many states a creditor may, before judgment on the merits of his claim, seize his debtor's property to secure it for the payment of a judgment. When this is done by court order, there is "state action" so that the due process protections of the Fourteenth Amendment of the United States Constitution are available to protect the debtor. A series of United States Supreme Court opinions provide that for prejudgment garnishment or replevin to pass constitutional muster, the debtor must be entitled to a hearing at which the probable validity of the creditor's claim can be tested. This hearing must be available to the debtor either before or immediately after garnishment or replevin. See Sniadach v. Family Finance Corp., 395 U.S. 337, 89 S.Ct. 1820, 23 L.Ed.2d 349 (1969); Fuentes v. Shevin, 407 U.S. 67, 92 S.Ct. 1983, 32 L.Ed.2d 556 (1972); Mitchell v. W.T. Grant Co., 416 U.S. 600, 94 S.Ct. 1895, 40 L.Ed.2d 406 (1974); North Georgia Finishing, Inc. v. Di-Chem, Inc., 419 U.S. 601, 95 S.Ct. 719, 42 L.Ed.2d 751 (1975).

A creditor who has taken a security interest in personal property can, on the debtor's default, take possession of the property without judicial process (if this can be done without breach of the peace) and sell it at public or private sale. (UCC §§ 9–503, 9–504) Although this procedure is authorized and implemented by Article 9 of the UCC and a number of other statutes in each state, most courts have held that seizure and sale under Article 9 is not "state action" and therefore the due process requirements that the debtor be given notice and opportunity to be heard at crucial stages of the process are not applicable. See, e.g., Adams v. Southern California First National Bank, 492 F.2d 324 (9th Cir.1973), cert. denied, 419 U.S. 1006, 95 S.Ct. 325, 42 L.Ed.2d 282 (1974). UCC § 9–504 requires notice to the debtor before the property is sold and orders the creditor to account to the debtor for any surplus of sale proceeds over indebtedness and costs of collection, but permits the creditor to buy at the public sale and in some circumstances at a private sale as well. Despite the protections of § 9–504, there have been many abuses of these self-help creditor remedies. The FTC has obtained agreements from the finance subsidiaries of the three largest United States automobile manufacturers requiring changes in the methods of accounting to debtors for surpluses. There is also evidence that the price at which repossessed automobiles are sold is almost always far below fair value. See Schuchman, Profit on Default, 22 Stan.L.Rev. 20 (1969).

The Wisconsin Consumer Act abolishes self-help repossession of consumer goods, requires judicial proceedings (Wis.Stat.Ann. §§ 425.205–425.206), and provides that in computing any deficiency (the remaining indebtedness after deducting the net proceeds of resales), the debtor must be credited with the "fair market value of the collateral." (Id. § 425.210).

Some consumer advocates have argued that a creditor should be made to choose between a judgment for the balance of the indebtedness and repossession of collateral; that if collateral is repossessed, the debt should be deemed satisfied and no deficiency judgments permitted. The U3C bars deficiency judgments if the goods repossessed had the price stated in the statute. (1968 Act § 5.103 ($1000 or less); 1974 Act § 5.103 ($1750 or less).

(3) *Debtor Harassment.* In addition to physical violence, harassing collection practices include telephoning the debtor repeatedly late at night and informing third persons, such as the debtor's employer, that a debt is owed. These practices are forbidden by federal statute when engaged in by a "debt collector" who collects debts due another. 15 U.S.C.A. §§ 1692–1692o. The U3C regulates similar conduct by the creditor. (1974 Act only, § 5.108(2) and (5), in force in 4 states as of January 1, 1991).

F. EDUCATION AND INFORMATION. The Truth-in-Lending Act of 1968 and Regulation Z promulgated under it by the Board of Governors of the Federal Reserve System had the goal of requiring disclosure to debtors of all factors bearing on the cost of credit and especially the annual percentage rate of interest charged. The theory was that debtors would then be able to make more intelligent decisions when comparison shopping for credit. Unfortunately the Act and Regulation were so complex that debtors were deluged with detailed "disclosures" that often buried essential information in a mass of marginal data. In addition, compliance was difficult and many creditors committed unintentional violations. The Truth-In-Lending Simplification and Reform Act of 1980 and the new Regulation Z promulgated under it seek to remedy these defects. 15 U.S.C.A. ch. 41(I); 12 C.F.R. Part 226. Debtor awareness of the annual percentage rate of interest has shown a steady increase since its disclosure was first required in 1968.

Another approach to helping consumers understand transactions in which they engage is "plain meaning" legislation. New York, for example, has enacted a statute that requires agreements concerning leasing of residential premises or sale of consumer goods or services to be "[w]ritten in a clear and coherent manner using words with common and every day meanings." In addition, the writing must be "[a]ppropriately divided and captioned by its various sections." The penalty for violation of the statute is "actual damages sustained plus a penalty of fifty dollars" and the statute may be enforced through a class action up to a total penalty of $10,000. Violation of the statute is not, however, a defense to enforcement of the agreement. N.Y.Gen. Obligations Law § 5–702 (McKinney 1989).

Legislation of this kind is addressed to a pervasive problem. Consumers frequently sign long, complicated contracts tendered to them on a "take it or leave it" basis by the party in a vastly superior bargaining position. The length of the document, the technical nature of its terms, and the consumer's inability to effect any change, all combine to discourage an attempt to read and understand all of the terms. Although this is true of most adhesion contracts, the problem is especially troublesome when it involves exclusions of coverage in insurance policies. The exclusions state circumstances in which the insurance coverage is not available. Often the insured is unaware of the exclusion until he makes a claim only to be told "sorry, wrong coverage." A proposal has been made that in order for an insurer to rely on an exclusion of coverage, the insurer must prove "that the provision was brought to the insured's attention before contract formation and that it was reasonable for the insurer to conclude from the transaction that the particular consumer actually assented to the purpose and effect of the provision." See Note, A Common Law Alternative to the Doctrine of Reasonable Expectations in the Construction of Insurance Contracts, 57 N.Y.U.L.Rev. 1175, 1199 (1982). Courts have applied a somewhat analogous rule to some problems of insurance coverage. For example, the insured is likely to expect that when he applies for life insurance and pays the first premium, he is covered as long as he continues to pay premiums. Insurers often contend that permanent coverage does not attach until the applicant is approved by the insurer and that until this occurs, the insurer is free to cancel coverage by notifying the insured. Courts have said that the right to reject the application and cancel the insurance must be clearly stated in the documents seen by the applicant and must also be called to his attention. See, e.g., Smith v. Westland Life Insurance Co., 15 Cal.3d 111, 123 Cal.Rptr. 649, 539 P.2d 433 (1975).

G. FRAUDULENT AND COERCIVE SALES PRACTICES. Fraudulent sales practices include, of course, false descriptions of the nature of the goods or services sold. Less obvious fraud includes bait and switch advertising and referral sales schemes. (For a discussion of bait and switch advertising, see supra page 425.) In a referral sale scheme, the buyer is offered a discount for providing the seller with names of other persons to whom subsequent sales are made. The referral scheme often combines aspects of chain-letter or other pyramid frauds because if each customer can get a discount only by providing the names of additional persons who subsequently buy, the available population will be exhausted after a few levels of sales and recommendations.

Another perceived evil is in-home selling. Although there are many reputable door-to-door sales businesses, sales in the buyer's home often can take on coercive elements. The buyer may be pressured into making an affirmative decision just to get rid of the unwanted salesman.

All of these sales practices are regulated or forbidden. The U3C forbids referral sales. (1968 Act § 2.411; 1974 Act § 3.309). The Federal Trade Commission has issued regulations covering door-to-door sales. There is a three-day "cooling off" period when the buyer may elect to cancel the transaction. The buyer must be notified of this cancellation option and be given a form that he may use to exercise this option. 16 C.F.R. § 429.1.

H. ENFORCEMENT. A major problem with consumer protection rules is how these rules are to be enforced. Typically, they can be used as the basis for a defense or a claim by a consumer in litigation brought by or against a creditor. But that alone is not likely to be effective because even without resort to inconvenient forums or cognovit clauses, the vast majority of consumers sued by creditors permit a default judgment to be entered against them. This default rate may be a reflection of the merits of the positions of the parties, but it is also likely that the inconvenience and expense of litigation is part of the explanation. Also, given the classic litigation model of one-on-one confrontation with each party paying his own attorney's fees, it is unlikely that a consumer would have the resources to take advantage of consumer protection rules; in addition, the amount at stake will usually not justify the expenditure even by a wealthy consumer.

One way to make litigation more feasible is to provide for recovery of attorney's fees if the consumer wins. Many state and federal statutes now do so. A related device is the consumer class action. If a person has lost a few dollars in a consumer transaction, the matter is unlikely to be worth pursuing. But if an action can be brought on behalf of thousands of consumers similarly situated, the resulting verdict may be large enough to attract able plaintiff's counsel, which in turn deters wrongful conduct. Much modern legislation contains provisions facilitating consumer class actions.

Another enforcement mechanism is to empower some public official, such as a state's attorney general, to sue to enjoin violations, invoke criminal penalties, and recover civil damages for the benefit of those affected. This was the procedure employed in Kugler v. Romain, supra page 756.

Many state and national agencies have been created to administer and enforce various aspects of consumer protection laws. Perhaps the best known is the Federal Trade Commission. Agency enforcement has the benefit of permitting continuity in policy development and the acquisition of expertise. Often, however, the agency has not been given the resources to carry out its responsibilities. In some instances the agency has developed such close working relations with the industry it is purporting to supervise that it becomes the industry's captive rather than its regulator.

Another important enforcement mechanism involves the establishment of informal forums in which disputes can be heard. Convenient consumer dispute resolution was given impetus by the Magnuson-Moss Warranty [and] Federal Trade Commission Improvement Act. The Act invites warrantors to set up informal dispute settlement mechanisms. If a warrantor provides a qualified means of dispute settlement, a consumer is barred from commencing a civil action under the Act without first resorting to that procedure. 15 U.S.C.A. § 2310. Thousands of merchants have taken advantage of this provision, most often by agreeing to submit to arbitration by a panel provided by the Better Business Bureau in the consumer's locality.

One of the most efficient methods of protecting consumers against unconscionable contract terms is to have a public agency draft a fair contract and require that it be the only form used. The drafting process should permit participation by representatives of all affected parties. This would be better than swatting unconscionable clauses one by one when they occur in privately drafted adhesion contracts. In the United States, required contract forms are common for insurance, but we have not made as much use of the technique as have other countries.

Chapter 8

CONDITIONS

IN RE CARTER'S CLAIM
Supreme Court of Pennsylvania, 1957.
390 Pa. 365, 134 A.2d 908.

Before CHARLES ALVIN JONES, C. J., and BELL, CHIDSEY, MUSMANNO, ARNOLD, BENJAMIN R. JONES and COHEN, JJ.

BENJAMIN R. JONES, JUSTICE.

This is an appeal from a judgment entered upon an arbitrator's award in a proceeding under the Act of 1927.

In June 1954 the Edwin J. Schoettle Co., a Pennsylvania corporation, and its six subsidiaries were available for purchase. Lester L. Kardon, interested in purchasing the company and five of its subsidiaries, opened negotiations for that purpose. The negotiations extended from June 24, 1954 to September 17, 1954, on which latter date the parties entered into a written agreement under the terms of which Kardon (hereinafter called the buyer) purchased all the issued and outstanding capital stock of Schoettle Co. and all its subsidiaries (hereinafter called sellers). The total purchase price set forth in the agreement of sale (excluding certain real estate) was $2,100,000 of which amount $187,863.60 was set aside under paragraph 11 of the agreement to be held by the Provident Trust Company of Philadelphia as escrow agent to indemnify the buyer against "the liabilities of sellers by reason of any and all provisions of this agreement."

The present litigation arises from the fact that the buyer has presented a claim against the escrow fund for $69,998.42 as a "liability" of the seller under the agreement. Payment of this claim having been disputed by the sellers, both parties, under the provisions of the agreement, submitted to arbitration and Judge Gerald F. Flood was selected as arbitrator. On October 26, 1956 Judge Flood, as arbitrator, and, after hearing, awarded to the buyer $3,182.88.[3] Buyer's motion to correct the arbitrator's award was dismissed by the Code of Common

---

3. The buyer's claim is based largely on the proposition that sellers had warranted the company's net worth. The amount allowed by the arbitrator—$3,182.88—represented an error in computing state taxes, additional taxes and water rent. This amount is undisputed as a proper claim against the fund.

Pleas No. 6 of Philadelphia County and judgment was entered in the amount of $3,182.88 in conformity with the arbitrator's award. From that judgment this appeal ensued.

The resolution of this controversy depends upon the interpretation of certain portions of the 25-page written agreement of September 17, 1954. The pertinent portions of this agreement are paragraphs 5(g), 9(a), 9(b), 9(c), 10(d), and 15, which read as follows:

"5. *Representations and Warranties.* Sellers *represent* and *warrant* as follows: [Emphasis supplied.] * * *

"5(g) *Absence of certain changes.* Since June 30, 1954, there have not been (i) any changes in Company's or its subsidiaries' financial condition, assets, liabilities, or businesses, other than changes in the ordinary course of business, none of which have been materially adverse, and changes required or permitted hereunder; (ii) any damage, destruction, or loss, whether or not covered by insurance, materially and adversely affecting the properties or businesses of Company and its subsidiaries as an entirety; (iii) any declaration, or setting aside, or payment of any dividend or other distribution in respect of Company's capital stock or that of any subsidiary (except that prior to the date hereof, Company has declared and paid a dividend of Sixteen and Two Thirds Cents ($.16⅔) per share on all issued and outstanding shares of its said capital stock), or any direct or indirect redemption, purchase, or other acquisition of any such stock; or (iv) any increase in the compensation payable or to become payable by Company or any subsidiary to any of their officers, employees, or agents, or any bonus payment or arrangement made to or with any of them. * * *

"9. *Conditions precedent.* All obligations of Buyer under this agreement are subject to the fulfillment, prior to or at the closing of each of the following *conditions:* [Emphasis supplied.]

"(a) *Financial condition at closing.* As of the time of closing the financial condition of the Company and its subsidiaries in the aggregate shall be no less favorable than the financial condition shown on the statements of said corporations dated June 30, 1954 and warranted to be true and complete in paragraph 5(e) hereof.

"(b) *Representations and warranties true at closing.* Sellers' representations and warranties contained in this agreement shall be true at the time of closing as though such representations and warranties were made at such time.

"(c) *Performance.* Sellers shall have performed and complied with all agreements and conditions required by this agreement to be performed or complied with by them prior to or at the closing. * * *

"10. *Indemnification.* Sellers shall indemnify and hold harmless Buyer, subject to the limitations of paragraph 11 hereof, against and in respect of: * * *

"(d) Any damage or deficiency resulting from any misrepresentation, breach of warranty, or nonfulfillment of any agreement on the part of Sellers, or any of them, under this agreement, or from any misrepresentation in or omission from any certificate or other instrument furnished or to be furnished to Buyer hereunder; * * *

"15. *Survival of representations.* All representations, warranties and agreements made by Sellers and Buyer in this agreement or pursuant hereto shall survive closing, subject to the provisions of paragraph 11 hereof."

The buyer (appellant) contends that the financial condition on the date of purchase—September 17, 1954—was less favorable than that reflected in the company's financial statement of June 30, 1954 and, therefore, he is entitled to reimbursement out of the escrow fund for the amount of the deficiency. Sellers (appellees) deny any reduction in the financial condition and further argue that, even if there were any reduction, buyer has no right to reimbursement under the agreement unless such reduction resulted from occurrences outside the ordinary course of business or which caused a materially adverse change in the company's financial condition. Actually the buyer's position is that paragraph 9(a), supra, constituted a "warranty" on the sellers' part that the financial condition of the company and its subsidiaries was not less favorable than demonstrated by the financial statement of June 30, 1954 and, therefore, sellers having breached the warranty the buyer is entitled to claim the difference between the net worth on June 30, 1954 and September 17, 1954. On the other hand, sellers take the position that their engagement under paragraph 9(a) constituted a "condition" and not a warranty and the buyer had simply the right to refuse a consummation of the sale if the "condition" was not fulfilled; when the buyer elected to consummate the sale it waived the "condition."

At the hearing before the arbitrator the buyer introduced certain evidence for the purpose of proving that it was the parties' intent that the sellers would warrant that the financial condition of the company and its subsidiaries would be no less favorable on the date of closing than on June 30, 1954. * * *

The language of the instant agreement is clear and unambiguous. The buyer's evidence would tend to prove that in the negotiations leading up to the integrated agreement it was intended that the sellers warrant the company's and its subsidiaries' financial condition, whereas the language of the agreement plainly expresses a contrary intent. The admission of such evidence would vary and change the language of the agreement and its exclusion was eminently proper under the circumstances.

This written agreement was carefully and meticulously prepared by able and competent counsel after long and thorough negotiations. Each general paragraph of the agreement is headed by a title descriptive of the contents of each paragraph. Paragraph 5, entitled "Representations and Warranties", expressly states that the sellers "represented and warranted" fifteen separate and carefully spelled out factual situations. Paragraph 9, entitled "Conditions precedent" expressly states that "All obligations of buyer under this agreement are subject to the fulfillment, prior to or at the closing, of each of the following *conditions.*" It is to be noted that included among the *"conditions"* was the financial condition of the company and its subsidiaries at the time of closing, that the fulfillment of the "conditions" was to take place not subsequent to but "prior to or at the closing" and that the buyer's obligations, not the sellers', were made subject to the fulfillment of the condition. This agreement, in distinct and indubitable language, distinguishes between such engagements on the sellers' part as constitute "Warranties" and such engagements as constitute "Conditions".

Assuming, arguendo, that the company and its subsidiaries' financial condition was less favorable on September 17, 1954 than the financial condition shown on the statement dated June 30, 1954, what under this agreement was the buyer's remedy? The buyer claims that such fact constituted a breach of warranty which gave to him the right to recover the amount of the reduced net worth, while the sellers claim that the buyer had the choice on September 17, 1954 either to accept the situation or to refuse to proceed under the agreement.

The buyer argues that it was impossible to ascertain at the date of closing whether or not the net worth of the company and its subsidiaries had been reduced, and that only by an examination after date of closing could this fact be ascertained and therefore, both parties must have intended that the buyer have a reasonable time after the date of closing to ascertain this fact. Such an argument not only finds no support in the wording of the agreement but, on the contrary, is in direct conflict with the express terms of the agreement. Such a contention would require that we read into the agreement that which is in direct variance with the clear and unambiguous language employed to express the parties' intent.

Neither the Sales Act of 1915 nor the Uniform Commercial Code— Sales Article— is applicable to this situation. The former legislation was repealed as of July 1, 1954 and this agreement was not executed until September 17, 1954. Under [§ 2–105(1)] of the Uniform Commercial Code—Sales, "investment securities"—that which was purchased and sold under this agreement—are expressly excluded. Comment 1 thereunder provides, inter alia: " 'Investment securities' are expressly excluded from the coverage of this Article. It is not intended by this exclusion, however, to prevent the application of a particular section of this Article by analogy to securities * * * when the reason of that section makes such application sensible and the situation involved is not covered by the Article of this Act dealing specifically with said securities (Art. 8)." * * *

The buyer urges that § 2–714, § 2–717 and § 2–720 of the Code gave him the right to recoup damages from the sellers even though it may have waived its right to rescind the contract. The arbitrator's answer to this contention is fully justified: "But this likewise does not apply to this contract. If A promises to deliver to B 1300 shares of A Co. stock but delivers only 1200 shares there is no injustice in allowing B to take the 1200 and sue for damages. But if A promises to deliver 1300 shares at a certain price, and B promises to pay a certain price for them, but the contract provides that B need not perform if the market price is lower than the sale price on the delivery date, there is no basis in law or justice in allowing B to take the shares and sue for the difference between sale price and market price. This is precisely the situation before me, and nothing in the Sales Act, the Uniform Commercial Code, or any of the cases cited lead to a different result from that which I have reached." In addition thereto, the instant situation does not call for the application of Article 2 to the sale and purchase of shares of capital stock.

In determining this controversy we have no need to draw a distinction between "warranties" and "conditions" generally—a field in which there is great confusion.[7] The parties themselves to this agreement have by its express terms drawn a clear distinction between the sellers' obligations in the nature of warranties and their obligations in the nature of conditions and among the latter have included the financial condition of the company and its subsidiaries. Sellers made no representation or warranty concerning the financial condition.

The buyer's next contention * * * [is] that the failure of a party to perform a condition may be treated as a warranty, allowing the other party to accept the defective performance and sue for the breach * * *.

The arbitrator concluded that to construe paragraph 9(a) as creative of a promise for the breach of which the buyer could recover damages—i.e., a warranty—would be inconsistent with paragraph 5(g).

---

7. Lord Abinger in Charter v. Hopkins, 4 M. & W. 399, has said "Two things have been confounded together. A warranty is an express or implied statement of something which the party undertakes shall be part of a contract; and, though part of the contract, yet collateral to the express object of it. But in many of the cases, some of which have been referred to, the circumstances of a party selling a particular thing by its proper description has been called a warranty, and a breach of such contract a breach of warranty, but it would be better to distinguish such cases as a noncompliance with a contract which a party has engaged to fulfill; as, if a man offers to buy peas of another, and he sends him beans, he does not perform his contract; but that is not a warranty; there is no warranty that he should sell him peas; the contract is to sell peas, and if he sell him anything else in their stead it is a nonperformance of it. So, if a man were to order copper for sheathing ships—that is, a particular copper, prepared in a particular manner—if the seller sent him a different sort, in that case he does not comply with the contract; and though this may have been ranged under the class of cases relating to warranties, yet it is not properly so."

With this conclusion we are in full agreement. The sellers in paragraph 5(g) represented and warranted, inter alia, there there had not been any changes in the financial condition of the company or its subsidiaries other than changes in the ordinary course of business, none of which had been materially adverse and were changes required or permitted under the agreement. Paragraph 9(a) covers an entirely different situation in that it referred to such changes in the financial condition of the company and its subsidiaries in the ordinary course of business which were materially adverse and not permitted under the agreement; if this situation arose the agreement specifically provided that the buyer was under no obligation to complete the purchase. A comparison of paragraph 5(g) with paragraph 9(a) clearly leads to this conclusion; to place upon paragraph 9(a) any other construction than that placed upon it by the arbitrator would amount to a redundancy.

A resolution of the instant controversy depends entirely upon an interpretation of the language of this agreement. The language employed by the parties is manifestly indicative of that which was intended and the meaning of the agreement—free as it is of ambiguity and doubt—is to be determined by what the agreement states. The parties carefully and scrupulously delineated between the sellers' undertakings which were intended to be "warranties" and those which were intended to be "conditions". It is crystal clear that the undertaking under paragraph 9(a) was simply a "condition" and not a "warranty" and once the buyer elected to accept this agreement the provisions of paragraph 9(a) ceased to be operative and the buyer had no right to recover any damages.

The judgment of the Court below is affirmed. Costs to be paid by appellant.

BELL and COHEN, JJ., dissent.

Typical words used for the creation of a condition are "on condition that," "provided that," and "if." One cannot use such words as a talismanic test for distinguishing between a condition and a promise, however, since rarely in the everyday world is language used by the parties with total precision. Indeed, the distinction between a condition and a promise is a slippery one under the best of circumstances, since persons using language of condition may not understand or intend to impose a condition. A person who is considering obligating himself to do some act in the future (the "obligor") normally wishes to obtain some benefit from the obligee in return. The obligor has three alternatives: (1) he may insist that the obligee promise to provide the desired benefit; (2) he may make receipt of the benefit a condition to his own obligation, or (3) he may insist that the obligee promise to provide the desired benefit and in addition make his own performance conditional on receipt of the benefit. From a legal standpoint significantly different results flow from these choices, yet it is likely that many persons are only dimly aware of the three alternatives, if aware of them at all.

As a result, the issue whether specific language should be classed as a condition, as a promise, or as both is normally a matter of interpretation and construction of language that is uncertain or ambiguous.

The issue whether specific language should be viewed as a condition or as a promise is colored by the fact that a condition often involves a substantial risk of loss or forfeiture to one party. The reason for this is that the non-occurrence of a condition completely discharges the obligor's duty, while if the language is construed as a promise, the obligor may have a claim against the obligee for breach of contract but normally cannot treat his duty as at an end. The extent to which a condition involves a risk of loss or forfeiture usually depends on when the condition is resolved; if it occurs (or does not occur) before either party has relied on its expected occurrence, the likelihood of a substantial loss is small. Where, however, the condition is not resolved until after one party has relied substantially, the probability is very high that treating language as a condition will cause significant injustice. As a result, the case law strongly prefers to treat unclear or imprecise language as promissory rather than as a condition. See Restatement, Second, Contracts §§ 84, 246, reprinted at pp. 311–312 supra.

It should be noted that this preference arises only in the context of contract construction and interpretation and does not resolve all problems of substantial loss or forfeiture arising from conditions. It does not, for example, deal with the situation of language that clearly creates a condition so that there is no room for the preference to operate. If truly agreed upon, such clear language should normally be enforced under basic principles of freedom of contract even where the consequence is hard on one party. On the other hand, it is not surprising that courts have broadened concepts of waiver or excuse to protect persons against forfeitures where the condition did not appear to be a central part of the bargained-for exchange.

RESTATEMENT, SECOND, CONTRACTS § 227:

(1) In resolving doubts as to whether an event is made a condition of an obligor's duty, and as to the nature of such event, an interpretation is preferred that will reduce the obligee's risk of forfeiture, unless the event is within the obligee's control or the circumstances indicate that he has assumed the risk.

(2) Unless the contract is of a type under which only one party generally undertakes duties, when it is doubtful whether

(a) a duty is imposed on an obligee that an event occur, or

(b) the event is made a condition of the obligor's duty, or

(c) the event is made a condition of the obligor's duty and a duty is imposed on the obligee that the event occur,

the first interpretation is preferred if the event is within the obligee's control.

(3) In case of doubt, an interpretation under which an event is a condition of an obligor's duty is preferred over an interpretation under which the non-occurrence of the event is a ground for discharge of that duty after it has become a duty to perform.

Illustrations:

1. A, a general contractor, contracts with B, a sub-contractor, for the plumbing work on a construction project. B is to receive $100,000, "no part of which shall be due until five days after Owner shall have paid Contractor therefor." B does the plumbing work, but the owner becomes insolvent and fails to pay A. A is under a duty to pay B after a reasonable time.

2. A, a mining company, hires B, an engineer, to help reopen one of its mines for "$10,000 to be payable as soon as the mine is in successful operation." $10,000 is a reasonable compensation for B's service. B performs the required services, but the attempt to reopen the mine is unsuccessful and A abandons it. A is under a duty to pay B $10,000 after the passage of a reasonable time.

3. A, a mining company, contracts with B, the owner of an untested experimental patented process, to help reopen one of its mines for $5,000 paid in advance and an additional "$15,000 to be payable as soon as the mine is in successful operation." $10,000 is a reasonable compensation for B's services. B performs the required services, but because the process proves to be unsuccessful, A abandons the attempt to reopen the mine. A is under no duty to pay B any additional amount. In all the circumstances the risk of failure of the process was, to that extent, assumed by B.

4. A contracts to sell and B to buy land for $100,000. At the same time, A contracts to pay C, a real estate broker, as his commission, $5,000 "on the closing of title." B refuses to consummate the sale. Absent a showing of a contrary intention, a court may conclude that C assumed this risk, and that A's duty is conditional on the sale being consummated. A is then under no duty to pay C.

HUDSON v. WAKEFIELD

Supreme Court of Texas, 1983.
645 S.W.2d 427.

KILGARLIN, JUSTICE.

Petitioners, Robert Hudson and Andy Wright (hereinafter referred to as "Purchasers") brought this suit to enforce specific performance of a contract for the sale of real property owned by Respondents, Marion and Jean Wakefield (hereinafter referred to as "Sellers"). The trial court granted Sellers' Motion for Summary Judgment on the grounds that the instrument on which specific performance was sought never attained the status of a contract because the check for earnest money was returned due to insufficient funds. The court of appeals affirmed. 635 S.W.2d 216. We reverse the judgments of the trial court and the court of appeals and remand this case for determination of the fact issue of whether a material breach has occurred.

The facts are as follows:

On March 18, 1981, Sellers entered into a written contract with Purchasers for the sale of a 186 acre tract of land in Freestone County. Pursuant to the terms of the contract, Purchasers paid $5,000 earnest money in the form of a check dated March 18, 1981, drawn on the First International Bank in Houston and payable to Freestone County Title and Abstract Company, Inc., said check being signed by Purchaser Robert A. Hudson. On March 24, 1981, the check and contract were delivered to the title company and on the following day the company manager, Betty Conovan, deposited Purchaser's check for collection in the Fairfield State Bank. On March 30, 1981, First International Bank in Houston returned the check to Fairfield State Bank with the notation "N.S.F." (not sufficient funds).[3] Sometime between April 7, 1981, and April 24, 1981, Conovan was advised by the Fairfield State Bank of the return of the check.

Sellers signed a contract to sell the same 186 acres to J.W. Robinson, their attorney, on March 19, 1981.[4] Thereafter, Purchasers' attorney wrote Sellers demanding specific performance of the contract with Purchasers. On April 7, 1981, Robinson and Sellers entered into a release of their March 19, 1981 contract. On April 8, however, Purchasers sued Sellers for specific performance. On April 24, 1981, Conovan wrote Sellers, advising them of the return of the earnest money check for reason of insufficient funds, and stated that the file was being closed. Four days later, attorney Robinson wrote Purchasers, advising them of the return of the earnest money check, that the contract was thereby terminated, and demanded a dismissal of the suit, with prejudice.

As soon as Purchasers found out about the insufficiency of the check, they took the following actions: (1) requested the title company to again present the check for payment, which the title company refused to do; (2) thereafter, had $5,000 wire transferred to Fairfield State Bank and asked the title company to draw on it, which the title company likewise refused to do; and (3) on May 28, 1981, tendered a $5,000 cashier's check, which the title company refused to accept.

The threshold question is whether the earnest money provision of the contract [5] amounted to a condition precedent or a covenant. Pur-

---

3. First International Bank V.P. Dunham stated in his affidavit that had the check been presented in the normal manner (regular clearing process) rather than for collection, it would have been paid because at all times Hudson had sufficient funds on deposit with the bank to cover the $5,000.00 check.

4. The contract between Sellers and their attorney has no effect upon our holding and is mentioned solely to explain why

Purchasers filed their suit for specific performance when they did.

5. Relevant portions of the contract are as follows:

Article IV

Purchaser's Obligations

The obligations of Purchaser hereunder to consummate the transaction contemplated hereby are subject to the satis-

chasers contend that rather than being a condition precedent, the earnest money provision of this particular instrument was but one of the many covenants of the parties and that Sellers were not entitled to back out of the agreement because of the return of the earnest money check. Sellers urge that the earnest money provision was a condition precedent to the formation of the contract. If they are correct, they must prevail. However, if, as Purchasers contend, the provision was but a covenant of the contract, then the granting of a summary judgment for Sellers was error.

For authority that the earnest money provision in the contract was a condition precedent, Sellers rely upon Slam Properties v. Pickett, 495 S.W.2d 381 (Tex.Civ.App.1973, writ ref'd n.r.e.), Bowles v. Fickas, 140 Tex. 312, 167 S.W.2d 741 (1943), and Antwine v. Reed, 145 Tex. 521, 199 S.W.2d 482 (1947). The earnest money provisions of the contracts in Bowles v. Fickas, supra, and Antwine v. Reed, supra, are distinguishable from those in the case at bar. In the first case, Fickas (purchaser) wrote a letter to Bowles, enclosing a copy of the proposed contract, and stated that if Bowles wished to accept the

faction of each of the following conditions (any of which may be waived in whole or in part by Purchaser at or prior to the closing).

Within 30 days after the date hereof, Seller, at Seller's sole cost and expense, shall have caused the title company to issue title report.

Said title report shall be subject only to the liens above described and to the following:

1. Any reservations of oil, gas or other minerals affecting the above described tract of land presently of record.

2. Any easements affecting the above described tract of land presently of record.

Seller shall deliver to Purchaser prior to closing an estoppel letter signed by the holders of any existing indebtedness secured by the above described property, stating that through November 7, 1980, that no default exists under either the Deed of Trust or mortgage [sic] notes or any instruments securing the payment of same; that all installments of principal and interest payable through November 7, 1980, that the next principal and interest payment on either note is May 1, 1981; the amount of the unpaid balance of each of the above described notes; and there have been no modifications or amendments to any of the Deeds of Trust or mortgage instruments.

Seller shall have performed, observed and complied with all of the covenants, agreements and conditions required by this agreement to be performed, observed and

complied with by him prior to or as of the closing. * * *

Article VII

Escrow Deposit

For the purpose of securing the performance of Purchaser under the terms and provisions of this agreement, Purchaser has delivered to Freestone County Title, Fairfield, Texas, the sum of $5,000.00 the Escrow Deposit, which shall be paid by the title company to Seller in the event Purchaser breaches this agreement as provided in Article IX hereof. At the closing, the Escrow Deposit shall be paid over to Seller and applied to the cash portion of the purchase price. * * *

Article IX

Breach by Purchaser

In the event Purchaser should fail to consummate the purchase of the property, the conditions to Purchaser's obligations set forth in Article IV having been satisfied and Purchaser being in default and Seller not being in default hereunder, Seller shall have the right to (1) bring suit for damages against Purchaser; or (2) receive the Escrow Deposit from the title company, such sum being agreed on as liquidated damages for the failure of Purchaser to perform the duties, liabilities and obligations imposed upon it by the terms and provisions of this agreement, and Seller agrees to accept and take said cash payment as its total damages and relief and as Seller's sole remedy hereunder in such event.

contract as drawn, she should sign same and instruct her bank to see to it that Fickas put up $1,000. After revising the contract, Bowles instructed her bank to hold the contract until the deal was closed, but after two things had occurred: (1) Fickas had signed the revised contract and (2) Fickas had put up $1,000 "forfeit." Fickas signed the contract but did not deposit the $1,000 earnest money. Approximately eighteen days later, Bowles declared the deal terminated and two days thereafter Fickas deposited $1,000 as earnest money with the bank. This Court observed:

> Under the facts as set out above, the thing which the bank was to hold in escrow for the parties was to be a contract. The instrument in question never acquired that character. The instrument remained what it was when it first came to the hands of the bank, namely, the offer or proposal of Mrs. Bowles to be bound by the terms specified in the instrument if Mrs. Fickas, in turn, signed the instrument and deposited the earnest money as prescribed in Mrs. Bowles' letter to the bank.

140 Tex. at 314, 167 S.W.2d at 742–43.

The distinction in Antwine v. Reed, supra, from the present case is much more pronounced. In *Antwine,* the parties never even had a meeting of the minds on how much the earnest money was to be as the space in the proposed contract for the insertion of the earnest money amount was left blank.

The language in Slam Properties v. Pickett, supra, closely resembles the language in the case at bar. In *Slam Properties,* the contract [6] provided for $6,000 as earnest money. Both seller and purchaser signed the contract and purchaser wrote a check for $6,000, giving it to his agent, who stated that she would deposit the check with the title company on Monday (the date of the signing occurring on a Saturday). On Monday, purchaser's agent did not tender the check to the title company, and on Tuesday, purchasers' agent advised seller that purchaser no longer wished to purchase the property. The Tyler court, relying on Bowles v. Fickas, supra, and Antwine v. Reed, supra, held that the instrument in question never acquired the character of a contract because the offer to sell

---

6. The significant provisions of the contract are:

The purchase price is $65,000.00; payable as follows: $6,000.00 cash, of which the Purchaser has deposited with Commercial Title the sum of $6,000.00 as earnest money and part payment, the receipt of which is hereby acknowledged by said deposit holder, and the balance is to be paid as follows:

Purchaser to be given ten days to secure financing in the amount of $42,000.00.

Seller agrees to accept a second lien note from the Purchaser, in the amount of $17,000.00 @ 8% interest for ten years, payable monthly, including principle (sic) and interest, starting one month after closing. Said note may be paid off in full, at anytime, without penalty.
* * *

Closing to be as soon as possible, but not later than five days after Purchaser arranges financing. * * *

495 S.W.2d at 382.

was conditioned upon the deposit of $6,000 with the title company, which was not done. 495 S.W.2d at 383.

In our opinion, the case cited by Purchasers, Cowman v. Allen Monuments, Inc., 500 S.W.2d 223 (Tex.Civ.App.1973, no writ), correctly states the law. In *Cowman,* the instrument entitled "Earnest Money Contract" provided that sellers agreed to sell and buyer agreed to buy the property described therein for the price and upon the terms set out. It further provided that the total sales price was "$12,500.00; payable as follows: $12,500.00 cash, of which buyer agrees to forthwith deposit with the State First National Bank of Texarkana, Arkansas, Escrow Agent, the sum of $1500.00 as earnest money, to bind this sale. * * *" Id. at 225. At the time the contract was signed, buyer's attorney made out a check in the amount of $1,500, payable to the sellers, which was placed in an envelope on which was written "only to be opened by Norman Russell, Allen Monument Contract," and such was delivered to the escrow bank. Sellers subsequently refused to convey and buyer filed suit for specific performance. Sellers contended that as the check was never converted to cash, buyer could have stopped payment on the check at any time.

The Texarkana court held that since this was simply a contract to sell real estate, which required an earnest money payment and was not an escrow agreement, the law of contracts and the equitable principles of specific performance controlled the case, rather than the law of escrows. Id. at 226. The court rejected the sellers' contention that the contract never became a binding contract because the earnest money had not been deposited as required. Finally, the court concluded that what was really at issue was whether or not the placing of a check for $1,500 rather than cash for $1,500 with the escrow agent was a breach of the contract so material as to authorize the sellers to repudiate the contract, which question is one of fact, to be determined by the trier of facts.

This Court held in Schwarz-Jordan, Inc. of Houston v. Delisle Construction Co., 569 S.W.2d 878, 881 (Tex.1978) that "[i]t is a rule of construction that a forfeiture by finding a condition precedent is to be avoided when possible under another reasonable reading of the contract." In order to determine whether a condition precedent exists, the intention of the parties must be ascertained and that can only be done by looking at the entire contract. A reading of the contract here leads to only one conclusion: that the earnest money was intended as a penalty for a breach, and not as a condition precedent to the contract. To the extent that Slam Properties v. Pickett, supra, is in conflict with this opinion, it is disapproved.

Having concluded that the earnest money provision in the contract was a covenant, and not a condition precedent, we reverse the judgments of the lower courts and remand the cause to the trial court to determine whether the return of the earnest money check because of insufficient funds was such a material breach of the contract as to warrant Sellers' repudiation of same.[7]

Dissenting Opinion by McGEE, J., in which CAMPBELL, J., joins.

McGEE, JUSTICE, dissenting.

Because I agree with the holding of the court of appeals in this case and the holding of the court in Slam Properties v. Pickett, 495 S.W.2d 381 (Tex.Civ.App.1973, writ ref'd n.r.e.), I respectfully dissent. In my opinion the purchasers' payment of five thousand dollars to the title company was a condition precedent to the formation of a binding contract.

Even if the provisions of the earnest money contract are construed as a covenant, the purchasers would not be entitled to specific performance as a matter of law. Assuming a contract had been formed, the failure of the purchasers' bank to honor the five thousand dollar check was a material failure of performance, or failure of consideration. As such, the seller's duty of performance under the contract was excused. See S & H Supply Co. v. Hamilton, 418 S.W.2d 489, 492 (Tex.1967) (Greenhill, J., dissenting).

CAMPBELL, J., joins in this dissent.

HAYMORE v. LEVINSON

Supreme Court of Utah, 1958.
8 Utah 2d 66, 328 P.2d 307.

CROCKETT, JUSTICE.

Plaintiffs Haymore recovered judgment for $2,739 for money payable under a contract by which they sold defendants Levinson a house. The essence of Levinsons' defense below and contention for reversal here is that there had been no "satisfactory completion" of the house as required by the contract.

The question involved is what the term "satisfactory completion" comprehends.

Plaintiff Arnold Haymore, a contractor and builder, was constructing the house in question at Holladay in Salt Lake County. In November of 1955, when it was well along toward completion, defendants contracted to purchase it for $36,000 on terms described therein. The provision pertinent here was that $3,000 of the purchase price was to be placed in escrow to be held until "satisfactory completion of the work" which referred to a list of items attached to the contract.

The Levinsons moved in and Haymore proceeded with the work, and when he finished, requested the release of the $3,000. The Levinsons stated that they were not "satisfied" with certain of the items and refused to release the money. After some discussion, Haymore agreed

---

7. Modern authorities now apply the maxim "de minimis non curat lex" so that what is required is merely substantial, and not literal, compliance with the terms of the contract.

to take care of another list of items which the Levinsons insisted must be completed. When he and his workman came to do this work, the Levinsons indicated dissatisfaction with this second list they had agreed upon and demanded still further work, to which Haymore would not agree. The Levinsons thereupon told him that unless he would agree to and do all the work they then requested and in a manner they required, he could do none; and when he refused, ordering him off the property, taking the position that they would not release the money until he fully satisfied their demands.

The defendants' position is in essence that the words "satisfactory completion of the work" are to be given a subjective meaning: i.e., that it is a matter of their choice and unless they are satisfied and so declare, the money is not payable; whereas the plaintiffs assert that it means only that the work must meet a standard reasonable under the circumstances.

The adjudicated cases recognize that contracts wherein one party agrees to perform to the satisfaction of the other fall into two general classes: the first is where the undertaking is to do something of such a nature that pleasing the personal taste, fancy or sensibility of the other, which cannot be readily determined by objective standards, must reasonably be considered an element of predominant importance in the performance. In such cases the covenant that something will be done to the satisfaction of the favored party ordinarily makes him the sole judge thereof and he may give or withhold his approval as he desires.

The other class of cases involves satisfaction as to such things as operative fitness, mechanical utility or structural completion in which the personal sensibilities just mentioned would not reasonably be deemed of such predominant importance to the performance. As to such contracts the better considered view, and the one we adhere to, is that an objective standard should be applied: that is, that the party favored by such a provision has no arbitrary privilege of declining to acknowledge satisfaction and that he cannot withhold approval unless there is apparent some reasonable justification for doing so.

Building contracts such as the one in question generally fall within the second class of contracts above discussed. In regard to them it is plain to be seen that giving the word "satisfactory" an entirely subjective meaning might produce unconscionable results. The favored party could, upon any whim or caprice, and without reason, refuse to acknowledge satisfaction and thereby escape his obligations under the contract. The ends of justice are obviously better served by the application of the objective standard which only requires the work to be completed in a reasonably skillful and workmanlike manner in accordance with the accepted standards in the locality. If, in the light of such standards, it would meet the approval of reasonable and prudent persons, that should be sufficient.

The above view is consonant with our recent holding that a clause in a contract for the furnishing of heat was to be within the lessor's "sole judgment," could not be arbitrarily applied to justify the furnishing of entirely inadequate heat, but was subject to a sensible interpretation in relation to the reasonable needs of the lessees under the circumstances. [13th and Washington Corp. v. Neslen, 123 Utah 70, 254 P.2d 847.]

The trial court correctly adopted and applied the standard to which we give our approval herein. In doing so it found that the plaintiff had completed the original list of items attached to the contract in a satisfactory manner, (except some minor deficiencies of a total value of $261 for which an offset in favor of defendants was allowed) and that there were no structural defects. * * *

In regard to items complained of as not being completed on the second list, which the plaintiff at one time agreed to fix, another principle of law is applicable. Assuming without deciding that the plaintiff became obligated to complete that list, the defendants prevented the plaintiff from further performing by ordering him off the property, and therefore cannot take advantage of the failure of performance.

Affirmed. Costs to respondents.

McDONOUGH, C.J., and WADE and HENRIOD, JJ., concur.

WORTHEN, J., concurs in the result.

———

MORIN BUILDING PRODUCTS CO. v. BAYSTONE CONSTRUCTION, INC., 717 F.2d 413 (7th Cir.1983). General Motors Corporation hired Baystone to build an addition to its Chevrolet plant in Muncie, Indiana. Baystone in turn hired Morin to supply and erect the aluminum walls for the addition. The contract provided that the exterior siding of the walls should be of "aluminum type 3003, not less than 18 B & S gauge, with a mill finish and stucco embossed surface texture to match finish and texture of existing siding." The contract further provided:

"[A]ll work shall be done subject to the final approval of the Architect or Owner's authorized agent, and his decision in matters relating to artistic effect shall be final, if within the terms of the Contract Documents.

"[S]hould any dispute arise as the quality or fitness of materials or workmanship, the decision as to acceptability shall rest strictly with the Owner, based on the requirement that all work done or materials furnished shall be first class in every respect. What is usual or customary in erecting other buildings shall in no wise enter into any consideration or decision."

General Motors' representative rejected the siding on the ground that, when viewed in bright sunlight from an acute angle, it did not give the impression of a uniform finish. Baystone removed Morin's siding and replaced it with siding provided by another subcontractor; Baystone refused to pay Morin the balance of the contract price of $23,000. The jury was instructed that, despite the language quoted above, an objective standard was applicable, and that the test "is not whether the owner was satisfied in fact, but whether the owner, as a reasonable person, should have been satisfied with the materials and workmanship in question." A judgment for Morin was affirmed (POSNER, C.J.):

"Suppose the manager of a steel plant rejected a shipment of pig iron because he did not think the pigs had a pretty shape. The reasonable-man standard would be applied even if the contract had an 'acceptability shall rest strictly with the Owner' clause, for it would be fantastic to think that the iron supplier would have subjected his contract rights to the whimsy of the buyer's agent. At the other extreme would be a contract to paint a portrait, the buyer having reserved the right to reject the portrait if it did not satisfy him. Such a buyer wants a portrait that will please him rather than a jury, even a jury of connoisseurs, so the only question would be his good faith in rejecting the portrait. *Gibson v. Cranage,* 39 Mich. 49 (1878).

"This case is closer to the first example than to the second. The building for which the aluminum siding was intended was a factory— not usually intended to be a thing of beauty. That aesthetic considerations were decidedly secondary to considerations of function and cost is suggested by the fact that the contract specified mill-finish aluminum, which is unpainted. There is much debate in the record over whether it is even possible to ensure a uniform finish within and among sheets, but it is at least clear that mill finish usually is not uniform. If General Motors and Baystone had wanted a uniform finish they would in all likelihood have ordered a painted siding. Whether Morin's siding achieved a reasonable uniformity amounting to satisfactory commercial quality was susceptible of objective judgment; in the language of the Restatement, a reasonableness standard was 'practicable.'

"But this means only that a requirement of reasonableness would be read into this contract if it contained a standard owner's satisfaction clause, which it did not; and since the ultimate touchstone of decision must be the intent of the parties to the contract we must consider the actual language they used. The contract refers explicitly to 'artistic effect,' a choice of words that may seem deliberately designed to put the contract in the 'personal aesthetics' category whatever an outside observer might think. But the reference appears as number 17 in a list of conditions in a general purpose form contract. And the words 'artistic effect' are immediately followed by the qualifying phrase, 'if within the terms of the Contract Documents,' which suggests that the 'artistic effect' clause is limited to contracts in which artistic effect is one of the things the buyer is aiming for; it is not clear that he was here. The other clause on which Baystone relies, relating to the quality or fitness of workmanship and materials, may seem all-encompassing, but it is qualified by the phrase, 'based on the requirement that all work done or materials furnished shall be first class in every respect'—and it is not clear that Morin's were not. This clause also was not drafted for this contract; it was incorporated by reference to another form contract (the Chevrolet Division's 'Contract General Conditions'), of which it is paragraph 35. We do not disparage form contracts, without which the commercial life of the nation would grind to a halt. But we are left with more than a suspicion that the artistic-effect and quality-fitness clauses in the form contract used here were not intended to cover the aesthetics of a mill-finish aluminum factory wall. * * *

"Lest this conclusion be thought to strike at the foundations of freedom of contract, we repeat that if it appeared from the language or circumstances of the contract that the parties really intended General Motors to have the right to reject Morin's work for failure to satisfy the private aesthetic taste of General Motors' representative, the rejection would have been proper even if unreasonable. But the contract is ambiguous because of the qualifications with which the terms 'artistic effect' and 'decision as to acceptability' are hedged about, and the circumstances suggest that the parties probably did not intend to subject Morin's rights to aesthetic whim."

RESTATEMENT, SECOND, CONTRACTS § 271:

§ 271. Impracticability as Excuse for Non–Occurrence of a Condition

Impracticability excuses the non-occurrence of a condition if the occurrence of the condition is not a material part of the agreed exchange and forfeiture would otherwise result.

Illustrations:

1. A contracts with B to repair B's building for $20,000, payment to be made "on the satisfaction of C, B's architect, and the issuance of his certificate." A properly makes the repairs, but C dies before he is able to give a certificate. Since presentation of the architect's certificate is not a material part of the agreed exchange and forfeiture would otherwise result, the occurrence of the condition is excused, and A has a claim against B for $20,000. Cf. Illustration 3 to § 225.

3. A, an insurance company, issues to B a policy of whole life insurance making it a condition of A's duty that premiums be paid annually. B is imprisoned in a foreign country for five years, and is unable to pay the premiums during that time. On his release, he tenders the overdue premiums, but A refuses to accept them. Since the annual payment of premiums is a material part of the agreed exchange, its non-occurrence is not excused because of impracticability even though forfeiture will result. B has no claim against A.

BURGER KING CORP. v. FAMILY DINING, INC.

United States District Court, Eastern District of Pennsylvania, 1977.
426 F.Supp. 485, aff'd mem., 566 F.2d 1168 (3d Cir.).

MEMORANDUM AND ORDER

HANNUM, DISTRICT JUDGE.

* * * [P]laintiff seeks a determination under the Declaratory Judgment Act, that a contract between the parties, by its own terms, is no longer of any force and effect. * * *

FACTS ESTABLISHED IN PLAINTIFF'S CASE

Plaintiff Burger King Corporation (hereinafter "Burger King") is a Florida corporation engaged in franchising the well-known Burger King Restaurants. In 1954, James W. McLamore, founder of Burger King Restaurants, Inc. (the corporate predecessor of Burger King) built the first Burger King Restaurant in Miami, Florida. In 1961 the franchise system was still relatively modest size having only about 60 or 70 restaurants in operation outside of Florida. By 1963, however, Burger King began to experience significant growth and was building and operating, principally through franchisees, 24 restaurants per year. It was also at this time that Burger King's relationship with defendant Family Dining, Inc., (hereinafter "Family Dining") was created.

Family Dining is a Pennsylvania corporation which at the present time operates ten Burger King Restaurants (hereinafter "Restaurant") in Bucks and Montgomery Counties in Pennsylvania. Family Dining was founded and is currently operated by Carl Ferris who had been a close personal friend of McLamore's for a number of years prior to 1963. In fact they had attended Cornell University together in the late 1940's. It would seem that this friendship eventually led to the business relationship between Burger King and Family Dining which was conceived in the "Burger King Territorial Agreement" (hereinafter "Territorial Agreement") entered on May 10, 1963.

In accordance with the Territorial Agreement Burger King agreed that Family Dining would be its sole licensee, and thus have an "exclusive territory," in Bucks and Montgomery Counties provided Family Dining operated each Restaurant pursuant to Burger King license agreements[1] and maintained a specified rate of development. Articles I and II of the Territorial Agreement * * * provide as follows:

I.

For a period of one year, beginning on the date hereof, Company will not operate or license others for the operation of any

---

1. Each Restaurant is opened pursuant to a separate Burger King license agreement.

BURGER KING restaurant within the following described territory hereinafter referred to as "exclusive territory," to-wit:

The counties of Bucks and Montgomery, all in the State of Pennsylvania

as long as licensee operates each BURGER KING restaurant pursuant to BURGER KING restaurant licenses with Company and faithfully performs each of the covenants contained.

This agreement shall remain in effect and Licensee shall retain the exclusive territory for a period of ninety (90) years from the date hereof, provided that at the end of one, two, three, four, five, six, seven, eight, nine and ten years from the date hereof, and continuously thereafter during the next eighty years, Licensee has the following requisite number of BURGER KING restaurants in operation or under active construction, pursuant to Licenses with Company:

One (1) restaurant at the end of one year;

Two (2) restaurants at the end of two years;

Three (3) restaurants at the end of three years;

Four (4) restaurants at the end of four years;

Five (5) restaurants at the end of five years;

Six (6) restaurants at the end of six years;

Seven (7) restaurants at the end of seven years;

Eight (8) restaurants at the end of eight years;

Nine (9) restaurants at the end of nine years;

Ten (10) restaurants at the end of ten years;

and continually maintains not less than ten (10) restaurants during the next eighty (80) years.

Licensee and company may mutually agree to the execution of a restaurant license to a person other than the Licensee, herein, if such restaurant license is executed same will count as a requisite number as set forth in paragraph above.

II.

If at the end of either one, two, three, four, five, six, seven, eight, nine or ten years from the date hereof, or anytime thereafter during the next eighty (80) years, there are less than the respective requisite number of BURGER KING operations or under active construction in the "exclusive territory" pursuant to licenses by Company, this agreement shall terminate and be of no further force and effect. Thereafter, Company may operate or license others for the operation of BURGER KING Restaurants anywhere within the exclusive territory, so long as such restaurants are not within the "Protected Area", as set forth in any BURGER KING Restaurant License to which the Licensee herein is a party.

The prospect of exclusivity for ninety years was clearly intended to be an inducement to Family Dining to develop the territory as prescribed and it appears that it had exactly this effect as Family Dining was to become one of Burger King's most successful franchisees. While Burger King considered Carl Ferris to be somewhat of a problem at various times and one who was overly meticulous with detail, it was nevertheless through his efforts which included obtaining the necessary financing and assuming significant risks, largely without assistance from Burger King, that enabled both parties to benefit from the arrangement.

On August 16, 1963, Family Dining opened the First Restaurant * * *. The second Restaurant was opened on July 2, 1965, * * * and the third Restaurant was opened October 19, 1966, * * *.

However, by April, 1968, Family Dining had not opened or begun active construction on a fourth Restaurant which, in accordance with the development rate, should have been accomplished by May 10, 1967, and it was apparent that a fifth Restaurant would not be opened by May 10, 1968, the date scheduled. On May 1, 1968, the parties entered into a Modification of the Territorial Agreement (hereinafter "Modification") whereby Burger King agreed to waive Family Dining's failure to comply with the development rate. There is nothing contained in the record which indicates that Burger King received anything of value in exchange for entering this agreement. However, McLamore testified that if the fourth and fifth Restaurants would be built nearly in compliance with the development rate for the fifth year he would overlook the year or so default in the fourth Restaurant. This attitude seems to be consistent with his overall view toward the development rate with respect to which, he testified, was "designed to insure the company of an orderly process of growth which would also enable the company to produce a profit on the sale of its franchises and through the collection of royalties that the restaurants would themselves produce."

The fourth Restaurant was opened on July 1, 1968, * * * and the fifth Restaurant was opened on October 17, 1968, * * *.

On April 18, 1969, Ferris forwarded a letter to McLamore pertaining to certain delays in site approval and relating McLamore's earlier statement that there would be no problem in waiving the development schedule for the sixth Restaurant. The letter expressed Ferris' concern regarding compliance with the development rate. By letter dated April 26, 1969, from Howard Walker of Burger King, Ferris was granted a month extension in the development rate. With respect to this extension McLamore testified that "It never crossed my mind to call a default of this agreement on a technicality."

On October 1, 1969, the sixth Restaurant was opened * * *. The seventh Restaurant was opened on February 2, 1970, ahead of schedule, * * *.

At this point in time Burger King was no longer a modest sized franchise system. It had become a wholly owned subsidiary of the Pillsbury Company and had, in fact, evolved into a complex corporate entity. McLamore was elevated to Chairman of the Board of Burger King and, while he remained the chief executive officer for a time, Arthur A. Rosewall was installed as Burger King's President. Ferris was no longer able to expect the close, one to one relationship with McLamore that had previously obtained in his dealings with the company. It seems clear that as a result Family Dining began to experience difficulties in its day to day operations with Burger King.

One of the problem areas which arose concerned site selection. In a typical situation when a franchisee would seek approval for a building site an application would be submitted to the National Development Committee comprised of various Burger King officials. Based on Ferris' prior showing regarding site selection it could be expected that he would have little difficulty in obtaining their approval. In McLamore's view, Ferris was an exceptionally fine franchisee whose ability to choose real estate locations was exceptional. However, in August, 1970, a Frankford Avenue location selected by Ferris was rejected by the National Development Committee. The reasons offered in support of the decision to reject are not entirely clear and it seems that for the most part it was an exercise of discretion. * * *

In his August 25, 1970, memo to the Carl Ferris file McLamore observed that Burger King "had sloppy real estate work involved in servicing him and that [Burger King was] guilty of many follow up delinquencies." This was during a time, as Burger King management was well aware, where it was one thing to select a location and quite another to actually develop it. That is, local governing bodies were taking a much stricter view toward allowing this type of development. It was also during this time, as McLamore's memo points out, Burger King realized that the Bucks-Montgomery territory was capable of sustaining substantially more Restaurants than originally thought.

Amidst these circumstances, the eighth Restaurant was opened ahead of schedule on October 7, 1970, * * *. And in December, 1971, Burger King approved Family Dining's proposed sites for two additional Restaurants in Ambler, Pennsylvania and Levittown, Pennsylvania.

In early 1972, Arthur Rosewell became the chief executive officer of Burger King. At this time it also became apparent that the ninth Restaurant would not be opened or under construction by May 10, 1972. On April 27, 1972, in a telephone conversation with McLamore, Ferris once again expressed his concern to Burger King regarding compliance with the development rate. Burger King's position at that time is evidenced by McLamore's Memo to the Carl Ferris file dated April 28, 1972, wherein he provides that "Ferris' territorial arrangement with the company is such that he must have his ninth store (he has eight open now) under construction next month. I indicated to him that, due to the fact that he was in the process of developing four sites at this time, the company would consider he had met, substantially, the requirements of exclusivity." McLamore testified that at that time he had in mind a further delay of 3 to 6 months.

In April, 1973, Burger King approved Family Dining's proposed site for a Restaurant in Warminster, Pennsylvania. However, as of May 10, 1973, neither the ninth or the tenth Restaurant had been opened or under active construction.

A letter dated May 23, 1973, from Helen D. Donaldson, Franchise Documents Administrator for Burger King, was sent to Ferris. The letter provides as follows:

Dear Mr. Ferris:

During a periodic review of all territorial agreements we note that as of this date your development schedule requiring ten restaurants to be open or under construction by May 10, 1973, has not been met. Our records reflect eight stores open in Bucks and/or Montgomery County, and one site approved but not manned.

Under the terms of your territorial agreement failure to have the required number of stores in operation or under active construction constitutes a default of your agreement.

If there are extenuating circumstances about which this office is not aware, we would appreciate your earliest advice.

It is doubtful that the Donaldson letter was intended to communicate to Ferris that the Territorial Agreement was terminated. * * *

It seems that throughout this period Burger King treated the matter as something of a "hot potato" subjecting Ferris to contact with several different Burger King officials. * * * [The first clear indication that Burger King considered the Territorial Agreement terminated was given Ferris by a letter dated November 6, 1973.] Burger King's corporate structure had become so complex that the question of who, when or where the decision was made could not be answered. The abrupt manner in which Burger King's position was communicated to Family Dining, under the circumstances, was not straightforward.

From November, 1973, until some point early in 1975, the parties attempted to negotiate their differences with no success. The reason for the lack of success is understandable given that Burger King from the outset considered exclusivity a non-negotiable item. It was during this period on September 7, 1974, that Family Dining began actual construction of the ninth Restaurant in Warminster, Pennsylvania.

Several months before the instant litigation was begun Family Dining informed Burger King that it intended to open a ninth Restaurant on or about May 15, 1975, on Street Road, Warminster, Pennsylvania. In February, 1975, Burger King notified Family Dining that a franchise agreement (license) had to be entered for the additional Restaurant without which Family Dining would be infringing Burger King's trademarks. A similar notice was given in April, 1975, in which

Burger King indicated it would retain counsel to protect its rights. Nevertheless Family Dining proceeded with its plans to open the Warminster Restaurant.

In May, 1975, Burger King filed a complaint, which was the inception of this lawsuit, seeking to enjoin the use of Burger King trademarks by Family Dining at the Warminster Restaurant. * * * On May 13, 1975, the parties reached an agreement on terms under which the Burger King trademarks could be used at the Warminster Restaurant. Pursuant to the agreement Burger King filed an amended complaint seeking the instant declaratory relief. Subsequently and also pursuant to this agreement Family Dining opened its tenth Restaurant in Willow Grove, Pennsylvania, the construction of which began on March 28, 1975.

DISCUSSION

Family Dining raises several arguments in support of its motion pursuant to Rule 41(b). One of its principal arguments is that the termination provision should be found inoperative because otherwise it would result in a forfeiture to Family Dining. For reasons which have become evident during the presentation of Burger King's case the Court finds Family Dining's position compelling both on legal and equitable grounds and is thus persuaded that the Territorial Agreement should not be declared terminated. * * * Inasmuch as termination is the only relief sought by Burger King, it follows that dismissal of the action is appropriate.

In bringing this suit Burger King maintains that the Territorial Agreement is a divisible contract wherein Family Dining promised to open or have have under active construction one new Restaurant in each of the first ten years of the contract in exchange for which Burger King promised to grant one additional year of exclusivity for each new Restaurant. This, to be followed by an additional eighty years of exclusivity provided the first ten Restaurants were built on time. In support Burger King relies on the opening language of Article I of the Territorial Agreement which provides that "[f]or a period of one year, beginning on the date hereof, Company will not operate or license * * *" It is thus argued that since Family Dining clearly failed to perform its promises the Court must, in accordance with the express language of Article II, declare the contract terminated. Burger King further argues that because Family Dining did not earn exclusivity beyond the ninth year, upon termination, it could not be found that Family Dining would forfeit anything in which it had an interest.

Contrary to the analysis offered by Burger King, the Court considers the development rate a condition subsequent, not a promise, which operates to divest Family Dining of exclusivity. Where words in a contract raise no duty in and of themselves but rather modify or limit the promisees' right to enforce the promise such words are considered to be a condition. Whether words constitute a condition or a promise is a matter of the intention of the parties to be ascertained from a reasonable construction of the language used, considered in light of the surrounding circumstances. Feinberg v. Automobile Banking Corporation, 353 F.Supp. 508, 512 (E.D.Pa.1973); Williston, Contracts, §§ 665, 666. It seems clear that the true purpose of the Territorial Agreement was to create a long-term promise of exclusivity to act as an inducement to Family Dining to develop Bucks and Montgomery Counties within a certain time frame. A careful reading of the agreement indicates that it raises no duties, as such, in Family Dining. Both Article I and Article II contain language which refers to ninety years of exclusivity subject to limitation. For instance, Article I provides in part that "[t] his Agreement shall remain in effect and licensee shall retain the exclusive territory for a period of ninety (90) years from the date hereof, provided that at the end of one, two * * *" Failure to comply with the development rate operates to defeat liability on Burger King's promise of exclusivity. Liability, or at least Family Dining's right to enforce the promise, arose upon entering the contract. The fact that Burger King seeks affirmative relief premised on the development rate and the fact that it calls for a specified performance by Family Dining tend to obscure its true nature. Nevertheless, in the Court's view it is a condition subsequent.

Furthermore, the fact that performance is to occur in installments does not necessarily mean that the contract is divisible. Once again, this is a question of the intention of the parties ascertained, if possible, from a reasonable interpretation of the language used. Continental Supermarket Food Service, Inc. v. Soboski, 210 Pa.Super. 304, 232 A.2d 216, 217 (1967). In view of the fact that there was a single promise of exclusivity to have a ninety year duration, assuming the condition subsequent did not occur by a failure to comply with the development rate, the Court believes, consistent with the views previously expressed herein, that the contract was intended to be entire rather than severable.

The question arises whether Burger King has precluded itself from asserting Family Dining's untimeliness on the basis that Burger King did not demand literal adherence to the development rate throughout most the first ten years of the contract. Nothing is commoner in contracts than for a promisor to protect himself by making his promise conditional. Ordinarily a party would be entitled to have such an agreement strictly enforced, however, before doing so the Court must consider not only the written contract but also the acts and conduct of the parties in carrying out the agreement. As Judge Kraft, in effect, provided in Dempsey v. Stauffer, 182 F.Supp. 806, 810 (E.D.Pa.1960), after one party by conduct indicates that literal performance will not be required, he cannot without notice and a reasonable time begin demanding literal performance.

In the early going Burger King did not demand that Family Dining perform in exact compliance with the development schedule. It failed to introduce any evidence indicating that a change in attitude had been communicated to Family Dining. At the time of the Donaldson letter

Family Dining's non-compliance with the development rate was no worse than it was with respect to the fourth and fifth Restaurants. The letter itself was sent by a documents administrator rather than a Burger King official and it seems to imply that the Territorial Agreement would not be terminated. Assuming that at some point between May and November, or even at the time of the Donaldson letter, Ferris realized literal performance would be required, the circumstances of this type of development are such that Burger King was unreasonable in declaring a termination such a short time after, if not concurrent with, notice that literal performance would be required.

Considerable time was consumed in negotiations between November, 1973, until shortly before suit although it appears that these efforts were an exercise in futility given Burger King's view on exclusivity. Moreover, it could be expected that Burger King would have sued to enjoin any further progress by Family Dining, during this lengthy period, just as it did when Family Dining attempted to get the ninth Restaurant under way. The upshot being that the hiatus in development from November, 1973, until active construction began on the ninth and tenth Restaurants is not fully chargeable to Family Dining.

Based on the foregoing the Court concludes that Burger King is not entitled to have the condition protecting its promise strictly enforced.

Moreover and more important, even though a suit for declaratory relief can be characterized as neither legal nor equitable, United States Fidelity & Guaranty Co. v. Koch, 102 F.2d 288, 290 (3d Cir.1939), giving strict effect to the termination provision involves divesting Family Dining of exclusivity, which, in the Court's view, would amount to a forfeiture. As a result the Court will not ignore considerations of fairness and believes that equitable principles, as well, ought to govern the outcome of this suit.

The Restatement, Contracts, § 302 provides:

"A condition may be excused without other reason if its requirement

(a) will involve extreme forfeiture or penalty, and

(b) its existence or occurrence forms no essential part of the exchange for the promisor's performance."

Taking the latter consideration first, it seems clear that throughout the early duration of the contract Burger King was more concerned with a general development of the territory than it was with exact compliance with the terms of the development rate. Burger King offered no evidence that it ever considered literal performance to be critical. In fact, the evidence indicates quite the contrary. Even though McLamore testified that he never contemplated a delay of the duration which occurred with the ninth and tenth Restaurants, he felt a total delay of approximately 19 months with respect to the fourth and fifth Restaurants was nearly in compliance. On the basis of his prior conduct and his testimony considered in its entirety his comments on this point command little weight.

Clearly Burger King's attitude with respect to the development rate changed. Interestingly enough it was sometime after Burger King realized Bucks and Montgomery Counties could support substantially more than ten Restaurants as had been originally thought. It was also at a time after Rosewall replaced McLamore as chief executive officer.

*   *   *

As previously indicated, the Court believes that if the right of exclusivity were to be extinguished by termination it would constitute a forfeiture. In arguing that by termination Family Dining will lose nothing that it earned, Burger King overlooks the risks assumed and the efforts expended by Family Dining, largely without assistance from Burger King, in making the venture successful in the exclusive territory. While it is true that Family Dining realized a return on its investment, certainly part of this return was the prospect of continued exclusivity. Moreover, this is not a situation where Burger King did not receive any benefit from the relationship.

In making the promise of exclusivity Burger King intended to induce Family Dining to develop its Restaurants in the exclusive territory. There is no evidence that the failure to fulfill the time feature of this inducement was the result of any intentional or negligent conduct on the part of Family Dining. And at the present time there are ten Restaurants in operation which was all the inducement was intended to elicit. Assuming all ten were built on time Burger King would have been able to expect some definable level of revenue, a percentage of which it lost due to the delay. Burger King did not, however, attempt to establish the amount of this loss at trial.

In any event if Family Dining were forced to forfeit the right of exclusivity it would lose something of incalculable value based on its investment of time and money developing the area, the significant risks assumed and the fact that there remains some 76 years of exclusivity under the Territorial Agreement. Such a loss would be without any commensurate breach on its part since the injury caused to Burger King by the delay is relatively modest and within definable limits. Thus, a termination of the Territorial Agreement would result in an extreme forfeiture to Family Dining.

In accordance with the foregoing the Court finds that under the law and based upon the facts adduced in Burger King's case, it is not entitled to a declaration that the Territorial Agreement is terminated.

*   *   *

CLARK v. WEST, 193 N.Y. 349, 86 N.E. 1 (1908). Plaintiff was the well known author of "Clark & Marshall on Corporations," a three volume work of 3,649 pages that enjoyed considerable commercial success; defendant was the publisher. This work had been published pursuant to a contract that provided that Clark agreed "to totally abstain from the use of intoxicating liquors during the continuance of this contract."

Clark was to be paid $2 per page, but if he "abstains from the use of intoxicating liquor and otherwise fulfills his agreements as hereinbefore set forth, he shall be paid an additional $4 per page." This additional $4 per page was also conditioned on sales of the completed work exceeding certain numbers, a requirement which concededly had been met. Clark was paid $2 per page and he filed suit for the additional $4 per page claiming that while "he did not totally abstain from the use of intoxicating liquor during the continuance of such contract, * * * such use * * * was not excessive and did not prevent or interfere with the due and full performance by the plaintiff" of his obligations under the contract. Plaintiff further alleged that defendant knew that plaintiff was not abstaining from the use of intoxicating liquor but at no time indicated that he would insist upon strict compliance with the contract; rather, "on the contrary, and with full knowledge of plaintiff's said use of intoxicating liquors, defendant repeatedly avowed and represented to the plaintiff that he was entitled to and would receive" the full royalty payment. Plaintiff finally alleged that he relied on defendant's representation by continuing the writing of the book. The court held that plaintiff could recover the additional $4 per page:

(1) The clause requiring abstention from the use of intoxicating liquor was a condition precedent and not the consideration for the additional payment of $4 per page:

> "The subject-matter of the contract was the writing of books by the plaintiff for the defendant. * * * The compensation for the work specified in the contract was to be $6 per page, unless the plaintiff failed to totally abstain from the use of intoxicating liquors during the continuance of the contract, in which event he was to receive only $2 per page. That is the obvious import of the contract construed in the light of the purpose for which it was made, and in accordance with the ordinary meaning of plain language. It is not a contract to write books in order that the plaintiff shall keep sober, but a contract containing a stipulation that he shall keep sober so that he may write satisfactory books. When we view the contract from this standpoint it will readily be perceived that the particular stipulation is not the consideration for the contract, but simply one of its conditions which fits in with those relating to time and method of delivery of manuscript, revision of proof, citation of cases, assignment of copyrights, keeping track of new cases and citations for new editions, and other details which might be waived by the defendant, if he saw fit to do so."

(2) As a condition precedent, it could be, and was, waived without any formal agreement to that effect and without the payment of additional consideration:

> "This, we think, is the fair interpretation of the contract, and it follows that the stipulation as to the plaintiff's total abstinence

was nothing more nor less than a condition precedent. If that conclusion is well founded there can be no escape from the corollary that this condition could be waived; and if it was waived the defendant is clearly not in a position to insist upon the forfeiture which his waiver was intended to annihilate. The forfeiture must stand or fall with the condition. If the latter was waived, the former is no longer a part of the contract. Defendant still has the right to counterclaim for any damages which he may have sustained in consequence of the plaintiff's breach, but he cannot insist upon strict performance. * * *

"The theory upon which the defendant's attitude seems to be based is that even if he has represented to the plaintiff that he would not insist upon the condition that the latter should observe total abstinence from intoxicants, he can still refuse to pay the full contract price for his work. The inequity of this position becomes apparent when we consider that this contract was to run for a period of years, during a large portion of which the plaintiff was to be entitled only to the advance payment of $2 per page, the balance being contingent, among other things, upon publication of the books and returns from sales. Upon this theory the defendant might have waived the condition while the first book was in process of production, and yet when the whole work was completed, he would still be in a position to insist upon the forfeiture because there had not been strict performance. Such a situation is possible in a case where the subject of the waiver is the very consideration of a contract (Organ v. Stewart, 60 N.Y. 413, 420), but not where the waiver relates to something that can be waived. In the case at bar, as we have seen, the waiver is not of the consideration or subject-matter, but of an incident to the method of performance. The consideration remains the same. The defendant has had the work he bargained for, and it is alleged that he has waived one of the conditions as to the manner in which it was to have been done. He might have insisted upon literal performance and then he could have stood upon the letter of his contract. If, however, he has waived that incidental condition, he has created a situation to which the doctrine of waiver very precisely applies.

"The cases which present the most familiar phases of the doctrine of waiver are those which have arisen out of litigation over insurance policies where the defendants have claimed a forfeiture because of the breach of some condition in the contract, but it is a doctrine of general application which is confined to no particular class of cases. A waiver has been defined to be the intentional relinquishment of a known right. It is voluntary and implies an election to dispense with something of value, or forego some advantage which the party waiving it might at its option have demanded or insisted upon * * *"

See UCC § 1–207, see also pages 307–308 supra.

———

It may be recalled that in the famous case of Jacob & Youngs, Inc. v. Kent, 230 N.Y. 239, 129 N.E. 889 (1921), described supra page 16, the owner had specified that only Reading pipe be used in a large country house being built for him by the plaintiff. Even though pipe of a different manufacture was used, Mr. Justice Cardozo ordered judgment for the plaintiff for the amount of the final payment of about $3,500 which had been withheld since there was little or no difference in value between the pipe used and Reading pipe. The case is usually cited as an example of the "substantial performance" doctrine, a doctrine applied in construction contracts which states that where there has been substantial although not full performance, the building contractor has a right to the unpaid balance of the contract price reduced by the owner's claim for damages based on the failure to perform fully. Obviously, where the substantial performance doctrine is applied, the court has concluded that the breach committed by the contractor is not material. Would the result in Jacob & Youngs, Inc. v. Kent be changed if the owner had specified in the contract that the final payment was expressly conditioned on the builder having fully performed covenant to use Reading pipe? A dictum in that case suggests that the answer is "yes." The court states, "This is not to say that the parties are not free by apt and certain words to effectuate a purpose that performance of every term shall be a condition of recovery." 129 N.E. at 891. Do you agree?

RESTATEMENT, SECOND, CONTRACTS § 229:

To the extent that the non-occurrence of a condition would cause disproportionate forfeiture, a court may excuse the non-occurrence of that condition unless its occurrence was a material part of the agreed exchange.

LARDAS v. UNDERWRITERS INSURANCE CO.

Supreme Court of Pennsylvania, 1967.
426 Pa. 47, 231 A.2d 740.

Before MUSMANNO, JONES, COHEN, EAGEN, O'BRIEN and ROBERTS, JJ.

OPINION

JONES, JUSTICE.

Nick D. Lardas, Constance Lardas, James Lardas, Evangelina Lardas, Constantin Lardas and Sophie Lardas, [Lardas] are the record owners of a warehouse facility located in West Deer Township, Allegheny County. This warehouse was used for "dead storage"[1] of equipment

---

1. Lardas' business required they have heavy painting, structural, scaffolding equipment. Such equipment was stored in the warehouse during the "in between jobs" periods.

used in Lardas' painting-contracting business. Underwriters Insurance Company, Home Insurance Company, National Union Fire Insurance Company and Fidelity Phenix Fire Insurance Company [Insurance Companies] insured the warehouse from loss by fire, the total coverage of all policies totalling $10,500.

On March 4, 1962, a fire of undetermined origin occurred which resulted in a total loss of the warehouse and caused damage in excess of the $10,500 policies' limits. Lardas first learned of the fire on or about July 15, 1962, when a letter was received from the Allegheny County Fire Marshal advising them the warehouse had been "gutted" by fire. Lardas immediately notified the Insurance Companies of the Fire Marshal's letter and their own lack of knowledge of the exact date of the fire.

The Insurance Companies sent an adjuster to investigate the fire and to initiate negotiations with Lardas and their counsel on the question of and the possible amount of liability. Prior to any active negotiations, however, the adjuster insisted upon Lardas executing nonwaiver agreements concerning any possible violation of the terms and conditions of the insurance contracts. On the advice of their counsel, Lardas executed such agreements. Active negotiations toward a possible settlement of the claim continued for a few months. Insurance Companies submitted their maximum offer of settlement in October 1962 which Lardas rejected in November 1962; this was the last offer by either party for settlement of the claims.

Upon failure of the Insurance Companies to pay Lardas' claims, the latter on March 28, 1963—1 year, 3 weeks and 3 days subsequent to March 4, 1962, when the fire occurred[2]—instituted an assumpsit action against the Insurance Companies to recover upon the insurance contracts. * * * The action was tried before a court without a jury and, after a trial, the court ordered the entry of a judgment in favor of the Insurance Companies. * * * From the entry of that judgment Lardas has appealed.

The Insurance Companies defended on four grounds: (1) no proof of loss was given within 60 days from the date of the fire; (2) no lawsuit was filed within one year from the date of the fire; (3) use of the premises by Lardas constituted an abandonment of the premises which increased the hazard; (4) Lardas had not given notice to the companies of the loss within a reasonably short time after the loss. The court below entered judgment on two grounds: (1) no proof of loss had been submitted within 60 days from the date of the fire; (2) no lawsuit was filed within one year from the date of the fire.

The insurance contracts—standard fire policies as required by law—provided, inter alia: "Suit. No suit or action on this policy for the recovery of any claim shall be sustainable in any court of law or equity unless all the requirements of this policy shall have been

---

2. The *exact* date of the fire is not in dispute.

complied with, and unless commenced within twelve months next after inception of the loss." That such a clause is valid and reasonable has been long recognized: Selden v. Metropolitan Life Ins. Co., 354 Pa. 500, 502, 503, 47 A.2d 687 (1946) and authorities therein cited. This is not a statute of limitation imposed by law; it is a contractual undertaking between the parties and the limitation on the time for bringing suit is imposed by the parties to the contract. That Lardas has breached this provision of the contracts is clear beyond question; the instant action was not instituted "within twelve months next after inception of the loss", i.e., March 4, 1962.

Lardas would excuse the breach of this policy provision in several ways. First, that Lardas' failure to commence suit within twelve months from date of the loss was not a breach of the insurance policy because the one year period began to run *when the insured had knowledge of the loss.* The fire occurred March 4, 1962. Lardas had knowledge of the fire on July 15, 1962, and commenced his suit on the insurance policies on March 28, 1963, or more than one year after the occurrence of the loss and eight months after knowledge of said loss. Certainly, Lardas had adequate opportunity and time to commence a lawsuit after he gained knowledge of the loss and prior to the policy limitation of "twelve months next after inception of the loss". Such language as to the time limitation is too plain and unequivocal to be subject to any ambiguity or misunderstanding. The period of twelve months, in fact the period of eight months, was not an unreasonable length of time in which to require the commencement of an action and " * * * it is lawful for the parties so to contract and such a provision is binding on them [citing authorities] ." Abolin v. Farmers American Mutual Fire Insurance Company, 100 Pa.Super. 433, 435 (1930). Lardas violated this requirement of the policies and such violation is sufficient to bar his claim. * * *

Lardas next contends that the Insurance Companies *waived* the requirement of commencement of a cause of action within twelve months after the inception of the loss or, at least, is estopped from defending the action upon the basis of that policy provision. The record unequivocally reveals that prior to *any* negotiations between the insurers and the insured, non-waiver agreements were executed by Lardas and such agreements preserved for the companies their rights to defend on the basis of any policy provisions. Furthermore, review of this record indicates that (a) the Insurance Companies did not in any manner mislead Lardas about the possibility of settlement—in fact in November, 1962, the parties broke off all settlement negotiations and (b) the Insurance Companies did not in any manner induce or persuade Lardas to refrain from commencing suit. From early November 1962 to March 28, 1963,—approximately five months—the parties did not have any effective contacts concerning the claims. Lardas has presented no factual basis upon which a finding of waiver or estoppel could be supported. * * *

The failure of Lardas to abide by the contract provision limiting a right of action on the policies to the twelve months period from the date of the inception of the loss constitutes an absolute bar to Lardas' claim. To hold otherwise, in the factual matrix of this litigation would render meaningless this provision of the contract to which Lardas bound themselves.

In view of the conclusion reached, we need not consider Lardas' other contentions on this appeal.

Judgment affirmed.

MUSMANNO, J., dissents.

BELL, C.J., did not participate in the decision of this case.

RESTATEMENT, SECOND, CONTRACTS § 230:

(1) Except as stated in Subsection (2), if under the terms of the contract the occurrence of an event is to terminate an obligor's duty of immediate performance or one to pay damages for breach, that duty is discharged if the event occurs.

(2) The obligor's duty is not discharged if occurrence of the event

(a) is the result of a breach by the obligor of his duty of good faith and fair dealing, or

(b) could not have been prevented because of impracticability and continuance of the duty does not subject the obligor to a materially increased burden.

(3) The obligor's duty is not discharged if, before the event occurs, the obligor promises to perform the duty even if the event occurs and does not revoke his promise before the obligee materially changes his position in reliance on it.

Illustrations:

1. A, an insurance company, insures the property of B under a policy providing that no recovery can be had if suit is not brought on the policy within two years after a loss. A loss occurs and B lets two years pass before bringing suit. A's duty to pay B for the loss is discharged and B cannot maintain the action on the policy.

2. The facts being otherwise as stated in Illustration 1, B lives in a foreign country and is prevented by the outbreak of war from bringing suit against A for two years. A's duty to pay B for the loss is not discharged and B can maintain an action on the policy when the war is ended.

3. The facts being otherwise as stated in Illustration 1, after the loss occurs, A tells B that it is not necessary to bring suit within two years, and B relies on the statement in refraining from suing for two years. A's duty to pay B for the loss is not discharged and B can maintain an action on the policy even after two years have passed.

The "condition" involved in *Lardas* is sometimes referred to as a "condition subsequent" on the ground that the non-occurrence of the event, i.e. bringing suit within one year, will extinguish an existing duty to pay for the loss. In contrast, conditions that qualify the existence of the duty itself are sometimes referred to as "conditions precedent." The time at which "precedent" or "subsequent" is being measured is obviously the time the duty arises. Since the non-occurrence of either a condition precedent or a condition subsequent means there is no obligation, little appears to hang on this distinction. The distinction, however, was believed important in resolving procedural questions relating to the burden of pleading and of proof, though it probably gave rise to more confusion than understanding in such procedural contexts. The Restatement, Second, Contracts abandons this distinction and uses the word "condition" to refer to all conditions precedent (as defined above); a condition subsequent is not referred to as a condition at all but as "an event [that terminates] an obligor's duty of immediate performance or one to pay damages for breach."

Along with "conditions precedent" and "conditions subsequent," the literature also contains references to "concurrent conditions," a term that is discussed in the following chapter.

Chapter 9

PROBLEMS OF PERFORMANCE

STEWART v. NEWBURY

New York Court of Appeals, 1917.
220 N.Y. 379, 115 N.E. 984.

CRANE, J. The defendants are partners in the pipe fitting business under the name of Newbury Manufacturing Company. The plaintiff is a contractor and builder residing at Tuxedo, N.Y.

The parties had the following correspondence about the erection for the defendants of a concrete mill building at Monroe, N.Y.:

"Alexander Stewart,
"Contractor and Builder,
"Tuxedo, N.Y., July 18, 1911.

"Newbury Mfg. Company, Monroe, N.Y.—Gentlemen: With reference to the proposed work on the new foundry building I had hoped to be able to get up and see you this afternoon, but find that impossible and am, in consequence, sending you these prices, which I trust you will find satisfactory.

"I will agree to do all excavation work required at sixty-five ($.65) cents per cubic yard.

"I will put in the concrete work, furnishing labor and forms only, at two and 05–100 ($2.05) dollars per cubic yard.

"I will furnish labor to put in reenforcing at four ($4.00) dollars per ton.

"I will furnish labor only to set all window and door frames, window sash and doors, including the setting of hardware for one hundred twelve ($112) dollars. As alternative I would be willing to do any or all of the above work for cost plus 10 per cent., furnishing you with first class mechanics and giving the work considerable of my personal time.

"Hoping to hear favorably from you in this regard, I am,

"Respectfully yours,
"[Signed] Alexander Stewart."

"The Newbury Mfg. Co.,
"Steam Fittings, Grey Iron Castings,
"Skylight Opening Apparatus,
"Monroe, N.Y.

"Telephone Connection.

"Monroe, N.Y., July 22, 1911.

"Alexander Stewart, Tuxedo Park, N.Y.—Dear Sir: Confirming the telephone conversation of this morning we accept your bid of July the 18th to do the concrete work on our new building. We trust that you will be able to get at this the early part of next week.

"Yours truly,
The Newbury Mfg. Co.,
"H.A. Newbury."

Nothing was said in writing about the time or manner of payment. The plaintiff, however, claims that after sending his letter, and before receiving that of the defendant, he had a telephone communication with Mr. Newbury and said: "I will expect my payments in the usual manner," and Newbury said, "All right, we have got the money to pay for the building." This conversation over the telephone was denied by the defendants. The custom, the plaintiff testified, was to pay 85 per cent. every 30 days or at the end of each month, 15 per cent. being retained till the work was completed.

In July the plaintiff commenced work and continued until September 29th, at which time he had progressed with the construction as far as the first floor. He then sent a bill for the work done up to that date for $896.35. The defendants refused to pay the bill and work was discontinued. The plaintiff claims that the defendants refused to permit him to perform the rest of his contract, they insisting that the work already done was not in accordance with the specifications. The defendants claimed upon the trial that the plaintiff voluntarily abandoned the work after their refusal to pay his bill.

On October 5, 1911, the defendants wrote the plaintiff a letter containing the following:

"Notwithstanding you promised to let us know on Monday whether you would complete the job or throw up the contract, you have not up to this time advised us of your intention. * * * Under the circumstances, we are compelled to accept your action as being an abandonment of your contract and of every effort upon your part to complete your work on our building. As you know, the bill which you sent us and which we declined to pay is not correct, either in items or amount, nor is there anything due you under our contract as we understand it until you have completed your work on our building."

To this letter the plaintiff replied the following day. In it he makes no reference to the telephone communication agreeing, as he testified, to make "the usual payments," but does say this:

"There is nothing in our agreement which says that I shall wait until the job is completed before any payment is due, nor can this be reasonably implied. * * * As to having given you positive date as to when I should let you know what I proposed doing, I did not do so; on the contrary, I told you that I would not tell you positively what I would do until I had visited the job, and I promised that I would do this at my earliest convenience and up to the present time I have been unable to get up there."

The defendant Herbert Newbury testified that the plaintiff "ran away and left the whole thing." And the defendant F.A. Newbury testified that he was told by Mr. Stewart's man that Stewart was going to abandon the job; that he thereupon telephoned Mr. Stewart, who replied that he would let him know about it the next day, but did not.

In this action, which is brought to recover the amount of the bill presented, as the agreed price and $95.68 damages for breach of contract, the plaintiff had a verdict for the amount stated in the bill, but not for the other damages claimed, and the judgment entered thereon has been affirmed by the Appellate Division.

The appeal to us is upon exceptions to the judge's charge. The court charged the jury * * *.

* * * [I]f there were no agreement as to payments, * * * the plaintiff would be entitled to part payment at reasonable times as the work progressed, and if such payments were refused he could abandon the work and recover the amount due for the work performed.

This is not the law. Counsel for the plaintiff omits to call our attention to any authority sustaining such a proposition and our search reveals none. In fact, the law is very well settled to the contrary. This was an entire contract. Ming v. Corbin, 142 N.Y. 334, 340, 341, 37 N.E. 105. Where a contract is made to perform work and no agreement is made as to payment, the work must be substantially performed before payment can be demanded. Gurski v. Doscher, 112 App.Div. 345, 98 N.Y.Supp. 588; affirmed 190 N.Y. 536, 83 N.E. 1125. * * *

The judgment should be reversed, and a new trial ordered; costs to abide the event.

HISCOCK, C.J., and COLLIN, CARDOZO, POUND, and ANDREWS, JJ., concur. CUDDEBACK, J., absent.

Judgment reversed, etc.

RESTATEMENT, SECOND, CONTRACTS § 234:

Illustrations:

9. A contracts to do the concrete work on a building being constructed by B for $10 a cubic yard. In the absence of language or

circumstances indicating the contrary, payment by B is not due until A has finished the concrete work.

10. The facts being otherwise as stated in Illustration 9, B promises to furnish a bond to secure his payment. No provision is made as to the time for furnishing the bond. No performance by A is due until B has furnished the bond. Although the doing of the concrete work by A requires a period of time and the furnishing of the bond by B does not, the circumstance that the bond is required to secure payment by B indicates that B must furnish the bond first.

R. G. POPE CONSTRUCTION CO. V. GUARD RAIL OF ROANOKE, INC.

Supreme Court of Virginia, 1978.
219 Va. 111, 244 S.E.2d 774.

COMPTON, JUSTICE.

In this construction contract case, the dispute is between the general contractor on a highway project and the guardrail subcontractor. The controversy stems from the refusal of the subcontractor to perform its agreement.

In June of 1971, plaintiffs R.G. Pope Construction Company, Inc. and Pope Paving Corporation (hereinafter sometimes collectively referred to as Pope) executed a written contract with the Commonwealth of Virginia, Department of Highways (hereinafter, Highway Department) for the construction of a 6.5-mile section of U.S. Route 58 in Russell County between Dickensonville and Hansonville. During the following month, Pope and defendant Guard Rail of Roanoke, Inc. signed a written subcontract in the amount of $103,086.85 calling for the defendant to furnish and install steel guardrail in connection with the project. The prime contract expressly stated that all the work on the project was to be completed by October 1, 1973. The site was not ready for erection of all of the guardrail pursuant to the subcontract until July of 1974. As the result of Guard Rail's refusal to perform at that time, due to a shortage of steel and increases in steel prices, Pope engaged another subcontractor to do the work, which commenced in August of 1974 at a cost of $132,071.90 more than the original subcontract price.

Subsequently in February of 1975, Pope proceeded by motion for judgment against Guard Rail and its surety, Fidelity & Deposit Company of Maryland, seeking damages against Guard Rail in the foregoing amount, and against the surety in the amount of its bond, for Guard Rail's alleged breach of contract. Guard Rail thereafter filed a counterclaim for $13,183.01 alleging lost profits as the result of an alleged breach of the subcontract by Pope.

After a jury trial lasting five and one-half days, the panel hung. The court below then discharged the jury and declared a mistrial. The respective parties thereafter renewed separate motions, earlier made during the course of the trial, to strike their adversary's evidence, Rule

1:11, and Pope also filed a motion for a new trial. The trial court, following consideration of additional memoranda of law and further argument of counsel, denied Pope's requests and granted the defendants' motions. Judgment was accordingly entered in favor of Guard Rail and the surety on Pope's original claim and in favor of Guard Rail against Pope in the amount sued for in the counterclaim. We granted Pope a writ of error to the August 1976 judgment order.

The documents comprising the agreement between Pope and the Highway Department included a proposal submitted by Pope in May of 1971, plans, and the Road and Bridge Specifications of the Highway Department contained in a 583-page manual. In the writings, Pope agreed to start work on the date specified in a Notice to Proceed and to complete all work in accordance with the plans and specifications "within the time limit set forth in the contract which is: October 1, 1973." The documents provided that "[t]ime is an essential element of the contract and it is important that the work be completed within the time specified." Under such a "fixed calendar date" contract, according to the agreement, the prime contractor must "take into consideration normal conditions considered unfavorable for the prosecution of the work and place sufficient men and equipment on the project to complete the work in accordance with the time limit." The contract also provided that extensions of time may be granted by the Highway Department "when a delay occurs due to unforeseen causes beyond the control of and without the fault or negligence of the Contractor." Under the agreement, if the work was not completed within the time limits, the Highway Department had the option of either permitting the prime contractor to continue with the work, assessing liquidated damages for each day of additional time consumed, or, take the prosecution of the work out of the contractor's hands, declaring him in default, and calling upon his surety for the satisfactory and expeditious completion of all work under the prime contract.

The subcontract was embodied in a printed form provided by Pope to Guard Rail. The subcontractor agreed "to furnish all labor, materials, equipment, and services as may be necessary to complete items of work on [the] project" relating to installation of the guardrail. In addition, Guard Rail acknowledged that it had "examined all the project plans, specifications, and other prime contract documents" and agreed to "assume and fulfill" all of Pope's obligations included in the prime contract, insofar as they applied to erection of guardrail. The subcontract further provided that Guard Rail would "prosecute the various portions of [its] work as directed by [Pope's] superintendent in order to assure orderly completion of the whole project within the contract time limit." The subcontract also required Guard Rail to "protect and maintain" its work until final acceptance by the Highway Department "or longer if so required by job specifications."

In a written "certification" executed on behalf of Guard Rail in September of 1971, the subcontractor acknowledged that "all stipulations of the 'Required Contract Provisions' of the Prime Contract" had been "physically incorporated" into the subcontract.

According to the evidence, one of the last items of work to be performed on a highway project is the installation of guardrail. This is because installation must occur in a continuous sequence, not piecemeal, after the highway shoulders and surface are completed. Unless such construction is at this final stage, serious problems of placement and alignment of the guardrail arise. The components of the device include a post, which is set in the ground; a block, attached to the post; and the rail, affixed to the block.

The record shows that the Highway Department notified Pope to proceed with construction on June 28, 1971. In the spring of 1973, Guard Rail entered into a contract with Syro Steel Company of Girard, Ohio, for Syro to furnish the guardrail components to enable defendant to perform the Pope subcontract. The testimony showed that Syro was not a steel manufacturer, but a fabricator and supplier which maintained an inventory of raw materials. The fabrication is accomplished about four weeks prior to the time the customer needs the product; the material is then placed on a truck when the customer calls for it and shipped directly to the job site to arrive at a time just before the rails are to be erected. In this instance, Syro, which had examined the relevant prime contract documents, calculated that Guard Rail would need its product in August of 1973. According to the record, installation of guardrail in this quantity takes about four to six weeks.

Knowing that the prime contract called for completion of the project by the fixed calendar date of October 1, 1973, Syro's quotation to Guard Rail was based on a "locked in" price, provided delivery took place anytime from August of 1973 to "early November" of that year. Syro's representative testified that if Guard Rail did not call for the material within that time period, a new contract at different prices would have to be negotiated between the supplier and the defendant.

The evidence shows that by September of 1972, Pope was delinquent in the amount of work completed on the project to a degree which was unacceptable to the Highway Department. Nevertheless, Pope indicated in its Monthly Progress Schedules, and other correspondence filed with the Department, that its work would be completed on schedule. Progress continued to slacken and, because of the delinquency, the Highway Department temporarily disqualified Pope in June of 1973 from bidding on future contracts with the Department. The rate of progress failed to improve. In August of 1973, Pope advised its surety, its bonding agency, its banker, and the Highway Department of Pope's "difficulty" in completing the job and stated that it needed "additional resources to bring [the project] to a rapid conclusion." Guard Rail, however, was not advised by Pope of its "problems." In September of 1973, the Highway Commissioner notified Pope that because progress on the project was "very unsatisfactory", the Department would annul the contract and turn the work over to Pope's surety company unless within ten days Pope took such steps as would "insure the completion of the work within a reasonable length of time." Thereafter, with the assistance of Pope's surety, a superintendent was put on the job and progress improved. The contract was not annulled and Pope was allowed to continue with the project.

In April of 1974, having received no direct communication from Pope about the project or any order from Pope to proceed with the performance of the subcontract (except an October 1972 directive to install 1100 feet of temporary railing), Guard Rail wrote Pope stating that the price it had quoted for the material had been "locked down" with the steel mill only until October of 1973 and declared that "[w]ith the steel situation the way it is," the subcontract "for this project must be renegotiated." The evidence showed that beginning in January of 1974, because of unanticipated economic conditions affecting the domestic steel industry, guardrail posts became "nonexistent." Syro's representative described the situation, which lasted to July of 1974, as "probably the worst shortage that the steel mills had ever placed upon fabricators." During that period, because of the short supply and great demand, prices for the guardrail components doubled and tripled.

Within two weeks after receiving the letter from Guard Rail, Pope wrote to the defendant that "the installation of this guard rail will begin during the month of May, 1974" and that "we will hereby expect you to fulfill the terms of your subcontract." Guard Rail refused to perform. Pope obtained another subcontractor to install the rails. The site was not ready for installation of all the rail until July of 1974 and the new subcontractor commenced work during August. The entire project was eventually completed by Pope in September of 1974.

Subsequently, the Highway Department, as a part of the process of ascertaining the amount Pope would be penalized for the overrun, allowed a 35-day extension on the contract time limit. It then assessed Pope with liquidated damages of $79,800 ($300 per day from November 5, 1973 until the project was completed).

Plaintiffs contend that the trial court erred in failing to sustain their motions to strike the defendants' evidence, or, in the alternative, that the court erred in refusing to award them a new trial. Plaintiffs argue, first, that Guard Rail breached its agreement by abandoning the subcontract prior to termination of the prime contract, without an excuse for non-performance. Plaintiffs say that the subcontract should not have been abandoned when it became more expensive to perform because economic hardship does not "form the basis of an excuse for non-performance."

Pope argues that Guard Rail could have avoided the situation which developed in January of 1974 by notifying Pope that its steel price was confirmed only until a specific date and by also notifying plaintiffs that it would refuse to perform after such date. Pope also argues that Guard Rail could have made an attempt to extend its contract with Syro, which it failed to do.

In addition, Pope emphasizes that the prime contract allowed material to be stockpiled on the project site and provided for reimbursement of its cost, less a standard ten percent retainage. Plaintiffs say that Guard Rail was under a positive duty to cooperate with the general contractor in the performance of the prime contract and thus should have ordered the steel in advance and stored it on the site until ready for use.

Pope further asserts that time was not of the essence of the subcontract and that "the subcontractor was continuously obligated under the express terms of its agreement to perform the general contractor's prime contract obligations as long as the prime contract remained viable and executory." Pope points out that the Highway Department extended the completion date to November 5, 1973, and continued to regard the general contractor's obligations under the prime contract as unaltered until September, 1974. Plaintiffs say: "Clearly the whole and cumulative effect of the quoted agreements of the parties was that [Guard Rail] was to assume and fulfill Pope's obligation for guardrail installation under the prime contract in the time and manner directed by Pope, and to direct and maintain said work until accepted by the [Highway Department] or longer if required by the job specifications."

In its alternative argument seeking a new trial, Pope says that even if Guard Rail was not obligated to perform its agreement until the ultimate termination of the prime contract, it still did not possess the "right to abandon at the expiration of the prime contract's original completion date, but was obligated to perform within a reasonable time." Pope argues that the determination of what was a reasonable time and whether the general contractor called for performance by the subcontractor within that time was purely a question of fact for the jury, and was not a matter of law for the court.

Finally, Pope contends that even if the time of performance is presumed to be a reasonable time, Guard Rail wrongfully abandoned the contract because timely notice of the intention to abandon was never given to Pope by the defendant. Pope asserts that "it does not follow that one party may suddenly without notice terminate the contract while the other party is in good faith attempting to perform it."

We are concerned here, of course, with contract performance.* Specifically, we are dealing with performances by each party to be exchanged under reciprocal promises. Guard Rail promised to do the work and Pope promised to pay the subcontract price. These bilateral promises implicated duties of performance by Pope as well as Guard Rail.

---

* In the view we take of the case it becomes unnecessary to decide whether, as Guard Rail argues, time was of the essence of the subcontract, or whether, as Pope argues, time was not of the essence and the defendant was obligated to perform either within a reasonable time or even until termination of the prime contract.

We hold that under these facts there was a material failure of performance by Pope which operated to discharge Guard Rail's duty to itself perform. Here, the defendant's performance of the duty to install guardrail was subject to certain conditions, the most important of which was the implied condition that a site would be available for such installation. The performance of Guard Rail's duty, subject to such conditions, did not become due unless the conditions occurred, or unless their nonoccurrence was excused. Restatement (Second) of Contracts [§ 225]. In this case such conditions, culminating in the requirement for availability of a site upon which to erect the guardrail, did not occur at a time when Guard Rail was able to perform nor was such nonoccurrence of the conditions excused, as we shall demonstrate. In fact, Pope actually unjustifiably prevented Guard Rail from performing its contract by conduct which caused the delay in completion of the project, rendering Pope liable to Guard Rail for damages. See Boggs v. Duncan, 202 Va. 877, 882, 121 S.E.2d 359, 363 (1961).

As the defendants contend, among the conditions precedent to Guard Rail's obligation to perform was the express duty upon Pope, according to the prime contract incorporated into the subcontract, to conduct the work "in such a manner and with sufficient materials, equipment and labor as are necessary to insure its completion in accordance with the plans and specifications within the time limit set forth in the contract." This gave rise to the implied duty upon Pope to do everything which was reasonably necessary to enable Guard Rail to perform within the time agreed. These general requirements gave rise to a significant implied duty upon Pope to provide a work site upon which Guard Rail could perform its promises according to the terms of the subcontract.

The evidence is without conflict that these conditions did not occur; the site was not ready for timely erection of the rail by October 1, 1973, the original contract completion date; it was not ready by November 5, 1973, the later-extended date; and it was not ready by May of 1974, the time when Pope called upon defendant to perform. There was no place ready to erect the guardrail until July 1974, according to all the evidence.

The main issue in the case then becomes: Was the nonoccurrence of these conditions excused? We think not. Ronald G. Pope, President of one plaintiff corporation and secretary-treasurer of the other, sought to excuse the delay by conclusory testimony unsupported by specific evidence. He testified that the delay was caused by "a considerable amount of bad weather, in excess of what we had in previous years"; by "unsuitable materials"; by "a lot of traffic" through the area which required time and manpower to control; and by "cement and fuel shortages". There was also evidence that Pope claimed that "economic difficulties due to ∗ ∗ ∗ increased prices" contributed to the delay.

But not only were these reasons unsupported by sufficient evidence at the trial, these excuses were all rejected by the Highway Department when it assessed, after the project was completed, the ultimate responsibility which Pope had under the prime contract.

The contract provided (emphasis added) that if the Highway Department "determines that the work was delayed because of conditions *beyond the control of and without the fault of the Contractor,* [it] may extend the time for completion as the conditions justify." The Department's Resident Engineer, whose duties included direct supervision of the construction of this project, testified, reciting specifics, that he could find no basis for recommending to the Department that even a one-day extension be granted to Pope. For example, he said that the amount of inclement weather did not justify any time extensions; that the percentage of "unsuitable material" was "relatively insignificant"; that Pope had admitted to the Department that "the fuel shortage had not actually interfered with his progress"; and that Pope never asked the Department for an extension based on "economic difficulties due to the increased prices." The Resident Engineer stated that at least three factors caused the 11-month delay: (1) Pope's "failure to prosecute the work diligently in the first year"; (2) Pope's "failure to provide engineering personnel on the project"; and (3) Pope's failure to provide adequate "supervision" on the job.

The Highway Department's District Engineer, under whose general supervision the project fell, was called as a witness by the plaintiffs. While stating that he "imagine[d] that fifty percent of the [highway] projects overrun in time", he said that in this instance Pope caused almost the entire period of delay and that such delay was due to conditions over which Pope had control. He testified that of the 35-day extension ultimately granted, any period exceeding eight days was a pure "gift" to Pope. He explained that officials in the Department above the district level, for reasons of fairness, frequently grant time extensions in addition to the amount recommended in the field when resulting liquidated damages would exceed the added expense incurred by the Department as the result of the overrun. So, he said, "to look at the 35 days and to say that this was the additional time of extension that was justified, is not necessarily true."

The evidence further showed that though Pope was continually short on cash and was otherwise undercapitalized, it entered into four major highway construction projects between 1970 and 1972. Pope was committed to complete eighteen million dollars' worth of such projects in two states (Virginia and Tennessee) within about three years' time. In a June 1973 letter to the Highway Department, Pope admitted that it was a "victim of ambition." The record shows that Pope lacked sufficient manpower, equipment or funds to meet the binding progress schedules. Finally, in order to obtain necessary capital, Pope sold "a substantial portion" of its equipment in February of 1974 and sold its "crushing operation" and asphalt plant three months later.

In sum, we believe that the plaintiffs' evidence, as a matter of law, utterly fails to show that any of the 266-day delay, which continued beyond the extended completion date of November 5, 1973 and for which the Highway Department asessed liquidated damages, was excusable. Thus, under these facts, and considering the early 1974 unavailability of steel and the concomitant significant price increase, Guard Rail was fully justified in April of 1974 in refusing to perform its subcontract because of Pope's uncured material failure to render its performance due at an earlier date. Restatement (Second) of Contracts [§ 237] supra.

In conclusion, we will comment upon plaintiffs' claim that Guard Rail should have stockpiled the material and their claims that, in effect, Guard Rail otherwise should have taken some positive action to extricate Pope from its difficulties either by notices to Pope or efforts to extend the Syro contract. These contentions are all without merit.

* * *

Accordingly, the plaintiffs' breach of contract action must fail and, because Pope prevented Guard Rail's performance of the contract, defendant's counterclaim must succeed.

For the foregoing reasons, we are of opinion that the trial court was correct in its several rulings on the respective post-trial motions. Consequently, the judgment below will be

Affirmed.

SAHADI v. CONTINENTAL ILLINOIS NATIONAL BANK & TRUST CO.

United States Court of Appeals, Seventh Circuit, 1983.
706 F.2d 193.

HARLINGTON WOOD, JR., CIRCUIT JUDGE.

This is an appeal from the district court's order granting partial summary judgment in favor of the defendant-appellee Continental Illinois Bank (the Bank) in an action alleging that the Bank breached its agreement with the plaintiff-appellant's business, Great Lakes and European Lines, Inc. (GLE), by calling a $7 million loan when GLE tendered interest payments less than one day after they were due. On appeal, the plaintiffs argue that the district court erred in granting summary judgment because there existed an array of genuine and material disputed factual issues concerning, *inter alia*, whether GLE's day-late tender of payment was a "material" breach of the underlying agreement warranting the Bank's calling of the loan, whether the Bank's conduct in accepting late interest payments under the predecessor loan agreement with GLE resulted in a waiver of its right to call the loan for the delayed tender without notice, and whether the Bank's calling of the loan without notice violated its duty of "good faith" under the Uniform Commercial Code and the common law. Because there existed a genuine factual dispute at least as to the question of whether there was a "material" breach of the agreement, we find that the district court's award of summary judgment to defendant on the question of breach was inappropriate, and we remand for a trial.

I.

Viewing the facts in the light most favorable to the plaintiffs, as we must, there emerges a story of financial brinkmanship and opaque dealing in which neither side emerges wholly blameless. GLE, an international shipping line, began its relationship with the Bank in 1976 with a $3 million loan, personally guaranteed by the Sahadis. The Bank increased its loan commitment to $11 million in 1977, a commitment upon which GLE relied in expanding its business, but which was repudiated by the Bank, to the detriment of GLE, when personal and institutional friction developed between the parties. The parties quickly reached a stalemate, with GLE threatening to sue the Bank for breach of its loan commitment and the Bank threatening to call the loans already extended. Meanwhile, GLE successfully interested another lender which conditioned its backing on GLE's settlement of its differences with the Bank.

Negotiations ensued in which, the evidence indicated, the Bank primarily sought to obtain release from the Sahadis and GLE of their claims stemming from the Bank's purported breach of its loan commitment, and to obtain further collateral from the Sahadis to secure their guarantee of the outstanding loan. The Bank also sought to have GLE's outstanding interest payments, which had been withheld during the several months of the dispute, brought up to date.

The negotiations resulted in two agreements executed on October 25, 1977. One agreement ran between the Sahadis and the Bank, completely releasing the Bank from any claims stemming from its failure to fulfill the loan commitment; it also extensively collateralized the Sahadis' guarantee of the Bank's outstanding loan to GLE. The other agreement, cross-referenced to the first and running between GLE and the Bank, provided in turn for the payment of interest and for the Bank's forbearance from demanding payment of the entire outstanding loan and accrued interest:

> 1. [The Bank] hereby agrees to forbear from demanding payment of the Liabilities during the period ending December 31, 1977, except for payment of current interest thereon as more fully set forth in clause (i) of paragraph 3 below.

The agreement went on to state:

> 3. Notwithstanding the foregoing, [the Bank] may demand payment in full of the Liabilities prior to December 31, 1977 if * * * (i) [GLE] shall fail to make payment of interest accrued on the Liabilities through September 30, 1977 on or before November 15, 1977.

This latter paragraph, as initially drafted, provided for October 7, 1977 as the deadline for the payment of accrued interest. This date was changed to November 15, 1977 at Sahadi's request with no objection by the Bank; moreover, there was no evidence that the precise date on which accrued interest was to be paid was ever a point of contention in the negotiations.

Despite the seeming air of reconciliation surrounding these agreements and despite the fact that the Bank had routinely accepted late interest payments from GLE under the underlying loan which the agreement modified, plaintiff's evidence established that after October 25, the Bank furtively prepared to take advantage of GLE's propensity for late payment to call the loan under the technical letter of the new agreement. Although the Bank sent a billing to GLE headquarters on November 9, 1977 reminding GLE of the interest due on November 15 and referring to the October 25, 1977 agreement, the letter made no mention of the Bank's intent to call the loan if payment did not arrive on the precise contractually specified date. In speaking with top GLE representatives on November 14 and 15, the Bank made no mention of its intent to call the loan.

Sahadi was reminded by a subordinate on November 14 of the November 15 interest payment date, but Sahadi responded that the payment should be delayed so that GLE monies in Chicago would be available to satisfy other immediate liabilities. As Sahadi noted in his affidavit, "There was no great significance attached to the payment of interest in this covenant; it did not occur to us that the bank would treat the interest payment date any differently than it had treated previous payment dates." On the morning of November 16, a GLE representative was queried by the Bank as to whether the interest payments had been made; when the GLE representative responded negatively but indicated that the payment would be made by the end of the week, the Bank representative responded that the matter could be discussed later that day. At that later meeting, the Bank presented the surprised GLE representative with notification that the loan was called. The GLE representative immediately offered to tender payment for the due interest from the company's account with the Bank, but the Bank refused.[1] The calling of the loan destroyed GLE and subjected the Sahadis to liability on the personal guarantee.

The Sahadis, indirectly as assignees of GLE, thereafter filed this action against the Bank, seeking release from their personal guarantee agreement and damages for the destruction of GLE. Chiefly, they contended that GLE's brief delay in tender of the November 15 interest payment did not amount to a "material" breach of the October 25 agreements justifying the Bank's cessation of forbearance, and that the Bank's conduct was in any case unjustified under principles of waiver and "good faith."

1. Although the company had earlier instructed the Bank that the latter was not to *automatically* withdraw funds from this account to cover interest due, there is no contention that the company's explicit tender of payment on November 16 from this account was ineffective.

In granting partial summary judgment to the Bank, the district court rejected the Sahadis' waiver argument, but did not directly address their "material" breach or "good faith" contentions, either of which, the Sahadis argued, required a trial to assess the conflicting evidence. Instead, the district court chose the alternative analytical framework of "ambiguity" and held that, since the November 15 date was not "ambiguous," there was no room for factual difference as to whether a brief delay in payment was permitted. After the district court denied the Sahadis' motion for reconsideration, this appeal followed.

II.

The limitations upon the use of summary judgment are stringent, and we may not affirm the district court's order unless the record reveals the absence of any genuine issue of material fact. Fed.R.Civ.P. 56(c). We cannot agree with the district court that under Illinois law, expressly made applicable in the agreements here, this record presents no issues of material fact requiring a full trial. While outstanding issues of material fact may well exist also in relation to the Sahadis' waiver and breach of "good faith" claims, we need not reach those questions here and so confine our analysis for the purposes of this appeal to the issues of "material" breach.

It is black letter law in Illinois and elsewhere that only a "material" breach of a contract provision by one party will justify nonperformance by the other party. See Janssen Bros. v. Northbrook Trust and Savings Bank, 12 Ill.App.3d 840, 299 N.E.2d 431, 434 (2d Dist. 1973); 5 Williston on Contracts §§ 675, 805 (3d ed. 1961); Restatement (Second) of Contracts § 229 (1979). Moreover, the determination of "materiality" is a complicated question of fact, involving an inquiry into such matters as whether the breach worked to defeat the bargained-for objective of the parties or caused disproportionate prejudice to the non-breaching party, whether custom and usage considers such a breach to be material, and whether the allowance of reciprocal nonperformance by the non-breaching party will result in his accrual of an unreasonable or unfair advantage. All of these issues must be resolved with reference to the intent of the parties as evidenced in large part by the full circumstances of the transaction, thus making these issues especially unsuited to resolution by summary judgment. Conrad v. Delta Airlines, Inc., 494 F.2d 914, 918 (7th Cir.1974); *Janssen Bros.*, 299 N.E.2d at 433.

The need for a complete factual inquiry into the underlying circumstances and commercial custom is especially acute where, as here, the purportedly breaching party claims that time was not of the essence of the contract. Even where the contract contains a provision, not present here, explicitly stipulating that "time is of the essence," the Illinois courts will inquire into the situation of the parties and the underlying circumstances to determine whether a delay in performance resulted in a "material" breach. *Janssen Bros.*, 299 N.E.2d at 434. The record in the case at bar discloses evidence that would permit a trier of fact to find that payment of the interest due precisely on November 15 was *not* "of the essence" of the agreement from the Bank's point of view. For example, Sahadi himself was allowed unilaterally to choose the payment date, and there was no contention in negotiations over the fixing of that date; the prejudice to the Bank's rights stemming from a payment delay of several hours was *de minimis* in view of the Bank's retention of the enhanced collateralization, its retention of the complete release of legal claims stemming from the reneged-upon loan commitment, and the Bank's clear knowledge that GLE had on hand in the Bank, and tendered, funds sufficient to satisfy the interest requirement; the Bank had previously accepted late payments in its course of dealings with GLE; and there was evidence that calling a loan for such a brief delay was without precedent in the banking community. Significantly, even the Bank conceded at oral argument on appeal, "The important thing * * * is not the date of the fifteenth in that sense; it's the fact of the promise." Whether or not these facts would be sufficient to prove non-materiality in light of all the other evidence adduced at trial, they at least raise a genuine issue as to whether the "promise" was in any important way defeated by the hours of delay in tender of payment. Indeed, it would be difficult to posit a set of alleged facts making summary resolution of the issue of "materiality" in favor of the defendant less appropriate.

The Bank launches three lines of attack against such a conclusion. First, it argues, the contract before us presents a uniquely attractive case for the rigid and summary application of time requirements because it contains a specific provision allowing the cessation of the Bank's forbearance if interest was not paid on or before November 15, 1977. However, this argument merely assumes what it seeks to prove: that the payment of interest on precisely the named date was an essential part of that specific provision, and that whether the precise day of payment was essential can be determined without the benefit of a full inquiry at trial.

The Illinois courts have rightly spurned such conclusory logic. In Janssen Bros. v. Northbrook Trust & Savings Bank, 12 Ill.App.3d 840, 299 N.E.2d 431 (2d Dist.1973), for example, a real estate contract specifically provided that time was of the essence and that if certain payments were not made by the named date, certain deeds would be automatically recorded and the purchase price refunded. 299 N.E.2d at 432. Notwithstanding this explicit recitation of the consequences of late payment, the court refused to undertake a wooden reading of the provision, let alone to do so through a summary procedure. Noting that even where the parties clearly intended to regard a specific payment date as crucial, "equity will refuse to enforce such a provision when to do so would be unconscionable or would give one party an unfair advantage over the other," id. at 434, the court also underscored that "summary procedure is not * * * suited to situations in which substantial questions are present relating to the formation and terms of a settlement agreement or its construction, and evidence or testimony is required to satisfactorily resolve the issue," id. at 433. Significantly, none of the Illinois cases cited by the Bank to illustrate the strict and summary application of explicit consequential provisions involve the enforceability of time requirements; rather, the provisions and defaults in those cases concern far more substantive matters, such as absolute failure to properly maintain and improve municipally granted property or the failure of a real estate purchaser to obtain required mortgage financing.[2] By contrast the Illinois case most directly on point, *Janssen Bros.,* supra, well expresses the special principles extended to the enforcement of time requirements even when attached to explicit termination provisions, in view of the fact that performance dates are by their nature accessory rather than central aspects of most contracts. See, e.g., Restatement (Second) of Contracts, § 229 and Illustrations 3 and 4 (1979).

The Bank contends alternatively that no room for a "materiality" analysis and its concomitant factual inquiry exists here because the payment of the interest on or before November 15 was an "express condition" of the Bank's forbearance, and thus its terms were required to be exactly fulfilled. This second argument, like the Bank's first, suffers from its conclusory assumption of what it seeks to prove—that the payment of the interest on the precise named date rather than payment of the interest in a reasonably prompt manner was of threshold importance to the completion of the contract. In short, asking whether a provision is a "condition" is similar to stating the "materiality" question: both seek to determine whether its performance was a *sine qua non* of the contract's fulfillment. And that determination may not be made through a mechanical process.

In general, contractual terms are presumed to represent independent promises rather than conditions. 3A Corbin on Contracts § 635 (1960); 5 Williston on Contracts §§ 665, 666 (1961). Determining whether this presumption may be upset entails a full inquiry into the "intention of the parties and the good sense of the case" including such

---

2. In addition, of the three Illinois cases cited by the Bank, we note that two—City of Belleville v. Citizen's Horse Railway, 152 Ill. 171, 38 N.E. 584 (1894) and People v. Central Union Telephone Co., 232 Ill. 260, 83 N.E. 829 (1900)—were decided in the salad days of American legal formalism whch were marked by an unprecedented adherence to the letter of contractual texts—a jurisprudential posture that has since been eclipsed by the kind of materiality approach embodied in *Janssen Bros.,* supra. See, e.g., Horwitz, The Transformation of American Law, 1780–1860 160–210, 253–69 (1977) (legal formalism in contract law described as attempt to displace customary fairness considerations from common law adjudication in favor of "objective" standards favoring economic rationalization); * * * In the third Illinois case cited by the Bank, Dodson v. Nink, 72 Ill.App.3d 59, 28 Ill.Dec. 379, 390 N.E.2d 546 (2d Dist.1979) the court considered the question of whether a variation in performance amounted to a cognizable breach of a termination clause "under the circumstances," emphasizing that the variation had placed a new substantive duty on the other party. 28 Ill.Dec. at 380–383, 390 N.E.2d at 547, 550. Such a fact-sensitive, contextual review is markedly different from the summary procedure the Bank would have us sustain here.

The non-Illinois cases cited by the Bank fail to persuade us for similar reasons. * * *

factors as whether the protected party can achieve its principal goal without literal performance of the contractual provision. So reluctant are courts to elevate a term to the status of a condition that the factual inquiry will often be undertaken in spite of the existence of explicit language, not present here, creating liability only "on condition" of the occurrence of a required, prior act. Rooks Creek Evangelical Lutheran Church v. First Lutheran Church, 290 Ill. 133, 129 N.E. 793, 795 (1919); 5 Williston on Contracts § 665 (1961) ("Especially words literally appropriate for conditions have not been given their natural meaning where the consequence would lead to injustice and a violation of the probable intent of the parties."). The Bank points to a confirmatory telex message from Sahadi stating that the Bank's forbearance was to be "on condition" that interest was paid by the named date, but such evidence is but one tile in the evidentiary mosaic; the law requires that the Sahadis be given the opportunity to present evidence that the parties only considered the payment of the interest, not its payment by an exact hour, to be the relevant "condition," if, indeed, that term as used in the telex is to be given its formal legal meaning. The Sahadis have been denied this opportunity by the district court's summary disposition.

Moreover, even if the payment of interest by the named date could be summarily construed as a necessary "condition," the district court would *still* be required to conduct a full-ranging factual inquiry into whether that condition had been "materially" breached or whether the technical breach was without "pecuniary importance." 5 Williston on Contracts § 805 at 839–40 (1961). Restatement (Second) of Contracts § 229 (1979) ("To the extent that the non-occurrence of a condition would cause disproportionate forfeiture, a court may excuse the non-occurrence of that condition unless its occurrence was a material part of the agreed exchange."); see also Restatement (Second) of Contracts § 229, Illustrations 3 and 4 (demonstrating that day-late payments are not "material" breaches).[3] At either level of the "promise/condition"

---

3. Contrary to the Bank's assertion, the "forfeiture" required to trigger the analysis of Restatement § 229 describes without strain the effect of a technical reading of the contract here. Comment (b) of that section defines a "forfeiture" as a "denial of compensation that results when the obligee loses his right to the agreed exchange after he has relied substantially, as by preparation or performance on the expectation of that exchange." Construing, as we must under Illinois law, both the Sahadi/Bank agreement and the simultaneous GLE/Bank agreement together as part of the same transaction, it is apparent that the Sahadis surrendered their legal claims against the Bank for its breach of the $11 million loan commitment and posted substantial additional collateral as a result of reliance upon the Bank's forbearance which is now sought to be negated through a technical interpretation. At the very least, this is the kind of circumstance which demands careful weighing of "the extent of the forfeiture by the obligee against the importance to the obligor of the risk from which he sought to be protected and the degree to which that protection will be lost if the nonoccurrence of the condition is excused to the extent required to prevent forfeiture." Restatement (Second) of Contracts § 229, comment b (1979). Moreover, we note that, the *Restatement* standard aside, under Illinois law, this inquiry may be undertaken even when the breach of a condition does not result in a "forfeiture." See *Janssen Bros.*, 299 N.E.2d at 434.

analysis, then, summary judgment would not be appropriate in this case.

The Bank finally contends that the factual elements and general principles of the "materiality" requirement are inapplicable to the kind of loan-calling provisions present here because, it argues, contracts involving commercial paper are more strictly and literally construed than are other contracts. The Illinois cases cited by the Bank, however, do not support this premise, for they state no more than that loan acceleration clauses are not inequitable *per se;* they do not consider whether such clauses may be enforced where there is a breach of an arguably incidental element of the clause such as exact time of payment. Moreover, we would decline to speculate that the materiality principles embodied in later Illinois cases like *Janssen Bros.,* supra, involving an arm's length corporate real estate transaction, would be held inapplicable by the Illinois courts to loan contracts like those present here.

CONCLUSION

Although we need not reach the question of whether summary judgment may properly be applied to plaintiffs' assertion of waiver and "good faith," we hold that such a procedure was an inappropriate short-cut in resolving the necessarily fact-bound, complex question of "material" breach. The "materiality" issue cannot be avoided. The holding that the deadline date for interest payments in the contract was "unambiguous" does not resolve the matter. The plaintiffs concede the existence of an unambiguous, contractually specified date, but this is merely the beginning, not the end, of the required factfinding analysis.

Reversed and Remanded.

WALKER & COMPANY v. HARRISON

United States Supreme Court of Michigan, 1957.
347 Mich. 630, 81 N.W.2d 352.

SMITH, JUSTICE.

This is a suit on a written contract. The defendants are in the dry-cleaning business. Walker & Company, plaintiff, sells, rents, and services advertising signs and billboards. These parties entered into an agreement pertaining to a sign. The agreement is in writing and is termed a "rental agreement." It specifies in part that:

> "The lessor agrees to construct and install, at its own cost, one 18'9" high × 8'8" wide pylon type d.f. neon sign with electric clock and flashing lamps * * *. The lessor agrees to and does hereby lease or rent unto the said lessee the said SIGN for the term, use and rental and under the conditions, hereinafter set out, and the lessee agrees to pay said rental * * *.

> "(a) The term of this lease shall be 36 months * * *.

"(b) The rental to be paid by lessee shall be $148.50 per month for each and every calendar month during the term of this lease; * * *.

"(d) Maintenance. Lessor at its expense agrees to maintain and service the sign together with such equipment as supplied and installed by the lessor to operate in conjunction with said sign under the terms of this lease; this service is to include cleaning and repainting of sign in original color scheme as often as deemed necessary by lessor to keep sign in first class advertising condition and make all necessary repairs to sign and equipment installed by lessor. * * *."

At the "expiration of this agreement," it was also provided, "title to this sign reverts to lessee." This clause is in addition to the printed form of agreement and was apparently added as a result of defendants' concern over title, they having expressed a desire "to buy for cash" and the salesman, at one time, having "quoted a cash price."

The sign was completed and installed in the latter part of July, 1953. The first billing of the monthly payment of $148.50 was made August 1, 1953, with payment thereof by defendants on September 3, 1953. This first payment was also the last. Shortly after the sign was installed, someone hit it with a tomato. Rust, also, was visible on the chrome, complained defendants, and in its corners were "little spider cobwebs." In addition, there were "some children's sayings written down in here." Defendant Herbert Harrison called Walker for the maintenance he believed himself entitled to under subparagraph (d) above. It was not forthcoming. He called again and again. "I was getting, you might say, sorer and sorer. * * * Occasionally, when I started calling up, I would walk around where the tomato was and get mad again. Then I would call up on the phone again." Finally, on October 8, 1953, plaintiff not having responded to his repeated calls, he telegraphed Walker that:

"You Have Continually Voided Our Rental Contract By Not Maintaining Signs As Agreed As We No Longer Have A Contract With You Do Not Expect Any Further Remuneration."

Walker's reply was in the form of a letter. After first pointing out that "your telegram does not make any specific allegations as to what the failure of maintenance comprises," and stating that "We certainly would appreciate your furnishing us with such information," the letter makes reference to a prior collateral controversy between the parties, "wondering if this refusal on our part prompted your attempt to void our rental contract," and concludes as follows:

"We would like to call your attention to paragraph G in our rental contract, which covers procedures in the event of a Breach of Agreement. In the event that you carry out your threat to make no future monthly payments in accordance with the agreement, it is our intention to enforce the conditions outlined under paragraph

G[1] through the proper legal channels. We call to your attention that your monthly rental payments are due in advance at our office not later than the 10th day of each current month. You are now approximately 30 days in arrears on your September payment. Unless we receive both the September and October payments by October 25th, this entire matter will be placed in the hands of our attorney for collection in accordance with paragraph G which stipulates that the entire amount is forthwith due and payable."

No additional payments were made and Walker sued in assumpsit for the entire balance due under the contract, $5,197.50, invoking paragraph (g) of the agreement. Defendants filed answer and claim of recoupment, asserting that plaintiff's failure to perform certain maintenance services constituted a prior material breach of the agreement, thus justifying their repudiation of the contract and grounding their claim for damages. The case was tried to the court without a jury and resulted in a judgment for the plaintiff. The case is before us on a general appeal.

Defendants urge upon us again and again, in various forms, the proposition that Walker's failure to service the sign, in response to repeated requests, constituted a material breach of the contract and justified repudiation by them. Their legal proposition is undoubtedly correct. Repudiation is one of the weapons available to an injured party in event the other contractor has committed a material breach. But the injured party's determination that there has been a material breach, justifying his own repudiation, is fraught with peril, for should such determination, as viewed by a later court in the calm of its contemplation, be unwarranted, the repudiator himself will have been

---

1. "(g) Breach of Agreement. Lessee shall be deemed to have breached this agreement by default in payment of any installment of the rental herein provided for; abandonment of the sign or vacating premises where the sign is located; termination or transfer of lessee's interest in the premises by insolvency, appointment of a receiver for lessee's business; filing of a voluntary or involuntary petition in bankruptcy with respect to lessee or the violation of any of the other terms or conditions hereof. In the event of such default, the lessor may, upon notice to the lessee, which notice shall conclusively be deemed sufficient if mailed or delivered to the premises where the sign was or is located, take possession of the sign and declare the balance of the rental herein provided for to be forthwith due and payable, and lessee hereby agrees to pay such balance upon any such contingencies. Lessor may terminate this lease and without notice, remove and repossess said sign and recover from the lessee such amounts as may be unpaid for the remaining unexpired term of this agreement. Time is of the essence of this lease with respect to the payment of rentals herein provided for. Should lessee after lessor has declared the balance of rentals due and payable, pay the full amount of rental herein provided, he shall then be entitled to the use of the sign, under all the terms and provisions hereof, for the balance of the term of this lease. No waiver by either party hereto of the nonperformance of any term, condition or obligation hereof shall be a waiver of any subsequent breach of, or failure to perform the same, or any other term, condition or obligation hereof. It is understood and agreed that the sign is especially constructed for the lessee and for use at the premises now occupied by the lessee for the term herein provided; that it is of no value unless so used and that it is a material consideration to the lessor in entering into this agreement that the lessee shall continue to use the sign for the period of time provided herein and for the payment of the full rental for such term."

guilty of material breach and himself have become the aggressor, not an innocent victim.

What is our criterion for determining whether or not a breach of contract is so fatal to the undertaking of the parties that it is to be classed as "material"? There is no single touchstone. Many factors are involved. They are well stated in section 275 of Restatement of the Law of Contracts in the following terms:

"In determining the materiality of a failure fully to perform a promise the following circumstances are influential:

"(a) The extent to which the injured party will obtain the substantial benefit which he could have reasonably anticipated;

"(b) The extent to which the injured party may be adequately compensated in damages for lack of complete performance;

"(c) The extent to which the party failing to perform has already partly performed or made preparations for performance;

"(d) The greater or less hardship on the party failing to perform in terminating the contract;

"(e) The wilful, negligent or innocent behavior of the party failing to perform;

"(f) The greater or less uncertainty that the party failing to perform will perform the remainder of the contract."

We will not set forth in detail the testimony offered concerning the need for servicing. Granting that Walker's delay (about a week after defendant Herbert Harrison sent his telegram of repudiation Walker sent out a crew and took care of things) in rendering the service requested was irritating, we are constrained to agree with the trial court that it was not of such materiality as to justify repudiation of the contract, and we are particularly mindful of the lack of preponderant evidence contrary to his determination. Jones v. Eastern Michigan Motorbuses, 287 Mich. 619, 283 N.W. 710. The trial court, on this phase of the case, held as follows:

"Now Mr. Harrison phoned in, so he testified, a number of times. He isn't sure of the dates but he sets the first call at about the 7th of August and he complained then of the tomato and of some rust and some cobwebs. The tomato, according to the testimony, was up on the clock; that would be outside of his reach, without a stepladder or something. The cobwebs are within easy reach of Mr. Harrison and so would the rust be. I think that Mr. Bueche's argument that these were not materially a breach would clearly be true as to the cobwebs and I really can't believe in the face of all the testimony that there was a great deal of rust seven days after the installation of this sign. And that really brings it down to the tomato. And, of course, when a tomato has been splashed all over your clock, you don't like it. But he says he kept calling their attention to it, although the rain probably washed some of the tomato off. But the stain remained, and they didn't come. I really can't find that that was such a material breach of the contract as to justify rescission. I really don't think so."

Nor, we conclude, do we. There was no valid ground for defendants' repudiation and their failure thereafter to comply with the terms of the contract was itself a material breach, entitling Walker, upon this record, to judgment. * * *

Affirmed. Costs to appellee.

———

The first Restatement of Contracts simply took the position that any material breach or non-performance of a promise by one party "discharges" the duty of the other party to perform his or her obligations. Restatement, First, of Contracts § 397. The list of factors set forth in § 275 [quoted in Walker & Co.] was the principal determinant in the all-important question of whether a breach was "material." These deceptively simple provisions hide major questions of strategy for counsel when contract performance has broken down, as in *Walker & Co.* If your client withholds his or her own performance without justification ["as viewed by a later court in the calm of its contemplation"], then your client has committed a material breach giving rise to liability and permitting the other party to withhold his performance. It is not enough that there merely be an irritating breach by the other party to justify withholding of performance. There is, furthermore, the question of waiver; one cannot take a material breach and put it in one's back pocket to use at some later date when it is convenient. What should you advise your client to do when there has been a relatively minor breach at the outset of contract performance, and your client believes that this minor breach is a harbinger of more serious breaches to come? What should you advise your client to do when neither party has begun to perform and your client is about to begin an expensive performance but is concerned that the other party may be unable or willing to perform?

The second Restatement of Contracts adopts a somewhat different approach than the first Restatement, though the basic strategic issues are largely the same. Restatement, Second, of Contracts § 237 states that "it is a condition of each party's remaining duties to render performances to be exchanged under an exchange of promises that there be no uncured material failure by the other party to render any such performance due at an earlier time." The use of the term "condition" in this section makes applicable § 225 of the second Restatement that "[u]nless it has been excused, the non-occurrence of a condition discharges the duty *when the condition can no longer occur.*" Thus, the possibility at least exists under the second Restatement that a defaulting party may cure a material breach under certain circumstances and the contract duties are then not discharged. But cf. Restatement, Second, Contracts § 242. Cure is a concept introduced expressly by the Uniform Commercial Code. See UCC § 2–508(1).

The Uniform Commercial Code, on the other hand, basically rejects the concept of a material breach in the "perfect tender rule" of UCC § 2–601, though as indicated earlier, the harshness of this provision is softened in various ways. See pp. 96–99, supra. See also UCC §§ 2–301, 2–503(1), 2–507, 2–511(1).

The Uniform Commercial Code also recognizes that a contract for sale imposes an obligation on each party that the other's expectation of performance will not be impaired, UCC § 2–609(1), and permits a party to take defensive steps if there is doubt whether that performance will occur. A person who has "reasonable grounds for insecurity" with respect to the other party's performance may demand additional security, and, if commercially reasonable, suspend his own performance. UCC § 2–609(2). Further, a seller may stop delivery of goods that are in transit if he learns that the buyer is insolvent or the buyer repudiates or fails to make a payment when due. UCC § 2–705(1). Should these provisions be extended to commercial contracts generally?

Chapter 10

THIRD PARTY BENEFICIARIES

In Dunlop Pneumatic Tyre Co. v. Selfridge & Co., A.C. 847, 853 [1915] Lord Haldane announced, "My Lords, in the law of England certain principles are fundamental. One is that only a person who is a party to a contract can sue on it. Our law knows nothing of a jus quaesitum tertio arising by way of contract. Such a right may be conferred by way of property, as for example, under a trust, but it cannot be conferred on a stranger to a contract as a right to enforce the contract in personam." The subject of this chapter is the extent to which this strict rule has been relaxed in the United States.*

In the first place, why should possible plaintiffs be restricted to the parties to a contract? All sorts of people may have an economic interest in the completion of a contract. Why should they not be able to sue to enforce the contract? Consider, for example, a contract to build a house. The local appliance dealer has a strong interest in seeing the contract performed. To a lesser extent, so does the paper hanger, the carpenter, the plumber, the local municipality (whose tax base will be increased thereby), and the local country club. Should all, or some, or none, of these persons have a right to sue to enforce the contract? Reflection should indicate that the various rules developed throughout earlier chapters of this book, including measurement of damages, consideration, interpretation, mistake, and so forth, assume that enforcement of the contract will be by one of the parties to the contract. If suits by third persons are permitted at all, it is imperative that some line be drawn around the class of plaintiffs that may maintain suit: otherwise chaos will result.

* Even in England the rule against the rights of third parties has been eroded, though more grudgingly than in the United States. See Farnsworth, Contracts 744–45 (2d Ed.1990).

CHOATE, HALL & STEWART v. SCA SERVICES, INC.

Supreme Judicial Court of Massachusetts, 1979.
378 Mass. 535, 392 N.E.2d 1045.

Before HENNESSEY, C.J., and QUIRICO, KAPLAN and ABRAMS, JJ.

KAPLAN, JUSTICE.

We hold on the facts of the case so far disclosed that the plaintiff, an "intended" beneficiary, of the "creditor" type, of a contract between the defendant (promisor) and another (promisee), may maintain this action to enforce the defendant's promise. In so deciding we make a long anticipated but relatively minor change in the law of the Commonwealth.

The plaintiff law partnership Choate, Hall & Stewart[1] commenced this action against the defendant SCA Services, Inc. (a company doing a waste disposal business), to recover fees for legal services performed for one Berton Steir. The claim is based on a provision of an agreement between the defendant and Steir (among others) by which the defendant undertook to pay legal fees incurred by Steir in circumstances and under conditions to be detailed below. * * *

[The promise by SCA to pay Steir's legal expenses was made in connection with the settlement of a controversy over control of SCA. Steir was a member of one faction consisting of four directors that comprised one half of the board of directors; the struggle for control had led to bitter recriminations and the filing of four lawsuits and an investigation by the SEC. As part of the settlement the Steir faction agreed to resign (turning undisputed control of the corporation over to the other faction).]

We come now to the further provision of the settlement contract which is in issue in the present case. By that provision, set out in the margin,[2] the defendant agreed to "continue to indemnify and hold harmless" each of the resigning directors for "all losses, liabilities or expenses" incurred by him resulting "from any acts or omissions to act * * * while a director, officer or employee of [the defendant] or any of its subsidiaries * * * and each of the [resigning directors] may

---

1. We use the collective designation of the partnership, as do the parties.

2. "SCA shall continue to indemnify and hold harmless each of the parties of the first part for any and all losses, liabilities or expenses, if any (other than * * *), suffered or incurred by such party arising out of or resulting from any acts or omissions to act by such party while a director, officer or employee of SCA or any of its subsidiaries prior to the effective date hereof and each of the parties of the first part may select his own counsel whose reasonable fees and out-of-pocket expenses will be paid on a current basis directly by SCA, all to the maximum extent permissible under Delaware law. SCA's current charter and by-law provisions with regard to indemnification will not hereafter be changed to terms which are in any respect less favorable to the parties of the first part. This obligation includes without limitation all legal and other fees and expenses incurred after the date hereof and arising from the Securities and Exchange Commission investigation of SCA, File No. HO–867."

select his own counsel whose reasonable fees and out-of-pocket expenses will be paid on a current basis directly by [the defendant], all to the maximum extent permissible under Delaware law." The obligation was expressly stated to include legal fees and expenses to arise from a then pending investigation of the defendant by the Securities and Exchange Commission.

The agreement was executed by the eight directors and the defendant. The plaintiff law firm had represented Steir throughout the preceding negotiations.

In pursuance of the agreement, the defendant twice paid the plaintiff its submitted statements of fees and expenses for representing Steir in the SEC matter. The defendant made the payments direct to the plaintiff, upon the plaintiff's statements addressed to the defendant, followed by Steir's letters of request to the defendant. The defendant pursuant to the agreement made similar payments direct to other attorneys representing Steir, as well as to attorneys retained by the other resigning directors.

But on the plaintiff's statements of March 1, and May 28, 1977, respectively for $18,345.34 and $10,137.03, the defendant refused payment. * * *

The plaintiff brought the present action on July 25, 1977, praying a declaratory judgment. * * *

The defendant's answer, besides denials, asserted [among other] * * * affirmative defenses that the plaintiff was not a party to the settlement agreement and therefore could not sue to enforce it; * * * The defendant moved for judgment on the pleadings on the first affirmative defense mentioned—that the plaintiff, not a party to the agreement, was disabled from suing to enforce it. Affidavits were filed on both sides with respect to the negotiation of the critical provision.

Treating the motion as one for summary judgment, the judge held for the defendant, applying Massachusetts law as to the standing of third-party beneficiaries. Thereupon the plaintiff moved to amend its complaint to substitute Steir for itself as plaintiff in the action and correspondingly as the party to the preliminary injunction. The motions were denied. * * *

2. *Suit by third-party beneficiary.* As recently observed in Falmouth Hosp. v. Lopes, 376 Mass. 580, 382 N.E.2d 1042 (1978), the law of the Commonwealth before the mid-nineteenth century looked with considerable favor on enforcement of a contract by an outsider for whose benefit it was made;[3] and that was the view generally taken in this country. But in Mellen v. Whipple, 1 Gray 317, 321 (1854), this court, impressed by English authority, wrote that "a plaintiff, in an action on a simple contract, must be the person from whom the consideration of the contract actually moved, and * * * a stranger

---

3. [The court cites eight cases decided between 1813 and 1849.]

to the consideration cannot sue on the contract. The rule is sometimes thus expressed: There must be a privity of contract between the plaintiff and defendant, in order to render the defendant liable to an action, by the plaintiff, on the contract." But an abstract notion of "privity" serves no better purpose here than elsewhere in the law: compare the attack on privity as a limiting conception in the tort law. Prosser, The Assault upon the Citadel, 69 Yale L.J. 1099 (1960). If privity requirements reflected a disinclination to compel a contracting party to meet in litigation a person with whom he had not chosen to do business, they were a reminder of a simple, neighborly society already on the way out, and now long vanished. See L.M. Friedman, Contract Law in America 121–122 (1965). At all events, American courts, under the inspiration of Lawrence v. Fox, 20 N.Y. 268 (1859), have held quite generally that "creditor" beneficiaries may sue on contracts to which they were not parties. Professor Corbin says: "If the promisee in a contract contemplates the present or future existence of a duty or liability to a third party and enters into the contract with the expressed intent that the performance contracted for is to satisfy and discharge that duty or liability, the third party is a creditor beneficiary" entitled to enforce the contract. 4 Corbin, Contracts § 787 at 95 (1951).

This court has in fact frequently recognized the right of suit of creditor beneficiaries fitting Corbin's description, but it has been in the form of "exceptions" to (or formulas of evasions of) the supposed general prohibitory rule of the *Mellen* case. Thus we have been able to find that the promisor had "in his hands money which, in equity and good conscience, belongs to" the creditor.[6] Or that the promisee could sue as "trustee" for the third party.[7] Or that the promisee's right of exoneration was an asset recoverable from the promisor by a creditor's suit in equity. Other exceptions, some of them statutory, were more particularized.[9] Scholars have catalogued and assembled the exceptions to show that despite our formal adherence to the *Mellen* doctrine, we have actually reached nearly the same results as other jurisdictions which have rejected it. But of some of the exceptions, it has been said, with justification, that they are "rationalization[s] after the event" with "obvious weaknesses" of analysis. 4 Corbin, *supra*, § 790 at 121. And there has been uncertainty as to the scope of various exceptions.

The rather confusing patchwork should be supplanted by the general rule now prevalent, which avoids circuity of action and is

---

6. The language appeared in Mellen v. Whipple, 1 Gray 317, 322 (1854).

7. See Boyden v. Hill, 198 Mass. 477, 85 N.E. 413 (1908); Grime v. Borden, 166 Mass. 198, 44 N.E. 216 (1896). A "trust" theory was also a basis for recovery by third parties in England, but this approach has been curtailed since 1930. See 1 Chitty, Contracts 1118–1121 (24th ed. 1977).

9. See G.L. c. 149, § 29A (enforcement of surety bond); G.L. c. 175, §§ 111, 125 (of

certain insurance policies); UCC [§ 2–318] (third party suit for breach of warranty); Johnson-Foster Co. v. D'Amore Constr. Co., 314 Mass. 416, 50 N.E.2d 89 (1943) (enforcement of explicit contractual provision for third party recovery); Palmer Sav. Bank v. Insurance Co., 166 Mass. 189, 44 N.E. 211 (1896) (suit by mortgagee against mortgagor's insurer).

calculated to accord with the probable intentions of the contracting parties and to respond to the reasonable reliance of the third party creditor. As we now adopt the general rule,[10] we need not pause to consider whether the present case can by any possibility be squeezed into one or other of the "exceptions"; the plaintiff shows a most restrained enthusiasm in trying to do this. We do not hesitate to apply a general rule "retroactively" to the present case, for we have repeatedly reserved the point whether we would repeal so much of Mellen v. Whipple as remained; the handwriting has long been on the wall. It happens, moreover, that no recent case has been cited in which the *Mellen* doctrine was used to deny recovery to a beneficiary of the creditor variety.

We have yet to consider in relation to the particular facts whether the plaintiff qualifies as a creditor beneficiary entitled to sue the promisor, or, on the contrary, is no more than an "incidental" beneficiary without such a right of suit. We search for indicia of intention against the background of the transaction. See Restatement (Second) of Contracts § [302]. The defendant argues that the contract provision was one for indemnification alone, and in such situations the third party has usually not been accorded a right of action against the indemnitor to recover the payments due the indemnitee. "The performance promised must be one that will in fact discharge the promisee's (or another party's) obligation to a third person; if it will not do this, the third person may be a creditor of the promisee but he is not a creditor beneficiary of the contract. Such is the case where the defendant has promised an obligor (or debtor) to indemnify him and save him harmless with respect to the obligation or debt." 4 Corbin, supra, § 787, at 102. This view is reflected in many decisions. Now it is true that the provision at bar says that the defendant is to "indemnify and hold harmless each of the parties" (resigning directors), and it may also be noted that Steir in his covering letters referred to "amounts which [the defendant] may reimburse me or pay for my account." The defendant would conclude that the expressed intent was to benefit Steir, not his attorneys, and any benefit flowing to the plaintiff should be regarded as "incidental."

This, however, would disregard the fact that the parties agreed the payments under the clause would be made "directly" to Steir's counsel. The defendant concedes that this language "changes the pocket into which the indemnification payments flow." The difference is not trivial. If payments were to be made to Steir, performance by the defendant would not discharge Steir's obligation to the plaintiff; the contrary is true when payments are to be made direct to the plaintiff, and it becomes very plausible to allow the plaintiff his action against the defendant. The distinction is taken in numerous decisions and in

10. The simultaneous existence of the statutory "exceptions" to be enforced while they stand will not, we think, create any material difficulties.

both Restatement of Contracts.[11] The result is not altered merely because words of indemnity have been used (herein company with the "directly" language). "The mere form of the words should not be conclusive * * *; surrounding facts may indicate that payment direct to the creditor was the kind of indemnification that the parties intended." 4 Corbin, supra, § 787, at 102. It is suggested (with affidavit support) that the indemnification wording shows the defendant intended to benefit Steir. That is true in a sense, but it is not inconsistent with an intention to benefit the plaintiff, and one rather clearly expressed.

We observe that our holding that the plaintiff has a locus standi on the facts disclosed by no means assures it ultimate recovery. As noted, the defendant in its answer has set out a number of defenses including the alleged illegality of the provision sued on, and its alleged procurement through misrepresentations. We do not reach the question of the soundness of any of the defenses or of their availability as against the plaintiff. See Restatement (Second) of Contracts [§ 309]; 4 Corbin, supra at § 818.

3. *Conclusion.* The summary judgment for the defendant will be reversed. We leave undisturbed the order denying the plaintiff's motions to substitute, as those motions were evidently made on the assumption, arguendo, that the plaintiff could not itself maintain the action, and the assumption is now held incorrect.[13] * * *

Judgment accordingly.

SEAVER v. RANSOM

New York Court of Appeals, 1918.
224 N.Y. 233, 120 N.E. 639.

POUND, J. Judge Beman and his wife were advanced in years. Mrs. Beman was about to die. She had a small estate, consisting of a house and lot in Malone and little else. Judge Beman drew his wife's will according to her instructions. It gave $1,000 to plaintiff, $500 to one sister, plaintiff's mother, and $100 each to another sister and her son, the use of the house to her husband for life, and remainder to the American Society for the Prevention of Cruelty to Animals. She named her husband as residuary legatee and executor. Plaintiff was

---

11. "B promises A to pay whatever debts A may incur in a certain undertaking. A incurs in the undertaking debts to C, D and E. If the promise is interpreted as a promise that B will pay C, D and E, they are intended beneficiaries * * *; if the money is to be paid to A in order that he may be provided with money to pay C, D and E, they are at most incidental beneficiaries." Restatement (Second) of Contracts [§ 302], Illustration 3. The same example appeared as Illustration 9 to Restatement of Contracts, § 133 (1932). (In the Second Restatement, the class of

"intended" beneficiaries engrosses as a subclass the "creditor" beneficiaries of the First Restatement.) * * *

13. Rights, if any, of the plaintiff, as third party beneficiary, or of the defendant, as promisor, to join Steir, as promisee, of course were not tested (nor was the right of Steir to intervene in the action). It may be convenient, where possible jurisdictionally and under procedural rules to have all three sides represented in the law suit. * * *

her niece, 34 years old in ill health sometimes a member of the Beman household. When the will was read to Mrs. Beman, she said that it was not as she wanted it. She wanted to leave the house to plaintiff. She had no other objection to the will, but her strength was waning, and, although the judge offered to write another will for her, she said she was afraid she would not hold out long enough to enable her to sign it. So the judge said, if she would sign the will, he would leave plaintiff enough in his will to make up the difference. He avouched the promise by his uplifted hand with all solemnity and his wife then executed the will. When he came to die, it was found that his will made no provision for the plaintiff.

This action was brought, and plaintiff recovered judgment in the trial court, on the theory that Beman had obtained property from his wife and induced her to execute the will in the form prepared by him by his promise to give plaintiff $6,000, the value of the house, and that thereby equity impressed his property with a trust in favor of plaintiff. Where a legatee promises the testator that he will use property given him by the will for a particular purpose, a trust arises. Beman received nothing under his wife's will but the use of the house in Malone for life. Equity compels the application of property thus obtained to the purpose of the testator, but equity cannot so impress a trust, except on property obtained by the promise. Beman was bound by his promise, but no property was bound by it; no trust in plaintiff's favor can be spelled out.

An action on the contract for damages, or to make the executors trustees for performance, stands on different ground. Farmers' Loan & Trust Co. v. Mortimer, 219 N.Y. 290, 294, 295, 114 N.E. 389. The Appellate Division properly passed to the consideration of the question whether the judgment could stand upon the promise made to the wife, upon a valid consideration, for the sole benefit of plaintiff. The judgment of the trial court was affirmed by a return to the general doctrine laid down in the great case of Lawrence v. Fox, 20 N.Y. 268, which has since been limited as herein indicated.

Contracts for the benefit of third persons have been the prolific source of judicial and academic discussion. Williston, Contracts for the Benefit of a Third Person, 15 Harvard Law Review 767; Corbin, Contracts for the Benefit of Third Persons, 27 Yale Law Review, 1008. The general rule, both in law and equity was that privity between a plaintiff and a defendant is necessary to the maintenance of an action on the contract. The consideration must be furnished by the party to whom the promise was made. The contract cannot be enforced against the third party, and therefore it cannot be enforced by him. On the other hand, the right of the beneficiary to sue on a contract made expressly for his benefit has been fully recognized in many American jurisdictions, either by judicial decision or by legislation, and is said to be "the prevailing rule in this country." Hendrick v. Lindsay, 93 U.S. 143, 23 L.Ed. 855. It has been said that "the establishment of this doctrine has been gradual, and is a victory of practical utility over theory, of equity over technical subtlety." Brantly on Contracts (2d Ed.) p. 253. The reasons for this view are that it is just and practical to permit the person for whose benefit the contract is made to enforce it against one whose duty it is to pay. * * *

In New York the right of the beneficiary to sue on contracts made for his benefit is not clearly or simply defined. It is at present confined: First. To cases where there is a pecuniary obligation running from the promisee to the beneficiary, "a legal right founded upon some obligation of the promisee in the third party to adopt and claim the promise as made for his benefit." Farley v. Cleveland, 4 Cow. 432, 15 Am.Dec. 387; Lawrence v. Fox, supra: Vrooman v. Turner, 69 N.Y. 280, 25 Am.Rep. 195. Secondly. To cases where the contract is made for the benefit of the wife (Buchanan v. Tilden, 158 N.Y. 109, 52 N.E. 724, 44 L.R.A. 170, 70 Am.St.Rep. 454) affianced wife (De Cicco v. Schweizer, 221 N.Y. 431, 117 N.E. 807, Ann.Cas. 1918C, 816), or child (Todd v. Weber, 95 N.Y. 181, 193, 47 Am.Rep. 20) of a party to the contract. The close relationship cases go back to the early King's Bench case (1677), long since repudiated in England * * *. The natural and moral duty of the husband or parent to provide for the future of wife or child sustains the action on the contract made for their benefit. "This is the farthest the cases in this state have gone," says Cullen, J., in the marriage settlement case of Borland v. Welch, 162 N.Y. 104, 110, 56 N.E. 556.

The right of the third party is also upheld in, thirdly, the public contract cases (Little v. Banks, 85 N.Y. 258; Pond v. New Rochelle Water Co., 183 N.Y. 330, 76 N.E. 211, 1 L.R.A. [N.S.] 958, 5 Ann.Cas. 504; 96 N.E. 409); where the municipality seeks to protect its inhabitants by covenants for their benefit; and, fourthly, the cases where, at the request of a party to the contract, the promise runs directly to the beneficiary although he does not furnish the consideration (Rector, etc., v. Teed, 120 N.Y. 583, 24 N.E. 1014). It may be safely said that a general rule sustaining recovery at the suit of the third party would include but few classes of cases not included in these groups, either categorically or in principle.

The desire of the childless aunt to make provision for a beloved and favorite niece differs imperceptibly in law or in equity from the moral duty of the parent to make testamentary provision for a child. The contract was made for the plaintiff's benefit. She alone is substantially damaged by its breach. The representatives of the wife's estate have no interest in enforcing it specifically. It is said in Buchanan v. Tilden that the common law imposes moral and legal obligations upon the husband and the parent not measured by the necessaries of life. It was, however, the love and affection or the moral sense of the husband and the parent that imposed such obligations in the cases cited, rather than any common-law duty of husband and parent to wife and child. If plaintiff had been a child of Mrs. Beman, legal obligation would have required no testamentary provision for her, yet the child could have enforced a covenant in her favor identical with the covenant of Judge Beman in this case. The constraining power of conscience is not regulated by the degree of relationship alone. The dependent or faithful niece may have a stronger claim than the affluent or unworthy son. No sensible theory of moral obligation denies arbitrarily to the former what would be conceded to the latter. We might consistently either refuse or allow the claim of both, but I cannot reconcile a decision in favor of the wife in Buchanan v. Tilden, based on the moral obligations arising out of near relationship, with a decision against the niece here on the ground that the relationship is too remote for equity's ken. No controlling authority depends upon so absolute a rule. * * * Kellogg, P.J., writing for the court below well said:

> "The doctrine of Lawrence v. Fox is progressive, not retrograde. The course of the late decisions is to enlarge, not to limit, the effect of that case."

The court in that leading case attempted to adopt the general doctrine that any third person, for whose direct benefit a contract was intended, could sue on it. The headnote thus states the rule. Finch J., in Gifford v. Corrigan, 117 N.Y. 257, 262, 22 N.E. 756. 6 L.R.A. 610, 15 Am.St.Rep. 508, says that the case rests upon that broad proposition; Edward T. Bartlett, J., in Pond v. New Rochelle Water Co., 183 N.Y. 330, 337, 76 N.E. 211, 213 (1 L.R.A. [N.S.] 958, 5 Ann.Cas. 504), calls it "the general principle"; but Vrooman v. Turner, supra, confined its application to the facts on which it was decided. "In every case in which an action has been sustained," says Allen, J., "there has been a debt or duty owing by the promisee to the party claiming to sue upon the promise." 69 N.Y. 285, 25 Am.Rep. 195. * * *

But, on principle, a sound conclusion may be reached. If Mrs. Beman had left her husband the house on condition that he pay the plaintiff $6,000, and he had accepted the devise, he would have become personally liable to pay the legacy, and plaintiff could have recovered in an action at law against him, whatever the value of the house. Gridley v. Gridley, 24 N.Y. 130; Brown v. Knapp, 79 N.Y. 136, 143; Dinan v. Coneys, 143 N.Y. 544, 547, 38 N.E. 715; Blackmore v. White, [1899] 1 Q.B. 293, 304. That would be because the testatrix had in substance bequeathed the promise to plaintiff, and not because close relationship or moral obligation sustained the contract. The distinction between an implied promise to a testator for the benefit of a third party to pay a legacy and an unqualified promise on a valuable consideration to make provision for the third party by will is discernible, but not obvious. The tendency of American authority is to sustain the gift in all such cases and to permit the donee beneficiary to recover on the contract. Matter of Edmundson's Estate (1918, Pa.) 103 Atl. 277, 259 Pa. 429. The equities are with the plaintiff, and they may be enforced in this action, whether it be regarded as an action for damages or an action for specific performance to convert the defendants into trustees for plaintiff's benefit under the agreement.

The judgment should be affirmed, with costs.

HOGAN, CARDOZO, and CRANE, JJ., concur. HISCOCK, C.J., and COLLIN and ANDREWS, JJ., dissent.

Judgment affirmed.

Contract Beneficiaries and the Restatements of Contracts

As the opinions in these two cases reflect, the issue of whether or not third persons should be permitted to enforce contracts made for their benefit, or from the performance of which they will receive a benefit, has troubled the courts. Would you characterize the judicial concern in these cases as theoretical or doctrinal, or as practical? In any event, at various times, in various jurisdictions, the rule has varied from allowing virtually all third persons to bring suit, to allowing no third person to bring suit, to allowing some narrowly defined classes of third persons to bring suit. In a way it is remarkable that this basic disagreement could remain unresolved in an important commercial state such as Massachusetts as late as 1979.

The confusion and uncertainty presented by third party beneficiary cases would appear to make them an appropriate area for prestigious restatements of the law to have considerable impact, and indeed they have. The analysis of the two restatements, however, differs in some respects.

The First Restatement of Contracts (1931), § 133(1) divided third party beneficiaries into three classes. A "donee beneficiary" was a person who would benefit from performance of a promise "if it appear[ed] * * * that the purpose of the promisee in obtaining the promise * * * [was] to make a gift to the beneficiary or to confer upon him a right against the promisor to some performance * * *." A "creditor beneficiary" was a person to whom "no purpose to make a gift appear[ed]" and "performance of the promise [would] satisfy an actual or supposed or asserted duty of the promisee to the beneficiary * * *." An "incidental beneficiary" was a person benefitted by a promise but who did not fall into either the category of "donee beneficiary" or "creditor beneficiary." Essentially the first Restatement provided that "donee beneficiaries" and "creditor beneficiaries" could enforce the promise for their benefit but "incidental beneficiaries" could not. This pattern obviously created considerable pressure on the definitions of "donee beneficiary" and "creditor beneficiary" because it was essential for the plaintiff to fit himself into one of these two categories if he was to prevail.

The Restatement, Second, of Contracts (1981) avoids the terms "donee beneficiary" and "creditor beneficiary" because they "carry overtones of obsolete doctrinal difficulties" (Introductory Comment to Chapter 14). Rather, the world of third party beneficiaries is divided into a class of "intended beneficiaries" (who have rights to enforce the promise made for their benefit) and "incidental beneficiaries" (who do not). A beneficiary is an "intended beneficiary" under § 302(1) "if recognition of a right to performance in the beneficiary is appropriate to effectuate the intention of the parties and either

> "(a) the performance of the promise will satisfy an obligation of the promisee to pay money to the beneficiary; or

> "(b) the circumstances indicate that the promisee intends to give the beneficiary the benefit of the promised performance."

Two questions may be raised about these definitions. First, is there any real difference between the tests of the First and Second Restatements? Second, are these definitions ultimately tautological or circular?

RESTATEMENT, SECOND, CONTRACTS § 302:

Illustrations:

1. A owes C a debt of $100. The debt is barred by the statute of limitations or by a discharge in bankruptcy, or is unenforceable because of the Statute of Frauds. B promises A to pay the barred or unenforceable debt. C is an intended beneficiary under Subsection (1)(a).

4. A, an insurance company, promises B in a policy of insurance to pay $10,000 on B's death to C, B's wife. C is an intended beneficiary under Subsection (1)(b).

5. C is a troublesome person who is annoying A. A dislikes him but, believing the best way to obtain freedom from annoyance is to make a present, secures from B a promise to give C a box of cigars. C is an intended beneficiary under Subsection (1)(b).

10. A, the operator of a chicken processing and fertilizer plant contracts with B, a municipality, to use B's sewage system. With the purpose of preventing harm to landowners downstream from its system, B obtains from A a promise to remove specified types of waste from its deposits into the system. C, a downstream landowner, is an intended beneficiary under Subsection (1)(b).

12. B contracts to build a house for A. Pursuant to the contract, B and his surety S execute a payment bond to A by which they promise A that all of B's debts for labor and materials on the house will be paid. B later employs C as a carpenter and buys lumber from D. C and D are intended beneficiaries of S's promise to A, whether or not they have power to create liens on the house. [Would C or D be "creditor beneficiaries" under the first Restatement?]

16. B contracts with A to erect an expensive building on A's land. C's adjoining land would be enhanced in value by the performance of the contract. C is an incidental beneficiary.

17. B contracts with A to buy a new car manufactured by C. C is an incidental beneficiary, even though the promise can only be performed if money is paid to C.

19. A contracts to erect a building for C. B then contracts with A to supply lumber needed for the building. C is an incidental beneficiary of B's promise, and B is an incidental beneficiary of C's promise to pay A for the building.

RESTATEMENT, SECOND, CONTRACTS § 304:

Comment:

e. * * * Where the promisee clearly manifests an intention to confer on the beneficiary a legal right to enforce the contract, recognition of the beneficiary's right rests on the same grounds as recognition of the promisee's right. In cases of doubt, the question whether such an intention is to be attributed to the promisee may be influenced by the likelihood that recognition of the right will further the legitimate expectations of the promisee, make available a simple and convenient procedure for enforcement, or protect the beneficiary in his reasonable reliance on the promise.

———

QUILTER v. WENDLAND, 403 S.W.2d 335 (Tex.1966). Mrs. Lutz opened three savings accounts of $5,000 each at Gibralter Savings Association in the names of herself and one of the three close relatives who are the plaintiffs in this case. Each account named Mrs. Lutz and the specified relative or relatives as joint tenants with the right of survivorship. Mrs. Lutz received the passbooks and signed and returned the signature cards but did not ask any of the relatives who were named as joint tenants to sign the appropriate signature card. Mrs. Lutz thereafter received the dividends until her death. Held, "We will assume without deciding that there is an incompleted gift here, but even so, the respondents are entitled to recover as third party beneficiaries to the contract that was completed between Mrs. Lutz and the savings association."

Three Justices dissented: "I cannot agree that the evidence supports a theory of recovery on a third party beneficiary contract. The evidence fails to show a completed contract between Mrs. Lutz and the Gibralter Savings Association. * * * Mrs. Lutz chose to establish a joint account but she did not complete the contract with the Savings Association. She never at any time relinquished control of the funds. Her acts prevented the respondents from withdrawing the funds during her lifetime. The respondents never acquired any title to the funds in the Savings Association during her lifetime, hence at her death the funds belonged to [her estate]." This dissent also refers to testimony by the responsible officer of Gibralter that if any of the respondents had sought to withdraw funds from the accounts in question during Mrs.

Lutz's lifetime, the savings association would have refused to do so since the respondents did not have the passbook and the association did not have a signature card signed by the relative.

RESTATEMENT, SECOND, CONTRACTS § 313:

(1) The rules stated in this Chapter apply to contracts with a government or governmental agency except to the extent that application would contravene the policy of the law authorizing the contract or prescribing remedies for its breach.

(2) In particular, a promisor who contracts with a government or governmental agency to do an act for or render a service to the public is not subject to contractual liability to a member of the public for consequential damages resulting from performance or failure to perform unless

(a) the terms of the promise provide for such liability; or

(b) the promisee is subject to liability to the member of the public for the damages and a direct action against the promisor is consistent with the terms of the contract and with the policy of the law authorizing the contract and prescribing remedies for its breach.

Illustrations:

1. B contracts with the United States to carry mail over a certain route. C, a member of the public, is injured by B's failure to perform his contract. B is under no contractual duty to C.

2. B, a water company, contracts with A, a municipality, to maintain a certain pressure of water at the hydrants on the streets of the municipality. A owes no duty to the public to maintain that pressure. The house of C, an inhabitant of the municipality, is destroyed by fire, owing to B's failure to maintain the agreed pressure. B is under no contractual duty to C.

3. A, a municipality, enters into a contract with B, by which B promises to build a subway and to pay damages directly to any person who may be injured by the work of construction. Because of the work done in the construction of the subway, C's house is injured by the settling of the land on which it stands. D suffers personal injuries from the blasting of rock during the construction. B is under a contractual duty to C and D.

5. A, a municipality, owes a duty to the public to keep its streets in repair. B, a street railway company, contracts to keep a portion of these streets in repair but fails to do so. C, a member of the public, is injured thereby. He may bring actions against A and B and can recover judgment against each of them.

J'AIRE CORP. v. GREGORY, 24 Cal.3d 799, 157 Cal.Rptr. 407, 598 P.2d 60 (1979). Gregory entered into a contract with the County of Sonoma to renovate the Sonoma County Airport terminal building, including improvements to the restaurant premises, the heating and air conditioning, and installation of insulation. J'Aire operated the restaurant under a lease from the County of Sonoma. Gregory did not complete the construction promptly with the result that the J'Aire restaurant suffered loss of business and resulting loss of profits. J'Aire sued on two theories: that it was a third party beneficiary of the contract between Gregory and the County, and that Gregory was liable in tort based upon negligence in completing the work within a reasonable time. Gregory demurred, and the trial court sustained the demurrer without leave to amend. J'Aire appealed solely on the dismissal of the claim based on the second theory. Held, the complaint states a cause of action in tort: "respondent had a duty to complete construction in a manner that would have avoided unnecessary injury to appellant's business, even though the construction contract was with the owner of a building rather than with appellant, the tenant." The court based its decision on the following:

"(1) The contract entered into between respondent and the county was for the renovation of the premises in which appellant maintained its business. The contract could not have been performed without impinging on that business. Thus respondent's performance was intended to, and did, directly affect appellant. (2) Accordingly, it was clearly foreseeable that any significant delay in completing the construction would adversely affect appellant's business beyond the normal disruption associated with such construction. Appellant alleges this fact was repeatedly drawn to respondent's attention. (3) Further, appellant's complaint leaves no doubt that appellant suffered harm since it was unable to operate its business for one month and suffered additional loss of business while the premises were without heat and air conditioning. (4) Appellant has also alleged that delays occasioned by the respondent's conduct were closely connected to, indeed directly caused its injury. (5) In addition, respondent's lack of diligence in the present case was particularly blameworthy since it continued after the probability of damage was drawn directly to respondent's attention. (6) Finally, public policy supports finding a duty of care in the present case. The wilful failure or refusal of a contractor to prosecute a construction project with diligence, where another is injured as a result, has been made grounds for disciplining a licensed contractor."

Justices Clark and Richardson concurred in the result.

MARKESINIS, DOCTRINAL CLARITY IN TORT LITIGATION: A COMPARATIVE LAWYER'S VIEWPOINT

25 Intl. Law 953, 963 (1991).

My reading of these cases is that they are really contract cases solved through tort: in England because of the strict doctrine of privity, in the U.S.A. because the advantages of the contractual approach have not seriously been considered; indeed, worse still, in the leading case of *J'Aire* the contractual cause of action was, *according to the plaintiff's lawyer,* abandoned at the Supreme Court level inter alia on the (unbelievable) grounds that "contracts were never [his] strong point in Law School"! So why not treat, where the facts allow it, the plaintiff (*O*) as a third-party beneficiary of the contract between *C* and *SC*? Deciding this on the intended beneficiary criteria should be clearer than applying the vaguer tort of negligence or saying that though the action is tortious it is shaped by the underlying contracts that may exist. In my solution, the plaintiff would get his action where, on occasion, tort doctrine has denied it to him. * * *

BIGGINS v. SHORE

United States Supreme Court of Pennsylvania, 1989.
565 A.2d 737.

FLAHERTY, JUSTICE.

This case requires us to reconsider our long-standing adherence to section 142 of the Restatement of Contracts, which makes a contractual gift to a donee beneficiary irrevocable upon execution of the contract, in contrast with section 311 of the Restatement (Second) of Contracts, which permits revocation of the gift at any time before the donee manifests reliance or acceptance. We hold that abandonment of Restatement § 142 would work an injustice on the parties in this case, and that there is no need to adopt Restatement (Second) § 311 merely to align ourselves with the "weight of authority" in other jurisdictions.

The facts are as follows. The appellee, Marie T. Biggins, is the widow of the late Robert A. Biggins, formerly a partner in the appellants' realty firm. On October 29, 1979, Biggins departed the firm and sold his interest to appellants Shore and Guerra. Paragraph 4 of the sales agreement recited the consideration Biggins was to receive for his share of the partnership:

4. The consideration for this sale, payable in cash to Biggins by S–G, is as follows:

(a) Eight Thousand ($8,000.00) Dollars upon execution of this Agreement, as earned draws.

(b) Six Thousand Nine Hundred Thirty-two ($6,932.00) Dollars on or before August 15, 1981.

(c) Eleven Thousand ($11,000.00) Dollars on or before August 15, 1982.

(d) Commencing June 1, 1980, S–G shall pay to Biggins for life the sum of Thirty-five ($35.00) Dollars on each settlement held on or after June 1, 1980 on any type of transaction, said sum to be paid within five (5) days after settlement. Upon the death of Biggins, the said Thirty-five ($35.00) Dollars payment shall continue and be paid to Marie T. Biggins for her life. In the event of the death of Biggins and Marie T. Biggins within six (6) years of the date of this agreement, the Thirty-five ($35.00) Dollars payment shall be paid to Robert G. Biggins, as Trustee for Anthony Biggins, Thomas Biggins and Jonathan Biggins. These payments to Robert G. Biggins shall continue for a period of six (6) years.

Paragraph 4(d) of the contract thus prescribed that part of the purchase price for Biggins's interest in the firm was to be paid to Biggins and his wife for life. Marie T. Biggins was therefore a third-party donee beneficiary under the sales agreement.

In 1982, however, Biggins drafted the following memorandum:

3 June 1982

To: Murray J. Shore and Angelo D. Guerra

From: Robert A. Biggins

Subject: Award of Options under an Agreement dated 26 October 1979 between Robert A. Biggins, Murray J. Shore and Angelo D. Guerra

(1) I hereby award you the following Options to be exercised by you within 30 days of notification of my death opting for either A or B Option.

(A) Keep in full force and effect Paragraph 4B, 4C and 4D under the above mentioned Agreement.

(B) Change Paragraph 4C of the Agreement to read: Upon the death of Biggins, pay the sum of (fifteen) $15.00 Dollars to St. Joseph's Preparatory School 18th and Girard Avenue, Philadelphia, Pa., on each settlement for a period of not less than (three) 3 years. Change Paragraph 4A and Paragraph 4C to read as follows: Any sums of money not paid to Robert A. Biggins under Paragraph 4B and 4C shall not be paid to the estate of Robert A. Biggins but a lump sum of $500.00 (Five Hundred) Dollars shall be paid to St. Joseph's Preparatory School if the sum payable to Robert A. Biggins shall excede [sic] $500.00. Any sums payable to Robert A. Biggins under $500.00 shall be paid to St. Joseph's Preparatory School.

(2) If you chose to exercise Option B, I hereby release you from all claims that may be brought against you and release you from from [sic] the obligations of Option A.

(3) All other Terms and Conditions of the Agreement shall remain in full force and effect.

My hand and seal affixed 3 June 1982.

                           s/ Robert A. Biggins

Biggins sealed the memorandum in an envelope marked "To be opened only at the death of Robert A. Biggins," and gave the envelope to his former partner, appellant Angelo D. Guerra. After Biggins died on May 17, 1984, Mr. Guerra's wife opened the envelope and found the memorandum. Appellants Shore and Guerra chose to make reduced payments to St. Joseph's under Option B of the memorandum rather than the payments to Biggins's widow under paragraph 4(d) of the original contract.

Mrs. Biggins brought suit to enforce her rights under the original contract. The appellants answered that the contract had been modified by the 1982 memorandum and that Mrs. Biggins was entitled to nothing. Mrs. Biggins responded that the alleged modification was ineffective, and moved for summary judgment, which was granted.

Superior Court affirmed, *Biggins v. Shore,* 365 Pa.Super. 237, 529 A.2d 487 (1987), holding that the rights of Mrs. Biggins, a donee beneficiary of the original contract, vested indefeasibly upon the execution of the contract and could not be destroyed by a subsequent modification of the contract by the contracting parties. The court based its holding on *Logan v. Glass,* 136 Pa.Super. 221, 7 A.2d 116 (1939), *aff'd per curiam,* 338 Pa. 489, 14 A.2d 306 (1940), which is a restatement of the long-standing rule that a donee beneficiary's contractual rights vest immediately, that they may not be modified by the contracting parties unless the power to modify has been expressly reserved in the contract, and that the donee beneficiary has a right of action to enforce the benefit conferred by the contract. This is the same rule expressed in the Restatement of Contracts, § 142.[2] Under this rule, Mrs. Biggins was clearly entitled to summary judgment, as the original 1979 contract reserved no power to modify her rights as donee beneficiary.

Appellants, however, would have us adopt instead the "modern" rule set forth in the Restatement (Second) of Contracts, § 311,[3] which

---

2. Restatement of Contracts, § 142, reads:

§ 142. VARIATION OF THE DUTY TO A DONEE BENEFICIARY BY AGREEMENT OF PROMISOR AND PROMISEE.

    Unless the power to do so is reserved, the duty of the promisor to the donee beneficiary cannot be released by the promisee or affected by any agreement between the promisee and the promisor, but if the promisee receives consideration for an attempted release or dis-

charge of the promisor's duty, the donee beneficiary can assert a right to the consideration so received, and on doing so loses his right against the promisor.

3. Restatement (Second) of Contracts, § 311 reads:

§ 311. Variation of a Duty to a Beneficiary

(1) Discharge or modification of a duty to an intended beneficiary by conduct of the promisee or by a subsequent agreement between promisor and promisee is

permits modification of the rights of a donee beneficiary prior to acceptance of or reliance on the gift, unless the contract specifically prohibits modification. In this way, the Restatement (Second) eliminates the distinction between creditor and donee beneficiaries, combining both categories under the designation "intended third party beneficiaries," and treats all intended third party beneficiaries in the same way that creditor beneficiaries were treated under the original Restatement. If we were to adopt the so-called modern rule, then summary judgment in favor of the appellee would be improper, and we would have to remand the case for a determination of whether Mr. Biggins's attempted modification or discharge of her rights was effective under Restatement (Second) of Contracts, § 311.

The rule embodied in the original Restatement has been the settled law of this Commonwealth for at least one hundred fifty-two years. A distinction between donee and creditor beneficiaries was recognized by this Court prior to 1837. In *Blymire v. Boistle*, 6 Watts 182 (1837), it was held that a creditor beneficiary could not sue upon a promisor's duty to indemnify a debtor-promisee, whereas a donee beneficiary could enforce a contract in which the promisor undertakes to confer a gratuitous benefit. The Court noted that "there appear to be reasons of substantial justice in favor of [the distinction], as well as the authority of decided cases." *Id.* at 184.

In the *Blymire* case, Blymire promised Gladstone to pay Gladstone's debt to Boistle. When Blymire failed to pay Boistle, Boistle sued on Blymire's promise to Gladstone, and obtained judgment against Blymire in the trial court. In reversing, this Court explained that Boistle, as a creditor beneficiary, still had a cause of action against Gladstone on the original debt, independent of the Gladstone–Blymire contract, and thus did not need a right of action against Blymire in order to be protected. Moreover, Gladstone, the promisee, had a right of action against Blymire for the indemnity promised. Were Boistle permitted to sue Blymire on the contract, Blymire would be liable both to Gladstone, the promisee, and to Boistle, the creditor beneficiary. In the words of the late Mr. Justice Sergeant:

> If then by this action Blymire is liable also to Boistle, he may be twice sued. Who should be preferred? or might not Blymire in one event, be compelled to pay both? The equity of the case would be, and chancery would decree, that Blymire should pay but once, and

ineffective if a term of the promise so provides.

(2) In the absence of such a term, the promisor and promisee retain power to discharge or modify the duty by subsequent agreement.

(3) Such a power terminates when the beneficiary, before he receives notification of the discharge or modification, materially changes his position in justifiable reliance on the promise or brings suit on it or manifests assent to it at the request of the promisor or promisee.

(4) If the promisee receives consideration for an attempted discharge or modification of the promisor's duty which is ineffective against the beneficiary, the beneficiary can assert a right to the consideration so received. The promisor's duty is discharged to the extent of the amount received by the beneficiary.

that the money should go to Boistle on his releasing Gladstone. But in two common-law suits against Blymire it might be difficult to effect this equity. The suits must, therefore, be by Gladstone against Blymire, and by Boistle against Gladstone, and thus Blymire would be released by one payment to Gladstone, and Gladstone exonerated by paying Boistle; unless one suit should be brought in the name of Gladstone for the use of Boistle against Blymire.

Id. In further explanation of the rule, the Court stated:

[W]hen a debt already exists from one person to another, a promise by a third person to pay such debt, being for the benefit of the original debtor, and to relieve him from the payment of it, he ought to have a right of action against the promisor for his own indemnity; and if the promisor were also liable to the original creditor, he would be subject to two separate actions at the same time, for the same debt, which would be inconvenient, and might lead to injustice.

Id. The converse of this rule, that a donee beneficiary does have a right of action against the promisor in a third-party beneficiary contract, *id.*, has been consistently applied, and has been justified by the fact that the donee beneficiary has no cause of action against the promisee, for there is no debt independent of the contract, as well as by the fact that in an action by the promisee against the promisor, the promisee might recover only nominal damages, he not being entitled to indemnification. ✱ ✱ ✱

It is therefore clear that the rule set forth in section 142 of the original Restatement is an accurate statement of the law which has long existed in Pennsylvania. *Logan v. Glass, supra,* did not "adopt" section 142 of the Restatement, but simply recognized the correspondence of the Restatement rule with the long-standing law of this Commonwealth.

In the face of the foregoing history and purpose of the rule, the appellants offer only one argument for us to abandon a concept which "has been rejected by the Restatement (Second) of Contracts and the weight of authority in this country." It is asserted that this case demonstrates "the need for, and equitable nature of" the modern rule, because the existing rule "may prevent perfectly proper readjustments in the light of misconduct of the beneficiary, the birth of children, or a family financial crisis." [See] Comment F to Restatement (Second) of Contracts § 311.

We disagree. The existing law permits a contracting party, if he intends to make readjustments, to reserve the power to do so when he enters the contract. Section 142 of the Restatement of Contracts begins: "*Unless the power to do so is reserved,* the duty of a promisor cannot be released ✱ ✱ ✱." In similar fashion, section 311 of the Restatement (Second) begins: "Discharge or modification of a duty to an intended beneficiary ✱ ✱ ✱ is ineffective *if a term of the promise so provides.*" In either case, the contracting parties are free to confer a benefit indefeasibly or not, as they wish. The difference, of course, is that in the absence of an express term in the contract, the existing rule makes the gift indefeasible whereas the Restatement (Second) permits modification.

Pennsylvania's existing rule, unlike the Restatement (Second) position, is consistent with the concept of a gift. When parties enter a contract which confers a gift, there is no reason to suppose that the gift may be withdrawn at a later date. The late Mr. Justice Kephart summarized the history of the rule permitting third party beneficiaries to enforce rights under contracts made for their benefit in *Greene County v. Southern Surety Co.*, 292 Pa. 304, 313, 141 A. 27, 31 (1927), where he concluded: "Whatever the objections to recovery by the sole beneficiary, they are insufficient to overcome the undoubted merit and justice of his cause." For us now to invert a rule of such ancient standing would work a substantial injustice in this case. Everyone connected with the contract at issue had a right to rely on the long-standing law which prevents discharge or modification of the gift in the absence of a specific reservation of the power to do so. To permit Biggins, from his grave, to destroy the annuity of his widow would not be equitable.

We see no sound reason to change the law and to adopt the new Restatement view; the Restatement (Second) affords no greater freedom of contract than exists at present. Contracting parties may continue to rely on the rule which has existed in Pennsylvania at least since 1837; if they do not intend to convey an indefeasible benefit, they need merely say so in the contract. Accordingly, we affirm the order of the Superior Court.

Order affirmed.

STOUT, FORMER JUSTICE, did not participate in the decision of this case.

LARSEN and McDERMOTT, JJ., concur in the result.

NIX, CHIEF JUSTICE, concurring.

I am not opposed to the adoption of section 311 of the Restatement of Contracts (Second). I would nonetheless limit its application to third party beneficiary contracts entered into after the adoption of such a change.[1] However, our longstanding firm adherence to the principles of law enunciated in *Blymire v. Boistle*, 6 Watts 182 (1837, Pa.) * * * together with the 150-year business practice in this Commonwealth of

---

1. As has been noted, the Restatement (Second) did not explain the reason for departing from the former rule. I agree with Mr. Justice Flaherty that the same result could have been obtained under the former Rule if the promisor had so desired by merely reserving the right to modify the contract. Nevertheless, because the Rule embraces a fundamental principle of contract law and a majority of the states have chosen to adopt it, it may be advantageous for a state with high interstate business activity, such as Pennsylvania, to be a part of that majority.

reliance upon that rule of law dictate against a precipitous change as is urged by the dissent.

While it possibly may be that Mr. Biggins did not fully understand the consequences of his actions, albeit he had been a successful realtor for a considerable period of time, sound jurisprudential concerns prevent use of an assumption of commercial naivete on the part of the donor/promisor here, as the basis for a radical departure from what is now a commercial tradition.

I therefore join the opinion of the Court.

ZAPPALA, J., joins this concurring opinion.

PAPADAKOS, JUSTICE, dissenting.

It is ludicrous to suggest that there was any actual reliance by either Mr. or Mrs. Biggins on either the new or the old Restatement rule at issue in this case. Neither were lawyers. Neither were counseled by lawyers at the time the critical events in this case occurred. Mr. Biggins merely adopted certain "homemade" and extremely inexact devices to arrange his financial affairs and we must now decide which is the sounder of two rules that ought to be applied to the facts at hand. I vigorously dissent from the view expressed by the majority that that choice depends solely or even principally on one's natural instinct not "to destroy the annuity of his [Biggins] widow * * *". Which rule a common law court applied or adopts should not depend on extra-judicial sympathy for an individual litigant, however justified. All persons must be equal before the Court, whatever their status. To do otherwise is to indulge in result oriented decision making that is ultimately destructive to the rule of law itself. It is wrong to pick a winner for extraneous reasons and then adopt a rule to reach the pre-chosen result. To do so, as I believe the Majority has done in this case, lends credence to the theories of "realists" like the late Judge Jerome Frank, and the modern "critical legal studies" radicals that ours is not a system of law at all, but merely one of individual preference.

The Majority have blinded themselves to the subtlety of the common law system. We are not a Civil Law court applying a pre-adopted Code. That does not mean, however, that we decide matters randomly, case by case, or, that we can never abandon a precedent once it is established. We are responsible for formulating the governing rules in many areas of our law and for fine tuning those rules and keeping them in accord with modern expectations. I am convinced that Section 311 of the Second Restatement is the better rule to adopt in this Commonwealth, even if only on a prospective basis. * * *

At first blush, it is not immediately apparent why this case should be resolved as a matter of contract law principle, and in particular the rules governing third-party beneficiaries. The law of powers, gifts, trusts, subrogation, or agency law principles might conceivably yield a more satisfactory analysis. In a leading law review article published some years ago, it was noted that:

> There are many cases in which transactions of this sort are treated by some courts as contracts between A and B which give to C a right to enforce it; and in which the right of C, if any, is to enforce his contractual right against A. Other courts insist that C's right is to be explained on principles of agency, although who is the principal and who the agent is often left in a safe obscurity. Other courts deny that these transactions are contracts at all, but insist that they are trusts, executed gifts and the like.[4]

The move toward uniform treatment of these cases as third-party beneficiary/contract law cases has been linked to the gradual acceptance in the country, after initial hesitancy, of third-party beneficiary doctrine. The history of the acceptance of third-party beneficiary doctrine in Pennsylvania, noting the longstanding right of third-party *donee* beneficiaries to sue to enforce a contract made for their benefit, is detailed in Mr. Justice Kephart's learned opinion in *Green County for Use of Crescent–Portland Cement Co. v. Southern Surety Co.*, 292 Pa. 304, 141 A. 27 (1927). He stated on behalf of this Court that "Whatever the objections to recovery by the sole beneficiary, they are insufficient to overcome the undoubted merit and justice of his cause." 141 A. at 31. Despite problems that have arisen in other jurisdictions, it would seem that Pennsylvania has long been willing to categorize the type of transaction at issue here as a third-party donee beneficiary problem, and to recognize that the beneficiary has enforceable rights. That is not to say that other areas of the law should not come into play and possibly overlap as in the instant case. They may. But it makes perfectly good sense to treat the rights of the parties here as essentially contractual in nature, arising from the original contract between Mr. Biggins and Appellants which made Mrs. Biggins a third-party beneficiary thereto. Moreover, the parties have, in fact, treated the rights and duties at issue in this case as being contractual in nature and falling into that framework of analysis. * * *

It is not readily apparent why the American Law Institute, in adopting the Second Restatement of Contracts, made * * * [the change it did]. The simplest explanation is that the rule applied in a majority of states on this point, at the time Section 311 was drafted, was (and continues to be) the opposite of that espoused in the First Restatement.[7] The problem with this explanation is that it is not the least bit helpful in persuading anyone that the minority rule currently applicable in Pennsylvania must or must not be abandoned. There is also some authority for the proposition that the Restatement rule was changed because, analytically, some courts had concluded that the

---

4. William H. Page, "The Power of Contracting Parties to Alter a Contract for Rendering a Performance to a Third Person," 12 Wisc.L.Rev. 141, at 151 (1937), hereinafter referred to as "Page."

7. See, A.L.I. Proceedings 1967, at pp. 323–324. See also, Note, "The Third Party Beneficiary Concept: A Proposal," 57 Colum.L.Rev. 406, at 418 ff. (1957) (hereinafter cited as "Columbia Note").

distinction drawn between third-party *donee* beneficiaries and third-party *creditor* beneficiaries was vague and unworkable, and did not cover certain intermediate situations, *e.g.*, where laborers and material-men sued on surety bonds to secure performance of building contracts.[8] Hence, the single category in the Second Restatement of "intended third-party beneficiaries." While there is certainly some merit in reducing two categories in our law down to one where possible, this reasoning is, nevertheless, of little help in resolving the question for it might well be that *all* cases should be treated as falling under the old rule governing *donee* beneficiaries rather than by now applying the old *creditor* beneficiary rule to all situations as is done in the Second Restatement. Little assistance is provided by the cases cited in Appellants' brief because they all apply the majority rule of § 311 of the Second Restatement while providing virtually no explanation as to why it is superior to the rule of the First Restatement.

Trust law, of course, is the opposite of the Second Restatement of Contracts. A settlor cannot revoke a trust if, by the terms of the trust, he did not reserve such a power.[10] The rule with respect to insurance companies for a long time has been likewise opposite to that of the Second Restatement of Contracts.[11]

The dominant idea that seems to have influenced a number of the revisions adopted in the Second Restatement of Contracts, including the one here at issue, was that of enhancing freedom of contract. Upon due reflection, I believe that that concept provides the key to understanding the advantages of Section 311 of the Second Restatement. Section 311 seems to conform to the ordinary expectations of uncounselled persons, like Mr. Biggins, who are arranging the expenditure of their own finances. The normal assumption is that when individuals sign a contract specifying how their own money is to be distributed, and one of the parties is merely an agent in some sense, as here, that the agreement can be changed, modified or altered in a confidential manner as suits exigent circumstances, at least before any third party becomes aware of it. A trust is a solemn undertaking creating property rights in a beneficiary. The ordinary view of a contract, however, is that the principal parties have the freedom to alter it from time to time

---

8. See, A.L.I. Proceedings 1967, at pp. 323–324; Columbia Note, *id.*, at pp. 421 ff.; see also, Page, *op. cit.*, at pp. 183–184.

10. Second Restatement of Trusts, §§ 330–331.

11. Comment c. to § 311 of the Restatement of Contracts Second reads as follows:

c. *Life insurance.* Partly on the basis of statutes, the rule was established in a number of states in the latter part of the nineteenth century that the ordinary life insurance policy in the form then in use belonged to the beneficiary the moment it was issued, and that the insured had

no power to transfer the right to any other person unless the power was reserved. That rule was not applied to fraternal benefit insurance, partly again because of statutes and partly because of charter and by-law provisions. Standard policy forms were revised to avoid the rule by reserving to the insured the power to change the beneficiary. Modern policies also provide for powers to surrender for cash, to borrow against the policy, and to assign the policy. Deletion of such a standard provision may manifest an intention that the power is not to exist.

to suit themselves. The rule of Section 311 better reflects these modern assumptions.

To make a third-party beneficiary contract irrevocable or incapable of modification under Section 311, *ab initio,* the contract must expressly so provide. This part of the rule also is superior to the First Restatement based on modern expectations. Requiring an express clause to make these kinds of contracts irrevocable also vivifies for the parties what the consequences are of their consensual agreement such that their minds cannot be changed later on. This has traditionally been one of the reasons that for an *inter vivos* gift to be effective, actual delivery is generally required—because it vivifies for the donor what the irrevocable step is that he is taking. The same rationale applies here.

For these reasons then, I believe that Section 311 of the Second Restatement is the better rule, best suited to modern commercial and contractual expectations. We should join the majority of our sister states and adopt this rule as the law in Pennsylvania. *Logan v. Glass, supra,* to the extent that it is contrary to Section 311 of the Second Restatement of Contracts, should be expressly overruled. By adopting Section 311 there would be no reliance expectations that would be upset by our doing so. Parties could still make third-party beneficiary contracts expressly irrevocable or incapable of modification if they so wished. By adopting Section 311 we would reduce the number of conceptual categories that encumber the contract law of this Commonwealth, but more importantly, we would be doing what is required by the merit and justice of the cause. * * *

Under the circumstances, I would vacate the summary judgment entered in favor of Mrs. Biggins in this case and the decision of the Superior Court affirming the same, and remand the matter directly to the Court of Common Pleas of Delaware County for further proceedings.

Chapter 11

ASSIGNMENT AND DELEGATION

C. H. LITTLE CO. v. CADWELL
TRANSIT CO.

Supreme Court of Michigan, 1917.
197 Mich. 481, 163 N.W. 952.

Suit by C.H. Little Company against the Cadwell Transit Company. Judgment for plaintiff and defendant brings error. Affirmed with costs.

MOORE, J. This suit was brought to recover damages for the breach of a contract made between the B. & O. Sand & Gravel Company and the defendant, which contract was assigned by the B. & O. Sand & Gravel Company to the plaintiff. It was agreed in open court that if plaintiff was entitled to recover anything it was the sum of $2,800.

* * *

[On April 3, 1912, the B & O Sand & Gravel Company entered into a written contract with Cadwell Transit Co. (Cadwell), the owner of a vessel called the C.W. Cadwell. The contract provided that Cadwell agreed to "carry sand and gravel in such quantities of approximately 500 cubic yards per week up to the capacity of the vessel, as might be required by the B & O Company." The price for carrying was 37 cents per yard for sand and 48, 50 or 52 cents per yard for gravel, depending on the distance from Detroit. Delivery was to be made at specified docks.

Performance under the contract continued until October 21, 1912, when B & O Company "assigned" the contract to the C.H. Little Co. Cadwell was notified of the assignment promptly and responded on October 25, 1912: "We hereby notify you that the said assignment is in breach of the said contract, as you have no right to assign the same. We hereby declare said contract forfeited. * * *" Cadwell refused to carry sand or gravel for the C.H. Little Co., and this suit was brought.]

Is the contract assignable? Counsel say it is not consistent with the rights and interest of the contracting party to be compelled, by assignment against his will, to deal with another who, for any reason,

862

was so objectionable that he would not originally have entered into contract relations with him. If, for example, the defendant had had business dealings with the plaintiff, and its experience had been such that, because of unfair dealings and disregard of contract obligations on the part of the plaintiff, the defendant would not again voluntarily have entered into contract relations with such company, it clearly would be grossly unjust to compel it, without its consent and at the instance of the obnoxious party to do so. * * *

The question of the assignability of contracts had the attention of this court in the case of Northwestern Lumber Co. v. Byers, 133 Mich. 534, 95 N.W. 529. That case came to this court from the circuit court of which Justice Stone, now of this court, was then presiding judge. He filed a written opinion in the case which reviewed the authorities so fully and accurately that it was adopted by this court. The case is so recent and so accessible that it is unnecessary to do more than refer to it.

The same question arose again in the case of Voigt v. Murphy Heating Co., 164 Mich. 539, 129 N.W. 701. In this case the bills were payable monthly, and the heating company had the right to require security for the payment of the steam expected to be consumed. It was claimed, as in the instant case, that the contract was personal and could not be assigned. This court held otherwise, and cited the case of Northwestern Lumber Co. v. Byers, 133 Mich. 534, 95 N.W. 529, and the last edition of the fifth volume of American and English Encyclopedia of Law and Practice, at pages 885, 886, and 906. It is difficult to see how the personal element entered into the contract involved here. What difference could it make to the defendant whether the sand and gravel were furnished by the B. & O. Sand & Gravel Company or by the plaintiff. * * *

Judgment is affirmed, with costs to appellee.

OSTRANDER, STONE, and STEERE, JJ., concur with MOORE, J.

KUHN, C.J. (dissenting). On the trial of this case an offer was made by the defendant to introduce testimony to show that at the time the contract was entered into, it would not have made such a contract with the C.H. Little Company, and that it would not have been willing to extend credit to that company. This testimony was excluded by the court. In my opinion this was clearly admissible under the rule announced in a case cited in the opinion of Mr. Justice Moore, Northwestern Cooperage & Lumber Co. v. Byers, 133 Mich. 534, 95 N.W. 529, where Mr. Justice Stone, then circuit judge, stated the rule to be as follows:

> "I think that the true doctrine is that where an executory contract is not necessarily personal in its character, and can, *consistent with the rights and interests of the adverse party,* be fairly and sufficiently executed as well by the assignee as by the original contractor, and when the latter has not disqualified him-

self for performance of the contract, it is assignable." (Italics mine.)

Exclusion of this testimony was clearly reversible error, but I am also satisfied that the court should have directed a verdict for the defendant upon the record as made, for the rule should be and is that a contracting party has the right to select and determine with whom he will contract, and cannot have another person thrust upon him without his consent. * * *

"A Chose in Action Is Not Assignable"

The early history of the law of assignments is a study of the struggle between commercial needs and legal conceptualism. From an early time, wealth consisted of land and chattels; intangibles were unknown or unimportant. Thus, while transfers of tangible property were recognized from an early time, attempted transfers of intangibles were generally ineffective. The most important exception to this principle were mercantile bills of exchange or promissory notes that were subject to a separate set of rules, "the law merchant," and which have come down to us today as negotiable instruments—primarily, promissory notes and checks drawn on banks. The common law attitude against assignability was encapsulated in the phrase "a chose in action is not assignable." Such a statement of course did not explain very much, nor, indeed, did it articulate the scope of the relevant principle since "chose in action" was a law-French phrase of imprecise meaning. "In its primary sense [the term chose in action] includes debts of all kinds, tort claims, and rights to recover ownership or possession of real or personal property; it has been extended to instruments and documents embodying intangible property rights, to such intangible property as patents and copyrights, and even to equitable rights in tangible property." Restatement, Second, Contracts § 316, comment a. (1979).

Assignments of contract rights were ordinarily viewed as ineffective at common law for two reasons. A contractual relationship was a personal one and the interjection of a third person, the assignee, into the relationship resulted in a contract different from what the parties had originally agreed upon. Further, there was a strong policy against fomenting litigation—maintenance and champerty—and assignments were viewed as being used primarily for the purpose of financing or stirring up litigation.

The common law attitude toward contract assignment began to change with the development of modern commercial transactions in which assignments serve an important economic function. As indicated by cases such as *C.H. Little*, the early notion had been completely eliminated by the twentieth century and was replaced by the presumption that intangible interests could be conveyed as readily as tangible property. The history of how this reversal of attitude came about need not be described in detail. As in other areas, an alternative device (enforcement through a power of attorney) was developed that permitted necessary transactions and enabled courts of equity to recognize the rights of assignees to maintain suit in the name of their assignors. This development was ultimately followed by recognition of courts of law of the validity of contract assignments. Traces of this early history linger in the procedural rules of some states, but most states have adopted statutes that permit the real party in interest (the assignee) to maintain an action in his or her own name.

The assignee is, of course, a stranger to the original contract, and his power to enforce the other party's contractual obligations appears to be the same as the enforcement power accorded a third party creditor beneficiary discussed in Chapter 10. The historical development in the two classes of cases, however, were quite different.

Does the old common law notion that choses in action are not assignable have any relevance today? As described below, there are some remaining limitations on the types of contract rights or duties that may be transferred, but these limitations are based on distinctly modern considerations and are exceptions from the general principle of free assignability. An important class of case in which the older concepts may be said to continue to have force is assignment of claims for personal torts, particularly claims for personal injuries. Such claims are generally not assignable today. Is this based on fear of fomenting litigation? On concern over the possibility that persons suffering personal injuries may be persuaded to sell their claims at less than "fair" value if such claims were generally assignable? Is the modern practice of attorneys representing such plaintiffs on the basis of contingent fees consistent with the prohibition against assignment of such "choses in action"?

"Assignment" and "Delegation"

Modern usage distinguishes between "assignment" and "delegation." Rights are said to be assigned while duties are delegated. Many early cases [like *C.H. Little*] refer to assignment of "the contract" without distinguishing between rights or duties; such usage is fundamentally ambiguous and should be avoided.

Assignment and delegation differ in one fundamental respect. An assignment is the transfer of a right by the owner to another person, which usually may be accomplished without the consent of the other party. In this sense, a duty cannot be assigned; the most that a person subject to a duty may do is to empower a substitute to perform on his behalf, but the obligor remains subject to the duty until it has been discharged by performance or otherwise. Hence, the word "delegation" is used.

See UCC § 2–210.

One other term should be mentioned. Where the obligation to perform a duty is delegated to a third person, the person originally subject to that duty is responsible for its performance. However, if the party to whom the duty is owed consents to the delegation and either expressly or impliedly agrees to look only to the substituted party for responsibility for performance, the person originally subject to the duty is released from further responsibility. This transaction of substitution is called a "novation."

RESTATEMENT, SECOND, CONTRACTS § 318:

Illustrations:

9. A borrows $50,000 from B and contracts to repay it. The contract provides that, if a corporation C is organized and assumes the debt under described conditions, A will be under no further obligation. C is organized and in good faith assumes the debt as provided. A is discharged.

10. A contracts with B to cut the grass on B's meadow. A delegates performance to C, who contracts with A to assume A's duty and perform the work. C begins performance with B's assent, but later breaks the contract. C is liable to B, but A is not discharged.

RESTATEMENT, SECOND, CONTRACTS § 317:

(1) An assignment of a right is a manifestation of the assignor's intention to transfer it by virtue of which the assignor's right to performance by the obligor is extinguished in whole or in part and the assignee acquires a right to such performance.

(2) A contractual right can be assigned unless

(a) the substitution of a right of the assignee for the right of the assignor would materially change the duty of the obligor, or materially increase the burden or risk imposed on him by his contract, or materially impair his chance of obtaining return performance, or materially reduce its value to him, or

(b) the assignment is forbidden by statute or is otherwise inoperative on grounds of public policy, or

(c) assignment is validly precluded by contract.

Comment:

d. *Material variation.* What is a material variation, an increase in burden or risk, or an impairment of the obligor's expectation of counter-performance under paragraph (2)(a) depends on the nature of the contract and on the circumstances. Both assignment of rights and delegation of performance are normal and permissible incidents of many types of contracts. See, for example, as to contracts for the sale of goods, [UCC § 2–210 Comment]. When the obligor's duty is to pay money, a change in the person to whom the payment is to be made is not ordinarily material. Compare [UCC § 9–318]. But if the duty is to depend on the personal discretion of one person, substitution of the personal discretion of another is likely to be a material change.

* * *

Illustrations:

3. B contracts to support A for the remainder of A's life. A cannot by assignment confer on C a right to have B support C.

4. B contracts to support A for the remainder of A's life. B commits a material breach of the contract, and A assigns his right of action to C. The assignment is effective.

5. B contracts to sell to A for three years 250 tons of ice a week, and A contracts to pay on delivery a stated price per ton. A assigns his right under the contract to C. The assignment is effective. C's right to delivery is conditional on payment, but payment by C satisfies the condition.

THE BRITISH WAGGON CO. AND THE PARK-GATE WAGGON CO. v. LEA & CO.

Queen's Bench, 1880.
5 Q.B.D. 149, 49 L.J.Q.B. (n.s) 321.

The judgment of the Court (Cockburn, C.J., and Manisty, J.) was delivered by

COCKBURN, C.J. This was an action brought by the plaintiffs to recover rent for the hire of certain railway waggons, alleged to be payable by the defendants to the plaintiffs, or one of them, under the following circumstances:—

By an agreement in writing of the 10th of February, 1874, the Parkgate Waggon Company let to the defendants, who are coal merchants, fifty railway waggons for a term of seven years, at a yearly rent of 600*l.* a year, payable by equal quarterly payments. By a second agreement of the 13th of June, 1874, the company in like manner let to the defendants fifty other waggons, at a yearly rent of 625*l.*, payable quarterly like the former.

Each of these agreements contained the following clause: "The owners, their executors, or administrators, will at all times during the said term, except as herein provided, keep the said waggons in good and substantial repair and working order, and, on receiving notice from the tenant of any want of repairs, and the number or numbers of the waggons requiring to be repaired, and the places where it or they then is or are, will, with all reasonable despatch, cause the same to be repaired and put into good working order."

On the 24th of October, 1874, the Parkgate Company passed a resolution, under the 129th section of the Companies Act, 1862, for the voluntary winding up of the company. Liquidators were appointed, and by an order of the Chancery Division of the High Court of Justice, it was ordered that the winding-up of the company should be continued under the supervision of the Court.

By an indenture of the 1st of April, 1878, the Parkgate Company assigned and transferred, and the liquidators confirmed to the British Company and their assigns, among other things, all sums of money, whether payable by way of rent, hire, interest, penalty, or damage, then due, or thereafter to become due, to the Parkgate Company, by virtue of the two contracts with the defendants, together with the benefit of the two contracts, and all the interest of the Parkgate Company and the said liquidators therein; the British Company, on the other hand covenanting with the Parkgate Company "to observe and perform such of the stipulations, conditions, provisions, and agreements contained in the said contracts as, according to the terms thereof were stipulated to be observed and performed by the Parkgate Company." On the execution of this assignment the British Company took over from the Parkgate Company the repairing stations, which had previously been used by the Parkgate Company for the repair of the waggons let to the defendants, and also the staff of workmen employed by the latter company in executing such repairs. It is expressly found that the British Company have ever since been ready and willing to execute, and have, with all due diligence, executed all necessary repairs to the said waggons. This, however, they have done under a special agreement come to between the parties since the present dispute has arisen, without prejudice to their respective rights. * * *

The main contention on the part of the defendants * * * was that, as the Parkgate Company had, by assigning the contracts, and by making over their repairing stations to the British Company, incapacitated themselves to fulfil their obligation to keep the waggons in repair, that company had no right, as between themselves and the defendants, to substitute a third party to do the work they had engaged to perform, nor were the defendants bound to accept the party so substituted as the one to whom they were to look for performance of the contract; the contract was therefore at an end.

The authority principally relied on in support of this contention was the case of Robson v. Drummond, [2 B. & Ad. 303] * * * [A] carriage having been hired by the defendant of one Sharp, a coachmaker, for five years, at a yearly rent, payable in advance each year, the carriage to be kept in repair and painted once a year by the maker—Robson being then a partner in the business, but unknown to the defendant—on Sharp retiring from the business after three years had expired, and making over all interest in the business and property in the goods to Robson, it was held, that the defendant could not be sued on the contract—by Lord Tenterden on the ground that "the defendant might have been induced to enter into the contract by reason of the personal confidence which he reposed in Sharp, and therefore might have agreed to pay money in advance, for which reason the defendant had a right to object to its being performed by any other person"; and by Littledale and Parke, JJ., on the additional ground that the defendant had a right to the personal services of Sharp, and to the benefit of his judgment and taste, to the end of the contract.

In like manner, where goods are ordered of a particular manufacturer, another, who has succeeded to his business, cannot execute the order, so as to bind the customer, who has not been made aware of the transfer of the business, to accept the goods. The latter is entitled to refuse to deal with any other than the manufacturer whose goods he intended to buy. * * * The case of Robson v. Drummond comes nearer to the present case, but is, we think distinguishable from it. We entirely concur in the principle on which the decision in Robson v. Drummond rests, namely, that where a person contracts with another to do work or perform service, and it can be inferred that the person employed has been selected with reference to his individual skill, competency, or other personal qualification, the inability or unwillingness of the party so employed to execute the work or perform the service is a sufficient answer to any demand by a stranger to the original contract of the performance of it by the other party, and entitles the latter to treat the contract as at an end, notwithstanding that the person tendered to take the place of the contracting party may be equally well qualified to do the service. Personal performance is in such a case of the essence of the contract, which, consequently, cannot in its absence be enforced against an unwilling party. But this principle appears to us inapplicable in the present instance, inasmuch as we cannot suppose that in stipulating for the repair of these waggons by the company—a rough description of work which ordinary workmen conversant with the business would be perfectly able to execute—the defendants attached any importance to whether the repairs were done by the company, or by any one with whom the company might enter into a subsidiary contract to do the work. All that the hirers, the defendants, cared for in this stipulation was that the waggons should be kept in repair; it was indifferent to them by whom the repairs should be done. Thus if, without going into liquidation, or assigning these contracts, the company had entered into a contract with any competent party to do the repairs, and so had procured them to be done, we cannot think that this would have been a departure from the terms of the contract to keep the waggons in repair. While fully acquiescing in the general principle just referred to, we must take care not to push it beyond reasonable limits. And we cannot but think that, in applying the principle, the Court of Queen's Bench in Robson v. Drummond went to the utmost length to which it can be carried, as it is difficult to see how in repairing a carriage when necessary, or painting it once a year, preference would be given to one coachmaker over another. Much work is contracted for, which it is known can only be executed by means of subcontracts; much is contracted for as to which it is indifferent to the party for whom it is to be done, whether it is done by the immediate party to the contract, or by someone on his behalf. In all these cases the maxim Qui facit per alium facit per se applies.

In the view we take of the case, therefore, the repair of the waggons, undertaken and done by the British Company under their contract with the Parkgate Company, is a sufficient performance by the latter of their engagement to repair under their contract with the defendants. Consequently, so long as the Parkgate Company continues to exist, and, through the British Company, continues to fulfil its obligation to keep the waggons in repair, the defendants cannot, in our opinion, be heard to say that the former company is not entitled to the performance of the contract by them, on the ground that the company have incapacitated themselves from performing their obligations under it, or that, by transferring the performance thereof to others, they have absolved the defendants from further performance on their part.

That a debt accruing due under a contract can, since the passing of the Judicature Acts, be assigned at law as well as equity, cannot since the decision in Brice v. Bannister[4] be disputed.

We are therefore of opinion that our judgment must be for the plaintiffs for the amount claimed.

RESTATEMENT, SECOND, CONTRACTS § 318:

(1) An obligor can properly delegate the performance of his duty to another unless the delegation is contrary to public policy or the terms of his promise.

(2) Unless otherwise agreed, a promise requires performance by a particular person only to the extent that the obligee has a substantial interest in having that person perform or control the acts promised.

(3) Unless the obligee agrees otherwise, neither delegation of performance nor a contract to assume the duty made with the obligor by the person delegated discharges any duty or liability of the delegating obligor. * * *

Illustrations:

2. A contracts to deliver to B coal of specified kind and quality. A delegates the performance of this duty to C, who tenders to B coal of the specified kind and quality. The tender has the effect of a tender by A.

5. A, a teacher employed in a public or private school, attempts to delegate the performance of his duties to B, a competent person. An offer by B to perform A's duties need not be accepted, and actual performance by B without the assent of the employer will create no right in either A or B to the salary stated in A's contract.

4. 3 Q.B.D. 569.

7. A contracts with B that A will personally cut the grass on B's meadow. A cannot effectively delegate performance of the duty to C, however competent C may be.

RESTATEMENT, SECOND, CONTRACTS § 322:

(1) Unless the circumstances indicate the contrary, a contract term prohibiting assignment of "the contract" bars only the delegation to an assignee of the performance by the assignor of a duty or condition.

(2) A contract term prohibiting assignment of rights under the contract, unless a different intention is manifested,

(a) does not forbid assignment of a right to damages for breach of the whole contract or a right arising out of the assignor's due performance of his entire obligation;

(b) gives the obligor a right to damages for breach of the terms forbidding assignment but does not render the assignment ineffective;

(c) is for the benefit of the obligor, and does not prevent the assignee from acquiring rights against the assignor or the obligor from discharging his duty as if there were no such prohibition.

Cf. UCC §§ 2–210(3); 9–318(4).

RESTATEMENT, SECOND, CONTRACTS § 323:

(1) A term of a contract manifesting an obligor's assent to the future assignment of a right or an obligee's assent to the future delegation of the performance of a duty or condition is effective despite any subsequent objection.

(2) A manifestation of such assent after the formation of a contract is similarly effective if made for consideration or in circumstances in which a promise would be binding without consideration, or if a material change of position takes place in reliance on the manifestation.

LANGEL v. BETZ

New York Court of Appeals, 1928.
250 N.Y. 159, 164 N.E. 890.

POUND, J. Plaintiff, on August 1, 1925, made a contract with Irving W. Hurwitz and Samuel Hollander for the sale of certain real property. This contract the vendees assigned to Benedict, who in turn assigned it to Isidor Betz, the defendant herein. The assignment contains no delegation to the assignee of the performance of the assignor's duties. The date for performance of the contract was originally set for October 2, 1925. This was extended to October 15, 1925, at the request of the defendant, the last assignee of the vendees. The ground upon which the adjournment was asked for by defendant was that the title company had not completed its search and report on the title to the property. Upon the adjourned date the defendant refused to perform. The vendor plaintiff was ready, able, and willing to do so, and was present at the place specified with a deed, ready to tender it to the defendant, who did not appear.

The plaintiff as vendor brought this action against the defendant assignee for specific performance of the contract. Upon the foregoing undisputed facts he has had judgment therefor.

The question is: "Can the vendor obtain specific performance of a contract for the sale of real estate against the assignee of the vendee, where the assignee merely requests and obtains an extension of time within which to close title?"

Here we have no novation, no express assumption of the obligations of the assignor in the assignment, and no demand for performance by the assignee.

The mere assignment of a bilateral executory contract may not be interpreted as a promise by the assignee to the assignor to assume the performance of the assignor's duties, so as to have the effect of creating a new liability on the part of the assignee to the other party to the contract assigned. The assignee of the vendee is under no personal engagement to the vendor where there is no privity between them. The assignee may, however, expressly or impliedly, bind himself to perform the assignor's duties. This he may do by contract with the assignor or with the other party to the contract. It has been held (Epstein v. Gluckin, 233 N.Y. 490, 135 N.E. 861) that, where the assignee of the vendee invokes the aid of a court of equity in an action for specific performance, he impliedly binds himself to perform on his part and subjects himself to the conditions of the judgment appropriate thereto. "He who seeks equity must do equity." The converse of the proposition, that the assignee of the vendee would be bound when the vendor began the action, did not follow from the decision in that case. On the contrary, the question was wholly one of remedy rather than right, and it was held that mutuality of remedy is important only so far as its presence is essential to the attainment of the ends of justice. This holding was necessary to sustain the decision. No change was made in the law of contracts nor in the rule for the interpretation of an assignment of a contract.

A judgment requiring the assignee of the vendee to perform at the suit of the vendor would operate as the imposition of a new liability on the assignee which would be an act of oppression and injustice, unless the assignee had, expressly or by implication, entered into a personal and binding contract with the assignor or with the vendor to assume the obligations of the assignor.

It has been urged that the probable intention of the assignee is ordinarily to assume duties as well as rights, and that the contract should be so interpreted in the absence of circumstances showing a contrary intention. The American Law Institute's Restatement of the

Law of Contracts (section 164) proposes a change in the rule of interpretation of assigned contracts to give as full effect to the assumed probable intention of the parties as the law permits. The following statement is proposed:

"Section 164. Interpretation of Words Purporting to Assign a Bilateral Contract and Effect of Acceptance of the Assignment by the Assignee.

"(1) Where a party to a bilateral contract which is at the time wholly or partially executory on both sides, purports to assign the whole contract, his action is interpreted, in the absence of circumstances showing a contrary intention, as an assignment of the assignor's rights under the contract and a delegation of the performance of the assignor's duties.

"(2) Acceptance by the assignee of such an assignment is interpreted, in the absence of circumstances showing a contrary intention, as both as assent to become an assignee of the assignor's rights and as a promise *to the assignor to assume the performance of the assignor's duties.*"

This promise to the assignor would then be available to the other party to the contract. Lawrence v. Fox, 20 N.Y. 268; 1 Williston on Contracts, § 412. The proposed change is a complete reversal of our present rule of interpretation as to the probable intention of the parties. It is, perhaps, more in harmony with modern ideas of contractual relations than is "the archaic view of a contract as creating a strictly personal obligation between the creditor and debtor" (Pollock on Contracts [9th Ed.] 232), which prohibited the assignee from suing at law in his own name and which denied a remedy to third party beneficiaries. "The fountains out of which these resolutions issue" have been broken up if not destroyed (Seaver v. Ransom, 224 N.Y. 233, 237, 120 N.E. 639, 2 A.L.R. 1187), but the law remains that no promise of the assignee to assume the assignor's duties is to be inferred from the acceptance of an assignment of a bilateral contract, in the absence of circumstances surrounding the assignment itself which indicate a contrary intention.

With this requirement of the interpretation of the intention of the parties controlling we must turn from the assignment to the dealings between the plaintiff and the defendant to discover whether the defendant entered into relations with the plaintiff whereby he assumed the duty of performance. The assignment did not bring the parties together, and the request for a postponement differs materially from the commencement of an action in a court of equity, whereby the plaintiff submits himself to the jurisdiction of the court or from a contractual assumption of the obligations of the assignor. If the substance of the transaction between the vendor and the assignee of the vendee could be regarded as a request on the part of the latter for a postponement of the closing day and a promise on his part to assume the obligations of the vendee if the request were granted, a contractual relation arising from an expression of mutual assent, based on the exchange of a promise for an act, might be spelled out of it; but the transaction is at least as consistent with a request for time for deliberation as to the course of conduct to be pursued as with an implied promise to assume the assignor's duties if the request were granted. The relation of promisor and promisee was not thereby expressly established, and such relation is not a necessary inference from the nature of the transaction. When we depart from the field of intention and enter the field of contract, we find no contractual liability; no assumption of duties based on a consideration.

Plaintiff contends that the request for an adjournment should be construed (time not being the essence of the contract) as an assertion of a right to such adjournment, and therefore as a binding act of enforcement, whereby defendant accepted the obligations of the assignee. Here again we have an equivocal act. There was no demand for an adjournment as a matter of right. The request may have been made without any intent to assert a right. It cannot be said that by that act alone the assignee assumed the duty of performance.

Furthermore, no controlling authority may be found which holds that a mere demand for performance by the vendee's assignee creates a right in the complaining vendor to enforce the contract against him. That question may be reserved until an answer is necessary.

The judgment of the Appellate Division and that of the Special Term should be reversed and the complaint dismissed, with costs in all courts.

CARDOZO, C.J., and CRANE, ANDREWS, LEHMAN, KELLOGG, and O'BRIEN, JJ., concur.

Judgments reversed, etc.

RESTATEMENT, SECOND, CONTRACTS § 328:

(1) Unless the language or the circumstances indicate the contrary, as in an assignment for security, an assignment of "the contract" or of "all my rights under the contract" or an assignment in similar general terms is an assignment of the assignor's rights and a delegation of his unperformed duties under the contract.

(2) Unless the language or the circumstances indicate the contrary, the acceptance by an assignee of such an assignment operates as a promise to the assignor to perform the assignor's unperformed duties, and the obligor of the assigned rights is an intended beneficiary of the promise.

Caveat: The Institute expresses no opinion as to whether the rule stated in Subsection (2) applies to an assignment by a purchaser of his rights under a contract for the sale of land.

Comment:

c. *Land contracts.* By virtue of the right of either party to obtain specific performance of a contract for the sale of land, such contracts are treated for many purposes as creating a property interest in the purchaser and thus as partially executed. The vendor's interest resembles the interest of a mortgagee under a mortgage given as security for the purchase price. An assignment of the vendor's rights under the contract is similar to an assignment of a right to payment for goods or services: ordinarily no assumption of the vendor's duties by the assignee is implied merely from the acceptance of the assignment.

When the purchaser under a land contract assigns his rights, the assignment has commonly been treated like a sale of land "subject to" a mortgage. In this view acceptance of the assignment does not amount to an assumption of the assignor's duties unless the contract of assignment so provides either expressly or by implication. A provision in the land contract that it will bind the "assigns" of the parties does not change this result. The assignee may, however, bind himself by later action such as bringing a suit for specific performance. Decisions refusing to infer an assumption of duties by the assignee have been influenced by doctrinal difficulties in the recognition of rights of assignees and beneficiaries. Those difficulties have now been overcome, and it is doubtful whether adherence to such decisions carries out the probable intention of the parties in the usual case. But since the shift in doctrine has not yet produced any definite change in the body of decisions, the Institute expresses no opinion on the application of Subsection (2) to an assignment by a purchaser under a land contract.

———

Cf. UCC § 2–210(4).

———

Assignments in the Modern Commercial Context
(Financing Transactions)

Assignments are important in modern commercial practice primarily since they are involved in many financing devices for business. Indeed, millions of dollars of loans are secured daily by assignments of accounts receivable, general intangibles, or the proceeds from contracts that have not been performed; these loans often provide essential working capital without which many large and profitable businesses as well as almost all small and marginal ones could not remain in operation. This widespread use of intangibles or accounts to finance business operations is largely a development of the twentieth century.

Secured financing is generally dealt with in Article 9 of the Uniform Commercial Code, a complex article that is the subject of an advanced course in commercial law in law schools. Everyone is familiar with some transactions that are governed by Article 9: perhaps the prototype transaction is the purchase of an automobile or other consumer goods "on time" whereby the seller retains a "security interest" (the Article 9 term for a lien) in the goods until the purchase price, together with interest and other charges, is paid in full. Article 9, however, also covers commercial financing by businesses of all types to the extent the financing is secured by personal property, tangible or intangible. Where the security consists of accounts or other intangibles, the distinction between a loan secured by the accounts and an outright sale of the accounts is vague and care must be taken in drafting the agreement to set forth clearly the rights and duties of "borrower" (or "seller") and "lender" (or "buyer"). The spectrum of possible transactions includes the following: (1) the borrower and lender negotiate a loan secured by a security interest in borrower's accounts, but the account debtors are not notified of the assignment and continue to make all payments to the borrower who then pays over part or all of the proceeds to lender to reduce the debt; (2) essentially the same loan is negotiated by borrower and lender except that account debtors are notified of the assignment and are directed to make all payments directly to the lender; (3) the seller sells its accounts to the buyer but guarantees that the face value of each account will be paid when due and agrees to reimburse the seller for any that are "bad" either by buying back the account or by other means such as making a direct payment to the seller (accompanied usually by a reassignment of the delinquent account); and (4) seller sells its accounts to the buyer with the buyer assuming all risks that the accounts may not be collectible (provided that the seller has made no misrepresentations about the status of the account or the transaction giving rise to it). The close similarity between transactions (2) and (3) particularly should be apparent. Section 9–102 makes Article 9 of the Uniform Commercial Code applicable not only to transactions "intended to create a security interest * * * in documents, instruments, general intangibles, chattel paper or accounts" but also to "any sale of accounts or chattel paper." The result is that in both kinds of transactions the lender or buyer will have to give public notice of his interest in the accounts if his interest is to prevail against certain third parties who also claim an interest in the accounts. An "account" is any right to payment for goods sold or leased or for services rendered not evidenced by a negotiable instrument or chattel paper "whether or not it has been earned by performance" [UCC § 9–106]. "Chattel paper" denotes a writing or writings which evidence both a monetary obligation and a security interest in or a lease of specific goods [UCC § 9–105(1)(b)].

Some types of commercial financing involve assignments of interests before they have matured into accounts receivable or chattel paper. A contractor may enter into commitments to deliver goods or do construction work with payment due only upon delivery or after the investment of substantial funds for research and development. If the contractor lacks the financial resources to carry the work until payments come due under the contract, he may borrow money from a lender to enable him to perform his contract; the lender usually will demand an assignment of the rights to the future payments due under the contract as security for his loan. This arrangement is unlike the traditional assignment of accounts receivable in that the right assigned is either a future right or a present right that is conditional upon future performance by the borrower of his obligations under the contract. It nevertheless is an "account" under the definition of UCC § 9–106. Before 1972, UCC § 9–106 defined "contract right" as "a right to payment under a contract not yet earned by performance." This separate definition was eliminated and the definition of "account" broadened primarily to eliminate technical problems of description of collateral.

These financing transactions, of course, developed before the Uniform Commercial Code was approved. The pre-UCC law had no difficulty in enforcing these arrangements as between assignor and assignee; problems arose, however, in situations where third party rights, including a bankruptcy trustee representing other creditors of the assignor, intervened. By and large these problems have been satisfactorily resolved by Article 9 of the Uniform Commercial Code, which addressed many of them squarely.

A good example is the problem of the assignment of future or present rights. The common law generally took the position that a person cannot sell or mortgage property that he does not possess and to which he has no title. A distinction was made between future and present rights, between a future right and a present right that was conditional upon a future event. In a famous dictum, a court stated that while an owner might sell the wool to be grown by his flock or the crop to be harvested from his field, "[t]he catch of fish expected to be made upon a voyage about to begin cannot be sold." Taylor v. Barton-Child Co., 228 Mass. 126, 117 N.E. 43, 44 (1917). [Compare Speelman v. Pascal, supra, page 165.] Needless to say, such a distinction was a subtle one, and considerable confusion existed as between future rights and present rights. What then was the status of a lender who financed a future fishing trip taking an assignment of the expected catch of fish? If that future catch of fish were assigned for a valuable consideration (as was certainly the case of the lender financing the trip), the courts recognized an "equitable assignment" so that the assignment would become effective when the property came into the ownership of the fisherman. Thus, the fisherman was bound by his assignment when the property came into existence. The problem that this created was that the assignee did not have a lien upon the future property before it came into existence, so that the assignee was an unsecured creditor in the event of the intervening bankruptcy of the assignor and could not claim priority even if thereafter the catch were sold profitably. Article 9 addresses this problem squarely by broadly validating after acquired property clauses. See UCC § 9–204. If the person financing the fishing trip files an appropriate financing statement and polices the disposition of the collateral, his or her security interest in the catch of fish will prevail over the claim of an intervening bankruptcy trustee.

See UCC §§ 9–203(1), 9–302, 9–303(1), 9–312(5)(a); 11 U.S.C.A. § 547(c)(5), (e)(3).

Another problem addressed by the common law in an inadequate way was the issue of priorities where a single debtor made successive assignments of the same accounts receivable or intangible assets to more than one creditor. While successive assignments might be fraudulent, they may also be innocent since two or more creditors may demand broad assignments of accounts (including future rights) that overlap in coverage and the debtor may not be aware of the overlap. The common law developed three different and competing principles for the situation where neither assignment was revocable or involved the receipt of a symbolic token of the account (such as a pass book): (1) the English rule (based on Dearle v. Hall, 38 Eng.Rep. 475 (Ch. 1827)) was that the second assignee prevailed if he was unaware of the first assignment, paid value, and gave notice first to the account debtor; (2) the New York rule was that the first in time was first in right; and (3) the four horsemen rule was that the first in time was first in right unless the second assignee obtained payment, recovered judgment, entered into a new contract with the account debtor, or received a tangible token or writing the surrender of which was required by the account debtor's contract.

Section 9–312 of the Uniform Commercial Code now largely solves the problem of competing claims to the same intangible collateral by a series of rules that depend in part on the nature of the security interests involved, the times of filing of competing financing statements (the first to file has priority over the later), and only in the event of a failure to file by both claimants does the New York rule apply. Section 9–312 does not solve all problems of priority since some assignments are not subject to Article 9, but it does solve virtually all problems arising in connection with commercial assignments. Where the Uniform Commercial Code is not applicable, the Restatement, Second, Contracts § 342 adopts a variation of the "four horsemen" rule described above.

IRRIGATION ASS'N v. FIRST NAT. BANK

Texas Court of Appeals, Fifth District, 1989.
773 S.W.2d 346, writ den.

HOWELL, JUSTICE.

In this case, we are called upon to probe the law of assignments and to decide the circumstances whereby a party who pays but who does not receive the bargained performance may demand the refund of his money, not only from his promisor but from the assignee of his promisor. Under the circumstances here present, we hold that the paying party may demand refund from the assignor-promising party but not from the assignee of the promising party.

Plaintiff-appellant Irrigation Association (Payor), a trade association, desired a prominent speaker for its convention and contracted with a booking agent, Mark Thompson, d/b/a International Program

Consultants (Assignor), for the appearance of former president Gerald Ford. The contract called for the payment of a $10,000 "deposit" in advance plus an additional payment at the time Mr. Ford made his appearance.

Before the advance payment or deposit came due, Assignor executed an assignment for collateral security purposes, to defendant-appellee First National Bank of Frisco (Assignee), of all of his contract rights. Thereafter, as instructed, Payor remitted the $10,000 deposit to Assignee Bank by means of a check payable jointly to Assignor and Assignee. Assignee credited part of the proceeds to Assignor's note; the remainder was credited to his deposit accounts.

For reasons not disclosed by the record but quite possibly attributable to Assignor, Mr. Ford never appeared. Payor's demands for a refund went unmet. Hence, Payor brought suit against both Assignor and Assignee. The trial court gave judgment against Assignor but denied judgment against Assignee. The judgment against Assignor is not contested in this appeal. Payor contends on appeal that it should have had a joint and several judgment against Assignee as well as Assignor. We overrule the contention and affirm the action of the trial court.

It is axiomatic that an assignee walks in the shoes of his assignor and that he takes the contract subject to all defenses which the opposing party might be able to assert against his assignor. This proposition has been applied by the Texas courts many times. *See Houchins v. Scheltz,* 590 S.W.2d 745, 750–51 (Tex.Civ.App.—Houston [14th Dist.] 1979, no writ) (assignee has no greater right to recover on contract than assignor) * * *.

However, the proposition in question almost universally arises in a defensive context. That is to say, when the assignee brings suit against the opposing party (generally referred to as the "contract debtor" meaning, in this case, Payor) to enforce rights conferred by the contract, the courts will almost universally agree that the said contract debtor may assert any defense that might have been asserted against the assignor, being one of the original contract parties.

The historic rule concerning assignments of contractual rights has been incorporated into section 9–318 of the Uniform Commercial Code as adopted in Texas. That section provides, in pertinent part:

> (a) Unless an account debtor [2] has made an enforceable agreement not to assert defenses or claims arising out of a sale * * * the rights of an assignee are subject to
>
> > (1) all the terms of the contract between the account debtor and assignor and any defense or claim arising therefrom * * *.

---

2. An account debtor includes a person who is obligated on an account. [UCC § 9–105(a)(1)]. An account is a right to payment for goods sold or leased or for services rendered * * * whether or not it has been earned by performance. UCC [§ 9–106].

The official comment states that the section is intended to make no substantial change in the common law rule. [UCC § 9–318], comment 1.

The case in hand and similar cases raise the question whether a rule of law that was fashioned as a shield against liability may also be employed as a spear by means of which an affirmative recovery may be secured. There is little authority squarely on point. * * *

[O]nly a limited number of cases in point are to be found and, as might be expected, they do not present a uniform view. At one time, the pre–UCC case of *Firestone Tire & Rubber Co. v. Central Nat'l Bank,* 159 Ohio St. 423, 112 N.E.2d 636 (1953), was the prevailing authority on the right of a payor to sue an assignee for a refund of money paid. In *Firestone,* the payor or contract debtor ordered sleds from Mr. Wood. Wood entered into a working capital agreement with the defendant bank. In accordance with instructions, Firestone remitted to the bank on the basis of invoices which were assigned to it. The bank applied a portion of this payment against Wood's debt and deposited the remainder to Wood's account. Subsequently, Firestone discovered that the invoices were fraudulent, and, inasmuch as Wood had taken bankruptcy, it sued the bank for refund of the amounts paid. Applying the rules relating to a party seeking to recover money paid under a mistake of fact, the Ohio Supreme Court stated that Firestone was not guilty of any negligence in failing to discover the fraud, and that the bank, by delivering the invoices to Firestone, unwittingly made a false representation that they were valid. Therefore, the court held that Firestone was entitled to recover the payments that it made directly to the bank except for the amount deposited to Wood's account and withdrawn by him. With regard to this amount, the court denied recovery on the basis that the bank had so changed its position that it would be unjust to require a refund.

In the wake of *Firestone,* several later post-UCC cases purporting to find support in *Firestone* and/or [§ 9–318] likewise held that a payor could obtain a refund from the assignee grounded upon non-performance by the assignor. * * *

During the present decade, the leading case, without doubt, is *Michelin Tires (Canada) Ltd. v. First Nat'l Bank,* 666 F.2d 673 (1st Cir. 1981). The payor or contract debtor in *Michelin* engaged a construction contractor with respect to its tire factory. The contractor assigned its contract rights to assignee bank as security for advances. The assignor contractor submitted several fraudulent claims for progress payments and the payor-contract debtor forwarded payment to the assignee bank in accordance with instructions. After the assignor contractor became bankrupt, the payor-contract debtor brought suit against the assignee bank to recover for overpayments occasioned by the fraudulent progress payment claims. The First Circuit held that neither [§ 9–318] nor the pre-existing Massachusetts law would allow recovery. *Firestone* and its progeny were expressly rejected.

The foregoing analysis brings out that the issue now before us primarily relates to the liability of banking organizations. Banks are the most commonly encountered assignees of contract rights, normally taking an assignment of the customer's contract rights as security for money loaned or advanced. Quite commonly, banks do not resort to this type of security arrangement until they become concerned about the ability of a borrower to perform his pre-existing obligations. *Michelin* observed:

> [Payor's] theory rests upon a construction of § 9–318 that would impose full contract liability on assignees of contract rights. Under this view, a bank taking an assignment of contract rights as security for a loan would also [be burdened with] a delegation of duties under the contract *and the risk of being held liable on the contract* in the place of its borrower.

Id. at 677 (emphasis added). *Michelin* further declared that "common sense requires that we not twist the 'precarious security' of an assignee into potential liability for his assignor's breach." *Id.* at 678 (footnote omitted). *Michelin* further observed that allowing affirmative suits against assignees for the recovery of payments to which the assignor was not entitled would " 'make every Banker, who has taken an assignment of accounts for security purposes, a deep pocket surety for every bankrupt contractor in the state to whom it had loaned money.' " *Id.* at 679 (quoting the dissenting opinion in *Benton State Bank* [v. Warren, 562 S.W.2d 74, 77 (1978)].

> We are unwilling to impose such an obligation on the banks of the Commonwealth without some indication that this represents a considered policy choice. By making the bank a surety, not only will accounts receivable financing be discouraged, but transaction costs will undoubtedly increase for everyone. The case at hand provides a good example. In order to protect themselves, [the assignee bank] would essentially be forced to undertake the precautionary measures that [Payor] attempted to use, independent observation by an intermediary and sworn certifications by the assignor. [Assignee bank] would have to supervise every construction site where its funds were involved to ensure performance and payment. We simply do not believe that the banks are best suited to monitor contract compliance. The party most interested in adequate performance would be the other contracting party, not the financier. Given this natural interest, it seems likely to us that while the banks will be given additional burdens of supervision, there would be no corresponding reduction in vigilance by the contracting parties, thus creating two inspections where there was formerly one. Costs for everyone thus increase, without any discernible benefit. It is also difficult to predict the full impact a contrary decision would have on the availability of accounts receivable financing in general.

Michelin, 666 F.2d at 679–80.

Since its delivery, *Michelin* has been widely, if not uniformly, followed. We reach the same result by employing a somewhat different analysis. With regard to [§ 9–318], we hold that this statute is inapplicable. It is only calculated to define the conditions under which *a contract debtor may resist an action* brought against him by the assignee for the recovery of amounts which are unpaid. Those who framed this statute simply did not undertake to define the conditions under which *an assignee may resist an action* brought against him by the contract debtor for the recoupment of amounts already paid. The latter situation brings different considerations into play, as discussed momentarily.

At the same time, we do not need to go as far as *Michelin* in order to decide this case. In the interest of judicial restraint, we decline to do so. We do firmly adopt what we consider to be the overriding principle to be gleaned from *Michelin*. Claims by the opposing contract party or contract debtor or payor demanding that an assignee return money already paid on grounds that the assignor has failed to perform the contract *constitute claims for restitution*. Claims for restitution are governed by *equitable principles*. *See Staats v. Miller,* 150 Tex. 581, 243 S.W.2d 686, 687–88.

We do not need to re-weigh the equities as they are recited in *Michelin*. We find the equities in the case at hand to be far stronger in favor of Assignee bank than the equities raised in favor of the assignee banks in *Michelin* or *Firestone* or any of the progeny discussed above.

The strongest contention that could have been made in favor of those payors or contract debtors would have been that, "If we had known in advance of the true facts, *i.e.,* that the claims upon which we have paid were false and no money was really owed, Section 9–318 would have entitled us to resist payment; therefore, we consider that we are entitled to a refund." *Our Payor cannot make this claim.* For such reason, it is not necessary for us to decisively choose between the *Michelin* and the *Firestone* lines.

Restating the matter in different terms, the distinction is that, at the time that Payor Irrigation Association forwarded its check to Assignee Bank, there was a valid, subsisting, matured obligation for payment. Payor had contracted to pay $10,000 in advance to Assignor looking only to the financial strength and reputation of Assignor for performance. Had there been no assignment, Payor would have been under obligation to pay the $10,000 to Assignor *at the exact time that it delivered its check to Assignee Bank.* Payor sustained no loss by virtue of the fact that it forwarded its check, as directed, to Assignee rather than to Assignor. Payor's right against Assignor remains intact, for whatever it may be worth.

Payor did not bargain for the financial strength and reputation of Assignee; it bargained only for the financial strength and reputation of Assignor. We hold that any sum which Payor could, under these circumstances, recover from Assignee Bank would amount to the grant of a windfall recovery to Payor.

Reverting to the facts of *Michelin,* we find that the *Michelin* assignee bank was far from spotless in its behavior. The assignee there knew of the precarious financial situation of the assignor contractor and engaged in a continuing series of maneuvers endeavoring to enforce the payment of its own debt in preference over others who were doing business with assignor, including payor Michelin. Nevertheless, the *Michelin* court held that the assignee bank had no responsibility to even inquire as to the validity of the signed invoices by means of which it received money from the payor. For such reason, we decline to decide if we would necessarily reach *Michelin* 's result on *Michelin* 's facts.

In the case before us, Assignee First National presents a much cleaner image. It was not dealing in fraudulent invoices, either intentionally or unintentionally. It only sought the payment of money which was actually, under the provisions of the contract which Payor willingly entered into, then and there, due and payable. The fact that Payor elected to enter into a contract which called for payment in advance of performance was a choice made by Payor, not by Assignee Bank.

In summary, we have before us a transaction involving three parties. If the defaulting party, the primary wrongdoer, is financially responsible, it is plain that he should bear the loss. However, as between the two remaining parties, both comparatively free of blame, we can find no equitable considerations militating in favor of a judgment that would transfer Payor's loss to Assignee Bank and make the loss into Assignee's loss. Assignee was every bit as blameless for the loss as was Payor, if not more so. We hold that Payor must look solely to the party to whom, in the first instance, it contracted to look for any default on the part of Assignor. We decline to transfer that loss to Assignee, an essentially blameless party.

The judgment of the trial court is AFFIRMED.

See part D(1) of the "Survey of Consumer Protection Issues" in Chapter 7, p. 774 supra.

Assignments in the Modern Commercial Context: Other Transactions

Assignments also arise in a non-financing context when a creditor desires to dispose of his claim to a third person. The creditor is often a bank or lending institution but also may be an individual or a business not regularly engaged in lending money. If the claim is not evidenced by a negotiable instrument—e.g., a promissory note—the transfer can be made only by an "assignment" which transfers the property of the creditor to the third person. The acquiring party takes subject to any defenses to which the holder was subject, which may include claims of fraud, breach of warranty, and similar matters. In addition, there is always the risk that the account debtor will be unable to pay off the assigned obligation even if he recognizes its validity and concedes he has no defense to it. Many such assignments are absolute in character and without recourse against the assignor if the account is uncollectible: in effect the assignee assumes all risk of collection. Collection agencies often purchase overdue accounts of businesses for "fifty cents on the dollar" on this basis and seek to compel the defaulting debtors to pay up; if the collection agency is successful, it keeps whatever it collects; if nothing can be collected it is the collection agency's loss. Similarly, a financially embarrassed business may assign an account to a creditor in full or partial settlement of an obligation. Such an assignment is not in the main stream of commercial financing transactions and is not within Article 9 of the Uniform Commercial Code. See UCC § 9–104(f).

Assignments of the nature described in the previous paragraph may also be made "with recourse," so that the assigning party warrants or guarantees that the assigned accounts are collectible.

Many obligations are reflected by "negotiable instruments" rather than by entries in the creditors' books or simple evidences of indebtedness (an "I.O.U."). Negotiable instruments are transferred by "negotiation" or "indorsement" rather than by "assignment" and are governed by a different set of rules than assignments generally. The law of negotiable instruments has long recognized that a "holder in due course" of a "negotiable instrument" takes free of many defenses that may exist between the original parties to the instrument. The extent to which defenses are cut off, and the meaning of the critical phrases "holder in due course" and "negotiable instrument," are themselves large subjects which are considered in advanced courses in commercial law. For a broad outline, see UCC §§ 3–104, 3–302, and 3–305. It is clear, however, that a person who takes a negotiable instrument by indorsement is typically in a better situation than as assignee who takes a nonnegotiable interest by assignment. But see UCC § 9–206(1), which makes a promise by a debtor not to assert a defense against an assignee enforceable unless the defense could have been asserted against a holder in due course of a negotiable instrument.

A transfer of a negotiable instrument by which the transferee becomes the holder is referred to as a "negotiation" rather than an "assignment." UCC § 3–201. However, a person disposing of a negotiable instrument may in some circumstances "assign" it without the transaction being treated as a negotiation, e.g., by conveying a portion of the instrument. UCC § 3–203(d). However, a statement such as "I hereby assign this note to X" is a negotiation of the note, not an assignment. UCC § 3–204(a).

CONSUMER CREDIT IN THE UNITED STATES: REPORT OF THE NATIONAL COMMISSION ON CONSUMER FINANCE

pp. 31–32, December 1972.

WAGE ASSIGNMENT

Wage assignment is a transfer by a debtor to a creditor of the debtor's right to collect all or a given part of his wages, earned and unearned. Traditionally, the wage assignment was irrevocable and was taken by the creditor as either payment or security for a debt. Its function, like self-help repossession, was to provide the creditor with a speedy method of collection without a hearing on the merits of the underlying claim.

Many states have restricted the right of the creditor to obtain wage assignments. The restrictions cover a full range. In some states, wage assignments are completely prohibited; in others they are limited to a given percentage of the debtor's earnings. Some states require that the assignment be accepted by the debtor's employer. * * *

In consumer credit transactions involving an amount financed exceeding $300, a creditor should not be permitted to take from the debtor any assignment, order for payment, or deduction of any salary, wages, commissions, or other compensation for services or any part thereof earned or to be earned. In consumer credit transactions involving an amount financed of $300 or less, where the creditor does not take a security interest in any property of the debtor, the creditor should be permitted to take a wage assignment but in an amount not to exceed the lesser of 25 percent of the debtor's disposable earnings for any workweek or the amount by which his disposable earnings for the workweek exceeds 40 times the Federal minimum hourly wage prescribed by section 6(a)(1) of the Fair Labor Standards Act of 1938 in effect at the time.

Wage assignments generally represent a potentially disruptive force to the wage earner, the family, and their pattern of living. The irrevocable wage assignment permits the creditor to reach the debtor's past and, in many cases, future earnings without a determination by the courts on the merits of the underlying claim. The Commission makes this recommendation despite findings from the cross-state econometric model that restrictions or prohibitions on the use of wage assignments would reduce the number and amount of credit union personal loans.

The Commission also recognizes that small unsecured loans which often serve a useful purpose would not be made available unless the creditor had an effective and inexpensive method of collecting in the event of default.

For many low income wage earners, the only pledgable, tangible asset is a paycheck. To deny the right to obtain credit based on that asset is to fail to recognize the individual's earning capacity and to withhold opportunity afforded more affluent members of society.

The *Survey* indicated that sales and consumer finance companies, as well as some small banks, relied to a significant extent on wage assignments to collect on defaulted obligations. The cross-state econometric analysis of the finance company sector of the personal loan market indicated that where wage assignments were prohibited or substantially restricted the number but not the dollar amount of loans made per family was reduced significantly. This suggests that restriction or prohibition of wage assignments has greatest impact on loans of $300 or less because significant reductions in the number of loans of this size would not necessarily have much impact on the total dollar amounts extended.

The unwillingness of lenders to make loans of this size without an effective and inexpensive method of collecting in the event of default is understandable. 'The small size loan is the most costly to make in relation to the amount lent, and unless creditors can collect without incurring additional expenses, such as attorneys' fees and court costs, they probably would not make such loans. The wage assignment device provides an inexpensive method of collection.

In view of its general opposition to wage assignments, the Commission believes they should be allowed only when the creditor extends credit on an unsecured basis, relying solely on the debtor's earning capacity. But, it also recommends that where a wage assignment is allowed and becomes operative due to default, if it should cause the debtor hardship because of an unexpected emergency, such as illness of the debtor or the family, the debtor should have the right to ask an appropriate court to stay the operation of the assignment until such time as it can be reinstated without causing undue hardship.

RESTATEMENT, SECOND, CONTRACTS:

Introductory Note to Chapter 15:

Government contracts. Federal statutes forbid the assignment of claims against the United States before the issuance of a warrant for payment, and the assignment of any public contract or order. Both statutes contain an exception, called the Assignment of Claims Act of 1940, permitting a single assignment to a financial institution where the contract does not forbid assignment and written notice is filed with appropriate Government officers and with any surety on a bond in connection with the contract. An assignment pursuant to the exception protects the assignee against liability to repay the United States, and in certain cases against setoff of a liability of the assignor to the United States.

Several jurisdictions also have limitations on the assignment of public contracts, or of particular types of public contracts. * * *

AMERICAN BRIDGE CO. OF NEW YORK v. CITY OF BOSTON

Supreme Judicial Court of Massachusetts, 1909.
202 Mass. 374, 88 N.E. 1089.

HAMMOND, J. This is an action of contract brought by the plaintiffs as assignees of all "the moneys now due or which may hereafter become due" to one Coburn, the assignor under two certain building contracts between him and the defendant, dated respectively July 16, 1901, and August 27, 1901. It is brought to recover the amount of two architect's certificates, one for $2,210 and the other for $3,085.50, each dated November 10, 1902. The case was heard upon the auditor's report (which was for the defendant) and certain exhibits by a justice of the superior court, sitting without a jury, who found for the plaintiffs for the full amount claimed; and it is before us upon exceptions taken by the defendant.

These exceptions raise the general question whether in this action the defendant may recoup for the damages sustained by the default of the assignor, which occurred after the defendant had notice of the assignment.

It is contended by the plaintiffs that these sums were due and payable at the time the defendant received notice thereof, that the plaintiffs' rights were fixed at the time of notice and could not be changed by the act of the assignor or of the defendant after notice, and consequently that the damages caused to the defendant by the default of the assignor in leaving his contract unperformed, although without any fault or collusion on the part of the defendant, cannot be recouped in this action. It is contended that the only remedy open to the defendant is by way of an action against the assignor.

Even if it be conceded in favor of the plaintiffs that the sums were due and payable at the time of the notice, and that the rights of the plaintiffs were fixed at that time, still the conclusion which the plaintiffs seek to draw by no means necessarily follows.

We are dealing, not with the right of set-off, but with that of recoupment—an entirely different right. The one is a creation of statute; the other exists at common law and not by statute. The one is applicable even where there are different contracts; the other arises only out of the same contract as that under which the claim of the plaintiffs arises. Confusion sometimes has been caused by a neglect to note the distinction between these two rights. The principles applicable to a case of set-off are in many respects different from those applicable to a case of recoupment, and some care is required not to be misled by apparent analogies.

The assignment of a chose in action conveys, as between the assignor and assignee, merely the right which the assignor then possesses to that thing; but as between the assignee and the debtor it does not become operative until the time of notice to the latter, and does not change the rights of the debtor against the assignor as they exist at the time of the notice.

It becomes necessary to consider the exact relation between the defendant and Coburn, the assignor, at the time of the notice. The auditor has found that written notice of the assignments were given to the defendant on November 14, 1902, before the service of any trustee process. At that time there does not seem to have been any default on the part of Coburn. At the time of the notice what were the rights between him and the defendant, so far as respects this contract? He was entitled to receive these sums, but he was also under an obligation to complete his contract. This right of the defendant to claim damages for the nonperformance of the contract existed at the making of the contract and at the time of assignment and of notice, and the assignees knew it, and they also knew that it would become available to the defendant the moment the assignor should commit a breach. Under these circumstances it must be held that the assignees took subject to that right. Coburn, the assignor, abandoned the work in a few days after the notice. This action was not brought until October 30, 1906, nearly four years after the breach.

Even if the sums were due and payable in November, 1902, at the time of the notice, still if this action had been brought by the assignor after the default, there can be no doubt that the defendant would have had the right to recoup the damages suffered by his default. And the assignees who seek to enforce this claim can stand in no better position in this respect than the assignor. The defendant is simply trying to enforce a right existing under the contract at the time of the notice, a right of which the assignees had knowledge, and since they have delayed suit for these sums, until after default, the defendant may recoup against them as it could have recouped against the assignor. It cannot without its own fault or consent be deprived of rights under the contract. Any other conclusion would make the contract different from that into which the defendant entered. * * *

Exceptions sustained.

At first blush, the notion that an assignee cannot obtain greater rights than his assignor should appear to be self-evident. Self-evident principles, however, are often dangerous. For one thing, as indicated above, the law of negotiable instruments has long recognized that a "holder in due course" of a "negotiable instrument" takes free of many defenses that may exist between the original parties to the instrument. For another, an obligor may undertake a greater obligation to an assignee than to the assignor by direct contract with the assignee, and he may confer on the assignor an agency power to bind him to such an agreement. See UCC § 9–206. These principles have wide potential application to transactions involving consumers, but their impact has been blunted by state legislation and the Federal Trade Commission rule eliminating the holder-in-due-course defense. See supra p. 774.

Chapter 12

STATUTES OF FRAUDS

SECTION 1: INTRODUCTION

A. IMPORTANCE

Contrary to a view commonly held by persons not trained in the law, an oral contract is enforceable unless a special statute requires that particular kind of contract to be in writing and signed by the person sought to be held liable on the contract. Such a statute is called a "statute of frauds." Although discussion of this topic is typically entitled "The Statute of Frauds", the plural is used in the title of this chapter to emphasize the fact that there are many varieties of such statutes both within a single state and in different states.

A contract that is subject to a statute of frauds (and thus must be evidenced by a signed writing) is referred to as "being within the statute." A contract that is not subject to a statute of frauds is said to be without or "not within" the statute. If a contract was originally within the statute but a court holds that the requirement of a writing has been met or may be dispensed with under one or more statutory or judicially created exceptions described below (e.g. by taking possession and making improvements in the case of land transactions) the contract is usually described as "having been taken out of the statute."

A statute of frauds imposes an additional legal requirement on the enforceability of agreements that are within the statute. A statute of frauds may make unenforceable an agreement that meets all the requirements of a binding contract other than a signed writing, e.g., offer, acceptance, consideration, capacity, etc. Further, a statute of frauds may prevent the enforcement of a contract even though the evidence is overwhelming that in fact an otherwise enforceable agreement was reached.

Illustrations:

1. Peter Smith orally offers to employ Mary Jones as a personal secretary for two years at $1,500 per month. Mary orally accepts only after extensive oral negotiation with respect to days off, the nature of the work to be performed, and all other relevant matters (upon which

Peter and Mary are in full agreement). Because an employment contract for two years is within the statute of frauds (see infra section 5), the agreement is not enforceable, even though there was total agreement on all aspects of the relationship and the simultaneous exchange of promises.

2. The foregoing negotiation takes place in front of ten disinterested witnesses, all of whom testify precisely as to the course of the negotiation and from whose testimony it is perfectly clear that full agreement was reached on all particulars. The contract is still unenforceable under the statute of frauds.

Statutes of fraud have generated much litigation. Professor Corbin, in his classic multi-volume treatise on contracts, devotes an entire volume to statutes of frauds. The purpose here is to provide a general understanding of the problems encountered in applying statutes of frauds. This chapter is intended to be read near the beginning of the course and reread as necessary when a statute of frauds problem is encountered in the course materials. Because both the wording of statutes of frauds and their application vary greatly from state to state, discussion in this chapter focuses on the general trend of decisions. For detailed understanding of a statute of frauds, you must turn to the law of the particular jurisdiction involved. Discussions of statutes of frauds, other than the one in volume 2 of Corbin on Contracts referred to above, include Restatement, Second, Contracts, chapter 5, and Williston on Contracts, chapters 16–21 (3d ed. Jaeger, 1960). White & Summers, Uniform Commercial Code sections 2–1 through 2–8 (3d ed. 1988) contains a useful discussion of statutes of frauds found within the Uniform Commercial Code, particularly § 2–201.

B. HISTORY

Modern American statutes of frauds descend from the English Statute of Frauds entitled "An Act for the Prevention of Frauds and Perjuries," 29 Charles II, ch. 3, enacted in 1677. Concern with perjury was especially keen at that time because a defendant in an action to enforce an alleged promise could not testify in his own defense and the judge had no power to set aside unreasonable jury verdicts. Two sections of that statute, sections 4 and 17, deal with matters relevant to this course:

"§ 4. * * * no action shall be brought whereby to charge any executor or administrator upon any special promise, to answer damages out of his own estate; (2) or whereby to charge the defendant upon any special promise to answer for the debt, default or miscarriages of another person; (3) or to charge any person upon any agreement made upon consideration of marriage; (4) or upon any contract or sale of lands, tenements or hereditaments, or any interest in or concerning them; (5) or upon any agreement that is not to be performed within the space of one year from the making thereof; (6) unless the agreement upon which such action shall be brought, or some memorandum or note thereof, shall be in writing, and signed by the party to be charged therewith, or some other person thereunto by him lawfully authorized."

"§ 17.   *   *   *   no contract for the sale of any goods, wares or merchandises, for the price of ten pounds sterling or upwards, shall be allowed to be good, except the buyer shall accept part of the goods so sold, and actually receive the same, or give something in earnest to bind the bargain, or in part of payment, or that some note or memorandum in writing of the said bargain be made and signed by the parties to be charged by such contract, or their agents thereunto lawfully authorized."

It is ironic that England repealed all but the land and surety provisions in 1954 while American courts continue to struggle with statutes of frauds dealing with all of the categories originally covered in sections 4 and 17. The United Nations Convention on Contracts for the International Sale of Goods (see supra, p. 36), provides that "[a] contract of sale need not be concluded in or evidenced by writing" (Article 11), but ratifying countries are permitted to exclude this provision (Articles 12, 96). The United States has ratified the Convention and has not excluded Article 11.

C. PURPOSES

As is true of any rule of law, sensible application of a statute of frauds must begin with an understanding of its purposes. The title to the original statute of frauds indicates that the requirement of a signed writing was first imposed as a protection against fraud and mistake, and certainly this purpose is the one most often referred to in judicial decisions. Two other reasons for requiring a signed writing are: (1) to assure deliberation before making a promise concerning important matters (a cautionary function); (2) to specify a method by which intention may be given legal effect (a channeling function). These other purposes may be involved in varying degrees depending on the particular statute in issue, and some statute of frauds decisions cannot be understood except in terms of the cautionary and channeling functions.

Does the requirement of statutes of frauds that an agreement be evidenced by a signed writing prevent fraud or does it encourage more fraud than it prevents? It should be clear on brief reflection that if statutes of fraud are literally applied, they have significant capacity for mischief since persons may well rely on oral promises without realizing that there is a further legal requirement before the promise is enforceable. In Illustrations 1 and 2, what happens if Mary Jones, in contemplation of her new employment with Peter Smith, gives up her former job, sells her home, and moves to a new city in order to be able to begin working for Peter Smith, only to learn thereafter that Peter Smith has changed his mind and is relying on the statute of frauds to avoid all liability to her? It is well established that recovery based on principles of restitution—theoretically independent of the contract—is not barred by a statute of frauds. See Boone v. Coe, supra page 110. Unless the concept of "unjust enrichment" is stretched to the breaking point, however, that principle alone is unlikely to help Mary. See infra section 2(B), indicating that only particular kinds of reliance on the defendant's oral promise will take the contract out of the statute or be compensated if the contract is not enforced.

Literal application of statutes of fraud may also give rise to inequitable results whenever an agreement within the statute is evidenced by a writing signed by one party but not by the other. Courts generally have enforced a contract against the party who signed it even though the statute of frauds would prevent enforcement against the nonsigning party. But see UCC § 2–201(2), discussed infra in section 3(B).

One aspect of the possible cautionary function of statutes of frauds should also be mentioned. A procedure performs an effective cautionary function only if it is applicable to important transactions and not applicable to unimportant ones. Unfortunately, to a substantial extent, the kinds of transactions within statutes of frauds are independent of the importance or size of the transaction.

Illustrations:

3. ABC Grading Company orally agrees to move 11,500,000 cubic yards of dirt and rock for construction of an airport. The contract price is $1.25 per cubic yard and the time for performance is 10 months. Under the statutes of most if not all states, this contract is not within any statute of frauds.

4. Emma Lou Glen is an elderly, wealthy widow. She orally agrees that she will pay $100,000 per month to Judy Dee, a palm reader and psychic, for investment advice over the next 10 months. This contract is also not within any statute of frauds in most if not all states; whether this contract can be avoided for undue influence, lack of competence, etc. is independent of the statute of frauds.

5. Johnny Desertrat owns 20 acres of land deep in the Mojave Desert. The land has no water and is worth no more than $1.00 per acre. Johnny orally agrees to exchange this land for a used automobile worth perhaps $25.00. This contract is within the statute and is unenforceable unless evidenced by a signed writing.

————

Many similar examples can be cited, particularly those arising under the provision of statutes of fraud relating to contracts not to be performed within one year, which is construed in a particularly bizarre manner. See infra section 5.

D. VARIETIES OF STATUTES

The primary focus of this chapter is on the five kinds of contracts dealt with in section 4 of the English statute and on contracts for the sale of goods. Discussion is in the order of importance of these provisions in modern cases rather than in the order stated in Sections 4 and 17.

There are many other statutes requiring a contract to be in writing and signed in order to be enforceable. Perhaps the most common are statutes derived from Lord Tenterden's Act, 9 Geo. IV, ch. 14, enacted in England in 1828. There statutes require a promise to be in writing and signed if it is to start the period of limitations running anew. It is fairly common to find statutes of frauds dealing with contracts to make a will or to pay a commission to a real estate or business opportunity broker. The statute of frauds for contracts for the sale of goods is UCC § 2–201. Several other provisions in the UCC also require a signed writing: §§ 1–206 (a statute of frauds for personal property not otherwise covered), 2–205 (firm offers), 2–209(2) (clause relating to modification or rescission), 5–104 (letters of credit), 8–319 (contract for sale of securities), and 9–203(1)(a) (creation of security interest).

SECTION 2: PERVASIVE PROBLEMS

A. INTRODUCTION

There are some problems that recur no matter what statute of frauds is in issue. It is useful to review first these pervasive problems. Many of them are discussed again in the context of a particular statutory provision.

B. AVOIDING INJUSTICE

Statutes of frauds may themselves be instruments of fraud. It is as likely that a dishonest person will falsely deny that an oral promise has been made as that he will allege a fictitious promise.

The pressure on a court to find an exception to the need for a signed writing is greatest when the plaintiff has relied on the oral agreement. In such a case, a court might have recourse to one of the well-established part-performance exceptions to the statute's writing requirement. Not all part-performance has been recognized as taking the contract out of the statute, but some forms of reliance have long been treated as eliminating the need for a signed writing. See, for example, section 4(C) infra, concerning part performance of contracts for the sale of land. Some statutes of frauds themselves specify forms of part performance that eliminate the need for a signed writing. See UCC § 2–201(3)(a) (specially manufactured goods).

Even if the plaintiff's part performance is not of a kind recognized as making the oral agreement enforceable, the plaintiff may be able to recover on a "restitution" theory for the reasonable value of any "benefit" conferred on the defendant. The traditional explanation for restitution recovery in this context is that payment to avoid unjust enrichment is not dependent on the existence of a contract and therefore does not violate the statute.

Unless the plaintiff's part performance benefits the defendant, mere reliance loss would not be enough for recovery under a restitution theory. Compensation for reliance losses would be a form of damages and flout the statute. See Boone v. Coe, supra p. 110. This distinction between unjust enrichment and mere reliance puts pressure on courts to find some form of "benefit" that will justify recovery. Courts are particularly likely to find that the plaintiff's reliance has benefitted the defendant when reliance is in the form of part performance of the oral agreement—so called "essential" reliance as distinguished from "incidental" reliance. See Farash v. Sykes Datatronics, Inc., supra p. 112. (The terms "incidental" and "essential" reliance were introduced in Fuller and Perdue, The Reliance Interest in Contract Damages, 46 Yale L.J. 52, 78 (1936)).

The Restatement, Second, Contracts § 139 would make straining to find a "benefit" unnecessary by recognizing all forms of reliance as sufficient to make a promise enforceable to the extent necessary to prevent injustice, "notwithstanding the Statute of Frauds."

RESTATEMENT, SECOND, CONTRACTS § 139:

(1) A promise which the promisor should reasonably expect to induce action or forbearance on the part of the promisee or a third person and which does induce the action or forbearance is enforceable notwithstanding the Statute of Frauds if injustice can be avoided only by enforcement of the promise. The remedy granted for breach is to be limited as justice requires.

(2) In determining whether injustice can be avoided only be enforcement of the promise, the following circumstances are significant:

(a) the availability and adequacy of other remedies, particularly cancellation and restitution;

(b) the definite and substantial character of the action or forbearance in relation to the remedy sought;

(c) the extent to which the action or forbearance corroborates evidence of the making and terms of the promise, or the making and terms are otherwise established by clear and convincing evidence;

(d) the reasonableness of the action or forbearance;

(e) the extent to which the action or forbearance was foreseeable by the promisor.

––––––––––

Whether reliance on an oral promise will avoid a statute of frauds defense, therefore, sometimes depends on the kind of reliance and sometimes on the rule in a particular state. To summarize: (1) some kinds of reliance have been widely recognized as substitutes for a signed writing; (2) some kinds of reliance are codified in the statute as sufficient to make an oral promise enforceable; (3) reliance that benefits the defendant may result in recovery on an unjust enrichment theory even if the oral agreement itself is not made enforceable, but in some states courts will reach further than in others to find a "benefit" when part performance has not increased the defendant's assets; (4) the Second Restatement and some states find any reliance sufficient to overcome a statute of frauds objection to the extent necessary to avoid injustice.

When, a statute of frauds specifies a form of reliance as an acceptable substitute for a signed writing (see, e.g., UCC § 2–201(3)(a) and (c)), the question arises whether there is any room for further judge-made exceptions. For UCC statutes of frauds, the answer in part depends on application of UCC § 1–103—are additional judicial exceptions to a signed writing "displaced by the particular provisions of this Act?"

Illustrations:

6. Buyer and Seller make an oral contract for the sale of a horse for $5,000. Buyer pays Seller the $5,000 and Seller accepts the money. The oral contract is now enforceable. See UCC § 2–201(3)(c).

7. Buyer and Seller make an oral contract for the sale of a horse for $5,000. Buyer buys feed for the horse. The oral contract is not enforceable under UCC § 2–201 (unless Seller "admits" that the contract was made, see § 2–201(3)(b)), and there is a split of authority whether Buyer's "incidental" reliance, even if substantial and foreseeable, makes the contract enforceable.

———

One substitute for a signed writing is almost universally recognized. Once the oral contract has been fully performed by both parties, one of them cannot undo it on the ground that he could not have been compelled to do what he has done.

Illustration:

8. A and B orally agree that A will work on B's farm for 13 months and that at the conclusion of this time, B will pay A $5,000 for A's services. A performs the work and B pays A as agreed. B then sues A to recover the money on the ground that a contract not to be performed within one year must be in writing and signed to be enforceable. B loses.

C. RESTITUTION

As indicated in the preceding section, even when an oral agreement is unenforceable because of a statute of frauds, the plaintiff will usually be compensated for benefits that part performance has conferred on the defendant. This recovery is necessary to avoid unjust enrichment.

Illustration:

9. Owner promises to convey Blackacre to Doctor if Doctor performs surgery on Owner. Doctor performs the surgery. Even a court that would not hold that this essential reliance took the contract out of the statute would permit Doctor to recover on a claim in "restitution" for the value of her services. There is a split of authority as to whether the oral promise and the value of Blackacre are admissible as evidence of that reasonable value. In some jurisdictions, evidence of the oral promise is not admissible if the services are otherwise subject to reasonable valuation.

———

Although suit may be brought to recover in restitution for benefits conferred in performance of a contract that is not enforceable because of the statute of frauds, the party seeking restitution is subject to any defense or counterclaim resulting from the claimant's failure to perform his part of the contract. Either party to the contract, however, is excused from further performance if he demands that the other sign a memorandum sufficient to take the contract out of the statute and this demand is refused.

RESTATEMENT, SECOND, CONTRACTS § 375:

Illustration:

4. A makes an oral contract to buy a tract of land from B for $100,000. Payment is to be made in $10,000 installments, conveyance to be made on the payment of the third installment. A pays $10,000 and then refuses to pay any more and sues B to recover in restitution the $10,000 that he has paid. If B signs a sufficient memorandum, A's refusal to pay is a defense to his action * * * and A cannot get restitution. If B refuses to sign a sufficient memorandum, A's refusal to pay is not a defense * * * and A can get restitution.

———

Sometimes a signed writing is so essential to the purpose of the statute that there is no recovery for services rendered in reliance on the oral promise. This is likely to be the result, for example, under a statute requiring that a promise to pay a commission to a real estate broker be in writing and signed.

D. OVERLAPPING PROVISIONS

Sometimes enforcement of an oral contract can be opposed under more than one statutory provision. When this occurs, two questions are likely to arise. First, if the contract is enforceable because of a specific exemption in one provision, is it nevertheless unenforceable under the other provision? Second, are acts that are sufficient to take the contract out of one provision also sufficient to take it out of the other? A common example of the first problem is an oral contract made today to lease Blackacre for one year beginning a month from now. This is both a contract for an interest in land and a contract not to be performed within one year from the making thereof. Many land statutes of frauds contain exceptions for oral leases of not longer than one year. If so, is the oral lease nevertheless unenforceable because not to be performed within one year? Most courts have held that once out of the land provision, the contract is also out of the one-year provision. An example of the second problem is a contract for the sale of goods over a period of two years. The defendant admits in a pleading that the contract was made. Are all statute of frauds objections removed by UCC § 2–201(3)(b) or does the one-year provision still prevent enforcement? Courts have disagreed on the answer.

E. THE KIND OF WRITING REQUIRED

Many questions concern the character of the writing needed to satisfy a statute of frauds. The original English statute required that "the agreement * * * or some memorandum or note thereof, shall be in writing." Some statutes require that the agreement itself be in writing and render a mere memorandum insufficient to satisfy the statute. Some statutory provisions expressly require that the writing recite the consideration; some expressly exclude such a requirement.

How complete and accurate must the agreement or memorandum be? UCC § 2–201(1) imposes minimal requirements for sales of goods. See infra part 3(A). Other statutes of frauds require more completeness and accuracy. For example, UCC § 2–201(1) does not require that the price of the goods be stated, but most courts would hold a memorandum of a contract to sell land insufficient if the price is not stated.

Illustrations:

10. A and B enter into an oral contract by which A promises to sell and B to buy 1,000 tons of A's number 4 grade coal at $100 per ton, B to pay the costs of transportation from A's coal yard, delivery on May 2, 1983, payment due 10 days after delivery. A and B sign a memorandum reading: "Sold today, 1,000 tons of coal." The memorandum is sufficient; all other terms may be established by oral testimony about the oral contract.

11. A and B enter into an oral contract by which A promises to sell a house to B for $170,000. A and B sign a memorandum reading: "A agrees to sell and B to buy the house and lot known as 2915 Smith Street, Austin, Texas. Payment in full and general warranty deed to be exchanged May 2, 1983, at 12 noon at Jones Title Company. Taxes to be prorated as of that date. Risk of loss does not pass from A to B until deed delivered." The memorandum is not sufficient because it omits the price.

Sometimes a claimant attempts to put together several writings in order to produce a sufficient memorandum. This presents no problem if each of the writings is signed, but suppose that some are not? A common requirement is that the unsigned writings must be referred to in the signed writings or otherwise clearly connected to those writings by, for example, being clipped to them or contained in the same envelope.

UCC § 1–201(46) defines "writing" as any "intentional reduction to tangible form." A tape recording has been held to qualify. Computer files also seem to meet this requirement.

RESTATEMENT, SECOND, CONTRACTS § 132:

Illustrations:

2. A and B make an oral contract within the Statute. A writes and signs a letter to B which is a sufficient memorandum except that it does not identify B. The deficiency may be supplied by the name and address on the envelope in which the letter arrives.

3. A and B make an oral contract within the Statute. A memorandum of the contract is made on two sheets of paper which are not connected physically, and A signs one of the sheets. The two sheets may be read together as a memorandum to charge A if an incomplete sentence on one is completed on the other, if the contract partially disclosed by one is clearly the same contract partially disclosed by the other, or if the fact that one is a continuation of the other is otherwise shown by clear and convincing evidence.

———

A sufficient memorandum need not be intended by its author as a memorandum of the agreement.

Illustration:

12. Buyer and Seller make an oral contract for the sale of 174 suits for $17,000. Buyer signs and sends a letter to Seller reading: "You cannot enforce our oral agreement for the sale of 174 suits because of the statute of frauds." The letter enables Seller to enforce the contract.

———

A contrary result may be reached under circumstances in which a statute's policy of protection against inconsiderate promises is more important. A repudiating memorandum, for example, may not be sufficient if the agreement is "made upon consideration of marriage."

There is no requirement that the defendant's memorandum be delivered to the plaintiff or anyone else. A memorandum discovered in defendant's files may be sufficient.

RESTATEMENT, SECOND, CONTRACTS § 133:

Illustration:

1. A and B enter into an oral contract for the sale of Blackacre. A writes and signs a letter to his friend C containing an accurate statement of the contract. The letter is a sufficient memorandum to charge A even though it is never mailed.

The requirement that the writing be "signed" can be satisfied in ways other than the typical signature at the end of the document. Initials, a stamp, even the letterhead may suffice. As stated in UCC § 1–201, comment 39: "The question always is whether the symbol was executed or adopted by the party with present intention to authenticate the writing." Although a computer file may qualify as a "writing," whether the file is "signed," depends on whether it contains "any symbol executed or adopted by a party with present intention to authenticate a writing." UCC § 1–201(36).

The signature may be by someone the defendant has authorized to sign for him. Unless the statute specifically provides, this authority need not be in writing. An auctioneer has irrevocable power to sign for both buyer and seller for a reasonable time on the day of sale.

If a signed writing that satisfied the statute has been lost or destroyed, its prior existence may be proven by oral evidence. This is a clear indication of how lightly courts typically regard the evidentiary purposes of the statute.

If the writing does not accurately state the terms of the contract, most courts permit it to be corrected by reformation when that remedy would otherwise be appropriate in cases not involving the statute of frauds. It seems somewhat inconsistent with the evidentiary purpose of the statute to say that an accurate writing is required, admit that a writing is not accurate, "reform" the writing on the basis of oral evidence as to its intended contents, and then hold that the reformed writing satisfies the statute. One explanation is that the requirements for reformation incorporate substitute protections against perjury. The remedy is equitable and therefore there is no jury in most states. The standard of proof is also usually increased, "clear and convincing evidence" being the typical formulation.

Illustration:

13. A and B orally agree that A will sell and B will buy Blackacre for $10,000. A delivers a deed to B that, because of a typographical error, purports to convey not only Blackacre but also land adjoining Blackacre. A can have the deed reformed to contain the correct description.

F. ORAL RESCISSION OR MODIFICATION

Assume that there is a signed agreement meeting the requirements of a statute of frauds. May that agreement be orally rescinded or modified? Oral rescission is usually held not to violate the statute if the rescission does not result in the retransfer of property that is the subject of the statute (e.g., goods or an interest in land). For example, an oral rescission of a contract for the sale of goods may not be effective if the buyer has already received the goods. If the seller still has the goods, even though title may have passed to the buyer (see UCC § 2–401(3)(b)) the oral rescission may be effective on the ground that by agreeing to the rescission the seller has "received and accepted" the goods (UCC § 2–201(3)(c)). UCC § 2–209(3) states that the requirements of § 2–201 "must be satisfied if the contract as modified is within its provisions." Because of § 2–201(3)(c) and § 2–209(4) & (5), § 2–209(3) is likely to prevent enforcement only of oral modifications or rescissions that are repudiated while executory and before the other party has relied.

RESTATEMENT, SECOND, CONTRACTS § 148:

Illustrations:

1. A and B enter into a written contract of employment for a term exceeding a year. Later they orally agree to rescind the contract. The oral agreement is effective and the written contract is rescinded.

2. A contracts to sell and B to buy a refrigerator for the price of $500, and the refrigerator is delivered and paid for. One week later A and B orally agree that if B is not satisfied after a week's further trial the transaction will be rescinded. There is no redelivery or repayment. The contract of rescission is unenforceable.

RESTATEMENT, SECOND, CONTRACTS § 149:

Illustrations:

1. A and B make a written contract that A will employ B for two years at $500 a month. At the time B begins work, they agree orally to substitute a contract for six months at $600 a month. The second contract is not within the Statute, is enforceable, and at once discharges the prior contract.

2. A and B make a written contract that A will repair and sell to B two specific appliances for $3,000. Later they agree orally to eliminate one appliance and to reduce the price. Whether the second contract is within the Statute depends on whether the reduced price is $500 or more. See UCC § 2–201.

6. A and B make an enforceable oral contract that A will work for B for 30 days at $20 a day. The next day A and B orally contract to

substitute employment for two years at $6,000 a year. The first contract remains enforceable; the second is not.

———

Illustration 6 to § 149 assumes that the parties do not intend the rescission of the old contract to be effective even though the new contract is unenforceable. This assumption would not be true under all circumstances.

SECTION 3: SALE OF GOODS

The most uniform of all statutes of frauds today is that for the sale of goods, thanks to the adoption of UCC § 2–201 in all states except Louisiana. Only a few states have changed the official text of § 2–201. Nebraska, for example, has added a provision to § 2–201(2) concerning contracts for the sale of grain.

A. UCC § 2–201(1): WHEN A WRITING IS REQUIRED AND WHAT KIND OF WRITING

The writing requirement is not triggered unless the "price" of the goods is $500 or more. The price need not be payable in money (see UCC § 2–304(1)). The section applies to "a contract for the sale of goods." As defined in § 2–106(1), this "includes both a present sale of goods and a contract to sell goods at a future time." Written evidence of a present sale is not needed under § 2–201(3)(c) if full payment has been made and accepted or all the goods have been received and accepted.

Section 2–201(1) makes few requirements concerning the completeness or accuracy of the writing. The writing must indicate that a contract has been made, name the parties, be signed by the party to be charged, and state a quantity. A literal reading of the last sentence of § 2–201(1) creates doubt that even the quantity need be stated. One reading of this ambiguous sentence is that if a quantity is stated, the contract cannot be enforced beyond that quantity, but that there is no need to state the quantity. Failure to state a quantity is not a statement that the quantity is zero. Comment 1, in the first and last paragraphs, however, states that a quantity term must appear, and this accords with the legislative history of the section. Omission of price or quality presents less serious danger of perjury than omission of the quantity. The price and quality may be compared with the market at the time of the agreement, but there is no similar check on the quantity. Although the parties must be identified, the writing need not indicate who is buyer and who is seller.

Sometimes the contract includes the seller's labor as well as materials. For example, the seller may promise to deliver and install carpeting. Is this a "contract for the sale of goods" under § 2–201(1)? Typically, courts have approached this question in terms of whether the goods or the labor form the predominant portion of what is bargained for. See supra p. 35.

An agreement that the buyer may return goods not resold by the buyer is treated as a separate contract for purposes of § 2–201 (see UCC § 2–326(4)).

B.   UCC § 2–201(2):   WRITTEN CONFIRMATION

If both buyer and seller are merchants, one need not have signed a writing if he or she receives a signed confirmation of the contract sent by the other and does not within 10 days after receiving the confirmation give written notice of objection to its contents. Notice is given when mailed (§ 1–201(26)). Section 2–104, comment 2 points out that almost every person in business is a "merchant" for the purpose of having sufficient knowledge and skill to answer mail. But the § 2–201(2) confirmation must affect the recipient in his mercantile capacity. A corporate officer buying goods for personal use is not a "merchant" under § 2–201(2).

Illustration:

14. Buyer and Seller orally agree on the sale of six dozen television sets at $1,000 per dozen to be delivered and paid for a dozen a month for the next six months. Seller signs and sends Buyer a letter confirming the sale and stating its terms. Buyer does not reply. The contract is enforceable.

––––––––

The only effect of § 2–201(2) "is to take away from the party who fails to answer the defense of the Statute of Frauds" (§ 2–201, Comment 3). The sender still must prove that a contract was made and the contract's contents, although failure of the recipient to object to the confirmation may assist the sender in carrying this burden. The failure of the recipient to object to a material addition to the oral agreement does not mean, as a few courts have incorrectly held, that the addition is part of the contract because of § 2–201(2) when it would not be part of the contract under § 2–207(2). See Itoh and Co. v. Jordan International Co. supra page 565.

C.   UCC § 2–201(3):   ENFORCEABILITY WITHOUT A SIGNED WRITING

This subsection contains three alternatives to a signed writing that make a contract for the sale of goods enforceable. The first and third are modifications of alternatives that existed in pre-UCC law and the second is new in most states.

(1) UCC § 2–201(3)(a): *Specially Manufactured Goods*

The first alternative concerns goods specially manufactured for the buyer and not suitable for sale to others in the ordinary course of the seller's business. A contract to sell such goods is enforceable if the seller has begun manufacture or made commitments to procure the goods under circumstances that indicate that the goods are for the buyer and before receiving notice of the buyer's repudiation.

Illustration:

15. Buyer, owner of the "Purple Club," makes an oral contract with Manufacturer for purchase of 5,000 square yards of purple carpet for $50,000. Manufacturer dyes 5,000 square yards of carpet purple. The contract is enforceable.

(2) UCC § 2–201(3)(b): Defendant's Admission

The contract is enforceable against a party who "admits in his pleading, testimony or otherwise in court that a contract for sale was made." This has been held to include admissions made during pre-trial discovery.

(3) UCC § 2–201(3)(c): Goods Delivered or Payment Made

The contract is enforceable if the goods have been received and accepted or payment for the goods has been made and accepted. But the contract is enforceable only as to that portion of the goods received or paid for. If only part of the price is paid, the contract is enforceable only as to "an apportionable part of the goods" § 2–201, Comment 2. If the buyer has received and accepted only part of the goods, he is liable for only a just proportion of the price (id.). Suppose the goods cannot be apportioned. For example, does a $100 down payment made and accepted toward purchase of a $10,000 automobile make the entire contract enforceable? Most courts have held that it does.

Illustration:

16. Buyer and Seller orally agree on the sale of six dozen television sets at $1,000 per dozen to be delivered and paid for a dozen a month for the next six months. Seller delivers one dozen sets and Buyer receives and accepts them. The contract is enforceable as to that dozen sets, but is not enforceable as to the remaining five dozen.

Under prior law, part payment or part delivery if accepted made the entire contract enforceable. Section 2–201(3)(c) therefore makes it more difficult to enforce an oral contract for the sale of goods.

D. OTHER ALTERNATIVES TO A SIGNED WRITING

The fact that § 2–201 in subsections 2 and 3 provides its own detailed alternatives to a signed writing raises the question whether a court may apply additional common law alternatives. The decisions have gone both ways.

SECTION 4: SALE OF LAND OR AN INTEREST IN LAND

A. INTEREST IN LAND

A contract for the sale of land or of an interest in land is one of the most common subjects of statutes requiring a signed writing. In this course we are concerned with an agreement to convey in the future rather than a present conveyance. (There are also likely to be formalities for a present conveyance. In the original English Statute of Frauds, sections 1 and 3 dealt with formalities for conveyances.)

The first question in dealing with a statute of frauds concerning an agreement to convey an interest in land is the meaning of "an interest in land." The answer is provided by the law of real property. An easement to enter upon and use land is an interest in property but a "mere" license to use realty is not. Both the promise to buy and the promise to sell land are within the statute, so long as the conveyance has not been made.

RESTATEMENT, SECOND, CONTRACTS § 125:

Illustrations:

3. A owes B $1,000. In consideration of B's promise to extend the time of payment three months, A promises orally that he will sell his land and apply the proceeds as far as necessary to pay the debt. A's promise to sell the land is within the Statute of Frauds.

4. A and B orally promise C a share in a partnership of which A and B are partners. C orally promises to contribute his services to the firm business. A and B own land as part of the partnership assets. The promises are within the Statute.

5. For consideration, A promises B to devise Blackacre to B. A's promise is within the Statute.

6. A promises B, his daughter, that he will die intestate so that B will inherit a share in a parcel of land. A's promise is not within the land contract provision of the Statute of Frauds. The contemplated transfer to B is a transfer by operation of law, not a transfer by virtue of the contract.

7. A orally promises B to share with him whatever proceeds A obtains from the sale of Blackacre. A's promise is not within the land contract provision of the Statute of Frauds.

9. A promises to support B during B's life in consideration of B's promise to convey Blackacre to A. A's promise is within the Statute of Frauds.

RESTATEMENT, SECOND, CONTRACTS § 127:

Illustration:

6.   A orally promises B to allow B to paste advertisements on A's wall during the ensuing month, in consideration of B's promise to pay A $100.   Neither promise is within the Statute of Frauds.

———

UCC § 2–107 marks distinctions between interests in land, not covered by Article 2, and goods, which are covered.   Under § 2–107(2) a contract for the sale of things attached to realty and capable of severance without material harm to the realty is a contract for the sale of goods.   The sale of crops and timber are examples.   A contract for the sale of minerals or a structure attached to realty is a contract for the sale of goods if the seller is to sever the subject of the sale from the realty.   See § 2–107(1).

B.   OVERLAPPING PROVISIONS

Most courts have held that if the agreement is taken out of the land section by a statutory or judge-made exception, it is also removed from other statutory writing requirements.   Land statutes of frauds typically exempt oral leases for a term not longer than one year.   An oral lease for one year to begin in the future is enforceable in most states even though it is a contract that cannot be performed within one year from the time it is made.   (Boone v. Coe, supra, p. 110, represents a minority view with regard to oral leases.)   Oral contracts that are not leases or contracts to lease are not taken out of the one year provision even though part of a lease transaction.

RESTATEMENT, SECOND, CONTRACTS § 125:

Illustration:

1.   A leases land to B under a written lease terminable at the end of any year by written notice given by either party.   During the third year of the lease, in consideration of a loan by B, A orally promises not to terminate the lease before the end of the fourth year.   The oral agreement is not a lease or contract to lease but is a contract not to be performed within a year and is within the one-year provision of a Statute of Frauds enacted in the original English form.

———

C.   PART PERFORMANCE MAKING CONTRACT ENFORCEABLE

Many cases focus on what acts make enforceable an oral agreement to convey an interest in land.   Two qualities of the acts in reliance on the oral promise to convey are important in deciding whether those acts are sufficient to take the contract out of the statute: the extent to which the acts are evidence of the oral agreement and the degree to which injustice may result if the party who has relied on the oral promise is not able to compel conveyance of the land. When part performance of a contract to convey an interest in realty takes the contract out of the statute, the contract is specifically enforceable and the claimant's full expectancy interest is protected. Part performance does not always have this effect. The claimant may be limited to compensation for benefits conferred on the land owner, or to reimbursement for reliance that conferred no benefit, or may have no remedy. There is a good deal of variation from state to state concerning when acts in reliance have one effect and when another. The statements in this section reflect the general trend of decisions.

The most generally recognized exception to the writing requirement occurs when the land has been conveyed. After conveyance, the promise to pay for the land is enforceable. A few courts have even enforced a promise to pay with other land.

RESTATEMENT, SECOND, CONTRACTS § 125:

Illustrations:

11. A promises B to transfer Blackacre to B, in consideration of B's promise to pay A $5,000. A tenders a deed of Blackacre to B and B accepts the deed. B's promise is no longer within the land contract provision of the Statute of Frauds.

12. A owes B $10,000. A promises to convey Blackacre to B in full settlement of the debt, and B promises to accept the conveyance in full settlement. A tenders to B a deed to Blackacre and B accepts the deed. The Statute of Frauds does not prevent enforcement of B's promise.

———

Oral settlement of a boundary dispute is enforceable when the adjoining land owners have marked the agreed boundary or relied on the agreement.

Many courts have recognized a special exception for promises to convey land in exchange for services rendered over a substantial period of time. Performing the services makes the promise to convey enforceable.

In most states, an oral agreement to sell land becomes specifically enforceable once the vendee has taken possession of the land with the vendor's assent and has paid at least part of the price or made improvements on the realty.

RESTATEMENT, SECOND, CONTRACTS § 129:

Illustrations:

1. A and B agree by an unsigned writing that A will sell Blackacre to B for $5,000. B pays the price to A as agreed, and A accepts the

payment but refuses to transfer the land as agreed. B is not entitled to specific performance, but can recover the amount of the payment.

2. A orally leases A's farm to B for five years, agreeing that B will repair the premises at prevailing wages to be credited on the rent. B takes possession of the farm and does $1,000 worth of repair work, using material furnished by A. A then seeks to evict B. B is entitled to $1,000 less the fair rental of the farm for the period of his occupancy, but is not entitled to specific performance or damages.

3. A and B make an oral agreement for the sale of Blackacre by A to B. With A's consent B takes possession of the land, pays part of the price, builds a dwelling house on the land and occupies it. Two years later, as a result of a dispute over the amount still to be paid, A repudiates the agreement. B may obtain a decree of specific performance.

5. A owns an unsightly vacant lot adjoining B's home in a residential suburb. A's agent and B orally agree that A will sell the lot to B for $1,500. B, a lawyer aware of the doctrine of part performance, expends $1,000 in grading and planting on the lot, but makes no payments and does not communicate with A for two years. A observes the grading and planting, but later denies concluding a contract or knowing that B claimed under a contract. B is not entitled to specific performance, since his actions are not unequivocally referable to a contract for sale and recovery of the value of the improvements is an adequate remedy.

SECTION 5: CONTRACTS NOT TO BE PERFORMED WITHIN ONE YEAR

A. AGREEMENTS WITHIN THE STATUTE

The reason the English Statute of Frauds included agreements "not to be performed within the space of one year from the making thereof" was "not to trust to the memory of witnesses for a longer term than one year" (Restatement, Second, Contracts § 130, comment a). The one-year provision has been construed so narrowly, however, that this purpose has not been realized. Many contracts that were expected to and in fact take longer than one year to perform, are not within the statute.

Most courts have held that for the statute to apply there cannot be any possibility that the agreement will be performed, as distinguished from prematurely discharged, within a year. An agreement to hire a 21-year-old athlete in perfect health for the rest of her life is not within the statute because she may die within the year. An agreement to hire a 90-year-old man on his death bed for 2 years is within the statute because it cannot be performed within one year although there is every likelihood that it will be prematurely discharged by impossibility of performance within one year when the man dies. It is not easy to distinguish between full performance and premature discharge. The result is likely to turn on whether the major purpose of the agreement can be satisfied within one year. An agreement to support a new-born infant until he is 21 is not within the statute because its purpose is fully satisfied if the child dies within one year. A few statutes, however, provide that an agreement measured by the life of one of the parties must be in writing and signed.

RESTATEMENT, SECOND, CONTRACTS § 130:

Illustrations:

1. A, an insurance company, orally promises to insure B's house against fire for five years, B promising to pay the premium therefor within the week. The contract is not within the Statute of Frauds, since if the house burns and the insurer pays within a year the contract will be fully performed.

3. A and B, a railway, agree that A will provide grading and ties and B will construct a switch and maintain it as long as A needs it for shipping purposes. A plans to use it for shipping lumber from adjoining land which contains enough lumber to run a mill for 30 years, and uses the switch for 15 years. The contract is not within the one-year provision of the Statute.

4. A orally promises B to sell him five crops of potatoes to be grown on a specified farm in Minnesota, and B promises to pay a stated price on delivery. The contract is within the Statute of Frauds. It is impossible in Minnesota for five crops of potatoes to mature in one year.

The one year does not begin to run until an agreement is made, ordinarily when the offer is accepted.

Illustration:

17. Diamond Jim makes an oral promise to give a reward of $5,000 to anyone who finds his lost ring. Finder tenders the ring to Jim 5 years later. The one-year statute does not apply. Jim may argue that the offer has lapsed by passage of time, but that is another matter and depends on a reasonable time to accept the offer, which contains no specific time limit.

The one year expires on midnight of the anniversary of the day on which the contract is made. This is in accord with the common-law rule that fractions of a day are not taken into account. Thus an oral contract to work for one year beginning the next day is not within the one-year statute because the year will not start until midnight of the day of contracting and will expire on midnight of the anniversary of that day.

B. PART PERFORMANCE

When one party has completed his part of the contract, the other party's promise can be enforced, even if the completed performance took longer than one year. This saves the trouble of substituting payment other than the one the parties have agreed upon. If, however, there has been only part performance by the promisee, an oral promise that cannot be performed within one year remains unenforceable. This is true even though the promisee's performance can or must be completed within a year.

RESTATEMENT, SECOND, CONTRACTS § 130:

Illustrations:

13. A sells and delivers goods to B in return for B's promise to pay $1,000 in six months, $1,000 in a year and $1,000 in eighteen months. B's promises are not within the one-year provision of the Statute.

15. A and B contract orally for A's employment by B at a stated salary for the ensuing two years. A works under the contract for 15 months when B discharges him without cause. The contract is not withdrawn from the operation of the Statute, and A may not recover damages for wrongful discharge. But A may recover any unpaid salary.

SECTION 6: ANSWER FOR THE DEBT OF ANOTHER

A. PROMISES WITHIN THE STATUTE

An oral promise to act as a surety—to pay another's debt if he does not—is unenforceable. It remains unenforceable even though there is consideration for the promise or it has been relied on by extending credit or forbearing collection. The promisor is not a surety, however, unless someone else is the principal obligor. If a donor buys merchandise for a gift, the donor's promise to the seller to pay is not within a "promise to answer for the debt of another." (It may, however, be a direct obligation that is unenforceable under UCC § 2–201.) The donee is not an obligor, and the donor promisor is not a surety. Much the same reasoning applies to the so-called "novation exception" to the surety provision. The oral promise of someone other than the original debtor to pay the debt, is enforceable if the creditor, as consideration for the promise, releases the original debtor from further liability.

A debtor who promises to indemnify his surety is not himself a surety. Moreover, the creditor need not be a mind reader. Even though the relationship between two parties is that of debtor and surety, the surety cannot invoke the protection of the statute of frauds unless the creditor had reason to know of the relationship when the debt was incurred. If, for example, the debtor and the surety promise at the same time to pay for some performance by the creditor, the creditor must have reason to know that one party is the debtor who has promised to hold the other harmless from any liability on the latter's promise as surety. The creditor will have reason to know that one party is acting as surety if the creditor should know that the creditor's performance will benefit only the debtor and not the surety.

RESTATEMENT, SECOND, CONTRACTS § 112:

Illustrations:

2. S promises C orally to guarantee the performance of any duty that D may incur to C within the ensuing year. Relying on this promise, C enters into contracts with D, by which D undertakes within the year to sell materials for a house and to act as supervising architect during its construction. D, without excuse, fails to perform his contract. S's promise is within the Statute of Frauds.

5. S obtains goods from C on this oral promise: "Charge them to D, and, if he does not pay for them, I will." S has no authority to charge the goods to D, and D makes no promise to pay for them. S's promise is not within the suretyship provision of the Statute of Frauds, since D is under no duty, and hence is not a principal obligor.

9. S, for consideration, orally promises E to pay a debt of E's son D to C, if D fails to pay it at maturity. S's promise is not within the Statute of Frauds because it was made to E, not to the creditor C.

11. D induces S to purchase goods from C. Though the purchase is for D's benefit, the goods are delivered by C to S, who afterwards turns them over to D. S orally promises C to pay for them. D, as part of the transaction, guarantees C that S will pay. C neither knows nor has reason to know that S is a surety. Though S is a surety as between himself and D, his promise is not within the Statute of Frauds. D's promise also is not within the Statute, since the duty to pay is in truth his.

RESTATEMENT, SECOND, CONTRACTS § 118:

Illustration:

1. I promises to indemnify S if he will guarantee I's obligation to C. I's promise is not within the Statute of Frauds. S's promise is.

A cautionary purpose is especially important in requiring a written promise to act as surety. This is the kind of promise that is likely to be made without appropriate deliberation. A written repudiation or reliance on an oral promise to execute a writing is not likely to take the surety's promise out of the statute.

RESTATEMENT, SECOND, CONTRACTS § 117:

Illustration:

1. In consideration of a loan by C to D, S orally promises C to execute a written instrument guaranteeing the debt. S's promise is within the Statute.

B. MAIN PURPOSE EXCEPTION

An important exception to the surety provision is the "main purpose rule." If the surety's promise is made primarily for her own economic advantage, the promise is not within the statute. Examples include a promise of payment if a creditor will forbear from seizing the debtor's property in which the surety has an interest inferior to the creditor's interest, a guaranty by one who sells her accounts receivable that the buyer will be able to collect the accounts, and a salesman who guarantees her customers' accounts. If the promise is made by a professional surety company, the premium paid for surety insurance is not sufficient to bring the promise within the main purpose exception.

RESTATEMENT, SECOND, CONTRACTS § 116:

Illustration:

1. D owes C $1,000. C is about to levy an attachment on D's factory. S, who is a friend of D's desiring to prevent his friend's financial ruin, orally promises C that if C will forbear to take legal proceedings against D for three months S will pay D's debt if D fails to do so. S has no purpose to benefit himself and C has no reason to suppose so. S's promise is not enforceable.

2. D owes C $1,000. C is about to levy an attachment on D's factory. S, who is also a creditor of D's, fearing that the attachment will ruin D's business and thereby destroy his own chance of collecting his claim, orally promises C that if C will forbear to take legal proceedings against D for three months, S will pay D's debt if D fails to do so. S's promise is enforceable.

3. D contracts with S to build a house for S. C contracts with D to furnish materials for the purpose. D, in violation of his contract with C, fails to pay C for some of the materials furnished. C justifiably refuses to furnish further materials. S orally promises C, that if C will continue to furnish D with materials that C had previously agreed to furnish, S will pay the price not only for the materials already furnished but also for the remaining materials if D fails to do so. S's promise is enforceable.

SECTION 7: PROMISE OF EXECUTOR OR ADMINISTRATOR

The promise of an executor or administrator of an estate to answer personally for the duty of the decedent is a specialized example of a promise to act as surety. The principles discussed in section 6.

Special forms of the novation and main purpose exceptions are likely to be present. The novation exception applies when the executor promises to pay the decedent's debt if the creditor does not file his claim in the estate administration. A common instance of the main purpose rule is the executor's promise to pay an estate debt if the creditor does not object to the promisor's appointment as executor.

SECTION 8: ON CONSIDERATION OF MARRIAGE

An oral promise is unenforceable if all or part of the consideration is marriage or a promise to marry. Not included within the statute, however, are the mutual promises of two persons to marry. (But many states have abolished the cause of action for breach of promise to marry.)

If the promise made on consideration of marriage is a promise other than one to marry the promisee, the statute applies.

RESTATEMENT, SECOND, CONTRACTS § 124:

Illustrations:

1. In consideration of A's promise to marry B, B orally promises to marry A and to settle Blackacre upon A. B's promise is within the Statute of Frauds.

2. B offers to marry A. To induce A to accept the offer, B orally promises to settle property upon A. A accepts the offer. Both promises to marry and B's promise to make a settlement are within the Statute of Frauds.

4. In consideration of A's marrying B, C orally promises A a settlement. C's promise is within the Statute of Frauds.

———

Cases must be distinguished in which marriage is the condition on which the promise is to be performed but not the consideration for the promise. If A and B exchange promises that each will give A's daughter $1,000 when she marries B's son, the consideration is the mutual promises of A and B, not the marriage. The promises are not within the statute.

Index

References are to Pages

†